SCHOOL OF ORIENTAL AND AFRICAN STUDIES
University of London

Please return this book on or before the last date shown

Long loans and One Week loans may be renewed up to 10 times
Short loans & CDs cannot be renewed
Fines are charged on all overdue items

Online: http://lib.soas.ac.uk/patroninfo
Phone: 020-7898 4197 (answerphone)

DEVELOPMENT MACROECONOMICS

FOURTH EDITION

DEVELOPMENT MACROECONOMICS

Pierre-Richard Agénor

Peter J. Montiel

Princeton University Press
Princeton and Oxford

Copyright © 2015 by Princeton University Press

Published by Princeton University Press, 41 William Street, Princeton, New Jersey 08540
In the United Kingdom: Princeton University Press, 6 Oxford Street, Woodstock, Oxfordshire OX20 1TW

press.princeton.edu

Jacket art © igor_shmel - Fotolia.com

Library of Congress Cataloging-in-Publication Data
Agénor, Pierre-Richard.
  Development macroeconomics / Pierre-Richard Agenor and Peter J. Montiel. – Fourth Edition.
      pages cm
  Includes bibliographical references and index.
  ISBN 978-0-691-16539-4 (cloth : alk. paper) – ISBN 0-691-16539-4 (cloth : alk. paper) 1. Developing countries–
Economic conditions.   2. Development economics.   3. Macroeconomics.   I. Montiel, Peter.   II. Title.
  HC59.7.A7422 2015
  330.9172′4–dc23
                    2014030689

British Library Cataloging-in-Publication Data is available

This book has been composed in Garamond Premier Pro

Printed on acid-free paper. ∞

Typeset by S R Nova Pvt Ltd, Bangalore, India
Printed in the United States of America

10 9 8 7 6 5 4 3 2 1

To our fathers, the late Frédéric and Pedro,
for their support and guidance

Part II: Financial Policies

6 A Framework for Monetary Policy Analysis 182

Part III: Inflation Stabilization and Applied Models for Monetary Policy Analysis

11 Analytical Issues in Disinflation Programs   381

Part IV: Financial Openness, Capital Flows, and Financial Crises

13 Financial Integration and Capital Flows 476

14 Exchange-Rate Crises and Sudden Stops 514

15 Banking Crises and Twin Crises   550

16 Sovereign Debt Crises   572

Part V: Growth, Structural Reforms, and Political Economy

19   The Political Economy of Adjustment   675

Preface to the Fourth Edition

A significant analytical literature began to develop in the early 1970s to address a succession of macroeconomic woes that afflicted developing countries. By the 1980s, this literature had reached a level of rigor and sophistication comparable to that characteristic of macroeconomic analysis for high-income countries. However, these developments were not typically reflected in standard textbooks in macroeconomics (or open-economy macroeconomics), where the analysis was generally conducted with analytical frameworks designed for high-income economies. When issues relevant to developing countries were raised, there was often no attempt to adapt the theoretical framework to the particular conditions and structural characteristics of such countries.

The first three editions of *Development Macroeconomics* attempted to fill this gap. Their objective was to present a coherent, rigorous, and comprehensive overview of the analytical literature in this area. They reviewed attempts to formulate and adapt standard macroeconomic analysis to incorporate particular features and conditions characteristic of developing economies, and used a variety of analytical models to examine macroeconomic policy issues of concern to those countries. The analytical material was supplemented with empirical evidence on behavioral assumptions as well as on the effects of macroeconomic policies in developing countries.

The third edition was published in 2008, and was largely written during 2006 and early 2007. At the time, the Great Moderation was still ongoing in high-income countries, and the first indications of trouble in the U.S. housing market were just beginning to appear. For most developing countries the decade of the 2000s had been a prosperous one up to that point, with many countries experiencing rapid growth, low inflation, and favorable performance in their external accounts. Those positive outcomes were the results of the structural and macroeconomic reforms implemented during the 1990s (described in earlier editions of this book) as well as a very favorable external environment. Macroeconomic stabilization issues therefore tended to move to the background of policy concerns, giving way to concerns with structural issues such as poverty and income distribution, unemployment, reform of the legal system and the civil service, and improvements in accountability and transparency of government operations.

The outbreak of the Global Financial Crisis (GFC), which originated in the United States and reached its trough in late 2008 and early 2009, changed this situation dramatically.[1] The increased commercial and financial openness that most developing countries had embraced during the reforms of the 1990s in the successful pursuit of improved efficiency and growth had as its flip side heightened exposure to external real and financial shocks, and the shocks of both types generated by the GFC proved to be severe indeed. Once again, international turbulence aggravated the stabilization challenge for developing countries, and once again stabilization issues moved to center stage. Issues such as the appropriate management of the domestic financial system, policy responses to capital inflows and outflows, the formulation of exchange-rate policy, and the pursuit of monetary and fiscal policy regimes that simultaneously achieve medium-term credibility and short-run flexibility, have once again moved to the center of the policy debate. As in the past, these issues have emerged in distinctive form among developing countries, where greater commercial openness, more fickle capital flows, less well-established macroeconomic institutions and policy regimes, and significantly less confidence in macroeconomic management have all combined to produce especially acute challenges.

The new macroeconomic challenges developing countries are facing have made this an appropriate time to introduce a new edition of this book. In addition to a general updating of both empirical and analytical material, the third edition has been substantially revised to reflect the changed environment in which developing countries now operate. The coverage of issues such as public debt and the management of capital inflows has been expanded. New sections and chapters have also been added on fiscal discipline, monetary policy regimes, currency, banking and sovereign debt crises, currency unions, and the choice of an exchange-rate regime. In addition, the coverage of stabilization programs has been expanded to incorporate important recent experiences. A new chapter has been added on dynamic stochastic general equilibrium models (DSGEs) with financial frictions, to reflect how the new focus on financial issues in macroeconomics in the wake of the GFC has started to reshape our profession's thinking on the role of such frictions in both generating as well as propagating macroeconomic shocks. We have also added new material on macroprudential regulation as a tool to simultaneously preserve financial and macroeconomic stability.[2]

Instructors and students can visit the book's website at http://press.princeton.edu/titles/10494.html to find supplemental materials relating to the text.

---

[1] See Gorton and Metrick (2012) for an overview of the key facts and mechanisms behind the GFC.

[2] As in previous editions, we have refrained from discussing issues pertaining specifically to the reforming socialist countries of Eastern Europe and the former Soviet Union. In many regards, these countries share common structural features with developing countries, and as time passes since their initial stages of transition, this has become ever more so. Their current policy concerns (such as the management of capital flows, the stability of their financial systems, and the design of their monetary and fiscal policy regimes) are increasingly the same as those faced by policymakers around the developing world. The majority of the policy lessons derived in the book have therefore now become as pertinent to these countries as they are to countries that did not previously experience central planning.

In preparing this new edition, we have continued to benefit from comments and suggestions made by various readers of the first three editions. We also owe a special and continuing debt to our coauthors, current and former colleagues, and students, most notably Joshua Aizenman, Koray Alper, Nihal Bayraktar, Keith Blackburn, Otaviano Canuto, Jerry Caprio, Karim El Aynaoui, Eduardo Fernandez-Arias, Alejandro Izquierdo, Henning Jensen, Mohsin Khan, Prachi Mishra, Kyriakos Neanidis, Emmanuel Pinto Moreira, Luiz Pereira da Silva, Eswar Prasad, Carmen Reinhart, Issouf Samake, Murat Ucer, Nadeem Ul Haque, Carlos Végh, and Devrim Yilmaz, although none of them bears any responsibility for the views expressed in the book. Financial support from the University of Manchester and Williams College is also gratefully acknowledged. Finally, we would like to express our appreciation to the publishers of the *Handbook of International Macroeconomics*, the former *IMF Staff Papers*, the *International Journal of Central Banking*, the *Journal of Development Economics*, the *Journal of Economic Dynamics and Control*, the *Journal of International Money and Finance*, the *Journal of Macroeconomics*, the *Journal of Money, Credit, and Banking*, *Open Economies Review*, *Oxford Economic Papers*, and Princeton Essays and Studies in International Finance, for permission to use material from some of our previous contributions.

DEVELOPMENT MACROECONOMICS

Introduction and Overview

Developing and transition economies—including those, like South Korea, which are now classified as developed—now account for more than half of world output (evaluated at purchasing power parity exchange rates), and the great majority of the countries monitored by the International Monetary Fund belong to the developing world. Thus, not only does most of the world's production take place in developing countries, but it is also true that country-specific macroeconomic policy formulation is usually carried out in a developing-country context. Despite this, much of modern macroeconomics has been developed to address circumstances and issues that arise in the context of industrial nations. The extent to which the analytical tools and models appropriate for the analysis of industrial-country macroeconomic problems are able to offer guidance for the formulation and conduct of macroeconomic policy in developing nations is thus an important issue for economists and policymakers alike.

1   Scope of Development Macroeconomics

The title of this book suggests that there is something intrinsically different about macroeconomics in developing nations. If the standard textbook treatment of macroeconomics developed for industrial countries were adequate to deal with macroeconomic phenomena in the developing world, there would be little justification for "development" macroeconomics. The title also suggests that macroeconomic phenomena in individual developing countries are sufficiently similar that it is meaningful to speak of a "development macroeconomics" rather than the macroeconomics of, say, Brazil, Cameroon, or Nepal. We are aware that both implications are problematic: many economists would subscribe to the notion that the standard tools and models of macroeconomics can be used in developing nations, and others would argue that Brazil, Cameroon, and Nepal have so little in common that the very notion of a "development" macroeconomics lacks meaning.

These views are sufficiently compelling that the burden of proof falls on us. The view that development macroeconomics is distinctive may sound suspiciously like an old and discredited claim from the 1960s that modern neoclassical (micro) economics is not relevant to developing countries, because these countries are somehow "different" in unspecified ways or because these "traditional" societies are populated by nonoptimizing—and nonrational—economic agents. The perspective adopted in this book should not be confused with that view. We do not believe that economic agents in developing countries behave differently from those in industrial economies in ways that are inconsistent with the rational optimizing principles of neoclassical microeconomics: rather, we believe that they behave similarly to their industrial-country counterparts, but operate in a different environment. Our perspective is that the standard analytical tools of modern macroeconomics are indeed of as much relevance to developing countries as they are to industrial countries, but that different models are needed to analyze familiar issues.

This is so because "structural" differences between developing and industrial nations make many popular industrial-country models less than ideally suited to the analysis of developing-country macroeconomic phenomena. The word "structural" is in quotes because we do not want to suggest that the characteristics that we have in mind are unchanging and not amenable to reform. But they are given at a moment in time, and thus have to be taken into account by macroeconomists who focus on such countries. These differences in macroeconomic environment can be identified explicitly.[1] Moreover, the structural features that distinguish developing from industrial economies are sufficiently widespread throughout the developing world that it is indeed meaningful to speak of a distinct family of "development" macroeconomic models. The task of development macroeconomics is to uncover the implications of these differences in macroeconomic structure for macroeconomic behavior and policy.

Having said this, we would not wish to overstate our case. Good macroeconomics in any environment takes into account the institutional framework in which an economy operates. Economists who work mainly with high-income countries are familiar with the implications that different wage-setting mechanisms, budgetary institutions, exchange-rate and monetary policy regimes, as well as financial sector structures, can have for macroeconomic analysis. Our claim is simply that there are systematic differences in phenomena of these types between industrial and developing countries, and that there are enough similarities regarding such phenomena among developing countries themselves that it is useful to attempt to provide a unified treatment of macroeconomic issues in such countries.

2 Some Special Topics

In addition to differences in structure, a number of specific macroeconomic issues that have concerned economists and policymakers in developing nations have not

---

[1] Among the distinctive aspects of development macroeconomics are the roles of terms of trade shocks (implying the relevance of a three-good model), imported capital and intermediate goods, partial financial openness, informal credit markets, public sector production, working capital, labor market segmentation, income inequality, instability of policy regimes, and volatility.

been of similar importance in the industrial world. Again, these issues have not been specific to single countries, but have come up in different developing nations at various times, and have therefore been of widespread interest in the developing world. In short, not only the nature of the models used, but also the purposes to which they have been applied, distinguish macroeconomics in developing countries from that in industrial countries.

- Stabilization of High Inflation

High inflation has been more common in the developing world than in the industrial world over the past three decades. The developing world has also witnessed several alternative approaches to price-level stabilization, ranging from orthodox money-based programs relying on tight fiscal and monetary policies and exchange-rate policy geared to external balance, to "heterodox" programs based on tight aggregate demand policies supplemented by an exchange-rate freeze as well as some form of wage and price controls. The evaluation of this experience and its lessons for future stabilization efforts in the developing world and elsewhere have been important topics of research.

- Inflation Targeting and Monetary Policy Regimes

Since the 1990s, many countries—both high-income and developing—have begun to conduct monetary policies by managing short-term interest rates so as to hit a publicly announced inflation target. The design and implementation of inflation targeting regimes are at the forefront of the policy agenda in many developing countries at present, where recurrent terms of trade shocks, exchange-rate management, and uncertainties about monetary transmission pose special challenges to the implementation of such regimes.

- Exchange-Rate Management

The vast majority of high-income countries either maintain floating exchange rates or belong to a monetary union. Floating exchange rates and monetary unions also exist in developing countries, but many such countries continue to actively manage their exchange rates in pursuit of price stability or enhanced external competitiveness. The issues of how to map specific country circumstances onto an optimal exchange-rate regime, and how to operate a managed exchange rate, continue to figure prominently in the policy agenda for developing countries.

- Benefits and Costs of Currency Unions

In recent years, there has been growing interest in developing countries in forming currency unions. Developing-country currency unions already exist in West Africa and the Caribbean, and have been discussed in the context of MERCOSUR (a trade arrangement in Latin America), of the Chiang Mai initiative in Southeast Asia, and the East African Community (EAC). The benefits and costs of forming currency unions are thus very much on the developing-country macroeconomic policy agenda.[2]

● Fiscal Rules and the Procyclicality of Fiscal Policy

There has been much debate in recent years on whether explicit fiscal rules may help to achieve and maintain fiscal discipline. Like inflation targeting, such rules have been used in high-income and developing countries alike. However, they may have an especially important role to play in developing countries due to the higher frequency of sovereign debt crises and the pronounced procyclicality of fiscal policy in such countries.

● Managing Capital Flows

Large capital flows— in the form of both inflows and outflows—have severely complicated macroeconomic management among developing countries both in the early 2000s and in the wake of the GFC. The causes of inflows and outflows, their welfare implications, and appropriate policy responses have been the subject of much recent attention in the developing-country literature.

● Financial Crises

Although currency crises have afflicted both industrial and developing countries as capital mobility has increased, these events have been both more frequent and more severe in the latter group of countries. This issue remains at the forefront of the research agenda in development macroeconomics. The roles of self-fulfilling expectations and policymakers' preferences, the links among currency, banking, and sovereign debt crises, and the predictive content of various economic indicators, in particular, have generated a sizable literature in the past few years.

● Financial Sector Reforms

Since the 1990s, a large number of developing countries have undertaken wide-ranging reforms to their financial systems designed to enhance the role of financial intermediaries in channeling domestic saving, as well as to give the real economy a more outward orientation. The relationship between these reforms and macroeconomic stabilization has been a recurrent focus of attention, and has come to the

---

[2]Ishiyama (1975) and De Grauwe (2012) provide reviews of the literature on this topic.

fore since the GFC in the form of macroprudential regulation, which needs to be structured to the specific characteristics of financial sectors in developing countries.

- The Functioning of Labor Markets

Macroeconomists have begun to appreciate the role that the various types of labor market structures observed in developing nations may play in the analysis of the transmission mechanism of policy shocks. Particularly important phenomena are the incidence of labor market segmentation, the role of government regulations (in setting, for instance, the minimum wages for different categories of workers or in designing unemployment benefit schemes), and the low degree of labor mobility across sectors in the short run.

- Public Capital and Growth

The impact of public investment and public capital on growth has been the subject of much attention in recent academic research and policy debates in the developing-country context. Much academic research (both empirical and analytical) has focused, in particular, on the effects of public infrastructure (see Agénor, 2012*b*). It is now increasingly recognized that infrastructure generates externalities that go much beyond those typically emphasized in the early literature—notably with respect to education and health outcomes.

- Political Aspects of the Macroeconomy

In all countries, political factors play a pervasive role in economic life. The recent literature in macroeconomics has recognized the need to take these factors into account in attempting to understand many macroeconomic phenomena, such as inflation inertia, the setting of policy instruments, and the sustainability of reform programs. The interactions between the political objectives of policymakers and the design of economic policy are critically important in developing countries undergoing macroeconomic reform and remains a major area of investigation.

3 Overview of the Book

The book is organized into five parts. The first part focuses on macroeconomic relationships and differences in market structure between developed and developing nations. Chapter 1 identifies the structural features that, in our view, distinguish most developing countries from the textbook industrial-country model, describes the accounting framework, and discusses some key aspects of macroeconomic modeling for developing countries. Chapter 2 focuses on behavioral functions, exploring in particular how the specification of standard forms of such functions must be altered to reflect structural features that are either specific to or more pronounced in the developing world. This includes liquidity constraints in aggregate consumption, credit and foreign exchange rationing as well as debt overhang effects on production and private investment, uncertainty and irreversibility effects on investment decisions, and the effects of currency substitution on money demand.

The second part of the book focuses on financial (fiscal, monetary, and exchange-rate) policies in developing countries. Chapter 3 examines the nature of the government budget and its implications for fiscal management, as well as the links among fiscal rules, fiscal discipline, and public investment. Chapter 4 continues the analysis of fiscal issues by exploring the effects of fiscal deficits on a variety of macroeconomic variables. We examine, in particular, the link between budget deficits and the current account, whether fiscal contractions can be expansionary, and the implications of fiscal policy for labor market dynamics. The chapter concludes with an examination of the role of labor market segmentation and sectoral wage rigidity in the transmission of fiscal policy shocks.

Chapters 5, 6, and 7 focus on monetary policy. In recent years, financial liberalization in many developing countries has considerably reduced the adverse effects of financial repression.[3] Chapter 5 begins by reviewing the key characteristics of financial systems in countries (mostly middle-income) that have "moved away" from financial repression, with a particular focus on the role of banks, the credit market, and asymmetric information. Alternative analytical approaches to modeling credit markets at the macroeconomic level are also discussed, with an emphasis on the role of collateral and its implications for risk premia and borrowing constraints. We also provide a broad overview of the monetary transmission mechanism and discuss the implications of dollarization.

We then develop in Chapter 6 a simple static framework for studying the monetary transmission mechanism under fixed and flexible exchange rates, in the context of a small open economy with imperfect capital mobility. The model is used to study a variety of policy and exogenous shocks. Although behavioral equations are not derived explicitly from optimization problems in that chapter, we view this model (given its inherent general equilibrium nature) as a very powerful tool for basic monetary policy analysis in middle-income countries. More rigorous, micro-based models may not be demonstrably better from that perspective, particularly when it comes to discussing real-world policy issues. Precisely because its mechanics are relatively straightforward, it can be adapted to address a number of issues beyond those discussed in this chapter.

Chapter 7 focuses on monetary policy regimes, macroeconomic stability, and financial stability. We begin with a thorough discussion of the principles and mechanics of inflation targeting. In addition, we compare inflation targeting with alternative regimes—monetary targeting, exchange-rate targeting, and especially nominal

---

[3]Most of the material in previous editions dealing with informal financial markets is included in Supplement A, available online.

income targeting. The performance of inflation targeting regimes and challenges to inflation targeting are then discussed. We then turn our attention to financial stability issues in the context of an inflation targeting regime and the relationship between monetary policy and macroprudential policy—a set of prudential rules that focus on mitigating systemic risk and ensuring financial stability. Since the global financial crisis of 2008–2009, the role of macroprudential regulation, and whether or not monetary policy should incorporate a financial stability objective, have been at the forefront of the policy agenda in many countries, developed and developing alike. We conclude with a discussion of some issues that are at the forefront of the research agenda on monetary policy, namely, the role of asymmetries and nonlinearities, the need to account for uncertainty in the monetary transmission process, and the design of interest rate rules aimed at promoting both macroeconomic and financial stability.

Chapters 8 and 9 discuss the choice of exchange-rate regime in developing countries. After a brief review of the evidence on exchange-rate regimes, Chapter 8 discusses the role of credibility—or the lack thereof—on inflation under a fixed exchange-rate regime. We then discuss the role of exchange-rate bands in addressing the trade-off between flexibility and credibility, and currency unions, in which a country surrenders to a supranational authority its ability to manipulate its exchange rate.

Additional criteria for choosing an exchange-rate regime are discussed in Chapter 9. We first focus on the role of the exchange-rate regime in the presence of stochastic shocks. We then examine the various channels (including balance sheet effects) through which changes in the nominal exchange rate may exert contractionary effects on output. To the extent that these effects are large, they would tend to militate against a high degree of exchange-rate flexibility. After discussing moral hazard problems associated with pegged exchange rates, we conclude the chapter with an assessment of the pros and cons of various exchange-rate regimes.

High inflation has been the central problem confronting many well-known stabilization episodes in the developing world. Accordingly, the third part of the book focuses on inflation stabilization issues—in light of the features of developing economies described previously—and the type of models currently in use for studying the impact of monetary policy on inflation.[4]

Chapter 10 presents alternative models of the inflationary process, focusing on differences between "orthodox" and "new structuralist" approaches, and examines the macroeconomic dynamics associated with monetary and exchange-rate policy rules in a context where international capital mobility is imperfect. Chapter 11 then discusses three important sets of issues that have arisen in the context of exchange-rate-based disinflation programs (the behavior of output, real interest rates, and

---

[4]Supplement B, available online, reviews attempts at stabilizing high inflation in developing countries. Stabilization attempts are classified into the categories of money-based and exchange-rate-based programs, and we draw on the voluminous existing literature to summarize experience with alternative approaches to stabilization, including the literature on "heterodox" programs.

real wages) and presents an extensive discussion of the role of credibility factors in disinflation programs. We examine, in particular, several alternative proposals to enhance the credibility of stabilization plans, and the choice between nominal anchors.

The recent global financial crisis has made it abundantly clear that macroeconomic analysis no longer can abstract from financial factors—there is increasing evidence, for both developed and developing countries, to suggest they tend to be an important source of, and a critical propagation channel for, a variety of macroeconomic shocks. The crisis has also led to a shift in the type of questions that are being asked in macroeconomics, and to be able to answer these questions requires an increased emphasis on financial aspects (Woodford, 2010). At the same time, central banks have had to rethink their role and the models that they use for policy, to account not only for financial factors but also for macroprudential regulation, as well as interactions between monetary and macroprudential policies. Indeed, understanding how macroprudential tools operate requires improved understanding of the monetary transmission mechanism, and this in turn requires models in which credit market imperfections take center stage. Equally important, however, is the fact that macroprudential policy regimes may alter the monetary transmission mechanism, and understanding why and how this occurs is critical to the conduct of monetary policy.

From that perspective, Chapter 12 provides an introduction to the type of dynamic stochastic general equilibrium (DSGE) models that many central banks around the world are either using or currently developing. We first present the basic structure of (nonfinancial) DSGE models and then go on to focus on ways to incorporate the type of credit market frictions that are typical of middle-income countries, as discussed in Chapter 5. In that context, we discuss how monetary and macroprudential policies interact to shape macroeconomic outcomes and mitigate the degree of procyclicality of the financial system. Extensions of these models to account for open-economy considerations and macroprudential regulation, as well as their limitations, are also discussed.

Part 4 of the book focuses on financial openness, capital flows, and financial crises. Chapter 13 examines the links between international financial integration and capital flows. We begin by discussing the potential benefits and costs associated with financial integration. We then discuss standard explanations that are offered to explain episodes of large capital inflows into developing countries and review both the macroeconomic challenges that they raise and the policy responses that may be undertaken by the recipient countries.

An important issue for developing countries is their vulnerability to "sudden stops," that is, abrupt reversals in capital inflows, and their potential to generate currency and banking crises. These issues are discussed in Chapters 14 and 15. The first part of Chapter 14 presents the *first-generation* model of speculative attacks and currency crises, which emphasizes the role of inconsistencies among fiscal, credit, and exchange-rate policies for the viability of a fixed exchange-rate regime.

After considering various extensions of this model, the *second-generation* family of currency crisis models, which emphasizes the role of policy trade-offs and self-fulfilling expectations, is discussed.[5] The third part examines *third-generation* models of currency crises, which give a key role to financial structure fragility and financial institutions. The last part of the chapter presents alternative models of sudden stops, that is, large and abrupt reversals in capital inflows. Chapter 15 discusses various models of banking crises, links between currency and banking crises, and early warning systems for predicting financial crises.

Chapter 16 turns to sovereign debt crises. The history of sovereign borrowing has been fraught with crises, and many prominent default episodes over the past three decades have involved governments in developing economies. In this chapter we consider several analytical and empirical issues related to this experience, such as the assessment of whether a government's fiscal program is sustainable (in the sense of being consistent with solvency), the incentives governments may face to adopt sustainable fiscal programs in the absence of legal mechanisms to compel them to service their debts, and the consequences of sovereign default for the domestic economy.

Part 5 of the book focuses on medium-term issues in development macroeconomics and the political economy of adjustment. Growth and its determinants are considered in Chapter 17. The chapter begins by providing a brief overview of the traditional neoclassical theory of growth, in which growth in income per capita is largely exogenous. The discussion is then extended to consider alternative channels for long-run growth—in particular, the roles of human capital and economies of scale, as emphasized in endogenous growth theories. The importance for growth of fiscal policy, financial factors (including inflation), volatility, and inequality are also examined.

Chapter 18 examines the macroeconomic effects of trade and financial liberalization, as well as of issues associated with the sequencing and speed of reforms. The impact of trade reform on the dynamics of the labor market and unemployment are discussed first, followed by an examination of financial liberalization in the form of interest rate deregulation and the removal of restrictions on credit allocation. We also discuss the implications of financial liberalization for financial stability. The chapter closes with a detailed account of the debate on the proper sequencing of the liberalization and reform measures in these areas, integrating analytical arguments and empirical evidence on alternative sequencing options and the optimal speed of reform.

Chapter 19 focuses on the role of political factors in the adoption and abandonment of stabilization and structural adjustment programs in developing countries. It summarizes the major findings of existing research and discusses various models of the political business cycle. In that context, it provides an analytical framework for examining the link between exchange-rate policy and electoral cycles—an issue that has not received much attention but may prove particularly relevant for some

---

[5] Supplement D, available online, reviews the evidence on currency crises that occurred in Mexico (December 1994), Thailand (July 1997)—the latter triggering a full-blown financial crisis in Asia—Brazil (January 1999), and Argentina (January 2002). For coverage of these and several other important currency crises, see Montiel (2013*b*).

developing countries. We also discuss the role of institutions and property rights, the design of fiscal rules, and the link between corruption and financial integration.

4   Some Methodological Issues

Our attempt to provide coverage of both theory and policy at an accessible level has inevitably involved simplification of what are sometimes complex and controversial issues. As a result of sacrificing generality in the interest of clarity and analytical convenience, the conclusions may sometimes appear less compelling than they would otherwise be. Proofs of complicated results are presented in some important cases; in other cases the general properties of relevant models are described and appropriate references to the literature are provided. The mathematical background required for this book includes standard algebra, differential equation systems, and basic dynamic optimization techniques.

Many of the models developed in the book are not derived from "first principles," but are included because they have proved useful in understanding some key macro-economic issues. As is well known, ad hoc macroeconomic models can be criticized on a number of grounds. First, such models yield results that may be sensitive to arbitrary assumptions about private sector behavior. Second, they are susceptible to the Lucas critique, according to which decision rules should be policy-invariant (Lucas, 1976). Third, without an explicit description of the preferences of different categories of agents and the budget constraints that they face, such models are strictly speaking un-suitable for making welfare comparisons. Fourth, they often ignore intertemporal re-strictions implied by transversality conditions, that is, appropriate restrictions on the solution path associated with the optimization process. In contrast, models in which individual behavior is derived from an explicit intertemporal optimization problem serve a variety of purposes. First, optimizing models are suggestive of assumptions under which aggregate behavioral relations often postulated are consistent with individual maximizing behavior. Second, because they are built up on the basis of preferences that are invariant with respect to policy change, they provide vehicles for policy analysis that are less vulnerable to the Lucas critique. Third, they provide a nat-ural setting in which welfare consequences of macroeconomic policies can be assessed.

However, optimizing models with representative agents are themselves subject to a number of criticisms. Heterogeneity and aggregation issues are often avoided in these models, leading in some circumstances to misleading results. Macroeconomic models based on "representative" firms and consumers, for instance, cannot ade-quately address issues that arise from imperfect information, where heterogeneity is crucial.[6] Money is often introduced into these optimizing models in rather ad hoc

---

[6]The recent literature in macroeconomics has recognized the shortcomings of this approach and the need to introduce two or more kinds of agents, such as liquidity-constrained versus non-liquidity-constrained agents. See Kir-man (1992), who argues that representative-agent models provide only *pseudo micro-foundations* to macroeconomic behavioral equations. See also Greenwald and Stiglitz (1987) and Stiglitz (1992).

ways, so their immunity to the Lucas critique is not complete. Most important, the results and insights derived from ad hoc models can often be shown to carry through in more complex, optimizing models. Our overall strategy therefore has been to eschew, wherever possible, attempts to recast the existing developing-country macroeconomic literature in an optimizing framework, thereby avoiding overly complicated mathematical models in favor of simpler models with clear policy implications. In our analytical discussion of disinflation policies and in models of public capital and economic growth, however, we introduce a series of models with behavioral functions explicitly derived from an optimizing framework, thus showing how this type of analysis can be fruitfully applied to the case of developing countries.

In macroeconomics in general, an important methodological issue is the treatment of money. The very existence of money remains a vexing question in monetary economics, and it is not our purpose to get involved in this debate. Rather, in the models examined here, various operational assumptions are used to introduce money, in line with much of the literature on the "new" open-economy macroeconomics.[7] In one approach that has been followed frequently, money is introduced directly as an argument in the utility function, because agents are assumed to derive utility from holding cash balances in the same way that they derive utility from consuming real goods. A second approach views money as being necessary for transactions and held before purchases of consumption goods takes place; this leads to the popular cash-in-advance constraint (see Stockman, 1989). A third approach is to view money as facilitating transactions by reducing shopping time and thus acting as a substitute for leisure. This leads to the specification of a transactions technology directly in the private agents' budget constraint. Our preference, based largely on tractability, is to adopt the money-in-the-utility-function approach when using optimizing models because of the restrictive implications of the cash-in-advance constraint (it imposes, in particular, a zero-interest-rate elasticity of money demand). There are conditions under which choosing a particular operational formulation matters little (Feenstra, 1985), although, in general, alternative assumptions about the function of money do affect the predictions of macroeconomic models.

Despite our efforts, we have been unable to ensure that the notation used in the book is uniform and consistent. In different parts of the book, the same symbol sometimes carries different meanings. However, differences in notation never occur within a single chapter, and thus there should be limited risk of confusion. Throughout the book, the derivative of a function of one variable is denoted with a prime, while (partial) derivatives of a function with several variables are indicated with subscripts. Finally, in standard fashion, the derivative of a variable with respect to time is denoted by a dot over the variable.

---

[7]See Obstfeld (2001) for a broad perspective on the new open-economy macroeconomics, Lane (2001) for a review of various models, and Ganelli (2005) for a contribution focusing on fiscal policy.

Chapter 1

Economic Structure and Aggregate Accounts

This chapter describes the structural features that, in our view, distinguish most developing countries from the textbook industrial-country model, and provides an overview of some general analytical features of developing-country macroeconomic models. It takes a model-based perspective, focusing on the general structure of macroeconomic models for developing countries, including the accounting framework, the level of commodity disaggregation, and the particular role of labor markets. Chapter 2 will focus on specific components of macroeconomic models, examining evidence on the properties of private behavioral functions in developing nations.

This chapter is divided into four sections. Section 1.1 identifies the distinctive aspects of development macroeconomics. It also documents a range of regularities in macroeconomic fluctuations for developing countries. Section 1.2 sets out a general accounting framework consisting essentially of budget constraints for each type of agent typically appearing in a developing-country macroeconomic model, and defines several concepts that will prove useful later on. In Section 1.3, we consider how economic structure can be imposed on these accounting relationships by reviewing three alternative approaches to commodity disaggregation in an open economy: the Mundell-Fleming model, the "dependent economy" model, and a three-good structure distinguishing exportables, importables, and nontraded goods. Almost all macroeconomic models for developing countries rely on some variant of one of these approaches. Each of these three production structures is analyzed in both classical and Keynesian modes.

Section 1.4 looks at the labor market, a market that plays a central analytical role in all macroeconomic models, and the functioning of which is widely accepted to depend on country-specific institutional factors, both in the industrial- and developing-country contexts. As emphasized in Section 1.3, labor markets play a key role in determining the properties of an economy's short-run aggregate supply function. Accordingly, in Section 1.4 we examine the structural features of labor markets in developing nations. We focus on the short-run implications of these features, emphasizing the role of wage rigidity and the nature of labor market segmentation.

1 Economic Structure and Macroeconomics

The structural characteristics that differentiate a "representative" developing economy from the textbook industrial-country model cover a wide spectrum, spanning most of the standard components of a macroeconomic model. Many of these features are not shared by all developing countries, and some may be found among industrial countries as well. Nevertheless, we will provide evidence in this section that the features described below—all of which can be readily recognized as affecting macroeconomic behavior—systematically differentiate developing countries *as a group* from the standard textbook representation of an industrial-country economy. They include the nature of openness to trade with the rest of the world in both commodities and assets, the nature of financial markets, the characteristics of fiscal institutions and the government budget, the properties of the economy's supply function, the degree of income inequality, the stability of policy regimes, and the degree of macroeconomic volatility.

1.1 ■ Openness to Trade in Goods and Assets

1. Developing economies, like small industrial countries, tend to be much more open to trade in goods and services than are the major industrial countries.

A standard measure of openness is the trade share, that is, the sum of the shares of exports and imports in GDP. By this measure, developing nations tend to be substantially more open than the major industrial countries.[1] Openness to this extent, of course, limits at the outset the applicability of the closed-economy textbook industrial-country model to the developing-country context. Very few developing nations can even approximately be described as closed economies by this measure.

2. Developing countries typically have little control over the prices of the goods they export and import—that is, they typically face exogenous terms of trade.

This characteristic tends to distinguish developing countries even from small industrial countries. The exogeneity of the terms of trade for developing economies

---

[1] This group consists of Canada, France, Germany, Italy, Japan, the United Kingdom, and the United States. It should be noted that the degree of openness of the smaller industrial countries (such as Belgium) is typically much higher.

is suggested both by their small share in the world economy and by the composition of their exports.

Very few developing countries account for a significant portion of the world market even for the commodities in which their exports are heavily specialized. Moreover, various studies confirm that, with limited exceptions for particular goods, these countries continue to have limited individual influence over the prices at which they buy and sell. Exogenous terms of trade call into question the usefulness, for the analysis of many macroeconomic policy issues in developing nations, of the open-economy model that continues to be widely used in the industrial-country context, the Mundell-Fleming model. This model assumes endogenous terms-of-trade determination, with the domestic economy completely specialized in the production of a good over which it exerts significant market power. Instead, the production structure most suitable for the analysis of developing-country macroeconomic phenomena is likely to be the Salter-Swan "dependent economy" model or (given that terms-of-trade changes tend to be very important for such countries) a three-good model consisting of exportables, importables, and nontraded goods. Such a production structure permits a distinction to be drawn between the exogenous terms of trade and an endogenous real exchange rate, which is the central intratemporal macroeconomic relative price in these economies.

The importance for many developing nations of primary-commodity exports with exogenously determined prices accounts for an important source of macroeconomic instability in these countries. Prices of primary commodities tend to fluctuate quite sharply. Consequently, developing countries have faced highly unstable terms of trade at various times over the past two decades, with large asymmetric effects; for instance, in a study of the behavior of the real prices of thirty-six world commodities over the period 1957–1999, Cashin et al. (2002) found that price slumps typically last a lot longer than price booms.[2] Episodes of drastic changes in the terms of trade for these countries have often been dominated by changes in oil prices, but at times nonfuel commodities also undergo sharp fluctuations in price. Coupled with the relatively large share of exports and imports in domestic economic activity, such fluctuations in export prices represent substantial exogenous changes in national income from one year to the next, and constitute an important source of macroeconomic volatility for such countries.

3. The extent of external trade in assets has tended to be more limited in developing than in industrial countries, though this situation has recently begun to change in dramatic fashion for an important group of developing economies.

---

[2]There is, however, continuous debate on whether there has been a secular deterioration in primary-commodity prices relative to prices of manufactured goods—the so-called Prebisch-Singer thesis. For alternative views on this issue, see Bleaney and Greenaway (1993b) and Reinhart and Wickham (1994).

Perfect capital mobility is often used as the standard textbook assumption for industrial countries. In developing countries, capital controls have long been the rule, and although their effectiveness is questioned, the degree of capital mobility that characterizes economies that do not retain such restrictions remains far less than is assumed in textbook industrial-country models. Thus, unlike standard macroeconomic modeling for industrial countries, in the developing-country case the assumption of perfect capital mobility is generally inappropriate. Evidence on this issue is discussed in Chapter 13 and used in Chapters 6 and 10 to formulate appropriate models of the monetary transmission process and for the analysis of stabilization policies in developing countries.

4. Greater integration with international financial markets exposes many middle-income countries to abrupt reversals in capital flows, which exacerbate macroeconomic volatility.

For many developing countries, a large stock of gross external debt presents important macroeconomic challenges. Among highly indebted low-income countries, the problem emerged essentially because of borrowing by the government. The existence of such debt therefore has important implications for the level and composition of public expenditure. But among countries that have recently become integrated with international capital markets, external debt has tended to be incurred by the private sector. In this context, the policy challenges involve coping with potential macroeconomic overheating associated with a sudden inflow of capital, as well as with vulnerability to macroeconomic volatility induced by abrupt reversals in capital flows. As suggested by Caballero (2000), possible factors behind the high degree of volatility experienced by many middle-income developing countries are greater, but still weak, links with international financial markets (which limit the ability to borrow and lend to smooth shocks) and insufficiently developed domestic financial systems (which limit the speed of resource reallocation following an adverse shock and may magnify contractions in output).

1.2 ■ Exchange-Rate Management

5. In contrast to the major industrial countries, the vast majority of developing countries have neither adopted fully flexible exchange rates nor joined monetary unions.

Industrial countries are typically modeled either as operating flexible exchange rates or as members of a currency union, whereas in developing countries, officially determined rates, adjusted by a variety of alternative rules (loosely referred to as "managed" rates) predominate. A brief description of the nature of exchange-rate regimes in individual developing countries is presented in Chapter 8.

Exchange-rate regimes in developing countries have evolved toward greater flexibility since the collapse of the Bretton Woods system in 1973. However, in practice this has meant either more frequent adjustments of an officially determined parity or the adoption of market-determined exchange rates with extensive official intervention. The prevalence of intermediate exchange-rate regimes implies that issues relating to the macroeconomic consequences of pegging, of altering the peg (typically in the form of a devaluation), and of rules for moving the peg are of particular importance in developing countries. These issues are discussed in Chapters 8 and 9.

1.3 ▪ Domestic Financial Markets

> 6. Financial systems in many developing nations have been the subject of extensive deregulation in recent years. However, they continue to be dominated by banks. They also remain fragile and often exacerbate macroeconomic and financial volatility.

Although several developing countries have recently developed very large equity markets, such markets (as well as secondary markets for securities) continue to be small or nonexistent in many of them. Financial markets in the vast majority of developing economies continue to be dominated by a single type of institution— the commercial bank. Thus, the menu of assets available to private savers is limited. Moreover, even where equity markets have developed, they tend to be dominated by a few closely held firms and exhibit very low turnover ratios.

The commercial banking sector in developing countries has traditionally been heavily regulated: it has often been subjected to high reserve and liquidity ratios as well as legal ceilings on interest rates together with sectoral credit allocation quotas. Over the last two decades, however, many countries have taken steps to deregulate their financial markets, resulting in enhanced competition, greater access to foreign banks, and improved efficiency. Rather than being legally imposed, as before, credit rationing in the developing world tends now to be endogenously generated by information asymmetries, as is commonly taken to be the case in industrial countries.

Nevertheless, the financial system remains, in many countries, underdeveloped. In spite of the more limited range of financial assets available to savers in developing nations, monetization ratios (as measured by the ratio of a monetary aggregate to nominal GDP) are generally lower for such countries than for industrial countries. In large part because of the nature of the financial system, but also because of some of the other features mentioned previously, the specification of standard textbook macroeconomic behavioral relationships (decision rules) may need to be modified in the developing-country context. In particular, it becomes necessary to incorporate the implications of credit rationing in private decision rules when such rationing is present. This affects, for instance, private consumption, investment, and asset demand functions. The incorporation of these phenomena has been treated in different ways—by including, for instance, quantity constraints in consumption and investment equations. These issues are taken up in Chapter 2.

Another issue relates to the fact that the institutional prerequisites for successful liberalization—in the form of appropriate regulatory and supervisory mechanisms—have frequently not been in place, resulting in enhanced macroeconomic instability and severe crises involving interactions between the balance of payments and the financial system. As discussed in Chapters 14 and 15, the weakness of the institutional framework in many developing countries has made both the frequency and depth of such crises much more extensive in such countries than in industrial countries.

1.4 ■ The Government Budget

7. The composition of the government budget differs markedly between industrial and developing countries.

In many developing nations, the state plays a pervasive role in the economy. This role is exercised through the activities of not just the nonfinancial public sector (consisting of the central government, local governments, specialized agencies, and nonfinancial public enterprises), but also of financial institutions owned by the government. Regarding the nonfinancial public sector itself, the government tends to play a more active role in production than is the case in most industrial nations, and the performance of public-sector enterprises is often central in determining the fiscal stance.

Unfortunately, systematic data on the size and performance of the consolidated nonfinancial public sector are not available for a large number of developing countries. Published information tends to refer to the finances of the central government only. Even so, existing studies suggest that the central government absorbs a smaller fraction of output in developing than in industrial countries, and that the composition of spending differs between the two groups of countries. Developing nations devote a substantially larger fraction of expenditures to general public services, defense, education, and other economic services (reflecting the role of government in production) than do industrial nations, whereas the latter spend somewhat more on health and substantially more on social security.

As for revenue, the main source of central government revenue is taxation, but the share of nontax revenue in total revenue tends to be much higher in developing than in industrial countries. The collection of tax revenue in developing countries is often hindered by limited administrative capacity and political constraints (Bird and Zolt, 2005). One consequence of this is that direct taxation plays a much more limited role in developing than in industrial nations; as noted by Bird and Zolt (2005), the tax structure in most developing countries is dominated by taxes on consumption, whereas in industrial countries, income taxes account for the largest share and taxes on foreign trade are negligible. Of direct taxes, the share of tax revenue raised from individual incomes (which often amount to withholding taxes on labor income in the formal sector) tends to be much larger than that from corporations in the developing world, whereas the reverse is true in the industrial world. In part, this is the result of high collection costs on capital income. Trade taxes consist primarily of import rather than export duties in developing countries and are used more extensively in the poorest countries.

The political and administrative constraints on tax collection in developing nations, coupled with the limited scope for the issuance of domestic debt in many such countries, has led to greater reliance on seigniorage, and therefore to higher levels of inflation (on average), than in industrial countries. With few exceptions, industrial countries tend to raise fairly low amounts (less than 1 percent of GDP) of seigniorage revenue, whereas many developing countries have traditionally collected significant amounts in this fashion. As a result, inflation rates in developing countries tend to be higher than those that prevail in the industrial world.

The macroeconomic implications of budget institutions—the set of rules and procedures by which government budgets are prepared, revised, and approved by the legislature—has attracted renewed interest, particularly in Latin America (see Grisanti et al., 1998, and Agénor and Yilmaz, 2011). Four dimensions, in particular, have been much discussed: (*a*) the nature (and credibility effects) of the constitutional rules that can be implemented to impose constraints on the size of the fiscal deficit, such as balanced-budget rules; (*b*) the procedural rules (whether "collegial" or "hierarchical") that guide the elaboration of the budget by the executive branch, its approval by the legislative branch, and its execution; (*c*) the transparency of the budgetary process; and (d) the implications of alternative fiscal rules for growth. It has been argued, for instance, that in a volatile environment asymmetric balanced-budget rules (which prevent borrowing in "bad" times but impose no saving in "good" ones) may be overly restrictive—possibly forcing a procyclical reaction to adverse economic shocks. By contrast, imposing an upper limit on the debt-to-output ratio may be desirable, especially as a means to ensure fiscal sustainability (see Chapter 3). It has also been suggested that, in Latin America, better budgetary institutions are associated with lower fiscal deficits and stocks of public debt, but that at the same time high inflation and the volatility of economic activity have tended to reduce the ability of the budgetary process to impose fiscal discipline (Aizenman and Hausmann, 1995).

1.5 ▪ Aggregate Supply and the Labor Market

8. The large direct role that the state has played in production in many developing countries implies that the size and efficiency of the public capital stock figures prominently in the aggregate (or sectoral, under the three-good classification suggested earlier) production function(s).

Nonfinancial public enterprises have been important economic actors in most of the developing world. Public capital represents a much larger share of the aggregate capital stock in such countries than in developed nations. Although reliable capital stock data are not available for such countries, existing data do indeed show that in many countries the public sector accounts for a sizable share of total investment. Given the important role that the public sector has played in the development process, the medium-term supply-side effects of government spending often cannot be ignored.

In recent years, the traditional role of the public sector as producer in developing countries has received new scrutiny, and several developing countries have undertaken massive privatizations of nonfinancial public enterprises. Because of the relatively large weight of public sector production in developing countries relative to that in industrial countries, the macroeconomic implications of such measures have been particularly important in the developing-country context.

9. Imported intermediate goods play an important role in the aggregate (or, under the three-good structure, sectoral) production function(s) in developing countries.

Imported intermediate goods play a prominent role in economic activity in the developing world. Such goods account for a sizable fraction of all developing-country imports. In some countries the share of energy and non-energy intermediate imports can even exceed 70 percent. As a result, the difference between the value of domestic production and domestic value added tends to be larger in developing than in industrial nations. Through the cost of imported intermediates, the exchange rate has an important influence on the position of the economy's short-run supply curve. The role of imported intermediate goods means not only that exchange-rate changes will have short-run supply effects, but also that, in the presence of foreign exchange rationing, the availability of foreign exchange may have a direct effect on the position of the economy's short-run supply curve. The role of intermediate goods in the formulation of open-economy macroeconomic models is discussed in Chapter 12.

10. Short-run supply functions in developing economies may be significantly affected by working-capital considerations.

Because of the underdeveloped nature of the financial system, firms in many developing countries tend to rely on bank credit to finance their working-capital needs (labor costs and imported intermediate goods) prior to the sale of output. The existence of these needs implies that shocks to official interest rates and credit availability may play an important supply-side role in the short run; they imply, for instance, that a contractionary monetary policy may have short-run stagflationary consequences. This issue is discussed further in Chapter 6.

11. Although labor market institutions vary substantially across developing
countries, the informal sector continues to play an important role in the
determination of wages and employment in many of them.

The nature of short-run wage-setting behavior represents one of the key differences between the major schools of modern macroeconomics, but most participants
in these disputes acknowledge that country-specific institutional differences (such as
the prevalence of staggered overlapping contracts in the United States or synchronized wage bargaining in Scandinavia) are important in determining the economy's
short-run supply behavior. In this context, the role of economy-wide backward
indexation mechanisms in the context of disinflation programs has received much
attention. Despite the importance of labor market institutions in wage formation,
however, the (limited) empirical evidence available on wage-setting behavior in
developing countries suggests that many of them are characterized by a high degree
of real wage flexibility (Horton et al., 1994; Agénor, 2006*b*).

There is also increasing recognition of the macroeconomic role played by the
informal urban sector, which can account for a sizable proportion (50–60 percent,
and in some cases even more) of economic activity and total employment in developing countries, particularly in some parts of Asia, the Middle East, and Sub-
Saharan Africa. A consequence of the formal-informal dualism is the segmentation
of the urban labor market, which plays a crucial role in explanations of urban poverty,
unemployment, and underemployment in developing countries.

1.6 ▪ Stability of Policy Regimes

12. Policy regimes tend to change much more frequently in developing
countries than in industrial countries.

High inflation has been a symptom of policy instability and has frequently
been associated with policy uncertainty. In large parts of the developing world—
particularly in Latin America and Africa—policy instability has been endemic.
In part, this has been the result of indigenous factors. Political instability has
characterized many developing countries from the time of their independence, and
multiparty democracies with free elections remain rare. Changes in government not
infrequently signal changes in ruling ideologies and correspondingly in economic
policy regimes.

Policy uncertainty has been an important factor in the macroeconomics of
development, in many instances triggering currency substitution, capital flight,
exchange-rate crises, and the collapse of private investment. Uncertainty regarding
the policy environment—or the anticipation of future policy reversals—is a feature
that frequently must be built into developing-country macroeconomic models and
the design of macroeconomic reform programs.

1.7 ■ Macroeconomic Volatility and Fluctuations

13. As a result of many of the phenomena described previously, the macroeconomic environment in developing countries is often much more volatile than that in industrial countries.

A critical feature of the macroeconomic environment in many developing countries is instability of macroeconomic outcomes. The roots of this macroeconomic instability are both external and internal. Volatility in the terms of trade and in international financial conditions is directly transmitted to small developing countries that are price takers in international markets for goods and services as well as for financial assets. Coupled with the inflexibility of domestic macroeconomic instruments and political instability resulting in frequent and discrete changes in policy regimes in weak institutional settings, the macroeconomic experience of many developing countries has tended to be punctuated by a series of crises. These have had implications for a broad range of macroeconomic phenomena. Components of the government's budget, for instance, tend to be much less stable in developing countries than is typically the case in industrial countries. Instability has also characterized macroeconomic relative prices such as the terms of trade and real exchange rate. Most important, macroeconomic instability has resulted in unstable growth rates of real output as well as of private consumption. There is also evidence that macroeconomic volatility in some countries (particularly in Latin America) may have been compounded by a procyclical fiscal policy response—a tendency for government expenditure and fiscal deficits to increase during periods of economic expansion and to fall during recessions (Gavin and Perotti, 1997). Overall, boom and bust phenomena tend to be much more common in developing than in industrial countries; the higher degree of macroeconomic volatility that results from such phenomena are correspondingly more costly in the former group of countries. Indeed, using small calibrated models of archetype economies with a single representative consumer, Pallage and Robe (2003) found that macroeconomic volatility may entail large welfare losses and that even if consumers are only moderately risk averse, eliminating these fluctuations altogether may be preferable, from a welfare perspective, to a permanent increase in consumption growth.

14. In part as a result of greater exposure to volatility, features of macroeconomic fluctuations in developing countries differ significantly from those characterizing industrial countries. In particular, supply-side and external shocks play a more prominent role.

A related issue is that the sources of macroeconomic fluctuations differ significantly between industrial and developing countries. Developing countries not only experience shocks that differ in type and amplitude from those experienced in industrial countries, but also the domestic macroeconomic environment in which these shocks play themselves out tends to be quite different in the developing-country setting from what is typically assumed in industrial-country macroeconomic analysis. Thus, both the sources of macroeconomic shocks and their propagation mechanisms are likely to differ in the developing world.

Agénor et al. (2000) provide a systematic attempt to document a wide range of regularities in macroeconomic fluctuations for a group of twelve developing countries with diverse experiences with structural change and for which quarterly data of reasonable quality could be assembled (Colombia, Chile, India, Korea, Malaysia, Mexico, Morocco, Nigeria, the Philippines, Tunisia, Turkey, and Uruguay). The data they use cover a wide range of macroeconomic variables and include industrial output, prices, wages, various monetary aggregates, domestic private sector credit, fiscal variables, exchange rates, and trade variables. The relationship between economic fluctuations in these countries and two key indicators that proxy for economic activity in industrial countries—an index of industrial-country output and a measure of the world real interest rate—are also examined.

To examine economic fluctuations at business cycle frequencies, it is necessary to decompose all macroeconomic series into nonstationary (trend) and stationary (cyclical) components, because certain empirical characterizations of the data, including cross-correlations, are valid only if the data are stationary. Agénor et al. (2000) use three alternative filters, to examine the robustness of their results: a modified version of the Hodrick-Prescott filter (see Hodrick and Prescott, 1997); the band-pass filter, developed by Baxter and King (1999) and extended by Christiano and Fitzgerald (2003); and a nonparametric detrending method.

In line with much of the literature, Agénor et al. (2000) measure the degree of comovement of a series y_t with industrial output x_t by the magnitude of the correlation coefficient $\rho(j)$, $j \in \{0, \pm 1, \pm 2, ...\}$. These correlations are between the stationary components of y_t and x_t, with both components derived using the same filter. A series y_t is said to be procyclical, acyclical, or countercyclical, depending on whether the contemporaneous correlation coefficient $\rho(0)$ is positive, zero, or negative. In addition, the series y_t is said to be strongly contemporaneously correlated if $0.26 \leq |\rho(0)| < 1$, weakly contemporaneously correlated if $0.13 \leq |\rho(0)| < 0.26$, and contemporaneously uncorrelated with the cycle if $0 \leq |\rho(0)| < 0.13$.[3]

The cross-correlation coefficients $\rho(j)$, $j \in \{0, \pm 1, \pm 2, ...\}$ indicate the phase-shift of y_t relative to the cycle in industrial output. Again, in line with the existing literature, y_t is said to lead the cycle by j period(s) if $|\rho(j)|$ is maximum for a positive j, to be synchronous if $|\rho(j)|$ is maximum for $j = 0$, and to lag the cycle if $|\rho(j)|$ is maximum for a negative j.[4] To establish which correlations are significantly different from zero, they use the following result, established by Kendall

---

[3]The approximate standard error of these correlation coefficients, computed under the null hypothesis that the true correlation coefficient is zero, and given the average number of observations per country in the sample, is about 0.13.

[4]The pattern of lead-lag correlations and, in particular, the lag at which the peak positive correlation occurs, could be interpreted as indicating the speed with which innovations in variable y_t are transmitted to real activity x_t.

and Stuart (1967, pp. 292–93): the statistic $\ln[(1 + \rho)/(1 - \rho)]/2$, where ρ is the bivariate correlation coefficient between detrended output and detrended x_t, has an asymptotically normal distribution with a variance equal to $1/(T - 3)$, where T is the number of observations. With 27 observations, for instance, this implies that positive correlations of 0.32 or larger are significantly different from zero at the 10 percent level, and of 0.48 or greater are significant at the 1 percent level.

Their main findings can be summarized as follows:

- Output volatility, as measured by standard deviations of the filtered cyclical component of industrial production, varies substantially across developing countries, but is on average much higher than the levels typically observed in industrial countries. This is consistent with the results in Neumeyer and Perri (2005) and Calderón and Fuentes (2014).[5] There is also considerable persistence (as measured by autocorrelation coefficients) in output fluctuations in developing countries.

- Activity in industrial countries has a positive but relatively weak influence on output in developing countries, in contrast to the results of Hoffman (2007). Real interest rates in industrial countries tend to be positively associated with output fluctuations in developing countries; these results are consistent with those of Ahmed (2003), Neumeyer and Perri (2005), and Uribe and Yue (2006), regarding the impact of U.S. interest rates.

- Government expenditure is countercyclical. Government revenues are acyclical in some countries, and significantly countercyclical in others, a phenomenon that appears difficult to explain. The ratio of government spending to government revenue is negatively correlated with the business cycle.

- The cyclical behavior of nominal wages varies markedly across countries and is not robust across filters. By contrast, the evidence strongly supports the assumption of procyclical real wages.

- There is no consistent relationship between the stationary components of the levels of output and prices, or the levels of output and inflation. Variations in the price level and inflation are countercyclical in a number of countries and procyclical in a few.

- Contemporaneous correlations between money (measured through various monetary aggregates) and output are broadly positive, but not very strong—in contrast to the evidence for many industrial countries.

- The contemporaneous correlations between the velocity of broad money and industrial output are strongly negative across all filters for almost all the countries in our sample. This result is in contrast to the weakly procyclical behavior of velocity observed in most advanced industrial countries.

---

[5] Pallage et al. (2006) estimate that the percentage volatility of per capita consumption in developing countries (excluding countries affected by civil wars) has typically been two to six times greater than in industrialized countries over the past three decades.

- Domestic credit and industrial output are positively associated for some countries. However, the strength of the relationship between credit and output is not always robust to the choice of detrending procedure. In some countries, there is a negative correlation between these two variables.

- There is no robust correlation between merchandise trade movements (as measured by the ratio of exports to imports) and output. For some countries, the contemporaneous correlations are negative (irrespective of the filter used), whereas for others the contemporaneous correlations are strongly positive—the latter result possibly indicating that industrial output fluctuations are driven by export demand and that merchandise imports are not as sensitive to domestic demand fluctuations as in industrial countries.

- Cyclical movements in the terms of trade are strongly and positively correlated with output fluctuations.

- There are no systematic patterns in the contemporaneous correlations between nominal effective exchange rates and industrial output; in addition, for a majority of the countries under study, these correlations are not significantly different from zero. Similar results are obtained for real effective exchange rates.

These results highlight the importance of external and supply-side shocks in driving business cycles in developing countries. They are in line with those for a number of industrial countries and those obtained by Hoffmaister and Roldós (1997, 2001), Hoffmaister et al. (1998), Kalulumia and Nyankiye (2000), Kose and Riezman (2001), Kose (2002), and Frankel et al. (2013).[6] Subsequent research by Claessens et al. (2011) and Calderón and Fuentes (2014) confirmed a strong correlation between financial cycles (as measured by credit growth and changes in asset prices) and the business cycle.[7] Of course, using cross-correlation coefficients as indicators for evaluating the empirical relevance of demand-oriented, versus supply-oriented, macroeconomic theories can be problematic.[8] The results are also not uniform across countries. In particular, whereas negative price-output correlations in some countries provide support for "real" or supply-side interpretations of business cycles, countries where price-output correlations are positive would tend to support demand-side interpretations.

---

[6]Raddatz (2007) appears to be the only study that departs from the consensus on the quantitative importance of external shocks in explaining output volatility; however, he focuses only on low-income countries.

[7]Claessens et al. (2011) found that recessions are longer and deeper when accompanied by financial disruptions—the average output decline in a recession rises from 5 percent if there is no concomitant credit crunch to 8.5 percent if there is one. Likewise, recessions associated with equity price busts result in a 6.8 percent decline in output, on average, versus a milder 3.3 percent fall in the absence of such busts. Both studies document the procyclicality of bank financial intermediation.

[8]More generally, covariation among a set of variables may depend not only on the nature of the shocks that perturb the economy, but also (under rational expectations) on how long the lag is between perception (announcement) and realization (implementation) of the shock.

1.8 ■ Income Inequality

15. The degree of income inequality tends to be much higher in developing than industrial countries. Income inequality has important implications not only for growth and development, but also for short-run macroeconomic fluctuations.

The high degree of inequality that characterizes the distribution of income in developing countries is well documented (see, for instance, Todaro and Smith, 2011), and much research on the economic effects of income inequality focuses on its implications for growth and long-term development. However, a highly unequal distribution of income may also have short-run macroeconomic implications. Countries characterized by high levels of income inequality tend to have a small and volatile tax base; this may translate into high volatility of (public) expenditure and output (Woo, 2005). Indeed, Woo (2011) found evidence that more unequal societies are more likely to resort to more procyclical fiscal policies.

Alternatively, as argued by Iyigun and Owen (2004), the degree of income inequality can affect private consumption variability when the ability to obtain credit depends on income. Essentially, when income plays a role in access to credit, the distribution of income contains information about the fraction of individuals who are credit-constrained and cannot smooth consumption. If credit is so abundant that only the lower class is shut out of credit markets and unable to smooth consumption through downturns, greater inequality (a smaller middle class) is likely to be associated with more volatility in consumption. In contrast, if the availability of credit is limited to such an extent that both the lower and middle classes are credit-constrained, a more unequal distribution of income is likely to result in smoother aggregate consumption. Put differently, when credit-constrained and -unconstrained individuals have different consumption smoothing abilities, the distribution of wealth and income can affect aggregate fluctuations because it determines the fraction of individuals who are credit-constrained.

Using cross-country panel data for the period 1969–1992, Iyigun and Owen found that greater income inequality is associated with less consumption variability when per capita income is low. By contrast, when per capita income is high, greater income inequality is associated with higher consumption variability. Thus, the distribution of income affects the short-run variability of consumption differently in high- and low-income countries—possibly because financial development and availability of credit are positively associated with higher levels of per capita income, as discussed in Chapter 18.

2   A General Accounting Framework

All macroeconomic models are based on an accounting framework that, in essence, describes the intratemporal budget constraints confronting all types of economic agents included in the model. The accounting framework does little more than specify the set of choices that can be made by each type of agent. The model is completed by adding decision rules governing such choices and equilibrium conditions reconciling the decisions made by different agents. In this section we describe a general accounting framework on which a large variety of particular developing-country macroeconomic models can be based. Our purpose is to adapt the standard industrial-country macroeconomic accounting framework to the developing-country characteristics described earlier.

The first step is to specify the list of agents involved. We shall discuss in turn the nonfinancial private sector, the nonfinancial public sector, the central bank, and the commercial banking system.

2.1 ▪ The Nonfinancial Private Sector

In describing the budget and balance sheet constraints faced by the nonfinancial private sector, a logical place to begin is the specification of the menu of assets available to private agents. This is, of course, a function of the degree of sophistication of the country's financial system. In several middle-income developing nations, small equity markets have been in existence for some time, and in some countries government bonds are sold to the nonbank private sector and are traded in secondary markets. In the rest of the developing world, however, these phenomena are exceptional. Moreover, the analysis of macroeconomic models with these features is familiar from standard industrial-country applications (see Buiter, 1980). Thus, the portfolio choices that will be described here are those that are relevant for developing countries with less-developed financial systems.

The nonfinancial private sector holds both financial and real assets. Financial assets consist of currency issued by the central bank CU, deposits issued by the commercial banks D^p,[9] net foreign assets EF^p (where E is the exchange rate expressed as the domestic-currency price of foreign currency and F^p is the foreign-currency value of these assets), and loans extended by households in informal markets, L^h. Liabilities of the sector consist of credit from banks, L^p, and loans received through informal markets. The sector's real assets consist of inflation hedges (typically real estate or gold), with price p_H and quantity $\bar{H}$.[10] In the absence of equity markets, physical capital is treated in the same manner as human capital—that is, as a nonmarketable asset that generates income available to finance consumption—but does not represent a component of households' marketable portfolios. Under these conditions, the nonfinancial private sector's marketable net

---

[9]Of course, in many macro models it is desirable to disaggregate deposits into demand and time deposits, because demand functions for these assets differ in general. For the purpose at hand, though, this distinction is unimportant, because both types of deposits are assets of the private nonfinancial sector and liabilities of the banking system.

[10]We shall assume that there is a fixed stock of these, given by $\bar{H}$, so that whereas the price of such hedges can vary over time, their quantity cannot.

worth Ω^p is:

$$\Omega^p = CU + D^p + EF^p + p_H \bar{H} - L^p. \tag{1}$$

Note that loans extended through the informal market do not affect net worth, because these loans are transacted entirely within the nonfinancial private sector and thus do not represent a claim by the sector on the rest of the economy.

Differentiating (1) with respect to time yields

$$\dot{\Omega}^p = C\dot{U} + \dot{D}^p + \dot{E}F^p + E\dot{F}^p + \dot{p}_H \bar{H} - \dot{L}^p. \tag{2}$$

The change in the marketable net worth of the nonfinancial private sector consists of the purchase of financial assets (financial saving, denoted S^p) plus capital gains:

$$\dot{\Omega}^p = S^p + \dot{E}F^p + \dot{p}_H \bar{H}. \tag{3}$$

From (2) and (3), S^p is given by[11]

$$S^p = C\dot{U} + \dot{D}^p + E\dot{F}^p - \dot{L}^p. \tag{4}$$

Finally, financial saving is the difference between disposable income and expenditure on consumption and investment:

$$S^p = Y + i_d D^p + i^* EF^p - i_c L^p - \tau^p - C^p - I^p. \tag{5}$$

Equation (5) indicates that disposable income consists of factor income Y plus net interest income (income from deposits and foreign assets minus interest payments on bank credit, where the respective interest rates are given by i_d, i^*, and i_c), minus net taxes τ^p. Private consumption is C^p, and private investment is I^p.

2.2 ■ The Public Sector

2.2.1 *The Nonfinancial Public Sector*

The nonfinancial public sector is typically a substantial net financial debtor. Its debt is owed to the central bank (L^{bg}),[12] to commercial banks (L^{cg}), and to foreigners

---

[11] Note that financial saving does not include the acquisition of inflation hedges. This is because their stock is fixed and they are held only by the nonfinancial private sector, so they cannot be acquired from agents outside the sector.

[12] L^{bg} denotes *net* credit to the public sector from the central bank. As such, it is the sum of public sector bonds held by the central bank plus bank credit in the form of, say, overdrafts, minus public sector deposits.

$(-EF^g)$.[13] The nonfinancial public sector's net worth, Ω^g, is thus given by

$$\Omega^g = EF^g - L^{bg} - L^{cg}. \tag{6}$$

The change in Ω^g over time obeys

$$\dot{\Omega}^g = \dot{E}F^g + E\dot{F}^g - \dot{L}^{bg} - \dot{L}^{cg}, \tag{7}$$

which consists of new borrowing by the nonfinancial public sector, $-S^g$, plus capital gains on net foreign assets:

$$\dot{\Omega}^g = S^g + \dot{E}F^g. \tag{8}$$

From equations (7) and (8), S^g consists of

$$S^g = E\dot{F}^g - \dot{L}^{bg} - \dot{L}^{cg}. \tag{9}$$

Total new borrowing by the nonfinancial public sector must be equal to the overall fiscal deficit:

$$-S^g = C^g + I^g + i_b L^{bg} + i_c L^{cg} - i^* EF^g - \tau^p - \tau^g, \tag{10}$$

where τ^g represents transfers from the central bank to the nonfinancial public sector and i_b the interest rate paid on loans received from the central bank.

2.2.2 The Central Bank

The central bank's balance sheet will prove to play a central role in many of the models examined in this book. Under present assumptions, it is given by

$$\Omega^b = ER^* + (L^{bg} + L^{bc}) - M, \tag{11}$$

where R^* represents net foreign assets of the central bank, L^{bc} credit from the central bank to commercial banks, and M high-powered money (or the monetary base), defined as the sum of currency held by the nonfinancial private sector and reserves of the commercial banking system held in the vaults of the central bank, RR:

$$M = CU + RR. \tag{12}$$

---

[13]The minus sign is introduced here because we shall adopt, for uniformity, the convention that the symbol F denotes a net claim on the rest of the world.

As with the other sectors, the change in Ω^b can be written as

$$\dot{\Omega}^b = E\dot{R}^* + \dot{E}R^* + (\dot{L}^{bg} + \dot{L}^{bc}) - \dot{M}, \tag{13}$$

or

$$\dot{\Omega}^b = S^b + \dot{E}R^*, \tag{14}$$

where S^b is given by

$$S^b = E\dot{R}^* + (\dot{L}^{bg} + \dot{L}^{bc}) - \dot{M}. \tag{15}$$

S^b is referred to as the "quasi-fiscal" surplus (or, when negative, deficit).[14] It is the difference between the central bank's earnings and its expenditures. The former consist of interest earnings on net foreign exchange reserves, credit to commercial banks, and net credit to the nonfinancial public sector; the latter consist of transfers to the government τ^g:

$$S^b = i^* E R^* + i_b(L^{bg} + L^{bc}) - \tau^g, \tag{16}$$

where, for simplicity, we assume that the central bank charges the same interest rate i_b on its loans to the government and to commercial banks.

Equation (15) can be rewritten in a useful way to derive the sources of base money growth:

$$\dot{M} = \dot{L}^{bg} + E\dot{R}^* - S^b + \dot{L}^{bc}. \tag{17}$$

Equation (17) indicates that the sources of base money growth consist of central bank financing of the nonfinancial public sector, balance-of-payments surpluses, quasi-fiscal deficits, and credit extended by the central bank to the private banking system.

2.2.3 The Consolidated Public Sector

The consolidated public sector consists of the nonfinancial public sector and the central bank. Using (6) and (11), the financial net worth of the consolidated public sector, Ω^{ps}, is given by

$$\Omega^{ps} = \Omega^g + \Omega^b = E(F^g + R^*) + (L^{bc} - L^{cg}) - M, \tag{18}$$

---

[14]A discussion of quasi-fiscal deficits is provided in Chapter 3.

which changes over time according to

$$\dot{\Omega}^{ps} = E(\dot{F}^g + \dot{R}^*) + (\dot{L}^{bc} - \dot{L}^{cg}) - \dot{M} + \dot{E}(F^g + R^*). \tag{19}$$

From (9) and (15), its financial saving consists of

$$S^{ps} = S^g + S^b = E(\dot{F}^g + \dot{R}^*) + (\dot{L}^{bc} - \dot{L}^{cg}) - \dot{M}, \tag{20}$$

so that (19) can alternatively be written as

$$\dot{\Omega}^{ps} = S^{ps} + \dot{E}(F^g + R^*). \tag{21}$$

The overall financial surplus of the consolidated public sector is given by, from (10) and (16):

$$S^{ps} = S^g + S^b = (\tau^p - C^g - I^g) + i_b L^{bc} + i^* E(F^g + R^*) - i_c L^{cg}. \tag{22}$$

Other useful concepts of the overall public sector accounts are the primary surplus (consisting of the non-interest portion of the overall public sector surplus) and the operational surplus, which excludes the inflation component of nominal interest transactions and thus consists of the primary surplus plus real interest payments. These concepts will be examined in more detail in Chapter 3.

2.3 ■ The Commercial Banking System

The commercial banks' financial net worth Ω^c is the difference between bank assets and liabilities that have already been identified:

$$\Omega^c = L^p + L^{cg} + RR - D^p - L^{bc}, \tag{23}$$

which changes over time according to

$$\dot{\Omega}^c = \dot{L}^p + \dot{L}^{cg} + R\dot{R} - \dot{D}^p - \dot{L}^{bc}. \tag{24}$$

Because commercial banks are assumed to hold neither foreign assets nor inflation hedges, the change in banks' net worth over time simply consists of

$$\dot{\Omega}^c = S^c = \dot{L}^p + \dot{L}^{cg} + R\dot{R} - \dot{D}^p - \dot{L}^{bc}, \tag{25}$$

and S^c is given by

$$S^c = i_c(L^p + L^{cg}) - i_d D^p - i_b L^{bc}. \tag{26}$$

2.4 ■ Aggregate Relationships

Summing (1), (18), and (23), the economy's aggregate net worth Ω consists of its net international indebtedness (net claims on foreigners, F) plus its stock of inflation hedges:

$$\Omega = \Omega^p + \Omega^{ps} + \Omega^c = E(F^p + F^g + R^*) + p_H \bar{H} = EF + p_H \bar{H}, \qquad (27)$$

which grows over time according to

$$\dot{\Omega} = E\dot{F} + \dot{E}F + \dot{p}_H \bar{H}. \qquad (28)$$

Equation (28) can be derived by either differentiating (27) or summing (2), (19), and (24). From (8), (21), and (25), it can also be written as

$$\dot{\Omega} = S^p + S^{ps} + S^c + \dot{E}F + \dot{p}_H \bar{H} = S + \dot{E}F + \dot{p}_H \bar{H}, \qquad (29)$$

where S represents national financial saving. Equations (28) and (29) imply

$$S = E\dot{F}, \qquad (30)$$

which indicates that national financial saving represents the net accumulation of claims on the rest of the world.

By summing (5), (22), and (26), S can also be expressed as

$$S = Y + i^* EF - (C^p + C^g) - (I^p + I^g), \qquad (31)$$

which indicates that national financial saving is the difference between gross national product, $GNP = Y + i^* EF$, and domestic absorption, $DA = (C^p + C^g) + (I^p + I^g)$, which is the current account of the balance of payments, CA. The negative of national financial saving as used here is what is commonly referred to as foreign saving (the current account deficit). Some familiar macroeconomic identities can be derived from (31). First, defining total absorption by the nonfinancial public sector as $G = C^g + I^g$, and replacing S by CA yields the national income accounting identity:

$$GNP = C^p + I^g + G + CA. \qquad (32)$$

Second, defining total national saving S_T (the sum of aggregate financial and real saving) as the difference between national income and total consumption ($S_T = GNP - C^p - C^g$) yields the flow-of-funds version of (32):

$$CA = S_T - (I^p + I^g), \qquad (33)$$

which is the standard identity linking total saving $(S_T - CA)$ to total investment $(I^p + I^g)$. Third, replacing S by its value in (30), we have, after sectoral disaggregation:

$$E\dot{R} = (GNP - C^p - I^p - G) - E(\dot{F}^p + \dot{F}^g). \tag{34}$$

Equation (34) is the familiar balance-of-payments identity, expressed in domestic-currency terms. The left-hand side corresponds to reserve accumulation by the central bank (the overall balance of payments). The first term on the right-hand side is the current account and the second is the capital account.

3 Production Structure in an Open Economy

To convert the set of identities described in the preceding section to a macroeconomic model, economic behavior and equilibrium conditions must be specified. First, however, the degree of sectoral disaggregation must be determined. As suggested in the introduction, most open-economy macroeconomic models adopt one of three basic options.[15] In this section we describe each of these in turn.

3.1 ▪ The Mundell-Fleming Model

The most common analytical framework adopted in modeling the production structure in open-economy models of industrial countries is the Mundell-Fleming framework.[16] This framework assumes that the economy specializes in the production of a single (composite) good, which is an imperfect substitute for the single (composite) good produced by the rest of the world. The law of one price holds for each individual good, so the domestic-currency price of the foreign good is equal to the foreign-currency (international) price (which we denote P^*) multiplied by the domestic-currency price of the foreign currency, E. Similarly, the foreign-currency price of the domestically produced good is its domestic-currency price, P, divided by the domestic-currency price of the foreign currency. Domestic residents demand both the domestic and foreign goods, as do foreign residents. Thus, the foreign good is the home economy's importable good, and the domestic good is its exportable good. The relative price of the foreign good in terms of the domestic good is referred to as

---

[15] A fourth option is the approach proposed by McCallum and Nelson (2000), in which imports are not treated as finished consumer goods but rather as intermediate goods, which are used (together with domestic intermediate goods) in the production of the domestic final good. As discussed in Chapter 12, this approach is particularly relevant for developing countries, where trade in raw materials accounts for a very large share of imports.

[16] See Mundell (1963) and Fleming (1962). The Mundell-Fleming model is presented in all standard texts on open-economy macroeconomics. For a particularly thorough description, see Frenkel and Razin (1987).

the domestic economy's terms of trade or its real exchange rate. The two terms are interchangeable in the Mundell-Fleming model.

The key property of the Mundell-Fleming model is that the domestic economy's terms of trade are endogenous, because the home country is small in the market for its importable good but large—in the sense of possessing some degree of monopoly power—in the market for its exportable good. The latter implies that changes in domestic demand for the exportable good will affect its relative price or level of production. The mechanism through which it does so, and the extent to which equilibrium is restored through relative price or output adjustments, depends on the exchange-rate system and the short-run supply function for the exportable good. To illustrate the determination of the terms of trade, we examine a simple short-run Mundell-Fleming model that focuses only on the production side of the economy, that is, the goods and labor markets. We consider only the case of fixed exchange rates.[17]

Let y represent output of the domestic good, a the level of domestic absorption, and b the trade balance, all measured in units of the domestic good. Also, let $z = E P^*/P$ denote the terms of trade. Because domestic and foreign goods are imperfect substitutes, the trade balance can be written as

$$b = b(\overset{+}{z}, \overset{-}{a}), \quad -1 < b_a < 0, \tag{35}$$

where the sign of the derivative with respect to the terms of trade assumes that the Marshall-Lerner condition holds.[18] The equilibrium condition of the market for domestic goods is given by

$$y = a + b(z, a). \tag{36}$$

The nature of the equilibrating mechanism depends on the supply side of the economy. In the short run, domestic output is determined by a production function that exhibits diminishing returns to labor:

$$y = y(n), \quad y' > 0, \quad y'' < 0, \tag{37}$$

where n is the level of employment. Let w denote the nominal wage, and ω the real wage in terms of the importable good. Then the real wage in terms of exportables is $w/P = (w/E P^*)(E P^*/P) = z\omega$, and labor demand n^d is given by

---

[17] See Dornbusch (1980) for a description of the Mundell-Fleming model under flexible exchange rates.

[18] That is, if $x = x(z, \cdot)$ and $m = m(z, a, \cdot)$ represent the behavior of real exports and real imports, respectively, so that $b = x - zm$, assuming $b_z > 0$ requires, at an initial value of $b = 0$, that $\eta_{xz} + \eta_{mz} - 1 > 0$, where η_{xz} and η_{mz} are demand elasticities for exports and imports, respectively.

the profit-maximizing condition

$$y'(n) = z\omega \Rightarrow n^d = n^d(z\omega), \tag{38}$$

where $n^{d'} = 1/y'' < 0$. Finally, labor market equilibrium requires:

$$n^d(z\omega) = \bar{n}, \tag{39}$$

where $\bar{n}$ is the exogenous supply of labor.

This model can be solved for z as a function of a under classical or Keynesian conditions. In the former case, the labor market clears, so (39) can be used to replace n by $\bar{n}$ in (37), leaving (36) in the form

$$y(\bar{n}) = a + b(z, a), \tag{40}$$

which determines z implicitly as a function of a. The effect on z of an increase in a is given by $dz/da = -(1 + b_a)/b_z$, which has a negative sign: an increase in domestic absorption increases the domestic price level, so that the terms of trade improve.[19] In the Keynesian mode, ω is exogenous and the labor market-clearing equation (39) does not hold. Substituting the demand for labor n^d from (38) into (37) allows us to write (40) in the form

$$y[n^d(z\omega)] = a + b(z, a), \tag{41}$$

which implies that, in this case, the relationship between z and a is $dz/da = (1 + b_a)/(\omega y' n^{d'} - b_z) < 0$, because the numerator is positive and the denominator negative. A change in domestic absorption has a smaller effect on the terms of trade in the Keynesian case (the denominator of dz/da is larger in absolute value) because a change in z elicits a supply as well as a demand response in this case, so a given change in z is more effective in eliminating excess demand in the market for domestic goods.

The simultaneous determination of internal and external balance in this model is illustrated in Figure 1–1. The CC schedule depicts the set of combinations of z and a compatible with equilibrium in the market for home goods that prevails when the model operates in classical mode. The slope of CC reflects the dependence of the terms of trade on domestic spending in the Mundell-Fleming model, as derived above. The BB schedule depicts the set of combinations of z and a compatible with a given trade balance outcome, say a sustainable trade balance level b_0. It is derived from (35). Its slope is positive and given by $-b_a/b_z$. Points above BB correspond to an improvement in the trade balance relative to b_0, and points below imply a deterioration relative to b_0. Equation (36) implies that the economy must always lie along CC, where the market for domestic goods clears. Given a level of absorption

---

[19]Given the solution for z, (39) determines the real wage in terms of importables, ω.

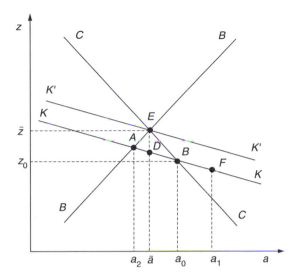

Figure 1–1 ▪ Internal and External Balance in the Mundell-Fleming Model

a_0, CC determines the value of z required to clear the market for domestic goods, and the negative slope of CC follows from the sign of dz/da, derived above. In the figure, the equilibrium value of the terms of trade corresponding to a_0 is z_0. The trade balance at point B corresponding to (a_0, z_0) exhibits a deficit in excess of b_0. Thus, in the classical case, B represents a point of internal, but not external, balance. The simultaneous achievement of external and internal balance, at point E, requires a reduction in domestic absorption from a_0 to $\tilde{a}$.

The commodity-market equilibrium schedule in the Keynesian mode is derived from (41). Its position depends on the initial value of the real wage measured in terms of importables, ω. Graphically, a change in ω causes the commodity-market equilibrium locus to shift vertically. The shift is downward for an increase in ω and upward for a reduction in ω. In both cases the magnitude of the shift is less than proportional to the change in ω.[20] The Keynesian commodity-market equilibrium locus that passes through the initial point B is labeled KK. Since z is more responsive to a in the classical than in the Keynesian mode, KK is depicted in the diagram as flatter than CC. In the Keynesian case internal balance may not hold at B since, although the goods market clears by assumption, the labor market equilibrium condition (39) may not hold.[21] Increasing absorption to a_1 would move the economy to F, achieving internal balance. However, this implies further departure from

---

[20]The magnitude of the shift is given by $dz/d\omega = -z/(\omega + b_z)$, so the proportional shift is $(dz/d\omega)(\omega/z) = -\omega/(\omega + b_z)$.

[21]For a given value of ω, there is a unique value of z that satisfies (39), so this equation holds only at a single point along KK, say at F. Along KK to the northwest of F, labor demand falls short of labor supply, and to the southeast of F, labor demand exceeds supply.

external balance. An adjustment of absorption to $\bar{a}$, as in the classical case, would fail to restore external balance (since the terms of trade would not deteriorate sufficiently) and move the economy further away from internal balance. Finally, external balance could be restored at point A, but this would move the economy further away from internal balance.

What is required in the Keynesian model is the simultaneous adjustment of absorption and the real wage in terms of importables. In the classical model, the latter is achieved through nominal wage flexibility. In the Keynesian model, it must be achieved by an adjustment in the nominal exchange rate. A reduction of absorption from a_0 to $\bar{a}$, coupled with a nominal exchange-rate depreciation sufficient to shift KK to $K'K'$, would simultaneously achieve external and internal equilibrium at point E.

3.2 ■ The "Dependent Economy" Model

The endogeneity of the terms of trade in the Mundell-Fleming model is inconsistent with the evidence cited earlier that developing countries tend to be small in the market for their exports, so that such countries in fact exert very little control over the world prices of their exports. If the terms of trade are instead taken as exogenous, but the Mundell-Fleming assumption of a single domestically produced good is retained, then domestic demand conditions would have no effect on either the price or output of the domestic good, since that good would effectively face an infinitely elastic world demand at a domestic-currency price determined by the law of one price. The only role for domestic demand in this case would be to determine the excess demand for the domestic good, and thus the trade balance.

This situation is unrealistic, because many domestic goods and services indeed cannot be sold abroad; transportation costs and commercial policies make such domestic goods uncompetitive in foreign markets. However, such goods and services may not be imported either, since trade barriers such as those mentioned may render their foreign equivalents uncompetitive in the domestic market. Goods and services of this type that can neither be sold nor bought abroad are referred to as nontraded. Nontraded goods are produced at home for sale at home.

The dependent economy model, according to Swan (1960) and Salter (1959), contains two domestic production sectors, one producing traded and the other non-traded goods. The traded goods sector consists of both importables and exportables. They can be aggregated into a single sector because the terms of trade are taken to be both exogenous, as suggested above, and constant, so that exportables and importables can be treated as a single Hicksian composite good. What matters for macroeconomic equilibrium is the total value of domestic production and con-sumption of traded goods, rather than either exportables or importables separately. Domestic residents are assumed to spend on both traded and nontraded goods.

As already indicated, in the dependent economy model the terms of trade are constant. The law of one price holds for traded goods, so in the small-country case the domestic economy faces infinitely elastic world demand for exportables and supply of importables at their respective world market prices. The key relative price in the dependent economy model is the real exchange rate, defined as the price of traded goods in terms of nontraded goods, or $z = P_T/P_N$, where P_T is the domestic-currency price of traded goods—measured in terms of exportables, importables, or any combination of these goods—and P_N is the price of nontraded goods. Production in each sector is described by a linearly homogeneous sectoral production function in capital and labor, but in the short run each sector's capital stock is fixed. Labor, on the other hand, is homogeneous and intersectorally mobile. In the short run, supply of output in each sector depends on employment in that sector:

$$y_h = y(n_h), \quad y_h' > 0, \; y_h'' < 0, \quad h = N, T, \tag{42}$$

where y_T and y_N denote, respectively, the value of domestic production of traded and nontraded goods, and n_T and n_N correspond to employment in each of the two sectors. Demand for labor from each sector is inversely related to that sector's product wage:

$$n_T^d = n_T^d(\omega), \quad n_N^d = n_N^d(z\omega), \quad n_T^{d\prime}, n_N^{d\prime} < 0, \tag{43}$$

where $\omega = w/P_T$ is the real wage in terms of traded goods. Substituting (43) in (42) yields the sectoral supply functions:

$$y_T^s = y_T^s(\omega), \quad y_N^s = y_N^s(z\omega), \quad y_T^{s\prime}, y_N^{s\prime} < 0. \tag{44}$$

Domestic demand for traded and nontraded goods is taken to depend on the relative prices of the two goods, given by the real exchange rate, and on total domestic absorption measured in terms of traded goods, a, given by

$$a = a_T + z^{-1}a_N. \tag{45}$$

Thus,[22]

$$a_T = a_T(\overset{-}{z}, \overset{+}{a}), \quad 0 < \partial a_T/\partial a < 1 \tag{46}$$

---

[22] As with the previous model, real absorption is taken as exogenous here for expository purposes. For a fully specified dependent economy model, see Montiel (1985), Buiter (1988), and Brock and Turnovsky (1994).

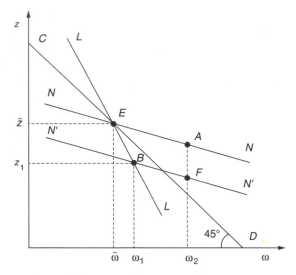

Figure 1–2 ▪ Classical Equilibrium in the Dependent-Economy Model

$$a_N = a_N(\overset{+}{z}, \overset{+}{a}), \quad 0 < \partial a_N/\partial a = 1 - \partial a_T/\partial a < 1. \tag{47}$$

The trade balance b is determined by the value of the domestic excess supply of traded goods:

$$b = y_T^s(\omega) - a_T(z, a). \tag{48}$$

Equilibrium in the nontraded goods market requires

$$y_N^s(z\omega) = a_N(z, a). \tag{49}$$

Finally, the labor market-clearing condition is given by

$$n_T^d(\omega) + n_N^d(z\omega) = \bar{n}. \tag{50}$$

Unlike the Mundell-Fleming model, the classical version of this model is not recursive. Rather than determining the real exchange rate first, and from that the real wage, the real exchange rate and the real wage must be solved together from conditions (49) and (50): that is, the equilibrium values of ω and z are those that simultaneously clear the labor and nontraded goods markets. The solution is portrayed graphically in Figure 1–2. The locus LL depicts the set of combinations of ω and z that satisfy the labor market equilibrium condition (50), and NN is the corresponding locus for the nontraded goods market (49). The slope of LL

is $-(n_N^{d'} + n_T^{d'})/n_N^{d'} < -1$, and that of NN is $-y_N^{''}n_N^{d'}/(y_N^{''}n_N^{d'} - \partial a_N/\partial z) > -1$ which, although greater than -1, is negative.[23] The line CD, with slope -1, is inserted in the figure for reference. To the right (left) of LL, the real wage is too high (low), and excess supply (demand) prevails in the labor market. Similarly, below (above) NN the real exchange rate is excessively appreciated (depreciated), and excess supply (demand) prevails in the market for nontraded goods. The equilibrium combination of z and ω is given by $(\bar{z}, \bar{\omega})$, where LL and NN intersect (point E).

Consider now the effects of an increase in absorption, a. The nontraded goods locus NN shifts down to a position like $N'N'$, because equilibrium in this market requires a more appreciated real exchange rate when aggregate spending is higher. The new equilibrium moves to B, with an appreciated real exchange rate and an increase in the real wage. Notice that, because B lies below CD, the proportional reduction in z exceeds the proportional increase in ω. This means that the product wage in the nontraded goods sector falls. Thus, labor is released from the traded goods sector and absorbed by the nontraded goods sector. For this reason, and because the appreciation of the real exchange rate shifts demand toward the traded good, the trade balance deteriorates.

The graphical analysis of the determination of internal and external balance can be conducted in a manner similar to that of the Mundell-Fleming model by solving (50) for ω in terms of z. The slope of this relationship is that of the LL locus in Figure 1–2—it is negative and greater than unity in absolute value. Substituting the resulting expression into (48) and (49) yields a pair of equations that determine the trade surplus and the nontraded goods market equilibrium as functions of z and a, in the manner of Figure 1–1.

The Keynesian form of this model takes ω to be exogenous. In Figure 1–2, if the initial value of ω is ω_2, the market for nontraded goods will clear at point A, and the labor market will be characterized by a situation of excess supply, because point A is to the right of LL. An increase in a would move the economy to point F, which would reduce the extent of excess supply in the labor market since the nontraded goods sector would expand, in this case not by drawing labor away from the traded goods sector but rather by absorbing unemployed workers. The analysis of internal and external balance in this case can use (49) and (50) as they are, treating ω as given. Because a nominal devaluation would alter ω, it would cause shifts in the Keynesian version of both (49) and (50) in z-a space.

3.3 ■ A Model with Three Goods

The dependent economy model incorporates an important developing-country stylized fact described earlier—the exogeneity in the terms of trade—but it does not capture another feature of such economies also mentioned previously: variability in

---

[23]Both slopes are calculated around initial values $z = \omega = 1$.

the terms of trade as a source of macroeconomic shocks. It does not do so, of course, because to aggregate exportables and importables into a composite good means that the terms of trade are taken as fixed. Allowing changes in the terms of trade, then, requires disaggregating the traded goods sector into separate exportables (identified with the symbol X) and importables sectors (symbol I); that is, it requires the use of a three-good model.

In this subsection we examine a simple version of such a model, one in which the exportable good is not consumed at home. This assumption would represent a reasonable approximation to reality in an economy whose exports are dominated by a primary commodity. As suggested earlier, despite an increase in the relative importance of manufactured goods in recent years, this continues to be the case in many developing countries.

In the three-good model, production takes place in three sectors, with sectoral production functions given by

$$y_h = y_h(n_h), \quad y_h' > 0, \ y_h'' < 0, \quad h = X, I, N. \tag{51}$$

Labor demand is given by

$$n_X^d = n_X^d(\omega\Theta^{-1}), \quad n_I^d = n_I^d(\omega), \quad n_N^d = n_N^d(z\omega), \tag{52}$$

with $n_h^{d'} < 0$. In this equation Θ denotes the terms of trade, given by P_X/P_I; z the real exchange rate measured in terms of importables, so that $z \equiv P_I/P_N$; and ω the real wage in terms of importables. P_X, P_I, and P_N represent the domestic-currency prices of exportables, importables, and nontraded goods, respectively. The first two are given by the law of one price, so that $P_X = EP_X^*$ and $P_I = EP_I^*$. By contrast, P_N is determined domestically.

In general, changes in the terms of trade can be expected to have sectoral resource reallocation effects on the supply side of the economy, of the type already seen in our discussion of the dependent economy model. In addition, however, because terms-of-trade changes affect a country's real income, they can be expected to have demand-side effects as well. To incorporate these effects in the simplest possible fashion, we shall assume that domestic absorption measured in terms of importables, denoted a, is given by

$$a = a(\overset{+}{\Theta}, \overset{+}{g}). \tag{53}$$

Thus, absorption depends positively on the terms of trade as well as on the shift parameter g. As in the previous section, sectoral supply functions can be derived by substituting the sectoral labor demand functions given in (52) into the sectoral production functions in (51). Equilibrium in the market for nontraded

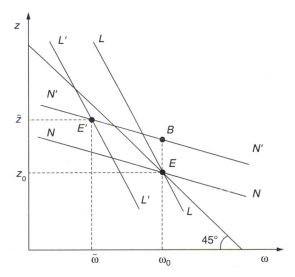

Figure 1–3 ■ Effects of a Negative Terms-of-Trade Shock in the Three-Good Model

goods requires

$$y_N(z\omega) = a_N(\overset{+}{z}, \overset{+}{a}), \quad 0 < \partial a_N/\partial a < 1. \tag{54}$$

The trade surplus measured in units of importables b is given by the domestic excess supply of traded goods:

$$b = \Theta y_X(\omega\Theta^{-1}) + y_I(\omega) - a_I(z, a). \tag{55}$$

Finally, the full employment condition is

$$n_X^d(\omega\Theta^{-1}) + n_I^d(\omega) + n_N^d(z\omega) = \bar{n}. \tag{56}$$

Like the others, this model can be analyzed in the classical or Keynesian mode. For a given value of the terms of trade, the analysis exactly duplicates that of the dependent-economy model and will not be repeated here. What distinguishes this model from the previous ones, however, is its ability to handle changes in the terms of trade. Accordingly, the rest of this section examines the effects of terms-of-trade changes on the real exchange rate and the real wage in the three-good model. In the classical mode, these variables are determined simultaneously by (54) and (56). The diagrammatic apparatus is presented in Figure 1–3, where the curves NN and LL depict (54) and (56), respectively, and the determination of equilibrium at point E is exactly as in Figure 1–2.

Consider now a deterioration in the terms of trade brought about by a reduction in P_X. In this case, Θ falls on impact. From (53), absorption also falls. This means that the real exchange rate must depreciate to maintain equilibrium in the market for nontraded goods; that is, the NN locus shifts up in Figure 1–3, to $N'N'$. At the same time, the product wage rises in the exportables sector, inducing this sector to shed labor as it contracts production. To maintain full employment at a given value of ω, the excess labor must be absorbed by the nontraded goods sector. This can happen only if z falls, so LL shifts down. The outcome, as shown in Figure 1–3, is a new equilibrium with a depreciated real exchange rate and reduced real wage, at point E'.

In the Keynesian case, the real wage in terms of importables cannot change. Thus, the new equilibrium is at point B, rather than E'. The situation is characterized by unemployed labor, since point B lies to the right of the labor market equilibrium locus $L'L'$. The real exchange rate depreciation in the Keynesian case is less than that in the classical case. To maintain full employment under Keynesian conditions requires a nominal devaluation that would reduce the real wage from ω to $\bar{\omega}$, thus moving the economy from point B to point E' along $N'N'$.

An important application of the model described in this section is to the "Dutch disease" phenomenon, which refers to the macroeconomic implications of the existence of a booming sector.[24] A "boom" in the present context can be represented by the reverse of the shock just analyzed, that is, an increase in P_X. In this case, the real exchange rate would *appreciate* (z would fall), and as a consequence ω would rise. The result would be a *contraction* of output in the importables sector. Because this outcome arises in part due to the larger spending on nontradables induced by the favorable income effects associated with the terms-of-trade shock, it will be more pronounced the larger such effects are. In developing countries, the "Dutch disease" phenomenon has often been aggravated by expansionary macroeconomic policy responses to favorable terms-of-trade shocks. Such responses have proved difficult to reverse when the shocks that induced them proved to be transitory.

4   The Structure of Labor Markets

The study of labor markets in development economics focuses traditionally on medium- and long-run issues, such as the determinants of rural-to-urban migration, the growth in the urban labor force and the associated rise in unemployment, and the effects of education on levels of earnings. Some contributions have recognized the crucial role that the structure of labor markets may play in determining the effects of trade reforms and structural adjustment policies.[25] However, labor markets also

---

[24]The term "Dutch disease" arose out of concern about de-industrialization in the Netherlands as a result of North Sea oil discoveries. A comprehensive survey of the literature on this issue is provided by Corden (1984).

[25]See, for instance, Edwards (1988), who emphasizes the role of labor reallocation across sectors.

play an important role in the transmission of macroeconomic policy shocks. The different effects of policy and external shocks in the classical and Keynesian versions of the models analyzed in the previous section, for instance, are entirely attributable to differing assumptions about the degree of nominal wage flexibility. More generally, the degree of wage inertia determines to a large extent the effect of fiscal, monetary, and exchange-rate policies on real output. In particular, as will be shown in Chapter 9, real wage resistance plays an important role in determining whether or not a nominal devaluation is contractionary. The purpose of this section is to examine the main empirical characteristics of labor markets in developing countries and highlight their macroeconomic implications, with a particular emphasis on the short-term determination of wages and the nature of labor market segmentation. We begin by outlining some structural features of these markets. We then examine the correlation among output, wages, and unemployment. We conclude by discussing the nature and sources of labor market segmentation in developing countries.

4.1 ■ Functioning of Labor Markets

Labor markets in developing nations differ in important ways from those operating in industrial countries. Key structural differences are the importance of the agricultural sector in economic activity (which implies that employment tends to display a marked seasonal pattern), the importance of self-employment, and irregular work activities. These structural differences imply that standard labor market concepts used in the industrial world (such as employment and unemployment) do not necessarily have the same meaning here and must be interpreted with care.

Development economists typically distinguish three sectors in the labor market in developing countries (see Agénor, 2006b). The first is the rural sector, which is characterized by a large share of self-employed persons and unpaid family workers. The second segment is the informal urban sector, characterized by self-employed individuals or small, privately owned enterprises producing mainly services and other nontradables. Activities in this sector rely mostly on the provision of labor services by owners and their families, but occasionally also on paid labor without any formal employment contract. Job insecurity is pervasive, wages are highly flexible, and workers get very few benefits from their employers. Legal minimum wage laws do not apply or are not enforced, and labor unions play a very limited role. The third segment of the labor market is the formal urban sector, consisting of medium and large enterprises (including state-owned firms) that hire workers on the basis of formal contracts. Workers and employers are subject to various labor market regulations. Employers, in particular, must provide a variety of benefits (such as a pension plan, health insurance, and relative job security) to their workers.[26] Labor unions often

---

[26]In some countries, the formal sector is not entirely confined to urban areas; wage earners bound by explicit contracts may also be employed in agriculture.

play an important role in the determination of wages, and legal minimum wage laws exist, albeit enforced with varying stringency across professions and countries.

A number of studies have attempted to identify the determinants of the size of the formal and informal sectors. Dabla-Norris et al. (2008) develop a general equilibrium model where the quality of the legal system (or the likelihood of detecting informal activity) manifests itself not only in better access to government-provided services, as in some other studies, but in enforcing better compliance with existing entry regulations. In particular, better legal quality implies a higher probability of detection of informal entrepreneurs who avoid entry regulation requirements, such as licensing fees and compliance with labor standards. Their cross-country regressions, based on firm-level data, highlight the importance of the quality of the legal system in explaining the size of the informal sector.[27] An important aspect of legal quality relates to the incidence of credit market imperfections, as measured by the cost of enforcement of financial contracts. Numerical experiments performed by Antunes and Cavalcanti (2007) suggest that these costs can be as important as regulation costs in explaining the size of the informal sector in developing countries.

Along the same line, Straub (2005) argued that the benefits of being formal can be viewed as consisting of access to two categories of public goods. First, those making production possible (as, for instance, police and judicial protection against crime) and/or enhancing productivity (such as public infrastructure). Second, those which, by ensuring the enforcement of property rights and contracts, secure access to specific markets, where they make interactions between private agents possible and more efficient. The effect of the second category of public goods is of particular importance in the credit market. His analysis shows that the decision of an entrepreneur to become formal or not depends on the amount of available initial capital (which affects the ability to pledge collateral), the relative efficiency of credit markets (as measured by the ability to recover loans through the judiciary), and the cost of registering formally. Other factors include the volatility of the economic environment and the existence of labor rigidities (such as minimum wage requirements or dismissal costs).

In many developing countries, agriculture still employs the great majority of the labor force in rural areas, and the "modern" sector is small. The functioning of rural and urban labor markets differs considerably in at least three respects. First, the heterogeneity and diversity of production in urban areas requires a wider variety of competence and skills among workers. Second, seasonal and climatic effects on production in urban areas are less pronounced than in rural areas. Third, urban production activities are more concentrated geographically than in rural agriculture.

---

[27] Auriol and Warlters (2005) suggest that high barriers to entry to the formal sector may be consistent with a deliberate government strategy for raising tax revenue. By generating market power, and hence rents, for the permitted entrants, market entry fees foster the emergence of large taxpayers. The rents can then be confiscated by the government through entry fees and taxes on profits. However, this view presumes that confiscation can occur at a low administrative cost—which is at variance with much of the evidence on tax collection costs in these countries (see Bird and Zolt, 2005).

As a result of the importance of the rural and urban informal sectors, the proportion of wage earners in total employment tends to be much lower than in the industrial world, although there are large variations across countries and regions. Wage employment (which tends to be positively correlated with the urbanization rate and the size of the public sector) accounts for about 10 percent of total employment in some low-income Sub-Saharan African countries, but as much as 80 percent in some middle-income Latin American countries. The share of informal sector employment in total urban employment is sizable in many developing countries—particularly in some parts of Asia, the Middle East, and Sub-Saharan Africa—and may vary between 40 and 60 percent (Agénor, 2006 *b*; and Schneider, 2011).

4.2 ■ Open and Disguised Unemployment

Available data on employment and unemployment in developing countries are not very reliable and often are not comparable across nations.[28] Another problem is that published measures of unemployment are based mostly on unemployed workers looking for jobs in the formal sector, and do not include underemployed workers in the informal and rural sectors—the so-called disguised unemployment. The effective excess supply of labor may thus be understated. In addition, open unemployment may show a rising trend despite strong employment growth, as industrialization combined with migration from rural to urban sectors frequently means that previously underemployed workers are registered as openly unemployed while they are looking for industrial jobs. The available evidence suggests, in fact, that underemployment is far more pervasive than open unemployment. In some countries, open and disguised unemployment vary anywhere from 25 to 60 percent of the labor force (Agénor, 2006*b*).

Data on the rate of output growth and the measured unemployment rate for developing countries indicate in some cases a relatively close inverse correlation for some countries, but also a rather weak relationship for others, and the correlation seems to vary erratically over time. The absence of a stable "Okun's law" (see for instance Blanchard and Fischer, 1989, pp. 8–9) may be the result of spillover effects across different segments of the labor market, as discussed below.

4.3 ■ Indexation and Wage Rigidity

From a macroeconomic perspective, a critical aspect of the functioning of labor markets is the degree of real wage rigidity. In developing countries, a variety of labor

---

[28]Most estimates are derived from labor force surveys and, less frequently, general censuses of population. The International Labor Office has devoted considerable effort to establishing adequate measures of unemployment in developing countries.

market regulations—minimum wages, indexation laws, employment-protecting measures such as labor tenure laws, restrictions on labor mobility, government-imposed taxes, and large, powerful trade unions—may inhibit real and nominal wage flexibility.[29] Although the relative importance of these factors varies considerably across regions, countries, and over time, an endemic feature has been implicit or explicit wage indexation. In high-inflation countries in particular, wage indexation is an essential feature of the labor market.

Indexation clauses, under normal circumstances, allow for adjustment of wages for productivity changes as well as past inflation. Procedures differ among countries and over time in three main respects: the interval between wage adjustments, the degree of indexation to inflation, and the nature of adjustments for productivity changes. In some countries, the law permits the productivity adjustment to be negotiated freely between workers and employers; in others, the adjustments are specified by the government. In some countries, the frequency of wage adjustments has tended to increase with the rate of inflation; many economists view the frequency itself as one of the structural elements in the inflationary process (see Dornbusch et al., 1990; Simonsen, 1983; and Parkin, 1991). In some cases the degree of indexation to inflation is a function of the wage level, with over-indexation at certain wage levels and under-indexation at others. The average degree of indexation has also been used as a means of altering inflationary expectations and reducing the inertial element in inflation, as was the case in Argentina (see Online Supplement B).

The manner in which indexation operates is important for the transmission of policy shocks to output, inflation, and unemployment. The traditional view of indexation suggests that it helps to insulate output and employment from monetary (demand) shocks, but not from real (supply) shocks.[30] A high degree of real wage rigidity would therefore insulate the real sector from aggregate demand shocks. However, a high degree of wage indexing at the sectoral level may also distort policy-induced price signals, such as a nominal devaluation, and may hamper the reallocation of resources. Moreover, indexed contracts are often viewed as the root cause of inflation persistence and stickiness of inflationary expectations. Institutional reforms aimed at reducing the degree of indexation of wages may thus be a critical component for ensuring the credibility and ultimate success of disinflation programs (see Chapter 11).

Despite the widespread existence of wage indexation, however, real wages in many countries seem to be more flexible than is generally assumed. Horton et al. (1994), in particular, summarize the findings of a large World Bank study on labor

---

[29] Labor unions, for instance, have long been viewed as the main culprits in explanations of wage rigidity in Latin America. Over the past few years, institutional reforms in some countries have greatly reduced their bargaining power and ability to impose wage settlements on employers.

[30] See Blanchard and Fischer (1989, pp. 523–25). Carmichael et al. (1985) provide a detailed discussion of wage indexation rules in an open-economy context. Most of the analytical literature assumes the existence of ex ante indexation. In practice, wage indexation is generally ex post, with the current wage adjusting to past changes in prices. Fischer (1988) examines the role of ex post wage indexation in the conduct of disinflation programs.

markets and adjustment in developing countries that provides quantitative evidence supporting the existence of a relatively high degree of real wage flexibility in Latin America and Asia; Agénor (2006*b*) reviews further evidence along these lines. The persistence of unemployment in many cases, therefore, cannot be attributed to excessive real wage rigidity but may result from aggregate demand effects associated with declining real wages and output market imperfections. The first type of effect is known as the Keynes-Kalecki effect (Taylor, 1991). It relies on the assumption that the propensity to save is considerably lower for wage earners than for profit recipients. To the extent that a fall in real wages is accompanied by a fall in the share of wages in national income, aggregate demand will also fall. Unemployment may therefore persist despite a substantial reduction in real wages. The second type of effect may occur as a result of imperfect competition in product markets, even if labor markets are competitive and real wages flexible (Layard et al., 1991). Unfortunately, empirical attempts at discriminating between these alternative hypotheses are scarce.

Although the prevalence of real wage rigidity may be questionable, there is a widespread consensus that nominal wage rigidity is a pervasive feature of the labor market in many developing countries. Nominal wage inertia results from a variety of factors, including lagged indexation, staggered and overlapping wage contracts, and slow adjustment in inflationary expectations. The existence of multiperiod labor contracts appears to be the prevalent source of nominal wage rigidity in some middle-income countries. We will develop a formal specification of nominal wage contracts that captures both backward- and forward-looking indexation rules in Chapter 11.

4.4 ■ Labor Market Segmentation

Labor market dualism in developing countries may be related to the sector of employment or the production structure (agriculture and industry, or traditional and modern), the geographic location of activities (rural and urban, as indicated earlier), the legal nature of activities (formal and informal), or the composition of the labor force (skilled and unskilled workers). These disaggregations do not in general correspond to the distinctions discussed earlier between tradable and non-tradable sectors or to the three-good production framework, but may prove useful for macroeconomic analysis. This is because a frequent implication of dualism is labor market segmentation, which can be defined as a situation where observationally identical workers receive different wages depending on their sector of employment. In particular, restrictions on occupational mobility between sectors—resulting from institutional barriers or other factors—may prevent workers in the "low-wage" segment from having full access to a job in the "high-wage" segment held by workers with similar qualifications, even if wages are fully flexible. If there were no barriers, workers in the low-wage sector would enter the high-wage sector and bid wages down in that sector, until sectoral earnings were equalized. Labor market segmentation may also be induced by the existence of sectoral wage rigidities, which lead to demand-constrained employment.

The best-known model of labor market segmentation in developing nations is the migration model of Harris and Todaro (1970). The main objective of the model is to explain the persistence of rural-to-urban migration, despite the existence of widespread urban unemployment in developing countries. A key element of the model is the equality of expected (rather than actual) wages as the basic equilibrium condition across the different segments of the labor market. Specifically, Harris and Todaro assume that rural workers, in deciding to migrate, compare the current wage in agriculture w_A to the expected urban wage w_U^a, which is calculated by multiplying the prevailing wage w_U—assumed fixed as a result of, say, minimum wage legislation—by the urban employment ratio, which measures the probability of being hired. In equilibrium, the Harris-Todaro hypothesis yields

$$w_A = w_U^a = w_U \frac{n_U}{n_U + L_U}, \tag{57}$$

where n_U is urban employment and L_U the absolute number of workers unemployed in urban areas. The Harris-Todaro model has been extended in a variety of directions over the years (see Agénor, 2006b). Particularly interesting developments have been the explanation of urban wage rigidity as a result of efficiency considerations rather than government regulations. According to these hypotheses, real wage cuts lower productivity because they directly reduce incentives to provide effort (Stiglitz, 1982), raise incentives to shirk, increase the quit rate (and thus turnover costs, as emphasized by Stiglitz, 1974), and reduce loyalty to the firm. For instance, workers' effort may depend positively on the wage paid in the current sector of employment (say, the urban sector), relative to the wage paid in other production sectors (the agricultural wage) or the reservation wage. In such conditions each firm will set its wage so as to minimize labor costs per efficiency unit, rather than labor costs per worker. The wage that minimizes labor costs per efficiency unit is known as the efficiency wage. The firm hires labor up to the point where its marginal revenue product is equal to the real wage it has set. A typical case, then, is that aggregate demand for labor, when each firm offers its efficiency wage, falls short of labor supply, so that involuntary unemployment emerges.[31] Efficiency wage theories are particularly useful for explaining why modern-sector firms pay more than the market-clearing wage in models with segmented labor markets. They predict the existence of noncompetitive wage differentials even in the absence of unions and other institutional constraints.

The importance of accounting for market segmentation and the degree of wage flexibility for a proper understanding of the effects of macroeconomic shocks on unemployment can be illustrated with a simple graphical analysis. Consider a small

---

[31] There is a voluminous literature on developed countries that views involuntary unemployment as the result of efficiency wages. See Blanchard and Fischer (1989) and Layard et al. (1991).

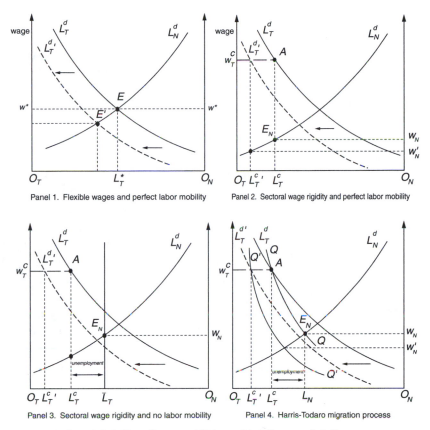

Panel 1. Flexible wages and perfect labor mobility

Panel 2. Sectoral wage rigidity and perfect labor mobility

Panel 3. Sectoral wage rigidity and no labor mobility

Panel 4. Harris-Todaro migration process

Figure 1–4 ▪ Labor Mobility, Sectoral Wage Rigidity, and Adjustment

open economy producing traded and nontraded goods using only labor, the supply of which is given. The determination of wages and employment under four different assumptions regarding labor market adjustment is shown in Figure 1–4. In all four panels the horizontal axis measures total labor available to the economy, $O_T O_N$. The vertical axis measures the wage rate in the economy, which is either uniform across sectors or sector-specific. The demand for labor in the traded (nontraded) goods sector is represented by the downward-sloping curve L_T^d (L_N^d). Consider first panel 1, which is based on the assumption that wages are perfectly flexible and labor perfectly mobile across sectors. The initial equilibrium position of the labor market obtains at point E, where the economy-wide wage rate is equal to w^*, labor employed in the traded goods sector is $O_T L_T^*$, and labor used in the production of nontraded goods is $L_T^* O_N$.

In panels 2, 3, and 4, the wage rate in the traded goods sector is fixed at w_T^c (above the economy-wide, market-clearing wage) whereas wages in the nontraded goods sector remain flexible.[32] The panels differ in the underlying assumptions regarding the degree of intersectoral labor mobility. In panel 2, labor can move freely across sectors, as in panel 1. Perfect labor mobility, together with wage flexibility in the nontraded goods sector, prevents the emergence of unemployment. The initial equilibrium obtains at point A in the traded goods sector, corresponding to an employment level of $O_T L_T^c$, and at point E_N in the nontraded goods sector, with wages equal to w_N and employment to $L_T^c O_N$. In panel 3, labor is completely immobile within the time frame of the analysis. The labor force in the traded goods sector is equal to $O_T \bar{L}_T$, while the supply of labor in the nontraded goods sector is measured by $\bar{L}_T O_N$. Since sectoral labor supply is completely inelastic and wages cannot adjust in the traded goods sector, unemployment will typically emerge in that sector. The situation depicted in panel 3 indicates that employment in the traded goods sector is equal to $O_T L_T^c$ and unemployment to $L_T^c \bar{L}_T$. Finally, panel 4 is an adaptation of the Harris-Todaro labor allocation mechanism, which assumes that equilibrium obtains when the wage rate in the nontraded goods sector is equal to the expected wage in the traded goods sector. The downward-sloping locus QQ is a rectangular hyperbola along which this equality holds, and is known as the Harris-Todaro curve (Corden and Findlay, 1975).[33] The intersection of the L_N^d curve with QQ determines the wage rate and the employment level in the nontraded goods sector, while the intersection of the L_T^d curve with the horizontal line drawn at w_T^c determines employment in the traded goods sector. The initial equilibrium is therefore also characterized by sectoral unemployment, which is equal to $L_T^c L_N$.

Suppose that the demand for labor in the traded goods sector falls, as a result of a macroeconomic shock—a reduction, say, in sectoral productivity—shifting the curve L_T^d to the left, while leaving the demand curve for labor in the nontraded goods sector unchanged. Let us also abstract, in this partial-equilibrium analysis, from induced effects of the shock on relative prices, income, and wealth. If wages are perfectly flexible and labor perfectly mobile across sectors, adjustment of the labor market leads to a fall in the overall wage rate in the economy and a reallocation of labor across sectors, leading the economy to a new equilibrium (point E' in panel 1) with full employment.

Consider now what happens in the presence of a sector-specific wage rigidity. If labor is perfectly mobile across sectors, the demand shock leads only to a reallocation of the labor force and a fall in wages in the nontraded goods sector (panel 2).

---

[32] The source of wage rigidity in the traded goods sector is deliberately left unspecified at this stage. A common rationale is the existence of a government-imposed minimum wage, which typically covers only the manufacturing sector. A different interpretation is provided in the general equilibrium model presented below.

[33] As indicated above, the expected wage in the traded goods sector is defined as the product of the actual wage in that sector times the probability of being hired, which is measured by the employment ratio: $w_T(L_T^d / O_T \bar{L}_T)$. The equilibrium condition of the Harris-Todaro model implies, therefore, that $w_N(O_T \bar{L}_T) = w_T L_T^d$. Since L_T^d is a decreasing function of w_T in general, the preceding condition defines the rectangular hyperbola QQ. The requirement that wage rates be equal to the marginal product of labor for $w_T = w_T^c$ is met only at points A and E_N on the QQ curve.

However, if workers cannot move across sectors, the reduction in demand leads to an increase in unemployment in the traded goods sector, with no effect on wages and employment in the nontraded goods sector (panel 3). With a labor allocation mechanism of the Harris-Todaro type, the shock reduces employment in the traded goods sector, as in the preceding case. However, the effect on the unemployment rate is now ambiguous. This is because the QQ curve shifts to the left following the shift in L_T^d since the fall in employment reduces the likelihood of being hired and, therefore, the expected wage in the traded goods sector. This implies that more workers would elect to seek employment in the nontraded goods sector, bidding wages down. Employment therefore increases in the nontraded goods sector, while wages fall. However, despite the reallocation of labor across sectors, in equilibrium unemployment may well increase in the traded goods sector. The thrust of the analysis, therefore, is that it is critically important to assess correctly the key features of the labor market in order to evaluate the implications of macroeconomic shocks on wages, employment, and the unemployment rate in the economy.[34] We will examine in Chapter 4 how labor market segmentation and relative wage rigidity induced by efficiency considerations alter the transmission of macroeconomic policy shocks.

An additional implication of labor market segmentation is that it offers a particularly clear interpretation of the apparent instability (discussed earlier) of Okun's law in developing countries. Agénor and Aizenman (1999a) provide an analytical framework, which is discussed in more detail in Chapter 4, that helps explain the mechanisms at work. Essentially, their analysis stresses the possibility that interactions between the formal and informal urban labor markets may be characterized by substitutability rather than complementarity in the short run, implying that the employment effects of macroeconomic policy shocks can be highly mitigated. In periods of weak output growth, for instance, skilled as well as unskilled workers laid off in the formal sector may seek employment in the informal sector where wages and labor productivity tend to be lower. Unless skilled workers' reservation wage is higher than the going wage for unskilled workers in the informal sector (as a result, for instance, of generous unemployment benefits in the formal sector), fluctuations in aggregate demand will translate into changes in average productivity rather than a rise in open unemployment.

---

[34]Note that the existence of unemployment in the situation depicted in panel 3 may be only a short-run phenomenon, if labor can adjust over time, so that the long-run outcome might be similar to that which obtains in panel 2.

Chapter 2

Behavioral Functions

The formulation of a complete macroeconomic framework suitable for policy analysis requires not only a description of the basic accounting identities or equilibrium conditions that must hold at the level of the aggregate economy, but also the specification of private agents' behavioral functions. A large literature aimed at formulating and estimating models of private agents' behavior in developing countries has emerged over the years. While the focus of the early literature—in this area as well as in many others—was the application of standard concepts and specifications used in the industrial world, more recent studies have been characterized by a systematic account (at the analytical as well as the empirical levels) of some of the specific structural features of developing countries.

This chapter examines the specification of and empirical evidence on aggregate behavioral functions in developing nations. The first part analyzes the formulation of consumption and savings functions, focusing in particular on the role of liquidity and credit constraints and the effect of interest rates on saving decisions. The second part discusses the determinants of private investment, emphasizing the role of credit rationing, macroeconomic instability, uncertainty and irreversibility effects, and the relationship between private capital formation and public investment. The third part examines the determinants of the demand for money. It distinguishes between conventional models, which emphasize the substitution effects between money and real goods, and more recent models that stress the role of currency substitution factors and financial innovation in the determination of the demand for real money balances.

1 Consumption and Saving

As in industrial countries, private consumption represents by far the largest component of aggregate demand in developing nations. Analytically, consumption occupies a strategic role in macroeconomic models, whether of industrial or developing countries. The effects of fiscal policy on aggregate demand, for instance, depend critically on the properties of the consumption function in any macroeconomic model. In developing nations the behavior of private consumption has also received attention because, in spite of the role of external resources, the bulk of domestic investment in almost all of these countries continues to be financed by domestic saving, an important determinant of which is private consumption. Moreover, because the current account deficit of the balance of payments is definitionally equal to the difference between domestic investment and domestic saving (see Chapter 1), private consumption behavior is central to the external adjustment process as well.

The standard model of household consumption widely used for industrial countries postulates a representative household devising a consumption plan that maximizes utility over its lifetime, subject to an intertemporal budget constraint.[1] With additively separable utility and no uncertainty, the household maximizes lifetime utility V as given by

$$V = \sum_{t=0}^{T} \frac{u(c_t)}{(1+\rho)^t},$$ (1)

where $u(\cdot)$ is a concave period utility function, c is real consumption, and ρ is a constant rate of time preference. Assuming a constant real interest rate r, the function V is maximized by choosing a path of consumption $\{c\}_{t=0}^{T}$ subject to

$$\sum_{t=0}^{T} \frac{u(c_t)}{(1+r)^t} \leq a_0 + \sum_{t=0}^{T} \frac{y_t}{(1+r)^t},$$ (2)

where a_0 is the household's initial wealth and y denotes disposable factor income. The first-order condition for an optimum is given by the Euler equation

$$u'(c_{t+1}) = \frac{1+\rho}{1+r} u'(c_t), \quad t = 1, ..., T-1.$$ (3)

Condition (3) states that the allocation of consumption across periods must be such that an extra unit of consumption would make the same contribution to lifetime utility no matter to what period it is allotted.[2] The consumption path that solves the household's optimizing problem is that satisfying (3), and for which (2) holds as an

---

[1]The presentation that follows abstracts from demographic factors, such as dependency rates. Rossi (1989) develops and tests an analytical framework that links dependency rates, consumption, and saving rates in developing countries. See also Loayza et al. (2000).

[2]If allotted to the present, lifetime utility would rise by u'; if allotted to the next period, it would yield $(1+r)$ units of future consumption and thus $(1+r)u'(c_{t+1})$ units of future utility, worth $[(1+r)/(1+\rho)]u'(c_{t+1})$ today.

equality, so no income is wasted. Heuristically, condition (3) determines the shape of the consumption path (the rate of growth of consumption) while (2), written as an equality, determines the height of the consumption path (the initial level of consumption).

The key property of this model of consumption is its implication that households will tend to smooth consumption; that is, consumption will not necessarily be tied to current income, as in the simple Keynesian consumption function (KCF). With diminishing marginal utility ($u'' < 0$) and fluctuating income, tying consumption too closely to current income would violate the Euler equation (3), since adjacent periods of high and low consumption would produce ratios of marginal utilities $u'(c_{t+1})/u'(c_t)$ that would exceed or fall short of $(1 + \rho)/(1 + r)$. The model also predicts that the effect of changes in income on current consumption depends on when such changes take place and how long they are expected to last, since these characteristics will determine the impact of the income change on the lifetime resources of the household. Finally, the model makes no prediction about the effects of changes in the interest rate on the consumption behavior of households that are net savers in the current period. For such households the substitution effect arising from consumption "tilting" toward the future, based on (3), would tend to depress current consumption, while the income effect arising from an easing of the intertemporal budget constraint (2) would tend to increase it. The net effect on consumption of a change in r would depend on the relative strength of these two effects, which in turn depends on properties of the utility function.

The application of this theory in the context of developing countries raises four issues. The first issue stems from whether households can effectively smooth consumption. This depends on access to unconstrained borrowing and lending, which may be inhibited by the possible existence of liquidity constraints preventing households from moving resources across periods. The second issue relates to the effective length of planning horizons. Even if households are able to smooth consumption over time, they may not choose to do so over sufficiently long periods to make much difference. The extent to which the model described above departs from the simple KCF thus depends on the length of the planning horizon, with greater differences for longer horizons. The relevance of Ricardian equivalence in particular applications, for instance, depends on the length of consumers' planning horizon (see below). The third issue relates to the empirical determination of the effects of interest rate changes on consumption. To test the theory, it is necessary to distinguish between the effect of higher interest rates on the *level* of current consumption, about which the theory makes no prediction, and the effect on the *growth* of consumption, which should be positively related to the interest rate. Finally, the question arises as to the effects of fiscal policy on private consumption. These effects depend not just on the issues already listed, but also on the possibility that public consumption may be an argument in the instantaneous utility function $u(\cdot)$ and, in the extreme, may be a close substitute for private consumption, so that "direct crowding out" of private by public consumption occurs.

Surveys by Gersovitz (1988), Deaton (1989, 1992), and Rosenzweig (2001) suggest a number of reasons that household consumption behavior in developing countries may differ from that in industrial countries. First, households in developing countries tend to have different demographic structures from those in industrial countries. The individual household tends to be larger and more generations tend to live together, sharing resources. This has several implications for consumption behavior. First, if resources are shared among the several generations within the household, there is no need for "hump" saving to finance retirement, since household income will tend to be sustained as a new working generation replaces the old. Second, with resources pooled among household members, the household provides insurance for individuals against certain types of risk (such as health risk) that may only be imperfectly insured against in the market, and that would otherwise have provided a motive for precautionary household saving. Third, the relationship between generations in a single household makes more plausible the intergenerational altruism required to extend the household planning horizon beyond the lifetime of the current working generation; that is, developing-country households may provide a closer approximation to the "dynastic" household of Barro (1974).

A second source of differences in consumption behavior between developed and developing countries relates to the observation that household incomes in the developing world may be more uncertain than those in industrial nations, for several reasons. These include the greater share of agricultural incomes in developing countries as well as macroeconomic instability arising from both external shocks (for instance, the variability in the terms of trade described in Chapter 1) and domestic macroeconomic policy shocks. This sort of uncertainty affects the entire household and cannot be diversified away by risk pooling within the household. Thus, as emphasized in particular by Deaton (1989) and Rosenzweig (2001), a precautionary saving motive may be more important in developing countries.

Caballero (1990) and Irvine and Wang (2001) study formally how increased uncertainty regarding future income may enhance the precautionary motive for saving, whereas Wang (2004) develops a model in which higher uncertainty about the *components* of future income (despite total income being observable) increases precautionary saving. In general, however, greater uncertainty need not imply higher saving in the model described here. In the presence of uncertainty, the household maximizes expected utility, and the Euler equation sets the marginal utility of current consumption equal to the expected value of the marginal utility of saving. The effect of uncertainty on current consumption will depend on the source of the uncertainty and the properties of the instantaneous utility function. If uncertainty concerns future income, for instance, a precautionary saving motive will exist only if marginal utility is convex (see Gersovitz, 1988).

A third source of differences may result from the widely observed phenomenon that many households in developing countries operate at near-subsistence income levels. This may strengthen the motive for consumption smoothing, because the consequences of a bad income draw in a given period would be catastrophic under such circumstances. Finally, differences in consumption behavior may also be the consequence of developing-country households' need to cope with the implications of financial repression (see Chapter 1). Thus, while their motive to smooth consumption may be strong, households may be restricted in their ability to transfer resources across time, both by an inability to borrow against future earnings and by very low real returns on current saving. To see how these factors play out in practice, we now examine the evidence on the behavior of private consumption in developing countries, focusing on the issues raised previously.

1.1 ■ Consumption Smoothing

As indicated above, given that the utility function is concave, consumption smoothing will be observed if households both plan consumption over multiple periods and have the means to transfer resources across periods. Thus, evidence that households smooth consumption suggests that both factors are present. This evidence takes several forms in developing countries.

First, because the alternative to smoothing consumption is to consume out of current income, evidence of consumption smoothing comes from tests of the permanent income hypothesis (PIH). A large number of such tests have been conducted for developing nations. These tests effectively consist of estimating the regression

$$c = a_0 + a_1 y_p + a_2(y - y_p) + u, \tag{4}$$

where c is real per capita consumption, y_p real per capita permanent income, y current per capita real income, and u a disturbance term. Under the PIH, consumption is equal to permanent income, so $a_1 = 1$ while $a_0 = a_2 = 0$. Under the KCF, in which consumption depends on current income and the permanent/transitory distinction is irrelevant, $a_1 = a_2$ and $a_0 > 0$. Equations of this type have been estimated at various times for developing countries—in the early literature by Bhalla (1980) and Wolpin (1982) for rural households in India, by Musgrove (1979) for urban households in three South American countries, and by Gan and Soon (1994) for Malaysia and Singapore. Overall, the results indicate that income decomposition matters; that is, the propensity to consume out of permanent income exceeds the propensity to consume out of current income. These results are thus consistent with the consumption-smoothing hypothesis. At the same time, however, the elasticity of consumption with respect to permanent income is not typically found to be unity, nor is the propensity to consume out of transitory income found to be zero. Thus, while evidence of this type supports consumption smoothing, the strict form of the PIH is not often supported by the data in developing nations. The rational expectations version of the PIH, discussed for instance by Abel (1990), has also been rejected in various studies, such as Gan and Soon (1994) and Zuehlke and Payne (1989).

A second type of evidence emerges from cross-country studies of saving behavior. If "hump" saving over the life cycle is indeed important, the theory suggests that countries experiencing rapid growth in per capita incomes should exhibit relatively high saving rates, because young cohorts engaging in "hump" saving will be more affluent than older cohorts with lower saving rates, and thus will account for a larger share of aggregate income. For a similar reason, countries with a larger share of the population in the peak earning years should exhibit larger saving rates. The cross-sectional evidence for developing countries is broadly consistent with these predictions (see, for instance, Fry, 1996; Loayza et al., 2000), suggesting that consumption smoothing over the life cycle may indeed be important in these countries.[3] Several authors have also produced time series evidence supportive of this mechanism, such as Lahiri (1989), who studied saving behavior in eight Asian developing countries, and Kwack and Lee (2005), who examined the experience of Korea over the period 1975–2002. In both studies, the youth and older age dependency ratios tend to reduce the saving rate.

A very different type of evidence has to do with responses to income shocks. As already suggested, changes in the terms of trade, typically emanating from changes in the prices of primary export commodities, have been quite large in many developing countries at various times. Because of the public sector's role in export production, these shocks are not always transmitted to household incomes. In cases where they have been, however, the response of household consumption is informative with respect to the prevalence of consumption smoothing. For instance, Bevan et al. (1993) analyzed the effects of the 1976–1979 coffee boom on farmers in Kenya. Unlike the situation in neighboring Tanzania, the increase in international coffee prices was passed on to small growers in Kenya, who thus experienced a windfall in income. The evidence reported by Bevan et al. indicates that this windfall, understood to be temporary because it was known to be caused by a frost in Brazil, was largely saved, as would be expected if peasant households sought to smooth consumption.

1.2 ■ Planning Horizon and Liquidity Constraints

The evidence suggesting that consumption smoothing takes place in developing countries implies that, on average, planning horizons extend beyond a single period and that at least some households are able to move resources intertemporally. More

---

[3]However, this evidence is not unambiguous. The direction of causality between saving rates and per capita income growth may run either way. Moreover, if life-cycle saving accounts for these results, then in fast-growing countries the age-consumption profile should be relatively more tilted toward the young than in slow-growing countries. Yet, as Deaton (1989) shows, this does not appear to have been the case in a sample of several developing countries for which such data were available.

direct evidence on the length of planning horizons and the prevalence of liquidity constraints is also available.[4] Haque (1988), for instance, devised an empirical test of the Yaari-Blanchard proposition, according to which the probability of dynastic extinction drives a wedge between the effective planning horizons of the public and private sectors (see Blanchard and Fischer, 1989, pp. 115–26) and tested it for a group of sixteen developing countries. In fifteen of the sixteen cases no such wedge could be detected, suggesting that the planning horizon of private households was effectively infinite. A similar result was derived by Leiderman and Razin (1988) for the case of Israel. This conclusion was reinforced by Haque and Montiel (1989), who generalized Haque's procedure to measure independently the length of household planning horizons and the share of total consumption attributable to liquidity-constrained "rule of thumb" consumers spending only out of current income. In a different sixteen-country sample from that of Haque, they were unable to reject the null hypothesis of infinite horizons in any country. Overall, then, the direct evidence on the length of household planning horizons in developing nations does not appear to be inconsistent with Deaton's suggestion that the "dynastic family" construct may be more relevant in the developing world than in industrial countries.

By contrast, the measured incidence of liquidity constraints appears to be substantially greater in developing countries.[5] Veidyanathan (1993), using a group of almost sixty countries and annual data covering three decades, finds that consumers in the developing world are subject to liquidity and borrowing constraints. Using panel data, Loayza et al. (2000) found that variables measuring liquidity constraints have a significant impact on household saving rates. The panel study by Haque and Montiel (1989) derived point estimates of the share of total consumption accounted for by households that simply spend their current incomes. For fourteen of their sixteen countries the estimated share exceeded 20 percent, and several cases exceeded 50 percent. These values are substantially larger than the typical estimate of 0.1 for the United States. The country-specific estimates derived by Haque and Montiel are of the same order of magnitude as regional estimates derived by Rossi (1988) using a Euler equation approach (see below). For low-income countries, Rossi's estimates were in the range 0.7–0.8; for middle-income countries, values were in the broader but still relatively high range of 0.2–0.8. As documented by Lee and Sawada (2010) in the case of Pakistan, credit market constraints may induce precautionary saving behavior.

It should be noted, however, that some economists have claimed that a close link between current income and consumption is not a good test of the presence of liquidity constraints. Zeldes (1989), for instance, has argued that if consumers

---

[4]Life-cycle models with borrowing constraints include Hubbard and Judd (1986) and Zeldes (1989). In both of these models, liquidity constraints are imposed exogenously in the form of simple non-negative wealth constraints.

[5]For industrial countries, there is some debate about the importance of these constraints (see Attanasio and Weber, 2010). Sarantis and Stewart (2003) for instance found that the existence of liquidity constraints and (to a lesser extent) precautionary saving are the major reasons why the basic RE-PIH (rational expectations permanent income hypothesis) model is rejected for most industrial countries.

face liquidity constraints, but are forward-looking, they would tend to smooth consumption *within* stages of their lives, these stages being defined endogenously by the level of consumption deemed sustainable without debt. Alternatively, Chah et al. (1995) have argued that, in life-cycle models, liquidity constraints yield very different predictions for the behavior of consumption of durable goods and nondurable goods—the timing of purchases of durables tend to be more affected, given that they provided services over an extended period of time. However, there have been few attempts to test these types of predictions using data for developing countries.

1.3 ■ Liquidity Constraints and Asymmetric Effects

Borrowing constraints may also help to explain an *asymmetric* consumption and savings response by private agents to income shocks. For instance, Agénor and Aizenman (2004) examine the possibility that *permanent* shocks to income may have an asymmetric effect on savings, depending on whether they are favorable or unfavorable. To explore this idea analytically, they consider a three-period model in which consumers (or households) are identical and live for three periods. Households may also be subject to borrowing constraints during some periods of their life when faced with bad shocks.

Suppose that the representative consumer has a quadratic utility function, and that both the rate of time preference and the real interest rate are set to zero. Specifically, assume that total utility over the life span of the typical household, V, is given by

$$V = u(c_0, c_1) + u(c_1, c_2) + u(c_2, c_3), \tag{5}$$

where

$$u(c_{h-1}, c_h) = c_h - 0.5\phi c_h^2 - 0.5\tau(c_h - c_{h-1})^2, \tag{6}$$

where c_h is consumption in period h and ϕ, $\tau \geq 0$. We assume that ϕ is small enough to ensure that in the relevant region, the marginal utility of consumption is positive. Equation (6) allows for the presence of habit formation—changes in the current level of consumption relative to the previous level entail disutility, proportional to τ. Prior to period 1, both income and consumption are stable, and were expected to remain such. Hence, the initial level of assets at period 1 is zero, and consumption is equal to income, y:

$$y_0 = c_0 = 1.$$

Suppose now that, at the beginning of period 1, there is a change in the underlying stochastic process of income. First, a permanent shock increases income by ε. Second, an adverse transitory shock (induced, for instance, by an adverse movement in the terms of trade) may occur in the second period with probability q, reducing second-period income by δ. Hence, the revised income path is anticipated to be

$$
y = \begin{cases}
y_h = 1 + \varepsilon, \quad h = 1, 2, 3 & \text{with prob. } 1 - q \\
y_1 = y_3 = 1 + \varepsilon, \quad y_2 = 1 + \varepsilon - \delta & \text{with prob. } q
\end{cases}. \tag{7}
$$

A convenient feature of the model described by (5) and (6) is that, in the absence of habit formation ($\tau = 0$), and with a well-functioning capital market, the consumer would behave according to the PIH described earlier. That is, if indeed consumers face an adverse transitory shock in period 2, they will borrow in that period in order to smooth their consumption path. A key issue, however, is whether borrowing is at all feasible. In what follows we evaluate the impact of credit constraints on savings by contrasting two scenarios: the first assumes that consumers have full access to the international capital market, whereas the second considers the case where consumers are unable to borrow, due for instance to perceptions of country risk.

With full access to the capital market, consumers borrow in period 2 in bad states of nature and repay fully in period 3. The representative consumer's problem is thus, with $x = 1 + \varepsilon$:

$$
\max_{s_1, s_2^L, s_2^H} \begin{cases}
u(1; x - s_1) \\
+ q \left[u(x - s_1; x - \delta + s_1 - s_2^L) + u(x - \delta + s_1 - s_2^L; x + s_2^L) \right], \\
+ (1 - q) \left[u(x - s_1; x + s_1 - s_2^H) + u(x + s_1 - s_2^H; x + s_2^H) \right]
\end{cases} \tag{8}
$$

where s_2^L (respectively s_2^H) denotes second-period savings if the adverse income shock is indeed positive (zero).

The first-order conditions of the above problem provide three linear equations in $s_1, s_2^L s_2^H$, from which we can infer that

$$
s_1 = \frac{\delta q (1 + 3\theta)(1 + \theta) + \varepsilon \theta (2 + 5\theta)}{3 + 14\theta(1 + \theta)}, \tag{9}
$$

where $\theta = \tau / \phi$ measures the relative importance of habit formation versus the diminishing marginal utility of consumption. Note that

$$
s_1 |_{\theta = 0} = \frac{\delta q}{3}, \tag{10}
$$

$$
s_1 |_{\theta \to \infty} = \frac{3\delta q + 5\varepsilon}{14}. \tag{11}
$$

Equation (10) corresponds to the case where habit formation is absent ($\theta = \tau = 0$). In these circumstances, saving in period 1 is determined simply by the difference between endowment, given by $x = 1 + \varepsilon$, and permanent income, given by

$$y_P = \frac{x + (x - q\delta) + x}{3} = x - \frac{\delta q}{3},$$

in line with the prediction of the PIH. Consumption in the first period will increase by the permanent increase in income, minus the expected value of the transitory shock, smoothed over the three periods of life. Equation (11) corresponds to the other extreme, where adjustment of consumption is extremely costly (or the marginal utility is constant). Note that habit formation implies that a fraction of the permanent shock is saved in the first period, in order to smooth the cost of adjustment across time. Applying the first-order conditions we infer that, in the absence of habit formation, second-period saving is[6]

$$s_2^L\big|_{\theta=0} = -\frac{\delta(3 - q)}{6} < 0. \tag{12}$$

Equation (12) indicates that if an adverse transitory shock does indeed reduce second-period income, households will borrow to smooth their consumption.

Suppose that the habit formation parameter ϕ and the permanent shock are not large enough relative to the transitory shock so that $s_2^L < 0$. Assume also, however, that borrowing is not feasible at all. In these circumstances, the maximization problem of the representative household becomes

$$\max_{s_1, s_2^H} \begin{cases} u(1; x - s_1) \\ +q\left[u(x - s_1; x - \delta + s_1) + u(x - \delta + s_1; x)\right] \\ +(1 - q)\left[u(x - s_1; x + s_1 - s_2^H) + u(x + s_1 - s_2^H; x + s_2^H)\right] \end{cases}. \tag{13}$$

---

[6]If there is no habit formation, and if the adverse shock does hit consumers in the second period, the revised permanent income would be

$$y_P = 0.5\, s_1\big|_{\theta=0} + \frac{(x - \delta) + x}{2} = x + \frac{(\delta q/3) - \delta}{2}.$$

Hence, savings would be

$$x - \frac{\delta q}{3} - \delta - \left[x + \frac{(\delta q/3) - \delta}{2}\right] = -\frac{\delta(3 - q)}{6}.$$

Solving this problem, we can infer that the presence of borrowing constraints modifies first-period savings to

$$\bar{s}_1 = \frac{\delta q (1 + 3\theta) + \varepsilon\theta}{(2 + 6\theta)(2 + 5\theta) - (1 - q)(1 + 4\theta)^2}(2 + 5\theta). \tag{14}$$

Hence, in the absence of habit formation,

$$\bar{s}_1|_{\theta=0} = \frac{\delta q}{2 - 0.5(1 - q)}. \tag{15}$$

Comparing (10) and (15), we find that first-period saving is higher under borrowing constraints, as the consumer is accumulating assets to reduce the expected hardship in the second period. It follows from these equations that

$$\bar{s}_1|_{\theta=0} - s_1|_{\theta=0} = \frac{\delta q (3 - q)}{3(3 + q)}, \quad \frac{\partial(\bar{s}_1 - s_1)}{\partial\theta} < 0.$$

Hence, the higher the probability of an adverse shock to second-period income, and the larger the magnitude of the shock, the greater will be the gap between the savings rates with and without borrowing constraints. In addition, greater habit formation (as measured by a higher θ) reduces the gap between the two saving rates.

Put differently, positive (negative) transitory income shocks are entirely saved (dissaved) as in the permanent income hypothesis. In addition, however, a fraction of permanent income should also be set aside during "good" times (that is, in period 1), if there is habit formation. Indeed, as can be inferred from (14), as long as $\theta > 0$, the permanent shock ε has a positive effect on first-period savings. Thus, the possibility of binding borrowing constraints in "bad" states of nature implies (under habit formation) an asymmetric response of savings to *permanent* income shocks.

It is worth noting that, in the foregoing discussion, we focused only on the case of an adverse transitory shock in the second period to simplify the analysis. If the transitory second-period shock is positive, the borrowing constraint will not bind. Thus, even if the transitory shock follows a symmetric distribution, the qualitative features of our analysis will continue to hold. We can illustrate this point with a simple example. Suppose that the second-period transitory shock is δ with a probability equal to one-half, and $-\delta$ with a probability one-half; suppose also that there is no habit formation ($\tau = 0$). All the other assumptions continue to hold. It is easy to verify that in these conditions

$$s_1|_{\theta=0} = 0, \quad \bar{s}_1|_{\theta=0} = \frac{\delta}{7}.$$

Consequently, first-period saving is zero in the absence of borrowing constraints, whereas it is positive in the presence of these constraints (in fact, proportional to the standard deviation of the transitory shock).

Agénor and Aizenman (2004) also show that loss aversion—captured by attaching an extra utility weight to bad states of nature—magnifies the increase in saving arising from the anticipation of future binding borrowing constraints induced by terms-of-trade shocks. The reason is that under loss aversion (a particular form of asymmetric utility preferences), individuals exhibit a larger degree of risk aversion to adverse shocks to income. As a result, they tend to save more in good times, increasing their consumption by less than the increase in income.

1.4 ■ Effects of Interest Rate Changes on Savings

As indicated earlier, the theory of consumption described in this section is compatible with either positive or negative effects of changes in interest rates on saving, depending on the strength of income and substitution effects. Nevertheless, the issue is important in developing countries, because one argument frequently adduced in support of financial liberalization is that higher real interest rates will tend to stimulate domestic saving.[7]

The traditional empirical approach to this issue has been the estimation of structural saving equations, in which the saving rate is regressed on a set of variables loosely motivated by the theory described above. While some authors have found evidence of positive interest rate effects on saving in developing countries using this approach, estimated effects tend to be small—or negative.[8] Loayza et al. (2000), for instance, found in some of their regressions that a 1 percentage point increase in the real interest rate raises the private saving rate by about 0.05 percent. In other regressions, however, they found a significant *negative* effect, suggesting that the income effect outweighs the substitution effect.

An alternative approach to testing the link between savings and interest rates is to estimate the intertemporal elasticity of substitution directly. If the instantaneous utility function exhibits constant relative risk aversion, the Euler equation (3) will relate the rate of growth of consumption to the difference between the real interest rate and the (constant) rate of time preference, with a factor of proportionality

---

[7] See Chapter 18. The case for liberalization does not rest solely on this argument, however, because whether saving increases or not, liberalization may affect the efficiency with which a given level of saving is allocated among potential investment opportunities.

[8] Empirical work on saving behavior in developing countries, and particularly on the relation between saving and interest rates, has been handicapped by severe limitations of data. Saving data, as a rule, are calculated as a residual item, either by taking the difference between gross national product and consumption expenditure or by subtracting the current account deficit (less net factor income from abroad) from gross domestic investment. In either case, the data on aggregate saving can be subject to substantial measurement errors. Furthermore, because nominal interest rates are often regulated, they tend to exhibit little or no variation for extended periods.

equal to the intertemporal elasticity of substitution. Estimation of the Euler equation can thus yield an estimate of the intertemporal elasticity of substitution. A negative interest rate effect on consumption requires that this elasticity be sufficiently large to generate a substitution effect that dominates the positive income effect of higher interest rates on net savers. This approach has the virtues that it estimates a "deep" parameter directly and that it relies on consumption data, which are available separately for the private sector.

Giovaninni (1985) estimated Euler equations for eighteen developing countries, finding a statistically significant intertemporal elasticity of substitution (averaging about 0.5) in only five cases. Rossi (1988) modified Giovaninni's procedure to allow for liquidity constraints and direct substitutability between private and public consumption. His generalized specification yielded larger estimates of the intertemporal elasticity of substitution for developing-country regions than had been found by Giovaninni for individual countries, but Rossi concluded that these were still too small to alter the implication that changes in real interest rates would have but weak effects on consumption.

In a subsequent study, Ogaki et al. (1996) provided estimates of the effects of real interest rates on saving using a large cross-section of countries. In their model, the intertemporal elasticity of substitution is made to vary with the level of wealth. They find strong support for the hypothesis that the sensitivity of saving to the interest rates rises with the level of income. In low-income countries, consumption appears to be more related to subsistence considerations than to intertemporal factors; as a result, estimates of the intertemporal elasticity of substitution are likely to be low. This is particularly so in countries where the share of necessities (most notably food) in total expenditure is large. The range of estimated values obtained by Ogaki et al. for the intertemporal elasticity of substitution is actually fairly large, varying from about 0.05 for Uganda and Ethiopia (the poorest countries in the sample) to a high of 0.6 for Venezuela and Singapore. Even the highest estimates remain, nevertheless, fairly small, suggesting that the effect of changes in interest rates on saving is likely to remain weak, even in the most advanced developing countries.

1.5 ■ Public and Private Consumption

The final issue to be addressed in this section is the possibility that public consumption could be a direct substitute for private consumption in developing countries. Much of the evidence, however, has failed to corroborate the hypothesis that public consumption directly affects private consumption levels; see, for instance, Haque (1988) and Rossi (1988). Moreover, Karras (1994), in a study covering a large number of developing countries, found that private and public consumption expenditure appear to be complementary rather than substitutes. Similar results are obtained by Chiu (2001) for Taiwan.

2   Private Investment

Private investment plays an important role in developing nations for the same reason that it does in industrial countries: investment determines the rate of accumulation of physical capital and is thus an important factor in the growth of productive capacity. In the developing world, the association of capacity growth with physical capital accumulation has, if anything, traditionally been viewed as closer than in industrial countries. Moreover, because investment is a forward-looking activity with irreversible aspects, it tends to be a volatile component of aggregate demand. We begin by reviewing the "conventional" determinants of investment and then turn our focus to uncertainty and irreversibility effects.

2.1 ■ Conventional Determinants

Empirical investment functions for industrial countries have relied on either a "stock" or a "flow" approach (see Abel, 1990). Under the stock approach (also referred to as the neoclassical or "flexible accelerator" approach), installed capital is assumed to be available at price p_k. Given a discount rate ρ and rate of depreciation δ, the rental price of capital is given by $\sigma = (\rho + \delta)p_k$. Let $\pi(k)$ denote the flow profit function, given by

$$\pi(k) = py[k, n(w/p, k)] - wn(w/p, k), \tag{16}$$

where p is the price of output, w the nominal wage, and $n(\cdot)$ the level of employment, derived from profit maximization conditioned on the existing capital stock. Then the optimal capital stock k^* will satisfy

$$\pi'(k^*) = \sigma. \tag{17}$$

Given an initial capital stock k_0, net investment represents a gradual adjustment of the actual to the desired capital stock, and gross investment is derived by adding to this an amount of replacement investment that is proportional to the initial capital stock. The flow model, by contrast, postulates the existence of a convex function $h(I)$ that measures the total cost (in units of output) of achieving the level of gross investment I. If the firm's objective is to maximize the present value $V(k)$ (using the discount rate ρ) of its profits $\pi(k)$ net of the costs of investment $ph(I)$, then at each moment the rate of investment must satisfy

$$h'(I^*) = q/p, \tag{18}$$

where $q = dV(k)/dk$ is the marginal value of installed capital at the current period, and q/p is the marginal value of "Tobin's q," the ratio of the value of installed capital to its replacement cost.

The determinants of investment in these specifications include, in the stock version, expected future values of aggregate demand, the user cost of capital (with the simple version above typically modified to reflect tax policies that affect investment), and the wage rate, as well as the initial capital stock. These interact in nonlinear forms suggested by the model. In the flow version, what matters is the marginal value of Tobin's q and the parameters of the adjustment-cost function.

2.2 ■ Reformulation of Theories

There are several reasons why investment theories developed for industrial countries may need to be reformulated to fit the circumstances typical of developing nations.[9]

2.2.1   Nature of the Financial System

First, the influence of financial variables on investment behavior makes the specification of investment functions heavily dependent on the institutional environment in the financial system. The typical absence of equity markets and limited development of corporate bond markets in the developing world imply that neither Tobin's q nor standard neoclassical "flexible accelerator" investment functions can be applied blindly in developing countries. Credit rationing may heavily influence the behavior of private investment in many of these countries. Mlambo and Oshikoya (2001), for instance, found that credit availability has a large effect on private investment in Africa, in line with several other studies. However, causation may not be unidirectional, given that actual credit flows may reflect the demand for credit by investing firms rather than a rationed supply (see Chapter 6).

2.2.2   Imported Goods

Second, given the importance of imported capital goods in the developing world, the relative price of these goods (or, in some countries, the degree of foreign exchange rationing) may also be important determinants of private investment behavior. Specifically, the role of imported intermediate goods in developing nations suggests that the specification of relative factor prices in empirical investment functions cannot be restricted to the wage rate and the user cost of capital, but must also take into account the domestic-currency price, as well as the availability, of such goods. If firms produce for local and foreign markets, as illustrated by Nucci and Pozzolo (2001), a real exchange-rate depreciation may then have opposite effects on investment: a positive effect through higher revenues, and a negative effect through higher costs. The net effect is ambiguous and depends on the firm's share of foreign sales to total sales, and the degree of reliance on imported inputs.

---

[9] Servén and Solimano (1993) provide an early overview of specification issues that arise in the formulation of investment functions in developing nations. See also Chhibber and Dailami (1993) and Rama (1993).

From a dynamic perspective, the importance of accounting for the role of imported capital goods in explaining investment behavior is demonstrated by Servén (1990), who studies the effect of a real exchange-rate devaluation on capital formation.[10] Servén shows that the long-run effect of a real devaluation on private capital formation is, in general, ambiguous. Whether the total capital stock rises or falls depends in particular on the effect of the real depreciation on the import content of capital goods. In the long run, the capital stock is likely to rise in the traded goods sector and fall in the nontraded goods sector. However, despite this long-run ambiguity, an anticipated real exchange-rate depreciation provides the incentive for an intertemporal reallocation of investment over time. When a real depreciation is expected, an investment boom is likely to develop if the import content of capital goods is high relative to the degree of capital mobility, because the expected depreciation induces a preemptive switch toward foreign goods. The boom is subsequently followed by a slump when the depreciation is effectively implemented, because the exchange-rate change is equivalent to the removal of a subsidy on investment. With high capital mobility, the anticipated depreciation promotes flight into foreign assets, and the opposite pattern occurs.

2.2.3   Debt Overhang Effects

A third factor that underlines the need to reformulate investment theories in the developing-country context results from the existence of a debt overhang in many countries, which has often been cited as a factor inhibiting private investment. The possibility that confiscatory future taxation will be used to finance future debt service may need to be reflected in the specification of private investment behavior.[11] Fitzgerald et al. (1994), Greene and Villanueva (1991), Oshikoya (1994), Schmidt-Hebbel and Muller (1992), Iyoha (2000), and Clements et al. (2003), all found a significant negative effect of the debt output ratio on investment, providing support for debt overhang effects. The evidence provided by Cohen (1993) suggests, however, that it may not be the *stock* of debt itself that directly affects private investment, but rather *debt service* that may reduce public investment—and thus private capital formation, through a complementarity effect (as discussed next).

2.2.4   Role of Public Capital

Fourth, the large role of the public capital stock suggests the need to incorporate complementarity-substitutability relationships between public and private capital

---

[10]The relationships between investment, the real cost of capital, and the real exchange rate are also analyzed by Cardoso (1993) and Faini and de Melo (1992). This issue is further examined in Chapter 9, in the context of our review of the contractionary effects of devaluation.

[11]See, for instance, Sachs (1989). However, Borensztein (1990) argued that credit rationing on international capital markets may have a more detrimental effect on domestic investment than the debt overhang, even in highly indebted countries.

into private investment decisions. The relationship between public and private investment takes on greater importance in the developing world than in industrial countries because of the larger role played by the government in the overall process of capital formation, particularly in core infrastructure (see Agénor, 2012*b*). Whether, on balance, public sector investment raises or lowers private investment is uncertain a priori. On the one hand, public sector investment can crowd out private investment expenditure if it uses scarce physical and financial resources that would otherwise be available to the private sector. The financing of public sector investment, whether through taxes, issuance of debt instruments, or inflation, can reduce the resources available to the private sector and thus depress private investment activity.[12] Moreover, the public sector may produce marketable output that competes with private output. On the other, public investment to maintain or expand infrastructure and the provision of public goods is likely to be complementary to private investment. Public investment of this type can enhance the prospects for private investment by raising the productivity of capital. There is no a priori reason to believe that public and private capital formation are necessarily substitutes or complements. Moreover, public investment may stimulate private output by increasing the demand for inputs and other services, and may augment overall resource availability by expanding aggregate output and saving. The net effect of public investment on private investment will depend on the relative impacts of these various effects.

Several studies reviewed in Agénor (2012*b*) found a positive effect of public investment on private capital formation. Other studies have found that public investment in infrastructure tends to be complementary to private investment, whereas increases in other types of government investment tend to crowd out the private sector. The complementarity between public and private investment has important implications for growth and employment when adjustment measures aimed at reducing the fiscal deficit take the form of severe cuts in public expenditure on infrastructure. Buffie (1992), for instance, has argued that this link may explain the protracted recession that was associated with adjustment programs in highly indebted Latin American countries, in the aftermath of the debt crisis of the early 1980s.

2.2.5 *Macroeconomic Instability and Uncertainty*

Finally, macroeconomic instability, often induced by political factors, has been identified in Chapter 1 as an important feature of the macroeconomic environment faced by developing countries, and the resulting uncertainty may have a large influence on private investment. Alesina and Tabellini (1989), for instance, have examined analytically the effect of political uncertainty on investment and capital flight in developing countries. Their analysis shows that the possibility of electing a

---

[12]To the extent that public sector projects are financed through concessional foreign lending, of course, the resources available to the private sector are not reduced.

government prone to tax capital and productive activities leads to a substitution of productive domestic investments in favor of consumption and capital flight, leading to a reduction of domestic output.

Several papers have found that indicators of macroeconomic instability exert significant negative effects on private investment. Rodrik (1991), for instance, provides evidence suggesting that uncertainty on the part of economic agents regarding the government's future intentions affects investment behavior in developing countries. Similar results have been obtained by Aizenman and Marion (1993), using a sample of forty developing countries and data covering the period 1970–1985. Larraín and Vergara (1993) have argued that real exchange-rate variability (a popular measure of macroeconomic instability) has an adverse effect on private capital formation. Evidence on the effect of external shocks and the debt overhang on private investment has also been found. Cardoso (1993) and Bleaney and Greenaway (1993a) have shown that fluctuations in the terms of trade (through their effects on real income and the profitability of the export sector) also affect private investment.

The tendency to delay irreversible investment in the face of uncertainty has also been much emphasized in the analytical literature on capital formation, most notably by Dixit and Pindyck (1994), and has been shown to exist even when investors are risk-neutral agents. When the future is uncertain, delay involves trading off the returns from investing now against the gains from being able to make a more informed decision in the future. We now turn to a more detailed discussion of this effect.

2.3 ■ Uncertainty and Irreversibility Effects

The key insight of Dixit and Pindyck (1994) is that under uncertainty there exists an "option value" to delay an investment decision in order to await the arrival of new information about market conditions.

Their key result can be illustrated in the following setup, which is adapted from Dixit and Pyndick (1994, chapters 4 and 5).[13] Consider the case of a monopolist who envisages making an investment whose present value is X. A sunk cost whose present value is S must be incurred. The investment is irreversible, in the sense that there is no possibility to scrap the value of capital in the future. Under a conventional net present value (NPV) criterion, the firm makes the investment if $X - S \geq 0$.

Suppose now that X varies over time and follows a geometric Brownian motion with drift:

$$dX = \alpha X dt + \sigma X dz, \qquad (19)$$

---

[13]See Bertola (1998) for a more complex model of irreversible investment by a firm facing uncertainty in technology, demand, and price of capital.

where α is the mean of dX and σ the standard deviation of dX. The term dz is the random increment of a Wiener process, and is such that

$$dz = \varepsilon_t \sqrt{dt}, \tag{20}$$

where ε_t follows a standard normal distribution (with zero mean and variance equal to unity), and is serially uncorrelated (that is, $\mathbb{E}(\varepsilon_i \varepsilon_j) = 0, \forall i, j$, for $i \neq j$).[14]

Equations (19) and (20) imply that future returns associated with the investment are log-normally distributed with an expected value given by $\mathbb{E}(X_t) = X_0 \exp(\alpha t)$, where X_0 is today's value of X, and a variance that grows exponentially with t. The monopolist will time its investment decision so as to maximize the expected present value of the option to invest, $F(X)$, given by

$$F(X) = \max \mathbb{E}(X_T - S) = X_0 \exp(-\rho T), \tag{21}$$

where X_T is the value of the investment at the (as yet) unknown future period in time T, at which the investment decision is made, and $\rho > \alpha$ is the discount rate.

Delaying the investment decision and holding the option is equivalent to holding an asset which pays no dividends but may gain in value as time passes. As shown by Dixit and Pyndick (1994, chapter 4), the fundamental condition for optimality (or Bellman equation), if the firm delays investment and holds the option, is given by

$$\rho F = \mathbb{E}(dF)/dt. \tag{22}$$

The left-hand side of (22) is the discounted normal rate of return that an investor would require from holding the option, whereas the right-hand side is the expected total return per unit of time from holding the option. If this condition holds, the firm is equating the expected return from delaying the investment with the opportunity cost of delay. In effect, (22) describes a no-arbitrage condition.

The next step is to calculate the total differential, dF. To do so, given that F is a continuous-time stochastic process, requires using Ito's lemma—the stochastic calculus equivalent of the chain rule for computing the derivative of a composite function. This gives

$$dF = F'(X)dX + \frac{1}{2}F''(X)(dX)^2. \tag{23}$$

---

[14]A Wiener process (also called a Brownian motion) is a continuous-time Markov stochastic process whose increments are independent, no matter how small the time interval. Specifically, if z_t is a Wiener process, then any change in z, Δz, corresponding to a time interval Δt, satisfies the following conditions: (a) the relationship between Δz and Δt is given by $\Delta z = \varepsilon_t \sqrt{\Delta t}$, where ε_t is a normally distributed random variable with mean zero and a standard deviation of 1; (b) ε_t is serially uncorrelated, that is, $\mathbb{E}(\varepsilon_t \varepsilon_s) = 0$ for $t \neq s$. Thus, the values of Δz for any two different intervals of time are independent, so z_t follows a Markov process. Letting the Δt's become infinitesimally small, the increment of the Wiener process can be written as in (20).

Substituting out for dX from (19) and taking expectations yields[15]

$$\mathbb{E}(dF) = \alpha X F'(X)dt + \frac{\sigma^2}{2} X^2 F''(X)dt. \tag{24}$$

Substituting (24) in the arbitrage condition (22) yields

$$\rho F(X) = \alpha X F'(X) + \frac{\sigma^2}{2} X^2 F''(X), \tag{25}$$

which represents a second-order differential equation in X.

If the firm follows the optimal investment rule, the value of the option to wait must satisfy (25). It addition, it must satisfy three boundary conditions:

$$F(0) = 0,$$

$$F(\bar{X}) = \bar{X} - S.$$

$$F'(\bar{X}) = 1.$$

The first condition indicates that if the value of the investment drops to 0, then (naturally enough) the value of the option to invest is zero. The second defines the net payoff at the value of X at which it is optimal to invest. The third is termed a *smooth pasting* condition and requires the function $F(X)$ to be continuous and smooth around the optimal investment timing point.

The solution of (25) subject to the conditions given above is

$$F(X) = a X^b, \tag{26}$$

where $a = (\bar{X} - S)/\bar{X}^b$, and

$$b = \frac{1}{2} - \frac{\alpha}{\sigma^2} + \sqrt{\left(\frac{\alpha}{\sigma^2} - \frac{1}{2}\right)^2 + \frac{2\rho}{\sigma^2}}. \tag{27}$$

By substituting (26) in the second and third boundary conditions, the payoff associated with the optimal investment timing is

$$\bar{X} = \frac{b}{b-1} S. \tag{28}$$

Because $b > 1$, we also have $b/(b-1) > 1$, so that $\bar{X} > S$. Thus, in the presence of uncertainty and irreversibility the standard NPV criterion, which consists of

---

[15] The term in dz disappears because its expectation is zero.

setting $\bar{X} = S$, no longer holds. From (27), it can also be established that the magnitude of the wedge between $\bar{X}$ and S is increasing with the degree of uncertainty about future returns (as measured by σ^2). Thus, increased uncertainty, by increasing the value of the option to wait, reduces investment.

In sum, the investment rule in the presence of irreversibility and uncertainty requires that expected profits be no less than the user cost of capital plus the opportunity cost of exercising the option to invest. This option has value because by delaying the decision, the investor can choose not to invest in future states of nature where it has become apparent that profits will be low; the expected future return from the investment therefore tends to be higher with delay than without. The option has no value if investment decisions can be reversed, because divestment can take place in low-profit states.[16]

Much of the empirical evidence, for both industrial and developing countries, suggests that uncertainty (at both the micro and macro levels) tends to lower investment rates. This suggests the existence of an irreversibility effect, whereby greater uncertainty raises the value of the "call option" to delay a commitment to investment. This effect appears to dominate any positive impact on investment stemming from the possibility that greater uncertainty, under certain circumstances, increases the marginal profitability of capital (see Caballero, 1991). Arguments of this type have been used to explain the low levels of investment observed in Sub-Saharan Africa in the 1980s and 1990s.[17] Oshikoya (1994), Servén (1997), and Mlambo and Oshikoya (2001) have found that instability, irreversibility, and uncertainty played a significant role in the poor investment performance of Sub-Saharan Africa during the past decades. In a more general study, based on panel data for fifty-nine industrial and developing countries over the period 1966–1992, Asteriou and Price (2005) also found that uncertainty (measured by the conditional variance of output) has a strong negative effect on private investment.

3 The Demand for Money

The specification of the demand for real money balances plays an important role in macroeconomic analysis for both theoretical and empirical purposes. At the analytical level, the money demand function is a key element in the formulation of many macroeconomic theories. From an operational point of view, the determination of a stable relationship between real balances and other macroeconomic variables is an essential requirement for the formulation of quantitative monetary

---

[16] As noted by Abel and Eberly (1999), however, irreversibility may either increase or decrease capital accumulation, because in addition to its adverse effect on the user cost of capital, there is a hangover effect, which arises because irreversibility prevents the firm from selling capital even when the marginal revenue product is low.

[17] Caballero (1999) and Carruth et al. (2002) provide a review of the evidence for industrial countries.

targets. The transmission mechanism of monetary policy shocks (and, more generally, macroeconomic management) depends on the variables that determine the demand for money balances.

The estimation of the demand for money in developing countries has generated a voluminous literature over the years, which has by and large followed advances in econometric and statistical methods—particularly the development of cointegration techniques and the estimation of long-run relationships in economics (see, for instance, Greene, 2003). We begin this section by discussing the existing evidence relating to the conventional specification of money demand models in developing countries, and we evaluate some of the more advanced econometric studies.[18] We then discuss the phenomenon of currency substitution and its effects on the demand for domestic real money balances. Because of the breadth of the existing literature on money demand in developing nations, we do not attempt to provide a comprehensive survey of existing studies. Rather, we focus our attention on general methodological issues that arise in this particular context, and we illustrate the discussion with some specific references.

3.1 ■ Conventional Models

Early models of money demand in developing countries typically included only real income as a scale variable and the rate of inflation as an opportunity cost variable. Domestic interest rates were excluded either because alternative financial assets were assumed not to be available, so that the choice of asset holdings was limited to either money or real assets, such as commodity inventories or consumer durable goods, or because government regulations associated with financial repression implied that such rates displayed little variation over time, so that their potential effect was difficult to determine econometrically (Khan, 1980).

Early studies that attempted to introduce nominal interest rates in money demand functions met with little success. Subsequent studies, however, have found a significant effect of interest rates on money demand in middle-income countries where the financial system had reached a relatively high degree of diversification and financial markets have begun to operate with relative freedom from government intervention and regulations. For instance, Arrau et al. (1995) and Reinhart and Végh (1995) report statistically significant effects of interest rate variables on the demand for real money balances, and so do Arize et al. (2005), in a study of eight developing countries for the period 1973–1999. In a study of the demand for money in Morocco, Hoffman and Tahiri (1994) found that a foreign interest rate can also serve as the relevant opportunity cost of holding domestic monetary assets. A similar result was obtained by Calvo and Mendoza (1996) for Mexico.

---

[18]Duca and VanHoose (2004) provide a survey of the literature on money demand pertaining to industrial countries.

Assuming a partial adjustment mechanism of actual to desired levels, the conventional money demand function can be expressed as:[19]

$$\ln m = \lambda a_0 + \lambda a_1 \ln y - \lambda a_2 i_t - \lambda a_3 \pi^a_{+k} + (1 - \lambda) \ln m_{-1} + u, \qquad (29)$$

where m denotes real money balances, y real income, i the nominal interest rate (or the opportunity cost of holding money), π^a_{+k} the expected inflation rate for k periods ahead, u a disturbance term, and $\lambda \in (0, 1)$ the speed of adjustment.

Estimation of (29) raises a host of econometric issues related to simultaneity, the choice of proxy variables for expectations, and so on.[20] Most studies of the conventional demand-for-money function in developing countries suggest that the expected inflation rate (often proxied by the actual inflation rate and measured in terms of consumer prices) is highly significant. This result stresses the importance of the substitution effects between real assets and real money balances.

In line with recent developments in econometric techniques, many recent studies of the demand for money in developing countries, based on the conventional specification described earlier as well as several variants of it, have used a two-step estimation approach (see Greene, 2003). Essentially, the first step consists of estimating the long-run determinants of the demand for money using cointegration techniques. In the second step, the "general-to-specific" approach to modeling dynamic time series is used to specify the short-run dynamics of money demand. This approach generates an error correction model that distinguishes between short-run disequilibrium and long-run equilibrium properties of the demand function for real money balances. The two-step approach has been followed by Asilis et al. (1993) for Bolivia and Ahumada (1992) for Argentina, as well as many others. This literature provides a much richer specification of the short-run dynamics than the simple partial adjustment framework used earlier, and typically yields regression equations that provide better predictions of the short-run behavior of real money holdings.[21] However, the long-run parameter estimates derived from this approach do not seem to vary significantly from those derived by less sophisticated techniques. In addition, problems are often encountered in explaining economically the excessively long lags that appear in estimated money demand equations.

Studies of the demand for money in developing countries have also aimed at integrating additional explanatory variables in the conventional specification.

---

[19] As shown by Goldfeld and Sichel (1990), an equation like (29) can be derived as the solution of an optimization problem in which agents minimize the loss resulting from a disequilibrium between actual and desired money balances, given the existence of adjustment costs. We assume here that the adjustment of the demand for money toward its equilibrium value occurs in real rather than nominal terms.

[20] Goldfeld and Sichel (1990) provide a comprehensive review of econometric issues that arise in the estimation of money demand models.

[21] Another implication of recent techniques is that they clarify the conditions under which the practice of renormalizing the money demand function using the inflation rate as the dependent variable, determined by the excess growth of nominal balances over real money demand, is a valid procedure (see, for instance, Darrat and Arize, 1990).

Arrau et al. (1995), for instance, attempted to capture the role of financial innovation, whereas Deutsch and Zilberfarb (1994) and Arize et al. (2005) accounted for the adverse effect of inflation variability (a proxy for the degree of macroeconomic stability) on money demand. But the issue that has captured the most attention, at the theoretical as well as the empirical level, has been the demand for domestic- versus foreign-currency holdings.

3.2 ■ Currency Substitution and Dollarization

Currency substitution—the process whereby foreign currency substitutes for domestic money as a store of value, unit of account, and medium of exchange—has become a pervasive phenomenon in many developing countries.[22] This phenomenon has been observed in countries that differ considerably in levels of financial development, in the degree of integration with the rest of the world, and in types of exchange-rate regimes and practices.

A large number of empirical studies of currency substitution in developing countries have been conducted over the past few years in order to isolate the causes of this phenomenon.[23] These studies have shown that the degree of currency substitution depends on a variety of factors. The transactions motive may be particularly important in small, very open economies. More generally, in countries where inflation and the nominal rate of exchange-rate depreciation are high, and where opportunities for portfolio diversification are limited or ceilings on domestic interest rates are present, assets denominated in domestic currency lose their capacity to provide an efficient hedge. If transactions costs incurred in switching from domestic-currency assets to foreign-currency assets are low, the degree of currency substitution tends to be high. In a study of six Asian countries during the period 1977–1996, Sharma et al. (2005), for instance, found that exchange-rate depreciation has a significant impact on the demand for domestic money, indicating a high degree of currency substitution.[24] Uncertainty about social and political developments, fear of expropriation of assets denominated in domestic currency, and the potential need to leave the country

---

[22]The term "dollarization" is also used in many Latin American countries. As suggested by Calvo and Végh (1996), this term should be taken to refer to the use of foreign currency as a unit of account and store of value, whereas "currency substitution" should be used to refer to a stage where, beyond dollarization, foreign money is also used as a medium of exchange.

[23]For a detailed list of references, see Agénor and Khan (1996), Calvo and Végh (1996), Giovannini and Turtleboom (1994), and Prock et al. (2003), who also discuss the evidence pertaining to industrial countries.

[24]In a context where both foreign money and foreign bonds are available, the demand for domestic money will depend negatively on the (expected) rate of exchange-rate depreciation through two different channels: substitution vis-à-vis foreign money (currency substitution per se) and substitution vis-à-vis the foreign bond (capital flight). For this reason, it has been argued that the significance of an expected exchange-rate depreciation term in the demand for domestic money does not provide a valid test for the presence of currency substitution. However, as shown by Freitas and Veiga (2006), if access to foreign bonds is constrained (through binding capital controls, for instance), and domestic and foreign monies are substitutes as means of payment, the procedure remains valid.

also tend to encourage holdings of foreign currency.[25] In countries where high and variable inflation rates and uncertainty about domestic policies have prevailed for a substantial period of time, a large proportion of domestic sales and contracts are transacted in foreign currency. An additional factor that may help explain the increase in currency substitution relates to technological advances in communication and financial management, which have substantially reduced the cost of transferring funds across country borders.

Foreign currency in developing countries is held either in the form of cash "under the mattress," as deposits in the domestic banking system, or as deposits in banks abroad. Estimates of the stock of foreign currency held by private citizens are extremely difficult to obtain, although some tentative estimates have been developed in particular cases. Information on foreign-currency-denominated deposits in domestic banks is much easier to obtain—available data are generally reported in the IMF's *International Financial Statistics*—given that such deposits are being allowed by a growing number of developing countries. The IMF also collects data on foreign-currency deposits held abroad by residents of a large number of developing countries.[26]

Both the short- and long-run consequences of an increase in the holdings of foreign currency are well recognized (Agénor and Khan, 1996).[27] In the short run, a rise in foreign-currency deposits held abroad, which is equivalent to a capital outflow, can have potentially destabilizing effects on domestic interest rates, the exchange rate, and international reserves. Such an outflow may create a shortage of liquidity in the domestic banking system, which in turn would exert upward pressure on domestic interest rates. The outflow would also tend to depreciate the domestic currency under a floating exchange-rate regime. If the government is committed to defending a particular exchange rate, it would deplete its reserves. Furthermore, when a country faces the possibility of a balance-of-payments crisis and immediate corrective policy action is not taken, residents of the country, foreseeing an eventual devaluation and higher inflation or the imposition of exchange controls, are likely to increase transfers abroad. Consequently, at the very time that foreign exchange resources are required by the country, funds are shifted abroad, accelerating the erosion of official reserves and precipitating the crisis (see Chapter 14). If the buildup of foreign-currency deposits abroad is permanent, that is, if the resources are effectively lost by the home country, there are several additional long-term effects. First, there is a reduction in available resources to finance domestic investment, leading in the short run to a reduction in activity and in the long run to a decline in the rate

---

[25]Poloz (1986) develops a model where currency substitution emerges as the result of a precautionary motive for holding cash balances.

[26]These data are defined as "cross-border bank deposits of nonbanks by residence of depositor" and are derived from reports on the geographic distribution of the foreign assets and liabilities of deposit banks prepared by the authorities of a large number of international banking centers.

[27]We will discuss in the following chapters the implications of dollarization and currency substitution for monetary and exchange-rate management in developing countries.

of capital formation, thus adversely affecting the country's growth rate.[28] Second, the shift to foreign-currency deposits abroad reduces the government's ability to tax all the income earned by its residents, mainly because governments have difficulty taxing wealth held abroad as well as income generated from that wealth. Third, as government revenues fall with the erosion of the tax base, there is an increased need to borrow from abroad (thereby increasing the foreign debt burden) or greater recourse to domestic monetary financing, which raises the long-run inflation rate.

Thus, the degree of currency substitution has important implications for many developing countries, especially for monetary policy (see Chapter 5). Formulating an accurate measure of foreign-currency holdings would require adding information on foreign-currency deposits held abroad by domestic residents to data on foreign-currency deposits held in domestic banks, as well as data on foreign-currency notes in circulation. The last component, however, is almost impossible to estimate with any degree of accuracy. Existing data on total foreign-currency deposits thus provide only a lower bound on the amount of foreign-money balances held by residents of developing countries.

A general and important methodological implication of the preceding discussion is that estimating appropriate, reduced-form behavioral functions requires explicit and careful derivation of the theory underlying the specification chosen. Too often in the past, econometric studies have consisted of adding variables in regression equations without a clear underlying analytical framework.

---

[28] Note that a switch from foreign-currency deposits held in the domestic banking system to deposits held abroad would also have an adverse effect on domestic credit and other macroeconomic variables in the short run and the long run. Rodríguez (1993) discusses the macroeconomic effects associated with a change in the location of foreign deposits.

Chapter 3

The Government Budget
and Fiscal Management

The assessment of the macroeconomic effects of public sector deficits has been the subject of an extensive literature, both in developed and developing countries. The relationship between fiscal deficits, money growth, and inflation, in particular, has long been a central element in the "orthodox" view of the inflationary process. Other important issues that have attracted attention include the role of alternative financing options in the behavior of real interest rates and the sustainability of fiscal deficits, the impact of public sector imbalances on the current account and the real exchange rate, the role of expectations about future fiscal policies in price dynamics, the extent to which bonds are considered "net wealth" by private agents—the so-called Ricardian equivalence proposition—and the design of fiscal rules. Although many of these issues are common to developed and developing countries, structural differences between these two groups—most important, as discussed in Chapter 1, differences in the structure of public finance, the degree of diversification of the financial system, and the nature of the institutional arrangements that prevail between the fiscal authorities and the central bank—have important implications for the terms of the debate and the importance of specific factors in almost every respect.

This chapter discusses the measurement and sustainability of fiscal deficits in developing countries, and the role of fiscal rules.[1] The government budget constraint is presented in Section 1, and alternative deficit concepts are derived. Section 2 examines some measurement issues that often arise in developing countries. We focus in particular on issues related to the measurement of so-called quasi-fiscal deficits, a still common phenomenon in many developing nations. Section 3 addresses the issue of contingent fiscal liabilities. Section 4 examines the role of seigniorage and the

---

[1]We thus focus on the stabilization aspects of fiscal policy and public finance and abstract from allocative and distributional issues, which are discussed, for instance, in Goode (1984).

inflation tax as sources of deficit finance. We also discuss in that section the nature of "financial repression" and present a public finance view of the trade-offs between conventional taxes, the degree of financial repression, capital controls, and the inflation tax as alternative financing options for budget deficits. Section 5 discusses the factors determining the sustainability of fiscal deficits (or, more generally, the solvency of the public sector) and the overall consistency of stabilization programs. Sections 6 and 7 focus on fiscal rules, first in relation to fiscal discipline, and second in relation to public investment and growth.

1   The Government Budget Constraint

When fiscal revenues fall short of current and capital expenditure (including interest payments on the public debt), the government incurs a deficit that may be financed in a variety of ways. The government budget constraint provides the linkage between taxes, expenditure, and alternative sources of financing of public imbalances. It is an essential tool for understanding the relationship between monetary and fiscal policies, and more generally the macroeconomic effects of fiscal deficits.

To derive this constraint, consider a small open economy operating under a predetermined exchange-rate regime. The central bank provides loans only to the general government, which includes local and central governments. In general, the government can finance its budget deficit by either issuing domestic bonds, borrowing abroad, or borrowing from the central bank. The consolidated budget identity of the general government can thus be written as

$$\dot{L} + \dot{B} + E\dot{F}^g = P(g - \tau) + iB + i^* E F^g + i_c L, \tag{1}$$

where L is the nominal stock of credit allocated by the central bank, B the stock of domestic-currency-denominated interest-bearing public debt, F^g the stock of foreign-currency-denominated interest-bearing public debt, g real public spending on goods and services (including current and capital expenditure), τ real tax revenue (net of transfer payments), i the domestic interest rate, i^* the foreign interest rate, $i_c \leq i$ the interest rate paid by the government on central bank loans, E the nominal exchange rate, and P the domestic price level.[2] Equation (1) abstracts from the existence of nontax revenue and foreign grants, although these components may be sizable in some developing nations. As discussed in Chapter 1, the proportion

---

[2]Our presentation of the budget constraint of the public sector abstracts from assets such as natural resources and publicly owned capital—components that may, in practice, be important in some countries. Buiter (1983) has argued that the exclusion of such assets and liabilities may give a misleading estimate of the government's net worth, as well as its present and future financial constraints. We also exclude from public resources the cash income derived from the public sector capital stock, as well as sales of public sector assets as a source of financing of the budget deficit (see the appendix to this chapter).

of nontax revenue in total fiscal resources tends to be much larger in developing countries than in industrial countries. For simplicity, we will nevertheless exclude nontax revenue and foreign grants in the discussion that follows.

The right-hand side of (1) shows the components of the general government deficit (expenditure, taxes, and interest due on domestic and foreign debt) and the left-hand side identifies the sources of financing of the fiscal imbalance. The government budget constraint thus indicates that the fiscal deficit is financed by an increase in interest-bearing domestic and external debt, or credit from the central bank.

The central bank balance sheet in this economy is given by

$$M = L + ER - \Omega, \tag{2}$$

where M is the nominal stock of base money (currency held by the public and reserves held by commercial banks), R the stock of foreign exchange reserves, and Ω the central bank's accumulated profits or, equivalently, its net worth. Equation (2) can be generalized to equation (11) of Chapter 1 by including central bank loans to commercial banks. Profits of the central bank consist of the interest received on its loans to the government, its interest earnings on foreign reserves, and capital gains resulting from the revaluation of reserves $\dot{E}R$. In the absence of operating costs, the counterpart of these profits is an increase in the central bank's net worth, the nominal value of which is also affected by capital gains arising from exchange-rate depreciation:

$$\dot{\Omega} = i^* ER + i_c L + \dot{E}R, \tag{3}$$

where, for simplicity, the interest rate earned on reserves is assumed to be the same as that paid on the government's foreign debt.

As in Chapter 1, obtaining the overall public sector deficit requires consolidating the general government budget constraint with that of the central bank. To do so, central bank profits need to be subtracted from the general government deficit, and the increase in its net worth must be deducted from the general government's increase in liabilities. Thus, from (1) and (3),

$$\dot{L} + \dot{B} + E\dot{F}^g - \dot{\Omega} = P(g - \tau) + iB + i^*E(F^g - R) - \dot{E}R. \tag{4}$$

From (2), $\dot{L} = \dot{M} - E\dot{R} - \dot{E}R + \dot{\Omega}$. Substituting this result in (4) yields

$$\dot{M} + \dot{B} + E(\dot{F}^g - \dot{R}) = P(g - \tau) + iB + i^*E(F^g - R).$$

Defining net public foreign debt as $F^* = F^g - R$ yields

$$\dot{M} + \dot{B} + E\dot{F}^* = P(g - \tau) + iB + i^*EF^*. \tag{5}$$

On the basis of (5), several commonly used budget concepts can be derived.[3] The first concept refers to the primary (noninterest) fiscal deficit. Measured in real terms, it is given by:

$$d_P = g - \tau. \tag{6}$$

The primary deficit is important for evaluating the sustainability of government deficits and the consistency among macroeconomic policy targets, as discussed below.

The second, most commonly used concept is that of the conventional fiscal deficit, which is equal to the primary deficit augmented by interest payments on the domestic and foreign debt of the public sector. Measured in real terms, the conventional fiscal deficit is defined as

$$d_C = g + i \left(\frac{B}{P} \right) + i^* \left(\frac{E F^*}{P} \right) - \tau. \tag{7}$$

Finally, the (inflation-corrected) operational fiscal deficit can be defined as

$$d_O = g + (i - \pi) \left(\frac{B}{P} \right) + i^* \left(\frac{E F^*}{P} \right) - \tau, \tag{8}$$

where π denotes the domestic inflation rate.[4]

The operational deficit deducts from the real conventional deficit the inflation component of interest payments on domestic debt. The rationale for this adjustment is the presumption that inflation-induced interest payments are tantamount to amortization payments in their economic impact; that is, they do not represent "new" income to asset holders and are willingly reinvested in government bonds, and therefore do not affect real aggregate expenditure. The operational deficit can be thought of as providing an approximate measure of the size of the deficit the government would face at a zero inflation rate.

In practice, the difference between alternative measures of fiscal balance can be substantial. Care must therefore be exercised in choosing a particular measure to assess the stance of fiscal policy.

2 The Measurement of Fiscal Deficits

The measurement of fiscal deficits in developing nations raises a host of conceptual and practical issues, which are compounded by the lack of uniformity among

---

[3]The most general concept of public sector deficit is the change in the government's net worth, which equals the expected present value of all taxes, including seigniorage revenue (to be discussed), plus the net value of current assets (including natural resources and fixed capital), less the current value of all noncontingent and contingent liabilities (Buiter, 1983). However, few attempts have been made to use this concept in practice.

[4]With zero world inflation, if the economy produces only one good and purchasing power parity holds in absolute and relative terms—so that $E = P$ and $\varepsilon = \pi$, where $\varepsilon \equiv \dot{E}/E$ denotes the devaluation rate—and if uncovered interest parity holds continuously (that is, $i = i^* + \varepsilon$), (8) simplifies to $d \equiv g + (i - \pi)[(B/P) + F^*] - \tau$.

countries.[5] For instance, the conventional deficit can be measured on a cash basis or an accruals (or payment order) basis. In the first case, the deficit is simply the difference between total cash-flow expenditure and fiscal revenue. In the second case, the deficit records accrued income and spending flows, regardless of whether they involve cash payments or not. Accumulation of arrears on payments or revenue is reflected by higher deficits when measured on an accrual basis compared with a cash-based measure.

Another important measurement problem arises in countries where controls on key public and private prices are pervasive. To the extent that expenditure is measured at official prices, the deficit may be largely underestimated. The appropriate solution in this case is to determine, for valuation purposes, an adequate "shadow" price for the goods or services whose prices are subject to government regulations. But this is often a daunting task, fraught with empirical and conceptual difficulties.

Determining the appropriate—that is, economically meaningful—degree of coverage of the "consolidated public sector," accounting for some of the operations performed by different public entities, can also be extremely difficult in practice. In that regard, a particularly important issue for developing nations relates to the treatment of central bank operations. In many countries, central banks perform a variety of "quasi-fiscal" operations, such as the implicit levy of taxes (either through the exchange-rate system, or through the imposition of unremunerated reserve requirements), the management of government subsidy programs, debt service and transfers, the provision of preferential credit, and emergency loans to the financial system or other industries experiencing liquidity or solvency problems.[6] Significant central bank losses related to these quasi-fiscal operations are common in developing countries. Operations performed by public financial intermediaries other than the central bank may also account for sizable quasi-fiscal deficits.

Quasi-fiscal deficits in developing countries may exceed conventional fiscal deficits in overall size. To the extent that these quasi-fiscal operations are similar to other budgetary activities, they should be included in a comprehensive measure of the public sector balance. The use of the consolidated nonfinancial public sector deficit, to the extent that it excludes the losses and gains of the central bank and other important public financial intermediaries from quasi-fiscal operations, may thus provide a distorted picture of the fiscal stance.

In practice, separating monetary and quasi-fiscal operations of central banks raises difficult methodological questions, such as the appropriate treatment of capital gains or losses resulting from valuation changes—arising, for instance, from the

---

[5] An overview of measurement problems that arise in assessing the size of fiscal deficits is provided by Blejer and Cheasty (1991).

[6] Implicit taxes on foreign exchange transactions are levied when exporters must surrender foreign-currency proceeds at prices lower than some importers can buy it from the central bank. The opposite also occurs frequently: central banks may subsidize certain sectors by selling foreign exchange at rates below the rate paid to exporters. In a broader economic sense, the "tax" levied or the "subsidy" provided can be measured in unit terms by the parallel market premium, when a well-functioning informal market for foreign exchange exists.

effect of exchange-rate fluctuations on the domestic-currency value of net foreign assets—or the proper way to estimate quasi-fiscal activities performed outside the central bank's profit-and-loss account. In some countries, exchange-rate or loan guarantees provided by the central bank remain completely off its balance sheet. In addition, governments and central banks typically use different accounting systems: government accounts are on a cash basis, whereas central bank accounts are on an accrual basis. The current budgetary practice, as pointed out by Robinson and Stella (1993) and Blejer and Cheasty (1991, pp. 1661–63), is such that, when a central bank operates profitably, it generally transfers a substantial portion of its profits to the government. However, when it operates at a loss, the central bank generally runs down its reserves (or prints money) rather than receiving a transfer from the government to cover all or part of the loss. Such an asymmetric practice may seriously bias the accuracy of a country's measured fiscal deficit when central bank losses are large. Symmetry needs to be restored and the full amount of the central bank loss must be included in the government accounts in order for the size of the fiscal deficit to be accurately assessed.

3   Contingent Liabilities

Quasi-fiscal activities may lead to the creation of contingent *implicit* liabilities, which can be defined as obligations that the government is expected to fulfill if specific conditions arise, although the required outlays are typically uncertain before the triggering event occurs. Good examples are the liabilities created by the need to support the financial system (when its stability appears to be at risk) or large public enterprises.

Governments in developing countries may also be faced with various types of contingent *explicit* fiscal liabilities, which can be broadly defined as obligations that the government is legally compelled to honor if the entity that incurred them in the first place cannot—or chooses not to—do so; examples are state guarantees of borrowing by parastatal enterprises or local government entities (Polackova, 1998).

Contingent liabilities, together with direct liabilities—both explicit and implicit, such as those assumed under pay-as-you-go social security schemes, and future recurrent costs of public investment projects—have grown at a rapid pace in many developing countries in recent years and have created significant fiscal risks in many countries. Because conventional measures of the fiscal stance (as discussed earlier) do not account properly for the expected future cost of all the contingent liabilities incurred by the government, they provide misleading indicators of its ability to pay and the sustainability of budget deficits.

Because of their potentially severe distortionary effects on the allocation of resources, eliminating or at least reducing the scope of quasi-fiscal activities has become a key objective of macroeconomic management. For political and other reasons, however, the first-best solution may be difficult to achieve in the short term. It then becomes important to bring such operations into the budget, by first identifying and quantifying them and subsequently by transforming them into explicit taxes and expenditures. Appropriate accounting of explicit and implicit contingent liabilities is thus essential for assessing the stance of fiscal policy. At the same time, however, this may be a very difficult task; as noted by Blejer and Cheasty (1991, p. 1667), the calculation of the expected cost of contingent liabilities may be complicated by moral hazard problems. The very fact that the government chooses to assume explicitly these liabilities may lead to changes in private sector behavior that may make the realization of the events against which liabilities are created more likely.

4   Seigniorage and Inflationary Finance

> A government can live for a long time . . . by printing paper money. That is to say, it can by this means secure the command over real resources, resources just as real as those obtained by taxation. The method is condemned, but its efficacy, up to a point, must be admitted . . . so long as the public use money at all, the government can continue to raise resources by inflation . . . What is raised by printing notes is just as much taken from the public as is a beer duty or an income tax. What a government spends the public pays for. There is no such thing as an uncovered deficit (John Maynard Keynes).[7]

Seigniorage is an important implicit tax levied by the government. Broadly defined, it consists of the amount of real resources appropriated by the government by means of base money creation. With the base money stock denoted M and the price level P, seigniorage revenue S_{rev} can be defined as

$$S_{rev} = \dot{M}/P = \mu m = \dot{m} + \pi m, \qquad (9)$$

where $\mu \equiv \dot{M}/M$ denotes the rate of growth of the monetary base and m real money balances. The first expression in (9) defines seigniorage as the change in the nominal money stock divided by the price level. The second expression defines total seigniorage as the product of the rate of nominal money growth and real balances held by the public. By analogy with the public finance literature, μ is often referred to as the tax rate and m, which is equal to the demand for cash balances under the assumption of money market equilibrium, as the tax base. The third expression in (9) expresses the value of resources extracted by the government as the sum of the

---

[7] Quoted by Dornbusch (1993, p. 19).

increase in the real stock of money $\dot{m}$ and the change in the real money stock that would have occurred with a constant nominal stock because of inflation, πm. The last expression represents the inflation tax, I_{tax}:

$$I_{tax} = \pi m, \tag{10}$$

so that

$$S_{rev} = I_{tax} + \dot{m}, \tag{11}$$

which implies that in a stationary state (with $\dot{m} = 0$), seigniorage is equal to the inflation tax.[8] To the extent that money creation causes inflation, thereby affecting the real value of nominal assets, seigniorage can be viewed as a tax on private agents' domestic-currency holdings.

4.1 ■ The Optimal Inflation Tax

While the inflation tax has long been recognized as an important source of government revenue (as suggested by the preceding quotation by John Maynard Keynes), Phelps (1973) was the first to emphasize that the inflation rate can be determined *optimally* by policymakers in a public finance context. To show how his analysis proceeds, consider an economy in which there are no commercial banks, so that base money consists only of real cash balances held by private agents. Suppose that the economy is in a steady-state equilibrium, where the rate of output growth is zero, expectations are fulfilled, and the inflation rate is constant at π^s.[9] From (10), inflation tax revenue is thus equal to

$$I_{tax} = \pi^s m. \tag{12}$$

Suppose that the money demand function follows the Cagan specification (see Blanchard and Fischer, 1989, pp. 195–96), so that real money balances vary inversely with the expected—and actual, in this case—inflation rate:

$$m = m_0 e^{-\alpha \pi^s}, \tag{13}$$

where m_0 denotes a constant. Combining (12) and (13) and setting, for simplicity, $m_0 = 1$ yields

$$I_{tax} = \pi^s e^{-\alpha \pi^s}. \tag{14}$$

---

[8] Many macroeconomists use the terms "seigniorage" and "inflation tax" interchangeably. As shown by (11), this is a rather regrettable habit.

[9] See Auernheimer (1974) for an explicit account of transitional effects in the determination of the optimal inflation rate.

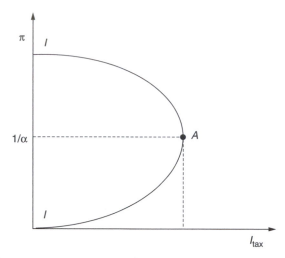

Figure 3–1 ▪ Inflation and Revenue from Inflationary Finance.

The right-hand side of (14) is depicted in Figure 3–1 as curve I, which defines the inflation tax Laffer curve. When $\pi^s = 0$, the revenue from the inflation tax is also zero. With an increase in the inflation rate, revenue rises (at a decreasing rate) at first and begins falling (at an increasing rate) beyond a certain point. Maximum revenue is reached when $dI_{tax}/d\pi^s = 0$, or, equivalently, when the absolute value of the elasticity of the demand for real money balances is unity (point A). For any given level of inflation tax revenue lower than that corresponding to point A, there are two equilibrium levels of inflation. The unique revenue-maximizing rate of inflation is thus equal to

$$\pi^s_{tax} = \alpha^{-1}, \tag{15}$$

which is the inverse of the semi-elasticity of the demand for money. Given a specific assumption about the formation of inflationary expectations, the parameter α can easily be estimated for individual countries (see, for instance, Rodríguez, 1991).

The analysis of the optimal inflation tax has been extended in a variety of directions. It has been recognized, for instance, that governments levy the inflation tax not only on currency holdings by the public, but also on noninterest-bearing required reserves that they impose on commercial banks (see Brock, 1989). Along different lines, Cox (1983) determines the revenue-maximizing rate of inflation (and the welfare cost associated with deficit finance) in a model where government bonds and privately issued bonds are imperfect substitutes. His analysis shows that traditional formulations (which view private debt and public debt as perfect substitutes) may considerably underestimate the revenue-maximizing rate of inflation. By contrast, Kimbrough (2006) finds that in a more general equilibrium framework with an explicit labor-leisure choice and money being held because it economizes on transactions costs, the revenue-maximizing inflation tax is lower than that implied by Cagan's rule.

The link between the inflation tax and currency substitution, which plays a pervasive role in many developing countries, has also been explored.[10] Végh (1989*a*) examines whether the use of inflationary finance is optimal in the presence of currency substitution. He shows, in particular, that the higher the degree of currency substitution, the higher the optimal inflation tax is for a given level of government spending. In addition to examining whether or not recourse to the inflation tax is optimal in the presence of currency substitution, some authors have studied the effect of currency substitution on the level (and variability) of inflation tax revenue. Khan and Ramírez-Rojas (1986), for instance, show that the revenue-maximizing rate of inflation is lower in the presence of currency substitution. The reason is that the elasticity of the demand for domestic real money balances is higher in this case, because the foreign currency also provides liquidity services. However, the conventional argument that a high degree of currency substitution reduces the yield of the inflation tax—because agents are able to reallocate the composition of their portfolios away from domestic-currency holdings—does not always hold. Brock (1984), in particular, has shown that when a reserve requirement is imposed on capital inflows—in addition to domestic deposits—inflation tax revenue may in fact increase when the economy becomes more open to world capital markets. Significant developments in the analysis of the optimal inflation tax have also focused on the introduction of collection lags and collection costs.

Finally, Easterly et al. (1995) have questioned the assumption of constant semi-elasticity of money demand with respect to inflation, as implied by the Cagan specification (13). Using an optimizing framework in which agents face a cash-in-advance constraint on consumption, they showed that (as long as the degree of substitutability between money and bonds in household portfolios is sufficiently high) the inflation semi-elasticity of money may in fact be increasing with inflation—an assertion that appears to be supported by the empirical evidence that they provide for a group of eleven high-inflation countries. They also showed that the seigniorage-maximizing rate of inflation (which they found to be about 266 percent per annum in their sample) varies inversely with the elasticity of substitution between money and bonds. However, further robustness tests regarding the assumed nonlinear relationship between money demand and inflation appears warranted.[11]

---

[10] See Calvo and Végh (1996) for a more detailed discussion of these issues.

[11] In their empirical estimates, Easterly et al. use a functional form for money demand of the type $\ln(m/y) = m_0 + \lambda \pi^\gamma$, where m is the money stock, y is output, and π is the inflation rate. The inflation semi-elasticity is thus given by $\partial \ln(m/y)\partial \pi = \gamma \lambda \pi^{\gamma-1}$, which is increasing in π if $\gamma > 1$. The seigniorage-maximizing inflation rate can be shown to be given by $\pi_{tax}^s = (-\gamma \lambda)^{-1/\gamma}/[1 - (-\gamma \lambda)^{-1/\gamma}]$, which implies that a finite π_{tax}^s exists only if $-\lambda \gamma > 1$. Otherwise, seigniorage would increase monotonically with π, no Laffer curve would exist, and π_{tax}^s would be infinite.

4.2 ■ Collection Lags and the Olivera-Tanzi Effect

An important element that ought to be considered in the debate over the optimal use of inflationary finance relates to the effects of inflation on the tax system—in particular, the link between inflation and the collection lag in conventional tax revenue. This factor, which has been emphasized by Olivera (1967) and more forcefully by Tanzi (1978), has become known as the Olivera-Tanzi effect. It plays an important role in the analysis of fiscal, monetary, and inflation dynamics in developing countries.[12]

Taxes are collected with lags in almost all countries. In industrial nations, average collection lags—which measure the time between the moment taxes due are calculated and the moment they are actually paid to the fiscal authority—vary from one month in some cases and for particular sources of taxation (such as income taxes that are withheld at the source) to six to ten months in other cases (such as indirect taxes). In developing countries, by contrast, average collection lags may be substantially higher. The share of revenue generated by taxes collected with progressive rates and withheld at the source is small, and taxes (such as import duties and excises) are often levied at specific rates. In such conditions an increase in the inflation rate will bring a fall in real conventional tax revenue, the extent of which will depend on the average collection lag and the prevalent tax burden, that is, the initial ratio of taxes to aggregate output. Formally, let n denote the average lag in collection of conventional taxes measured in months, and let π_M denote the monthly inflation rate. The real value of conventional tax revenue at an annual inflation rate of π^s is given by (Tanzi, 1978, p. 426):

$$Tax(\pi^s) = \frac{Tax(0)}{(1+\pi_M)^n} = \frac{Tax(0)}{(1+\pi^s)^{n/12}}, \tag{16}$$

where $Tax(0)$ denotes the real value of conventional taxes at a zero inflation rate. Thus, in the presence of collection lags ($n > 0$), inflation lowers the real value of conventional tax revenues.

Using (14) and (16), total government revenue T is equal to

$$T = \pi^s e^{-\alpha\pi^s} + \frac{Tax(0)}{(1+\pi^s)^{n/12}}. \tag{17}$$

---

[12]Olivera (1967), in an attempt to provide an explanation of chronic inflation in Latin America in the 1960s, argued that as a result of fiscal lags, nominal revenues are fixed in the short run, so that their real value falls with inflation. Dutton (1971) and Aghevli and Khan (1978) were also among the first to emphasize the tax-inflation nexus.

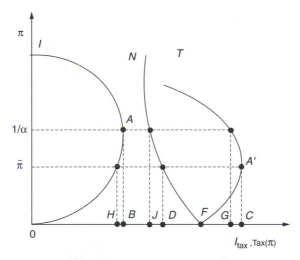

Figure 3–2 ▪ Inflation, Inflationary Finance, and Total Tax Revenue
Source: Adapted from Tanzi (1978. p. 428).

Setting the derivative of (17) with respect to π^s equal to zero gives the value of the inflation rate that maximizes total real revenue, $\tilde{\pi}$:

$$dT/d\pi = (1 - \alpha\tilde{\pi})e^{-\alpha\tilde{\pi}} - \left(\frac{n}{12}\right)\frac{Tax(0)}{(1 + \tilde{\pi})^{1+n/12}} = 0, \qquad (18)$$

which is a nonlinear equation in $\tilde{\pi}$. A graphical determination of the solution is depicted in Figure 3–2. Curve I represents, as before, the inflation tax Laffer curve. Curve N represents revenue from conventional taxes, which depends negatively on inflation and is maximized at a zero inflation rate (point F). Curve T represents the horizontal sum of curves I and N and gives total revenue. As the figure shows, the total revenue-maximizing rate of inflation $\tilde{\pi}$ is lower than the rate that maximizes revenue from the issuance of money, $1/\alpha$ [see (15)]. At that level of inflation, revenue from the inflation tax is equal to OB (which is equal to JG) and conventional tax revenue is equal to BG (which is also equal to OJ). Total tax revenue, by contrast, is maximized at rate $0 < \tilde{\pi} < 1/\alpha$. Compared to its value at the rate $1/\alpha$, revenue from conventional taxes rises from OJ to OD; but because inflation is positive, revenue from conventional taxes is now lower (by the quantity $OF - OD$, that is, DF) compared to the case where inflation is zero. Similarly, the contribution of the inflation tax to total revenue, equal to OH, is now lower (by the quantity HB) than what it would be at the rate $1/\alpha$.

In fact, the fall in conventional revenue resulting from an increase in inflation may be large enough to outweigh the increase in revenue from the inflation tax, yielding an overall *decline* in total real revenue. This can be seen also in Figure 3–2; at $\tilde{\pi}$, total revenue is maximized and given by OC; beyond $\tilde{\pi}$, higher inflation rates

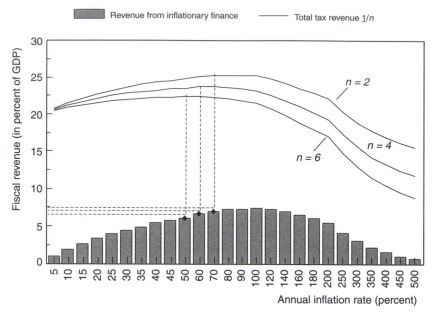

Figure 3–3 ▪ Inflation, Inflationary Finance, and Tax Revenue
Source: Adapted from Tanzi (1978, pp. 433 and 446).
$1/n$ denotes the collection lag, in months. The calculations reported assume that $\alpha = 1$ and that the ratio of money to GDP and the ratio of total tax revenue to GDP (both at a zero inflation rate) are equal to 20 percent.

would tend to reduce total revenue, because increases in revenue from the inflation tax are insufficient to compensate for the fall in revenue from conventional taxes. At $\pi = 1/\alpha$, for instance, $OG < OC$. The simulation results provided by Tanzi (1978, 1988) show that this outcome is indeed entirely plausible, under reasonable parameter configurations. Some of Tanzi's results are shown in Figure 3–3. When the collection lag is two months, the total revenue-maximizing rate of inflation is equal to 70 percent. When the collection lag rises to six months, the revenue-maximizing inflation rate drops to 50 percent. In that case, inflating at a rate of 70 percent would increase revenue from the inflation tax (from 6.1 percent of GDP to 7 percent), but total tax revenue would fall.[13]

An important implication of the Olivera-Tanzi effect is that it makes clear the distinction between the seigniorage-maximizing inflation rate and the revenue-maximizing inflation rate. But how relevant is this effect in practice? Choudhry (1991) reports estimates (based on a sample of eighteen developing countries) of collection lags for different components of fiscal revenue. The average collection lag

---

[13]In the simulations reported in Figure 3–3, the inflation rate is assumed to be directly under the control of the monetary authority; that is, the feedback effect from money creation to prices is taken to be instantaneous. In practice this assumption may not be warranted and may bias the results considerably.

appears to be about six months for total revenue but varies widely among the different categories of revenue. The lag is higher than average for income taxes (about seven months for individual income, and fourteen months for profits and capital gains), taxes on domestic goods and services (about nine months), import duties (eight months), and nontax revenue—such as transfers from public enterprises (about twelve months). In addition, these lags appear to vary considerably across countries. In several cases, the econometric estimates indicate that the erosion of fiscal revenue would have substantially offset the resources generated by an increase in the yield of the inflation tax, and would have resulted in a fall in net revenue. Thus, in countries where collection lags are high, raising the inflation tax may be counterproductive, as a result of the Olivera-Tanzi effect.[14]

The conventional inflation tax Laffer curve depicted in Figure 3–1 appears to be well supported by the empirical evidence on countries with moderate inflation. Easterly and Schmidt-Hebbel (1994) have drawn attention to the fact that conventional estimates of revenue-maximizing inflation rates may be biased—upward in high-inflation countries, downward in low-inflation countries—by misspecification of the demand function for real money balances as being of constant semi-elasticity with respect to inflation, when in fact the semi-elasticity may fall as inflation rises.[15] More generally, the available evidence suggests that, at least in high-inflation countries, the rate of inflation has been higher than the rate that maximizes steady-state revenue from the inflation tax. The public finance motive for inflationary finance does not seem to explain cases of chronic high-inflation countries, although the acceleration of inflation observed in Latin America after the outbreak of the debt crisis in 1982 is consistent with a greater need to finance external and internal obligations with internal resources.[16] Thus, if imperfect information or lags in the adjustment of inflationary expectations are ruled out, an alternative explanation for the existence of chronically high inflation must be found. The lack of credibility and the time inconsistency problem faced by policymakers, which is discussed at length in Chapter 11, may provide such a rationale.

---

[14]Dixit (1991) has argued that, in general, it is not only the optimal level of the inflation tax that is affected by the presence of collection lags, but the whole tax structure. In such conditions the collection costs associated with alternative, conventional taxes, rather than the revenue yielded by the different taxes, may become a critical consideration. In particular, the presence of lags may raise the excess burden of income taxes, warranting greater reliance on the inflation tax than would be the case in the absence of collection lags. See, however, Mourmouras and Tijerina (1994) for an evaluation of Dixit's conjecture.

[15]See the discussion of Easterly et al. (1995) above.

[16]Dornbusch and Fischer (1993) and Dornbusch et al. (1990) adopt the conventional view that the revenue motive does not explain high inflation in developing countries. It should be noted, however, that based on the evidence provided by Phylaktis and Taylor (1992, 1993) for the Taiwanese hyperinflation of 1945–1949 as well as for some recent episodes of high inflation in Latin America (Argentina, Bolivia, Brazil, Chile, and Peru), the assumption that the average inflation rate that prevailed during the 1970s and 1980s was equal to the revenue-maximizing rate $1/\alpha$ cannot be rejected.

4.3 ■ Collection Costs and Tax System Efficiency

The use of inflationary finance for financing government spending and fiscal deficits
has been justified by a variety of arguments. The early debate on the desirability of
inflationary finance focused on the welfare cost of alternative options for financing
public expenditure (see Bailey, 1956; and Auernheimer, 1974). However, as pointed
out by Aghevli (1977), if alternative revenue sources are not readily available, a
comparative analysis is of little relevance. In most developing economies, the tax
base is inadequate, the share of small-income earners is disproportionately large,
and evasion is endemic, preventing the imposition of a high tax burden on the
population. Tax administration is weak, inefficient, and often subject to a large degree
of corruption (Goode, 1984). In such conditions the appropriate comparison is
between the total cost of inflationary finance—taking into account the distortions
introduced into the tax system itself by inflation, as emphasized by Tanzi (1978)—
and the benefits, in terms of additional consumption in the future, derived from a
higher level of government expenditure.

The effect of the efficiency of the tax system on the optimal inflation tax rate
can be illustrated using a simple framework. Suppose that the government faces the
budget constraint

$$g - \theta \iota y = \pi m,$$

where g denotes government spending, $0 < \iota < 1$ the conventional income tax rate,
$0 < \theta < 1$ a coefficient that reflects the efficiency of the tax system (that is, the
fraction of tax liabilities actually collected), and y the tax base. The wedge $(1 - \theta)\iota$
represents unit collection costs, which are wasted by the inefficiencies of the tax
system. The government's objective is to maximize potential revenue ιy with respect
to the conventional tax rate and the inflation rate, subject to the budget constraint
given above. Given this objective, as shown by De Gregorio (1993), a reduction in the
efficiency of the tax system (a fall in θ) leads in general to an increase in the optimal
inflation rate and a fall in the inflation tax base. The effect on the optimal tax rate is
ambiguous, but the share of income tax revenues falls as the share of revenue from the
inflation tax in total resources increases. Thus, even when the optimal conventional
tax rate increases, it will not outweigh the effects of the fall in efficiency on the
revenue collected from the income tax.

The trade-off between explicit direct taxation and the inflation tax has been
shown to persist in more general settings, notably by Aizenman (1987) and Végh
(1989b). Both authors argue that a decline in the efficiency of the tax system raises the
inflation rate.[17] Végh, in particular, examines the relationship between government

---

[17] Along the same lines, Fishlow and Friedman (1994) have shown that a high degree of income tax evasion (which
typically increases with the rate of inflation) will raise the inflation rate required to fund a given level of the fiscal
deficit.

spending and inflationary finance in a model where alternative, conventional taxes (such as the consumption tax) are subject to increasing marginal collection costs. As a result, the inflation tax is shown to depend positively on the level of government spending. An improvement in the efficiency of tax collection would therefore reduce the government's reliance on the inflation tax as a source of revenue.

Other work has attempted to identify the effect of political factors on the efficiency of the tax system, in addition to institutional constraints, such as the degree of competence of public administration. In most developing nations, high-income earners have considerable political power, making it difficult for the government to enforce tax laws. A formal analysis of the relationship between tax system efficiency—measured by the extent to which seigniorage is used as a source of fiscal revenue—political instability, and economic structure has been provided by Cukierman et al. (1992). Their analysis indicates that the efficiency of the tax system in developing countries is highly correlated with the composition of output (countries with a large agricultural sector, for instance, tend to rely more on seigniorage than countries with large mining and manufacturing sectors) and with the degree of instability and polarization of the political system. The degree of openness to foreign trade and the rate of urbanization also have significant effects on tax system efficiency. Thus, in addition to structural and administrative factors, countries that are more politically unstable tend to rely more on the inflation tax as a source of government revenue.[18]

4.4 ■ Financial Repression and the Inflation Tax

The term "financial repression" is used by analysts who take their lead from McKinnon (1973) and Shaw (1973). These authors presented the first systematic attempts at taking into account some of the specific characteristics of financial markets in developing countries. According to McKinnon (1973), the financial system in most developing countries is "repressed" (kept small) by a series of government interventions that have the effect of keeping very low (and often at negative levels) interest rates that domestic banks can offer to savers. To a large extent, the motivation for this set of interventions is a fiscal one; the government wants to actively promote development but lacks the direct fiscal means to do so, because of either a lack of political will or administrative constraints. It uses the financial system to fund development spending in two ways. First, by imposing large reserve and liquidity requirements on banks, it creates a captive demand for its own non-interest-bearing and interest-bearing instruments, respectively. Thus, it can finance its own high-priority spending by issuing debt. Second, by keeping interest rates low through the imposition of ceilings on lending rates, it creates an excess demand for credit. It then requires the banking system to set aside a fixed fraction of the credit available to

---

[18] However, the ability of the political-weakness approach to explain persistence of seigniorage financing has been questioned by Cukierman (1992).

priority sectors. This system has implications both for economic efficiency and for the distribution of income.

The combination of low rates of return on assets and high reserve requirements implies that even a competitive banking system will be forced to offer low interest rates on its liabilities. In many developing countries the combination of low nominal deposit interest rates and moderate to high inflation has often resulted in negative real rates of return on domestic financial assets, with an adverse effect on saving and the financial intermediation process. If the rate of return available in the domestic financial system represents the relevant intertemporal relative price in the economy, whether saving falls or rises will depend on the familiar trade-off between income and substitution effects in consumption (see Chapter 2). Regardless of the direction of the effect on saving, however, interest rate ceilings introduce a wedge between the social and private rates of return on asset accumulation, thereby distorting intertemporal choices in the economy. Moreover, the portfolio effects of such ceilings are conducive to financial disintermediation, as savers are induced to switch from the acquisition of claims on the banking system to accumulation of real assets, assets traded in informal markets, and foreign assets.

Assets such as gold and real estate play important roles in the financial decisions of households in many such countries. The induced incentive to hold real assets, however, does not imply the achievement of high levels of investment. The reason is that, although the notional demand for investment may be high, many prospective investors will be unable to secure financing. Their own prospective savings may be inadequate to finance large projects; the formal financial system may not have the resources available, due to government absorption of a large part of the small pool of savings intermediated through commercial banks and other financial institutions; and the high potential costs of doing business in informal markets, as well as the costs of evading capital controls, may render financing through these channels uneconomical. Finally, in the absence of rationing through the price system, there is no assurance that those investment projects that *are* financed through the formal financial system will necessarily yield higher returns than those that are not.

The consequences of financial repression for the distribution of income arise because this system transfers resources from actual and potential savers, as well as from excluded borrowers, to favored borrowers who are able to acquire resources at the contracted interest rates. The most important of the latter, of course, is the public sector itself. In addition, however, enterprises in priority sectors and well-connected individuals will tend to benefit from privileged access.[19] Benefits also accrue to the beneficiaries of the additional public spending made possible by this source of financing for the public sector, as well as to potential taxpayers who would be affected by the replacement of the "financial repression tax" by more conventional taxes.

---

[19] Because financial repression creates an economic rent for favored borrowers, a secondary efficiency loss arises from the rent-seeking activities stimulated by the existence of such rents.

The foregoing discussion did not provide a general rationale for the existence of financial repression and its association with capital controls. Why do countries choose to repress their financial systems and impose impediments to capital mobility, in view of the inefficiencies that the use of such policy instruments typically entail? We adopt the view here that accounting for the fiscal aspects of such measures is essential to understanding governments' motivations in adopting them. Specifically, we view the determination of the degree of financial repression and the intensity of capital controls as a fiscal issue involving a choice between alternative taxation instruments subject to appropriate constraints. We begin by considering the optimal choice between financial repression and the inflation tax in a model where the policymaker's objective is to maximize seigniorage, given the portfolio structure of private agents. We then consider a more general framework in which conventional taxes and capital controls are used as additional taxation instruments by the government.

The trade-off between the inflation tax and the degree of financial repression can be illustrated in a simple framework adapted from Brock (1989).[20] Consider a closed economy in which private agents hold cash balances and bank deposits, with the former asset bearing a zero rate of interest. Output is taken as given and is normalized at zero for simplicity. Banks are subject to a fractional reserve requirement on deposits. Asset demand functions for cash m and bank deposits d can be written in general form as[21]

$$m = m(\overset{-}{i_L}, \overset{+}{i_L - i_D}),\qquad(19)$$

$$d = d(\overset{+}{i_L}, \overset{-}{i_L - i_D}),\qquad(20)$$

where i_L denotes the nominal lending rate and i_D the deposit rate. If banks face no operating costs, the zero-profit condition yields

$$i_L = i_D/(1 - \mu), \quad 0 < \mu < 1,\qquad(21)$$

where μ denotes the required reserve ratio. For simplicity, assume that the asset demand functions take the form

$$\ln m = \alpha_0 - \alpha i_L, \quad \ln d = \beta_0 - \beta(i_L - i_D) = \beta_0 - \beta\mu i_L.\qquad(22)$$

---

[20]Bencivenga and Smith (1992) and Roubini and Sala-i-Martin (1995) examine the determination of the optimal degree of financial repression in a growth context. The latter study, however, treats inflation as a proxy for financial repression, an assumption that is not very useful for our purpose here.

[21]Brock (1989) shows how the asset demand equations (19) and (20) can be derived from a simple optimization problem in which cash balances and deposits provide liquidity services that reduce transactions costs.

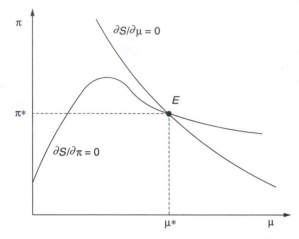

Figure 3–4 ▪ Seigniorage, Reserve Ratio, and the Inflation Tax
Source: Adapted from Brock (1989. p. 113).

Assume that the real interest rate is constant and set equal to zero. Thus, $i_L = \pi$, where π denotes the (actual and expected) inflation rate. The policymaker's objective is to maximize inflation tax revenues, which are given by

$$S_{rev} = \pi(m + \mu d),\qquad(23)$$

with respect to the inflation rate and the reserve ratio μ.[22] Brock (1989, pp. 111–12) shows that solving this maximization problem yields

$$\partial S_{rev}/\partial \mu = 0 \;\Rightarrow\; \pi\mu = 1/\beta,\qquad(24)$$

$$\partial S_{rev}/\partial \pi = 0 \;\Rightarrow\; \pi = \frac{1}{\alpha} + \frac{\beta\mu d}{\alpha m}\left(\frac{1}{\beta} - \pi\mu\right).\qquad(25)$$

Equation (25) indicates that when the reserve ratio is zero, the revenue-maximizing inflation rate is equal to $1/\alpha$, as derived earlier. If both instruments are used, however, the optimal inflation rate may be either higher or lower than $1/\alpha$. Figure 3–4 shows graphically the determination of the optimal values of both policy instruments, which are obtained at the intersection of the two curves defined by (24) and (25). Because, in general, $\bar{\mu} > 0$, there exists an optimal degree of financial repression, which is traded off (within a given range) with the optimal inflation tax in order to raise the demand for money—the inflation tax base.

---

[22]McKinnon and Mathieson (1981) discuss the case where the policymaker's objective is to minimize the inflation rate (instead of maximizing inflation tax revenue) with respect to the required reserve ratio.

In practice, reserve requirements that are unremunerated or remunerated at a fixed rate may represent a large share of the revenue from seigniorage. Another source of revenue from financial repression is the implicit subsidy from which the government benefits by obtaining access to bank financing at below-market interest rates, and the implicit tax—collected through the banking system—on private sector bank deposits that are remunerated at below-market interest rates. This source of the financial repression tax may be complementary to the inflation tax rather than substitutable, as discussed in the case of reserve requirements. This may occur, in particular, if the menu of financial assets available to portfolio holders is limited, and if real interest rates are sufficiently negative to increase the demand for real money balances, that is, the inflation tax base (Giovannini and de Melo, 1993).

Repression of the domestic financial system in developing countries is almost always accompanied by controls on international capital movements, in order to prevent restrictions on domestic financial intermediaries from being bypassed by recourse to foreign intermediaries. To the extent that the imposition of restrictions on capital mobility forces agents to hold more domestic-currency balances than they would prefer to hold (thus raising the base of the inflation tax), capital controls may be viewed as imposing a tax on asset holders, whose costs and benefits must be traded off with other taxes, explicit and implicit. A unifying framework for understanding the use of financial repression, capital controls, and the inflation tax in developing countries thus requires a model in which policymakers are faced with some type of constraint on the use of regular taxes.

To illustrate the basic implications of such a framework, consider a portfolio structure similar to that described above, with the addition of imperfectly substitutable foreign bonds. In such a setting, capital controls can be modeled as an explicit tax on foreign interest income or as a tax on purchases of foreign assets.[23] The key aspect of the taxation system that needs to be taken into account is the existence of collection and enforcement costs, which, as for instance in Aizenman (1987) and Végh (1989b), can be assumed to be an increasing and convex function of the level of revenue. By contrast, other forms of taxation at the disposal of the government—financial repression and the inflation tax, which are implicit taxes, and capital controls—have low collection costs. The government's problem then consists of maximizing either inflation tax revenue, an overall revenue target—in order to finance, say, a "minimum" level of public expenditure—or, as in the normative models of Aizenman (1987) and Végh (1989b), the representative consumer's indirect utility subject to its budget constraint. A general prediction of this approach is that capital controls, financial repression, and the inflation tax must be used concurrently with regular taxes when collection or enforcement costs on the latter source of revenue are sufficiently large. An increase in collection costs may also reduce the use of

---

[23] Aizenman (1986) models capital controls in the context of a dual exchange-rate regime under which controls generate a wedge between the exchange rates applied for current and capital account transactions. Capital controls can also be modeled as a surrender requirement on some categories of exports at a more appreciated exchange rate.

regular taxes relative to other tax instruments, whereas an increase in the deficit target (resulting from, say, a rise in government spending) may lead to a more intensive use of all taxation instruments. The first prediction accords well with the intuitive idea that in an optimal tax structure, the highest tax rates are imposed on activities that carry the lowest collection costs.

The unified public finance framework highlighted in the foregoing discussion helps to emphasize the fiscal considerations underlying the simultaneous existence of conventional taxes, financial repression, capital controls, and the inflation tax. Of course, reserve requirements are often changed as a result of purely monetary considerations (to reduce, for instance, excess liquidity in the economy), while capital controls are often imposed to prevent speculative attacks and the eventual collapse of a fixed exchange rate (see Chapter 14). Nevertheless, in a long-run context the fiscal view may be the most sensible approach to understanding the setting of these policy instruments in developing countries. One of the important implications of this approach is that the decision to impose a high degree of financial repression, far from being an aberration, may be the outcome of an optimally determined taxation structure. In such conditions, successful financial liberalization requires the simultaneous implementation of appropriate fiscal reforms, an issue to which we will return in Chapter 18.

5   Policy Consistency and Solvency

The flow budget identity of the government derived earlier does not highlight the dynamic nature of the financing constraint that the public sector typically faces. Governments cannot indefinitely accumulate domestic and foreign debt. They therefore face an *intertemporal* budget constraint, which also imposes restrictions on the paths followed by different components of the budget identity. In addition, the flow budget constraint imposes consistency requirements on the overall formulation of macroeconomic policy targets that must be taken into account in the design of stabilization programs. The first part of this section examines how the solvency constraint can be derived to evaluate the sustainability of fiscal policy. The second part analyzes the requirements imposed by financing constraints on the formulation of macroeconomic policy objectives.

5.1 ■ The Intertemporal Solvency Constraint

As shown in (5), the consolidated public sector deficit can be defined in real terms as

$$\frac{\dot{M}}{P} + \frac{\dot{B}}{P} + \frac{E\dot{F}^*}{P} = g + i\left(\frac{B}{P}\right) + i^*\left(\frac{EF^*}{P}\right) - \tau. \qquad (26)$$

Equation (26) can be rewritten in terms of the behavior over time of stocks and flows per unit of output, which yields

$$\frac{\dot{M}}{Py} + \dot{b} + z\dot{f}^* = g - \tau + (i - \pi - n)b + (i^* + \varepsilon - \pi - n)zf^*, \qquad (27)$$

where lower-case letters represent the corresponding upper-case quantities expressed as a proportion of nominal output (that is, $b \equiv B/Py$, for instance), n the rate of growth of real output, $z = E/P$ the real exchange rate, and ε the devaluation rate. The quantity $\dot{M}/Py$ is seigniorage as a fraction of output.[24]

Let $d'_p = (g - \tau)/y$ measure the primary public sector deficit as a fraction of output, and let seigniorage as a share of output be equal to $s = \dot{M}/Py$. Total public debt as a fraction of output can be defined as $\Delta = b + zf^*$.

Using the identity $d(zf^*)/dt \equiv z\dot{f}^* + \hat{z}zf^*$, where $\hat{z}$ denotes the rate of depreciation of the real exchange rate, (27) can be written as

$$\dot{\Delta} = (r - n)\Delta + d'_p + (i^* + \hat{z} - r)zf^* - s, \qquad (28)$$

where r is the domestic real interest rate. Defining the augmented primary deficit as

$$d = d'_p + (i^* + \hat{z} - r)zf^* \qquad (29)$$

yields

$$\dot{\Delta} = (r - n)\Delta + d - s, \qquad (30)$$

which indicates that the difference between the (augmented) primary deficit plus interest payments on the existing debt and seigniorage revenue must be financed by domestic or foreign borrowing.

Integrating forward, (30) yields the public sector's intertemporal budget identity:

$$\Delta = \mathbb{E}_t \int_t^\infty (s_k - d_k)e^{-\int_t^k (r_h - n_h)dh} dk + \lim_{k \to \infty} \mathbb{E}_t \Delta e^{-\int_t^k (r_h - n_h)dh}, \qquad (31)$$

where $\mathbb{E}_t$ denotes the expectations operator, conditional on information available at period t. The government is solvent if the expected present value of the future resources available to it for debt service is at least equal to the face value of its initial stock of debt. Under these circumstances, the government will be able to service its debt on market terms. Solvency thus requires that the government's prospective fiscal

---

[24]If purchasing power parity holds (so that $z \equiv 1$) and uncovered interest parity prevails, (27) becomes $\dot{M}/(Py) + \dot{b} + \dot{f}^* = g - \tau + (r - n)(b + f^*)$, where $r = i - \pi$ denotes the real interest rate. We will focus, however, on the more general formulation in (27).

plans satisfy the present-value budget constraint

$$\Delta \le \mathbb{E}_t \int_t^\infty (s_k - d_k) e^{-\int_t^k (r_b - n_b) db} dk,$$

or equivalently,

$$\Delta \le PV(s, t, r - n) - PV(d, t, r - n), \tag{32}$$

where

$$PV(x, t, r - n) = \mathbb{E}_t \int_t^\infty x_k e^{-\int_t^k (r_b - n_b) db} dk$$

denotes the present value at time t of flow x, discounted at the instantaneous rate of discount $r - n$. Equation (32) indicates that public debt must be equal at most to the present value as of time t of seigniorage revenue minus the present value as of time t of future (augmented) primary deficits. These conditions imply the transversality condition

$$\lim_{k \to \infty} \mathbb{E}_t \Delta e^{-\int_t^k (r_b - n_b) db} \le 0. \tag{33}$$

Equation (33) indicates that, as of time t, the expectation of the present value of the consolidated (domestic and foreign) future public debt cannot be positive in the limit.

Equation (33) implies that, ultimately, the debt/output ratio must grow at a rate *below* the real interest rate minus the rate of growth of output. This restriction rules out an indefinite Ponzi game: the government cannot pay forever the interest on its outstanding domestic and foreign debt simply by borrowing more. At some point the debt must be serviced by reducing primary deficits or by increasing seigniorage revenue.

The solvency restriction—or, equivalently, the government's intertemporal budget constraint—ensures only that the existing debt is ultimately serviced (by current and future primary surpluses or by current and future seigniorage); it does not imply that the debt is actually paid off (Buiter, 1989a). A logical implication of the foregoing analysis is that solvency is ensured even if the debt/output ratio grows at a positive rate, as long as this rate remains below the long-run value of the difference between the real interest rate and the real growth rate. A government may thus be solvent despite the fact that its real outstanding debt and even its debt/output ratio are growing without bound. If the real interest rate remains below the growth rate of output forever ($r < n$, for all t), condition (33) will not be binding: the government will be able in each period to service the existing debt by further borrowing, engaging in an "honest" Ponzi scheme. We will, however, assume that this condition does not hold for an indefinite period of time, thus excluding Ponzi games.[25] Solvency requires, eventually, positive values for $s - d$, the difference between seigniorage revenue and the augmented primary deficit. Although running a conventional surplus is not necessary to ensure solvency, positive operational surpluses are eventually required in the absence of seigniorage revenue. More generally, to ensure solvency requires reducing the augmented primary deficit (by reducing government expenditure, increasing net current revenue, or shifting the composition of the public debt between internal and external debt) or increasing the present value of future seigniorage.

For different paths of $r - n$ and for a given present value of seigniorage revenue, the size of the primary surplus required to stabilize the debt/output ratio can in principle be calculated. Alternatively, by treating debt and primary surpluses as exogenous, the level of seigniorage revenue required for ensuring solvency can be calculated for different values of $r - n$. Depending on the assumed form of the money demand function, such an option also has implications for the inflation rate. In practice, however, the use of the solvency constraint to determine a sustainable path of fiscal policy is fraught with difficulties, which result in particular from the uncertainty about future revenue and expenditure flows. As a result, few attempts have been made to evaluate the sustainability of fiscal deficits in light of the solvency constraint. For industrial countries, Uctum and Wickens (2000), Bravo and Silvestre (2002), and Arghyrou and Luintel (2007) represent some useful applications; for developing countries, Buiter and Patel (1992) for India, and Haque and Montiel (1994) for Pakistan, are among the few studies available. Most of these tests for fiscal sustainability are performed by analyzing cointegration between public expenditures and revenues, both measured as ratios to GDP.

Perhaps more important, solvency is a weak criterion with which to evaluate the sustainability of fiscal policy (Buiter, 1985). Several alternative fiscal policy rules can be consistent with a given intertemporal constraint, but not all of them are necessarily sustainable in the long run.[26] As discussed below, the sustainability of alternative fiscal strategies must be evaluated in the context of the overall macroeconomic policy mix, taking into account all macroeconomic targets.

5.2 ▪ Financing Constraints and Policy Consistency

Macroeconomic programs typically consist of specifying targets for inflation, output growth, domestic and foreign borrowing, and the overall balance of payments. The

---

[25] The condition $r > n$ is the requirement that the economy be dynamically efficient in closed-economy macroeconomics (see Blanchard and Fischer, 1989, pp. 103–64). Although the real interest rate may remain below the growth rate for substantial periods of time in fast-growing economies (such as the newly industrialized countries of Asia), this cannot be the case indefinitely.

[26] See Spaventa (1987). In addition, as shown by Bohn (1990), rules that appear sustainable in a perfect foresight world may not be feasible in a stochastic environment.

existence of such targets imposes restrictions on the use of alternative sources of financing of the public sector deficit. The government budget constraint thus determines a "financeable" or sustainable level of the fiscal deficit given the authorities' policy targets. If the actual deficit exceeds its sustainable level, one or all macroeconomic targets must be abandoned, or fiscal policy adjustment must take place. For instance, for a given size of the fiscal deficit, the government budget constraint allows the derivation of an "equilibrium" inflation rate for which no fiscal adjustment is required. However, given a fixed exchange-rate regime, limited foreign reserves determine the path of central bank credit to the government and, through the budget constraint, the size of the primary deficit. Ignoring the consistency requirement between fiscal policy, inflation, and credit growth implied by a fixed exchange rate would lead, as discussed in Chapter 14, to recurrent speculative attacks and eventually to a collapse of the exchange-rate regime.

A convenient accounting framework for the analysis of consistency requirements between fiscal deficits, inflation, output growth, and the balance of payments in a small open economy is provided by the government budget identity derived above.[27] The essential analytical tool is provided by (28). For instance, whether a given fiscal policy path is sustainable can be determined by projecting the future course of the debt/output ratio for given predictions about the evolution of money demand (using one of the alternative specifications discussed in Chapter 2), the desired inflation rate, the real interest rate, and the growth rate of the economy. If the analysis shows the debt/output ratio to be rising continually, eventually violating the solvency constraint, fiscal adjustment or adjustment in other targets is required.

If the policy target is to maintain a fixed debt/output ratio for both internal and external debt, real debt cannot grow faster than real output. Using (28) together with an inflation target (and therefore a given level of revenue from money creation) yields the primary deficit plus interest payments on domestic and foreign debt. Given the level of the primary deficit, it is possible to determine the inflation rate at which revenue from the inflation tax covers the difference between the government's financing needs and its issuance of interest-bearing debt. A similar strategy would lead to the determination of the appropriate path of foreign and domestic borrowing, given primary deficit and inflation targets. Whatever the "closure rule" chosen, the resulting path of policy variables will depend on assumptions about the behavior of the predetermined variables (domestic output growth, the real exchange rate, foreign inflation, and foreign real interest rates), as well as the estimated form of the demand for real money balances.

Consistency checks among the different objectives of macroeconomic policy and their financing implications are an essential aspect of the design of macroeconomic reform programs. However, the fact that a given path of fiscal policy is sustainable,

---

[27] Anand and van Wijnbergen (1989) provide a detailed description of the methodological issues involved in deriving deficit levels that are consistent with internal and external debt strategies, an inflation target, and alternative exchange-rate arrangements. Budina and van Wijnbergen (2008) introduce uncertainty in that setting.

given other macroeconomic targets, does not imply that it is necessarily the optimal choice (Fischer and Easterly, 1990). For instance, a financeable fiscal deficit may be large enough to crowd out private investment. Reducing the debt/output ratio would be an appropriate policy choice in such conditions since it would "crowd in" private capital expenditure and allow the economy to sustain a higher growth rate of output.

6   Fiscal Rules and Fiscal Discipline

There has been much debate in recent years on whether explicit fiscal frameworks may help to achieve and maintain fiscal discipline, thereby safeguarding fiscal solvency. Fiscal rules, in particular, have taken the form of maintaining fixed targets for the deficit (variously defined) and/or public debt ratios to GDP. Such rules have been used in industrial and developing countries alike (García, 2012). Brazil for instance introduced a Fiscal Responsibility Law in May 2000 that prohibits financial support operations among different levels of government and requires that limits on the indebtedness of each level of government be set by the Senate.

A common criticism of standard deficit rules (including balanced budget rules) is that they are inflexible (to the extent that they are defined irrespective of the cyclical position of the economy) and tend to be procyclical.[28] Studies based on fiscal constraints in U.S. states, such as Fatás and Mihov (2006), have indeed shown that while balanced budget rules have proved effective in limiting the size of deficits and the volatility of spending, they have also imposed costs to the states' economies because of the large (downward) adjustment in government spending that is required during recessions.[29] Similar results have been shown to hold in cross-country studies of industrial countries (see Lane, 2003).

In response, deficit rules have been refined and are now often applied either to a cyclically adjusted deficit measure (such as the structural budget deficit) or an average over the economic cycle. Chile, for instance, introduced in early 2000 a structural surplus rule (of 1 percent of GDP) that allows for limited deficits during recessions.[30] By doing so, advocates claim, these rules may allow the operation of automatic stabilizers and possibly provide some room for discretionary policy within the cycle.

---

[28] Another criticism of budget rules that take the form of strict limits on the overall fiscal deficit-to-GDP ratio is that they may end up discouraging public investment. See Agénor and Yilmaz (2011) for a more detailed discussion.

[29] The evidence provided by Canova and Pappa (2006), which is also based on the experience of U.S. states, does not support the existence of a close link between fiscal constraints and (lack of) volatility—the reason being, in their view, that these constraints have not been properly enforced.

[30] See Rodríguez et al. (2007). The budget is adjusted not only for the effects of the business cycle on public finances, but also for fluctuations in the price of copper—Chile's main export commodity.

However, this increased flexibility comes at a cost, because the benchmark against which fiscal performance is to be judged is made more complicated—especially if estimates of potential output are frequently revised, as is often the case. In turn, this increases the scope to bypass the rules, making them potentially harder to enforce and undermining their credibility. In countries with a poor (or uneven) track record of policy consistency, lack of credibility may lead to higher interest rates, thereby exacerbating debt sustainability problems.

7   Fiscal Rules, Public Investment, and Growth

Another criticism of budget rules that take the form of strict limits on the overall fiscal deficit-to-GDP ratio is that they may discourage public investment. A fiscal rule that caps the overall budget deficit puts both current and investment spending on an equal footing in the measurement of the deficit. The danger, then, is that whenever the rule becomes binding, the government will choose to cut those spending categories that are politically less costly to alter. If the political cost of postponing or abandoning investment projects is lower than the political cost of constraining current expenditure—as is often the case in practice—an overall deficit rule will entail a built-in bias against public investment, which in turn may have an adverse effect on economic growth (see Chapter 17).

The existence of this bias has led a number of economists, most notably Blanchard and Giavazzi (2004), to advocate reliance on a *golden rule*, whereby the focus is on maintaining a current balance (that is, current revenues less current expenditures) or surplus, with capital expenditures being financed from government savings and borrowing. Under the Blanchard-Giavazzi rule, governments should borrow in net terms on a continuous basis only to the extent that this net borrowing finances net public investment, that is, gross investment less capital depreciation (which counts as current spending).[31] This rule therefore would allow gross borrowing for the purpose of refinancing maturing debt, thereby leaving net debt unaffected. Moreover, to the extent that public investment boosts the economy's production capacity on a permanent rather than just temporary basis, it would affect welfare of not only the present generation but also future generations. Thus, intergenerational equity provides a rationale to spread the costs of public investment over both current and future generations, by financing investment through government borrowing instead of current tax revenues. By implementing a golden rule—or, more specifically, by allowing no new borrowing in net terms to finance current spending—the outstanding debt stock of any country would, over time, become fully backed by the public capital stock.

---

[31] Musgrave (1939) was an early proponent of a rule aimed at excluding capital outlays from the operating budget, while including depreciation of the government capital stock.

Despite its intuitive appeal, the golden rule has attracted much criticism.[32] First, advocates of the golden rule have generally emphasized the need to exclude capital expenditure on *infrastructure* from the fiscal deficit rule. In countries with large infrastructure gaps, certain projects (such as roads, ports, or airports) may indeed have rates of return that are so high, and a degree of complementarity with private investment (see Chapter 2) that is so tight, that they justify receiving priority in the design of a public investment program. However, in other countries investment in human capital (education and health) may be an equally important priority, in part because it may have a larger impact on growth. Excluding public investment in "core" infrastructure only (as opposed to investment in schools and hospitals) from fiscal targets would create a bias against these other components of public investment.

Second, if applied to *gross* public investment—as opposed to *net* investment, as advocated by Blanchard and Giavazzi (2004)—the golden rule could turn into an obstacle to deficit and debt reduction. Given the ratio of public investment as a share of GDP, the long-run equilibrium level of government debt could be quite high, especially in an environment of low inflation. This, in turn, could push interest rates and debt service to unsustainable levels. To prevent this from happening, a concomitant limit on public debt may also prove necessary.

Third, the golden rule is not a good guide to fiscal policy if some components of current expenditure—such as on operation and maintenance that keeps existing infrastructure in good condition, or spending that contributes to health outcomes and the accumulation of human capital—can promote growth more effectively than capital expenditure per se. This may be particularly so if the golden rule creates a moral hazard problem, in the sense that the possibility of borrowing without limits to finance investments lowers the care that must be taken when evaluating the costs and benefits of each project. Put differently, components of recurrent expenditure, such as spending on schools and hospitals, may be equally important to maintain the quality of the services produced by the capital stock in those categories. The same issue arises if the focus on current spending entails a bias against operations and maintenance, that is, the expenditure required to keep the existing physical infrastructure in good working order.

The implication of the foregoing discussion is that alternative fiscal rules may have an ambiguous effect on fiscal performance and economic growth. The key question is where should one draw the line in imposing a deficit rule. As noted earlier, current spending on education and health enhances human capital. In addition to infrastructure investment, excluding current spending on education and health may be costly from a growth and fiscal stability perspective. At the same time, however, public capital in infrastructure may have a sizable impact on health and education outcomes (see Chapter 17). If these externalities are sufficiently strong, a rule that

---

[32] See Agénor and Yilmaz (2011) and the references therein for a more detailed discussion.

includes some bias toward investment in infrastructure only may still lead to higher growth rates—despite some degree of inefficiency in the investment process itself.

Appendix
Fiscal Effects of Privatization

In many developing countries, the operation of state-owned enterprises (SOEs) is a significant component of the government budget. The role of SOEs expanded in many cases after independence. The economic role of the state was perceived to be important, both for ideological reasons as well as due to the alleged productivity of public goods (infrastructure, health, education) in development. Favorable terms of trade and low international interest rates in the 1970s gave a huge boost to debt-financed public investment in LDCs. However, SOEs have become a drain on the budget in many countries, partly as a result of poor investments and various structural problems. Privatization, in many cases, has become an attractive way to help cope with fiscal deficits.[33] Indeed, privatizing is one way that the government can achieve a credible fiscal adjustment. Credibility in this case comes from the fact that the source of the deficit was the location of the enterprise in the public sector, and re-nationalizing it would be costly. Thus, the government can "lock in" a (present and) future fiscal adjustment by divesting itself of the enterprise.

The main point regarding the fiscal effects of privatization is that they are not generally equal to privatization revenues, essentially because measuring fiscal effects in that way fails to take into account the (positive or negative) effects on the government's budget of keeping the enterprise.

To show this, recall from the earlier discussion that (in the absence of debt financing) the government budget constraint can be written as

$$-d_P + (\pi + n)m = (r - n)\Delta, \tag{A1}$$

where $-d_P$ is the primary surplus, π the inflation rate, m real money balances, r the real interest rate, n the rate of growth of output, and Δ the stock of public debt.

For simplicity, suppose that the government owns only one SOE. Splitting $-d_P$ up into the portion contributed by the SOE and the rest of the primary surplus, p^s, yields

$$-d_P = p^s + (r_G - n)k_G, \tag{A2}$$

---

[33]Arguments for privatization, however, are not just fiscal; efficiency may often be the most important consideration. Structural problems make it better to run many firms privately, even if in principle public ownership is compatible with economic efficiency. Even if a public firm is profitable, the economy may be better off having it in the private sector, if the latter can produce an even higher return.

where k_G is the SOE's capital stock valued at replacement cost relative to GDP, and r_G is the ratio of the SOE's net income (profits minus depreciation) to its capital stock, k_G. The quantity $r_G - n$ is what the government receives on a permanent basis as a result of the SOE maintaining a capital-output ratio k_G (because each period the SOE has to plow back nk_G into investment).

Using (A2), the public sector budget constraint can be written as:

$$p^s + (r_G - n)k_G + (\pi + n)m = (r - n)\Delta. \tag{A3}$$

The drain on the budget is larger, of course, the smaller $r_G - n$ is. This puts pressure on p^s.

How do we know if it is (fiscally) a good idea to sell k_G? To answer this question we have to ask in what direction p^s would have to move in order for the above equation to continue to hold if the government sold k_G. As a first pass, let us consider first what would have to happen to p^s if k_G were to be simply given away. Then there would be no privatization revenue, but privatization would still have a fiscal effect: the government would lose a permanent flow of income as long as $r_G > n$. This makes the point that the fiscal implications of privatization are not limited to the direct revenue effect.[34]

Consider now the case where the government sells k_G, and suppose that the private rate of return to capital is $r_P - n$. Then the private sector would pay

$$Q = (r_P - n)/(r - n),$$

for k_G. If $(r_P - n) < 0$, then no one will buy the SOE's capital. Now suppose that the stock of debt is constant at Λ; the public sector budget constraint (A3) can be rewritten as:

$$\frac{p^s + (r_G - n)k_G + (\pi + n)m}{r - n} = \Delta.$$

If the private sector pays Q, then the effect of the sale is to replace $(r_G - n)k_G/(r - n)$ on the left-hand side by Qk_G. Thus, the fiscal impact of the sale is given by:

$$\frac{\Delta p^s}{r - n} = -\left(Q - \frac{r_G - n}{r - n}\right)k_G.$$

---

[34] A more general issue is whether privatization proceeds should be viewed as a form of revenue or as a form of financing, similar to a bond issue. See MacKenzie (1998).

This means that the government's fiscal position will be eased (the required adjustment in p^s will be negative) as long as $r_P > r_G$, because this will make the term inside the parentheses positive. The lessons are the following:

- The SOE can be sold only if the private sector can make it profitable.
- The government may be (fiscally) better off selling it even if the SOE is profitable.
- The fiscal benefit to the government from the sale will be

  - less than the sale price if $r_G - n > 0$;
  - negative if $r_P < r_G$;
  - equal to the sale price if $r_G - n = 0$;
  - more than the sale price if $r_G - n < 0$.

Going back to the credibility issue, the important point is that by selling a loss-making enterprise, the government can "lock in" a future fiscal adjustment. It can increase the primary surplus today *and* tomorrow at the same time, so creditors do not have to rely on promises of future fiscal actions that may not be kept by the same or a different government. That is, it can adjust in a present value sense *today*.

Two additional points are worth noting. First, it is important that the actual impact of privatization on the budget be measured correctly. The key question is, by how much is the sustainable non-SOE primary surplus affected by privatization? The answer is given by

$$\Delta p^s = -(r - n)\left(Q - \frac{r_G - n}{r - n}\right)k_G.$$

That is, the present value benefit has to be amortized to calculate the impact on the sustainable primary surplus.

Second, whether privatization is worth pursuing does not depend solely on its fiscal implications. It depends, more generally, on whether the resources involved yield a greater *social* return in public or private sector use. But whenever their return is greater, the decision to keep the resources in the public sector or transfer them to the private sector will invariably have fiscal implications, and these have to be taken into account when analyzing public sector solvency.

Chapter 4

Macroeconomic Effects of Fiscal Policy

A key starting point for understanding the macroeconomic effects of fiscal policy is the economy's aggregate resource or saving-investment constraint discussed in Chapter 1, which shows how conventional public deficits, $I^g - S^g$, are financed by surpluses from the private sector, $S^p - I^p$, and the rest of the world, CA, where CA is the current account deficit:[1]

$$D = I^g - S^g = (S^p - I^p) + CA. \tag{1}$$

The nature of the effects of large public deficits on the macroeconomy thus depends on the components of this equation that actually adjust. In turn, adjustment depends on the scope for domestic and foreign financing, the degree of diversification of financial markets (which determines to some extent the choice between money or bond financing), and the composition of the deficit. Expectations about future government policies also play an important role in the transmission of fiscal policy.

This chapter provides a broad perspective on the macroeconomic effects of fiscal policy. We first examine the theoretical applicability of the Ricardian equivalence proposition and review the empirical evidence related to developing countries. The linkage between fiscal deficits, monetary policy, and inflation is then explored, using a closed-economy model in which the government faces a solvency constraint and must adjust the overall policy stance at a well-defined date in the future. The impact of public sector deficits on real interest rates and private investment (through crowding-out effects) is examined in Section 3, using an optimizing model of a small open economy with zero capital mobility. Section 4 focuses on the relation between fiscal deficits and the current account. Section 5 considers the possibility that fiscal

---

[1] Equation (1) is derived by decomposing national saving, S (as defined in Chapter 1), into its private and public components, denoted by S^p and S^g, respectively, and rearranging terms.

contractions may actually be expansionary. Section 6 studies the dynamic effects of fiscal policy on output and the labor market.

1   Ricardian Equivalence

The Ricardian equivalence proposition states that deficits and taxes are equivalent in their effect on consumption (Barro, 1974). Lump-sum changes in taxes have no effect on consumer spending, and a reduction in taxes leads to an equivalent increase in saving. The reason is that a consumer endowed with perfect foresight recognizes that the increase in government debt resulting from a reduction in taxes will ultimately be paid off by increased future taxes, the present value of which is exactly equal to the present value of the reduction in current taxes. Taking the implied increase in future taxes into account, the consumer saves today the amount necessary to pay them tomorrow. Ricardian equivalence implies, in particular, that fiscal deficits have no effect on aggregate saving or investment or consequently, through the economy-wide saving-investment identity presented above, on the current account of the balance of payments.

The conditions required for Ricardian equivalence to hold are the existence of effectively infinite planning horizons, certainty about future tax burdens, perfect capital markets (or the absence of borrowing constraints), rational expectations, and nondistortionary taxes. The restrictive nature of these assumptions has been demonstrated by various authors. In particular, the debt neutrality proposition has been shown to break down if agents have finite horizons, capital markets are imperfect, or uncertainty and distributional effects play a pervasive role in individuals' consumption and savings decisions.[2]

The available evidence for developing and industrial countries has failed so far to provide much support for the Ricardian equivalence hypothesis. The evidence from industrial countries appears to be largely inconclusive (see Romer, 2000*b*, and Riccuiti, 2003). In developing countries where financial systems are underdeveloped, capital markets are highly distorted or subject to financial repression, and private agents are subject to considerable uncertainty regarding the incidence of taxes, many of the considerations necessary for debt neutrality to hold are unlikely to be valid. As alluded to in Chapter 2, the empirical evidence has indeed failed to provide much support for the Ricardian equivalence proposition. Haque and Montiel (1989) reject the null hypothesis of debt neutrality for fifteen out of a group of sixteen developing countries. Veidyanathan (1993), and the empirical studies reviewed by Easterly and Schmidt-Hebbel (1994), for the most part also fail to detect any significant effects of public deficits on private consumption. Both Haque and Montiel and

---

[2] See Leiderman and Blejer (1988) and Riccuiti (2003) for extensive discussions of the conditions under which debt neutrality fails to hold. Barro (1989) offers a more sympathetic view.

Veidyanathan suggest that consumers in developing countries are subject to liquidity and borrowing constraints.

2 Deficits, Inflation, and the "Tight Money" Paradox

> Milton Friedman's famous statement that inflation is always and everywhere a monetary phenomenon is correct. However, governments do not print money at a rapid rate out of a clear blue sky. They generally print money to cover their budget deficit. Rapid money growth is conceivable without an underlying fiscal imbalance, but it is unlikely. Thus rapid inflation is almost always a fiscal phenomenon. (Fischer and Easterly, 1990, pp. 138–39)

The relationship between fiscal deficits and inflation has been the focus of considerable attention in development macroeconomics. We will examine below some of the empirical and analytical issues that arise in this context—in particular, the role of policy expectations and financing constraints. Chapter 11 will examine further the link between fiscal deficits and money growth in the inflationary process.

One common explanation for the inflationary consequences of fiscal deficits in developing nations is the lack of sufficiently developed domestic capital markets that can absorb newly issued government debt. At the level of any particular country, there may be no clear short-term link between fiscal deficits and inflation. The correlation may even be negative during extended periods of time. The emergence of a positive correlation in the long run is also not a clear-cut phenomenon. Using data spanning 107 countries over 1960–2001 and dynamic panel techniques that explicitly distinguish between short- and long-run effects, Catão and Terrones (2005) found a strong link between inflation and fiscal deficits in high-inflation countries, but not in low-inflation cases. In a study of ninety-one countries over the period 1960–2006, Lin and Chu (2013) found that fiscal deficits have a strong impact on inflation in high-inflation episodes, and a weak impact in low-inflation episodes.

Various arguments have been proposed to explain the absence of a close correlation between budget deficits and inflation in the short run. First, an increase in fiscal deficits may be financed by issuing bonds rather than money; although such a policy is not sustainable as a result of the government's solvency constraint (as discussed in Chapter 3), it may imply a weak relation in the short run between deficits and inflation. Second, a change in the composition of the sources of deficit financing over time (in particular, a substitution of domestic financing for foreign financing) may lead to higher inflation without substantial changes in the level of the consolidated public sector deficit. Third, the correlation may be low if the money demand function is unstable, if expectations are slow to adjust, or if inertial forces (such as the existence of staggered wage contracts) prevent the economy from adjusting rapidly to changes in inflationary pressures.

A fourth and particularly appealing argument relies on the existence of strong expectational effects linked to perceptions about future government policy. Private agents in an economy with high fiscal deficits may at different times form different expectations about how the deficit will eventually be closed. For instance, if the public believes at a given moment that the government will attempt to reduce its fiscal deficit through inflation (thus eroding the value of the public debt), current inflation—which reflects expectations of future price increases—will rise. If, at a later time, the public starts believing that the government will eventually introduce an effective fiscal adjustment program to lower the deficit, inflationary expectations will adjust downward and current inflation—reflecting, again, expectations about the future behavior of prices—will fall (Drazen and Helpman, 1990).

A particularly well-known example of the role of expectations about future policy is provided by the "monetarist arithmetic," or the so-called tight money paradox. In a seminal contribution, Sargent and Wallace (1981) have shown that when a financing constraint forces the government to finance its budget deficit through the inflation tax, any attempt to lower the inflation rate today, even if successful, will require a higher inflation rate tomorrow. For a given level of government spending and "conventional" taxes, the reduction in revenue from money creation raises the level of government borrowing. If a solvency constraint (of the "no Ponzi game" type discussed in the previous chapter) imposes an upper limit on public debt, the government will eventually return to a rate of money growth high enough to finance not only the same primary deficit that prevailed before the initial policy change, but also the higher interest payments due to the additional debt accumulated as a result of the policy change. Solvency and macroeconomic consistency thus impose constraints on policy options in attempts to reduce the inflation rate. In the discussion that follows we present the Sargent-Wallace result, following Liviatan (1984, 1986).[3]

2.1 ■ The Analytical Framework

Consider a closed economy with a zero rate of population growth ($n = 0$) and in which the representative household's flow budget constraint is given by

$$\dot{m} + \dot{b} = (1 - \iota)(y + \tau + rb) - c - \pi m, \qquad (2)$$

where m denotes real money balances, b the stock of indexed government bonds held by the public, y output (assumed exogenous), τ net lump-sum transfers from the government, c consumption expenditure, π the inflation rate, and r the constant real

---

[3]The analytical framework used by Sargent and Wallace is based on an overlapping generations model with a number of restrictive assumptions. Liviatan's formulation is more general. It should also be noted that the question addressed by Sargent and Wallace was the anticipation of a once-and-for-all increase in the level of the nominal money stock, rather than in the rate of money growth, as is done here.

interest rate.[4] $0 < \iota < 1$ is the proportional income tax rate, which, for simplicity, is assumed to be levied on all components of gross income. Real wealth a can be defined as

$$a = m + b + (1 - \iota) \int_t^\infty (y + \tau) e^{-(1-\iota)rb} \, db.$$

Assuming that transfers are also constant over time yields

$$a = m + b + (y + \tau)/r. \tag{3}$$

The demand functions for goods and money are defined as

$$c = \kappa a, \quad \kappa > 0 \tag{4}$$

$$m = (\rho - \kappa)a/i, \quad \rho > \kappa \tag{5}$$

where $i = (1 - \iota)r + \pi$ denotes the net nominal interest rate and ρ the rate of time preference, which is assumed here to equal the after-tax real interest rate:[5]

$$\rho = (1 - \iota)r.$$

The equilibrium condition in the goods market is given by

$$c = y - g, \tag{6}$$

where g, non-interest government spending, is assumed constant over time. The government budget constraint can be written as

$$\dot{m} + \dot{b} = g - \iota y + (1 - \iota)(\tau + rb) - \pi m. \tag{7}$$

Finally, the dynamics of the real money stock are given by

$$\dot{m} = (\mu - \pi)m, \tag{8}$$

where $\mu \equiv \dot{M}/M$ denotes the rate of growth of the nominal money stock.

---

[4] See Fernández (1991) for an analysis of the Sargent-Wallace monetarist arithmetic with an endogenous real interest rate.

[5] Liviatan derives (4) and (5) from an explicit optimization setup. The condition $\rho = (1 - \iota)r$ ensures a stationary solution for consumption. Note that the interest elasticity of real money balances is equal to unity; see Drazen (1985) for the general case.

In the steady state $\dot{m} = \dot{b} = 0$, so that using (2) to (8) yields, with $r = \rho/(1-\iota)$,

$$\tilde{c} = y - g, \tag{9}$$

$$\tilde{m} = \frac{\rho - \kappa}{(1-\iota)\rho + \mu}\{\tilde{m} + \bar{b} + r^{-1}(y + \tau)\}, \tag{10}$$

$$g - \iota y + (1-\iota)(\tau + r\bar{b}) = \tilde{m}, \tag{11}$$

and $\pi^* = \mu$. There are only two independent equations in this system, which can be used to determine the steady-state values of the inflation rate (or, equivalently, the rate of growth of the nominal money stock) and real money balances for a given level of the stock of bonds, or the solutions for real money holdings and bonds for a given inflation rate. Whatever the "closure rule" chosen, however, it is useful to note for what follows that consumption and the real interest rate are independent of the rate of growth of the nominal money stock across steady states. This is implied for the real interest rate by the assumption that $r = \rho/(1-\iota)$, and for consumption by the market-clearing condition which requires that $\tilde{c} = y - g$.

2.2 ■ Constant Primary Deficit

Consider a temporary reduction in the rate of money growth during the time interval $(0, T)$, with the primary government deficit held constant at $\bar{d}$, which is equal to:

$$\bar{d} = g - \iota y + (1-\iota)\tau. \tag{12}$$

After T, the stock of real government bonds is assumed to remain constant at the level it attained at period T. Therefore, during the interval $(0, T)$ μ is exogenous and b endogenous, while for $t \geq T$ the stock of bonds remains constant at the level b_T^+, and μ becomes endogenous.[6]

Examining the effects of this policy rule on the dynamics of inflation and real money balances proceeds in two stages. First, substituting (8) in (7) yields

$$\dot{b} = (1-\iota)rb - \mu m - z_b, \tag{13}$$

---

[6]The assumption that there exists an upper bound on the stock of real bonds b_T^+ that private agents are willing to hold seems to ignore that the stock of domestic debt can tend to infinity without violating the government's solvency constraint, as long as all interest income received by the public can be taxed away in a lump-sum fashion (McCallum, 1984). However, if lump-sum taxation is not feasible, bond financing of fiscal deficits and debt accumulation cannot continue indefinitely (Erbas, 1989). To the extent that private agents perceive correctly the constraints that the government faces, they will also anticipate any attempt to stabilize the level of public debt in the future.

where $z_b = (1 - \iota)(y + \tau) - c$. Because output and public spending are constant, private consumption is also constant, at $(y - g)$ from (6), along the equilibrium path. Hence z_b is also constant.

Given that, from (8), $\pi m = \mu m - \dot{m}$, (4) and (5) imply, given the definition of the nominal interest rate, that

$$\dot{m} = [\mu + (1 - \iota)r]m + z_m, \quad z_m = -\left(\frac{\alpha - \kappa}{\kappa}\right)(y - g), \qquad (14)$$

where z_m is also constant. From (4), a constant level of consumption implies that real wealth must be constant along the equilibrium path, so that $\dot{m} + \dot{b} = 0$. This condition can be verified by adding (13) and (14), using (3) and (4).

Suppose that, starting at a steady state where $\mu = \mu^b$, the monetary authority reduces the rate of money growth unexpectedly at time $t = 0$ to a value $\mu^s < \mu^b$ over the interval $(0, T)$. Although the price level is fully flexible, real money balances will not jump at $t = 0$ because m_0 is determined, from (4) and (5), by the requirement that consumption remain constant and by the fact that b_0 cannot jump on impact.[7] It follows from (14) that a reduction in the rate of growth of the nominal money stock implies $\dot{m}_0 < 0$, so that real money balances will be declining over time. Solving (14) yields

$$m = \tilde{m}(\mu^s) + [m_0 - \tilde{m}(\mu^s)]e^{[(\mu^s + (1 - \iota)r)t]}, \qquad (15)$$

where $m_0 < \tilde{m}(\mu^s) = -z_m/[\mu^s + (1 - \iota)r]$. Equation (15) indicates that real money balances will be declining at an increasing rate over the interval $(0, T)$. From (4), (5), and (6),

$$\pi = \left(\frac{\alpha - \kappa}{\kappa}\right)(y - g)m^{-1} - (1 - \iota)r, \quad 0 < t < T, \qquad (16)$$

implying that the inflation rate increases continuously over the interval $(0, T)$.

The solution for $t \geq T$ is obtained as follows. During the interval $(0, T)$, b must be rising because $\dot{m} < 0$ and $\dot{m} + \dot{b} = 0$. Because the latter condition must continue to hold for $t \geq T$ and the stock of bonds must remain constant at b_T^+ for $t \geq T$, we must have $\dot{m} = 0$ for $t \geq T$. Real money balances must therefore remain constant at, say, m_T^+ for $t \geq T$. The condition $\dot{m} = 0$ for $t \geq T$ is satisfied by adjusting discontinuously the rate of money growth at T so as to satisfy (14):

$$\dot{m}_T = 0 = [\bar{\mu} + (1 - \iota)r]m_T^+ + z_m. \qquad (17)$$

---

[7]However, as shown by Liviatan (1986), the constancy of real money balances on impact does not necessarily hold under more general conditions, particularly if money and real goods are either substitutes or complements, or if consumption is highly sensitive to changes in the real interest rate.

Since $\dot{m} < 0$ for $0 < t < T$, (17) implies that $\bar{\mu}$ must be raised above μ^s. Moreover, since $m_T^+ < m_0$, it follows that

$$\mu^s < \mu^b < \bar{\mu}, \tag{18}$$

which indicates that the reduction in the money growth rate during the interval $(0, T)$ below its initial value must be followed at T by an increase beyond the initial value.

It can also be shown using (16) that in the post-adjustment steady-state inflation remains constant at π_T^+ and that

$$\pi_T^+ > \pi_0, \quad t \geq T, \tag{19}$$

which indicates that the steady-state inflation rate that prevails beyond T is higher than in the initial steady state. The increase in the inflation rate occurs during the interval $(0, T)$, because no jump can occur at time T as a result of perfect foresight.

The thrust of the analysis is thus that a temporary reduction in the rate of money growth raises the inflation rate both during and after the policy change. Intuitively, a temporary reduction in nominal money growth is offset by an increase in bond finance. Thus, after the temporary policy is removed, higher interest payments require that seigniorage revenue be higher to finance the deficit, and this, in turn, requires a higher inflation rate. The expectation of higher inflation in the future implies higher inflation even while the contractionary policy is in place, because otherwise price level jumps would give rise to arbitrage profits.

2.3 ▪ Constant Conventional Deficit

Consider now what happens if it is the deficit inclusive of interest payments (that is, the conventional deficit) that remains fixed, rather than the primary deficit. Using (11), (12) is therefore replaced by

$$\bar{d} = g - \iota y + (1 - \iota)(\tau + rb). \tag{20}$$

For (20) to hold continuously with b endogenous, we assume that the government makes compensatory adjustments in transfer payments to households, τ. Because public spending and output are constant, the financing rule implies that $\tau + rb$ is constant at, say, Λ. We will also assume in the following analysis that the rate of population growth n is positive (and constant), instead of zero.[8]

---

[8] The assumption of a nonzero population growth rate is necessary to avoid degenerate dynamics in the present case.

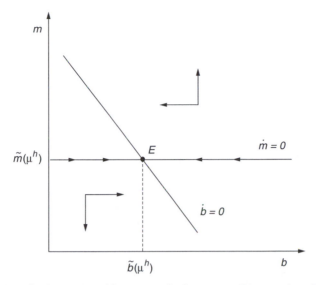

Figure 4–1 ▪ Steady-State Equilibrium with Constant Conventional Deficit
Source: Adapted from Liviatan (1984, p. 13).

Equations (3)–(6) and (8) now yield, using (20),

$$\dot{b} = -nb - \mu m + z'_b, \quad z'_b \equiv (1 - \iota)(y + \Lambda) - (y - g), \tag{21}$$

and (14) is unchanged. For μ given, (14) and (21) form a differential equation system in b and m whose steady-state equilibrium is a saddlepoint. The slope of the saddlepath coincides in the present case with the slope of the $[\dot{m} = 0]$ curve, as shown in Figure 4.1. The steady state is reached at point E, for a given value of $\mu = \mu^b$. Real balances may now jump on impact since endogenous transfers ensure that wealth, and therefore consumption, remains constant initially. Varying μ and maintaining $\dot{m} = \dot{b} = 0$ permits the derivation of alternative long-run equilibrium values of real money balances and the stock of bonds. Alternatively, for a given value of b, treating m and μ as endogenous allows us to derive the steady-state relation between real holdings of money and bonds. This relationship is given by

$$m = (nb - z'_b - z_m)/(1 - \iota)r. \tag{22}$$

Equation (22) is represented by line MM in Figure 4.2. The initial long-run equilibrium with $\mu = \mu^b$ obtains at E in the figure.

Consider now, as before, a reduction of the money growth rate from μ^b to μ^s over the interval $(0, T)$. The new steady-state solution associated with (14) and (21) and $\mu = \mu^b$ obtains at point E', which is also located on MM. On impact, real money balances increase, in association with a fall in both the price level and the initial steady-state inflation rate, and the system jumps from point E to point A.

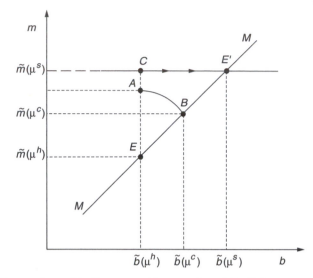

Figure 4–2 ▪ Dynamics with Constant Conventional Deficit
Source: Adapted from Liviatan (1984, p. 14).

The economy then follows a divergent path over $(0, T)$, moving over time from point A to point B located on curve MM, which is reached exactly at period T. If at that moment the policymaker raises the rate of growth of the money stock to some value $\mu^c > \mu^s$ and freezes the stock of bonds at b_T^+, point B will represent a steady-state equilibrium.[9] During the transition period, real balances fall while the stock of bonds and the inflation rate rise. However, at point B real balances remain above their original equilibrium level $\tilde{m}(\mu^b)$, implying that the inflation rate will remain permanently below its initial steady-state level. Consequently, a *temporary* reduction in the money growth rate leads to a *permanent* reduction in the inflation rate. Essentially, the difference from the previous case results from the fact that when the primary deficit is held constant, the increase in interest payments on the public debt is financed by the inflation tax and is therefore inflationary. By contrast, when the overall deficit is held constant, the increase in interest payments on government debt is financed by a rise in taxes, which leads to a lower reliance on the inflation tax.

In the preceding framework, defining "tight" monetary policy as a reduction in the rate of growth of the nominal money stock leads to a system that is dynamically unstable during the interval $(0, T)$. The solvency constraint eventually requires a freeze of the stock of government bonds. Consequently, for $t \geq T$, the economy is "stuck" with a smaller stock of money, a larger stock of bonds, and a permanently higher rate of inflation. Liviatan (1986) shows that this dynamic instability disappears if a "tight monetary policy" is defined as a reduction in the *share* of money

---

[9]By a chain of reasoning similar to that developed above, it can be shown that we must also have $\dot{m} = 0$ for $t \geq T$. Thus, the second stage of the monetary experiment must also correspond to a steady state.

financing of the government deficit over the interval $(0, T)$. In this formulation, the ratio of money financing to bond financing γ is exogenous, whereas the rate of growth of the nominal money stock is endogenous. Monetary tightening is now defined as a temporary reduction in γ. Liviatan shows that the modified model is saddlepath stable, provided that the initial share of money financing is not too small. He also shows that with a constant primary deficit, a temporary monetary tightening leads to an immediate but temporary increase in inflation, whereas a permanent tightening leads to an immediate and permanent increase in inflation. The first result differs from the Sargent-Wallace paradox derived earlier, where tighter money was defined as a reduction in the money growth rate. However, the result regarding conventional deficits derived above persists: if the deficit is defined as including interest payments on the public debt, the Sargent-Wallace paradox is reversed.

A further generalization can be obtained if the deficit target is written as

$$\tilde{d} = g - \iota y + (1 - \iota)\tau + \Theta r b,$$

where $0 < \Theta < 1$. The case of constant primary deficit thus obtains for $\Theta = 0$, while the constant overall deficit case obtains for $\Theta = 1$. Assuming that the composition of deficit finance γ is again the policy parameter, Liviatan (1988) demonstrates that a policy trade-off emerges in the choice of the optimal combination (γ, Θ). In particular, he shows that there exists a value Θ^* such that for $\Theta < \Theta^*$ an increase in the money-to-bond ratio is deflationary, while for $\Theta > \Theta^*$ an increase in γ is inflationary. At any given level of inflation there exists a trade-off between γ and Θ, which is negative when $\Theta < \Theta^*$ and positive when $\Theta > \Theta^*$.

The lack of a close correlation between fiscal deficits and inflation may be compounded by the existence of uncertainty about the type of policy instruments that policymakers are expected to use to close the budget deficit. Suppose that the government increases public spending today and finances the resulting budget deficit by issuing bonds. As argued above, this policy is not sustainable and requires future measures to close the deficit and satisfy the intertemporal government budget constraint. However, the public is not sure whether the government will opt to increase taxes, use money financing, or use a combination of the two options. Kawai and Maccini (1990) have examined the effects of this type of uncertainty in a closed economy.[10] Their analysis shows that if "pure" money finance is anticipated to be used in the future, then inflation usually displays a strong, positive correlation with fiscal deficits. However, if tax finance is anticipated to be used, inflation and deficits may be positively or negatively correlated. These results are important to interpret the empirical findings of Fischer et al. (2002), according to which there appears to exist no significant long-run relationship between fiscal deficits and inflation.

---

[10] See also Drazen and Helpman (1990). Kawai and Maccini use a Blanchard-Yaari framework in which households have uncertain lifetimes (see Blanchard and Fischer, 1989, pp. 115–26). Their analysis also has important implications for the correlation between deficits and real interest rates, which are discussed next.

3 Deficits, Interest Rates, and Crowding Out

In countries where the financial system is relatively developed and interest rates are market determined, the reliance on domestic debt financing of government fiscal deficits may exert a large effect on real interest rates. In Colombia, for instance, large public deficits during the period 1983–1986 seem to have been the primary factor behind the sharp increase in real interest rates during that period (Easterly and Schmidt-Hebbel, 1994). A rise in domestic public debt may also increase the risk of default and reduce private sector confidence in the sustainability of the fiscal stance, leading to high real interest rates and further fiscal deterioration, a potentially destabilizing mechanism (see Fishlow and Morley, 1987; Agénor et al., 2006).

A weak empirical association between fiscal deficits and real interest rates may result from central bank regulations that prevent a complete adjustment of nominal interest rates to market levels. It may also result from expectations about future, rather than current, fiscal policy. We present in the following discussion a simple macroeconomic model that allows us to capture the dynamics of real interest rates induced by policy expectations.

3.1 ■ Expectations, Deficits, and Real Interest Rates

Consider a small open economy in which there are only three categories of agents: households, the government, and the central bank. Domestic production consists of a tradable consumption good and is assumed fixed at y during the time frame of the analysis. Purchasing power parity holds continuously and world prices are normalized to unity, implying that the domestic price level is equal to the nominal exchange rate, which is devalued at a constant, predetermined rate ε by the central bank. Households hold two categories of assets in their portfolios: domestic money, and an indexed government bond. Domestic money bears no interest, but the transactions technology is such that holding cash balances reduces liquidity costs associated with purchases of consumption goods. Capital is perfectly immobile internationally.[11] The government consumes final goods, collects income taxes, and pays interest on the outstanding stock of bonds. It finances its fiscal deficit by issuing bonds or by borrowing from the central bank. Finally, agents are endowed with perfect foresight.

The representative household maximizes discounted utility over an infinite horizon:

$$\int_t^\infty [u(c,m)]e^{-\rho t}dt, \qquad (23)$$

---

[11] The assumption of zero capital mobility is not well founded empirically. It is, however, a convenient simplification here and will be relaxed when we discuss stabilization policy in Chapter 10, using essentially an extension of the present framework.

where $\rho > 0$ denotes the rate of time preference (assumed constant), c consumption, m real money balances, and $u(\cdot)$ the instantaneous utility function, which is strictly concave and satisfies the Inada conditions. For simplicity, we will assume that the function is separable in c and m, and is of the form

$$u(c,m) = \frac{c^{1-\eta}}{1-\eta} + \chi \ln m, \quad \chi > 0$$

where η, the coefficient of relative risk aversion, is positive and different from unity.[12]

Real financial wealth of the representative household a is given by

$$a = m + b, \tag{24}$$

where b denotes the real stock of indexed government bonds. The flow budget constraint gives the actual change in real wealth as the difference between ex ante savings and capital losses on real money balances:

$$\dot{a} = (1 - \iota)(y + \tau + rb) - c - \varepsilon m, \tag{25}$$

where r denotes the real interest rate, τ lump-sum transfers from the government, and $0 < \iota < 1$ the proportional income tax rate. For simplicity, taxes are levied on gross income at a uniform rate.

Using (24), (25) can be written as

$$\dot{a} = (1 - \iota)ra + (1 - \iota)(y + \tau) - c - im, \tag{26}$$

where $i = (1 - \iota)r + \varepsilon$ denotes the net nominal interest rate.

Households treat y, r, ε, and τ as given and maximize (23) subject to (26) by choosing a sequence $\{c, m, b\}_{t=0}^{\infty}$. The Hamiltonian for this problem can be written as[13]

$$H = u(c,m) + \lambda \left\{ (1 - \iota)ra + (1 - \iota)(y + \tau) - c - im \right\},$$

where λ, the costate variable associated with the flow budget constraint, can be interpreted as measuring the marginal utility of wealth. The required optimality conditions are given by

$$c^{-\eta} = \lambda, \quad \chi/m = \lambda i, \quad \dot{\lambda}/\lambda = \rho - (1 - \iota)r,$$

---

[12]See Blanchard and Fischer (1989, pp. 43–44). With $\eta = 1$, the function $u(\cdot)$ becomes
$$u(c,m) = \ln c + \chi \ln m.$$

[13]See, for instance, Beavis and Dobbs (1990) for a discussion of the solution procedure for this type of optimization problem.

together with the transversality condition

$$\lim_{t \to \infty} \left(e^{-\rho t} a \right) = 0.$$

Noting that $\dot{\lambda} = -\eta \dot{c}^{\eta-1}$, the optimality conditions can be rewritten as

$$\chi c^{\eta} / m^{\phi} = i, \tag{27}$$

$$\dot{c}/c = \sigma [(1 - \iota)r - \rho], \tag{28}$$

where $\sigma = 1/\eta$ measures the intertemporal elasticity of substitution in consumption.

Equation (27) equates the marginal rate of substitution between consumption and real money balances to the nominal interest rate, which measures the opportunity cost of holding money. Equation (28) shows that the dynamics of consumption are determined by the difference between the after-tax real interest rate and the rate of time preference. We will examine in more detail the role of σ in determining the dynamic path of consumption in Chapter 10.

Equation (27) can be written as

$$m = \chi c^{\eta} / i, \tag{29}$$

which relates the demand for money inversely to the nominal interest rate and positively to the level of transactions. The nominal money stock must satisfy

$$M = D + ER, \tag{30}$$

where D measures the stock of domestic credit—extended by the central bank to the government—and R the foreign-currency value of net foreign assets held by the central bank. Changes in the real credit stock d are given by

$$\dot{d} = (\mu - \varepsilon)d, \tag{31}$$

where μ denotes the rate of nominal credit growth. Assuming for simplicity that net foreign assets and loans to the government do not bear interest, net profits of the central banks consist only of capital gains on reserves $\dot{E}R$, which are transferred to the government. In real terms, the government budget constraint is thus given by

$$\dot{d} + \dot{b} = g - \iota y + (1 - \iota)(\tau + rb) - \varepsilon m, \tag{32}$$

where g denotes non-interest public spending, assumed constant.

Combining (26), (30), (31), and (32) gives the overall budget constraint of the economy, which determines the evolution of the balance of payments:

$$\dot{m} = y - c - g. \tag{33}$$

Using (29), the equilibrium condition of the money market can be solved for the equilibrium nominal interest rate:

$$i = i(\overset{+}{c}, \overset{-}{m}),$$

which in turn yields the real interest rate:

$$r = [i(c, m) - \varepsilon]/(1 - \iota). \tag{34}$$

Equation (34) indicates that an increase in consumption requires an increase in the real interest rate to maintain equilibrium of the money market. A rise in the real money stock, resulting from either an expansion of domestic credit or an accumulation of net foreign assets, lowers the real interest rate. Finally, an increase in the devaluation rate requires a compensating reduction in the real interest rate.

Suppose that the central bank expands nominal credit at the same rate as the rate of inflation ($\mu = \varepsilon$). As a result, $\dot{d} = 0$. To ensure long-run solvency and eliminate Ponzi games, let us further assume that the government foregoes the issuance of bonds to finance its fiscal deficit ($\dot{b} = 0$) and instead adjusts the level of net transfers to households to balance the budget. Equation (32) therefore becomes

$$\tau = (1 - \iota)^{-1}(\iota y - g + \varepsilon m), \tag{35}$$

where for simplicity the constant real stocks of domestic credit and bonds are normalized to zero. Seigniorage revenue is thus equal to εm.

Equations (28), (33), and (34) form a first-order differential equation system in c and m. Using a linear approximation in the neighborhood of the steady state, this system can be written as:

$$\begin{bmatrix} \dot{c} \\ \dot{m} \end{bmatrix} = \begin{bmatrix} \sigma i_c & \sigma i_m \\ -1 & 0 \end{bmatrix} \begin{bmatrix} c - \tilde{c} \\ m - \tilde{m} \end{bmatrix},$$

where a '~' is used to denote steady-state values. Alternatively, note that from (34) we have $c = \Phi(r, m)$, with $\Phi_r, \Phi_m > 0$. As a result, $\dot{c} = \Phi_r \dot{r} + \Phi_m \dot{m}$. Combining this result with (28) and (33) yields $\dot{m} = y - \Phi(r, m) - g$, that is, with $y = g = 0$:

$$\dot{c} = \Phi_r \dot{r} - \Phi_m \Phi(r, m) = \sigma \Phi(r, m)[(1 - \iota)r - \rho].$$

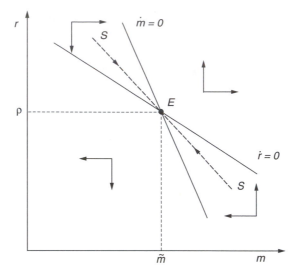

Figure 4–3 ■ Steady-State Equilibrium with Zero Capital Mobility

This equation can be rewritten as

$$\dot{r} = \Lambda(\overset{+}{r}, \overset{+}{m}).$$

The dynamic system in c and m can thus also be expressed in terms of r and m:

$$\begin{bmatrix} \dot{r} \\ \dot{m} \end{bmatrix} = \begin{bmatrix} \Lambda_r & \Lambda_m \\ -\Phi_r & -\Phi_m \end{bmatrix} \begin{bmatrix} r - \tilde{r} \\ m - \tilde{m} \end{bmatrix}. \tag{36}$$

Given the solution of this system, the behavior of consumption and from (35) the path of real transfers over time can be calculated. We assume in what follows that the condition for the system (36) to be saddlepath stable holds; that is, that the determinant of the matrix of coefficients is negative ($\Phi_r \Lambda_m - \Lambda_r \Phi_m < 0$). As shown in Figure 4.3, this condition requires that the slope of the $[\dot{m} = 0]$ locus be steeper than the slope of the $[\dot{r} = 0]$ locus. The saddlepath SS has a negative slope, and the steady-state equilibrium obtains at point E. As indicated by (28), the real after-tax interest rate must be equal to the rate of time preference at point E.

Suppose that the economy is initially in a steady-state equilibrium, and consider a fiscal policy shock brought about by a permanent, unanticipated increase in government spending. The adjustment process is shown in Figure 4.4. The increase in public expenditure generates on impact an excess demand for goods, which—domestic production being constant—requires a concomitant fall in private consumption to keep $\dot{m} = 0$. The effect is to shift the $[\dot{r} = 0]$ and $[\dot{m} = 0]$ loci to the left by the same amounts, as shown in the figure. The real interest rate jumps downward from point E to point A located on the new saddlepath $S'S'$, and begins rising along $S'S'$ toward the new steady state, point E'. Private consumption falls on impact, but not all the

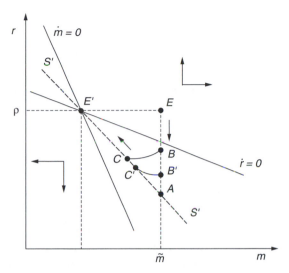

Figure 4–4 ▪ Permanent and Temporary Increases in Government Spending with Zero Capital Mobility

way to its steady-state level, so the economy runs a current account deficit during the transition period, and foreign reserves fall.

Consider now the case where the increase in government spending is announced at $t = 0$ to occur at period T in the future. Qualitatively, the long-run effects are similar to those described above. In the short run, however, the dynamics of the real interest rate will depend on the horizon T. If the horizon is very distant in the future, the real interest rate will jump downward to a point such as B, and will continue to fall along the divergent path BC during the interval $(0, T)$. The economy will reach the new saddlepath $S'S'$ (at point C) exactly at the moment the increase in public expenditure is implemented. By contrast, if the horizon is short, the real interest rate will begin rising immediately after the initial downward drop to point B, along the divergent path $B'C'$. The new saddlepath will be reached exactly at period T, as before.

The thrust of the preceding analysis is that real interest rates will tend to fluctuate in reaction not only to actual fiscal policy shocks, but also to expected changes in the fiscal stance. For instance, to the extent that agents correctly anticipate an increase in, say, public spending, the real interest rate will begin adjusting immediately, with little effect occurring when the policy measure is effectively implemented. The correlation between fiscal deficits and real interest rates can therefore be weak in the short run.

Expectations may be related not only to perceived changes in policy instruments per se, but also and more generally to the financing mix that the government may choose in the future. For instance, the government may initially raise the level of public expenditure and finance the ensuing deficit by issuing bonds during an interval of time $(0, T)$. At the same time, it may announce its intention to either reduce net transfers to households or scale down expenditure on final goods to balance the budget, in such a way that the real stock of bonds is maintained constant at a level b_T^+ beyond period T. A formal analysis of the effect of an alternative policy sequence on the behavior of real interest rates is provided by Kawai and Maccini (1990) in a model where inflation is endogenously determined. In their framework, the government runs a fiscal deficit (brought about by a tax cut or an increase in government spending) using bond finance for a transitory period, and closes it at a given date in the future by either raising taxes or using money finance.[14] When agents anticipate the latter option to be used, the expected inflation rate will rise and translate into an immediate increase in nominal interest rates. This induces asset holders to reduce their money balances and shift into bonds, thereby reducing the real interest rate. Thus, although current deficits and nominal interest rates are positively correlated, there is an inverse relation between current public deficits and real interest rates. Depending on the state of policy expectations, larger fiscal deficits may paradoxically lower real interest rates. Furthermore, to the extent that uncertainty about the financing option that the government will use in the future to close the fiscal gap varies over time, the correlation between current deficits and interest rates can be subject to large fluctuations.

3.2 ■ Deficits, Investment, and Crowding Out

In the model of the last subsection, the government did not borrow from domestic credit markets. However, in countries where interest rates are relatively flexible, large public deficits that are financed by borrowing from domestic credit markets will exert upward pressure on real interest rates and thus reduce private investment and output. In financially repressed economies where the structure of interest rates is determined by government fiat, excessive domestic borrowing may also lead to crowding out of private sector expenditure, by entailing a direct reduction of the amount of credit allocated by the banking system (see Chapter 2). In addition, if working capital needs are financed by bank credit, tighter restrictions on the availability of loans may lead to higher interest rates, which may in turn lead to an increase in prices if financial costs have a large effect on pricing decisions.[15] Large fiscal deficits may thus have, in addition to an inflationary impact, a negative output effect. The adverse effect of large fiscal deficits may, however, be mitigated if they reflect predominantly an increase in public investment and if, as discussed in Chapter 2, private and public investment are complementary rather than substitutes. Thus, in general, whether fiscal deficits have

---

[14]The subjective probability that monetization will be used in the future is assumed exogenous in the Kawai-Maccini framework. In a different setting, Masson (1985) relates this probability to the size of the deficit relative to output.

[15]This result was highlighted by new structuralist economists—see, for instance, Taylor (1983) and van Wijnbergen (1982)—in their discussion of the stagflationary effects of monetary policy.

a negative effect on private investment, output, and growth depends to a large extent on the sources of the deficit and the composition of government expenditure.

4 Budget Deficits and the Current Account

The relation between fiscal deficits and the current account can be understood by looking at the financing identity derived in (1) and assuming for a moment that net private saving is given. In such conditions, a close correlation would exist between fiscal deficits and current account deficits. The implication is that a reduction in the availability of external financing requires fiscal adjustment.[16]

Several analytical models have attempted to link fiscal deficits, external deficits, and the real exchange rate. Carlos Rodríguez (1991), for instance, develops an analytical framework that captures several mechanisms through which fiscal policies affect private spending and the accumulation of foreign assets. The external deficit determines the real exchange rate that is consistent with the clearing of the market for nontraded goods. An important implication of such models is that the effect of deficits—or, more generally, fiscal policy—on the current account and the real exchange rate depends not only on the level but also on the composition of public expenditure (see Montiel, 1986; Khan and Lizondo, 1987).[17]

An alternative way to view the link between fiscal deficits and the current account is through expectations about future policy, as emphasized in the previous subsections on real interest rates and the tight money paradox. Suppose the government runs a bond-financed fiscal deficit for a limited period of time. The dynamics of the economy during the transition period depend on whether the public expects the government to switch in the future to a tax finance regime or to a money finance regime (Kawai and Maccini, 1995). If tax finance is expected to be used to close the deficits in the future, then current fiscal deficits will be associated with a current account deficit. On the contrary, if money finance—or seigniorage—is primarily anticipated to be used, then fiscal deficits may be associated with current account surpluses. "Twin deficits" therefore arise only when private agents anticipate that the government will raise taxes in the future to eliminate current fiscal deficits.

The available empirical evidence seems to suggest the existence of a positive relation between large fiscal deficits and large external imbalances. Khan and Kumar

---

[16]The assumption of Ricardian equivalence—the independence of private consumption and investment from the government's mix of borrowing and tax financing—reviewed earlier implies the absence of any relation between fiscal deficits and the current account. With debt neutrality, deficit reductions brought about through tax increases would lead to an equal reduction in private saving, leaving the current account unchanged. Likewise, permanent cuts in public spending would merely result in an equal increase in private consumption and no effect on the current account balance. However, it was shown earlier that the evidence supporting the debt neutrality proposition is weak.

[17]Intertemporal effects may also alter the impact of government spending on the real exchange rate, as shown in a more general context by Frenkel and Razin (1992, chapter 11).

(1994) for instance, using data for forty-two countries covering the 1970s and 1980s, found that fiscal deficits have a highly significant effect on the behavior of the current account.[18]

5   Expansionary Fiscal Contractions

As discussed in more detail in subsequent chapters, macroeconomic adjustment in developing countries often involves substantial cuts in fiscal deficits. The conventional or "Keynesian" view of fiscal contractions is that they tend to have negative effects on output, notably through their adverse effect on aggregate demand. However, research on the experience of small industrial countries in the late 1980s (most notably Denmark in 1983–1986 and Ireland in 1987–1989) has led to an alternative view, which contends that a credible program of government spending cuts may stimulate private demand—sufficiently so perhaps to offset the direct effects of the fiscal contraction, so that the net effect of fiscal consolidation can be positive rather than negative.

Several different theories have been advanced to explain how fiscal contractions could be expansionary. The first, the *expectations view*, suggests that reductions in government spending can be expansionary due to their effects on private sector expectations concerning taxation (see Barry and Devereux, 1995, 2003; and Sutherland, 1997). If forward-looking consumers and investors anticipate long-run tax reductions because of cuts in expenditure today, then they may increase expenditure now and so offset the direct effects of the fiscal contraction. Alternatively, if tax increases unexpectedly stabilize debt now, thereby avoiding a later, more painful, stabilization involving larger increases, then the change in expectations could prove expansionary. Such an outcome is most likely when economies have high debt-output ratios. Indeed, Barry and Devereux (2003) show that the expansionary effect is highly nonlinear; the negative impact of government spending on output becomes larger, the higher the share of government spending in output. Put differently, when the share of government spending in output is very high to begin with, government spending cuts may have substantially positive effects on activity.[19]

An alternative approach, the *labor market view*, stresses the effect of the composition of fiscal adjustment (whether the deficit reduction is achieved through tax increases or through spending cuts) on the economy through the labor market and production costs. This view suggests that fiscal adjustment that results from cutting public spending, especially transfers and the government wage bill, rather

---

[18]The results of Khan and Kumar show a positive impact of fiscal deficits on current account imbalances when the regression is run for the 1970s only, with no significant effect appearing for the 1980s. However, the stock of external debt appears to be highly significant in the 1980s. These results may reflect the fact that fiscal deficits were financed mainly by foreign capital flows during the 1970s, which then fueled a large buildup of external debt.

[19]By implication, as noted by Choi and Devereux (2006), fiscal policy may be less expansionary in an environment of high real rates because of an adverse effect on expectations about future taxes.

than increasing taxes, are more likely to be successful (in the sense of reducing the debt-to-GDP ratio) and expansionary. They induce a moderation in the wage claims by unions, stimulating employment, capital accumulation, and growth.

The empirical evidence available to date on expansionary fiscal contractions relates mostly to industrial countries. Giavazzi et al. (2000), Alesina and Perotti (1997), Perotti (1999), and Giavazzi et al. (2005) perform multicountry analyses of consumption and savings and show, by and large, that expenditure cuts tend to have non-Keynesian effects on consumption. Alesina and Perotti (1997), in a study of a wide range of fiscal adjustment experiences, found that the adjustment programs most likely to succeed in stabilizing debt levels are those that cut expenditure as opposed to those that focus on raising taxes. Moreover, they argued that expenditure reduction programs succeed not because they reduce deficits by more, but rather because they lead to higher growth. In a study of large fiscal contractions in seventeen industrial countries, Ardagna (2004) found that expectations about the stance of future fiscal policy as well as the composition of fiscal adjustment are both important elements for understanding the growth effects of stabilization—with the latter being more robust than the former. This study therefore provides greater support to the labor market view.[20]

The possibility that fiscal contractions may be expansionary has important potential implications for the design of adjustment programs in developing countries. Essentially, it implies that there is no dynamic trade-off associated with stabilization, between higher costs (in terms of lower output and higher unemployment) now versus greater benefits tomorrow (in terms of lower inflation). From a political economy perspective, non-Keynesian effects may enhance the feasibility of adjustment programs (see Chapter 19). Unfortunately, to this date the evidence is insufficient to draw firm conclusions for developing countries. In a study focusing on private consumption behavior in forty countries (of which nineteen are industrialized and twenty-one are developing countries) over the period 1970–2000, Schclarek (2007) found no evidence that favors the hypothesis of expansionary fiscal consolidations. Studies by Hogan (2004) and Perotti (2013) himself have also cast some serious doubt on the validity of the expansionary fiscal consolidation hypothesis for industrial countries.

6   Fiscal Adjustment and the Labor Market

As noted in Chapter 1, the nature and extent of labor market segmentation in developing countries have been subjects of much discussion over the years, particularly in the context of urbanization policy and migration between rural and urban areas.

---

[20]Building on these results, Ardagna (2007) analyzes the effects of fiscal policy in a general equilibrium model with a detailed structure of the labor market.

As noted in Chapter 2, Harris and Todaro (1970) showed that the existence of a binding minimum wage in the urban sector can lead, even if the rural labor market is competitive, to a persistent wage differential between the rural and urban sectors and to the emergence of unemployment in equilibrium. Moreover, expansion of labor demand or real wage restraint in the urban sector may not restore full employment and may even increase unemployment.

Much attention has been focused on the role of labor market segmentation in the context of trade and structural reform.[21] The implications of various types of dualism or segmentation of labor markets for the short-run determination of output and employment in an open developing economy have also received increased attention in the existing literature. This section discusses some of these implications, focusing in particular on the role of imperfect labor mobility for the effectiveness of macroeconomic policy shocks.[22] It presents a dynamic, general equilibrium model with an informal sector, heterogeneous labor, minimum wage legislation, and imperfect mobility across sectors.

We first present the model, which incorporates several important features: a large informal sector, public sector production and employment, labor market segmentation (induced by government regulations and wage-setting agents), a heterogeneous and imperfectly mobile labor force, and wage and price flexibility in the informal economy. After deriving the dynamic form of the model and its steady-state solution, we then examine the short- and long-run effects of a permanent reduction in government spending on nontraded goods.

6.1 ▪ The Model

Consider a small open economy in which three categories of agents operate: firms, households, and the government. The nominal exchange rate is depreciated at a predetermined rate by the government. The economy consists of two major segments: the formal economy, and the informal sector. Goods produced in the formal economy consist of exportables and are only sold abroad.[23] Firms in the informal economy produce a nontraded good, which is used only for final consumption. The price of this good is flexible, and adjusts to eliminate excess demand. The capital stock in each production sector is fixed within the time frame of the analysis. The labor

---

[21] See Chapter 18. Edwards (1988), for instance, examines the relationships between terms-of-trade disturbances, tariffs, and the labor market, under alternative assumptions about wage formation and labor mobility.

[22] Demekas (1990) is one of the first studies to examine the implications of labor market segmentation in a general equilibrium framework. The analysis that follows draws, in part, on the models developed by Agénor and Aizenman (1999a) and Agénor and Santaella (1998). See Turnovsky and Basher (2009) for an alternative optimizing model with imperfect labor mobility.

[23] The absence of an import-competing sector in the formal economy can be rationalized along the lines suggested by Agénor and Aizenman (1999a), who assume that the efficiency losses induced by government-imposed barriers to foreign trade—which are not explicitly modeled here—are initially so high that goods that were once importables have effectively become nontraded goods.

force (which is also constant) is heterogeneous and consists of skilled and unskilled workers. Production of the nontraded good and government services requires only unskilled labor, whereas production of exportables requires both labor categories.

A minimum wage for unskilled labor imposed by government fiat exists, but is enforced only in the formal sector. Firms in that sector determine employment levels so as to maximize profits. They also set the wage rate for skilled labor in the formal sector (measured in terms of the domestic price of exportables) on the basis of efficiency considerations, taking into account workers' opportunity earnings.[24] By contrast, wages of unskilled workers in the informal sector are fully flexible.

As a result of relocation and congestion costs, mobility of the unskilled labor force between the formal and the informal sectors is imperfect. Migration flows are determined by expected income opportunities, along the lines of Harris and Todaro (1970).[25] Specifically, the supply of unskilled workers in the formal sector is assumed to change gradually over time as a function of the expected wage differential across sectors. Wage and employment prospects are based on prevailing conditions in the labor market. In the informal sector, which absorbs all unskilled workers who do not queue up for employment in the formal sector, wages adjust continuously to equilibrate supply and demand for labor.

Household consumption is a function of wealth, which consists of holdings of tradable bonds. Households supply labor inelastically and consume, in addition to the nontraded good produced in the informal sector, an imported final good which is imperfectly substitutable for the home good. The government consumes also both nontraded and imported goods, and finances its spending by levying lump-sum taxes on households.

6.1.1 *The Formal Economy*

As indicated above, production in the formal economy consists of exportable goods. Suppose that the world price of exportables is exogenous and normalized to unity. The domestic price of exportables is thus equal to the nominal exchange rate, E. The production technology in the exportable sector is given by

$$y_X = y_X(en_S, n_U), \tag{37}$$

where y_X is output of exportables, n_S and n_U employment levels of skilled and unskilled labor (measured in natural units), and e effort. Production of exportables takes place under decreasing returns to labor, so that, in particular, $\partial y_X / \partial n_U > 0$,

---

[24]See Agénor (2006*b*) for a discussion of the literature that views involuntary unemployment as the consequence of efficiency wages.

[25]See the discussion in Chapter 1. Note that in the present setup the Harris-Todaro framework is used to explain migration flows between the (urban) informal sector and the (urban) formal sector, rather than migration between the rural and the urban sectors.

and $\partial^2 y_X / \partial n_U^2 < 0$. We also assume that skilled and unskilled labor are Edgeworth complements, so that $\partial^2 y_X / \partial n_S \partial n_U > 0$.

Following Agénor and Aizenman (1999a), the effort function is defined by

$$e = 1 - \left(\frac{\Omega}{\omega_S} \right)^\gamma, \quad \gamma > 0, \tag{38}$$

where ω_S denotes the product wage for skilled workers in the exportable sector, and $\Omega < \omega_S$ the reservation wage—or alternatively the opportunity cost of effort. Equation (38) indicates that an increase in the wage earned by skilled workers in the formal sector relative to their reservation wage raises the level of effort. Effort is also concave in ω_S.

Let ω_m^* be the real minimum wage (measured in terms of the price of exportables) earned by unskilled workers in the export sector. Assuming that firms incur no hiring or firing costs, the decision problem is thus

$$\max_{n_S, \omega_S, n_U} \Pi_X = y_X \left\{ n_S [1 - \left(\frac{\Omega}{\omega_S} \right)^\gamma], n_U \right\} - \omega_S n_S - \omega_m^* n_U.$$

The first-order conditions for this optimization problem are:[26]

$$\left(\frac{\partial y_X}{\partial n_S} \right) [1 - \left(\frac{\Omega}{\omega_S} \right)^\gamma] = \omega_S, \tag{39}$$

$$\left(\frac{\partial y_X}{\partial \omega_S} \right) \left(\frac{\Omega}{\omega_S} \right)^\gamma = \gamma^{-1} n_S, \tag{40}$$

$$\partial y_X / \partial n_U = \omega_m^*, \tag{41}$$

Optimality conditions (39) and (40) can be solved to yield:

$$\omega_S = \delta \Omega, \quad \delta \equiv (1 + \gamma)^{1/\gamma} > 1, \tag{42}$$

which indicates that, in equilibrium, firms in the formal sector set the efficiency wage for skilled workers at a higher level than the opportunity cost of effort. A graphical determination of the efficiency wage is shown in Figure 4.5.

---

[26]Equation (39) yields the *Solow condition*, which indicates that in equilibrium the elasticity of effort with respect to the product wage must be equal to unity.

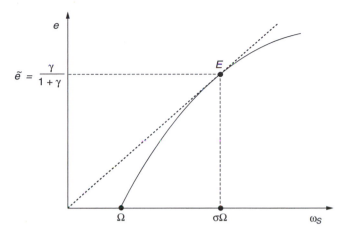

Figure 4–5 ■ Productivity and Wages in the Format Sector
Source: Adapted from Agénor and Santaella (1998, p. 272).

Equations (38) and (42) imply that in equilibrium effort is constant at

$$\tilde{e} = 1 - \delta^{-\gamma} \equiv \gamma/(1+\gamma).$$

Suppose now that skilled workers' reservation wage depends on an exogenous component, Ω_0, as well as on the real wage in the informal economy, ω_N—both measured in terms of the price of exportables:

$$\Omega = \omega_N^\theta \Omega_0^{1-\theta}, \tag{43}$$

where $0 \le \theta < 1$. For simplicity, we will assume further that $\Omega_0 = 1$. As shown below, whether θ is zero or positive plays a critical role in the dynamics associated with fiscal adjustment policies.

Equation (43) can be substituted in (42) to give the optimal value of ω_S:

$$\omega_S = \delta \omega_N^\theta. \tag{44}$$

Substituting (43) and (44) in (39) and (40), and solving the resulting equation together with (41) yields the demand functions for skilled and unskilled labor in the formal sector:

$$n_S^d = n_S^d(\overset{-}{\omega}_N, \overset{-}{\omega}_m^*), \quad n_U^d = n_U^d(\overset{-}{\omega}_N, \overset{-}{\omega}_m^*). \tag{45}$$

An increase in the informal sector wage reduces the demand for both skilled and unskilled labor in the formal sector. In order to generate the optimal level of effort, a rise in ω_N increases the efficiency wage paid to skilled workers in the formal sector. This increase reduces directly the demand for skilled labor and, as a result of gross complementarity, the demand for unskilled labor as well. An increase in the minimum wage reduces not only the demand for unskilled workers but also the demand for skilled workers for similar reasons.

Substituting (42) and (45) in (37) yields

$$y_X^s = y_X^s(\overset{-}{\omega}_N, \overset{-}{\omega}_m^*), \tag{46}$$

which indicates that an increase in either the minimum wage for unskilled workers or the market-clearing wage in the informal sector reduces output of exportables.

6.1.2 The Informal Sector

Technology for the production of the nontraded good in the informal sector is characterized by decreasing returns to labor:

$$y_N = y_N(n_N), \quad y_N' > 0, \ y_N'' < 0, \tag{47}$$

where y_N denotes output and n_N the quantity of labor employed in the informal economy. Producers maximize profits given by $z^{-1}y_N - \omega_N n_N$, where ω_N denotes the real wage in the informal sector (measured in terms of the price of exportable goods) and z the relative price of exportables in terms of home goods, hereafter the real exchange rate. Profit maximization yields the familiar equality between marginal revenue and marginal cost, $\omega_N = y_N'/z$, from which labor demand can be derived as

$$n_N^d = y_N'^{-1}(\omega_N z) = n_N^d(\omega_N z), \quad n_N^{d\prime} < 0, \tag{48}$$

where $\omega_N z$ measures the product wage in the informal sector. Substituting (48) in (47) yields the supply function for goods produced in the informal sector:

$$y_N^s = y_N^s(\omega_N z), \quad y_N^{s\prime} < 0. \tag{49}$$

Suppose, again for simplicity, that only one (representative) firm operates in each sector. Using (46) and (50), net factor income, y (measured in terms of exportables), can be defined as

$$y = y_X^s + z^{-1}y_N^s. \tag{50}$$

6.1.3 Consumption and Wealth

There is only one household whose members consist of all workers. The household's total consumption expenditure, c (measured in terms of the price of exportables), is assumed to be related positively to financial wealth, B^*:[27]

$$c = \alpha B^*, \quad \alpha > 0. \tag{51}$$

The household's financial wealth consists only of holdings of an internationally traded bond, which evolve over time according to

$$\dot{B}^* = i^* B^* + y - c - \tau, \tag{52}$$

where i^* is the bond interest rate (assumed constant) and τ lump-sum taxes imposed by the government.

The household consumes imported goods (in quantity c_I) as well as home goods (in quantity c_N). Assuming that the utility derived from consuming these goods is well represented by a Cobb-Douglas function, the allocation of total consumption expenditure is given by

$$c_I = (1 - \delta)c, \quad c_N = \delta z c, \quad 0 < \delta < 1, \tag{53}$$

where δ measures the share of home goods in total expenditure.

6.1.4   Market for Informal Sector Goods

The equilibrium condition of the nontraded goods market can be written, using (49), (51), and (53), as:

$$y_N^s(\omega_N z) = \alpha \delta z B^* + g_N, \tag{54}$$

where g_N denotes public consumption of nontraded goods. Equation (54) will be solved below for z.

6.1.5   The Informal Labor Market

As indicated earlier, the demand for labor in the informal sector is derived from profit maximization and is given by (48); in addition, the supply of unskilled workers in the formal sector, denoted n_U^s, is predetermined at any moment in time. Thus, the supply of unskilled labor in the informal sector is also given at any point in time.

In line with the "luxury unemployment" hypothesis (Horton et al., 1994), suppose that skilled workers who are unable to obtain a job in the formal sector prefer to remain unemployed rather than seek employment in the informal economy.[28] The

---

[27]The use of a consumption function that depends only on wealth is adopted for simplicity and tractability. An alternative model with some of the same features as the present one and with optimizing households is developed in Agénor (2005) and, with perfect labor mobility, in Agénor and Aizenman (1999a).

[28]See Agénor (2006b) for a review of the evidence on skilled unemployment in developing countries. In general, of course, whether skilled workers who are not successful in applying for a job in the formal sector decide to seek employment (as unskilled workers) in the informal economy depends on factors such as the efficiency of on-the-job search activities, demotivation effects, and the degree of support from relatives.

equilibrium condition of the labor market in the informal economy is thus given by

$$n_U^p - n_U^s = n_N^d(\omega_N z), \tag{55}$$

where n_U^p denotes the constant number of unskilled workers in the labor force. Solving this equation yields:

$$\omega_N = \kappa(\overset{-}{z}, \overset{+}{n_U^s}), \quad \kappa_z = -1, \tag{56}$$

which indicates that a depreciation of the real exchange rate has a negative effect on the informal sector wage (which is such that the product wage remains constant), whereas an increase in the number of workers seeking employment in the formal economy has a positive effect.

The mechanism through which unskilled workers migrate across sectors follows the formulation of Harris and Todaro (1970), and relates movements of labor to the expected wage differential between sectors. Because there is no job turnover in the public sector, the expected wage in the formal economy is thus equal to the minimum wage weighted by the probability of being hired in the formal sector. Assuming that hiring is random, this probability can be approximated by the ratio of currently employed workers to those seeking employment, n_U^d/n_U^s. The expected wage in the informal economy is simply the going wage, since there are no barriers to entry in that sector. Thus, the supply of unskilled workers in the formal sector evolves over time according to

$$\dot{n}_U^s = \beta \left\{ \frac{\omega_m^* n_U^d}{n_U^s} - \omega_N \right\}, \quad \beta > 0, \tag{57}$$

where β denotes the speed of adjustment. This equation shows that an increase in the informal sector wage ω_N has two effects on migration flows. On the one hand, it raises the expected return from working in the informal sector, thereby reducing the incentive to migrate. On the other, it raises ω_S and (through gross complementarity) reduces the demand for unskilled labor in the export sector [see (44) and (45)]. In turn, this lowers the hiring probability and expected income in the formal economy. The net effect is therefore negative ($\partial \dot{n}_U^s / \partial \omega_N < 0$).

The absence of on-the-job search in the informal sector in the present setup can be justified in a variety of ways. An important consideration is the existence of informational inefficiencies, which may result from the absence of institutions capable of processing and providing in a timely manner relevant information on job opportunities to potential applicants. As a result, search activities for unskilled workers in the formal sector may require, literally speaking, waiting for job offers at factory gates.

6.1.6 *Government*

The government consumes both home and imported goods, and finances its expenditure through the revenue derived from lump-sum taxes on households:

$$\tau - g_I - z^{-1}g_N = 0, \tag{58}$$

where g_I denotes government imports.

6.2 ▪ Dynamic Structure

In order to examine the dynamic properties of the model described in the previous section, it is convenient to rewrite it in a more compact form. As shown below, the dynamics of the model can be formulated in terms of the size of the unskilled labor force seeking employment in the formal economy and households' holdings of traded bonds.

By definition, $c = c_I + z^{-1}c_N$. Substituting this result in the representative household's budget constraint [see (52)] yields, together with the equilibrium condition for the nontraded goods market [(54)], (50), and the government budget constraint [(58)]:

$$\dot{B}^* = i^*B^* + y_X^s - c_I - g_I,$$

which can be rewritten as, using (46), (51), and (53):

$$\dot{B}^* = [i^* - \alpha(1 - \delta)]B^* + y_X^s(\omega_N, \omega_m^*) - g_I. \tag{59}$$

To determine the short-run market-clearing solutions of the real exchange rate and real wages in the informal sector (measured in terms of the price of exports), we substitute (56) for ω_N in the equilibrium condition of the market for nontraded goods [(54)] to solve for z, for given values of B^* and n_U^s. The result is

$$z = z(\overset{-}{n_U^s}, \overset{-}{B^*}; \overset{-}{g_N}). \tag{60}$$

An increase in the supply of unskilled labor in the formal sector, for instance, creates an excess demand for labor in the informal economy, thus putting upward pressure on wages there. As a result, output in the informal sector falls and the real exchange rate must appreciate (z must fall) to maintain market equilibrium. An increase in holdings of traded bonds stimulates consumption of home goods and also requires a real appreciation to maintain equilibrium between supply and demand.

Substituting (60) in (56) yields:

$$\omega_N = \omega_N(\overset{+}{n^s_U}, \overset{+}{B^*}; \overset{+}{g_N}).\tag{61}$$

Substituting (51), (53), and (61) in (59) yields

$$\dot{B}^* = [i^* - \alpha(1-\delta)]B^* + y^s_X(n^s_U, B^*; g_N) - g_I,\tag{62}$$

with $\partial y^s_X/\partial n^s_U = \partial y^s_X/\partial B^* = 0$ if $\theta = 0$.

Finally, substituting (45) for n^d_U and (61) for ω_N in (57) yields:

$$\dot{n}^s_U = \beta\Psi(\overset{-}{n^s_U}, \overset{-}{B^*}; \overset{-}{g_N}).\tag{63}$$

Equation (63) shows, in particular, that an increase in the number of job seekers in the formal sector dampens migration flows, as a result of two effects. On the one hand, it reduces directly the probability of finding employment in the formal economy, and thus expected income there. On the other, it leads to an increase in the informal sector wage—that is, the opportunity cost of queueing—which in turn further lowers (as discussed earlier) expected income in, and incentives to migrate to, the formal sector.

Equations (62) and (63) represent the dynamic equations of the system, defined in terms of the size of the unskilled labor force in the formal sector and holdings of traded bonds valued in foreign currency terms. Using a linear approximation around the steady state yields

$$\begin{bmatrix} \dot{n}^s_U \\ \dot{B}^* \end{bmatrix} = \begin{bmatrix} \beta\Psi_{n^s_U} & \beta\Psi_{B^*} \\ \partial y^s_X/\partial n^s_U & \Lambda \end{bmatrix}\begin{bmatrix} n^s_U - \tilde{n}^s_U \\ B^* - \tilde{B}^* \end{bmatrix},\tag{64}$$

where

$$\Lambda = i^* - \alpha(1-\delta) + (\partial y^s_X/\partial B^*).$$

Assuming that the world interest rate is sufficiently small ensures that $\Lambda < 0$. Necessary and sufficient conditions for the differential equation system described by (64) to be locally stable is that the trace of its matrix of coefficients, $\mathbf{A}$, be negative, and that its determinant be positive:

$$\text{tr}\mathbf{A} = \Lambda + \beta\Psi_{n^s_U} < 0,$$

$$\det\mathbf{A} = \beta[\Lambda\Psi_{n^s_U} - \Psi_{B^*}(\partial Y^s_X/\partial n^s_U)] > 0.$$

The first condition is always satisfied; the second condition will be assumed to hold, and is interpreted graphically below.

6.3 ■ Steady-State Solution

The steady-state solution of the model is obtained by $\dot{B}^* = \dot{n}_U^s = 0$ in (62) and (63). More directly, (57) implies that in the steady state the current account must be in equilibrium, that is, the surplus of the services account, $i^* \bar{B}^*$, must be matched by a trade deficit, $\bar{c}_I + g_I - \bar{y}_X^s$:

$$i^* \bar{B}^* = \bar{c}_I + g_I - \bar{y}_X^s. \tag{65}$$

Equation (59) also implies that the ratio of wages earned by unskilled workers in the formal and informal sectors (hereafter the unskilled wage ratio) must be equal in the long run to the inverse of the employment ratio of that category of labor in the private formal economy:

$$\omega_m / \tilde{\omega}_N = \tilde{n}_U^s / \tilde{n}_U^d. \tag{66}$$

This result indicates that, as long as the minimum wage is higher than the informal sector wage ($\omega_m > \tilde{\omega}_N$), unskilled unemployment will emerge in equilibrium.[29]

Finally, from the steady-state solutions of B^* and n_U^s, the equilibrium values of the "short-run" variables, the real exchange rate, and the real wage in the informal economy, can be derived by using (60) and (61).

A graphical depiction of the steady-state equilibrium is shown in Figure 4.6 for $\theta > 0$. The locus $B^* B^*$ gives the combinations of B^* and n_U^s for which bond holdings remain constant, whereas the locus LL depicts the combinations of B^* and n_U^s for which the size of the unskilled labor force seeking employment in the formal sector does not change over time. The second condition for stability described earlier requires $B^* B^*$ to be steeper than LL. The steady-state equilibrium obtains at point E. In general, the possibility of cycles in the adjustment process cannot be excluded; for simplicity, we will focus in what follows only on non-cyclical paths. If the economy's initial position is at, say, point A—characterized by a positive differential between the expected wage in the formal and the informal sectors, and a current account deficit—the transition toward the steady state will be characterized by a gradual increase in bond holdings and in the size of the unskilled labor force in the formal sector. If $\theta = 0$, the curve $B^* B^*$ is vertical, because in that case y_X^s becomes independent of ω_N—and thus of n_U^s.

---

[29] In our setting, the condition that the minimum wage be higher than the market-clearing wage is in fact necessary to avoid a corner solution—or a situation in which no unskilled worker has the incentive to seek employment in the formal economy.

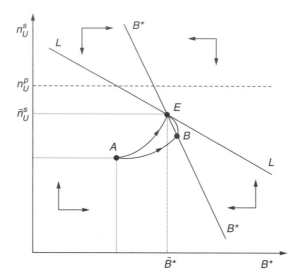

Figure 4–6 ■ Steady-State Equilibrium

A partial, long-run equilibrium position of the labor market is depicted in Figure 4.7. Panel A depicts the demand functions for labor in the formal sector. The demand curve for skilled labor n_S^d is downward sloping, because it is negatively related to ω_S, the wage earned by skilled workers. The demand for unskilled labor in the formal economy is the downward-sloping curve n_U^d, because skilled and unskilled workers are gross complements. The supply of unskilled workers in the formal sector n_U^s, given by the long-run solution of (57), is proportional to total demand for labor in that sector times the unskilled wage ratio. As noted earlier, if that ratio is greater than unity, n_U^s will be greater than n_U^d and unskilled unemployment will emerge; this is the case shown in Panel B. By subtracting n_U^s from the total supply of unskilled workers n_U^p, Panel B also allows us to determine the supply of labor (and thus actual employment) in the informal economy. Given the labor demand curve in the informal sector n_N^d, the market-clearing wage is determined at point C in Panel C.[30] The positive relationship between the skilled workers' wage and the informal sector wage (for $\theta > 0$) is displayed as curve WW in Panel D. Thus, unemployment of both categories of labor prevails in equilibrium—despite the existence of wage flexibility in the informal sector. Skilled unemployment is given in Panel A by the distance between the supply of skilled labor n_S^p and the equilibrium point on the demand curve n_S^d. Unskilled unemployment is given by the difference in Panel B between total supply n_U^s and demand for labor in the formal sector n_U^d. Thus,

---

[30]From (46) and (56), n_N^d is a function of z. From the equilibrium condition of the market for nontraded goods [(54)], $z = z(\omega_N, \cdot)$, where $|z'_{\omega_N}| < 1$. Substituting this result in (56) shows that the n_N^d curve is downward-sloping in the ω_N-n_U space.

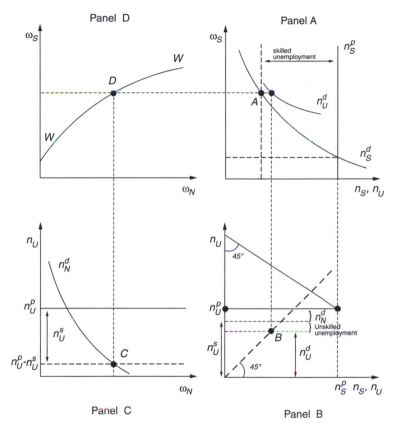

Figure 4–7 ▪ Labor Market Equilibrium

"quasi-voluntary" unemployment of skilled workers and "wait" unemployment of unskilled workers emerge in equilibrium.[31]

6.4 ▪ Government Spending Cut

We now turn to an analysis of the impact and steady-state effects of a permanent cut in government spending on home goods, g_N, on output, the sectoral composition of employment, and unemployment.

In general, the long-run effects of the shock on holdings of traded bonds and the supply of unskilled labor in the formal sector are ambiguous.[32] Figure 4.8 illustrates

---

[31] Because there is no unemployment benefit scheme in the present framework, unemployed workers in the long run are implicitly assumed to either turn to a subsistence activity (home production) or to rely on relatives for their survival.

[32] Formally, the steady-state effects of this shock on the size of the unskilled labor force in the formal sector and the stock of bonds can be derived from (62) and (63), with $\dot{B}^* = \dot{n}_U^s = 0$. and solving for B^* and n_U^s as a function of g_N.

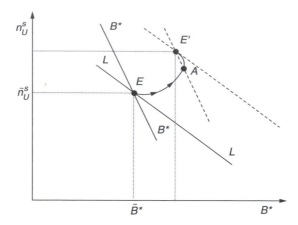

Figure 4–8 ▪ Reduction in Government Spendings on Home Goods

one possible outcome, which corresponds to the case where θ is not too large. Both B^*B^* and LL shift to the right. In the new steady state, holdings of traded bonds and the supply of unskilled labor in the formal sector are both higher.

The initial effect (for n_U^s and B^* given) of a reduction in government spending on home goods is a discrete real depreciation, which maintains equilibrium between supply and demand for these goods [(60)]. The real depreciation implies that ω_N must fall on impact [(56)]. The movement in z and ω_N must be in opposite directions and exactly offset each other, in order to maintain the product wage $z\omega_N$ in the informal sector constant. This is so because labor supply (and thus employment) in the informal economy cannot change on impact, with n_U^s adjusting only slowly over time. On impact, given that total consumption [as shown by (51)] cannot change, consumption of imported goods cannot change either [see (53)]. At the same time, the fall in informal sector wages tends to lower the efficiency wage in the formal sector, leading to an increase in the demand for both categories of labor and thus an expansion in output of exportables. Thus, the current account moves into surplus ($\dot{B}^* > 0$), as illustrated in Figure 4.8. The impact effect on the flow of unskilled workers seeking employment in the formal economy is also positive ($\dot{n}_U^s > 0$). The reason is that a fall in ω_N lowers expected income in the informal sector; at the same time, it raises expected income in the formal sector, because it raises the demand for unskilled labor in that sector, as implied by (45). Thus, the change in the expected income differential [which determines the initial effect on $\dot{n}_U^s$, as shown in (57)] is unambiguously positive.

The transitional dynamics are also illustrated in Figure 4.8. The adjustment process consists of two phases. In the first, holdings of traded bonds and the supply of unskilled labor in the formal sector are both increasing; in the second, holdings of traded bonds begin falling (after reaching point A) although the supply of unskilled labor in the formal sector continues to increase. The reason for this two-phase adjustment process is that during the first phase, the real exchange rate appreciates continuously [as implied by (60)], thereby leading to a gradual increase in informal sector wages and the efficiency wage over time. As a result, output of exportables falls over time, leading to an increase in the trade deficit that eventually becomes large enough to create a current account deficit as well. In the long run, nevertheless, as depicted in the figure, the stock of foreign bonds and the supply of unskilled workers in the formal sector are both higher (point E'). Whether the real exchange rate appreciates or depreciates in the steady state (and thus whether informal sector wages are higher or lower) cannot be determined a priori. Thus, the long-run effect of the shock on the unskilled wage ratio—which, as indicated earlier, is equal to the inverse of the steady-state private employment ratio—and the level of unskilled unemployed is also ambiguous.

Chapter 5

Financial Markets and the Monetary Transmission Mechanism

A key economic feature that differentiates developed and developing countries is the structure of their financial systems.[1] The menu of assets available to private savers in developing countries from the formal financial system is often limited to cash, demand deposits, time deposits, and sometimes government securities acquired in a primary market.

In addition to being limited in scope, the financial system is often also limited in size and geographic distribution. Many private individuals thus have limited access to commercial banks, which are by far the dominant organized financial institutions—often operating under oligopolistic market structures and a high degree of concentration. Other specialized institutions exist, but they typically conduct a very small portion of total financial intermediation in the economy. Secondary securities and equities markets either remain nonexistent or are very limited in scope, so that bank credit and internally generated funds provide the bulk of financing for private firms.[2]

This chapter examines the nature of differences in the financial structure between developed and developing countries and their implications for the transmission mechanism of monetary policy. Section 2 provides a description of some of the main features of the financial system in developing countries, with particular attention to the role of banks in the financial intermediation process. Section 3 provides an overview of the monetary transmission mechanism in countries where the financial structure is relatively diversified, a well-functioning secondary market

---

[1] Papademos and Modigliani (1983) present a macroeconomic framework that integrates most types of assets found in the financial systems of industrial countries.

[2] By contrast, the role of bank credit in corporate capital structure varies considerably across industrial countries. While bank credit amounts to a relatively small share of total indebtedness of private nonfinancial corporations in the United States, it represents a much more significant source of finance in Europe and Japan. See the data appendix in the IMF's *Global Financial Stabilty Report*, September 2013.

for government securities exists, and asset prices tend to be market-determined. Section 4 discusses the implications of dollarization for monetary policy.

1   Financial Structure and the Role of Banks

Because monetary policy operates through financial markets, the instruments of monetary policy, the mechanisms through which they affect the real economy, as well as the magnitude of these impacts, all depend on the structure of the domestic financial system. Beyond this general observation, it is worth noting two more specific links between the financial structure and monetary policy. First, at least in the context of liberalized financial systems, monetary policy has become the policy tool of choice for countercyclical purposes. Its substantial advantage over fiscal policy is its potential flexibility. However, as has become increasingly apparent in recent years, regardless of the details of how monetary policy effects are transmitted to the real economy, the very feasibility of using tight monetary policy—and thus the flexibility of this instrument—depends on the soundness of the domestic financial system. To the extent that financial development is associated with a healthier financial system, an important contribution of financial development is to permit monetary policy to be used in a flexible manner. Second, the external and internal dimensions of the financial structure may interact in ways that have important implications for the effectiveness of monetary policy. In particular, the effectiveness of sterilized foreign exchange market intervention depends on the strength of arbitrage links between the domestic and foreign financial sectors, as well as among domestic financial assets.

In most developing countries (low- and middle-income alike), banks continue to dominate the financial system (see Mohanty et al., 2006; Agénor and Pereira da Silva, 2013; and Mishra et al., 2013). Other specialized institutions exist in many cases, but they typically account for only a very small portion of total financial intermediation in the economy. Bank deposits remain the most important form of household savings, and bank loans (together with retained earnings) are the most important source of finance for firms, both for working capital needs and for investment in fixed capital. The overwhelming proportion of bank loans is, in fact, allocated to firms in many developing countries and is short term in nature—although in recent years consumer credit has expanded at a rapid pace in many of them. Equity markets and corporate bond markets have increased in size in many developing countries in recent years; but stock market capitalization remains low compared with advanced industrial countries and equity finance remains confined to the largest firms. Similarly, corporate bond markets remain quite narrow, concentrated, and relatively illiquid.

From the perspective of monetary policy, it is thus essential to account for the central role that banks play in the economy. In general, banks have three main functions. First, they transform the short-term, liquid deposits held by households (or asset holders) into illiquid liabilities issued by firms. Second, they screen potential borrowers and monitor actual borrowers on behalf of depositors. Third, they facilitate transactions between agents (firms and workers, buyers and sellers) by providing payment services.

In many middle-income countries, banks are now less subject to government-imposed restrictions—such as binding legal ceilings on lending rates, high reserve ratios and liquidity requirements, and restrictions on their portfolio composition designed to direct resources toward favored sectors.[3] Reserve requirements remain important for prudential reasons, or for sterilizing large inflows of capital (see Chapter 13), but they are less motivated by the need to finance large fiscal deficits, as in the past.[4]

The nature of banking operations and their degree of sophistication in many middle-income countries have been transformed in recent years by privatization and cross-border acquisitions. However, the financial systems in most of these countries continue to lag behind developments in industrial markets. In particular, and despite some exceptions, the expansion of nonbank financial intermediaries (hedge funds, commodities funds, private equity groups, and money market funds), the shift toward the "originate and distribute" model of banking, and the development of off-balance sheet instruments, have not reached the same importance as they have in advanced economies. Indeed, apart from a few countries, nonbank financial intermediaries are not highly developed. Data compiled by Ghosh et al. (2014) for instance on the importance of shadow banking show that the sector is large only in a few developing countries, such as the Philippines and Thailand.[5]

Another important feature of financial systems in middle-income countries (although not all of them) is that supervisory capacity is often weak and the ability to enforce prudential regulations limited. In many of these countries, bank supervisors lack the ability to assess the effectiveness of banks' risk management practices, especially the adequacy of capital in relation to the risks that they undertake. The lack of expertise in the supervisory agency is especially problematic for those countries

---

[3]Liquidity requirements specify that banks must hold specific types of government securities, in amounts proportional to their deposit liabilities, over and above required reserves.

[4]In theory, other considerations may be important. Di Giorgio (1999), for instance, shows that the optimal reserve requirement rate depends on the degree of financial sector efficiency (as measured by verification costs). Castiglionesi (2007) develops a model in which reserve requirements are also chosen optimally, so as to ensure that the central bank has enough liquidity in case of an adverse shock that could trigger a banking crisis, while at the same time taking into account the need to avoid diverting too many resources from profitable lending and investment opportunities.

[5]Shadow banking comprises a set of activities, markets, contracts, and institutions that operate partially (or fully) outside the traditional commercial banking sector, and, as such, are either lightly regulated or not regulated at all (see Pozsar et al., 2010). In industrial countries, alternatives to conventional bank finance include invoice factoring or discounting (where a business borrows money against its invoices), asset-based financing (where money is borrowed against assets such as a plant or machinery), peer-to-peer and consumer-to-business lending (in which individuals agree to lend money to each other or to businesses through an online money exchange). New lending models also involve providing cash advances to businesses (e.g., restaurants and hotels) that derive much of their income from credit card sales. However, most of these new lending models haven't reached a mass of borrowers that is critical enough to be considered serious alternatives to bank finance.

that aim to allow banks to rely on historical data and internal models for the determination of credit risk estimates and capital requirements. Lack of supervisory capacity affects the ability to assess other risks as well, such as market and interest rate risks. In addition, inadequate prudential supervision creates systemic fragility and may precipitate (or compound) bank runs and currency crises, as discussed in Chapter 15. The persistence of weaknesses in the environment in which banks operate also complicates the conduct of monetary policy. As discussed later, these weaknesses distort the transmission mechanism of monetary policy because banks that are less capable of controlling their balance sheets will be less responsive to changes in interest rates. Moreover, as discussed in Chapter 7, banking problems may reduce the scope for tightening liquidity and raising interest rates to reduce price pressures in an inflation targeting regime.

2   Asymmetric Information and Credit

A key feature that distinguishes the credit market from other markets for goods or financial assets is that the interest rate charged by a given bank on a loan contract to a given borrower typically differs from the return the lender expects to realize on the loan, which is equal to the product of the contractual interest rate and the probability that the borrower will actually repay the loan. Because of imperfect or asymmetric information between banks and their borrowers—that is, a situation in which borrowers have greater information about their own default risk than do lenders—this probability is almost always less than unity. A seminal analysis by Stiglitz and Weiss (1981) showed that in the presence of asymmetric information, credit rationing may emerge endogenously, instead of resulting from government-imposed restrictions, as in a regime of financial repression.

We begin this section by presenting the Stiglitz-Weiss analysis. We then consider an alternative approach, based on costly state verification, due to Townsend (1979) and Williamson (1986). We illustrate the usefulness of this approach by using a stochastic model proposed by Agénor and Aizenman (1998, 1999b). The analysis remains partial equilibrium in nature; in Chapter 12 we will consider how the costly state verification model can be embedded in a full-blown general equilibrium model. We then examine more specifically the role of binding collateral constraints in an important model developed by Kiyotaki and Moore (1997).[6]

---

[6]See Freixas and Rochet (1997) for a survey of models of credit markets with adverse selection and credit rationing. Another approach to credit market imperfections, as discussed by Wasmer and Weil (2004), involves assuming the existence of search frictions (as in some models of the labor market). However, we find it hard to argue that "locating" credit, which involves stochastic matching between creditors and borrowers, is a key source of financial sector imperfections.

2.1 ■ The Stiglitz-Weiss Model of Credit Rationing

The key idea that underlies the analysis in Stiglitz and Weiss (1981) is that the probability of repayment may be negatively related to the contractual interest rate; that is, as the interest rate on the loan increases, the probability of repayment may decline. The repayment probability for some borrowers may actually fall by more than the increase in the contractual interest rate if the latter rises beyond a certain level—implying that the expected return to the bank on loans to these borrowers may actually diminish as a result of further increases in the contractual rate. Because the bank has no incentive to lend in such conditions, it will stop lending completely to these borrowers—even if they are willing to accept higher contractual interest rates. There is, therefore, credit rationing.

The Stiglitz-Weiss model can be described as follows. Consider an economy populated by a bank and a group of borrowers, each of whom has a single, one-period project in which he (or she) can invest. Each project requires a fixed amount of funds, L; in the absence of any endowment, L is also the amount that each borrower must obtain to implement the project.[7] Each borrower i must pledge collateral in value $C_i < L$. All agents are risk-neutral profit maximizers.

Assume also that each project i requiring funding has a distribution of gross payoffs, $F(R_i, \theta_i)$, where R_i is the project's return (assumed constant across projects) and θ_i a parameter that measures the riskiness of the project. All projects yield either R_i (if they succeed) or 0 (if they fail); the borrower cannot, in any case, affect R_i. Although projects differ in risk, they all have the same mean return, R; thus, if p_i denotes the probability that the project yields R_i, then

$$p_i(\theta_i)R_i + [1 - p_i(\theta_i)] \cdot 0 = R, \tag{1}$$

for all i, where $p_i' < 0$. A higher value of θ is taken to represent an increase in risk. More precisely, an increase in θ captures an increase in the variance of the project's return, while leaving its mean constant. Shifts in θ are thus assumed to be mean preserving.[8] The assumption $p_i' < 0$ captures the idea that riskier projects are less likely to succeed.

Borrower i receives the fixed amount of loans, L, at the contractual interest rate r and defaults on the loan if the project's return R_i plus the value of the collateral C_i are insufficient to repay the loan (that is, $R_i + C_i < (1+r)L_i$). The bank therefore receives either the full contractual amount $(1+r)L_i$ or the maximum possible, $R_i + C_i$, in case of default. Assuming that lenders face no collection or enforcement costs—an assumption that will be further discussed below—the return to the bank is

---

[7]The absence of endowment rules out the possibility for the borrower to invest his or her own funds or to raise funds by other means—such as equity issues or promissory notes.

[8]See Varian (1992, p. 186) for a simple example of a mean-preserving distribution.

given by the smaller of these two values:

$$\min\{R_i + C_i; (1+r)L\}.$$

Because the project yields a zero return if it fails, the return to the borrower is given by

$$\max\{R_i - (1+r)L; -C_i\}.$$

Stiglitz and Weiss show that for a given contractual interest rate, r, there is a critical value of θ, say $\bar{\theta}$, such that an agent will borrow to invest if, and only if, $\theta > \bar{\theta}$; that is, the interest rate serves as a screening device. They also show that an increase in the interest rate triggers two types of effects: (a) an adverse selection effect (which translates into a rise in the threshold value $\bar{\theta}$), resulting from the fact that by increasing the riskiness of the pool of applicants, less risky borrowers drop out of the market; and (b) an adverse incentive effect, or moral hazard effect, which occurs because other borrowers are induced to choose projects for which the probability of default is higher—in turn because riskier projects are associated with higher expected returns. This has a negative effect on the lender's expected profit, which may dominate the positive effect of an increase in the contractual interest rate.

The first result, $\partial\bar{\theta}/\partial r > 0$, implies that the direct, positive effect of an increase in the contractual interest rate on the bank's expected (mean) rate of return on its loans, ρ (defined as the product of the contractual interest rate and the probability of repayment), may be partly offset by the negative effect due to the increase in the riskiness of the pool of borrowers. If the latter effect indeed dominates, the mean return to the lender ρ will not be monotonically related to r and credit rationing may occur in equilibrium. Note that the difference between the moral hazard effect and the adverse selection effect is simply that in the former case lenders choose the contractual interest rate to affect the actions of their borrowers (to get them to avoid riskier projects), whereas in the latter they do so to affect the quality of the pool of borrowers (to avoid causing borrowers with less risky projects to leave the market). Otherwise, the reasoning is essentially the same—in each case lenders are trying to channel funds into safer projects.

The above results can be illustrated with the help of Figure 5.1. The northeast panel in the figure shows the demand for loans, L^d, and the supply of loanable funds, L^s, both as functions of the contractual loan rate, r. The demand for loans is depicted, in a standard fashion, as a downward-sloping function of the loan interest rate. By contrast, the supply of funds is taken to be positively related to the loan interest rate only up to a certain interest rate level, $\tilde{r}$. As indicated earlier, increases in the interest rate beyond the bank-optimal rate $\tilde{r}$ trigger adverse selection and adverse incentive effects, which, by reducing the expected rate of return to the bank, lead to decreasing amounts of credit offered to borrowers. Thus, the relationship between the interest rate and the supply of loanable funds turns negative, and the value of L^s decreases to the right of $\tilde{r}$. Put differently, the supply curve of loans has a concave shape.

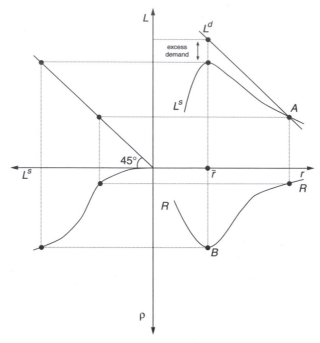

Figure 5–1 ▪ Interest Rate Determination in the Stiglitz–Weiss Credit Rationing Model
Source: Adapted from Stiglitz and Weiss (1981, p. 397).

As noted earlier, the expected rate of return to the bank, ρ, is the product of the contractual interest rate and the probability of repayment. Owing to the adverse selection and adverse incentive effects associated with a rise in the interest rate, the repayment probability declines by more than the increase in the interest rate beyond the threshold level of the contractual rate, $\tilde{r}$. The relationship between ρ and the contractual rate of interest is thus non-monotonic, as illustrated by curve RR in the southeast panel of Figure 5.1. Moreover, RR has a more pronounced concave shape than L^s.

A higher expected rate of return raises the incentive to lend; there is, therefore, a positive relationship between ρ and the supply of loanable funds, as depicted in the southwest panel of Figure 5.1. The northwest panel shows a 45-degree line mapping of the equilibrium loan amount and the supply curve of loans, L^s. The value of the contractual interest rate that ensures equality between demand and supply of loans is obtained at point A in the northeast panel; however, the credit-rationing equilibrium (characterized by an excess demand for loans) occurs at the interest rate $\tilde{r}$, where the expected return to the bank, ρ, is at its maximum level. Again, the market-clearing interest rate is not optimal for the bank, because at that level bank profits are less than at $\tilde{r}$. It is also inefficient, because borrowers with high repayment probabilities drop out and are replaced by those with high default risk. By contrast, the non-market-clearing rate $\bar{r}$ is both optimal and efficient, because bank profits are at a maximum level and risky borrowers are rationed out.[9]

Thus, under imperfect information, lending rates that are below market-clearing levels can be observed even in competitive credit markets. Such non-market-clearing lending rates reflect an efficient response to profit opportunities. The implication of this analysis is that increases in official interest rates, beyond a certain level, can be counterproductive. Even in a situation where there exists an excess demand for loans, and even if there is some degree of competition among banks, borrowers may face limits on their ability to borrow and banks may charge an interest rate below the level that would clear the market. It may not be optimal for the bank to raise interest rates to the market-clearing level, because at that rate the bank's expected profit is less than that achieved at the credit-rationing level, and borrowers with high repayment probabilities tend to drop out and are replaced by those with high default risks.

The Stiglitz-Weiss hypothesis of equilibrium credit rationing is helpful to understand why in some developing countries bank credit is severely rationed (in addition to the distortions in credit allocation induced by government regulations), with bank lending rates unresponsive to excess demand for credit. For instance, the degree of riskiness of projects (as measured by the coefficient θ above) may be endogenously related to the level of economic activity—which itself depends on the amount of loans available. This link creates a channel through which credit rationing can be exacerbated and may display persistence over time.

The Stiglitz-Weiss model suffers, however, from several limitations. The first is the assumption that lenders are completely unable to assess the degree of riskiness of potential borrowers. If interest rate increases do indeed lead to riskier projects being funded, banks have incentives to invest in screening technologies in order to acquire information about the risk characteristics of their customers. This is particularly plausible in a dynamic context, even though screening may be hampered somewhat by high-risk borrowers attempting to mimic low-risk borrowers.

A second issue relates to the assumption that all projects have the same mean return [see (1)]. As shown by De Meza and Webb (1987), if on the contrary projects differ in expected return, rationing would not emerge in equilibrium. The reasoning is as follows. Suppose in the above framework that all projects have the same payoff R if successful, but that they differ in terms of their probability of success, which is assumed to be private information for the borrowers.

As before, suppose that unsuccessful projects have a zero return. Thus, projects with a higher probability of success have a higher mean expected return than those with a lower success probability. Banks prefer to lend to borrowers whose projects have a higher probability of success; but now, as the contractual lending rate is

---

[9]Stiglitz and Weiss also show that it is possible to have, in a situation in which there are several groups of observationally distinguishable borrowers, complete exclusion of some groups from the credit market—despite the fact that the expected productivity of their investments may be higher than those of the groups that actually receive credit.

increased, it is projects with the lower success probabilities that are withdrawn from the market. Hence, there is a "favorable" selection effect, as opposed to an adverse selection effect, and the quality of the pool of loan applications actually improves as a result of the rise in interest rates. The relationship between the expected return to the bank, ρ, and the contractual rate is now monotonic; banks gain from both the higher debt repayments on successful projects and the improvement in the quality of potential applications as r rises. They will therefore set the contractual interest rate at the market-clearing level and rationing will not occur.

A third issue relates to the role of collateral, C, in the model. Wette (1983) showed that adverse selection effects similar to those emphasized by Stiglitz and Weiss may result if lenders attempt to raise mean returns by increasing the collateral required from borrowers. Higher collateral requirements may thus reduce the bank's expected profit and lead to equilibrium rationing. Bester (1985) argued, however, that if lenders can vary both collateral requirements and the contractual loan rate to screen loan applicants, the possibility of a rationing equilibrium disappears. The reason is that by manipulating both instruments, lenders can induce borrowers (whose willingness to pledge collateral tends to vary inversely with the degree of riskiness of their project) to self-select themselves into low- and high-risk groups. In a subsequent contribution, Stiglitz and Weiss (1992) argued that even if banks are able to manipulate interest rates and collateral, rationing may still emerge in equilibrium if borrowers are subject to decreasing absolute risk aversion. In such conditions, collateral and the degree of riskiness of borrowers will be positively correlated.

A fourth issue relates to the fact that in the Stigliz-Weiss model, the credit rationing equilibrium is obtained under the assumption that firms have projects with fixed borrowing requirements. De Meza and Webb (2006) have argued that in a rationing equilibrium, the borrower's marginal cost of funds is infinite, so reducing the loan size is almost always worthwhile. This is true whether the origin of rationing is moral hazard or adverse selection. In this alternative credit-rationing equilibrium, internal funds will be at a premium and entrepreneurs will have a strong incentive to cut back current expenditure to reduce borrowing. Moreover, if the project can be scaled down or delayed, there will always be an incentive to do so. Divisible projects, or saving opportunities, imply that banks will never be at the turning point of their return function, but rather on the increasing segment of this function. Hence the competitive credit market will generally clear, and rationing will not be observed.

A fifth issue relates to the role of collection and verification costs, to which we now turn.

2.2 ■ Costly State Verification Models

As noted earlier, the asymmetry of information in the Stiglitz-Weiss model is purely ex ante: although projects differ in their distributions of return before implementation, lenders can observe (costlessly) actual (or ex post) outcomes. An alternative approach, developed notably by Townsend (1979) and Williamson (1986), is to assume that projects are ex ante identical but only borrowers are able to observe the project returns costlessly. This ex post asymmetry of information also gives rise to a moral hazard problem, in the sense that borrowers have an incentive to declare a project return that is low enough to default on the loan, although the return may in fact be higher than needed to pay off the debt. To prevent this, lenders must commit themselves to incur ex post monitoring and enforcement costs to (*a*) verify the outcome of all the projects for which borrowers declare themselves bankrupt; and (*b*) legally enforce the terms of the loan contract (notably seizure of collateral) if the borrower chooses to default. As shown by Williamson (1986), in such conditions it is the positive relationship between the contractual interest rate and expected monitoring and enforcement costs that may generate a nonmonotonic relationship between the expected return to the lender ρ and the contractual lending rate r, thereby creating the possibility of credit rationing. The reason is that the higher the contractual lending rate, the more likely is any borrower to genuinely suffer bankruptcy and the more likely is the lender to incur monitoring and enforcement costs. By raising contractual interest rates to the market-clearing level, the bank might incur a rise in these costs that may offset the direct benefits of the higher price on credit and actually lead to a reduction in expected returns to lending, as in the Stiglitz-Weiss framework. Again, because banks have no incentive to lend in such conditions, credit rationing will emerge in equilibrium.

To illustrate the implications of the costly state verification approach, consider a simplified version of the static analytical framework developed by Agénor and Aizenman (1998, 1999*b*), which highlights the impact of productivity and external cost of credit shocks on domestic output.[10] We first consider the link between bank credit and the supply side, and then derive the curve linking the contractual interest rate and the cost of funds. Finally, we study the impact of an increase in intermediation costs on employment and output.

2.2.1   *Bank Credit and the Supply Side*

Consider an economy in which risk-neutral banks provide intermediation services to domestic producers, who demand credit to finance their production plans. Production is subject to a random productivity shock. The realized value of the productivity shock is revealed to banks only at a cost. If a producer chooses to default on its loan repayment obligations, the bank seizes any collateral set as part of the loan contract, plus a fraction κ of realized output. Seizing involves two types of costs: first, verifying the net worth of the project is costly; second, enforcing repayment requires costly recourse to the legal system.

---

[10] Agénor and Aizenman (2006) present a dynamic application that highlights the impact of intermediation costs and volatility on investment.

Suppose that all producers are similar ex ante, and that the production technology is such that output requires borrowing equal to the wage bill, wL_i, where w is the wage rate (assumed constant) and L_i is labor employed by producer i. Spending wL_i by producer i yields output of

$$y_i = (1+\varepsilon_i)L_i^{\beta}, \quad |\varepsilon_i| \leq U < 1, \quad i = 1, \ldots n, \tag{2}$$

where $0 < \beta < 1$, and ε_i is the realized productivity shock.[11] Equation (2) implies decreasing returns to labor.

Producers cannot issue claims on future output or their capital stock, and can pledge collateral only in quantity $Q_i < wL_i$. Let r_L^i be the contractual interest rate; producer i will default if repayment in the event of default, $\kappa(1+\varepsilon_i)L_i^{\beta} + Q_i$, is less than contractual repayment, $(1+r_L^i)wL_i$:

$$\kappa(1+\varepsilon_i)L_i^{\beta} + Q_i < (1+r_L^i)wL_i. \tag{3}$$

Let ε_i^* denote the highest value of the productivity shock leading to default, that is

$$\kappa(1+\varepsilon_i^*)L_i^{\beta} + Q_i = (1+r_L^i)wL_i, \tag{4}$$

which implies that

$$\varepsilon_i^* = \frac{(1+r_L^i)wL_i - Q_i}{\kappa L_i^{\beta}} - 1. \tag{5}$$

This equation shows that, for ε_i^* to be negative, expected output, L_i^{β} times κ, must exceed contractual repayment.

If default never occurs, the bank's revenue on its loan to producer i, Π_i, is equal to $(1+r_L^i)wL_i$, and ε_i^* is set at the lower end of the support $(\varepsilon_i^* = -U)$. In case of default, Π_i is given by the producer's repayment plus the collateral that is seized minus the state verification and contract enforcement cost, C_i:[12,13]

$$\Pi_i|_{default} = \kappa(1+\varepsilon_i)L_i^{\beta} + Q_i - C_i. \tag{6}$$

---

[11]Note that there is no aggregate risk in our model. All firms are identical and the productivitiy shock ε_i is uncorrelated among them.

[12]C_i is a lump-sum cost paid by banks in order to identify the productivity shock ε_i, and to enforce proper repayment. The analysis would be more involved if some costs were paid *after* obtaining the information about ε_i. In these circumstances, banks would refrain from forcing debt repayment when the realized productivity is below an "enforcement threshold." We also ignore all other real costs associated with financial intermediation.

[13]Alternatively, C could be assumed to increase with the level of a firm's output, that is, $C_i = c_i y_i$, as for instance in Greenwald and Stiglitz (1993). This assumption, as well as a variety of others, would not change qualitatively the results discussed below; what is necessary is that the cost function be convex in y_i.

Banks have access to an elastic supply of funds (up to a given ceiling) at a real cost of r_C, which is independent of i. For the moment, it is assumed that the demand for credit is never constrained (see the discussion below). Banks are risk neutral, and compete in a manner akin to monopolistic competition. This assumption about market structure is captured by postulating a markup pricing rule, whereby banks demand the expected yield on their loans (net of enforcement costs) to be $\theta(1+r_C)$, where $\theta \geq 1$ is taken to be constant. Consequently, the contractual interest rate on loans to producer i is determined by the break-even condition:

$$\theta(1+r_C)wL_i = \int_{\varepsilon_i^*}^{U} [(1+r_L^i)wL_i]f(\varepsilon_i)d\varepsilon_i$$

$$+ \int_{-U}^{\varepsilon_i^*} [\kappa(1+\varepsilon_i)L_i^\beta + Q_i - C_i]f(\varepsilon_i)d\varepsilon_i, \qquad (7)$$

where $f(\varepsilon_i)$ is the density function of ε_i. For simplicity, and given that producers are assumed to be identical (with, in particular, $C_i = C$), the sub-index i will be dropped in what follows.

Equation (7) can be rewritten as

$$\theta(1+r_C)wL = (1+r_L)wL$$

$$- \int_{-U}^{\varepsilon^*} [(1+r_L)wL - \kappa(1+\varepsilon)L^\beta - Q]f(\varepsilon)d\varepsilon - C\int_{-U}^{\varepsilon^*} f(\varepsilon)d\varepsilon.$$

Substituting (4) for $(1+r_L)wL$ in the second term on the right-hand side of the above equation and rearranging yields the interest rate spread as

$$1+r_L = \theta(1+r_C) + \frac{\kappa L^\beta \int_{-U}^{\varepsilon^*}(\varepsilon^*-\varepsilon)f(\varepsilon)d\varepsilon}{wL} + \frac{C\int_{-U}^{\varepsilon^*}f(\varepsilon)d\varepsilon}{wL}. \qquad (8)$$

Equation (8) shows that the (gross) contractual interest rate is determined by a markup rule, which exceeds the bank's net return on its funds by the sum of two terms. The first term, $\kappa L^\beta \int_{-U}^{\varepsilon^*}(\varepsilon^*-\varepsilon)f(\varepsilon)d\varepsilon/wL$, is the expected revenue lost due to default in bad states of nature. The second term, $C\int_{-U}^{\varepsilon^*}f(\varepsilon)d\varepsilon/wL$, measures the expected state verification and contract enforcement costs. Note that collateral affects the markup equation (8) through ε^*; a higher collateral increases the cost of default, thereby reducing the frequency of defaults (ε^* falls). Consequently, higher collateral reduces the interest rate spread.

The *contractual* repayment obligation for the producer is $(1+r_L)wL$. However, the *expected* repayment depends on the realized state of nature, and thus on the value of ε; it is given by

$$\int_{\varepsilon^*}^{U} [(1+r_L)wL]f(\varepsilon)d\varepsilon + (\kappa L^\beta + Q)\int_{-U}^{\varepsilon^*}(1+\varepsilon)f(\varepsilon)d\varepsilon.$$

The first term indicates the repayment if the realized productivity shock is above ε^*; the second, the value of output that is seized if the realized productivity shock is too low ($\varepsilon < \varepsilon^*$).

The producer's expected net income is thus equal to

$$E \max\left\{(1+\varepsilon)L^\beta - (1+r_L)wL,\ (1-\kappa)(1+\varepsilon)L^\beta - Q\right\},$$

which can be rewritten as expected output, L^β, minus expected repayment in "good" and "bad" states of nature:

$$L^\beta - \int_{\varepsilon^*}^{U} [(1+r_L)wL]f(\varepsilon)d\varepsilon - \int_{-U}^{\varepsilon^*}[\kappa(1+\varepsilon)L^\beta + Q]f(\varepsilon)d\varepsilon. \qquad (9)$$

Applying (7), we can simplify (9) to

$$L^\beta - \theta(1+r_C)wL - C\int_{-U}^{\varepsilon^*}f(\varepsilon)d\varepsilon. \qquad (10)$$

2.2.2   The Cost of Funds–Contractual Interest Rate Curve

Suppose that the shock ε follows a uniform distribution, so that $-U \leq \varepsilon \leq U$. Solving (8) therefore yields the quadratic equation

$$1+r_L = \theta(1+r_C) + \frac{U\kappa L^\beta}{wL}\Phi^2 + \frac{C}{wL}\Phi, \qquad (11)$$

where Φ, the probability of default (with $C\Phi$ therefore measuring the expected cost of financial intermediation), is given by:

$$\Phi = \int_{-U}^{\varepsilon^*}f(\varepsilon)d\varepsilon = \frac{U+\varepsilon^*}{2U}. \qquad (12)$$

The second term of (11) illustrates how producers pay for the information asymmetry through the banks' markup rule. Combining (4), (10), and (11), the contractual interest rate can be solved for as a function of the banks' cost of funds. In general, this curve is nonlinear, and in the case of a uniform distribution for ε it is

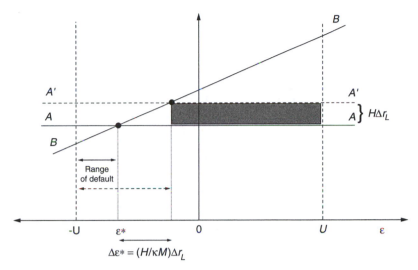

Figure 5–2 ■ Interest Rate and Expected Repayment with Costly State Verification
Source: Agénor and Alzeman (1999b, p. 205).

quadratic:

$$\theta(1+r_C) + \Psi g(r_L)^2 + \frac{C}{wL}g(r_L) - (1+r_L) = 0, \tag{13}$$

where $\Psi = U\kappa L^\beta / wL$ and, with $Q_j = 0$ for simplicity,

$$g(r_L) = \frac{1}{2} - \frac{1}{2U} + \frac{1+r_L}{2\Psi}.$$

It can be inferred from (13) that

$$\frac{dr_L}{dr_C} = -\frac{\theta}{\Phi + (C/2wL\Psi) - 1}. \tag{14}$$

Further insight regarding (14) can be inferred from Figure 5.2, which relates repayment to the value of the productivity shock, ε. Curve BB (respectively AA) corresponds to the left-hand side (respectively right-hand side) of (3). The intersection of these curves determines ε^*. The probability of repayment is determined by the length of the segment $U\varepsilon^*$, normalized by $2U$. Curve $A'A'$ corresponds to a marginal increase in the contractual interest rate by Δr_L. A higher interest rate affects the bank's expected repayment in two opposite directions. On the one hand, expected repayment increases by the shaded area (which represents the increase in the value to be repaid in good states of nature, at a given level of the demand for loans) normalized by $2U$—an area which is also equal to the probability of repayment, $1 - \Phi$, because Φ is the probability of default—times $wL\Delta r_L$. On the other, expected repayment falls as a result of the increase in expected intermediation costs, which is equal to C times $[(d\varepsilon^*/dr_L)/2U]\Delta r_L$.[14] The net increase in expected repayment is thus given by

$$\left\{ (1 - \Phi)wL - \frac{C}{2U}\frac{d\varepsilon^*}{dr_L} \right\} \Delta r_L.$$

From (5), $d\varepsilon^*/dr_L = wL/\kappa L^\beta > 0$. Substituting this result in the above expression yields

$$\left\{ (1 - \Phi) - \frac{C}{2U\kappa L^\beta} \right\} wL\Delta r_L. \tag{15}$$

Hence, the condition for observing $\Delta r_L/\Delta r_C > 0$ is that, for $\Phi = 0$:

$$1 - \frac{C}{2U\kappa L^\beta} > 0,$$

or equivalently $C/2U < \kappa L^\beta$. Thus, if the foregoing condition is satisfied, we will observe an upward-sloping portion for the contractual interest rate/cost of loanable funds curve.

Suppose that this condition is met. If $\kappa L^\beta(1 - U) + Q < \theta(1 + r_C)wL$, then (given the definition of ε_i^* given above) $U + \varepsilon_i^* > 0$ and the probability of default, Φ, will be positive. In these circumstances the interest rate/cost of credit curve is backward bending, as shown in Figure 5.3. In this figure, point M is reached when the term in brackets in (15) is zero.

With a low level of bank funding costs, if we also have $\kappa L^\beta(1 - U) + Q > \theta(1 + r_C)wL$, then Φ, the probability of default, will be zero—as is the case along the portion KL in Figure 5.3 where, as implied by the break-even condition (11) with $\Phi = 0$,

$$1 + r_L = \theta(1 + r_C).$$

Thus, with no probability of default, the contractual interest rate reflects the banks' cost of funds, adjusted for the markup rate.

At a high enough level of the banks' funding cost (and thus of the contractual lending rate), producers will default in the worst states of nature, as is the case if

$$r_C \geq \tilde{r}_C = \frac{\kappa L^\beta(1 - U) + Q}{\theta wL} - 1.$$

---

[14]Recall from the previous discussion that $\Phi = (U + \varepsilon^*)/2U$. By implication, we have $d\Phi/dr_L = (2U)^{-1}d\varepsilon^*/dr_L$.

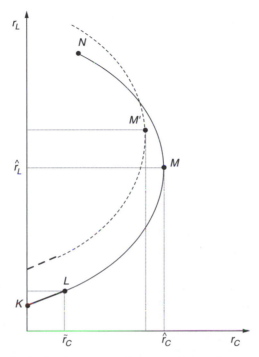

Figure 5–3 ▪ Cost of Funds–Contractual Interest Rate Curve
Source: Agénor and Alzeman (1999b, p. 207).

The point at which $r_C = \tilde{r}_C$ corresponds to point L in Figure 5.3. Beyond $\tilde{r}_C$, a further increase in the banks' funding cost would increase the probability of default, leading to an increasing risk premium and a higher contractual rate, moving along portion LM. Equation (14) implies that, moving above point L, the slope of the curve increases as the probability of default rises. At a high enough cost of funding, the economy would reach point M (at which point $r_C = \hat{r}_C$), where further rises in the banks' funding cost would make the project unfeasible. This will happen because a higher contractual lending rate reduces the probability of repayment, and at point M further increases in this rate raise the probability of default at a rate that is high enough to reduce expected repayment. It can be verified that interest rates at point M are given by

$$\hat{r}_L = \frac{\kappa L^\beta(1+U)+Q-C}{wL} - 1, \quad \hat{r}_C = \frac{(C^2/4U\kappa L^\beta)+\kappa L^\beta - C}{w\theta L} - 1. \quad (16)$$

Equation (16) implies that higher domestic volatility—an increase in U—would shift point M upward and to the left. This is confirmed by the dotted curve in Figure 5.3, with point M shifting to point M'.

It can be inferred from (16) that

$$sg\left(\frac{d\hat{r}_C}{dC}\right) = sg\left(\frac{C}{2U\kappa L^\beta} - 1\right) < 0,$$

given the condition derived earlier for generating an upward-sloping portion for the curve linking r_L and r_C. Thus, higher enforcement and verification costs lower the threshold level of the funding cost above which lending becomes unfeasible.

In general, given that changes in the cost of funds affect expected repayment in two opposite directions (as discussed earlier), there are two domestic contractual rates associated with each level of r_C. The high interest rate is also associated with a low probability of repayment. If competitive forces are sufficiently strong, they will prevent the inefficient equilibrium associated with operating on the backward-bending portion of the curve (segment MN).

As noted earlier, banks are assumed to operate only (as a result of efficiency considerations) on the upward-sloping portion of this curve. It can be verified that if $C/2U > \kappa L$, a credit ceiling will be reached at the lowest level of loans associated with default. In these circumstances the supply curve has an inverted L shape. This would occur if verification costs are too large to be recovered, in which case banks would not supply credit levels that would lead to default in some states of nature.

2.2.3   Intermediation Costs, Employment, and Output

To analyze the implications of the foregoing analysis for employment and output, suppose now that each (identical) producer chooses the level of employment L that maximizes *expected* profits, which is given not by the difference between L^β and contractual repayment, $(1+r_C)L$, but rather by (10), which, using (12), can be written as

$$L^\beta - \theta(1+r_C)wL - C\Phi. \tag{17}$$

Thus, with a zero probability of default ($\Phi = 0$), enforcement costs have no effect on profits. Differentiating the above expression with respect to L and setting the result to zero gives

$$\beta L^{\beta-1} - \theta(1+r_C)w - C\frac{d\Phi}{dL} = 0,$$

that is, using (5) and (12):

$$\beta L^{\beta-1} - \theta(1+r_C)w - C(1-\beta)\frac{(1+r_L)w}{\kappa L^\beta} = 0, \tag{18}$$

which determines the optimal demand for labor.[15] It is easy to establish from this expression (using the implicit function theorem) that the demand for labor is inversely related to contract enforcement and verification costs ($dL/dC < 0$). Thus, an increase in intermediation costs also has an adverse effect on output.

Collateral considerations can easily be introduced in the costly state verification approach.[16] Essentially, with ex post asymmetric information, collateral diminishes the (inefficient) amount that must be liquidated in the case of default, and therefore increases welfare. More specifically, Aizenman and Powell (2003) introduced collateral in the model described earlier and showed that, by increasing the cost of default and lowering the threshold value of the productivity shock, higher collateral reduces the premium of the lending rate over the banks' cost of borrowing.

2.3 ■ Net Worth and Borrowing Constraints

An alternative approach to modeling credit restrictions is to assume that borrowing constraints are tied in some way to the net worth of the potential borrower. An influential approach along these lines is the one developed by Kiyotaki and Moore (1997). In their paper they construct several versions of their "credit cycle" model, differing in complexity and in the particular dynamic mechanisms that they want to highlight. In what follows we present a simplified version of their basic framework.

Consider an economy where there are two production sectors and two categories of firms, a constrained sector (with type C-entrepreneurs) and an unconstrained sector (with type U-entrepreneurs). Types are distinguished by the technology available for producing a perishable good. Both technologies use land and labor inputs at time t to produce output at $t + 1$, but differ crucially in the nature of their labor inputs. The labor input of U-entrepreneurs can be guaranteed ahead of time, independently of any debt they might have. In contrast, C-entrepreneurs cannot commit to work. This exposes potential lenders to the risk of default, because it is assumed that no good is produced without the C-entrepreneurs' labor input. If a C-entrepreneur's debt becomes too onerous, it will be in his interest to withdraw his labor and default on his loan. As a result, lenders will require loans to C-entrepreneurs to be backed by collateral.

In general, the amount of collateral required depends on the specifics of the bargaining process that follows default. Kiyotaki and Moore argue that C-entrepreneurs will capture the entire difference between their debt and the liquidation value of their

---

[15]Note that r_L is taken as given by each producer in determining optimal employment. The reason is that we assume the existence of a large group of ex ante homogeneous producers, all of whom are charged the same interest rate by lenders. As shown earlier, r_L is determined in equilibrium by a break-even condition that internalizes all the information about the distribution of the idiosyncratic shocks.

[16]See Coco (2000) for an overview of the literature on collateral, albeit with a focus on industrial countries.

land, so that lenders will require the full (expected) value of their land as collateral.[17] In other words, a C-entrepreneur cannot take out a loan for more than the (expected) value of his current land holdings. This constraint makes the equilibrium sequential and is responsible for all the model's dynamics.[18]

In their basic framework, Kiyotaki and Moore make three unconventional assumptions that facilitate the analysis. First, they abstract from issues of risk-sharing by assuming that preferences are linear in consumption. Second, they assume that C- and U-entrepreneurs have different rates of time preference. In particular, C-entrepreneurs are assumed to be less patient than U-entrepreneurs, so that in equilibrium C-entrepreneurs are borrowers and U-entrepreneurs are lenders. Third, they impose a technological upper bound on the savings rate of C-entrepreneurs (by assuming that some of their output cannot be traded) and impose parameter restrictions ensuring a corner solution for their savings decisions. Thus, savings dynamics play no role in the basic framework.

Even with these simplifying assumptions, the model remains quite complex and yields potentially rich dynamic interactions between asset prices and aggregate economic activity. However, the basic framework has a couple of unattractive features that Kiyotaki and Moore address in an extended version. First, there is no aggregate investment. The total supply of land is fixed, and dynamics take the form of reallocations of land between C- and U-entrepreneurs. Second, leverage ratios are unrealistically high, being equal to the reciprocal of the gross interest rate. Such high-leverage ratios then yield implausibly large impulse responses to unanticipated shocks. In addition, the lack of aggregate investment makes these responses rather transitory.

Kiyotaki and Moore remedy these shortcomings by introducing reproducible capital into the model. This capital is used together with land and labor as production inputs, and is augmented through investment (given as a fraction of output). It consists of specific assets, and hence cannot be used as collateral. This reduces leverage ratios and dampens the economy's response to shocks. By assuming that in any given period only a fraction of C-entrepreneurs have the opportunity to invest in reproducible capital, Kiyotaki and Moore are also able to draw out the economy's response to shocks. Moreover, they show that this extended model can potentially have (stable) complex roots and thus produce cyclical responses to shocks.[19]

---

[17] Because C-entrepreneurs cannot commit to pay dividends either, introducing an equity market would not help them raise capital. However, in some versions of Kiyotaki and Moore's model, there may be an advantage to setting up a rental market in land.

[18] See also Kiyotaki (1998) for a discussion. There are of course other ways of introducing financial market imperfections. Perhaps the most common approach is to assume asymmetric information, as discussed earlier. However, basing debt on the "inalienability of human capital" rather than on moral hazard or adverse selection simplifies matters considerably in dynamic settings.

[19] A third version of the model is developed in the appendix to their paper, which is designed to show that none of the substantive results from their basic framework depend on its unconventional preference and technology assumptions.

Both C- and U-entrepreneurs face a constant probability of dying, $1 - p$, where p is the probability of surviving from one period to the next. Each period, new cohorts of entrepreneurs are born, each of size $1 - p$, so that by the law of large numbers the economy's total population remains constant at 2. Although the assumption of geometrically distributed lifetimes is demographically unrealistic, it greatly facilitates aggregation, because marginal propensities to save are independent of age.

All entrepreneurs are endowed with perfect foresight and maximize the expected present discounted value of utility from consumption, c_t, conditional on surviving each successive period. Preferences of each type of entrepreneur are assumed to be identical and concave, so that each entrepreneur's problem is

$$\max_{c_t} U = \mathbb{E}_t \sum_{j=0}^{\infty} (\beta p)^j \ln c_{t+j}, \tag{19}$$

where β is the discount factor and $\mathbb{E}_t$ the expectations operator. For tractability, the instantaneous utility function is taken to be logarithmic. Labor is supplied inelastically, so that leisure does not enter the utility function.

Entrepreneurs are distinguished by their production technologies. C-entrepreneurs have a linear technology. Thus, if we denote the time t aggregate land holdings of C-entrepreneurs by H_t^C and output at time $t + 1$ by Y_{t+1}^C, we have

$$Y_{t+1}^C = a H_t^C, \qquad a > 0. \tag{20}$$

Production by U-entrepreneurs, Y_{t+1}^U, is subject to diminishing returns; assuming a quadratic technology yields

$$Y_{t+1}^U = F(H_t^U) = b_1 H_t^U - \frac{b_2}{2}(H_t^U)^2, \quad b_1, b_2 > 0, \tag{21}$$

where H_t^U represents land holdings by U-entrepreneurs. The total land supply is taken to be fixed at $\bar{K}$, so that market clearing requires $\bar{H} = H_t^C + H_t^U$ for all t. Hence, the model's dynamics take the form of reallocations of land between the two types of entrepreneurs. To guarantee an interior steady-state allocation of land requires imposing the following parameter restrictions: $b_1 > a > pa > b_1 - b_2\bar{H}$. This set of inequalities indicates that if U-entrepreneurs hold all the land, the marginal product of land in the C-sector is greater than in the U-sector, whereas if C-entrepreneurs hold all the land, then the marginal product of land in the U-sector is greater.

At the start of each period, exchange takes place in four markets: (*a*) a spot commodity market in which output is bought and sold; (*b*) a real estate market in which land is exchanged; (*c*) a domestic bond market in which both types of entrepreneurs borrow and lend among themselves; and (*d*) an international capital market that absorbs the difference between domestic production and domestic expenditure. Domestic output is assumed to be the numéraire, with its price normalized to unity. The time t price of a unit of land is denoted q_t, and the (constant) gross world interest rate is R (both expressed in units of the domestic good).

Entrepreneurs solve the maximization problem in (19) subject to a sequence of budget constraints. Suppose that entrepreneurs are not born with any endowment; if b_t denotes the time t debt of either type of entrepreneur, then these constraints take the following form (in the aggregate):[20]

$$q_t(H_t^C - H_{t-1}^C) + Rb_{t-1} + c_t = pa\,H_{t-1}^C + b_t, \qquad (22)$$

for C-entrepreneurs, and

$$q_t(H_t^U - H_{t-1}^U) + Rb_{t-1} + c_t = p\left\{b_1 H_{t-1}^U - \frac{b_1}{2}(H_{t-1}^U)^2\right\} + b_t, \qquad (23)$$

for U-entrepreneurs.

The right-hand sides of these constraints are the sources of time t funds, which consist of current production of surviving entrepreneurs and issues of new debt. The left-hand sides are the uses of time t funds, given by land purchases, debt repayments, and consumption expenditure.

The key ingredient of the model is a constraint limiting the debt, b_t, of C-entrepreneurs. This constraint arises from their inability to commit to work, along with the assumption that no output is produced without labor. Kiyotaki and Moore argue that with perfect foresight no C-entrepreneur will be able to take out a loan that exceeds the present value of his current land holdings, given that lenders recognize the incentive to default if debt were to exceed that value. If land prices are not stochastic, the future value of collateral is $q_{t+1}H_t^C$. Assuming for simplicity that C-entrepreneurs are able to borrow up to the (expected) present value of their land, the borrowing constraint will take the binding form:

$$Rb_t = q_{t+1}H_t^C, \qquad (24)$$

where R appears rather than R/p, because when a C-entrepreneur dies, his land remains. Put differently, borrowing must be equal to the present discounted value of land at $t + 1$.

---

[20]Mortality risk implies that the interest rate on individual loans is R/p. However, in the aggregate, this risk is fully diversifiable, so the sectoral budget constraints are as shown in (22) and (23).

Using (24) to substitute out for b_t in the (aggregate) budget constraint of C-entrepreneurs (22) yields:

$$z_t H_t^C + c_t = (pa + q_t)H_{t-1}^C - Rb_{t-1}, \tag{25}$$

where $z_t = q_t - q_{t+1}/R$ can be described as the "user cost of capital" at t, or alternatively here, the required down payment on a fully mortgaged unit of land.

Solving (19) subject to the constraint (25) yields the following decision rule for C-entrepreneurs' investment expenditure on land:

$$H_t^C = \frac{\beta p}{z_t} pa H_{t-1}^C. \tag{26}$$

This equation shows that C-entrepreneurs spend a fixed fraction βp of their time t net worth on land. The remaining fraction, $1 - \beta p$, is spent on consumption.

Equation (26) is one of the two fundamental equations of the model. The second fundamental equation summarizes optimal behavior of U-entrepreneurs. Because U-entrepreneurs do not face borrowing constraints, their land purchases are based on a no-arbitrage condition. In particular, U-entrepreneurs must be indifferent between lending and buying land (or, alternatively, between borrowing and selling land). This will be the case when the following equality holds:

$$\frac{F'(H_t^U)}{z_t} = \frac{R}{p}. \tag{27}$$

The left-hand side of (27) is the rate of return from buying a unit of land, whereas the right-hand side is the return from lending (recall that a mortality risk premium is charged on individual loans).

Using the market-clearing condition $\bar{H} = H_t^C + H_t^U$, and the definition of z_t in (25), equations (26) and (27) can be reduced to two equations in the two unknown stochastic processes, q_t and H_t^C. Substituting out for z_t in (26) using (27) yields the following nonlinear difference equation that determines the equilibrium path of C-entrepreneurs' land holdings:

$$\frac{p}{R}F'(\bar{H} - H_t^C)H_t^C - \beta p^2 a H_{t-1}^C = 0. \tag{28}$$

Two results summarize the essential properties of this equation. The first is that there exists a unique positive steady-state allocation of land. If the world interest rate satisfies the restriction $R\beta > 1$, and the parameters of the production function $F()$ satisfy the restrictions given above, then in the steady state farmers' land holdings are:

$$\bar{H}^C = \frac{\beta Rpa - (b_1 - b_2\bar{H})}{b_2}. \tag{29}$$

The proof of this proposition is straightforward. From (21), $F'(\bar{H} - H_t^C) = b_1 - b_2(\bar{H} - H_t^C)$. Hence, the left-hand side of (28) is quadratic. To solve for the steady state, set $H_t^C = H_{t-1}^C = \bar{H}^C$. This gives $pR^{-1}[b_1 - b_2(\bar{H} - \bar{H}^C)]\bar{H}^C - \beta p^2 a \bar{H}^C = 0$, which can be rearranged as $b_1 - b_2(\bar{H} - \bar{H}^C) - \beta Rpa = 0$. Solving this equation gives (29), where $\bar{H}^C > 0$ if $R\beta > 1$ and (as stated above) $pa > b_1 - b_2\bar{H}$.

The second result is obtained by linearizing (28) around $\bar{K}^C$. It implies that in the neighborhood of the steady state, farmers' land holdings follow a stationary first-order autoregressive process, given by:

$$H_t^C = H_0^C + \lambda H_{t-1}^C, \tag{30}$$

where

$$\lambda = \frac{\beta Rpa}{2\beta Rpa - (b_1 - b_2\bar{H})} < 1, \qquad H_0^C = \frac{b_2\bar{H}^2}{b_1 - b_2\bar{H} + 2b_2\bar{H}^C}. \tag{31}$$

Once the equilibrium process of H_t^C is determined, (27) can be used to derive the equilibrium process of q_t. In the neighborhood of the steady state, land prices are also driven by a stationary first-order autoregressive process:

$$q_t = \bar{q} + \left(\frac{pb_2}{R - \lambda}\right)H_t^C = \left\{(1 - \lambda)\bar{q} + \left(\frac{pb_2}{R - \lambda}\right)\bar{H}^C\right\} + \lambda q_{t-1}, \tag{32}$$

where

$$\bar{q} = \frac{p(b_1 - b_2\bar{H})}{R - 1} - \frac{pb_2 H_0^C}{(R - \lambda)(1 - \lambda)}.$$

Indeed, from (27) $z_t = q_t - q_{t+1}/R = (p/R)F'(\bar{H} - H_t^C) = (p/R)[b_1 - b_2(\bar{H} - H_t^C)]$. Iterating forward (that is, applying a transversality condition on land prices), plugging in for H_t^C from (30) and evaluating the resulting present discounted value gives (32).

As shown by Kiyotaki and Moore, as long as $R < 1/\beta p$, the presence of borrowing constraints implies that in the steady state the rate of return in the constrained sector exceeds the rate of return in the unconstrained sector.[21] This discrepancy is a key feature of the model; it implies that marginal reallocations of land have first-order consequences for output and asset prices. In addition, the parameter λ increases when borrowing constraints become tighter. Thus, from (30) and (32), tighter borrowing constraints both magnify and prolong the economy's response to shocks.

---

[21]Indeed, the steady-state rate of return in the C-sector is $a/\bar{z}$, that is, given that from (26), $\bar{z} = \beta p^2 a$, $a/\bar{z} = 1/\beta p^2$. By contrast, C-entrepreneurs are free to equate margins, so their steady-state rate of return is the market rate, R/p. Thus, $1/\beta p^2 > R/p$ holds if $R < 1/\beta p$.

The Kiyotaki–Moore model described earlier is based on a number of "non-standard" assumptions—such as the assumption that C-entrepreneurs have a linear technology [see (20)]. These assumptions are not innocuous. Cordoba and Ripoll (2004) extend the model to consider standard preferences and technologies. Using empirically plausible calibrations, they find that the quantitative significance of collateral constraints as an amplification mechanism of shocks is much more limited than in the original model. In addition, Krishnamurthy (2003) showed that this mechanism is not robust to the introduction of markets that allow firms to hedge against common shocks.

3   The Monetary Transmission Mechanism: Overview

Greater monetary policy autonomy imparted by the recent shift toward more flexible exchange-rate regimes has led to renewed focus on the monetary transmission mechanism in developing countries. This section provides a review of the main channels through which monetary policy decisions are transmitted to aggregate demand and the supply side in a small open developing economy.[22] We will focus throughout on the case of a country with a sufficiently developed financial system, where the operational target for monetary policy is a short-term policy rate, that the central bank controls by affecting the supply of liquidity to commercial banks.[23] Specifically, we will assume that the supply of liquidity by the central bank is perfectly elastic at the official rate.

3.1 ■ The Pass-Through of Policy Rates to Market Rates

Before reviewing the transmission channels of monetary policy per se, a key issue is the extent to which changes in short-term official rates affect market interest rates. If the pass-through of policy rates to short-term market interest rates is complete and rapid, then a representative market rate (for instance, the overnight interbank rate, the money market rate, or the three-month Treasury bill rate) can be regarded as the policy instrument itself.

In developing countries, however, due to various types of market imperfections, the pass-through is not always complete and may not occur very quickly. In general, stickiness in bank lending rates in any given economy depends on the country's financial structure, which in turn depends on factors such as the degree of

---

[22]For a more detailed overview of the transmission channels of monetary policy in developing countries, see Agénor (2004b, chapter 4) as well as Mishra et al. (2013). We do not discuss in what follows how trade credit (upon which small firms may be particularly reliant) affects the monetary transmission mechanism; see Mateut (2005) for a broad overview.

[23]See Laurens (2005) for a discussion of the various policy instruments that modern central banks use to implement monetary policy.

development of financial markets, the degree of competition within the banking system, and the ownership structure of financial intermediaries. For instance, the lower the degree of competition in the credit market is, the more limited alternative sources of finance are, and the lower the elasticity of the demand for loans is, the more limited will be the response of lending rates to changes in policy and money market rates. At the same time, the more transitory the change in the money market rate is perceived to be, the less responsive will lending rates be. In countries where the banking system continues to be dominated by state-owned banks, political pressure (or sheer inefficiency) may also delay adjustments in lending rates. The response of the money market rate itself may be limited as well if the interbank market for loans is not sufficiently competitive or if the adjustment in the policy rate is perceived as temporary in nature. By implication, it is possible for the response of bank deposit and lending rates to changes in official rates to be *asymmetric*. Chong et al. (2006), for instance, found that in Singapore, bank interest rates adjust less rapidly when they are below their long-term equilibrium level than when they are above; thus, a monetary policy contraction may take a longer time to affect the economy than an expansionary monetary policy.

In addition, the level of short-term interest rates affects only a fraction of the financing of aggregate spending by households and firms. The private sector may also finance expenditure through retained earnings (as is often the case in developing countries) and, to a lesser extent, at longer-term rates through the banking system or the capital market. The cost of borrowing from these sources is only indirectly influenced by short-term interest rates.

Overall, the impact of changes in policy rates on the cost of finance depends on the degree of substitutability between different forms of finance, the pass-through of changes in these rates to short-term market interest rates (including bank lending and deposit rates), and the impact of changes in short-term interest rates on long-term rates. In turn, the degree of substitutability between different forms of finance depends on the structure and functioning of financial markets.

Available studies, such as Disyatat and Vongsinsirikul (2003) and Archer (2006), suggest that policy rates affect short-term market interest rates with significant lags. This finding is important for assessing the role and impact of monetary policy; it indicates that the transmission mechanism of monetary policy decisions may be enhanced by structural measures aimed at strengthening competition among financial intermediaries. Nevertheless, it will be assumed in what follows that changes in the policy interest rate are transmitted to a significant extent (even after some delay) to market interest rates.

A synoptic view of the transmission channels of monetary policy for a small open developing country operating under fixed and flexible exchange rates is provided in Figures 5.4 and 5.5. These channels can be classified into interest rate effects, nominal exchange-rate effects, asset price and balance sheet effects, credit availability effects, and expectations effects. Balance sheet effects and credit availability effects are often referred to as the credit channel (see Bernanke and Gertler, 1995).

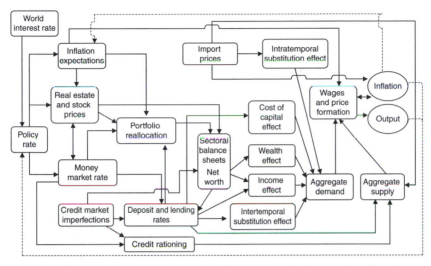

Figure 5–4 ▪ The Transmission Process of Monetary Policy under Fixed
Exchange Rates
Source: Adapted from Agénor (2004*a*, p. 133).

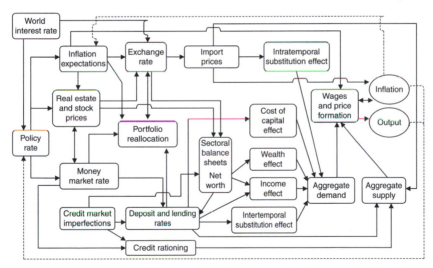

Figure 5–5 ▪ The Transmission Process of Monetary Policy under Flexible
Exchange Rates
Source: Adapted from Agénor (2004*b*, p. 133).

This essentially relies on the view that the functioning of the credit market is
hindered by asymmetries in information between borrowers and lenders, as discussed
earlier. In a dynamic perspective, there are also, of course, feedback effects from the
behavior of key macroeconomic aggregates (output and inflation) to policy decisions
and expectations, which are shown as dotted lines in the figures.

3.2 ■ Interest Rate Effects

Changes in interest rates initiated by monetary policy decisions affect both aggregate demand and aggregate supply. With respect to aggregate demand, four channels of transmission can be distinguished.

The first is a *cost of capital effect*, on purchases of durable consumption goods, investment in housing, business investment on plant and equipment, as well as inventories. If firms must borrow to finance capital formation, a rise in real bank lending rates induced by an increase in nominal policy rates would raise the cost of capital and tend to lower investment and output. The second is a *wealth effect* on household expenditure. An increase in official rates that translates into higher domestic interest rates would tend to reduce the present value of the future income stream from real assets and fixed-coupon financial assets. This, in turn, would tend to lower their price and reduce the value of these assets in households' portfolios. The resulting reduction in private wealth would reduce private expenditure.

The third is an *income effect*, which can be positive or negative depending on whether households are net debtors or creditors toward the banking system. If households are net creditors, an increase in official interest rates that translates into higher deposit rates would lead to higher disposable income and higher spending. The greater the degree of substitutability between bank deposits and central bank loans as sources of funds for commercial banks is, the larger will be the effect of changes in official rates on deposit rates. The fourth is an *intertemporal substitution effect* on consumer spending; a rise in real interest rates, for instance, induces households to substitute cheaper future consumption for more expensive current consumption. Because a rise in interest rates also exerts a positive income effect (as noted previously), which tends to offset the adverse effect of intertemporal substitution on spending, the net impact on private expenditure is in general ambiguous.

With respect to aggregate supply, there are also several effects. First, there is a *labor supply effect*. To the extent that a rise in interest rates leads households to lower the demand for leisure and increase their supply of labor, a temporary rise in potential output may result. Second, there is a *cost effect*, which may be particularly important in developing countries. If firms are net debtors with respect to the banking system, higher lending rates induced by higher refinancing costs for the banks will raise production costs, as formally described in Subsection 5.2. This would be the case, for instance, if firms must pay their workers prior to the sale of output and therefore borrow from the banking system. In such conditions, the effective cost of labor includes the lending rate.

The net, direct effect of changes in policy interest rates on output will thus in general depend on whether the supply-side effect is expansionary or contractionary, and on whether it is mitigated or exacerbated by aggregate demand effects. If, for instance, the wealth effect is expansionary but takes some time to operate, an increase in interest rates may well induce a recession. In addition, the effect on inflation would depend on the process of wage and price formation. If wages and prices are sticky in the short run, and therefore do not respond rapidly to excess supply of labor and excess demand for goods and services, changes in policy interest rates will affect inflation only gradually.

3.3 ■ Exchange-Rate Effects

Under flexible exchange rates, policy-induced changes in the nominal exchange rate are an important transmission channel through which monetary policy affects both inflation and output (see Figure 5.5). Typically, for a given expected inflation rate, the immediate impact of an increase in domestic interest rates is an inflow of capital and an appreciation of the nominal exchange rate. In turn, the exchange rate has both direct and indirect macroeconomic effects.

First, there is a direct effect on inflation via the cost of imported goods. This is usually the most rapid transmission channel from monetary policy to inflation in an open economy. An appreciation of the real exchange rate, for instance, lowers the domestic price of imports and has a direct downward effect on the price of import-competing goods. The pass-through of lower import prices to final demand prices, by contrast, may be spread over time.[24] Second, there is an indirect effect on inflation via changes in aggregate demand and expenditure, themselves resulting from movements in the relative prices of tradable and nontradable goods. This is an intratemporal substitution effect.[25] For instance, an increase in the relative price of nontradable goods (a real appreciation) would tend to lower demand for these goods and put downward pressure on inflation. However, in countries that are net importers of capital goods (as is often the case in the developing world), the real appreciation may also stimulate private investment by lowering the domestic price of investment goods. This transmission channel may eventually have an impact on inflation and economic activity, although it may occur more gradually.

Finally, there is a direct supply-side effect resulting from the impact of changes in the domestic-currency price of imported inputs (such as oil) on the production of tradables and nontradables. A depreciation of the nominal exchange rate, for instance, raises the domestic-currency price of imported intermediate products and may lead to a contraction in domestic output in both sectors if perfect substitutes for these inputs do not exist at home.

Estimates of the pass-through of exchange-rate changes into domestic inflation are provided by Agénor (2002), Gagnon and Ihrig (2004), Ghosh (2013), Ho and McCauley (2003), Carranza et al. (2009), with the latter study focusing on highly dollarized economies. Agénor (2002) found that the strength of the pass-through is regime-dependent, in the sense that it varies with the phase of the business cycle; the pass-through is weaker during recessions. Gagnon and Ihrig (2004) found that

---

[24]Lower consumer prices will tend to moderate wage demands and would thus also affect inflation gradually.

[25]Of course, the intratemporal substitution effect could result instead from a change in import prices measured in *foreign* currency, as shown in Figure 5.3.

the reduction in the pass-through of exchange-rate changes into domestic inflation observed since the 1980s in industrial countries appears to have resulted from increased emphasis on inflation stabilization in these countries. During the period 1971–2003, countries that had the highest declines in either the level or the standard deviation of inflation (viewed as a consequence of greater responsiveness of central bank policies to expected price changes) were also the countries with the largest declines in estimated rates of pass-through. Ghosh (2013), in a study of nine Latin American countries during the period 1970–2010, found that low inflation and a low degree of trade openness tend to mitigate the magnitude of the pass-through effect. He also found that the degree of exchange rate pass-through has declined in the past decade—a result that can be attributed to the changing composition of a country's imports away from raw materials and energy imports toward manufacturing goods that have more competitive markets, and the practice of *local-currency pricing*, that is, setting of prices in the currency of the destination market.

3.4 ■ Asset Prices and Balance Sheet Effects

As noted earlier, changes in asset prices—mainly the price of land and the exchange rate, given the relatively low degree of development in markets for securities in most developing countries—can have large effects on the value of assets such as housing and holdings of foreign bonds, which in turn may affect spending by changing the perceived value of wealth.[26] For instance, exchange-rate movements induced by policy changes in interest rates may have large valuation effects, depending on the structure of indebtedness of agents in the economy. A depreciation would reduce wealth in a country with a net foreign-currency liability position. The balance sheet effects of exchange-rate fluctuations can in fact be far more significant than their effect on consumption expenditure and aggregate demand induced by perceived changes in wealth.

Changes in the value of real assets tend to occur early in the transmission process, both because asset prices tend to adjust faster than prices of goods and services, and because asset prices are inherently more sensitive to changes in interest rates and to changes in expectations; assets are generally held for the purpose of substituting consumption across periods or as hedges against anticipated movements in prices. As a result, they may carry considerable information about how agents perceive future economic developments. Asset prices, however, are also influenced by a variety of factors other than monetary policy in the short run. This raises the issue of whether, and to what extent, monetary policy should respond to short-term changes in asset prices—a particularly important topic in the context of industrial countries, where changes in equity prices tend to have large wealth effects (see Cecchetti et al., 2000).

---

[26]This wealth effect may also influence the ability to borrow, as in the Kiyotaki-Moore framework presented earlier.

Deteriorating balance sheets operate primarily on spending and aggregate demand in the short run, although in the longer run they may affect aggregate supply as well by inhibiting capital formation. Significant feedback and magnification effects are also likely. First, there may be feedback to asset prices, as declining spending and income, together with forced asset sales, lead to further decreases in asset values. Second, declining sales and employment imply continuing weakening of cash flows and, hence, further declines in spending. Alternatively, the magnification effect may operate through the external finance premium.

3.4.1 Net Worth and the Finance Premium

The external finance premium can be defined as the wedge between the cost of funds raised externally (the bank lending rate for most firms in developing countries) and the opportunity cost of internal funds (or retained earnings), which could be an interest rate on government bonds, the bank deposit rate, or the foreign rate of interest. This premium depends inversely on the borrower's collateralizable net worth relative to the obligation on the loan.[27] Collateralizable net worth includes net financial assets and also any tangible physical assets (such as buildings or machinery) that may be pledged as collateral.

3.4.2 The Financial Accelerator

Because the premium for external funds affects the overall price of funds that the borrower faces (the lending rate), credit market imperfections affect consumption and investment decisions—regardless of whether rationing prevails or not (see again Figures 5.4 and 5.5). Changes in firms' net worth have an additional impact on the financing premium and hence the cost of capital. Rising asset prices, for instance, will improve firms' balance sheets, inducing banks to charge a lower finance premium on loans, hence lowering the cost of capital and stimulating investment.[28] Thus, balance sheet effects are propagated through a financial accelerator mechanism.

Models incorporating a mechanism of this type include Bernanke and Gertler (1989), Bernanke et al. (2000), Gertler (1992), and Gertler et al. (2007).[29] In all of these models, procyclical movements in borrowers' financial positions lead to countercyclical movements of the premium on external funds. The net effect is a financial accelerator, which amplifies the cyclical fluctuations in borrowers' spending.[30] For instance, in the model of Bernanke and Gertler (1989), the agency

---

[27]Using data for corporate bond markets, Mizen and Tsoukas (2012) offer evidence for Indonesia, Korea, and Thailand that balance sheet indicators of creditworthiness affect the external finance premium.

[28]See Hubbard (1998) for a simple diagrammatic illustration of the link between net worth, the external premium, and investment.

[29]Iacoviello (2005) extends the Bernanke et al. setup to account for collateral constraints on firms tied to real estate values, as in Kiyotaki and Moore (1997).

[30]Fountas and Papagapitos (2001) provide indirect evidence that the financial accelerator matters for predicting output fluctuations in some European countries (France, Germany, Italy, and the United Kingdom) by using, as

costs of financial intermediation drive a wedge between the internal cost of funds and the cost of external (monitored) financing. Single-period exogenous shocks, by increasing these agency costs, can lead to declines in investment and therefore in future output. Similarly, in the model of Bernanke et al. (2000), the effects of asset price changes are transmitted to a very significant extent through their effects on the balance sheets of households, firms, and financial intermediaries. Firms or households may use assets they hold as collateral when borrowing, in order to mitigate information and incentive problems that would otherwise limit their ability to obtain credit. Under such circumstances, a decline in asset values (for instance, a fall in home equity values) reduces available collateral and impedes potential borrowers' access to credit. Financial intermediaries, which must maintain an adequate ratio of capital to assets, can be deterred from lending, or induced to shift the composition of loans away from bank-dependent sectors (such as small business) by declines in the values of the assets they hold.

As discussed earlier, in Kiyotaki and Moore (1997), collateralizable net worth also plays a key role in lowering the costs of lending; and by restricting the aggregate supply of credit, negative shocks to net worth also lower production. In their model, land is used as collateral for working capital loans (which are intermediate inputs in the production process). A negative shock to the economy that lowers output will also result in a fall in the price of land, thereby reducing the value of collateral and magnifying the initial negative shock as banks restrict their loans for working capital.

The financial accelerator mechanism is more applicable to small borrowers because it is this group that may face a particularly high premium for external funds. There are a variety of reasons why this may be true. One possibility is that bankruptcy costs are proportionately greater for small borrowers, due to the existence of fixed costs in evaluation and monitoring. Another possibility is that large borrowers have proportionately greater collateralizable net worth.[31] Moreover, unobservable idiosyncratic risk, which is a key determinant of the severity of the incentive problem, is likely to be proportionately greater for small borrowers, who are on average less well diversified.

The analytical framework presented in the next chapter will make clear how the financial accelerator operates; Chapter 12 will also highlight how this mechanism is embedded in current dynamic stochastic general equilibrium models with financial frictions. However, we can already note that the propagation mechanism that characterizes the financial accelerator is useful to understand why exchange-rate devaluations can be contractionary in some of the developing countries that have experienced financial crises. A devaluation (or a sharp initial depreciation) of the currency has a direct effect on the balance sheets of firms. If firms are indebted in

---

a measure of the external finance premium, the interest rate spread between corporate bonds and government securities.

[31] In Gertler (1992), net worth is a function of the borrower's discounted future earnings. To the extent that small firms have shorter expected horizons, their net worth is likely smaller in proportion to their current investments.

foreign currency, a devaluation raises the debt burden measured in domestic-currency terms. At the same time, because assets are typically denominated in domestic currency, there is no concomitant increase in the value of firms' assets. A devaluation therefore leads to a deterioration in firms' balance sheets and a decline in net worth, which, in turn, worsens the adverse selection problem because effective collateral has fallen, thereby providing less incentives to lend.[32] In turn, the decline in lending tends to affect investment and economic activity negatively. A case in point is the East Asia crisis (see online Supplement D). As a result of large interest differentials between domestic- and foreign-currency loans, banks and corporations in these countries accumulated a significant volume of unhedged foreign-currency-denominated debt in the early 1990s. The large devaluations that occurred in the region after the Thai baht crisis of mid-1997 raised the domestic-currency value of these debts, weakening bank and corporate balance sheets, and inducing a collapse in credit and output.

It should be noted, however, that the idea that credit market distortions magnify the effect of economic shocks has been subject to some criticism. As argued by House (2006), when these distortions are the result of adverse selection problems, the financial accelerator may have a stabilizing, rather than destabilizing, effect. In his framework, the total amplification effect associated with credit market distortions can be decomposed into three separate channels. A shock that increases internal funds, for instance, affects investment in three different ways. First, the increase in internal funds causes the premium on borrowed funds to fall. In turn, the lower premium induces firms to invest more. This is the "agency cost" channel emphasized in much of the existing literature. Second, because borrowers internalize more of the costs and benefits of their investment projects when their net worth is higher, the level of investment is closer to the efficient level. This may cause investment to either increase or fall. In the latter case, financial market imperfections tend to mitigate the effect of the shock. Third, the allocation of investment becomes more efficient when internal funds rise. Investment increases for projects with high expected returns and falls for projects with low expected returns. Thus, even if the total volume of investment is unchanged, shocks are amplified because investment is allocated more appropriately. The total effect on investment is the sum of these three effects. If the second effect is negative and dominates the other two effects, credit market imperfections will have a stabilizing (albeit inefficient) effect on the economy.

3.5 ■ Credit Availability Effects

The bank lending channel of monetary policy depends on the fact that bank loans and funds raised in capital markets are not perfect substitutes. Certain types of

---

[32] The decline in net worth may also increase moral hazard incentives for firms to take on greater risk because they have less to lose if the loans do not perform.

borrowers, particularly small firms, lack or do not have access to capital markets and rely on banks, which have the capability to monitor and screen these borrowers' activities. But this capability is imperfect—borrowers have more information on their ability to repay a loan than do banks, as noted previously—so that banks also use nonprice rationing devices, such as security checks, credit risk evaluation, and collateral requirements, as part of the loan approval process. When monetary policy is tightened and bank liquid reserves fall, the supply of bank lending is reduced partly through these devices, because banks internalize the fact that raising lending rates alone may have adverse selection effects, as illustrated earlier by the Stiglitz-Weiss model. Borrowers who are dependent on banks will then be particularly affected. The balance sheet effects described earlier can reinforce this result, through their effect on collateralizable net worth.

For developing countries, few studies have attempted to assess the strength of the credit channel of monetary policy. Disyatat and Vongsinsirikul (2003), for instance, provide evidence on the importance of this channel for Thailand. More generally, however, it has not yet conclusively been established (at the very least for developing countries) that credit availability effects are a critical channel for monetary policy. In practice, there are important identification problems that arise in addressing this issue. In particular, it is empirically difficult to distinguish between tight credit conditions caused, on the one hand, by a reduction in bank liquid reserves, and, on the other, by a decline in the creditworthiness of potential borrowers—that is, to discriminate between the bank lending channel and balance sheet effects.

3.6 ▪ Expectations

Changes in expectations (most importantly of inflation and movements in nominal exchange rates) may magnify the transmission channels described earlier, depending on the degree of credibility of the policy change and its perceived duration. For instance, a rise in interest rates that is perceived to be only temporary (due mostly to transitory pressures on the nominal exchange rate) may have no effect on private behavior. Similarly, an interest rate hike may have no impact on private spending because activity is low and unemployment is high, and agents expect the monetary authorities to eventually reverse their course of action to avoid compounding the effects of a recession on employment (see Chapter 11). But to the extent that a policy change is perceived as credible, its impact on the economy may be magnified by a change in expectations. Again, suppose that higher interest rates do indeed lower investment and consumption, and that agents understand that the fall in aggregate demand will eventually reduce inflation. With forward-looking price expectations, the policy change may lead to an immediate fall in inflation, as a result, for instance, of lower wage demands in today's labor contracts.

4   Dollarization

Dollarization refers to a situation in which a foreign currency is used as a unit of account, store of value, and a medium of exchange, concurrently with the domestic currency (Giovannini and Turtelboom, 1994).[33] A common measure of the degree of dollarization, the share of foreign-currency deposits in total domestic bank deposits, shows that dollarization has at times been pervasive in many countries.[34]

4.1 ▪ Determinants of Dollarization

Dollarization seems to be associated with periods of economic instability and high inflation. Using a large sample of countries for the period 1990–2001, Nicoló et al. (2005) found that—controlling for the impact of relevant regulations—the macroeconomic policy environment (as measured by the rate of inflation) and the institutional structure are key determinants of cross-country variations in deposit dollarization. In addition, allowing de facto dollarization appears to promote a deeper domestic financial system only in inflationary economies; put differently, dollarization tends to moderate the adverse effect of inflation on financial depth.

   Dollarization can thus be viewed as an endogenous response by domestic agents attempting to avoid the inflation tax and capital losses on assets denominated in domestic currency (see Chapter 3).[35] At the same time, of course, it responds to portfolio diversification needs—which may exist even at relatively low inflation rates.

4.2 ▪ Persistence of Dollarization

The evidence suggests that, even after sharp reductions in inflation, dollarization can remain relatively high. Several explanations have been offered to explain the persistence of a high degree of dollarization in a low-inflation environment. Guidotti and Rodríguez (1992) suggested that transaction costs incurred in switching from one currency to the other—justified by the assumption of economies of scale in the use of a single currency—imply that there is a range of inflation rates within which the degree of dollarization is likely to remain unchanged. Put differently, a reversal of dollarization after stabilization would tend to be slow if there are no

---

[33]Calvo and Végh (1996) suggested the use of the term "dollarization" (or "asset substitution") to refer to the use of foreign currency as a store of value, and the term "currency substitution" to refer to a stage where, beyond dollarization, foreign money is also used as a medium of exchange or a unit of account. In practice, however, the terms currency substitution and dollarization are often used interchangeably.

[34]Using foreign-currency deposits to measure the degree of dollarization can seriously underestimate the pervasiveness of the problem; if the risk of confiscation of foreign-currency assets held in domestic banks is high, agents may hold their cash outside banks, literally "under the mattress." Foreign-currency deposits may also be held abroad.

[35]Note, however, that in some countries, like Brazil, macroeconomic instability has led not to dollarization but rather to the development of a variety of indexed financial assets.

significant benefits associated with switching back to the domestic currency as a means of payment.

Other contributions explain the persistence of dollarization without relying on the existence of transactions costs. One explanation is proposed by Freitas (2004), who develops a small open economy model where domestic and foreign currencies are perfect substitutes as means of payment. Foreign residents are not allowed to hold the domestic currency (that is, currency substitution is asymmetric) and domestic money holdings are subject to a minimum constraint (which reflects, for instance, the fact that transactions involving the government cannot be settled in foreign currency). Even without transactions costs, dollarization hysteresis prevails; the demand for foreign currency does not necessarily decline when inflation falls (following, for instance, the implementation of a disinflation program).

A second explanation that does not rely on transactions costs was offered by McNelis and Rojas-Suárez (1996). They emphasized the fact that the degree of dollarization depends not only on expectations of inflation and exchange-rate depreciation, but also on the risk (or volatility) associated with these variables. Whereas during periods of high inflation the risk component tends to be dominated by the level of inflation itself, in periods of low inflation (or post-stabilization episodes) risk factors become more important. Everything else equal, increased risk (or volatility) of prices and exchange rates would induce asset holders to switch away from domestic currency and toward foreign currency. Thus, reducing the degree of dollarization requires not only a reduction in the levels of expected inflation and exchange-rate depreciation, but also a reduction in the volatility of these variables.

A third explanation of hysteresis effects in dollarization is proposed by Duffy et al. (2006). In their model, there are two production technologies, and the more efficient one is subject to a fixed cost of operation. Arbitrage equates the returns on productive capital and on the foreign currency—both of which can be used to store value. High inflation (which fosters dollarization in the first place) undermines financial intermediation, leading to the adoption of a less efficient production technology—which in turn makes a "dollarization trap" possible. The reason is that the exogenously given return on foreign currency pins down the return on productive capital, thus making the capital stock and output independent of inflation. A sustained disinflation increases (instead of reducing) foreign-currency holdings, rather than the capital stock. The only way to exit from the low-growth trap is to reduce inflation below a threshold level.

4.3 ▪ Dollarization and Macroeconomic Management

Dollarization may be beneficial to the extent that it leads to an increase in the flow of funds into the banking system, thereby promoting financial intermediation. Moreover, a low degree of dollarization (as measured by the share of foreign-currency accounts in domestic banks) may merely reflect "normal" portfolio diversification needs. However, high degrees of dollarization may significantly complicate the conduct of monetary and exchange-rate policies.

First, dollarization involves a loss of seigniorage revenue, because the demand for domestic base money is lower than otherwise. This reduction in the base of the inflation tax can lead to higher inflation—which may in turn lead to a further reduction in holdings of domestic money balances (see Chapter 3). The outcome may be an inflationary spiral, with full dollarization as the ultimate outcome. Evidence provided by Edwards and Magdenzo (2006), however, suggests that in fact inflation has been significantly lower in dollarized economies compared with nondollarized countries.

Second, dollarization affects the choice of assets that should be included in the monetary aggregates that are used by policymakers as indicators of monetary conditions or target variables. Aggregates including foreign-currency cash and deposits are relevant if the use of foreign currency as a medium of exchange tends to distort the link between domestic money and inflation. There may be less reason to consider comprehensive measures if dollarization represents asset diversification, with no implications for aggregate demand and inflation. In fact, the difficulty of interpreting the behavior of monetary aggregates including and excluding foreign-currency deposits is one of the reasons that has driven some countries to adopt inflation targeting, as discussed later.

Third, dollarization (in the form of foreign-currency deposits in domestic banks) essentially indexes deposits to the exchange rate. Because the domestic-currency value of foreign-currency deposits rises proportionately with exchange-rate depreciation, monetary aggregates tend to accommodate inflationary pressures. To the extent that loans extended against foreign-currency deposits are denominated in domestic currency, the ensuing currency mismatch may weaken banks' balance sheets if the exchange rate depreciates and if lending rates cannot be adjusted to absorb the loss on loan principal measured in foreign-currency terms. These weaknesses can force the central bank to intervene, and the increase in liquidity can exacerbate inflationary pressures.

Fourth, dollarization affects the choice of an exchange-rate regime (see Chapter 9), because it may lead to short-term foreign-currency liabilities that are high relative to foreign exchange reserves. In such conditions, an increase in foreign-currency deposits held in domestic banks may increase the vulnerability of the banking system and the official exchange rate to abrupt reversals in market sentiment and capital flows. At the same time, dollarization may entail a high degree of volatility in a floating exchange rate, as a result of large and unpredictable shifts in the use of domestic and foreign currencies for transactions purposes.[36] Empirical evidence

---

[36] Besancenot and Vranceanu (2007) highlight an alternative channel through which dollarization exacerbates exchange-rate volatility. They develop a model in which firms finance themselves by borrowing dollars, while their income is denominated in domestic-currency units. They show that governments aiming to adopt fully flexible exchange-rate regimes should first reduce their dollar liabilities.

provided by Nicoló et al. (2005) does suggest that, whether risk in the banking system is measured by the mean ratio of non-performing loans, the volatility of deposits, or a proxy for the probability of bank default, dollarization appears to heighten solvency and liquidity risks (in part because of currency mismatches), thereby making financial systems more fragile. A high degree of dollarization appears therefore to promote financial instability.

Although the foregoing discussion suggests that dollarization may have adverse consequences for macroeconomic management, outright restrictions aimed at reducing holdings of foreign assets are likely to prove ineffective due to the ability of asset holders to evade them through informal currency markets (see Supplement A). In addition, as argued by Chang and Velasco (2002), if policymakers have low credibility and dollarization can serve as an effective discipline device, it can actually improve welfare. More important, high degrees of dollarization are generally not a cause, but rather a symptom, of underlying financial imbalances and weaknesses. Thus, measures aimed at reducing dollarization—such as, for instance, the creation of an interest rate wedge in favor of domestic-currency deposits, the imposition of higher reserve requirement rates on foreign-currency deposits, or legal and institutional measures to foster the use of domestic currency over foreign means of payment in domestic transactions, particularly those involving the public sector—are unlikely to be effective in an unstable macroeconomic environment. Reversing (or at least containing) financial dollarization requires a credible monetary policy framework and measures to strengthen the institutional and regulatory environment.

5   Macroprudential and Monetary Policies

The global financial crisis has led to renewed calls for central banks to consider more systematically potential trade-offs between the objectives of macroeconomic stability and financial stability, and the extent to which the central bank's policy loss function (and therefore its interest rate response) should account explicitly for a financial stability goal.[37] The issue is not new; it has long been recognized, for instance, that an increase in interest rates aimed at preventing the development of inflationary pressures may, at the same time, heighten uncertainty and foster volatility in financial markets. The debate was initially focused on the extent to which monetary policy should respond to perceived misalignments in asset prices, such as real estate and

---

[37]The concept of financial stability has remained surprisingly elusive in the existing literature. Financial stability is usually perceived as a negative concept, involving the absence of something unwanted. Indeed, two common definitions are "financial stability is the absence of an adverse impact on the real economy from dysfunction in the financial system, or risk thereof," and "financial stability is the absence of financial crises, and a financial crisis is defined as a sequence of events, or the risk thereof, that impairs credit intermediation or capital allocation" (see Goodhart, 2006).

equity prices.[38] In that context, several observers argued that trying to stabilize asset prices per se is problematic for a number of reasons—one of which being that it is almost impossible to know for sure whether a given change in asset values results from changes in underlying fundamentals, nonfundamental factors, or both. By focusing on the *implications* of asset price movements for credit growth and aggregate demand, the central bank may be able to focus on the adverse effects of these movements—without getting into the tricky issue of deciding to what extent they represent changes in fundamentals.

Another lesson from the global financial crisis is that financial regulation and supervision must adopt a *macroprudential* perspective to identify weaknesses in the financial system and mitigate systemic risk. This issue, and the related question of whether monetary and macroprudential policies are substitutes or complements, will be discussed in more detail in Chapter 7.

---

[38] See Agénor and Pereira da Silva (2013) for references to the literature.

Chapter 6

A Framework for Monetary Policy Analysis

As discussed in the previous chapter, credit market imperfections play a central role in the monetary transmission mechanism. When there is imperfect information, for instance, the strength of firms' balance sheets becomes a major factor in the determination of the availability and price of external funds. And because alternative forms of borrowing from financial intermediaries are no longer perfect substitutes, firms face a nontrivial choice of external finance. In addition, some firms may be particularly dependent on bank finance, because their characteristics prevent them from accessing alternative markets for funds (such as corporate paper or bond markets). This gives rise to the bank lending channel, which is particularly important in developing countries.

Despite the widespread recognition that the credit channel is an important mechanism through which monetary policy affects the economy, there are very few tractable models for monetary policy analysis that account explicitly for the credit market and its imperfections. An early attempt to separate the credit and bond markets in the standard IS-LM model was proposed by Bernanke and Blinder (1988), whose analysis was subsequently extended to an open economy in various contributions. But monetary policy in many of these models is defined in terms of changes in the stock of liquidity, whereas in practice central banks use a short-term interest rate as their instrument.

Indeed, as pointed out by Romer (2000a), one of the basic assumptions of the IS-LM model is that the central bank targets the money supply, while most central banks nowadays pay little attention to monetary aggregates in conducting monetary policy. Romer's approach is to replace the LM curve, together with the assumption that the central bank targets the money supply (or, more specifically, the supply of liquid reserves to commercial banks), by the assumption that it follows a real interest rate rule. However, this is not necessarily a good characterization of monetary policy either. Central banks, in practice, set nominal, not real, interest rates. In the short run, they cannot respond to changes in expected inflation, and therefore cannot control real interest rates. Moreover, there is no distinction in Romer's model between the official (policy) rate and market-determined interest rates, which depend on the behavior of banks (lenders) and private agents (borrowers and depositors). This requires modeling credit market imperfections as well as private financial decisions.

Drawing on Agénor and Montiel (2006, 2007), this chapter presents a simple framework for monetary policy analysis in small open economies. The model accounts explicitly for an important source of imperfection in credit markets, namely, limited enforceability of contracts. We do not derive behavioral relations explicitly from first principles; instead, in the IS-LM tradition, we postulate these relations and provide some background rationalization and intuitive arguments. The reason for doing so is that we view our model as essentially a way to communicate results from other, more fully articulated, stochastic macroeconomic models where credit market imperfections play a prominent role—such as those dwelling on the costly state verification approach or those based on borrowing constraints in the tradition of Kiyotaki and Moore, as discussed in the previous chapter. As in some of these models, we relate the risk premium (defined as a markup over funding costs) charged by banks to borrowers' net worth—but we do so in a relatively straightforward manner, without bringing explicitly into the picture the stochastic shocks that may lead borrowers to default.

The chapter is organized as follows. Section 1 presents the basic model, under fixed exchange rates. After describing the structure of the model and its solution, we study the impact of a variety of policy experiments, including changes in the refinance and reserve requirement rates, as well as exogenous shocks. Section 2 considers the case of a flexible exchange rate and illustrates the behavior of the model with the same set of policy and exogenous shocks, for comparative purposes. Section 3 discusses three extensions of the analysis, sterilization policies, working capital needs, and dynamics.

1   The Basic Model: Fixed Exchange Rates

In line with the foregoing discussion, key features of the basic model are the assumption that banks' funding sources are perfect substitutes and that lending rates are set as a premium over the cost of borrowing from the central bank. The premium is a function of firms' collateralizable net worth. Thus, credit market imperfections in our setting mean that access to loans is more costly for firms with a weak financial position (as measured by their net worth), as opposed to weak (usually small) firms being denied access outright to bank loans. Put differently, we do not account explicitly for credit rationing or binding borrowing constraints as in the Kiyotaki-Moore tradition (see Chapter 5). Loan supply and the provision of liquidity by the central bank are perfectly elastic at the prevailing official rate.

In addition, and as discussed further in Chapter 13, capital mobility is imperfect, allowing the domestic bond rate to be determined from domestic macroeconomic equilibrium conditions, rather than being tied to the world interest rate. After solving the model, we present a variety of policy experiments, including changes in the refinance and reserve requirement rates, central bank auctions, exogenous shifts in the premium and contract enforcement costs, and changes in public spending and the world interest rate.

1.1 ■ Structure of the Model

Consider a small open economy producing a (composite) good that is imperfectly substitutable for foreign goods. Domestic output is fixed within the time frame of the analysis, but its price is determined endogenously. The production structure is thus in the Mundell-Fleming tradition. As discussed in Chapter 1 and elsewhere in this book, a dependent-economy framework or a three-good structure would normally be a more appropriate starting point for developing countries; however, because our focus is on monetary transmission rather than real sector phenomena, we retain it here for simplicity.

There are five markets in the economy (for currency, bank deposits, credit, bonds, and goods), and four categories of agents: households, commercial banks, the government, and the central bank. The nominal exchange rate, E, is fixed. Because the economy is small, the world price of foreign goods is taken as exogenous.

1.1.1 *Household Portfolio Allocation*

Households supply labor inelastically, consume the domestic and foreign goods, and hold four categories of assets: domestic currency (which bears no interest), deposits with the banking system, foreign-currency deposits held abroad, and land (whose supply is fixed and normalized to one). All assets are imperfect substitutes in household portfolios.[1] Foreigners do not hold domestic assets. Total household wealth, A^H, is thus defined as:

$$A^H = BILL + D + 1 \cdot Q + E \cdot D^*, \tag{1}$$

where $BILL$ is currency holdings, D (D^*) domestic (foreign) bank deposits, and Q the price of land. It will be useful to define the financial component of household

---

[1]Substitution across assets can be impeded by a variety of factors, such as heterogeneous information, institutional constraints, and government-induced distortions. As discussed in more detail in Chapter 13, the empirical evidence for most developing countries suggests that the assumption of perfect substitutability between domestic and foreign assets is rejected even for assets that differ only in a single dimension, such as the currency of denomination or maturity.

wealth as:

$$F^H = A^H - Q = BILL + D + E \cdot D^*. \tag{2}$$

Because the nominal exchange rate is fixed at $E = \bar{E}$, and because we distinguish between beginning- and end-of-period stocks, total financial wealth at the beginning of the period, F_0^H, is predetermined.

Asset demand equations are as follows. The demand for currency is assumed to be related negatively to the opportunity cost of holding it (measured by the interest rate on bank deposits):

$$\frac{BILL}{D} = v(i_D), \tag{3}$$

where i_D is the interest rate on bank deposits and $v' < 0$. Households view currency only as an alternative to domestic deposits; thus, given that there is no direct rate of return on currency, only the interest rate i_D enters in (3).[2]

The real demand for deposits in domestic banks is taken to depend positively on exogenous output, $\bar{Y}$, and the bank deposit rate, as well as negatively on the rate of return on alternative assets, that is, the interest rate on foreign deposits and the expected rate of increase in the price of land, $\hat{q}$:

$$\frac{D}{P} = d(i_D, i^*, \hat{q}, \bar{Y}), \tag{4}$$

where P is the cost-of-living index, i^* the interest rate on deposits held abroad, d_{i_D}, $d_Y > 0$, and d_{i^*}, $d_{\hat{q}} < 0$. The nominal exchange rate is assumed to be credibly fixed, so that the expected depreciation rate is zero. The expected rate of change of land prices is taken to be exogenous. Using (3), we will assume that

$$\frac{\eta_D}{\eta_v} > \frac{BILL}{BILL + D} = \frac{v}{1 + v}, \tag{5}$$

where $\eta_D = P d_{i_D} i_D / D = d_{i_D} i_D / d > 0$ and $\eta_v = -v' i_D / v > 0$. That is, the ratio of the interest elasticity of demand for deposits to that of the currency-deposit ratio exceeds the share of currency in the total money stock, given by $BILL + D$. When this condition is satisfied, an increase in the deposit interest rate will raise the total demand for money (that is, $\partial(BILL + D) / \partial i_D > 0$).

The demand function for land is given by:

$$Q = q(i^*, \hat{q})(A^H - BILL - D),$$

---

[2]We do not account explicitly for the expected rate of inflation by assuming that its effect on the demand for currency and the demand for deposits is exactly the same.

or, given that $A^H = F^H + Q$,

$$Q = \frac{q(i^*, \hat{q})}{1 - q(i^*, \hat{q})}(F^H - BILL - D), \tag{6}$$

where $q_{i^*} < 0$ and $q_{\hat{q}} > 0$. Thus, because $F^H - BILL - D = \bar{E} \cdot D^*$, the demand for land is proportional to foreign-currency deposits as long as i^* and $\hat{q}$ are constant. In turn, the demand for foreign-currency deposits can be derived residually from (1) and (6).

1.1.2 Commercial Banks

Banks allocate their investable assets (that is, assets net of required reserves) between bank loans and government bonds. They can borrow reserves from the central bank in order to match their assets and liabilities, but cannot borrow abroad. Assets of the commercial banks consist of credit extended to firms, L^F, reserves held at the central bank, RR, and government bonds, B^B. Bank liabilities consist of deposits held by households, D, and borrowing from the central bank, L^B. The balance sheet of the representative commercial bank can therefore be written as:

$$L^F + RR + B^B = D + L^B, \tag{7}$$

where all variables are measured in nominal terms. Reserves held at the central bank do not pay interest and are determined by:

$$RR = \mu D, \tag{8}$$

where $\mu \in (0, 1)$ is the required reserve ratio.

Banks set both deposit and lending interest rates. They are indifferent to the source of their domestic-currency funds—or, equivalently, they view domestic-currency deposits and loans from the central bank as perfect substitutes (at the margin).[3] Accordingly, the deposit rate on domestic currency-denominated deposits, i_D, is set equal to the cost of funds provided by the central bank, i_R corrected for the (implicit) cost of holding reserve requirements on deposits:

$$1 + i_D = (1 + i_R)(1 - \mu). \tag{9}$$

---

[3]With *imperfect* substitution between borrowed reserves and deposits, the deposit rate could be specified as a positive function of both the cost of borrowing from the central bank and returns on bank assets. Alternatively, a wedge between i_D and i_R, reflecting the degree of competition or the cost of servicing deposits, could also be introduced. See Freixas and Rochet (1997, p. 57) for a discussion of an arbitrage condition similar to (9).

The supply of deposits by commercial banks is perfectly elastic at the rate i_D.[4]

Other than the central bank, commercial banks are the only holders of domestic government debt. The interest rate that banks demand to be paid on government bonds, i_B, is set as a premium over their marginal cost of funds. Given that central bank liquidity is perfectly elastic at the prevailing refinance rate, this cost is simply i_R:

$$1 + i_B = (1 + \theta_B)(1 + i_R), \tag{10}$$

and θ_B is the risk premium on government bonds. We assume that this premium is increasing in the ratio of the stock of such bonds in the possession of banks to the maximum debt that the government's fiscal plans can support, $B^{\max}$.[5] Thus:

$$\theta_B = \theta_B(B^B / B^{\max}), \quad \theta'_B > 0. \tag{11}$$

The domestic loan rate, i_L, is set at a premium over the prevailing interest rate on government bonds, which represents the rate of return on alternative assets:

$$1 + i_L = (1 + \theta_L)(1 + i_B), \tag{12}$$

where the risk premium θ_L on lending to firms is inversely related to the ratio of firms' assets (the value of their beginning-of-period physical capital stock, K_0, which is taken as given, times P_D, the price of the domestic good) over their liabilities, that is, beginning-of-period domestic borrowing, L_0^F:

$$\theta_L = \theta_L \left(\frac{\kappa P_D K_0}{L_0^F}; x_P \right), \tag{13}$$

where x_P is a shift parameter, whereas $\theta_{L_{K/L^F}} < 0$ and $\theta_{L_{x_P}} > 0$. As in Agénor et al. (2006), the coefficient $\kappa \in (0, 1)$ in (13) measures the proportion of assets that can effectively be used or pledged as collateral; $\kappa P_D K_0$ therefore measures firms' "collateralizable" wealth.[6]

The view that underlies this specification is that the risk premium charged by banks reflects the perceived risk of default on their loans to domestic firms, as discussed in the previous chapter. The higher the value of firms' physical assets,

---

[4]Note that if banks have excess liquidity, they may not adjust deposit rates upward in response to an *increase* in the official rate (as postulated in (9)), in order to avoid attracting more deposits. In other words, there may be asymmetric behavior in price-setting behavior by banks.

[5]Because we do not explicitly account for the government budget constraint, and given the static nature of our model, we take $B^{\max}$ as given. A more thorough treatment would of course treat $B^{\max}$ as endogenous, relating it to variables affecting the government's intertemporal budget constraint (see Chapter 3).

[6]Although we treat κ as constant, it is worth noting that in a more general setting it could be made countercyclical, to reflect the fact that banks are more willing to lend when firms' cash flows are high or, equivalently, that banks are prone to excessive lending during booms. Countercyclical movements in κ could also result from procyclical changes in the intensity of competition among banks.

relative to domestic liabilities, the higher the proportion of total lending that banks can recoup in the event of default. This reduces the risk premium and the cost of borrowing. Thus, in the present setting, firms are not subject to "strict" rationing, based on their ability to pledge collateral; banks provide all the liquidity that firms need at the prevailing lending rate. Nevertheless, because both K_0 and L_0^F are predetermined, the risk premium varies inversely with the price of the domestic good, P_D. This introduces a "financial accelerator" in the effects of monetary policy.

With interest rates set as above, commercial banks' total holdings of government bonds are determined by central bank policies. Specifically, holdings of government bonds by commercial banks are determined by the difference between the total stock of bonds outstanding, $\bar{B}$, which is exogenous (given the time frame of the analysis), and bonds held by the central bank, B^C:

$$B^B = \bar{B} - B^C. \tag{14}$$

Given the commercial banks' interest rate-setting behavior, their stock of loans outstanding is determined by firms' demand for credit, to be described below.[7] With B^B and L^F determined in this way, (7) implies that borrowing from the central bank must be determined residually:

$$L^B = L^F + RR + B^B - D.$$

Using (4) and (8), this equation becomes:

$$L^B = L^F + B^B - (1 - \mu)d(i_D, i^*, \hat{q}, Y)P. \tag{15}$$

1.1.3 Central Bank

The central bank ensures the costless conversion of domestic-currency holdings into foreign currency at the officially determined exchange rate, E. It also supplies reserves elastically to commercial banks at the fixed official (or refinance) rate, i_R. Because banks set their deposit rate on the basis of this official rate, monetary policy operates largely through the effects of the refinance rate on the banking system's cost of funds. And because the supply of liquidity is perfectly elastic at rate i_R, base money is endogenous; it responds passively to shocks to banks' liquidity needs—which are themselves related to banks' asset pricing decisions, the central bank's auctions of government bonds, and the demand for credit by domestic firms.

The balance sheet of the central bank consists, on the asset side, of loans to commercial banks, L^B, foreign reserves, R^* (in foreign-currency terms), and

---

[7]Note that in the present setting bank profits are not necessarily zero, but rather given by $i_L L^F + i_B B^B - i_D D - i_R L^B$. For simplicity, we assume that these profits are retained as an off-balance sheet item by banks, rather than distributed to households. In a full dynamic setting, this would of course be unsatisfactory, and the impact of retained profits on banks' net worth would need to be explicitly accounted for.

government bonds, B^C. On the liability side, it consists only of the monetary base, MB:

$$E \cdot R^* + B^C + L^B = MB. \tag{16}$$

The monetary base is also the sum of currency in circulation and required reserves:

$$MB = BILL + RR, \tag{17}$$

which implies, using (8), that the supply of currency is

$$BILL^s = MB - \mu D. \tag{18}$$

In this framework, which is intended to realistically represent the financial structure of many developing countries, the central bank has three monetary policy instruments at its disposal: the refinance rate, i_R, the amount of government bonds that it retains on its books rather than auctioning them off to the banking system, B^C, and the required reserve ratio, μ. With the central bank following an interest rate rule, the monetary base will be entirely passive, so the model does not contain an LM curve as such. We shall consider later on the case where the central bank controls the path of the monetary base.

1.1.4 *Price Level and the Real Sector*

The cost of living, P, is defined as a geometrically weighted average of the price of the domestic good, P_D, and the price of imported final goods, $E P_M^*$, where P_M^* is the foreign-currency price of the good (assumed exogenous):

$$P = P_D^{1-\delta}(E P_M^*)^\delta, \tag{19}$$

where $\delta \in (0, 1)$ is the share of spending by households on imported goods. Setting $P_M^* = 1$, this equation becomes

$$P = P_D z^\delta, \tag{20}$$

where $z = E/P_D$ is the real exchange rate.

Real consumption expenditure by households, C, measured in units of the domestic good, is assumed to depend on the resources available to households in the form of human as well as physical capital and wealth, and on intertemporal relative prices. Because our model is not explicitly intertemporal, we capture the contribution of human and physical capital by allowing consumption to depend positively on disposable income and on the real value of financial wealth. To capture the effects of intertemporal relative prices, we allow it to depend negatively on real rates of return on the assets held by households (domestic deposits, foreign deposits, and land). We treat the partial effects of each of these rates of return on present consumption as being identical.[8] Thus, consumption spending can be written as:

$$C = \alpha_1(\bar{Y} - T) - \alpha_2[(i_D - \pi^a) + (i^* - \pi^a) + (\hat{q} - \pi^a)] + \alpha_3(A^H/P_D), \quad (21)$$

where T denotes lump-sum taxes, π^a is the expected inflation rate, $\alpha_1 \in (0, 1)$ the marginal propensity to consume out of disposable income, and $\alpha_2, \alpha_3 > 0$.

The desired capital stock by firms, K^d, is inversely related to the real lending rate, $i_L - \pi^a$. Real investment spending by domestic firms, I, is taken to be a linear function of the difference between the desired stock and the actual stock, K_0:

$$I = K^d(i_L - \pi^a) - K_0 = I(i_L - \pi^a; K_0), \quad (22)$$

where $I_1 = I_{i_L - \pi^a} < 0$. In what follows we assume that all investment must be financed by bank loans. Thus, with the beginning-of-period stock of loans given by L_0^F, new loan demand from commercial banks is equal to[9]

$$L^F = L_0^F + P_D I. \quad (23)$$

Let $X(z)$ denote exports, which are positively related to the real exchange rate, so that $X' > 0$. The supply of domestic goods to the domestic market is thus $\bar{Y} - X(z)$. The equilibrium condition of the market for domestic goods is thus given by

$$\bar{Y} - X(z) = (1 - \delta)C + I + G, \quad (24)$$

where G is government spending on domestic goods.

1.2 ▪ Model Solution

A macroeconomic equilibrium in our model requires simultaneous equality between supply and demand in the markets for five financial assets (domestic currency, domestic deposits, government bonds, commercial bank loans, and central bank credit), for the model's single traded real asset (land), and for domestic goods. By Walras' Law, the six asset market equilibrium conditions are not independent; one of them can be derived residually from the other equations, and can therefore be eliminated. Given the assumption that the central bank fixes the policy interest

---

[8]As is well known, life-cycle models would predict a relationship between wealth and consumption rather than income. However, as noted in Chapter 2, liquidity-constrained consumers would indeed tend to adjust consumption as a function of (disposable) income.

[9]Internal finance could be added to the model by simply assuming that retained earnings are a constant fraction χ of total output, $\bar{Y}$; new borrowing by firms would thus be $P_D(I - \chi \bar{Y})$. This, however, would not greatly alter much the results of our policy experiments, given that output is exogenous.

rate i^R and supplies all the credit demanded by banks at that rate, the market for central bank credit is always in equilibrium. We derive the equilibrium conditions for domestic deposits, government bonds, and commercial bank loans from the asset pricing decisions of the commercial banks, and analyze the equilibrium condition in the market for land separately. We choose therefore to eliminate the equilibrium condition for the market for currency.

To solve the model, then, consider first the determination of the price of land. Substituting (3), (4), and (19) in (6) yields

$$Q = \frac{q(i^*,\hat{q})}{1-q(i^*,\hat{q})}[F^H - [1+v(i_D)]d(i_D, i^*, \hat{q}, \bar{Y})P_D^{1-\delta}E^\delta],$$

that is,

$$Q = Q(P_D; i_R, \mu, B^B, ...),\tag{25}$$

where, given assumption (5),

$$Q_1 = \frac{\partial Q}{\partial P_D} = -\left(\frac{q}{1-q}\right)(1-\delta)(1+v)d\cdot z^\delta < 0,$$

$$Q_2 = \frac{\partial Q}{\partial i_R} = -\left(\frac{q}{1-q}\right)(1-\mu)\left(\frac{D}{i_D}\right)\eta_v(1+v)\left(\frac{\eta_D}{\eta_v} - \frac{v}{1+v}\right) < 0,$$

$$Q_3 = \partial Q/\partial\mu = \left(\frac{q}{1-q}\right)\left(\frac{D}{i_D}\right)\eta_v(1+v)\left(\frac{\eta_D}{\eta_v} - \frac{v}{1+v}\right)(1+i_R) > 0,$$

$$Q_4 = \partial Q/\partial B^B = 0.$$

Thus, an increase in the domestic price level reduces the price of land, because it causes households to reallocate their portfolios into currency and deposits and away from land. The partial equilibrium effect of an increase in the refinance rate on the price of land is also negative, because a higher refinance rate raises banks' deposit rate, thus inducing households to shift their portfolios away from both currency and land, which has the effect of reducing the price of land. However, an increase in the required reserve ratio raises the price of land, because it reduces the deposit interest rate and causes households to switch out of deposits and into land. Holdings of government bonds by commercial banks are determined residually from (14) and have no direct effect on the price of land.

Turning to the loan interest rate, from (10) to (13) we can write:

$$i_L = \left[1 + \theta_L \left(\frac{\kappa P_D K_0}{L_0^F}; x_P\right)\right]\left[1 + \theta_B \left(\frac{B^B}{B^{\max}}\right)\right](1 + i_R) - 1. \qquad (26)$$

This equation is essentially the model's financial market equilibrium condition. It determines the equilibrium loan rate as a function of the arbitrage conditions that determine the banks' equilibrium allocation of funds. The effects on the equilibrium loan rate of changes in the domestic price level and in the monetary policy variables controlled by the central bank are given by:

$$\frac{\partial i_L}{\partial P_D} = \left(\frac{\kappa K_0}{L_0^F}\right)\theta_L'(1 + \theta_B)(1 + i_R) < 0,$$

$$\frac{\partial i_L}{\partial i_R} = (1 + \theta_L)(1 + \theta_B) > 0,$$

$$\frac{\partial i_L}{\partial \mu} = 0,$$

$$\frac{\partial i_L}{\partial B^B} = \left(\frac{\theta_B'}{B^{\max}}\right)(1 + \theta_L)(1 + i_R) > 0.$$

Thus, the equilibrium loan rate falls as the domestic price level rises. This reflects a "financial accelerator" effect. In nominal terms, an increase in the domestic price level raises the value of firms' collateralizable net worth relative to their stock of outstanding loans, which are fixed in nominal value (alternatively, in real terms, the real value of their outstanding loans falls relative to that of their real collateral). The implication is that banks are willing to accept a lower risk premium, thus reducing the loan rate. By contrast, an increase in the refinance rate raises the cost of funds for banks, and because the loan rate reflects this cost of funds plus the markup factor $(1 + \theta_L)(1 + \theta_B)$, this induces an increase in the lending rate. An increase in the required reserve ratio has no effect on the loan rate: with the marginal cost of funds set by the refinance rate, its only effect is to lower the deposit rate. Finally, a reduction in central bank holdings of government bonds requires that more of these bonds be held by commercial banks. Because this increases the stock of government debt in private hands relative to the government's debt-servicing capacity, the effect is to increase the risk premium on government debt as well as on loans to private firms, resulting in a higher lending rate.

Turning to the real sector, using (19), (21), and (22), setting $C_0 = 0$, and assuming that financial wealth is measured at the beginning of the period, we can write the goods market equilibrium condition, (24), as:

$$\bar{Y} = (1 - \delta)\left\{\alpha_1(\bar{Y} - T) - \alpha_2[(i_D - \pi^a) + (i^* - \pi^a) + (\hat{q} - \pi^a)]\right. \quad (27)$$

$$\left. + \; \alpha_3\left(\frac{F_0^H + Q}{P_D}\right)\right\} + I(i_L - \pi^a; K_0) + G + X(E/P_D).$$

Using (9) to solve for i_D and substituting (25) for Q, this equation implicitly defines a set of combinations of the loan interest rate and the domestic price level that are consistent with equilibrium in the market for domestic goods, given by:

$$i_L = i_L(P_D; i_R, \mu, B^B, ...), \quad (28)$$

where

$$\frac{\partial i_L}{\partial P_D} = -\left\{(1 - \delta)\alpha_3\left[\frac{Q_1}{P_D} - \left(\frac{F_0^H + Q}{P_D^2}\right)\right] - X'\left(\frac{z}{P_D}\right)\right\}/I_1 < 0,$$

$$\frac{\partial i_L}{\partial i_R} = (1 - \delta)\left[\alpha_2(1 - \mu) - \alpha_3\left(\frac{Q_2}{P_D}\right)\right]/I_1 < 0,$$

$$\partial i_L/\partial \mu = -(1 - \delta)\left[\alpha_2(1 + i_R) + \alpha_3\left(\frac{Q_3}{P_D}\right)\right]/I_1 > 0,$$

$$\partial i_L/\partial B^B = 0.$$

Equations (26) and (28) can be solved together for the equilibrium values of the loan interest rate i_L and the price of domestic goods P_D. The solution can be depicted graphically as in Figure 6.1. Both equations trace out curves with negative slopes in i_L-P_D space. However, it is easy to show that under standard dynamic assumptions, local stability requires the goods-market equilibrium curve derived from (28), labeled *GG* in Figure 6.1, to be steeper than the financial-market equilibrium curve derived from (26), labeled *FF*. Thus, the economy's equilibrium values of i_L and P_D are determined at the point of intersection of the relatively flat *FF* curve and relatively steep *GG* curve, as shown in Figure 6.1.

Once the equilibrium values of the loan interest rate and the price of domestic goods are determined, the remaining endogenous variables in the model can be pinned down in straightforward fashion. It is worth noting, in particular, how the financial side of the model is solved. Given the equilibrium value of the loan interest rate and the domestic price level, the scale of nominal investment by domestic firms is determined. In turn, this determines the flow of new loan demand from commercial banks. Thus, the scale of new loans is determined on the demand side of the market,

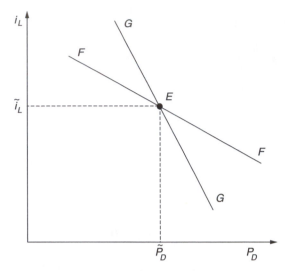

Figure 6–1 ▪ Goods and Financial Market Equilibrium under Fixed Exchange Rates
Source: Agénor and Montiel (2006).

given the loan interest rates set by the banking system. Banks finance these loans by borrowing from the central bank at the policy interest rate i_R, and in turn the central bank finances its loans to commercial banks by issuing new base money. Like the supply of loans to firms, then, that of loans to banks is determined on the demand side of the market, given the price-setting behavior of the lender.

Note also that changes in official foreign reserves (which are endogenous under fixed exchange rates) play no direct role in defining the equilibrium. In principle, the balance-of-payments equilibrium condition requires that

$$E^{-1}P_D[X(z) - \delta C] + i^*(D_0^* + R_0^*) - (D^* - D_0^*) - (R^* - R_0^*) = 0,$$

where D_0^* and R_0^* are the beginning-of-period stocks of household deposits abroad and official reserves, respectively. Given the definition of the monetary base [see (16)], changes in foreign reserves affect the monetary base one-to-one in the absence of sterilization—and, from (18), the supply of currency. However, given (3), which fixes the demand for currency in proportion to the demand for domestic bank deposits, and Walras' Law (which was used to eliminate the equilibrium condition of the market for currency), (18) plays no direct role in the solution of the model. Thus, official reserves may take on any value required to ensure external balance. At the same time, however, an equilibrium with, say, continuous losses in official reserves would not be sustainable (see Chapter 14). Because we do not require reserves to remain constant, and given our treatment of expectations and the supply side, our concept of equilibrium remains essentially short run in nature.

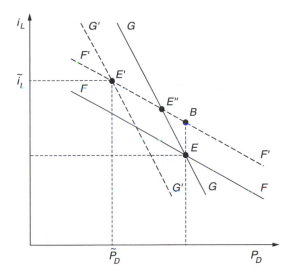

Figure 6–2 ■ Increase in the Central Bank Refinance Rate
Source: Agénor and Montiel (2006).

1.3 ■ Policy and Exogenous Shocks

To illustrate the functioning of our framework, we consider several experiments: an increase in the official rate, i_R; central bank auctions, leading to a change in B^B; an increase in the required reserve ratio, μ; exogenous shifts in the premium, x_P, and contract enforcement costs, κ; and changes in public spending, G, and the world interest rate, i^*.

1.3.1 *Increase in the Refinance Rate*

As indicated earlier, changes in the refinance rate are intermediated through the banking system to the bond rate as well as to loan interest rates. As shown in the discussion of the goods-market equilibrium condition (28), an increase in the refinance rate reduces demand for domestic goods because it is passed on directly by banks to the deposit rate. This exerts both interest rate and wealth effects on consumption. An increase in the deposit interest rate directly induces consumers to increase saving and thus reduce spending on domestic goods. It also induces them to switch away from other assets—including land—and into deposits, thereby depressing land prices. The lower land prices represent a reduction in household wealth, which reinforces the depressing effects of higher deposit interest rates on consumption. The upshot is that to maintain equilibrium in the domestic goods market at an unchanged value of P_D, the loan interest rate would have to fall. Thus, GG shifts downward, as in Figure 6.2.

At the same time, the increase in the refinance rate increases banks' borrowing costs, inducing them to increase their loan interest rates, given that those rates are set as a markup over banks' cost of funds. Consequently, *FF* shifts upward. The implication, as shown in Figure 6.2, is that an increase in the refinance rate results in an increase in the equilibrium loan interest rate as well as a reduction in the price of domestic goods. The deflationary effects of this policy are transmitted through three channels: direct interest rate effects on consumption, wealth effects on consumption arising from a reduced portfolio demand for land, and direct interest rate effects on investment arising from the increase in banks' borrowing costs.

It is worth noting that the final increase in the loan interest rate is more than proportionate to the increase in banks' cost of funds, that is, $di_L/di_R > 1$. The increase in i_L resulting strictly from the increase in banks' cost of funds corresponds to the upward shift in *FF* in Figure 6.2. It is depicted at point *B*. However, the increase in the equilibrium value of the loan interest rate would be larger than this, even if the *GG* curve did not shift down at the same time—that is, in the absence of the downward shift in *GG*, the new equilibrium would have been at E'', rather than *B*. This additional effect on the loan rate represents the influence of the financial accelerator: the reduction in the price of domestic goods increases the real value of firms' debt to banks, reducing the portion of this debt that is covered by collateralizable real assets and thus increasing the risk of lending to firms. This reduction in the domestic price level thus causes banks to further increase the loan interest rate. This effect is accentuated as the result of the downward shift in *GG*, because the shift in *GG* magnifies the effect of the policy on the domestic price level. As in more sophisticated models of credit market imperfections, the financial accelerator imparts a countercyclical pattern to changes in loan rates.

1.3.2   *Central Bank Auctions*

Another common monetary policy tool used by central banks in middle-income developing countries is the auctioning of government bonds to commercial banks. To examine the macroeconomic effects of this policy instrument, consider the consequences of a central bank auction that raises the stock of government bonds, B^B, that must be held by commercial banks. Because this measure has no effect on bank deposit rates, it does not affect the rates of return faced by domestic households on the assets they hold in their portfolios. Consequently, there is no incentive for households to reallocate portfolios, and no impact effect on household demand for land. The implication is that land prices are not a vehicle for monetary transmission in this case and the position of the goods-market equilibrium curve *GG* is undisturbed.

However, the additional bonds held by commercial banks increase the risk associated with this asset, because the government's debt-servicing capacity (as measured by B^{max}) remains unchanged. Consequently, banks increase the premium θ_B that they demand for holding government bonds. Because the loan interest rate is

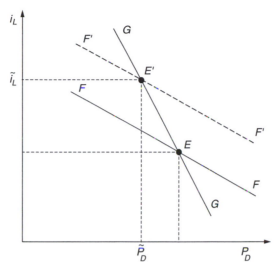

Figure 6–3 ▪ Bond Auction by the Central Bank
Source: Agénor and Montiel (2006).

determined as a markup over the interest rate on government bonds, the lending rate demanded by banks in order to continue to hold the amount of loans outstanding increases as well, shifting the *FF* curve upward, as in Figure 6.3. The upshot is that the economy moves to the northwest along a stationary *GG* curve from a point like *E* to one like *E'*: the loan interest rate rises and the price of domestic goods falls. Note that the transmission mechanism is somewhat different in this case than in the previous one: neither direct interest rate nor wealth effects on consumption are part of the monetary transmission mechanism. Instead, monetary policy works through the adverse effects of higher loan rates on investment spending by domestic firms.

Although changes in land prices do not play any direct role in the monetary transmission process in this case, land prices do not remain unchanged. As a result of the reduction in the domestic price level, households engage in portfolio reallocations from currency and deposits to land and foreign assets. Consequently, in equilibrium, land prices are actually higher. The role of real asset prices in this case, then, is to actually weaken the effect of monetary policy on the real economy—although this effect, which is already captured in the slope of the *GG* curve, cannot offset the overall deflationary effect of the bond auction.

1.3.3 *Increase in the Required Reserve Ratio*

The third monetary policy instrument included in our model is the required reserve ratio μ. An increase in that ratio makes deposits less attractive to banks as a source of funding, and causes them to lower the deposit interest rate. This affects the goods market both directly, because the lower deposit rate discourages saving and stimulates consumption, as well as indirectly, as the lower deposit rate causes households to

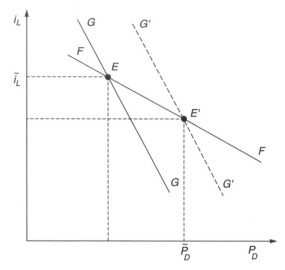

Figure 6–4 ■ Increase in the Required Reserve Ratio
Source: Agénor and Montiel (2006).

reallocate their portfolios away from deposits and into real assets such as land, causing land prices to rise and stimulating consumption through a wealth effect. Because both effects tend to increase demand for domestic goods, a higher loan rate is required to clear the goods market. Thus, *GG* shifts upward. By contrast, under the assumption that the central bank stands ready to supply funds to banks perfectly elastically at the policy rate i_R, the increase in reserve requirements has no effect on banks' marginal cost of funds. Consequently, the *FF* curve is unaffected by this policy. The upshot, as shown in Figure 6.4, is that an increase in the required reserve ratio is actually inflationary.

As already mentioned, the explanation for this seemingly counterintuitive result is that, under our assumed monetary policy regime, changes in reserve requirements have no effect on banks' cost of funds. Because the central bank stands ready to provide the funds desired by banks at the given policy rate i_R, increases in reserve requirements leave banks' cost of funds—and therefore their lending rates—unaffected while *lowering* the interest rate that represents the opportunity cost of current versus future consumption, as well as of holding real assets as opposed to financial ones.

1.3.4 *Shifts in the Risk Premium and Contract Enforcement Costs*

Our model also allows us to analyze the effects of non-policy financial shocks on the economy. Consider, for instance, the effects of changes in banks' perceived risks of lending to private firms. We can capture this in the model in the form of a change

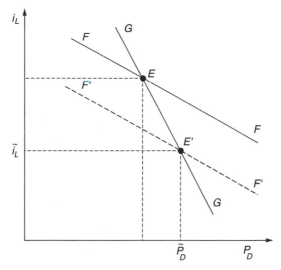

Figure 6–5 ▪ Reduction in Contract Enforcement Costs
Source: Agénor and Montiel (2006).

in the risk parameter x_P.[10] If the risks that banks perceive as associated with lending to private firms were to increase (as represented by an upward shift in x_P), banks would demand a higher risk premium. Just as in the case of central bank auctions, this would have no effect on the goods-market equilibrium condition or the *GG* curve, but would shift the *FF* curve upward, reflecting the increase in the loan rate required for banks to extract a larger risk premium. Again, the macroeconomic results are as depicted in Figure 6.3: the equilibrium loan interest rate rises, and the price of domestic goods falls. A financial accelerator is at work once again: an increase in the loan interest rate is required to offset the initial shift in perceived risk, because the rise in the real value of loans outstanding lowers the collateral offered by firms, increasing banks' intermediation costs.

An alternative type of financial shock is a reduction in contract enforcement costs, an item that is now on the financial reform agenda in many developing countries. Such a reduction would in effect increase the proportion of firms' real assets that is collateralizable, and can be captured in our model in the form of an increase in κ. The improved quality of collateral reduces banks' intermediation costs and allows them to charge a lower premium. Thus, the markup on lending to firms θ_L is reduced and *FF* shifts downward, as in Figure 6.5. This is clearly an inflationary effect, as the domestic price level rises and the loan interest rate falls.

Note that in this case the financial accelerator magnifies the reduction in the loan rate, because the increase in the domestic price level reduces the real value of firms'

---

[10]In developing countries—even in those that have undertaken financial liberalization in a sustained fashion—bank spreads remain high, much higher than in industrial countries. As noted, for instance, by Barajas et al. (1999) and Chirwa and Mlachila (2004), this often reflects—in addition to lack of competition and, in some cases, high inflation—high monitoring costs as well as contract enforcement costs.

loans, and thus increases the effective value of their collateral over and above what is achieved through the reduction in contract enforcement costs.

1.3.5   *Changes in Public Expenditure and World Interest Rates*

It is straightforward to extend the analysis to the case of real shocks. For instance, a fiscal policy shock in the form of a bond-financed increase in government spending on domestic goods would shift GG to the right, increasing the domestic price level and reducing the loan interest rate.[11] The latter might seem counterintuitive, but recall that the central bank follows an accommodative monetary policy under our assumptions, keeping the refinance rate i_R fixed and rediscounting freely to meet banks' demands for funds. Thus, the supply of funds to banks is perfectly elastic, and in the absence of financial accelerator effects the loan interest rate would remain unchanged. The effect on the loan rate thus arises purely from the financial accelerator effect, which in this case acts to reduce the loan rate—because the higher domestic price level reduces the real value of firms' outstanding debt to banks.

Similarly, a change in world interest rates has a straightforward effect in the model. An increase in i^*, for instance, has no direct effect on the economy's financial market equilibrium, because banks are assumed to neither borrow nor lend abroad. Households, however, do have access to foreign assets, and the higher foreign deposit rate induces them to shift their portfolios out of domestic and into foreign assets. This implies a reduced demand for land, and a fall in the price of land. As a result, GG shifts to the left, the price of domestic goods falls, and the loan interest rate rises as a result of financial accelerator effects.

2   Flexible Exchange Rates

We now consider the case of flexible exchange rates. Because the structure of the model remains very similar to the one presented earlier, we provide only a parsimonious presentation of some of the equations that were previously introduced and focus on explaining differences with the fixed exchange-rate case.

2.1 ▪ Model Structure

Total household financial wealth is again defined as:

$$A^H = BILL + D + Q \cdot 1 + E \cdot D^*, \tag{29}$$

---

[11] Given our timing convention, the increase in government spending in the current period translates into an increase in the outstanding stock of public bonds only in the next period. There are, therefore, no contemporaneous wealth effects. Alternatively, one could analyze the case where the increase in spending is financed by a rise in lump-sum taxes, T.

where E is now endogenously determined. This equation can be rewritten as

$$A^H = (BILL + D + Q_0 + E_0 \cdot D^*) + (Q - Q_0) + (E - E_0)D^*,$$

that is, using (29),

$$A^H = A_0^H + (Q - Q_0) + (E - E_0)D_0^*, \tag{30}$$

where E_0 is the beginning-of-period values of the nominal exchange rate, and D_0^* the beginning-of-period stock of foreign exchange deposits. The term A_0^H represents the predetermined component of household financial wealth and $(Q - Q_0) + (E - E_0)D_0^*$ is the endogenous component.

The demand for currency and real demand for domestic-currency deposits are given as in (3) and (4), which are repeated here for convenience:

$$\frac{BILL}{D} = v(i_D), \tag{31}$$

$$\frac{D}{P} = d(i_D, i^* + \varepsilon, \hat{q}, \bar{Y}), \tag{32}$$

where $v' < 0, d_1, d_4 > 0 \ d_2, d_3 < 0$, and $\eta_D/\eta_v > v/(1 + v)$.

Demand for land and foreign-currency deposits is also as given in (6),

$$\frac{E \cdot D^*}{Q + E \cdot D^*} = f(i^* + \varepsilon, \hat{q}),$$

or

$$E \cdot D^* = \frac{f(i^* + \varepsilon, \hat{q})}{1 - f(i^* + \varepsilon, \hat{q})}Q = h(i^* + \varepsilon, \hat{q})Q, \tag{33}$$

where $f_1 > 0, f_2 < 0$, and $h = f/(1 - f)$, so $h_1 > 0, h_2 < 0$.

We will now assume, however, that households face costs in adjusting their stocks of foreign-currency deposits. While these costs could be motivated in a variety of ways, a simple assumption is that the country in question maintains (imperfect) restrictions over capital outflows, which have the effect of throwing "sand in the wheels" of the mechanism through which households adjust their stocks of foreign-currency deposits. As a result, these adjustments are not instantaneous. Specifically, we will assume that they occur gradually over time, in such a way that capital outflows during each period, denoted ΔD^*, are proportional to the gap between households' desired stock of foreign exchange deposits and the actual stock they inherit from the previous period:

$$\Delta D^* = \lambda(D^* - D_0^*),$$

that is, using (33),

$$\Delta D^* = \lambda[h(i^* + \varepsilon, \hat{q})Q/E - D_0^*]. \tag{34}$$

The parameter $\lambda > 0$ is an indicator of the severity of adjustment costs, with $\lambda = 1$ indicating the absence of such costs, and $\lambda = 0$ a situation where such costs are prohibitive, eliminating private capital movements altogether.

Under these conditions, the *effective* demand for foreign-currency deposits becomes:

$$E \cdot D^* = \lambda h(i^* + \varepsilon, \hat{q})Q + (1 - \lambda)E \cdot D_0^*. \tag{35}$$

In turn, the effective demand for land can be derived residually from (29) as

$$Q = A^H - BILL - D - E \cdot D^*,$$

that is, using (31), (32), and (35),

$$Q = A_0^H + (Q - Q_0) + (E - E_0)D_0^* - (1 + v)Pd(\cdot) - \lambda h(\cdot)Q - (1 - \lambda)E \cdot D_0^*.$$

Rearranging terms yields

$$Q = \frac{A_0^H - Q_0 - [1 + v(i_D)]Pd(i_D, i^* + \varepsilon, \hat{q}, \bar{Y}) + (\lambda E - E_0)D_0^*}{\lambda h(i^* + \varepsilon, \hat{q})},$$

or equivalently

$$Q = Q(i_D, i^* + \varepsilon, \hat{q}, \bar{Y}, E; A_0^H). \tag{36}$$

Because the supply of land is exogenous, this equation also represents the equilibrium condition in the market for land. It therefore determines the equilibrium value of Q. It has the following properties:

$$Q_1 = -\frac{Pd\eta_v(1 + v)}{i_D \lambda h}\left(\frac{\eta_D}{\eta_v} - \frac{v}{1 + v}\right) < 0,$$

$$Q_2 = -\frac{Q\lambda h_1 + (1 + v)Pd_2}{\lambda h} < 0,$$

$$Q_3 = -\frac{Q\lambda h_2 + (1+v)P d_3}{\lambda h} > 0,$$

$$Q_4 = -\frac{(1+v)P d_4}{\lambda h} < 0,$$

$$Q_5 = D_0^*/h > 0,$$

$$Q_6 = 1/\lambda h > 0.$$

The intuition for these results is as follows. An increase in the deposit rate shifts households into money (bills and domestic bank deposits), with no effect on their choice between land and foreign deposits; it must therefore result, other things equal, in a decline in their demand for land and a decrease in the equilibrium price of land. An increase in the rate of return on foreign deposits, by contrast, has two effects on the demand for land: first, by causing the demand for money to contract, it increases demand for all non-monetary assets, including land; second, it reduces the demand for land by causing households to switch from land into foreign-currency deposits. The net effect on the demand for land is thus ambiguous in principle. However, if land is a closer substitute for foreign deposits than for money, the second effect must dominate. Because this assumption is plausible, we assign a negative sign to Q_2.

Next, an increase in the expected rate of increase in land prices unambiguously raises the demand for land, drawing resources out of both money holdings and foreign-currency deposits. Thus, an expected future increase in the price of land raises its current price. Higher domestic income, by contrast, induces households to hold more money for transactions purposes, reducing the demand for land as an asset and lowering its price. A depreciation of the exchange rate creates a capital gain on foreign-currency deposits, which increases household wealth and therefore also the demand for, and equilibrium price of, land. The magnitude of this effect depends on the initial composition of household portfolios. If households initially hold their desired ratio of foreign-currency deposits to land, so that $E_0 D_0^*/Q_0 = h$, then $Q_5 E_0/Q_0 = 1$, that is, the equilibrium land price and the nominal exchange rate change in the same proportion. Finally, an increase in initial household wealth raises the demand for land, because in the absence of wealth effects on the demand for money, the additional resources are devoted to holding land and foreign-currency deposits. The result is an increase in the equilibrium price of land.

The equations characterizing the behavior of commercial banks are the same as before, as described by (8) to (15). We summarize them here for convenience:

$$RR = \mu D, \tag{37}$$

$$1 + i_D = (1 + i_R)(1 - \mu), \tag{38}$$

$$1 + i_B = (1 + \theta_B)(1 + i_R), \tag{39}$$

$$\theta_B = \theta_B(B^B / B^{\max}), \quad \theta'_B > 0, \tag{40}$$

$$1 + i_L = (1 + \theta_L)(1 + i_B), \tag{41}$$

$$\theta_L = \theta_L\left(\frac{\kappa P_D K_0}{L_0^F}; x_P\right), \tag{42}$$

$$B^B = \bar{B} - B^C, \tag{43}$$

$$L^B = L^F + B^B - (1 - \mu)d(i_D, i^* + \varepsilon, \hat{q}, \bar{Y})P. \tag{44}$$

Using (11), (12), and (13), the banks' loan rate can be written as:

$$i_L = \left[1 + \theta_L\left(\frac{\kappa P_D K_0}{L_0^F}; x_P\right)\right][1 + \theta_B(B^B / B^{\max})](1 + i_R) - 1,$$

or equivalently

$$i_L = i_L(P_D; B^B, i_R, x_P, ..), \tag{45}$$

with $i_{L1} < 0$, $i_{L2} > 0$, $i_{L3} > 0$, and $i_{L4} > 0$. This equation has the same properties as (26).

The central bank's balance sheet is now given by

$$E \cdot R^* + (B^C + L^B) = MB + (E - E_0)R^*, \tag{46}$$

where the term $(E - E_0)R^*$ on the liability side represents capital, which consists solely of capital gains or losses on foreign exchange reserves arising from fluctuations in the market exchange rate relative to the reference rate, E_0.

As in (17), the monetary base is the sum of currency in circulation and required reserves. This implies, using (37), that the supply of cash is given again by (18).

As before, the central bank can manipulate three instruments to conduct monetary policy: the refinance rate, i_R, holdings of government bonds, B^C, and the required reserve ratio, μ. In addition, now it also has an exchange-rate policy instrument in the form of its holdings of foreign exchange, R^*.

Equations characterizing the price level and the real sector, (20) to (24), are the same as before, and we summarize them here for convenience:

$$P = P_D z^\delta, \tag{47}$$

$$C = \alpha_1(\bar{Y} - T) - \alpha_2[(i_D - \pi^a) + (i^* - \pi^a) + (\hat{q} - \pi^a)] + \alpha_3(A^H/P_D), \tag{48}$$

$$I = I(i_L - \pi^a; K_0), \tag{49}$$

$$L^F = L_0^F + P_D I. \tag{50}$$

$$\bar{Y} - X(z) = (1 - \delta)C + I + G. \tag{51}$$

Regarding the balance of payments, assume for now that official foreign reserves are constant at $R_0^* = 0$. We close the model by specifying the economy's balance-of-payments equilibrium condition as:

$$E^{-1} P_D[X(z) - \delta C] + i^* D_0^* - (D^* - D_0^*) = 0,$$

where D_0^* is the beginning-of-period stock of household deposits held abroad. Given that $E/P_D = z$, this condition becomes

$$z^{-1}[X(z) - \delta C] + i^* D_0^* - \Delta D^* = 0. \tag{52}$$

2.2 ■ Solution

In solving the model, and as in the previous section, we will take the expected rate of change in land prices, the expected rate of inflation, and the expected rate of depreciation all to be exogenous. There are three key endogenous variables in the model: the banks' lending rate, i_L, the price of domestic goods, P_D, and the real exchange rate, z. To solve it we will express the domestic goods market clearing condition (51) and the balance-of-payments equilibrium condition (52) as functions of these three variables, and then use (45) to eliminate the lending rate from these equations. The model thus collapses to two equations—an *internal balance* condition describing equilibrium in the domestic goods market, and an *external balance* condition describing balance-of-payments equilibrium—which can be solved for the two unknowns, z and P_D.

Consider first the internal balance condition. Substituting the consumption function (48) and the investment function (49) in (51), the goods-market equilibrium condition can be written as the requirement that the excess demand for domestic goods be equal to zero:

$$(1-\delta)\left\{\alpha_1(\bar{Y}-T)-\alpha_2[(i_D-\pi^a)+(i^*+\varepsilon-\pi^a)+(\hat{q}-\pi^a)]\right.$$

$$\left.+\alpha_3(A^H/P_D)\right\}+I(i_L-\pi^a;K_0)+G+X(z)-\bar{Y}=0.$$

Using (30), (36), (38), (40), and (41), this condition becomes:

$$(1-\delta)\left\{\alpha_1(\bar{Y}-T)-\alpha_2[((1+i_R)(1-\mu)-1-\pi^a)+(i^*+\varepsilon-\pi^a)+(\hat{q}-\pi^a)]\right.$$

$$+(\alpha_3/P_D)[A_0^H+Q(i_D,i^*+\varepsilon,\hat{q},Y,zP_D;A_0^H)-Q_0+(zP_D-E_0)D_0^*\}$$

$$+I\left\{\left[1+\theta_L\left(\frac{\kappa P_D K_0}{L_0^F};x_P\right)\right]\left[1+\theta_B\left(\frac{B^B}{B^{\max}}\right)\right](1+i_R)-1-\pi^a;K_0\right\}$$

$$+G+X(z)-\bar{Y}=0.$$

This equation expresses the internal balance condition as a function of the endogenous variables z and P_D. Note that the effect of a change in the real exchange rate, z, on the excess demand for domestic goods is given by

$$\alpha_3(1-\delta)(Q_5+D_0^*)+X'>0.$$

This expression consists of two parts: a wealth effect on consumption of domestic goods, given by $\alpha_3(1-\delta)(Q_5+D_0^*)$, and a competitiveness effect, given by X'. The wealth effect arises from the fact that, given the price of domestic goods, a real exchange-rate depreciation is the equivalent of a depreciation in the *nominal* exchange rate. This nominal depreciation both creates a capital gain on foreign-currency deposits and results in an increase in the price of land [see (34)]. The total effect on household wealth is given by $Q_5+D_0^*$, and the resulting increase in consumption demand for domestic goods is $\alpha_3(1-\delta)(Q_5+D_0^*)$. As indicated earlier, the sum of the wealth and competitiveness effects is positive: a real exchange-rate depreciation, holding the price of domestic goods constant, increases excess demand.

The effect of an increase in the price of domestic goods on the excess demand for such goods, holding the real exchange rate constant, is somewhat more complicated. It is given by:

$$\frac{\alpha_3(1-\delta)}{P_D}\left[(Q_5+D_0^*)z-\left(\frac{A_0^H}{P_D}\right)\right]+I_1\theta_{L_1}\left(\frac{\kappa K_0}{L_0^F}\right)(1+\theta_B)(1+i_R).$$

The first term in this expression is negative: it captures the wealth effects on consumption of an increase in the price of domestic goods, holding the real exchange rate constant. When the price of domestic goods rises at an unchanged value of the real exchange rate, the nominal exchange rate must depreciate in the exact same proportion as the increase in the price of domestic goods. As we have just seen, this gives rise to a capital gain on foreign deposits and land. On the assumption that households initially hold their desired foreign-currency deposits-land ratio, the increase in the price of land is proportional to the exchange-rate depreciation. This implies that the real value of land and foreign-currency deposits remains unchanged. Thus, the net effect on the real value of household financial wealth, given by $[(Q_5 + D_0^*)z - A_0^H/P_D]/P_D$, is determined by the effects of the price level increase on total real money balances, which are negative.[12]

The second term is the "financial accelerator" effect. Recalling that $I_1 < 0$ and $\theta_{L_1} < 0$, this term is positive: an increase in the domestic price level increases the collateralizable net worth of domestic firms, thus lowering their external finance premium, reducing banks' lending rate, and increasing investment. This, in turn, raises the excess demand for domestic goods. We will assume for now that the role of this effect is to ameliorate, but not reverse, the negative effects on the excess demand for domestic goods of an increase in the price of such goods that operate through wealth effects. In what follows, however, we will highlight how the properties of the model are affected by this financial accelerator effect.

Putting together the effects on the excess demand for domestic goods of changes in the real exchange rate and of the price of domestic goods, we can derive an internal balance locus drawn in z-P_D space. On the assumption just made that wealth effects on consumption dominate financial accelerator effects on investment, the internal balance locus must have a positive slope, as in the curve labeled IB in Figure 6.6: the positive effects on the excess demand for domestic goods arising from a real depreciation must be offset by negative effects arising from an increase in the domestic price level. The slope of IB is given by

$$\left. \frac{dz}{dP_D} \right|_{IB} = -\frac{\alpha_3(1-\delta)P_D^{-1}[(Q_5 + D_0^*)z - P_D^{-1}A_0^H] + I_1\theta_{L_1}i_L}{\alpha_3(1-\delta)(Q_5 + D_0^*) + X'} > 0.$$

Note that, because financial accelerator effects weaken the effects of increases in P_D on the excess demand for domestic goods, these effects make the internal balance locus flatter than it would otherwise be—that is, a larger increase in the domestic price level is required to restore internal balance after a real depreciation than would be required if financial accelerator effects were absent.

---

[12]To see this, recall that if $h = E_0 D_0^*/Q_0$, $Q_5 = D_0^*/h = Q_0/E_0$. Substituting in the first term above yields $(Q_5 + D_0^*)z - A_0^H/P_D = (Q_0 + ED_0^* - A_0^H)/P_D = -(BILL + D)/P_D$.

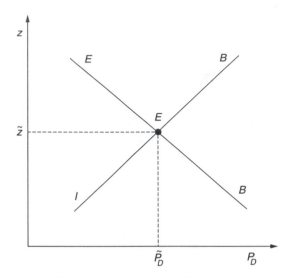

Figure 6–6 ▪ Goods and Financial Market Equilibrium under Flexible Exchange Rates
Source: Agénor and Montiel (2007).

Next, consider the external balance condition. Substituting the consumption function (48) and capital flows equation (34) into the balance-of-payments equilibrium condition (52), the external balance condition can be written as:

$$z^{-1}[X(z) - \delta\{\alpha_1(\bar{Y} - T) - \alpha_2[(i_D - \pi^a) + (i^* + \varepsilon - \pi^a) + (\hat{q} - \pi^a)]$$

$$+\alpha_3(A^H/P_D)\}] + i^* D_0^* - \lambda[h(i^* + \varepsilon, \hat{q})Q/E - D_0^*] = 0.$$

Substituting for the deposit interest rate from (38), for household financial wealth from (30), and for the price of land from (36), and replacing the nominal exchange rate E by zP_D, the external balance condition becomes:

$$z^{-1}\{X(z) - \delta[\alpha_1(\bar{Y} - T) - \alpha_2[\{(1+i_R)(1-\mu) - 1 - \pi\} + (i^* + \varepsilon - \pi^a)$$

$$+(\hat{q} - \pi^a)] + \frac{\alpha_3}{P_D}[A_0^H + (Q((1+i_R)(1-\mu) - 1, i^* + \varepsilon, \hat{q}, Y, zP_D; A_0^H)$$

$$-Q_0) + (zP_D - E_0)D_0^*]\} + i^* D_0^* - \lambda\left[\frac{h(i^* + \varepsilon, \hat{q})}{zP_D}Q\right.$$

$$\times \left.\left\{(1+i_R)(1-\mu) - 1, i^* + \varepsilon, \hat{q}, Y, zP_D; A_0^H\right\} - D_0^*\right] = 0.$$

Again, this condition can be described as an equation in the two endogenous variables z and P_D.

To derive the external balance locus, consider first the effects of a real exchange-rate depreciation on the country's external balance. This effect is given by:

$$z^{-1}\left(X' - \frac{TB}{z}\right) - z^{-1}\delta\alpha_3(Q_5 + D_0^*) - \left(\frac{\lambda h}{z^2 P_D}\right)(Q_5 z P_D - Q), \qquad (53)$$

where $TB = X - \delta C$ is the initial trade balance. This expression can be decomposed into three parts, corresponding to the three terms above. The first term captures the conventional Marshall-Lerner expenditure-switching effect. This term will be positive unless the country runs a large initial trade surplus $(TB > zX')$ and the elasticity of substitution in demand for the country's exports is relatively small. We assume the conventional positive sign here.

The second term captures an expenditure-increasing effect arising from the wealth effects created by depreciation-induced capital gains on foreign-currency deposits and land. The negative sign on this term arises because the increase in spending induced by these capital gains results in an increase in imports and thus causes the trade balance to deteriorate.

The third term arises from the effect of exchange-rate depreciation on capital outflows. A depreciation of the nominal exchange rate simultaneously increases households' demand and supply of foreign-currency deposits. The latter effect arises because an exchange-rate depreciation increases the domestic-currency value of deposits held abroad proportionately. The former arises because the increase in the domestic-currency value of foreign-currency deposits increases the price of land, which in turn raises the demand for foreign-currency deposits. However, if households initially hold their desired composition of land and foreign-currency deposits, as we have been assuming (that is, if $E_0 D_0^*/Q_0 = h$), then it is easy to show that these effects exactly offset each other, so $Q_5 z P_D - Q = 0$ and the third term vanishes. In what follows we will consider the reference case to be one in which expenditure-switching effects are dominant, giving the expression in (53) a positive sign. However, as before, we will consider the implications of this condition failing to hold for the experiments to be conducted later.

Finally, consider the effects on the balance of payments of an increase in the price of domestic goods, P_D. The total effect is given by:

$$-\frac{\delta\alpha_3}{z P_D}\left[(Q_5 + D_0^*)z - \frac{A_0^H}{P_D}\right] - \left(\frac{\lambda h}{z P_D^2}\right)(Q_5 z P_D - Q).$$

The first term captures the expenditure-reducing effects of an increase in the price of domestic goods, operating through a negative real balance effect, on the country's trade balance. This effect is the same as that described in the derivation of the *IB* curve. In this case, the reduction in domestic consumption implies a reduced demand for imports and thus an improvement in the balance of payments, giving the first term a positive sign.

The second term is similar to that discussed immediately above in deriving the effects of a real exchange-rate depreciation. It vanishes under the maintained assumption that $E_0 D_0^* / Q_0 = h$. The upshot is that an increase in the price of domestic goods, at a given value of the real exchange rate, must improve the balance of payments, essentially because of adverse real-balance effects on the demand for imports.

Putting together the effects on the external balance condition of changes in z and P_D, it follows that an increase in the price of domestic goods must be offset by an appreciation in the real exchange rate for the balance of payments to remain in equilibrium. That is, the external balance locus, labeled EB in Figure 6.6, must have a negative slope. This slope is given by:

$$\left. \frac{dz}{dP_D} \right|_{EB} = \frac{\delta \alpha_3 [(Q_5 + D_0^*) z - A_0^H / P_D] / P_D}{(X' - TB/z) - \delta \alpha_3 (Q_5 + D_0^*)} < 0.$$

Putting together the internal and external balance loci, as in Figure 6.6, the model can be solved for the equilibrium values of the real exchange rate and the price of domestic goods. To understand how the model works, the next section analyzes the effects on this equilibrium of a variety of policy and exogenous shocks.

2.3 ■ Policy and Exogenous Shocks

In this section, to illustrate the functioning of the model under flexible exchange rates, we undertake the same set of experiments as those conducted under fixed exchange rates.

2.3.1 *Increase in the Refinance Rate*

As indicated earlier, changes in the refinance rate are intermediated through the banking system to the bond rate as well as to the loan interest rate. Because it is passed on directly by banks to the deposit rate, an increase in the refinance rate exerts both interest rate and wealth effects on consumption.

An increase in the deposit interest rate directly induces consumers to increase saving and thus reduce spending on domestic goods. It also induces them to switch away from nonmonetary assets—including land—and into deposits, thereby depressing land prices. The lower price of land represents a reduction in household wealth, which reinforces the adverse effect of higher deposit rates on private consumption. In addition, the higher refinance rate is passed on by banks to the loan rate (given the fixed markup on government bonds), which reduces investment by domestic firms.

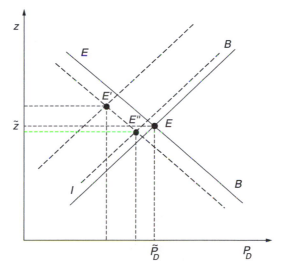

Figure 6–7 ■ Increase in the Central Bank Refinance Rate
Source: Agénor and Montiel (2007).

The upshot is that to maintain internal balance at an unchanged value of P_D, the real exchange rate would have to depreciate. Thus, *IB* shifts upward, as illustrated in Figure 6.7.

An increase in the refinance rate has three effects on the external balance condition. First, through its effect on the deposit rate, it directly reduces consumption spending, thus lowering the demand for imports and improving the trade balance. Second, by exerting downward pressure on the price of land, it reduces household wealth, with negative indirect effects on consumption; these effects, as we have just seen, reinforce the direct effect. These two effects together cause an increase in the refinance rate to improve the trade balance, for given values of z and P_D.

At the same time, the reduction in the price of land caused by the increase in the refinance rate reduces household demand for foreign-currency deposits, so households are led to repatriate capital. The resulting capital inflow reinforces the positive effects of the increase in the refinance rate on the trade balance, with the result that the three channels all combine to improve the balance of payments. Consequently, to restore external balance, the real exchange rate has to appreciate, that is, *EB* shifts down. The upshot is that the price of the domestic good must fall—the increase in the refinance rate is deflationary—but the effect of this policy on the real exchange rate is ambiguous. As shown in Figure 6.7, depending on the magnitude of the shift in *IB* for a given shift in *EB*, the economy may move from the initial position E to a point such as E' (corresponding to a depreciation) or E'' (corresponding to an appreciation).

Because the effect of the financial accelerator mechanism is to flatten out the *IB* curve, it is easy to show that the stronger the financial accelerator effect is, the more

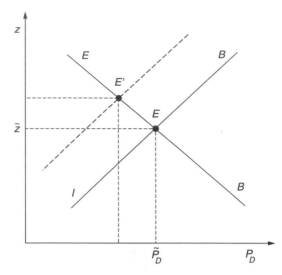

Figure 6–8 ■ Bond Auction by the Central Bank
Source: Agénor and Montiel (2007).

powerful will be the contractionary effect of the increase in the refinance rate on the domestic economy—that is, the larger the drop in the price of the domestic good. A stronger financial accelerator effect, everything else equal, also makes it more likely that the real exchange rate will depreciate in response to an increase in the refinance rate.

2.3.2 *Central Bank Auctions*

As before, a central bank auction that leads to an increase in the stock of government bonds B^B held by commercial banks does not affect the rates of return faced by households on the assets they hold in their portfolios, and thus has no impact effect on household demand for land, implying that land prices are not a vehicle for monetary transmission.

However, because more government bonds must now be held by banks, they increase the premium θ_B that they demand for holding such bonds. Because the loan interest rate is determined as a markup over the interest rate on government bonds, the lending rate demanded by banks in order to continue to hold the amount of loans outstanding increases as well. Because this reduces the investment demand for domestic goods, *IB* shifts upward, as shown in Figure 6.8. However, on our maintained assumption that investment demand is wholly devoted to the purchase of domestic goods, this shock has no effect on the external balance locus. The domestic price level must fall—making this a contractionary shock—and the real exchange rate must depreciate. It is easy to show that a stronger financial accelerator effect will tend to magnify both of these results.

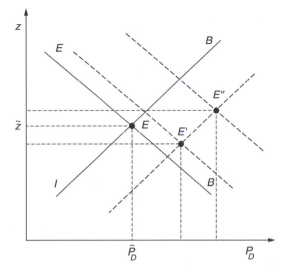

Figure 6–9 ▪ Increase in the Required Reserve Ratio
Source: Agénor and Montiel (2007).

2.3.3 *Increase in the Required Reserve Ratio*

An increase in the required reserve ratio, μ, makes deposits less attractive to banks as a source of funding and causes them to lower the deposit interest rate. This affects the goods market both directly, because the lower deposit rate discourages saving and stimulates consumption, as well as indirectly, as the lower deposit rate causes households to reallocate their portfolios away from deposits and into real assets such as land. The result is that land prices rise and household consumption is stimulated through a wealth effect. Because both effects tend to increase demand for domestic goods, a more appreciated real exchange rate is required to clear the goods market.

Unlike in the case of a change in the refinance rate, this policy has no effect on the loan rate or investment spending, because under the monetary policy regime under consideration, it does not change commercial banks' marginal cost of funds. The positive effects on consumption cause *IB* to shift downward (see Figure 6.9). Because changes in the required reserve ratio affect the external balance condition only through the term $(1 + i_R)(1 - \mu) - 1$, the effects of an increase in that ratio on the *EB* curve are exactly the opposite of those of an increase in the refinance rate considered above: the external balance locus shifts upward.

The net result is that the price of domestic goods increases, but effects on the real exchange rate are ambiguous, with possibly a real appreciation in the new equilibrium (a move from point E to point E'') if the shift in *EB* is large enough. In short, increases in the required reserve ratio are inflationary.

The explanation for this seemingly counterintuitive result is that, as previously mentioned, changes in required reserve ratios have no effect on banks' cost of funds under our assumed monetary policy regime. Because the central bank stands ready to provide the funds desired by banks at the given policy rate i_R, increases in reserve requirements leave banks' cost of funds—and therefore their lending rates—unaffected, while at the same time *lowering* the interest rate that represents the opportunity cost of current versus future consumption, as well as of holding real assets as opposed to financial ones. The induced substitution of current for future consumption and the higher level of private consumption induced by capital gains on real assets are the mechanisms through which inflationary effects are transmitted to the real economy.

2.3.4   *Shifts in the Risk Premium and Contract Enforcement Costs*

An increase in banks' perceived risk of lending to private firms, as captured by an upward shift in the parameter x_P, induces banks to demand a higher risk premium. Just as in the case of central bank auctions, this would increase banks' lending rate, cause domestic investment to contract, and shift *IB* upward.

Again, the macroeconomic results are as depicted in Figure 6.8: the real exchange rate depreciates, and the price of domestic goods falls. The presence of a financial accelerator once again magnifies these effects: the increase in the loan interest rate is larger than that required to offset the initial shift in perceived risk, because the rise in the real value of loans outstanding lowers the collateral offered by firms, increasing banks' intermediation costs.

An increase in κ, resulting from a reduction in contract enforcement costs, raises the proportion of firms' real assets that can be pledged as collateral. In turn, the improved quality of collateral reduces banks' intermediation costs and allows them to charge a lower premium. Thus, the markup on lending to firms, θ_L, is reduced, and *IB* shifts downward, as in Figure 6.10. This is clearly inflationary, as the domestic price level rises and the real exchange rate appreciates.

Note that in this case the financial accelerator magnifies the reduction in the loan rate, because the increase in the domestic price level reduces the real value of firms' loans, and thus increases the effective value of their collateral over and above what is achieved through the reduction in contract enforcement costs per se.

2.3.5   *Changes in Public Expenditure and World Interest Rates*

An increase in government spending on domestic goods shifts *IB* downward while leaving the *EB* unchanged, increasing the domestic price level and causing the real exchange rate to appreciate. It is straightforward to show that, contrary to what standard "crowding out" considerations might suggest, the loan interest rate would actually *fall* in this case. The reason is that the central bank follows an accommodative monetary policy under our assumptions, keeping the refinance rate i_R fixed and rediscounting freely to meet banks' demands for funds. Thus, the supply of funds to banks is perfectly elastic, and in the absence of financial accelerator effects the loan interest rate would remain unchanged. The effect on the loan rate thus arises purely from the financial accelerator effect, which in this case acts to reduce

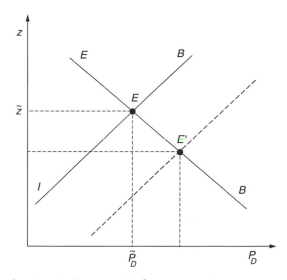

Figure 6–10 ▪ Reduction in Contract Enforcement Costs
Source: Agénor and Montiel (2007).

the loan rate because the higher domestic price level reduces the real value of firms' outstanding debt to banks.

Changes in world interest rates have more complicated effects. An increase in i^*, for instance, has no direct effect on commercial banks or the government, because neither financial intermediaries nor the government are assumed to borrow or lend abroad. Households, however, do have access to foreign assets in the form of deposits, and the higher foreign deposit rate induces them to shift their portfolios out of domestic and into foreign assets. This implies a reduced demand for land, with a concomitant fall in its price. Together with a direct negative effect on consumption spending arising from the substitution of future for present consumption, the result is that the demand for domestic goods contracts, causing *IB* to shift upward. The shift in the external balance locus, however, is ambiguous. The reduction in domestic absorption caused by the effects just described, together with an increase in interest earnings on (beginning-of-period) foreign-currency deposits, cause the current account to improve. However, the increased returns available on foreign-currency deposits induce a capital outflow, leaving the overall effect on the balance of payments ambiguous. If impediments to capital outflows (as measured by λ) are sufficiently strong, such inflows will be muted and the net effect on the balance of payments will be positive, causing *EB* to shift downward. In this case the effect on the domestic economy must be deflationary (the price of the domestic good must fall), but effects on the real exchange rate are ambiguous, as illustrated in Figure 6.11 (move from *E* to either *E'* or *E"*).

However, if capital outflows are sufficiently large, this result could be reversed. Indeed, if these outflows are strong enough to cause the increase in the world interest rate to induce an incipient *deficit* in the balance of payments, *EB* would shift upward. If so, the real exchange rate always depreciates; and if the shift in *EB* is sufficiently

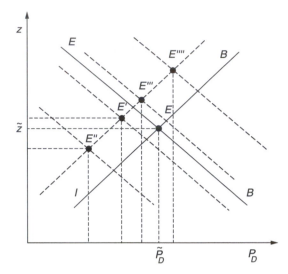

Figure 6–11 ▪ Increase in the World Interest Rate
Source: Agénor and Montiel (2007).

large, the shock could be inflationary (move from E to E'''', as opposed to E''', in Figure 6.11). This effect would be driven in this case by a depreciation of the real exchange rate that improves the competitiveness of domestic producers and creates positive wealth effects on consumption.

The impact of the various shocks on consumption, investment, aggregate demand for the domestic good (defined as the sum of household and public spending on the domestic good, investment, or equivalently as output minus exports), the lending rate, and the risk premium, are shown in Table 6.1. The table shows that all "domestic" shocks affect these variables in the same direction, regardless of the exchange-rate regime—with the exception of the real exchange rate. A shock to the world interest rate, by contrast, has well-defined effects only on private consumption (with the same qualitative impact under both regimes); under flexible exchange rates, the effect on all the other variables is ambiguous, as discussed earlier.

3   Extensions

The basic framework developed in the previous sections can be extended in a number of important and interesting ways. In this section, we consider three issues: sterilization policies, the link between output and working-capital needs, and dynamics of prices and interest rates.[13]

---

[13] Agénor and Montiel (2006) also consider the case of credit targeting, that is, the case where the central bank restricts the supply of credit to commercial banks.

Table 6.1 ▪ Comparison of Shocks under Fixed and Flexible Exchange Rates

Change in	Effect on	Fixed	Flexible
Increase in refinance rate	Aggregate demand	-	-
	Consumption	-	-
	Investment	-	-
	Lending rate	+	+
	Risk premium	+	+
	Price of domestic good	-	-
	Real exchange rate	+	?
Central bank auction	Aggregate demand	-	-
	Consumption	+	+
	Investment	-	-
	Lending rate	+	+
	Risk premium	+	+
	Price of domestic good	-	-
	Real exchange rate	+	+
Rise in required reserve ratio	Aggregate demand	+	+
	Consumption	+	+
	Investment	+	+
	Lending rate	-	-
	Risk premium	-	-
	Price of domestic good	+	+
	Real exchange rate	-	?
Rise in the risk premium	Aggregate demand	-	-
	Consumption	+	+
	Investment	-	-
	Lending rate	+	+
	Risk premium	+	+
	Price of domestic good	-	-
	Real exchange rate	+	+
Rise in world interest rate	Aggregate demand	-	?
	Consumption	-	-
	Investment	-	?
	Lending rate	+	?
	Risk premium	+	?
	Price of domestic good	-	?
	Real exchange rate	+	?

3.1 ▪ Sterilization

An interesting aspect of our model concerns its implications for the behavior of the monetary base, and the consequences of that behavior for the macroeconomic effects of monetary sterilization. Exploring these issues illustrates well the importance of grounding an understanding of monetary transmission in the specific context of a country's financial structure. As we shall show in this section, the failure to do so can prove highly misleading not only in interpreting the stance of monetary policy in developing countries, but also in monetary policy design in general.

To illustrate these points, consider the determination of the monetary base in our model. Using (3), (4), and (8) in (17) yields

$$MB = [v(i_D) + \mu]d(i_D, i^*, \widehat{q}, Y)P_D^\delta E^{1-\delta}. \tag{54}$$

To see what this equation implies, suppose that $\eta_D/\eta_v > v/(v + \mu)$, where $\eta_D = Pd_{i_D}i_D/D$ and $\eta_v = -v'i_D/v$ as before; the demand for monetary base is thus an increasing function of the deposit interest rate, other things equal.[14] This has some important implications.

Consider the model of Section 2, in which the central bank sets a policy value of the refinance rate and makes the supply of credit to the banking system perfectly elastic at that rate. In that setting, contractionary monetary policy consists of an increase in the policy-determined central bank lending rate, as shown in Section 4.1. But because by (9) the deposit interest rate paid by commercial banks is an increasing function of the refinance rate, (54) implies that the tighter monetary policy must be associated with an *increase* in the monetary base at the initial value of the domestic price level.

What differentiates this case from the standard industrial-country story about monetary transmission, in which *reductions* in the monetary base are associated with higher domestic interest rates, is that the interest rate through which aggregate demand is affected in this case (specifically, the deposit rate, because it is through the deposit rate that bank lending rates and land prices are affected by monetary policy) is not an interest rate on an asset that substitutes for money in household portfolios. In fact, just the opposite is true: the interest rates that rise under tight monetary policy include the own rate of return on holding money, whereas the interest rates on money substitutes are unaffected. This is why a monetary tightening is associated with an increase in the monetary base on impact (that is, at a given value of the domestic price level). Whether the monetary base turns out to be higher or lower in the new macroeconomic equilibrium that emerges after the monetary contraction, however (that is, after the domestic price level is allowed to adjust), cannot be determined unambiguously in our model. It depends on the net effect of two offsetting influences: the increase in the deposit interest rate and decrease in the domestic price level. By (54), the former increases the demand for base money whereas the latter reduces it, leaving the net effect dependent on a variety of elasticities in the model.

This analysis has at least two important implications. First, because a monetary tightening could be associated with an increase in the monetary base and a monetary expansion with a reduction in the base, the stance of monetary policy in an economy

---

[14]Because $\mu < 1$, the assumption $\eta_D/\eta_v > v/(v + \mu)$ ensures that condition (5) holds.

such as the one we are examining cannot be inferred from the behavior of the monetary base. As just shown, the impact of monetary policy on the monetary base may be either in the same or in the opposite direction as its impact on aggregate demand. Second, consider the effects of a policy of monetary sterilization. In principle, the central bank could use any of its three instruments to stabilize the monetary base in response to shocks: the refinance rate i_R, lending to banks L^B, and changes in its stock of government bonds B^C.

For concreteness, suppose that the central bank varies i_R so as to stabilize the monetary base; in other words, consider sterilization within the context of the model of Section 2. Again for concreteness, suppose that the shock in question is an increase in the foreign interest rate, i^*. We saw in Section 2.5 that, holding the policy rate i^R constant, an increase in the foreign interest rate would cause the GG curve to shift to the left and the price of domestic goods to fall. In other words, this shock has a contractionary effect on aggregate demand. From (54), the combination of a higher rate of return on foreign assets and lower domestic price level cause the monetary base to contract, because they combine to reduce the demand for deposits. The contraction in the monetary base stems from a combination of capital outflows as households switch from domestic deposits to foreign assets, as well as reduced commercial bank borrowing from the central bank, because the lower domestic price level increases bank lending rates and reduces firms' demand for loans. To sterilize these effects and stabilize the monetary base, the central bank would be led, by (54), to try to induce an increase in the demand for deposits by increasing deposit interest rates. It could do this by raising its refinance rate. But as shown earlier, this policy also has contractionary effects on aggregate demand. Thus, rather than stabilize the economy in response to real shocks, sterilization does exactly the opposite: in order to stabilize the monetary base, it destabilizes aggregate demand. The upshot is that when the economy's financial structure is as described here, the conventional wisdom based on the familiar Poole-type analysis of the optimal choice of monetary policy instruments is stood on its head: in response to real shocks, interest rate targeting is superior to monetary targeting.

3.2 ■ Working-Capital Needs

In the foregoing discussion, output was assumed to be exogenous. We now extend the analysis to endogenize the supply side and introduce a cost channel for monetary policy, by accounting for a direct effect of lending rates on firms' production costs (which must be incurred prior to the sale of output), as for instance in Greenwald and Stiglitz (1993), Edwards and Végh (1997), Gupta (2005), Agénor (2006a), and Christiano et al. (2004). As noted in the previous chapter, this is a common feature of developing economies, and there is some evidence that this effect may be important also in industrial countries.[15]

---

[15] See, for instance, Ravenna and Walsh (2006) for the United States, and Gaiotti and Secchi (2006) for Italy.

Suppose that firms have no direct access to world capital markets. To finance their working-capital needs, which consist solely of labor costs, they must borrow from commercial banks.[16] Total production costs faced by the representative firm are thus equal to the wage bill plus the interest payments made on bank loans. For simplicity, we will assume that loans contracted for the purpose of financing working capital (which are short term in nature, in contrast to those made for capital accumulation), are provided at a fixed markup (normalized to unity) on the cost of borrowing from the central bank, at the rate i_R.

Formally, the maximization problem faced by the representative firm can be written as

$$\max_{y} P_D Y - WN - i_R L^F, \tag{55}$$

where y denotes output, W the nominal wage, N the quantity of labor employed, i_L the nominal (contractual) lending rate charged by commercial banks, and L the nominal amount of loans obtained from commercial banks.

The production function takes the Cobb-Douglas form

$$Y = N^{\alpha} K_0^{1-\alpha}, \tag{56}$$

where $\alpha \in (0, 1)$. The firm's financial constraint is given by

$$L^F \geq L_0^F + W \cdot N + P_D I, \tag{57}$$

where as before I denotes investment.

Constraint (57) will be assumed to be continuously binding, because the only reason for firms to demand loans is to finance labor costs and capital accumulation.

Solving problem (55) subject to (56) and (57), taking i_R and I as given, yields the first-order condition $\alpha P_D N^{\alpha-1} K_0^{1-\alpha} - (1 + i_R)W = 0$. Thus, labor demand can be written as

$$N^d = [\alpha K_0^{1-\alpha}/(1 + i_R)(W/P_D)]^{1/(1-\alpha)}, \tag{58}$$

which can be substituted in (56) to give

$$Y^s \equiv [\alpha/(1 + i_R)(W/P_D)]^{\alpha/(1-\alpha)} K_0. \tag{59}$$

This equation shows that supply of the domestic good is inversely related to the effective cost of labor, $(1 + i_R)(W/P_D)$.

---

[16] As before, there is no domestic substitute for bank loans, so that firms cannot issue equities or bonds (claims on their capital stock) to finance their working-capital needs.

Using (57) and (58), the firm's demand for credit is now given by

$$L^F = WN^d + P_D I. \tag{60}$$

The nominal wage is assumed to be fully indexed on the overall price index, P, defined in (20):

$$W = P = P_D z^\delta. \tag{61}$$

The real wage is thus fixed in terms of the cost-of-living index. However, the *product* wage, W/P_D, which determines firms' employment decisions, is equal to

$$W/P_D = z^\delta,$$

which in turn can be substituted into (58) to give $N^d = N(z; i_R)$, with N_1^d, $N_2^d < 0$. Similarly, using (59) yields

$$Y^s = Y(z; i_R), \tag{62}$$

with Y_1^s, $Y_2^s < 0$. Output is thus negatively related to the real exchange rate and to the official interest rate. It is worth noting that a similar result would obtain under fixed exchange rates if we had assumed instead (in standard Keynesian fashion) that it is the *nominal* wage that is fixed at $\tilde{W}$. The product wage would then be $(\tilde{W}/E)z$, implying again a negative relationship between the real exchange rate and output.

We will also assume that profits are distributed at the end of the period, after the sale of output. Assuming that profits in the previous period are zero, setting $\pi^a = 0$, and using (61), the consumption function therefore takes the form, instead of (21),

$$C = \alpha_1 z^\delta N(z; i_R) - \alpha_2 (i_D + i^* + \hat{q}) + \alpha_3 (A^H/P_D), \tag{63}$$

with (62) substituted in the equilibrium condition (24).

Without going through all the previous derivations, it is relatively easy to see the implications of this change. As long as the official interest rate remains constant, the model behaves in exactly the same way as before; the reason is that $Y^s - X$, whether output is endogenous or not, remains negatively related to z.

Matters are now different, however, when it comes to examining the impact of an increase in the official rate. The key difference now is that output falls on impact, because of the direct effect of i_R on firms' borrowing costs. This is essentially the Cavallo-Patman effect, emphasized by New Structuralist economists (see Taylor, 1983, and van Wijnbergen, 1982). If aggregate supply falls by more than aggregate demand, a situation of excess demand for the domestic good may result, thereby leading to *higher* prices, as opposed to lower prices, as in the previous case. Graphically, in Figure 6.2 curve GG would be upward sloping and would shift to the right, instead of the left. If this shift is sufficiently large, the new equilibrium will be characterized by both higher prices and a higher lending rate—implying a lower level of aggregate demand for the domestic good.

Thus, by introducing the cost channel, the model can explain why monetary policy may have stagflationary effects. As noted earlier, this is a key insight of the New Structuralist models developed most notably by Taylor (1983) and van Wijnbergen (1982), in the context of their criticism of stabilization programs in developing countries. But the positive correlation between policy interest rates and inflation has also been observed in industrial countries, and the cost channel emphasized here has been proposed as an explanation of this "price puzzle" (see, for instance, Chowdhury et al., 2006).

3.3 ■ Dynamics of Prices and Interest Rates

A dynamic extension of the framework described in the previous sections—albeit in a closed-economy context—was provided by Agénor and Pereira da Silva (2014). The extended model (which also accounts for the cost channel described in the previous subsection) has two key sources of dynamics. The first is the assumption that prices adjust gradually to disequilibria between aggregate demand and aggregate supply, in line with the backward-looking specification proposed by Fuhrer and Moore (1995). The second is a simple partial adjustment mechanism in either the bank loan rate or, more important from a policy perspective, the central bank refinance rate. The rule followed by the central bank is akin to a Taylor rule, as discussed in the next chapter. The model also assumes that commercial banks engage in costly monitoring to reduce the credit risk in their loan portfolios. This leads to an endogenous determination of the risk premium embedded in loan rates, which varies inversely with the ratio of collateral to investment loans. However, in contrast to the framework described earlier, collateral is measured in terms of a fraction of output, not physical capital. Even though balance sheet effects are not explicitly introduced, changes in collateral-loan ratios may still generate a financial accelerator effect—induced not by changes in asset prices but rather by endogenous adjustment in factor prices and borrowing costs. At the same time, the analysis shows that the transitional dynamics associated with an autonomous change in the refinance rate are quite complex; long-term effects on the economy may differ substantially from the short-term effects.

The analysis can be extended in other directions as well, to address a number of issues beyond those discussed in this chapter. First, the Mundell-Fleming one-good production structure was adopted for tractability; instead, a tradable-nontradable structure, or a three-good structure (as described in Chapter 1), could be used. As documented by Tornell and Westermann (2003), in several middle-income countries there is a pronounced asymmetry in size and financing opportunities available to firms across tradables and nontradables sectors. Firms in the tradables sector tend to be large and have access to world capital markets (in addition to domestic loans), because they can either pledge export receivables as collateral, or can get guarantees from closely linked firms. By contrast, firms in the nontradables sector tend to be smaller on average, are more dependent on bank credit, and may face borrowing constraints.

Second, in the framework described earlier, firms can borrow only from domestic banks. While this is appropriate for many lower middle-income countries, direct foreign borrowing by firms could also be accounted for, as for instance in Gertler et al. (2007); Céspedes et al. (2003, 2004); Elekdag et al. (2006); and Tovar (2005). By endogenizing the foreign interest rate through a markup equation similar to the one used earlier, one could examine the net worth effects associated with changes in the domestic-currency value of foreign debt, in the presence of currency mismatches. A nominal depreciation, in this context, could trigger a vicious cycle: by increasing the domestic-currency value of foreign liabilities, it may lead to a deterioration in borrowers' net worth. The resulting increase in the premium on foreign borrowing, by raising the domestic cost of borrowing, may in turn exacerbate fluctuations in investment, activity, and capital flows.

Alternatively, it could be assumed that firms borrow directly only from domestic financial intermediaries, with these intermediaries in turn borrowing at a premium on world capital markets, as for instance in Agé nor and Aizenman (1998).[17] This two-level financial structure may actually provide a better characterization of borrowing opportunities for some middle-income developing countries, where direct access to international capital markets is typically available to only a small group of large firms. These issues are further discussed in Chapter 12.

---

[17]Disyatat (2004) also considers foreign borrowing by domestic banks.

Chapter 7

Inflation Targeting, Macroeconomic Stability, and Financial Stability

There is growing acceptance among both policymakers and economists that the pursuit of price stability (defined as maintaining a low and stable rate of inflation) is the main medium- to long-run goal of monetary policy. The first reason is the recognition that a high and variable inflation rate is socially and economically costly. These costs include price distortions, lower savings and investment (which inhibits growth), hedging (into precious metals or land), and capital flight (into foreign assets).

The second is that experience has shown that short-term manipulation of monetary policy instruments to achieve other goals—such as higher output and lower unemployment—may conflict with price stability. The attempt to achieve these conflicting goals tends to generate an inflationary bias in the conduct of monetary policy without, in the end, achieving systematically higher output and employment.

To achieve the goal of price stability, monetary policy was for a long time conducted by relying on intermediate targets such as monetary aggregates or exchange rates. During the 1990s, however, several industrial and developing countries began to focus directly on inflation itself. This approach to the problem of controlling inflation through monetary policy is known as inflation targeting.[1] It essentially makes inflation—rather than output or unemployment—the primary goal of monetary policy. It also forces the central bank to predict the future behavior of prices, giving it the opportunity to tighten policies before sustained inflationary pressures develop.

The purpose of this chapter is to discuss various analytical issues associated with the implementation of inflation targeting in developing countries.[2] Many of these countries have adopted floating exchange rates in recent years and must therefore

---

[1] As discussed below, two major reasons why countries chose to implement inflation targeting over alternative monetary policy frameworks were exchange-rate crises and money demand instability.

[2] Much of the material presented in this chapter draws on Agénor (2002) and Agénor and Pereira da Silva (2013). The first paper also discusses operational requirements for inflation targeting.

find another nominal anchor to guide domestic monetary policy. Whether inflation targeting has a wider applicability to developing economies has indeed been a matter of debate in recent years. It has been argued, for instance, that poor data on prices and real sector developments, the absence of reliable procedures for forecasting inflation, the difficulty of maintaining de facto independence for the central bank, and the lack of an anti-inflationary history may preclude the establishment of a transparent framework for conducting monetary policy and therefore any attempt at inflation targeting. However, others (including Mishkin and Schmidt-Hebbel, 2007) have adopted a more favorable position, at least for the case of countries where the financial system is sufficiently developed to permit the use of indirect instruments of monetary policy.

Section 1 presents a basic analytical framework for inflation targeting in a closed economy, based on the important work of Svensson (1997). A closed-economy setting provides a good starting point for understanding the nature of an inflation targeting regime. Section 2 extends the model to consider the case of an open economy, to highlight the role of the exchange rate in monetary policy transmission (see Chapter 5). Section 3 begins with a comparison between inflation targeting and both money supply and exchange-rate targeting regimes, and highlights the risks associated with pursuing implicit exchange-rate targets. It also compares inflation targeting with an alternative regime, nominal income targeting. Section 4 identifies basic requirements for implementing an inflation targeting framework, namely, central bank independence, the absence of implicit targeting of the exchange rate, and transparency in the conduct of monetary policy. Section 5 examines the design of interest rate rules in practice. The last section focuses on some further analytical issues in the design of inflation targeting regimes, namely the role of asymmetric policy preferences and uncertainty about behavioral parameters.

1   Basic Framework: Closed Economy

Following Svensson (1997, 2003), consider a closed economy producing one (composite) good. The economy's structure is characterized by three equations, where all parameters are defined as positive:

$$\pi_t - \pi_{t-1} = \alpha_1 y_{t-1} + \alpha_2 g_{t-1} + \varepsilon_t, \tag{1}$$

$$y_t = \beta_1 y_{t-1} - \beta_2 (i_{t-1} - \pi_{t-1}) + \beta_3 g_{t-1} + \eta_t, \quad \beta_1 < 1, \tag{2}$$

$$g_t = \gamma g_{t-1} + v_t, \quad \gamma < 1, \tag{3}$$

where $\pi_t \equiv p_t - p_{t-1}$ is the inflation rate at t (with p_t denoting the logarithm of the price level), y_t, the output gap (defined as the logarithm of the ratio of actual to potential output), g_t a measure of fiscal impulse (say, government spending), i_t the nominal interest rate (taken to be under the direct control of the central bank), and ε_t, η_t, and v_t are i.i.d. shocks. Equation (1) indicates that changes in inflation are positively related to the cyclical component of output and the fiscal impulse, in both cases with a lag of one period.[3] Equation (2) relates the output gap positively to its value in the previous period and government spending, and negatively to the real interest rate—with a one-period lag in the case of the latter two variables. Finally, (3) states that government spending follows a first-order autoregressive process.

In this model, policy actions (changes in the nominal interest rate) affect output with a one-period lag and, as implied by (1), inflation with a two-period lag.[4] The lag between a change in the policy instrument and inflation will be referred to in what follows as the *control lag* or *control horizon*.

Depending on the central bank's policy loss function, two regimes can be distinguished: strict and flexible inflation targeting. We consider them in turn.

1.1 ▪ Strict Inflation Targeting

Under strict inflation targeting, the central bank's period-by-period policy loss function, L_t, is a function only of deviations of actual inflation from its target value, $\bar{\pi}$:[5]

$$L_t = \frac{(\pi_t - \bar{\pi})^2}{2}.$$ (4)

The central bank's policy problem in period t is to choose a sequence of current and future interest rates, $\{i_h\}_{h=t}^{\infty}$ so as to minimize the expected sum of discounted squared deviations of actual inflation from its target value, U_t:

$$\min U_t = \mathbb{E}_t \left\{ \sum_{j=0}^{\infty} \delta^j \frac{(\pi_{t+j} - \bar{\pi})^2}{2} \right\},$$ (5)

where $\delta \in (0, 1)$ denotes a discount factor and $\mathbb{E}_t$ the expectations operator conditional upon the central bank's information set at period t.

---

[3] Instead of being linear as in (1), the output-inflation relationship may have a convex shape, that is, positive deviations of aggregate output from potential (or booms) may be more inflationary than negative deviations (recessions) are disinflationary. See Schaling (2004) for a discussion of the implications of this nonlinearity under inflation targeting.

[4] Note that introducing a forward-looking element (as in the New Keynesian models discussed, for instance, by Fuhrer (1997) in (1) would imply that monetary policy has some effect on contemporaneous inflation, altering the properties of the model significantly.

[5] Svensson (1999) and Vestin (2006) discuss the arguments in favor of specifying the target in terms of the *level* of prices, as opposed to their rate of change. An alternative to (strict) consumer-price targeting is producer-price targeting; see Sutherland (2006) and Agénor and Pereira da Silva (2013) for a discussion in an open-economy context.

The most direct way to solve this optimization problem is by applying dynamic programming techniques. The problem can, however, be recast in a simpler form, which allows a more intuitive derivation of the optimal path of the policy instrument. To begin with, note first that, because the nominal interest rate affects inflation with a two-period lag, π_{t+2} can be expressed in terms of period t variables and shocks occurring at $t+1$ and $t+2$. Equation (1) can be written as

$$\pi_{t+2} = \pi_{t+1} + \alpha_1 y_{t+1} + \alpha_2 g_{t+1} + \varepsilon_{t+2}.$$

Updating (2) and (3) in a similar manner and substituting the results in the above expression yields

$$\pi_{t+2} = (\pi_t + \alpha_1 y_t + \alpha_2 g_t + \varepsilon_{t+1}) + \alpha_1 [\beta_1 y_t - \beta_2 (i_t - \pi_t) + \beta_3 g_t + \eta_{t+1}]$$

$$+ \alpha_2 (\gamma g_t + v_{t+1}) + \varepsilon_{t+2},$$

that is

$$\pi_{t+2} = a_1 \pi_t + a_2 y_t + a_3 g_t - a_4 i_t + z_{t+2}, \tag{6}$$

where

$$z_{t+2} = \varepsilon_{t+2} + \varepsilon_{t+1} + \alpha_1 \eta_{t+1} + \alpha_2 v_{t+1},$$

$$a_1 = 1 + \alpha_1 \beta_2, \quad a_2 = \alpha_1 (1 + \beta_1), \quad a_3 = \alpha_1 \beta_3 + \alpha_2 (1 + \gamma),$$

and $a_4 = \alpha_1 \beta_2$.

Thus, the interest rate set at t will affect inflation in $t+2$ and beyond, but not in t and $t+1$; similarly, the interest rate set at $t+1$ will affect inflation in $t+3$ and beyond, but not in $t+1$ and $t+2$; and so on. The solution to the optimization problem described earlier can therefore be viewed as consisting in assigning the nominal interest rate at t $(t+1)$ so that the expected inflation at $t+2$ $(t+3)$ is equal to the target rate, and so on. Formally, the central bank's optimization problem becomes that of minimizing period by period L_t with respect to i_t:

$$\min_{i_t} L_t = \frac{\delta^2}{2} \mathbb{E}_t (\pi_{t+2} - \bar{\pi})^2. \tag{7}$$

Note that, from standard statistical results,[6]

$$\mathbb{E}_t (\pi_{t+2} - \bar{\pi})^2 = (\pi_{t+2|t} - \bar{\pi})^2 + V(\pi_{t+2}), \tag{8}$$

---

[6]Let x be a random variable, and $\bar{x}$ its mean; the standard result referred to in the text is $\mathbb{E}(x - \bar{x})^2 = (Ex - \bar{x})^2 + V(x)$, that is, the expected squared value of the deviation of a random variable from its mean equals the square of the bias plus the variance of that variable.

where $\pi_{t+2|t} = \mathbb{E}_t \pi_{t+2}$. This expression indicates that the central bank's optimization problem can be viewed equivalently as minimizing the sum of expected future squared deviations of inflation from target (the squared bias in future inflation, $(\pi_{t+2|t} - \tilde{\pi})^2$) and the variability of future inflation, $V(\pi_{t+2})$. This decomposition (8) will prove useful for the discussion later on of the role of uncertainty.

The first-order condition of problem (7) is given by

$$\delta^2 \mathbb{E}_t \left\{ (\pi_{t+2} - \tilde{\pi}) \frac{\partial \pi_{t+2}}{\partial i_i} \right\} = -\delta^2 a_4 (\pi_{t+2|t} - \tilde{\pi}) = 0,$$

with the last result following from (6). This condition therefore implies

$$\pi_{t+2|t} = \tilde{\pi}. \tag{9}$$

Equation (9) shows that, given the two-period control lag, the optimal policy for the central bank is to set the nominal interest rate such that the expected rate of inflation for $t + 2$ (relative to $t + 1$) based on information available at t be equal to the inflation target.

To derive explicitly the interest rate rule, note from (6) that, because $\mathbb{E}_t z_{t+2} = 0$, $\pi_{t+2|t}$ is given by

$$\pi_{t+2|t} = a_1 \pi_t + a_2 y_t + a_3 g_t - a_4 i_t, \tag{10}$$

which implies that

$$i_t = \frac{-(\pi_{t+2|t} - \pi_t) + \alpha_1 \beta_2 \pi_t + a_2 y_t + a_3 g_t}{a_4}.$$

This result shows that, in particular, because interest rate changes affect inflation with a lag, monetary policy must be conducted in part on the basis of forecasts; the larger the amount by which the current inflation rate—which is predetermined up to a random shock, as implied by (1)—exceeds the target, the higher the interest rate. The fact that the inflation forecast can be considered an *intermediate policy target* is the reason why Svensson (1997) refers to inflation targeting as inflation *forecast* targeting. The use of conditional inflation forecasts as intermediate targets in the policy rule is optimal, given the quadratic structure of policy preferences.

The inflation forecast can readily be related to the current, observable variables of the model. To do so requires setting (10) equal to $\tilde{\pi}$ and solving for i_t:

$$i_t = \frac{-\tilde{\pi} + a_1 \pi_t + a_2 y_t + a_3 g_t}{a_4}.$$

Given the definitions of the a_b coefficients derived above, this expression can be rewritten to give the following explicit form of the central bank's reaction function:

$$i_t = \pi_t + b_1(\pi_t - \bar{\pi}) + b_2 y_t + b_3 g_t, \tag{11}$$

where

$$b_1 = \frac{1}{\alpha_1 \beta_2}, \quad b_2 = \frac{1 + \beta_1}{\beta_2}, \quad b_3 = \frac{\alpha_1 \beta_3 + \alpha_2(1 + \gamma)}{\alpha_1 \beta_2}.$$

Equation (11) indicates that it is optimal for the central bank to adjust the nominal interest rate upward to reflect current inflation as well as the difference between current and desired inflation rates, increases in output, and government spending. As emphasized by Svensson (1997, p. 1119), the reason why current inflation appears in the optimal policy rule is not because current inflation is a policy target but because it helps (together with output and government spending) predict future inflation, as implied by (10). It is also important to note that rule (11) is *certainty-equivalent*: the same interest rate rule would be optimal in the absence of shocks. Although the central bank cannot prevent temporary deviations of actual inflation from its target value, it can ensure that the effects of such shocks do not persist over time.[7]

In equilibrium, *actual* inflation in $t + 2$ will deviate from the inflation forecast $\pi_{t+2|t}$ and the inflation target, $\bar{\pi}$, only by the forecast error z_{t+2}, due to shocks occurring within the control lag, after the central bank has set the interest rate to its optimal value

$$\pi_{t+2} = \pi_{t+2|t} + z_{t+2},$$

or

$$\pi_{t+2} - \bar{\pi} = z_{t+2}. \tag{12}$$

The fact that, even by following an optimal instrument setting rule the central bank cannot prevent deviations from the inflation target resulting from shocks occurring within the control lag, is important in assessing the performance of inflation targeting regimes in practice.

1.2 ■ Policy Trade-Offs and Flexible Targeting

Consider now the case where the central bank is concerned not only about inflation but also about the size of the output gap. Specifically, suppose that now the policy loss function (4) is given by

$$L_t = \frac{(\pi_t - \bar{\pi})^2}{2} + \frac{\lambda y_t^2}{2}, \quad \lambda > 0, \tag{13}$$

---

[7]This, of course, results from the fact that shocks have been assumed to be i.i.d. In practice, however, shocks are often persistent; this has important implications under uncertainty.

where λ measures the relative weight attached to cyclical movements in output.[8] The expected sum of discounted policy losses is now given by

$$U_t = \mathbb{E}_t \left\{ \sum_{j=0}^{\infty} \delta^j \frac{(\pi_{t+j} - \bar{\pi})^2 + \lambda y_{t+j}^2}{2} \right\}. \tag{14}$$

Suppose, for simplicity, that government spending has no effect on inflation or the output gap, that is, $\alpha_2 = \beta_3 = 0$. As shown by Svensson (1997, 1140–43), the first-order condition for minimizing (14) with respect to the nominal interest rate can be written as

$$\pi_{t+2|t} = \bar{\pi} - \frac{\lambda}{\delta \alpha_1 \kappa} y_{t+1|t}, \tag{15}$$

where κ is given by

$$\kappa = \frac{1}{2} \left\{ 1 - \mu + \sqrt{(1+\mu)^2 + 4\lambda/\alpha_1^2} \right\},$$

and

$$\mu = \frac{\lambda(1-\delta)}{\delta \alpha_1^2}.$$

Condition (15) requires the inflation forecast $\pi_{t+2|t}$ to be equal to the inflation target $\bar{\pi}$ only if the one-period ahead expected output gap is zero ($y_{t+1|t} = 0$). In general, as long as $\lambda > 0$, $\pi_{t+2|t}$ will exceed (fall short of) $\bar{\pi}$ if the output gap is negative (positive). The higher λ (the relative weight on output fluctuations in the policy loss function) is, the larger will be the impact of the expected output gap on the inflation forecast.[9]

A more intuitive formulation of the optimality condition (15) can be obtained by noting that, from (1), with $\alpha_2 = 0$ and $\mathbb{E}_t \varepsilon_{t+1} = 0$,

$$y_{t+1|t} = \frac{\pi_{t+2|t} - \pi_{t+1|t}}{\alpha_1}.$$

---

[8] Note that, because the target level of the output gap is zero, there is no built-in inflationary bias in this specification; see the discussion in Chapter 11.

[9] The policy loss function (13) can be further extended to account for interest rate smoothing by adding the squared value of changes in i_t. As shown by Svensson (1997), an instrument smoothing objective would also make the inflation forecast deviate from the inflation target in order to reduce costly fluctuations in interest rates.

Substituting this result in (15) and rearranging terms yields

$$\pi_{t+2|t} - \bar{\pi} = c(\pi_{t+1|t} - \bar{\pi}), \quad c = \frac{\lambda}{\lambda + \delta\alpha_1^2\kappa} < 1. \tag{16}$$

This expression indicates that the deviation of the two-period inflation forecast from the inflation target is proportional to the deviation of the one-period forecast from the target; when $\lambda = 0$, $c = 0$ and the previous result [see (9)] holds. The implication of this analysis is that, when cyclical movements in output matter for the central bank, it is optimal to adjust *gradually* the inflation forecast to the inflation target. By doing so, the central bank reduces fluctuations in output. As also shown by Svensson (1997, 1143–44), the higher the weight on output in the policy loss function (the higher λ) is, the more gradual the adjustment process will be (the larger c will be).

The interest rate rule can be derived explicitly by noting that, from (1) and (2),

$$\pi_{t+1|t} = \pi_t + \alpha_1 y_t, \quad \pi_{t+2|t} = \pi_{t+1|t} + \alpha_1 y_{t+1|t},$$

$$y_{t+1|t} = \beta_1 y_t - \beta_2(i_t - \pi_t).$$

Substituting the first and third expressions in the second yields

$$\pi_{t+2|t} = \pi_t + \alpha_1(1 + \beta_1)y_t - \alpha_1\beta_2(i_t - \pi_t). \tag{17}$$

Equating (17) and (15) and rearranging terms implies that

$$i_t = \pi_t + b_1'(\pi_t - \bar{\pi}) + b_2' y_t, \tag{18}$$

where

$$b_1' = \frac{1-c}{\alpha_1\beta_2}, \quad b_2' = \frac{1-c+\beta_1}{\beta_2},$$

from which it can be verified that $b_1' = b_1$ and $b_2' = b_2$ when $\lambda = 0$ (and thus $c = 0$). Equation (18) indicates that the optimal instrument rule requires, as before, the nominal interest rate to respond positively to current inflation and the output gap, as well as the excess of current inflation over the target. However, an important difference between reaction functions (11) and (18) is that the coefficients of (18) are smaller, due to the positive weight attached to cyclical movements in output in the policy loss function.[10] This more gradual response implies that the (expected) length

---

[10] Note also that in both cases the parameters characterizing the optimal policy rule continue to be independent of variances of the shocks affecting inflation and output. This is because certainty equivalence holds in both cases.

of adjustment of current inflation to its target value, following a disturbance, will take longer than the minimum two periods given by the control horizon. The time it takes for expected inflation to return to target following a (permanent) unexpected shock is known as the *implicit targeting horizon* or simply as the *target horizon*. Naturally, the length of the implicit target horizon is positively related not only to the magnitude of the shock and its degree of persistence but also to the relative importance of output fluctuations in the central bank's objective function.

Thus, the central bank's output stabilization goal has a crucial effect not only on the determination of short-term interest rates but also on the *speed* with which the inflation rate adjusts toward its target after a shock. It can also be shown that policy preferences also affect the *variability* of output and inflation. It can be established that the variance of inflation is increasing with λ, whereas the variance of the output gap is decreasing with λ. Intuitively, the larger the weight attached by the central bank to output-gap stabilization, the lower its variability, and the larger the volatility of inflation. Flexible inflation targeting therefore entails a trade-off between inflation variability and output-gap variability. By varying the relative weight attached by the central bank to the two policy goals in its loss function, it is possible to derive an "optimal policy frontier" (or optimal trade-off curve), which can be defined (following Fuhrer, 1997, 226) as the set of efficient combinations of inflation variability and output variability attainable by policymakers.[11] The slope of the output-inflation variability frontier is also related to the slope of the aggregate supply curve: the flatter the aggregate supply curve, the larger the increase in output variability that accompanies a reduction in inflation variability; and the higher the relative weight attached to output fluctuations in the policy loss function, the longer it will take for inflation to converge to its target value following a shock.

2   Inflation Targeting in an Open Economy

As discussed in Chapter 5, in an open economy the exchange rate is an essential component of the transmission mechanism of monetary policy; it affects the target variables of monetary policy (inflation and the output gap) through a variety of channels. There is a direct exchange-rate channel via the impact of prices of imported final goods on domestic consumer prices with a relatively short lag in general. There are also two indirect channels, operating through both aggregate demand and aggregate supply. By altering the real exchange rate, the nominal exchange rate affects aggregate demand, typically with a lag (due to the time it takes for consumers to respond to relative price changes); this affects the output gap and subsequently

---

[11]Of course, the existence of a long-run trade-off between the *variances* of output and inflation does not imply a long-run trade-off between the *levels* of these variables. In the present setting, such a trade-off only exists in the short run.

inflation itself.[12] The exchange rate may also affect aggregate supply (with or without a lag), because costs of production may depend on the cost of imported intermediate inputs, whereas nominal wages may depend on (actual or expected) changes in consumer prices caused by exchange-rate changes. In turn, the exchange rate is affected by interest rate differentials, foreign disturbances, and expectations of future exchange rates and risk premia that depend on domestic factors, such as the size of the domestic public debt or the degree of credibility of the inflation target.

The importance of the exchange rate in transmitting the effects of changes in both policy interest rates and exogenous disturbances to inflation implies that, analytically, there are at least two issues that must be addressed when studying inflation targeting rules in an open-economy setting. The first (discussed in Chapter 5) relates to the direct pass-through from exchange-rate changes to inflation. If this effect is strong, as noted by Mishkin and Savastano (2001, p. 433), the central bank cannot afford an attitude of "benign neglect" toward currency depreciations.

Suppose that, as in Ball (1999), the log of the nominal exchange rate, z_t, enters the aggregate supply and demand equations (1) and (2) as follows:[13]

$$\pi_t - \pi_{t-1} = \alpha_1 y_{t-1} + \alpha_2 g_{t-1} + \alpha_3(z_{t-1} - z_{t-2}) + \varepsilon_t,$$

$$y_t = \beta_1 y_{t-1} - \beta_2(i_{t-1} - \pi_{t-1}) + \beta_3 g_{t-1} + \beta_4 z_{t-1} + \eta_t,$$

with the exchange rate determined by

$$z_t = -\phi i_t + \zeta_t,$$

where ζ_t is an error term that captures, for instance, shocks to foreign interest rates. With a one-period lag, a depreciation raises inflation as well as aggregate demand; the former represents the pass-through effect and the second the intratemporal substitution effect (see Chapter 5). The exchange rate itself is assumed to be negatively related to the nominal interest rate, because an increase in domestic interest rates leads to capital inflows, and thus an appreciation.

Using (4) and solving as before, the optimal interest rate rule becomes, instead of (11),

$$i_t = \pi_t + b_1(\pi_t - \bar{\pi}) + b_2 y_t + b_3 g_t + b_4 z_t,$$

where $b_4 > 0$. If exchange-rate fluctuations have a large effect on aggregate demand (through β_4) and aggregate supply (through α_3, because the pass-through is high),

---

[12] The effect of exchange-rate changes on aggregate demand may also depend on the structure of indebtedness of the economy. For instance, in a country with a large foreign debt, currency fluctuations may have important wealth and balance sheet effects, possibly offsetting their direct effects on aggregate demand.

[13] Guender (2006) provides an explicit derivation of a New Keynesian open-economy version of the Phillips curve in which the *real* exchange rate appears.

the weight on the exchange rate in the modified Taylor-rule, b_4, may be quite high. However, as stressed by Mishkin and Savastano (2001, p. 434), this is not inconsistent with inflation targeting: it simply results from the fact that in this type of regime, the central bank should care about exchange-rate fluctuations (given their role in the transmission mechanism), just as it should care about output fluctuations. This result also holds under flexible targeting.

As pointed out by Mishkin and Savastano (2001, p. 439), it is possible that the pass-through from exchange-rate changes to prices be regime-dependent. After a sustained period of achievement of (low) inflation targets under a high degree of exchange-rate flexibility, the information content of the exchange rate in the expectations-formation process and price-setting behavior may well fall significantly—regardless of how open the economy is. This view seems to be corroborated by the results of Ca' Zorzi et al. (2007), who found a positive correlation between average inflation and the degree of pass-through to consumer prices, and only a weak empirical relationship between import openness and the strength of the pass-through.

In any case, responding too heavily and too frequently to movements in the nominal exchange rate entails two main problems. The first is that this may destabilize output. The reason is the effect of changes in the nominal exchange rate on inflation through tradable prices. Because it is the fastest channel from monetary policy to inflation in this model, large movements in the exchange rate can produce excessive fluctuations in output by inducing large changes in interest rates.

The second problem is that a strong and systematic interest rate response runs the risk of transforming the nominal exchange rate into an alternative anchor for monetary policy that takes precedence over the inflation target. From the perspective of the public, this could have an adverse effect on expectations; to mitigate this risk, the central bank may try to improve transparency in clarifying the role of the exchange rate (and its ability to affect aggregate demand and supply) in the determination of policy interest rates. In practice, what this means is convincing the public that the central bank's goal is only to smooth abrupt or potentially destabilizing fluctuations in the exchange rate in the short term, and not to prevent it (through systematic intervention) from adjusting to changes in fundamentals over longer horizons. In turn, improved transparency will help signal that the inflation target, and not the exchange rate, remains the primary nominal anchor of the economy.

The second issue is whether targeting inflation in nontradable prices only would be more appropriate than targeting aggregate inflation. The instantaneous policy loss function given by (13) assumes that the central bank targets *aggregate* inflation, π_t. To analyze this issue, consider for instance a shock unrelated to fundamentals that causes a persistent depreciation of the nominal exchange rate—say, a large and sustained outflow of short-term capital due to an adverse shift in confidence (Bharucha and Kent, 1998). The immediate effect is an increase in inflation in the traded goods sector. If, for instance, firms producing home goods use imported intermediated inputs (or if nominal wages are indexed to the overall price level), inflationary pressures will also develop in the nontradable goods sector and prices there may also rise, compounding the initial increase in tradable prices. Targeting aggregate inflation may involve substantial adjustment in the interest rate and increased volatility in output. By contrast, if the central bank is targeting only nontradable inflation, the adjustment of the interest rate would be of a lower magnitude, and output and nontradable inflation would be less variable—albeit at the cost of greater variability in the nominal exchange rate and aggregate inflation.

Devereux et al. (2004) also examined the choice among inflation targets using a two-sector, three-good model of a middle-income country where firms face binding borrowing constraints on the financing of investment (which occurs through international capital markets). They compare three alternative rules: a fixed exchange-rate rule and two types of inflation targeting rules (focusing on overall inflation and nontradable inflation). Their results show that the degree of exchange-rate pass-through is an important factor in the welfare ranking of alternative rules. In particular, in an economy with a very high pass-through, targeting nontradable inflation appears to be the best strategy. By contrast, in a low pass-through economy, targeting overall inflation is the most desirable policy.

In general, however, whether nontradable inflation targeting is strictly preferable to aggregate inflation targeting depends on the *nature* of the shocks hitting the economy, in addition to their relative size. In fact, targeting nontradable inflation may produce undesirable outcomes when the economy is subject to shocks other than to the exchange rate. For instance, in response to demand or supply shocks, a central bank with a nontradable inflation target is likely to attempt to restore inflation to its targeted path rapidly. This would occur through large adjustments in the interest rate—which would entail greater volatility in the exchange rate and aggregate inflation. Thus, whereas an aggregate inflation target may induce excessive volatility in the interest rate (and thus output) to offset exchange-rate shocks, a nontradable inflation target may induce excessive volatility in the exchange rate as the policy instrument is adjusted to offset supply or demand shocks. Indeed, in the simulation results presented by Bharucha and Kent (1998), neither aggregate inflation targeting nor nontradable inflation targeting produced consistently lower volatility in both product and financial markets across all types of shocks.

3   Comparison with Other Regimes

Price stability as a medium- to long-term goal can be achieved, in principle, not only by focusing directly on the final objective itself, the inflation rate or the price level, but also by adopting either a pegged nominal exchange rate or a monetary target as an intermediate goal. A third option is nominal income targeting. This section reviews these three alternative frameworks for monetary policy and compares them with inflation targeting.

3.1 ▪ Monetary Targeting

Monetary targeting presumes the existence of a stable relationship between one or more monetary aggregates and the general level of prices. When this is the case, monetary policy can be directed at a particular rate of growth in the monetary aggregate (the intermediate objective) compatible with low inflation. Specifically, monetary targeting requires adequate knowledge of the parameters characterizing the demand for money. In an economy undergoing rapid financial liberalization, however, these parameters (notably the interest elasticity of money demand) may be highly unstable. In such conditions money ceases to be a good predictor of future inflation; that is, the relation between the intermediate target and the final objective becomes unstable. Similarly, in a context of disinflation, the demand for money may be subject to large and unpredictable shifts; as a consequence, the information content of money for future inflation will be very low.

Both arguments suggest that relying on monetary aggregates can be potentially risky. In addition, suppose that monetary targeting is viewed as minimizing money growth variability around the money-growth target—a characterization that is fairly adequate if the policy loss is quadratic. As shown by Svensson (1997), this policy goal may be in conflict with the objective of minimizing inflation variability; that is, there often is a conflict between stabilizing inflation around the inflation target and stabilizing money growth around the monetary target. In fact, monetary targeting will in general imply greater inflation variability than inflation targeting. By inducing higher volatility in interest rates, it also leads to increased variability in output (Clarida et al., 1999).[14]

Another argument relates to the ability to precommit under uncertainty. Gersbach and Hahn (2006) consider a model where the public is unsure about the precision of the central bank's information on future inflation, as well as the nature of the central bank's information on the future link between money growth and inflation. They show that inflation targets are better suited for the central bank to commit to low inflation. This occurs despite the fact that, under inflation targeting, the central bank cannot perfectly commit to a certain target value (as is the case under monetary targeting), because there may be unforeseen shocks affecting the future value of inflation. The key reason is that inflation targets are more closely related to future inflation and thus make it easier for the central bank to commit to price stability.

In recent years, several industrial countries have indeed adopted inflation targeting after abandoning (or being abandoned by) their monetary targets due to increased

---

[14] See McCallum (1999) for a further discussion of the lack of efficiency of monetary targeting.

distortions in the link between the money supply and overall prices, as documented for instance by Estrella and Mishkin (1997).[15] It is worth noting, however, that although some researchers have claimed that the relationship between monetary aggregates and prices has also weakened in developing countries (see, for instance, Mishkin and Savastano, 2001, for Latin America), systematic formal evidence on this issue remains limited (particularly for the late 1990s) and subject to different interpretations. The study by Arrau et al. (1995), for instance, showed that the alleged instability in money demand documented in several studies focusing on developing countries during the 1980s may well have been the result of an omitted variable, namely financial innovation.

De Grauwe and Polan (2005) studied the relationship between money growth and inflation for a large group of countries, using both cross-section and panel data. They found a strong positive relation between the growth rate of money and inflation, in the long run, but this relation is not proportional. This lack of proportionality is not due to a systematic relationship between money growth and output growth. In low-inflation countries, money growth and output growth are independent in the long run, whereas in high-inflation countries, an increase in the growth of money leads to an increase in both inflation and velocity; as a result, the estimated coefficient of money growth typically exceeds unity in these countries. They also found that the strong link between money growth and inflation is almost wholly due to the presence of high-inflation or hyperinflation countries in the sample. The relation between inflation and money growth for low-inflation countries (on average less than 10 percent per year over 30 years) is weak, if not absent.[16] Finally, velocity tends to increase with the rate of inflation.

The implication of this study is that in low-inflation environments, money growth is not a useful signal of inflationary conditions, because it is dominated by "noise" originating from velocity shocks. By implication, the use of the money stock as a guide for steering policies toward price stability is not likely to be useful for countries with a history of low inflation.

3.2 ■ Exchange-Rate Targeting

Many countries (particularly in the developing world) have viewed pegging their nominal exchange rate to a stable low-inflation foreign currency as a means to achieve domestic price stability, through a "disciplining mechanism" with two dimensions. First, to the extent that higher domestic relative to foreign inflation results in a real

---

[15] It has also been argued that, in practice, the lack of stability and predictability in the assumed relationships between interest rates and the target monetary aggregate, and between the monetary target and inflation, have been well recognized in those countries that have pursued monetary targeting.

[16] As argued by Mendizábal (2006), the low correlation between money growth and inflation found in cross-country studies could result from pooling together countries with very dissimilar transactions technologies. Once differences in transactions costs across countries are accounted for, the correlation may turn out to be higher.

exchange-rate appreciation, the demand for domestic goods would fall and induce a cyclical downswing that would put downward pressure on domestic prices. Second, to the extent that wage- and price-setting decisions anticipate these consequences of wage and price increases being too high, they would make higher domestic inflation less likely to occur in the first place. In a sense, countries that target their exchange rates (against an anchor currency) attempt to "borrow" the foreign country's monetary policy credibility.

In addition, a key advantage of the exchange rate relative to, say, the money supply is that it is more visible, and therefore easier for the public to gather and interpret information about. In turn, this makes the exchange rate a better anchor for "tough" (anti-inflation) governments to convey credibility, as argued by Canavan and Tommasi (1997), because the signaling effect regarding the government's true preferences is stronger. This is an important consideration for countries that have attempted to stabilize from high inflation by pegging their exchange rate (see Chapter 11).

However, the experience of recent years has shown that in a world of high capital mobility and unstable capital movements, conventional pegged exchange rates have proved fragile (see Chapter 14). Most important, simply pegging the exchange rate did not prove to be a substitute for maintaining monetary stability and credibility at home. In fact, recent experiences suggest that exchange-rate pegs can be sustainable only when they are credible, and credibility is to a large extent determined by domestic macroeconomic policies. From that perspective, an inflation targeting regime may operate better than an exchange-rate targeting framework. It may even be argued that, to the extent that the domestic currency in many developing countries has been attacked because the central bank had an implicit or explicit exchange-rate objective that was not perceived to be credible, the adoption of inflation targeting may lead to a more stable currency if it signals a clear commitment to macroeconomic stability and a freely floating exchange rate.

It is worth emphasizing that a key characteristic of inflation targeting regimes compared to other approaches to controlling inflation is that the adjustment of policy instruments relies on a systematic assessment of *future* (rather than past or current) inflation, as opposed to an arbitrary forecast.[17] Under this regime, the central bank must explicitly quantify an inflation target and establish precise mechanisms to achieve this target. This implies that there is an important *operational* difference between an inflation targeting regime, on the one hand, and monetary and exchange-rate targeting, on the other.[18] Changes in monetary policy instruments usually affect

---

[17] In practice, central banks typically use an unchanged-interest rate assumption in deriving inflation forecasts, that is, expected inflation is derived conditional on the interest rate not being changed throughout the forecast-feedback horizon. See Leitemo (2006) for a discussion of the properties of this approach.

[18] Note also that there is an important difference between exchange-rate targeting and monetary targeting, in the sense that while it is possible to deviate temporarily from monetary targets if the underlying relationships appear to have changed, it is generally not possible to depart temporarily from an exchange-rate peg (or a target band, for that matter) without there being a loss of credibility and possibly a currency crisis.

the money supply and the exchange rate faster than inflation itself; as discussed earlier, this leads to the existence of a control lag and a reaction function that relates the policy instrument to an inflation forecast. The implication is that the credibility of an inflation targeting regime depends not on achieving a publicly observable, intermediate target that is viewed as a leading indicator of future inflation (as is the case under monetary or exchange-rate targeting), but rather on the credibility of a *promise* to reach the inflation target in the future. This in turn depends on whether the public believes that the central bank will stick resolutely to the objective of price stability. Credibility and reputation of the monetary authorities may therefore play an even more crucial role in dampening inflation expectations under inflation targeting. At the same time, because performance can only be observed ex post, the need for transparency and accountability becomes more acute under inflation targeting, in order to help the public assess the stance of monetary policy and determine whether deviations from target are due to unpredictable shocks rather than policy mistakes.

3.3 ■ Nominal Income Targeting

Nominal income targeting (NIT) is typically viewed as an alternative to flexible inflation targeting (FIT). The focus on nominal income growth is often motivated by uncertainty regarding estimates of the output gap. To illustrate the difference between the two regimes for optimal monetary policy, we consider the model in Frisch and Staudinger (2003), which consists of a forward-looking Phillips curve relation and a forward-looking aggregate demand equation, as in Clarida et al. (1999) and Svensson (2003). Thus, the model is in contrast to the backward-looking specification used earlier. Specifically, the model consists of the following equations:

$$\pi_t = \mathbb{E}_t \pi_{t+1} + \alpha_1 y_t + \varepsilon_t, \quad \alpha_1 > 0, \tag{19}$$

$$y_t = \beta_1 \mathbb{E}_t y_{t+1} - \beta_2 (i_t - \mathbb{E}_t \pi_{t+1}) + \eta_t, \quad \beta_1, \beta_2 > 0, \tag{20}$$

where $\mathbb{E}_t \pi_{t+1}$ ($\mathbb{E}_t y_{t+1}$) is the expected inflation rate (output gap) of the next period based on the information available in period t.[19] The processes driving the disturbance terms η_t and ε_t are given by:

$$\varepsilon_t = \rho_\varepsilon \varepsilon_{t-1} + \nu_t. \tag{21}$$

$$\eta_t = \rho_\eta \eta_{t-1} + \zeta_t. \tag{22}$$

---

[19] In an appendix to their paper, Frisch and Staudinger (2003) examine the case of a two-period control lag, as in the simplified Svensson model presented earlier. The qualitative conclusions remain the same as those discussed below.

Both disturbances follow a first-order autoregressive process, with $0 \leq \rho_\varepsilon, \rho_\eta \leq 1$; v_t and ζ_t are i.i.d. random variables with zero mean and constant variance σ_v^2 and σ_ζ^2, respectively. For $\rho_\varepsilon = \rho_\eta = 0$, the shocks are purely transitory (as before), whereas for $\rho_\varepsilon = \rho_\eta = 1$ both shocks follow a random walk process. The model also assumes no lag between changes in the output gap and inflation, and no lag between changes in the (real) interest rate and the output gap.

The central bank's policy objective is, as in (14):

$$\min_{i_t} U_t = \mathbb{E}_t \left\{ \sum_{j=0}^{\infty} \delta^j \left[\frac{(\pi_{t+j} - \tilde{\pi})^2 + \lambda y_{t+j}^2}{2} \right] \right\}, \tag{23}$$

where δ is a discount factor, $\tilde{\pi}$ the inflation target, and λ measures the relative weight on the output gap.

Setting $\beta_1 = 1$ for simplicity, and substituting (20) in (19) yields

$$\pi_t = \mathbb{E}_t \pi_{t+1} + \alpha_1 [\beta_1 \mathbb{E}_t y_{t+1} - \beta_2 (i_t - \mathbb{E}_t \pi_{t+1}) + \eta_t] + \varepsilon_t. \tag{24}$$

Because i_t affects only y_t and π_t, the optimization problem boils down to solving a period-t problem only:

$$\min_{i_t} \left[\frac{(\pi_t - \tilde{\pi})^2 + \lambda y_t^2}{2} \right],$$

subject to (24). The optimality condition is

$$y_t + \frac{\alpha_1}{\lambda} (\pi_t - \tilde{\pi}) = 0, \tag{25}$$

from which it can be seen that $\pi_t = \tilde{\pi}$ under strict inflation targeting ($\lambda = 0$). Using (19) and (20), it can be established that

$$\beta_2 i_t = (\alpha_1 \Phi + \beta_2) \mathbb{E}_t \pi_{t+1} + \alpha_1 \Phi \varepsilon_t - \alpha_1 \Phi \tilde{\pi} + \eta_t + \mathbb{E}_t y_{t+1}, \tag{26}$$

where $\Phi = 1/(\lambda + \alpha_1^2)$. It can be noted that the coefficient on expected inflation is larger than unity: following a shock to that variable, the central bank must raise the nominal interest rate so as to ensure an increase in the real interest rate.

Substituting this optimal condition back into (24) yields

$$\pi_t = \Phi \lambda (\mathbb{E}_t \pi_{t+1} + \varepsilon_t) + \alpha_1^2 \Phi \tilde{\pi}. \tag{27}$$

This equation can be solved by using the method of undetermined coefficients (see Minford and Peel, 2002). Conjecturing a solution of the form

$$\pi_t = \kappa_1 \bar{\pi} + \kappa_2 \varepsilon_t, \tag{28}$$

implies that $\pi_{t+1} = \kappa_1 \bar{\pi} + \kappa_2 \varepsilon_{t+1}$, so that, using (21):

$$\mathbb{E}_t \pi_{t+1} = \kappa_1 \bar{\pi} + \kappa_2 \mathbb{E}_t \varepsilon_{t+1} = \kappa_1 \bar{\pi} + \kappa_2 \rho_\varepsilon \varepsilon_t.$$

Substituting this expression in (28) and rearranging terms yields

$$\pi_t = (\alpha_1^2 + \lambda \kappa_1)\Phi \bar{\pi} + \lambda(1 + \kappa_2 \rho_\varepsilon)\Phi \varepsilon_t. \tag{29}$$

Equating coefficients in (28) and (29) yields

$$\kappa_1 = (\alpha_1^2 + \lambda \kappa_1)\Phi, \quad \kappa_2 = \lambda(1 + \kappa_2 \rho_\varepsilon)\Phi,$$

which can be rearranged to give

$$\kappa_1 = 1, \quad \kappa_2 = \frac{\lambda}{\lambda(1 - \rho_\varepsilon) + \alpha_1^2}.$$

Thus, the solution for π_t is

$$\pi_t = \bar{\pi} + \lambda \theta \varepsilon_t, \tag{30}$$

where

$$\theta = \frac{1}{\lambda(1 - \rho_\varepsilon) + \alpha_1^2}.$$

Substituting (30) in (25) yields

$$y_t = -\left(\frac{\alpha_1}{\lambda}\right)(\pi_t - \bar{\pi}) = -\left(\frac{\alpha_1}{\lambda}\right)\lambda \theta \varepsilon_t,$$

that is

$$y_t = -\alpha_1 \theta \varepsilon_t. \tag{31}$$

From (21) and (30), $\mathbb{E}_t \pi_{t+1}$ is given by

$$\mathbb{E}_t \pi_{t+1} = \kappa_1 \bar{\pi} + \lambda \theta \mathbb{E}_t \varepsilon_{t+1} = \bar{\pi} + \lambda \theta \rho_\varepsilon \varepsilon_t, \tag{32}$$

whereas from (21) and (31):

$$\mathbb{E}_t y_{t+1} = -\alpha_1 \theta \rho_\varepsilon \varepsilon_t. \tag{33}$$

Combining (26), (32), and (33) yields the interest rate rule:

$$i_t = \bar{\pi} + \frac{(\alpha_1 + \beta_2 \lambda \rho_\varepsilon)}{\beta_2} \theta \varepsilon_t + \frac{\eta_t}{\beta_2}. \tag{34}$$

The complete solution of the model consists therefore of (30), (31), and (34).

These equations show that a demand shock (a rise in η_t) entails no trade-off between inflation and output; as implied by (30) and (31), the shock is entirely eliminated by the optimal monetary policy. Indeed, as shown in (34), the nominal interest rate rises by η_t/β_2 to perfectly offset the shock.

In the case of a supply shock, however, a trade-off exists between output and inflation. From (30) and (31), a rise in ε_t, for instance, lowers output and raises prices. The "slope" of the trade-off depends on λ, as before: under strict inflation targeting ($\lambda = 0$), the shock has no effect on inflation (which in this case remains tied to $\bar{\pi}$) and the drop in the output gap is maximized, whereas in the opposite case ($\lambda \to \infty$, or "strict" output targeting), the output gap does not change, but the inflationary effect is maximized.

The interest rate rule (34) implies that, as long as $\lambda < \infty$, the optimal policy response is an increase in the real interest rate—that is, the nominal interest rate must rise by more than the increase in the inflation rate.[20]

We now consider nominal income targeting. Equations (19) and (20) are the same as before, but the loss function is now

$$\min_{i_t} U_t = \mathbb{E}_t \left\{ \sum_{j=0}^{\infty} \delta^j \left[\frac{[(y_{t+j} - y_{t+j-1}) + \pi_{t+j} - \Theta]^2}{2} \right] \right\}, \tag{35}$$

where Θ is the target growth rate of nominal income (assumed exogenous). The first-order condition is now

$$y_t - y_{t-1} + \pi_t = \Theta,$$

which implies that the nominal interest rate has to be chosen such that nominal income growth equals its target value in every period.

---

[20] In models as simple as the one considered here, a forward-looking rule in which the nominal interest rate responds more than proportionately to increases in expected inflation ensures also that the behavior of the economy is determinate. However, this is not necessarily the case in more general models; see Carlstrom and Fuerst (2005).

Combining this condition with (19) and (20) yields

$$\beta_2 i_t = (\Phi' + \beta_2)\mathbb{E}_t\pi_{t+1} + \Phi'\varepsilon_t - \Phi'\Theta - \Phi'y_{t-1} + \mathbb{E}_t y_{t+1} + \eta_t, \qquad (36)$$

where $\Phi' = 1/(1+\alpha_1)$. Again, the coefficient on expected inflation is larger than unity.

Substituting (36) in (20) yields

$$y_t = \Phi'y_{t-1} - \Phi'\mathbb{E}_t\pi_{t+1} - \Phi'\varepsilon_t + \Phi'\Theta. \qquad (37)$$

Again using the method of undetermined coefficients, we can postulate a solution for π_t and y_t of the form

$$\pi_t = \kappa_{11}y_{t-1} + \kappa_{12}\varepsilon_t + \kappa_{13}\Theta, \qquad (38)$$

$$y_t = \kappa_{21}y_{t-1} + \kappa_{22}\varepsilon_t + \kappa_{23}\Theta. \qquad (39)$$

From (38), shifting the time index one period, substituting for y_t from (39), and taking expectations yields

$$\mathbb{E}_t\pi_{t+1} = \kappa_{11}\kappa_{21}y_{t-1} + (\kappa_{12}\rho_\varepsilon + \kappa_{11}\kappa_{22})\varepsilon_t + (\kappa_{13} + \kappa_{11}\kappa_{23})\Theta.$$

Substituting this expression in (19), respectively in (37), and comparing with (38), respectively (39), yields

$$\kappa_{11} = (\kappa_{11} + \alpha_1)\kappa_{21},$$

$$\kappa_{21} = (\kappa_{12}\rho_\varepsilon + \kappa_{11}\kappa_{22}) + 1 + \alpha_1\kappa_{22},$$

$$\kappa_{13} = \kappa_{13} + \kappa_{11}\kappa_{23} + \alpha_1\kappa_{23},$$

$$\kappa_{21} = \Phi'(1 - \kappa_{11}\kappa_{21}),$$

$$\kappa_{22} = -\Phi'(\kappa_{12}\rho_\varepsilon + \kappa_{11}\kappa_{22} + 1),$$

$$\kappa_{23} = -\Phi'(\kappa_{13} + \kappa_{11}\kappa_{23} - 1).$$

Solving this system yields

$$\kappa_{11} = -A,$$

$$\kappa_{12} = (A + 1 - \rho_\varepsilon)[(1 - \rho_\varepsilon)^2 - \alpha_1 \rho_\varepsilon],$$

$$\kappa_{13} = 1,$$

$$\kappa_{21} = 1 + A,$$

$$\kappa_{22} = -\kappa_{12},$$

$$\kappa_{23} = 0,$$

where $A = (\alpha_1 - \sqrt{\alpha_1^2 + 4\alpha_1})/2 < 0$ and $1 + A > 0$. Substituting these results in (38) and (39) gives[21]

$$\pi_t = -Ay_{t-1} + \frac{A + (1 - \rho_\varepsilon)}{(1 - \rho_\varepsilon)^2 - \alpha_1 \rho_\varepsilon} \varepsilon_t + \Theta, \tag{40}$$

$$y_t = (1 + A)y_{t-1} - \frac{A + (1 - \rho_\varepsilon)}{(1 - \rho_\varepsilon)^2 - \alpha_1 \rho_\varepsilon} \varepsilon_t + \Theta, \tag{41}$$

$$i_t = \zeta_1 y_{t-1} + \frac{\zeta_2}{\beta_2(1 + \alpha_1)} \varepsilon_t + \Theta + \frac{\eta_t}{\beta_2}, \tag{42}$$

where

$$\zeta_1 = \frac{\Phi'}{\beta_2}[A + \alpha_1(1 + A)^2 - A\beta_2(1 + A)(1 + \alpha_1)],$$

$$\zeta_2 = 1 + \frac{A + (1 - \rho_\varepsilon)}{(1 - \rho_\varepsilon)^2 - \alpha_1 \rho_\varepsilon}[\{\beta_2(1 + \alpha_1) - \alpha_1\}(A + \rho_\varepsilon) - (1 + \alpha_1)\}].$$

From (40) and (41), it can be seen that the effects of a demand shock are fully absorbed under NIT; neither the output nor the inflation rate are affected. As shown in (42), the nominal rate rises sufficiently to fully offset the demand shock. This is also the case under FIT, as shown earlier.

---

[21]Given that y_{t-1} appears in these solutions, the issue of dynamic stability arises now, in contrast to the case of FIT. Frisch and Staudinger show that, because $1 + A \in (0, 1)$, the model is always stable.

By contrast, a supply shock cannot be neutralized under NIT. As shown by (40) and (41), a positive shock to ε_t leads to exactly offsetting changes in inflation (which increases) and the output gap (which falls).

To compare the two regimes, a natural criterion is to focus on the variance of inflation and output. Under FIT, (30) and (31) yield

$$\sigma_\pi^2\big|_{FIT} = \frac{\lambda^2 \sigma_\varepsilon^2}{[\lambda(1-\rho_\varepsilon)+\alpha_1^2]^2}, \ \sigma_y^2\big|_{FIT} = \frac{\alpha_1^2 \sigma_\varepsilon^2}{[\lambda(1-\rho_\varepsilon)+\alpha_1^2]^2},$$

whereas under NIT (40) and (41) yield

$$\sigma_\pi^2\big|_{NIT} = \sigma_y^2\big|_{NIT} = \frac{[(1-\rho_\varepsilon)+A]^2 \sigma_\varepsilon^2}{[(1-\rho_\varepsilon)^2 - \alpha_1 \rho_\varepsilon]^2}.$$

A comparison of these results shows that $\sigma_\pi^2\big|_{FIT} < \sigma_\pi^2\big|_{NIT}$ requires

$$\lambda < -\frac{[(1-\rho_\varepsilon)+A]\alpha_1^2}{\alpha_1 \rho_\varepsilon + A(1-\rho_\varepsilon)}.$$

The right-hand side of the above expression is positive, so it imposes an upper bound on λ. Thus, FIT gives a lower variability of inflation only if the degree of "flexibility" is not too high.

Similarly, it can be established that the condition $\sigma_y^2\big|_{NIT} < \sigma_y^2\big|_{FIT}$ requires

$$\lambda < \frac{\alpha_1(1-\rho_\varepsilon)^2 - \alpha_1^2(1+A)}{A(1-\rho_\varepsilon) + (1-\rho_\varepsilon)^2},$$

which indicates that unless the degree of flexibility under FIT is sufficiently high, the variability of the output gap will be smaller under NIT.

In sum, for both targeting regimes, optimal monetary policy response entails an interest rate that responds to both demand and supply shocks. In addition, a positive shock to expected inflation leads in both cases to an increase in the nominal interest rate that must be large enough to entail a rise in the real interest rate. Second, both strategies imply the same response to a demand shock—a complete offset through interest rates, which leaves inflation and the output gap unchanged. Third, if the shock is a supply disturbance, there is a significant difference between the performance of the two strategies. If the central bank follows inflation targeting, the policymakers face a trade-off between inflation and output stabilization. This trade-off depends on the preference parameter attached to output stabilization relative to inflation stabilization. A large value of λ implies an accommodative monetary policy, that is, strong output stabilization at the expense of high inflation, whereas a small value implies low inflation at the expense of high output losses, that is, a non-accommodative policy.

A broad implication of the foregoing analysis is that there are conditions under which nominal income targeting may perform better than inflation targeting—although not uniformly so. Using a closed-economy model with both sticky wages and prices, Kim and Henderson (2005) found that nominal income growth targeting dominates inflation targeting (from a welfare perspective), for a range of plausible parameter values. Numerical simulation results by Jensen (2002) also show that when shocks causing an inflation-output gap trade-off in monetary policy are important, nominal income growth targeting performs better, in the sense that it leads to more stable inflation than under inflation targeting—essentially by creating greater inertia in official interest rates.

However, more research on comparing these alternative strategies may be warranted, particularly in an open-economy context. Guender and Tam (2004) offer a contribution in that direction. Using an extended version of the small open economy model in Turnovsky (1983), and using a range of empirically plausible parameter values, they found that strict adherence to a nominal income targeting rule may cause excessive fluctuations in the exchange rate and thus in the overall price level. The higher the degree of openness, or the stronger the sensitivity of aggregate supply to changes in the real exchange rate, the more pronounced these fluctuations are. Inflation targeting appears therefore preferable for a small open economy, particularly for those that are highly dependent on imported intermediate goods.

4   Basic Requirements for Inflation Targeting

There are five basic requirements for implementing an inflation targeting regime. The first is a high degree of central bank independence (not so much in choosing the inflation target itself but rather in the choice and manipulation of policy instruments), the second the absence of a de facto targeting of the nominal exchange rate (or, equivalently, the predominance of the inflation target), the third a sufficiently strong financial system, the fourth increased transparency and accountability, and the fifth the technical ability to forecast inflation. In what follows we discuss in more detail the first four requirements.

4.1 ■ Central Bank Independence and Credibility

Inflation targeting requires that the central bank be endowed by the political authorities with a clear mandate to pursue the objective of price stability and, most important, a large degree of independence in the *conduct* of monetary policy—namely, in choosing the instruments necessary to achieve the target rate of inflation, as opposed to choosing the target itself.[22] This implies, in particular, the ability to resist political pressures to stimulate the economy in the short term.

Inflation targeting calls not only for a high degree of central bank independence, but also for a sufficient degree of credibility—or, more properly, an adequate anti-inflation reputation (see Chapter 11). Independence, credibility, and reputation are of course related but may evolve differently over a given period of time. In countries where the financial system is perceived to be highly vulnerable (to, say, exchange-rate shocks, as discussed below) and the central bank is perceived to be likely to inject liquidity to prevent a full-blown crisis, the credibility of an announced inflation may be seriously undermined—even if the central bank is deemed independent. Lack of confidence in the policymakers' commitment to (or ability to maintain) low inflation may be one of the reasons why inflation tends often to display a strong degree of persistence in developing countries.[23] But establishing credibility or improving reputation, particularly in countries with a history of high inflation and macroeconomic instability, is a difficult process. Analytically, it has been shown—most notably by Walsh (1995)—that inflation targets can be used as a way of overcoming credibility problems because they can mimic optimal performance incentive contracts; and by increasing the accountability of monetary policy, inflation targeting may reduce the inflation bias inherent in discretionary policy regimes. Moreover, as argued by Walsh (1999), the public announcement of inflation targets may itself help to improve the credibility of the central bank when its policy preferences are uncertain.

4.2 ■ Absence of Fiscal Dominance

Fiscal dominance exists when fiscal policy considerations play an overwhelming role in monetary policy decisions. In countries where systematic reliance on seigniorage as a source of revenue is high (a situation that characterizes countries where government borrowing from the central bank is large), fiscally induced inflationary pressures will undermine the effectiveness of monetary policy by forcing, for instance, the central bank to maintain low interest rates in an attempt to prevent unsustainable public debt dynamics.

An unsustainable fiscal policy may hinder the effectiveness of monetary policy—to the point that an increase in interest rates can have a perverse effect on inflation. Indeed, as argued by Blanchard (2004), if the initial level of public debt is high, an increase in the real interest rate may increase the probability of default on that debt, making domestic government debt less attractive and leading to a real

---

[22]Some countries have indeed followed a contractual approach to inflation targeting; the government sets an inflation target in a contract with the central bank, and gives the central bank operational independence so that it can manipulate its policy instruments to achieve the agreed target.

[23]Inflation persistence may also be the result of overlapping and asynchronized wage and price contracts. See Chapter 11.

depreciation—rather than an appreciation, as in the conventional case. In such conditions, inflation targeting can clearly have perverse effects: a rise in the real interest in response to higher inflation leads to a real depreciation which, in turn, may lead to a further increase in inflation.

4.3 ■ Absence of de facto Exchange-Rate Targeting

Adopting a low and stable inflation rate as the main objective of monetary policy requires in principle the absence of any commitment to a particular value of the exchange rate, as is the case under a floating exchange-rate regime. In practice, however, in many of the developing countries that have opted for a de jure flexible exchange rate, monetary authorities have continued to pay considerable attention to the value of the domestic currency—often adopting a de facto target path or band. There are various reasons for the central bank to be concerned with nominal exchange-rate movements, even when its degree of independence (and thus its ability to commit itself only to the pursuit of price stability) is high. As noted earlier, the exchange rate has a direct impact on inflation and plays a key role in transmitting monetary policy shocks to prices. If the pass-through effect is indeed high, the central bank may be tempted to intervene in the foreign exchange market to limit currency fluctuations. A high degree of nominal exchange-rate instability may also be of concern to policymakers to the extent that it translates into a high degree of variability in the real exchange rate and distorted relative price signals to domestic producers. Another important reason is that in (partially) dollarized economies, large fluctuations in exchange rates can lead to banking and financial instability by inducing large portfolio shifts between domestic- and foreign-currency-denominated assets. Finally, in countries where the corporate and banking sectors hold large foreign-currency liabilities, exchange-rate depreciations can have significant adverse effects on their balance sheets (see Chapters 5 and 9).[24]

When limiting (or preventing) exchange-rate fluctuations is a stated or an implicit policy target, it usually will be very difficult for the central bank to convey to the public its intention to give priority to price stability over other objectives of monetary policy in a credible and transparent manner. Private agents are likely to discount public pronouncements heavily; and the lack of credibility will translate into higher inflation expectations. Thus, the absence of (implicit or explicit) commitment to a particular level for the exchange rate—or, equivalently, giving the inflation target unambiguous priority over other policy objectives—is an important prerequisite for adopting inflation targeting. In fact, a credible commitment to an inflation targeting regime in developing economies, by enhancing macroeconomic and financial stability, may well provide a greater degree of stability to a flexible nominal exchange rate

---

[24] It should be noted, however, that these last two points can also be viewed as calling for adequate regulation and supervision of the domestic banking system, as opposed to representing arguments in favor of a rejection of inflation targeting as a policy regime.

than a pegged arrangement that is subject to recurrent speculative pressures (and possibly frequent crises and forced devaluations) due to perceived inconsistencies in macroeconomic policy.

4.4 ■ Healthy Financial System

To implement an inflation targeting regime, it is essential to have a banking system that is sufficiently healthy. Weaknesses in the banking system (in the form, for instance, of a large proportion of nonperforming loans) may constrain the ability of the central bank to manipulate interest rates. Following a positive shock to inflation, for instance, the central bank may be unable to raise its policy rate because of the fear that higher market rates can lead to higher default among banks' borrowers and therefore put further pressure on banks' balance sheets. The ability of the central bank to conduct an independent monetary policy may also be hampered if weaknesses in the financial system require repeated injections of liquidity to support ailing banks. Improving loan-loss provision ratios, and aggressive recapitalization programs, may often need to precede (or be part of) an orderly transition toward inflation targeting.

4.5 ■ Transparency and Accountability

Openness and transparency in the conduct of monetary policy are important ways to improve credibility in an inflation targeting framework. By making the central bank publicly accountable for its decisions, they raise the incentive to achieve the inflation target and therefore enhance the public's confidence in the ability of the monetary authorities to do so. And by exposing to public scrutiny the process through which monetary policy decisions are taken, they may lead to improved decision-making by the central bank and enhanced credibility. The fact, for instance, that monetary authorities must announce policy changes and explain the reason for these changes to the public may increase the effectiveness of monetary policy under inflation targeting. By reducing uncertainty about the central bank's preferences, transparency may lead to a lower expected rate of inflation and a lower propensity to respond to supply shocks.[25]

To illustrate these arguments, consider for instance the model in Faust and Svensson (2001), where the central bank's goals and intentions (in terms of its desired levels of inflation and employment) are unobservable to the public and must be inferred from policy outcomes. Transparency is defined solely in terms of the unobservable portion of the inflation control error. They show that increased transparency is generally good, in the sense that it makes the private sector expectations and the

---

[25] See Geraats (2014) for an overview of the literature. Some of the studies reviewed show indeed that improvements in transparency have helped to anchor private sector inflation expectations. Comparable studies, however, are not available for developing countries.

central bank's reputation and credibility more sensitive to its actions. As a result, the central bank's incentive to act discretionarily (that is, to initiate inflation surprises to achieve its desired level of employment) is dampened, inducing it to follow a policy that is closer to the socially optimal one.

However, it is possible also for greater transparency to have an adverse effect on inflation through changes in expectations. Eijffinger and Tesfaselassie (2007) study disclosure policy when a central bank has private information on the future (as opposed to current) state of the economy. They show that the effects of advance disclosure depend on the presence of uncertainty about policy targets when the shock occurs. With uncertainty about policy targets, disclosure is harmless to current outcomes, owing to the strong dependence of inflation expectations on policy actions, which induces the central bank to focus exclusively on price stability. By contrast, if the central bank's targets are common knowledge, disclosure of future shocks impairs stabilization of current inflation and output.

In practice, a potential problem with accountability in an inflation targeting framework is related to the difficulty of assessing performance only on the basis of inflation outcomes. The reason is that (as indicated earlier) there is a lag between policy actions and their impact on the economy; it is thus possible (or tempting) for the central bank to blame "unforeseen" or totally unpredictable events for inadequate performance, instead of taking responsibility for policy mistakes. To mitigate this risk, in inflation-targeting countries the central bank is usually required to justify its policy decisions and publicly explain differences between actual outcomes and inflation targets.[26] Openness and transparency have been promoted also by the regular publication of an *Inflation Report*, which sets out the central bank's analysis of recent economic developments, and a forecast of inflation (as well as other variables, including output) over the coming year or years. However, although in practice the most transparent central banks tend to be all inflation targeters, inflation targeting appears to be neither a necessary nor a sufficient condition for transparency (see Geraats, 2014).

Accountability has been promoted by providing public explanations (in the form of a public letter from the governor of the central bank to the government) of the reason(s) why the rate of inflation deviated from the target by more than a given percentage on either side, how long these deviations are expected to persist, and what policies the central bank intends to implement to bring inflation back to target.

5   Performance of Inflation Targeting Regimes

Empirical research on the performance of IT regimes has followed two main methodological approaches, both of which involve a before-after comparison. The first

---

[26]The distinction between goal independence and instrument independence, alluded to earlier, implies that the latter is essential for accountability of the monetary authorities.

approach has focused on macroeconomic outcomes following the adoption of these regimes, compared to non-IT countries. In that context, the debate has focused mainly on whether the adoption of IT has contributed to substantial declines in average inflation, lower inflation volatility, and general macroeconomic stability (including greater fiscal discipline), compared to those countries that have maintained a different monetary policy regime. The second approach has focused on central bank behavior under IT and non-IT. The key issue in that context has been the extent to which the adoption of IT has changed central bank behavior in a substantive way, and in particular responses to inflation and output gaps, but also, in some cases, with respect to exchange rates or asset prices. In most cases, the methodology has involved estimating simple and augmented interest rate rules.

Agénor and Pereira da Silva (2013) provided a thorough examination of the formal empirical evidence on the performance of IT regimes in major developing countries. Empirical studies based on the first approach suggest that IT regimes in these countries have been fairly successful—even more so, in several regards, than in industrial countries. Except for periods of severe external shocks, IT countries were successful in meeting their targets, and the output sacrifice ratio (the percentage fall in output resulting from a one-percentage-point reduction in inflation) was lower after the adoption of IT in these countries compared with other groups. Indeed, the level of expected inflation fell in many IT developing countries (relative to the control group), and both the variability of expected inflation and the average absolute forecast error (controlling for the level and variability of past inflation) fell significantly. Inflation persistence also declined in IT countries—a result that is consistent with the view that IT has played a role in strengthening the effect of forward-looking expectations on inflation, hence weakening the degree of inflation inertia. The reduction in volatility and the degree of persistence of inflation expectations also suggests that IT has been associated with improved credibility of monetary policy. However, there appears to be no consensus across studies on whether IT has contributed to a reduction in output volatility.

There is also limited evidence that IT may have been associated with reduced fiscal imbalances—possibly because lower inflation expectations tend to reduce interest rates and weaken the adverse effects of debt service on the budget, or because IT has been associated with greater fiscal discipline—and a lower pass-through effect. However, the evidence on these two issues (especially the first) is less conclusive. In addition, even though the pass-through effect may have weakened, in many developing countries it continues to play a central role in the monetary transmission mechanism.

Empirical studies based on the second approach (policy reaction functions) suggest that IT central banks in many developing countries have become more responsive to deviations in actual inflation from target—improving, in so doing, prospects for macroeconomic stability. From that perspective, the fact some studies found a positive effect of asset prices and/or exchange rates in interest rate rules does not necessarily reflect a deliberate attempt to target asset prices or the exchange rate, but rather an indirect response to the impact that these variables have on aggregate demand.

Overall, and regardless of the methodology used, most recent studies reach similar conclusions; the adoption of an IT regime in developing countries has led to lower average inflation rates and reduced inflation volatility compared to a control group of non-IT countries, and possibly to a lower exchange rate pass-through. Operating procedures of IT central banks have also become more responsive to inflation gaps. Although in achieving these outcomes most developing countries benefited from the period of "Great Moderation" in world inflation, as well as from deep structural reforms, the IT regime may have led to important institutional changes in the conduct of macroeconomic policy.

However, despite its performance during the past decade, and the continued acceptance that the main medium- to long-run goal of monetary policy is the pursuit of price stability, Agénor and Pereira da Silva (2013) identify several challenges to IT regimes in middle-income countries. These challenges include:

(*a*) mitigating the risk of fiscal dominance in some countries where public debt-to-GDP ratios remain high and future fiscal liabilities associated with health care and pensions spending loom large, therefore affecting inflation expectations today;

(*b*) managing terms-of-trade shocks, which have often proved to be quite persistent, feeding into domestic prices through wage indexation and sustained increases in inflationary expectations;

(*c*) mitigating exchange-rate volatility, given the role of the exchange rate in the monetary transmission mechanism (see Chapter 5);

(*d*) maintaining credibility, which can be lost quickly and take significant time to be restored;

(*e*) addressing financial stability concerns.

Challenge (*e*) will be addressed in the next section. Regarding (*c*), adopting an IT regime requires (as noted earlier) the absence of any commitment to a particular value of the exchange rate, and therefore to let the currency float freely (apart from smoothing interventions). In practice, however, in many developing countries that have opted for a de jure flexible exchange rate, monetary authorities have continued to pay considerable attention to the value of the domestic currency—often adopting a de facto target path or band. There are various reasons for the central bank to be concerned with nominal exchange-rate movements, even when its degree of independence (and thus its ability to commit itself only to the pursuit of price stability) is high. As noted earlier, the exchange rate has a direct impact on inflation and plays a key role in transmitting monetary policy shocks to prices. If the pass-through effect is indeed high, the central bank may be tempted to intervene on the foreign exchange market to limit currency fluctuations.

A high degree of nominal exchange-rate instability may also be of concern to policymakers to the extent that it translates into a high degree of variability in the real exchange rate and distorted relative price signals to domestic producers. Another important consideration is that in dollarized economies large fluctuations in exchange rates can lead to banking and financial instability by inducing portfolio shifts between domestic- and foreign-currency-denominated assets. Finally, in countries where the corporate and banking sectors hold large foreign-currency liabilities, exchange-rate depreciations can have significant adverse effects on their balance sheets. The higher the degree of financial sector integration with global markets, the higher the probability for corporations and banks to access foreign-currency resources. Despite adequate financial regulation and supervision and the availability of hedging instruments, sudden reversals of flows and exchange-rate volatility can have damaging effects on the real economy.

When limiting exchange-rate fluctuations is a stated or an implicit policy target, it will usually be difficult for the central bank to convey to the public its intention to give priority to price stability over other objectives of monetary policy in a credible and transparent manner. Private agents are likely to discount and/or get confused by public pronouncements; in turn, lack of credibility will translate into higher inflation expectations. Thus, the absence of (implicit or explicit) commitment to a particular level for the exchange rate—or, equivalently, giving the inflation target unambiguous priority over other policy objectives—is in principle important for the functioning of an IT regime. In practice, however, this has not been the case in developing countries.

Almost from the moment they adopted IT, many developing countries started to develop a so-called fear of floating, which has led policymakers to take deliberate policy actions to stabilize the exchange rate (Calvo and Reinhart, 2002). The reasons for a country to fear floating exchange rates and currency volatility are varied—they include underdeveloped markets for foreign exchange (which limits the availability of hedging instruments), a short history of stable inflation, high exchange rate pass-through (as discussed earlier), adverse effects on competitiveness, the existence of a large debt in foreign currency, balance sheet effects, and the fact that excessive currency appreciation may exacerbate risk-taking behavior by financial intermediaries.[27] The latter effects can be powerful enough to dominate other effects of the exchange rate through more standard channels.

In addition to fear-of-floating considerations, there is a clear theoretical rationale for monetary policy to react to the exchange rate in developing countries that are highly vulnerable to terms-of-trade shocks and have underdeveloped financial systems. In such situations, stabilizing domestic output in the face of external shocks may prove difficult. Indeed, both Aghion et al. (2009) and Aizenman et al. (2011) argued that in such environments it is optimal for the central bank to pursue an interest rate rule that accounts for movements in the real exchange rate. Céspedes et al. (2004), Morón and Winkelried (2005), and Cavoli and Rajan (2006) also suggest that there may be some benefit from including the exchange rate in the reaction function of an IT central bank in financially vulnerable economies. In the same vein, Roger et al. (2009) and Garcia et al. (2011) found that for financially

---

[27] Ghosh (2013) for instance found that in countries where the exchange rate pass-through is high, the degree of exchange rate flexibility tends to be weaker.

robust economies, putting a small weight on exchange-rate smoothing is beneficial in handling risk premium shocks, with no significant adverse consequences for inflation or output performance. For financially vulnerable economies, some exchange-rate smoothing is found to be even more beneficial, largely reflecting perverse effects of demand shocks on exchange-rate movements.

Regarding (*d*), as discussed earlier the credibility of an IT regime depends on the credibility of a promise to reach the inflation target in the future. Establishing the credibility of an IT regime has therefore proved elusive in some cases—occurring only over an extended time frame, keeping inflationary expectations and risk premia high in the process. In countries where the preference for output and employment stability is perceived to be high to begin with, or to increase significantly when the unemployment rises above a threshold level, the credibility of an announced inflation target may be significantly undermined. Lack of confidence in the policymakers' commitment to (or ability to maintain) low inflation may be one of the reasons why inflation tends often to display a strong degree of persistence in developing countries (see Agénor and Bayraktar, 2010); low credibility tends to impart a strong backward-looking component to inflation expectations. Indeed, an important lesson of the experience of developing countries during the past two decades, as discussed in the previous section, is that uncertainty about the central bank's preferences over output and inflation may adversely affect credibility, and that price shocks may have large asymmetric effects on credibility. Overshooting the inflation target (possibly out of excessive concern for limiting short-run output losses) may be highly costly in terms of lost credibility, in contrast to undershooting, that is, inflation below target. In addition, credibility depends not only on the level of deviations from target, but also on how long these deviations last.

6   Inflation Targeting and Financial Stability

The global financial crisis triggered by the collapse of the subprime mortgage market in the United States was a clear reminder that although financially integrated markets have benefits, they also carry substantial risks, with potentially large real economic consequences. Increasing interconnectedness of financial institutions and markets, and more highly correlated financial risks, has intensified cross-border spillovers and has led to renewed emphasis on the need to strengthen prudential regulation and supervision of financial institutions. It has been recognized that in many countries, reducing the risk of financial instability and the procyclicality of financial markets requires improvements not only in *micro* prudential regulation, accounting standards, and capital requirement rules, but also a greater focus on *macro*prudential regulation, that is, a system-wide dimension to financial regulation. Along these lines, on September 12, 2010, the Basel Committee on Banking Supervision released a new capital framework which not only strengthens the definition of capital but also recommends the implementation of both a capital conservation buffer and a countercyclical capital buffer, with the latter ranging from 0 to 2.5 percent of risk-weighted assets (see Basel Committee on Banking Supervision, 2011). At the same time, there has been a vigorous debate about whether central banks should consider more explicitly financial stability objectives in the conduct of monetary policy.

Indeed, several observers have argued that when setting interest rates, central banks should consider more systematically the potential trade-offs that may arise between the objectives of macroeconomic stability and financial stability. A common argument to support this view is that the very achievement of price stability (which translates into relatively low interest rates) may be associated with an increased risk of financial instability: by inducing excessively optimistic expectations about future economic prospects, or by increasing incentives to take on more risk, low and stable rates of inflation may foster the development of asset price bubbles. Thus, price stability—defined as maintaining a low and stable rate of inflation—may not be a sufficient condition for financial stability, and monetary policy must internalize potential risks to economic stability and act preemptively, rather than "mop up" after a crisis has erupted. From that perspective, macroprudential policy and monetary policy are complements in pursuing financial stability.[28]

In the context of developing countries, there is much merit in considering augmenting a conventional interest rate rule by adding a measure of the private sector credit growth gap, defined as the difference between the actual growth rate of that variable and a "reference" or "equilibrium" growth rate. By doing so monetary policy would help to counter accelerator mechanisms that generate excessively rapid growth in credit and asset prices, which are common manifestations of financial imbalances. Indeed, a large body of evidence has documented that excessively rapid credit growth tends to go hand-in-hand with a tendency to underprice risks in good times (especially during episodes of large capital inflows), and a deterioration in lending origination standards and credit quality.[29] In turn, the weakening of lending standards tends to increase financial fragility during a downturn. In such conditions, monetary policy—possibly in combination with some sector-specific macroprudential tools, such as loan-to-value and debt-to-income ratios—could help to mitigate procyclicality and thereby address the time dimension of systemic risk, through its effect on the economy-wide cost of borrowing.

However, when a country is confronted with a sudden flood of private capital, that is, large inflows induced by changes in external market conditions (see Chapter 13), the scope for responding to the risk of macroeconomic and financial instability through monetary policy is limited because higher domestic interest rates vis-à-vis interest rates in advanced economies may simply exacerbate the flood of private capital. Put differently, monetary policy loses its effectiveness and other instruments must be used to manage capital flows and mitigate their destabilizing effects on the

---

[28] Agénor and Pereira da Silva (2013) provide an extensive discussion of the recent literature on this issue.

[29] See Chapter 1, as well as Claessens et al. (2011) and Calderón and Fuentes (2014).

domestic economy. Indeed, if financial imbalances are related to excessive credit growth, and if credit growth is fueled by capital inflows (as is often the case in developing countries), a comprehensive policy response could involve the use of both macroprudential tools and—at least temporarily—capital controls, or, to use a more politically correct term now, following the paradigm shift at the International Monetary Fund (2012), capital flow management (CFM) measures. Some types of capital controls (e.g., exposure limits on foreign-currency borrowing, or reserve requirements on foreign-currency deposits in domestic banks) are tantamount to prudential measures—which are especially important when gross capital inflows are intermediated through the regulated financial system. For instance, in the aftermath of the recent global financial crisis, several countries in Latin America imposed or intensified CFM measures. As discussed in Chapter 13 the evidence suggests that the effectiveness of any given measure gets eroded over time, as markets find new ways to circumvent the legislation. Nevertheless, temporary effectiveness may well be all that policymakers need, when faced with sudden floods and neither monetary policy nor macroprudential policy can respond quickly.

7 Some Other Analytical Issues

Analytical and operational aspects of inflation targeting regimes continue to generate a large amount of research, in industrial and developing countries alike. How best to measure core inflation, for instance, continues to be actively discussed (see Silver, 2006). This section focuses on three issues of debate in the analytical literature on the design and operation of an inflation targeting regime. The first relates to the implications of asymmetries in policy preferences and the second to uncertainty (regarding the variables to be measured, behavioral parameters, and policy lags).[30]

7.1 ▪ Non-Quadratic Policy Preferences

The central bank's instantaneous policy loss functions (4) and (13) were taken to be symmetric; positive output gaps, for instance, were considered to be just as costly as negative output gaps. Adopting this approach can be justified because of its tractability. In general, however, the short-run cost of disinflation may matter a great deal to the central bank and may lead to a situation where a higher weight is attached to negative output gaps—for instance by adding a term that is linear in $-y_t$ in (13). As a result, even if there is no long-run trade-off between output and inflation, the optimal inflation rate may be greater than $\tilde{\pi}$. One reason why preferences with respect to inflation and/or output gaps may be asymmetric is because some central

---

[30]Svensson (2010) discusses a range of other relevant issues, such as transparency and the nature of forecasts to be published.

bankers are accountable to elected political officials; they may therefore have greater aversion to recessions than to expansions.

More fundamentally, Orphanides and Wieland (2000) questioned the use of a quadratic objective function for policymakers in the analysis of inflation targeting regimes. They begin by noting that in practice most inflation-targeting central banks specify a *target band* as opposed to *point targets*; they then argue that the existence of a target range implies a nonlinear optimal policy rule.

A simple way to specify policy preferences that are consistent with a target band is to write the instantaneous loss function, instead of (13), as:

$$L_t = \frac{(\pi_t - \bar{\pi})^2}{2} + \frac{\lambda y_t^2}{2} + \frac{\chi \, |y_t|}{2}, \tag{43}$$

where $\chi > 0$. As shown by Orphanides and Wilcox (2002), this specification implies an asymmetric policy response: as long as inflation is relatively close to target, the optimal interest rate policy is simply to stabilize output. Otherwise, policy should keep inflation within a range (that varies positively with λ), and then wait for favorable supply shocks (positive shocks to ε_t) to move it closer to the desired value $\bar{\pi}$.

Orphanides and Wieland (2000) considered in fact a more general specification than (43), namely, a *zone-quadratic* policy loss function, that is, a loss function that assigns a quadratic loss to inflation deviations outside an explicit target band and a (near) zero loss as long as inflation fluctuates within the band. Put differently, the zone-linear Phillips curve implies that inflation is essentially stable for a range of output gaps and changes outside that range. As a consequence, if the central bank assigns some weight to fluctuations in output (as is generally the case in practice), the output objective will dominate during periods when inflation is within the band and will lose (some) importance when inflation is outside the band. They argued that this specification of policy preferences is consistent with the often-observed tendency of central banks to show overwhelming concern with inflation only when it is beyond some range.

Using numerical analysis, Orphanides and Wieland also found that, with non-quadratic preferences (and a nonlinear inflation-output trade-off, as discussed later), uncertainty due to unexpected shocks has important effects on the *width* of the target band and on the relative size of the policy response inside and outside the band. In particular, the optimal policy rule under uncertainty does not call for a mechanical response only when inflation falls outside the band. Instead, it is optimal to respond to inflation deviations already within the band and continue to do so more aggressively if inflation continues to evolve outside the desired range.[31]

---

[31] In addition, they showed that in the case where the Phillips curve is linear, the width of the band increases with the variance of shocks to inflation.

It is worth noting that the degree of asymmetry in preferences is not the only consideration for choosing the width of an inflation target band. Alexius (1999), for instance, discusses an escape clause contract whereby the central bank follows a simple inflation rule in normal times and resorts to discretionary policy if the economy is hit by a major supply-side shock. The interval within which the central bank keeps the inflation at the target value depends on the cost of breaking the rule. More generally, Erceg (2002) argued that the desired width of an inflation target band should depend on the economy's underlying structural characteristics and exposure to shocks—such as the degree of nominal wage rigidity and the variability of terms of trade and domestic productivity disturbances.

7.2 ■ Uncertainty and Optimal Policy Rules

From the perspective of the design of policy rules under inflation targeting, it is convenient analytically to distinguish between four sources of uncertainty:

- Uncertainty about some of the *determinants* of inflation, which relates to the fact that some economic series are unobservable and must be estimated. One obvious example in the present case is the measurement of potential output in the calculation of the output gap. Potential output is very often approximated by trend output, but alternative detrending techniques may sometimes give large discrepancies.[32,33]
- Uncertainty about the *parameters* of the model, which can be interpreted in two ways: either the underlying model itself is uncertain, or the "true" model is deterministic but policymakers do not know it for sure and must estimate it. Econometric techniques normally provide a sense of the degree of uncertainty that accompanies empirical estimates, because they yield not only point estimates of parameters but also their variances and covariances.
- Uncertainty about the *transmission lag* and the *timing* of policy actions. The transmission lag depends on a variety of economic and institutional factors, such as the degree of development of financial markets and the intensity of competition on both the supply and demand sides, the degree of trade openness, and the composition of private agents' financial wealth.[34]

---

[32] Note that the error in measuring potential output is not necessarily problematic if it takes an additive form and is uncorrelated over time.

[33] A related problem is the significant revisions in economic time series (due to changes in seasonal adjustment factors, re-definitions, and so on) that often occur after a preliminary release of data—particularly those dealing with the real sector. Large revisions in the variables entering the instrument rule, in particular, may complicate the use of preliminary data as a basis for policy decisions.

[34] As discussed earlier, there are lags in the response of aggregate demand to changes in interest rates, and lags in the response of inflation to the output gap. There are also lags in the response of inflation expectations to policy changes, as well as the response of inflation to changes in inflation expectations. In addition, as noted previously, there are lags in the response of aggregate demand to changes in relative prices induced by exchange-rate changes, and lags in supply response to exchange-rate-induced movements in the domestic price of imported inputs.

- Uncertainty about the *nature* and *degree of persistence* of shocks that the economy is subject to, that is, whether the shocks are on the supply or demand side of the economy, and whether they are temporary or permanent.

In general, whereas some of these sources of uncertainty cause optimal policy to become more cautious, others may have the opposite effect. To illustrate these results and their implications for inflation targeting, it is sufficient to consider two analytical examples: uncertainty about parameters and uncertainty about the degree of persistence of macroeconomic variables, including inflation.

In a seminal paper, Brainard (1967) argued that when the policymaker is uncertain about the effect of its actions, it may be optimal to adopt a more gradual policy stance than under certainty (or, more generally, under certainty equivalence, which holds in a linear model with a quadratic loss function and additive shocks). To illustrate the implications of Brainard-type uncertainty, consider again Svensson's model of strict inflation targeting described earlier [see (1)–(5)]. To simplify the analysis, suppose that output affects inflation immediately, $\alpha_1 = 1$, $\beta_1 = 0$, that there are no supply shocks ($\varepsilon_t = 0$ for all t), and that $\alpha_2 = \beta_3 = 0$. The behavioral equations of the model therefore become

$$\pi_t - \pi_{t-1} = \alpha_1 y_t, \tag{44}$$

$$y_t = -\beta_2(i_{t-1} - \pi_{t-1}) + \eta_t, \tag{45}$$

where the demand shock η_t is once again an additive, serially uncorrelated shock with zero mean. Substituting (45) in (44) yields

$$\pi_{t+1} = \gamma_1 \pi_t - \gamma_2 i_t + \eta_{t+1},$$

where $\gamma_1 = (1 + \alpha_1 \beta_2)$ and $\gamma_2 = \alpha_1 \beta_2$. Assuming the same intertemporal loss function as before [(5)] and setting for simplicity the target $\bar{\pi} = 0$, the optimal interest rate rule can be shown to be

$$i_t = \frac{\gamma_1}{\gamma_2} \pi_t. \tag{46}$$

As noted earlier, this rule is *certainty equivalent*: the same interest rate rule would be optimal in a world with no uncertainty about aggregate demand shocks. But suppose now that the central bank does not know for sure the values of γ_1 and γ_2; all that is known is that these parameters are drawn from independent, normal distributions with means $\bar{\gamma}_1$ and $\bar{\gamma}_2$ and variances σ_1^2 and σ_2^2, respectively. In this case, as shown by Brainard, the optimal instrument rule becomes

$$i_t = \frac{\bar{\gamma}_1 \bar{\gamma}_2}{\bar{\gamma}_2^2 + \sigma_2^2} \pi_t. \tag{47}$$

This equation shows that as uncertainty about the parameters in the transmission process of policy shocks increases (that is, as σ_2^2 rises), the optimal instrument response to movements in current inflation becomes smaller.[35] The fundamental reason for this result is the following. As shown earlier [see (8)], the per-period loss function can be decomposed into the sum of the squared expected deviation of each variable from its target (or the squared bias), and the conditional variance of that variable. With additive uncertainty, the variance is independent of the policy rule, and so policy decisions aim only at minimizing expected deviations in inflation. By contrast, under uncertainty about the parameters of the model, the variance of (future) inflation depends on the level of nominal interest rates; in particular, large movements in the policy instrument in response to deviations between actual and targeted inflation tend to reduce *bias*, as implied by the first term in (8)—at the cost, however, of increasing the *variance* of inflation, the second term in (8). The central bank will therefore internalize this effect by choosing a lower optimal level of interest rates.[36] A similar result would hold in a more general, linear-quadratic setting in which the central bank pursues several policy objectives simultaneously.

Whether preferences are symmetric or not also matters under uncertainty. Dolado et al. (2002) found that, in the absence of certainty equivalence, when the central banker associates a larger loss to positive than to negative inflation deviations, uncertainty also induces a more prudent behavior by the monetary authorities, which is reflected in the inclusion of the conditional variance of inflation as an additional argument in the interest rate rule.

However, studies such as those of Soderstrom (2002) or Kimura and Kurozumi (2007) have shown that uncertainty about deep parameters in the economy can lead to a more, rather than less, aggressive policy than under certainty. In Soderstrom (2002), for instance, it is uncertainty about the degree of *persistence* of inflation itself that may lead to this result. Without full information regarding inflation persistence, a cautious monetary policy may result in inflation not approaching the target at the desired rate, or even diverging from the target. The central bank can lower this risk by implementing large adjustments in interest rates, thereby reducing uncertainty regarding the path of inflation. This more aggressive policy leads to the expectation

---

[35]Note that as σ_2^2 tends to zero, (47) becomes identical to (46).

[36]It is important to note, however, that Brainard himself qualified this result by showing that it does not necessarily hold when the *covariance* between parameters (the policy multiplier, in his example) and the additive disturbance is sufficiently negative.

that inflation will return to target more quickly, so that the implicit targeting horizon is shortened.[37]

The sharp differences in these results suggest that more quantitative research is needed to fully understand the impact of uncertainty on policy rules under inflation targeting. In particular, it may well be that the impact of uncertainty on the optimal policy rule depends on which parameter, or which behavioral relationship, is being considered in a structural model. Put differently, uncertainty about particular parameters may be of relatively limited importance for the conduct of monetary policy, whereas others may have an unduly large effect on the setting of policy instruments. Identifying which parameter(s) matter(s) may well be model specific.

---

[37]Note that if the central bank cares only about stabilizing inflation, the implicit targeting horizon is already as short as possible (that is, equal to the control lag). In this case, it is not affected by uncertainty about the persistence of inflation.

Chapter 8

Choosing an Exchange-Rate Regime I: Credibility, Flexibility, and Welfare

T he role of exchange-rate policy in macroeconomic adjustment has been the subject of renewed controversy in the past few years. The traditional arguments involved in choosing between fixed and flexible exchange-rate regimes have been reexamined in light of the credibility and reputational effects that formal arrangements may provide. The sources and implications of inconsistencies that may arise between the exchange-rate regime and other macroeconomic policy instruments have also been the subject of considerable attention. Theoretical and empirical studies have emphasized the perverse effect that devaluations may exert on output, even when they lead to an improvement in the trade balance. Finally, the move toward inflation targeting regimes, with lingering concerns about volatility and competitiveness, in several countries has raised a variety of questions related to the broader macroeconomic implications of such policy choices.

This chapter and the next discuss some conceptual issues associated with the choice of an exchange-rate regime in developing countries.[1] Section 1 of this chapter provides a typology of exchange-rate regimes, whereas Section 2 provides an overview of the evolution of exchange-rate regimes in developing countries in recent decades. Section 3 examines the role played by credibility considerations in the adoption of an exchange-rate regime. Section 4 discusses the role of exchange-rate bands, as a "solution" to the trade-off between credibility and flexibility. Finally, Section 5 discusses the decision to adhere to a monetary union and examines its welfare effects.

---

[1] Chapter 14 examines the factors underlying currency crises.

1   Basic Typology

A basic typology of exchange-rate arrangements currently in operation in developing countries involves classifying them as pegged regimes, flexible regimes, and band regimes.[2]

Pegged regimes come in several forms: currency boards, whereby the currency is (in principle) irrevocably fixed and the base money stock is backed by official foreign reserves; adjustable pegs, in which the currency is fixed against a foreign currency and is seldom changed; and crawling pegs, whereby the currency is initially fixed but policymakers subsequently adjust the exchange rate at regular intervals to take into account changes in inflation differentials or the state of the trade balance. The rate of crawl can be either a well-defined (nondiscretionary) feedback rule or discretionary. In all of these regimes, the currency may be fixed against either a single foreign currency or alternative baskets of currencies (often tailor-made ones, relying on partner-country trade weights).

Under a pure currency board, the base money stock is fully backed by foreign reserves; the currency board only prints money against the reserve currency at a fixed exchange rate. Money issued by the currency board is also fully convertible on demand (at the fixed exchange rate) into the reserve currency, and vice versa. By definition, the ratio of the base money stock to the stock of foreign currency reserves is given by the exchange rate between the domestic currency and the reserve currency.[3]

In *flexible regimes*, the exchange rate is allowed to fluctuate in response to changes in demand and supply of foreign exchange. If the central bank does not intervene in the market for foreign exchange, the regime is a free float; otherwise, it is a managed float.

Band regimes involve the announcement of a central exchange rate together with a fluctuation band (which may or may not be symmetric) around that rate. The central exchange rate is itself managed in some fashion—being, for instance, fixed or crawling. The implicit commitment of the central bank is to intervene actively at the margins of the band to prevent the exchange rate from moving outside the band. The implementation of a band also requires the adoption of a set of rules to guide foreign exchange market intervention, if any, within the band.

2   Evolution of Exchange-Rate Regimes

The forms of exchange-rate arrangements in developing countries have tended to evolve systematically over time. Immediately after the collapse of the Bretton Woods

---

[2] A fourth category, multiple exchange-rate regimes, is ignored in what follows, given that such regimes are now seldom used.

[3] By contrast, deposits in private domestic banks are not backed by the currency board's foreign exchange reserves; these are liabilities of private banks.

system, most developing nations were pegging their exchange rates against a single currency. Over the subsequent decades, the proportion of peggers to a composite of currencies increased, but their overall number fell substantially.[4] Fixed exchange rates, whether pegged to a single currency or a composite, remain dominant in some parts of Sub-Saharan Africa, most notably among the fourteen member countries of the CFA Franc Zone, which maintained a fixed parity against the French franc since 1948, and against the Euro since 1999.[5] Small, highly open Caribbean islands also continue to peg their exchange rates.

In more recent years, however, flexible arrangements have become more common. Although a number of developing countries continue to fix their exchange rates (and at the same time maintain extensive capital controls on residents), a growing number of them (mostly middle-income) have moved toward a policy of managed floating, in which their exchange rates are determined largely by market forces, albeit with frequent central bank intervention. In Latin America, in particular, and South East Asia, the number of countries operating a managed float or an independently floating regime increased significantly. Bubula and Otker-Robe (2002) document the shift toward greater flexibility between 1990 and 2001 in developing countries and the concomitant reduction in the proportion of intermediate regimes (such as conventional pegged exchange-rate systems or band regimes with narrow margins). Among these countries, the share of floating regimes rose from 13.2 percent to 34.6 percent.

Similarly, Levy-Yeyati and Sturzenegger (2005) constructed a de facto classification of exchange-rate regimes based on data on exchange rates and international reserves from all IMF-reporting countries over the period 1974–2000. Specifically, they classify exchange-rate regimes on the basis of the behavior of three variables: changes in the nominal exchange rate, the volatility of these changes, and the volatility of international reserves.[6] They found that the number of intermediate regimes (including conventional pegs) indeed showed a tendency to fall over time, to the benefit of more flexible arrangements. They also found that many countries that claim to float do not allow their nominal exchange rate to move freely, a pattern that Calvo and Reinhart (2002) referred to as "fear of floating" (see Chapter 7).

---

[4]The move from pegging to a single currency to the use of basket pegs may have been the outcome of an attempt to dampen the impact of external sources of real exchange instability arising from large fluctuations among the real exchange rates of industrial countries in the post–Bretton Woods period. For a further discussion, see Aghevli et al. (1991).

[5]The CFA Franc Zone consists of two separate groups of Sub-Saharan African countries and the Comoros. The first group includes the seven members of the West African Monetary Union (Benin, Burkina Faso, Côte d'Ivoire, Mali, Niger, Senegal, and Togo), whose central bank (the BCEAO) has responsibility for conducting a common monetary policy. The second group consists of the six members of another common central bank, the BEAC (Cameroon, the Central African Republic, Chad, the Congo, Equatorial Guinea, and Gabon). Each of the two groups and the Comoros maintain separate currencies: the Franc de la Communauté Financière Africaine for the countries of the West African Monetary Union, the franc de la Coopération Financière en Afrique Centrale for the BEAC countries, and the Comorian franc for the Comoros. The currencies of the two groups and the Comoros, however, are commonly referred to as the CFA franc.

[6]See Tavlas et al. (2008) for a review of the literature on the distinction between de jure and de facto classifications of exchange-rate regimes.

Thus, in practice, many countries classified as "managed floaters" or "independent floaters" intervene heavily to manage their exchange rates; true floating remains the exception rather than the norm. The near absence of truly free floating is an important difference between developing and industrial countries. This phenomenon may reflect the limited level of financial development achieved by the former group. One reason, as discussed in the previous chapter, may be the strength of the "pass-through" effect from exchange-rate changes to prices, or the lack of competition on the foreign exchange market. Nevertheless, because free floats remain rare, and (heavily) managed floats often behave like fixed exchange-rate regimes, understanding the criteria that determine the choice of an exchange-rate regime remains a critical issue in macroeconomic management.

3   Policy Trade-Offs and Credibility

Policymakers in developing countries typically face a dilemma when using the exchange rate as a policy instrument. Although a nominal depreciation may improve the trade balance and the balance of payments, it is usually associated with a rise in the price level, which may turn into inflation and ultimately erode external competitiveness. Conversely, keeping the exchange rate fixed to stabilize prices in the presence of a large current account deficit is often not a viable option if the country faces a shortage of foreign exchange reserves or an external borrowing constraint. Nevertheless, as argued in the previous section, the exchange rate continues to be used as a policy instrument in developing countries, many of which are moving away from pegging to a single currency to more flexible exchange-rate arrangements, such as composite pegs.[7]

Despite this notable evolution toward the discretionary use of the exchange rate as a policy tool, a variety of arguments have recently been proposed in favor of adopting a fixed exchange-rate regime.[8] The debate has recently focused on the role of the exchange rate as an anchor for the domestic price level and on the "credibility effect" that a fixed rate may attach to a disinflation program when the commitment to defend the parity is clearly established.[9] Without central bank credibility, private

---

[7]In addition to the reasons adduced in the previous section, some countries may have opted for more flexible arrangements in order to "disguise" the depreciation of the domestic currency, enabling governments to avoid the political costs of announced devaluations.

[8]These arguments relate, in particular, to the role of exchange-rate stability in the promotion of trade flows and foreign investment. See Aghevli et al. (1991) for a review of the literature on the choice of an exchange-rate regime, and Levy-Yeyati et al. (2010) for empirical evidence on the determinants of that choice.

[9]This literature has developed to a large extent from Barro and Gordon's (1983) seminal work on monetary policy, which emphasizes the interdependence between the behavior of private, forward-looking agents and centralized policymakers. In this context, credibility issues emerge because of an incentive for policymakers to pursue a strategic advantage and seek short-run gains by reneging on previously announced policies, leading to time inconsistency problems. For a survey of this literature, see Cukierman (1992).

agents will continue to expect a high inflation rate, and this will increase the cost of any attempt to stabilize domestic prices. Establishing credibility means convincing the public that the central bank will not deviate from its exchange rate or money supply target in order to secure short-term benefits associated with surprise inflation. This requires that the public be convinced that the authorities have some incentive to refrain from introducing monetary surprises.[10] It has been argued that by acting as a constraint on macroeconomic policies, a fixed exchange rate may enhance the credibility of the central bank's commitment to maintaining a low and stable rate of money growth.

This section examines arguments favoring a fixed exchange-rate regime that are based on inflation problems caused by policymakers' lack of credibility. Drawing on Agénor (1994), we first present a simple model that allows us to establish the basic time inconsistency proposition, and to determine the degree of credibility of a fixed exchange rate by examining how the policymaker is induced to behave under alternative policy rules. We then focus on how the "devaluation bias" generated by the time inconsistency problem faced by the policymaker can be alleviated by building up "reputation" or by the need to signal policy commitment. Finally, we examine the costs and benefits of joining an international monetary arrangement in which the country surrenders the power to alter the exchange rate.

3.1 ■ Time Inconsistency and Exchange-Rate Policy

Consider a small open economy producing traded and nontraded goods. The economy's exchange rate is determined by a policymaker whose preferences relate to external competitiveness and price stability. The foreign-currency price of traded goods is determined on world markets. Agents in the nontraded goods sector set their prices so as to protect their position relative to the traded goods sector, and to respond to domestic demand shocks. Prices in the nontraded goods sector are set *before* the policymaker sets the exchange rate.[11] The domestic rate of inflation, π, is given by

$$\pi = \delta\pi_N + (1-\delta)(\varepsilon + \pi_T^*), \quad 0 < \delta < 1, \tag{1}$$

where ε denotes the rate of devaluation of the nominal exchange rate, π_N the rate of increase in the price of nontradables, π_T^* the rate of increase in the foreign-currency price of tradables, and $1 - \delta$ the degree of openness. The government's loss function, L^g, depends on deviations of the rate of depreciation of the real exchange rate from a

---

[10]Credibility issues are further discussed in Chapter 11, in the context of disinflation programs.

[11]Without this assumption, there would be no incentive for the authorities to adjust the exchange rate. Price stickiness may result from a variety of factors. The existence of "menu costs," for instance, may prevent agents from revising nontradable prices immediately following a nominal exchange-rate adjustment.

target rate Θ, and the inflation rate:

$$L^g = -\alpha[(\varepsilon + \pi_T^* - \pi_N) - \Theta] + \lambda\pi^2/2, \quad \alpha, \lambda \geq 0. \qquad (2)$$

The stated objective reflects the assumption that the authorities would welcome an improvement in competitiveness, which results from a depreciation of the real exchange rate. The rate of change of the real exchange rate enters the loss function linearly, because the authorities are assumed to attach a negative weight to a real appreciation relative to their target.[12] The government's objective is to minimize its loss function given by (2).

Agents in the nontraded goods sector change prices in reaction to fluctuations in the (expected) domestic price of tradable goods, and to an exogenous demand disturbance to their sector d_N, which occurs at the beginning of the period and becomes known immediately. Their loss function is therefore taken to be

$$L^p = [\pi_N - (\varepsilon^a + \pi_T^*) - \phi d_N]^2/2, \quad \phi \geq 0, \qquad (3)$$

where ε^a denotes the expected rate of depreciation of the exchange rate. The price setters' objective is to minimize L^p.

When the authorities decide whether or not to devalue the exchange rate, they know prices set in the nontraded goods sector. Substituting (1) in (2) and setting $\pi_T^* = 0$ for simplicity, the optimal rate of adjustment of the nominal exchange rate, conditional on π_N, is given by[13]

$$\varepsilon = \frac{\delta}{1-\delta}\left[\frac{\alpha}{\lambda\delta(1-\delta)} - \pi_N\right]. \qquad (4)$$

From (3), the optimal rate of inflation in the nontradable goods sector from the perspective of agents in that sector is

$$\pi_N = \phi d_N + \varepsilon^a. \qquad (5)$$

In a discretionary regime (defined as one in which the private sector and the policymaker take each other's behavior as given when making their own decisions), the equilibrium values of the nontradable inflation rate and the rate of devaluation $(\tilde{\pi}_N, \tilde{\varepsilon})$ are found by imposing rational expectations $(\varepsilon^a = \varepsilon)$ on the part of agents in

---

[12]Note that, in this one-period setup, the real exchange-rate target could be expressed equivalently in level form; the rate of change formulation used here is simply easier to work with analytically.

[13]Equation (4) would not be independent of Θ if the cost of deviations from the real exchange-rate target in the loss function (2) were quadratic. Moreover, the policymaker may be concerned not only with competitiveness of the tradable sector but also with the beneficial effects of a real appreciation—in the form, for instance, of a reduction on the relative cost of imported intermediate goods.

the nontraded goods sector and solving (4) and (5) simultaneously. This yields

$$\tilde{\pi}_N = (\kappa + \phi d_N)/\Omega \geq 0, \tag{6}$$

$$\tilde{\varepsilon} = (\kappa - \upsilon\phi d_N)/\Omega \gtrless 0, \tag{7}$$

where $\upsilon = \delta/(1-\delta)$, $\Omega = \upsilon/\delta \geq 1$, and $\kappa = \alpha\upsilon/\lambda\delta(1-\delta) > 0$.

Equations (6) and (7) indicate that, in the absence of demand shocks, the optimal discretionary policy requires a positive rate of devaluation and results in a positive rate of inflation in the nontradable sector. When demand shocks are present, that is, $d_N \neq 0$, whether the rate of devaluation $\tilde{\varepsilon}$ is positive or negative depends on the relative importance of the real-exchange-rate target and the inflation objective in the government's loss function. When the latter predominates—that is, when λ is "high," when α is "low," or, more generally, when $\alpha/\lambda < \delta(1-\delta)\phi d_N$—the optimal policy may call for an appreciation of the nominal exchange rate.

Substituting (6) and (7) in (1)–(3) yields the solutions for the inflation rate and the policymaker's loss function under discretion:

$$\tilde{\pi} = \kappa/\Omega, \tag{8}$$

$$\tilde{L}^g = \alpha(\phi d_N + \Theta) + \lambda(\kappa/\Omega)^2/2. \tag{9}$$

Equation (8) indicates that the economy's inflation rate is independent of the demand shock and increasing with the relative weight attached to competitiveness in the policymaker's loss function, α/λ. Inflation is positive because, if it were zero, the policymaker would always have an incentive to devalue. This is because, from (2), at zero inflation the gain from enhanced competitiveness outweighs the loss from higher inflation. Knowing this, private agents would adjust π_N upward [see (5)], which implies that overall inflation must be positive. Thus, the policymaker incurs a net loss unless d_N takes on a large negative value, which simultaneously improves competitiveness and reduces the rate of increase in nontradable prices.

Consider now the case in which the government is able to commit to a predetermined exchange rate. Formally, this means that in minimizing its loss function, it takes into account the effect of its announced policy on private sector behavior, on the assumption that the private sector believes that the government will not renege. Rather than solving (2) for a given value of π_N, the government substitutes (5) into (2) and minimizes with respect to ε ($= \varepsilon^a$). In this case the government will announce and maintain a devaluation rate of $\varepsilon = -\delta\phi d_N$. In general, because d_N is known to the government when setting the devaluation rate, the optimal policy requires offsetting the demand shock; only when $d_N \equiv 0$ is a fixed exchange rate ($\varepsilon = 0$) optimal.[14]

---

[14]However, the government would be subject to a credibility problem, yielding as outcome the discretionary equilibrium, if it merely announces a fixed exchange rate. For the new equilibrium to emerge, the commitment must be perceived as binding. We assume this can be achieved for the moment and will return to this issue later.

If the private sector believes the announcement and acts on that basis, (5) yields $\bar{\pi}_N = (1-\delta)\phi d_N$ which in turn implies $\bar{\pi} = 0$ and

$$\bar{L}^g = \alpha(\phi d_N + \Theta), \tag{10}$$

or, if $d_N \equiv 0$,

$$\bar{L}^g = \alpha\Theta. \tag{11}$$

From (9) and (10), $\bar{L}^g \leq \tilde{L}^g$. Thus, the no-devaluation equilibrium gives a value of the loss function that is less than that obtained under the noncooperative, discretionary regime. This reflects the fact that the policymaker is not able to achieve the gain in competitiveness sought in the discretionary regime, because price setters simply increase nontradable prices accordingly. Thus, a binding commitment entails a gain in the form of a lower inflation rate with no loss in competitiveness.[15]

Consider now the case where the government announces at the beginning of the period its intention to maintain the exchange rate fixed (that is, $\varepsilon = 0$), but decides to deviate from this policy and to implement a discretionary change once price decisions have been made. If price setters believe the zero-devaluation announcement, they will choose $\ddot{\pi}_N = \phi d_N$. Substituting this result in (4), the optimal rate of devaluation chosen by the policymaker becomes

$$\ddot{\varepsilon} = \kappa - \upsilon\phi d_N. \tag{12}$$

The minimized value of the policymaker's loss function under this "cheating" regime is

$$\ddot{L}^g = -\alpha[\kappa - \phi d_N/(1-\delta) - \Theta] + \lambda\ddot{\pi}^2/2, \tag{13}$$

where $\ddot{\pi} = (1-\delta)\kappa$.

For $d_N \equiv 0$, and for λ sufficiently small, it can be verified that $\ddot{L}^g < \bar{L}^g < \tilde{L}^g$.[16] The discretionary solution produces (ex post) the largest loss for the authorities. Because the loss is lower when the government succeeds in "fooling" the private sector than when it commits itself without reneging, there is an incentive to deviate from the fixed exchange-rate target if price setters can be made to believe that the current parity will be adhered to, so that, for $d_N \equiv 0$, $\ddot{\varepsilon} = \kappa > \tilde{\varepsilon} = \kappa/\Omega > \bar{\varepsilon} = 0$. However, although the rate of depreciation is *higher* under cheating than under discretion, the overall inflation rate is the same under both regimes ($\bar{\pi} = \ddot{\pi}$), because the rate of inflation in the nontradable sector is *lower* when price setters are fooled than in the

---

[15] However, if the effect of the demand shock on nontradable prices is large enough, the loss under precommitment can exceed that obtained under discretion, that is, $\bar{L}^g > \tilde{L}^g$.

[16] For positive demand shocks, the loss under cheating will always be less than that obtained under discretion ($\ddot{L}^g < \tilde{L}^g$), whatever the value of d_N.

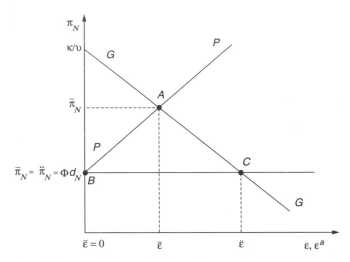

Figure 8–1 ▪ Credibility and Commitment: Alternative Equilibria
Source: Agénor (1994, p. 7).

discretionary regime (for $d_N \equiv 0$, $\ddot{\pi}_N = 0$, and $\tilde{\pi}_N = \kappa/\Omega > 0$). Moreover, under discretion, the rate of depreciation of the real exchange rate is zero ($\bar{\varepsilon} - \tilde{\pi}_N = 0$). The authorities are incapable of altering the real exchange rate by a nominal devaluation. By contrast, if the private sector can be successfully misled by the fixed-exchange-rate announcement, $\ddot{\varepsilon} - \tilde{\pi}_N = \kappa$. Such a strategy, however, entails reputational costs, an issue we examine below.

The three different solutions are represented in Figure 8.1.[17] In the $\pi_N - \varepsilon$ space, the locus PP reflects the reaction function of the private sector [given by (4)] and has a positive slope, while GG depicts the policymaker's reaction function under discretion [given by (5)] and has a negative slope. The noncooperative equilibrium is located at the intersection of curves GG and PP, that is, at point A. The precommitment solution obtains at point B, while the "cheating" solution obtains at point C. The discretionary solution is characterized by a "devaluation bias." Private agents know that once they set prices of nontradables, the policymaker has the incentive to devalue so as to depreciate the real exchange rate and improve the balance of payments. They therefore set prices at a higher level, to the point where they believe the authorities are unwilling to trade off a higher inflation rate for a more depreciated real exchange rate. The precommitment solution, although not the best possible, provides a better outcome than the discretionary alternative. This provides an argument in favor of a fixed exchange rate, assuming the commitment can be made binding and perceived as such by price setters.[18]

---

[17]The figure assumes that $\alpha/\lambda > \delta(1 - \delta)\phi d_N$, which ensures that $\bar{\varepsilon} > 0$.

[18]Note that this is an argument for a zero rate of crawl under a predetermined exchange rate, not an argument for a predetermined rate in lieu of a flexible one.

3.2 ■ Credibility of a Fixed Exchange Rate

Precommitment to a preannounced zero-devaluation rule can be successful only if the authorities incur some penalty if they deviate from the rule. One form that this penalty can take is that if the government were to depart from the preannounced rule, the public would not believe its announcements in the following period(s), and the economy would revert to the discretionary equilibrium. In such a context, a zero-devaluation rule—that is, a fixed exchange-rate target—is credible if the temptation to deviate from the rule is less than the discounted value of the "punishment" associated with reversion to the discretionary equilibrium. Following Barro and Gordon (1983) and Horn and Persson (1988), the degree of credibility of a fixed exchange rate, C, can be defined as the difference between the present value of the punishment $(\ddot{L}^g - \bar{L}^g)$ and the temptation $(\tilde{L}^g - \bar{L}^g)$:

$$C = (\ddot{L}^g - \bar{L}^g) - \frac{\gamma}{1-\gamma}(\tilde{L}^g - \bar{L}^g), \qquad (14)$$

where γ is a discount rate.

Substituting (9), (10), and (13) in (14) and setting $d_N \equiv 0$, it can be shown that a necessary condition for the degree of credibility of a fixed exchange rate to be positive is

$$\tilde{\pi} \geq 2\alpha(1-\gamma)/\lambda(1-\delta) > \bar{\pi} = 0. \qquad (15)$$

Equation (15) indicates that a fixed exchange rate can be credible only if the inflation rate that would obtain in a discretionary regime is high enough to "discourage" any attempt to devalue. Using (8), it can be shown that (15) requires, in turn, $\gamma \geq 0.5$. A fixed exchange rate, under perfect information about the policymaker's preferences, is the optimal strategy, provided that the future costs of higher inflation are not sufficiently discounted so as to fall short of the current gain from a depreciation of the real exchange rate resulting from a devaluation. Credibility requires that the short-term benefits from a nominal devaluation be foregone in order to secure the gain from low inflation over the long term.[19]

3.3 ■ Reputation, Signaling, and Commitment

We now consider how reputational factors and signaling considerations may help mitigate the time inconsistency problem faced by the policymaker in choosing an exchange-rate policy.[20]

---

[19] An increase in the degree of openness (as measured by a fall in δ) reduces the temptation to devalue, since it increases the effect of exchange-rate changes on overall inflation, and thus increases the punishment. The net effect on exchange-rate credibility of an increase in openness is therefore unambiguously positive.

[20] A more detailed discussion of these issues is provided in Agénor (1994).

Following Rogoff (1989), let us assume that there is a continuum of types of policymakers that differ with respect to the cost incurred from reneging on a fixed exchange-rate commitment. As time proceeds, private beliefs are updated on the basis of observed exchange-rate policy: the longer the policymaker sticks to a fixed exchange rate, the lower is the expected rate of devaluation. But if the policymaker deviates even once from the fixed exchange-rate target, private agents will raise devaluation expectations (to the discretionary level) for the indefinite future. A sequential process of this type leads agents to revise continually upward the threshold level of cost below which they assume the government has an incentive to renege—provided, of course, that no devaluation occurs. As a result, devaluation expectations tend to fall over time. Although agents may never discover the "true" value of the cost attached to reneging by the policymaker, the behavior of expectations creates an incentive to commit to a fixed exchange-rate rule. "Reputation" is thus viewed as a mechanism leading to a progressively lower expected rate of depreciation.[21] In this context, a government facing a relatively low cost of reneging may be tempted to devalue very early in its term in office. But if the policymaker's horizon is long enough (or if the discount rate is low enough), the temptation to devalue is lowered because of the costs resulting from high devaluation expectations.

The implication of the preceding analysis is that even policymakers who are concerned with a balance-of-payments target may tend, at the start of their term in office, to act as if they are not in order to maintain the impression (among private agents) that inflation is their primary target and thereby lower expectations. Policymakers of this type may, nevertheless, devalue near the end of their term in an attempt to improve competitiveness and raise output. A nominal devaluation will "work," in this context, as long as the policymaker has a reputation of being a "pegger" or as long as the cost of reneging on the exchange-rate commitment is not too large. The critical element on which this result rests is the public's lack of information about the policymaker: even if the authorities are committed to maintaining a fixed exchange rate, private agents cannot know this with certainty. Complete credibility in this context is impossible to achieve. This line of reasoning also suggests, however, that reputational factors can help mitigate the time inconsistency problem. A government that is more concerned about a balance-of-payments target retains an incentive to avoid the discretionary outcome early in its term of office because doing so secures more favorable price behavior on the part of private agents.

Consider now a situation in which there are only two types of policymakers, who differ in the relative weights they attach to the "internal" target (inflation) and the "external" target (the real exchange rate). Policymakers of the first type, labeled D-policymakers ("devaluers"), attach a value both to low inflation and to a more depreciated real exchange rate. The second type, labeled P-policymakers ("peggers"),

---

[21] In Barro's (1986) framework, reputation is explicitly defined in probabilistic terms. However, his model has the unattractive feature of involving a phase of randomizing strategy by the policymaker. See Rogoff (1989) for a discussion of Barro's analysis.

attach a lower weight to the real exchange rate in its loss function. Price setters do not know the type of government currently in office, but they have a prior probability that it is type P. As time proceeds, private agents observe the exchange-rate policy and revise their assessment of the policymaker's type.

In the presence of imperfect information about policymakers' preferences, as shown by Vickers (1986), a policymaker who cares more about inflation can signal this preference to the private sector by inducing a temporary recession. Policymakers with relatively greater concern about output and employment are unwilling to bear this cost, so the signal successfully conveys the policymaker's preference for low inflation. In the context of the above framework, Vickers's analysis suggests that even a government concerned more about inflation (that is, a P-type policymaker) may have an incentive to devalue by less than it would otherwise find optimal, in order to signal its preferences to the public. One way for the P-type government to reveal its identity might be to select an exchange-rate policy that the D-type policymaker would not find optimal to replicate. Such a policy would not, of course, be without cost for the P-type policymaker, but could be a credible signaling device under some circumstances.

Assume, for simplicity, that the policy horizon is limited to two periods. The precise conditions under which the P-government will depart from the optimal, perfect-information response in the first period in order to successfully reveal its type can readily be established (see Agénor, 1994). By devaluing by less than it would find otherwise optimal, an anti-inflation government is able to signal immediately and unambiguously its commitment to price stability to private agents, and is able to secure the gain from lower inflation expectations in the second period.

This result provides an interesting argument in support of an exchange-rate freeze in stabilization programs, of the type that has been observed in many developing countries over the past three decades (see online Supplement B). Fixing the exchange rate (or, more generally, lowering the rate of depreciation of the exchange rate) may prove successful in signaling the anti-inflationary commitment of the policymaker, and will therefore enhance the credibility of a stabilization program. Indeed, an extension of the argument suggests that it may ultimately be beneficial for a government to *revalue* its currency to convey unambiguous information about its policy preferences. Chile, for instance, revalued its currency twice in 1977, in an attempt to demonstrate the government's resolve to fight inflation.

There are, however, situations in which signaling considerations either are not important for or are incapable of mitigating the time inconsistency problem faced by policymakers operating under a fixed exchange-rate regime. For instance, both types of policymakers may have a high rate of time preference, in which case the optimal solutions obtained under perfect information and uncertain preferences may not be very different from each other. Intuitively, this is because D-type policymakers have a reduced incentive to masquerade as P-type. If price setters understand that the future is heavily discounted, P-policymakers need not send an overly "strong" signal to distinguish themselves from D-type policymakers.

Another situation, which is often relevant for developing countries, may be that, when implementing a disinflation program, a country is faced with a large current account deficit and a financing constraint. If the deficit is unsustainable and perceived as such by private agents, a "high" rate of depreciation will appear inevitable and will undermine any signaling attempt. Finally, there are other ways for a P-type government to send signals that would enable the public to clearly identify its preferences: such signals may be sent via the removal of capital controls, a drastic cut in the budget deficit, or the appointment of a "conservative" central banker. The benefits and costs of alternative signaling strategies are further discussed in Chapter 11, in the context of disinflation programs.

4   Credibility vs. Flexibility: Role of Bands

When the exchange rate is officially determined, it plays dual macroeconomic roles which are often in conflict with each other. In general, as emphasized in the previous section, changes in the nominal exchange rate influence an economy's price level as well as its real exchange rate. Potential policy conflicts may arise when a given change in the nominal exchange rate causes one of these variables to move in the direction desired by policymakers, and the other in the opposite direction. As discussed earlier, a familiar example consists of a nominal devaluation undertaken to facilitate real exchange-rate depreciation, which simultaneously has the undesired effect of increasing the domestic price level.

This policy trade-off applies fairly generally, because it will arise whenever some other nominal variable is fixed in the economy, so there is no dichotomy between an economy's real and nominal sectors. Even when domestic prices are fully flexible, so that relative price adjustment can take place without nominal exchange-rate changes—that is, through changes in the nominal prices of nontraded goods— the nominal and real roles of the nominal exchange rate will not generally be independent. The reason is that in this case the value of the domestic price level may indirectly influence the equilibrium relative price of traded goods—at least in the short run—through wealth effects (operating through components of private wealth such as the monetary base and nonindexed government debt). The conflict arises in even more acute form when domestic nontraded goods prices are sticky. In those circumstances, achieving adjustments in the real exchange rate while retaining the nominal anchor role of the nominal rate may require undesirable changes in the domestic price level (to achieve a real appreciation) or a temporary slowdown in economic activity (to achieve a real depreciation).

4.1 ▪ Rationale for Bands

The extreme form of a fixed or flexible exchange-rate regime essentially opts for one policy objective at the expense of another. Under fixed exchange rates, the nominal exchange rate is used to provide a nominal anchor for the economy, and relative price adjustments rely on the domestic wage-price mechanism. Under flexible exchange rates, the nominal exchange rate provides the adjustment in relative prices, while the economy's nominal anchor is provided by the money supply. In the pure forms of these arrangements, of course (that is, currency boards and flexible rates with money supply targets), the exchange rate is not actively managed and therefore ceases to function as a policy instrument. Thus, the potential policy conflict is addressed in such cases by the choice of regime. Countries that do actively manage nominal exchange rates, however, have to confront this policy dilemma, and increasingly have sought to devise institutional mechanisms that would preserve some degree of exchange-rate flexibility to promote relative price adjustment while retaining the role of the exchange rate as nominal anchor.

Announced exchange-rate bands are one such mechanism that has often been adopted by developing countries. This arrangement involves the announcement of a central parity, which is itself managed in some fashion, together with a range of fluctuation around that parity. The implicit commitment of the authorities is to intervene actively at the margins of the band, to prevent the exchange rate from moving outside those margins. The implementation of a band also requires the adoption of a set of rules to guide foreign exchange market intervention, if any, within the band.

By combining some features of fixed and flexible exchange rates, bands attempt to combine the virtues of both systems. Relative to fixed exchange rates (that is, parities without bands), exchange-rate bands allow the exchange rate to facilitate *temporary* relative price adjustments and preserve some degree of monetary autonomy, the extent of which depends on the width of the band. Whether these benefits will materialize depends on how the band is managed. If the authorities seek to keep the exchange rate very close to the central parity, or allow it to get stuck at the top or bottom of the band, then the band will behave like a fixed exchange rate, both with respect to relative price adjustments as well as to monetary autonomy. Relative to completely flexible rates (that is, nonbinding "bands" without central parities), exchange-rate bands can in principle provide a nominal anchor for the domestic price level, as well as limit the range of fluctuation of nominal exchange rates. Again, whether they achieve both of these objectives depends on how bands are managed. If the central parity is specified in terms of the behavior of the *real* exchange rate, for instance, the economy's nominal anchor will have to be provided by the money supply, as in the case of flexible rates. Whether the band succeeds in stabilizing the exchange rate, on the other hand, depends on its credibility.

The classic analysis of the stabilizing effect that a credible exchange-rate band can exert on exchange-rate fluctuations was provided in Krugman's target zone model. Krugman (1991) showed that a band that is perfectly credible, and for which intervention takes place only at the upper and lower margins, will tend to exhibit a *honeymoon effect*—that is, for a given value of the "fundamentals," the nominal exchange rate will be closer to the central parity than it would have been

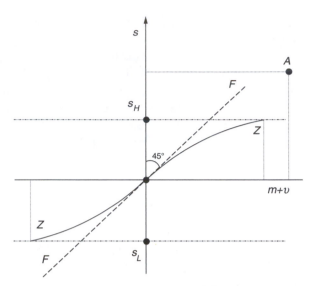

Figure 8–2 ▪ Krugman's Basic Target Zone Model
Source: Adapted from Svensson (1992, p. 123).

under flexible exchange rates even without intervention, meaning that the presence of the announced band is itself stabilizing.[22] The reason for this result is that, near the limits of the band, even with zero expected change in the fundamentals, the likelihood of intervention to prevent movement outside the band will cause agents to expect the exchange rate to revert toward the central parity, essentially because a fundamentals-driven movement in the exchange rate that tends to have this effect (that is, that drives the exchange rate toward the central parity) will be permitted to be fully realized, whereas one that has the opposite effect (that is, that tends to drive the exchange rate outside the band) will not. Such an expectation will itself restrict fluctuations in the exchange rate. Krugman also shows that the sensitivity of the exchange rate to the fundamentals diminishes as the exchange rate approaches the limits of the band (a property known as *smooth pasting*).[23] Thus, according to the Krugman model, in a situation in which the relationship between the exchange rate and the fundamentals would be linear, the announcement of a band would instead make it S-shaped (see Figure 8.2 in the appendix), with the exchange rate lying below the corresponding flexible-rate value when changes in the fundamentals drive it above the central parity, and above the flexible-rate value when

---

[22] A brief formal description of Krugman's target zone model is provided in the appendix to this chapter.

[23] This property arises because as the exchange rate approaches the margins of the band, the expected change in the fundamentals becomes discontinuous (due to the fact that anticipated intervention—itself a fundamental—offsets the effects of other fundamentals that would tend to drive the exchange rate outside the band), while the expected change in the exchange rate cannot be discontinuous (otherwise arbitrage opportunities would be created). This means that the exchange rate must be insensitive to the fundamentals at the margins of the band [see Svensson (1992)].

changes in the fundamentals drive it below the central parity. The upshot is that the implementation of a credible band will, in and of itself, tend to have a stabilizing effect on exchange-rate movements.

4.2 ■ Bands and Monetary Policy Credibility

Aside from the credibility of the band itself, a separate issue is how the implementation of a (credible) band affects the Barro-Gordon problem examined earlier in this chapter. Specifically, the question is the following: if "tying one's hands" by pegging to a low-inflation currency can make an anti-inflationary policy stance credible, thereby avoiding the socially inferior discretionary outcome, is this beneficial outcome lost when a fixed exchange rate is replaced by a band?

The target zone literature has only recently begun to address this issue, since research based on Krugman's target zone model tended to restrict the scope of monetary policy to the management of the band (by altering the fundamentals at the margins to safeguard the band or by undertaking intramarginal intervention in the form of "leaning against the wind"). To consider the implications of a band for the anti-inflationary credibility of monetary policy, it is necessary to model the latter as directed to the standard Barro-Gordon objectives (that is, to allow the monetary authorities to behave strategically), while constrained by the requirements of maintaining the band, rather than that of maintaining an absolutely fixed exchange rate.

Coles and Philippopoulos (1997) generalized the Barro-Gordon analysis to the case of bands. They argue that in this context, optimal monetary policy strategies depend on the position of the exchange rate within the band. They consider two cases: a deterministic case in which the partner country's inflation rate is nonstochastic, and a case in which the "center" country's inflation rate is subject to random shocks. In the deterministic case, the typical Barro-Gordon result emerges when the exchange rate lies initially inside the target zone, that is, the monetary authorities overinflate until the exchange rate reaches the upper margin of the band. Once there, domestic inflation matches foreign inflation, as under fixed exchange rates. This result suggests that, from the perspective of resolving time-inconsistency issues, a target zone would be inferior to a fixed exchange rate with very narrow bands. However, this conclusion does not carry over to the case in which the partner country experiences stochastic inflation shocks. The reason is that if the center country experiences a negative inflation shock, this may constrain domestic inflation by moving the exchange rate immediately to the top of the band, whereas if it experiences a positive inflation shock, the domestic economy does not necessarily have to follow it (as it would under a fixed exchange rate), because the exchange rate can appreciate into the interior of a sufficiently wide band (and would indeed do so if the realized foreign inflation rate exceeds the autarkic Barro-Gordon domestic "inflation bias"). Coles and Philippopoulos show that, in the face of unstable partner-country inflation, a band would therefore tend to stabilize the domestic inflation rate relative to what would happen under fixed exchange rates and thus may potentially dominate both fixed and flexible exchange rates on welfare grounds.

As shown by Cukierman et al. (2004), the degree of credibility matters also for the width of the band. Using a stochastic model, they derive the optimal exchange-rate band in terms of the underlying distribution of shocks to the current and capital accounts of the balance of payments and in terms of the commitment reputation of policymakers.

4.3 ▪ Experience with Bands

In theory, then, credible bands have the potential to stabilize exchange-rate fluctuations relative to what would be observed under flexible exchange rates, as well as to stabilize domestic inflation relative to what would be observed under fixed exchange rates. How have exchange-rate bands performed in practice in developing countries? Bands have often been implemented in the aftermath of exchange-rate-based stabilization programs.[24] They thus represent the "flexibilization" stage of such programs. Although many of these bands share this common background, the choices that individual countries have made in managing their bands have been rather different. These choices cover five dimensions. First, the definition of the central parity must be stated in terms of some currency or basket of currencies, so the first choice that must be made concerns the currency composition of the reference basket.

Second, if the domestic rate of inflation exceeds the rate of inflation of trading partners and is expected to continue to do so, then an unalterably fixed central parity is not an option, and a choice must be made between frequent discrete realignments of the central parity and the adoption of a crawling central parity.

Third, the mode of accommodation of the central parity to permanent shocks affecting the "fundamental" determinants of the equilibrium real exchange rate has to be determined. Aside from the issue of identifying the relevant set of fundamentals and the expected duration of changes in these variables, this also requires quantifying the required extent of adjustment in the real exchange rate and designing the adjustment path for the central parity.

Fourth, the permitted range of fluctuation of the exchange rate around the central parity (that is, the width of the band) has to be determined. Finally, the rules governing foreign exchange intervention inside the bands need to be established.

As summarized by Helpman et al. (1994), lessons from experience with exchange-rate bands in developing countries are as follows. First, the adoption of a band is a commitment to limited nominal exchange-rate flexibility, not to a specific choice of nominal anchor. Bands are thus compatible with a variety of different weights that may be attached by the authorities to competitiveness and

---

[24]See Helpman et al. (1994) and Williamson (1996) for a review of some experiences with bands.

price stability objectives. Differences in such weights will be reflected in differences in the management of the central parity. This means that bands may be—and have been—associated with a variety of real exchange-rate experiences. In countries where inflation stabilization had been an important objective, the exchange-rate band tended to be associated with fairly continuous real appreciation. In others, where external competitiveness was crucial during the early years of the band, the real exchange rate depreciated. These differences suggest that the crawling nature of the central parity is an important clue to the survival of bands in many of the countries that adopted them.

Second, moving to a band from a fixed rate, or to a band with a crawling central parity from one with a fixed parity, was not associated with an acceleration of inflation. Thus, the additional exchange-rate flexibility was not obviously associated with a loss of price stability. This finding is consistent with the view that flexibility can enhance credibility.

Nonetheless, the adoption of a band does not represent a magic solution to credibility problems. Several of the experiences with bands were characterized by periods in which expectations of realignment—associated with the behavior of "fundamentals" such as the performance of the real economy, the stock of foreign exchange reserves, and the path of the real exchange rate—emerged. This implies that active management of the central parity to keep it in line with the equilibrium real exchange rate is indispensable to preserve the bands when capital mobility is high. Adjustment of the central parity in line with perceived changes in the fundamentals was indeed undertaken in successful applications of exchange-rate bands. At the same time, failed attempts suggest that circumstances may not always lead the authorities to react quickly enough and to adjust parities by appropriate magnitudes.

5   Currency Unions

Instead of choosing its own exchange-rate policy, a country may purely and simply surrender to a supranational authority its ability to manipulate the exchange rate and join a currency union. Although in the past decades the move toward currency unions has occurred mostly among industrial countries (such as the creation of the Euro area in 1999), it is an issue worth considering for developing countries as well, because the issue is being debated (at least in preliminary form) in several corners of the world. In Africa, countries that are part of the Southern African Development Community (SADC) announced in August 2006, at a meeting in Lesotho, their intention to form a monetary union by 2016 and to adopt a single currency by 2018.[25] Members of the Economic Community of Western African States (ECOWAS, which includes

---

[25] SADC consists of fourteen countries, namely, Angola, Botswana, Democratic Republic of Congo, Lesotho, Malawi, Mauritius, Mozambique, Namibia, Seychelles, South Africa, Swaziland, Tanzania, Zambia, and Zimbabwe.

countries belonging to the CFA Franc Zone, like Benin and Senegal, but also Ghana and Nigeria) announced their intention to form the West African Monetary Zone (consisting of Gambia, Ghana, Guinea, Liberia, Nigeria, and Sierra Leone), as a first step toward a wider monetary union with the West African part of the CFA Franc Zone (which includes Benin, Burkina Faso, Côte d'Ivoire, Mali, Niger, Senegal, and Togo), to produce a single currency for all ECOWAS countries.[26] We will discuss both the credibility and welfare effects of currency unions.

5.1 ▪ Credibility Effects of Monetary Unions

A possible way to attach credibility to a fixed exchange-rate regime (and signal the policymaker's commitment to low inflation) would be for the authorities to surrender the power to alter the exchange rate. This could be achieved, for instance, by forming a monetary union under which a group of countries adopt a common currency and fix their parity against a major currency; for developing countries, the CFA Franc Zone (as noted earlier) and the East Caribbean Currency Area provide examples of such an arrangement. One way for a government to establish credibility for an anti-inflationary policy, as discussed in Chapter 11, is to appoint a "conservative" central banker, highly averse to inflation (Rogoff, 1985). It has been argued that membership in a monetary union plays an equivalent role: it allows member countries, in effect, to appoint a "strong" central banker, establishing credibility by linking a country's monetary policy to the anti-inflationary preferences of the dominant central bank. By "tying their hands" when joining a fixed exchange-rate arrangement, therefore, "weak" policymakers can combat inflationary expectations more effectively (Giavazzi and Pagano, 1988). In these circumstances it may be desirable for the authorities to adopt an institutional arrangement that imposes large—political or otherwise—costs on reneging on such precommitment. The important general point emphasized in this line of reasoning is that, to be credible, such monetary arrangements must be based on institutional features that make it costly to alter the exchange rate.

There are, however, costs associated with foregoing the use of the exchange rate as a policy instrument, particularly in the presence of large external shocks. The credibility of a country's commitment to the "rules of the game" of a monetary union, and thus the extent to which membership in a union can overcome time inconsistency problems, must depend on the nature of such costs. We briefly examine these issues by extending the model developed previously so as to capture the institutional and macroeconomic constraints imposed by an international monetary arrangement.

---

[26]However, whether these monetary zones can be considered optimal remains a controversial issue. See, for instance, Boughton (1993) for a discussion of the CFA Franc Zone, and Karras (2007) for a broader perspective on the optimality of a common currency for Sub-Saharan Africa.

Consider again the model presented in Section 3 and suppose that a country must decide whether or not to keep its exchange rate fixed within the framework of a monetary union with its major trading partner.[27] Suppose, moreover, that inflation in the partner country is positive (that is, $\pi_T^* > 0$). Both the policymaker and private agents learn about changes in foreign prices immediately after their occurrence, and make their decisions afterward. For simplicity, let $d_N \equiv 0$. The discretionary solution is now given by

$$\tilde{\pi}_N = \kappa / \Omega \geq 0, \tag{16}$$

$$\tilde{\varepsilon} = \kappa / \Omega - \pi_T^* \gtrless 0, \tag{17}$$

which yields an overall inflation rate equal to

$$\tilde{\pi} = \tilde{\pi}_N = \kappa / \Omega, \tag{18}$$

and a constant real exchange rate $(\tilde{\varepsilon} + \pi_T^* - \tilde{\pi}_N = 0)$. The associated loss for the policymaker is

$$\tilde{L}^g = \lambda (\kappa / \Omega)^2 / 2. \tag{19}$$

If the authorities decide to keep the nominal exchange rate fixed, and if their commitment to such a policy is assumed by price setters $(\bar{\varepsilon} = 0, \bar{\pi}_N = \bar{\pi} = \pi_T^*,$ so that $\bar{\varepsilon} + \pi_T^* - \bar{\pi}_N = 0)$, the loss function is equal to

$$\bar{L}^g = \lambda (\pi_T^*)^2 / 2. \tag{20}$$

A comparison of (19) and (20) shows that the loss under a (credible) commitment to maintain the exchange rate fixed is higher than under discretion when $\pi_T^* > \kappa / \Omega$—in which case the government may decide to renege on its commitment to a fixed parity. When the foreign price shock is small, its direct inflationary impact is limited, and the rate of appreciation of the nominal exchange rate required to offset its impact in the discretionary regime is also small. If the commitment to the fixed exchange rate is credibly enforced, the rate of appreciation of the real exchange rate is the same under both regimes. But the overall effect on inflation under precommitment is π_T^* (because prices of nontradables are adjusted upward) while under discretion it is κ / Ω.

The analysis suggests that, for a policymaker concerned with both inflation and competitiveness, the desirability of "tying one's hands" as a solution to the time inconsistency problem depends on what one's hands are tied to. When union members have stable, low inflation rates, precommitment to a fixed exchange rate

---

[27] The foreign country is assumed not to face time inconsistency problems.

may help demonstrate domestic resolve to maintaining financial discipline. But when the economy is subject to large nominal shocks, the credibility gain may be outweighed by the cost of lost autonomy.

In practice, exchange-rate arrangements involving a peg typically incorporate an "escape clause" or a contingency mechanism that allows members to deviate from the declared parity under exceptional circumstances.[28] To examine this issue in the present setting, suppose that π_T^* is now a random variable that follows a uniform distribution over the interval $(0, c)$ and is realized *after* private agents make their price decisions. Suppose also that the domestic country maintains a fixed parity when foreign price shocks are "small" but is allowed to alter the fixed exchange rate discretionarily if the foreign price shock is "large." The probability that the contingency mechanism will be invoked is therefore $q = \Pr(\pi_T^* \geq \mu)$, where $0 \leq q \leq 1$, and μ denotes a given threshold. Under the assumption regarding the distribution of π_T^*, this probability is given by

$$q = \Pr(\pi_T^* \geq \mu) = \int_\mu^c (1/c)\,d\pi_T^* = (c - \mu)/c. \tag{21}$$

Price setters form expectations prior to the realization of the foreign price shock. If they are aware of the policy rule followed by the authorities, the expected rate of depreciation of the exchange rate will be given by

$$\varepsilon^a = q\,E(\varepsilon \mid \pi_T^* \geq \mu) + (1 - q) \cdot 0,$$

or[29]

$$\varepsilon^a = \frac{q}{1 + \upsilon q}(\kappa - \Omega\bar{\pi}_T^*), \tag{22}$$

where $\bar{\pi}_T^* = E(\pi_T^* \mid \pi_T^* \geq \mu) = (c + \mu)/2$. Suppose that, for the sake of argument, $\bar{\pi}_T^* \leq \kappa/\Omega$ so that $\varepsilon^a \geq 0$. Equation (22) indicates that when $q = 0$ the expected rate of depreciation is also zero. By contrast, when $q = 1$, the expected rate of depreciation is $\varepsilon^a = \kappa/\Omega - \bar{\pi}_T^*$, a solution that can be interpreted as the rate that would prevail in the purely discretionary regime examined above with a stochastic foreign inflation rate.[30] In general, as long as there is a positive probability less than one that the contingency mechanism will be invoked, the expected rate of

---

[28] A case in point is the Bretton Woods system. The properties of monetary policy rules combining discretionary and state-contingent mechanisms have been discussed by Flood and Isard (1989).

[29] Minimizing (2) and (3) with $d_N = \Theta = 0$ with respect to π_N and ε, respectively, and substituting for π_N in the first equation yields $\varepsilon = \kappa - \upsilon\varepsilon^a - \Omega\pi_T^*$. Taking the conditional expectation of this equation and solving for ε^a yields (22).

[30] Strictly speaking, it is the unconditional expectation of the rate of foreign inflation (rather than π_T^*) that determines the anticipated rate of devaluation in the purely discretionary regime. The difference, however, is small if c is large and can be abstracted from for simplicity.

depreciation is lower than under pure discretion because $q < 1$. The discretionary exchange-rate policy when the escape clause is activated is given by[31]

$$\bar{\varepsilon} = \frac{\kappa + \Omega \upsilon q \bar{\pi}_T^*}{1 + \upsilon q} - \Omega \pi_T^*, \tag{23}$$

which is lower than the value that would prevail under pure discretion, obtained by setting $q = 1$ in (23), because devaluation expectations are lower. An implication of (23) is that the higher q is—or, equivalently, the lower μ is—the more effective the contingency mechanism will be in mitigating the devaluation bias of the discretionary regime ($\partial \bar{\varepsilon}/\partial q < 0$). A high value of q does, however, generate real costs in circumstances in which foreign price shocks turn out to be "small." To illustrate this result, note that in a purely discretionary regime, the *actual* (ex post) change in the real exchange rate, using (22) and (23) with $q = 1$ and noting that $\tilde{\pi}_N = \varepsilon^a + \pi_T^*$, is given by

$$\bar{\varepsilon} + \pi_T^* - \tilde{\pi}_N = -\Omega(\pi_T^* - \bar{\pi}_T^*), \tag{24}$$

which essentially reflects unanticipated changes in the foreign inflation rate. By contrast, in a regime where the possibility to invoke an escape mechanism exists, the actual rate of depreciation of the real exchange rate is determined by the size of the foreign price shock. If the realized value of π_T^* is sufficiently large to trigger the contingency mechanism, (22) and (23) imply

$$\bar{\varepsilon} + \pi_T^* - \tilde{\pi}_N = \frac{\kappa(1 - q) + q\Omega^2 \bar{\pi}_T^*}{(1 + \upsilon q)} - \Omega \pi_T^*, \tag{25}$$

which indicates, by comparison with (24), that the real rate of depreciation is lower than under pure discretion. However, if π_T^* turns out to be "small," the authorities will maintain the nominal exchange rate fixed. The change in the real exchange rate will in this case be given by $(\pi_T^* - \tilde{\pi}_N)$, that is, $-\varepsilon^a$. Equation (22) indicates therefore that in "normal circumstances," a high probability of using the contingency mechanism may have a negative effect on competitiveness, because nontradable prices are set at a level that may be higher than they would be if instead $\varepsilon^a = 0$. This suggests, therefore, that if escape mechanisms are to be considered as part of an exchange-rate arrangement, q should not be "too high"; that is, the threshold above which a discretionary adjustment of the exchange rate is allowed should not be excessively low.

---

[31]Equation (23) is obtained by substituting (22) in the equation for ε derived previously, $\varepsilon = \kappa - \upsilon \varepsilon^a - \Omega \pi_T^*$.

5.2 ▪ Welfare Effects of Optimum Currency Areas

Since the seminal contribution of Mundell (1961), the literature on optimum currency areas (OCAs) has proposed a variety of criteria for choosing which countries should participate in a currency union. These criteria generally include similarity of inflation rates, the degree of factor mobility, the openness and size of the economy, the degree of commodity diversification, the degree of price and wage flexibility, the extent of integration in goods markets, the correlation between economic shocks across countries, the degree of fiscal integration, and the political will to integrate. Another argument for a single currency area is that it offers risk-sharing benefits when capital markets are limited in their ability to facilitate consumption insurance (Ching and Devereux, 2003).[32]

Bayoumi (1994) was one of the first to develop a formal OCA model, obtaining some of the key insights (expressed informally in some previous papers) regarding the role of openness, diversification, labor mobility, and correlation of economic shocks. In what follows, we provide a concise presentation of his model and use it to discuss the welfare effects of currency unions.

5.2.1   *The Model*

The general equilibrium OCA model presented by Bayoumi (1994) has four main features. First, there is downward nominal wage rigidity; whereas wages can increase in periods of excess demand, they cannot fall below a certain threshold in periods of excess supply. Second, the model has no financial assets and no government. Third, each country is assumed to be fully specialized in the production of a specific (or regionally differentiated) good, implying that there are no differential shocks to industries within a country.

Formally, suppose that there are n countries, each of which has the same underlying structure but produces a different good. Each country has a fixed amount of labor available that can be used to produce its particular good; thus, there is no labor mobility across countries (for the moment). The production function for country i is

$$Y_i = L_i^\alpha \exp(\varepsilon_i), \quad 0 < \alpha < 1, \tag{26}$$

where Y_i is output, L_i is labor, and ε_i a normally distributed, zero-mean disturbance. In logs, this equation is

$$y_i = \alpha l_i + \varepsilon_i. \tag{27}$$

Suppose that the maximum quantity of labor available in any country is 1, so that $L_i \leq 1$. Country 1 is different from the other countries in that the productivity

---

[32]See De Grauwe (2012) for an overview. Agénor and Aizenman (2011) consider the role of capital market imperfections as a separate criterion of optimality.

disturbance ε_1 is always equal to 0, and hence, the full employment level of output Y_1 is 1 (or $y_1 = 0$). The price of output in country 1, P_1, is used as the numéraire, so $P_1 = 1$.

The labor market is competitive; the wage, $W_i E_i$, where W_i is the wage in local currency and E_i the bilateral exchange rate with country 1, is equal to the marginal product of labor. In logs,

$$w_i + e_i = \ln \alpha + \varepsilon_i - (1 - \alpha)l_i + p_i. \qquad (28)$$

Nominal wage rigidity is assumed to be asymmetric. Specifically, the response of the wage measured in terms of the price of local goods, W_i, depends upon the state of excess demand in the labor market when the wage is at a "normal" level, $\omega = \alpha P_i$, defined as the wage in local prices that ensures full employment when there is no productivity shock ($\varepsilon_i = 0$) and the exchange rate E_i is normalized to 1. If there is excess demand for labor at this point, the nominal wage is raised to the level that is consistent with full employment ($L_i = 1$). By contrast, if labor demand is below the full employment level when $W_i = \omega$, the wage is assumed to remain at this high level, and some labor is unemployed. This specification of the labor market has important implications for the choice of an exchange-rate regime. If the country has a nominal exchange rate that is free to adjust in response to underlying disturbances, the wage will always be at the normal level, and the exchange rate will adjust to ensure that full employment prevails. By contrast, when adjustments in the nominal exchange rate are precluded because the country is part of a currency union, the functioning of the labor market will imply some loss in output through unemployment.

Each country chooses its exchange rate, E_i; and if i chooses an exchange rate that differs from j, the ratio E_i/E_j differs from unity. However, flexibility entails (proportional) transactions costs, which are captured by assuming that goods that are exported from country j shrink by a factor $(1 - T)$ upon arrival to country i. For simplicity, the cost T is assumed to be the same for all trade transactions. By contrast, if countries i and j choose to form a currency union, the ratio E_i/E_j is constant and fixed at unity. Assuming no transportation costs between countries, the transaction cost T is then assumed to be zero.

With no cross-border ownership of production units, income in each country is equal to nominal output, $P_i Y_i$. Consumption in each country is over all goods; the utility function is assumed to take the form

$$U_i = \sum_{j=1}^{N} \beta_{ij} \ln(C_{ij}) - \phi, \qquad (29)$$

where C_{ij} is consumption of good j in country i, $\beta_{ij} > 0$, and ϕ is a constant term, which is set (to simplify later calculations) equal to $\sum_{j=1}^{N} \beta_{ij} \ln(\beta_{ij})$. There are also two restrictions on the coefficients β_{ij}, $\sum_{j=1}^{N} \beta_{ij} = 1$ (which implies that β_{ij} is the proportion of income in country i that is spent on good j), and $\sum_{i=1}^{N} \beta_{ij} = 1$ (which ensures that the aggregate demand for each good is symmetrical, and hence that all countries have the same level of income). Given the specification of utility, demand for good j from country i is given by

$$Y_{ij} = \beta_{ij} \frac{P_i Y_i}{P_j}. \tag{30}$$

Given that $\sum_{i=1}^{N} \beta_{ij} = 1$, total demand for good j (at the point of production) is thus given by

$$\sum_{i=1}^{N} Y_{ij} = Y_j = \frac{1}{P_j} \sum_{i=1}^{N} \beta_{ij}(P_i Y_i) = \frac{1}{P_j},$$

which therefore implies that income in every single country, $P_i Y_i$, is equal to unity.

If the two countries are not in a currency union, then the quantity of goods consumed in country i is less than the volume of goods demanded at the point of production j, as a result of transactions costs. From (30), consumption of good j in country i is

$$C_{ij} = \beta_{ij} \frac{(1 - T_i) P_i Y_i}{P_j} = \beta_{ij} \frac{(1 - T_i)}{P_j}, \tag{31}$$

where $T_i = T$ for countries outside the currency union and zero for member countries.[33]

5.2.2   Equilibrium

Consider first the case in which there is no currency union, that is, all countries allow their currencies to float against each other. As a result of full exchange-rate flexibility, nominal wages in local goods, W_i are set at the normal level ω. Full employment implies that $y_i = \varepsilon_i = e_i$. From (31), it follows that

$$c_{ij} = \ln \beta_{ij} + \ln(1 - T_i) + \varepsilon_j,$$

so that

$$U_i = \sum_{j=1}^{N} \beta_{ij} \varepsilon_j - \sum_{j \neq i}^{N} \beta_{ij} \tau, \tag{32}$$

where $\tau = \ln(1 - T)$.

---

[33]Note that the consumption for good j in country i is $P_j / (1 - T_i)$. Consumption prices for good j can differ across countries because of transactions costs; they are only equalized at the point of production.

Because the exchange rate in each country is able to respond to the country-specific productivity disturbance, there is full employment and hence output at the point of production is maximized. However, the existence of separate currencies involves a cost in transferring goods not produced in the country from one currency to another. This cost rises with β_{ij}, the proportion of good j in region i's consumption bundle.

Consider now the case in which the first two countries, denoted 1 and 2, choose to form a currency union, whereas (for simplicity) all other countries continue to float against each other. The exchange rate for the union, e_{12}, is equal to the geometric average of the exchange rate of the individual countries in the free float analyzed above. Thus,

$$e_{12} = \frac{e_1 + e_2}{2}.$$

The normal wage, ω, implies excess demand for labor in the country with the larger shock and too little demand for labor in the other country. Let 1 be the country with excess demand and 2 be the one with the shortfall. Output and wages in the two countries are then

$$y_1 = \varepsilon_1, \quad w_1 = \ln \omega + \frac{(\varepsilon_1 - \varepsilon_2)}{2},$$

$$y_2 = \varepsilon_2 - \alpha \frac{(\varepsilon_1 - \varepsilon_2)}{2(1-\alpha)}, \quad w_2 = \ln \omega.$$

Thus, in country 1, where excess demand for labor prevails, the wage rises and labor remains fully employed. By contrast, in country 2 the wage stays at the normal level ω and output falls below its full employment level. The equilibrium for the other countries remains unchanged.

5.2.3   Welfare Effects

The welfare effects of the currency union can now be calculated from the difference between the level of utility achieved under the new equilibrium and the level defined by (32). For countries 1 and 2, and for region h outside the union, we have

$$\Delta U_1 = \beta_{12}\tau - \alpha\beta_{12}\frac{(\varepsilon_1 - \varepsilon_2)}{2(1-\alpha)}, \quad \Delta U_2 = \beta_{21}\tau - \alpha\beta_{22}\frac{(\varepsilon_1 - \varepsilon_2)}{2(1-\alpha)},$$

$$\Delta U_h = -\alpha\beta_{h2}\frac{(\varepsilon_1 - \varepsilon_2)}{2(1-\alpha)}.$$

In the first two equations (which show the impact on members of the currency union), the first term measures the welfare gain associated with eliminating the transactions costs with the other country. This gain depends upon the size of these costs (as measured by τ) and the importance in the home country's consumption bundle of the good produced by the other country (β_{12} or β_{21}). The second term is the loss in welfare associated with the lower output in region 2 because of the lower flexibility of real wages caused by the currency union. This depends upon the importance of good 2 in each country's consumption (as measured by β_{12} and β_{22}) and upon the size of the difference between the two productivity shocks, $\varepsilon_1 - \varepsilon_2$.

Within the union, each country has a 50 percent chance of facing excess demand for labor and a 50 percent chance of facing a shortage of demand for labor. The expected value of the change in welfare for a member of the union (say, country 1) is thus

$$E(\Delta U_1) = \beta_{12}\tau - \gamma\beta_{11}E(\varepsilon_1 - \varepsilon_2 \mid \varepsilon_1 < \varepsilon_2)\Pr(\varepsilon_1 < \varepsilon_2)$$

$$-\gamma\beta_{12}E(\varepsilon_2 - \varepsilon_1 \mid \varepsilon_1 > \varepsilon_2)\Pr(\varepsilon_1 > \varepsilon_2),$$

which is equal to

$$E(\Delta U_1) = \beta_{12}\tau - \gamma 2\Phi(0)\frac{\beta_{11}}{2}\sqrt{\sigma_1^2 + \sigma_2^2 - 2\sigma_{12}} - \gamma 2\Phi(0)\frac{\beta_{12}}{2}\sqrt{\sigma_1^2 + \sigma_2^2 - 2\sigma_{12}},$$

or equivalently

$$E(\Delta U_1) = \beta_{12}\tau - \gamma\Phi(0)(\beta_{11} + \beta_{12})\sqrt{\sigma_1^2 + \sigma_2^2 - 2\sigma_{12}}, \tag{33}$$

where $\gamma = \alpha/2(1-\alpha)$, $\Phi(0)$ is the density function of a standard normal variate with mean 0 and standard deviation 1, σ_i^2 is the variance of the productivity disturbance in country i, and σ_{12} is the covariance between ε_1 and ε_2.[34]

Equation (33)—which can be easily generalized to the case of a union with more than two countries, as shown by Bayoumi (1994)—illustrates the gains and losses involved in joining a currency union. The first term shows the gain in welfare from the lower transactions costs associated with trade with the other member of the union. This depends upon the degree to which domestic households desire the goods from the other country, β_{12}. The expected costs of joining a currency union depend upon the importance in consumption of all goods produced in the currency union, $\beta_{11} + \beta_{12}$, and on the variance of the difference between the underlying disturbances. This variance in turn depends upon both the sizes of the underlying disturbances and the correlation between these disturbances, that is, the expected size of asymmetric disturbances.

---

[34]The expected value of a standard normal variable $\varepsilon \sim N(0, \sigma^2)$, given that $\varepsilon > X$, is $\sigma f(X)/F(X)$, where $f(\cdot)$ and $F(\cdot)$ are respectively the density function and the cumulative density function of a standard $N(0, 1)$ normal distribution.

Similarly, it can be shown that the expected value of the change in welfare for a country h outside the union is

$$E(\Delta U_h) = -\gamma \Phi(0)(\beta_{h1} + \beta_{h2})\sqrt{\sigma_1^2 + \sigma_2^2 - 2\sigma_{12}},\qquad(34)$$

which indicates that the currency union reduces welfare for all countries outside of the union, with the largest reductions occurring in those countries whose consumption is most closely connected with the currency union. The intuition underlying this result is as follows. The gains from lower transactions costs are limited to countries within the union. However, the losses from a currency union, in the form of lower output caused by lower real wage flexibility, affect all regions through their trade patterns. Hence, while the welfare gains are limited to those countries within the currency union, the welfare losses affect all countries and depend, among other things, upon the suitability of the union itself in terms of the size and correlation of the underlying productivity disturbances. This result, however, is not general; lower transactions costs could benefit not only union members (as is the case in the present framework), but also countries outside the union.

Suppose now that labor is mobile across countries of the union. Specifically, assume that all labor that is offered employment within a country stays in that country. If labor is not employed, it can move to another country in the union. However, there are costs to this movement. As a result, the rise in effective labor in the region receiving the workers is only a proportion δ of labor that is not employed in the depressed region (the initial model can be thought of as having $\delta = 0$). Hence, if in the initial equilibrium with no labor mobility employment in region i is 1 and in region 2 is $1 - \theta$, the new equilibrium involves effective employment levels of $1 + \delta\theta$ and $1 - \theta$, respectively.

If θ is small, then $\ln(1 + \theta)$ can be approximated by θ. For a two-country union, the resulting equilibrium is

$$y_1 = \varepsilon_1 + \frac{\alpha\delta(\varepsilon_1 - \varepsilon_2)}{2(1 - \alpha)}, \quad w_1 = \ln\omega + \frac{(1 - \delta)(\varepsilon_1 - \varepsilon_2)}{2},$$

$$y_2 = \varepsilon_2 - \alpha\frac{(\varepsilon_1 - \varepsilon_2)}{2(1 - \alpha)}, \quad w_2 = \ln\omega.$$

The equilibrium for country 2, where labor is not fully employed, is the same, because the level of employment is unchanged. However, output (and employment) in country 1, the country with the excess demand for labor, is now higher because labor has moved to this country from the depressed country.[35] This flow of labor

---

[35] The approximation $\ln(1 + \theta) \simeq \theta$ slightly underestimates the rise in aggregate output because it failed to account for the fact that labor is moving from a low-productivity country to a high-productivity one.

reduces the fall in aggregate output for the union, thus lowering the costs of the union for all.

More formally, the expected changes in utility for a union member (say, country 1) and for country h outside it are now given by

$$E(\Delta U_1) = \beta_{12}\tau - \gamma(1 - \delta)\Phi(0)(\beta_{11} + \beta_{12})\sqrt{\sigma_1^2 + \sigma_2^2 - 2\sigma_{12}}. \qquad (35)$$

$$E(\Delta U_h) = -\gamma(1 - \delta)\Phi(0)(\beta_{h1} + \beta_{h2})\sqrt{\sigma_1^2 + \sigma_2^2 - 2\sigma_{12}}. \qquad (36)$$

A comparison of (33) and (35), and (34) and (36), shows that the gains from the union remain unchanged. However, the losses in utility resulting from lower output are reduced by a factor of $1 - \delta$. Hence, labor mobility lowers the costs associated with a currency union, both inside and outside the union. Indeed, in the extreme case of perfect mobility ($\delta = 1$), there are no output costs associated with forming a currency union.

In the foregoing discussion, as well as in much of the early literature on OCAs, optimality criteria are taken as given. Recent research, however, has emphasized that some of these criteria may be endogenous, as a result of the very existence, and integrating effects, of a currency union. For instance, it has been argued that similarity of inflation rates may be promoted by participating in a currency union, and that a high degree of convergence should not necessarily be viewed as a precondition for entry. Fiscal discipline may also be a *consequence* of joining a union, and the degree of labor mobility and wage-price flexibility may respond endogenously to the elimination of currency fluctuations. Similarly, entry into a currency union may strengthen international trade linkages over time, and therefore increase the benefits of joining the union in the first place. Indeed, to the extent that the degree of trade openness increases as a result of greater trade within the union, business cycles may become more synchronous, thereby obviating the need for countercyclical movements in interest rates.[36] The key issue in this context is whether increased integration leads to greater diversification or instead increased specialization, which would make countries more dissimilar. In theory, closer trade ties could result in national business cycles becoming more idiosyncratic, if they result in countries becoming more specialized in goods in which they have a comparative advantage. Countries would then become more sensitive to industry-specific shocks. However, if common shocks (domestic or external) tend to predominate, or if intra-industry trade accounts for most of the trade, then business cycles may indeed become more similar across countries experiencing greater trade integration.

---

[36] See Alesina and Barro (2002); Glick and Rose (2002); and Tenreyro and Barro (2007). However, Calderón et al. (2002) found that the impact of trade integration on business cycle synchronization is much lower for developing countries than it is for industrial countries.

Finally, it is worth noting that the recent crisis in the Euro Area, triggered by the sovereign debt crisis in Greece, and then spreading to Ireland, Spain, and Cyprus, contains a number of lessons for the formation and viability of currency unions in other parts of the world. Most important, a currency union may be difficult to maintain without effective measures to ensure fiscal discipline on all union members, without mechanisms to limit real exchange-rate overvaluation, current account deficits, and the build-up of foreign debt, and without union-wide institutions to supervise financial systems and maintain financial stability (Beetsma and Giuliodori, 2010; Obstfeld, 2013). In particular, as argued by De Grauwe and Ji (2014), the loss of the ability to back up public debt by issuing money makes self-fulfilling liquidity crises, degenerating into full-blown solvency crises, possible. A full discussion of these issues is beyond the scope of this book; however, one aspect of the Euro Area crisis, the link between banking crises and sovereign debt crises, will be addressed in Chapter 16 in view of their recurrent feature in developing countries.

Appendix
Krugman's Target Zone Model

A basic version of Krugman's model of a target zone (Krugman, 1991) can be presented as follows. Consider an economy with fixed output and flexible prices. Under continuous time, and with purchasing power parity holding, the equilibrium condition of the money market can be written as

$$s = m + \upsilon + \alpha \mathbb{E}(ds \mid \Omega)/dt, \tag{A1}$$

where s is the log of the nominal exchange rate, m the log of the nominal money stock, $\mathbb{E}$ the expectations operator, Ω the information set on which expectations are formed, and υ a "catch-all" variable (velocity, say) that captures determinants of money demand other than the expected change in the exchange rate, $\mathbb{E}(ds \mid \Omega)/dt$. The coefficient α can be interpreted as the semi-elasticity of money demand. The nominal money stock is assumed to be a policy variable.

Suppose that the shift variable, υ, follows a Brownian motion (the continuous-time analog of a random walk). Let us consider the behavior of the exchange rate under alternative exchange-rate regimes.

Under a freely floating regime, m is constant; from (A1), the exchange rate therefore also follows a Brownian motion process and the expected change in the exchange rate, $\mathbb{E}(ds \mid \Omega)/dt$, is zero. Graphically, this implies that the exchange rate is located along the 45-degree line FF in Figure 8.2, which relates s linearly to fundamentals, $m + \upsilon$.

Under a fixed exchange-rate regime, in order to maintain s constant, policymakers must alter the money stock m so as to offset changes in υ. The expected change in the exchange rate in this case is again zero, but the graph of s against $m + \upsilon$ is concentrated at a single point, such as point A in Figure 8.2.

Under the (basic) target zone regime, the central bank's policy is to maintain the exchange rate within the lower and upper limits of the band, s_L and s_H, by changing the level of the money stock, m. However, intervention is only *marginal*; it occurs only when the exchange rate reaches the lower or upper edge of the band. In the first case, the money supply is reduced, in the second it is increased.[37] As long as the exchange rate is inside the band, there is no intervention and the money supply is constant.

Suppose that the target zone is symmetric and perfectly credible—in the sense that agents believe that the lower and upper edges of the band will remain fixed forever, and that the exchange rate will always remain within the band. Suppose also that there is no drift in the process characterizing υ.[38] The exchange rate is thus also a Brownian motion without drift, and its expected future change is zero. Formally, the solution of the model in this particular case is a nonlinear, S-shaped relationship between the exchange rate and the fundamentals given by

$$s = m + \upsilon + A\left\{\exp[\alpha(m + \upsilon)] - \exp[-\alpha(m + \upsilon)]\right\}, \qquad (A2)$$

where $\alpha = \sqrt{2/\theta\sigma^2}$, with σ^2 the variance of the innovation in the fundamentals and A is a constant term. This curve, denoted ZZ in Figure 8.2, is pasted smoothly onto the upper and lower edges of the target zone. The S-shape feature of ZZ characterizes two main features of the Krugman model: the *honeymoon effect* and the *smooth-pasting conditions*.

The honeymoon effect captures the idea that, in a plot of s against fundamentals $m + \upsilon$ (as in Figure 8.2) under a fully credible target zone regime, s will lie on a curve that is *less steep* than the 45-degree line FF corresponding to the freely floating regime (with $s = m + \upsilon$). The reason is that if s is near the top edge of the band (above the central parity), the probability that the exchange rate will touch the edge of the band and therefore trigger exchange market intervention by the central bank is higher. As a result, the probability that the exchange rate will appreciate is higher than the probability that it will depreciate further. Thus, market participants will bid the exchange rate down to a level below the one it would be at if the probability of intervention were zero, which implies that the level of s must indeed be below the 45-degree line FF. Similar reasoning reveals that when s is closer to the lower edge of the band, it must be above FF; that is, more depreciated than the value that would prevail in a floating rate regime. The slope of ZZ is thus less than unity at

---

[37] In the basic target zone model, intervention is assumed to be unsterilized because it affects the exchange rate through changes in the supply of money.

[38] As pointed out by Svensson (1992, p. 122), the assumption that υ follows a Brownian motion without drift implies essentially that (*a*) the realized distribution of υ is continuous over time and discrete jumps cannot occur; and (*b*) changes in υ over any fixed time interval are distributed as a normal random variable with a zero mean and a variance that is proportional to the time interval's length.

all times. Consequently, the honeymoon effect implies that a credible target zone is stabilizing in the sense that (for any given range of fluctuations in the fundamentals) the exchange rate is more stable than the underlying fundamentals; the range of variation in the exchange rate is thus smaller than under a freely floating regime.

The smooth-pasting conditions are essentially boundary conditions for the solution of the basic target zone model. These conditions—which determine the value of the constant A in (A2)—imply that in the $s - (m + v)$ space, the permissible exchange-rate path must "paste" smoothly onto the upper and lower edges of the band. This result is again fairly intuitive: if the exchange rate were simply to hit the edge of the band at an angle, market participants would be offered a one-sided bet, because they know that the central bank would intervene to bring the rate back into the band. Because market participants would start taking positions *in anticipation* of the one-way bet before it occurred, this will tend to work against the influence of the fundamentals as the edges of the band are approached, for instance, a currency depreciating because of weak fundamentals will be brought near the edge of the band in anticipation of official support. Thus, the exchange rate becomes increasingly less responsive to movements in the fundamentals as the edges of the bands are approached and, in the limit, the slope of ZZ, which measures the responsiveness of the exchange rate to the fundamentals, tends to zero.

The basic target zone model presented above has been extended in various directions to account for imperfect credibility, sticky prices, intra-marginal intervention (that is, intervention aimed at returning the exchange rate to a specified target value within the band) and so on; see Svensson (1992) for a detailed account. For instance, incorporating intra-marginal, "leaning-against-the-wind" intervention substantially reduces the impact of the smooth-pasting conditions. This is because, as s approaches the edges of the band, the central bank is already known to be intervening. The perceived probability of hitting the edge of the band is therefore lower than under marginal intervention. The probability of a riskless arbitrage opportunity occurring will therefore be lower and the slope of the ZZ curve relating the exchange rate to the fundamentals will be closer to a straight line, with smooth pasting occurring only when the exchange rate is very close to the edges of the band.

As another extension of the basic target zone model, Werner (1995) considered the case in which the probability of a realignment is an increasing function of the distance of the exchange rate from the central parity, as a percentage of the width of the band. His analysis showed that the relationship between short-term interest rate differentials and the exchange rate inside the band may be nonlinear, being at first positive and eventually negative. By contrast, the model predicts no correlation between the exchange rate within the band and long-term interest rate differentials.

Finally, in the target zone model presented earlier, changes in the stochastic processes driving the fundamentals are associated with changes in the steepness of the S-curve—therefore changing the stabilizing or "honeymoon effects" of the band. By contrast, Driffill and Sola (2006) present a more general framework in which the fundamentals driving exchange-rate movements are treated as a two-state process.

The exchange rate is then allowed to switch randomly from one state (as defined by its rate of drift and innovation variance) to another.

Their analysis shows that, in contrast to the standard one-regime model, expected changes in the process that drives fundamentals may exert powerful effects on the sustainability of the exchange rate. Depending on the original state of the economy, these changes may result in either a significant gain in the stabilizing effects of the exchange-rate band, or an attack-type crisis where the policymaker is forced to implement a discrete intervention to sustain the band. The model also provides an explanation, based on fundamentals, for large changes in the exchange rate that are not associated with discernible contemporaneous changes in the fundamentals.

Chapter 9

Choosing an Exchange-Rate Regime II: The Role of Shocks, Contractionary Effects, and Moral Hazard

s indicated in the previous chapter, although many developing countries maintain a fixed parity against either a single currency or an announced basket of currencies, a growing number of them (particularly middle-income countries) are moving toward more flexible exchange arrangements. In this chapter we continue to examine the various criteria that may guide countries in choosing an exchange-rate regime. We examine, in particular, the role of shocks, the contractionary effects on real output that exchange-rate changes may entail, and moral hazard effects associated specifically with fixed exchange-rate regimes.[1] The possibility of contractionary effects is relevant for all types of exchange-rate regimes, and we discuss a number of (demand and supply) channels through which such effects may arise.

1 Role of Shocks

A widely used criterion for evaluating exchange-rate regimes focuses on their effectiveness as "automatic stabilizers," that is, the extent to which the exchange-rate regime succeeds in insulating the domestic economy from the effects of stochastic shocks, given an unchanged stance of macroeconomic policies. While in principle the insulation properties of the foreign exchange-rate regime could be evaluated with respect to the volatility that shocks may induce on a variety of domestic macroeconomic variables, the concern has most commonly been with the behavior

---

[1]We do not examine how optimal inflation tax considerations may affect the choice between exchange-rate regimes (as suggested by Fischer, 1983) because we do not believe that the argument is empirically important.

of real output, following the classic closed-economy analysis of Poole (1970). To give the flavor of the standard analysis of this issue, in this section we examine a simple model due to Genberg (1989).

1.1 ▪ Model Specification

Genberg follows the traditional literature by formulating the analysis of the insulating properties of the exchange-rate regime using a simple IS-LM model. The domestic economy is assumed to be small, completely specialized in the production of a single good that is an imperfect substitute for the good produced by the rest of the world, and perfectly integrated with international financial markets. It is subject to a variety of domestic shocks, arising in domestic goods and financial markets as well as in the wage-setting behavior of domestic workers, and is also subject to external shocks that affect the prices of foreign goods as well as world interest rates. These shocks are modeled as white noise processes that may or may not be correlated with each other.

Aggregate demand for the domestic good depends negatively on the domestic real interest rate and positively on the real exchange rate. It can therefore be expressed as:

$$y = -\alpha r + \beta(s + p^* - p) + u^{yd}, \tag{1}$$

where y is the log of domestic real output, r is the domestic real interest rate, s is the log of the nominal exchange rate (price of foreign currency in terms of domestic currency), p^* is the log of the foreign-currency price of the foreign good, p is the log of the domestic-currency price of the domestic good, and u^{yd} is a white-noise domestic aggregate demand shock. α and β are both positive parameters. The supply of the domestic good is a decreasing function of the product wage, and is given by:

$$y = -\theta(w - p) + u^{ys}, \tag{2}$$

where w is the log of the domestic nominal wage, u^{ys} is a white-noise domestic aggregate supply shock (for instance, a transitory productivity shock), and θ is a positive parameter. The actual nominal wage, in turn, deviates randomly from the contractually specified wage w^c:

$$w = w^c + u^w, \tag{3}$$

where the contractual wage is indexed to the nominal exchange rate:[2]

$$w^c = \varepsilon s + u^{wc}. \tag{4}$$

---

[2] A more elaborate treatment would involve alternative assumptions about the form of wage indexation. See, for instance, Turnovsky (1983), whose analysis shows that if the nominal wage is fully indexed to a weighted average of domestic and foreign prices, exchange-rate changes become totally ineffective as a tool to stabilize output.

The positive parameter ε is an index of the degree of of ex post indexation to the nominal exchange rate, with no indexation if $\varepsilon = 0$ and full indexation if $\varepsilon = 1$.

Because the model assumes perfect capital mobility, the domestic nominal interest rate i is given by uncovered interest parity:

$$i = i^* + (\bar{s} - s) + u^r. \tag{5}$$

Here i^* is the foreign nominal interest rate, $\bar{s}$ is the log of the expected future nominal exchange rate, and u^r can be interpreted as a white-noise shock to a mean-zero risk premium. The expected future nominal exchange rate corresponds to the equilibrium value of the nominal exchange rate in the absence of shocks, and because all the shocks in the model are white noise, the future nominal exchange rate reverts to a constant equilibrium value after one period, making $\bar{s}$ exogenous. Domestic money market equilibrium requires that the domestic nominal interest rate also satisfies:

$$i = -\lambda m + \lambda p + \gamma y + u^{md}, \tag{6}$$

where λ and γ are positive parameters and u^{md} is a money demand shock. Finally, the domestic real interest rate is given by:

$$r = i - (\bar{p} - p), \tag{7}$$

where $\bar{p}$ is the expected future price level, which is exogenous for the same reason as $\bar{s}$.

The assumption of perfect capital mobility means that domestic and foreign bonds are identical, so there is no distinction between central bank intervention in the foreign exchange market and in the domestic bond market. Exchange-rate regimes are therefore characterized by the extent to which interventions in the international bond market—and therefore changes in the domestic money supply—are influenced by an exchange-rate target. Because this is in principle a continuous variable, the analysis treats foreign exchange regimes as lying along a spectrum depending on the extent to which monetary policy is constrained by the objective of stabilizing the nominal exchange rate. The general specification for money supply determination is:

$$m = -\delta s + u^{ms}, \tag{8}$$

where u^{ms} is a white-noise money supply shock. The parameter δ, which measures the extent to which the money supply reacts to changes in the exchange rate, identifies the exchange-rate regime. The case $\delta = 0$ corresponds to a clean float with monetary targeting. In this case the domestic economy enjoys full monetary autonomy and uses it to set an exogenous target for the money supply. On the other hand, if $\delta \longrightarrow \infty$ the exchange rate is fixed, the domestic economy has no monetary autonomy, and

u^{ms} disappears from the model. In intermediate cases with finite positive values of δ (that is, with $0 < \delta < \infty$), the central bank "leans against the wind," intervening to moderate but not eliminate exchange-rate fluctuations. In this case, the central bank allows a limited degree of exchange-rate flexibility, in return for which it achieves a limited degree of monetary autonomy. However, δ may also be negative. In this case, which can be dubbed a "super float," the central bank not only does not use monetary policy to stabilize the exchange rate, but because it instead uses monetary policy to pursue domestic objectives, is actually led to magnify exchange-rate movements.

The objective of the analysis is to determine the optimal value of δ, where optimality is defined as minimizing the variance of real output.

1.2 ■ Model Solution

In solving the model, Genberg adopts the normalizations $i^* = u^{i^*}$ and $p^* = u^{p^*}$, choosing units such that in the absence of shocks, $y = p = s = w = w^c = i = m = 0$. Equivalently, the variables in the model are expressed as deviations from their expected equilibrium values. To solve the model, it is convenient to reduce it to IS and LM curves drawn in $s-y$ space. To do so, first substitute (3) and (4) into (2) and then solve for p to express the aggregate supply equation as:

$$p = (1/\theta)y + \varepsilon s + [(u^w + u^{wc}) - (1/\theta)u^{ys}], \tag{9}$$

or

$$p = (1/\theta)y + \varepsilon s + u^l,$$

where $u^l = u^{wc} + u^w - 1/\theta u^{ys}$ is a composite aggregate supply shock. Next, use the uncovered interest parity relationship to write the real interest rate as:

$$r = p - s + (u^{i^*} + u^r) = p - s + u^i, \tag{10}$$

where $u^i = u^{i^*} + u^r$ is a composite external financial shock. Substituting this equation into the goods market equilibrium condition produces:

$$y = -\alpha(p - s + u^i) + \beta(s + p^* - p) + u^{yd},$$

or

$$y = -(\alpha + \beta)p + (\alpha + \beta)s + (u^{yd} + \beta u^{p^*} - \alpha u^i),$$

that is

$$y = -(\alpha + \beta)p + (\alpha + \beta)s + (u^y - \alpha u^i), \tag{11}$$

where $u^y = u^{yd} + \beta u^{p^*}$. The error term in this equation combines the aggregate demand shock, an external price shock, and the composite external financial shock, with the first two combined into the goods market demand-side shock u^y. Using the aggregate supply relationship (9) we have:

$$y = -(\alpha + \beta)[(1/\theta)y + \varepsilon s + u^l] + (\alpha + \beta)s + (u^{yd} + \beta u^{p^*} - \alpha u^i),$$

or

$$[1 + (\alpha + \beta)/\theta)]y = (\alpha + \beta)(1 - \varepsilon)s - (\alpha + \beta)u^l + (u^{yd} + \beta u^{p^*} - \alpha u^i),$$

that is

$$y = (\alpha + \beta)(1 - \varepsilon)s - (\alpha + \beta)u^l + u^y - \alpha u^i. \tag{12}$$

This yields the economy's IS curve, which is affected by goods market demand-side shocks, goods market supply-side shocks, and external financial shocks. To derive the LM curve, substitute the uncovered interest parity condition, the money supply equation, and the aggregate supply equation into the money market equilibrium condition. The result is:

$$-s + (u^{i^*} + u^r) = -\lambda(-\delta s + u^{ms}) + \lambda((1/\theta)y + \varepsilon s + u^l) + \gamma y + u^{md}. \tag{13}$$

Solving this for s produces:

$$(1 + \lambda\varepsilon + \lambda\delta)s = -(\gamma + \lambda/\theta)y + (u^{i^*} + u^r) + \lambda u^{ms} - u^{md} - \lambda u^l \tag{14}$$

$$= -(\gamma + \lambda/\theta)y + u^i + u^m - \lambda u^l,$$

where $u^m = \lambda u^{ms} - u^{md}$ is a composite money market shock.

Finally, substituting the LM equation into the IS equation and simplifying, a reduced-form equation for y can be derived that expresses the deviation of domestic real output from its equilibrium value as a function of aggregate demand shocks u^y, aggregate supply shocks u^l, money market shocks u^m, and external financial shocks u^i:

$$\Psi y = -(x + \lambda)u^l + \frac{1}{\alpha + \beta}xu^y + \left(1 - \frac{\alpha}{\alpha + \beta}x\right)u^i + u^m, \tag{15}$$

where

$$\Psi = \gamma + \frac{\lambda}{\theta} + \frac{1 + \frac{\alpha + \beta}{\theta}}{\alpha + \beta}x, \quad x = \frac{1 + \lambda\varepsilon + \lambda\delta}{1 - \varepsilon}. \tag{16}$$

Note that the intervention parameter δ enters these equations through the variable x, and x is an increasing function of δ. Assuming that the four types of shocks are mutually uncorrelated, the implied variance of y is given by:

$$var(y) = \frac{1}{\Psi^2}\left\{(x+\lambda)^2\sigma_l + \frac{1}{(\alpha+\beta)^2}x^2\sigma_y + \left(1 - \frac{\alpha}{\alpha+\beta}x\right)^2\sigma_i + \sigma_m\right\}. \quad (17)$$

The problem of choosing the optimal regime is now reduced to that of minimizing the variance of y with respect to x, and then inferring the optimal value of δ from the optimal value of x according to:

$$\delta^* = \frac{1-\varepsilon}{\lambda}x^* - \left(\frac{1}{\lambda} + \varepsilon\right). \quad (18)$$

Four main results can be derived from this framework.

First, suppose that money market shocks are the dominant source of stochastic shocks in the domestic economy. In the limit, suppose that $\sigma_l = \sigma_y = \sigma_i = 0$, so that all shocks are monetary. In that case, minimizing the variance of y requires maximizing Ψ^2. Because Ψ is a positive linear function of x, Ψ^2 goes to infinity as x goes to infinity. But because x is a positive linear function of δ, this implies letting δ become infinitely large, that is, fixing the exchange rate. Thus, when money market shocks dominate, fixing the exchange rate minimizes the variance of domestic output. Indeed, because $1/\Psi^2$ goes to zero under fixed exchange rates, fixing the exchange rate in this case stabilizes output perfectly.

Second, and alternatively, suppose that goods market shocks are dominant, so $\sigma_l = \sigma_i = \sigma_m = 0$. In this case, it is easy to see from (18) that minimizing the variance of y requires minimizing $(x/\Psi)^2$, which implies setting $x = 0$. From (8), the optimal degree of intervention is therefore equal to:

$$\delta^* = -\left(\varepsilon + \frac{1}{\lambda}\right). \quad (19)$$

Thus, allowing some degree of exchange-rate flexibility is not only optimal in this case, but the central bank should actually reinforce nominal exchange-rate movements, expanding the domestic money supply when the exchange rate depreciates. A pure float (without monetary intervention that reinforces exchange-rate movements) is optimal in this case only if there is no wage indexation ($\varepsilon = 0$) and the interest rate semi-elasticity of the demand for money is very low (λ is high), so that the LM curve is vertical.

Third, the case where the dominant source of shocks is fluctuations in international financial conditions (either the world interest rate or the risk premium), so that $\sigma_l = \sigma_y = \sigma_m = 0$, illustrates the sensitivity of the verdict on regime optimality to other behavioral parameters in the economy. In this case, the optimal regime is chosen by minimizing $[\{1 - \alpha x/(\alpha + \beta)\}/\Psi]^2$, so it implies setting $x = 1 + \beta/\alpha$. The implied solution for δ is:

$$\delta^* = \frac{1 - \varepsilon}{\lambda}(1 + \beta/\alpha) - \left(\varepsilon + \frac{1}{\lambda}\right). \tag{20}$$

Note that this implies more exchange-rate stabilization than in the previous case, when the main source of volatility was aggregate demand shocks. The optimal degree of exchange-rate stabilization increases with the real exchange-rate elasticity of aggregate demand β and decreases with the interest rate elasticity of aggregate demand α. Note that if β is sufficiently large or α is sufficiently small so that $\alpha/(\alpha + \beta)$ is close to zero, then the coefficient of σ_i in (18) approaches unity. By analogy with the case of domestic monetary shocks, fixing the exchange rate is optimal in this case. On the other hand, if β is sufficiently small and α is sufficiently large so that $\alpha/(\alpha + \beta)$ is near unity, the optimal value of x approaches unity as well, in which case the optimal degree of intervention is given by:

$$\delta^* = -\varepsilon\left(1 + \frac{1}{\lambda}\right), \tag{21}$$

which again goes beyond a clean float to suggest magnification of exchange-rate movements by monetary policy. However, in the absence of wage indexation, ε is zero. In that case, $\delta^* = 0$ and the optimal regime is a clean float.

Finally, consider the case where domestic supply shocks dominate, so $\sigma_y = \sigma_i = \sigma_m = 0$. Optimal policy in this case requires choosing δ so as to minimize $[(x + \lambda)/\Psi]^2$, which implies setting $x = -\lambda$. The optimal degree of intervention becomes:

$$\delta^* = -\left(1 + \frac{1}{\lambda}\right). \tag{22}$$

Again, in general it is optimal for the central bank to reinforce exchange-rate movements that are driven by supply shocks. Because λ is positive, it is optimal to refrain from doing so only if the interest rate semi-elasticity of the demand for money is zero, so the LM curve is vertical in s-y space.

Overall, this analysis suggests that from the perspective of providing automatic stabilization to domestic output, fixed exchange rates will rarely be optimal. Fixing the exchange rate is an optimal strategy only when domestic money market shocks dominate. Because stabilization of domestic real output is a cherished objective of policymakers, and because the simple framework in which these results were derived is a workhorse open-economy model in policy circles, this analysis has provided a powerful argument in support of floating exchange rates.[3]

There is some evidence to corroborate the view that flexible exchange-rate regimes are able to "buffer" real shocks better than fixed regimes. Broda (2004) for instance used a sample of seventy-five developing countries for the period 1973–1998 to assess whether the response of real output, real exchange rates, and inflation to terms-of-trade shocks differs systematically across exchange-rate regimes. He found that the behavior of both output and the real exchange rate differed significantly. Under fixed exchange-rate regimes, negative terms-of-trade shocks are followed by large and significant losses in terms of growth, whereas the real exchange rate begins to depreciate only after two years. By contrast, under flexible regimes, output losses are smaller and real depreciations are large and immediate. Edwards and Levy-Yeyati (2005) also found that terms-of-trade shocks get amplified in countries that have more rigid exchange-rate regimes; therefore, flexible exchange-rate arrangements appear to be better able to accommodate real external shocks.[4] In a panel study of forty-two developing countries, Hoffman (2007) found that flexible exchange-rate regimes are better able to mitigate the volatility of domestic output and the real exchange rate induced by shocks to world output and interest rates. Thus, all three studies support the view that output volatility tends to be smaller under flexible exchange rates, as predicted by the foregoing analysis.

However, stabilization of economic activity is not the only objective that can be sought through the choice of exchange-rate regime, and the relative virtues of floating the exchange rate are not as readily apparent with respect to other macroeconomic objectives. Indeed, an extensive analytical literature has analyzed the links between the type of disturbances that an economy is subject to and the optimal choice of an exchange-rate system, as well as the optimal degree of exchange-rate flexibility (or foreign exchange market intervention), taking into account the possibility of conflicts among various policy objectives—such as the minimization of the variance of not only real output, but also the price level or real expenditure (see, for instance, Collard and Dellas, 2005). As pointed out by Van Gompel (1994) in his overview, there are very few robust results that emerge from the literature.

2 | Contractionary Effects

One reason for the absence of robust results is that the effects of exchange-rate changes depend on the structure of the economy. In this section we illustrate this point by examining a variety of channels through which an exchange-rate

---

[3] Mundell (1961) initially applied similar reasoning to the analysis of optimum currency areas (see Chapter 8).

[4] They also find evidence of an asymmetric response to terms-of-trade shocks; the output response is larger for negative than for positive shocks.

depreciation may actually exert contractionary effects on economic activity, in contrast with the model of the last section.[5]

Consider a small open economy that operates under a fixed-exchange-rate system. We adopt a "dependent economy" framework in which traded and nontraded goods are produced using homogeneous, intersectorally mobile labor; sector-specific capital; and imported inputs. Production costs may also be affected by the need to finance working capital. Wage determination is crucial for the issue discussed here, and we shall allow for a variety of mechanisms to determine the nominal wage. Households hold money, capital, and foreign securities and issue debt to each other.

This analytical framework is quite general, and consistent with the setup considered in various other places in this book. The first two parts of this section consider the separate effects of a nominal devaluation on aggregate demand for, and supply of, domestic output, and the last part reviews the empirical evidence on the contractionary effects of devaluation in developing countries.

2.1 ■ Effects on Aggregate Demand

In a small open economy producing traded and nontraded goods, the demand curve facing the traded goods sector is given by the law of one price:

$$P_T = E P_T^*,$$

where P_T is the domestic-currency price of traded goods, E is the nominal exchange rate (units of domestic currency per unit of foreign currency), and P_T^* is the foreign-currency price of traded goods, which we take to be unity. Aggregate real demand for nontraded goods, which we denote d_N, consists of the sum of domestic consumption c_N, investment I_N, and government demand g_N for such goods:

$$d_N = c_N + I_N + g_N.$$

We now examine the effects of devaluation on the components of this equation. Consumption and investment demand are treated separately, and government demand is incorporated in the discussion of the government budget constraint in the subsection on consumption (under the heading "Effects Through Changes in Real Tax Revenue"). Finally, we consider the impact on the domestic interest rate, which affects both consumption and investment demand.

2.1.1 *Consumption*

Consider first the effects of devaluation on consumption demand for nontraded goods. We will adopt a fairly general ad hoc specification of household behavior, in

---

[5]The analysis in this section draws heavily on Lizondo and Montiel (1989).

which demand for nontraded goods depends on the real exchange rate $z = P_T/P_N$, where P_N is the domestic-currency price of nontraded goods; on real factor income received by households, y, net of real taxes paid by them, tax; on real household financial wealth, a; and on the real interest rate $i - \pi^a$, where i is the domestic nominal interest rate and π^a the expected inflation rate. Possible distributional effects on aggregate consumption are captured by a shift parameter, denoted Θ. Consumption demand for nontraded goods thus takes the general form[6]

$$c_N = c_N(z, y - tax, i - \pi^a, a; \Theta). \tag{23}$$

We now examine the effects of devaluation on each of the arguments of c_N.

Relative Price Effects. A nominal devaluation brings about changes in relative prices that affect the demand for domestically produced goods. Within the "dependent economy" framework adopted in this section, it is necessary to distinguish the relative price effect on the demand for traded goods and for nontraded goods. The *total* (domestic and foreign) demand for domestically produced traded goods is perfectly elastic and therefore is not affected by relative price changes. Although the domestic demand for these goods is affected by relative prices, an important effect for balance-of-payments purposes, it is the total demand that is relevant for output and employment in this sector. But changes in relative prices that affect the domestic demand for nontraded goods will affect the total demand for these goods, since both demands are the same by definition. A devaluation therefore will have a relative price effect on the demand for domestically produced goods through its effect on the demand for nontraded goods. A real depreciation of the domestic currency (that is, an increase in the relative price of traded to nontraded goods), with real income held constant, will increase the demand for nontraded goods, and vice versa. This implies a positive partial derivative c_{Nz} in (23).[7]

Real Income Effects. Devaluations also produce changes in real income that affect the demand for domestically produced goods. These real-income changes can be decomposed into those resulting from changes in relative prices at the initial level of output and those resulting from changes in output at the new relative prices. Because we are discussing effects on the demand for domestic output, we will be interested primarily in the change in real income at the initial level of output, which provides the impact effect. Effects occurring through the endogenous change in output (that

---

[6]Although (23) is an ad hoc specification of aggregate consumption behavior, it mimics to some extent the consumption behavior implied by an optimizing model; that is, one in which intertemporal utility is additively separable, the rate of time preference is constant, and instantaneous utility is of the constant relative risk aversion family.

[7]This substitution effect, present in most models, is excluded in some analyses of contractionary devaluation—such as Krugman and Taylor (1978)—by the assumption that consumers demand only nontraded goods.

is, Keynesian multiplier effects) are omitted here, since the purpose of the analysis is precisely to investigate the factors that determine the qualitative direction of such changes.

To analyze the income effect, we need some definitions. The price level will be denoted by P, with

$$P = E^\delta P_N^{1-\delta}, \quad 0 < \delta < 1 \tag{24}$$

where δ is the share of traded goods in consumption.[8] Real income measured in units of the consumption bundle is equal to

$$y = y_N z^{-\delta} + y_T z^{1-\delta}, \tag{25}$$

where y_N is the production of nontraded goods and y_T is the production of traded goods.

The effect of a real devaluation on real income for a given level of output is ambiguous. Differentiating (25) with respect to z, with y_N and y_T kept constant, yields

$$dy/dz = z^{-1}(\alpha - \delta)(y_N z^{-\delta} + y_T z^{1-\delta}), \tag{26}$$

where α is the share of traded goods in total output:

$$\alpha = z y_T / (y_N + z y_T). \tag{27}$$

Equation (26) shows that the impact effect on real income depends on whether traded goods have a higher share in consumption or in income. Clearly, a variety of results are possible. Assume, for instance, that there is no expenditure on investment goods, so that consumption and expenditure are the same, and suppose that there is no public sector expenditure, so that $c_N = y_N$. In this case the net effect on real income depends on whether consumption of traded goods is higher or lower than y_T—that is, on whether there is a trade deficit or a trade surplus. If there is a deficit, then $\delta > \alpha$, and real income declines with a real devaluation. The reason is that the goods whose relative price has increased (traded goods) have a higher weight in consumption than in income. Introducing investment and public expenditure naturally complicates these simple results.

For models with traded and nontraded goods, besides the ambiguous effect on real income derived here for given levels of output, the demand for nontraded goods may also increase because of a higher level of output of traded goods. In general, the production of traded goods will increase as long as the price of its input

---

[8]Implicitly, therefore, we are assuming that the consumers' utility function is of the Cobb-Douglas form. See Chapter 10.

does not rise by the full amount of the devaluation. As shown later, whether the latter condition holds will depend on the degree of wage indexation, the stance of inflationary expectations, and other factors.

Effects through Imported Inputs. The presence of imported inputs is an additional factor that may have a negative effect on the demand for domestically produced goods after a devaluation. The reason is that, under certain conditions, imported inputs make it more likely that the real income effect of a devaluation, discussed previously, will be negative.

The modification that imported inputs introduce in the previous analysis is that they must be subtracted from domestic output to obtain national income. A real devaluation therefore affects real income not only through the channels mentioned previously, but also through changes in the real value of imported inputs.

There are two opposing effects of a real devaluation on the real value of imported inputs. On the one hand, a real devaluation increases the relative price of imported inputs in terms of the basket of consumption, thereby increasing the real value of the initial volume of imported inputs. On the other hand, if the price of labor does not increase by the full amount of the devaluation, the relative price of imported inputs increases, and domestic producers have an incentive to substitute labor for imported inputs, thus reducing the volume of imported inputs. Clearly, the net effect of these two opposing forces depends, among other things, on the degree of factor substitutability in production and on the extent to which a devaluation is transmitted to wages.

Assuming that traded goods are produced with a fixed amount of specific capital and with labor, and that nontraded goods are produced with an imported input and labor according to a CES production function with elasticity of substitution σ, Lizondo and Montiel (1989) show that the effect of a real devaluation on real income identified in (26) is modified in the presence of imported inputs by the inclusion of an additional term given by

$$z^{-\delta} J_N [\sigma - (1 - \delta)], \tag{28}$$

where J_N is the volume of imported intermediate goods used in the nontradable sector. The presence of imported inputs will thus contribute to a reduction in real income when $(1 - \delta) > \sigma$. It is clear that the net effect is ambiguous, and a variety of results are possible. For instance, if there is no substitution in production (as in Krugman and Taylor, 1978), $\sigma = 0$ and the net effect is necessarily negative.

In summary, the net effect on real income due to the presence of imported inputs is ambiguous. It is more likely to be negative the lower the elasticity of substitution between imported inputs and primary factors, and the higher the share of nontraded goods in the price index.

Income Redistribution Effects. Another factor frequently mentioned as a possible cause for a decline in the demand for domestically produced goods after a devaluation is the redistribution of income from sectors with high propensity to spend on goods of this type to sectors with a lower propensity. Alexander (1952) recognized the possibility that redistribution of income may affect expenditure, and included it as one of the direct effects of devaluation on absorption. He discussed redistribution of income in two directions, both associated with an increase in the price level: first, from wages to profits because of lags in the adjustment of wages to higher prices, and second, from the private to the public sector because of the existing structure of taxation. If profit recipients have a lower marginal propensity to spend than the private sector, absorption will decline for a given level of real income. Note, however, that whereas Alexander was interested in the effects on the trade balance and therefore examined the behavior of total expenditure, the focus here is on the demand for domestic output.

Of the two types of redistribution mentioned above, we will examine here the shift of income from wages to profits, leaving the shift from the private to the public sector to be discussed later. The redistribution from wages to profits was examined formally by Díaz-Alejandro (1963, 1965) and Krugman and Taylor (1978), and in both models the only impact effect of a devaluation is to redistribute a given level of real income from wages to profits because of an increase in prices, with nominal wages kept constant. Both show that this may cause a reduction in the demand for domestic output if the marginal propensity to spend on home goods is lower for profit recipients than for wage earners.

However, this is not the only type of income redistribution effect between workers and owners of capital that can be associated with a devaluation. For instance, in a model with traded and nontraded goods, flexible wages, and sector-specific capital, a real devaluation would reduce real profits in the nontraded goods sector, increase real profits in the traded goods sector, and have an ambiguous effect on real wages. Real wages would increase in terms of nontraded goods but would decline in terms of traded goods. Sectoral considerations may therefore become important, and it is not clear a priori what the effect of this type of redistribution would be on the demand for the domestically produced good. Cooper (1971) mentioned the possibility of redistribution from the factors engaged in purely domestic industries to the factors engaged in export- and import-competing industries, and he recognized that, although in some cases this may have reduced demand, under different circumstances this may induce a spending boom. Furthermore, in the longer run, when all factors of production are mobile, the redistribution of income may depend on technological considerations. For instance, in a Heckscher-Ohlin world, real wages and profits in terms of either of the two goods depend, with intersectorally mobile labor and capital, on factor intensities. A real devaluation will increase real payments to factors used intensively by the traded goods sector and will reduce real payments to the other factor. All these considerations imply that the pattern of redistribution may change over time as the economy adjusts to the new situation after a devaluation. It seems natural to think of the redistribution of income as a dynamic process encompassing the various situations mentioned above. First, nominal wages are fixed for some period after a devaluation, then wages adjust to the new price level and workers move among occupations while capital remains sector-specific, and, finally, capital also moves to the sectors with higher returns.

Besides the theoretical issues mentioned above, there remains the question of how important the effect on the demand for domestic output of redistribution from wages to profits is likely to be. Alexander (1952) emphasized that what is important is the marginal propensity to spend, so that even if profit recipients have a lower marginal propensity to consume than wage earners, higher profits may stimulate investment, and the redistribution of income may therefore result in increased absorption. Díaz-Alejandro (1963), however, argued that investment expenditure is even more biased toward traded goods than consumption expenditure, and because investment expenditure is undertaken by profit recipients, the demand for domestically produced goods is likely to decline. Even if this proposition about the relative marginal propensities to spend on domestic output by workers and owners of capital is accepted, the next question is how important is the redistribution of income that will lead to a change in the pattern of aggregate expenditure. On this issue the evidence does not provide firm support for the hypothesis of redistribution against labor. Using data from thirty-one devaluation episodes, Edwards (1989b) showed that in fifteen cases there was no significant change in income distribution, whereas in eight cases the share of labor in GDP declined significantly, and in seven other instances it increased significantly.

Effects through Changes in Real Tax Revenue. To the extent that devaluation affects the real tax burden on the private sector, thus redistributing income from the private to the public sector, changes in real tax revenue represent a separate channel through which a contractionary effect on economic activity may result. This effect may operate through the demand for domestic output or through its supply, and in the former case through private consumption expenditure or through private investment. Up to the present, only the effect of devaluation on the real tax burden faced by consumers has figured prominently in the literature, and here we shall focus on this effect.

As discussed in Chapter 1, many governments in developing countries derive a substantial proportion of their revenues from import and export taxes. Thus, as argued by Krugman and Taylor (1978), a nominal devaluation that succeeds in depreciating the real exchange rate will increase the real tax burden on the private sector by increasing the real value of trade taxes, for given levels of imports and exports.[9] This effect depends, however, on the presence of ad valorem rather than

---

[9]This result will continue to hold, after allowing for quantity responses on the part of imports and exports, as long as the price elasticity of demand for imports is not too large. It can readily be demonstrated in a model in which traded goods are differentiated into exportables and importables, as in Khan and Montiel (1987).

specific taxes on foreign trade. To the extent that nominal devaluation results in increases in the domestic price level, the presence of specific taxes would reverse the effect emphasized by Krugman and Taylor, because the real value of nonindexed specific taxes would fall as a consequence of the increase in the general price level brought about by a nominal devaluation.

The latter is, of course, simply a specific instance of the Olivera-Tanzi effect discussed in Chapter 3, which surprisingly has played only a limited role in the literature on contractionary devaluation. This effect is present when lags in tax collection or delays in adjusting the nominal value of specific taxes cause the real value of tax collections to fall during periods of rising prices. To the extent that nominal devaluations are associated with at least temporary bursts of inflation, the Olivera-Tanzi effect should be expected to be operative during the immediate post-devaluation period when prices are rising. Because the real tax burden would fall as a consequence of this effect, devaluation would exert an expansionary short-run effect on aggregate demand through this channel.

A third channel through which devaluation may affect aggregate demand by its effects on the real tax burden borne by households is that of discretionary tax changes caused by the effect of an exchange-rate adjustment on government finances. To clarify this point, let us suppose that, other than trade taxes, all taxes are levied on households in lump-sum fashion. To incorporate the two channels discussed above, let us write the government's real tax receipts, denoted T_r, as

$$T_r = T_r(\overset{+}{z}, \overset{-}{\pi}, \overset{+}{\tau}),$$

where τ is a parameter that captures the effects of discretionary taxes and π is the inflation rate. The first two terms in the function $T_r(\cdot)$ capture the trade tax and Olivera-Tanzi effects. The government's budget constraint takes the form

$$T_r(z, \pi, \tau) \equiv g_N z^{-\delta} + g_T z^{1-\delta} + i^* z^{1-\delta} F^g - z^{1-\delta}(\dot{L}^g/E + \dot{F}^g), \qquad (29)$$

where g_T and g_N denote government spending on traded and nontraded goods, respectively; i^* the foreign nominal interest rate; F^g net public external debt; and L^g the stock of net government liabilities to the central bank.[10]

The first point to be made from identity (29) is that, in the Krugman-Taylor case, the increase in the real value of trade taxes attendant on a real devaluation cannot be the end of the story. As identity (29) makes clear, this increase in $T_r(\cdot)$ must be offset somewhere else within the government budget, because identity (29) must hold at all times. The effect of an increase in real trade taxes on aggregate demand will depend on the nature of this offset. If, for instance, the offset takes the form of a *reduction* in discretionary taxes τ, leaving real tax receipts $T_r(\cdot)$ unchanged, the contractionary

---

[10] As in Chapter 4, we assume here that the government does not borrow directly from the public.

effect on aggregate demand will disappear altogether. Other possible offsets will differ in their consequences for aggregate demand, in ways that are explored below.

A nominal devaluation that results in a real depreciation may potentially affect each of the entries on the right-hand side of identity $T_r(\cdot)$. Among these, several authors have noted the importance of the existence of a stock of foreign currency-denominated external debt in affecting the possible contractionary effects of a nominal devaluation (see Gylfason and Risager, 1984; van Wijnbergen, 1986; and Edwards, 1989b). In all of these cases, however, the external debt has been treated as if it were owed by the *private* sector.[11] In many countries, however, most external debt in developing countries continues to be owed by the public sector. Indeed, currency substitution and capital flight have probably made the private sector in many developing countries a net *creditor* in foreign-currency terms. The sectoral allocation of debt can be ignored, and all debt treated as private debt, only in the case of complete Ricardian equivalence, which is discussed below. For the moment, we examine the implications of public external debt in the absence of Ricardian equivalence.[12]

If the public sector is a net external debtor, a real devaluation will increase the real value of interest payments abroad. As identity (29) indicates, the government can finance such increased debt-service payments by increased taxation, reduced spending, or increased borrowing from the central bank or from abroad. The effects on aggregate demand will depend on the mode of financing. If the government chooses to increase discretionary taxes, the effects on aggregate demand would be contractionary because private disposable income would fall. This is implicitly the effect captured by van Wijnbergen (1986), Edwards (1989b), and Gylfason and Risager (1984) in treating all debt as private debt and in deducting interest payments from private disposable income. The effect on private consumption would be similar to that of an increase in discretionary taxes arising from any other cause. As a second alternative, increased real debt-service payments could be financed by a reduction in government spending on goods and services. If this takes the form of reduced spending on *nontraded* goods, the contractionary effects on aggregate demand would exceed those associated with tax financing unless the propensity to spend out of taxes approached unity. In contrast, if spending reductions fall on *traded* goods, the contractionary effects would be nil, because the small-country assumption ensures that government demand would be replaced by external demand. Finally, the increased real debt-service payments could be financed by borrowing, either from the central bank or from abroad. In this case, with the exchange rate fixed at its new level, contractionary effects would again fail to appear because the counterpart to the increased flow of credit to the government would simply consist of an outflow of foreign reserves in the former case, and of increased government external debt in the latter, with no impact on aggregate demand in either case.

---

[11] If such debt were in fact owed by the private sector, of course, F^g would not appear in identity (29).

[12] It was argued in Chapter 4 that this is the empirically relevant case for most developing countries.

In addition to the effect on real interest payments, devaluation would affect the real value of government expenditures on goods and services. Because the real value of spending on traded goods rises while that on nontraded goods falls, the total effect depends on the composition of government spending between traded and nontraded goods. Should the net effect be an increase in real spending, the same financing options as before would present themselves. This would be the case if government spending were heavily weighted toward traded goods. In the alternative case, a *reduction* in discretionary taxes may ensue, for instance, with corresponding expansionary effects on aggregate demand.

Finally, the effect of a devaluation on discretionary taxes will also depend on the monetary policy regime in effect. This channel is captured by the last term on the right-hand side of identity (29). If the central bank pegs the flow of credit to the government in *nominal* terms, the rise in prices that attends a nominal devaluation will reduce $\dot{L}^g/P$ and call for an adjustment in the government budget, possibly through a discretionary tax increase. If the flow $\dot{L}^g$ is adjusted to accommodate the price increase, however, no further changes in the budget will emanate from this source. The last option we consider is that in which real valuation gains on the central bank's stock of foreign exchange reserves are passed along to the government. In this case $\dot{L}^g/P$ could *increase*, and the financing options would include an expansionary tax reduction.

Wealth Effects. Because an increase in wealth can be expected to increase household consumption, a devaluation can also affect the demand for domestically produced goods through its effects on real wealth. If the level of domestic expenditure depends on real wealth, and private sector asset holdings are not indexed to the domestic price level, a devaluation changes the real value of existing wealth and thus affects the demand for home goods.

Nominal wealth is often taken to coincide with the nominal stock of money, thus converting the wealth effect into a real cash balance effect. Alexander (1952) emphasized this channel when analyzing the consequences a devaluation would have for absorption. He noted that a devaluation would increase the price level and thus reduce the real stock of money. This reduction would in turn have two types of effects, both tending to reduce absorption: a direct effect, when individuals reduce their expenditures in order to replenish their real money holdings to the desired level; and an indirect effect, when individuals try to shift their portfolios from other assets into money, thus driving up the domestic interest rate in the absence of perfect capital mobility. We will be concerned in the present discussion only with the direct effect; the other effect is included in our discussion of the interest rate at the end of this section.

The real cash balance effect has been widely recognized and incorporated in the literature on contractionary devaluation. For instance, Gylfason and Schmid (1983), Hanson (1983), Islam (1984), Gylfason and Radetzki (1991), Buffie (1986a), and

Edwards (1989*b*) take this effect into account by including real cash balances directly as an argument in the expenditure function or indirectly through the use of a hoarding function. In all these cases a devaluation, by increasing the price level in the presence of a given initial nominal stock of money, reduces real cash balances, thereby exerting a contractionary effect on demand.

This unambiguous result must be modified if the private sector holds other types of assets whose nominal value increases with a devaluation. For instance, assume that the private sector holds foreign-currency-denominated assets in an amount F^p. Then real wealth would be equal to

$$a = \frac{M}{P} + \frac{EF^p}{P} = z^{1-\delta}\left(\frac{M}{E} + F^p\right). \tag{30}$$

The percentage change in real wealth from a nominal devaluation would then be equal to

$$\hat{a} = (1-\delta)\hat{z} - \lambda\varepsilon, \tag{31}$$

where λ is the ratio of domestic money to private sector wealth and ε the devaluation rate. Because $\hat{z}$ is bounded above by ε (unless the price of nontraded goods declines with a devaluation, which we do not consider), (31) has the following implications. If domestic money is the only asset in the portfolio of the private sector, $\lambda = 1$, a devaluation necessarily has a negative effect on real wealth and on demand. This was the case considered above. This is *a fortiori* the case if the private sector is a net debtor in foreign currency, so $\lambda > 1$. Alternatively, if the private sector is a net creditor in foreign currency, the result is ambiguous. The source of the ambiguity is that, although the real value of the stock of domestic money declines because of the increase in the price level, the real value of the stock of foreign assets increases as long as the domestic price level does not rise by the full amount of the devaluation. The effect on the demand for domestic goods may thus be positive or negative. It is more likely to be negative the higher the share of traded goods in the price index δ, the lower the real depreciation $\hat{z}$, and the higher the share of domestic money in private sector wealth λ.

2.1.2   *Investment*

The effects of a devaluation on private demand for nontraded goods also depend on investment demand for this category of goods emanating from both the traded and nontraded goods sectors. For simplicity, suppose that the capital stock in each sector consists of traded and nontraded goods combined in fixed proportions. A unit of capital in the traded goods sector consists of γ_N^T units of nontraded goods and γ_T^T units of traded goods, whereas in the nontraded goods sector capital consists of γ_N^N nontraded goods and γ_T^N traded goods. Then the prices of a unit of capital in the traded goods sector P_{KT} and in the nontraded goods sector P_{KN} are given by

$$P_{KT} = \gamma_N^T P_N + \gamma_T^T E, \tag{32}$$

$$P_{KN} = \gamma_N^N P_N + \gamma_T^N E. \tag{33}$$

Suppose, as indicated above, that output in each sector is produced by using capital, labor, and imported inputs. The marginal product of capital in the two sectors is therefore given by[13]

$$m_K^T = F_K^T(w/\overline{E}; \overline{K}_T), \tag{34}$$

$$m_K^N = F_K^N(w/\overline{P_N}, \overline{z}; \overline{K}_N), \tag{35}$$

where w denotes the nominal exchange rate.

In the short run, the capital stock is fixed. By the first-order conditions for profit maximization, an increase in the product wage will reduce demand for labor. The ensuing increase in the capital intensity of production will cause the marginal product of capital to fall. A similar effect results from an increase in the real cost of imported inputs, z. Note that this variable does not enter (34), because the price of imported inputs in terms of traded goods is not affected by devaluation.

Because the demand for investment goods is inherently forward looking, today's demand for investment in each sector will depend on the anticipated future paths of w, E, P_N, and the nominal interest rate i. Under rational expectations, these paths can be generated only by the full solution of a model. Because we do not present such a solution here, we will examine the issues involved under the assumption that all relative prices are expected to remain at their post-devaluation levels. Under this assumption, the sectoral net investment functions can be expressed as

$$\hat{K}^T = q_T \left\{ \frac{Em_K^T/P_{KT}}{i + \eta - \pi_{KT}} - 1 \right\}, \quad q_T(0) = 0, \; q_T' > 0$$

$$= q_T \left\{ \frac{EF_K^T(w/E; K_T)P_{KT}}{i + \eta - \pi_{KT}} - 1 \right\}, \tag{36}$$

---

[13]The signs of the partial derivatives with respect to w/E, w/P_N, and z in (34) and (35) assume that factors of production are complementary in the sense that an increase in the use of one factor increases the marginal productivity of the other factors.

$$\hat{K}^N = q_N \left\{ \frac{P_N m_K^T / P_{KN}}{i + \eta - \pi_{KN}} - 1 \right\}, \quad q_N(0) = 0, \ q_N' > 0$$

$$= q_N \left\{ \frac{P_N F_K^N(w/P_N, z; K_N) P_{KN}}{i + \eta - \pi_{KN}} - 1 \right\}, \tag{37}$$

where π_{Kh} denotes the rate of increase in the price of capital in sector h.

Net investment demand in each sector depends on the ratio of the marginal product of capital to the real interest rate. Gross investment demand is the sum of net investment and replacement investment, where depletion is assumed to take place at the uniform rate $\mu > 0$ in both sectors. Equations (36) and (37) can now be combined with replacement investment to yield the total investment demand for nontraded goods:

$$I_N = I_N^T + I_N^N \tag{38}$$

$$= \gamma_N^T q_T \left\{ \frac{E F_K^T(w/E; K_T) P_{KT}}{i + \eta - \pi_{KT}} - 1 \right\} K_T + \mu(\gamma_N^T K_T + \gamma_N^N K_N)$$

$$+ \gamma_N^N q_N \left\{ \frac{P_N F_K^N(w/P_N, z; K_N) P_{KN}}{i + \eta - \pi_{KN}} - 1 \right\} K_N.$$

The effects of a real devaluation on the investment demand for nontraded goods can now be examined.

Both Branson (1986) and Buffie (1986*b*) have emphasized that, because a substantial portion of any new investment in developing countries is likely to consist of imported capital goods, a real depreciation will raise the price of capital in terms of home goods, discouraging new investment and exerting a contractionary effect on aggregate demand. As is evident from (38), this analysis is valid only in the case of investment demand that originates in the nontraded goods sector. The situation is precisely the opposite in the traded goods sector, where a real depreciation *lowers* the real supply price of capital measured in terms of output. In this sector, therefore, this effect operates to stimulate investment, so the net effect on investment demand for nontraded goods of changes in the supply price of capital is ambiguous in principle.

A second channel through which devaluation affects the investment demand for nontraded goods operates through real profits. The analysis of this channel has to be model-specific to a greater extent than the previous one because it will depend, for instance, on the extent to which product markets are assumed to clear, that is, on whether firms operate on their factor demand curves. The exposition above assumes that they do. In this case the return to capital is its marginal product, which depends on the initial stock of capital, on the product wage, and, in the case of the nontraded goods sector, on the real exchange rate, which determines the price of imported inputs. The effects of changes in product wages on profits, and therefore on investment spending, were emphasized by van Wijnbergen (1986), Branson (1986), and Risager (1988). Both van Wijnbergen and Branson contrasted the case of fixed nominal wages with that in which there is some degree of wage indexation. By contrast, Risager examined the effect on investment of holding the nominal wage constant over some fixed initial contract length and then restoring the initial real wage.

The basic result of these studies is that a devaluation may raise or lower the product wage on impact depending on the nature and degree of wage indexation. With rigid nominal wages, the product wage would fall on impact, and investment would increase in the short run, even if the original product wage were expected to be restored in the future (Risager, 1988). With indexation that gives significant weight to imports, however, the product wage could rise, thereby dampening investment. A common result in "dependent economy" models with some nominal wage flexibility, however, is that a nominal devaluation results in a *reduction* in the product wage in the traded goods sector and an *increase* in the product wage in the nontraded goods sector (see, for instance, Montiel, 1987). In this case, investment would be stimulated in the former and discouraged in the latter, with ambiguous effects on total investment demand for nontraded goods.

In the presence of imported inputs, a third channel will be operative. The marginal product of capital in the nontraded goods sector will be affected by a real devaluation through the higher real costs of such inputs (van Wijnbergen, 1986; Branson, 1986). The effect is unambiguously contractionary, because the depressing effect on profits in the nontraded goods sector is not offset by positive effects on profits in the sector producing traded goods.

Note that, in the case of a real depreciation that lowers the product wage in the traded goods sector and raises it in the nontraded goods sector, the three effects analyzed above (that is, the effects on the real cost of capital, the product wage, and the cost of imported inputs) together tend to increase investment in the traded goods sector and to decrease it in the nontraded goods sector. If these effects are sufficiently strong, total investment demand for nontraded goods must increase when capital is sector-specific. In this case, an increase in investment demand in the traded goods sector can be met only through new production. It cannot be offset by negative *gross* investment in the nontraded goods sector. Thus, whenever a devaluation has a disparate effect on sectoral investment incentives sufficient to increase investment in the traded goods sector by more than the initial level of gross investment in the nontraded goods sector, total investment must rise, no matter how adverse the incentives for investment in the nontraded goods sector may be.

As a final point, note that, to the extent that firms hold foreign-currency debt, a depreciation can increase domestic firms' leverage, which in turn may put upward pressure on borrowing costs (in line with the models discussed in

Chapters 5 and 6) and constrain investment. The fall in investment could trigger a fall in overall domestic demand and output. Thus, a traditional argument in favor of flexible exchange rates—that they insulate output better from real shocks, because the exchange rate can adjust and stabilize demand for domestic goods through expenditure switching—is weakened in the presence of high foreign-currency debt. This is consistent with the results of Towbin and Weber (2013), who found that flexible exchange rates do not insulate output better from external shocks if foreign indebtedness is high.

2.1.3 *Nominal Interest Rates*

An increase in the real interest rate can be expected to reduce private consumption of nontraded goods as well as investment spending on nontraded goods by both the traded and nontraded goods sectors. Although the expected-inflation component of the real interest rate is treated as exogenous here, in this subsection we examine the effects of devaluation on the nominal interest rate. To analyze those effects, it is useful to distinguish between the current effect of an anticipated (future) devaluation and the contemporaneous effect of a previously unanticipated devaluation. Both shocks will be analyzed here. The effect of a devaluation on the nominal interest rate will depend, of course, fundamentally on the characteristics of the economy's financial structure, and many of the diverse results derived in the literature can be traced to different assumptions about these characteristics. We begin by describing a fairly general framework (consistent with that described in Chapters 1 and 3) from which various special cases can be derived.

Suppose that domestic residents can hold financial assets in the form of money, domestic interest-bearing assets, and interest-bearing claims on foreigners (denominated in foreign exchange). Assume further that the domestic interest-bearing assets take the form of loans extended by households to other entities in the private sector (other households and firms). The effects of a devaluation on the nominal interest rate charged on these loans, whether it is a previously unanticipated current devaluation or an anticipated future devaluation, depend critically on the degree of capital mobility (that is, on the extent to which domestic loans are regarded by households as perfect substitutes for foreign assets) and on the severity of portfolio adjustment costs. We will assume that portfolio adjustment is costless and distinguish two cases, based on whether domestic loans and foreign assets are perfect or imperfect substitutes.[14]

---

[14]As indicated in Chapter 5, the assumption of imperfect substitutability is empirically relevant for a large number of developing countries.

If loans and foreign assets are imperfect substitutes, equilibrium in the loan market may be given by the fairly general formulation[15]

$$h\left[\overset{-}{i}, \overset{+}{i^* + \varepsilon^a}, \overset{+}{y}, \overset{-}{\frac{M + EF^p}{P}}; \overset{+}{x}\right] = 0, \qquad (39)$$

where $h(\cdot)$ is the real excess demand function for loans; i the nominal interest rate on loans; $i^* + \varepsilon^a$ the nominal rate of return on foreign assets, consisting of the foreign nominal interest rate i^* plus the expected rate of depreciation of the domestic currency ε^a; y real income; $(M + EF^p)/P$ real household financial wealth; and x a vector of additional variables that have been included in the real loan excess demand function in the contractionary devaluation literature (see below). An increase in i has a negative own-price effect on excess loan demand, whereas an increase in $i^* + \varepsilon^a$ raises excess demand for loans as borrowers switch to domestic sources of finance while lenders seek to place more of their funds in foreign assets. An increase in domestic real income causes lenders to increase their demand for money, which they finance in part by reducing their supply of loans, thereby increasing excess demand in the loan market. Finally, other things being equal, an increase in private financial wealth both reduces borrowers' need for outside financing and provides lenders with surplus funds, which they can place in both loans and foreign assets after satisfying their own demands for money. This effect reduces excess demand in the loan market.

Now consider the effect of a devaluation on the nominal interest rate i at a given initial level of real income y and price of nontraded goods P_N, with $\varepsilon^a = 0$. In the case of a previously unanticipated devaluation, the effect on the domestic interest rate will depend, as can be seen from (39), on the composition of household financial wealth. Whether the real excess demand for loans rises or falls depends on whether real household financial wealth increases or decreases. The devaluation will lower the real money stock but will raise the real value of foreign assets and liabilities. If a large share of household financial wealth is devoted to the holding of cash balances or if households are net debtors in foreign currency, and if traded goods have a large weight in private consumption (so that the price level P registers a strong increase), the former effect will dominate; real private financial wealth will fall, the real excess demand for loans will increase, and the domestic interest rate will rise. This result will be reversed, however, if foreign assets dominate households' balance sheets or if traded goods carry a small weight in domestic consumption (or both). In van Wijnbergen's (1986) model, for instance, households hold no foreign assets; thus, a nominal devaluation raises the domestic interest rate. In contrast, Buffie (1984a) derived opposite conclusions precisely because he assumed that households hold a substantial portion of their wealth in assets denominated in foreign exchange.

---

[15]This analysis could equivalently be conducted in the context of the money market.

When the partial derivative h_i, evaluated at $i = i^* + \varepsilon^a$, approaches negative infinity, domestic loans and foreign assets become perfect substitutes in private portfolios. In this case, (39) is replaced by

$$i = i^* + \varepsilon^a, \tag{40}$$

so that uncovered interest parity holds continuously. Under these conditions, a previously unanticipated current devaluation will have no effect on the domestic nominal interest rate. This is the assumption that appears in the models of Turnovsky (1981) and Burton (1983).

The effects of an anticipated future devaluation are straightforward. In the case of imperfect substitutability, this is represented by an increase in ε^a in (39), with the level of the exchange rate held constant. The domestic nominal interest rate thus rises. If the own-price effect h_i exceeds the cross-price effect $h_{i^*+\varepsilon^a}$, the increase will be lower than the anticipated devaluation. In the case of perfect substitutability, however, the domestic interest rate will rise by the full amount of the anticipated devaluation, as indicated in (40).

The literature on contractionary devaluation has placed a substantial emphasis on the importance of "working capital" in developing countries as a source of loan demand, following a key tenet of the new structuralist school (see Chapter 5). This introduces effects of a previously unanticipated current devaluation that were not included in the preceding analysis. These effects can be captured by defining the variable x in (39) as

$$x = x(\overset{+}{w}, \overset{+}{E}, \overset{-}{P_N}). \tag{41}$$

The variable x now becomes an index of real working capital requirements, which are taken to depend on the wage bill and on purchases of imported inputs (see the last part of Subsection 1.1.1). An increase in x increases the demand for loans, an effect that explains the positive sign of h_x in (39). Real working capital requirements are assumed to increase when the nominal wage or the domestic-currency price of traded goods (or both) increases, and they are assumed to fall when the price of nontraded goods rises. The positive sign of x_E is in keeping with the standard assumption in the literature on contractionary devaluation. Note, however, that this sign places restrictions on the share of imported inputs in variable costs and on the elasticity of substitution between labor and imported inputs.

Because a previously unanticipated current devaluation is represented by an increase in E and is also likely to increase nominal wages, the real excess demand for loans will rise, putting upward pressure on the domestic interest rate. Thus, taking working capital into account may cause the impact on nominal interest rates to be positive even if foreign assets figure prominently in private sector balance sheets. Working capital considerations, therefore, do enhance the likelihood that devaluation will be contractionary. Note, however, that these considerations become irrelevant if domestic loans and foreign assets are perfect substitutes—in which case (40) applies—and do not affect the analysis of an anticipated future devaluation.

2.2 ■ Effects on Aggregate Supply

In addition to affecting demand, as described in the previous discussion, a devaluation also affects the supply of domestically produced goods. The production cost of those goods in domestic currency is likely to increase as the prices of the factors of production rise in response to a devaluation. This can be thought of as an upward shift in the supply curve for those goods, which, together with a downward-sloping demand curve, would result in a lower level of output and a lower real depreciation than otherwise would be the case. A devaluation may cause an upward shift in the supply curve through three separate channels: increases in nominal wages, the use of imported inputs, and increases in the cost of working capital.

2.2.1   Effects on the Nominal Wage

In this subsection we will examine the effect of a devaluation on the nominal wage in the context of a general model from which specific results appearing in the literature can be derived as special cases. We assume again a "dependent economy" setup, take capital to be sector-specific and fixed in the short run, and allow both sectors to employ imported inputs. With all variables in logarithms, the aggregate demand for labor is

$$
\begin{aligned}
n^d &= n_0 - d_1(w - e) - d_2(w - p_N) - d_3(e - p_N), \\
&= n_0 - (d_1 + d_2)(w - e) - (d_2 + d_3)z, \tag{42}
\end{aligned}
$$

where n_0, d_1, d_2, and d_3 are positive parameters. An increase in the product wage measured in terms of traded goods reduces the demand for labor in the traded goods sector both by reducing output in that sector and by encouraging the substitution of imported inputs for labor. The magnitude of d_1 depends on the share of labor employed in the traded goods sector, on the labor intensity of production in that sector, and on the elasticity of substitution between labor and imported inputs in the production of traded goods. The sign and magnitude of d_2 are determined similarly except, of course, that the nontraded goods sector is involved. Finally, d_3 captures the effect on the demand for labor in the nontraded goods sector of an increase in the price of imported inputs. The demand for labor falls because of a decrease in the level of output, but it increases as labor is substituted for imported inputs. The negative sign in (42) will hold when substitution elasticities are sufficiently small that the former effect dominates the latter. The magnitude of d_3 depends on this substitution elasticity, on the labor intensity of output in nontraded goods, and on the share of the labor force employed in that sector.

Turning to aggregate supply, we assume the current nominal wage to be given by

$$w = \bar{w} + s_1(n - n_0) + s_2 p^a + s_3(p - p^a) \tag{43}$$
$$= \bar{w} + s_1(n - n_0) + s_3 e - s_3(1 - \delta)e + (s_2 - s_3)[e^a - (1 - \delta)z^a],$$

where $\bar{w}$, s_1, s_2, and s_3 are positive parameters, all variables are again in logarithms, and expectations of current values are formed one period ago. In the contract described by (43), the current nominal wage w consists of an exogenous component $\bar{w}$ (taken hereafter to be zero, for simplicity) plus an endogenous component that depends on the level of employment n relative to its "natural" or full-employment level n_0, on price expectations for the contract period formed when the contract was signed, and on the degree of indexation (s_3) to unanticipated price shocks ($p - p^a$).

When alternative restrictions are imposed, various special cases can be derived from (43):

- Exogenous nominal wages follow from $s_1 = s_2 = s_3 = 0$.
- Predetermined nominal wages with Fischer-type contracts (see Fischer, 1985; Blanchard and Fischer, 1989, pp. 415–16) are implied by $s_2 = 1$ and $s_1 = s_3 = 0$.
- Wage indexation to the current price level in its simplest form can be imposed by setting $s_1 = 0$ and $s_2 = s_3$. As a special case, fixed real wages follow from $s_1 = 0$ and $s_2 = s_3 = 1$.
- The simple Phillips curve, without expectations, is derived with $s_2 = s_3 = 0$. If employment was dated one period ago, the nominal wage would be predetermined. If, as in (43), the *current* value of employment matters, then the nominal wage is endogenous.
- A neoclassical labor market model can be produced by imposing the restriction $s_2 = s_3 = 1$.
- Finally, the Friedman-Phelps version of the Phillips curve (see Blanchard and Fischer, 1989, pp. 572–73) emerges from $s_2 = 1$ and $s_3 = 0$.

In this subsection, we will impose only the restrictions that $s_2 = 1$ and $s_3 < 1$, so that perfectly anticipated inflation has no effect on workers' real wage demands and the degree of indexation to current prices is only partial. Substituting (42) in (43) and simplifying, the equilibrium nominal wage implied by this more general model is

$$w = e^a - \frac{1 - \delta + \Omega_{23}}{1 + \Omega_{12}} z^a + \frac{s_3 + \Omega_{12}}{1 + \Omega_{12}}(\bar{e} - e^a) - \frac{s_3(1 - \delta) + \Omega_{23}}{1 + \Omega_{12}}(z - z^a), \quad (44)$$

where $\Omega_{12} = s_1(d_1 + d_2)$, and $\Omega_{23} = s_1(d_2 + d_3)$.

This formulation immediately leads to several important observations. First, in assessing the effects on the nominal wage of an exchange-rate depreciation, the extent to which a nominal depreciation translates into a real depreciation is crucial. The equilibrium nominal wage after a devaluation is determined simultaneously with the equilibrium real exchange rate as shown in (44). The second observation is that, in the absence of perfect indexation (that is, as long as $s_3 < 1$), it is important to distinguish, in assessing the effects of devaluation on the nominal wage, whether a current devaluation was previously anticipated or not. If, as seems likely, the effect on the *real* exchange rate of an anticipated devaluation is smaller than that of an unanticipated devaluation, the impact of an anticipated devaluation on the nominal wage will exceed that of an unanticipated parity change.[16]

The third important observation, however, is that in neither case must the nominal wage necessarily increase. This highlights the importance of an integrated treatment of the labor market in assessing the likelihood that devaluation can be contractionary. To clarify this point, we adopt the working assumption that the price of nontraded goods is constant on impact. This simplifies (44), which can now be written as

$$w = e^a - \frac{\delta + s_1(d_1 - d_3)}{1 + \Omega_{12}} e^a + \frac{s_3 \delta + s_1(d_1 - d_3)}{1 + \Omega_{12}}(\bar{e} - e^a). \tag{45}$$

Note that if $d_3 > d_1$, the effects of both an anticipated and an unanticipated devaluation could be negative. To see how this possibility can arise, note from (42) that if $d_3 > d_1$, an increase in the nominal exchange rate E will *lower* the demand for labor, given wages and the price of nontraded goods. The reason is that an increase in demand in the traded goods sector is offset by reduced demand in the nontraded goods sector. The latter, in turn, arises from the effect of an increase in the price of imported inputs, which reduces the level of output and therefore the demand for labor in that sector. This effect will be dominant if the share of labor in the nontraded goods sector is large, if that sector is relatively intensive in its use of imported inputs, and if the elasticity of substitution of labor for imported inputs in that sector is small. Note that, regardless of whether d_3 exceeds d_1 or not, the presence of imported inputs in the nontraded goods sector tends to dampen the increase in the nominal wage that would tend to accompany a devaluation. This effect acts as an offset to the contractionary effect of a devaluation on the supply of nontraded goods that operates through the imported input channel (see the next subsection).

As a final observation, note from (44) that if $d_1 > d_3$, then as long as a nominal depreciation (whether anticipated or unanticipated) results in a less-than-proportional real depreciation ($0 < dz/de < 1$), the increase in the nominal wage will be no greater than the increase in the price of traded goods and no less than the

---

[16]To derive this result, express z^a as a function of e^a and $(z - z^a)$ as a function of $(\bar{e} - e^a)$ in (44), and assume that the condition $dz^a/de^a \le d(z - z^a)/d(\bar{e} - e^a)$ holds.

increase in the price of nontraded goods. That is, the product wage will fall in the traded goods sector and rise in the nontraded goods sector.[17]

2.2.2 *Imported Inputs*

In the event of a devaluation, the price of imported inputs increases by the same percentage as the exchange rate, driving up the costs of production of domestically produced goods. The magnitude of this increase in costs depends on technological factors and on the extent to which the price of other factors of production responds to the devaluation. To illustrate these relationships, we will use a specific example (see Schmid, 1982).

Assume an economy that produces and consumes traded and nontraded goods. Nontraded goods are produced with imported inputs and "value added," according to a CES production function with elasticity of substitution σ. Value added, in turn, is produced with a fixed amount of specific capital and with labor according to a Cobb-Douglas production function. The share of labor in value added is denoted by γ. Nominal wages are assumed to be determined exogenously and to increase by a given amount as a result of the devaluation. The return on capital, in contrast, is endogenous and varies so as to clear the market for that factor.

In analyzing the effect of a devaluation on the supply of nontraded goods, we investigate the increase in costs, or supply price, for a given level of output. This is the upward shift in the supply curve of those goods. The percentage increase in the supply price is

$$\pi_N = \theta_J \varepsilon + \theta_w \hat{w} + \theta_k \hat{r}, \tag{46}$$

where ε is the percentage of the nominal devaluation, $\hat{w}$ is the exogenous increase in nominal wages, and $\hat{r}$ is the endogenous increase in the return on capital. Because labor and capital are combined according to a Cobb-Douglas production function, we have, because the capital stock is constant,

$$\hat{r} = \hat{w} + \hat{n}.$$

Cost minimization for a given level of production implies

$$\hat{n} = \sigma \theta_J \{\theta_w + \theta_J [\sigma(1 - \gamma) + \gamma]\}^{-1}(\varepsilon - \hat{w}),$$

and therefore

$$\hat{r} = \hat{w} + \sigma \theta_J \{\theta_w + \theta_J [\sigma(1 - \gamma) + \gamma]\}^{-1}(\varepsilon - \hat{w}). \tag{47}$$

---

[17]The change in w can be obtained by differentiating (44) with respect to e^a or $(\bar{e} - e^a)$, imposing $dz^a/de^a < 1$ or $d(z - z^a)/d(\bar{e} - e^a) < 1$. The change in the price of traded goods is unity, whereas that for nontraded goods can be obtained from the definition of the real exchange rate, which implies, using logarithms, that $p_N = \bar{e} - z$.

Equation (47) is useful for examining the effect of the devaluation and the adjustment of wages on the return to capital. If wages increase by the full amount of the devaluation ($\hat{w} = \varepsilon$), the return to capital will also increase by the same amount. The reason is simple. At the initial rate of return of capital, there is an incentive to substitute value added for imported inputs, and within value added to substitute capital for labor. The amount of capital is constant, however, and thus its rate of return increases—until the initial ratio of nominal wages to the rate of return of capital is restored, so that the initial desired capital/labor ratio is also restored. At the end, $\hat{r} = \hat{w} = \varepsilon$, and the same combination of inputs is used to produce the given level of output. A value of $\hat{r}$ different from $\hat{w}$ would not be an equilibrium value. For instance, assume that $\hat{r} < \hat{w}$. Then the desired capital-labor combination would be higher, which together with a fixed capital stock implies lower employment, which in turn implies lower value added. For a given level of output, this implies a higher level of imported inputs. But this change in the use of factors is inconsistent with the change in factor prices. Because the rate of return on capital increased by less than the nominal wage, the price of value added increased by less than the price of imported inputs, so we should expect a decline (instead of an increase) in the intensity of the use of imported inputs.

If wages do not increase by the full amount of the devaluation, (47) indicates that the return on capital increases by more than nominal wages. The reason is that if the rate of return on capital increases only by the same amount as nominal wages, producers will want to use the same capital/labor ratio. Because the capital stock is fixed, this implies a constant level of employment. But because the price of value added would decline relative to the price of imported inputs, there would be an excess demand for capital and labor. These excess demands are satisfied by an increase in the use of labor and a further increase in the return to capital.

Using (47) to replace $\hat{r}$ in (46), and remembering that $\gamma \theta_k = (1 - \gamma)\theta_w$ because capital and labor are combined according to a Cobb-Douglas function to produce value added, yields

$$\pi_N = \varepsilon - \gamma(1 - \theta_J)[\gamma(1 - \theta_J) + \sigma(1 - \gamma) + \gamma]^{-1}(\varepsilon - \hat{w}). \qquad (48)$$

Therefore, if wages increase by the full amount of the devaluation, the supply curve shifts upward by the same percentage as the exchange-rate change. If wages do not increase by the full amount of the devaluation, the supply curve shifts upward by less than the exchange rate, but by more than the increase in wages, since in this case the return to capital increases more than wages, as discussed above. In this case it is also clear from (48) that the increase in the supply price will be larger the larger is the share of imported inputs in total costs and, for a given share of imported inputs, the larger is the share of capital in value added. The increase in the supply price will also be larger the smaller is the elasticity of substitution between imported inputs and value added.

Equation (48) assumes that value added is produced by capital and labor according to a Cobb-Douglas production function. Therefore, it is assumed that the elasticity of substitution between labor and capital is equal to unity. If instead a CES function were assumed for the production of value added, when $\hat{w} < \varepsilon$ the increase in the supply price would be larger the lower the elasticity of substitution between labor and capital. The reason is that the lower the elasticity, the higher must be the increase in the return to capital needed to induce producers to increase the employment of labor necessary to compensate for a lower use of imported inputs.

The use of imported inputs in the production of traded goods does not offer new insights because the price of this type of input moves together with the price of output. Even if we assume the same structure of production as the one assumed above for nontraded goods, the level of output will depend on the product wage, or the ratio of nominal wages to the exchange rate. Consequently, if wages increase by less than the full amount of the devaluation, output of traded goods will increase (if working-capital considerations are ignored), and vice versa.

2.2.3 Effects through Working-Capital Costs

Several authors of the new structuralist school, notably Taylor (1983) and van Wijnbergen (1983), emphasized that a nominal devaluation could exert contractionary effects on the supply of domestic output by increasing the cost of working capital, that is, by financing labor costs and purchases of imported inputs (see Chapter 6). To examine how this effect could operate, consider first the nontraded goods sector. The need to finance working capital arises from an asynchrony between payments and receipts, much the same as the motivation sometimes used in justifying households' demand for money (see Blanchard and Fischer, 1989, chapter 4). Suppose that, in the nontraded goods sector, to finance a real wage bill $\omega_N n_N$—where $\omega_N = w/P_N$ is the product wage in that sector—and a real imported input bill $z O_N$ the firm is led to hold real stocks of loans outstanding in the amount of $h^n(i, w_N n_N)$ for real wages and $h^o(i, z O_N)$ for imported inputs.[18] The representative firm's profits are thus given by

$$\Pi_N = P_N y_N(n_N, O_N) - w n_N - E O_N - i P_N h^n(\cdot) + i P_N h^o(\cdot), \qquad (49)$$

and the first-order conditions for profit maximization are

$$dy_N/dn_N = \omega_N[1 + i h^n_{\omega_N n_N}(\cdot)], \qquad (50)$$

$$dy_N/dO_N = z[1 + i h^o_{\omega_N n_N}(\cdot)]. \qquad (51)$$

---

[18] A negative interest rate effect on loan demand is included by analogy with the households' transactions demand for money but is not necessary for the following analysis. Both loan demand and the cost of holding loans in (49) should depend on the expected *real* interest rate measured in terms of nontraded goods. Because we are treating expected inflation as exogenous, however, the expected inflation component of the real interest rate is suppressed here for notational convenience.

These equations can be solved for labor and imported input demand functions:

$$n_N^d = n_N^d(\overset{-}{\omega}_N, \overset{?}{z}, \overset{-}{i}),\tag{52}$$

$$O_N^d = O_N^d(\overset{?}{\omega}_N, \overset{-}{z}, \overset{-}{i}).\tag{53}$$

Substituting these equations in the short-run production function for nontraded goods yields the short-run supply function for nontraded goods:

$$y_N^s = y_N^s(\overset{-}{\omega}_N, \overset{-}{z}, \overset{-}{i}).\tag{54}$$

Repeating this exercise for the traded goods sector yields a traded goods supply function:

$$y_T^s = y_T^s(\overset{-}{\omega}_T, \overset{-}{i}),\tag{55}$$

where $\omega_T \equiv w/E$.

The presence of the costs of financing working capital has two important supply consequences that affect the likelihood of contractionary devaluation. The first of these is the Cavallo-Patman effect discussed in Chapter 6: an increase in loan interest rates adds to the costs of financing working capital and shifts the output supply curve upward. This effect is captured in the negative sign of the partial derivative of i in (54) and (55). The magnitude of the effect depends on the properties of the functions h^n and h^o.[19] There are several important implications of this effect. First, the Cavallo-Patman effect will appear in conjunction with a previously unanticipated current devaluation only if capital mobility is imperfect. If domestic and foreign interest-bearing assets are perfect substitutes, the domestic nominal interest rate will not be affected by a devaluation of this type, and no Cavallo-Patman effect will materialize. Second, if domestic interest rates *do* rise, then the Cavallo-Patman effect represents the only channel through which devaluation may exert contractionary effects in the traded goods sector. Finally, the Cavallo-Patman effect represents a second channel, in addition to the effects of interest rate changes on aggregate demand, through which an anticipated future devaluation could affect current output. In the case where domestic and foreign interest-bearing assets are imperfect substitutes, an anticipated future devaluation would *stimulate* current production in the traded goods sector by lowering the expected real interest rate (measured in terms of traded goods). Whether current output of nontraded goods rises or falls will depend on whether

---

[19]For given values of i, $w_N n_N$, and $z O_N$, the smaller their elasticities with respect to the interest rate, the larger the upward displacement of the output supply curves caused by an increase in i. Also, larger values of the partial derivatives with respect to real labor costs and the real cost of imported inputs will magnify these upward supply shifts.

the anticipated devaluation lowers or raises the expected real interest rate in terms of nontraded goods.

The second important consequence of the financing of working capital is the effect of working-capital costs on the *elasticities* of the sectoral short-run supply curves given by (54) and (55).[20] This effect is captured by the cross-partial derivatives of these supply equations. The presence of working-capital costs is likely to *reduce* short-run supply elasticities in both sectors because of the increase in marginal costs associated with the need to finance additional working capital. In the presence of a real exchange-rate depreciation, this reduction in supply elasticities will be unfavorable with respect to economic expansion in response to devaluation in the traded goods sector, but the reduction may be either favorable or unfavorable with respect to activity in the nontraded goods sector, depending on whether demand for such goods contracts or expands in response to devaluation.

2.2.4   *Effects through Balance Sheets*

As noted in Chapter 5, exchange-rate movements (induced by policy decisions or exogenous domestic and external shocks) may have large valuation effects, depending on the structure of indebtedness of agents in the economy, that is, the degree of "liability dollarization." Suppose that domestic firms are highly indebted in foreign currency (perhaps as a result of moral hazard problems, as discussed next) whereas their assets are denominated in domestic currency, and that banks set their short- and long-term lending rates on the basis of a risk premium that depends on borrowers' net assets (as formally analyzed in Chapter 6). In such conditions, a depreciation, in the absence of adequate currency hedging, would increase the domestic-currency value of firms' foreign liabilities and reduce their net worth, thereby raising borrowing costs and triggering a contraction in investment and output, as argued above. Qualitatively similar results are derived by Cook (2004) in an alternative model in which firms finance capital accumulation by issuing foreign-currency debt.

Contractionary effects may also result from "liability dollarization" by financial intermediaries. Choi and Cook (2004) develop a model in which banks borrow abroad (in foreign currency) to extend domestic-currency loans. The resulting currency mismatch exposes their balance sheets to exchange-rate fluctuations. The banks' cost of borrowing on international financial markets depends on their net worth. Thus, an unexpected nominal exchange-rate depreciation negatively affects banks' balance sheets, increases the country's default-risk premium and firms' borrowing costs, and potentially offsets the standard expansionary effects of depreciation on output. Liability dollarization among firms and financial intermediaries figures prominently in "third generation" models of currency crises, which are taken up in Chapter 14.

---

[20]The working capital-supply side nexus was discussed in Chapters 5 and 6.

3   An Assessment

The choice of an exchange-rate regime and its impact on economic performance remains one of the most controversial topics in development macroeconomics. The criteria reviewed in this chapter and the last suggest that in practice such a choice entails a trade-off between a number of conflicting goals. Both types of regimes have strengths and weaknesses, and while attempts to follow "in between" solutions such as bands can in theory provide a middle ground, in practice they turn out to be merely temporary.

Conventional arguments in favor of a fixed exchange rate, for instance, are that it provides a nominal anchor to prices, has often been instrumental in helping to bring down inflation (as discussed in Chapters 10 and 11), and that it may help promote fiscal discipline or contribute to maintaining it once achieved. The ability to control the nominal exchange rate under a peg to a low-inflation currency may lead to improved credibility and lower inflation, despite the fact that policymakers retain the ability to devalue unexpectedly (Herrendorf, 1997, 1999). Because the exchange rate is a highly visible price, it can be monitored more easily than other variables and may allow rapid gains in credibility. Pegging to a low-inflation country can also help to signal the government's commitment to price stability and generate credibility gains, in the form of lower expectations of inflation and devaluation. There is indeed evidence suggesting that countries that have opted for pegged exchange rates tend to have lower inflation. Consistent with several other studies, Coudert and Dubert (2005), for instance, found that fixed exchange-rate regimes tended to be associated with a better performance than floating regimes in terms of inflation in a sample of ten Asian countries over the period 1990–2001.[21] The complete loss of monetary sovereignty that joining a currency union entails may be highly beneficial in some countries, to the extent that it also ensures greater independence of monetary policy from political influence (Grubel, 2005). Finally, the degree of nominal rigidities may not be independent of the exchange-rate regime choice; a peg, in particular, could increase the degree of internal price flexibility, by the very fact that the use of the exchange rate as a mechanism for adjustment is precluded. Nominal demand facing firms tends to be more volatile under a fixed exchange rate, and this may induce more firms to adjust prices at a higher frequency (Devereux, 2006).

However, some of these benefits have proved to be elusive. In developing countries, the credibility gain associated with pegging to a low-inflation country may be quite limited; building credibility and establishing a firm commitment to price stability instead has often required significant institutional reforms, such as granting independence to the central bank and forbidding automatic financing of fiscal deficits (see Chapter 11), and/or adopting inflation targeting (see Chapter 7).

---

[21] However, endogeneity bias, by which countries with low inflation are more likely to choose a pegged exchange rate, cannot be excluded.

The quantitative importance of the "price flexibility" effect of pegs alluded to earlier remains unclear. The evidence on the disciplinary effect of a fixed exchange rate on fiscal policy appears also inconclusive, as argued by Tornell and Velasco (1998). In fact, if the monetary authority can fully commit to an exchange-rate peg but fiscal policy lacks credibility—in the sense that the fiscal authority cannot commit to an optimal rule—a fixed exchange rate may give the fiscal authority an incentive to borrow abroad, in order to reduce unemployment caused by wage rigidity (Cook and Devereux, 2006b). This "overborrowing" phenomenon was also emphasized by McKinnon and Pill (1999) and Burnside et al. (2001).

Moreover, while nominal exchange-rate stability is important, some degree of flexibility is also necessary to avoid excessive real appreciation and offset the impact of destabilizing shocks. Pegging may in fact prevent real exchange-rate adjustment in response to domestic and external shocks, as documented by Broda (2004) and Hoffman (2007), and this may explain why some studies suggest that in developing countries less flexible exchange-rate regimes are associated with greater output volatility (Levy Yeyati and Sturzenegger, 2003). In addition, Bleaney and Fielding (2002), using a sample of eighty developing countries and data for 1980–1989, found that (after controlling for other factors) countries with managed exchange rates enjoyed lower inflation but suffered higher output *and* inflation variability than those with floating rates. Overall, there is also consistent evidence that less flexible exchange-rate regimes are associated with *slower* growth. Using data for 183 countries for 1974–2000, Edwards and Levy-Yeyati (2005) found that, after controlling for other factors, countries with more flexible exchange-rate regimes grew faster than countries with fixed exchange rates. Similar results are obtained by Levy-Yeyati and Sturzenegger (2003) and Coudert and Dubert (2005). At the same time, fixing the exchange rate and surrendering the power to alter its value may be costly if fiscal policy lacks short-term flexibility. As documented by Shambaugh (2004), based on a sample of more than one hundred industrial and developing countries for 1973–2000, interest rates in countries with pegged exchange rates and open capital markets tend to follow closely those in the base country; they therefore cannot pursue an autonomous monetary policy, as implied by the open-economy trilemma (Obstfeld, 2001).[22]

By contrast, a flexible exchange rate gives national monetary authorities greater independence in choosing their inflation objective, and provides a (partial) solution to the moral hazard problems created by a fixed exchange rate.[23] A float allows greater freedom in responding to exogenous shocks, and so greater stability of output (and inflation) than under pegged rates, at the expense of higher mean inflation. By purposely leaving some scope for unexpected exchange-rate movements and avoiding

---

[22]More generally, the open-economy trilemma that a country cannot simultaneously achieve exchange-rate stability, capital market openness, and monetary sovereignty. Choosing, say, to peg an exchange rate means choosing to give up some degree of monetary sovereignty, capital market openness, or both. See Popper et al. (2013) for a more detailed discussion and some empirical evidence.

[23]For a dissenting view, see McKinnon and Schnabl (2005).

implicit exchange-rate guarantees, policymakers can induce domestic borrowers to internalize (at least some of) the costs of failing to hedge appropriately their foreign-currency liabilities. In the case of Chile for instance, Cowan et al. (2005) found that the switch to a floating exchange-rate regime in late 1999 was indeed accompanied by reduced currency exposure. By eliminating implicit exchange-rate insurance, in a sense, the switch forced firms to internalize exchange-rate risk—thereby reducing vulnerability of corporate balance sheets to exchange-rate fluctuations.

Nevertheless, a flexible exchange-rate regime is not a panacea. It may not prevent a real exchange-rate appreciation (in periods of surges in capital inflows in particular, as discussed in Chapter 13) and it may be characterized by excessive volatility—possibly exacerbated by a high degree of dollarization, as noted in Chapter 5—with possibly adverse effects on trade flows (Klein and Shambaugh, 2006). In contrast to Chile, and as documented by Parsley and Popper (2006), Asia-Pacific firms remain significantly exposed to fluctuations in one or more of the four major currencies (the U.S. dollar, the euro, the yen, and the British pound). Moreover, the degree of foreign exchange exposure has not diminished over time—suggesting that hedging options remain limited. Large (unhedged) foreign-currency liabilities by domestic firms, as well as significant contractionary effects of exchange-rate changes on output, would both militate against a high degree of exchange-rate flexibility—key reasons perhaps for the common practice (documented in the previous chapter) of heavy management of currencies in developing countries.[24] Indeed, if corporate debts are denominated in foreign currency whereas the value of corporate assets depends on local currency (or, more generally, if corporate revenues increase with the relative price of goods produced domestically), sharp and unexpected currency movements may lead to financial instability, implying that while flexible exchange rates are destabilizing, a fixed exchange rate can enhance welfare by stabilizing banks' balance sheets. Indeed, as illustrated by the simulation results of Gertler et al. (2007), if firms hold a large foreign-currency debt and financial accelerator effects are strong (in the sense that the market value of domestic assets is the primary determinant of collateralized lending), a fixed exchange-rate regime may dominate over a large range of structural parameters.[25]

The thrust of this analysis is that because considerations regarding the choice of an exchange-rate regime are likely to change over time, policymakers should adopt a flexible view of what is the appropriate exchange-rate regime for their country. In practice, unfortunately, this principle has proved difficult to implement; too often countries have failed to adapt or change their exchange-rate regimes in a timely

---

[24]However, it should be noted that in a study of twenty-five countries, Rajan and Chen (2002) found that currency depreciations have significant contractionary effects on output only when they occur in the context of currency crises, not during "normal" (non-crisis) times.

[25]However, as argued by Chang and Velasco (2006), liability dollarization may be endogenous. When choosing the amounts of debt to issue as domestic and foreign currencies, borrowers are likely to take into account the risk-return characteristics of these securities. If so, exchange-rate policy depends on portfolio choices, and vice versa. This may lead to equilibrium outcomes that entail either fixed or flexible exchange rates.

manner—and have done so only upon being forced by markets to adjust abruptly and in some cases at a very high cost (see Chapter 14). Using a sample of fifty-five exits, involving both developed and developing countries, Asici et al. (2008) found indeed that countries tend to wait too long to leave a pegged exchange-rate regime. In the same vein, Aizenman and Glick (2008) found that exits from pegged exchange-rate regimes during the past two decades have often been accompanied by crises, and that the cost of a regime change (as measured by output losses) increases with the duration of the peg before the crisis.

Chapter 10

Inflation and Short-Run Dynamics

Since the monetarist-structuralist controversy of the early 1960s, the nature of the mechanisms underlying the dynamics of inflation has been the subject of a voluminous theoretical and empirical literature in developing countries. Key aspects of the debate in recent years have been the interactions—and the lack of consistency—between fiscal, monetary, and exchange-rate policies; structural factors (such as the degree of capital mobility and the existence of wage and price inertia); credibility problems; and the stance of expectations regarding future policies.

This chapter examines alternative models of the inflationary process and studies the short-run macroeconomic dynamics associated with monetary and exchange-rate policies. The first part begins by contrasting two models of inflation: the "orthodox" or "monetarist" model, which focuses on the interactions between fiscal deficits, money creation, and inflation; and the "new structuralist" model, which emphasizes the links between food bottlenecks, income distribution, and social conflicts over the determination of real wages. We then point out that although these models are traditionally viewed as competing explanations of the inflationary process, they can in fact be combined in a way that casts doubt on the policy prescriptions that would emerge from simple structuralist models. The second part of the chapter focuses on the short- and long-run effects of monetary and exchange-rate policy rules. It begins with a presentation of an optimizing one-good model with imperfect capital mobility, which is then extended to a two-sector, three-good framework. In addition to imperfect capital mobility, the extended model captures a number of structural features that have been shown in previous chapters to play an important macroeconomic role in the developing world (such as nominal wage rigidity and price-setting behavior) and thus provides a useful conceptual framework for the analysis of stabilization policies in developing countries.

1   Models of the Inflationary Process

The "orthodox" view of the inflationary process holds that the primary cause of inflation in developing countries is the recourse to money creation by governments faced with limited borrowing options (both domestically and internationally) for financing large fiscal deficits. By contrast, new structuralists in the tradition of Cardoso (1981) and Taylor (1983, 1991) view inflation as resulting essentially from the worker-capitalist conflict over the distribution of income between real wages and profits.

We begin by presenting the orthodox view, highlighting the role of inflationary expectations and the potentially destabilizing role of fiscal rigidities. We follow by discussing the new structuralist approach to inflation. We then show how the two models can be merged, by introducing the government budget constraint in the new structuralist model. An analysis of the effect of food subsidies on the behavior of inflation in the integrated model highlights the potentially misleading predictions that may result from the omission of financing constraints in simple new structuralist models.[1]

1.1 ■ Inflation, Money, and Fiscal Deficits

Consider a closed economy with exogenous output. Suppose that the demand for money function takes the Cagan semilogarithmic form used in analyzing inflationary finance in Chapter 3:

$$m = \exp(-\alpha\pi^a), \quad \alpha > 0, \tag{1}$$

where $m \equiv M/P$, with M representing the base money stock and P the price level. The expected inflation rate is π^a. The government cannot issue bonds to the public and finances its primary budget deficit d entirely through seigniorage:

$$d = \dot{M}/P = \mu m, \tag{2}$$

where $\mu \equiv \dot{M}/M$. Combining (1) and (2) implies

$$d = \mu \exp(-\alpha\pi^a). \tag{3}$$

Equation (3) specifies how the primary fiscal deficit affects the equilibrium rate of growth of the money stock, and hence the equilibrium inflation rate. However, to the extent that the demand for real money balances is inversely related to the expected

---

[1]To simplify the presentation, we consider throughout this section a closed economy. Extending the results to an open economy, although not a trivial matter, would not affect qualitatively the most salient conclusions derived here.

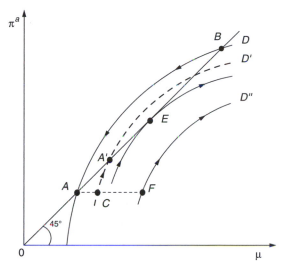

Figure 10–1 ■ Seigniorage and Dual Inflation Equilibria
Source: Adapted from Bruno and Fischer (1990, p. 355).

rate of inflation, the possibility of multiple solutions to (3) arises. As shown later, and in line with our discussion in Chapter 3, the existence of a "seigniorage Laffer curve" implies that there are two steady-state rates of inflation that generate any given amount of seigniorage.

Equation (3) is plotted in Figure 10.1, which is adapted from Bruno and Fischer (1990). Curve D depicts the combinations of μ and π^a for which the primary deficit is constant. Because (3) indicates that $d = \mu$ when the expected inflation rate is zero, the deficit is measured by the distance between the origin and the intercept of the D curve on the μ-axis. Because the government budget constraint is binding at any given moment in time, the economy is always located on the D curve.

Differentiating (1) with respect to time yields, since $\dot{m} \equiv \dot{M}/P - \pi m$,

$$\mu - \pi = -\alpha \dot{\pi}^a, \tag{4}$$

so that in the steady state, with $\dot{\pi}^a = 0$,

$$\pi = \pi^a = \mu. \tag{5}$$

Equation (5) is represented by the 45° line in Figure 10.1. As depicted in the figure, the D curve and the 45° line intersect twice. There are therefore two potential steady-state positions, that is, two inflation rates at which the primary fiscal deficit is financed through revenue from the inflation tax: a low-inflation equilibrium (point A) and a high-inflation equilibrium (point B). At point A the elasticity of the demand for real money balances is less than unity, whereas at point B it is greater than unity.

Suppose for a moment that the size of the primary deficit is constrained by the amount of revenue that can be generated through money creation. As shown in Chapter 3, the inflation rate that maximizes steady-state seigniorage revenue is equal to $\pi^s = 1/\alpha$, and the corresponding level of revenue is given by

$$d^s = \exp(-1)/\alpha.$$

Assume now that the primary deficit the government wishes to finance is fixed at an arbitrary level $\tilde{d}$. Depending on the size of the deficit target, there may be zero, one, or two equilibria. Because the government cannot obtain more than d^s in the long-run equilibrium, there is no steady state if $d > d^s$. For $\tilde{d} = d^s$ or $\tilde{d} < 0$, there is a unique steady state. For $0 < \tilde{d} < d^s$, there are two steady states, and the economy may be "stuck" at the high-inflation equilibrium (point B). To see under what conditions these long-run outcomes obtain, we consider two alternative assumptions about the formation of inflation expectations.

1.1.1 Adaptive Expectations

Consider first the case where inflation expectations are characterized by a first-order adaptive process:

$$\dot{\pi}^a = \beta(\pi - \pi^a), \quad \beta > 0. \tag{6}$$

Combining (4), (3), and (6) determines—together with an appropriate initial condition—the time path of actual and expected inflation, for a given primary fiscal deficit. From (4) and (6), changes in expected inflation are determined by

$$\dot{\pi}^a = \beta(\mu - \pi^a)/(1 - \alpha\beta),$$

whereas the actual inflation rate is

$$\pi = (\mu - \alpha\beta\pi^a)/(1 - \alpha\beta),$$

which implies again that in the steady state (which involves $\dot{\pi}^a = 0$), $\pi = \pi^a = \mu$.

If the speed of adjustment β is low enough (that is, $\beta < 1/\alpha$), $\dot{\pi}^a > 0$ for all points located below the 45° line, whereas $\dot{\pi}^a < 0$ for all points located above that line (see figure). This implies that point A is a stable equilibrium, whereas B is unstable. Thus, starting from any point to the left of B, the economy will converge to point A, whereas if it starts from any point to the right of B it will tend to diverge from it—ending up in hyperinflation.[2] The government prints money at an

---

[2] As shown by Evans and Yarrow (1981), similar results continue to hold if the adaptive mechanism is a second-order error-learning process of the type $\ddot{\pi}^a = \beta_1(\dot{\pi} - \dot{\pi}^a) + \beta_1(\pi - \pi^a)$, where $\beta_1, \beta_2 > 0$.

ever-increasing rate, preventing the expected inflation rate from ever coinciding with the actual rate of increase in prices. Although real money balances (the inflation tax base) are reduced at an increasing rate, the pace at which the government is printing money is so rapid that it is still able to finance its deficit.[3]

Suppose that the economy is initially at the stable low-inflation equilibrium (point A), and consider the effect of an increase in the fiscal deficit. Suppose first that the increase is "small," so that curve D shifts to the right to D' but continues to intersect the 45° line twice. The increase in the fiscal deficit thus leads to an instantaneous jump in the rate of money growth—as well as the actual inflation rate—from point A to C, and from then on to a gradual increase in both the actual and the expected inflation rate from point C to A'. The horizontal shift from A to C at the moment the deficit increases occurs because the adaptive expectations hypothesis implies that the expected inflation rate cannot jump in response to shocks.

Once expectations begin to adjust, the demand for real money balances—which depends, as shown in (1), only on π^a—starts falling. To compensate for the reduction in the inflation tax base, the government must print money at an accelerated pace, until the new equilibrium is reached. A similar result obtains if the shift in the D curve is such that there exists only one point of intersection with the 45° line (point E). By contrast, if the increase in the fiscal deficit is large, curve D may not intersect the 45° line at all (curve D''). There is thus no steady state, and inflation will keep increasing continually. The economy jumps from point A to point F and follows a hyperinflationary path, moving to the northeast along the curve D''.

If bonds can be used as an additional source of financing of the fiscal deficit, dual equilibria will still obtain if the government fixes the interest rate, but a unique steady-state inflation rate is attained when the government sets a nominal anchor for the economy—for instance, by fixing the rate of growth of the nominal money stock.[4] The existence of dual equilibria is thus a consequence of the government's choice of monetary and fiscal policy rules, given the process through which inflationary expectations are formed. This result has implications for the choice of a nominal anchor in disinflation programs, which is discussed in the next chapter.

1.1.2   *Perfect Foresight*

Consider now the case where inflation expectations are rational, an assumption that can be implemented here by setting $\beta \to \infty$ in (6) and allowing expected and actual prices to jump on impact. In this case, it can be shown that point B is now a stable equilibrium, whereas A is unstable. Stability requires the elasticity of the demand for real balances to *exceed* unity at point B. Moreover, because the initial expected rate of

---

[3]When the speed of adjustment of expectations is very high, the low-inflation equilibrium becomes unstable while the high-inflation equilibrium becomes stable. As noted by Bruno and Fischer (1990), if the speed of adjustment of expectations rises with the rate of inflation, both equilibria may be stable.

[4]See Bruno and Fischer (1990). As shown by Lee and Ratti (1993), dual equilibria may still emerge with regard to other variables of the economy, such as the levels of real money balances, real bond holdings, and real interest rates.

inflation can now jump on impact, all points located on curve D are potential short-run equilibria. An increase in the fiscal deficit leads in this setting to an instantaneous jump to a new equilibrium, but there is no guarantee that the economy will be at any particular position on the curve $D'D'$ (at, say, point A'). Inflation, without displaying any sign of instability, may thus be unnecessarily high under perfect foresight.

The above discussion seems to suggest that large budget deficits may lead to hyperinflation only when private agents have adaptive expectations, that is, when they make systematic errors in predicting future inflation. Because the assumption of adaptive expectations is difficult to defend in situations where inflation is high or tends to follow an unstable path, this would seem to make hyperinflation unlikely in the orthodox model. Bruno and Fischer (1990) and Kiguel (1989), however, have shown that large budget deficits may lead to hyperinflation even under perfect foresight, if there is sluggish adjustment toward equilibrium in the money market.

Following Kiguel, assume that the money market adjusts gradually according to

$$\dot{m}/m = \kappa(\ln m^d - \ln m), \quad \kappa > 0, \tag{7}$$

where m^d denotes desired real balances, given by (1), and κ the speed of adjustment. Equation (7) can equivalently be written as

$$\pi = \mu - \kappa(\ln m^d - \ln m), \tag{8}$$

which indicates that the inflation rate adjusts one-for-one with the rate of growth of the nominal money stock, but adjusts only partially in response to differences between the desired and actual levels of real money balances. The inflation rate is therefore sticky (but not predetermined), whereas real balances are predetermined at any point in time.

Solving for the logarithm of money demand from (1) and using the identity $\dot{m} \equiv \dot{M}/P - \pi m$ in (8) yields

$$\dot{m} = \frac{\kappa}{\alpha\kappa - 1}(\alpha d + m \ln m). \tag{9}$$

Equation (9) is plotted in Figure 10.2 for a value of the deficit equal to d_0 and $\kappa < 1/\alpha$. There are two equilibria, one unstable (point A) and one stable (point B). When the speed of adjustment is very high ($\kappa \to \infty$), (9) becomes

$$\dot{m} \simeq d + \alpha^{-1}m \ln m,$$

which, for $\dot{m} \simeq 0$, gives a curve similar to D in Figure 10.1.

Consider now what happens when the policymaker increases the primary deficit to $d_1 > d_0$. The schedule $[\dot{m} = 0]$ moves down, so much so that it may no longer intersect the horizontal axis. Put differently, there may be no stationary value of

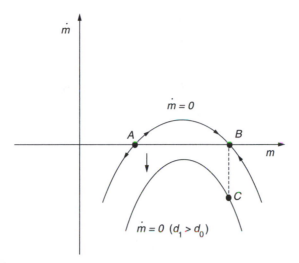

Figure 10–2 ■ Fiscal Deficits and Inflation with Gradual Adjustment of the Money Market
Source: Kiguel (1989, p. 152).

the inflation rate that ensures adequate revenue from the inflation tax to finance a deficit equal to d_1. In such conditions the behavior of the system will be unstable, characterized by decreasing real money balances and rising rates of inflation. Too large a deficit can therefore lead to a hyperinflationary path, as argued above in the case of adaptive expectations. Under perfect foresight, the potential instability in the inflation process depends crucially on the assumption of sluggish adjustment in the money market. The increase in money growth required to finance a higher deficit creates a temporary excess supply in the money market, which leads to an increase in inflation. The higher inflation rate exerts two conflicting effects on the equilibrium of the money market. On the one hand, it reduces the supply of real money balances, which tends to reequilibrate the market. On the other, it leads to a fall in the demand for real money balances, which tends to amplify the initial disequilibrium. When the system does not possess a stable long-run equilibrium, the latter effect dominates the former, and the resulting outcome is accelerating inflation, with a continuous increase in the rate of expansion of the nominal money stock.[5] As shown by Kiguel (1989), the possibility that the economy may follow an unstable inflationary path becomes even more likely if, as a result of the Olivera-Tanzi effect, discussed in Chapter 3, the erosion in tax revenue results in a positive relation between the primary fiscal deficit and the inflation rate. The importance of the Olivera-Tanzi effect in hyperinflation episodes has been emphasized also by Dornbusch (1993).

---

[5]Because $\dot{m} = d - \pi m$, seigniorage is constant along the unstable path. At the stationary equilibrium where $\dot{m} = 0$, seigniorage equals the inflation tax.

To summarize, money financing of fiscal deficits may lead, depending on the mechanism through which expectations are formed and the speed of adjustment of the money market, to multiple steady-state equilibria. Governments can therefore find themselves operating at an unnecessarily high inflation rate. The key message of the analysis, however, is that hyperinflation is an unstable process that emerges as a result of large, unsustainable fiscal deficits financed by money creation. Consequently, an essential feature of stabilization programs in countries undergoing hyperinflation must be a significant fiscal adjustment.

In small, open developing countries, an additional factor that may affect inflation directly in the short run is the exchange rate. A nominal depreciation affects directly the domestic-currency price of import-competing goods and exportables. An indirect effect may also result, as indicated in Chapter 9, if the cost of imported inputs (such as oil and semifinished goods) affects pricing decisions directly (see below). In addition, a depreciation of the exchange rate may also affect inflation by raising nominal wages, through implicit or explicit indexation mechanisms.[6] In such conditions, a real exchange-rate depreciation is likely to lead to inflationary pressures. The evidence provided by Darrat and Arize (1990), Dornbusch et al. (1990), Jorgensen and Paldam (1986), and Montiel (1989) supports the view that the exchange rate plays an important role in the short-run behavior of inflation in some chronic-inflation countries of Latin America. However, it is worth emphasizing that such evidence is not inconsistent with the presumption that fiscal deficits play a key role in the long run, as argued by the orthodox "fiscal view."

The model developed by Rodríguez (1978) provides a theoretical framework for explaining this type of result. If the fiscal deficit is financed through credit creation by the central bank, as is often the case in developing countries, the monetary expansion will lead to an increase in prices and a progressive erosion of foreign reserves, which will eventually trigger a devaluation if the central bank has limited access to borrowing in international capital markets (see Chapter 14). A devaluation-inflation spiral may develop, in the absence of corrective measures aimed at reducing the deficit. Thus, while the "proximate" cause of inflation may appear to be exchange-rate adjustment, the "ultimate" factor responsible for both inflation and exchange-rate depreciation may stem from fiscal rigidities.

1.2 ■ Food Supply and the Wage-Price Cycle

By contrast with the orthodox focus on the fiscal deficit, the link between inflation, food supply, and competing claims for the distribution of income is at the heart of the new structuralist approach to inflation. This section presents a modified

---

[6]In turn, the initial depreciation of the exchange rate may result from an external shock, such as a deterioration in the terms of trade or a sudden increase in external debt payments. Dornbusch (1993) has argued that in Argentina in the early 1980s, for instance, deteriorating terms of trade aggravated the external debt shock and forced a depreciation of the real exchange rate.

version of a model developed by Cardoso (1981), which provides a particularly clear formalization of the new structuralist view.

Consider a closed economy producing two goods: an agricultural good, whose production level is denoted y_A, and a manufactured good, whose production level is y_I. Food supply in the agricultural sector is given in the short run at $\tilde{y}_A$, while output is demand determined in the industrial sector. The equilibrium conditions in both markets are given by

$$\tilde{y}_A = c_A^d(\overset{+}{y}, \overset{-}{\theta}), \quad \theta \equiv P_A/P_I,$$

$$y_I = c_I^d(\overset{+}{y}, \overset{+}{\theta}) + g,$$

where $c_A^d(\cdot)$ denotes food demand, which in general depends positively on real factor income y and negatively on the relative price of agricultural goods, θ. $c_I^d(\cdot)$ represents private expenditure on manufactured goods, which depends positively on income and the relative price. g measures autonomous government expenditure on industrial goods. Real factor income, measured in terms of industrial goods, is defined as

$$y = \theta \tilde{y}_A + y_I.$$

Assume, without loss of generality, that the direct effect of changes in θ on demand is zero and let $0 < \alpha < 1$ denote the marginal propensity to consume. Measuring the proportion of consumption spent on agricultural goods by $0 < \delta < 1$, the equilibrium condition of the food market can be written as

$$\theta \tilde{y}_A = \delta \alpha y = \delta \alpha (\theta \tilde{y}_A + y_I), \tag{10}$$

while the market-clearing condition for industrial goods is

$$y_I = (1 - \delta)\alpha(\theta \tilde{y}_A + y_I) + g. \tag{11}$$

To examine the dynamic adjustment process and the behavior of inflation, assume for the moment that prices of industrial goods remain constant and that output in the industrial sector responds gradually to excess demand for manufactured goods:

$$\dot{y}_I = \upsilon_I[\alpha(1 - \delta)(\theta \tilde{y}_A + y_I) + g - y_I], \quad \upsilon_I > 0. \tag{12}$$

Similarly, agricultural prices respond gradually to the excess demand for food:

$$\dot{P}_A/P_A = \upsilon_A[\delta \alpha(\theta \tilde{y}_A + y_I) - \theta \tilde{y}_A], \quad \upsilon_A > 0. \tag{13}$$

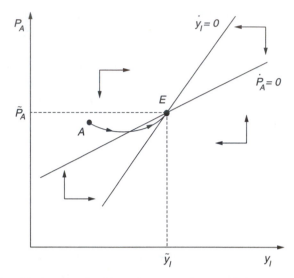

Figure 10–3 ■ Equilibrium in the New Structuralist Model

The rate of change in agricultural prices is thus equal to the rate of change in the relative price, $\dot\theta/\theta$, since prices of industrial goods remain constant.

Equations (12) and (13) constitute a system that determines the dynamic behavior over time of production in the industrial sector and agricultural prices:

$$
\begin{bmatrix} \dot P_A \\ \dot y_I \end{bmatrix} = \begin{bmatrix} -\upsilon_A(1-\alpha\delta) & \upsilon_A\alpha\delta \\ \upsilon_I\alpha(1-\delta) & -\upsilon_I(1-\alpha(1-\delta)) \end{bmatrix} \begin{bmatrix} P_A \\ y_I \end{bmatrix}, \tag{14}
$$

where, for simplicity, $g = 0$, and industrial prices are normalized to unity. For stability, the trace of the coefficient matrix must be negative and its determinant positive.

The equilibrium of the economy is shown in Figure 10.3. The curve $[\dot P_A = 0]$, which determines the combinations of industrial output and relative price that maintain equilibrium in the food market, has a positive slope, given by $dP_A/dy_I|_{\dot P_A=0} = \alpha\delta/(1-\alpha\delta)$. Points located to the left of this curve are associated with excess supply of food and falling prices, while points located to the right of it indicate excess demand and rising food prices. The curve $[\dot y_I = 0]$ represents the equilibrium condition for the industrial good market. This curve also has a positive slope, given by $dP_A/dy_I|_{\dot y_I=0} = [1-\alpha(1-\delta)]/\alpha(1-\delta)$. Points situated to the left of $[\dot y_I = 0]$ indicate excess demand for industrial goods and rising output, while points located to the right of $[\dot y_I = 0]$ indicate an excess supply of manufactured goods and falling output. To ensure stability, the $[\dot{y}_I = 0]$ curve must be steeper than the slope of the $[\dot{P}_A = 0]$ curve.[7] The steady-state equilibrium of the economy obtains at point E.

Suppose, for instance, that the initial position of the economy is at point A in Figure 10.3, which represents an excess supply of food and an excess demand for manufactured goods. The increase in output in the industrial sector dampens excess demand for manufactured goods while increasing income and the demand for agricultural products—reducing excess supply in that sector. The stability condition ensures that the income effect generated by the increase in industrial output does not exacerbate the initial excess demand in the market for industrial goods. Thus, in this basic framework, food prices fall at first and then rise, while industrial output rises continuously over time until the long-run equilibrium is reached. There is no tendency toward instability—because we assumed that industrial prices remain constant and we abstracted from workers' behavior.

Suppose now that firms in the industrial sector set prices as a fixed markup γ over labor costs. Assuming for simplicity that the unit labor requirement for industrial output is normalized to unity, industrial prices are given by

$$P_I = (1 + \gamma)w, \quad \gamma > 0. \tag{15}$$

Suppose also that workers have a constant real wage target ω^*, which implies that nominal wages are determined by

$$w = \tilde{\omega}P, \tag{16}$$

where P denotes the consumer price index, defined as

$$P = P_A^\delta P_I^{1-\delta}, \quad 0 < \delta < 1. \tag{17}$$

Using (15), (16), and (17) yields the "required" relative price, consistent with workers' real wage target:

$$\theta^* = [(1 + \gamma)\omega^*]^{-1/\delta}. \tag{18}$$

The rate of change of nominal wages is assumed to be determined by the difference between the required price ratio θ^* and the actual ratio θ so that, using (15), the rate of change of industrial prices π_I is equal to

$$\pi_I = \dot{w}/w = \kappa(\theta - \theta^*), \quad \kappa > 0, \tag{19}$$

where κ measures the speed of wage adjustment. θ^* is thus the relative price at which wage inflation is zero and industrial prices remain constant. Using (13) and (19) in

---

[7] For the system in (14) to be stable requires the matrix of coefficients on the right-hand side to have a positive determinant (to ensure that the roots are of the same sign) and a negative trace (to ensure that they are both negative). The condition on the trace always holds; the condition on the slopes stated in the text ensures that the determinant is indeed positive.

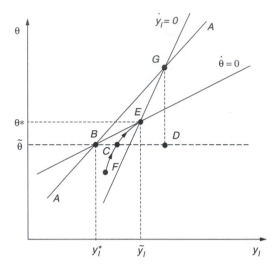

Figure 10–4 ▪ The Wage-Price Cycle in the New Structuralist Model
Source: Adapted from Cardoso (1981, p. 275).

the definition of θ yields

$$\dot{\theta}/\theta = \upsilon_A[\alpha\delta(\theta\tilde{y}_A + y_I) - \theta\tilde{y}_A] - \kappa(\theta - \theta^*). \qquad (20)$$

Figure 10.4 presents a diagrammatic solution of the system consisting of (12), (13), and (20). Curve AA is identical to curve $[\dot{P}_A = 0]$ defined previously, and gives combinations of the relative price and industrial output that ensure continuous equilibrium in the food market. The curves $[\dot{y}_I = 0]$ and $[\dot{\theta} = 0]$ are both upward sloping, with the former having a steeper slope to ensure stability. The slope of the AA curve is by construction also steeper than the slope of the $[\dot{\theta} = 0]$ curve. The two curves intersect at point B, where the actual relative price ratio is equal to the required relative price θ and the food market is in equilibrium. Curves $[\dot{y}_I = 0]$ and $[\dot{\theta} = 0]$ intersect at point E, which determines a value of the relative price $\tilde{\theta} > \theta^*$. Finally, curves $[\dot{y}_I = 0]$ and AA intersect at point G.

None of the points B, E, or G represent a long-run equilibrium in this economy. Suppose that the economy is initially at point G, where the food and industrial goods markets are both in equilibrium but real wages are lower than the desired level— or, equivalently, the actual relative price is higher than the required level. Nominal wages therefore increase, raising industrial prices and lowering the relative price of agricultural goods. The negative income effect reduces output in the industrial sector. At point B, real wages are at their desired level and the market for food is in equilibrium, but the economy is characterized by excess demand for manufactured goods. Industrial production begins rising, but as the economy moves away from point B (toward, say, point C), the increase in income exerts upward pressure on the relative price of food products.

If the economy is initially in a position such as point F, corresponding to a situation of excess demand in the food market, the upward pressure on agricultural prices is accompanied by a rise in nominal wages, which, in turn, leads to an increase in industrial prices and higher output in that sector. But as long as the excess demand for food remains large relative to the difference between the actual and the desired real wage, nominal wages and thus industrial prices will continue to increase less rapidly than agricultural prices, so that the relative price θ will rise over time. The upward pressure on the relative price leads to excess demand for manufactured goods, and industrial output rises. The economy therefore moves toward point E, where the curves $[\dot{y}_I = 0]$ and $[\dot{\theta} = 0]$ intersect, and both industrial output and the relative price remain constant.

But at that point, excess demand for agricultural products—resulting from the increase in income linked to output expansion in the industrial goods sector—maintains upward pressure on their price. Moreover, since the real wage is lower than desired, both nominal wages and industrial prices will continue to rise. Thus, there is no stable long-run equilibrium in this model because it is overdetermined. The relative price that corresponds to equilibrium in goods markets is inconsistent with the relative price that satisfies workers' claims on income. The outcome may be a self-perpetuating inflationary process, which may be exacerbated if the speed of adjustment of wages to changes in the price ratio increases over time.[8]

A stable, long-run equilibrium can be achieved in the above setting by various government policies. A reduction, for instance, in government spending g that is large enough to shift the $[\dot{y}_I = 0]$ curve to the left—until it intersects the AA and $[\dot{\theta} = 0]$ curves at point B—would halt the inflationary spiral, at the cost of lower industrial output. An incomes policy that would bring a reduction in the markup coefficient γ could also increase the target relative price θ^* toward $\tilde{\theta}$ and eliminate the inflationary cycle. Price controls could also prevent capitalists in the industrial sector from raising their prices and maintain the relative share of profits in national income, without necessarily leading to a reduction in output (see the appendix to Chapter 11). Nevertheless, the general implication of the analysis remains that when workers' desired real wage is high relative to the level compatible with long-run equilibrium, inflation stabilization is impossible to achieve without a shift in income distribution.

1.3 ■ A Structuralist-Monetarist Model

A crucial and generally implicit assumption in new structuralist models of inflation, including the modified version of Cardoso's model developed above, is that monetary policy fully accommodates changes in the price level. We now present an integrated

---

[8]In an extension of her analysis to an open economy, Cardoso (1981) argues that a devaluation of the real exchange rate has only a temporary effect on the trade balance but may generate a wage-price cycle similar to the one described here.

framework that accounts explicitly for money supply dynamics in the new structuralist model developed above. This extension provides a link with the orthodox approach described earlier and allows us to qualify some of the policy prescriptions commonly advocated by new structuralist economists. The link between prices, money, and fiscal deficits is captured by introducing food subsidies in the model and accounting for the government budget constraint.[9]

In the presence of a subsidy at the rate $0 < s < 1$, the consumer price index is defined as

$$P = [(1-s)P_A]^d P_I^{1-\delta}. \tag{21}$$

Suppose that the government levies a uniform tax on factor income at the rate $0 < \iota < 1$. Its expenditures consist of demand for industrial goods (in quantity g) and food subsidies. The government budget constraint can be written as

$$\dot{M} = P_I g + s P_A \tilde{y}_A - \iota(P_A \tilde{y}_A + P_I y_I),$$

which, in real terms, is equivalent to

$$\dot{m} = g + (s - \iota)\theta \tilde{y}_A - \iota y_I - \pi_I m, \tag{22}$$

where m denotes real money balances measured in terms of industrial prices. Assuming that the demand for food products is a positive function of real money balances yields the equilibrium condition of the food market in the presence of food subsidies:

$$(1-s)\theta \tilde{y}_A = \alpha\delta(1-\iota)(\theta \tilde{y}_A + y_I) + \lambda\delta m, \tag{23}$$

where α is now the propensity to consume out of disposable income, and $0 < \lambda < 1$. The left-hand side of this expression denotes the post-subsidy value of the supply of food, measured in terms of industrial goods.[10] The last term on the right-hand side measures a real balance effect.

The dynamics of output adjustment in the market for manufactures is now given by

$$\dot{y}_I = \upsilon_I[\alpha(1-\delta)(1-\iota)(\theta \tilde{y}_A + y_I) + \lambda(1-\delta)m + g - y_I]. \tag{24}$$

Assuming that workers pursue a real wage target as before, the required relative price is now given by

$$\theta^* = (1-\iota)^{-1}[(1+\gamma)\omega^*]^{-1/\delta}. \tag{25}$$

[9]The analysis follows Parkin (1991) and Srinivasan et al. (1989). For an analysis of food subsidies and inflation in a conventional new structuralist framework, see Taylor (1979, pp. 73–83).

[10]We assume in the following analysis that $s < 1 - \alpha\delta(1-\iota)$, to ensure that, for a given level of industrial output, a rise in the relative price of food reduces excess demand for agricultural goods.

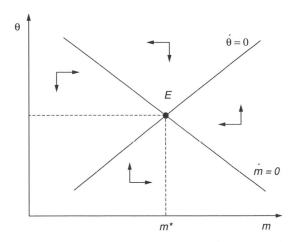

Figure 10–5 ▪ Equilibrium with Money and Food Subsidies in the New Structuralist Model
Source: Srinivasan et al. (1989).

After appropriate substitutions, the behavior of the relative price is determined by

$$\dot{\theta}/\theta = \upsilon_A \left[\frac{\alpha\delta}{1-s}(\theta\tilde{y}_A + y_I) + \frac{\lambda}{1-s}m - \theta\tilde{y}_A \right] - \kappa(\theta - \theta^*). \qquad (26)$$

Using (19), (22) can be approximated in the vicinity of the initial position (at $t = 0$) by

$$\dot{m} \simeq g + [(s - \iota)\tilde{y}_A - \kappa m_0]\theta - \iota y_I + \kappa(\theta_0 - \theta^*)m. \qquad (27)$$

Equations (24), (26), and (27) constitute a dynamic system in y_I, θ, and m. Instead of analyzing the complete system, let us assume that output adjustment in the market for industrial goods is instantaneous—that is, $\upsilon_I \to \infty$. Solving (24) for y_I with $\dot{y}_I = 0$ and substituting the result in (26) and (27) thus yields a system of two differential equations in θ and m.

A graphical presentation of the equilibrium is shown in Figure 10.5. The locus $[\dot{\theta} = 0]$ is positively sloped, since an increase in money holdings raises demand for agricultural and manufactured goods, requiring an increase in the relative price of food to maintain equilibrium. Under the assumption that $(s - \iota)\tilde{y}_A > \kappa m_0$, the locus $[\dot{m} = 0]$ is negatively sloped. In this case, stability is ensured.[11] In this setup, it can be shown that the long-run effect of an increase in the subsidy rate on inflation is

---

[11] If $(s - \iota)\tilde{y}_A < \kappa m_0$, stability requires that the slope of the $[\dot{m} = 0]$ curve be steeper than that of the $[\dot{\theta} = 0]$ curve.

ambiguous (see Parkin, 1991; Srinivasan et al., 1989). On the one hand, the increase in subsidy payments increases government spending and reduces the wedge between the actual price ratio and its required level—thus slowing down wage inflation— which tends to raise real money balances. On the other hand, higher activity in the industrial sector raises income tax revenue and reduces the fiscal deficit, exerting a downward pressure on money growth. It can be shown, nevertheless, that if the subsidy rate is high enough initially, then raising it further leads to higher money growth and inflation. Moreover, if wages are fully flexible, increasing subsidies on food is always inflationary.

The thrust of the preceding analysis is thus that once the link between subsidies, fiscal deficits, and monetary policy is properly taken into account, predictions of new structuralist models that ignore asset accumulation and the government budget constraint may require qualifications. In particular, an increase in subsidies may be inflationary, regardless of the specific assumption made regarding wage formation. More generally, the foregoing discussion suggests that combining orthodox and new structuralist models of inflation may provide new insights into the inflationary process. The emphasis on social conflict and income distribution may be important in understanding the chronic aspects of inflation in some countries, whereas accounting for the monetary effects of deficit financing is essential to understanding in most cases the transmission mechanism of policy shocks to inflation.

2   Dynamics of Alternative Policy Rules

A key aspect of the debate on the choice between money-based and exchange-rate-based stabilization programs is the dynamic path that different policy choices imply for inflation, output, and the current account. We present in this section two optimizing models that allow a rigorous analysis of the dynamics of stabilization policies in developing countries. The usefulness of these models results from their ability to capture some of the salient structural features of developing economies emphasized in previous chapters—particularly the role of imperfect asset substitutability, and nominal wage inertia—and their explicit microeconomic foundations. We begin by considering a one-good framework and then extend the analysis to a two-sector, three-good setting in which we endogenously determine the behavior of inflation and the real exchange rate.

2.1 ■ A One-Good Framework

The evidence discussed in Chapter 13 suggests that neither extreme of zero or perfect capital mobility appears to characterize the vast majority of developing countries. More relevant is an intermediate case in which domestic and foreign assets are imperfectly substitutable in private agents' portfolios. In what follows we present an analytical framework that captures this important feature of financial behavior in developing countries.[12]

Consider a small open economy in which there are four types of agents: producers, households, the government, and the central bank. All firms and households are identical, and their number is, for simplicity, normalized to unity. Domestic output consists of a tradable good produced using only labor, which is supplied in fixed quantity n^s. Wages are perfectly flexible, so that domestic production is fixed during the time frame of the analysis. Purchasing power parity holds continuously. Under a regime of predetermined exchange rates, the domestic currency is depreciated at a constant rate by the central bank, whose stock of foreign assets adjusts to equilibrate supply and demand for foreign exchange. Under a regime of flexible exchange rates, foreign reserves of the central bank are constant and the rate of credit growth is predetermined.

Households hold two categories of assets in their portfolios: domestic money and domestic government bonds. As in the model with zero capital mobility developed in Chapter 4, domestic money bears no interest. The household borrows on world capital markets subject to a rising risk premium, as discussed below. Foreigners do not hold domestic assets. The domestic interest rate adjusts to maintain equilibrium in the money market, while (as a result of the small-country assumption) the real rate of return on foreign bonds is determined on world capital markets. The government consumes goods and services, collects lump-sum taxes, and pays interest on its domestic debt. It finances its budget deficit either by issuing domestic bonds or by borrowing from the central bank.[13]

2.1.1   *Households*

The household's discounted lifetime utility is given as

$$\int_0^\infty \left\{ \frac{c^{1-\eta}}{1-\eta} + \chi \ln m \right\} e^{-\rho t} dt, \quad \rho, \chi > 0, \tag{28}$$

where ρ again denotes the constant rate of time preference, and c consumption. The instantaneous utility function takes the same form as in Chapter 4.

Nominal wealth of the representative household A is given by

$$A = M + B - EL^*,$$

---

[12]The model developed here is adapted from Agénor (1997) and represents an extension of the model with zero capital mobility developed in Chapter 3 to analyze the relationship between fiscal deficits, policy expectations, and real interest rates. Agénor (2006*a*) introduces commercial banks in a related setting.

[13]The assumption that the government may finance its fiscal deficit in part by issuing bonds may not be appropriate for all developing countries. It is, however, relevant for several upper-middle-income countries of Latin American and Asia. In any case, we do not focus on bond financing here.

where M denotes the nominal money stock, B the stock of government bonds, and EL^* the domestic-currency value of the stock of foreign bonds, with E denoting the nominal exchange rate and L^* the foreign-currency value of foreign borrowing by the household. Letting $m \equiv M/E$ denote real money balances and $b \equiv B/E$ the real stock of government bonds, real wealth can be defined as

$$a = m + b - L^*. \tag{29}$$

The flow budget constraint is given by

$$\dot{a} = y + ib - c - \tau - (i^* + \theta)L^* - (m + b)\varepsilon,$$

where y denotes domestic output (which is constant at $y(n^s)$), τ the real value of lump-sum taxes, i the domestic nominal interest rate, and $\varepsilon \equiv \dot{E}/E$ the predetermined rate of depreciation of the exchange rate. The term $-(m + b)\varepsilon$ accounts for capital losses on the stocks of money and domestic bonds resulting from changes in the exchange rate.

The term $i^* + \theta$ measures the cost of borrowing on world capital markets and consists of an exogenous, risk-free interest rate i^* and a risk premium θ, which is defined as

$$\theta = \theta(L^*, \cdot), \quad \theta_{L^*} > 0 \tag{30}$$

where the premium is assumed to be positively related to L^*.[14] Thus, domestic households are able to borrow more on world capital markets only at a higher rate of interest. This assumption captures the existence of individual default risk: the domestic agent's borrowing options are restricted by his or her capacity to repay.[15] Of course, the premium may also depend on various household characteristics other than the level of borrowing (such as the composition of the household), or factors such as market sentiment toward the country in question—in effect, a country-specific risk factor that reflects foreign lenders' idiosyncratic perceptions of the country's creditworthiness. It could also be related to macroeconomic variables, as for instance in Razin and Sadka (2004), where the risk premium on world capital markets is taken to depend on the fiscal stance (as measured by the primary surplus). For simplicity, we will abstract from these other factors at this stage.

---

[14]It is also plausible to assume that the premium is convex in L^* (so that $\theta_{L^*L^*} > 0$), and that for L^* sufficiently high a binding borrowing constraint is eventually reached. In what follows, it is assumed that the economy operates on the upward-sloping portion of the supply curve of funds, rather than at any absolute borrowing ceiling, and that θ is continuously differentiable in that range.

[15]See Agénor (1997) for a more detailed discussion. The assumption that the (household-specific) premium depends positively on the agent's level of debt—rather than the economy's total debt—leads naturally to the assumption that agents internalize the effect of their borrowing decisions on θ, as discussed below.

Using (29), the flow budget constraint can be rewritten as

$$\dot{a} = y + ra - c - \tau - (i^* + \theta - r)L^* - im, \tag{31}$$

where $r = i - \varepsilon$ denotes the domestic real rate of interest.

Households treat y, ε, i^*, i, and τ as given and maximize (28) subject to (30) and (31) by choosing a sequence $\{c, m, b, L\}_{t=0}^{\infty}$. The required optimality conditions are given by

$$m^d = \chi c^{\eta}/i \tag{32}$$

$$i = (i^* + \theta + \varepsilon) + L^*\theta_{L^*}, \tag{33}$$

$$\dot{c}/c = \sigma(r - \rho), \tag{34}$$

together with the transversality condition $\lim_{t \to \infty} (e^{-\rho t}a) = 0$.

Equation (32) is the money demand function, and is obtained from the condition that the marginal rate of substitution between money balances and consumption be equal to the opportunity cost of holding money—the nominal interest rate on domestic government bonds. Equation (34) is the conventional Euler equation, which shows that consumption rises or falls depending on whether the domestic real interest rate exceeds or falls below the rate of time preference.

Equation (33) is an arbitrage condition that determines implicitly the demand for loans. To understand its derivation, consider first the case where households face no risk premium on world capital markets ($\theta = 0$). In that case, clearly, optimality requires $i = i^* + \varepsilon$. Suppose, for instance, that $i > i^* + \varepsilon$; agents would then borrow unlimited amounts of funds on world capital markets and reap a net profit by buying government bonds. On the contrary, with $i < i^* + \varepsilon$, a corner solution would obtain, with households not borrowing at all from foreign lenders. Equilibrium (with a positive level of foreign debt) therefore requires equality between the marginal return i and the marginal cost of funds (measured in domestic-currency terms), $i^* + \varepsilon$.

Suppose now, as assumed above, that the premium rises with the level of private debt. Optimality requires, as before, that households borrow up to the point where the marginal return and the marginal cost of borrowing are equalized. Here, however, although the marginal return is again equal to the rate of return on domestic bonds, the marginal cost of borrowing is given by $i^* + \theta + \varepsilon$ plus the increase in the cost of servicing the existing stock of loans induced by the marginal increase in the risk premium (itself resulting from the marginal increase in borrowing), $L^*\theta_{L^*}$.

Since θ is a function of L^*, the optimal level of borrowing can be obtained from (33) by taking a linear approximation to θ, so that

$$L^* = (i - i^* - \varepsilon)/\gamma, \tag{35}$$

where $\gamma = 2\theta_{L^*} > 0$. Equation (35) indicates that foreign borrowing is positively related to the difference between the domestic interest rate and the sum of the safe world interest rate and the devaluation rate. Moreover, the demand for foreign loans is proportional to the differential $i - i^* - \varepsilon$, with a proportionality factor that depends on the sensitivity of the risk premium to the level of private debt.

2.1.2 Government and the Central Bank

There are no commercial banks in the economy, and the central bank lends only to the government. The nominal money stock is therefore equal to

$$M = D + ER^*, \tag{36}$$

where D denotes the stock of domestic credit allocated by the central bank to the government, and R^* the stock of net foreign assets, measured in foreign-currency terms. Changes in the real credit stock $d \equiv D/E$ are given by

$$\dot{d} = (\mu - \varepsilon)d, \tag{37}$$

where μ denotes the rate of growth of the nominal credit stock.

The central bank receives interest on its holdings of foreign assets and its loans to the government. For simplicity, we assume that the interest rate paid by the government on central bank loans is equal to the market rate of interest on domestic bonds. Real profits of the central bank are therefore equal to

$$\Pi^{cb} = (i^* + \varepsilon)R^* + id, \tag{38}$$

where εR^* measures real capital gains on reserves.

The government's revenue sources consist of lump-sum taxes on households and transfers from the central bank. It consumes goods and services and pays interest on its domestic debt. It finances its budget deficit by borrowing from the central bank or issuing bonds.[16] In nominal terms, the flow budget constraint of the government can be written as

$$\dot{B} + \dot{D} = E(g - \tau - \Pi^{cb}) + i(B + D),$$

where g denotes noninterest government spending, assumed exogenous. In real terms, and using (38), we have

$$\dot{d} + \dot{b} - \varepsilon m = g + rb - i^* R^* - \tau. \tag{39}$$

---

[16]We thus exclude the possibility that the government may borrow abroad.

Equation (39) indicates that government spending plus net interest payments on the domestic debt, minus lump-sum taxes, and interest income on reserves, must be financed by issuance of bonds, an increase in real domestic credit, or seigniorage revenue. Solving (39) yields the government's intertemporal budget constraint, which equalizes the present value of government purchases of goods and services to initial holdings of net assets plus the present value of lump-sum taxes subject to the solvency requirement

$$\lim_{t \to \infty} b e^{-rt} = 0.$$

As discussed in Chapter 4, the solvency constraint rules out indefinite Ponzi games by the government.

2.1.3 *Money Market Equilibrium*

To close the model requires specifying the equilibrium condition of the money market:

$$m^s = m^d.$$

Given (32), the above equation can be solved for the market-clearing domestic interest rate:

$$i = i(\overset{+}{c}, \overset{-}{m}), \tag{40}$$

which shows, as noted in Chapter 4, that the equilibrium nominal interest rate depends positively on private consumption and negatively on the stock of real cash balances.

2.1.4 *Dynamic Form*

Substituting (31), (36), and (39) in the household's flow budget constraint (29) give the economy's consolidated budget constraint:

$$\dot{L}^* - \dot{R}^* = i^*(L^* - R^*) + \theta L^* + c + g - y, \tag{41}$$

which determines the behavior over time of the total stock of foreign debt. Specifically, (41) indicates that the counterpart to the current account deficit, which is given as the sum of the trade deficit $c + g - y$ and net interest payments on the outstanding foreign debt $i^*(L^* - R^*) + \theta L^*$, is the change in net external liabilities. Integrating (41) yields (under the assumption that the safe world interest rate remains constant over time) the economy's intertemporal budget constraint

$$L_0^* - R_0^* = \int_0^\infty e^{-i^*}(y - c - g - \theta L^*)dt + \lim_{t\to\infty} e^{-i^*t}(L^* - R^*).$$

To satisfy the economy-wide intertemporal budget constraint, the second term on the right-hand side in the above expression must be zero. Thus, this constraint can be written, with i^* constant over time, as:

$$L_0^* - R_0^* = \int_0^\infty e^{-i^*t}(y - c - g - \theta L^*)dt,$$

which indicates that the current level of foreign debt must be equal to the discounted stream of the excess of future output over domestic absorption $(c + g)$, adjusted for the loss in resources induced by capital market imperfections.

Equations (34), (35), (37), (39), (40), and (41) describe the evolution of the economy along any perfect foresight equilibrium path. The system can be rewritten as:

$$L^* = [i(c, m) - i^* - \varepsilon]/\gamma, \tag{42}$$

$$\dot{c}/c = \sigma[i(c, m) - \varepsilon - \rho], \tag{43}$$

$$\dot{L}^* - \dot{R}^* = i^*(L^* - R^*) + \theta(L^*)L^* + c + g - y, \tag{44}$$

$$\dot{d} + \dot{b} + \varepsilon m = g + rb - i^*R^* - \tau, \tag{45}$$

$$\dot{d} = (\mu - \varepsilon)d, \tag{46}$$

$$m = d + R^*. \tag{47}$$

Equations (42)–(47) represent a differential equation system with six endogenous variables, c, b, L^*, R^*, d, and m. It is worth noting that the capital account and the overall balance of payments are defined in terms of changes in the level of private foreign debt and official reserves that occur over time. These definitions do not capture transactions that occur discretely under a regime of predetermined exchange rates, such as those that may reflect an instantaneous conversion of foreign currency loans for domestic cash balances. Specifically, although the economy's overall stock of foreign debt $L^* - R^*$ is predetermined, official reserves and private foreign borrowing may jump in response to sudden movements in domestic interest rates. An instantaneous shift in private indebtedness on world capital markets is thus associated, under a regime of predetermined exchange rates, with an offsetting movement in the level of official foreign reserves held by the central bank.

In what follows, we will assume that the government foregoes the issuance of bonds to finance its deficit ($b = 0$), and instead either borrows from the central bank or varies lump-sum taxes to balance its budget. Given this assumption, the model can be operated in different modes, depending on the "closure rule" chosen: the rate of devaluation can be treated as predetermined, or the rate of growth of the nominal credit stock can be viewed as predetermined. Regardless of the particular mode chosen, the steady-state solution is obtained by setting $\dot{c} = \dot{L}^* = \dot{R}^* = \dot{d} = 0$ in the above system. As can readily be shown from (43) and (46), in the long-run equilibrium the real domestic interest rate must be equal to the rate of time preference:

$$\tilde{r} = \tilde{i} - \varepsilon = \rho, \tag{48}$$

and the rate of domestic credit growth must be equal to the devaluation rate:

$$\mu = \varepsilon. \tag{49}$$

Real money balances are thus equal to

$$\tilde{m} = \tilde{m}(c, \rho + \varepsilon). \tag{50}$$

However, alternative closure rules lead to different transitory dynamic paths, as we now show.

2.1.5   Devaluation Rule

Under a constant rate of devaluation ($\varepsilon = \varepsilon^b$), the rate of growth of the credit stock must be endogenous if taxes cannot be adjusted to finance the fiscal deficit ($\tau = \tau_0$). Setting, for simplicity, the constant stock of government bonds equal to zero, (45) implies that the evolution of the real stock of credit over time is given by

$$\dot{d} = g - i^* R^* - \tau_0 - \varepsilon^b m. \tag{51}$$

The path of $\dot{d}$ given by (51) can be substituted in (46) to determine μ:

$$\mu = \varepsilon^b + \dot{d}/d.$$

From (47), $\dot{m} = \dot{d} + \dot{R}^*$. Substituting (51) in this expression yields

$$\dot{m} = \dot{R}^* + g - i^* R^* - \tau_0 - \varepsilon^b m,$$

or, using (44):

$$\dot{m} = \dot{L}^* + y - c - \tau_0 - (i^* + \theta)L^* - \varepsilon^b m. \tag{52}$$

Because the stock of government bonds is normalized to zero, (29) implies that

$$m = a + L^*, \tag{53}$$

which can be substituted in (42) to give

$$L^* = [i(c, a + L^*) - i^* - \varepsilon^b]/\gamma.$$

Taking a linear approximation to the function $i(\cdot)$ yields

$$L^* = (i_c c + i_m a - i^* - \varepsilon^b)/(\gamma - i_m),$$

or equivalently

$$L^* = \Phi(\overset{+}{c}, \overset{-}{a}; \overset{-}{\varepsilon^b}), \tag{54}$$

where, setting $\beta \equiv 1/(\gamma - i_m) > 0$:

$$\Phi_c = \beta i_c, \quad \Phi_a = \beta i_m, \quad \Phi_\varepsilon = -\beta.$$

Substituting (54) in (53) implies that

$$m = a + L^* = h(\overset{+}{c}, \overset{+}{a}; \overset{-}{\varepsilon^b}), \tag{55}$$

where

$$h_c = \Phi_c, \quad h_a = 1 + \Phi_a < 1, \quad h_\varepsilon = \Phi_\varepsilon.$$

Substituting (55) in (43) yields

$$\dot{c} = \sigma c \{i[c, h(c, a, \varepsilon^b)] - \varepsilon^b - \rho\} = G(\overset{+}{c}, \overset{-}{a}; \overset{-}{\varepsilon^b}), \tag{56}$$

where

$$G_c = \sigma \bar{c} \beta \gamma i_c, \quad G_a = \sigma \bar{c} i_m h_a, \quad G_\varepsilon = -\sigma \bar{c} \beta \gamma.$$

Finally, substituting (54) and (55) in (52) and rearranging yields

$$\dot{a} = \dot{m} - \dot{L}^* = y - c - \tau_0 - [i^* + \theta(\Phi(c, a; \varepsilon^b))]\Phi(c, a; \varepsilon^b) - \varepsilon^b h(c, a; \varepsilon^b),$$

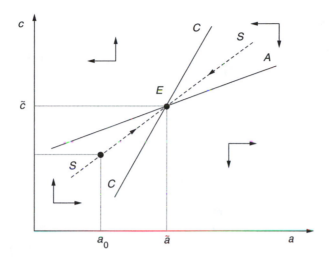

Figure 10–6 ▪ Equilibrium in the One-Good Model

or equivalently

$$\dot{a} = \Psi(\overset{-}{c}, \overset{+}{a}; \overset{+}{\varepsilon^{b}}), \tag{57}$$

where, with a '~' denoting initial steady-state values:

$$\Psi_{c} = -1 - (\bar{\theta} + \bar{L}^{*}\theta_{L^{*}})\Phi_{c}, \quad \Psi_{a} = -(\bar{\theta} + \bar{L}^{*}\theta_{L^{*}})\Phi_{a} - \varepsilon^{b}h_{a},$$

$$\Psi_{\varepsilon} = -(\bar{\theta} + \bar{L}^{*}\theta_{L^{*}})\Phi_{\varepsilon^{b}} - \tilde{m},$$

where we assume that ε^{b} and $\tilde{m}$ are sufficiently small.

Taking a linear approximation of (56) and (57) around the initial steady state yields the following system in c and a:

$$\begin{bmatrix} \dot{c} \\ \dot{a} \end{bmatrix} = \begin{bmatrix} G_{c} & G_{a} \\ \Psi_{c} & \Psi_{a} \end{bmatrix} \begin{bmatrix} c - \tilde{c} \\ a - \tilde{a} \end{bmatrix}. \tag{58}$$

Consumption is a forward-looking variable, whereas financial wealth is predetermined at each moment in time, with an initial value a_0. The determinant of the system (58) is given by $G_{c}\Psi_{a} - G_{a}\Psi_{c}$, which must be negative for the system to be saddlepoint stable.

A diagrammatic solution of the model is presented in Figure 10.6. The locus CC (along which $\dot{c} = 0$) is upward sloping and so is the locus AA, along which $\dot{a} = 0$. Saddlepath stability requires CC to be steeper than AA. The saddlepath SS, which also has a positive slope, is the unique path leading to the steady-state equilibrium (point E).

Suppose that the economy is initially in a long-run equilibrium position. Consider the effect of a permanent, unanticipated reduction in the devaluation rate from ε^b to $\varepsilon^s < \varepsilon^b$, with no discrete change in the level of the exchange rate. Using the steady-state solutions, it is readily established that a reduction in the devaluation rate raises $\tilde{a}$ and lowers $\tilde{c}$. From (42) and (48), the steady-state level of private foreign borrowing is given by

$$\tilde{L}^* = (\rho - i^*)/\gamma, \tag{59}$$

which is independent of the devaluation rate. But because $\tilde{a}$ rises, it must be the case that $\tilde{m}$ rises. The reason is that from (48) the nominal interest rate must be equal in the steady state to the rate of time preference plus the devaluation rate; it therefore falls in the same proportion as the devaluation rate—thereby reducing the opportunity cost of holding money and raising the demand for cash balances.

On impact, the reduction in the devaluation rate raises private foreign borrowing at the initial level of domestic interest rates. Because private financial wealth cannot change on impact, this portfolio shift must be offset by a rise in real money balances. This instantaneous adjustment takes place through purchases of foreign currency assets by the central bank (the counterpart to the inflow of capital associated with foreign borrowing) accompanied by a discrete increase in the domestic money stock. Consumption falls to place the economy on the convergent trajectory toward the new steady state. Because the real money stock rises and consumption falls, the domestic nominal interest rate falls—but by less than the devaluation rate, implying a rise in domestic real interest rates. The increase in foreign borrowing raises the risk premium faced by private agents on world capital markets. As a result, the services account of the balance of payments deteriorates. At the same time, however, the reduction in private consumption leads to an improvement in the trade balance. The net effect on changes in private financial wealth, as can be inferred from (57), is positive ($\dot{a}_0 > 0$). The rate of growth of the nominal credit stock falls on impact.

Because the shock is permanent, the adjustment path to the new steady state is monotonic. The transitional dynamics are illustrated in Figure 10.7. The economy is initially at point E; the reduction in the rate of devaluation shifts both CC and AA to the right. Because private wealth is predetermined, consumption jumps downward from point E to point B, located on the new saddlepath $S'S'$, and begins rising afterward. The nominal interest rate must rise over time to allow the real interest rate to return to its initial steady-state value. This increase leads to a reduction in private foreign borrowing (capital outflows), which returns to its initial value. During the transition the current account remains in surplus (in part because the reduction in foreign borrowing lowers the risk premium and improves the services account), which is large enough to compensate for the capital account deficit. Over time, therefore, the central bank's holdings of foreign assets and the real money stock increase. As a result of both the increase in real money balances and the reduction in foreign borrowing, private financial wealth rises over time. Assuming that the

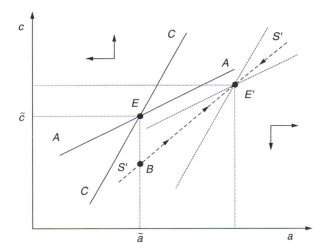

Figure 10-7 ▪ Reduction in the Devaluation Rate in the One-Good Model

risk-free rate is not too large, the rate of nominal credit growth falls gradually over time toward the lower devaluation rate. The new steady state is reached at point E'.

2.1.6 Credit Growth Rule

Under a constant nominal-credit rule ($\mu = \mu^b$), foreign reserves of the central bank remain constant ($\dot{R}^* = 0$), and the devaluation/inflation rate is determined endogenously. Setting, for simplicity, the constant level of official reserves equal to zero (so that $m = d$), (42) yields

$$\varepsilon = i(c, d) - i^* - \gamma L^* = \varepsilon(\overset{+}{c}, \overset{-}{d}, \overset{-}{L^*}),$$

which can be substituted out in (46) to give[17]

$$\dot{d} = [\mu^b - \varepsilon(c, d, L^*)]d. \tag{60}$$

Equation (60) determines changes in the real credit stock. Because $\dot{R}^* = 0$, (44) can be written as

$$\dot{L}^* = [i^* + \theta(L^*)]L^* + c + g - y, \tag{61}$$

which determines changes in private external borrowing over time. In contrast to the previous case, therefore, private foreign borrowing is predetermined at any point in

---

[17]Given that the nominal credit stock grows at a predetermined rate, the solution for the *level* of the nominal exchange rate obtains once the path of the real credit stock is known.

time. To ensure solvency of the public sector, we assume that lump-sum transfers are continually adjusted to maintain fiscal equilibrium—so that, from (45) and (46), and with $\dot{b} = b = 0$, $\tau = g - \mu^b d$.

The dynamic system now therefore consists of (43), (60), and (61). From (42), $i - \varepsilon = \gamma L^* + i^*$; substituting this result in (43) yields

$$\dot{c}/c = \sigma(i - \varepsilon - \rho) = \sigma(\gamma L^* + i^* - \rho) = \Gamma(\overset{+}{L^*}).$$

The dynamic system is thus

$$\begin{bmatrix} \dot{c} \\ \dot{d} \\ \dot{L}^* \end{bmatrix} = \begin{bmatrix} 0 & 0 & \Gamma' \\ -\varepsilon_c \tilde{d} & -\varepsilon_d \tilde{d} & -\varepsilon_{L^*} \tilde{d} \\ 1 & 0 & \Theta \end{bmatrix} \begin{bmatrix} c - \tilde{c} \\ d - \tilde{d} \\ L^* - \tilde{L}^* \end{bmatrix}, \tag{62}$$

where $\Theta = i^* + \tilde{\theta} + \tilde{L}^* \theta_{L^*}$.

Consumption and the real stock of credit are both jump variables, so to ensure saddlepath stability, system (62) must possess two positive roots and one negative root. In turn, sufficient conditions for this result are that the determinant of the matrix of coefficients in (62) be negative (which ensures either one or three negative roots) and that its trace be positive (which ensures at least one positive root). Both conditions always hold, because the trace is equal to $\Theta - \varepsilon_d \tilde{d} > 0$ and the determinant is equal to $\varepsilon_d \tilde{d} Q' < 0$.

Consider now a reduction in the rate of expansion of the nominal credit stock, from μ^b to $\mu^s < \mu^b$. In the long run, as shown earlier, private foreign borrowing is determined only by the difference between the rate of time preference and the risk-free world interest rate, and thus does not change [see (59)]. Because output is constant, this result implies, using (61), that consumption also does not change. And from (60), the devaluation rate must fall in the same proportion as the nominal credit growth rate, to ensure that the real credit stock is constant in the steady state. As a result, the domestic nominal interest rate also falls in the same proportion as the nominal credit growth rate.

But because consumption does not change, the reduction in the opportunity cost of holding money is unambiguously associated with an increase in real money balances—or, equivalently, given that official reserves are constant, an increase in the real credit stock. And because the stock of nominal credit does not change, the nominal exchange rate must undergo a step appreciation (a discrete fall in prices). There are, therefore, *no transitional dynamics*. The economy jumps immediately to a new steady state, with no effect on consumption, the current account, private foreign borrowing, or the domestic real interest rate. The rate of depreciation falls instantaneously to the lower level of the credit growth rate. The nominal interest rate falls also in the same proportion as the credit growth rate, and is associated with a steady-state increase in real money balances, resulting from an appreciation of the nominal exchange rate.[18]

The thrust of the foregoing discussion, then, is that exchange rate and monetary rules may lead to very different adjustment paths for the main variables under imperfect capital mobility. Models based on the monetary approach to the balance of payments—such as the one developed by Calvo and Rodríguez (1977)—typically possess a "dynamic equivalence" property, in the sense that the steady-state solutions and the adjustment paths associated with a monetary rule or an exchange-rate rule are identical. In the model developed here, although either rule can be used to attain a long-run inflation rate target—given the solvency constraint of the public sector— the behavior of the economy during the transition period is completely different.[19] Under a credit growth rule, there is no transitional adjustment as such; the economy jumps immediately to the new steady state. Under an exchange-rate rule, by contrast, there are two types of adjustments: those that occur through time and those that occur instantaneously, in order to maintain portfolio balance. Depending on the constraints that policymakers face in the short run, the nature of the transitional dynamics may determine the adoption of one rule as opposed to the other; the implication of this result for the choice of a nominal anchor in disinflation programs will be examined in the next chapter.

2.1.7   *Dynamics with Alternative Fiscal Policy Rules*

The adjustment path induced by monetary and exchange-rate policy shocks depends, among other factors, on the financing rules that policymakers adopt to close the fiscal deficit. Consider, for instance, a situation in which the government (as before) does not issue bonds, and the central bank sets the rate of growth of nominal credit equal to the rate of exchange rate depreciation ($\mu = \varepsilon$). The government then adjusts lump-sum taxes endogenously to close the fiscal deficit. In this setting, monetary policy and exchange-rate policy cannot be distinguished. This financing rule nevertheless satisfies the transversality condition of the public sector given above and is therefore sustainable. Because the credit rule implies that $\dot{d} = 0$, (45), with $\dot{b} = b = 0$, can be solved for the endogenous level of lump-sum taxes:

$$\tau + \varepsilon m = g - i^* R^*, \tag{63}$$

---

[18]Turnovsky (1985) obtains qualitatively similar results.

[19]Auernheimer (1987), Kiguel (1987), and Velasco (1993) also develop models in which the adjustment path depends on the prevailing policy rule. In particular, Kiguel develops a model with an endogenous real sector and imperfect capital mobility and shows how the path of the real exchange rate varies under alternative policy rules. Velasco (who assumes zero capital mobility) argues that the rise in real interest rates during the transition to the steady state determines the sustainable size of the primary (noninterest) fiscal deficit, leading to nonequivalence also in the long run.

where εm represents again inflation tax revenue. As a result of this rule, $\dot{m} = \dot{R}^*$; that is, changes in the real money stock reflect only changes in the central bank's net foreign assets.

An analysis of the above model under the financing rule (63) is provided by Agénor (1997). In particular, Agénor shows that the short- and long-run dynamics associated with a permanent, unanticipated reduction in the rate of devaluation-credit growth rate are qualitatively similar to those described earlier in our discussion of a reduction in the devaluation rate with credit financing of the budget deficit.

Yet another fiscal rule would be to assume that, following an initial policy adjustment, the central bank finances its deficit during a transitory period through bond or money financing, with the promise to switch at a future date to either a lower level of government expenditure or tax financing. This type of rule was examined in Chapter 4 in the context of a closed economy, in our discussion of the "monetarist arithmetic."

2.2 ■ A Three-Good Model with Flexible Prices

We now extend the analysis to consider the case where the economy produces two goods: a nontradable good that is used only for final domestic consumption, and an exportable good whose output is entirely exported.[20] The capital stock in each sector is fixed, while labor is homogeneous and perfectly mobile. Households and the government consume home goods and an imperfectly substitutable importable good, which is not produced domestically. Prices in the home goods sector and nominal wages are perfectly flexible.

2.2.1 *Households*

The consumption decision of households follows a two-stage process. They first determine the optimal level of total consumption given their budget constraint, and then allocate the optimal amount between consumption of home and importable goods.[21]

Under the assumption that labor is supplied inelastically, the representative household's discounted lifetime utility remains as given in (28), where c is now an index of total consumption expenditure and real money balances m are measured in terms of the price of the consumption basket, P.

---

[20] All other assumptions of the one-good model—particularly regarding the structure of private portfolios—are maintained in the present framework, which follows Agénor (1997). For simplicity and clarity, we abstract from the existence of an import-competing sector. Such an extension would, however, be useful for analyzing terms-of-trade shocks, as discussed in Chapter 1. A three-good model with an import-competing sector is presented in Hinkle and Montiel (1999).

[21] Precise conditions for the two-stage budgeting process of the type considered here to be well defined are given in Deaton and Muellbauer (1980).

Real financial wealth of the representative household is also defined as in (29):

$$a = m + b - l^*, \tag{64}$$

with a and b measured in terms of the price of the consumption basket, and real foreign indebtedness l^* now defined as $l^* \equiv EL^*/P$. The flow budget constraint is now given by

$$\dot{a} = y + ib - c - \tau - (i^* + \theta)l^* - \varepsilon l^* - \pi a, \tag{65}$$

where net factor income y is derived below, and $\pi \equiv \dot{P}/P$ is the overall inflation rate. The term $-\pi a$ accounts for capital losses on total wealth resulting from inflation, whereas the term εl^* represents the increase in the domestic-currency value of external liabilities resulting from exchange-rate devaluation.

Using (64), (65) can be written as

$$\dot{a} = ra + y - c - \tau - (i^* + \theta + \varepsilon - i)l^* - im, \tag{66}$$

where $r = i - \pi$ denotes the domestic real rate of interest.

In the first stage of the consumption decision process, the household treats π, ε, y, i, i^*, and τ as given, internalizes again the effect of his or her borrowing decisions on θ, and maximizes (28) subject to (30) and (66) by choosing a sequence $\{c, m, b, L^*\}_{t=0}^{\infty}$.[22] The optimality conditions are similar to those derived before:

$$m^d = \chi c^{\eta}/i = m(\overset{+}{c}, \overset{-}{i}) \tag{67}$$

$$i = (i^* + \theta + \varepsilon) + L^* \theta_{L^*}, \tag{68}$$

$$\dot{c}/c = \sigma(r - \rho), \tag{69}$$

together with the transversality condition $\lim_{t \to \infty}(e^{-\rho t}a) = 0$. Using again a linear approximation to θ, (68) yields a demand function for foreign loans similar to (35):

$$L^* = (i - i^* - \varepsilon)/\gamma. \tag{70}$$

The properties of (67) and (70) are essentially the same as those described in the previous section. An important new element in the present setting, however, is that the intertemporal Euler equation (69) implies that overall expenditure growth

---

[22] The assumption that the household chooses the foreign-currency value of foreign loans is adopted for simplicity. Note, however, that it is natural to retain the assumption that the risk premium depends on the foreign-currency value of private foreign borrowing, given that it reflects the behavior of foreign lenders.

depends on the real rate of interest measured in terms of the price of the consumption basket. Thus, as emphasized notably by Dornbusch (1983), even in the absence of capital market imperfections ($\gamma \to 0$), the presence of nontradable goods prevents equalization of domestic and foreign real interest rates. Put differently, differential changes in the relative price of nontradable goods across countries imply different real rates of return even when nominal rates of return are equal.

In the second stage of the consumption decision process, the representative household maximizes a homothetic sub-utility function $V(c_N, c_I)$, subject to the static budget constraint

$$P_N c_N + E c_I = P c,$$

where P_N denotes the price of the home good, and c_I (c_N) expenditure on the importable (nontradable) good. Because the foreign-currency price of the importable good is normalized to unity, the domestic-currency price is simply the nominal exchange rate.

Let z be the relative price of the importable good in terms of the home good, that is $z \equiv E/P_N$. Because the representative household's intratemporal preferences are homothetic, the desired ratio between home and importable goods depends only on their relative price, and not on overall expenditure. Thus:

$$V_{c_N}/V_{c_I} = z^{-1}.$$

Suppose that the sub-utility function is Cobb-Douglas, so that

$$V(c_N, c_I) = c_N^{\delta} c_I^{1-\delta}/[\delta^{\delta}(1-\delta)^{1-\delta}],$$

where $0 < \delta < 1$ denotes the share of total spending falling on home goods. The desired composition of spending is thus

$$c_N/c_I = \delta z/(1-\delta),$$

which can be substituted in the intratemporal budget constraint, $c = z^{\delta}(c_I + c_N/z)$, to give

$$c_N = \delta z^{1-\delta} c, \quad c_I = (1-\delta)z^{-\delta} c. \tag{71}$$

From the indirect sub-utility function, the appropriate definition of the consumer price index P is thus (Samuelson and Swamy, 1974):[23]

$$P = P_N^{\delta} E^{1-\delta} = E z^{-\delta}, \tag{72}$$

---

[23] Strictly speaking, the cost-of-living index should also include the opportunity cost of holding real money balances, that is, the domestic nominal interest rate. For simplicity, this component is ignored.

so that the inflation rate is

$$\pi = \varepsilon - \delta \dot{z}/z. \tag{73}$$

2.2.2 Output and the Labor Market

Technology for the production of tradable and nontradable goods is characterized by decreasing returns to labor:

$$y_h = y(n_h), \quad y_h' > 0, \; y_h'' < 0 \quad h = N, X \tag{74}$$

where y_h denotes output of good h, and n_h the quantity of labor employed in sector h. From the first-order conditions for profit maximization, the sectoral labor demand functions can be derived as

$$n_X^d = n_X^d(w_X), \quad n_N^d = n_N^d(zw_X), \quad n_X^{d\prime}, n_N^{d\prime} < 0, \tag{75}$$

where w_X is the product wage in the exportable goods sector. Nominal wages are perfectly flexible, so that w_X can be solved for from the equilibrium condition of the labor market:

$$n_X^d(w_X) + n_N^d(zw_X) = n^s,$$

where n^s denotes the supply of labor, which is again taken to be constant. This equation implies that the equilibrium product wage is negatively related to the real exchange rate:

$$w_X = w_X(z), \quad w_X' < 0, \; |w_X'| < 1. \tag{76}$$

Substituting this result in (74) and (75), and noting that $d(zw_X)/dz = 1 + w_X' > 0$, yields the sectoral supply equations:

$$y_h^s = y_h^s(z), \quad y_X^{s\prime} > 0, \; y_N^{s\prime} < 0. \tag{77}$$

2.2.3 Central Bank and the Government

As before, there are no commercial banks in the economy, and the central bank does not provide credit to domestic agents. The real money supply is thus equal to

$$m^s = z^\delta R^*. \tag{78}$$

Real profits of the central bank, $(i^* + \varepsilon)z^\delta R^*$, are fully transferred to the government. With lump-sum financing, and setting the constant real stock of government bonds to zero, the government budget constraint can be written as

$$\tau = z^{\delta}(g_I + g_N/z) - z^{\delta}(i^* + \varepsilon)R^*, \tag{79}$$

where g_I and g_N denote government spending on importable and nontradable goods, respectively.

2.2.4 Market-Clearing Conditions

To close the model requires specifying the equilibrium conditions for the home goods market and the money market, the latter being solved for the market-clearing interest rate. The former condition is given by

$$y_N^s = \delta z^{1-\delta} c + g_N, \tag{80}$$

and, from (67) and (78), the market-clearing interest rate is given as before by (40).

2.2.5 Dynamic Form

Real factor income y (measured in terms of cost-of-living units) is given by

$$y = z^{\delta}(y_X^s + y_N^s/z). \tag{81}$$

Equations (64) and (78) yield

$$a = z^{\delta}(R^* - l^*).$$

Although $R^* - l^*$ is predetermined, the real exchange rate can change in discrete fashion; net financial wealth a (or, equivalently, the domestic-currency value of the economy's stock of foreign assets) can therefore also jump on impact.

Using the above definition of a and (73) yields:

$$\dot{a} = z^{\delta}(\dot{R}^* - \dot{L}^*) + (\varepsilon - \pi)a.$$

Substituting the above results, together with (71), (79), (80), and (81) in (65) yields

$$\dot{L}^* - \dot{R}^* = i^*(l^* - R^*) + \theta(l^*, \cdot)L^* + (1 - \delta)z^{-\delta}c + g_I - y_X^s, \tag{82}$$

which represents the consolidated budget constraint of the economy. As before, integrating (82) yields, subject to the transversality condition $\lim_{t \to \infty}(L^* - R^*)e^{-i^*t}$, the economy's intertemporal budget constraint.

From (71) and (80), the short-run equilibrium real exchange rate is obtained as

$$z = z(\bar{c}; \bar{g}_N), \tag{83}$$

where

$$z_c = \delta/[y_N^{s\prime} - \delta(1-\delta)\bar{c}], \quad z_{g_N} = 1/[y_N^{s\prime} - \delta(1-\delta)\bar{c}].$$

Equations (40), (69), (70), (73), (78), (82), and (83) describe the behavior of the economy over time. These equations can be summarized as follows:

$$L^* = [i(c, m) - i^* - \varepsilon]/\gamma, \tag{84}$$

$$\dot{c}/c = \sigma[i(c, m) - \varepsilon + \delta\dot{z}/z - \rho], \tag{85}$$

$$z = z(c; g_N), \tag{86}$$

$$\dot{D} = i^* D + \theta(L^*)L^* + (1-\delta)z^{-\delta}c + g_T - y_X^s(z), \tag{87}$$

$$m = z^\delta R^*, \tag{88}$$

with (79) determining residually lump-sum taxes and $D = L^* - R^*$ denoting again net external debt.

To condense the dynamic form into a system involving only c and D, note that from (88):

$$m = z^\delta(L^* - D), \tag{89}$$

or, using (84):

$$m = z^\delta \left\{ [i(c, m) - (i^* + \varepsilon) - \gamma D]/\gamma \right\}. \tag{90}$$

Substituting (86) in (90) yields

$$m = z(c; g_N)^\delta \beta \left\{ i_c c - (i^* + \varepsilon) - \gamma D \right\}, \quad \beta \equiv 1/(\gamma - i_m), \tag{91}$$

so that

$$m = \varphi(\overset{?}{c}, \bar{D}; i^* \bar{+} \varepsilon, \bar{g}_N), \tag{92}$$

where

$$\varphi_c = \beta(i_c + \delta\gamma z_c \bar{R}^*), \quad \varphi_D = -\beta\gamma, \quad \varphi_{i^*+\varepsilon} = -\beta, \quad \varphi_{g_N} = \beta\delta\gamma z_{g_N} \bar{R}^*.$$

Substituting (92) in (85) yields

$$\dot{c}/c = \sigma \left\{ i[c, \varphi(c, D; i^* + \varepsilon, g_N)] - \varepsilon + \delta \dot{z}/z - \rho \right\}. \tag{93}$$

Suppose that changes in g_N occur only in discrete fashion. Equation (86) therefore implies that $\dot{z} = z_c \dot{c}$, with $z_c < 0$. Substituting this result in (93) yields a dynamic equation which can be written as

$$\dot{c} = G(\overset{+}{c}, \overset{+}{D}; \overset{+}{i}^*, \overset{-}{\varepsilon}, \overset{+}{g_N}), \tag{94}$$

where, with $\Delta = \sigma \bar{c}/(1 - \sigma \bar{c} \delta z_c) > 0$:[24]

$$G_c = (i_c + i_m \varphi_c)\Delta, \quad G_D = i_m \varphi_D \Delta,$$

$$G_{i^*} = i_m \varphi_{i^*+\varepsilon} \Delta, \quad G_\varepsilon = (i_m \varphi_{i^*+\varepsilon} - 1)\Delta, \quad G_{g_N} = i_m \varphi_{g_N} \Delta.$$

Substituting (92) into (84) yields

$$L^* = \lambda(\overset{+}{c}, \overset{+}{D}; \overset{-}{i}^* + \varepsilon, \overset{+}{g_N}), \tag{95}$$

where

$$\lambda_D = i_m \varphi_D/\gamma = -i_m \beta, \quad \lambda_{i^*+\varepsilon} = -\beta,$$

$$\lambda_c = (i_c + i_m \varphi_c)/\gamma = \beta(i_c + i_m \delta z_c \bar{R}^*), \quad \lambda_{g_N} = i_m \varphi_{g_N}/\gamma.$$

Finally, using (95), (87) can be written as

$$\dot{D} = \Psi(\overset{+}{c}, \overset{+}{D}; \overset{?}{i}^*, \overset{-}{\varepsilon}, \overset{+}{g_N}) - g_I, \tag{96}$$

where

$$\Psi_c = -z_c[y_X^{s\prime} + \delta(1 - \delta)\bar{c}] + (1 - \delta) + (\bar{\theta} + \bar{L}^* \theta_{L^*})\lambda_c,$$

$$\Psi_D = i^* + (\bar{\theta} + \bar{L}^* \theta_{L^*})\lambda_D, \quad \Psi_\varepsilon = (\bar{\theta} + \bar{L}^* \theta_{L^*})\lambda_{i^*+\varepsilon},$$

$$\Psi_{g_N} = -z_{g_N}[y_X^{s\prime} + \delta(1 - \delta)\bar{c}] + (\bar{\theta} + \bar{L}^* \theta_{L^*})\lambda_{g_N},$$

$$\Psi_{i^*} = \bar{D} + (\bar{\theta} + \bar{L}^* \theta_{L^*})\lambda_{i^*+\varepsilon}.$$

---

[24]Note that $i_c + i_m \varphi_c = \gamma \beta(i_c + i_m \delta z_c \bar{R}^*) > 0$; thus, G_c is positive regardless of whether m_c is positive or negative. Note also that $i_m \varphi_{i^*+\varepsilon} - 1 = -\beta \gamma < 0$.

In general, the partial derivative Ψ_{i^*} is ambiguous. On the one hand, an increase in the risk-free rate raises debt-service payments in proportion to the initial stock of foreign debt; on the other, the premium-related component of external debt service also falls along with the demand for foreign loans by private agents. The net effect on the current account (and thus the rate of accumulation of foreign debt) cannot be ascertained a priori. In the discussion that follows, and in order to focus the discussion on the case of a highly indebted economy, it will be assumed that the net effect is positive ($\Psi_{i^*} > 0$); that is, a rise in the risk-free world interest rate (at given levels of debt and consumption) increases the current account deficit.

Equations (94) and (96) again form a dynamic system in c and D, which can be linearized around the steady state and written as

$$\begin{bmatrix} \dot{c} \\ \dot{D} \end{bmatrix} = \begin{bmatrix} G_c & G_D \\ \Psi_c & \Psi_D \end{bmatrix} \begin{bmatrix} c - \tilde{c} \\ D - \tilde{D} \end{bmatrix}. \tag{97}$$

Saddlepath stability requires $G_c \Psi_D - G_D \Psi_c < 0$. The steady-state solution is obtained by setting $\dot{c} = \dot{D} = 0$ in (94) and (96). From (73), the steady-state inflation rate and the rate of inflation in nontradable prices are thus equal to the devaluation rate:

$$\tilde{\pi} = \tilde{\pi}_N = \varepsilon. \tag{98}$$

As before, in the steady state the current account must be in equilibrium:

$$y_X^s(\tilde{z}) - (1 - \delta)\tilde{z}^{-\delta}\tilde{c} - g_I = i^*\tilde{D} + \theta(\tilde{L}^*, \cdot)\tilde{L}^*. \tag{99}$$

The real (consumption-based) interest rate is again equal to the rate of time preference [see (48)], and the household's steady-state level of foreign borrowing is given by (59).

The steady-state equilibrium is depicted in Figure 10.8. The NN curve in the northwest quadrant depicts combinations of private consumption c and the real exchange rate z that are consistent with equilibrium in the market for nontradable goods [(83)], whereas the LL curve in the southwest quadrant depicts combinations of the product wage in the exportable goods sector w_X and the real exchange rate that are consistent with labor market equilibrium [(76)]. The interpretation of the CC and DD curves in the northeast quadrant is similar to the description provided in the previous subsection. In particular, points located to the right of CC represent situations where the domestic real interest rate is higher than the rate of time preference, consumption is increasing, and the real exchange rate is appreciating to eliminate excess supply of nontradable goods. Conversely, points located to the left of CC represent situations of falling consumption, excess supply of home goods, and a depreciating real exchange rate. Saddlepath stability requires again that the CC curve be steeper than the DD curve.

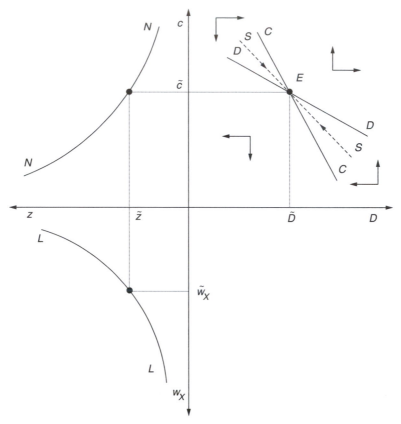

Figure 10–8 ▪ Equilibrium in the Three-Good Model
Source: Agénor (1997, p. 31).

2.2.6   *Policy Experiments*

To illustrate the functioning of the model, consider first a tax-financed, permanent increase in g_N. Such a shock has no long-term effect on the domestic nominal interest rate, which remains equal to the rate of time preference plus the devaluation rate [see (48)]. It also has no effect on foreign borrowing by the private sector, which depends, as indicated by (59), only on the difference between the world risk-free interest rate and the rate of time preference. At the initial level of the real exchange rate, private consumption must fall to maintain equilibrium of the market for nontradable goods. Real money balances must therefore fall, as shown by (50), because domestic interest rates do not change. The reduction in private consumption is proportionally less than the increase in government expenditure, so that total domestic spending on home goods rises and the real exchange rate appreciates to maintain equilibrium in the home goods market.

Although the real appreciation tends to reduce output of tradable goods, the trade-balance surplus (which, again, matches the initial deficit of the services account)

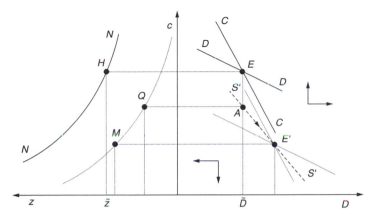

Figure 10–9 ■ Increase in Government Spending on Home Goods
Source: Agénor (1997, p. 40).

must rise to maintain external balance, because the economy's stock of debt D increases, and the services account deteriorates. This increase in debt results from a reduction in net foreign assets held by the central bank R^* (since holdings of foreign assets by the private sector, L^*, do not change), which accommodates the fall in the demand for real money balances.

On impact, private consumption falls—to an extent that depends on the degree of intertemporal substitution—because the increase in government spending raises households' lifetime tax liabilities and thus reduces their lifetime wealth. But the real exchange rate may now either appreciate or depreciate, depending on whether total spending on nontradable goods rises or falls. If the degree of intertemporal substitution in consumption σ is sufficiently low, private consumption will change relatively little on impact, and total spending will increase, thereby leading to an appreciation of the real exchange rate on impact.

Figure 10.9 illustrates the adjustment path to a permanent increase in g_N in the case where the degree of intertemporal substitution is indeed low enough to ensure that the real exchange rate appreciates on impact. Curves CC and DD both shift to the left in the northeast panel.[25] The NN curve in the northeast panel shifts inward. Private consumption jumps downward from point E to point A located on the new saddlepath $S'S'$, and the real exchange rate jumps from point H to point Q located on the new NN curve. At the initial level of interest rates and official reserves, the real money stock falls on impact; the reduction in money demand induced by the fall in consumption is matched by a reduction in supply, resulting from the valuation effects on the domestic-currency value of official reserves associated with

---

[25]As noted by Agénor (1997), the movement of the CC locus shown in the figure is drawn under the empirically plausible assumption that valuation effects (which account for the indirect effect of government spending on changes in private consumption, through its impact on the real exchange rate) are not too large.

the appreciation of the real exchange rate. If valuation effects are not too large, the fall in private consumption leads to a reduction in the domestic nominal interest rate, despite the upward pressure induced by the reduction in money supply. Private foreign indebtedness therefore falls, and the economy registers an outflow of capital. Because the stock of foreign debt cannot change on impact, official reserves must fall concomitantly. The current account moves into deficit ($\dot{D}_0 > 0$) and—as a consequence of the steady-state increase in the stock of debt and the monotonicity of the adjustment path to the new equilibrium—remains in deficit throughout the transition process.[26] Private consumption continues to fall over time, and the real exchange rate depreciates. Because the domestic nominal interest rate falls on impact, it must be rising during the transition to the new long-run equilibrium in order to restore the equality between the real interest rate and the rate of time preference. Thus, private foreign indebtedness increases over time and the economy experiences net capital inflows, which continue until private borrowing on world capital markets returns to its initial value.

Consider now an unanticipated reduction in the devaluation rate, ε.[27] Suppose first that the shock is permanent. As formally shown in the Appendix to this chapter, the reduction in ε in this case has no long-run effects on the real interest rate or private foreign borrowing. But, although the real interest rate remains equal to the rate of time preference in the new steady state, the nominal interest rate falls in the same proportion as the devaluation rate. The reduction in the opportunity cost of holding money raises the demand for domestic cash balances. The official stock of net foreign assets must therefore increase; and because private foreign borrowing does not change, the economy's external debt must be lower in the new steady state, implying that the initial deficit in the services account is also lower. To maintain external balance, the initial trade surplus must fall—or equivalently private consumption must rise. The increase in private expenditure leads to a real exchange-rate appreciation and raises further the demand for domestic cash balances.

On impact, consumption falls because the immediate effect of the reduction in ε is to increase the real interest rate, thereby creating an incentive for the household to shift consumption toward the future. The reduction in ε also leads to a discrete increase in private demand for foreign loans, thereby requiring an offsetting increase in official reserves (and thus a rise in the real money stock) which is such that the economy's stock of debt remains constant on impact. Because consumption falls

---

[26]The services account unambiguously improves, because the premium-related component of external debt service falls—as a result of both the reduction in private foreign borrowing and the reduction in the risk premium itself. For the current account to move into deficit on impact therefore requires the trade balance to deteriorate sufficiently to outweigh the improvement in the services account. And because private consumption falls, the reduction in output of tradable goods (resulting from the appreciation of the real exchange rate) must exceed the drop in consumption.

[27]Of course, because the initial steady state is in the present setting characterized by full employment (wages are fully flexible), it is not clear what the costs of inflation (and thus the benefits of disinflation) are. Given the illustrative nature of the exercise, however, it is sufficient to assume the existence of implicit distortions associated with the initial inflation-devaluation rate.

and the real money stock rises, the net impact effect on the nominal interest rate is unambiguously negative.[28]

The fall in consumption requires a depreciation of the real exchange rate to maintain equilibrium between supply and demand for home goods. As a result of the reduction in private spending and the expansion of output of tradables induced by the depreciation of the real exchange rate, the trade balance surplus increases. At the same time, the negative income effect associated with the increase in the premium-related component of interest payments (itself resulting from the increase in private foreign borrowing) raises the initial deficit of the services account. The current account nevertheless improves, and external debt falls ($\dot{D}_0 < 0$). Because the shock is permanent, the current account remains in surplus throughout the adjustment process. Consumption begins increasing, and the real exchange rate appreciates. The real interest rate rises toward its initial steady-state level, given by the rate of time preference.

The upper panel of Figure 10.10 illustrates the dynamics of this shock. Both CC and DD shift to the left. Consumption jumps downward from point E to point A on impact, and begins rising afterward. The economy's stock of foreign debt falls continuously during the transition to the new steady state, which is reached at point E'.

The case where the reduction in ε is temporary is illustrated in the lower panel of Figure 10.10. Again, because the shock is temporary, the optimal smoothing response for the representative household is to reduce consumption by less than he or she would if the shock was permanent. Depending on the length of the interval $(0, T)$, two adjustment paths are possible. If the duration of the shock is short, private consumption will jump downward from point E to point A', and will begin to increase until reaching point B' on the original saddlepath at T. The trade balance will improve only slightly, since the short duration of the shock gives agents little incentive to alter their consumption path. The current account will therefore move into deficit (as a result of the deterioration in the services account), and external debt will increase until the shock is reversed. Thereafter, consumption will continue to increase, with the current account moving into surplus, until the economy returns to the original equilibrium point E.

On the contrary, if the duration of the shock is sufficiently long, private consumption will jump from point E to point A, and will start to increase until point F on the original saddlepath is reached at T. Thereafter, consumption starts falling along the original saddlepath SS, eventually reaching the original equilibrium point E. Whereas the current account remains in surplus during the first phase of the adjustment process (between A and B), it moves into deficit afterward (between points B and F). Point B is reached before period T. Thereafter, with consumption

---

[28]If the degree of capital mobility (as measured by γ) is sufficiently high, the nominal interest rate will fall approximately by the same amount as the devaluation rate.

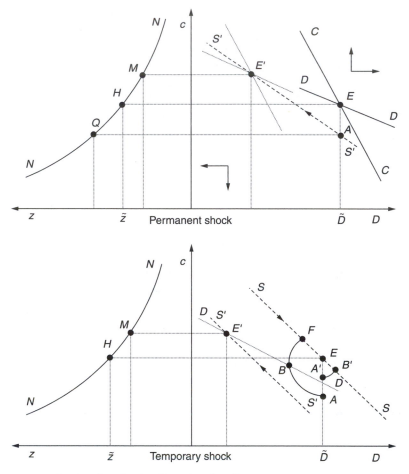

Figure 10–10 ▪ Reduction in the Devaluation Rate
Source: Agénor (1997, p. 43).

falling between points F and E, the current account remains in deficit, and external debt increases.[29]

It is important to emphasize the difference between the long-run predictions of the model under perfect and imperfect world capital markets. In the former case (which corresponds to $\gamma \to 0$), the uncovered interest parity condition $i = i^* + \varepsilon$ holds continuously, and private foreign borrowing can take any value a priori. The increase in the demand for real cash balances induced by the reduction in the opportunity cost of holding money is achieved through an instantaneous increase

---

[29]The initial drop and subsequent increase in expenditure predicted by the model is consistent with the "U-shaped" behavior of private consumption observed after the implementation of the July 1985 stabilization program in Israel, which was based in part on an exchange-rate freeze; see Helpman and Leiderman (1988, p. 27, and their figure 3).

in both money holdings and foreign indebtedness: the representative household increases borrowing on world capital markets, generating thereby a capital inflow which is monetized by exchanging the foreign exchange for domestic currency at the central bank (whose foreign reserves therefore increase) in such a way that the economy's net stock of debt remains constant. There are no real effects, and the adjustment process displays no dynamics; the economy jumps instantaneously to the new steady state. Although the composition of the economy's net external debt changes (with the share of official foreign reserves increasing), the stock of debt itself does not and neither do real variables.

By contrast, with capital market imperfections (that is, with $\gamma > 0$), the long-run value of private foreign borrowing is "pinned down" by the difference between the world risk-free interest rate and the rate of time preference, and therefore cannot vary across steady states in response to a change in the devaluation rate. Thus, the increase in real cash balances induced by the reduction in the opportunity cost of holding money cannot take place directly through a once-and-for-all inflow of capital and an increase in private foreign indebtedness, as described above. For official reserves to expand, as before, and for the money supply to match the increased demand for money, requires now a sequence of current account surpluses. In turn, because higher official reserves imply a reduction in the economy's net external debt (private foreign borrowing remaining constant), the lower deficit in the services account must be accompanied by a lower trade surplus, that is, higher private consumption. Thus, with imperfect world capital markets, the adjustment process to a reduction in the devaluation rate displays transitional dynamics as well as real effects in the long run.

2.3 ■ Extensions

The two-sector model developed above can be further extended to account for other features deemed relevant for developing countries. We consider here the existence of imported intermediate inputs and price stickiness in the nontraded goods sector.

2.3.1 *Imported Intermediate Inputs*

Suppose, for instance, that output of nontraded goods is produced using labor n_N and imported intermediate materials O_N according to a fixed-coefficients technology. The production function is thus given by[30]

$$y_N = \min(n_N, \alpha O_N),$$

where the parameter $1/\alpha$ measures the amount of intermediate materials that must be combined with a unit of labor to produce a unit of the domestic good. Constant returns to scale prevail in the nontraded goods sector according to this formulation.

---

[30] A similar formulation is adopted by Obstfeld (1986*a*).

Factor demand functions are given by

$$n_N^d = y_N, \quad O_N^d = \alpha^{-1} y_N.$$

Assuming that the world price of imported inputs is equal to unity, in equilibrium the price of home goods would be given by the zero-profit condition:

$$p_N = w + \alpha^{-1} E,$$

which implies that $w/E = z - \alpha^{-1}$. If intermediate imports are treated as final tradable goods, modifications of the current account equation are straightforward.

2.3.2 Sticky Prices

In the basic three-good model presented earlier, we assumed that prices of nontraded goods were perfectly flexible. Although this assumption is convenient as a benchmark case, it is not necessarily well-supported by the evidence; in fact, a number of economists would adopt the view that the degree of price inertia can be substantial in the short run. We now discuss briefly how the three-good model developed previously can be modified to introduce sticky prices.

Of course, because prices of exportables are given on world capital markets, we only need to focus on price formation in the home goods sector. Accordingly, suppose now that the price of the nontraded good P_N is predetermined and adjusts only gradually in response to disequilibrium in the market for these goods. Specifically, consider the price adjustment equation:

$$\pi_N \equiv \dot{P}_N/P_N = \beta[\delta z^{1-\delta} c + g_N - y_N^s] + \varepsilon, \quad \beta > 0, \tag{100}$$

where β denotes the speed of adjustment. In the limiting case of $\beta = 0$ the model operates in a "Keynesian" mode with fixed prices, whereas the case of perfect price flexibility considered earlier corresponds to $\beta \to \infty$. In general, the assumption of sticky prices carries with it some underlying rationing mechanism and the possibility of various rationed equilibria.[31] However, this issue will not be pursued here.

Because by definition $\dot{z}/z = \varepsilon - \pi_N$, using (100) yields

$$\dot{z}/z = \varepsilon - \beta(\delta z^{1-\delta} c + g_N - y_N^s) - \varepsilon = \Phi(\overset{-}{c}, \overset{-}{z}; \overset{0}{\varepsilon}, \overset{-}{g_N}), \tag{101}$$

---

[31] Firms, for instance, will typically increase output only as long as the marginal cost (the going real wage) does not exceed the prevailing product price. An alternative model of price stickiness, due to Calvo (1983), will be discussed in Chapters 11 and 12.

where, in particular, $\Phi_c = -\beta\delta$. Thus, in contrast to the case of perfect price flexibility, the relationship is not between the *rates of change* of the real exchange rate and consumption, but between the rate of change of z and the *level* of c.

In addition to (101), the other equations of the dynamic system are, as derived earlier:

$$L^* = [i(c,m) - i^* - \varepsilon]/\gamma, \qquad (102)$$

$$\dot{c}/c = \sigma[i(c,m) - \varepsilon + \delta\dot{z}/z - \rho], \qquad (103)$$

$$\dot{D} = i^*D + \theta(L^*)L^* + (1-\delta)z^{-\delta}c + g_I - y_X^s(z), \qquad (104)$$

$$m = z^\delta R^*, \qquad (105)$$

$$L^* = \Lambda(c, D; i^* + \varepsilon), \qquad (106)$$

where, as shown previously, $\Lambda_c, \Lambda_D > 0$, and $\Lambda_{i^*+\varepsilon} < 0$.

Eliminating L^* as before using (102) and (105) yields

$$m = z^\delta \left\{ [i(c,m) - (i^* + \varepsilon) - \gamma D]/\gamma \right\},$$

which can be written as

$$m = \varphi(\overset{+}{c}, \overset{+}{z}, \overset{-}{D}; i^* \overset{-}{+} \varepsilon),$$

where as before $\varphi_D = -\beta\gamma$ and $\varphi_{i^*+\varepsilon} = -\beta$, and now

$$\varphi_c = \beta i_c, \quad \varphi_z = \delta\bar{R}^*, \quad \varphi_{g_N} = 0.$$

Substituting this result in (103) yields

$$\dot{c}/c = \sigma\{i[c, \varphi(c, z, D, i^* + \varepsilon)] - \varepsilon + \delta\dot{z}/z - \rho\},$$

so that, using (101):

$$\dot{c} = G(\overset{?}{c}, \overset{-}{z}, \overset{+}{D}; \overset{+}{i^*}, \overset{-}{\varepsilon}, \overset{-}{g_N}), \qquad (107)$$

with now $\Delta = \sigma\bar{c} > 0$:[32]

$$G_c = (i_c + i_m\varphi_c + \delta\Phi_c)\Delta, \quad G_z = (i_m\varphi_z + \delta\Phi_z)\Delta, \quad G_D = i_m\varphi_D\Delta,$$

$$G_{i^*} = i_m\varphi_{i^*+\varepsilon}\Delta, \quad G_\varepsilon = (i_m\varphi_{i^*+\varepsilon} - 1)\Delta, \quad G_{g_N} = \delta\Phi_{g_N}\Delta.$$

---

[32]Note again that $i_m\varphi_{i^*+\varepsilon} - 1 = -\gamma\beta < 0$, and that in the case where $\bar{R}^*$ is small, $G_{g_N} \to 0$.

Although $i_c + i_m \varphi_c > 0$, the sign of G_c is in general ambiguous. G_z is also ambiguous. If the speed of adjustment β is sufficiently high (as will be assumed below), $G_c, G_z < 0$.

Equations (104) and (106) yield

$$\dot{D} = \Psi(\overset{+}{c}, \overset{-}{z}, \overset{+}{D}; \overset{?}{i^*}, \overset{-}{\varepsilon}) - g_I, \tag{108}$$

where Ψ_D, Ψ_{i^*}, and Ψ_ε are as given earlier:

$$\Psi_D = i^* + (\bar{\theta} + \bar{L}^* \theta_{L^*})\Lambda_D, \quad \Psi_\varepsilon = (\bar{\theta} + \bar{L}^* \theta_{L^*})\Lambda_{i^* + \varepsilon},$$

$$\Psi_{i^*} = \tilde{D} + (\bar{\theta} + \bar{L}^* \theta_{L^*})\Lambda_{i^* + \varepsilon},$$

and now

$$\Psi_c = (1 - \delta) + (\bar{\theta} + \bar{L}^* \theta_{L^*})\Lambda_c, \quad \Psi_z = -y_X^{s\prime} - \delta(1 - \delta)\bar{c},$$

with $\Psi_{i^*} > 0$ assumed positive as before.[33]

Equations (101), (107), and (108) represent a dynamic system in c, z, and D. As before, linearizing the model around the steady state gives

$$\begin{bmatrix} \dot{c} \\ \dot{z} \\ \dot{D} \end{bmatrix} = \begin{bmatrix} G_c & G_z & G_D \\ \Phi_c & \Phi_z & 0 \\ \Psi_c & \Psi_z & \Psi_D \end{bmatrix} \begin{bmatrix} c - \tilde{c} \\ z - \tilde{z} \\ D - \tilde{D} \end{bmatrix}. \tag{109}$$

To examine the local stability properties of the linearized system, note that the determinant of the system's matrix of coefficients $\mathbf{A}$ may be written as

$$|\mathbf{A}| = -\Phi_c(\Psi_D G_z - \Psi_z G_D) + \Phi_z(\Psi_D G_c - \Psi_c G_D),$$

from which it can be established, assuming that Ψ_D is initially close to zero, that $|\mathbf{A}| > 0$. Because $|\mathbf{A}|$ is equal to the product of the system's characteristic roots, there are either two roots with negative real parts or no negative root. Suppose that the speed of adjustment β is sufficiently high to ensure that the trace of the system's matrix of coefficients $\text{tr}\mathbf{A}$, given by

$$\text{tr}\mathbf{A} = G_c + \Phi_z + \Psi_D,$$

is negative. Because $\text{tr}\mathbf{A}$ is equal to the sum of the system's characteristic roots, there must be at least one root with a negative real part. It can therefore be concluded

---

[33]Note that now $\Psi_{g_N} = 0$.

that there are exactly two roots with negative real parts. Thus, because z and D are predetermined state variables, the system is saddlepath stable.

With two predetermined variables and one jump variable, it is not straightforward to apply standard phase diagram techniques, although the solution technique proposed by Dixit (1980) can be useful in this case to assess impact effects on consumption (see, for instance, Agénor, 1998a). One can also solve the model numerically to examine the short- and long-run effects of the type of shocks that we considered previously. Cook and Devereux (2006a), for instance, study the quantitative impact of an exogenous rise in the country risk premium in an open-economy model with sticky prices, imported intermediate goods, and flexible exchange rates.

Various other extensions are possible, depending on the issue at hand. These include the introduction of sticky wages (as in Rhee, 2008), a positive supply effect of government expenditure (as in Kimbrough, 1985, and Chapter 17), private investment and capital accumulation (in line with our discussion in Chapter 3), or a banking system (as discussed in Chapter 6).[34] The analysis could also be extended to account for habit formation and durable goods, as in Ikeda and Gombi (1999), Karayalcin (2003), Mohsin (2006), and Mansoorian and Neaime (2003). The first three studies focus on the current account effects of fiscal policy, whereas the third discusses (as in this chapter) the dynamic effects of a change in the devaluation rate. But some of these extensions could come at the cost of making the model overly complex and difficult to solve analytically. Again, a numerical solution may become necessary.

Appendix
Impact and Steady-State Effects

This appendix establishes the impact and steady-state effects of a reduction in ε in the three-good model with flexible prices.

Consider first a permanent shock. The equation of the saddlepath, SS, of the dynamic system (109) is given by

$$c - \bar{c} = \kappa(D - \tilde{D}), \tag{A1}$$

where $\kappa \equiv (\nu - \Psi_D)/\Psi_c = G_D/(\nu - G_c) < 0$ and ν denotes the negative root of (97). κ is the slope of the saddlepath SS.

---

[34]Dixon and Kara (2006) provide a general framework that accounts for various sources of wage stickiness and for understanding its relation with inflation persistence. Ascari (2003) focuses on the relation between wage stickiness and output persistence. He also discusses differences between wage and price stickiness.

From (94) and (96), it can be established that

$$d\tilde{c}/d\varepsilon = (\Psi_\varepsilon G_D - \Psi_D G_\varepsilon)/\Omega, \tag{A2}$$

$$d\tilde{D}/d\varepsilon = (\Psi_c G_\varepsilon - \Psi_\varepsilon G_c)/\Omega, \tag{A3}$$

where $\Omega = G_c \Psi_D - G_D \Psi_c < 0$ to ensure saddlepath stability, and (as discussed in the text) $G_\varepsilon, \Psi_\varepsilon < 0$. To show that $d\tilde{c}/d\varepsilon > 0$ requires showing that $\Psi_\varepsilon G_D - \Psi_D G_\varepsilon < 0$ or that

$$\Psi_\varepsilon/\Psi_D < G_\varepsilon/G_D = (i_m \varphi_{i^*+\varepsilon} - 1)/i_m \varphi_D = 1/i_m,$$

or equivalently

$$(\tilde{\theta} + \tilde{L}^* \theta_{L^*})\lambda_{i^*+\varepsilon} < i_m^{-1} \left[i^* + (\tilde{\theta} + \tilde{L}^* \theta_{L^*})\lambda_D \right].$$

With $\lambda_D = -i_m \beta$ and $\lambda_{i^*+\varepsilon} = -\beta$ (with $\beta \equiv 1/(\gamma - i_m)$):

$$-\beta(\tilde{\theta} + \tilde{L}^* \theta_{L^*}) < i_m^{-1} \left[i^* - i_m \beta(\tilde{\theta} + \tilde{L}^* \theta_{L^*}) \right],$$

or $i^* > 0$, which always holds. From the equilibrium condition of the home goods market:

$$d\tilde{z}/d\varepsilon = z_c d\tilde{c}/d\varepsilon < 0. \tag{A4}$$

From the steady-state condition (48), $d\tilde{\imath}/d\varepsilon = 1$. From (50):

$$d\tilde{m}/d\varepsilon = m_c d\tilde{c}/d\varepsilon + m_i < 0,$$

and from (A4), with $\tilde{z} = 1$:

$$d\tilde{R}^*/d\varepsilon = d\tilde{m}/d\varepsilon + \delta\tilde{m}(d\tilde{z}/d\varepsilon) < 0.$$

This result implies, because $d\tilde{L}^*/d\varepsilon = 0$, that

$$d\tilde{D}/d\varepsilon = -d\tilde{R}^*/d\varepsilon > 0.$$

To determine the impact effects of a reduction in ε, note that from (A1) and because $dD_0/d\varepsilon = 0$:

$$dc_0/d\varepsilon = d\tilde{c}/d\varepsilon - \kappa(d\tilde{D}/d\varepsilon),$$

which implies that, using (A2), (A3), and the definition of κ:

$$dc_0/d\varepsilon = \left[\Psi_\varepsilon(G_D + \kappa G_c) - \nu G_\varepsilon\right]/\Omega,$$

or equivalently, because $G_D + \kappa G_c = \kappa\nu$:

$$dc_0/d\varepsilon = -\nu(G_\varepsilon - \kappa\Psi_\varepsilon)/\Omega > 0. \tag{A5}$$

Thus, from the equilibrium condition of the market for nontradable goods,

$$dz_0/d\varepsilon = z_c\,dc_0/d\varepsilon < 0, \tag{A6}$$

and from (77), output of nontradable (exportable) goods falls (rises) on impact. From the equilibrium condition of the money market

$$di_0/d\varepsilon = (i_c + i_m\varphi_c)(dc_0/d\varepsilon) + i_m\varphi_{i^*+\varepsilon} > 0, \tag{A7}$$

because $i_c + i_m\varphi_c$ and $i_m\varphi_{i^*+\varepsilon}$ are both positive. It can be established that $di_0/d\varepsilon \to 1$ when $\gamma \to 0$, and that $di_0/d\varepsilon < 1$ for $\gamma > 0$.

Finally, from (84), and given that $di_0/d\varepsilon < 1$:

$$dL_0^*/d\varepsilon = \gamma^{-1}\left\{(di_0/d\varepsilon) - 1\right\} < 0.$$

Because $dD_0/d\varepsilon = 0$, $dR_0^*/d\varepsilon = dL_0^*/d\varepsilon < 0$. Thus, using (A7), and with $\tilde{z} = 1$:

$$dm_0/d\varepsilon = d(z_0^\delta R_0^*)/d\varepsilon = \delta\tilde{R}^*(dz_0/d\varepsilon) + dR_0^*/d\varepsilon < 0.$$

Consider now a temporary reduction in ε. The general solution of system (97) can be written:

for $0 \le t \le T$,

$$D = \tilde{D}_{t\le T} + C_1 e^{\nu_1 t} + C_2 e^{\nu_2 t}, \tag{A8}$$

$$c = \tilde{c}_{t\le T} + \kappa_1 C_1 e^{\nu_1 t} + \kappa_2 C_2 e^{\nu_2 t}, \tag{A9}$$

and for $t \ge T$,

$$D = \tilde{D}_0 + C_1' e^{\nu_1 t} + C_2' e^{\nu_2 t}, \tag{A10}$$

$$c_t = \tilde{c}_0 + \kappa_1 C_1' e^{\nu_1 t} + \kappa_2 C_2' e^{\nu_2 t}, \tag{A11}$$

where $v_1(= v)$ denotes the negative root and v_2 the positive root of the system, and $\kappa_h = G_D/(v_h - G_c)$, $h = 1, 2$. The four arbitrary constants C_1, C_2, C_1', and C_2' are determined under the assumptions that (*a*) $C_2' = 0$ (for the transversality condition to hold); (*b*) D evolves continuously from its initial given value $\tilde{D}_0 = D_0$, so that $D_0 = \tilde{D}_{t \leq T} + C_1 + C_2$; and (*c*) the time paths for c and D are continuous for $t > 0$. In particular, at time $t = T$, the solutions for (A8) and (A10); and (A9) and (A11) must coincide, yielding two more equations which, together with the above condition on D_0, uniquely determine the solution for C_1, C_2, and C_1'. The solutions are given by:

for $0 \leq t \leq T$,

$$D = \tilde{D}_{t \leq T} - \chi \Delta (D_0 - \tilde{D}_{t \leq T}) e^{v_1 t} + \chi v_1 (v_2 - G_c)(D_0 - \tilde{D}_{t \leq T}) e^{v_2(t-T)},$$

$$c = \tilde{c}_{t \leq T} - \chi \Delta \kappa_1 (D_0 - \tilde{D}_{t \leq T}) e^{v_1 t} + \chi v_1 G_F (D_0 - \tilde{D}_{t \leq T}) e^{v_2(t-T)},$$

and for $t \geq T$,

$$D = D_0 - \chi (D_0 - \tilde{D}_{t \leq T}) e^{v_1 t} \left\{ \Delta - v_2 (v_1 - G_c) e^{-v_1 T} \right\},$$

$$c = \tilde{c}_0 + \kappa_1 (D - D_0),$$

where

$$\chi = 1/G_c (v_2 - v_1), \quad \Delta = -\chi + v_1 (v_2 - G_c) e^{-v_2 T}.$$

Chapter 11

Analytical Issues in Disinflation Programs

The repeated failure of disinflation attempts in developing countries, particularly in Latin America, has given rise to a voluminous literature aimed at explaining the mechanisms through which program collapse may occur. While the early literature focused on the role of policy inconsistencies and inertial mechanisms (such as backward-looking implicit or explicit wage indexation, and adaptive inflationary expectations), more recent developments have highlighted the role of credibility and its interactions with expectations regarding the sustainability and political feasibility of government stabilization policies.

This chapter focuses on a selected, but representative, set of issues that have been considered in the recent literature. Section 1 focuses on two issues that have drawn much attention in recent discussions on exchange-rate-based stabilization programs: the boom-recession pattern of output and the behavior of real interest rates at the inception of such programs. We discuss the various interpretations of these phenomena that have been advanced in the literature, particularly the role of expectations about future government policies, and provide an assessment of alternative views. Section 2 examines the role of credibility factors in the formulation and design of stabilization programs. We review alternative mechanisms that have been suggested to enhance the credibility of such programs, including the adoption of a shock therapy approach for "signaling" purposes, the use of multiple nominal anchors, increased central bank independence, and recourse to foreign assistance.

1   Topics in Exchange-Rate-Based Programs

The empirical evidence on stabilization programs reviewed in online Supplement B indicates that although the use of the exchange rate as a key nominal anchor brought hyperinflation to a halt with a relatively small output cost, success in using the exchange rate has been more limited in chronic-inflation countries. The Southern

Cone tablita experiments of the late 1970s, in particular, were associated with a slow reduction in the inflation rate and an appreciation of the real exchange rate.

In addition, such programs have often been accompanied by an initial expansion in economic activity, followed by a significant contraction. In the exchange-rate-based stabilization program implemented in Morocco in 1990, for instance, an initial expansion followed by a significant slowdown was also discernible. Output grew at an annual rate of more than 10 percent in 1990 (compared with 1.5 percent in 1989) but dropped to -2.4 percent in 1991, -4.1 percent in 1992, and -0.2 percent in 1993. The boom-recession cycle seems to have been observed in both successful and eventually unsuccessful stabilization attempts, and has attracted much interest from development macroeconomists.

The behavior of real interest rates in exchange-rate-based stabilization programs has also been the subject of some scrutiny. While real interest rates declined at the inception of the program in the Southern Cone tablita experiments of the late 1970s, they rose sharply in the heterodox programs of the 1980s implemented in Argentina, Brazil, Israel, and Mexico (Végh, 1992; Rebelo and Végh, 1997). In addition, while real interest rates showed a tendency to increase gradually over time in the early experiments, no discernible pattern seems to have emerged in the more recent programs.

This section discusses a variety of analytical models that have attempted to explain the behavior of output and real interest rates in exchange-rate-based stabilization programs. A key aspect of some of these models is the emphasis on the dynamic effects associated with imperfectly credible policy announcements, or more generally the effect of varying expectations about present and future government policies. We begin by examining alternative interpretations of the boom-recession puzzle and then focus on explanations of the behavior of real interest rates.

1.1 ■ The Boom-Recession Cycle

The first attempt at explaining the expansion-recession cycle that appears to characterize exchange-rate-based disinflation programs (in particular the tablita experiments) was proposed by Rodríguez (1982). An alternative explanation was developed by Calvo and Végh (1993a, 1993b). A key feature of the latter approach is its emphasis on the interactions between the lack of credibility (modeled as a temporary policy) and intertemporal substitution effects in the transmission of policy shocks to the real sphere of the economy.[1] We first present the Rodríguez model and then provide a detailed account of the Calvo-Végh "temporariness" model, before evaluating the key features of both models.

---

[1] The role of intertemporal substitution in consumption—simply put, that agents are sensitive to changes in the relative price of consuming now rather than later—was also emphasized by Obstfeld (1985), whose contribution is discussed later.

1.1.1 *Expectations, Real Interest Rates, and Output*

The model developed by Rodríguez (1982) explains the behavior of output in exchange-rate-based programs implemented in a small open economy where the exchange-rate path is preannounced, the money supply is endogenous, expectations follow a backward-looking process, and capital is perfectly mobile internationally.

The basic structure of the model is as follows. The domestic rate of inflation π is given by

$$\pi = \delta\pi_N + (1-\delta)\varepsilon, \quad 0 < \delta < 1, \tag{1}$$

where, for simplicity, the rate of increase in world tradable prices is set to zero. Inflation in nontraded goods prices π_N depends on the expected behavior of prices in that sector π_N^a and excess demand for nontradables d_N:

$$\pi_N = \pi_N^a + \upsilon'd_N, \quad \upsilon' > 0. \tag{2}$$

Equations (1) and (2) yield

$$\pi = \pi^a + \upsilon d_N, \quad \upsilon = \delta\upsilon', \tag{3}$$

where $\pi^a = \delta\pi_N^a + (1-\delta)\varepsilon$. Price expectations are revised using an adaptive process similar to that specified in the first section of Chapter 10 [equation (6)]:

$$\dot{\pi}^a = \beta(\pi - \pi^a), \quad \beta > 0. \tag{4}$$

Aggregate supply is assumed constant at $\bar{y}$, and aggregate spending c varies inversely with the expected real interest rate $r = i - \pi^a$, where i denotes the nominal interest rate and $c' < 0$. Excess demand for tradable goods, d_T—which is equal to the trade-balance deficit—is assumed to depend negatively on the relative price of these goods, defined as $z = E/P$.[2] Excess demand for nontradables is therefore given by

$$d_N = c(r) - \bar{y} - d_T(z) = d_N(\overset{+}{z}, \overset{-}{r}). \tag{5}$$

Substituting (5) into (3) yields

$$\pi - \pi^a = \upsilon d_N(z, r), \tag{6}$$

which indicates that unexpected movements in inflation are positively related to the real exchange rate and negatively to the real interest rate.

---

[2]Note that the relative price in Rodríguez's model is *not* the real exchange rate, because the price index P is a weighted average of the prices of traded and nontraded goods. However, this has no substantial effect on the results, and we will refer to z as the real exchange rate here.

At any moment in time, the real exchange rate z is given. Over time, it changes according to

$$\dot{z}/z = \varepsilon - \pi. \tag{7}$$

Finally, the domestic nominal interest rate i is given by the constant world interest rate i^* plus the devaluation rate ε:

$$i = i^* + \varepsilon. \tag{8}$$

To express the model in a compact form, differentiate the real interest rate with respect to time and use (4) and (6), so that[3]

$$\dot{r} = -\dot{\pi}^a = -\beta \upsilon d_N(z, r). \tag{9}$$

Using (8) and the definition of the real interest rate to substitute out for the expected inflation rate in (6) yields

$$\pi = i^* + \varepsilon - r + \upsilon d_N(z, r). \tag{10}$$

Finally, substituting (10) in (7) yields

$$\dot{z}/z = r - i^* - \upsilon d_N(z, r). \tag{11}$$

Equations (9) and (11) constitute a differential equation system in the real interest rate and the real exchange rate. For given levels of these variables, (10) determines the inflation rate.

The steady-state equilibrium of the model is represented in Figure 11.1. The locus $[\dot{r} = 0]$ is obtained from (9) and determines the combinations of the real interest rate and the real exchange rate for which there is no excess demand in the nontraded goods market ($d_N = 0$). It has a positive slope because a real depreciation creates an excess demand for home goods, which requires an increase in the real interest rate to restore equilibrium. Values of r and z above (below) the curve correspond to excess demand for (supply of) nontraded goods, implying that the real interest rate will tend to fall (rise). The locus $[\dot{z} = 0]$, which is derived from (11), is also positively sloped and determines the combinations of the real interest rate and the real exchange rate for which the latter variable remains constant. Values of z above (below) the curve imply that domestic inflation exceeds the devaluation rate, so that the real exchange rate will tend to appreciate (depreciate).

---

[3] In deriving (9), the devaluation rate is assumed constant over time, so that, by (8), the domestic nominal interest rate is constant as well.

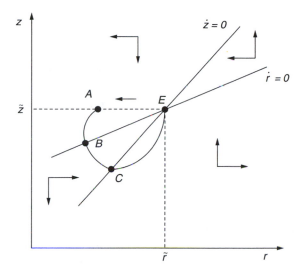

Figure 11–1 ■ Equilibrium and Adjustment in the Rodriguez Model

Equations (9) and (11) imply that, in the steady state (characterized by zero excess demand), the domestic real interest rate must be equal to the world interest rate, whereas (10) implies that the long-run inflation rate is equal to the predetermined devaluation rate:

$$\tilde{r} = i^*, \quad \tilde{\pi} = \varepsilon.$$

Given that neither z, nor r, can jump on impact, the system consisting of (9) and (11) is (locally) stable if and only if the coefficient matrix (assuming $\tilde{z} = 1$) defined by

$$\mathbf{M} = \begin{bmatrix} -\beta v(\partial d_N/\partial r) & -\beta v(\partial d_N/\partial z) \\ 1 - v(\partial d_N/\partial r) & -v(\partial d_N/\partial z) \end{bmatrix}$$

has a positive determinant and a negative trace:

$$\det \mathbf{M} = \beta v(\partial d_N/\partial z) > 0,$$

$$\mathrm{tr}\mathbf{M} = -v[(\partial d_N/\partial z) + \beta(\partial d_N/\partial r)] < 0.$$

The condition on the determinant of $\mathbf{M}$ is always satisfied, but the condition on the trace of $\mathbf{M}$ does not necessarily hold. It depends on whether the positive effect of a real exchange-rate depreciation on excess demand offsets the negative effect of an increase in the real interest rate on private demand for nontradable goods, as well as on the speed of adjustment of expectations, β. Assuming that the real exchange-rate effect is large relative to the real interest rate effect, or that β is low, ensures that

$\mathrm{tr}\mathbf{M} < 0$. The long-run equilibrium of the economy, which obtains at point E in Figure 11.1, is thus (locally) stable.

Consider now a reduction in the rate of devaluation from ε^b to $\varepsilon^s < \varepsilon^b$. The results of this experiment are also shown in Figure 11.1. The change in the devaluation rate does not affect the position of the curves $[\dot{r} = 0]$ and $[\dot{z} = 0]$, and therefore has no effect on the long-run equilibrium levels of the real exchange rate and the real interest rate. However, the reduction in ε reduces the real domestic interest rate on impact because, with the expected inflation rate given, it leads to a one-to-one reduction in the nominal interest rate. On impact, the system moves, therefore, from point E to a short-run equilibrium position such as point A, given that the real exchange rate is predetermined. The initial fall in the real interest rate generates an excess demand for home goods. The reduction of the devaluation rate tends to reduce prices, but the emergence of excess demand tends to raise them; the net effect on the inflation rate is nevertheless positive, as indicated by (10) and (8). The actual inflation rate subsequently rises above the expected rate, which also begins to rise gradually. The increase in the expected rate of inflation reduces the real interest rate further over time, leading in the first phase to a gradual process of appreciation of the real exchange rate, as domestic inflation exceeds the devaluation rate. In the second phase, however, the excess demand for nontraded goods generated by the fall in the real interest rate begins to dampen the rate of real exchange-rate appreciation, leading eventually—assuming that the stability conditions given above hold—to an elimination of excess demand. Equilibrium of the nontraded goods market is restored at point B—a point at which [as implied by (6)] actual and expected inflation rates are equal. Nevertheless, the real exchange rate continues to appreciate for a while, because at B the domestic rate of inflation (actual and expected) still exceeds the devaluation rate. This leads to an excess *supply* of nontraded goods. From (6), $d_N < 0$ implies $\pi^a > \pi$ so that, from (4), $\dot{\pi}^a < 0$ and the expected inflation rate begins to decline. This, in turn, leads to a gradual increase in the real interest rate (movement from B to C). At point C the rate of change of the real exchange rate is zero (the inflation rate is equal to the devaluation rate), but excess supply continues to prevail. Expected and actual inflation therefore continue to fall, leading to a depreciation of the exchange rate (which stimulates the demand for home goods and thus reduces excess supply) and a further rise in the real interest rate. In the long run, therefore, the economy returns to its initial equilibrium position at point E. The new steady-state value of the inflation rate is, by contrast, equal to $\varepsilon^s < \varepsilon^b$.

The adjustment process following a permanent reduction in the devaluation rate is thus characterized by a period of excess demand, that is, a short-run boom. In the Rodríguez model, the expansion of demand occurs as an inevitable consequence of the assumption of backward-looking expectations. The initial reduction in the devaluation rate leads to a fall in the nominal interest rate and a downward jump in the real interest rate—because the expected inflation rate is a predetermined variable—and hence to an increase in the demand for nontraded goods. This expansion of demand in the home goods sector puts upward pressure on domestic prices.

The ensuing appreciation of the real exchange rate dampens the expansion of demand and eventually dominates the initial expansionary effect, leading to a contraction in demand.[4] Thus, for the system to return to its initial equilibrium position, the initial boom must be followed by a demand contraction induced by the progressive appreciation of the real exchange rate in the second phase of the adjustment process, which results from the domestic inflation rate exceeding the devaluation rate.

1.1.2   *The Temporariness Hypothesis*

In several important contributions, Calvo and Végh (1993*a*, 1993 *b*) have provided an alternative explanation of the boom-recession cycle observed in exchange-rate-based stabilization programs, based on rigorous optimizing foundations and forward-looking expectations. The analytical structure developed by Calvo and Végh is of interest in its own right and, although it represents in several regards a less general framework than the three-good model developed in Chapter 10, is worth considering in detail.[5]

As in the Rodríguez model, consider a small open economy producing traded and nontraded goods. The representative household maximizes the discounted lifetime sum of utility, with instantaneous utility separable in both goods:

$$\int_0^\infty \ln(c_T, c_N)e^{-\rho t}dt, \quad \rho > 0, \tag{12}$$

where c_N (c_T) denotes consumption of nontraded (traded) goods. Households face a cash-in-advance constraint, given by

$$z^{-1}c_N + c_T \geq \alpha^{-1}m, \quad \alpha > 0, \tag{13}$$

where the real exchange rate is defined as $z = E/P_N$.[6] m denotes real money balances measured in terms of traded goods.

Households hold a stock b^p of internationally traded bonds, which bears a constant nominal and real rate of interest i^* determined on world capital markets. Real financial wealth in terms of traded goods, a, is thus $a = m + b^p$.

---

[4]Dornbusch (1982) obtains a similar result in a model with sticky prices and rational expectations, which suggests that the assumption of adaptive expectations may not be the key element explaining the boom-recession pattern in the Rodríguez model (see the following discussion). Note that if prices are flexible, the real exchange rate can appreciate on impact, so that the initial net output effect of the reduction of the devaluation rate may be ambiguous. This is essentially the result obtained by Fischer (1986) in a model with rational expectations and staggered contracts.

[5]The Calvo-Végh framework represents, in many regards, an extension of the cash-in-advance model presented by Calvo (1986). We refrain in what follows from discussing the role of currency substitution in their framework despite the importance of this feature in many developing countries, as noted in Chapter 5; see Calvo and Végh (1993*b*). Calvo (2007) extends the Calvo-Végh analysis to consider a class of interest rate rules that are formally equivalent to a devaluation rule.

[6]As before, the foreign-currency price of the traded good is set to unity for simplicity.

The intertemporal resource constraint faced by the consumer, which equates lifetime resources to lifetime expenditures, is given by

$$a_0 + \int_0^\infty (z^{-1}y_N + y_T + \tau)e^{-\rho t}dt = \int_0^\infty (z^{-1}c_N + c_T + im)e^{-\rho t}dt, \qquad (14)$$

where y_N denotes output of nontraded goods (which is determined below), y_T the exogenous level of output of traded goods, τ real transfers from the government, and i the domestic nominal interest rate, which, assuming that the uncovered interest parity condition holds, is given by

$$i = i^* + \varepsilon, \qquad (15)$$

where ε denotes, as before, the devaluation rate.

Households take as given a, y_T, y_N, τ, i, and z and maximize (12) subject to the cash-in-advance constraint (13)—holding with equality—and the lifetime resource constraint (14) by choosing a sequence $\{c_N, c_T, m\}_{t=0}^\infty$. Assuming that the subjective discount rate is equal to the world interest rate ($\rho = i^*$), the first-order conditions for this optimization problem are given by

$$1/c_T = \lambda(1 + \alpha i), \qquad (16)$$

$$c_N = zc_T, \qquad (17)$$

where λ can be interpreted, as before, as the marginal utility of wealth. Equation (16) equates the marginal utility of consumption of traded goods to the product of the marginal utility of wealth and their real effective price, which is defined as consisting of their direct, market price (equal to unity) and the opportunity cost of holding α units of money necessary to carry out the transaction, αi. Equation (17) equates the ratio of consumption of nontraded and traded goods (the inverse of the ratio of their marginal utilities) to the relative price of traded goods.

Output of nontraded goods is demand determined. The rate of change of inflation in the nontraded good sector, π_N, is assumed to be *negatively* related to excess demand in that sector, which is defined as the difference between actual output (itself determined by the demand side of the market) and its long-run level, $\bar{y}_N$:

$$\dot{\pi}_N = -\Theta(c_N - \bar{y}_N) = \Theta(\bar{y}_N - zc_T), \quad \Theta > 0, \qquad (18)$$

where the second equality follows from (17). The price mechanism specified in (18) follows the model of staggered prices and wages developed by Calvo (1983).[7] It relies

---

[7] Calvo's formulation was extended to account for partial wage indexation by Ambler and Cardia (1992).

on the assumption that firms in the nontraded goods sector determine the prices of their products in a nonsynchronous manner, taking into account the expected future path of demand and of the average price prevailing in the economy. At any moment in time, only a small subset of firms may change their individual prices. The price level is thus a predetermined variable at any given period, but inflation can jump, because it reflects changes in individual prices set by firms. When excess demand develops in the nontraded goods sector, for instance, some firms increase their individual prices and inflation rises. However, because the subset of firms that have yet to adjust their prices to excess demand diminishes quickly, inflation in home goods prices decreases over time. Hence, the change in the home goods inflation rate is inversely related to excess demand for nontraded goods.

Formally, suppose that there exists a large number (technically, a continuum) of firms in the nontraded goods sector, indexed in the interval between 0 and 1. Thus, the total number of firms in that sector is normalized to unity. Each firm produces a nonstorable good at a zero variable cost, the quantity of which is demand determined. The probability of receiving the price signal n periods from now is $\delta \exp(-\delta n)$, where $\delta > 0$. Under perfect foresight, the price set by the firm as of period t is given by

$$V = \delta \int_{t}^{\infty} [p_N(s) + \kappa E_N(s)] e^{-\delta(s-t)} ds, \quad \kappa > 0 \tag{19}$$

where V is the (logarithm of) the price quoted at t, $p_N(s)$ the (logarithm of) the price index for nontraded goods (which is defined below) at period s, and $E_N(s)$ denotes excess demand at period s for nontraded goods, defined as $E_N = c_N - \tilde{y}_N$. If the price-change signal is independent across firms, the proportion of prices set at time s that have not been modified as of time t is given by $\delta e^{-\delta(t-s)}$. The (logarithm of the) price index for nontraded goods is defined as the weighted average of prices currently quoted. Thus,

$$p_N = \delta \int_{t}^{\infty} V_s e^{-\delta(s-t)} ds. \tag{20}$$

In the above formulation, p_N, given by past price quotations, is a predetermined variable at time t. In contrast, V may jump when an unexpected change takes place. Along paths where p_N and E_N are uniquely determined, however, V is a continuous function of time. Differentiating (20) with respect to time yields

$$\pi_N = \delta(V - p_N), \tag{21}$$

where $\pi_N \equiv \dot{p}_N$.[8] It is important to note that (21) holds at any point in time; in particular, it holds at those points in time at which E_N is not continuous.

---

[8]Note that, because of the law of large numbers, π_N is nonstochastic.

Hence, anticipated discontinuities in π_N cannot take place even in the presence of anticipated discontinuities in E_N. This is an important consideration when temporary changes in policy are considered.

At points in time where E_N is continuous, (19) can be differentiated to yield

$$\dot{V} = \delta(V - p_N - \kappa E_N). \tag{22}$$

Differentiating (21) with respect to time yields $\dot{\pi}_N = \delta(\dot{V} - \pi_N)$. Substituting (21) and (22) in this expression and setting $\Theta = \delta^2 \kappa > 0$ implies that, at points in time at which E_N is continuous,

$$\dot{\pi}_N = -\Theta E_N = -\Theta(c_N - \bar{y}_N),$$

which is the form shown in (18).

As a result of staggered price setting in the nontraded goods sector, the real exchange rate is predetermined in the short run. Differentiating $z = E/P_N$ with respect to time yields:

$$\dot{z}/z = \varepsilon - \pi_N. \tag{23}$$

Closing the model requires a specification of the government's behavior. Under the assumption that the government buys no goods and redeems back to households the interest income on the central bank's net foreign assets and the revenue from money creation, the present value of government transfers is given by

$$\int_0^\infty \tau e^{-\rho t} dt = b_0^g + \int_0^\infty (\dot{m} + \varepsilon m) e^{-\rho t} dt, \tag{24}$$

where b_0^g denotes the government's initial stock of bonds.

Combining (14), (15), and (24); defining the total stock of bonds in the economy as $b = b^p + b^g$; and imposing the transversality condition $\lim_{t \to \infty} e^{-\rho t} b = 0$ yields the overall resource constraint:

$$b_0 + y_T/\rho = \int_0^\infty c_T e^{-\rho t} dt, \tag{25}$$

where b_0 denotes the economy's initial stock of bonds.

Equation (25) equates the present value of tradable resources to the present value of purchases of traded goods. Assuming further that transfers are used to compensate households for the depreciation of real money balances yields the economy's current account balance:[9]

$$\dot{b} = y_T + i^* b - c_T. \tag{26}$$

Finally, as in the two-sector, three-good framework developed in Chapter 10 and the Rodríguez model described earlier, the overall inflation rate is written as a weighted average of the devaluation rate and the rate of inflation in home goods prices:

$$\pi = \delta \pi_N + (1 - \delta)\varepsilon, \quad 0 < \delta < 1, \tag{27}$$

where the weight δ depends on the share of home goods in total consumption expenditure.

The dynamics of the model are determined by (18), (23), and (26). Because output of traded goods is exogenous and consumption of traded goods depends, from (16), only on the marginal utility of wealth—which varies over time solely as a result of unexpected shocks[10]—and the domestic interest rate, the system is recursive.[11] For a given path of c_T and ε, (18) and (23) form the interdependent block, which can be written as

$$\begin{bmatrix} \dot{z} \\ \dot{\pi}_N \end{bmatrix} = \begin{bmatrix} 0 & -\tilde{z} \\ -\Theta \tilde{c}_T & 0 \end{bmatrix} \begin{bmatrix} z \\ \pi_N \end{bmatrix} + \begin{bmatrix} \tilde{z}\varepsilon \\ \Theta \tilde{y}_N - \tilde{z} c_T \end{bmatrix}. \tag{28}$$

The first row of (28) indicates that, for the real exchange rate to remain constant over time, the rate of inflation in home goods prices must be equal to the devaluation rate. The second row indicates that consumption of nontraded goods must be equal to long-run output for the rate of inflation in home goods prices to remain constant over time. Because $\tilde{c}_T = \tilde{y}_N/\tilde{z}$, the determinant of the matrix of coefficients is $-\Theta \tilde{y}_N < 0$. The system is therefore saddlepath stable.

Reduction of ε: Full Credibility. As before, suppose that at time t the government announces an immediate and permanent reduction in the rate of devaluation from an initial value of ε^h to $\varepsilon^s < \varepsilon^h$. The permanent nature of the shock is interpreted by Calvo and Végh as indicating that the announcement carries full credibility, in the sense that private agents are convinced that the devaluation rate will indeed remain at its lower level in the indefinite future.

---

[9]The household's flow budget constraint is given by $\dot{m} + \dot{b}^p = z^{-1}(y_N - c_N) + y_T + i^* b^p - \tau - c_T - \varepsilon m$, whereas the government flow constraint is $\dot{m} - \dot{b}^g = \tau - i^* b^g - \varepsilon m$. Setting $\tau = \varepsilon m$ in the above equation yields $\dot{m} = \dot{b}^g - i^* b^g$. Substituting these results in the consumer's flow constraint and setting $c_N = y_N$ yields (26).

[10]From the intertemporal budget constraint and the optimality conditions, the equilibrium shadow price of wealth can be derived as a function of predetermined or exogenous variables only.

[11]The assumption that output of traded goods is exogenous may appear far-fetched, given that the real exchange rate is endogenous. However, it may be justified by low trade elasticities in the short run. Endogenizing y_T would break the recursiveness of the model.

Through the interest parity condition [equation (15)], the reduction in the devaluation rate leads to a concomitant fall in the nominal interest rate. Because the exchange-rate adjustment carries full credibility, private agents will expect the nominal interest rate to remain forever at its lower level. Although the reduction in the domestic interest rate is equivalent to a fall in the effective price of consumption, the fact that the exchange-rate adjustment is expected to last forever implies that private agents have no incentives to engage in intertemporal consumption substitution. Because tradable resources do not change, consumption of traded goods remains constant over time. From the system (24), it follows that, because c_T is not affected by permanent changes in the rate of devaluation, a fall in π_N that exactly matches the fall in ε immediately moves the system to a new steady state. The overall inflation rate of the economy, which is a weighted average of the inflation rate of home goods and that of traded goods [equation (27)], also falls instantaneously to its new level, ε^s. Therefore, a permanent, unanticipated reduction in the devaluation rate—or, in the Calvo-Végh interpretation, a fully credible exchange-rate-based stabilization program—reduces the inflation rate instantaneously at no real costs and is thus superneutral.[12] Moreover, this result holds also if the system starts away from an initial steady-state position.[13]

An important property of the Calvo-Végh model is that the immediate downward jump in inflation and the absence of real effects associated with a reduction in the devaluation rate that is perceived to be permanent occurs despite the existence of staggered price setting by individual forward-looking firms. Price level rigidity does not, by itself, imply stickiness in the inflation rate.[14]

Reduction of ε: Imperfect Credibility. Consider now the case where the government announces at t a reduction in the devaluation rate, but the public believes that the exchange-rate adjustment will be reversed at some period T in the future. Formally,

$$\begin{cases} \varepsilon = \varepsilon^s & \text{for } t_0 \le t < T, \\ \varepsilon = \varepsilon^b > \varepsilon^s & \text{for } t \ge T. \end{cases}$$

---

[12] In the presence of currency substitution, a permanent reduction in the devaluation rate has a real effect on impact. As shown by Calvo and Végh (1993a), it leads to a substitution away from foreign-currency holdings and to a positive wealth effect that stimulates consumption expenditure and output. The inflation rate in home goods prices can also rise on impact. The model, however, cannot predict a subsequent recession in that case.

[13] This would not be the case if the rate of time preference was assumed endogenous (regardless of whether the instantaneous utility function is separable in consumption and real money balances), as implied by Obstfeld's (1981) analysis. The increase in real money balances associated with a permanent reduction in the devaluation rate would in this case raise the level of instantaneous utility and make private agents more impatient. The increase in consumption would lead to a current account deficit.

[14] In a substantially different framework that emphasizes staggered price and wage setting, Ball (1994) has shown that under full credibility a fast disinflation (a large reduction in the rate of money growth) causes a boom rather than a recession. In Ball's model, as is the case here, the inflation rate is free to jump in spite of price level inertia.

Calvo and Végh interpret the belief that the policy is temporary as arising from lack of credibility—an interpretation to which we return later.[15] The dynamic behavior of consumption, the current account, the real exchange rate, and the inflation and real interest rates associated with a temporary exchange-rate policy are illustrated in Figure 11.2. The temporary reduction in the devaluation rate implies, by (15), that the nominal interest rate is lower in the interval $(0, T)$. Consequently, the effective price of traded goods is also lower during the interval $(0, T)$ and consumption of traded goods jumps upward [see (16)], to a level higher than initial permanent income (given by $y_T + i^* b_0$). However, because the intertemporal resource constraint of the economy [(25)] must be satisfied for all equilibrium paths, consumption of traded goods must subsequently (for $t \geq T$) fall below initial permanent income and remain forever at that lower level. The upward jump in consumption of traded goods leads on impact to a current account deficit. During the interval $(0, T)$, the deficit continues to increase (despite the fact that consumption of traded goods remains constant) as a result of a reduction over time of interest receipts on foreign bonds. When, at time T, the policy is abandoned, the current account jumps into balance and the stock of foreign bonds remains permanently at a lower level than initially.

The effect of the reduction in the devaluation rate on the path of home goods prices is, on impact, ambiguous. On the one hand, a lower rate of exchange-rate depreciation dampens the rate of inflation in home goods prices. On the other, the increase in aggregate demand tends to raise inflation. The net effect in general is a reduction in the rate of inflation in home goods prices, but by less than the rate of devaluation.[16] After the initial fall, inflation in home goods prices rises continuously, assuming that the horizon T is large enough, in anticipation of the expected resumption of the higher devaluation rate. At time T, the policymaker must decide whether to abandon the program (thus validating the public's expectations) or maintain the devaluation rate at the lower level. If the authorities indeed abandon the program, inflation in home goods prices will continue to increase toward its initial level, as shown in Figure 11.2. If, however, the authorities decide to maintain the lower-devaluation-rate policy, then inflation in home goods prices will jump downward at time T and converge from below toward ε^s.

Qualitatively, the overall inflation rate follows the same adjustment path during the interval $(0, T)$ as inflation in home goods prices. The Calvo-Végh model thus predicts that a temporary reduction in the devaluation rate (interpreted as a reflection of a lack of credibility) will lead to inflation inertia. Moreover, the more

---

[15] Intertemporal optimizing models in which the rate of time preference must be set equal to a (constant) world interest rate for stability purposes ($\rho = i^*$, as is the case here) are subject to subtle analytical problems when it comes to studying the impact of temporary shocks; see Schubert and Turnovsky (2002) for a discussion.

[16] In the absence of the aggregate demand effect, inflation in home goods prices would fall by the same proportion as the rate of devaluation, as occurs with a permanent shock. The overall inflation rate would also fall one-to-one with the devaluation rate.

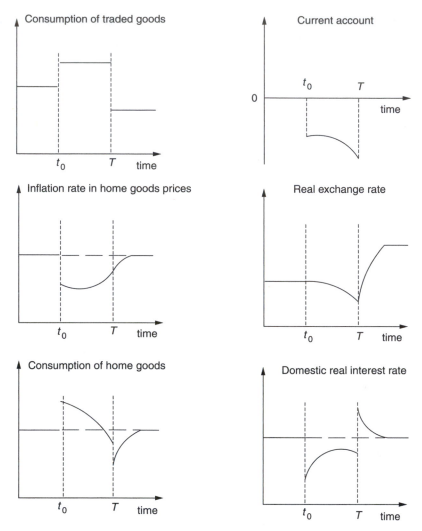

Figure 11–2 ▪ Dynamics of the Calvo-Végh "Temporariness" Model with Imperfect Credibility
Source: Calvo and Végh (1993*b*, p. 17).

temporary the exchange-rate policy, or the lower its degree of credibility, the lower the initial fall in the inflation rate.

Because the inflation rate in home goods prices remains systematically above the devaluation rate, the real exchange rate appreciates during the interval $(0, T)$. At time T, regardless of whether the exchange-rate policy is reversed or not, the real exchange rate begins to depreciate. If at that moment the lower-devaluation policy is not abandoned—and if private agents become convinced that it will be adhered to in the indefinite future—inflation in home goods prices falls below the devaluation rate, generating the real depreciation.

The domestic real interest rate, defined as the difference between the nominal interest rate and the rate of inflation in home goods prices, falls on impact, because the rate of inflation in nontraded goods prices drops by less than the devaluation rate and the concomitant fall in the nominal interest rate. It begins rising at first and then falls during the transition, jumping upward when the horizon T is reached, as a result of the jump in the nominal interest rate. Because domestic inflation increases gradually over time, the real interest rate falls monotonically thereafter toward its unchanged steady-state value given by the world interest rate.

Because the relative price of home goods in terms of traded goods cannot change on impact, the increase in the consumption of traded goods leads to a proportional rise in the consumption of home goods [see (17)]. The gradual appreciation of the real exchange rate leads to a reduction over time of private expenditure on home goods. If the horizon is sufficiently far in the future, a recession may set in well before T is reached. If the horizon is short, output will remain above its full-employment level throughout the transition period. At time T, consumption of both traded and nontraded goods jumps downward. After T, the real exchange rate begins to depreciate toward its long-run value, stimulating consumption of home goods. There is, therefore, an initial consumption boom followed later on, possibly before time T is reached, by a contraction. The smaller T is—or, according to the interpretation given above, the lower the credibility of the disinflation policy—the more pronounced are the intertemporal substitution effects, and the larger is the initial rise in the consumption of traded and home goods.

1.1.3   An Assessment

To a large extent, the explanation of the expansion-recession cycle provided by Rodríguez relies on an arbitrary specification of behavioral functions and expectations formation. Although plausible under certain conditions, the assumption of purely backward-looking expectations process appears untenable in the context of economies undergoing a comprehensive macroeconomic adjustment program—although there is evidence for the exchange-rate-based stabilization episodes of Brazil, Israel, Mexico, and Turkey during the 1990s that suggests that the behavior of nontradables inflation was characterized by a strong backward-looking component.[17]

As shown by Calvo and Végh (1994), however, Rodríguez's results also obtain if prices are sticky and expectations are forward-looking. Nevertheless, the predictions of the Rodríguez model can be substantially altered once behavioral functions are derived from a well-defined microeconomic optimization process, rather than simply postulated. Using an optimizing framework similar in many regards to the one

---

[17] See Celasun (2006). In the same vein, Burstein et al. (2005) found that for five middle-income countries (Argentina, Brazil, Mexico, Korea, and Thailand) large nominal devaluations were associated with large real depreciations because prices of nontradables tend to adjust slowly. This explains why overall inflation tends to be relatively low despite large movements in the nominal exchange rate.

described above, Calvo and Végh (1994) have argued that even in the presence of backward-looking price expectations—as embodied in wage contracts, for instance—a permanent reduction in the devaluation rate may have a contractionary effect, rather than an expansionary effect as predicted by Rodríguez. Essentially, this result is obtained because the appreciation of the real exchange rate has an ambiguous effect on output. On the one hand, the real appreciation has a negative impact because it increases the relative price of home goods. On the other, it stimulates output because it leads to a reduction in the domestic, consumption-based real interest rate.[18] Whether or not the latter effect dominates depends on whether the intertemporal elasticity of substitution (which measures the degree to which agents are willing to shift consumption across periods) is larger than the intratemporal elasticity of substitution between traded and home goods. Hence, the existence of backward-looking expectations may not be sufficient to explain the observed initial expansion in output. At the same time, however, Celasun (2006) showed that the introduction of backward-looking pricing behavior in a numerical version of the Calvo-Végh model yields a real appreciation in the first stage of an exchange-rate-based stabilization that is a lot more significant than what the "pure" Calvo price equation would generate.[19]

The Calvo-Végh framework provides a conceptually appealing formulation of the major mechanisms at work in the behavior of output in exchange-rate-based disinflation programs. In contrast to Rodríguez, who assumes backward-looking expectations, Calvo and Végh emphasize the role of forward-looking behavior and expectations of future policy reversals. Moreover, the Calvo-Végh framework can be extended to account for uncertainty about the date of the policy reversal—along the lines of Drazen and Helpman (1988, 1990), for instance—and thus may provide an explanation of the volatile behavior of aggregate variables in programs that lack credibility. The U-shaped time profile of inflation predicted by the Calvo-Végh model appears to correspond relatively well to the evidence observed in several exchange-rate-based stabilization attempts that ended in failure (see online Supplement B). In addition, the prediction of a growing current account deficit may be the only sign that the stabilization program is unsustainable in this type of model: Talvi (1997) has emphasized the fact that the initial consumption boom and buoyant domestic activity may lead to a significant increase in tax revenue and an actual fiscal surplus that may persist until the collapse of the fixed exchange rate that underlies the program. This aspect of the model is in contrast with the predictions of conventional models of balance-of-payments crises, as discussed in Chapter 14.[20]

---

[18] While the real interest rate determines the level of aggregate demand in the Rodríguez model, it determines only its rate of growth in the formulation of Calvo and Végh (1994).

[19] Calvo et al. (2003) provide a generalization of Calvo's staggered pricing model that generates inflation inertia.

[20] A practical implication of Talvi's analysis is the importance of focusing on a cyclically adjusted measure of a country's fiscal position in order to assess the sustainability of a stabilization program.

The ability of the Calvo-Végh temporariness hypothesis to explain the boom-recession puzzle depends on the extent to which the degree of intertemporal substitution can explain the large observed changes in private consumption expenditure. However, the available evidence on the intertemporal channel emphasized by Calvo and Végh does not appear to provide strong support for the theory. Estimates by Ostry and Reinhart (1992), Reinhart and Végh (1995), and especially Ogaki et al. (1996) for both low- and middle-income countries (including Argentina, Brazil, Chile, Israel, and Mexico) suggest the elasticity of substitution is relatively low but nevertheless statistically different from zero.[21]

In principle, even with low intertemporal elasticities of substitution, observed movements in interest rates may be large enough to generate substantial changes in consumption. But while many of the stabilization programs implemented in the mid-1980s (whether ultimately successful or not) were accompanied by a substantial fall in nominal interest rates, the evidence is less compelling with regard to other episodes—particularly the Southern Cone experiments. Reinhart and Végh (1995) have examined this hypothesis using a simulation analysis and have shown that, despite low elasticities, predicted changes in consumption match reasonably well the actual changes in the four heterodox programs implemented in the 1980s (particularly Brazil, Mexico, and Israel), but accuracy is poor for the tablita experiments. The overall evidence thus does not seem to provide overwhelming support for the view that lack of credibility—modeled as a policy adjustment subject to a future reversal—and intertemporal factors explain output behavior in exchange-rate-based programs.[22]

However, whether the intertemporal elasticity of substitution is small or large may be less important than the above discussion suggests. The results obtained by Calvo and Végh depend also in a crucial manner on the assumption that money and consumption are Pareto-Edgeworth complements. In their framework, the representative household (which faces a constant real rate of interest) attempts to keep the marginal utility of consumption constant over time. To do so, the household must change the path of consumption if the devaluation rate, and therefore the opportunity cost of holding money, is expected to increase at a well-defined future date. The direction of this change depends on whether consumption goods and real money balances are substitutes or complements. If consumption of traded goods and real money balances are Pareto-Edgeworth complements, then private agents will consume more when the nominal interest rate is temporarily lower, leading

---

[21] A limitation of existing studies attempting to estimate intertemporal elasticities of substitution is the absence of a distinction between durable and nondurable goods. This is likely to bias econometric estimates against the temporariness hypothesis.

[22] Calvo and Végh (1993*a*) have shown that, in addition to the intertemporal channel, lower nominal interest rates—induced by a reduction in the devaluation rate—can also lead to higher consumption if households face liquidity constraints such that cash is needed to meet interest payments. Such constraints affect consumption both by further reducing the effective price of goods consumed and by lowering the consumption-based real interest rate. There is, however, no clear evidence supporting this effect.

to a deterioration of the current account. This is the case that Calvo and Végh consider, implicitly, by introducing money through a cash-in-advance requirement. By contrast, if consumption of traded goods and real money balances are Pareto-Edgeworth substitutes, a temporary fall in nominal interest rates will raise money demand and induce a *reduction* in consumption expenditure. A temporary reduction in the devaluation rate leads in this case to a transitory current account surplus, rather than a deficit.[23]

Another difficulty in the Calvo-Végh framework is that the dynamic effects of an imperfectly credible policy depend—in addition to consumer preferences and price-setting rules—critically on the degree of temporariness, that is, the duration of the interval during which the policy is in effect. This feature of the model is a common one in the literature on temporary policy. However, because the period at which the policy is believed to be discontinued is given, credibility is exogenous. As discussed in the next section, a key aspect of credibility is precisely the endogenous interactions between policy decisions, economic outcomes, and the degree of confidence that private agents attach to policymakers' commitment to disinflate. Accounting for the existence of uncertainty regarding the degree of temporariness of an exchange-rate-based stabilization program is also important; Mendoza and Uribe (1996), using numerical simulation of a two-sector small open economy, with no price or wage rigidities, show that uncertainty about the duration of the program (a realistic feature of the vast majority of actual experiments) may be sufficient to lead to a boom-recession cycle, a deteriorating current account, and a real exchange-rate appreciation. At the same time, Venegas-Martínez (2001) showed that the central result of the temporariness hypothesis (namely, a consumption boom if an exchange-rate-based stabilization is expected to be temporary) continues to hold in a stochastic model of a small open economy in which agents have expectations of devaluation driven by a mixed diffusion-jump process—a common specification in the analysis of exchange-rate behavior.

Two more general points can be made concerning the previous models of the boom-recession cycle. First, instead of modeling exchange-rate policy as a sequence of jumps in the rate of devaluation, an alternative approach would be to consider a gradual reduction in the devaluation rate—an approach that is perhaps more in line with the Southern Cone tablita experiments (see online Supplement B). Obstfeld (1985) studied the dynamics associated with this type of policy, using an optimizing framework with continuous market clearing and perfect foresight. He emphasized, as do Calvo and Végh, the importance of intertemporal substitution effects in consumption generated by a gradual and permanent (and thus fully credible) reduction in the devaluation rate. Such a policy increases real money balances, and, if money and consumption are substitutes, consumption rises on impact and falls over time. Initially, the real exchange rate appreciates and a current account deficit emerges.

---

[23]This limitation of the Calvo-Végh temporariness framework is essentially similar to that highlighted by Calvo (1986) and Obstfeld (1985), in a different context.

Later on in the program, a real depreciation occurs, and a gradual reduction of the deficit takes place. As before, however, Obstfeld's predictions depend crucially on the treatment of money and consumption in households' utility function. Specifically, in Obstfeld's analysis, the consumer's utility function belongs to the constant relative-risk aversion class and is defined by

$$u(c, m) = \begin{cases} (c^\alpha m^{1-\alpha})^{1-\eta}/(1-\eta) & \text{if } \eta < 1 \text{ or } \eta > 1 \\ \alpha \ln c + (1-\alpha) \ln m & \text{if } \eta = 1 \end{cases},$$

where $0 < \alpha < 1$ and the elasticity of intertemporal substitution σ is equal to $1/\eta$. This formulation implies that the intratemporal elasticity of substitution between consumption and money is equal to unity. When $\eta < 1$, consumption and money are Edgeworth-Pareto complements (that is, $u_{cm} > 0$), while when $\eta > 1$ they are substitutes $(u_{cm} < 0)$.[24] If money and real goods are complements rather than substitutes, the economy's short- and long-run responses to a gradual reduction in the devaluation rate are completely reversed, just as in the Calvo-Végh model.

Another analysis of a gradual lowering of the devaluation rate is provided by Roldós (1995), who models money also through a cash-in-advance constraint—an assumption that is functionally equivalent to postulating complementarity between money and consumption in households' utility functions. A gradual, fully credible reduction in the devaluation rate in the model entails, as in Obstfeld's setting, a real exchange-rate appreciation and sustained current account deficits. However, an important feature of the model developed by Roldós (as in Lahiri, 2001, and Agé nor and Pizzatti, 2005) is the emphasis on the supply-side effects of exchange-rate policy. An initial boom occurs only when the intertemporal elasticity of substitution in labor supply is larger than that in consumption; it occurs in both production sectors—tradables and nontradables—as real wages fall. The reduction in inflation raises the marginal value of wealth, raising the opportunity cost of leisure and inducing an increase in labor supply in the initial phase of the program. The further reduction over time in the rate of inflation leads to additional increases in labor supply. Contrary to what happens in the Calvo-Végh framework, a recession does not occur later on.[25] The emphasis on intertemporal substitution in labor supply rather than consumption provides a potentially useful interpretation of the Mexican stabilization experiment (as well as some other exchange-rate-based experiences reviewed in online Supplement B), which was not accompanied by an early recession. However, no rigorous testing of this channel has yet been developed, and its empirical importance is therefore unclear.

---

[24] If the utility function $u(c, m)$ is nonseparable, ensuring that consumption and real money balances are normal goods requires $U_{mm}U_c - U_{cm}U_m < 0$ and $U_{cc}U_m - U_{cm}U_c < 0$.

[25] This is not surprising because Roldós considers only the case where the adjustment of the devaluation rate is fully credible, or permanent.

The second point relates to the fact that neither the Rodríguez nor the Calvo-Végh model of the boom-recession cycle incorporates durable goods, although an anticipated collapse of a stabilization program is likely to have more pronounced real effects in the presence of durable goods. Intuitively, an anticipated increase in the inflation rate and the opportunity cost of purchases immediately would induce an increase in spending on durable goods, an accumulation of inventories by firms, and investment in capital goods (machines and equipment, very often imported from abroad, as argued in Chapter 1), thereby causing a large increase in absorption. Buffie and Atolia (2012) study the dynamics of exchange-rate-based stabilization programs in a model with both durable and nondurable consumption. In numerical simulations that assume the rate of crawl decreases from 100 percent to zero for three years, weak credibility triggers a large, double-digit spending boom and a sharp real appreciation. Moreover, although durable goods comprise only 20 percent of consumption, they account for 70–90 percent of the increase in total spending. Durables also lead in the bust phase of the cycle, strongly overshooting their steady-state level after the program collapses. In short, volatile swings in durables spending drive the entire boom-bust cycle.

Moreover, exchange-rate-based stabilization programs may be subject to "hysteresis" effects in the presence of durable goods (Matsuyama, 1991).[26] In such conditions, a temporary reduction in the devaluation rate may have a permanent effect, because such a change alters the initial condition for some later moment when the policy is abandoned and the "old" policy is put back in place.[27] Understanding the dynamics of durable goods induced by expectations of relative price changes is thus a critical element in assessing the real effects induced by intertemporal substitution in stabilization programs.

A source of real sector dynamics in exchange-rate based stabilization programs that also needs to be explored further relates to the wealth effects of these programs. An early study of these issues was developed by Helpman and Razin (1987). Their analysis was based on the Blanchard-Yaari framework which, as mentioned in Chapter 4, assumes finite-lived individuals—so that Ricardian equivalence does not hold. They showed that an unexpected exchange-rate freeze generates capital gains (due to the reduction in the inflation tax) for agents currently alive. The unexpectedly appreciated exchange rate increases the real value of nominal asset holdings, such as money balances. Because agents have a finite horizon, this wealth effect is not fully offset by future tax liabilities. Thus, an exchange-rate freeze brings about an increase in private consumption and a deterioration of the current account. The increase

---

[26] A dynamic system is said to exhibit hysteresis if the steady state depends on initial conditions.

[27] The fact that the steady state may depend on initial conditions in optimizing models with infinite-lived agents and a constant discount rate has not been discussed in much detail in the existing literature. In particular, its implications for the evaluation of temporary shocks have received relatively little consideration (see Turnovsky and Sen, 1991). Note that in models where the equality between the discount rate and the world interest rate is dropped—as, for instance, in Obstfeld (1981) and the optimizing models presented in Chapter 10—hysteresis would generally not emerge.

in future tax liabilities in this framework is due to the loss of reserves attached to the freeze in the exchange rate, which translates into an increase in debt and debt service; future reductions in the budget deficit are therefore expected by means of an increase in taxes. The consumption effect stems from a tilt in the consumption profile that results from finite lifetimes. As time goes by, the share of the population that benefits from the capital gain declines while the share that is subject to tax liabilities increases, resulting in an eventual decline in consumption. The end result is a temporarily higher consumption level, a worsening current account, reserve losses, and an increase in government debt.[28] However, the empirical importance of this theory in explaining the business cycle associated with exchange-rate-based stabilization remains to be fully established.

Finally, Burstein et al. (2003) have argued that costs associated with the distribution of tradable goods (transportation, wholesaling, and retailing) are important to understand the dynamics of the real exchange rate during exchange-rate-based stabilizations. Accounting for these costs implies that (unlike the specification adopted earlier) relative PPP does not hold for (retail) prices of tradable goods. Because distribution costs are intensive in services (such as labor) that may fluctuate quite significantly during and after stabilization, they imply that movements in the price of tradables may be as important as changes in the price of nontradables in explaining movements in the real exchange rate.

1.2 ■ The Behavior of Real Interest Rates

As mentioned in the introduction, the divergent behavior of real interest rates in exchange-rate-based stabilization programs implemented during the 1970s and 1980s has received relatively little attention in the literature on macroeconomic adjustment in developing countries. We examine here two alternative models aimed at explaining this apparent puzzle. The first focuses on lack of credibility and the presence of additional nominal anchors, and the second on expectations about future fiscal policy shocks.

1.2.1 *Credibility, Nominal Anchors, and Interest Rates*

Analytical models designed to explain the boom-recession cycle associated with exchange-rate-based programs provide unambiguous predictions regarding the initial movement of real interest rates. In the Rodríguez model, for instance, a permanent, fully credible reduction in the devaluation rate leads to an immediate fall in real

---

[28]Related work can also be found in Helpman and Leiderman (1988), and Drazen and Helpman (1988, 1990). These papers view stabilization as a two-stage program. The first stage is exchange-rate management with few other adjustments, and the second stage is either a fiscal adjustment or an abandonment of the exchange-rate policy. These models assume infinitely lived individuals, but Ricardian equivalence does not hold due to distortions resulting from expectations of the different forms of budgetary adjustment. Real effects in the first period will therefore vary depending on the kind of fiscal tool that is expected to be used in the second stage to adjust the budget.

interest rates, because price expectations are predetermined at any moment in time. Similarly, in the Calvo-Végh "temporariness" framework described above, an imperfectly credible exchange-rate stabilization leads to an unambiguous fall on impact in the domestic real interest rate. To reconcile their theoretical construct with the diverging pattern observed in the 1970s and 1980s, Calvo and Végh (1993*b*) argue that if money is used as an additional anchor, as a result of the imposition of capital controls or the adoption of a credit target, then real interest rates may rise rather than fall at the inception of an imperfectly credible exchange-rate-based program. If, for instance, capital controls are in place, the money stock becomes predetermined. An increase in domestic money demand associated with a reduction in the devaluation rate requires an accommodating upward adjustment in interest rates. Given that the devaluation rate falls on impact, real interest rates will generally rise.

This line of argument may prove useful for understanding the sharp increase in real interest rates that occurred at the beginning of the Israeli stabilization of the mid-1980s. The restrictive credit policy adopted by the authorities at the inception of the program is widely believed to have been the major factor behind the rise in real interest rates.[29] However, there does not appear to be much evidence suggesting that credit policy was significantly different in the programs implemented in the 1970s and 1980s in Latin America. Capital controls apparently were not intensified at the inception of those programs either.

An issue that has not been fully appreciated in the recent literature relates to the fiscal implications of an exchange-rate-based stabilization program, and the fact that an exchange-rate adjustment is typically only one element of an overall stabilization package comprising trade, financial, and fiscal reforms designed to reduce inflation and improve the current account. An unanticipated reduction in the devaluation rate leads to a deterioration of the financial position of the public sector, through the loss of seigniorage and the increase in the real cost of servicing fixed-rate debt issued when nominal interest rates were high (Velasco, 1993). Eventually, the government must correct the fiscal deficit thus created via changes in its policy instruments, such as the rate of growth of domestic credit, lump-sum transfers to private agents, income tax rates, or spending cuts. In a forward-looking world, expectations about the nature of the instruments that the policymakers are likely to implement will have immediate effects on the behavior of real interest rates.[30]

1.2.2 *Expectations, Fiscal Adjustment, and Interest Rates*

We examine here, using the one-good model with imperfect capital mobility developed in Chapter 10, the implications of a two-stage stabilization program for the

---

[29] See online Supplement B and Patinkin (1993). The restrictive credit stance was brought about by an increase in the discount rate and the level of reserve requirements on bank deposits, and the tightening of restrictions on short-term capital flows.

[30] The link between anticipations about future policies and current policy outcomes was emphasized in Chapter 4, in our discussion of the short-term interactions between fiscal deficits, inflation, and the current account.

behavior of real interest rates. We will consider the specification in which lump-sum taxes are endogenously adjusted to balance the budget.

Assume that the economy begins at $t = 0$ in a steady state, characterized by a "high" devaluation rate and a "high" level of government spending, g^h. At $t = 0$ the government decides to reduce the devaluation rate from ε^h to $\varepsilon^s < \varepsilon^h$. At the same time that the reduction in the devaluation rate is implemented, the government announces its intention to permanently reduce public expenditure from g^h to g^s in the future, at period T or some time after T. The new level of spending g^s is common knowledge. However, the public does not entirely believe the policy announcement, and attributes only a given probability $0 < \alpha < 1$ that the reduction in spending will be effectively implemented. The coefficient α can thus be viewed as a measure of the degree of credibility of the fiscal component of the stabilization program. A value of α close to unity indicates that agents are almost certain that the policy reform will eventually be carried out, while a value close to zero indicates that the public has little confidence in the government's intention to reduce spending.

The level of spending that is expected to prevail after T is thus equal to $\alpha g^s + (1 - \alpha)g^h$ (which is lower than g^h as long as α is positive), and this is the value of spending that affects the dynamics of the economy for $t \geq T$. As shown by Agénor (1998b), the solution of the dynamic system yields a "quasi" steady state, because it is associated with a policy shock that may or may not occur at T or afterward. Once period T is reached, either the policy is implemented or agents start believing it will never be. Uncertainty eventually disappears, and α becomes unity or zero. Thus, there would normally be a jump in all variables at some moment after period T, after which the economy will begin converging to its "final" steady state. We will here discuss only the quasi-steady state, because the focus of attention is the short-run behavior of real interest rates. The solution of the model during the adjustment period $0 < t < T$ is such that the transition that takes place at T is perfectly anticipated.

The impact effect of a program consisting of an immediate reduction in the rate of devaluation and the announcement of a future reduction of spending on private consumption is in general ambiguous. To understand the short-run dynamics of real interest rates, consider the two polar cases: α close to zero and α positive. The case in which α is close to zero corresponds to the case of a permanent, unanticipated reduction in the devaluation rate only at $t = 0$, as described in Chapter 10. Thus (assuming that the degree of intertemporal substitution is sufficiently low, as indicated earlier), the announcement of a future fiscal adjustment that carries little credibility implies that the real interest rate is likely to fall on impact. By contrast, if α is close to unity, and if the initial reduction in the devaluation rate is not too large, it can be shown that the real interest rate will rise on impact. The larger α is, the larger will be the increase in the real interest rate.

The thrust of the foregoing analysis is thus that, as long as α is positive, the behavior of real interest rates at the inception of a two-stage exchange-rate-based stabilization program of the type discussed here is indeterminate. Depending on the degree of confidence in fiscal reform (as well as the degree of intertemporal substitution, the size of the initial exchange-rate adjustment, and the likely reduction in public spending), real interest rates may rise or fall. In practice, therefore, real interest rate fluctuations will reflect not only the type of policies that agents expect the government to implement in the future but also changes in the perceived ability of policymakers to stick to their announcements. An empirical test of the importance of the time profile of fiscal policy as emphasized here is, of course, difficult to implement because expectations of future policy changes are not observed by the econometrician. Nevertheless, the adjustment mechanism described in the foregoing discussion may have played an important role in the contrasting pattern, noted in the introduction to this chapter, in the behavior of real interest rates in the exchange-rate-based stabilization programs implemented in the 1970s and 1980s. As emphasized by many economists, lack of credibility has been a pervasive factor in the short-run dynamics associated with these experiments. However, although most observers have emphasized imperfect credibility of exchange-rate adjustment per se, the analysis developed here has focused on the fiscal dimension of the credibility issue in these programs. In the above setting, the initial exchange-rate adjustment is fully credible, in the sense that it is perceived to be permanent. What suffers from a lack of credibility is the announcement of a future spending cut. Our analysis thus suggests that, even when the exchange-rate policy component of an exchange-rate-based stabilization program is fully credible, large fluctuations in real interest rates may be observed in the course of the adjustment process if the degree of confidence in the fiscal policy component of the program varies over time.[31]

1.3 ▪ Disinflation and Real Wages

As discussed in online Supplement B, various forms of wage policy have been used in stabilization programs implemented in developing countries. Argentina's Austral Plan of June 1985 was preceded by a 22 percent increase in wages and a subsequent freeze. When prices kept rising—although at a much slower pace—the authorities raised nominal wages by 8.5 percent by the end of the year and then adopted quarterly wage adjustments. Israel's stabilization plan of July 1985 granted a 50 percent compensation for that month's inflation, and then froze wages for three months in a trilateral agreement between the government, the entrepreneurs' association, and the workers' federation, the Histadrut. Subsequent adjustments provided partial compensation for previous inflation of 4 percent or more. At the inception of Bolivia's August 1985 plan, the government granted bonuses and then froze wages. Later, it reduced restrictions on laying off workers, eliminated wage indexation, and set a very low minimum wage. Brazil's Cruzado plan of February 1986 established an initial bonus of 8 percent of wages for all workers. At the same

---

[31] The variability of real interest rates may also result from uncertainty regarding the date at which the disinflation effort is expected to collapse. This result would follow from those established by Drazen and Helpman (1988, 1990).

time, the minimum wage was increased by 16 percent. Nominal wages were not frozen, and annual (instead of semiannual) wage negotiations were restored. Wages were to be automatically adjusted when inflation reached 20 percent. This trigger was activated for the first time in December 1986, when the Cruzado Plan collapsed—in part as a result of excessive increases in public sector wages. As in Israel, Mexico's stabilization program implemented in end 1987-early 1988 also relied on a collective agreement (the Pacto) between labor, employers, and the government. Thus, while in some cases initial wage increases were followed by a unilateral wage freeze in the public sector (eventually followed by further adjustments, such as in Bolivia), in other cases wage fixing and adjustments were based on a more or less implicit social contract between workers and the state (the cases of Argentina and Brazil) or an explicit agreement between workers, entrepreneurs, and the government, as in Israel and Mexico.

The behavior of real wages in disinflation programs in developing countries has received surprisingly little attention. Studies of exchange rate-based programs have tended to focus on explaining the behavior of output on the basis of intertemporal effects associated with consumption behavior, with little emphasis on the supply-side effects of stabilization. However, as noted by Agénor (1998a), the *long-term* effects of stabilization policy may depend on the nature of wage contracts. A reduction in the rate of nominal devaluation may lead in the long run to a contraction in output of tradables with backward-looking nominal wage contracts, but to an expansion in activity with forward-looking contracts.

The short-run dynamics of real wages in an exchange rate-based stabilization program also depend crucially on the nature of wage contracts. If nominal wage contracts are backward-looking, a reduction in price inflation would lead at first to an increase in the real wage followed by a gradual reduction over time, as contracts begin to reflect the lower path of the inflation rate. However, the initial increase in the real wage may exacerbate the costs associated with stabilization.[32] Indeed, a critical lesson from the experience of several Latin American countries in the early 1980s (Chile in particular) is that combining a fixed nominal exchange rate with backward-looking wage indexation in stabilization programs leads to inflation inertia and results in an accelerating real appreciation of the exchange rate, as well as an unsustainable widening of the current-account deficit, often culminating in a balance-of-payments crisis and an exchange-rate collapse.

If wage contracts are forward-looking, an anticipated future reduction in inflation that carries full credibility may lead either to an immediate fall in the real wage (if nominal wages are adjusted immediately to reflect the lower future path of prices) or a temporary increase in the real wage (if contracts cannot be renegotiated instantaneously). By contrast, if price and wage setters do not believe that the future

---

[32]The inverse relationship between the inflation rate and the real wage emerges only if the frequency of readjustments remains constant. If this frequency falls as a result of lower inflation, the correlation between prices and real wages may be positive.

reduction in prices will take place—for instance because the announcement of the future policy shift is not credible, or because agents expect the initial disinflation measures to be reversed in the future—nominal wages will not adjust, and the real wage may show little response. In fact, if future economic conditions are expected to deteriorate, the real wage may rise immediately—despite initial corrective measures.

A simple analytical model with backward- and forward-looking wage contracts helps to illustrate these ideas.[33] Suppose that the economy produces a nonstorable good, which is an imperfect substitute for the foreign good. Domestic output y is inversely related to the real product wage, $\omega = w/P$, where w denotes the nominal wage and P the price of the domestic good:

$$y = y(\omega), \quad y' < 0. \tag{29}$$

Consumption c depends positively on income and negatively on the expected *long-run* value of the relative price of the domestic good, z^*:

$$c = c(\overset{+}{y}, \overset{-}{z^*}), \quad 0 < c_y < 1. \tag{30}$$

The value z^* must be consistent with the relative price for which the market for domestic goods clears in the long run:

$$c[y(\bar{\omega}), z^*] = y(\bar{\omega}),$$

from which we have, using (29):

$$z^* = c_{z^*}^{-1}(1 - c_y)y'\bar{\omega} = \Phi(\bar{\omega}), \tag{31}$$

with $\Phi' > 0$. Thus, an increase in the long-run value of the real wage, by increasing excess demand for the domestic good (because it reduces output supply by more than it reduces consumption), leads to an increase in the long-run expected relative price.

Suppose that changes in the inflation rate π depend *positively* on excess demand for goods (in contrast to the Calvo-Végh model) and the rate of depreciation of the real exchange rate, given by the difference between the nominal depreciation rate and the inflation rate:

$$\dot{\pi} = \kappa(c - y) + \theta(\varepsilon - \pi), \tag{32}$$

where $\kappa, \theta > 0$.

---

[33]The analysis in Agénor (1998a) shows that short-run results qualitatively similar to those obtained here also hold in a (more complex) intertemporal setting.

The nominal wage w is set under two alternative contract mechanisms. Under the first scheme, wage contracts are backward-looking and depend only on past levels of prices:

$$w = \rho \int_{-\infty}^{t} e^{-\rho(t-k)} P_k dk,$$

where ρ is a discount rate. Differentiating this equation with respect to time yields

$$\dot{w} = -\rho(w - P). \tag{33}$$

Under the second scheme, nominal wage contracts are assumed to be forward-looking and to depend on future prices:

$$w = \rho \int_{t}^{\infty} e^{\rho(t-k)} P_k dk,$$

implying that

$$\dot{w} = \rho(w - P). \tag{34}$$

Given the definition of the real wage, its rate of change over time can be written, under backward-looking contracts, as

$$\dot{\omega}/\omega = -\rho \left(1 - \frac{1}{\omega}\right) - \pi,$$

and, under forward-looking wage contracts, as

$$\dot{\omega}/\omega = \rho \left(1 - \frac{1}{\omega}\right) - \pi.$$

The steady-state solution is characterized by $\dot{\omega} = \dot{\pi} = 0$ and goods-market equilibrium. Thus, under both types of contracts, inflation and the rate of growth of nominal wages must be equal to the devaluation in the long-run equilibrium. Taking a linear approximation around the steady state yields, with backward-looking contracts:

$$\begin{bmatrix} \dot{\omega} \\ \dot{\pi} \end{bmatrix} = \begin{bmatrix} -\rho/\tilde{\omega} & -\tilde{\omega} \\ \kappa(1 - c_y)y' & -\theta \end{bmatrix} \begin{bmatrix} \omega - \tilde{\omega} \\ \pi - \varepsilon \end{bmatrix} + \begin{bmatrix} 0 \\ \kappa c_{z^*}z^* + \theta\varepsilon \end{bmatrix}, \tag{35}$$

where $\tilde{\omega} = (1 + \varepsilon/\rho)^{-1}$ denotes the steady-state level of the real wage. With forward-looking contracts, the system is given by

$$\begin{bmatrix} \dot{\omega} \\ \dot{\pi} \end{bmatrix} = \begin{bmatrix} \rho/\tilde{\omega} & -\tilde{\omega} \\ \kappa(1 - c_y)y' & -\theta \end{bmatrix} \begin{bmatrix} \omega - \tilde{\omega} \\ \pi - \varepsilon \end{bmatrix} + \begin{bmatrix} 0 \\ \kappa c_{z^*}z^* + \theta\varepsilon \end{bmatrix}, \tag{36}$$

where $\tilde{\omega} = (1 - \varepsilon/\rho)^{-1}$.

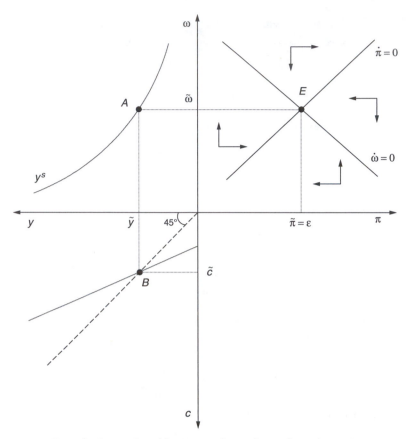

Figure 11–3 ▪ Steady-State Equilibrium with Backward-Looking Contracts

Stability of the dynamic system (35) with backward-looking contracts requires that the determinant of the matrix **A** of coefficients be positive, and that its trace be negative:

$$\det \mathbf{A} = \theta \rho / \bar{\omega} + \bar{\omega} \kappa (1 - c_y) y' > 0, \quad \mathbf{tr} \mathbf{A} = -(\theta + \rho / \bar{\omega}) < 0.$$

The first condition is satisfied if κ is not too large. In the system (36) with forward-looking contracts, given that the real wage is now a jump variable, saddlepath stability requires that the determinant of the matrix of coefficients be negative:

$$\det \mathbf{A} = -\theta \rho / \bar{\omega} + \bar{\omega} \kappa (1 - c_y) y' < 0.$$

This condition (which always holds) is interpreted graphically in Figure 11.4.

Figure 11.3 shows the long-run equilibrium of the model under backward-looking contracts. In the northeast panel, curve $\dot{\pi} = 0$ shows the combinations of the inflation rate and the real wage for which the inflation rate does not change over time, whereas curve $\dot{\omega} = 0$ shows the combinations of π and ω for which the

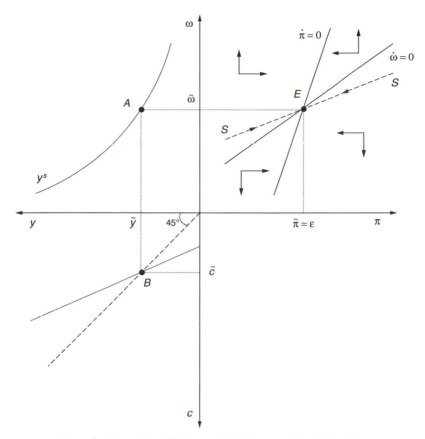

Figure 11–4 ▪ Steady-State Equilibrium with Forward-Looking Contracts

real wage does not change. Curve y^s in the northwest quadrant shows the inverse relationship between output and the real wage [equation (29)]. The consumption function [equation (30)] is represented in the southwest panel (for a given value of the long-run expected relative price z^*). The long-run equilibrium values of inflation and the real wage are obtained at point E, with output determined at point A and consumption (which equals output) determined at point B.

In a similar manner, Figure 11.4 shows the long-run equilibrium under forward-looking contracts. Curve $\dot{\omega} = 0$ is now upward-sloping in the northeast quadrant. Saddlepath stability $(\det \mathbf{A} < 0)$ requires that the curve $\dot{\pi} = 0$ be steeper than the curve $\dot{\omega} = 0$. The saddlepath, denoted SS, has a positive slope.

Consider now the effect of a disinflation program that takes the form of a permanent, unanticipated reduction in the devaluation rate, from ε^b to $\varepsilon^s < \varepsilon^b$. The dynamics under backward-looking contracts are shown in Figure 11.5. The curve $\dot{\pi} = 0$ shifts to the left. Neither inflation nor the real wage changes on impact. Whereas the real wage rises monotonically throughout the adjustment process (which takes the economy from point E to point E'), inflation either may fall

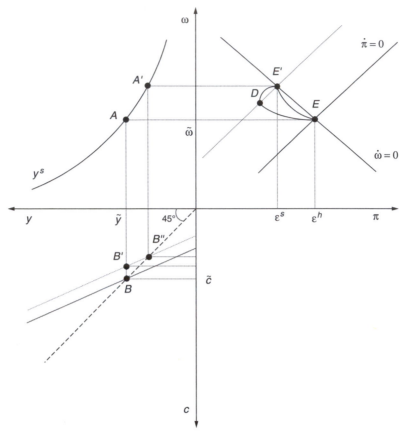

Figure 11–5 ■ Reduction in the Devaluation Rate with Backward-Looking Contracts

continuously or may fall at first and increase in a second stage. Mimicking the path of real wages, output falls continuously from point A to A' in the northwest quadrant. The expected long-run relative price z^* falls immediately to reflect the long-run increase in the real wage, thereby shifting the consumption function downward—in such a way that equilibrium of the market for domestic goods is maintained in the long run (point B''). The fall in consumption on impact (from point B to point B'), with output unchanged at its initial steady-state value, tends to create excess supply of domestic goods, thereby increasing the downward pressure on the inflation rate resulting from the reduction in the devaluation rate.

By contrast, with forward-looking contracts, agents discount the future reduction in inflation back to the present. As illustrated in Figure 11.6, the real wage jumps downward immediately to a point such as A on the new saddlepath $S'S'$ and continues to fall toward its lower steady-state level, which is also reached at E'. Inflation in this case always falls continuously. Mimicking again the path of real

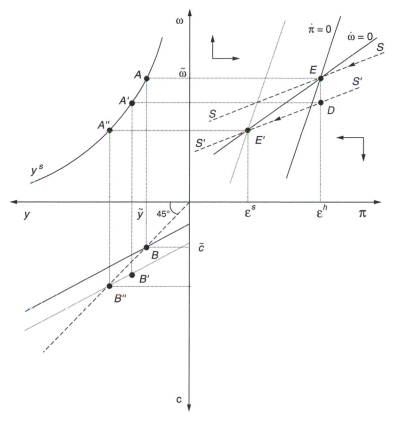

Figure 11–6 ■ Reduction in the Devaluation Rate with Forward-Looking Contracts

wages, output increases on impact from point *A* to *A'* in the northwest quadrant, and continues to increase until it reaches point *A''*. The expected long-run relative price z^* now increases to reflect the long-run reduction in the real wage, thereby shifting upward the consumption function (with consumption rising from point *B* to point *B'*) and ensuring that goods-market equilibrium holds in the long run (point *B''*). Here, because both consumption and output rise on impact, the net effect on excess demand cannot be determined a priori. If the sensitivity of consumption to the expected long-run relative price is sufficiently small, the net effect will be negative, thereby reinforcing the deflationary effect of the reduction in the devaluation rate on impact.

Thus, while the adjustment process to a cut in the devaluation rate leads to a gradual increase in real wages with backward-looking contracts, it leads to an initial downward jump followed by a continuous fall in real wages with forward-looking contracts. However, the evidence regarding the evolution of real wages in the exchange-rate-based stabilization programs reviewed in online Supplement B provides a mixed picture. At the inception of the tablita experiments of the late 1970s in Latin America, real wages either remained stable (Uruguay) or rose, whereas they fell in the heterodox experiments of the mid-1980s in Israel and Mexico.[34] The extent to which such movements can be viewed as reflecting backward- or forward-looking behavior and/or lack of credibility cannot be assessed without appropriate econometric methods. Unfortunately, despite the importance of this issue for stabilization policy, there have been very few attempts at estimating the degree to which wage formation is backward- or forward-looking in developing countries.

2 Role of Credibility in Disinflation Programs

The repeated failure of disinflation programs in developing countries has often been attributed to private agents' lack of confidence in the ability of governments to persevere in reform efforts and to maintain a consistent set of policies over time.[35] Moreover, a tradition of failed stabilization attempts suggests that the credibility problem each new anti-inflation program must confront becomes more severe over time, adding to the downward rigidities that characterize the inflationary process.

The most direct means policymakers can use to publicize their intention to refrain from adopting inflationary policies is, of course, to announce an inflation target. But because the inflation rate is not under the direct control of the authorities, an inflation target not linked to specific policy commitments that can be readily monitored will not be credible to private agents. Establishing the credibility of macroeconomic policies at the outset of a disinflation program is therefore crucial. By altering the formation of price expectations, a credible disinflation policy may substantially reduce the short- and medium-term output and employment costs of restrictive monetary and fiscal policies. For instance, a credible freeze of the exchange rate may reduce anticipations of future inflation, lower nominal interest rates, and consequently dampen the recessionary effect of a restrictive monetary policy. Establishing a reputation for responsible policymaking is particularly important in countries where failed stabilization attempts have created deep-rooted skepticism and a lack of confidence in the willingness or capacity of policymakers to reduce inflation.

A variety of mechanisms aimed at establishing or enhancing policy credibility and the reputation of policymakers have been considered. A key feature of this

---

[34] A sharp initial fall in real wages also occurred in many money-based programs, such as the program implemented in Bolivia in August 1985.

[35] The lack of policy credibility as a source of inflation persistence has been emphasized by various authors, including Blejer and Liviatan (1987), Dornbusch (1991), Sargent (1983), van Wijnbergen (1988), and Végh (1992). As discussed above, lack of credibility is also a key determinant of the short- and long-run dynamics associated with stabilization programs.

literature is that private agents interact strategically with policymakers and determine their behavior on the basis of their expectations about the likely course of current and future policies (Cukierman, 1992). The purpose of this section is to examine the implications of this literature for the formulation and design of disinflation programs in developing countries. The first part presents an overview of alternative sources of credibility problems. The second part examines alternative mechanisms aimed at alleviating such problems in stabilization programs, including the adoption of a shock therapy approach for signaling purposes, the use of price controls as an additional nominal anchor, increased central bank independence or adherence to a monetary union, and recourse to conditional foreign assistance. The concluding part summarizes the main policy implications of the analysis and provides some final remarks.

2.1 ■ Sources of Credibility Problems

A central notion that pervades the recent literature on macroeconomic policy credibility is that when the public lacks confidence in the ability of policymakers to carry out a newly announced stabilization program, disinflation becomes more difficult to achieve. However, "lack of confidence" and "imperfect credibility" have been defined in a variety of ways in the existing literature, depending in part on the issue under consideration. In the context of disinflation programs, the first important aspect of the credibility problem relates to the program itself, specifically, to the policy measures around which it is formulated and the degree to which they are consistent and sustainable. Other relevant aspects, which relate to policymakers' interactions with private agents, emerge as a result of various assumptions concerning the behavior and "characteristics" of those implementing an otherwise consistent program (such as the structure of policy preferences and the reputation of the policymakers themselves), the information structure, and the policy environment.

2.1.1 *Internal Inconsistency*

First, a credibility problem may emerge when the public perceives that a stabilization program is inconsistent with other policies being pursued simultaneously. A disinflation program that does not include measures to limit the public sector budget deficit will typically lack credibility because private agents will understand its inconsistent nature. The Brazilian Cruzado Plan implemented in 1986, for instance, lost credibility rapidly because private agents quickly realized the inflationary implications of the expansionary fiscal stance the authorities adopted at the outset (see Agénor and Taylor, 1993). In addition, inconsistencies in the *overall* formulation of an economic reform program or an inappropriate sequencing of policy measures may hurt the credibility of the stabilization effort, even if the components of the reform program are internally consistent.

2.1.2   *Time Inconsistency*

Second, the lack of credibility may result from a time-inconsistency dilemma faced by policymakers: their optimal ex post strategy may differ from their ex ante strategy. For instance, once nominal wages are set by the private sector, the authorities may find it tempting to disinflate less than they had promised to, in order to generate output gains (Barro and Gordon, 1983). This result obtains because the policymaker is concerned about both inflation and unemployment, and faces an expectations-augmented Phillips curve. The policymaker wants all agents to expect low inflation, in order to exploit a favorable trade-off between inflation and unemployment. But an announcement of a policy of low inflation is not credible. Once expectations are formed, the policymaker has an incentive to renege on the announcement in order to reduce unemployment. Private agents understand the incentive to renege and therefore do not believe the policy announcement in the first place.

A similar time-inconsistency problem emerges in a small open economy opting for a fixed exchange-rate arrangement, as discussed in Chapter 8. By fixing the exchange rate, and therefore the domestic price of tradable goods, the policymaker's aim is to reduce inflationary expectations embodied in prices set in the nontradable sector of the economy. However, price and wage setters understand the policymaker's incentive to deviate from the fixed exchange-rate announcement and to devalue the currency in order to depreciate the real exchange rate and stimulate output, and therefore will not fully believe the initial announcement.

The policymaker's incentive to inflate need not be based on employment considerations, as in the Barro-Gordon model. It may also arise as a result of the policymaker's desire to reduce the real value of the nominal public debt, or because of seigniorage considerations. A simple model that stresses the role of inflation in financing government deficits was developed by Barro (1983).[36] Suppose that the government's objective function takes the form

$$L = \theta \mu m^d(\pi^a) - \exp(\kappa_1 \pi + \kappa_2 \pi^a), \tag{37}$$

where all coefficients are defined as positive. μ denotes the rate of growth of the nominal money stock, π the actual rate of inflation, π^a the expected rate of inflation, $m^d(\cdot)$ money demand, and $\mu m^d(\cdot)$ revenue from money creation—that is, seigniorage (see Chapter 3). The first term in the loss function (37) represents the benefit the government derives from inflation, which is assumed to be proportional to revenue from money creation. The second term captures two different kinds of costs associated with inflation. The term in π reflects menu costs (that is, costs associated with changes in nominal prices) or costs associated with collection lags, resulting

---

[36]The formulation used in the subsequent analysis is adapted from Cukierman (1992). Similar models have been developed by Bruno (1991) and Kiguel and Liviatan (1994). Heymann and Sanguinetti (1994) consider explicitly the role of government spending and the Olivera-Tanzi effect in the determination of the optimal discretionary inflation rate.

from the Olivera-Tanzi effect discussed in Chapter 3. The term in π^a reflects the usual distortionary costs of perfectly anticipated inflation.

The demand for real money balances is of the Cagan type and is given by

$$m^d(\pi^a) = \exp(-\alpha\pi^a). \tag{38}$$

Once expectations are set, $m^d(\pi^a)$ is given and the money market equilibrium condition implies that $\pi = \mu$. The government's problem, then, is to maximize (37) subject to (38) with respect to μ.

We now consider two regimes: discretion and rules. Under discretion, the government is unable to convince private agents that it will follow a precise course of action in the future. Because it cannot make a binding commitment, it minimizes (37) subject to (38) with π^a given. The solution implied by this behavior is therefore given by

$$\theta \exp(-\alpha\pi^a) - \kappa_1 \exp(\kappa_1\pi + \kappa_2\pi^a) = 0.$$

In equilibrium, $\mu = \pi = \pi^a$, so that the solution is

$$\mu^D = \pi^D = (\alpha + \kappa_1 + \kappa_2)^{-1} \ln(\theta/\kappa_1) > 0. \tag{39}$$

The rates of inflation and monetary growth can therefore be higher than the seigniorage-maximizing rate $1/\alpha$ derived in Chapter 3, if θ/κ_1 is large enough.

In the "rules" regime, the government can make a binding—and therefore credible—commitment about its future behavior. It will therefore internalize the effect of its current decisions on future price expectations formed by private agents in choosing its optimal policy. Imposing the equilibrium condition $\pi = \pi^a$ in the loss function (37), the government's decision problem becomes

$$\max_{\mu} L = \theta\mu m^d(\mu) - \exp[(\kappa_1 + \kappa_2)\mu] \tag{40}$$

subject to (38). The solution yields, using the approximation $\ln(1 - \alpha\mu) \cong -\alpha\mu$ for $\alpha\mu$ small enough,

$$\mu^R = \pi^R = (2\alpha + \kappa_1 + \kappa_2)^{-1} \ln[\theta/(\kappa_1 + \kappa_2)], \tag{41}$$

which can be less than the revenue-maximizing rate $1/\alpha$. It is apparent from (39) and (41) that $\mu^D > \mu^R$, which implies that the inflation rate and the rate of monetary expansion are higher under discretion than under rules.[37] The reason is that, under

---

[37]It can also be shown that $L(\pi^D) - L(\pi^R) > 0$, which indicates that the rules regime is Pareto-superior to the discretionary regime.

rules, the government internalizes the consequences of its actions on the formation of private agents' expectations. By making a credible commitment to foresaking discretionary actions, the policymaker is able to dampen inflationary expectations and hence achieve lower inflation.

Thus, the general implication of models that highlight the time-inconsistency dilemma is that when policymakers have an ex post incentive to renege on their promises, rational agents will discount announcements of future policy actions or assurances regarding the continuation of present policies. Accordingly, inflation will be more difficult to reduce and will instead tend to display persistence over time.

2.1.3 Asymmetric Information

A third source of credibility problems is incomplete or asymmetric information about policymakers themselves: private agents may not be able to assess how serious the incumbents really are about fighting inflation (Barro, 1986). At the outset of a stabilization program, private agents do not entirely believe the authorities' commitment to disinflate, and need time to verify the new policy stance and assess the "true" intentions of policymakers. Imperfect information of this sort may be particularly prevalent in some developing countries, where policymakers tend to change rapidly, generating confusion about policy objectives and the preferences of the incumbents.

Imperfect monitoring abilities prevent private agents from detecting those preferences, unless the policymakers go public. If policymakers have the incentive to do so, they can exploit this informational advantage. The implication is, however, that imperfect monitoring capability reduces the scope for building reputation by policymakers, particularly if private agents learn only gradually, through a backward-induction process (see, for instance, Cukierman, 1992). Without a reputation for being "serious" or "tough," policymakers may find it difficult to dampen inflationary expectations.

2.1.4 Policy Uncertainty and Stochastic Shocks

A fourth source of credibility problems in disinflation programs is the uncertainty surrounding the policy environment and the predictability of policy measures. In a stochastic world, even if a program is coherently formulated and time consistent—in the sense that policymakers have no incentive to depart ex post from the preannounced policy measures—exogenous shocks large enough to throw the program "off track" may occur (Dornbusch, 1991; Orphanides, 1992). Under such circumstances, reputable policymakers may not be able to dampen price expectations and bring credibility to a stabilization program, because of the high probability that large shocks will force them to deviate from their targets. Such shocks may be external in nature (such as sharp changes in a country's terms of trade or world interest rates) but may also result from the policy environment itself, especially when the authorities have imperfect control over policy instruments. For instance, the announcement of a fiscal target will not be fully credible if the government does not adequately control the level of government expenditure, if tax revenues are subject to considerable variability, induced by either deterministic or stochastic factors (such as seasonal patterns or abrupt weather changes). Private agents will understand the implications of this lack of control over policy instruments and will accordingly assess the probability that the policy target will not be met.[38] The lower the degree of precision in the manipulation of policy instruments, the more likely it is that private agents will anticipate the possibility of a future collapse of the stabilization effort, and the more rigid downward the inflation rate will usually be. Thus, the lack of policy predictability may create doubts about the sustainability of the reform process and affect the degree of credibility of an otherwise consistent and viable program.

2.1.5 *Political Uncertainty*

Finally, a credibility problem may emerge when the public perceives that policymakers will be unable to implement their program because its political base may crumble, as may occur when the government is built on a coalition of parties with different ideological orientations or when the government's legitimacy is in doubt. Although private agents may believe in the government's economic objectives and policy intentions, they will also evaluate the political feasibility of potentially painful macroeconomic reforms. The less cohesive political forces are, or the greater the strength of vested interests, the more severe the credibility problem. Moreover, lack of political consensus will often lead agents to expect policy reversals. This uncertainty about future policies, in turn, has drastic implications for the long-term effects of stabilization plans. Strategies believed to be sustainable are likely to elicit both economic and political responses that will reinforce the reform process, while strategies believed to be reversible will have the opposite effect.

In practice, it has proved difficult to provide evidence, even retroactively, regarding the particular type of credibility problem a given program or policymaker faces. Most researchers have worked under the general premise that a credible disinflation program will translate into a change in the process driving a key variable (prices, money demand, nominal wages, or interest rates, for instance), while a program that lacks credibility will often have no discernible effect.[39] Although there has been some substantial methodological progress,[40] the paucity of robust quantitative techniques creates serious problems in gauging the practical importance of alternative sources of

---

[38] In a sense, the lack of credibility results from the inability of policymakers to precommit to particular actions in response to different states of the environment. Although, in principle, fully contingent mechanisms might eliminate this source of credibility problem, in practice they are hard to formulate.

[39] This assertion does not necessarily hold. In exchange-rate-based stabilization programs, as argued by Calvo and Végh (1993*b*) and Végh (1992), lack of credibility may translate initially into large real effects, rather than a sharp reduction in inflation.

[40] See Agénor and Taylor (1993) for a discussion of alternative methods.

credibility problems and makes it difficult to devise appropriate policy responses or undertake corrective measures. These practical difficulties, however, make it all the more important to strengthen the design of disinflation programs.

2.2 ■ Enhancing the Credibility of Disinflation Programs

A variety of proposals have been made for enhancing credibility in the context of disinflation programs. One line of inquiry has focused on ways to increase the credibility (or, in this case, the consistency) of the reform program itself by devising appropriate contingency clauses. The second and broader line has focused on ways to increase the reputation of the policymakers implementing the program. This subsection deals primarily with the second line of investigation, discussing the conceptual basis of some of these proposals and evaluating their practical policy implications. First, the appropriateness of a shock therapy approach to stabilization as a way to signal the policymakers' *type* to the public and build their reputation is examined. The role of price controls as an additional nominal anchor is then discussed. Third, institutional reforms, such as an increase in the degree of autonomy of the central bank or adhesion to a monetary union, are evaluated. Finally, the role of external agencies and conditional foreign assistance in alleviating the lack of credibility is discussed.[41]

2.2.1 *Signaling and Sustainability*

It is often argued that policymakers must make a sharp break with the past to demonstrate their commitment to price stabilization (Rodrik, 1989). This means that the authorities not only must refrain from accommodating inflation at the outset in order to sustain the stabilization effort (and eventually to succeed in controlling inflation), but that they may have to take more drastic measures than they would otherwise choose. Such a course of action may be all the more necessary when a series of unsuccessful attempts has rendered the public highly skeptical about the policymakers' ability and commitment to disinflate, or when the private sector has no yardstick for evaluating policymakers' actions. In such cases, "biting the bullet" by accepting a recession can be perceived by the private sector as a test of the authorities' determination to maintain low inflation (Vickers, 1986). In an economy where inflation is fueled by monetary financing of excessive government spending,

---

[41] The discussion throughout focuses on countries where policymakers must deal with high inflation, rather than hyperinflation. Kiguel and Liviatan (1992) have argued that credibility is easier to establish in the latter case. In chronic-inflation countries, where inertial mechanisms, such as staggered contracts, and implicit or explicit indexation, are well developed, the public tends to view disinflation programs as postponable, thus reducing their credibility. By contrast, the very nature of hyperinflation often leads private agents to believe that the process is not sustainable.

an overadjustment in the fiscal sector can also provide an important signal about the authorities' commitment to keep the budget deficit under control.[42]

However, using overly restrictive monetary and fiscal policies in an attempt to convey signals about the preferences of policymakers to the public may exacerbate the credibility problem, instead of helping to alleviate it. First, excessively harsh policy measures may create expectations that such decisions are not sustainable and will eventually be reversed. As discussed in more detail below, overadjustment (excessive cuts in public spending, for instance) may increase unemployment and undermine political support for painful reforms. Second, if uncertainty about incumbent policymakers relates to their ability to commit themselves to preannounced policies (and not to the authorities' relative concern for output expansion), the optimal behavior may be to partially accommodate inflationary expectations rather than adopt an overly restrictive monetary policy stance (Cukierman and Liviatan, 1991). In effect, when there is a perceived probability that the incumbent government may deviate from its preannounced policy stance, inflationary expectations are subject to an upward bias; because policymakers (whether viewed as "weak" or "strong") dislike recessions, it is optimal for the incumbents to partially accommodate these expectations.[43] Similarly, even in the absence of uncertainty about policymakers themselves, the existence of labor contracts with backward-looking wage indexing clauses may lead to partial accommodation (De Gregorio, 1995). More generally, the signaling argument for a "big bang" approach to stabilization rests on the assumption that the behavior of policymakers depends primarily on their policy preferences, that is, the weight they attach to price stability relative to output. In practice, however, policy decisions are also affected by the state of the economy, which depends in turn on the overall policy stance. To the extent that the output loss associated with a shock therapy approach has an adverse effect on the reelection prospects of the incumbent policymakers, it may weaken credibility by raising the expectation that actual policies will be relaxed eventually (Blanchard, 1985). Even a "tough" policymaker cannot ignore the cost associated with high unemployment, particularly when policies have persistent effects (Drazen and Masson, 1994).

In an environment where reforms create severe short-term costs for large segments of the population, there are temptations to reverse—or at least deviate from—the initial program objectives, particularly when incumbents cannot easily precommit (as in democratic regimes) future governments to a specific path of adjustment. Even if price stabilization is in the country's long-run interest, shortsightedness (such

---

[42]The imposition of price controls and the appointment of a "conservative" central banker (options to be discussed further) have also been advocated as signaling mechanisms. Only the use of orthodox policy instruments for signaling purposes is considered for the present.

[43]In addition, when the perceived characteristics (that is, policy preferences) of policymakers differ widely across the different "types," signaling simply may not be the optimal strategy (Andersen, 1989). Even if such characteristics are not too dissimilar, signaling in Vickers's (1986) framework may still not be optimal. This applies particularly when policymakers heavily discount future gains and do not find it worthwhile to bear the immediate costs of a sharper disinflation policy.

as the exclusive concern of the incumbents with their reelection prospects) may induce policymakers to alter or abandon their initial reform program.

Moreover, in the context of stabilization plans where fiscal deficits are the root cause of inflation, signaling options may be more limited than is often thought. In such cases, structural fiscal reforms (such as broadening the tax system, privatizing public enterprises, or altering the distribution of public sector wages and salaries to enhance control of government spending) are often called for to make attempts at controlling the fiscal deficit credible. But such reforms cannot be implemented overnight, and can only slowly enhance credibility.

It is the persistence over time that matters in establishing the reputation of policymakers, rather than the degree of restrictiveness of the policy measures implemented at the outset of a stabilization program. Macroeconomic adjustment measures that are not regarded as politically and economically sustainable (within the limits imposed by a democratic regime) cannot be credible and may lead to self-fulfilling failure (Buffie, 1998). A critical element in ensuring sustainability is the proper sequencing of stabilization measures in the context of the overall reform effort in an attempt to minimize the distortions that often accompany such programs. For instance, in some cases microeconomic adjustment and institutional changes may need to precede macroeconomic policy reforms to ensure that the overall reform strategy is consistent and to convey credibility to the stabilization package. The proper sequencing of policy actions in the structural and macroeconomic spheres may prove crucial in convincing private agents that stabilization will eventually be achieved. To some extent, ensuring the irreversibility of macroeconomic reforms ensures their sustainability. Sequencing adjustment measures in such a way to make it costly for future policymakers to reverse decisions already undertaken by a reform-minded government enhances the credibility of a disinflation program.

2.2.2 *Price Controls*

The evidence reviewed in online Supplement B indicates that price controls have been used repeatedly (in fact, since the early 1960s) in disinflation programs implemented in developing countries, despite their well-known microeconomic costs.[44] A typical argument provided by policymakers—or their advisors—for the use of price ceilings is the notion that the persistence of inflation results from the existence of lagged wage indexation and backward-looking expectations. The presence of inertial factors means that attempts to combat inflation exclusively through restrictive monetary and fiscal policies will lead to strong recessive effects, which make it impossible for such policies to be continued beyond the short term. More recent theoretical arguments, however, justify the temporary use of price controls as a "transition" mechanism to a low-inflation equilibrium (Bruno and Fischer, 1990), as a coordination device (Dornbusch and Simonsen, 1988), as a way to secure political

---

[44]Depending on market structure, however, price controls may lead to an expansion in output in the short run, as emphasized by Helpman (1988). See the Appendix to this chapter for a discussion of this result.

gains and generate political support (Jonung, 1990), and—most in line with our interest here—as a way to enhance credibility.[45]

The use of price controls (in addition to the money supply or the exchange rate) as a nominal anchor for enhancing credibility has been emphasized by Blejer and Liviatan (1987) and Persson and van Wijnbergen (1993). In Blejer and Liviatan's analysis, the lack of credibility stems from the severe asymmetry of the information available to the public and that held by policymakers. At the outset of a stabilization program, private agents do not entirely believe the authorities' commitment to disinflate, and need time to verify the new policy stance. A price freeze gives policymakers a period during which they can convince the public—by adopting, and sticking to, restrictive monetary and fiscal policies—of the seriousness of their policy targets.[46] Persson and van Wijnbergen provide a game-theoretic analysis of the mechanisms that enable controls to assist in establishing credibility, building on the signaling model developed by Vickers (1986). In their framework, policymakers must signal their willingness to accept a recession in order to gain credibility that they will not resort to inflationary measures or give in to pressure to reverse their policy stance. The temporary use of price and wage controls (in addition to a restrictive monetary policy) allows policymakers to reduce the cost of signaling their commitment to disinflate.

The most frequently cited example of a successful application of price controls is the Israeli stabilization of 1985, during which all nominal variables—including the exchange rate—were frozen (see online Supplement B). In addition to a sharp fiscal contraction (including a cut in subsidies) and an up-front devaluation, the government announced not only a credit freeze but also its intention to maintain the exchange rate fixed, with the understanding that the unions would temporarily suspend COLA clauses and freeze wages for a few months. Agreement on the latter was, in turn, made conditional on the introduction of price ceilings. The tripartite agreement between the government, employers, and trade unions formed the basis for a sharp reduction in inflation. The short-run gains, in terms of a quick reduction in inflation and enhanced government credibility resulting from the successful application of price controls, outweighed the distortions created by the price ceilings.[47]

In addition to the many practical problems associated with the imposition and removal of price controls (such as the enforcement mechanism and the length of

---

[45] Kiguel and Liviatan (1992), for instance, have argued that in high-inflation economies, staggered price setting is not the prime cause of persistence. In such economies, contracts are of a very short duration and are highly synchronized. Inertia, in their view, stems mainly from credibility and coordination problems.

[46] By bringing the rate of inflation down quickly, price and wage controls lead to an improvement in the fiscal deficit in real terms (as a result of a reverse Olivera-Tanzi effect), adding credibility to the fiscal component of adjustment.

[47] Bruno (1991) argued that the freeze of all nominal variables, other than the exchange rate, was short-lived and that significant changes in relative prices took place only a few months after the initial shock, primarily a real wage increase and a real appreciation. Yet the authorities were successful in maintaining a lower inflation rate, suggesting that the signaling of serious intentions and precommitment by the government constituted the most important benefit of the synchronized freeze in the early stage of the stabilization effort.

the flexibilization stage), the debate on whether price controls improve credibility is far from settled. In the Blejer-Liviatan (1987) framework, for instance, the use of price and wage controls can be counterproductive, because a freeze does not enable the public to learn whether sufficient fiscal restraint has been achieved, that is, whether inflation has really been stopped or has only been temporarily repressed. In fact, controls may lengthen the time required for expectations to adjust to a new equilibrium. In addition, the credibility-enhancing effect of price controls may vanish if policymakers are unwilling or unable to control all prices in the economy, and if forward-looking price setters in the "free," uncontrolled sector understand the incentives to depart from a preannounced price control policy in an attempt to reduce the macroeconomic costs associated with a price freeze (Agénor, 1995). Paradoxically, the imposition of price controls in such a framework may lead to inflation inertia.

To illustrate this result, consider an economy that produces a large number of homogeneous goods, a proportion of which (such as goods produced by public enterprises) are subject to direct price controls by the policymaker. As discussed in Helpman (1988) and van Wijnbergen (1988), the economy possesses noncompetitive markets and price-setting firms in the "free" sector. The policymaker, who faces an incentive to reduce inflation through the imposition of direct price controls, has an informational advantage over the private sector—due, for instance, to a better monitoring capacity—and sets controlled prices *after* the realization of shocks to the economy. A reduction in the rate of inflation is assumed to increase political support while the deadweight loss from excess demand—resulting from misallocation and resources devoted to nonprice rationing—reduces support, because aggregate real income is reduced. Price ceilings are chosen so as to maximize political support from holding prices down, against the opposition resulting from this deadweight loss. When prices are set below equilibrium, there are incentives for sellers to evade controls, so the policymaker must enforce the ceilings—at a nonprohibitive cost—to make them effective. Firms in the uncontrolled or free sector restrain price increases, beyond the expected increase in controlled prices, to avoid more stringent controls in the future.

Let p^c denote the logarithm of an index of the subset of prices set by the policymaker in period t, and let $\tilde{p}^c \geq p^c$ be the equilibrium price, that is, the market-clearing price in the absence of price controls. The deadweight loss D due to price ceilings—the loss of (Marshallian) consumer and producer surpluses when excess demand and nonprice rationing result in a misallocation or waste of resources—can be approximated by

$$D = \eta(p^c - \tilde{p}^c)^2, \quad \eta > 0, \tag{42}$$

which assumes that the deadweight loss is greater the larger the (squared) deviation between actual and equilibrium prices.[48] The rate of change of the market-clearing

---

[48]This type of measure, however, provides only a lower bound on the deadweight loss because it assumes that quantities produced at controlled prices are obtained by the consumers who value them most, and because it excludes the cost of resources devoted to nonprice rationing.

price is assumed to be determined by

$$\tilde{\pi}_c = c + \upsilon, \tag{43}$$

where $\tilde{\pi}_c \equiv \tilde{p}^c - p^c_{-1}$, c is a constant term, and υ a stochastic demand shock, which is assumed to be serially uncorrelated with zero mean and constant variance. The probability distribution from which υ is drawn is assumed to be common knowledge.

Price setters in the "free" sector set prices p^f so as to protect their relative position and without knowing the realized value of υ, so that

$$\pi_f \equiv p^f - p^f_{-1} = E_{-1}\pi_c, \tag{44}$$

where $E_{-1}x$ denotes the conditional expectation of x based on information available up to the end of time $t - 1$.[49]

Setting $\pi \equiv p - p_{-1}$, the rate of change of the domestic price level can be defined by

$$\pi = \delta\pi_c + (1-\delta)\pi_f, \quad 0 \le \delta \le 1, \tag{45}$$

where δ denotes the intensity of price controls, that is, the proportion of goods on which the authorities impose price controls.

Whereas agents in the flexible-price sector set prices without knowing the realized value of the demand shock, the policymaker sets controlled prices *after* observing the shock. The policymaker is assumed to use controlled prices to offset some of the effect of υ on the deadweight loss—for instance, by unexpectedly raising these prices when υ turns out to be positive.

The policymaker's preferences entail a trade-off between inflation and the deadweight loss resulting from excess demand and price controls. Specifically, the policymaker aims at minimizing the expected loss function

$$L = E(D + \theta\pi^2), \quad \theta > 0,$$

or, using (42) and (43),

$$L = E[\eta(\pi_c - \tilde{\pi}_c - \upsilon)^2 + \theta\pi^2]. \tag{46}$$

Under discretion, the policymaker chooses a rate of increase of controlled prices such that the difference between political support resulting from a reduction in the inflation rate and political opposition resulting from the deadweight loss is maximized. Formally, π_c is chosen in each period so as to minimize (46) subject to (45),

---

[49]The information set up to $t - 1$ is common to the policymaker and the private sector and is assumed to include all relevant data on the policymaker's incentives and constraints.

without regard to the announced policies, and with private sector expectations taken as given. In the discretionary regime, the rate of change of controlled prices is therefore given by

$$\pi_c = \frac{\eta}{\eta + \delta^2 \theta} \left\{ \tilde{\pi}_c + \upsilon - \frac{\delta \theta (1 - \delta)}{\eta} \pi_f \right\}. \tag{47}$$

Equation (47) indicates that, under discretion, the reaction function of the policymaker calls for setting controlled prices at a level below the equilibrium level, leading to a deadweight loss. The reason for this is, of course, the inflationary cost of an increase in controlled prices. The degree of accommodation of demand shocks is inversely related to the relative inflation-aversion coefficient θ/η. Also, the higher the (predetermined) level of prices in the free sector, the lower the rate of change of controlled prices.

Consider now the case (referred to as the "commitment" regime in what follows) in which the policymaker adopts a price-setting rule that takes the form[50]

$$\pi_c = \phi_0 \tilde{\pi}_c + \phi_1 \upsilon. \tag{48}$$

The authorities select values of ϕ_0 and ϕ_1 that minimize the unconditional expectation (46) subject to (48) and, from (44) and (48), $\pi_f = E_{-1}\pi_c = \phi_0 \tilde{\pi}_c$. The optimal values can be shown to be[51]

$$\phi_0 = \eta/(\eta + \theta), \quad \phi_1 = \eta/(\eta + \delta^2 \theta), \tag{49}$$

where $\phi_0 > 0$, and $\phi_1 < 1$. A comparison of (47) and (49) shows that under rule (48) the policymaker accommodates demand shocks to the same extent as under discretion, but systematic changes in the equilibrium price are accommodated to a lesser extent. This is because, under commitment, the policymaker can infer the endogenous response of price setters in the free sector through price expectations.

The (ex post) mean value of the inflation rate in the commitment regime is given by

$$E\pi = \phi_0 \tilde{\pi}_c + \phi_1 \delta \upsilon,$$

and the (unconditional) expected loss is

$$L^C = [\eta(\phi_1 - 1)^2 + \theta(\delta\phi_1)^2]\sigma_\upsilon^2 + [\eta(\phi_0 - 1)^2 + \theta\phi_0^2]\tilde{\pi}_c^2, \tag{50}$$

where σ_υ^2 denotes the variance of υ.

---

[50] In a linear-quadratic setting such as the one considered here, the optimal rule will also be linear as in (48).

[51] Note that the choice of the policy rule is assumed to be made before the realization of the demand shock, although the actual level of controlled prices is set after observing υ.

Under discretion, controlled prices are set by (47). Under rational expectations, the optimal solution is such that

$$\pi_f = \kappa \bar{\pi}_c, \quad 0 < \kappa < 1, \tag{51}$$

$$\pi_c = \kappa \bar{\pi}_c + \lambda \upsilon, \quad 0 < \lambda < 1, \tag{52}$$

where $\lambda = \eta/(\eta + \delta^2\theta) = \phi_1$ and $\kappa = \eta/(\eta + \delta\theta)$.[52] Under both discretion and commitment, a complete price freeze ($\pi_c = 0$) is optimal when the weight on inflation in the policymaker's loss function is very high, that is, $\theta \to \infty$.

The (ex post) mean value of the inflation rate under discretion is given by

$$E\pi = \kappa \bar{\pi}_c + \lambda \delta \upsilon,$$

with an (unconditional) expected loss given by

$$L^D = [\eta(\lambda - 1)^2 + \theta(\delta\lambda)^2]\sigma_\upsilon^2 + [\eta(\kappa - 1)^2 + \theta\kappa^2]\bar{\pi}_c^2. \tag{53}$$

A comparison of (53) and (50) shows that, because $\kappa > \phi_0$, $L^D > L^C$. The nature of this result can be explained as follows. Unless there is a binding arrangement forcing the policymaker to adjust prices so as to maintain equality between supply and demand, there exists a temptation to lower controlled prices below their equilibrium level in order to dampen inflationary expectations and reduce overall inflation. However, once the demand shock is realized, expectations are formed, and prices are set in the rest of the economy, the policymaker has an incentive to raise controlled prices and reduce the deadweight loss—or political cost—associated with the ceilings. Private agents understand this incentive and will expect the authorities to follow the discretionary regime, no matter what regime is announced. As a result, in equilibrium prices in the uncontrolled sector are set at a higher level than they would be if the commitment regime was fully credible—at $\kappa \bar{\pi}_c$ instead of $\phi_0 \bar{\pi}_c$ [(51)]. Inflation is therefore higher under imperfect credibility and entails an additional policy loss.[53]

The above result helps explain why inflation may remain positive under a partial freeze. The conventional explanation of this phenomenon follows the lines of Paus (1991), who considers Peru's experience during the Emergency Plan implemented

---

[52]Note that π_f in (51) differs from π_c in (52) only by the last term, since demand shocks cannot be anticipated by price setters in the flexible price sector. They fully take into account the systematic component of the price control policy, which implies that the policymaker's objective of reducing the deadweight loss creates only inflation and no real gains.

[53]This result assumes that the rule followed in the commitment regime is the outcome of an optimization process. If the authorities adopt an ad hoc rule—of the type $\pi_c = 0$, for instance—there will be no reason, in general, for the private sector to suspect that the authorities will depart from it, since the optimization process, from which the incentive to renege stems, has been eschewed. The outcome of this is thus unclear and may not yield any definite ranking between "commitment" and "discretionary" regimes. However, because the policymaker has chosen a policy arbitrarily, private agents will eventually realize that there is nothing preventing the choice of a different policy in an equally arbitrary way in the future.

in 1985–1986. In her view, the attempt to slow down inflation by holding back adjustments in government-determined prices led to a growing deficit of the non-financial public sector. The increase in the deficit had an expansionary effect on money supply, which maintained inflationary pressures. The rationale proposed here, by contrast, does not rely on the existence of an accommodative monetary stance. Price setters in the "free" sector understand the incentive that the policymaker has to raise controlled prices after private sector pricing decisions are taken—the reduction in the deadweight loss that ceilings entail. Therefore, they raise prices by more than they would have had they been convinced of the policymaker's commitment to the preannounced price rule. Consequently, the extent of "inflation inertia" results from the lack of credibility of price ceilings, and is in general inversely related to the proportion of prices subject to control.[54,55]

If the policymaker could make a binding commitment to a price-setting rule in the controlled sector, inflation would be lower under a partial freeze. However, unilateral commitments usually lack credibility. Along the lines of our discussion in Chapter 8 on exchange-rate policy, mechanisms that entail reputational forces (and "punishment" strategies) may provide a commitment technology that could alleviate the time-inconsistency problem discussed above, and may provide a substitute for a binding agreement.

In practice, price controls have often been used as a substitute for, rather than a complement to, monetary and fiscal adjustment, as in the populist programs reviewed in online Supplement B. While price controls have often been effective in bringing down inflation quickly in the short run, in many cases the initial success has proved difficult to sustain, due to a lack of persistence in macroeconomic policy reforms. Private agents have quickly realized that attempts to legislate prices down would not be very effective, and this has often led to a rapid resurgence of inflation. In Argentina, Brazil, and Peru, experiments with stabilization packages involving wage and price controls during the 1980s failed largely because of the policymakers' inability to sustain the fiscal and monetary discipline required to make the short-run drop in inflation sustainable. Under Alan García in Peru, wage and price controls were used as substitutes for, rather than complements to, more orthodox measures. Real wages were allowed to rise substantially, and there was little success in bringing public spending under control. When pressure on prices ultimately forced the relaxation of controls, a new spiral of inflation began. Brazil provides a similar example. As documented in online Supplement B, the authorities implemented three anti-inflation programs in the late 1980s that relied to an important extent on price

---

[54]As a result, $\partial(L^D - L^C)/\partial\delta < 0$. Note that, from (49), (51), and (52), under a complete freeze $\delta = 1$ and $\phi_0 = \kappa$, so that the discretionary and commitment regimes yield the same outcome. This follows trivially from the fact that, with comprehensive ceilings, the inflationary bias of a discretionary regime disappears.

[55]Agénor (1995) shows, in addition, that the intensity of price controls can be chosen so as to minimize the loss associated with a discretionary monetary policy. But this results in the effective imposition of price ceilings only if the cost of enforcing them is not too high, or if the weight attached to price distortions in the policymaker's loss function is sufficiently small.

controls: the Cruzado Plan in 1986, the Bresser Plan in 1987, and the Verano Plan in 1989. However, because the price freeze was not accompanied by adequate macroeconomic policy reforms, the rate of inflation jumped after a brief period of reduced inflation. After the collapse of the Bresser and Verano plans, inflation came back with a vengeance, leading many observers to conclude that the repeated use of price controls had diminished their effectiveness, as economic agents were able to anticipate the price increases that would follow the flexibilization stage.

2.2.3   *Central Bank Independence*

A possible way for policymakers facing credibility problems to demonstrate their capacity for and unequivocal commitment to reform is to appoint a "conservative" central banker with a well-known dislike for inflation, and whose day-to-day control over monetary policy is relatively free from political pressure or interference from key ministers in the incumbent government (Rogoff, 1989). An independent central bank with a clear and well-publicized mandate to maintain price stability provides an institutional mechanism that may reduce incentives to deviate from rules.

A similar idea, discussed in Chapter 8, is for a high-inflation country to join a monetary union with a fixed exchange-rate mechanism and surrender the power to conduct an independent monetary policy. By transferring its monetary and exchange-rate policy autonomy to a reputable central bank, a high-inflation country can "borrow" credibility and thus signal its own commitment to price stability, thereby reducing—relative to a purely domestic strategy—the cost of disinflation measured in terms of output and employment losses. In the context of developing countries, where central bank financing of fiscal deficits is often the root cause of inflation, this argument carries considerable weight.[56]

Appointment of an independent central banker may remove the temptation to rely on monetary expansion to secure a short-term output gain, reduce the incentive to rely on the inflation tax, and "force" the government to implement fiscal reform.[57] In addition, the political difficulties associated with stabilization programs may be less severe when the policymaking decision process is relatively centralized and insulated from pressures from various interest groups. This argument helps to emphasize the importance of institutional reforms in enhancing the credibility of macroeconomic adjustment programs.

Several empirical studies have shown that central bank independence contributes significantly to explaining cross-country variations in the rate of inflation. Countries with central banks enjoying the highest degree of autonomy seem to have the lowest levels and variability of inflation, although this should not necessarily

---

[56]The evidence presented by Cukierman (1992) suggests that there has been a substantial degree of accommodation of inflation in the behavior of central bank credit in developing countries, compared with industrial countries.

[57]Note that, as argued by McCallum (1997), it is not necessarily appropriate to presume that central banks will, in the absence of any tangible precommitment technology, inevitably behave in a "discretionary" fashion that implies an inflationary bias.

reflect a causal relationship.[58] Institutional reforms aimed at enhancing central bank autonomy have been implemented in a number of countries in the past two decades.

However, the extent to which policymakers should "tie their hands" by appointing a reputable anti-inflation central banker (or policymaker) to convince the public of their commitment to carrying out a domestic disinflation program remains a subject of controversy. Central bank independence is only one of several institutional devices that can be implemented to ensure price stability and enhance the credibility of macroeconomic policy. Although replacing discretionary actions with a rule-based policy framework implemented by an independent (domestic or foreign) central bank may help reduce the perception of arbitrariness and thereby strengthen confidence in the policymaking process, the signaling effect of such a change in the policy regime may be weak if secrecy prevails in the institution's day-to-day operations. Moreover, if the quality of fiscal institutions (as measured by the government's ability to collect revenue through formal tax channels) is weak, appointing a Rogoff-style conservative central banker may do little good for the credibility of the overall macroeconomic policy framework (Huang and Wei, 2006).

More important, perhaps, adhering to the rigid rules implemented by a domestic or foreign central bank may lead to suboptimal outcomes (compared with contingent rules) in an economy subject to random shocks. The trade-off between credibility and flexibility emphasized by Drazen and Masson (1994) and Neut and Velasco (2004), for instance, implies that appointing a more conservative central banker, as suggested by Rogoff, may actually lower credibility and raise expectations of inflation. Escape clauses for discretionary actions may be necessary, although extreme care must be taken in defining the conditions under which such clauses should be triggered, in order to avoid negative side effects.[59]

It it also worth noting that, as pointed out by Stella (2005), central bank credibility depends in part on the bank's financial strength. In many developing countries, however, central banks often lack sufficient capital; in such conditions, recapitalization may often be a key step to enhance credibility.

Finally, as emphasized by Swinburne and Castello-Blanco (1991), central bank independence cannot, by itself, guarantee the credibility of monetary policy. This depends on the overall stance of macroeconomic policy. For instance, if the fiscal policy adopted by the ministry of finance is viewed as inconsistent with the monetary institution's disinflation target, credibility is impossible to achieve, even with an independent central bank.

---

[58] See Cukierman (1992), the overview by Hayo and Hefeker (2002), and the updated results by Dincer and Eichengreen (2014). Central bank independence in empirical studies is measured in terms of a variety of factors, including the appointment mechanisms for the governor and the board of directors, the turnover of central bank governors, the approval mechanism for conducting monetary policy (the extent to which the central bank is free from involvement from the government or parliament), statutory requirements of the central bank regarding its basic aim and financing of the budget deficit (including whether or not interest rates are levied on deficit financing), and the existence of a ceiling on total government borrowing from the central bank.

[59] See Lohmann (1992) and the discussion in Chapters 8 and 14.

2.2.4   *External Enforcement and Foreign Assistance*

Requests for foreign assistance have traditionally been viewed as the result of a need to generate financial resources and, to a lesser extent, of the existence of cross-conditionality clauses in some bilateral agreements. It has been recognized subsequently that credibility problems may also be an important element in explaining why countries engaged in stabilization programs may seek the involvement of foreign institutions and subject themselves to external enforcement. By making foreign assistance conditional on specific policy targets, policymakers may be able to enhance their reputation. An external agent with a reputation for being "tough" can provide a commitment mechanism for enforcing programs, increase private agents' confidence in the intentions of the authorities, and—by increasing, through the threat of sanctions, the cost of deviating from a prespecified inflation target—help reduce inflation (Cukierman and Liviatan, 1992). In a sense, this argument simply extends the conservative banker approach discussed above, and is therefore related to the signaling argument underlying the shock therapy approach to macroeconomic reforms. The difference here is that conditionality wields a threat—no support for restructuring the country's external debt, for instance—that can strengthen the determination of the policymakers to enforce the agreement.[60] An external agency can sustain an effective threat beyond the probable life of a single government, and can also enforce a worse outcome compared with an appointed central banker if the agreement collapses.

Dornbusch and Fischer (1986) have emphasized that, in the pre–World War II stabilization episodes, foreign loans—or the prospect of receiving them—served more as a signal than as an inherent necessity. Typical examples are the loan by the League of Nations to Austria in 1922 and the Polish loan of 1927. Recent formal evidence supports the existence of a credibility factor in explaining why governments relied on foreign enforcement during the stabilization programs implemented in European countries in the 1920s (Santaella, 1993). Regarding recent stabilization episodes, it has been argued that one of the factors that helped to establish quickly the credibility of the 1985 Israeli program was the increase in U.S. foreign aid, which raised the public's confidence in the program in general and, in particular, in the government's ability to peg the exchange rate and successfully withstand possible speculative attacks against the Israeli currency (Cukierman, 1988; Patinkin, 1993).

However, a variety of potential difficulties arise in judging the credibility-enhancing effect of foreign assistance. First, political considerations are often perceived (rightly or wrongly) as playing a critical role in deciding whether particular countries should receive external financial support. As a result, the enforcement mechanism that foreign assistance provides may be insufficient to help domestic private agents assess the policymakers' "type," that is, whether policymakers are genuinely concerned about meeting their disinflation target. Second, by relaxing

---

[60]Foreign assistance is usually contingent on a series of actions that must take place before loans are disbursed, in order to gauge the policymakers' commitment to macroeconomic reforms.

the economy-wide budget constraint, such assistance may lead the government to expand its redistributive role, which can exacerbate distortions and endogenously weaken the program (Rodrik, 1989). Third, if the degree of conditionality attached to foreign aid is too tight, uncertainty about external support may rise, leading to delays in stabilization and increasing the likelihood that the program will collapse (Orphanides, 1996). This scenario may occur, in particular, if foreign capital plays an important role in determining the level of domestic economic activity. To the extent that the conditions attached to foreign assistance appear excessively stringent, inflationary expectations will remain high, depressing aggregate demand and increasing unemployment. In turn, the rise in unemployment may weaken political support and affect the viability of the disinflation effort.

2.2.5 Sequencing and Political Support

The design and subsequent implementation of a disinflation program require policymakers to make some decisions regarding the distribution of income. In the absence of a broad political consensus in support of the program, such decisions are difficult to make, and the stabilization plan will accordingly be more difficult to implement. For a program to be viable, the size and composition of distributional effects of the macroeconomic reforms must be politically acceptable. The credibility of stabilization programs depends heavily on the degree of political cohesion in the country and the legitimacy and popular support enjoyed by the government.

Political factors play a crucial role in both the shock therapy and gradual approaches to stabilization discussed earlier, in the context of signaling arguments aimed at enhancing credibility. The political trade-off can be summarized in the following terms. On the one hand, drastic measures may help generate credibility in the reform process quickly, particularly when they are implemented during a new administration's "honeymoon" with the public, during which the population is perhaps more willing to accept the costs associated with painful measures. In addition, the initial benefits of sharp adjustment may outweigh the costs that would be associated with the persistence of inflation at a higher level, as well as other social and economic costs that would result from the policy shock. On the other hand, overly costly policy decisions, from a social and economic point of view, run the risk of causing the political consensus to collapse and may lead to a policy reversal at a later stage.

A gradualist strategy may also lack credibility for precisely the same reason that a shock therapy approach may not be credible: future governments may be tempted to adopt discretionary policy reversals. However, the costs in terms of output and employment may be lower with a credible gradual approach than with a shock therapy approach, allowing policymakers to maintain the social and political consensus necessary to sustain the reforms.[61] From the perspective of credibility,

---

[61] In principle, the cost associated with maintaining austerity over a prolonged period under a gradual approach may be as high as the short-term cost associated with a shock therapy approach if output recovers rapidly in the aftermath of stabilization. In practice, however, future benefits are often heavily discounted by private agents, in a sense forcing policymakers to focus on short-run costs.

circumstances under which a shock therapy approach to stabilization is preferable to a more gradual strategy are therefore likely to vary across countries and over time.

Although broad political support is essential to the sustained success of macroeconomic reforms,[62] it is often difficult to establish a political consensus at the outset of a disinflation program.[63] As argued earlier, in situations where newly elected political leaders enjoy a period of widespread popularity, economic shock treatments have a higher probability of being accepted than prolonged adjustment programs. In general, however, political support tends to dissipate rather quickly if expenditures on basic programs such as education, health, and social services are cut to meet fiscal targets or if unemployment rises in the short term to very high levels. For any given country, the optimal speed of macroeconomic adjustment will depend on a variety of economic and political factors (such as the structure of the economy, the policymaker's preferences, and the degree of political consensus). Although in practice it is extremely difficult to determine the "optimal" pace of reform, it has been argued that two general points need to be taken into account in designing stabilization programs. First, as argued before, it is crucial to sequence macroeconomic and structural reforms in a way that minimizes the short-term drop in output.[64] Second, it may also be important to devise a compensatory scheme for those affected the most, that is, to put in place social safety nets that include (among other options) targeted subsidies on essential food products or cash transfers to vulnerable groups, to protect those least able to absorb the costs of macroeconomic adjustment (low-income families, pensioners, and unemployed workers). The latter appears to be one of the main lessons of the recent literature on the political economy of stabilization programs (Haggard and Kaufman, 1989).[65]

Nevertheless, while equity provides a strong rationale for targeting specific groups in the population, programs that attempt to avoid imposing severe economic costs on those groups deemed vulnerable may not necessarily be more credible (even if the social safety net is cost effective), because the targeted groups may not be the most politically influential in the country. Targeting specific groups for protection may impose substantial short-term costs on other groups that enjoy greater political power and could undermine the credibility and sustainability of the program as much as—and perhaps more than—ignoring the needs of the vulnerable groups altogether. As argued by Alesina and Drazen (1991), as groups attempt to shift to each other the

---

[62] Patinkin (1993), for instance, emphasizes the crucial role played by the "national-unity government" formed in September 1984 in the success of the Israeli stabilization program of 1985.

[63] However, as argued by Drazen and Grilli (1993), periods of very high inflation—or, more generally, periods of severe economic crises, as emphasized by Williamson and Haggard (1994)—create incentives for the resolution of social conflict and thus facilitate the introduction of economic reforms. By contrast, policies aimed at reducing the cost of inflation (such as widespread indexation mechanisms) may raise the inflation rate and lead to delays in the adoption of reforms.

[64] Obviously, if policymakers are not prepared to accept any short-term contraction in output and employment—because of, say, electoral reasons—credibility will be impossible to achieve.

[65] As argued by Haggard (1991, p. 248), "Compensating losers . . . may prove less costly than political opposition that undermines programs." Of course, the design of the safety net program itself is important. Expenditures associated with these mechanisms should not prevent macroeconomic stabilization.

burden of stabilization, the consequence may be serious delays in the stabilization effort, leading eventually to a complete collapse.

2.3 ■ Policy Lessons

Most economists agree that policymakers can speed up disinflation and reduce potential costs of doing so by achieving credibility early in the program. However, mere pronouncements about monetary and fiscal policies are not credible, because private agents understand that policymakers have obvious incentives to make false announcements and because the public is not likely to pay attention to statements not backed by concrete measures. An anti-inflationary reputation can only be gained by establishing a track record of consistent low-inflation policies; these, in turn, require the formulation of credible programs. The implementation of a credible disinflation program helps provide an anchor for price expectations, leads to a reduction in the large risk premiums that tend to maintain interest rates at very high levels, and limits the recessionary effects of restrictive monetary and fiscal policies. Although some of the analytical results of the recent literature on credibility are sensitive to particular assumptions (concerning the structure of the economy, the specification of preferences of policymakers and private agents, and the existence of informational asymmetries), and despite the limitations of the empirical literature on existing credibility models, some tentative conclusions and broad policy lessons can be drawn from the preceding discussion for the formulation and design of disinflation programs.

The alternative options that have been put forward have not created a consensus among economists regarding the optimal way to convey credibility to a disinflation program or to enhance the reputation of policymakers. For instance, it has often been argued that to reduce inflationary expectations effectively in accordance with the disinflationary goal (and thereby facilitate the transition to low inflation), a newly implemented policy must not only appear credible but must be accompanied by clear signals informing the public of the government's actions. In that regard, an overadjustment in the fiscal sector is sometimes viewed as providing an unambiguous signal regarding the policymakers' commitment to continue with stabilization. However, credibly reducing budget deficits often requires the implementation of structural measures to broaden the tax system, privatize state enterprises, and break up monopolies. Such measures take time and have high political costs. In addition, measures that appear too harsh are often perceived as unsustainable.[66] It is the persistence rather than the scope of the initial policy measures that matters. Policy discontinuities represent the most serious obstacle to establishing credibility. Proper sequencing between structural and macroeconomic reforms is also important, as

---

[66] In a sense, attempting to establish credibility via signaling is a "razor's edge" problem: measures that are not "bold" enough will not do, but measures perceived to be excessively harsh will generate expectations of future reversals.

microeconomic and institutional changes often need to precede macroeconomic reforms to ensure success and convey credibility. In particular, although central bank independence does not obviate the need to ensure close coordination among policymakers in a decentralized regime, it helps establish confidence in the goal of price stability.

In a similar vein, it has been argued that because orthodox programs often reduce inflation slowly in chronic-inflation countries, an outcome likely to undermine support for stabilization, imposing price controls at the outset of a program may be beneficial. By reducing inflation quickly, price controls may provide policymakers with "breathing space" before the introduction of additional fiscal and monetary measures aimed at strengthening the stabilization effort. However, the argument does not carry much weight if the freeze is not complete and price setters are forward-looking agents. In addition, countries have typically used price controls as substitutes for fiscal adjustment, leading in many cases to a collapse of the stabilization effort and a resurgence of inflation. Institutional reforms aimed at eliminating inertial mechanisms (such as wage indexation laws and financial indexation provisions) remain essential to breaking persistent inflation in chronic-inflation countries.

To support a stabilization plan, policymakers often have recourse to foreign assistance, through a conditional bilateral agreement between an external agency and the government. Conditional foreign assistance serves two functions. The first is to make credits conditional on the implementation of macroeconomic policy reforms, and the second is to provide a signal about the seriousness of the program and thus lend credibility to policymakers. However, the second dimension may not be operative if political considerations are believed to have played an overwhelmingly important role in the decision to provide foreign aid. The first function can actually reduce credibility if the degree of conditionality is so tight that private agents are led to believe that the authorities cannot meet their policy targets. In terms of its impact on credibility, then, conditionality may not provide an unambiguous mechanism to ensure the success of stabilization programs.

Finally, though many economists believe that stabilization programs should be accompanied by social safety nets aimed at protecting the most vulnerable groups from the effects of macroeconomic reforms, programs that contain such features are not necessarily more credible than others, because the targeted groups may not have much political influence on, say, the reelection prospects of the incumbent.

The public must be clearly informed, at the inception of a stabilization program, that a new economic regime is being introduced. This understanding will help to ensure that the behavior of the private sector will reinforce the reform process, in turn increasing the program's credibility. Policy measures must accordingly be structured to indicate early on that major changes are being introduced. Although signaling a break with past inflationary policies may require a significant tightening in monetary and fiscal policies, emphasis should be placed on hard-to-reverse structural actions that clearly demonstrate the direction of the reforms, rather than on excessively stringent macroeconomic policies. Such structural policies should aim at eliminating the principal causes of fiscal imbalances, because the persistence of fiscal deficits makes it less likely that subsequent reforms will be successful. Finally, the fact that stabilization often creates only long-run benefits (which are often discounted by short-sighted agents) means that the prevailing economic conditions should have some bearing on the performance of the strategy. A program that performs well in a number of alternative possible situations seems preferable to one designed for a specific scenario. Consequently, contingencies may need to be considered more systematically in the formulation of disinflation programs. Most important, perhaps, is the need to integrate political factors into the design of stabilization programs. Understanding the endogenous interactions among credibility, macroeconomic policy decisions, and the political environment may be the key challenge that program designers face at the present time.

3   Disinflation and Nominal Anchors

The evidence reviewed in online Supplement B suggests that, in several instances, fixing the exchange rate was a key factor in stopping hyperinflation. Under less extreme circumstances, is the exchange rate to be preferred to, say, a nominal money target? Our discussion in Chapter 10 of the dynamic effects associated with alternative stabilization rules and the foregoing review of sources of credibility problems provide essential elements for the choice of a nominal anchor in disinflation programs. We will focus, in particular, on the choice between an exchange rate and a money supply rule, which represent the two major alternative types of orthodox stabilization programs.

The choice among alternative anchors in stabilization programs depends, in general, on four major considerations: the nature of the shocks that are likely to affect the economy during the disinflation process, the degree of controllability of the different policy instruments, the dynamic adjustment path of the economy that the use of such instruments induces, and the intrinsic degree of credibility of the respective choices.[67] These factors are not independent, as the discussion in the previous section suggests.

The role of stochastic disturbances in choosing between the exchange rate and the money supply as a nominal anchor was examined by Fischer (1986) in a model of an open economy with staggered labor contracts. Fischer shows that, in general, the choice between fixing the money stock or the nominal exchange rate depends on the nature and degree of persistence of the shocks that are likely to affect the economy as

---

[67] An additional factor that needs to be accounted for in discussing the choice among nominal anchors in developing countries is the existence of currency substitution. This issue is discussed at length by Calvo and Végh (1996), who suggest that the existence of a high degree of currency substitution may lead to the adoption of an exchange-rate rule.

well as the degree of wage indexation. For instance, when disturbances arise primarily in the real sector, prices tend to be more stable during the disinflation process when the exchange rate is fixed. Under either strategy, however, wage rigidity increases the output cost of disinflation. While Fischer's analysis is based on ex ante indexation, in practice, wage indexation is generally ex post, with the current wage adjusting to past changes in prices.[68]

In a subsequent contribution, Fischer (1988) examined the role of ex post wage indexation in the conduct of disinflation programs based on a reduction of the money stock. Indexation, ex ante or ex post, speeds up the response of the economy to disinflation. In the early stages of the stabilization program, ex post indexation reduces the extent of the recession caused by a permanent, unanticipated reduction in the growth rate of the money stock, but tends to have a long-term recessionary effect. Although Fischer does not examine the implications of ex post indexing for exchange-rate-based disinflation programs, a likely result is that it also increases the long-run output cost in such programs. In any case, however, stochastic shocks are, by definition, difficult to predict in practice, so that basing the choice of a nominal anchor on expected disturbances only may not be an optimal strategy. According to this criterion, unless the variability and the likelihood of occurrence of some category of shocks are deemed very low, a superior approach would probably be to use both anchors.

The extent to which policymakers are able to control their policy instruments can be an important consideration in choosing between monetary and exchange-rate rules. In general, the central bank cannot directly control the money supply, whereas fixing the exchange rate can be done relatively fast and without substantial costs. As argued earlier, the perception by the public of a lack of precision in instrument manipulation may affect the credibility of the disinflation program. On such grounds, then, fixing the exchange rate rather than the money stock may appear preferable. However, policymakers must also be able to convince private agents that they will be able to defend the declared parity. If agents lack confidence in the authorities' ability to do so, speculative attacks will occur, eventually forcing the abandonment of the fixed exchange rate (see Chapter 14). Imposing controls on foreign exchange transactions may not be an appropriate remedy, if rationing in the official market leads to the emergence of a parallel market with a more depreciated rate—because the "signal" that is supposed to be conveyed to price setters by fixing the official exchange rate will be distorted. This problem has, in fact, been a recurrent one in stabilization programs in developing countries.

More important, perhaps, is the fact that the choice of a nominal anchor affects the adjustment path of the economy, and therefore the ultimate outcome of the stabilization program. As illustrated in the one-good model with imperfect capital mobility developed in the previous chapter, the transitory dynamics associated with

---

[68] As a result, the real wage tends to rise when the inflation rate is reduced—for instance, at the beginning of a disinflation program. See Simonsen (1983).

monetary and exchange-rate rules will usually differ in significant ways. Similarly, in the Calvo-Végh "temporariness" framework described earlier, exchange-rate-based stabilization programs may lead to an initial expansion and a recession later on, while money-based programs are characterized invariably by an initial contraction in output.[69] Another example of the importance of considering, in choosing among nominal anchors, the dynamic path induced by alternative policy options is provided by Bruno and Fischer (1990). They consider an extended version of the "orthodox" model of inflation developed in the first section of Chapter 10 and assume that bonds can be used, in addition to money, as a source of financing of the fiscal deficit. Their analysis suggests that dual equilibria exist if the government attempts to fix the real exchange rate, but a unique equilibrium can be attained if the government sets a nominal anchor for the economy—for instance, by fixing the rate of growth of the nominal money stock or the rate of depreciation of the nominal exchange rate. In such conditions, the equilibrium that obtains under perfect foresight is saddlepoint stable, while the inflationary process is globally stable (with slow adaptive expectations) under a fixed nominal rate of exchange depreciation. Similar results obtain from the use of a rule through which the nominal exchange rate is adjusted adaptively to the inflation rate. Thus, by ensuring that policy pursues an appropriate nominal target, the government can avoid the costs of operating at an inflation rate that is higher than the fundamentals require it to be.[70] Lächler (1988) provides yet another example of how the choice of a nominal anchor affects the dynamic path of the economy during adjustment.

The consideration of credibility factors in choosing among alternative nominal anchors is perhaps the most crucial of all, because it interacts with the adjustment path and the degree of controllability of policy instruments. In our discussion of real-interest-rate dynamics, for instance, the degree of credibility of fiscal policy announcements was shown to play a critical role in the short-run behavior of the economy in exchange-rate-based stabilization programs. In the Calvo-Végh framework discussed above, credibility, or the lack thereof, plays an important role in the choice between monetary and exchange-rate targets. In their setup, a key problem that emerges when the exchange rate is used as a nominal anchor is the real appreciation that ensues when the inflation rate in home goods prices is rigid downward—as in the two-sector model with backward-looking wage contracts and markup pricing presented earlier—as a result, in part, of the initial expansion of output that

---

[69] As shown by Rhee (2008) in a related model, however, a credible money-based disinflation may produce a sustained expansion in domestic output after the initial contraction. Conversely, using a New Keynesian model with nominal and real frictions (of the type discussed in Chapter 12), Ascari and Ropele (2013) found that disinflations under *both* a money supply rule and an interest rate rule involve a long-lasting decline in output under full credibility. Under imperfect credibility—captured by assuming that inflation expectations are a weighted average between rational expectations and the initial steady-state level of inflation that the central bank would eventually restore in case of reneging the disinflation—the slump in output is magnified and the length of the transitional dynamics is increased in both cases.

[70] However, as argued by Lee and Ratti (1993), this may occur at a higher interest rate level than necessary, with a potentially adverse output effect.

often accompanies these programs. This may immediately weaken the credibility of a policy aimed at fixing the exchange rate, because agents will anticipate future nominal devaluations aimed at realigning relative prices. By contrast, in money-based stabilizations there is an immediate recession, which may weaken endogenously the credibility of the program, if the short-term output and employment cost are high. When the lack of credibility is pervasive, the choice between money and the exchange rate may not matter a great deal; inflation will remain high regardless of the anchor. An exchange-rate rule is, however, more successful in reducing inflation if there is some degree of credibility in the program; in this case, the initial expansion and the upward pressure on the real exchange rate are dampened. Nevertheless, under such a policy regime large intertemporal substitution effects may result, which are conducive to large current account deficits. If policymakers are unable to finance the surge in imports, and rationing ensues in the official market for foreign exchange, fluctuations in the parallel market exchange rate may severely distort the signal that a fixed exchange rate was intended to convey to price setters.

Appendix
Output Effects of Price Controls

We examine here, using a diagrammatic presentation, how differences in market structure and intensity of price controls influence the levels of output following the imposition of price ceilings. The analysis, which follows Helpman (1988), contrasts the effects of price controls on output under competitive and monopolistic markets. We focus on the case where only output prices are controlled, with input prices remaining constant.

Figure 11.7 depicts a single industry under competitive and monopolistic market structures. Panel 1 in the figure describes the competitive industry, with a large number of producers and consumers. MC is the marginal cost or supply curve and D the demand curve of the industry, with the equilibrium price p_E and quantity q_E determined at the intersection of the two curves (point C). Suppose now that the government sets the price at p_C, below the equilibrium price p_E. At the controlled price level, there is excess demand for the good equivalent to AB. The quantity actually transacted in the market is given by the supply function (at point A). Output is thus supply determined in this regime.

Panels 2, 3, and 4 in the figure describe a monopolistic industry, where there is only one firm facing a multitude of consumers. In all three panels, the marginal revenue curve MR is below the demand curve D, and equilibrium corresponds to the intersection of the marginal revenue and marginal cost curves, at point E (in contrast to point C under competitive conditions). The equilibrium price p_E corresponds to point B on the demand curve. The three panels illustrate the familiar result

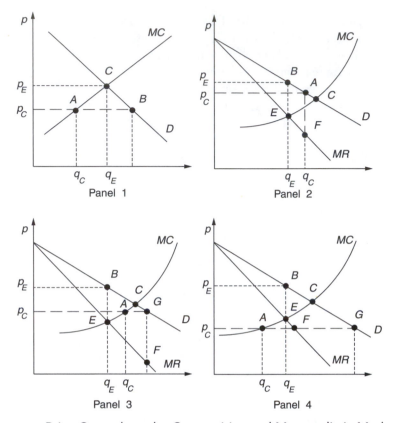

Figure 11–7 ▪ Price Controls under Competitive and Monopolistic Markets

that a monopolistic market structure leads to higher prices and lower output levels compared with market competition. However, the panels differ in the intensity of price controls imposed by the government. The implications of such differences are crucial to a proper understanding of the output effects of price controls.

First, consider the case where the controlled price p_C is set at a level below the equilibrium price p_E, but above the equilibrium price that would prevail in a competitive market (panel 2). Under this scenario, the marginal revenue curve becomes horizontal at the level p_C up to point A on the demand curve and then drops to F, coinciding with MR for higher output levels. Profit maximization motives lead the firm to supply the entire amount demanded at the controlled price. This result is valid for all price ceilings above point C and below point B. Hence, price controls lead to an expansion in output.

In the second case, the controlled price is set at a level below the equilibrium price that would prevail under both competitive and monopolistic market structures (panel 3). At the controlled price p_C, the marginal revenue curve becomes horizontal up to point G on the demand curve and then drops to F, coinciding with MR

for higher output levels. Output is determined at point A, where the marginal revenue curve intersects the marginal cost curve. Point G represents the quantity demanded at the controlled price. Output is now supply determined and there is excess demand (corresponding to AG), as in the competitive setting. The imposition of price controls also leads to an expansion of output, from q_E to q_C.

In the third case, the controlled price is set at a lower level than under the second case, that is, below the intersection of the marginal revenue and marginal cost curves (panel 4). At the controlled price p_C, point A represents the intersection of the marginal revenue curve (the horizontal line originating at p_C) with the marginal cost curve, while point G corresponds to the quantity demanded. Once again, output is supply determined and there is excess demand in an amount equivalent to AG. However, the imposition of price controls leads now to a fall in output (from q_E to q_C).

Therefore, depending on the intensity of price controls, there are three possible outcomes under a monopolistic market structure. In the first scenario, as long as the price ceiling is above the competitive equilibrium price, there is no excess demand, output is demand determined, and controls lead to an expansion in output. In the second and third scenarios, where the controlled price is set at lower levels, there is excess demand, output is supply determined, and shortages develop. However, while output rises in the second scenario, the third implies a fall in production. In general, therefore, the output effects of price controls depend on market structure, as well as on the severity of these controls, and on the structure of production costs.

The above results are obtained in a partial-equilibrium setting, where ceilings are imposed only on output prices while input prices are held constant; interactions among markets are also ignored. An equi-proportional reduction in all input and output prices for any given industry would leave output unchanged in that industry regardless of market structure.[71] Furthermore, when general equilibrium considerations are introduced, a uniform reduction in prices may affect output through its effects on both aggregate demand and aggregate supply. The effect of price controls on aggregate supply of final output will depend, in general, both on market structure as discussed above and on how much input prices are reduced relative to the price of final output. With regard to aggregate demand, the fall in the general price level may increase real money holdings and stimulate aggregate demand through the real balance effect. To the extent that inflationary expectations are dampened by controls, interest rates will fall and the demand for real money balances will increase. With a given nominal money stock, the increase in money demand will lead to further downward pressure on prices. However, to the extent that price controls reduce expected real income, they may have a negative effect on aggregate demand. Thus, the net effect of an increase in the overall price level on aggregate output may be positive or negative, depending on the initial conditions. In general, the effect of price controls on aggregate output will depend on the size of the competitive sector relative

---

[71]The foregoing analysis would nevertheless remain valid as long as output prices were lowered more than input prices.

to the monopolistic sector, as well as on the structure of production costs and the extent and intensity of price controls across industries.

The output effects of price controls will also depend on whether parallel goods markets exist. Excess demand in official markets tends to spill over to informal markets, leading to a rise in prices there as well as an increase in output. As argued in the main part of this chapter, if the domestic price level depends on official as well as parallel market prices, the very purpose of controls (a reduction in the rate of inflation) may be defeated by the existence of such markets.

Chapter 12

Dynamic Stochastic Equilibrium Models with Financial Frictions

Because of the complex nature of interactions across markets and over time that tend to prevail in a fully dynamic setting, it generally proves intractable to investigate an economy's full general-equilibrium response to exogenous and policy shocks analytically. Qualitative analysis is often possible only in highly parsimonious models. To go beyond qualitative results and explore the quantitative effects of shocks, a numerical model of the economy is indispensable. For this reason calibrated general equilibrium models have become a valuable research and policy tool for macroeconomists, in industrial and developing countries alike. Constructing such models, and ensuring that they are immune to the Lucas critique, has proved to be challenging; but once such a model is in hand, it can serve as a powerful research and policy tool, because it allows the researcher to conduct *ceteris paribus* experiments in macroeconomics, thereby avoiding the need to confront the difficult, and generally ambiguous, issues of identification that often plague empirical hypothesis testing.

Early applied macro-modeling emphasized the use of large-scale simultaneous-equations (LASSIE) models. The Lucas Critique argued that LASSIE models were not truly structural for the purpose of econometric policy evaluation. This gave rise to a new agenda focused on developing optimization-based rational-expectations equilibrium models based on first principles that would be immune to this critique. The first version of such models were the Real Business Cycle (RBC) models (see for instance Wickens, 2011, chapter 16). Today's vintage of quantitative macro-economic models, known as Dynamic Stochastic General Equilibrium (DSGE), have evolved from the core RBC model but with important modifications, incorporating a wide range of real and financial frictions. New Keynesian elements were introduced, including nominal price and wage rigidities, within an imperfectly competitive framework. Such models are *classical* in that money is neutral in the long run, but *Keynesian* in that monetary policy has short-run real effects. For this reason, DSGE models are also known as (optimization-based) New Keynesian models.

This chapter provides a review of a particular class of DSGE models, those focusing on financial frictions, especially credit market imperfections. These imperfections have figured prominently in the research agenda of macroeconomists since the global financial crisis. The first section reviews the main features of DSGE models. The second section presents a benchmark model without a financial sector. The third discusses different approaches to modeling financial issues and extends the analysis to introduce a financial system and financial frictions, while at the same time accounting for physical capital accumulation. Section 4 discusses log-linearization, calibration, and estimation issues with DSGE models. Various extensions, aimed in particular at introducing open-economy features and macroprudential regulation, are discussed in Section 5. Throughout, our focus is on the theoretical structure of DSGE models, rather than estimation issues or the extent to which these models approximate the volatility and comovement of economic time series.[1]

1 Main Features of DSGE Models

In basic DSGE models, behavioral equations for private agents are all derived by forward-looking agents solving intertemporal optimization problems.[2] A representative household maximizes its utility subject to a household budget constraint, and a representative firm maximizes profits.[3] The government collects taxes and spends on goods and services, subject to its intertemporal budget constraint and the central bank sets monetary policy by following an interest rate rule. Money is often introduced through the utility function (as in Chapter 5 for instance), a cash-in-advance constraint (see Chapter 11), or a shopping time or transaction costs restriction.[4] DSGE models are stochastic in nature; every period, random exogenous events perturb the equilibrium conditions in each block, injecting uncertainty in the evolution of the economy.

The dependence of current choices on future uncertain outcomes makes these models dynamic and assigns a central role to agents' expectations in the determination of current macroeconomic outcomes. Private agents are usually assumed to form their expectations rationally, although more recent developments tend to depart from that benchmark (see Section 5). Explicit microfoundations and model-consistent expectations allow DSGE models to study long-run equilibrium and

---

[1] Outcomes of estimation—namely, the possibility of recovering the structural shocks that drive economic fluctuations as well as the historical behavior of variables that are relevant for policy but are not directly observable—are an important area of research, but well beyond the scope of this book.

[2] For an overview of DSGE methodology and models (without financial frictions) for monetary policy analysis, see Christiano, Trabandt, and Walentin (2010).

[3] In more advanced models, a category of households (*hand-to-mouth consumers*) may be assumed to be subject to liquidity constraints and/or myopic horizons, which implies that their consumption is tied to current income.

[4] The nominal return to money is zero. Under the assumption of complete markets or with a riskless bond yielding positive nominal returns, the constraint on agents to hold money is a source of inefficiency.

short-run dynamics in a unified framework. The stochastic nature of these models, as well as their general equilibrium nature (which is key to capturing the interaction between policy actions and agents' behavior), allows one to examine the effects and relative importance of various shocks on the economy, interactions between nominal and real aggregates, the transmission process of macroeconomic policy, and the implications of alternative policy rules for macroeconomic and financial stability.

In addition, DSGE models account for nominal price and wage rigidities, along with monopolistically competitive product and (in some contributions) labor markets. Imperfect competition in the differentiated goods market leads to a markup distortion and results in a less efficient level of output, and asynchronous price or wage adjustment leads to relative price distortions and short-run non-neutrality of money, which in turn generate nominal-real interactions and create a role for monetary policy. DSGE models may also incorporate an array of other rigidities, including real rigidities—such as habit formation in consumption and hours worked, adjustment costs in capital or labor input, fixed costs in production, labor hoarding and variable capacity utilization—and, most important for our purpose, financial frictions.

2   A Basic Model

Simple DSGE models are built around three interrelated blocks: a demand block (which determines current activity as a function of the ex ante real interest rate and expectations about future real activity), a supply block (which determines inflation as a function of current activity and expectations of future inflation), and a monetary policy equation (with output and inflation fed from the demand and supply blocks).[5] The equations that define these blocks are derived from microfoundations: explicit assumptions about the behavior of the main economic actors in the economy— households, firms, and the government. These agents interact in markets that clear every period, which leads to the "general equilibrium" feature of the models. The central bank raises the nominal interest rate when the economy is overheating or when inflation rises, and lowers it when activity is weak and deflationary pressures prevail. By adjusting the interest rate, monetary policy in turn affects real activity and, through it, inflation. In what follows we present a simple model, which for the moment excludes capital accumulation and abstracts from financial markets (both issues are addressed in the next section).

Consider a closed economy populated by four classes of agents: a representative household; a representative final-good producing firm (FG producer, for short); a

---

[5]In good times, when the level of activity is high, firms must increase wages to induce employees to work longer hours. Higher wages increase marginal costs, putting pressure on prices and generating inflation. Moreover, the higher inflation is expected to be in the future, the higher is this increase in prices, thus contributing to a rise in inflation today.

continuum of intermediate firms (IG producers), indexed by $j \in (0, 1)$; and a central bank. The household consumes the final good and supplies labor to IG producers. Each of these producers is a monopolist in the production of a particular intermediate good j, for which it is thus able to set the price. Production of intermediate goods requires only labor. The FG producer packages the differentiated goods produced by the IG producers and sells the finished product to households in a perfectly competitive market. Wages are fully flexible and adjust to clear the labor market.[6] The central bank sets the nominal interest rate.

The remainder of this section describes the problem faced by each economic agent, shows the corresponding optimization conditions, and interprets the shocks that perturb these conditions. Together with market-clearing conditions, these relationships completely characterize the equilibrium behavior of the economy.[7]

2.1 ■ Household

The representative household's discounted lifetime utility is given by

$$U_t = \mathbb{E}_t \sum_{s=0}^{\infty} \Lambda^s \left\{ \frac{C_{t+s}^{1-\eta}}{1-\eta} - \int_0^1 \frac{\eta_L}{1+\psi} (N_{t+s}^j)^{1+\psi} dj \right\}, \tag{1}$$

where $\Lambda \in (0, 1)$ is a constant discount factor, C_t real consumption, N_t^j labor supplied (in terms of hours) to IG firm j, $\eta > 0$ the inverse of the elasticity of intertemporal substitution, ψ the inverse of the Frisch elasticity of labor supply and $\eta_L > 0$ a preference parameter, which measures the relative weight of the disutility of labor.[8] $\mathbb{E}_t$ is the expectations operator, conditional on information available up to period t.[9]

The representative household enters period t holding B_{t-1} one-period government bonds and receiving $i_{t-1}^B B_{t-1}$ in interest income, where i_t^B is the nominal rate of return on these bonds. During period t the household receives $W_t \int_0^1 N_t^j dj$ total nominal factor payments from supplying N_t^j units of labor at the economy-wide nominal wage rate W_t (which is taken as given) to each IG producer $j \in (0, 1)$. Further, the household receives nominal dividends from each IG firm, aggregating

---

[6]The assumption of complete wage flexibility at the aggregate level is a reasonable approximation for developing countries with a large informal sector; see Chapter 1.

[7]Supplement C provides all details about these derivations.

[8]The Frisch elasticity of labor supply captures the elasticity of hours worked with respect to the wage rate, given a constant marginal utility of wealth. Put differently, the Frisch elasticity measures the substitution effect of a change in the wage rate on labor supply.

[9]In some models, *habit formation* is introduced by writing the term in consumption as $\ln(C_{t+s} - \eta_C C_{t+s-1})$, or $C_{t+s}/C_{t+s-1}^{\eta_C}$, where $\eta_C \in (0, 1)$. As a result of this habit, consumers are unhappy if their current consumption is low, but also if it falls much below the level of their consumption in the recent past.

to $J_t^I = \int_0^1 J_t^{I,j} dj$. The household uses its funds to purchase new bonds, B_t, and to consume an amount C_t by buying output from the final goods sector at price P_t.[10]

The flow budget constraint of the household is thus given by

$$P_t C_t + B_t = (1 + i_{t-1}^B) B_{t-1} + W_t \int_0^1 N_t^j dj + J_t^I - P_t T_t, \qquad (2)$$

where T_t is a lump-sum tax in real terms.

The household chooses sequences of consumption, C_{t+s}, labor, N_{t+s}^j, $j \in (0, 1)$, and bonds, B_{t+s}, for $s = 0, 1, ...\infty$, so as to maximize (1), subject to the constraint (2) and for B_{t-1} given.[11] Prices, wages, the bond interest rate and lump-sum taxes are also taken as given when solving this problem.

Its solution is obtained by forming the Lagrangian

$$\mathcal{L}_t = \mathbb{E}_t \sum_{s=0}^{\infty} \Lambda^s \left\{ \frac{C_{t+s}^{1-\eta}}{1-\eta} - \int_0^1 \frac{\eta_L}{1+\psi} (N_{t+s}^j)^{1+\psi} dj \right.$$

$$\left. -\lambda_{t+s} \left[C_{t+s} + \frac{B_{t+s}}{P_{t+s}} - (1 + i_{t+s-1}^B) \left(\frac{B_{t+s-1}}{P_{t+s}} \right) - \frac{W_{t+s}}{P_{t+s}} \int_0^1 N_{t+s}^j dj - \frac{J_{t+s}^I}{P_{t+s}} + T_{t+s} \right] \right\},$$

where λ_t is a Lagrange multiplier associated with the household budget constraint.

The first-order conditions with respect to C_t, N_t^j and B_t are given by

$$\frac{\partial \mathcal{L}_t}{\partial C_t} : \frac{1}{C_t^{\eta}} = \lambda_t, \qquad (3)$$

$$\frac{\partial \mathcal{L}_t}{\partial N_t^j} : \frac{\eta_L (N_t^j)^{\psi}}{\lambda_t} = \frac{W_t}{P_t}, \qquad (4)$$

$$\frac{\partial \mathcal{L}_t}{\partial B_t} : \lambda_t = \Lambda \mathbb{E}_t \lambda_{t+1} (1 + i_t^B) \left(\frac{P_t}{P_{t+1}} \right), \qquad (5)$$

for $t = 0, 1, ...\infty$ and $\forall j \in (0, 1)$, together with the sequence of budget constraints (2).

---

[10]In this basic model, prices are measured in terms of a unit of account called "money," but the economy is otherwise cashless. Money (and credit) will be explicitly introduced later on.

[11]The household also faces a set of nonnegativity constraints on consumption and labor supply. However, the functional forms used to describe tastes and technologies guarantee that the household's choices of these variables will always be positive.

These conditions yield a fully state-contingent plan for the household's choice variables—how much to work, consume, and save in the form of bonds—looking forward from the planning date $t = 0$ and into the foreseeable future. At any point in time, the household is naturally uncertain about the way in which this future will unfold. However, the household is assumed to be aware of the kind of shocks that might affect its decisions and, crucially, to know the probability with which these shocks might occur. The household can therefore form expectations about future outcomes, which partly determine its current choices. Expectations are assumed to be rational—an issue to which we return later on. The optimal plan, then, is a series of rules on how to behave in response to the realization of each shock, given expectations about the future, rather than a one-time decision on exactly how much to work, consume, and save on each future date.

Combining (3) and (5) yields the standard Euler equation (see Chapter 2),

$$\frac{1}{C_t^{\eta}} = \Lambda \mathbb{E}_t \left[\left(\frac{1}{C_{t+1}^{\eta}} \right) \left(\frac{1+i_t^B}{1+\pi_{t+1}} \right) \right], \tag{6}$$

where $1 + \pi_{t+1} = P_{t+1}/P_t$. This condition establishes a negative relationship between the interest rate and desired current consumption that defines the demand side of the model: desired consumption today decreases when the (gross) real interest rate increases, when expected future consumption decreases, and when households become more patient.

Condition (4) represents the labor supply decision. Combining (3) and (4) yields

$$N_t^j = \left[\frac{C_t^{-\eta}}{\eta_L} \left(\frac{W_t}{P_t} \right) \right]^{1/\psi}, \tag{7}$$

which shows that labor supply is related negatively to consumption and positively to the real wage. Households are willing to work more hours when wages are higher— at least for differences in wages modest enough to have no significant effect on their income.[12] Large wage changes, in fact, would trigger an income effect and lead the now richer workers to curtail their labor supply. The reason is that workers with higher income could afford more consumption, which would lead to a drop in the marginal utility of consumption, and thus to a decrease in labor supply at any given wage level.

2.2 ■ Output and Price Formation

A key feature of DSGE models is the introduction of price-setting frictions. These frictions are introduced in order to accommodate the evidence of inertia in aggregate

---

[12] Labor supply is upward sloping because people dislike working an extra hour more intensely when they are already working a lot rather than when they are working little.

inflation. For these frictions to exist, firms must have the power to set prices, and this in turn requires the presence of monopoly power. To create an environment in which there is monopoly power, without contradicting the fact that actual economies have a very large number of firms, DSGE models usually build on the Dixit-Stiglitz (1977) production framework, with its very large number of price-setting monopolist firms.

As noted earlier, there are two types of firms: monopolistic, intermediate-goods (IG) producers, which set prices, indexed by $j \in (0, 1)$, and a final good (FG) producer, which simply aggregates the output of the IG producers into the final consumption good.

The final good, Y_t, is divided between private consumption, government consumption, and investment. It is produced by assembling a continuum of imperfectly substitutable intermediate goods Y_{jt}, with $j \in (0, 1)$:

$$Y_t = \left\{ \int_0^1 [Y_{jt}]^{(\theta-1)/\theta} dj \right\}^{\theta/(\theta-1)}, \tag{8}$$

where $\theta > 1$ is the elasticity of demand for each intermediate good, as in Dixit and Stiglitz (1977).

The FG producer sells its output at a perfectly competitive price. Taking as given the intermediate-goods prices P_{jt} and the final-good price P_t, it chooses the quantities of intermediate goods, Y_{jt}, that maximize its profits. The maximization problem of the FG producer is thus

$$Y_{jt} = \arg\max P_t \left\{ \int_0^1 [Y_{jt}]^{(\theta-1)/\theta} dj \right\}^{\theta/(\theta-1)} - \int_0^1 P_{jt} Y_{jt} dj.$$

The first-order conditions yield demand for each variety of good j:

$$Y_{jt} = \left(\frac{P_{jt}}{P_t} \right)^{-\theta} Y_t, \quad \forall j \in (0, 1). \tag{9}$$

Imposing a zero-profit condition leads to the following final good price:

$$P_t = \left\{ \int_0^1 (P_{jt})^{1-\theta} dj \right\}^{1/(1-\theta)}. \tag{10}$$

Each IG firm produces a distinct, perishable good, using only labor. Because the intermediate goods substitute imperfectly for one another in producing the finished good, each IG producer sells its output in a monopolistically competitive market. Thus, firm j sets the price P_{jt} for its output, subject to the requirement that it satisfy the representative FG producer's demand, taking P_t and Y_t as given.

Production technology involves constant returns in labor:

$$Y_{jt} = A_t N_{jt}, \tag{11}$$

where N_{jt} is total labor hours, $\alpha \in (0, 1)$, and A_t a common technology shock, which captures unexpected changes in productivity. A common assumption is that this shock follows a first-order autoregressive process:

$$A_t = A_{t-1}^{\rho_A} \exp(\xi_t^A), \tag{12}$$

where $\rho_A \in (0, 1)$ and $\xi_t^A \sim \mathbf{N}(0, \sigma_{\xi^A})$.

IG producers solve a two-stage problem. In the first stage, taking the real wage rate $\omega_t = W_t / P_t$ as given, they rent labor in a perfectly competitive factor market so as to minimize real costs. The unit real marginal cost is thus

$$mc_t = \frac{\omega_t}{A_t}, \tag{13}$$

which does not depend on the IG firm index.

In the second stage, each IG producer chooses a sequence of prices P_{jt} so as to maximize discounted real profits. In DSGE models, two approaches have been commonly adopted to formalize the price formation mechanism: the Rotemberg (1982) approach and the Calvo (1983) and Yun (1996) approach. The former emphasizes "menu costs" and is consistent with a symmetric equilibrium, whereas the latter (discussed in Chapter 11 in a continuous-time setting) assumes that firms change their prices only infrequently and produces relative-price dispersion among firms.

In the Rotemberg approach, IG firms incur a convex cost in adjusting nominal prices, of the form

$$PAC_t^j = \frac{\phi_F}{2} \left(\frac{P_{jt}}{\bar{\pi}^G P_{jt-1}} - 1 \right)^2 Y_t, \tag{14}$$

where PAC_t^j is the price adjustment cost incurred by IG firm j at time t, $\phi_F \geq 0$ the adjustment cost parameter, which determines the degree of price stickiness, and $\bar{\pi}^G = 1 + \bar{\pi}$ is the gross steady-state inflation rate. As argued by Rotemberg (1982), the adjustment cost seeks to account for the negative effects of price changes on the customer-firm relationship. These negative effects increase in magnitude with the size of the price change and with the overall scale of economic activity, Y_t.[13]

---

[13] See Gagnon (2009) for some evidence on menu costs and the frequency of price adjustment. This specification can be generalized by introducing a quadratic cost of adjustment in the price *level*, in addition to inflation; see Ireland (2001) for instance.

The costs of price adjustment make each IG producer's problem dynamic; rather than maximizing its profits period-by-period, each firm j acts to maximize its total market value.

The second-stage optimization problem is thus

$$\{P_{jt+s}\}_{s=0}^{\infty} = \arg\max \mathbb{E}_t \sum_{s=0}^{\infty} \Lambda^s \lambda_{t+s} \left(\frac{J_{jt+s}^I}{P_{t+s}} \right), \tag{15}$$

where nominal profits at t, J_{jt}^I, are defined as

$$J_{jt}^I = (P_{jt} - P_t mc_t)Y_{jt} - P\,AC_t^j,$$

and mc_t is defined in (13). In (15), $\Lambda^s \lambda_{t+s}$ is the multiplier on the representative household's budget constraint at period $t+s$. Because IG firms are owned by households (to whom they transfer their profits), the firm's discount factor for period-$t+s$ profits is $\Lambda^s \lambda_{t+s}$, where λ_{t+s} is the marginal utility value (in terms of consumption) of an additional currency unit of profits at $t+s$.

Firms maximize profits subject to the production function (11) and to the additional constraint that they must satisfy the demand for their product by the FG producer at every point in time, as given in (9); substituting that expression for Y_{jt} above yields

$$\{P_{jt+s}\}_{s=0}^{\infty} = \arg\max \mathbb{E}_t \sum_{s=0}^{\infty} \Lambda^s \lambda_{t+s} \left[\left(\frac{P_{jt+s}}{P_{t+s}} \right)^{1-\theta} - mc_{t+s} \left(\frac{P_{jt+s}}{P_{t+s}} \right)^{-\theta} \right.$$

$$\left. - \frac{\phi_F}{2} \left(\frac{P_{jt+s}}{\bar{\pi}^G P_{jt+s-1}} - 1 \right)^2 \right] Y_{t+s}.$$

Taking $\{mc_{t+s}, P_{t+s}, Y_{t+s}, \lambda_{t+s}\}_{s=0}^{\infty}$ as given, the first-order condition for this maximization problem is:

$$(1-\theta)\lambda_t \left(\frac{P_{jt}}{P_t} \right)^{-\theta} \frac{Y_t}{P_t} + \theta\lambda_t \left(\frac{P_{jt}}{P_t} \right)^{-\theta-1} \frac{mc_t Y_t}{P_t} - \lambda_t \phi_F \left\{ \left(\frac{P_{jt}}{\bar{\pi}^G P_{jt-1}} - 1 \right) \right.$$

$$\left. \times \frac{Y_t}{\bar{\pi}^G P_{jt-1}} \right\} + \Lambda \phi_F \mathbb{E}_t \left\{ \lambda_{t+1} \left(\frac{P_{jt+1}}{\bar{\pi}^G P_{jt}} - 1 \right) \left(\frac{P_{jt+1}}{\bar{\pi}^G P_{jt}^2} \right) Y_{t+1} \right\} = 0, \tag{16}$$

which gives the adjustment process of the nominal price P_{jt}. Essentially, this condition requires that at the optimum, a small change in prices must have a zero effect on the present discounted value of profits.

When prices are fully flexible ($\phi_F = 0$), this condition boils down to the simple markup rule:

$$\frac{P_{jt}}{P_t} = \frac{\theta}{\theta - 1} mc_t,$$

which shows that the real price is a fixed markup (also known as Lerner's formula) over the real marginal cost. Thus, in a symmetric equilibrium, this equation implies that the real marginal cost is the reciprocal of the markup:

$$mc_t = (\theta - 1)/\theta. \tag{17}$$

In the Calvo-Yun approach, in every period only a fraction $1 - \xi$ of firms is free to reset its nominal price while the remaining fraction maintains its old price, that is, $P_{jt} = P_{jt-1}$. Firms that are able to set an optimal price at t, denoted P_{jt}^O, maximize again the discounted stream of expected future profits, taking into account that periods $s = 1, 2...$ from now there is a probability ξ^s that they will be forced to retain the price chosen today. The objective function of each of these firms is therefore again (15), with nominal profits defined now as

$$J_{jt}^I = (P_{jt} - P_t mc_t)Y_{jt}.$$

Using (9) to substitute for Y_{jt} in this expression, the maximization problem becomes

$$\{P_{jt+s}^O\}_{s=0}^\infty = \arg\max \mathbb{E}_t \sum_{s=0}^\infty \Lambda^s \lambda_{t+s} \xi^s \left(\frac{P_{jt+s}}{P_{t+s}} - mc_{t+s} \right) \left(\frac{P_{jt+s}}{P_{t+s}} \right)^{-\theta} Y_{t+s},$$

subject to the production function (11). In this expression, the interpretation of $\Lambda^s \lambda_{t+s}$ is the same as before. The presence of ξ^s reflects the fact that IG firms are only concerned with future scenarios in which they are not able to reoptimize the price chosen in period t.

The first-order condition of this problem is

$$\mathbb{E}_t \sum_{s=0}^\infty (\xi \Lambda)^s \lambda_{t+s} Y_{t+s} P_{t+s}^{\theta-1} \left[P_{jt}^* - \left(\frac{\theta - 1}{\theta} \right) \left(\frac{w_{t+s}}{A_{t+s}} \right) \right] = 0,$$

or equivalently

$$P_{jt}^O = \frac{\theta}{\theta - 1} \frac{\mathbb{E}_t \sum_{s=0}^\infty (\xi \Lambda)^s \lambda_{t+s} P_{t+s}^\theta Y_{t+s} mc_{t+s}}{\mathbb{E}_t \sum_{s=0}^\infty (\xi \Lambda)^s \lambda_{t+s} P_{t+s}^{\theta-1} Y_{t+s}}, \tag{18}$$

where $(1 - \theta)/\theta$ is again the desired markup—the markup that the firm would charge if prices were flexible—over marginal cost. Thus, optimizing firms set their price as a markup over their marginal cost. However, this relationship holds in expected present discounted value, rather than every period, because a price chosen at time t will still be in effect with probability ξ^s in period $t+s$. Rational monopolists facing a more rigid demand optimally charge a higher markup, and thus higher prices, because their customers are less sensitive to changes in the latter. We assume that this sensitivity—the elasticity of demand—and thus the desired markup, are constant. Again, when $\xi = 0$ (18) implies that P_{jt}^O is a fixed markup over marginal cost:

$$P_{jt}^O = \frac{\theta}{\theta - 1} mc_t P_t.$$

Given that a fraction ξ of firms maintains the old price, $P_{jt} = P_{jt-1}$, the aggregate price level can be defined as a weighted average of newly set prices and of the past price index, P_{t-1}:

$$P_t = [(1 - \xi)(P_t^O)^{1-\theta} + \xi P_{t-1}^{1-\theta}]^{1/(1-\theta)}. \tag{19}$$

2.3 ■ Government

Government purchases of the final good, in quantity G_t, are a fixed fraction of real output:

$$G_t = \phi_G Y_t, \tag{20}$$

where $\phi_G \in (0, 1)$.

Government bonds are in zero supply. The government budget constraint thus simply equates spending and lump-sum taxes:

$$G_t = T_t. \tag{21}$$

2.4 ■ Market-Clearing Conditions

The equilibrium condition of the goods market depends on the price formation mechanism. Under Rotemberg pricing, this condition is, with Y_t denoting total output,

$$y_t = Y_t = C_t + G_t + 0.5\phi_F(\pi_t - 1)^2 Y_t,$$

or equivalently, using (20),

$$Y_t = \left[\frac{1}{1 - \phi_G - 0.5\phi_F(\pi_t - 1)^2} \right] C_t = \Psi_t C_t. \tag{22}$$

Under Calvo pricing, this condition takes the form:

$$Y_t = \frac{C_t}{1 - \phi_G}. \tag{23}$$

The equilibrium condition of the labor market is

$$\int_0^1 N_t^i di = N_t^S = \frac{Y_t}{A_t}, \tag{24}$$

where N_t^S is labor supply, and labor demand is obtained by inverting the production function (11) to find the amount of labor (the only factor of production for now) needed to produce Y_{jt}, and taking into account that under symmetry $Y_{jt} = Y_t$. Substituting from (7) in (24) implies that the real wage ω_t, and thus from (13) the marginal cost, is proportional to aggregate output.

Further, under the Calvo-Yun approach, and using (20) and aggregate demand (23), this expression becomes

$$N_t^S = \frac{C_t}{(1 - \phi_G)A_t}.$$

Suppose for a moment that $\phi_G = 0$. In the Rotemberg approach, the cost of nominal rigidities creates an inefficiency wedge between aggregate consumption and aggregate output ($C_t < Y_t$), given that $\Psi_t > 1$; part of the output is "eaten up" by the price adjustment cost. In the Calvo model, instead, $C_t = Y_t$; the cost of nominal rigidities (that is, nominal price dispersion), creates a wedge between aggregate employment and aggregate output [as given in (8)], which makes aggregate production less efficient. Both of these wedges are nonlinear functions of inflation. They are minimized at one when steady-state inflation is zero, whereas both wedges increase as trend inflation rises above zero.

In the Calvo-Yun approach, prices are staggered because firms charging prices at different periods will set different prices. Then, in each given period t, there will be a distribution of different prices. Price dispersion, which is caused by the interaction of inflation with price-setting frictions, results in an inefficiency loss in aggregate production. The reason is that with price dispersion, the price mechanism ceases to allocate resources efficiently, as too much production is done in firms with low prices and too little in the firms with high prices.[14] In the Rotemberg approach, firms can change their price in each period, subject to the payment of the adjustment cost. Therefore, all the firms face the same problem, and thus will choose the same price and output. In other words the equilibrium is symmetric ($P_{jt} = P_t$ and $Y_{jt} = Y_t$). Given this symmetry, the aggregate production function features no inefficiency due to price dispersion in the Rotemberg approach; however, the adjustment cost must enter the aggregate resource constraint, thereby creating an inefficiency wedge

---

[14] Yun (1996) derived a simple formula that characterizes the loss of output due to price dispersion.

between output and consumption. At the same time, the fact that some firms may not change prices for an extended period of time in the conventional Calvo-Yun approach may introduce an implausibly large persistence in the price level after shocks, and may result (as discussed later) in misleading welfare implications.

2.5 ▪ Interest Rate Rule

In most DSGE models, monetary policy is modeled as a *Taylor rule*, which relates the policy interest rate, i_t^R, to deviations in inflation and output from their targets. The central bank then provides uncollateralized loans (at the discretion of the commercial bank) through a standing facility. As discussed in Chapter 5, standing facilities are commonly used in both high- and middle-income countries to create (narrow) corridors to bound departures of short-term money market interest rates from target, with open-market operations used for the secondary objective of smoothing liquidity and moderating interest rate fluctuations. These facilities make the quantity of central bank cash endogenous, by providing unlimited access—subject to collateral requirements and institutional rules on who is eligible to maintain current balances with the central bank—to extra cash at the posted interest rate. For simplicity, we abstract from collateral requirements (typically low-risk and low-yield assets such as government securities), open-market operations, and consider a zero-width band around the target rate.

In addition, the central bank also puts some weight on (that is, smoothes out) variations in the interest rate. The interest rate rule takes therefore the form

$$1 + i_t^R = (1 + i_{t-1}^R)^\rho \left[(\tilde{r} + \pi^T) \left(\frac{Y_t}{\tilde{Y}} \right)^{\phi_Y} \left(\frac{\pi_t}{\pi^T} \right)^{\phi_\pi} \right]^{1-\rho} \exp(\epsilon_t^M), \qquad (25)$$

where $\tilde{r}$ and $\tilde{Y}$ are the initial steady-state values for the real interest rate and output, whereas π^T is the inflation target.[15] This reaction function captures the possibility that, depending on the shocks impinging on the economy, the central bank may need to internalize a trade-off between activity and inflation in setting interest rates.

The monetary policy shock ε_t^M, follows a first-order autoregressive process:

$$\epsilon_t^M = \epsilon_{t-1}^{\rho_\epsilon} \exp(\xi_t^\epsilon),$$

where $\rho_\epsilon \in (0, 1)$ and $\xi_t^\epsilon \sim \mathbf{N}(0, \sigma_{\xi^\epsilon})$ is a serially uncorrelated random shock with zero mean. It captures any deviation of the observed nominal interest rate from the value suggested by the rule.

---

[15] Rather than the steady-state value of output, DSGE models often use the *frictionless* or *efficient* level of output, which corresponds to the level of activity that would prevail if prices were fully flexible, to calculate the output gap. The rule could also include output *growth*, instead of the output gap, given that in practice the former often provides a better fit with the actual policy than the latter.

This rule implies that, if inflation and output rise above their baseline levels, the nominal interest rate is raised over time above its own baseline, $r_t^e + \pi_t^T$, by amounts dictated by the parameters ϕ_π and ϕ_Y and at a speed that depends on the coefficient ρ. The higher policy rate dampens aggregate demand and mitigates pressure on marginal costs and inflation. In this respect, π^T and $\bar{Y}$ can be regarded as targets of monetary policy—the levels of inflation and output that the central bank considers consistent with its mandate—and therefore do not elicit either a restrictive or a stimulative policy.

2.6 ■ The Log-Linearized Form

As shown in Supplement C, a log-linear approximation to (6) yields, setting $\phi_G = 0$ again, using the goods market-clearing condition, the equality between the bond rate and the policy rate $i_t^B = i_t^R$, and after some manipulations,

$$\hat{Y}_t = \mathbb{E}_t \hat{Y}_{t+1} - (\hat{i}_t^R - \mathbb{E}_t \hat{\pi}_{t+1}) + \varepsilon_t, \tag{26}$$

where $\widehat{x} = (x_t - \bar{x})/\bar{x}$, and $\bar{x}$ denotes a steady-state value. Thus, $\hat{\pi}_{t+1}$ and $\hat{Y}_t$ are log-deviations of inflation and output from their steady-state values, respectively; and ε_t is a random shock. This aggregate demand equation is dynamic and forward looking, as it involves current and future expected variables. In particular, it establishes a link between current output and the entire future expected path of real interest rates, as can be seen by solving the equation forward, $\hat{Y}_t = -\mathbb{E}_t \sum_{s=0}^{\infty} (\hat{i}_{t+s}^R - \hat{\pi}_{t+s+1} - \varepsilon_{t+s})$. Through this channel, expectations of future monetary policy directly affect current economic conditions.

Under Rotemberg pricing, (16) yields a New Keynesian Phillips curve—a relationship between current inflation, future expected inflation, and real marginal cost—of the form

$$\widehat{\pi}_t = \left(\frac{\theta - 1}{\phi_F}\right) \widehat{mc}_t + \Lambda \mathbb{E}_t \widehat{\pi}_{t+1} + u_t, \tag{27}$$

where u_t is a markup shock. The sensitivity of inflation to changes in the marginal cost, $(\theta - 1)/\phi_F$, depends negatively on the price adjustment cost parameter ϕ_F, as well as on the parameter θ.

In similar fashion, under Calvo-Yun pricing, (18) yields a New Keynesian Phillips curve of the form

$$\hat{\pi}_t = \chi \widehat{mc}_t + \Lambda \mathbb{E}_t \hat{\pi}_{t+1} + u_t, \tag{28}$$

where

$$\chi = \frac{(1 - \xi)(1 - \xi\Lambda)}{\xi(1 + \omega\theta)},$$

where again u_t is a markup shock and ω is the elasticity of the marginal disutility of work. The sensitivity of inflation to changes in the marginal cost, χ, depends negatively on the frequency of price adjustment ξ, as well as on other structural parameters.

A comparison of (27) or (28) shows that the two models are identical up to the coefficient on the marginal cost. Thus, it is possible to draw a relationship between the Rotemberg adjustment cost ϕ_F and the Calvo-Yun parameter ξ by imposing the condition $\phi_F = (\theta - 1)\xi/(1 - \xi)(1 - \Lambda\xi)$, which then implies the same first-order dynamics of the two models in the case of zero steady-state inflation (see Lombardo and Vestin, 2008).

Thus, despite the differences in their conceptual underpinnings, to a first-order approximation the Rotemberg and Calvo-Yun models are equivalent and, as shown by Roberts (1995), imply the same reduced-form New Keynesian Phillips curve. Furthermore, both models deliver the result, discussed in Chapter 11, of immediate adjustment of the economy to the new steady state following a disinflation, despite nominal rigidities in price-setting. However, the *nonlinear* disinflation dynamics implied by the two pricing models are very different; the properties of the Rotemberg model appear to be more robust to nonlinearities (Ascari and Rossi, 2011).

From (13), changes in marginal cost are given by

$$\widehat{mc}_t = \widehat{\omega}_t - \widehat{A}_t, \tag{29}$$

where, as noted earlier, $\widehat{\omega}_t$ is proportional to aggregate output deviations, $\hat{Y}_t$.

Equation (27) or (28), together with the expression for marginal costs (29), provides the relationship between inflation and real activity that defines the supply block of the model. Because the labor market equilibrium condition relates changes in the real wage with changes in output, marginal cost depends also on the level of aggregate activity, in addition to productivity shocks; higher economic activity leads to higher wages and marginal costs. Thus, firms increase their prices, boosting aggregate inflation.

Another important feature of the Phillips curve (27) or (28) is that it is forward-looking, just as the Euler equation (26) is. As in that case, therefore, we can iterate (28), for instance, forward to obtain $\pi_t = \mathbb{E}_t \sum_{s=0}^{\infty} \Lambda^s (\xi \widehat{mc}_{t+s} + u_{t+s})$. This highlights how inflation today really depends on the entire future expected path of marginal costs, and through those, of real activity. But this path depends in turn on expectations about interest rates, and thus on the entire future course of monetary policy.

A log-linear approximation to the policy rule (25) gives

$$\widehat{i_t^R} = \rho \widehat{i_{t-1}^R} + (1 - \rho)\left[\phi_Y \widehat{Y_t} + \phi_\pi \widehat{\pi_t^T}\right] + \epsilon_t^M. \tag{30}$$

What is typically referred to as the (core) New Keynesian model consists of the aggregate demand equation (26), the aggregate supply (or inflation) equation (27) or (28), after substituting for $\widehat{mc}_t$ from (29), and (30). The use of this model for policy evaluation is discussed extensively by Clarida et al. (1999), Woodford (2003), Galí (2008), and Christiano, Trabandt, and Walentin (2010). However, as it stands, in the model, money is a *side show*—monetary policy can be conducted without implicitly introducing money. The central bank fixes "the" nominal interest rate and provides all the liquidity that agents desire at that rate. Put differently, the money market, as well as other financial markets and prices on these markets, are ignored. We next extend the core model to account explicitly for these markets, as well as financial frictions and capital accumulation. As it turns out, these modifications (which are related in our framework) bring important new dimensions to DSGE models. In particular, the dichotomy between the real and the financial sides disappears, and the dynamics of the money market regain an important role.

3   Financial Frictions in DSGE Models

As noted in the Introduction of this book, the recent global financial crisis has made it abundantly clear that financial factors (including credit market imperfections) tend to be an important source of aggregate fluctuations, and a critical propagation channel of a variety of macroeconomic shocks. To understand the role of these factors, DSGE models have been developed in a number of directions. We begin with a brief discussion of the main approaches that have been proposed in the literature to account for financial frictions and subsequently extend the basic framework presented earlier.

3.1 ▪ Accounting for Financial Frictions

As discussed in Chapter 5, middle-income developing countries typically face a range of financial market imperfections. These include the predominance of banks in the financial structure, severe asymmetric information problems and a weak judiciary (which combine to encourage highly collateralized lending), the inability to diversify risk, the absence of financial safety nets, and a high degree of exposure and vulnerability to domestic and external shocks. In that chapter, two models of credit market imperfections were also discussed: the costly state verification (CSV) model of Townsend (1979) and S. Williamson (1986), and the model of collateral constraints of Kiyotaki and Moore (1997), which restricts borrowing to a fraction of assets. Many developments in the recent DSGE literature on financial frictions have built on the financial accelerator mechanism of Bernanke et al. (2000), hereafter BGG, which is itself based on the CSV model (see Brunnermeier et al., 2012).

At the heart of the BGG model are agency problems between borrowers and lenders, which are solved with appropriate contracting schemes; in turn, this introduces a role for leverage, risk, and spreads. The key mechanism relies on interacting production technologies with asymmetric information. The acquisition of capital is financed from both entrepreneurial net worth and external funds. Using the CSV approach, BGG assume that capital goods producers can easily observe the returns to their individual projects, but lenders must incur a cost to do so. This agency problem is solved with an optimal contract that entails a trade-off between monitoring costs and default probabilities, and implies an external finance premium that depends on the entrepreneur's leverage ratio. It therefore provides a novel amplification and propagation mechanism of productivity shocks.

The BGG framework emphasizes the role of the external finance premium, which was defined in Chapter 5 as the wedge between the cost of funds raised externally (the bank lending rate for most firms in developing countries) and the opportunity cost of internal funds. In both the KM and the BGG frameworks, variations in asset prices are key in determining borrowing behavior, as they affect either the price (via the finance premium) or the quantity (via collateralization) of funds available to borrowers. DSGE models developed in recent years have built on both channels. It has been argued that KM-style agency costs and BGG-style financial accelerators need not be confined to the household and corporate decision problem, respectively.

Brzoza-Brzezina et al. (2013) calibrated and compared the KM model of collateral constraints with the BGG model of external finance premia. They found that in general the business cycle properties of the external finance premium framework are more in line with the empirical evidence. However, the BGG framework suffers from several limitations. First, it assumes that investors lend directly to borrowers, without the intervention of financial intermediaries. In reality, a sizeable fraction of financial flows are channeled by banks, and a large body of work has attempted to uncover explicitly how the banking sector affects economic fluctuations in a general equilibrium environment.[16] A first strand of this literature considers perfectly competitive banking sectors in which the production processes of loans and deposits are costly and interest rates are determined by zero-profit conditions. Prominent examples of this approach are Goodfriend and McCallum (2007) and Christiano, Motto, and Rostagno (2010). The former considers banks that produce loans using collateral and monitoring, and identifies the external finance premium with the marginal cost of loan production. The presence of collateral in the production function generates a banking accelerator similar to the financial accelerator: monetary expansions that increase the value of the collateralizable assets reduce the external finance premium for given bank deposits. It also generates a *banking attenuator*, by which the increase in spending increases the demand for bank deposits and the premium for a given collateral value. Which effect dominates depends on the calibration.

---

[16]Although individual entrepreneurs are risky, banks themselves are not. We suppose that banks lend to a sufficiently diverse group of entrepreneurs that the uncertainty that exists in individual entrepreneurial loans washes out across all loans. Extensions of DSGE models that introduce risk into banking have been developed, but it is not clear (at the time of this writing at least) that the added complexity is justified.

A number of papers have analyzed the implications of imperfect competition in the banking sector on economic fluctuations. In some studies, banks owe their market power to switching costs. When setting interest rates, they face a trade-off between higher current profits and lower future market share. This generates countercyclical spreads which amplify the effects of productivity shocks on the economy. Andrés and Arce (2012) consider a monetary economy where spatial monopolistic competition in the banking sector interacts with collateral constraints on borrowers. Stronger banking competition affects cyclical fluctuations through two channels: higher leverage ratios (which increase short-run volatility of house prices, consumption and output) and lower lending margins (which weaken the transmission mechanism). The leverage effect dominates the lending margins' effect following a monetary policy shock, and conversely after a credit-crunch shocks. Gerali et al. (2010) analyze the effects of sluggish adjustment in nominal loan and deposit rates on cyclical fluctuations. In their model a continuum of banks compete à la Dixit-Stiglitz (as in the previous section) and are subject to costly adjustment of nominal loan rates.

In an important contribution, Christiano, Motto, and Rostagno (2010) have argued that, in addition to the BGG financial accelerator effect, there is a second, complementary channel through which changes in net worth can be propagated: the *Fisher deflation effect*. This effect presupposes that debt contracts are formulated in *nominal* terms. As a result (negative) surprises to the price level can alter ex post the real burden of the debt that the borrower will have to bear when the contract eventually matures. Indeed, in their framework debt contracts embody an important nominal rigidity: although loans to entrepreneurs are state contingent, banks' obligations to households are expressed in nominal terms. As a result, the opportunity cost perceived by the bank when lending to entrepreneurs at time t is not contingent on time $t+1$ shocks.[17] Fluctuations in the cost of borrowing reflect therefore two general equilibrium mechanisms. The first is the "pure" BGG-type financial accelerator effect identified earlier, which makes the contractual loan rate dependent on the net worth that borrowers can pledge to secure loans. The second is due to the fact that, with nominal contracts and state-contingent loans to entrepreneurs, surprises to the price level can alter ex post the real burden of entrepreneurial debt. Christiano, Motto, and Rostagno (2010) show that the pure accelerator mechanism and the Fisher deflation effect reinforce each other in the case of shocks that move the price level and output in the same direction, but tend to cancel each other out in the case of shocks that move the price level and output in opposite directions.

Agénor and Alper (2012) offer another contribution to the literature on New Keynesian models with credit market imperfections, but from a substantially different perspective. Although they follow a reduced-form approach in deriving default probbilities, the model that they propose allows monetary policy to generate a

---

[17] See Meh et al. (2009) for a discussion of this source of nominal rigidity.

financial accelerator effect, as in the BGG model. Building on the static framework described in Chapter 6, it combines the cost and balance sheet channels of monetary policy with an explicit analysis of the link between collateralizable wealth and bank pricing behavior. Because borrowers' ability to repay is uncertain, lending is collateralized and borrowers' net worth affects the terms of credit through a risk premium that banks incorporate in lending rates. Moreover, at the (premium-inclusive) prevailing lending rate, the supply of funds by financial intermediaries is perfectly elastic. Thus, in contrast to models in the Kiyotaki-Moore tradition, net worth does not impose a (continuously binding) constraint on borrowing.[18] As in standard DSGE models, the central bank conducts monetary policy by fixing a short-term interest rate, using a Taylor-type rule. To ensure that the actual interest rate remains close to target (or fluctuates only within a small band), the amount of liquidity that it provides in the market for overnight funds is adjusted endogenously. In addition, Agénor and Alper account explicitly for the fact that the central bank's supply of liquidity is perfectly elastic at the target interest rate. As a result, banks are unconstrained in their lending operations—which, together with deposits and reserve requirements, determine residually their liquidity needs. The central bank refinance rate represents the marginal cost of funds, upon which monopolistic banks set deposit rates; by contrast, the lending rate is set as a markup over the risk-free government bond rate, which represents the opportunity cost of lending. Because changes in bank borrowing affect the monetary base and the supply of currency, and the bond rate clears the money market, changes in the refinance rate exert both direct and indirect effects on the structure of bank rates. In turn, changes in the bond rate and bank rates affect aggregate demand and supply. Put differently, in the model money affects the dynamics of real variables—even under the assumption of separability between consumption and monetary assets in household utility.[19] Thus, compared to the existing literature, which often considers only a single interest rate or only a narrow spectrum of interest rates, while ignoring the implications of a perfectly elastic supply of central bank liquidity at the prevailing official rate, the Agénor-Alper setting offers a more complete perspective on interest rate determination and the monetary transmission mechanism. The model is developed in the next section.

3.2 ■ Extending the Basic Framework

Compared to the basic framework, there are now two new agents: a capital goods (CG) producer and a single commercial bank. The CG producer uses capital as

---

[18]Although the model does not account for endogenous credit rationing, it is compatible with *exogenous* rationing: it could be assumed for instance that small-scale firms, which operate in the informal sector (as is often the case in developing countries), are rationed out of the financial system entirely. See Beck and Demirguc-Kunt (2006) for a more detailed discussion and some evidence.

[19]Fundamentally, monetary aggregates matter for the model's dynamics because the velocity of money is not constant.

collateral against which it borrows from the bank to buy the final good for investment purposes and to produce capital. It then rents capital to IG producers. The bank also supplies credit to IG producers, who use it to finance their short-term working capital needs. Its supply of loans is perfectly elastic at the prevailing lending rate.

The maturity period of both categories of bank loans and the maturity period of bank deposits by unconstrained households is the same. In each period, loans are extended prior to activity (production or investment) and paid off at the end of the period. At the end of each period, the bank is liquidated and a new bank opens at the beginning of the next; thus, all its profits are distributed. As before, the central bank supplies liquidity elastically to the bank and sets its refinance rate solely in response to deviations of inflation from its target value and the output gap, as in standard Taylor-type rules.

The representative household's discounted lifetime utility is now given by, instead of (1),

$$U_t = \mathbb{E}_t \sum_{s=0}^{\infty} \Lambda^s \left\{ \frac{C_{t+s}^{1-\eta}}{1-\eta} - \int_0^1 \frac{\eta_L}{1+\psi} (N_{t+s}^j)^{1+\psi} dj + \eta_x \ln x_{t+s} \right\}, \qquad (31)$$

where x_t is a composite index of real monetary assets and $\eta_x > 0$ is a preference parameter. As noted in Chapter 5, rather than a money-in-the-utility function approach, a cash-in-advance approach or a liquidity cost approach (as in Kimbrough, 1992, for instance) could be used with qualitatively equivalent results. The only difference here is that we must think of "money" in terms of a composite monetary asset consisting of both cash balances and real bank deposits.

The composite monetary asset is generated by combining real cash balances, m_t, and real bank deposits, d_t, respectively (both at the beginning of period t), through a Cobb-Douglas function:

$$x_t = (m_t)^v d_t^{1-v}, \qquad (32)$$

where $v \in (0, 1)$.

Nominal wealth of the household at t is given by $M_t + D_t + B_t$, where $M_t = P_t m_t$ is nominal cash holdings, $D_t = P_t d_t$ nominal bank deposits, and B_t holdings of one-period nominal government bonds. The household enters period t with M_{t-1} holdings of cash, principal and interest on bank deposits at the rate contracted in $t-1$, $(1+i_{t-1}^D)D_{t-1}$, where i_t^D is the interest rate on deposits, and principal and interest payments on maturing government bonds, $(1+i_{t-1}^B)B_{t-1}$.

As before, the household supplies labor to IG firms, for which it receives factor payment of $\omega_t N_t$, where ω_t is, as before, the economy-wide real wage. It receives all the profits made by the IG producers, $J_t^I = \int_0^1 J_{jt}^I dj$, and the CG producer, J_t^K, in the form of lump-sum payments.[20] In addition, it receives all the profits of the bank, J_t^B.

The household's budget constraint is thus

$$P_t C_t + B_t + D_t + M_t = (1 + i_{t-1}^B) B_{t-1} + P_t \omega_t \int_0^1 N_t^j dj + (1 + i_{t-1}^D) D_{t-1}$$

$$+ M_{t-1} + J_t^B + J_t^I + J_t^K - P_t T_t. \tag{33}$$

The representative household maximizes lifetime utility (31) with respect to C_{t+s}, N_{t+s}^j, for $j \in (0, 1)$, m_{t+s}, d_{t+s}, and B_{t+s}, taking as given period-$t - 1$ variables as well as P_{t+s} and T_{t+s}, and subject to (32) and (33), for $s = 0, 1, \ldots \infty$. The solution yields equations (3)–(5) as before, and thus the Euler equation (6) again, together with

$$m_t = \frac{\eta_x \nu C_t^\eta (1 + i_t^B)}{i_t^B}. \tag{34}$$

$$d_t = \frac{\eta_x (1 - \nu) C_t^\eta (1 + i_t^B)}{i_t^B - i_t^D}, \tag{35}$$

for $t = 0, 1, \ldots \infty$. Equation (34) relates the real demand for cash positively with consumption and negatively with the opportunity cost of holding money, measured by the interest rate on government bonds. Similarly, (35) relates the real demand for deposits positively with consumption and the deposit rate, and negatively with the bond rate.

Production of the final good is given again by equations (8)–(10). However, the problem of the IG producers needs to reformulated.

3.2.1 Intermediate Good Producers

IG producers now use not only labor but also capital, in quantity K_{jt}:

$$Y_{jt} = A_t N_{jt}^{1-\alpha} K_{jt}^\alpha, \tag{36}$$

where $\alpha \in (0, 1)$. At the beginning of the period, each IG producer rents capital from the CG producer, at the same price r_t^K.[21]

Each firm j must borrow the amount $L_{jt}^{F,W}$ from the bank at the beginning of the period to pay wages in advance, that is, before production and sales have

---

[20] As noted earlier, the FG firm makes zero profits.

[21] The capital stock is predetermined in the aggregate, but profit maximization ensures that it is efficiently allocated across IG producers.

taken place:

$$L_{jt}^{F,W} = P_t \omega_t N_{jt}, \tag{37}$$

for all $t \geq 0$. As in Chapter 6, loans contracted for the purpose of financing working capital (which are short-term in nature) do not carry any risk, and are therefore made at a rate that reflects only the marginal cost of borrowing from the central bank, i_t^R. These loans are repaid at the end of the period.

As before, IG producers solve a two-stage problem. In the first stage, taking input prices as given, they rent labor and capital in perfectly competitive factor markets so as to minimize real costs:

$$N_{jt}, K_{jt} = \arg\min[(1 + i_t^R)\omega_t N_{jt} + r_t^K K_{jt}],$$

subject to $Y_{jt} = 1$. In standard fashion (see Supplement C), the first-order conditions equate the marginal products of capital and labor to their relative prices, r_t^K and $(1 + i_t^L)\omega_t$, respectively, implying that the capital-labor ratio is

$$\frac{K_{jt}}{N_{jt}} = \left(\frac{\alpha}{1-\alpha}\right)\left[\frac{(1 + i_t^R)\omega_t}{r_t^K}\right].$$

The real marginal cost is now

$$mc_t = \frac{\left[(1 + i_t^R)\omega_t\right]^{1-\alpha}(r_t^K)^\alpha}{A_t \alpha^\alpha (1-\alpha)^{1-\alpha}}, \tag{38}$$

which as before does not depend on j. Because firms also incur a financing cost for the payment of wages, the marginal cost of labor also includes borrowing costs, $i^R \omega_t$.

In the second stage, each IG producer chooses a sequence of prices P_{jt} so as to maximize discounted real profits. The optimization problem yields the adjustment process defined either by (16) under the Rotemberg approach, or by (18) under the Calvo-Yun approach.

3.2.2 Capital Good Producer

The CG producer owns all the capital in the economy and uses a linear technology to produce capital goods. At the beginning of the period, it buys an amount I_t of the final good from the FG producer. It combines these goods and the existing capital stock to produce new capital goods, K_{t+1}, which therefore accumulate as follows:

$$K_{t+1} = I_t + (1 - \delta_K)K_t - \frac{\Theta_K}{2}\left(\frac{K_{t+1}}{K_t} - 1\right)^2 K_t, \tag{39}$$

where $K_t = \int_0^1 K_{jt}dj$, $\delta_K \in (0, 1)$ is a constant rate of depreciation, and $\Theta_K > 0$ a parameter that measures the magnitude of adjustment costs. The new capital stock is then rented to IG producers, at the rate r_t^K.

Investment goods must be paid in advance; to purchase final goods, the CG producer must borrow from the bank:

$$L_t^{F,I} = P_t I_t. \tag{40}$$

At the end of the period, loans are paid in full with interest. Thus, the total (interest-inclusive) cost of buying final goods for investment purposes is given by $(1 + i_t^L)P_t I_t$, where i_t^L is the lending rate.

Repayment is uncertain and occurs with probability $q_t^F \in (0, 1)$. If loans are repaid in full, the total (interest-inclusive) cost of buying final goods for investment purposes is $(1 + i_t^L)P_t I_t$, where i_t^L is the lending rate. If there is default, which occurs with probability $1 - q_t^F$, the CG producer loses the collateral that it pledges to secure the loan; collateral is given by $\kappa P_t K_t$, where $\kappa \in (0, 1)$ is defined as a share of the capital stock that is pledged as collateral to the lender. As discussed in Chapter 6, coefficient κ can be viewed as a measure of efficiency of enforcement of debt contracts (see Djankov et al., 2008) or an inverse measure of anti-creditor bias in the judicial system (see Cavalcanti, 2010). Thus, the CG producer repays $(1 + i_t^L)P_t I_t$ with probability q_t^F and loses the collateral used to secure the loan with probability $1 - q_t^F$; expected repayment is $q_t^F(1 + i_t^L)P_t I_t + (1 - q_t^F)\kappa P_t K_t$.

The CG producer chooses the level of the capital stock (taking the rental rate, the lending rate, and the price of the final good as given) so as to maximize the value of the discounted stream of dividend payments to the household:

$$\{K_{t+s}\}_{s=0}^{\infty} = \arg\max \sum_{s=0}^{\infty} \mathbb{E}_t \left[\Lambda^s \lambda_{t+s} \left(\frac{J_{t+s+1}^K}{P_{t+s}} \right) \right], \tag{41}$$

where $\mathbb{E}_t[\Lambda^s \lambda_{t+s}(J_{t+s+1}^K / P_{t+s})]$ denotes discounted expected real profits at the end of period $t + s$, defined as

$$\mathbb{E}_t \left[\Lambda^s \lambda_{t+s} \left(\frac{J_{t+s+1}^K}{P_{t+s}} \right) \right] = \mathbb{E}_t \left\{ \Lambda^s \lambda_{t+s} \left[r_{t+s}^K K_{t+s} - [q_{t+s}^F(1 + i_{t+s}^L)I_{t+s} \right. \right.$$
$$\left. \left. + (1 - q_{t+s}^F)\kappa K_{t+s}]] \right\}.$$

Because the CG producer is owned by the household (to whom they transfer their profits), the discount factor for period-$t + s$ profits is again $\Lambda^s \lambda_{t+s}$. For simplicity, the stock of capital is valued at the price of the final good.

The first-order condition for maximization yields

$$
\mathbb{E}_t r_{t+1}^K = q_t^F (1 + i_t^L) \mathbb{E}_t \left\{ \left[1 + \Theta_K \left(\frac{K_{t+1}}{K_t} - 1 \right) \right] \left(\frac{1 + i_t^B}{1 + \pi_{t+1}} \right) \right\}
$$
$$
+ \mathbb{E}_t \left\{ (1 - q_{t+1}^F) \kappa - q_{t+1}^F (1 + i_{t+1}^L) \left\{ 1 - \delta + \frac{\Theta_K}{2} \left[\left(\frac{K_{t+2}}{K_{t+1}} \right)^2 - 1 \right] \right\} \right\},
$$
$$
\tag{42}
$$

which shows that the expected rental rate of capital is a function of the current and expected loan rates, the current and one-period ahead repayment probability, and the share of the capital stock used as collateral. The future values of the first two variables enter because of their effect on adjustment costs in the next period.

Without borrowing in advance (which takes out the interest component $i_t^L P_t I_t$ from profits), with no adjustment costs ($\Theta_K = 0$), and with full repayment ($q_t^F = 1$), this equation gives the standard arbitrage condition

$$
1 + \mathbb{E}_t r_{t+1}^K = \mathbb{E}_t \left(\frac{1 + i_t^B}{1 + \pi_{t+1}} \right) + \delta_K,
$$

which shows that the CG firm produces capital up to the point where the (expected) gross rental rate is equal to the (expected) gross real interest rate on government bonds, plus depreciation.

3.2.3 Commercial Bank

At the beginning of period t, the bank collects deposits D_t from the household. Funds are used for loans to the CG producer and IG producers, which use them to buy goods for investment purposes and pay labor in advance, respectively. Using (37) and (40), total lending, L_t^F, is equal to

$$
L_t^F = \int_0^1 L_t^{F,W} dj + L_t^{F,I} = P_t(\omega_t N_t + I_t), \tag{43}
$$

where $N_t = \int_0^1 N_t^j dj$ is aggregate labor demand by IG producers.

Upon receiving household deposits, and given its loans, the bank borrows from the central bank, L_t^B, to fund any shortfall in resources. At the end of the period, it repays the central bank, at the interest rate, i_t^R. It also holds unremunerated required reserves at the central bank, RR_t.[22] The bank's balance sheet is thus

$$L_t^F + RR_t = D_t + L_t^B. \tag{44}$$

The required level of reserves is determined by:

$$RR_t = \mu D_t, \tag{45}$$

where $\mu \in (0, 1)$ is the reserve requirement ratio.

Using (45), and given that L_t^F and D_t are determined by private agents' behavior, the balance sheet constraint (44) can be used to determine borrowing from the central bank:

$$L_t^B = L_t^F - (1 - \mu)D_t. \tag{46}$$

The bank is risk-neutral and chooses both the deposit and lending rates so as to maximize the present discounted value of its real profits:[23]

$$\{i_{t+s}^D, i_{t+s}^L\}_{s=0}^{\infty} = \arg\max \mathbb{E}_t \sum_{s=0}^{\infty} \Lambda^s \lambda_{t+s} \left(\frac{J_{t+s+1}^B}{P_{t+s}} \right),$$

where $\mathbb{E}_t(J_{t+s+1}^B/P_{t+s})$ denotes expected real profits at the end of period $t+s$. Because the bank is liquidated and debt is redeemed at the end of each period, this optimization program boils down to a period-by-period maximization problem, subject to the loan demand functions from the IG and CG producers, (37) and (40), and the balance sheet constraint (46).

Expected profits can be defined as

$$\mathbb{E}_t \left(\frac{J_{t+1}^B}{P_t} \right) = (1 + i_t^R) \left(\frac{L_t^{F,W}}{P_t} \right) + q_t^F (1 + i_t^L) \left(\frac{L_t^{F,I}}{P_t} \right) + (1 - q_t^F) \kappa K_t$$

$$+ \mu d_t - (1 + i_t^D) d_t - (1 + i_t^R) \left(\frac{L_t^B}{P_t} \right).$$

As defined earlier, the second term in this expression on the right-hand side, $q_t^F (1 + i_t^L) P_t^{-1} L_t^{F,I}$, represents expected repayment on loans to the CG producer

---

[22] For simplicity, the commercial bank holds no government bonds.

[23] To simplify matters, we solve only for the loan rate applicable to the CG producer. In principle, even if loans to IG producers carry no risk and are extended at the marginal cost of funds (the refinance rate), it should be assumed that the bank also determines it as part of its optimization problem—in which case the elasticity of the demand for working capital loans would affect the markup over the refinance rate. For simplicity, it has been assumed directly that the cost of these loans is only i_t^R.

if there is no default. The third term represents what the bank expects to earn in case of default, that is, real "effective" collateral.

The fourth term, μd_t, represents the reserve requirements held at the central bank and returned to the bank at the end of the period (prior to its closure). The term $(1 + i_t^D)d_t$ represents repayment of deposits (principal and interest) by the bank, whereas the term $(1 + i_t^R)P_t^{-1}L_t^B$ represents gross repayments to the central bank.

The bank internalizes the fact that the demand for loans by the CG producer (supply of deposits by unconstrained households) depends negatively (positively) on the lending (deposit) rate, as implied by (35) and (39), and takes the repayment probability of the CG producer, the value of collateral, prices and the refinance rate as given. The first-order conditions for maximization give

$$i_t^D = \left(1 + \frac{1}{\eta_D}\right)^{-1} (1 - \mu)i_t^R, \tag{47}$$

$$1 + i_t^L = \frac{1 + i_t^R}{(1 + \eta_F^{-1})q_t^F}, \tag{48}$$

where η_D is the interest elasticity of the supply of deposits to the deposit rate and η_F the interest elasticity of the CG demand for loans (or investment) to the lending rate.

Equation (47) shows that the equilibrium deposit rate is set as a markup over the refinance rate, adjusted (downward) for the implicit cost of holding reserve requirements. Equation (48) indicates that the gross lending rate depends negatively on the repayment probability and positively on the marginal cost of borrowing from the central bank, at the gross rate $1 + i_t^R$.

The repayment probability q_t^F is taken to depend positively on the effective collateral-CG loan ratio (which mitigates moral hazard on the part of borrowers) and the cyclical position of the economy (as measured by the output gap):

$$q_t^F = \left(\frac{\kappa P_t K_t}{L_t^{F,I}}\right)^{\varphi_1} (y_t^G)^{\varphi_2}, \tag{49}$$

with $\varphi_i > 0 \ \forall i$ and $y_t^G = Y_t / \bar{Y}_t$ is the output gap, with $\bar{Y}_t$ denoting the frictionless level of aggregate output (which obtains when $\theta = 0$). This semi-reduced-form approach to modeling the loan spread, which was used in Chapter 6, has been adopted in some other contributions. In Agénor and Pereira da Silva (2014), the repayment probability is endogenously determined as part of the bank's optimization process. Specifically, they assume that the bank can affect the repayment probability on its loans by expending effort to select (ex ante) and monitor (ex post) its borrowers; the higher the effort, the safer the loan. Assuming that the cost of monitoring depends (inversely) not only on the collateral-investment loan ratio but also on the cyclical position of the economy yields a specification similar to (49).

At the end of the period, the bank pays interest on deposits and repays with interest loans received from the central bank. Because the bank closes down, there are no retained earnings; all profits are rebated lump-sum to (unconstrained) households.

3.2.4 Central Bank

The central bank's assets consist of loans to the commercial bank, L_t^B, whereas its liabilities consists of currency supplied to (unconstrained) households and firms, M_t^s, and required reserves RR_t; the latter two make up the monetary base. The balance sheet of the central bank is thus given by

$$L_t^B = M_t^s + RR_t. \tag{50}$$

Using (45), (50) yields

$$M_t^s = L_t^B - \mu D_t. \tag{51}$$

Any income made by the central bank from loans to the commercial bank is transferred to the government at the end of each period.

As before, monetary policy is operated by fixing the refinance rate, as in (25), and provides an infinite supply of loans through a standing facility.

3.2.5 Government

The government budget constraint is now given by

$$P_t T_t + i_{t-1}^R L_{t-1}^B = (1 + i_{t-1}^B) B_{t-1} + P_t G_t, \tag{52}$$

where the term $i_{t-1}^R L_{t-1}^B$ represents interest income that the central bank makes from its lending to the commercial bank. Government purchases are fixed as in (20).

In a symmetric equilibrium, firms producing intermediate goods are identical. Thus, $K_{jt} = K_t$, $N_{jt} = N_t$, $Y_{jt} = Y_t$, $P_{jt} = P_t$, for all $j \in (0, 1)$. Equilibrium conditions must be satisfied for the credit, deposit, goods, and cash markets.[24] Because the supply of loans by the commercial bank, and the supply of deposits by households, are perfectly elastic at the prevailing interest rates, the markets for loans and deposits always clear. As before, equilibrium in the goods markets requires that production be equal to aggregate demand. With Rotemberg pricing, for instance, and using (20),

---

[24] By Walras' Law, the equilibrium condition of the market for government bonds can be eliminated.

the supply-demand equilibrium condition takes now the form

$$Y_t = C_t + G_t + I_t + \frac{\phi_F}{2}\left(\frac{1+\pi_t}{1+\tilde{\pi}} - 1\right)^2 Y_t. \tag{53}$$

The equilibrium condition of the market for cash is given by

$$M_t^s = M_t + M_t^F, \tag{54}$$

where M_t^s is defined in (51) and $M_t^F = \int_0^1 M_{jt}^F dj$ denotes cash holdings by IG firms and the capital producer. Suppose that bank loans to these agents are made only in the form of cash; we therefore have $L_t^F = M_t^F$.[25] Thus, (54) can be written as, using (51),

$$L_t^B - \mu D_t = M_t + L_t^F.$$

Using (46) to eliminate L_t^B in the above expression yields

$$M_t + D_t = 0.$$

As before, the equilibrium condition of the labor market is given as $N_t^S = \int_0^1 N_t^i di$ and bonds are in zero net supply.

The steady-state solution of the model is derived in Supplement C. With an inflation target π^T equal to zero, the steady-state inflation rate $\tilde{\pi}$ is also zero. In addition to the results discussed earlier (the steady-state value of the marginal cost, for instance, is given by $(\theta - 1)/\theta$), the steady-state value of the repayment probability is

$$\tilde{q}^F = \left\{\frac{\kappa \bar{P}\bar{K}}{\bar{L}^{F,I}}\right\}^{\varphi_1},$$

whereas steady-state interest rates are given by

$$\tilde{i}^B = \tilde{i}^R = \frac{1}{\Lambda} - 1 = \tilde{r},$$

$$\tilde{i}^D = \left(1 + \frac{1}{\eta_D}\right)^{-1}(1-\mu)\tilde{i}^R,$$

and

$$1 + \tilde{i}^L = \frac{\Lambda^{-1}}{(1+\eta_F^{-1})\tilde{q}^F}.$$

---

[25] See Agénor and Alper (2012) for a further discussion. Note also that this cash transits only briefly through IG and CG producers, who use it to pay wages and buy investment goods at the beginning of the period.

From these equations it can be shown that $\tilde{i}^B > \tilde{i}^D$. From (39), and given that from (42) $\bar{K} = \tilde{I}/\delta_K$, the steady-state level of the rental rate of capital is determined by

$$\tilde{r}^K = \tilde{q}(1 + \tilde{i}^L)(\Lambda^{-1} - 1 + \delta_K) + (1 - \tilde{q})\kappa,$$

which shows that the cost of borrowing has a direct effect on the rental rate.[26]

4   Calibration and Estimation

Recently developed second- or higher-order model solution methods make it possible to conduct more accurate welfare analysis of alternative monetary policy options.

    In the early literature, DSGE models were calibrated, rather than estimated. To a significant extent, calibration remains the tool of choice for small, exploratory models aimed at understanding a particular transmission channel. This is also often the only option when dealing with developing countries where data are scarce. However, DSGE models are more frequently estimated with historical data, using Bayesian methods. These methods have been the subject of major advances in recent years; they are used to characterize the posterior distribution of a model's parameters. This distribution combines the model's likelihood function with prior information on the parameters (see Schorfheide, 2011). To show that the estimated model provides a good fit to the data, researchers compare the second moments (in terms of standard deviations) implied by the estimated model with those measured in the data. Useful applications include Christiano, Motto, and Rostagno (2010) for industrial countries, and Lee and Rhee (2013) for Korea.

5   Extensions

From the perspective of developing countries, the introduction of financial frictions is of particular importance. There are also other important extensions to consider: heterogeneous agents and alternative expectational schemes; open-economy considerations; and macroprudential regulation.[27]

---

[26]Without borrowing in advance, and with no adjustment costs ($\Theta_K = 0$), the standard result obtains: $\tilde{r}^K = \beta^{-1} - (1 - \delta_K)$.

[27]Other challenges include uncertainties that policymakers face about the economic structure or the current state of economy, the nature and sources of shocks, the accuracy of available data, and accounting for labor market distortions and unemployment (see Christiano et al., 2011).

5.1 ■ Heterogeneous Agents and Expectations

As noted in Chapter 2, liquidity constraints are pervasive in developing countries; households are often unable to borrow to smooth consumption over time. As a result, consumption tends to follow movements in current income closely. A number of DSGE models incorporate this feature by distinguishing between optimizing households and liquidity-constrained (or hand-to-mouth) consumers, who do not participate in asset markets and follow a rule of thumb which involves consuming all their after-tax disposable wage income in each period. This departure from the representative agent framework helps to explain better the volatility of consumption in response to shocks (see for instance Agénor et al., 2013). However, most of these models keep the proportion of constrained households exogenous; future research needs to explain this factor endogenously.

In DSGE models, expectations about the future are the main channel through which policy affects the economy and therefore are a crucial determinant of today's outcomes. These expectations are rational in the sense that they are pinned down by the same mechanism that generates outcomes today. Therefore, output and inflation tomorrow, and thus their expectations as of today, depend on monetary policy tomorrow in the same way as they do today—taking into account what will happen from then on into the infinite future. At the same time, the management of expectations can be a more effective tool for stabilizing inflation than actual movements in the policy rate; this result is consistent with the increasing focus on central bankers' pronouncements of their future actions.

However, recent research on DSGE models has emphasized departures from pure forward-looking assumptions about expectations and aimed at adopting more realistic assumptions about rationality and expectations formation (see Woodford, 2013). Many models have (re-)introduced adaptive learning or partially backward-looking schemes, of the type discussed in Chapter 10. The evidence for middle-income countries does suggest that inflation expectations incorporate a strong backward-looking component (see Agénor and Bayraktar, 2010). Heterogeneity in expectations helps to better explain the persistence of inflation.

5.2 ■ Open-Economy Considerations

Open-economy extensions of DSGE models are particularly important for policy analysis in developing countries, given the range and magnitude of the external shocks that these countries face (see Chapter 1). Here again, the recent literature has to a large extent followed both the KM and BGG traditions. Lee and Rhee (2013) for instance provide a simple extension of the BGG model. Other applications include Choi and Cook (2004), Cook (2004), Cook and Devereux (2006a), Elekdag et al. (2006), Gertler et al. (2007), Leblebicioglu (2009), Christiano et al. (2011), Aysun and Honig (2011), Chang and Fernández (2013), and Agénor et al. (2014).

Agénor et al. (2014), in particular, highlight the role of banks in transmitting external financial shocks and the risk that capital flows, intermediated directly through the banking system, may lead to the formation of credit-fueled bubbles and foster financial instability. To conduct their analysis, they begin with the closed-economy model with credit market imperfections described earlier. A key feature of that model is a direct link between house prices and credit growth, via the impact of housing wealth on collateral and interest rate spreads. They extend that model in several directions.

First, the country produces a continuum of intermediate goods, which are imperfect substitutes to a continuum of imported intermediate goods. In line with the approach proposed by McCallum and Nelson (2000), imports are not treated as finished consumer goods but rather as intermediate goods, which are used (together with domestic intermediate goods) in the production of the domestic final good. This approach is particularly relevant for middle-income countries, where trade in raw materials accounts for a very large share of imports.[28] The final good is consumed by the household and the government, used for investment (subject to additional costs) by the CG producer, or exported. There is monopolistic competition in intermediate goods markets; each intermediate good is produced or imported by a single firm.

Second, they consider an open economy where capital is imperfectly mobile internationally, an assumption that accords well with the evidence reviewed in Chapter 13. Domestic private borrowers, as in the one- and three-good models developed in Chapter 10, face an upward-sloping supply curve of funds on world capital markets and internalize the effect of capital market imperfections in making their portfolio decisions. Thus, unlike New Keynesian models of the type developed by Kollman (2001), Caputo et al. (2006), Adolfson et al. (2008, 2014), Demirel (2010), and others, the external risk premium depends on the *individual's* borrowing needs, not the economy's overall level of debt. As a result of these imperfections, the domestic bond rate continues to be determined by the equilibrium condition of the money market, instead of foreign interest rates (as implied by uncovered interest rate parity under perfect capital mobility). Third, they consider a managed float and imperfect pass-through of nominal exchange-rate changes to domestic prices. Both features are well supported by the evidence (see Chapters 5 and 8).

Fourth, banks borrow on world capital markets, and their borrowing decisions affect the terms at which they obtain funds. At the same time, domestic agents (in particular, capital good producers), borrow only from domestic banks. These assumptions are in contrast to many contributions in the existing literature, where it is usually assumed that firms (or their owners, households) borrow directly on

---

[28] In Brazil, for instance, the average share of intermediate goods (including oil) in total imports amounted to 64 percent during 2006–2009; for Turkey, it exceeded 68 percent for the same period. As noted by McCallum and Nelson (2000), an advantage of this approach is that it avoids the assumption (implied by the tradable-nontradable dichotomy) that export and import goods are perfectly substitutable in production. However, here the relevant price index for produced goods is *not* the same as the consumer price index.

world capital markets subject to a binding constraint determined by their net worth. A sudden drop in the world risk-free rate induces banks to borrow more in foreign currency. This reduces their domestic borrowing from the central bank. Nevertheless, the inflow of foreign exchange is such that the monetary base expands, and this requires a lower bond rate to maintain equilibrium in the money market. The drop in the bond rate raises real estate prices, which increases the value of collateral that firms can pledge and lower the loan rate, thereby stimulating investment. Capital inflows may therefore generate an economic boom that is magnified by a financial accelerator effect, through their impact on collateral values, banks' balance sheets, and loan pricing decisions.[29] Fifth, the central bank does not engage in sterilization activities but it accumulates foreign-currency reserves based on a rule that depends on the volume of imports and net foreign-currency liabilities of the private sector.[30] The model also accounts for macroprudential regulation, an issue that we discuss next.

5.3 ▪ Macroprudential Regulation

The recent crisis in global financial markets has led to a substantial number of proposals aimed at strengthening the financial system and at encouraging more prudent lending behavior in upturns. Many of these proposals aim to mitigate the alleged procyclical effects of the Basel II capital standards, introduced in 2004 and which involved setting capital requirements on the basis of asset quality rather than only on asset type, as in the Basel I Accord introduced in 1988. Indeed, it has been argued that because of the backward-looking nature of its risk estimates (based on past loss experience) Basel II induces banks to hold too little capital in economic upswings and too much during downturns. Thus, it does not restrain lending sufficiently in boom times, while it restrains it too much during recessions. By raising capital requirements in a countercyclical way, regulators could help to slow credit growth and choke off asset price pressures before a crisis occurs. The new Basel III Accord adopted in November 2010 incorporates a proposal to implement a countercyclical capital buffer ranging from 0 to 2.5 percent of risk-weighted assets (see Basel Committee on Banking Supervision, 2011). The Accord also proposes a number of other macroprudential tools, including dynamic provisions, a leverage ratio, and a net funding ratio.

---

[29]Note that, in practice, nonbank firms have also benefited extensively from the current global excess liquidity conditions, which poses other complex problems of financial disintermediation, supervision, balance sheet imbalances, and risks to financial instability. These issues are not considered by Agénor et al., but nevertheless pose critical challenges to policymakers.

[30]As documented by Aizenman and Glick (2009), even though the degree of sterilization (as measured by offset coefficients) has increased in recent years in many middle-income countries, it remains imperfect—especially in Latin America. Note also that in thin and imperfect financial markets, sterilized intervention often drives up interest rates on the securities used for intervention—and this often results in even greater capital inflows. The policy may therefore not be sustainable, in addition to being costly.

The use of macroprudential tools raises a host of issues, both independently and in conjunction with monetary policy, as discussed in Chapter 7. To promote financial stability, how should countercyclical bank capital requirement rules be designed? Instead of adding a cyclical component to prudential regulation, shouldn't policymakers use monetary policy to constrain credit growth directly? To what extent should regulatory policy and monetary policy be combined to ensure both macroeconomic and financial stability? Put differently, are these policies complementary or substitutes? How large are the gains, in terms of reductions in macroeconomic and financial volatility, associated with the introduction of policy measures aimed at mitigating procyclical swings in credit conditions?[31] Quantitative studies of these issues are important for a number of reasons. Regarding the design of countercyclical bank capital rules, several observers have noted that there are indeed significant potential practical problems associated with their implementation—including the period over which relevant financial indicators (credit growth rates, for that matter) should be calculated. More important perhaps is the possibility that these rules may operate in counterintuitive ways, depending on the degree of financial sector imperfections. In particular, in countries where bank credit plays a critical role in financing short-term economic activity, a rule that constrains the growth in overall credit could entail a welfare cost. At the same time, of course, to the extent that it succeeds in reducing financial volatility and the risk of a full-blown crisis, it may also enhance welfare. The net benefits of countercyclical bank capital rules may therefore be ambiguous in general and numerical evaluations become essential.

With these issues in mind, the analysis of the use of macroprudential tools (especially countercyclical capital requirements) in DSGE models with financial frictions has proceeded at a fairly rapid pace in recent years; a partial review is provided in Galati and Moessner (2013). From the perspective of developing countries, Agénor et al. (2013, 2014) provide a useful analysis. Agénor et al. (2013) focus on a closed economy and examine the role of both monetary policy and a countercyclical capital regulation rule, and evaluate their implications for macroeconomic stability and financial stability—defined in terms of the volatility of nominal income, on the one hand, and the volatility of a measure of potential financial stress, on the other. They do so under a Basel II-type regime, with endogenous risk weights on bank assets. Regarding the role of monetary policy, the key issue is whether a central bank with a preference for output and price stability can improve its performance with respect not only to these two objectives but also to financial stability, by responding to excessive movements in credit and/or asset prices in addition to fluctuations in prices and activity.

To conduct their analysis, they extend the DSGE model described in Agénor et al. (2012). Important features of that model are that it accounts explicitly for a variety of credit market imperfections, and bank capital regulation. A housing

---

[31] See Athanasoglou et al. (2014) for an overview of the literature on procyclicality in banking.

sector is introduced and the role of real estate as collateral examined. Specifically, they establish a direct link between house prices and credit growth via their impact on collateral values and interest rate spreads on loans: higher house prices enable producers to borrow and invest more, by raising the value of the collateral that they can pledge and improving the terms at which credit is extended. This mechanism is consistent with the evidence suggesting that a large value of bank loans to (small) firms, in both industrial and developing countries, is often secured by real estate. To capture financial instability, they focus initially on the behavior of real house prices. This is also in line with the literature suggesting that financial crises are often preceded by unsustainable developments in the real estate sector and private sector credit (see Chapters 14 and 15).

They examine the implications of two alternative policy rules for economic stability: a standard Taylor-type interest rate rule augmented to account for credit growth, and (in line with the Basel III regime) a countercyclical regulatory rule that relates capital requirements also to credit growth. Their numerical experiments show that even if monetary policy can react strongly to inflation deviations from target, combining a credit-augmented interest rate rule and a countercyclical capital regulatory rule may be optimal for promoting overall economic stability. The greater the degree of interest rate smoothing, and the stronger the policymaker's concern with macroeconomic stability, the larger is the sensitivity of the regulatory rule to credit growth gaps.

This analysis is then extended to an open-economy setting in Agénor et al. (2014) to consider the role of bank regulation as a policy to mitigate the adverse effects of sudden floods in capital flows, induced by external financial shocks. The reason is that absorbing large amounts of capital inflows while preserving an independent monetary policy and maintaining macroeconomic and financial stability at home has proved to be a challenge. As discussed in Chapter 13, sudden floods of private capital have been a source of macroeconomic instability in many developing countries, as a result of rapid credit and monetary expansion (due to the difficulty and cost of pursuing sterilization policies), real exchange-rate appreciation, and widening current account deficits. In particular, the surge in capital flows to Latin America between early 2009 and mid-2011 induced booms in credit and equity markets in many countries and raised concerns about asset price bubbles and financial fragility.[32]

At the same time, the scope for responding to the risk of macroeconomic and financial instability through monetary policy may be limited, because higher domestic interest rates vis-à-vis zero interest floors prevailing in advanced economies may exacerbate the flood of private capital. Other measures must be considered; these include direct taxes on fixed income and equity inflows, foreign exchange market

---

[32]Under a flexible exchange rate, growing external deficits tend to bring about a currency depreciation, which may eventually lead to a realignment of relative prices and induce self-correcting movements in trade flows. However, sharp swings in capital flows make it more difficult for the central bank to strike a balance between its different objectives; in turn, this may lead to exchange rate volatility.

intervention, and, more recently, macroprudential tools. Again, Agénor et al. (2014) focus on countercyclical capital buffers and the extent to which they allow policy-makers to internalize potential trade-offs between the objectives of macroeconomic stability and financial stability (measured on the basis of the volatility of asset prices, domestic credit, and bank foreign borrowing).

Their quantitative experiments, using a calibrated version of the model for a middle-income economy, shows that a sudden flood in foreign capital, induced by a drop in the world risk-free interest rate, generates pressure on asset prices and an economic boom, the magnitude of which depends on bank pricing behavior and the nature of the regulatory regime. They also found that countercyclical capital regulation—in a setting where the central bank cannot raise interest rates due to the risk of exacerbating capital inflows—may be quite effective at promoting both macro-economic and financial stability. However, the marginal gain in terms of reduced volatility may exhibit diminishing returns—essentially because regulatory-induced volatility in capital holdings translates into volatility in lending and other macroeco-nomic and financial variables, including foreign bank borrowing and the exchange rate. In the end, an aggressive countercyclical capital regulatory rule may do little to reduce the volatility of capital flows. These results suggest that countercyclical capital buffers may need to be supplemented by other, more targeted, macroprudential instruments, such as loan-to-value and debt-to-income ratios. Understanding how these instruments interact, and more generally the interactions between financial frictions and the nature of the regulatory regime, are only some of the issues that need to be addressed in the context of future research on DSGE models.

Chapter 13

Financial Integration
and Capital Flows

T he degree of integration of financial markets around the world increased significantly during the late 1980s and 1990s. A key factor underlying this process has been the increased globalization of investments seeking higher rates of return and the opportunity to diversify risk internationally. At the same time, many countries have encouraged inflows of capital by dismantling restrictions and controls on capital outflows, deregulating domestic financial markets, liberalizing restrictions on foreign direct investment, and improving their economic environment and prospects through the introduction of market-oriented reforms. Indeed, many developing and transition economies in East Asia, Latin America, and Eastern Europe removed restrictions on international financial transactions, at the same time that they relaxed regulations on the operation of domestic financial markets and moved away from regimes of financial repression.

The increase in the degree of integration of world capital markets has been accompanied by a significant rise in private capital flows to developing countries. Foreign direct investment to these countries started growing in the 1980s and expanded at an accelerated rate after 1990, whereas portfolio flows have fluctuated significantly. Short-term, cross-border capital flows have also become more responsive to changes in relative rates of return, as a result of technological advances and increased linkages among capital markets.

Financial openness is often regarded as providing important potential benefits. Access to world capital markets, as noted earlier, expands investors' opportunities for portfolio diversification and provides the potential for achieving higher risk-adjusted rates of return. From the point of view of the recipient country, there are potentially large benefits as well. It has been argued that access to world capital markets allows countries to borrow to smooth consumption in the face of adverse shocks, and that the potential growth and welfare gains resulting from such international risk sharing can be large and permanent (Obstfeld, 1994). At the same time, however, it has been recognized that the risk of volatility and abrupt reversals in capital flows in the context of a highly open capital account may represent a significant cost. Concerns associated with such reversals were heightened by a series of recent financial crises (see online Supplement D). Although misaligned fundamentals played a very important role in all of the above crises (in the form of either overvalued exchange rates, excessive short-term foreign borrowing, or growing fiscal and current account imbalances), they have called attention to the inherent instability of international financial markets and the risks that cross-border financial transactions can pose for countries with relatively fragile financial systems and weak regulatory and supervisory structures. From that perspective, a key issue has been to identify the policy prerequisites that may allow countries to exploit the gains, while minimizing the risks, associated with financial openness.

This chapter begins with a selective review of the recent analytical and empirical literature on the benefits and costs of international financial integration.[1] Section 2 discusses explanations that are often offered to explain episodes of capital inflows into developing countries. Section 3 examines the policy challenges posed by these inflows and the policy options available to the recipient countries. The Appendix discusses alternative ways to measure the degree of financial integration or, more specifically, the degree of capital mobility.

1 ■ Benefits and Costs of Financial Integration

This section provides a selective review of the recent analytical and empirical literature on the benefits and costs of international financial integration, to identify some key policy lessons for small open economies. The first part reviews analytical arguments related to the benefits and costs of integration.[2] The second part provides an assessment of the empirical evidence on the benefits and costs of financial integration, highlighting in the process areas in which this evidence appears to lack robustness.

1.1 ■ Potential Benefits

Analytical arguments supporting financial openness (or, equivalently, an open capital account) revolve around four main considerations: the benefits of international risk

---

[1] Section 1 draws largely from Agénor (2012a), whereas Section 3 draws heavily on Montiel (1996). We do not discuss capital flows from developing to industrial countries; see von Hagen and Zhuang (2014) for a formal analysis.

[2] The benefits and costs of financial integration can be viewed either from the point of view of individual investors (such as, for instance, the opportunity for international risk diversification, as indicated earlier) or from the point of view of the countries initiating the process of integration. This chapter focuses solely on the second perspective, ignoring in the process issues such as the "home-bias puzzle" often observed in the behavior of private capital flows. See Coeurdacier and Rey (2013).

sharing for consumption smoothing; the positive impact of capital flows on domestic investment and growth; enhanced macroeconomic discipline; and increased efficiency, as well as greater stability, of the domestic financial system associated with foreign bank penetration.

1.1.1   Consumption Smoothing

Access to world capital markets may allow a country to engage in risk sharing and consumption smoothing, by allowing the country to borrow in "bad" times (say, during a recession or a sharp deterioration in the country's terms of trade) and lend in "good" times (say, in an expansion or following an improvement in the country's terms of trade). By enabling domestic households to smooth their consumption path over time, capital flows can therefore increase welfare. This countercyclical role of world capital markets is particularly important if shocks are temporary in nature. Bekaert et al. (2006) found that financial liberalization (in the form of equity market liberalization and capital account openness) is indeed associated with lower consumption growth volatility. Countries that have more open capital accounts experience a greater reduction in consumption growth volatility after equity market openings. They also find that financial liberalizations are associated with declines in the ratio of consumption growth volatility to GDP growth volatility, suggesting improved risk sharing. In the same vein, and using a novel methodology, Suzuki (2014) found that both the OECD and the non-OECD countries in his sample appear to benefit from financial integration in terms of consumption risk sharing and smoothing.

1.1.2   Domestic Investment and Growth

The ability to draw upon the international pool of resources that financial openness gives access to may also affect domestic investment and growth. In many developing countries, the capacity to save is constrained by a low level of income. As long as the marginal return from investment is at least equal to the cost of (borrowed) capital, net foreign resource inflows can supplement domestic saving, increase levels of physical capital per worker, and help the recipient country raise its rate of economic growth and improve living standards. These potential benefits can be particularly large for some types of capital inflows, most notably foreign direct investment (FDI).

In addition to this direct effect on growth, FDI may also have significant indirect long-run effects. FDI may facilitate the transfer or diffusion of managerial and technological know-how—particularly in the form of new varieties of capital inputs, as in Grossman and Helpman (1991)—and improve the skills composition of the labor force as a result of "learning by doing" effects, investment in formal education, and on-the-job training. In addition, as suggested by Markusen and Venables (1999), although the increased degree of competition in the product and factor markets induced by FDI may tend to reduce profits of local firms, spillover effects through linkages to supplier industries may reduce input costs, raise profits, and stimulate domestic investment.

FDI also has a risk-sharing advantage over other capital flows. As argued by Albuquerque (2003), this advantage results from the fact that although imperfect enforcement of financial contracts and expropriation risk lead to endogenous financing constraints and the emergence of a default premium on all types of capital flows, FDI is harder to expropriate than other flows (as it involves the use of intangible assets of the multinational company, such as human and organization capital, and technological advances). This translates into a lower default premium on FDI and lower sensitivity to changes in a country's financing constraint. The important point is that countries (particularly those that are financially constrained) should indeed borrow more through FDI—but not because it is more productive or less volatile.

To highlight the complementarity (through productivity effects) between FDI and skilled human capital in the growth process, consider, following Borensztein et al. (1998), an economy in which the source of technological progress is an increase in the number of varieties of capital goods available to producers, which consist of local and foreign firms. Suppose also that the economy produces a single final consumption good using the following technology:

$$Y = S^{\alpha} K^{1-\alpha}, \tag{1}$$

where $\alpha \in (0, 1)$, S is the economy's endowment of skilled labor (assumed given), and K is the stock of physical capital, which is itself a composite of a continuum of different varieties of capital goods, each one denoted by $x(j)$:

$$K = \int_{0}^{N} \left[x(j)^{1-\alpha} dj \right]^{1/(1-\alpha)}, \tag{2}$$

with N denoting the total number of varieties. Physical capital accumulation therefore takes place through an increase in the number of varieties of capital goods produced domestically.

Suppose that there are two types of firms producing capital goods: foreign firms, which produce $n^* < N$ varieties, and domestic firms, which produce the other $N - n^*$ varieties. Specialized firms produce each variety j of capital goods and rent it out to producers of final goods at a rate $m(j)$. The optimal demand for each variety j is thus determined by equating the rental rate and the marginal productivity of j in the production of the final good:

$$m(j) = (1 - \alpha) S^{\alpha} x(j)^{-\alpha}. \tag{3}$$

An increase in the number of varieties of capital goods available to producers is assumed to require the adaptation of technology available in more advanced countries. This adaptation to local needs requires a fixed setup cost, F, which is assumed to depend negatively on the ratio of foreign firms operating domestically to the total number of firms, n^*/N. Thus, $F = F(n^*/N)$, with $F' < 0$.[3] This assumption captures the idea that foreign firms make it easier to adopt the more advanced technology required to produce new varieties of capital, by bringing in the "knowledge" already available elsewhere.

In addition to this fixed cost, once a capital good is introduced, its owner must spend a constant maintenance cost per period of time. This is equivalent to assuming that production of $x(j)$ involves a constant marginal cost equal to unity and that capital goods depreciate fully. Assuming that the interest rate r that firms face is constant, profits for the producer of a variety j, denoted $\Pi(j)$, are given by

$$\Pi(j) = -F + \int_0^\infty [m(j)x(j) - x(j)] \exp(-rs)ds. \tag{4}$$

Maximization of (4) subject to (3) yields the equilibrium level of production of each capital good:

$$x(j) = S(1-\alpha)^{2/\alpha},$$

which shows that, given the assumption of symmetry among producers, the level of production of the different varieties of capital is the same.[4] Assuming free entry, it can be shown that the zero-profit condition implies that

$$r = \phi S/F, \tag{5}$$

where $\phi \equiv \alpha(1-\alpha)^{(2-\alpha)/\alpha} > 0$.

To close the model requires specifying savings decisions, which determine the process of capital accumulation. Suppose that households face a rate of return also equal to r and that they maximize a standard intertemporal utility function given by the discounted present value of consumption, C. It can be shown (see, for instance, Chapter 4, Section 3) that the optimal solution for the rate of growth of consumption, g_C, is:

$$\mathbf{g}_C = \sigma(r - \rho), \tag{6}$$

---

[3] Borensztein et al. (1998) also discuss a second possible effect on F, namely, the possibility of a "catch-up" effect in technological progress reflecting the fact that it may be cheaper to imitate products already in existence than to create new ones at the cutting edge of innovation. This notion is implemented in their model by assuming that setup costs depend positively on the number of capital varieties produced domestically, compared to those produced abroad.

[4] Substituting the optimal level of production into (3) yields the constant equilibrium rental rate, $m(j) = 1/(1-\alpha)$, as a markup over maintenance costs.

where ρ is the rate of time preference and σ measures the intertemporal elasticity of substitution. In a stationary state, the rate of growth of consumption must be equal to the rate of growth of output, g. Substituting (5) in (6) therefore yields the economy's growth rate:

$$\mathbf{g} = \sigma[\phi S/F(n^*/N) - \rho]. \tag{7}$$

Equation (7) shows that FDI, as measured by the fraction of capital goods produced locally by foreign firms in the total number of these goods, n^*/N, has a positive effect on the economy's long-term growth rate. The reason is that FDI reduces the cost of introducing new varieties of capital, thereby increasing the rate at which these goods are introduced. Moreover, the effect of FDI on the economy's growth rate is positively related to the existing stock of skilled labor employed in production—this is the complementarity effect mentioned earlier.

1.1.3 *Enhanced Macroeconomic Discipline*

It has also been argued that by increasing the rewards of good policies and the penalties for bad policies, the free flow of capital across borders may induce countries to follow more disciplined macroeconomic policies and thus reduce the frequency of policy mistakes. To the extent that greater policy discipline translates into greater macroeconomic stability, it may also lead to higher rates of economic growth, as emphasized in the recent literature on endogenous growth. A related argument is that external financial liberalization can act as a "signal" that a country is willing (or ready) to adopt "sound" macroeconomic policies, for instance by reducing budget deficits and foregoing the use of the inflation tax (Bartolini and Drazen, 1997). From that perspective, an open capital account may also encourage macroeconomic and financial stability, ensuring a more efficient allocation of resources and higher rates of economic growth.

1.1.4 *Banking System Efficiency and Financial Stability*

An increasingly common argument in favor of financial openness is that it may increase the depth and breadth of domestic financial markets and lead to an increase in the degree of efficiency of the financial intermediation process, by lowering costs and "excessive" profits associated with monopolistic or cartelized markets. In turn, improved efficiency may lead to lower markup rates in banking, a lower cost of investment, and higher growth rates (see Baldwin and Forslid, 2000). More generally, Levine (1996) has argued that foreign bank penetration may

- improve the quality and availability of financial services in the domestic market, by increasing the degree of bank competition and enabling the application of more sophisticated banking techniques and technology (such as more advanced risk management systems), which may improve efficiency by reducing the cost of acquiring and processing information on potential borrowers;

- serve to stimulate the development of the domestic bank supervisory and legal framework, if the local foreign banks are supervised on a consolidated basis with their parent;

- enhance a country's access to international capital, either directly or indirectly through parent banks;

- contribute to the stability of the domestic financial system (and reduced volatility in capital flows) if, in periods of financial instability, depositors may shift their funds to foreign institutions that are perceived to be more sound than domestically owned banks, rather than transferring assets abroad through capital flight.

In addition, foreign banks may also contribute to an improvement in the overall quality of the loan portfolios of domestic banks if they are less susceptible to government pressure to lend to "preferred" borrowers—as may be the case with domestic financial institutions, particularly those in which the state is involved.

1.2 ■ Potential Costs

The experience of the past two decades has led economists and policymakers to recognize that, in addition to the potential benefits just discussed, open financial markets may also generate significant costs. These costs include a high degree of concentration of capital flows and lack of access to financing for small countries, either permanently or when they need it most; an inadequate domestic allocation of these flows, which may hamper their growth effects and exacerbate preexisting domestic distortions; the loss of macroeconomic stability; procyclical movements in short-term capital flows; a high degree of volatility of capital flows, which relates in part to herding and contagion effects; and risks associated with foreign bank penetration.

1.2.1 *Concentration of Capital Flows and Lack of Access*

There is ample historical evidence to suggest that periods of "surge" in cross-border capital flows tend to be highly concentrated in a small number of recipient countries. The dramatic increase in capital inflows in the early 1990s, for instance, was directed to only a small number of large, middle-income countries of Latin America and Asia (see Fernández-Arias and Montiel, 1996). The share of total private capital flows going to low-income countries actually fell during the 1990s (from levels that were already quite low), whereas the share going to the top ten recipients increased significantly. Little foreign capital is directed to Sub-Saharan African countries, and most of what flows to the region continues to be limited to a few countries with significant natural resources (see Basu and Srinivasan, 2002). The capital inflow episode that started in 2003, and gathered pace in 2006–2007, displays the same features, with a considerable share of total flows going to just two countries (China and India). Thus, a number of developing countries (particularly the small ones) may simply be "rationed out" of world capital markets—regardless of how open their capital account is.[5]

1.2.2 Domestic Misallocation of Capital Flows

Although the inflows of capital associated with an open capital account may raise domestic investment, their impact on long-run growth may be limited (if not negligible) if such inflows are used to finance speculative or low-quality domestic investments—such as investments in the real estate sector. Low-productivity investments in the nontradables sector may reduce the economy's capacity to export over time and lead to growing external imbalances.

The misallocation of capital inflows may in part be the result of preexisting distortions in the domestic financial system. In countries with weak banks (that is, banks with low or negative net worth and a low ratio of capital to risk-adjusted assets) and poor supervision of the financial system, the direct or indirect intermediation of large amounts of funds by the banking system may exacerbate the moral hazard problems associated with (explicit or implicit) deposit insurance. That is, lenders may engage in riskier and more concentrated (or outright speculative) loan operations.

An example of how asymmetric information problems can affect the benefits of capital inflows is provided by Razin et al. (2000), who focus on the impact of FDI flows. They argue that through FDI and the transfer of control that it entails, foreign investors may gain inside information about the productivity of the firm(s) that they are investing in. This gives them an informational advantage over less informed domestic investors (whose holdings of shares may be insufficient to give them corporate control)—an advantage that they may be tempted to exploit by retaining the high-productivity firms and selling the low-productivity ones to partially informed domestic savers. This type of adverse selection problem can lead to over-investment by foreign direct investors. Moreover, asymmetric information can interact with economic behavior in such a way as to affect the response of capital flows to shocks. Gopinath (2004) for instance showed that in an economy where foreign investors do not have adequate information about returns associated with investment projects, they engage in costly search to evaluate different projects. This search friction generates an asymmetric response in capital flows, with a gradual inflow and gradual project creation in response to positive shocks and a sharp outflow and sharp project destruction in response to negative shocks.

---

[5] Imrohoroglu and Kumar (2004) develop a model in which financial intermediation costs help to explain why capital tends to flow from rich countries to middle-income countries, rather than capital-scarce, poor countries (where apparent rates of return may be higher).

1.2.3   Loss of Macroeconomic Stability

The large capital inflows induced by financial openness can have undesirable macro-economic effects, including rapid monetary expansion (due to the difficulty and cost of pursuing sterilization policies), inflationary pressures (resulting from the effect of capital inflows on domestic spending), real exchange rate appreciation, and widening current account deficits.

As formally established by Aghion et al. (2004*b*), capital account liberalization (and the capital inflows that it leads to) may be particularly destabilizing in economies at an intermediate level of financial development—as opposed to countries that are either very developed financially or underdeveloped. The reason essentially is that, at high levels of financial development, borrowing constraints on firms' investment become less binding, whereas at low levels of financial development, firms cannot borrow much to begin with.

1.2.4   Procyclicality of Short-Term Flows

As noted earlier, small developing economies are often rationed out of world capital markets. Moreover, among those countries with a greater potential to access these markets (such as oil producers), the availability of resources may be asymmetric. These countries may indeed be able to borrow only in "good" times, whereas in "bad" times they tend to face credit constraints. Access may thus be procyclical. Clearly, in such conditions, one of the alleged benefits of accessing world capital markets, the ability to borrow to smooth consumption in the face of temporary adverse shocks, is simply a fiction. Pro cyclicality may, in fact, have a perverse effect and increase macroeconomic instability: favorable shocks may attract large capital inflows and encourage consumption and spending at levels that are unsustainable in the longer term, forcing countries to over-adjust when an adverse shock hits.

There are essentially two reasons that may explain the procyclical behavior of short-term capital flows. First, economic shocks tend to be larger and more frequent in developing countries, reflecting these countries' relatively narrow production base and greater dependence on primary commodity exports. A common adverse shock to a group of countries may cause a deterioration in some countries' creditworthiness, as a result of abrupt changes in risk perception. This can lead borrowers who are only marginally creditworthy to be "squeezed out" of world capital markets. Second, asymmetric information problems may trigger herding behavior (as further discussed later) because partially informed investors may rush to withdraw "en masse" their capital in response to an adverse shock whose economic consequences for the country are not fully understood.

1.2.5   Herding, Contagion, and Volatility of Capital Flows

A high degree of financial openness may be conducive to a high degree of volatility in capital movements, a specific manifestation of which is large reversals in short-term flows associated with speculative pressures on the domestic currency. The possibility of large reversals of short-term capital flows raises the risk that borrowers may face costly "liquidity runs," or "sudden stops," as discussed later. The higher the level of short-term debt is relative to the borrowing country's international reserves, the greater the risk of liquidity runs will be. High levels of short-term liabilities intermediated by the financial system also create risks of bank runs and systemic financial crises.

In general, the degree of volatility of capital flows is related to both actual and perceived movements in domestic economic fundamentals, as well as external factors, such as movements in world interest rates.[6] The volatility of capital flows can have sizable real effects. Suppose, for instance, that foreign investors seek high-return investment projects in a developing country. As in Gopinath (2004), suppose also that these investors are constrained in their investment decisions by the need to determine the idiosyncratic type of each potential project through a time-consuming evaluation process and face an endogenously determined adjustment hazard, that is, a nonzero probability that the investment will not be successful. Thus, each investor has an incentive to search for a project with high idiosyncratic returns, and investment decisions will incorporate the option value to waiting (see Chapter 2). By implication, at any point in time, both "project creation" (when new projects get activated by foreign investors) and "project destruction" (when foreign investors withdraw from projects) may be observed. But, in response to a deterioration in fundamentals (resulting for instance from an adverse productivity shock), previously good matches may now provide inadequate returns and one may observe a sudden rise in "project destruction," which in turn may generate an asymmetrically sharp contraction in output. Search frictions in entry and exit decisions of investors may therefore magnify the impact of abrupt reversals in capital flows on output.

More generally, the fact that investor sentiment (particularly that of highly leveraged, speculative trading institutions, such as hedge funds) is constantly changing in response to new information creates the potential for markets to overshoot on a scale that can generate financial crises with very large economic and social costs. Short-term portfolio flows, in particular, tend to be very sensitive to herding among investors and contagious factors.[7] Although investor herding is seen by some as evidence of irrationality, some recent literature suggests differently. Herding can be a "rational" response in the presence of several effects (Devenow and Welch, 1996):

- payoff externalities, which are related to the fact that the payoff to an agent (investor) adopting a specific action may be positively related to the number of other agents adopting the same action;

---

[6]Smith and Valderrama (2009) have argued that some of the observed volatility of capital flows may be an equilibrium outcome, which reflects (optimal) financing decisions by firms that are subject to borrowing constraints. However, at this time there is little to substantiate that claim.

[7]See Chari and Kehoe (2004) for a model of herding behavior.

- principal-agent considerations, which result from the fact that a portfolio manager, in order to maintain or improve his or her reputation when markets are imperfectly informed, may prefer either to "hide in the herd" to avoid evaluation and criticism, or to "ride the herd" to generate reputational gains;

- information cascades, which are due to the fact that (small) agents that are only beginning to invest in a country may find it optimal to ignore their own information and follow the behavior of larger and more established investors.

In any case, whether rational or irrational, herding behavior often translates into large movements into and out of certain types of assets and exacerbates fluctuations in asset prices and capital movements.

Volatility of capital flows can also result from contagion effects.[8] Financial contagion may occur when a country suffers massive capital outflows triggered by a perceived increase in the vulnerability of a country's currency by international investors, or, more generally, a loss of confidence in the country's economic prospects, as a result of developments elsewhere (see Masson, 2000). It may also occur through two other channels, with indirect effects on the volatility of capital flows: terms-of-trade shocks or competitiveness effects. An example of the former effect is provided by the events that followed the Asia crisis, which led to a sharp reduction in the demand for imports by crisis-stricken countries and a sharp drop in world commodity prices. By increasing the degree of uncertainty regarding the short-term economic prospects of a country, terms-of-trade shocks may translate into financial contagion—as appeared to have happened in the case of Chile in late 1997 and early 1998. Changes in the terms of trade may also create contagion through collateral-based credit constraints (see Paasche, 2001). As an example of the latter effect, the sharp depreciation of the Thai baht that began in July 1997 put pressure on the currencies of neighboring countries that maintained a pegged exchange rate, in part because it implied a large loss of competitiveness for these countries (see Chapter 14).

Chang and Majnoni (2002) develop a model in which both fundamentals and self-fulfilling beliefs may cause contagion. In their model, the probability of a financial crisis in any given country depends on foreign investors' beliefs about the distribution of its fundamentals, and also on "animal spirits" or sunspots—which are independent across countries. In this setting, contagion occurs if a crisis in one country leads investors to rationally and adversely update their beliefs about fundamentals in other countries. However, purely expectational crises may still be contagious; this is the case if investors cannot determine whether the originating crisis has been caused by weak fundamentals or animal spirits. Their analysis carries some important lessons. First, it implies that a country is more vulnerable to contagion if its fundamentals

---

[8]For an overview of the literature on contagion and a comparison of alternative definitions, see Pericoli and Sbracia (2003).

(in particular its financial position) are weak. Second, how contagious a crisis is depends on the amount of information the crisis-stricken country releases. If information is sufficient for investors, then they can discern whether the crisis is caused by fundamentals or beliefs; a fundamentals-driven crisis will tend to be more contagious than a beliefs-driven crisis and will be more contagious than when information is less complete. The policy implication is that better information would not eliminate contagion. Instead, more transparency would make some kinds of crises more contagious and some others less so.

1.2.6 *Risk of Entry by Foreign Banks*

Although foreign bank penetration can yield several types of benefits (as discussed earlier), it has some potential drawbacks as well. First, foreign banks may ration credit to small firms (which tend to operate in the nontradables sector) to a larger extent than domestic banks, and concentrate instead on larger and stronger ones (which are often involved in the production of tradables). If foreign banks do indeed follow a strategy of concentrating their lending operations only to the most creditworthy corporate (and, to a lesser extent, household) borrowers, their presence will be less likely to contribute to an overall increase in efficiency in the financial sector. More important, by leading to a higher degree of credit rationing to small firms, they may have an adverse effect on output, employment, and income distribution.

Second, entry of foreign banks, which tend to have lower operational costs, can create pressures on local banks to merge in order to remain competitive. The process of concentration (which could also arise as foreign banks acquire local banks) could create banks that are "too big to fail" or "too political to fail"—as monetary authorities may fear that the failure of a single large bank could seriously disrupt financial markets and lead to social disruptions. Although these potential problems could be mitigated through enhanced prudential supervision or an outright ban on mergers that are perceived to increase systemic risks sharply, they may lead to an undesirable extension of the scope and cost of the official safety net. A too-big-to-fail problem may, in turn, increase moral hazard problems: knowing the existence of an (implicit) safety net, domestic banks (particularly those in which the state is involved) may be less careful in allocating credit and screening potential borrowers. Concentration could also create monopoly power that would reduce the overall efficiency of the banking system and the availability of credit. In particular, a high degree of banking system concentration may adversely affect output and growth by yielding both higher interest rate spreads (with higher loan rates and lower deposit rates relative to competitive credit and deposit markets) and a lower amount of loans than in a less concentrated, more competitive system.

Third, entry of foreign banks may not lead to enhanced stability of the domestic banking system, because their presence per se does not make systemic banking crises less likely to occur—as may happen if the economy undergoes a severe and persistent recession, leading to a large increase in default rates and a rise in nonperforming loans, and because they may have a tendency to "cut and run" during a crisis. To some extent, the latter effect could again be mitigated by strengthening prudential supervision in domestic markets and improving information sharing between supervisors in industrial and receiving countries. In practice, however, countries have very few options to prevent foreign banks from, say, cutting lines of credit to domestic borrowers in a crisis.

1.3 ■ Assessing the Evidence

The foregoing discussion suggests that, from a purely analytical point of view, it cannot be established a priori whether the benefits of financial openness are likely to outweigh its potential costs. One must therefore resort to the empirical evidence to determine if, on balance, unambiguous conclusions can be drawn. At the outset, it is important to note that the task is far from being straightforward, although some of the historical evidence for smaller industrial countries appears to suggest substantial net benefits. The reason is that to quantify the gains countries can reap from international financial integration would require, to be rigorous, a fully articulated model in which the counterfactual of financial autarky could be simulated. So far there has been no such ambitious attempt.

Agénor (2012a) provided a selective review of the evidence, both formal (econometric) and informal (country experiences), focusing on the determinants of the volatility and procyclicality of capital flows, the impact of the degree of financial openness and capital flows on domestic investment and growth, the macroeconomic effects of large capital inflows (dwelling mostly on the experience of the early 1990s), and the effect of foreign bank entry on the performance and stability of the domestic financial system. On balance, several conclusions can be drawn from this review.

First, there is evidence that international financial integration during the 1980s and 1990s has been accompanied in many developing countries by an increase in consumption volatility relative to output volatility—in contrast to what risk-sharing arguments would have predicted. A possible explanation for this result is provided by Levchenko (2005), who develops a model of a country with poorly developed financial markets (which therefore precludes efficient risk sharing domestically). The analysis shows that when risks are purely idiosyncratic, that is, perfectly insurable within the domestic economy, opening up to international markets reduces the amount of risk sharing attained at home and raises the volatility of consumption. When risk is purely aggregate in nature, the underdeveloped financial system prevents the pooling of aggregate risk across agents for the purposes of insurance in the international markets. Put differently, all agents do not have equal access to international markets. Thus, while the volatility of consumption decreases with opening in this case, it does so by much less than in a model with no capital market frictions.

Second, several studies suggest that short-term capital flows tend to be more unstable than longer-term flows (such as FDI), and thus more conducive to financial crises. Albuquerque (2003), for instance, provides evidence showing that FDI flows tend to be less volatile (or more persistent) than other types of capital flows. There is also evidence that short-term capital flows to developing countries tend to be procyclical, whereas medium- and long-term capital flows appear to be weakly countercyclical or acyclical. By itself, procyclical behavior may not be a cause for concern if it results from changes in demand in the developing countries themselves. In practice, however, it often arises from external, supply-side factors, such as a sudden change in the country's terms of trade, which raises the risk perceptions of lenders; it tends therefore to magnify the impact of a shock.

Third, studies examining the impact of international financial integration on domestic investment and growth—based either on a direct measure of the impact of capital account liberalization, derived from qualitative information on restrictions on capital movements, or on the level of capital flows as a proxy measure for the degree of financial openness—provide mixed support. Arteta et al. (2001), for instance, found some evidence of a positive link between the index of capital account openness and growth, but only when countries are already sufficiently open commercially and face limited macroeconomic imbalances. This is an important result because it brings to the fore the issue of sequencing of reforms. The evidence also suggests that the relationship between financial integration (as proxied by the size of FDI flows) and growth may be bidirectional: capital inflows may have a positive effect on growth, but growth in turn may tend to stimulate the inflow of FDI. This highlights the possibility of a "virtuous circle" between capital flows and growth-enhancing policies. It also implies, as emphasized by Edison et al. (2004), that studies of the impact of FDI on growth that do not account for the endogenous nature of capital flows (that is, the fact that FDI can itself be influenced by the economy's growth rate) are likely to produce estimated coefficients that are subject to significant bias. Edison et al. (2002) do account for endogeneity, as well as a host of other potential econometric problems. Using advanced panel data econometric techniques, these authors failed to find a robust, independent effect of FDI and various other measures of international financial openness on growth. By contrast, Edison et al. (2004), using various empirical measures to gauge the presence of controls on capital account transactions and the liberalization of equity markets, found a positive and significant effect of capital account openness and stock market liberalization on economic growth for middle-income countries but not for poor or rich countries. Along the same line, using panel data for 108 countries over the period 1980–2000, Chinn and Ito (2006) found that a higher level of capital account openness spurs equity market development only if a threshold level of legal development has been attained.[9] Both of these results are consistent with the view that poorer countries do not have the legal, social, and political institutions necessary to fully reap the benefits of capital account liberalization.

---

[9] They also found banking system development to be a precondition for equity market development.

Fourth, it is important to account for microeconomic evidence on the effects of FDI. This evidence suggests that private capital flows may enhance productivity, particularly in countries with a relatively skilled labor force and a well-developed physical infrastructure. More generally, microeconomic evidence is important in judging the impact of capital flows on the quality of domestic investment. Indeed, one lesson from the Asia crisis is that high aggregate ratios of capital formation to GDP can mask a sharp decline in the productivity of these investments.

Fifth, it should be noted that few existing econometric studies test for the existence of an adverse effect of the volatility of capital flows (as opposed to their level) on investment and growth. As emphasized in the literature on uncertainty and irreversibility (see Chapter 2), uncertainty about the availability of external finance in the future may deter investment, particularly in projects that have long gestation periods. At the same time, it must be recognized that the volatility of capital flows is itself endogenous, because it may arise not only from external shocks but also from domestic factors. In such conditions, modeling the sources of volatility is essential.

Sixth, the experience of the early to mid-1990s (as discussed by Calvo et al., 1996, and Fernández-Arias and Montiel, 1996) reveals that several large recipients of capital inflows suffered from some, or a combination of some, of the potential problems identified earlier—namely, a rapid increase in liquidity, inflationary pressures, real exchange-rate appreciation, and growing external imbalances. That was particularly the case in the main recipient countries in Latin America (compared to those in Asia), as a result of various factors. The deterioration in competitiveness weakened the credibility of the fixed exchange rate in some of these countries and raised doubts about their sustainability. The domestic liquidity expansion that resulted from large inflows may also have been a factor behind the credit boom, and subsequent deterioration in banks' balance sheets, that some of these countries experienced during the period.

Finally, entry by foreign banks (which increased dramatically in the 1990s, to the point where in some major Latin American countries more than half of total bank assets are now controlled by foreign institutions) continues to raise significant questions. From the point of view of international financial integration, two important questions that arise in this context are, as noted earlier, what impact has foreign entry had on the profitability and efficiency of domestic banks, and whether it has improved the financial system's ability to respond to large domestic and external shocks. The evidence on these issues, and more generally on the net benefits of foreign bank penetration, remains ambiguous. In some countries, increased penetration of foreign banks in the domestic banking system (as measured by the relative importance of foreign banks in either the total number of banks, or total assets, of the banking system) appears to be associated with a reduction in both profitability and overhead costs for domestic banks. By contrast, the effect on net interest margins (that is, the ex post spread between lending and deposit rates), which can be viewed as a measure of the efficiency of financial intermediation, is not always significant. There is also evidence that foreign banks lend less to small- and medium-sized enterprises, possibly leading to credit rationing (particularly to small firms in the nontradables sector) and greater concentration in the allocation of credit. Finally, some recent episodes appear to indicate that foreign banks may indeed "cut and run" during crisis periods, thereby contributing to domestic financial instability and increased volatility in the availability of credit.

The foregoing discussion therefore suggests that it is difficult to make broad statements regarding the benefits and costs of international financial integration. Although in principle financial openness allows countries to use international capital markets to diversify and hedge against idiosyncratic adverse shocks (particularly when those shocks are temporary), in practice, this alleged benefit is often a mirage for many developing countries—which often gain access to these markets (if at all) only in "good" times. Moreover, if international capital markets are prone to over-exuberance in good times and excess pessimism or herding (leading to sudden withdrawals of capital) in bad times, the benefits of capital inflows can be completely offset by large and sudden outflows that may put an already weak domestic financial system under stress. In such conditions, financial integration may increase the risks of costly financial crises, instead of reducing them. The empirical evidence suggests that international capital markets can be prone to sharp shifts in sentiment regarding a country's short- and longer-term economic prospects. The discipline that they exercise over government policies, although beneficial in some respects, can be excessive.

Nevertheless, despite creating the possibility of costly crises, and despite the fact that the existing empirical evidence does not allow blanket generalizations, global financial integration and the increase in FDI flows that it may lead to, hold potentially significant benefits in terms of higher domestic investment and economic growth rates. These "dynamic gains" are likely to be magnified in economies where, to begin with, the stock of human capital is high enough to take advantage of complementarity effects between technology and skills. The key issue for both national and international policymakers is therefore not to choose between openness and autarky, but rather to design policies that help to minimize the short-term risks, and maximize the longer-run gains, of financial openness. From the point of view of domestic policymakers, there has been renewed emphasis on the importance of macroeconomic discipline, information disclosure, and enhanced banking sector supervision. Avoiding real exchange-rate misalignment, limiting fiscal imbalances and preventing an excessive buildup of domestic debt, maintaining a monetary policy consistent with low inflation, and ensuring that the ratio of unhedged short-term foreign-currency debt over official reserves remains sufficiently low, are all preventive measures that are likely to reduce the risk that sudden changes in market sentiment may turn into large capital outflows and precipitate a financial crisis. Strengthening supervision and prudential regulation, fostering risk management capacities in banks and nonfinancial firms, and designing (possibly contingent) countercyclical macroprudential policies, are also important. The stronger economic fundamentals are, the longer the track record of macroeconomic discipline, the less susceptible the country will be to potentially volatile flows, and thus the lower will be the probability of a financial crisis.

2 Determinants of Capital Inflows

Explanations of surges in capital inflows to developing countries typically bring to the fore two categories of factors, dubbed "push" and "pull" factors. "Pull" factors are those that attract capital from abroad as a result of changes in regulation and improvements in the risk-return characteristics of assets issued by developing-country debtors, whereas "push" factors are those that operate by reducing the attractiveness of lending to industrial-country debtors. This section describes in more detail these two determinants of capital inflows.

2.1 ■ "Pull" Factors

Domestic or pull factors (macroeconomic stabilization and structural reforms) may play an important role in driving capital flows. Capital account liberalization (an important component of structural adjustment programs in many developing countries) may provide a strong incentive to invest or repatriate capital. Fiscal adjustment (entailing large cuts in budget deficits, through reductions in public expenditure and tax reform) may lower inflationary expectations and act as an important signal about the commitment to achieving and maintaining macroeconomic stability and may be instrumental in attracting capital flows.[10]

The welfare implications of capital flows driven by "pull" factors depend on whether these reflect the removal of a previously existing distortion, an exogenous change in an undistorted environment, or the introduction of a new distortion. For instance, if social risk-return trade-offs in the domestic economy are improved by economic reform, the capital inflows attracted by higher domestic returns would be welfare-enhancing, because they reflect wealth-increasing borrowing for the financing of new high-yield domestic investment opportunities that were not previously available and/or welfare-enhancing financing for consumption smoothing motivated by reform-induced increases in national wealth. Similarly, the characteristics of claims on domestic agents acquired by external lenders may have improved as a result of the removal of distortions that created gaps between social and private rates of return. For instance, if debt-overhang problems created a gap between social and private rates of return in a heavily indebted country, then resolution of such problems

---

[10]It should also be noted, however, that there are instances where it is large fiscal *imbalances* themselves, coupled with a relatively tight monetary policy stance (and consequent upward pressures on domestic real interest rates), that have led to large inflows of (short-term) capital. A notable example is Turkey in the early 1990s (see Agénor et al., 1997).

may allow private rates of return to reflect social returns more accurately and thus help to create the incentive for a renewed flow of capital.

Even an exogenous change in domestic portfolio preferences may trigger welfare-enhancing capital inflows. A domestic money-demand shock, for instance (in the form of an increase in money demand), could attract capital inflows by causing the prices of domestic interest-bearing assets to fall. In this case, the capital inflow makes it possible to accommodate the shift in domestic portfolio preferences and would again be welfare-enhancing.

On the other hand, as argued by Dooley (1996), the adoption of fixed exchange rates and deposit guarantees in the context of a liberalized but poorly supervised financial sector may create an opportunity for foreign lenders to reap high and secure private rates of return that do not reflect social returns on the resources that they transfer to the borrowing economy. This is a case of a "pull" factor that is welfare-reducing.

2.2 ■ "Push" Factors

The most widely cited "push" factor driving capital inflows to developing countries is a deterioration in the risk-return characteristics of assets issued by industrial-country debtors. This could happen, for instance, in response to cyclical factors that temporarily depress rates of return on assets in the lending country. Akinci (2013) found that global financial risk—measured by fluctuations in U.S. corporate bond spreads, the U.S. high-yield corporate spreads, and the U.S. stock market volatility index—and country spread shocks contribute significantly to macroeconomic fluctuations in a group of middle-income countries (Argentina, Brazil, Mexico, Peru, South Africa, and Turkey). Interdependence between economic activity and the country spread is a key mechanism through which global financial shocks are transmitted between industrial and developing countries.

An alternative "push" factor with different implications for policy has to do with changes in financial structure in capital-exporting countries. The increased role of institutional lenders such as mutual and pension funds as financial intermediaries, as well as the increased importance of securitization, may represent a secular change that favors lending to emerging markets for portfolio diversification reasons. If so, and given the fact that emerging markets continue to carry a relatively small share in the portfolios of institutional lenders, the sustainability implications would be very different from those associated with cyclical factors. To the extent that flows to developing countries since the early 1990s have been driven by structural "push" factors of this type, flows are likely to be sustained at high levels for an extended period of time.

The three-good model developed in Chapter 10 can be used to assess the effects of a reduction in world interest rates (or "push" factors, as discussed in the text) on capital flows, asset accumulation, and the real exchange rate (see Agénor, 1998c).

Specifically, the model can be used to examine both permanent and temporary reductions in the world safe interest rate, i^*.

In the setting described earlier, the long-run effects of a permanent reduction in i^* are a reduction in consumption, a depreciation of the real exchange rate, and an increase in foreign debt. The initial effect of the reduction in the cost of borrowing in world capital markets is an increase in private foreign indebtedness. At first sight, the net effect of the shock on external debt service—and thus the services account— would appear ambiguous, for two reasons. First, as noted in Chapter 10, a reduction in i^* has two types of partial effects: on the one hand, at the initial level of the economy's stock of foreign debt, it lowers interest payments; on the other, because the increase in private foreign borrowing raises the premium-related component $\theta \tilde{L}^*$, it tends to increase interest payments to foreign creditors. As indicated earlier, the former effect is assumed to dominate the latter, so that the services account tends to improve. Second, because the economy's stock of debt also increases, debt service at the initial risk-free rate tends also to increase. The latter effect dominates the former, so that the net effect is a deterioration of the services account.

To maintain external balance in the long run, the initial trade surplus (which matches the initial deficit in the services account) must therefore increase. In turn, at the initial level of the real exchange rate (and thus output of tradables), consumption must fall. This leads to a depreciation of the real exchange rate, which stimulates output of tradable goods and further improves the trade balance. Because the nominal interest rate remains constant at $\rho + \varepsilon$ (as shown earlier), real money balances fall also, as do official reserves. With foreign borrowing by private agents increasing, and net foreign assets held by the central bank falling, the economy's external debt unambiguously rises.

On impact, a permanent reduction in the world interest rate raises private spending and leads to an appreciation of the real exchange rate. The reason is that the wealth and intertemporal effects associated with this shock operate in the same direction: the reduction in i^* not only encourages agents to save less and consume more today (the intertemporal effect), but it also lowers the debt burden and generates a positive wealth effect.[11] The effect of a reduction in the risk-free world interest rate is in general ambiguous, because while it lowers interest payments on the economy's total foreign debt (which is given on impact), it also increases private foreign indebtedness, thereby raising directly and indirectly the premium-related component of external debt service. Again, from the discussion in Chapter 10, it is assumed that the net effect is an improvement in the services account on impact.

Although the trade balance and the services account move in opposite directions (the former deteriorates, whereas the latter improves), the net effect is a

---

[11] As discussed by Agénor (1998c), if the economy is initially a net creditor with respect to the rest of the world, the impact effect of a reduction in the risk-free rate on consumption is ambiguous, because wealth and intertemporal effects operate in opposite directions.

current-account deficit on impact—and thus an increase in external debt. The economy experiences an inflow of private capital matched by an increase in official reserves, which is such that the economy's stock of debt remains constant on impact. Because both consumption and the real money stock increase, the net effect on domestic interest rates is in general ambiguous. If the degree of intertemporal substitution is sufficiently low (so that consumption increases relatively little), the domestic interest rate will rise on impact.

The dynamic path of consumption, debt, and the real exchange rate are illustrated in the upper panel of Figure 13.1 (see the graphical description of the model in Chapter 10). Both CC and DD shift to the right, but the former shifts algebraically by more than the latter. Consumption jumps upward from point E to point A, and the real exchange rate appreciates from H to L. Because of the permanent nature of the shock and the monotonic nature of the adjustment process, the current account remains in deficit (with the economy's external debt increasing) throughout the transition period; consumption falls toward its new, lower steady-state level, and the real exchange rate depreciates—both effects contributing to a gradual reversal of the initial deterioration in the trade deficit.

The lower panel of Figure 13.1 illustrates the dynamics of a temporary reduction in the world interest rate. Because the expected duration of the shock matters for the adjustment path, consider first the case where the period of time, T, during which i^* falls is sufficiently large. The economy follows the path labeled $EABF$, with consumption jumping upward on impact, and falling continuously afterward—until reaching point F at period T. Because the shock is known to be temporary, the optimal response for households is to increase consumption on impact by less than they would if the shock were permanent. The real exchange rate depreciates gradually (from L to M'), after an initial step appreciation. The current account moves into deficit during the first phase of the transition process; however, the real depreciation of the currency and the reduction in consumption lead progressively to a restoration of external balance (at point B, where $\dot{D} = 0$). Afterward, the economy generates a current account surplus, and the stock of debt declines continuously over time, until the initial equilibrium (point E) is reached.

Suppose now that the length of time, T, during which the world interest rate falls is relatively short. In that case, the economy follows the path labeled $EA'B'$, which is characterized (as before) by an initial upward jump in consumption and a real appreciation. Consumption then starts falling, reaching the original saddlepath at point B' at T. Throughout the period during which the risk-free interest rate falls, the economy registers a current account surplus, that is, a reduction in external debt. After T, the economy remains on the original saddlepath (between B' and E), and the stock of debt rises over time.

Intuitively, the reason that the adjustment path depends on the length of the period during which world interest rates fall is as follows. If the duration of the shock is sufficiently long, agents have an incentive to substitute intertemporally and to increase consumption on impact by a relatively large amount; the negative

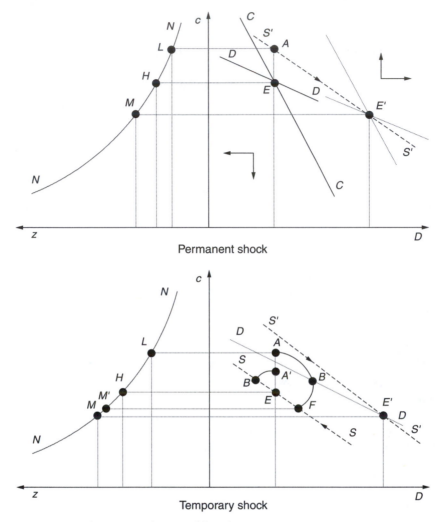

Figure 13–1 ▪ Reduction in the World Risk-Free Interest Rate
Source: Agénor (1997, p. 30).

effect on the trade balance in that case outweighs the positive effect on the services account, so that the current account moves into deficit and external debt increases. By contrast, if the reduction in the world interest rate is expected to be short-lived, agents will not adjust their consumption path by much. The improvement in the services account will therefore outweigh the deterioration in the trade balance, and the current account will move into surplus, with external debt falling throughout the period during which the shock is in place.

Finally, among "push" factors, one may also consider the fact that large inflows may reflect increased financial integration due to the removal or barriers impeding cross-border capital flows. Such barriers may arise either as the result of policy choices or of technological conditions affecting, for instance, information costs. As mentioned before, capital account liberalization had been widely adopted as the outcome of explicit policy decisions in both industrial and developing countries at the onset of the capital-inflow episode of the 1990s. Although it may seem that the removal of such distortions is unambiguously welfare-enhancing, this may not be so if previously existing restrictions reflected a second-best response to other distortions in the economy—for instance, the financial market distortions mentioned above.

2.3 ■ Assessing the Evidence

In practice, determining the relative roles that various factors may have played during an episode of capital inflow is difficult. A key issue is whether the inflow episode originates in the creditor or debtor countries.

Fernández-Arias (1996) provides a useful analytical framework within which to consider this issue. Capital flows are assumed to potentially occur in the form of transactions in various classes of assets, indexed by s, where $s = 1, ...n$. The domestic return on an asset of type s is decomposed into a "project" expected return D_s and a "country creditworthiness" adjustment factor C_s, which is bounded between zero and one. The project return depends inversely on the vector $\mathbf{F}$ of net flows to projects of all types (based on a diminishing marginal productivity argument), while the creditworthiness factor is a negative function of the vector of the end-of-period stocks of liabilities of all types, denoted $\mathbf{S}$. Voluntary capital flows (components of the vector $\mathbf{F}$) are determined by the arbitrage condition:

$$D_s(d, \mathbf{F})C_s(c, \mathbf{S}_{-1} + \mathbf{F}) = R_s(R), \tag{8}$$

where R_s is the opportunity cost of funds of type s in the creditor country, taken to depend on creditor-country financial conditions (proxied by the long-term risk-free external interest rate R), while c and d are shift factors associated with country creditworthiness and with the domestic economic climate, respectively. The convention adopted is that the functions D_s, C_s, and R_s are increasing in these shift parameters. Notice that in this framework capital flows will be determined by c, d, and R—that is, by domestic factors that operate at the project and country levels, as well as by external financial factors. The assumptions made above imply that the components of the vector $\mathbf{F}$ are increasing in d and c, but decreasing in R and $\mathbf{S}_{-1}$.

The country creditworthiness factor c is taken as reflecting the expected present value of resources available for external payments. If such resources grow at rate $\mathbf{g}$ from an initial value W, c is given by:

$$c = W/(R - \mathbf{g}). \tag{9}$$

When creditworthiness is sufficiently low, the solution to (8) above may entail extremely low capital inflows or capital outflows (negative values of various components of **F**) of a magnitude that imply transfers of resources that the country is unwilling to undertake. In this case, voluntary capital flows of such types would cease, and the condition would become an inequality no longer determining the corresponding (involuntary) capital flows. This observation is important for explaining how inflows could be externally driven, yet not uniform across developing countries. In a world in which some countries are creditworthy and others are not, a reduction in R would generate increased capital flows only for those countries that met the creditworthiness requirement.

For the inflow episode of the early 1990s, studies such as Calvo et al. (1996), Fernández-Arias (1996), Dooley, Fernández-Arias, and Kletzer (1994), and Fiess (2003) provided strong support for the role of R in determining **F**, though more recent research has suggested that the country-specific factor d and the "mixed" factor c also played important roles. Similar results have been found for the 1990s as a whole; in a study of private portfolio investment to four Asian and five Latin American countries over the period 1989–2002, Baek (2006), for instance, found that in Asia these flows were predominantly "pushed" by investors' appetite for risk (measured on the basis of excess returns) and other external factors; favorable domestic economic conditions had a negligible role. By contrast, in Latin America, portfolio flows were partly "pulled" by strong economic growth and partly "pushed" by foreign financial factors—but not by the market's attitude toward risk.

However, other studies, such as Schadler et al. (1993), argued that while foreign phenomena may have been important, such influences cannot be regarded as dominant, essentially for two reasons. First, they noted that the timing, persistence, and intensity of inflows has varied considerably across countries that have received inflows, suggesting that investors have responded to changes in country-specific factors over time. Second, they pointed out that surges in capital inflows have not been universal within regions of developing countries, so that external creditors have clearly exercised some cross-country discrimination in the allocation of funds.

The analytical framework described above is helpful in sorting out these issues. The reduced-form solution for **F** from (8) for country i takes the form

$$\mathbf{F}_i = F(c_i, d_i, R; \mathbf{S}_{-1}), \tag{10}$$

which implies

$$\mathbf{F}_i = F_c dc_i + F_d dd_i, F_R dR + F_S d\mathbf{S}_{i-1}. \tag{11}$$

The partial derivatives of F depend on the country-specific values of c, d, and $\mathbf{S}_{-1}$, as well as on R. This means that cross-country differences in capital-inflow variations are perfectly compatible with a primary role for the "push" factor R. Differences in the timing and persistence of changes in capital inflows, on the other hand, do indeed suggest a role for changes in "pull" factors. By estimating directly (10), Hernández and Rudolf (1994) provided evidence supporting a role for domestic factors in attracting capital inflows. Similarly, the World Bank (1997) suggests that the factors driving inflows in the early 1990s changed over time, and in particular that domestic factors may have played a more prominent role during 1994–1995, compared to 1990–1993.

More recent studies on the importance of push and pull factors as determinants of capital flows include Forbes and Warnock (2012), Fratzscher (2012), Okada (2013), Ahmed and Zlate (2014), and Ghosh et al. (2014). Fratzscher (2012), employing a dataset of high-frequency portfolio capital flows for fifty countries, found that common shocks—key crisis events as well as changes to global liquidity and risk—have exerted a large effect on capital flows both during the recent global financial crisis and in the subsequent recovery. However, these effects have been highly heterogeneous across countries, with a large part of this heterogeneity being explained by differences in the quality of domestic institutions, country risk, and the strength of domestic macroeconomic fundamentals. Comparing and quantifying these effects shows that common factors ("push" factors) were overall the main drivers of capital flows during the crisis, while country-specific determinants ("pull" factors) have been dominant in accounting for the dynamics of global capital flows in 2009 and 2010, in particular for middle-income countries. Ahmed and Zlate (2014) document not only the role of interest rate differentials but also global risk factors.

In sum, much of the evidence suggests that both "push" factors (especially changes in U.S. interest rates) and "pull" factors affect capital flows to developing countries, with the relative importance of each set of factors varying over time. "Push" factors seem to be particularly important during large episodes of inflows. Of course, the importance of "push" factors does not preclude the relevance of "pull" phenomena. For instance, a fall in interest rates in industrial countries, in addition to improving the relative rate of returns in favor of developing economies, may also improve the creditworthiness of some debtor countries and stimulate further inflows. More generally, while "push" factors may help to explain the timing and magnitude of a capital inflow episode, "pull" factors may be necessary to explain the geographic distribution of flows during that particular time. Differences in capital inflow levels across countries and within countries across time point to the importance of specific country (or period) characteristics for foreign capital absorption.

At the same time, it is important to recognize that at the individual country level, the identification of the factors underlying a surge in capital inflows matters considerably for policy formulation. It may be tempting to take the view that flows attracted to the recipient country by domestic "pull" factors do not present a policy problem, because they represent a restoration of creditworthiness, whereas flows "pushed" out of the source countries are an external shock that can easily be reversed and thus call for a policy response. This would be incorrect, however. Because both categories of factors can incorporate a wide variety of domestic and foreign phenomena, the policy implications associated with "push" and "pull" factors depend on the specific "pull" or "push" phenomena that are at work, rather than on whether the origin of the shock is domestic or external.

3　Managing Capital Inflows: Policy Options

What can countries do to manage capital movements during large inflow episodes? This is a particularly challenging task for countries that maintain an officially determined nominal exchange rate at the inception of the inflow episode. The macroeconomic challenge relates to the fact that large inflows may result in overheating—that is, an excessive expansion of aggregate demand, resulting in an increase in domestic inflation and an appreciation of the real exchange rate. The mechanism through which inflows could have this effect is as follows: with a predetermined exchange rate, large capital inflows are likely to generate an overall balance-of-payments surplus. To avoid an appreciation of the nominal exchange rate, the central bank would have to intervene in the foreign exchange market to buy the excess supply of foreign currency at the prevailing exchange rate. *Ceteris paribus*, this would result in an expansion of the monetary base. Base expansion would lead to growth in broader monetary aggregates, which would fuel an expansion of aggregate demand. This, in turn, would put upward pressure on the domestic price level. With the nominal exchange rate fixed, rising domestic prices would imply an appreciation of the real exchange rate.

This causal chain can be broken at various points by policy intervention. One useful way to organize the menu of policies available to the authorities to resist the emergence of overheating is thus according to where the intervention occurs along the chain of transmission described above. Accordingly, policy interventions can be classified as follows:

- Policies designed to restrict the net inflow of capital, either by restricting gross capital inflows or promoting gross capital outflows. Such policies include the imposition of administrative controls on capital inflows as well as the elimination of a variety of restrictions on capital outflows. They may also include the widening of exchange-rate bands with the intention of increasing uncertainty.
- Policies that seek to restrict the net foreign exchange inflow (reserve accumulation) by encouraging a current account offset to a capital account surplus. Trade liberalization and nominal exchange-rate appreciation would have this effect. In the limit (flexible exchange rates), the latter could avoid any foreign exchange accumulation whatsoever.
- Policies that accept the reserve accumulation associated with a balance-of-payments surplus, but attempt to ameliorate its effects on the monetary base. These amount to sterilized intervention, as well as attempts to limit recourse to the central bank's discount window.

- Policies that accept an increase in the base, but attempt to restrain its effects on broader monetary aggregates. Increases in reserve requirements and quantitative credit restrictions are examples of such policies.
- Policies that accept a monetary expansion, but attempt to offset expansionary effects on aggregate demand that could result in inflation and/or real exchange rate appreciation. This refers essentially to fiscal contraction.

3.1 ■ Restrictions on Gross Inflows

Though the imposition of capital controls—or, to use a more politically correct term now, following the paradigm shift at the International Monetary Fund (2012), *capital flow management* (CFM) *measures*—is controversial, a case for imposing them can be made on welfare grounds. The key requirement for controls to improve welfare is the presence of a preexisting distortion that creates an excessive level of foreign borrowing. This could happen, for instance, when the act of foreign borrowing itself creates externalities. If the costs of default on an international loan contract are shared by domestic agents other than the borrowing agent, then individual acts of foreign borrowing have negative external effects in the domestic economy. Because individual domestic agents do not internalize such effects, they will tend to overborrow (Aizenman, 1989). Capital controls, in the form of a tax on foreign borrowing, would effectively cause agents to internalize the costs that their external borrowing decisions impose on others. As such, they would represent a first-best policy intervention.

A variety of second-best cases can also be made for capital controls (Dooley, 1996). These emerge when the negative welfare consequences of a preexisting domestic distortion that cannot be removed are magnified by external borrowing. Distortions in the domestic financial system, for instance, may cause resources borrowed from abroad to be allocated in socially unproductive ways in the domestic economy. If the distortion causing the problem cannot be removed, a second-best option may be to limit foreign borrowing.

Beyond the issue of optimality, the use of capital controls faces the question of feasibility. Many economists have questioned the feasibility of direct intervention with capital flows, on the view that controls may be easily evaded (Ariyoshi et al., 2000). Testing this proposition is complicated by the fact that the efficacy of controls is likely to depend on a wide range of factors, including whether controls are imposed on inflows or outflows, whether controls have been imposed previously, whether their coverage is comprehensive or partial, and a host of other considerations. The upshot is that the effectiveness of controls is likely to differ both across countries as well as over time, making it difficult to draw general conclusions.[12]

---

[12]The incentive to evade depends on differences between foreign and domestic rates of return, and thus on financial policies abroad and at home. The feasibility of evasion, in turn, depends on the structure of trade (which affects the scope for under- and over-invoicing), on that of the domestic financial system (which affects the possibility

Dooley (1996) concluded his survey of the existing evidence on the efficacy of controls by arguing that controls can be effective in the sense of preserving some degree of domestic monetary autonomy (that is, influencing interest differentials). But he found little evidence that controls have helped governments meet policy objectives or improve economic welfare in the ways outlined above. A more recent review of the evidence by Agénor and Pereira da Silva (2013) suggests that capital controls appear to have had little effect (or, at best, a small effect) on the overall *level* of capital flows although they may have had some success in altering the *composition* of these flows. Empirical studies include both country-specific studies, such as Edwards and Rigobon (2009), and cross-country studies, such as Montiel and Reinhart (1999), Binici et al. (2010), and Ostry et al. (2012).

Edwards and Rigobon (2009) focus on Chile, a country whose experience with capital controls has been studied extensively. They concentrate on the country's experience during the 1990s—a period during which controls on capital inflows coexisted with an exchange rate band aimed at managing the nominal exchange rate. They found that although these controls helped to increase the unconditional volatility of the nominal exchange rate, they also made it less sensitive to external shocks. Some economists have argued that Chile-style controls on inflows have three important effects: (a) they reduce the degree of vulnerability to external shocks; (b) they result in lower exchange rate volatility; and (c) they help avoid the extent of currency appreciation during episodes of capital inflows.

In a study covering seventy-four countries during 1995–2005, Binici et al. (2010) estimated a model of capital flows with four categories: equity-like flows (including FDI) and debt for both capital inflows and capital outflows. The estimated effects of capital controls vary markedly with the type of controls imposed: they are binding on capital outflows (debt, equity and FDI); have no apparent effect on capital inflows of various types; and are less effective in low and middle-income countries. Moreover, there are no apparent substitution effects so that controls on debt and equity outflows change the volume and composition of capital flows as well as the net flow of capital in each asset class. The large differences across asset categories in the effects of capital controls suggest that the common use of aggregate capital control indicators can be misleading. While the overall qualitative pattern across asset categories is similar for countries at different income levels, low and middle-income countries appear to be less successful at enforcing capital account restrictions, particularly regarding debt instruments. This may be associated with weaker institutional ability to enforce controls.

In the same vein, Ostry et al. (2012), using a large cross-country dataset for fifty-one countries over the period 1995–2008, found that capital controls were associated with a lower proportion of (potentially more volatile) portfolio debt in total external

---

of evasion by altering the channels of financial intermediation), and the efficacy of policing mechanisms. Such factors explain why the efficacy of controls is likely to differ across countries and over time.

liabilities. However, the ability to implement them in many developing countries remains limited. In particular, in countries that have pursued trade integration but did not sufficiently increase resources spent on monitoring and enforcement of capital controls, the effectiveness of these controls has eroded quickly due to increased opportunities for capital flight.

In sum, there is still no general consensus on critical questions regarding the efficacy of capital controls. Although they do not seem to affect very much the level of capital inflows, they do appear to be effective in tilting foreign liabilities toward long-term maturities. This compositional effect is important because it means that capital controls can make a country less vulnerable to a sudden reversal in capital flows (see Chapter 14).

3.2 ■ Encouragement of Gross Outflows

The relevant issues are efficacy and optimality in the case of liberalizing restrictions on outflows, although these issues arise in a somewhat different way. First, in parallel with the previous case, restrictions on *outflows* may not be effective. But even if outflow restrictions are effective, their removal may not have the desired effect of reducing net inflows, because the very act of removing such restrictions may attract additional inflows.

Two sets of arguments have been adduced to suggest how this could happen. Labán and Larraín (1997) have pointed out that the presence of effective controls on outflows renders inflows irreversible. If future policies affecting the return on loans to domestic agents are uncertain, the option to keep funds abroad while the uncertainty is resolved becomes valuable, and foreign creditors may thus refrain from lending in this situation. Removing the outflow restrictions eliminates the irreversibility, and thus increases the relative return on domestic lending by eliminating the value of the option to wait. Alternatively, Bartolini and Drazen (1997) have argued that, because controls on outflows are often maintained for fiscal reasons (to facilitate the collection of financial repression taxes), their removal is interpreted by foreign investors as a signal that future capital taxation is less likely, thereby inducing capital inflows.

3.3 ■ Trade Liberalization

From a macroeconomic perspective, trade liberalization lowers the domestic currency price of importables directly, and may lower the price on nontradables indirectly (through a substitution effect). As indicated previously, to the extent that it induces a trade deficit, it absorbs some of the foreign exchange generated by the capital inflow, easing monetary pressures as well. The most controversial issue that arises with respect to trade liberalization as a means to restrict the net inflow of foreign exchange concerns efficacy. Because the trade balance is the difference between domestic saving and investment, the effect of trade liberalization on the trade balance depends on how saving and investment are affected. Both theory and evidence suggest that the effects of trade liberalization on the trade balance are ambiguous, depending on a host of structural characteristics of the domestic economy as well as on the nature of the liberalization program. The former include the importance of nontraded goods, sectoral factor intensities, the nature of accompanying fiscal policies, and the extent of labor market rigidities. The latter include the incidence of tariffs (whether they fall on intermediate or final goods) and their projected future paths.

For instance, Ostry (1991) shows that if temporary tariffs on intermediate goods are reduced, and tradables are more intensive in both intermediate and capital goods than nontradables, then the effect of the liberalization program will be to increase saving and reduce investment, thereby unambiguously improving the trade balance. The reduction in tariffs on intermediates will result in a short-run real appreciation as the traded goods sector expands, absorbing resources from the nontraded sector. This real appreciation will cause agents to expect a larger real depreciation over time, because future trade policy is left unaffected. Consequently, the real interest rate rises, and consumption tilts toward the future, increasing domestic saving. In turn, the increase in future consumption causes a future real appreciation which, relative to the undisturbed equilibrium, shifts capital from the traded to the nontraded sector in the future. Because the traded sector is relatively capital-intensive, the implication is a reduction in today's aggregate investment. With saving higher and investment lower, the trade balance unambiguously improves.

While this example may appear contrived, it merely illustrates the general principle that it is indeed quite possible in theory for a trade liberalization to improve the trade balance. The experience of liberalizing countries, as discussed in Chapter 18, suggests that this result is more than a theoretical curiosity.

3.4 ■ Exchange-Rate Flexibility

The alternative of inducing a current account offset to capital inflows through nominal exchange-rate flexibility, by contrast, raises issues that concern optimality, rather than efficacy. The potential inflationary implications of capital inflows can be completely avoided by refraining from intervention in the foreign exchange market. Permitting a (temporary) appreciation of the nominal exchange rate in response to a favorable external interest rate shock (by restricting the scale of foreign exchange intervention) will dampen and possibly reverse the expansionary effect of the foreign shock on domestic aggregate demand, by appreciating the real exchange rate. A capital inflow arising from a reduction in external interest rates becomes a *deflationary* shock under fully flexible exchange rates. This outcome will be desirable if domestic macroeconomic conditions are such that policymakers seek to avoid stimulating aggregate demand. Thus, to the extent that capital inflows are permitted to materialize, the desirability of foreign exchange intervention depends in part on the requirements for macroeconomic stability.

The trade-off, however, concerns the implications for domestic resource allocation. If the authorities allow the nominal exchange rate to appreciate in response to capital inflows, the profitability of the traded goods sector will obviously be affected adversely. Aside from possible political economy considerations, policymakers may have two reasons to be concerned with this outcome: first, if the capital inflow is believed to be temporary, an appreciation of the official exchange rate may tend to aggravate the effects of any previously existing domestic distortions biasing domestic resource allocation away from the traded goods sector (and causing the "shadow" value of foreign exchange to exceed its official value).[13] Second, with temporary capital inflows, the associated real exchange-rate appreciation will also be temporary, and any costly resource reallocations induced by changes in relative sectoral profitability between the traded and nontraded goods sectors would later have to be reversed. Because such costs represent fixed costs from the perspective of private agents, the associated resource reallocations would not be undertaken unless the incentives for doing so were perceived to be long-lasting. Because private agents will find it in their best interest to avoid the costs of transitory resource reallocation, the noise introduced into relative price signals by allowing excessive nominal exchange-rate variability may reduce the efficiency of resource allocation.

The preceding discussion treats the exchange rate as an instrument of short-run stabilization policy. However, the exchange rate also plays another role in small open economies—that of nominal anchor (see Chapter 8). Indeed, this role is often prominent in stabilization programs, and institutional arrangements have often been devised to enhance the credibility of the anchor. Where the exchange rate plays such a role, the issues are whether institutional arrangements are sufficiently flexible to allow the rate to move and, if so, whether perceptions of the authorities' anti-inflationary commitment would indeed be jeopardized by an appreciation of the nominal rate (albeit one which may later need to be reversed, if the inflow is temporary). The concern would be that even an appreciation may convey the signal that the exchange rate is not immutable.

3.5 ■ Sterilization

The monetary authorities can seek to avoid aggregate demand stimulus with a fixed exchange rate through sterilized foreign exchange intervention. The use of this policy raises a number of feasibility issues. First, by keeping domestic interest rates higher than they otherwise would be, sterilization will tend to magnify the cumulative capital inflow. The higher the degree of capital mobility, the larger will be the

---

[13]If the inflow is permanent, the associated real appreciation may be matched by an appreciation of the equilibrium real exchange rate, and thus would not necessarily increase the wedge between the "shadow" exchange rate and its official value.

accumulation of reserves associated with sterilized intervention. Second, sterilized intervention has quasi-fiscal costs, because the central bank exchanges high-yielding domestic assets for low-yielding reserves. The magnitude of these costs will be greater the higher the degree of capital mobility and the larger the gap between domestic and foreign rates of return. Thus, the fiscal feasibility of this policy is also at issue.[14] Third, even if sterilization succeeds in limiting domestic monetary expansion, it may not insulate the economy from the effects of capital inflows. This would be true under two sets of circumstances:

- If domestic interest-bearing assets are perfect substitutes among themselves, insulation would fail if the shock that triggers the inflows affects domestic money demand. In this case, with shifting money demand but fixed supply, domestic interest rates would change;
- if domestic interest-bearing assets are imperfect substitutes, then a capital inflow may be associated with a shift in the composition of demand for domestic interest-bearing assets, as well as with an increase in the total demand for such assets. In this case, unless the composition of domestic assets emitted in sterilization operations matches that demanded by creditors, the structure of domestic asset returns would be altered.

In both cases a portfolio reallocation may result; in the presence of wealth effects, this may affect aggregate demand and prices.

In recent years foreign exchange intervention appears to have increased in many developing countries. Aizenman and Glick (2009) have argued that a key reason why central banks have tried to sterilize capital flows more aggressively in recent years is because they have attached a greater weight on mitigating exchange-rate volatility—possibly to facilitate the attainment of their inflation targets.

The empirical evidence discussed in the Appendix to this chapter, which suggests that most developing countries continue to be characterized by imperfect capital mobility, implies that sterilized intervention remains a viable policy option for these countries. By and large, studies that have examined the effectiveness of sterilization directly have supported this conclusion. However, recent capital account liberalization in many developing countries may have changed this situation, increasing the effective degree of financial integration for the liberalizing countries. Thus, whether sterilization remains viable after liberalization is an open empirical question.

---

[14]Kletzer and Spiegel (2004) develop a framework in which sterilization costs are explicitly accounted for in the intertemporal government budget constraint. Their analysis shows that increases in sterilization costs tend to lead to a greater degree of flexibility (or accommodation) in the nominal exchange rate, in response to capital inflows.

3.6 ■ Policies to Influence the Money Multiplier

If for fiscal or other reasons sterilization is incomplete, the implication of a foreign exchange inflow is an expansion in the monetary base. Monetary expansion can still be avoided by a commensurate reduction in the money multiplier achieved through an increase in reserve requirements or other restrictions on credit expansion by the banking system. Feasibility issues arise here in several forms: first, increases in reserve requirements may have little effect if banks are already holding excess reserves. Second, if reserve requirements are changed selectively for different components of banks' liability portfolios, then their effects could be evaded as bank creditors shift to assets not affected by changes in reserve requirements. Finally, even if changes in reserve requirements are applied broadly across bank liabilities, domestic credit expansion could materialize through nonbank institutions (disintermediation). The scope for doing so, and thus for avoiding an increase in domestic aggregate demand, depends on the sophistication of the domestic financial system.

With regard to optimality, measures directed at the money multiplier avoid quasi-fiscal costs, but do so through implicit taxation of the banking system. The economic implications of this tax will depend on how the tax burden is ultimately shared among bank shareholders, their depositors, and their loan customers. Nonetheless, the likely effect of this policy is to shrink the domestic financial system, an outcome that runs counter to the trend toward financial liberalization in most reforming economies, and which may have adverse implications for economic growth.

3.7 ■ Fiscal Contraction

If domestic monetary expansion is not avoided, or if an expansionary financial stimulus is transmitted outside the banking system, the stabilization of aggregate demand will require a fiscal contraction. Feasibility and optimality issues arise in this context as well. Concerning feasibility, fiscal policy may simply prove too inflexible to be available as a tool to respond to fluctuations in capital movements. The budgetary process in most countries may not be able to respond sufficiently quickly, and lags in response may indeed aggravate the stabilization problems created by volatile capital movements. Second, even if fiscal policy can be changed, the desired effects on domestic demand (and thus on the real exchange rate) will be forthcoming—that is, the policy will be effective—only if expenditure cuts fall on nontraded goods.

From the perspective of optimality, similar issues arise in the case of fiscal adjustment as in that of exchange-rate changes—that is, should fiscal policy be designed to anchor long-run expectations of inflation and taxation, or should policy have countercyclical objectives? In principle these goals are not mutually exclusive, because short-run deviations from the medium-term fiscal stance can be designed to achieve stabilization objectives. The problem is, however, that if government credibility is lacking, adherence to the medium-term stance in the face of shocks may be the surest way to achieve it. In a nutshell, the issue is whether the achievement of fiscal credibility is compatible with the adoption of feedback rules for fiscal policy.[15] Finally, if the stabilization objective is adopted, changes in marginal tax rates in response to temporary capital inflows should be avoided, because fluctuations in such rates would distort intertemporal choices.

3.8 ■ Macroprudential Regulation

In the past two decades many MICs have continued to open their capital account, and greater integration with world capital markets has been accompanied by a substantial rise in private capital flows to these countries. As noted earlier, while foreign direct investment has often been driven by longer-term prospects (push factors), short-term, cross-border capital flows are highly responsive to changes in relative rates of return, including movements in interest rates in advanced economies and changes in risk perception among global investors (pull factors).

From the perspective of financial stability, the main source of concern with short-term capital inflows is their *gross*, rather than *net*, size, because of the risk that these flows (intermediated directly or indirectly through the banking system) may lead to the formation of credit-fueled bubbles. Forbes and Warnock (2012) found that in recent years the size and volatility of gross flows in many countries have increased, while net capital flows have been more stable. Broner et al. (2013) also found that gross capital flows are very large and volatile, relative to net capital flows. In addition, they found that gross capital flows are procyclical: during expansions, foreigners invest more domestically and domestic agents invest more abroad; during crises, total gross flows collapse and there is a retrenchment in both inflows by foreigners and outflows by domestic agents.

Among gross flows, bank-related flows are especially important, because of their potential direct impact on credit expansion and their role in transmitting international shocks: for instance, deteriorations in the balance sheet of domestic banks can push them to sell external assets or to recall external loans to comply with internal rules or with prudential regulations such as capital requirements or maximum leverage ratios.[16] In the recent wave of capital flows, bank-related flows have been particularly large. As argued by Bruno and Shin (2012), these capital flows reflect the interaction of the supply and demand for wholesale funding between global and local banks. When local and global banks interact in the market for wholesale bank funding, the liabilities of local banks serve as the assets of the global

---

[15]Note that, if such a rule were to be applied symmetrically, it would imply that capital outflows should elicit an *expansionary* fiscal response.

[16]Krugman (2008) refers to such international financial contagion as the "International Finance Multiplier;" changes in asset prices are transmitted internationally through their effects on the balance sheets of banks and other highly leveraged financial institutions. See Herrmann and Mihaljek (2013) for some formal evidence on the role of bank lending flows in transmitting financial shocks across borders.

banks, and the lending by global banks is the supply of wholesale funding, while the borrowing by local banks is its demand.

The volatility associated with short-term capital flows is a major concern because the financial system in many developing countries is highly vulnerable to external disturbances—even more so now to global financial cycles, as a result of increased international financial integration. Abrupt reversals in short-term capital movements tend to exacerbate financial volatility—particularly in countries with relatively fragile financial systems, weak regulatory and supervisory structures, and policy regimes that lack flexibility. Galindo et al. (2010), using a cross-country dataset covering seventeen countries in Latin America between 1996 and 2008, found that financial integration, despite contributing to a deepening of domestic credit markets, amplifies the impact of international financial shocks on domestic aggregate credit and interest rate fluctuations. The more recent surge in capital flows to developing countries—caused in part by the post-crisis global excess liquidity generated by the expansionary monetary policies of advanced reserve currency-issuing countries—has also induced booms in credit and equity markets, real appreciation, in many of these countries and raised concerns about asset price bubbles and financial fragility (Agénor and Pereira da Silva, 2013).

To mitigate the rapid increases in liquidity, aggregate demand pressures, real exchange-rate appreciation, growing external imbalances, and financial volatility associated with large capital inflows, a number of countries have implemented or strengthened a variety of macroprudential policies (see Tovar et al., 2012, and Claessens et al., 2013). Some of these policies—limitations on foreign currency exposures for banks that end up affecting mostly non-residents—operate in such a way that they can be considered a capital flow management tool (International Monetary Fund, 2012).[17] Ostry et al. (2012) also examined the extent to which macroprudential policies can enhance financial stability in response to large capital inflows. They construct indices of foreign currency (FX)-related prudential measures and domestic prudential measures. They found that FX-related prudential measures (just like capital controls, as noted earlier) are associated with a lower proportion of FX lending in total domestic bank credit, and with a lower proportion of portfolio debt in total external liabilities. Other prudential policies appear to help restrain the intensity of aggregate credit booms. Moreover, experience from the global financial crisis suggests that macroprudential and capital control policies in place during the boom enhanced economic resilience during the bust. From that perspective, macroprudential tools and capital controls have proved to be largely complementary policies.

---

[17] In addition, as noted by Claessens et al. (2013, p. 158), the use of macroprudential policies can also affect the need for capital controls. For instance, by reducing the demand for loans, caps on loan-to-value (LTV) ratios can reduce bank demand for wholesale funding, some of which may be in the form of foreign borrowing. Consequently, an LTV cap can indirectly reduce the need for imposing capital controls.

Appendix
Measuring the Degree of Financial Integration

Capital controls continue to prevail in many developing countries, but their effectiveness has often been questioned. At one extreme, if such controls are effective and the economy is completely closed, external financial intermediation is ruled out. Thus, domestic interest rates can be influenced by domestic monetary, fiscal, and other shocks.[18] At the other extreme, if controls are completely ineffective and perfect capital mobility prevails (meaning that nonmonetary domestic financial assets are perfect substitutes for their foreign counterparts and that portfolio adjustment is instantaneous, possibly despite the presence of formal capital controls), the interest rate on domestic financial assets must be equal to the uncovered-parity foreign rate, that is, the exogenous foreign interest rate plus the expected rate of depreciation of the domestic currency. The marginal cost of funds in the economy would then be given by the uncovered parity rate and would be unaffected by domestic policies and shocks, except to the extent that these affect the expected rate of depreciation of the domestic currency.

In practice, of course, the degree of financial openness differs both across countries and over time. Drawing on Montiel (1994) and Willett et al. (2002), this Appendix reviews some of the evidence on measuring the degree of capital mobility, which takes the form of indications of the size of gross capital flows, tests of interest parity conditions, tests of the effectiveness of sterilization, and correlations between savings and investment.

The Magnitude of Gross Flows

To the extent that the size of capital flows is indicative of the degree of financial integration, evidence on past episodes of substantial capital movements in and out of developing countries can be brought to bear on the issue. Specifically, one can measure the gross stocks of financial claims between developing countries and external financial markets to which capital flows have given rise. Some studies have found that private capital flight amounts to a large fraction of the external debt of a number of countries, with capital flight itself linked to portfolio considerations.[19]

---

[18] When the intensity of capital controls is high, parallel markets for foreign exchange tend to emerge (see Agénor, 1992). The macroeconomic implications of these markets (together with informal credit markets) were discussed in previous editions of this book; this material is now summarized in Annexes, available upon request.

[19] Various methodologies can be used to measure capital flight (see Cuddington, 1986). The most common is the "residual" approach, which identifies capital flight with net inflows of capital and net outflows (current account deficit plus the central bank's increase in reserves). An alternative method identifies capital flight as unreported capital outflows, that is, those flows that are hidden from domestic authorities. This approach consists in (a) estimating the stock of total private claims on foreigners, and (b) substracting the reported claims imputed from annual reported income, so as to obtain the stock of "unreported" holdings. Total claims are defined as cumulative capital outflows, plus errors and omissions, plus the discrepancy between two measures of external debt—that

The gross-flow evidence indicates therefore that some countries have exhibited a substantial amount of at least de facto financial openness.

Tests of Interest Parity Conditions

Tests of interest parity conditions are the most common approach to the measurement of financial integration for industrial countries (see Dooley and Isard, 1980, for an early study). In brief, if i denotes the domestic interest rate on an asset of a given type, i^* the interest rate on the corresponding foreign asset, and ε the expected rate of depreciation of the domestic currency, then the differential return, d, between holding the domestic and foreign assets, without hedging the exchange risk in forward markets, is given by $d = i - i^* - \varepsilon$. Under perfect capital mobility, expected returns on domestic and foreign assets should be equalized, so d should be zero. This situation is referred to as one in which uncovered parity holds. However, d is not directly observable; it depends on the unobserved expectation ε. If that expectation is formed rationally, then uncovered interest parity implies that $E(d/\Omega) = 0$, where Ω is the information set used in forecasting ε. Thus, d should not be correlated with any information contained in Ω. Joint tests of uncovered interest parity and rational expectations thus entail testing whether d is correlated with variables in Ω. However, a problem with standard tests of uncovered interest parity is the "peso problem"—a situation in which a nonzero probability of a future parity change produces a forward discount on the domestic currency (Krasker, 1980). This implies that rejection of the null hypothesis does not necessarily invalidate the assumption of perfect capital mobility.[20]

As argued by Willett et al. (2002), the use of covered interest parity tests is of limited value to assess the degree of capital mobility. While deviations from parity are clear evidence of limited capital mobility, the converse does not hold. Thus, covered parity is a necessary but not sufficient condition for perfect capital mobility. Their own estimate is that the degree of capital mobility in developing countries is not that high.

Several applications of these tests have been conducted for developing countries; see, for instance, Khor and Rojas-Suárez (1991) and Faruqee (1992). By and large, the results suggest that although the degree of integration with external financial markets may have increased in recent years for many developing countries, domestic interest rates depart substantially from their covered parity.

---

reported by the World Bank and that derived from cumulative recorded balance-of-payments liabilities. Chang et al. (1997) have shown, however, that in practice these methodologies do not lead to large measurement discrepancies.

[20] An alternative approach, developed by Edwards and Khan (1985) and extended by Haque and Montiel (1991) and Reisen and Yeches (1993), is criticized by Willett et al. (2002).

Tests of Monetary Autonomy

Under perfect capital mobility, the "offset coefficient" that relates changes in the stock of domestic assets of the central bank to changes in reserve flows normally takes a value of -1, because any expansion of the domestic assets of the central bank will give rise to an offsetting capital outflow, leaving the stock of money unchanged and implying a loss of monetary autonomy. A separate strand of investigation of the capital mobility issue in developing countries tests for this loss of monetary autonomy. By and large, early empirical studies based on this approach—such as Cumby and Obstfeld (1983), Kamas (1986), and Rennhack and Mondino (1988)—found that in some cases perfect capital mobility does not hold for some countries; slow portfolio adjustment and imperfect asset substitutability allowed them to retain at least some short-run monetary autonomy during that period, with an offset coefficient significantly less than unity.

An implication of maintaining some scope for independent monetary policy is, of course, that policy-induced changes in domestic financial aggregates will affect macroeconomic variables other than the capital account. Thus the identification of domestic macroeconomic effects arising from monetary policy shocks under fixed exchange rates provides an indirect confirmation of the retention of at least some degree of monetary autonomy. Some studies have found indeed that domestic interest rates are significantly affected only by domestic factors, with little evidence of a role for foreign interest rates.

Saving-Investment Correlations

An influential paper by Feldstein and Horioka (1980) argued that the degree of capital mobility among industrial countries could be tested by examining the degree of correlation between saving and investment rates, with the reasoning that under perfect capital mobility domestic saving and investment rates should be uncorrelated. Several investigators (including Dooley et al., 1987) who have constructed such tests included a number of developing countries in their cross-section samples and considered the effect of including such countries on their results. Surprisingly, these authors concurred in finding that the inclusion of developing nations reduced the strength of the saving-investment correlation in their samples. This was unexpected, because these countries were perceived ex ante as less integrated with world capital markets than industrial countries. The same methodology, with similar results, was used by Wong (1990) to look at a cross-section sample of forty-five developing countries. Khalkhali and Dara (2007) applied a varying coefficients error-correction approach to twenty-three industrial countries over the period 1970–2003 and found evidence of a close relationship between saving and investment, both in the short and the long run, with the long-run relationship appearing to be stronger for the more open economies. By contrast, they found no evidence that countries that are more open to trade are also more open in terms of capital flows, that is, the degree of capital mobility does not appear to be positively related to trade openness. Finally, in a study of Mexico's experience during the period 1960–2002, Payne (2005) found that savings and investment are cointegrated (suggesting low capital mobility in the long run), but there is also evidence of structural instability following the debt crisis that the country experienced in the early 1980s.

Overall, the existing evidence for developing countries suggests that few, if any, developing countries can be considered to be financially closed. At the same time, while many of these countries should be regarded as financially open, perfect capital mobility does not hold.

Chapter 14

Exchange-Rate Crises and Sudden Stops

T he sources and implications of inconsistencies that may arise between the exchange-rate regime and other macroeconomic policy instruments have been the subject of considerable attention in recent years. The currency crises that have occurred since the early 1990s (particularly in Mexico, as discussed below) have led to a resurgence of interest in models of speculative attacks and exchange-rate crises. Two strands appear to dominate the literature at present. "Conventional" models tend to emphasize inconsistencies between fiscal, monetary, and exchange-rate policies and the role of speculative attacks in "forcing" the abandonment of a currency peg.

More recent models, by contrast, emphasize the vulnerability of exchange-rate systems even in the presence of consistent macroeconomic policies and sound market fundamentals. They explicitly account for policymakers' preferences and the trade-offs that they face in their policy objectives. In this setting, an exchange-rate "crisis" (a devaluation or a switch to a floating-rate regime) is viewed as an ex ante optimal decision for the policymaker. These models also highlight the role of self-fulfilling mechanisms, multiple equilibria, and credibility factors. For instance, an arbitrary increase in inflation expectations (induced by a perceived incentive to relax monetary and fiscal policies in the face of persistent unemployment) may raise domestic interest rates to such an extent that the cost of preserving the peg (foregoing the possibility to stimulate output by raising prices and lowering real wages) becomes so large that the authorities may find it optimal to devalue or abandon altogether a fixed exchange-rate regime. Market expectations may thus take on the characteristics of self-fulfilling prophecies. Another line of reasoning, which has led to the so-called third-generation models of currency crises, emphasize the role of balance sheet factors and financial sector weaknesses in triggering speculative attacks.

This chapter is organized in five parts. The first part studies how macroeconomic policy inconsistencies may lead to recurrent speculative attacks and ultimately to the collapse of a fixed exchange rate. The second part examines the second-generation models of currency crises. It begins by considering a simple model that illustrates the interactions between policymakers' preferences (in the presence of an inflation-unemployment trade-off) and self-fulfilling expectations. It then considers the links between credibility and reputation (as discussed in Chapter 11) and the decision to devalue. The third part discusses briefly recent attempts to integrate first- and second-generation models of currency crises. The fourth part examines third-generation models of currency crises.[1] The final part discusses the characteristics of sudden reversals in capital inflows, namely, sudden stops.

1 Currency Crises: Conventional Approach

A fundamental proposition of open-economy macroeconomics is that the viability of a fixed exchange-rate regime requires maintaining long-run consistency between monetary, fiscal, and exchange-rate policies. "Excessive" domestic credit growth leads to a gradual loss of foreign reserves and ultimately to an abandonment of the fixed exchange rate, once the central bank becomes incapable of defending the parity any longer. Over the past decade a large formal literature has focused on the short- and long-run consequences of incompatible macroeconomic policies for the balance of payments of a small open economy in which agents are able to anticipate future decisions by policymakers. In a pioneering paper, Krugman (1979) showed that under a fixed exchange-rate regime, domestic credit creation in excess of money demand growth may lead to a sudden speculative attack against the currency that forces the abandonment of the fixed exchange rate and the adoption of a flexible-rate regime. Moreover, this attack will always occur *before* the central bank would have run out of reserves in the absence of speculation, and will take place at a well-defined date.

This section examines the implications of the literature on balance-of-payments crises for understanding the collapse of exchange-rate regimes in developing countries.[2] We first set out a single-good, full-employment, small open-economy model that specifies the basic theoretical framework used for analyzing balance-of-payments crises. We then summarize some important extensions of this framework, namely, the nature of the post-collapse exchange-rate regime, the output and current account implications of an anticipated exchange-rate crisis, and the role of external borrowing and capital controls.

---

[1] Online Supplement D reviews experiences with currency crises in Mexico, Thailand, Brazil, and Argentina; see also Montiel (2013*b*). Although our focus in this chapter is on crises, it should be noted that a number of countries managed to exit pegged exchange-rate regimes in an orderly manner; see Agénor (2004*a*) and Asici et al. (2008) for a discussion and some formal empirical evidence on the conditions for a successful exit.

[2] This section draws to a large extent on Agénor and Flood (1994). See Goldstein and Razin (2013) for an overview of alternative models of currency crises.

1.1 ▪ The Basic Model

Consider a small open economy whose residents consume a single, tradable good. Domestic supply of the good is exogenous, and its foreign-currency price is fixed (at, say, unity). The domestic price level is equal, as a result of purchasing-power parity, to the nominal exchange rate. Agents hold three categories of assets: domestic money (which is not held abroad), and domestic and foreign bonds, which are perfectly substitutable. There are no private banks, so that the money stock is equal to the sum of domestic credit issued by the central bank and the domestic-currency value of foreign reserves held by the central bank. Foreign reserves earn no interest, and domestic credit expands at a constant nominal growth rate. Finally, agents are endowed with perfect foresight.

The model is defined by the following set of equations:

$$m - p = y - \alpha i, \quad \alpha > 0, \tag{1}$$

$$m = \gamma d + (1 - \gamma)R, \quad 0 < \gamma < 1, \tag{2}$$

$$\dot{d} = \mu > 0, \tag{3}$$

$$p = e, \tag{4}$$

$$i = i^* + \dot{e}. \tag{5}$$

All variables, except interest rates, are measured in logarithms. m denotes the nominal money stock, d domestic credit, R the domestic-currency value of foreign reserves held by the central bank, e the spot exchange rate, p the price level, y exogenous output, i^* the foreign interest rate (assumed constant), and i the domestic interest rate.

Equation (1) relates the real demand for money positively to real income and negatively to the domestic interest rate. Equation (2) is a log-linear approximation to the identity defining the money stock as the stock of reserves and domestic credit, which grows at the nominal rate μ [see (3)]. Equations (4) and (5) define, respectively, purchasing-power parity and uncovered interest parity.

Setting $\delta = y - \alpha i^*$ and combining (1), (4), and (5) yields

$$m - e = \delta - \alpha \dot{e}, \quad \delta > 0. \tag{6}$$

Under a fixed exchange-rate regime, $e = \bar{e}$ and $\dot{e} = 0$, so that

$$m - \bar{e} = \delta, \tag{7}$$

which indicates that the central bank accommodates any change in domestic money demand through the purchase or sale of foreign reserves to the public.[3] Using (2) and (7) yields

$$R = (\delta + \bar{e} - \gamma d)/(1 - \gamma), \tag{8}$$

and, using (3),

$$\dot{R} = -\mu/\Theta, \quad \Theta \equiv (1 - \gamma)/\gamma. \tag{9}$$

Equation (9) indicates that if domestic credit expansion is excessive [that is, if it exceeds the rate of growth of the demand for money, which depends on δ as shown in (7), and is assumed here to be zero], reserves are run down at a rate proportional to the rate of credit expansion. Any finite stock of foreign reserves will therefore be depleted in a finite period of time.

Suppose that the central bank announces at time t that it will stop defending the current fixed exchange rate after reserves reach a lower bound, R_l, at which point it will withdraw from the foreign exchange market and allow the exchange rate to float freely thereafter. With a positive rate of domestic credit growth, rational agents will anticipate that, without speculation, reserves will eventually fall to the lower bound, and will therefore foresee the ultimate collapse of the system. To avoid losses arising from an abrupt depreciation of the exchange rate at the time of collapse, speculators will force a crisis *before* the lower bound on reserves is reached. The issue is thus to determine the exact moment at which the fixed exchange-rate regime is abandoned or, equivalently, the time of transition to a floating-rate regime.

The length of the transition period can be calculated by using a process of backward induction, which has been formalized by Flood and Garber (1984). In equilibrium and under perfect foresight, agents can never expect a discrete jump in the level of the exchange rate, because a jump would provide them with profitable arbitrage opportunities. As a consequence, arbitrage in the foreign exchange market requires the exchange rate that prevails immediately after the attack to equal the fixed rate prevailing at the time of the attack. Formally, the time of collapse is found at the point where the "shadow floating rate," which reflects market fundamentals, is equal to the prevailing fixed rate. The shadow floating rate is the exchange rate that would prevail with the current credit stock if reserves had fallen to the minimum level and the exchange rate were allowed to float freely. As long as the fixed exchange rate is more depreciated than the shadow floating rate, the fixed-rate regime is viable; beyond that point, the fixed rate is not sustainable. The reason is that if the shadow floating rate falls below the prevailing fixed rate, speculators would not profit from driving the government's stock of reserves to its lower bound and

---

[3]Because capital is perfectly mobile, the stock of foreign reserves can jump discontinuously as private agents readjust their portfolios in response to current or anticipated shocks.

precipitating the adoption of a floating-rate regime, because they would experience an instantaneous capital loss on their purchases of foreign currency. On the other hand, if the shadow floating rate is above the fixed rate, speculators would experience an instantaneous capital gain. Neither anticipated capital gains nor losses at an infinite rate are compatible with a perfect-foresight equilibrium. Speculators will compete with each other to eliminate such opportunities. This type of behavior leads to an equilibrium attack, which incorporates the arbitrage condition that the pre-attack fixed rate should equal the post-attack floating rate.

A first step, therefore, is to find the solution for the shadow floating exchange rate, which can be written as

$$e = \kappa_0 + \kappa_1 m, \tag{10}$$

where κ_0 and κ_1 are as-yet-undetermined coefficients and, from (2), $m = \gamma d + (1 - \gamma) R_l$ when reserves reach their lower level.[4]

Taking the rate of change of (10) and noting from (2) that under a floating-rate regime $\dot{m} = \gamma \, \dot{d}$ yields

$$\dot{e} = \kappa_1 \gamma \mu. \tag{11}$$

In the post-collapse regime, therefore, the exchange rate depreciates steadily and proportionally to the rate of growth of domestic credit. Substituting (11) in (6) yields, with $\delta = 0$ for simplicity,

$$e = m + \alpha \kappa_1 \gamma \mu. \tag{12}$$

Comparing (12) and (10) yields

$$\kappa_0 = \alpha \gamma \mu, \quad \kappa_1 = 1.$$

From (3), $d = d_0 + \mu t$. Using the definition of m given above and substituting in (12) yields

$$e = \gamma (d_0 + \alpha \mu) + (1 - \gamma) R_l + \gamma \mu t. \tag{13}$$

---

[4] In general, the exchange-rate solution can be derived—assuming no bubbles—by using the forward expansion of (6) and the definition of m when reserves reach their minimum level:

$$e = (\gamma / \alpha) \int_t^\infty [d_h + (1 - \gamma) R_l - \delta] \exp[(t - h)/\alpha] dh,$$

or by using (3),

$$e = (\gamma / \alpha) \int_t^\infty [d + (k - t)\mu + (1 - \gamma) R_l - \delta] \exp[(t - h)/\alpha] dh,$$

which expresses the shadow floating exchange rate as the "present discounted value" of future fundamentals. Integrating this expression by parts yields (13).

The fixed exchange-rate regime collapses when the prevailing parity, $\bar{e}$, equals the shadow floating rate, e. From (13) the exact time of collapse, t_c, is obtained by setting $\bar{e} = e$, so that

$$t_c = [\bar{e} - \gamma d_0 - (1-\gamma)R_l]/\gamma\mu - \alpha,$$

or, because, from (2) and (7), $\bar{e} = \gamma d_0 + (1-\gamma)R_0$,

$$t_c = \Theta(R_0 - R_l)/\mu - \alpha, \tag{14}$$

where R_0 denotes the initial stock of reserves.

Equation (14) indicates that the higher the initial stock of reserves, the lower the critical level, or the lower the rate of credit expansion, the longer it will take before the collapse occurs. With no "speculative" demand for money, $\alpha = 0$, and the collapse occurs when reserves are run down to the minimum level. The interest rate (semi-)elasticity of money demand determines the size of the downward shift in money balances and reserves that takes place when the fixed exchange-rate regime collapses and the nominal interest rate jumps to reflect an expected depreciation of the domestic currency. The larger α is, the earlier the crisis.[5]

The analysis implies, therefore, that the speculative attack always occurs before the central bank would have reached the minimum level of reserves in the absence of speculation. Using (8) with $\delta = 0$ yields the stock of reserves just before the attack (that is, at t_c^-):[6]

$$R_{t_c^-} \equiv \lim_{t \to t_c^-} R_{t_c} = (\bar{e} - \gamma d_{t_c^-})/(1-\gamma),$$

where $d_{t_c^-} = d_0 + \mu t_c^-$, so that

$$R_{t_c^-} = [\bar{e} - \gamma(d_0 + \mu t_c^-)]/(1-\gamma). \tag{15}$$

Using (14) yields

$$\bar{e} - \gamma d_0 = \gamma\mu(t_c^- + \alpha) + (1-\gamma)R_l. \tag{16}$$

Finally, combining (15) and (16) yields

$$R_{t_c^-} = R_l + \alpha\mu/\Theta. \tag{17}$$

---

[5]Note also that the larger the initial proportion of domestic credit in the money stock (the higher γ), the sooner the collapse. γ, however, appears in our reduced form as an artifact of log-linearization, and is used in the model mainly to convert the exogenous credit growth rate to a money supply growth rate.

[6]R is discontinuous at time t_c. It is positive as approached from below and jumps down to its critical level R_l at t_c.

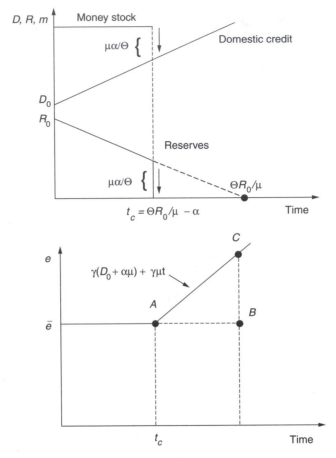

Figure 14–1 ▪ The Process of a Balance-of-Payments Crisis
Source: Agénor and Flood (1994, p. 230).

Figure 14.1 illustrates the process of a balance-of-payments crisis, under the assumption that the minimum level of reserves is zero.[7] The top panel of the figure portrays the behavior of reserves, domestic credit, and the money stock before and after the regime change, and the bottom panel displays the behavior of the exchange rate. Prior to the collapse at t_c, the money stock is constant, but its composition varies because domestic credit rises at the rate μ and reserves decline at the rate μ/Θ. An instant before the regime shift, a speculative attack occurs, and both reserves and the money stock fall by $\alpha\mu/\Theta$. Because $R_l = 0$, the money stock is equal to domestic credit in the post-collapse regime.

As shown in the bottom panel of Figure 14.1, the exchange rate remains constant at $\bar{e}$ until the collapse occurs. The path continuing through AB and

---

[7]Recall that R denotes the logarithm of the stock of foreign reserves, so it is simply an accounting convention to set $R_l = 0$.

then taking a discrete exchange-rate jump BC corresponds to the "natural collapse" scenario ($\alpha = 0$). With speculation, the transition occurs earlier, at A, preventing a discrete change in the exchange rate from occurring. Speculators, who foresee reserves running down to their critical level, avoid losses that would result from the discrete exchange-rate change by attacking the currency at the point where the transition to the float is smooth, that is, where the shadow floating exchange rate equals the prevailing fixed rate.[8]

1.2 ▪ Extensions to the Basic Framework

The literature on balance-of-payments crises has refined and extended the basic theory presented above in a variety of directions. This subsection examines some of the areas in which this literature has developed. It first considers alternative assumptions regarding the post-collapse exchange-rate regime, focusing on the case of a (perfectly anticipated) temporary post-collapse period of floating followed by repegging. We then discuss the real effects of an exchange-rate collapse, and the role of foreign borrowing and the imposition of capital controls as policy measures aimed at postponing (or preventing) the occurrence of a balance-of-payments crisis.[9]

1.2.1 Sterilization

A key assumption of the Krugman-Flood-Garber model is that the money supply falls, in line with money demand, at the moment the currency attack takes place. However, if reserve losses are completely sterilized, such a discrete jump will *not* take place. This case has been studied by Flood et al. (1996). Their analysis shows that the fixed exchange-rate regime is not viable under full sterilization; as long as agents understand that the central bank plans to sterilize an eventual speculative attack, they will attack *immediately*. To see this, consider the money market equilibrium condition (6) with $\delta = 0$. If the money stock is constant as a result of sterilized intervention (at, say, $m = m_S$) and the exchange rate is fixed, this condition becomes

$$m_S - \bar{e} = 0,$$

whereas, in the post-attack floating-rate regime, with $\dot{e} = \mu$:

$$m_S - e = -\alpha\mu.$$

---

[8]This analysis can be easily extended to consider the case where the precollapse regime is a crawling-peg arrangement. See, for instance, Connolly and Taylor (1984).

[9]Areas that have received much attention in recent years are the link between banking and exchange-rate crises, on the one hand, and banking and sovereign debt crises, on the other. The analytical issues involved are examined in Chapters 15 and 16.

Subtracting the second expression from the first yields

$$e - \bar{e} = \alpha\mu > 0.$$

Thus, if the money supply does not change when the attack takes place, the shadow exchange rate (consistent with money market equilibrium) will always exceed the prevailing fixed exchange rate, thereby provoking an immediate attack. By adding a risk premium to the above model, Flood et al. (1996) show that the extended model with sterilization can be compatible with a fixed exchange rate. Essentially, the risk premium adjusts to keep the demand for money constant, just as sterilization maintains money supply constant. A feature of their analysis is that because the money supply does not change, and the exchange rate cannot jump (although its rate of change, $\dot{e}$, does), the domestic interest rate cannot jump either—in contrast to the standard framework.

1.2.2 *Alternative Post-Collapse Regimes*

The focus of the early theoretical literature on balance-of-payments crises has been on the transition from a fixed exchange rate to a post-collapse floating rate. Various alternative scenarios are, however, suggested by actual experience. Following the breakdown of the fixed-rate system, the central bank can devalue the currency, implement a dual-exchange-rate arrangement, or adopt a crawling-peg regime. In general, the timing of a crisis depends on the particular exchange-rate arrangement that agents expect the central bank to adopt after a run on its reserve stock has forced the abandonment of the initial fixed rate. We will examine, for illustrative purposes, the case in which, after allowing the currency to float for a certain period of time, the central bank returns to the foreign exchange market and fixes the exchange rate at a new, more depreciated level (Obstfeld, 1984).

Suppose that the length of the transitory period of floating, denoted by T, and the level $\bar{e}_H > \bar{e}$ to which the exchange rate will be pegged at the end of the transition, are known with certainty.[10] The time t_c at which the speculative attack occurs is calculated, as before, by a process of backward induction. However, this principle now imposes two restrictions rather than one. First, as before, the initial fixed rate $\bar{e}$ must coincide with the relevant shadow floating rate, that is, $\bar{e} = e_{t_c}$. Second, at time $t_c + T$, the preannounced new fixed rate $\bar{e}_H$ must also coincide with the interim floating rate, $\bar{e}_H = e_{t_c+T}$.[11] The last requirement acts as a terminal condition on the exchange-rate differential equation.

In the foregoing discussion, when the central bank's policy was assumed to involve abandonment of the fixed rate and adoption of a permanent float thereafter,

---

[10]Note that the new fixed exchange rate, to be viable, must be greater than (that is, more depreciated) or equal to the rate that would have prevailed had there been a permanent postcrisis float.

[11]As before, this is implied by the absence of arbitrage profits, which rules out anticipated discrete changes in the exchange rate.

the shadow floating rate was given by (12). Now, under a transitory floating regime, the shadow rate is given by

$$e = \kappa_0 + \kappa_1 m + C \exp(t/\alpha), \quad t_c \leq t \leq t_c + T \qquad (18)$$

where C is an undetermined constant.[12] The complete solution must therefore specify values for both t_c and C. These values are obtained by imposing $\bar{e} = e_{t_c}$ and $\bar{e}_H = e_{t_c+T}$ on (18).[13] The solutions for t_c and C are

$$t_c = (\bar{e} - \alpha\gamma\mu - \gamma d_0 - \Omega)/\gamma\mu, \qquad (19)$$

$$C = \Omega \exp(-t_c/\alpha), \qquad (20)$$

where $\Omega = [(\bar{e}_H - \bar{e}) - \gamma\mu T]/[\exp(T/\alpha) - 1]$.

Equation (19) indicates that the collapse time is linked to the magnitude of the expected devaluation $(\bar{e}_H - \bar{e})$ and the length of the transitional float.[14] Crises occur earlier the greater the anticipated devaluation: equation (19) shows that the higher the anticipated post-devaluation exchange rate, the sooner the speculative attack occurs $(\partial t_c/\partial \bar{e}_H < 0)$.[15] The relationship between the collapse time and the length of the floating-rate interval depends, in general, on the parameters of the model; it is negative for small T and positive for large T. If the transitional float is sufficiently brief, therefore, a speculative attack on the domestic currency will occur as soon as the private agents realize that the current exchange rate cannot be enforced indefinitely.

1.2.3 Real Effects of an Anticipated Collapse

Existing evidence suggests that balance-of-payments crises are often associated with large current account movements during the periods preceding, as well as during the periods following, such crises. Typically, large external deficits tend to emerge as agents adjust their consumption pattern, in addition to adjusting the composition of their holdings of financial assets, in anticipation of a crisis. As suggested by the experience of Argentina, Chile, and Mexico reviewed below, for instance, movements in the real exchange rate and the current account can be quite dramatic.

---

[12]The last term in (18) represents a *speculative bubble* component, which was ruled out from the solution (13) by imposing the transversality condition $C = 0$. Imposing the terminal condition $\bar{e}_H = \bar{e}_{t_c+T}$ now requires $C \neq 0$.

[13]Formally, because $\kappa_0 = \alpha\gamma\mu$ and $\kappa_1 = 1$, these restrictions are given by

$$\bar{e} = \alpha\gamma\mu + \gamma(d_0 + \mu t_c) + C \exp(t_c/\alpha),$$

$$\bar{e}_H = \alpha\gamma\mu + \gamma[d_0 + \mu(t_c + T)] + C \exp[(t_c + T)/\alpha].$$

Direct manipulation of these equations yields the solutions for C and t_c given in (19) and (20).

[14]Note that (19) and (20) yield a solution for the collapse time that is equivalent to (17) with $R_l = 0$ and for $T \to \infty$, since in that case $\Omega \to 0$ and $(1 - \gamma)R_0 = \bar{e} - \gamma d_0$.

[15]If $\bar{e}_H$ is high enough, it is possible that $t_c \leq 0$. In this case, the speculative attack occurs at the moment speculators learn that the fixed exchange rate cannot be defended indefinitely.

Such movements may provide an explanation of why speculative attacks are often preceded by a period during which official foreign reserves are lost at accelerating rates. Financial crises are also characterized by large output costs—typically an abrupt recession. Using data for 157 countries for the period 1970–2006, Edwards (2011) found that currency crises have a significantly negative effect on GDP growth. Using panel data covering the period 1975–1997, Hutchison and Noy (2005), for instance, found that currency crises lead to reductions in output of about 5–8 percent over a two- to four-year period. Hong and Tornell (2005), using data for more than one hundred developing countries, found that, following a currency crisis, it takes less than three years for the *growth rate* of output to return fully to its pre-crisis average. The *level* of output, however, remains below its initial trend for a substantial period of time, suggesting that the effects of the shocks underlying a crisis are highly persistent.[16]

A convenient framework for examining the real effects of exchange-rate crises was developed by Willman (1988), who assumes that domestic output is demand-determined, positively related to the real exchange rate, and inversely related to the real interest rate.[17] The trade balance depends positively on the real exchange rate but is negatively related to aggregate demand. Prices are set as a markup over wages and imported input costs. In one variant of the model, nominal wages are determined through forward-looking contracts.[18] Under perfect foresight, an anticipated future collapse will affect wages immediately and, therefore, prices, the real exchange rate, output, and the trade balance. At the moment the collapse occurs, inflation jumps up, the rate of depreciation of the real exchange rate jumps down, and the real interest rate falls. As a result, output increases while the trade balance deteriorates. But because wage contracts are forward-looking, anticipated future increases in prices are discounted back to the present and affect current wages. Consequently, prices start adjusting before the collapse occurs. The real interest rate falls gradually and experiences a downward jump at the moment the collapse takes place, as indicated above. The decline in the (ex post) real interest rate has an expansionary effect on domestic activity before the collapse occurs. However, output also depends on the real exchange rate. The steady rise in domestic prices results in an appreciation of the domestic currency, which has an adverse effect on economic activity and may outweigh the positive output effect resulting from a lower real interest rate. If relative price effects are strong, the net impact of an anticipated collapse on output may well be negative. The continuous loss of competitiveness, unless it is associated with a fall in aggregate demand (and thus downward pressure on the demand for imports), implies that the trade balance deteriorates in the periods preceding the collapse of

---

[16]There is also evidence to suggest that low output growth may increase the likelihood of a currency crisis; see Licchetta (2011), whose study covers forty countries over the period 1980–2004.

[17]Other models focusing on real exchange-rate effects of an anticipated collapse include those of Claessens (1991), Connolly and Taylor (1984), Connolly (1986), Calvo (1987b), and Veiga (1999).

[18]A formulation of wage contracts similar to the one proposed by Willman was used in Chapter 11.

the fixed exchange-rate regime. The trade deficit increases further at the moment the crisis occurs and, in association with a gradual depreciation of the real exchange rate, returns afterward to its steady-state level. The gradual appreciation of the real exchange rate until the time of collapse and the subsequent depreciation predicted by Willman's model account fairly well for the real exchange-rate movements observed during crisis episodes in countries such as Argentina in the early 1980s, as discussed below.

The role of intertemporal substitution effects in understanding the real effects of exchange-rate crises has recently been clarified by Kimbrough (1992), who uses an optimizing framework in which money reduces transactions costs. Kimbrough shows that the effects of an anticipated speculative attack on the behavior of the current account depends crucially on the difference between the interest elasticity of the demand for money and the intertemporal elasticity of substitution in consumption. If the latter exceeds the former, an anticipated speculative attack raises consumption and real balances at the moment agents realize that the fixed exchange rate will eventually collapse, and leads to a continued deterioration of the current account until the attack actually takes place. By contrast, if the interest elasticity of the demand for money exceeds the intertemporal elasticity of substitution in consumption, the outcome is an initial reduction in consumption and real money balances, and an immediate and continued improvement in the current account until the time of the speculative attack and the collapse of the fixed exchange rate. An implication of Kimbrough's analysis is that anticipated speculative attacks may not be associated with similar real effects in all countries and at all times. Nevertheless, as discussed below for the case of several Latin American countries, speculative attacks and impending balance-of-payments crises have often been associated in practice with large current account deficits.

1.2.4 *Borrowing, Capital Controls, and Crisis Postponement*

Countries facing balance-of-payments difficulties often have recourse to external borrowing to supplement the amount of reserves available to defend the official parity, or impose restrictions on capital outflows in an attempt to limit losses of foreign exchange reserves. In the basic model developed above, it is assumed that there is a critical level, known by everyone, below which foreign reserves are not allowed to be depleted. However, such a binding threshold may not exist. A central bank facing a perfect capital market can, at least in principle, increase foreign reserves at its disposal by short-term borrowing. Negative (net) reserves are therefore also feasible.

In fact, perfect access to international capital markets implies that, at any given point in time, central bank reserves can become negative without violating the government's intertemporal solvency constraint. Unlimited access to borrowing could therefore postpone or avoid a regime collapse. The rate of growth of domestic credit cannot, however, be permanently maintained above the world interest rate, because it would lead to a violation of the government budget constraint

(Obstfeld, 1986*b*). In this sense, an over-expansionary credit policy would still ultimately lead to the collapse of a fixed exchange-rate regime.[19] Moreover, even with perfect capital markets, the timing of borrowing matters considerably for the nature of speculative attacks. Suppose that the interest cost of servicing foreign debt exceeds the interest rate paid on reserves. If borrowing occurs just before the fixed exchange rate would have collapsed without borrowing, the crisis is likely to be postponed. If borrowing occurs long enough before the exchange-rate regime would have collapsed in the absence of borrowing, the crisis would occur earlier. The reason the collapse is brought forward is, of course, related to the servicing cost of foreign indebtedness on the public sector deficit, which raises the rate of growth of domestic credit (Buiter, 1987).

In practice, most developing countries face borrowing constraints on international capital markets. The existence of limited access to external financing has important implications for the behavior of inflation in an economy where agents are subject to an intertemporal budget constraint. Consider, for instance, a country that has no opportunity to borrow externally and in which the central bank transfers its net profits to the government. If a speculative attack occurs, the central bank will lose its stock of reserves, and its post-collapse profits from interest earnings on those reserves will drop to zero. As a consequence, net income of the government will fall and the budget deficit will deteriorate. If the deficit is financed by increased domestic credit—a typical situation for a developing country with limited access to domestic and external borrowing—the post-collapse inflation rate will exceed the rate that prevailed in the pre-collapse fixed exchange-rate regime, raising inflation tax revenue to compensate for the fall in interest income (van Wijnbergen, 1991).

As indicated earlier, capital controls have often been used to limit losses of foreign exchange reserves and postpone a regime collapse. Such controls have been imposed either permanently or temporarily after the central bank had experienced significant losses, or at times when the domestic currency came under heavy pressure on foreign exchange markets.[20] With permanent controls, as shown by Agénor and Flood (1994), the higher the degree of capital controls, the longer it will take for the fixed exchange rate to collapse. This is because controls dampen the size of the expected future jump in the domestic nominal interest rate and the associated shift in the demand for money.

The effect of temporary capital controls on the timing of a balance-of-payments crisis was studied by Bacchetta (1990), who showed that temporary restrictions on capital movements may have pronounced real effects. In a perfect-foresight world, agents will anticipate the introduction of controls as soon as they realize the

---

[19]The relation between speculative attacks and the solvency of the public sector in an economy with interest-bearing debt has also been examined by Ize and Ortíz (1987).

[20]In developing countries, capital controls have often been of a permanent nature; see, for instance, Edwards (1989*a*) for Latin American countries. Temporary controls have typically been used in industrial countries, notably in Europe.

fundamental inconsistency between the fiscal policy and the fixed exchange rate. However, it is now critical to distinguish the case in which the timing of the policy change is perfectly anticipated and the case in which it is not. If controls take agents by surprise, capital outflows will increasingly be replaced by higher imports once such controls are put in place, leading eventually to a deterioration in the current account until a "natural" collapse occurs. The accelerated rate of depletion of foreign reserves through the current account will therefore precipitate the crisis, defeating the initial objective of controls. If capital controls are preannounced, or if agents are able to "guess" correctly the exact time at which controls will be introduced, a speculative attack may occur just before the controls are imposed, as agents attempt to readjust their portfolios and evade restrictions. Such an attack will, again, defeat the very purpose of capital controls and may in fact precipitate the regime collapse (Dellas and Stockman, 1993). These results are consistent with the empirical estimates of Glick and Hutchison (2005), based on panel data regressions for sixty developing countries for the period 1975–1997, which suggest that restrictions on capital flows typically do not appear to effectively insulate countries from speculative attacks and currency crises. In the same vein, Esaka (2010) examined the link between de facto exchange rate regimes and the incidence of currency crises in eighty-four countries from 1980 to 2001; he found that hard pegs with capital account liberalization have a significantly lower probability of currency crises than intermediate regimes with capital controls and free floats with capital controls.

1.2.5 *Interest Rate Defense*

The standard model of currency crises described earlier implicitly assumes that the central bank remains passive while official foreign reserves dwindle. In practice, central banks typically defend pegs aggressively by raising short-term interest rates (see Montiel, 2003). Contributions by Lahiri and Végh (2003) and Flood and Jeanne (2005) have amended the conventional model of speculative attacks, which is based on perfect capital mobility (and thus "ties" the domestic interest to the foreign rate under the fixed exchange-rate regime) to feasibility and optimality of interest rate hikes in delaying currency crises. To do so, both studies introduce frictions in the degree of substitution between assets.

In the model of Lahiri and Végh (2003), interest rate policy operates in conflictive ways. By raising demand for domestic, interest-bearing liquid assets, higher interest rates tend to delay the crisis. At the same time, however, higher interest rates increase public debt service and may signal higher future inflation (if the ensuing deficit cannot be closed by higher taxes), which tends to bring forward the crisis. Depending on the conditions, it is feasible to delay the crisis, but raising interest rates beyond a certain point may actually hasten it. It is thus optimal to engage in some active interest rate defense, but only up to a certain point. In Flood and Jeanne (2005), increasing the domestic currency interest rate before a speculative attack makes domestic assets more attractive as a result of an asset substitution effect, but weakens the domestic currency by increasing the government's fiscal liabilities.[21] Thus, an interest rate defense can be successful only if the initial level of public debt is not too large.

In contrast to the above contributions, Drazen and Hubrich (2006) suggest that the benefit of high interest rates to fend off speculative attacks stems mainly from the signal that they provide—rather than from their direct impact on the profitability of speculation. As discussed in more detail later, by raising interest rates, policymakers may signal their commitment to fixed exchange rates, but it may also signal weak fundamentals. Hence, while raising interest rates may lead to the expectation that future rates will be high, it may also increase the probability speculators assign to a collapse of the pegged exchange rate. The net effect may therefore be ambiguous.[22]

Indeed, as documented by Montiel (2003) and subsequent studies, a strong relationship between interest rates and speculative attacks has proved difficult to establish. Goderis and Ioannidou (2008) found that for low levels of short-term corporate debt (an indicator that captures balance sheet vulnerabilities, as emphasized in third-generation models of currency crises, as discussed later), raising interest rates lowers the probability of a successful attack. Using a dataset that covers fifty-four countries from March 1964 through December 2005, Grier and Lin (2010) found strong evidence that raising interest rates prior to a currency crisis has significantly different impacts in different country groups: it significantly reduces the probability of speculative attacks in countries that have a de facto hard peg, but increases it in de facto soft-pegging countries. In a study of twenty-four countries over the period 1986–2009, Eijffinger and Karataşa (2012) found that while increased interest rates in the aftermath of a currency crisis depreciate the currency in industrial countries, there is no robust effect for developing countries. If the crisis is accompanied by financial sector problems, tight monetary policy has detrimental effects on the domestic currency of these economies.

1.2.6   *Other Directions*

There are many other directions in which the theory of balance-of-payments crises has been extended, particularly in the areas of uncertainty (over the critical threshold of reserves, for instance, or the credit policy rule) and regime switches (see Agénor and Flood, 1994). The introduction of uncertainty on domestic credit growth provides a channel through which the sharp increases in domestic nominal interest rates

---

[21] To generate imperfect substitutability between domestic and foreign assets, Flood and Jeanne assume that holding foreign bonds generates disutility. This assumption is rather arbitrary and far from intuitive. A more attractive approach would be to introduce individual risk, along the lines of the model discussed in Chapters 10 and 13. This would yield a formulation similar to (5) in their paper.

[22] In general, as discussed by Hnatkovska et al. (2013), the relationship between the exchange rate and short-term interest rates may be non-monotonic. Small increases in the nominal interest rate appreciate the currency, whereas larger increases depreciate the currency. A possible reason is that higher interest rates increase money demand and hence appreciate the currency but also raise the fiscal deficit and depress output, both of which tend to depreciate the currency.

that typically precede an exchange-rate crisis can be explained.[23] But beyond being consistent with rising interest rates prior to the crisis, the introduction of uncertainty in collapse models has several additional implications. First, the transition to a floating-rate regime becomes stochastic, implying that the collapse time is a random variable that cannot be determined explicitly, as before. Second, there will, in general, always be a nonzero probability of a speculative attack in the next period, a possibility that in turn produces a forward discount on the domestic currency—the so-called peso problem (Krasker, 1980). Available evidence indeed suggests that the forward premium—or, as an alternative indicator of exchange-rate expectations in developing countries, the parallel market premium—in foreign exchange markets tends to increase well before the regime shift. Third, the degree of uncertainty about the central bank's credit policy plays an important role in the speed at which reserves of the central bank are depleted (Claessens, 1991). In a stochastic setting, reserve losses exceed increases in domestic credit because of a rising probability of regime collapse, so that reserve depletion accelerates on the way to the regime change. As indicated above, such a pattern has often been observed in actual crises.

Early models of balance-of-payments crises have been generally limited to the consideration of an exogenous rate of credit growth that has been, often implicitly, taken to reflect "fiscal constraints." The apparently ineluctable nature of a regime collapse that such an assumption entails runs into a conceptual difficulty—namely, why is it that policymakers do not attempt to prevent the crisis by adjusting their fiscal and credit policies? For instance, there is nothing in the basic model developed above that requires the central bank to float the currency and abandon the prevailing fixed exchange rate at the moment reserves hit their critical lower bound. Instead, the central bank could choose to change its credit policy rule (before reserves are exhausted) to make it consistent with a fixed exchange-rate target. Some recent models of balance-of-payments crises have indeed considered endogenous changes of this type in monetary policy. Drazen and Helpman (1988) and Edwards and Montiel (1989), in particular, have emphasized that the assumption that the authorities choose to adjust the exchange rate instead of altering the underlying macroeconomic policy mix can provide only a temporary solution. Ultimately, if the new exchange-rate regime is inconsistent with the underlying fiscal policy process, there will be a need for a new policy regime.

Finally, an area that has received much attention in the recent literature is the possibility of multiple equilibria. Instead of assuming, as in the basic Krugman-Flood-Garber model, that credit policy is exogenous, several authors have explored the implication of an endogenous credit policy rule. Specifically, Obstfeld (1986b) has examined the case where domestic credit growth is consistent with the indefinite viability of the fixed exchange rate as long as the regime is maintained ($\mu = 0$), but

---

[23]There have been many applications of the stochastic model of exchange-rate crises. See, in particular, Cumby and van Wijnbergen (1989) for Argentina; and Blanco and Garber (1986), Connolly and Fernández (1987), and Goldberg (1994) for Mexico.

contingent on the collapse of the fixed exchange rate, the loss of discipline causes the domestic credit growth rate to increase ($\mu \geq 0$). In such a setting, multiple equilibria may emerge. The fixed exchange rate can survive indefinitely if asset holders believe that it will not collapse. By contrast, if private agents believe that a collapse will occur, the run on official reserves will bring the regime down, triggering the contingent shift in domestic credit growth, and validating the attack. Formally, consider the case where $\mu = 0$ in the basic framework developed previously. From (14), $t_c = \infty$, and the regime survives indefinitely. Suppose that, contingent on a collapse of the fixed exchange rate, agents expect credit growth to be $\mu_c > 0$ and that $\Theta(R_0 - R_l)/\mu_c < \alpha$, so that $t_c < 0$. Then an immediate attack will take place; the post-attack solution for the floating rate will jump upward, or at least start depreciating sufficiently rapidly to ratify the sudden reduction in the domestic money stock. Thus, private agents' beliefs about the viability of the fixed exchange rate become a key element in determining the timing of the crisis. Shifts across alternative equilibria may be self-fulfilling: the economy may switch from an equilibrium in which devaluation expectations are low and the peg is sustainable, to an equilibrium in which devaluation expectations are high and the peg becomes impossible to defend.

Models of currency crises with multiple equilibria have been extended in various directions in recent years. The next section discusses the main features of these models.

2 Policy Trade-Offs and Self-Fulfilling Crises

A key feature of the recent literature on currency crises has been, in addition to a focus on multiple equilibria, an explicit modeling of policymakers' preferences and policy rules. In this setting, policymakers are viewed as deriving benefits from pegging the currency—by, say, "importing" the anti-inflation bias of the foreign central bank—but as also facing other policy objectives—such as the level of unemployment and domestic interest rates. Thus, depending on the circumstances that they face, policymakers may find it optimal to abandon the official parity.

According to this approach, the occurrence of an exchange-rate "crisis" is not related to the existence of a sufficient level of reserves. Rather, the abandonment of the peg is the result of the implementation of a *contingent rule* for setting the exchange rate. Each period, the policymaker considers the costs and benefits associated with maintaining the peg for another period, and must decide, given the relative weights attached to each policy objective, whether or not to abandon it. This decision typically is viewed as depending on the realization of a particular set of domestic or external shock(s). For a given cost associated with abandoning the currency peg, there exists a range of values for the shock(s) that makes maintaining the peg optimal. However, for sufficiently large realizations of the shock(s), the loss in flexibility associated with the discretionary use of the exchange rate may exceed the loss incurred by abandoning the peg; in such circumstances, it is optimal for the policymaker to operate a regime switch.

2.1 ■ Example Based on Output-Inflation Trade-Offs

A tractable framework that allows understanding the main features of models with "rational" or optimizing policymakers and the role of self-fulfilling factors is the model developed by Obstfeld (1996), which emphasizes trade-offs between output (or unemployment) and inflation.[24]

Suppose that the government's loss function is given by

$$L = (y - \tilde{y})^2 + \theta \Delta e^2 + c, \quad \theta > 0 \tag{21}$$

where y is (the log of) output, $\tilde{y}$ the policymaker's output target, e (the log of) the exchange rate, and c a fixed cost associated with changes in the official parity. Output is determined by an expectations-augmented Phillips curve

$$y = \bar{y} + \alpha(\varepsilon - \varepsilon^a) - u, \tag{22}$$

where $\bar{y}$ is the "natural" (or long-run) level of output, $\varepsilon \equiv \Delta e$, ε^a domestic price-setters' expectation of ε, and u is a zero-mean shock. As in Barro-Gordon type models, we assume that $\tilde{y} > \bar{y}$.

Price setters form their expectations prior to observing the shock u. By contrast, the policymaker chooses e after observing the shock. A devaluation bears a cost of c^d, and a revaluation cost of c^r.

Begin by ignoring the term c in (21). With ε^a predetermined, the policymaker chooses

$$\varepsilon = \frac{\alpha(\tilde{y} - \bar{y} + u) + \alpha^2 \varepsilon^a}{\alpha^2 + \theta}, \tag{23}$$

which implies a level of output equal to

$$y = \bar{y} + \frac{\alpha^2(\tilde{y} - \bar{y}) - \theta u - \alpha \theta \varepsilon^a}{\alpha^2 + \theta},$$

and a policy loss of (with the superscript D for discretionary):

$$L^D = \frac{\theta}{\alpha^2 + \theta}(\tilde{y} - \bar{y} + u + \alpha \varepsilon^a)^2.$$

---

[24]See Agénor and Masson (1999) for an alternative loss function in the context of a model of credibility and reputational factors.

If the government foregoes the use of the exchange rate (so that $\Delta e = 0$), the policy loss is instead, substituting (22) in (21),

$$L^F = (\tilde{y} - \alpha \varepsilon^a - u - \bar{y})^2.$$

Consider now the fixed cost c. When fixed costs exist, (23) holds only when u is so large that $L^D + c^d < L^F$, or so low that $L^D + c^r < L^F$. A devaluation (revaluation) thus takes place for $u > u^d$ $(< u^r)$, where

$$u^d = \frac{1}{\alpha}\sqrt{c^d(\alpha^2 + \theta)} - (\tilde{y} - \bar{y}) - \alpha \varepsilon^a,$$

$$u^r = -\frac{1}{\alpha}\sqrt{c^r(\alpha^2 + \theta)} - (\tilde{y} - \bar{y}) - \alpha \varepsilon^a.$$

Suppose that u is uniformly distributed in the interval $(-\nu, \nu)$. The rational expectation of next period's ε, given price-setters' expectation ε^a, is given by

$$E\varepsilon = E(\varepsilon \mid u < u^r)\,\Pr(u < u^r) + E(\varepsilon \mid u > u^d)\,\Pr(u > u^d),$$

or, using (23):

$$E\varepsilon = \frac{\alpha}{\alpha^2 + \theta}\left[\left(1 - \frac{u^d - u^r}{2\nu}\right)(\tilde{y} - \bar{y} + \alpha \varepsilon^a) - \frac{u^{d2} - u^{r2}}{4\nu}\right]. \qquad (24)$$

In full equilibrium, $E\varepsilon = \varepsilon^a$. Equation (24) is shown in Figure 14.2. As shown by Obstfeld (1996), the slope of the curve describing the relationship between $E\varepsilon$ and ε^a is given by, setting $\Delta = \alpha^2 + \theta$:

$$\frac{dE\varepsilon}{d\varepsilon^a} = \begin{array}{ll} \alpha^2 \Delta^{-1} & \text{for } u^r > -\nu \\ \alpha^2 \Delta^{-1}[\frac{\alpha}{2} + \frac{\alpha}{2\nu}(\tilde{y} - \bar{y} + \alpha \varepsilon^a)] & \text{for } u^r = -\nu \,. \\ \alpha^2 \Delta^{-1} & \text{for } u^d = -\nu \end{array}$$

There are, therefore, three possible equilibria (or, more precisely, three equilibrium expected depreciation rates) in this model, corresponding to three different probabilities of devaluation and realignment magnitudes—conditional on a devaluation taking place. These equilibria are denoted by points A, B, and C in the figure. Once ε^a is sufficiently high for u^d to remain at $-\nu$, the government's reaction function is given by (23) and the expected depreciation rate is the same as under a flexible exchange-rate regime—obtained by setting $\varepsilon = \varepsilon^a$ in (23):

$$\varepsilon = \varepsilon^a = \frac{\alpha(\tilde{y} - \bar{y} + u)}{\theta}.$$

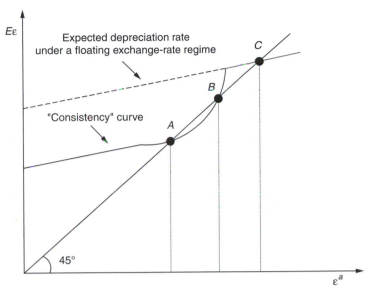

Figure 14–2 ■ Multiple Equilibria in a Model of Self-Fulfilling Exchange Rate Crisis
Source: Adapted from Obstfeld (1996, p. 1043).

To ensure that equilibrium C in Figure 14.2 exists, a necessary condition for multiplicities to exist, requires the restriction

$$\theta^{-1}\Delta(\bar{y} - \tilde{y}) - \nu \geq \alpha^{-1}\sqrt{c^d \Delta},$$

a condition that can be interpreted as indicating that if private agents form an expectation of the average depreciation rate of the floating exchange rate, then it will materialize—as long as the fixed devaluation cost is not too high. Thus, as long as market expectations gravitate around a nonzero depreciation rate, the policymaker will be unable to enforce its preferred equilibrium (which involves zero depreciation). Furthermore, a small random event could shift the exchange rate from a position where it is vulnerable to only very "bad" realizations of the shock, to one where output is so low (in the absence of a devaluation) that even small shocks will induce the policymaker to devalue the currency.

2.2 ■ Public Debt and Self-Fulfilling Crises

The role of public debt in generating self-fulfilling currency crises is highlighted in several contributions, most notably by Cole and Kehoe (1996) and

Velasco (1996, 1997).[25] The Cole-Kehoe model, in particular, emphasizes the role of a short average term of a country's public external debt in allowing a potentially temporary loss of investor confidence to produce a severe and persistent economic crisis. The implication of their analysis is that financial crises (of the type that occurred in Mexico in December 1994, as discussed later) can be avoided if governments diversify the term structure of their debt sufficiently to ensure that only a small portion of it matures during any particular interval of time.

In the Cole-Kehoe model, the government inherits a certain amount of foreign debt that it must either retire, refinance, or repudiate.[26] They focus on the case in which the initial stock of public debt is so large that it is either not feasible to repay it in one period or can be immediately retired only at the cost of a very significant loss in welfare. However, repudiating the debt, although costly (it may permanently reduce the productivity of the economy), may be preferable to retiring or refinancing the debt under some circumstances. The government, moreover, cannot credibly commit itself to refusing to repudiate the debt at a future date if repudiation turns out to be the "best" strategy at that date.

Cole and Kehoe show that if the initial debt is large enough, it is possible for the model to admit multiple equilibrium outcomes, depending on the nature of foreign lenders' expectations. If foreign lenders expect the government to be able to service its debts, then government bonds will sell at a moderate price and it will be optimal for the government to refinance them rather than repudiate them. If, on the other hand, lenders believe, for whatever reason(s), that the government will not be able to service its debts, then they will be unwilling to lend to the government. Under such conditions the government cannot possibly refinance its debt and it may be optimal to repudiate it rather than accept the large (and possibly infeasible) loss in consumption that would be necessary to extinguish foreign liabilities out of the country's current income. Thus, foreign lenders' expectations that the government will not be able to service its debt are self-fulfilling; when lenders hold this expectation, the government becomes unwilling or unable to service its debt. This situation can arise *stochastically*; that is, there can be equilibria in which lenders expect the government to be able to repay its debts, in which case the government refinances them and no crisis occurs, but occasionally lenders may expect the government to be unable to repay, in which case the government cannot refinance the debt and chooses to repudiate it, producing a crisis. Formally, these "bad" states of nature are tied to adverse realization of a spurious indicator variable—a sunspot, that is, a seemingly minor random event, such as the resignation of some key economic minister.

---

[25] See also Corsetti and Maćkowiak (2006) for a discussion of how external nominal shocks can cause fiscal imbalances and undermine currency stability, and how fiscal and interest rate policies interact to determine the magnitude and timing of speculative attacks.

[26] For the purpose of this discussion, it is important to distinguish between repudiating a debt, which is a decision not to repay any portion of it at any future date, and defaulting on a debt, a broader term that could include not only repudiation but also such actions as repaying only part of the principal or interest on the debt or unilaterally extending the term of the debt. When Cole and Kehoe use the term *default*, they are actually talking about repudiation.

There can be only one crisis, however, because after the government has repudiated its debt (thereby losing its reputation) it no longer has the option to borrow.

In the Cole-Kehoe model, a financial crisis can occur at a particular date only if the amount of debt that needs to be rolled over at that date is fairly large. As a result, changing the maturity structure of the debt can prevent crises from occurring. If the government refinances its initial debt by issuing bonds with varying maturities, then only a fraction of it would need to be refinanced at any particular future date. Under such conditions, even if lenders are led to believe (whatever the reason may be) that the government is going to be unable to refinance its debt, the government can retire maturing debt out of its current income without incurring welfare costs large enough to give it the incentive to repudiate its debt. Under these conditions an equilibrium in which self-fulfilling beliefs by lenders that the government will fail to repay does not exist and a crisis cannot occur.

2.3 ■ Role of Credibility and Reputation

The role of credibility and reputational factors in models of currency crises with optimizing policymakers (through their effect on exchange-rate expectations) has been emphasized by Drazen and Masson (1994). The notion of credibility on which these models focus consists of two elements: an assessment of the policymaker's "type" (which would be termed reputation), and (given the type of policymaker) an assessment of the probability that a policymaker will actually decide to stick to announced policies in the presence of adverse shocks. In the context considered here, the policy commitment is to maintain an exchange-rate peg in the face of shocks to reserves.

As argued by Drazen and Masson (1994), resisting a currency crisis can actually undermine, rather than enhance, the credibility of a pegged exchange rate. High interest rates, for instance, may signal the government's commitment to the peg and thus enhance credibility, but at the same time it may also worsen fundamentals, making the economy more vulnerable to adverse shocks. Thus, the most rigid policy is not necessarily optimal; in an uncertain economic environment, and if shocks are persistent, there may be a trade-off between credibility and flexibility.[27]

A straightforward application of these ideas is a study by Irwin (2004), on whether a currency board necessarily provides a durable basis for a fully binding and credible commitment to fix the exchange rate. Irwin develops a model in which a currency board is abandoned when the (political) cost of maintaining the peg is sufficiently high. A credibility problem exists because agents have incomplete information about the magnitude of this cost. If policymakers face a high cost of devaluation, they will maintain the currency board, but at the expense of higher unemployment. This tends to reduce the credibility of the exchange-rate peg. At the same time, because the public learns about the true devaluation cost by observing

---

[27] Neut and Velasco (2004) propose a related argument, albeit in a different framework.

actual exchange-rate behavior, maintaining the currency board will help to improve its credibility. If the first effect dominates, fundamentals will tend to deteriorate over time. Specifically, if unemployment is persistent, the credibility problem will be compounded, and the pressure to devalue and abandon the currency board will increase over time. Ultimately, even a policymaker who faces a very high cost of devaluation can be forced to devalue. In a sense, this conclusion is similar to Drazen and Masson (1994) regarding the sustainability of conventional pegs.

A more substantial extension of the Drazen-Masson framework is given by Benigno and Missale (2004), who account explicitly for public debt, using a three-period stochastic setting that emphasizes output-inflation trade-offs. In their model, the decision to devalue or maintain the peg depends on the realization of an output shock. Because of uncertainty, a devaluation leads to unexpected inflation, which increases output, both through a standard price-output effect and through the reduction of the distortionary taxes associated with nominal debt service. Whether the exchange-rate regime gains or loses credibility after a successful defense cannot be determined a priori. On the one hand, resisting a crisis enhances the credibility of the government and thus the expectation that the peg will be maintained. This "signaling" effect is important when there is substantial uncertainty about the government's cost of devaluation and when the level of public debt is low. On the other, defending the parity and refraining from inflationary financing increases the debt burden, hence the likelihood of a forced future devaluation. This "debt-burden" effect is important when the debt is large and there is little uncertainty about the government's cost of devaluation. Which effect prevails depends on the relative importance of the government's reputation and the fundamentals.

When the government's preferences are publicly known, only the fundamentals matter; a devaluation always increases the probability that a future defense of the new parity will succeed. In this case the probability of a first-period devaluation increases with the size of the public debt and with the share of it that is short-term—as in models of self-fulfilling crises. By contrast, when the government's preferences are not publicly known, the decision to devalue may reveal a weak government heading to further devaluation, which generates inflationary expectations and higher interest rates. This creates an incentive to defend the fixed parity both for a tough government, to signal its type, and for a weak one, in order to appear tough. Thus, reputation motives increase the probability that the parity will be maintained.

2.4 ■ Other Sources of Policy Trade-Offs

Various other sources of policy trade-offs have been discussed in the recent literature on self-fulfilling crises. Some, in particular, rely either directly or indirectly on the (adverse) effects of higher interest rates. For instance, banks may come under pressure if market interest rates rise unexpectedly. To avoid a costly bailout, the policymaker may want to implement a quick devaluation. Or, with sticky domestic prices, a hike in nominal interest rates may imply hikes in short-term real rates, and these may generate self-fulfilling devaluation pressures (see Ozkan and Sutherland, 1998).

The very existence of (implicit) government guarantees may also lead to a self-fulfilling financial crisis. As argued by Burnside (2004), by taking on a contingent liability, the government can actually increase the probability with which the underlying event takes place. For instance, in the face of (credible) government guarantees, banks' behavior may change in such a way that the banking system becomes more fragile—perhaps by inducing banks to take on more exchange-rate risk. Thus, the government becomes more likely to incur the fiscal cost associated with bank failures. And incurring this fiscal cost, in turn, makes the probability of bank failures higher. Further, as shown in Burnside (2004) and Burnside et al. (2004), this raises the likelihood of self-fulfilling speculative attacks. If agents come to believe that the exchange-rate regime will collapse, they will speculate against local currency, ultimately causing the central bank to float the exchange rate. The central bank's decision to float, in turn, will lead to depreciation of the currency—in anticipation of the government choosing to print money—which will ultimately lead to the failure of unhedged banks. These bank failures will, in turn, require the government to honor its bailout guarantee. When it does so by printing money, it validates the speculative attack.

In all of these models, "fundamentals," viewed as reflecting the policymaker's preferences and the economy's structure, affect the multiplicity of equilibria. But the policymaker is incapable of enforcing its preferred equilibrium, should market expectations focus on an inferior one. Further, "sunspots" could shift the exchange rate from a position where it is vulnerable to only very bad realizations of a shock—a phenomenon with very low ex ante probability—to one where output is so low absent devaluation that even "small" shocks will induce the authorities to devalue or to adopt a floating-rate regime.

Finally, it is worth noting that the role of (incomplete) information in self-fulfilling models of currency crises has been a matter of much debate. In an important contribution, Morris and Shin (1998) considered the case where speculators, having a uniform prior probability distribution over the state of fundamentals, update it according to the observation of a private signal. Lack of common knowledge is thus the driving force of their model. They show that the indeterminacy of equilibria that characterizes models of self-fulfilling currency crises can be completely removed, once a small degree of uncertainty about the true fundamentals is introduced. Put differently, multiplicity in their analysis is the consequence of assuming that fundamentals are common knowledge among market participants; if, instead, traders observe the relevant fundamentals with a small amount of idiosyncratic noise, a unique equilibrium can be selected.

Heineman and Illing (2002) extended the analysis of Morris and Shin to consider a broader class of probability distributions. They also show that increased transparency (in the sense of providing more precise information about fundamentals, namely, government policy) may reduce the likelihood of speculative attacks. Sbracia and Zaghini (2001) extend their analysis to examine the role of the distribution of agents' beliefs about fundamentals. They show that currency crises can be triggered by "small" changes in the distribution of agents' beliefs, even without any underlying deterioration of the fundamentals. Hellwig et al. (2006) extend their analysis to consider explicitly domestic asset markets and interest rates. By comparing the solution when fundamentals are common knowledge with the solution when traders have idiosyncratic, noisy signals, they find that (in contrast to Morris and Shin) arguments for multiplicity remain valid even in the presence of incomplete, heterogeneous information. The source of multiplicity, however, is not a coordination problem (as postulated in Morris and Shin) but rather the nonmonotonicity of trading strategies (which does not depend on the fact that private signals are noisy).

3   A "Cross-Generation" Framework

Flood and Marion (1999) have recently proposed a "cross-generation" framework for the analysis of currency crises. They argue that the key difference between the "old" and the "new" approaches is that the former assumes that the commitment to a fixed exchange is *state invariant*, whereas in the latter it is *state dependent*—a feature that captures well the evidence suggesting that policymakers respond to various objectives.

One way of linking the two generations of models, as suggested by Flood and Marion (1999), is to make the threshold level of reserves in the conventional approach a function of a variable that captures the state of the business cycle (such as the level of unemployment and the rate of inflation). Endogenizing R_l (rather than assuming it is fixed as in the standard model) has the implication that the policymaker may affect the behavior of the shadow exchange rate over time (and thus the size of the exchange-rate jump upon which a speculative attack depends) through its choice of the level of reserves that it wants to commit to defend the parity—or equivalently, the level at which it chooses to abandon it.[28] Although the potential profits to be realized by speculators remain the driving force behind speculative attacks in this framework, the state of the economy also influences the timing of currency crises—as in the new generation models.

Another attractive property of the cross-generation framework proposed by Flood and Marion is that it restricts the apparently large degree of arbitrariness (associated with self-fulfilling factors) that characterizes the timing of speculative attacks in second-generation models. There are ranges in which multiple equilibria do occur, but this happens only if (some of) the fundamentals are sufficiently out of line. From the point of view of policymakers, this appears to be a more sensible prediction

---

[28] Strictly speaking, the choice of the threshold level of reserves is the choice of the parameters linking R_l to the variable capturing the state of the economy.

than simply emphasizing the role of "sunspots." Nevertheless, more research remains necessary to fully reconcile the two generations of models.

4   Third-Generation Models

Third-generation models of currency crises give a key role to financial structure fragility and financial institutions. From a modeling perspective, there are three main approaches. A first approach, sketched by Krugman (1998), involves moral-hazard-driven investment, which leads to overinvestment, overborrowing, and eventually to the collapse of the banking system. A second approach, promoted by Chang and Velasco (2000a, 2000b, 2001) and Goldstein (2005), explains abrupt reversals in inflows as a by-product of bank runs due to an internationally illiquid banking sector (see Chapter 15). A self-fulfilling loss of confidence of depositors and foreign investors forces financial intermediaries to liquidate their investments prematurely.

A third approach stresses the balance sheet implications of currency depreciation. Third-generation models of currency crises have in common the idea that the crisis can be seen as a result of an adverse shock (real or financial) that was amplified by credit market imperfections, and more specifically a financial accelerator mechanism. Specifically, credit-constrained firms with a high proportion of debt denominated in foreign currency are vulnerable to a self-fulfilling fear of insufficient collateral, as this expectational shift triggers a capital outflow that causes a real devaluation. Krugman (1999), Caballero and Krishnamurthy (2001), and Aghion et al. (2001, 2004a) have spearheaded this approach.

In the models developed by Aghion et al., for instance, the key source of (self-fulfilling) currency crises is the interplay between credit or balance sheet constraints faced by private domestic firms—of the type discussed in Chapter 5, in reference to the Kiyotaki-Moore model—and the existence of nominal price rigidities. The possibility of multiple equilibria, including a currency crisis equilibrium with low output and a depreciated domestic currency, results from the following mechanism: if nominal prices are sticky in the short run, a currency depreciation leads to an increase in the foreign-currency debt repayment obligations of firms, and thus to a fall in profits in the current period—which lowers firms' net worth and their borrowing capacity. Tighter credit constraints tend to reduce investment and output in the next period, which in turn lowers the demand for the domestic currency and leads to a depreciation. Arbitrage in the foreign exchange market then implies that the currency must depreciate in the current period as well. Thus, the currency depreciation becomes self-fulfilling. In general, multiple short-run equilibria are possible; a currency crisis occurs either when expectations change or when a real shock shifts the economy to the "bad" equilibrium with low output. Nevertheless, the primary source of crises is the deteriorating balance sheets of private firms. Gertler et al. (2007) found that balance sheet effects help to explain the output contraction that occurred following the East Asian currency crisis. Similarly, using data on Mexican firms in the aftermath of the December 1994 peso crisis, Aguiar (2005) found that firms with heavy exposure to short-term foreign currency debt before the devaluation experienced a marked drop in investment after the currency was floated. This effect is particularly significant for exporters, which borrowed disproportionately in foreign currency. Weak balance sheets therefore explain much of the recessionary impact of the currency depreciation.

Another contribution along these lines is by Paasche (2001), who extended the Kiyotaki-Moore model of credit cycles to a three-country setting and studied how crises are transmitted internationally. Two of the countries are small and their domestic firms, which produce a differentiated commodity that they export to a large country, face credit constraints. Moreover, the small countries have no direct economic linkages; the only link between them is the elasticity of substitution in the consumption of their exports by the large country. A productivity shock to one of the small countries triggers an adverse term-of-trade shock to the other which is then amplified by credit constraints—possibly triggering large capital outflows and a sharp deterioration in the current account. Domestic financial frictions may therefore explain the transmission of contagious shocks between small open economies, even in the absence of direct trade or financial linkages.

This class of models is also useful to understand the impact of monetary policy on output in the presence of credit constraints. In Christiano et al. (2004) and Devereux and Poon (2004), for instance, the firms' borrowing constraint is not binding in "normal" times; it becomes binding only in "crisis" times. In both cases, the optimal response of monetary policy in response to shocks varies across states of nature. In particular, as shown in the first paper, following an unexpected tightening of external collateral constraints, a cut in official interest rates can either lead to an expansion (because higher asset prices induced by the interest rate cut lead to an improvement in firms' balance sheets, and thus a weaker constraint on borrowing) or a contraction (because a depreciation lowers the demand for imported intermediate goods, and thus employment and output). In a related paper, Aghion et al. (2000) also find that the impact of an interest rate cut on economic activity in an open-economy model is ambiguous.

5   Sudden Stops

For developing countries, financial integration has been associated not just with surges of capital inflows (as discussed in the previous chapter), but also with large reversals in short-term capital flows. For instance, in the wake of the Asia crisis, although FDI remained remarkably stable, short-term capital inflows from BIS-reporting banks to developing countries fell from $43.5 billion in 1997 to $8.5 billion in 1998. Volatility in capital inflows has also tended to translate into exchange-rate instability (under flexible exchange rates) or large fluctuations in official reserves (under a pegged exchange-rate regime), and greater volatility in domestic equity markets. Financial volatility may have led to adverse real effects as well—nominal exchange-rate volatility, in particular, may hamper the expansion of exports if hedging options available to domestic producers are limited.

While both first- and second-generation crisis models (reviewed earlier) predict a switch from domestic currency-denominated assets to foreign currency-denominated ones (or from foreign currency- to domestic currency-denominated liabilities), neither type of model predicts that the emergence of a crisis is necessarily associated with a sudden inability on the part of domestic agents to engage in external borrowing. However, Calvo (1998) noted that the currency crises in Mexico in 1994 and Asia in 1997–1998 were characterized by precisely such a loss of access to foreign funds, which he referred to as "sudden stops" of capital inflows. A sudden stop is a sharp, discontinuous fall in net capital flows (including foreign exchange reserve depletion) into a country. Because this phenomenon is not a necessary concomitant of either first- or second-generation currency crisis, it calls for a different modeling approach.

Models of sudden stops have sought to explain several empirical regularities associated with this phenomenon (Montiel, 2013a). First, among emerging market economies sudden stops have tended to be accompanied by large real exchange-rate depreciations. By contrast, large real exchange-rate depreciations and capital flow reversals are not closely associated with each other among industrial countries. Second, sudden stops have tended to come in bunches, affecting simultaneously countries with very different characteristics. Third, sudden stops have generally been accompanied by severe output contractions, large reductions in current account deficits, sharp increases in domestic interest rates, and substantial losses of foreign exchange reserves, often culminating in exchange regime transitions.[29] Hutchison and Noy (2006), for instance, using panel data for twenty-four developing countries over the period 1975–1997, found that sudden-stop crises have a large negative, but short-lived, impact on output growth over and above that found with currency crises: a currency crisis typically reduces output by about 2–3 percent, whereas a sudden stop reduces output by an additional 6–8 percent in the year of the crisis, and by 13–15 percent over a three-year period. The cumulative output loss of a sudden stop is even larger, around 13–15 percent over a three-year period. Edwards (2004) also found that current account reversals generally have a large adverse impact on output, and that the effect is larger in countries that are relatively closed to trade and characterized by greater exchange-rate fixity. Vulnerability to sudden stops seems to be reduced by "real" openness (measured as a large share of output devoted to production of traded goods), as well as by the absence of domestic liability dollarization.[30]

---

[29] See Guidotti et al. (2004).

[30] See Calvo et al. (2004). In the same vein, Mendoza and Smith (2002) define three key features of sudden stops: sharp reversals in capital inflows and current account deficits; large downward adjustments in domestic production and absorption, and collapses in asset prices and in the relative prices of nontradable goods relative to tradables.

In a subsequent study of eighty-three sudden-stop crises in sixty-six countries over the period 1980–2003, Hutchison et al. (2010) found that contractionary monetary and fiscal policies during a financial crisis are linked to larger economic downturns. Expansionary fiscal policy is associated with smaller output losses following a sudden stop, but expansionary monetary policy has no discernible correlation with these losses. Joyce and Nabar (2009), in a study based on a broad sample of countries over the period 1976–2002, found that sudden stops have a significant adverse impact on investment only if they are accompanied by a systemic banking crisis.[31]

A number of studies have also documented a positive relation between the increasing international capital flows due to greater integration with world financial markets and vulnerability to sudden reversals in capital flows. For instance, Broto et al. (2011) found that since 2000, global factors have become increasingly significant relative to country-specific drivers in determining the volatility of capital inflows into several MICs, whereas Dufrénot et al. (2011) found that stress indicators in U.S. financial markets in the aftermath of the subprime crisis caused abrupt changes in stock market volatility in several Latin American countries. Agosin and Huaita (2012) defined a sudden flood (or capital boom, in their terminology) as an episode where (gross) capital inflows are larger than one standard deviation above the historical mean and represent at least five percentage points of GDP.[32] Sudden stops are defined in symmetric fashion. Using a sample of mostly MICs over the period 1976–2003, they found that sudden floods are good predictors of subsequent sudden stops. Moreover, the probability of a sudden stop increases dramatically the longer the preceding capital boom. Thus, sudden stops may not be due to a (current or expected) deterioration in domestic macro fundamentals, but rather could represent downward overreactions to previous periods of positive "overreaction" in capital flows.[33]

From a modeling perspective, the discontinuity in capital flows associated with sudden stops can come about either as the result of a switch among multiple equilibria or as the outcome of a discontinuity in the relationship between capital flows and fundamentals in a model in which equilibrium is unique. In this section we briefly describe the structure of models with multiple equilibria, before examining in some

---

[31] They argue that whereas output growth may pick up quickly after a crisis if exports drive the recovery, investment may remain persistently low. Tracking the path of output in the immediate aftermath of a crisis will lead to an incomplete and misleading assessment of the effects of the crisis. If investment does not bounce back, the robustness of the recovery and the prospects for long-run growth could be severely compromised.

[32] This is a rather stringent definition. In Balakrishnan et al. (2012), for instance, an episode of large net private capital flows is defined as a period of two or more quarters during which these flows (as a share of GDP) are larger (by 1 standard deviation) than their historical trend—taken to be an eight-quarter moving average—or above the 75th percentile of their distribution over the whole sample.

[33] A possible explanation for this effect is that large capital inflows bring about some adverse endogenous changes in macroeconomic fundamentals in some dimension (such as a deterioration of the current account deficit, an appreciation of the real exchange rate, an excessive rise in bank credit to the private sector, or a progressive mismatch in the balance sheets of firms and banks that borrow in foreign currency) that eventually triggers a massive withdrawal of capital. Put differently, booms create the seeds of their own destruction.

detail a model in which the economy's equilibrium is unique, yet small changes in the fundamentals can nevertheless trigger discontinuous changes in capital flows that result in currency crises.

5.1 ■ Alternative Models

5.1.1 *Models with Multiple Equilibria*

In the original paper calling attention to the sudden-stop phenomenon, Calvo (1998) argued that sudden stops can come about through a self-fulfilling mechanism, in which capital inflows cease because creditors fear that they will not be repaid, while the cessation of capital inflows itself creates the conditions that make repayment unlikely. In this formulation, causation from a sudden stop of capital inflows to debt repayment difficulties operates through the real exchange rate. To see how this works, note that the balance-of-payments identity implies that a sudden stop of capital inflows requires an exactly offsetting increase in the current account surplus. In turn, the current account balance (CA) consists of the trade balance plus the sum of other factor and nonfactor payments (N), while the trade balance is the excess of domestic production of traded goods (Y^T) over domestic demand for such goods (D^T). Thus, the current account balance can be written as:

$$CA = Y^T - D^T + N. \tag{25}$$

It follows that current account adjustment in response to a sudden stop could in principle be achieved through a reduction in domestic demand for traded goods, leaving real output unchanged. However, as noted by Calvo, this is unlikely to happen in the real world, because in the absence of a change in the real exchange rate, a drop in domestic demand for traded goods would have to be brought about through a reduction in domestic absorption, which means that it is likely to be accompanied by a similar drop in demand for nontraded goods. The latter would require a real depreciation in order to maintain equilibrium in the nontraded goods market.

To examine what determines the size of the required change in the real exchange rate, in a later paper Calvo et al. (2004) postulated the following relationship between the demand for nontraded goods and that for traded goods:

$$d^N = \alpha + \beta e + \gamma d^T, \tag{26}$$

where d^N is the log of the domestic demand for nontraded goods, e is the log of the real exchange rate (price of traded goods in terms of nontraded goods), and d^T is the log of the domestic demand for traded goods (that is, $d^T = \log(D^T)$), α, β, and γ are positive parameters, where γ can be interpreted as the ratio of nontraded to traded goods in domestic absorption. If an initial current account deficit has to be completely eliminated by a sudden stop in capital inflows, then holding Y^T and Y^N

constant, the proportionate size of the adjustment in domestic absorption of traded goods is given by: $\Delta d^T / d^T = CA/d^T < 0$, because $CA < 0$.

Taking first differences in (26), and holding demand for nontraded goods constant, this means that the change in the real exchange rate must satisfy $0 = \beta \Delta e + \gamma CA/d^T$, or

$$\Delta e = -\frac{\gamma}{\beta} \frac{CA}{d^T}, \tag{27}$$

that is, the required real exchange-rate depreciation is larger the larger the initial current-account deficit, the smaller the elasticity of substitution in demand between traded and nontraded goods, and the larger the marginal propensity to absorb nontraded goods.

The intuition behind the last of these properties is that to achieve a given size of adjustment in the trade balance, the contraction in domestic absorption will have to be larger the smaller the share of this contraction falls on traded goods. The larger the contraction in domestic absorption, the larger the resulting excess supply of nontraded goods at the original real exchange rate, and therefore the larger the required change in the real exchange rate.[34]

To link the depreciation of the real exchange rate to debt-servicing difficulties, note that if the "sudden stop" was unanticipated, the real exchange-rate adjustment that accompanies it must have been so as well. In the presence of liability dollarization in the balance sheets of domestic agents (whether the government, banks, or firms), such an unanticipated change in the real exchange rate may create widespread reductions in net worth and potential insolvencies. Calvo claims that widespread bankruptcies in the domestic economy lower the marginal product of capital and thus make it unlikely that firms will be able to service their debt. They do so because they destroy specific human capital, partly by interfering with the fulfillment of implicit contracts within firms (which undermine the incentive structure inside the firm), and partly by diverting human capital to financial transacting, as the result of a reduction in inter-enterprise credit that is likely to accompany widespread bankruptcies. Because specific human capital is complementary to physical capital, the marginal product of physical capital is reduced, making it harder for firms to service their debt and justifying the cutoff of credit.

Although the details differ, a variety of other multiple-equilibrium models of the sudden-stop phenomenon follow similar lines (see for instance Montiel, 2013a). Specifically, these models tend to emphasize the interaction of real exchange-rate depreciation with liability dollarization in linking sudden stops to debt-servicing difficulties.

---

[34] Using a calibrated model with costly labor adjustment for Mexico, Kehoe and Ruhl (2009) found that sudden stops are also associated with substantial resource reallocation between the tradable and nontradable sectors.

5.1.2 A Sudden Stop as a Unique Equilibrium

An alternative modeling framework explains sudden stops as the outcome of a discontinuous transition between unique equilibria. In this section we will examine a simple model of this type due to Calvo (2003). An interesting feature of this model is that the sudden stop is both "real" (that is, it arises from goods-market rather than financial-market phenomena) and demand-driven, rather than supply-driven. In other words, it reflects a reduced *demand* for external funds on the part of domestic agents, rather than a reduced supply of such funds from external creditors. Nonetheless, the model is able to reproduce many of the features of the currency crises of the late 1990s, including steep output collapses, reduced growth rates, sharp real exchange-rate depreciations, and reserve depletion potentially associated with exchange-rate regime transitions.

Consider a small open economy that uses traded capital K to produce a single traded good Y with a linear production technology:

$$Y_t = \alpha K_t, \tag{28}$$

where α is the marginal product of capital.[35] The government taxes away a fraction τ of the economy's output, so that firms' cash flow S is equal to after-tax profits minus new investment $\dot{K}$:

$$S_t = \alpha(1 - \tau)K_t - \dot{K}_t = [\alpha(1 - \tau) - z_t]K_t, \tag{29}$$

where $z_t = \dot{K}/K$ is the rate of growth of the capital stock. If the international real interest rate is equal to r and the value of the initial capital stock K_0 is set equal to unity, the value of the firm is given by:

$$V = \int_0^\infty [\alpha(1 - \tau) - z_t]K_t e^{-rt} dt = \int_0^\infty [\alpha(1 - \tau) - z_t]_t e^{\int_0^t (r - z_s)ds} dt. \tag{30}$$

The firm maximizes its value by choosing the time path of z_t. Because the optimal value of z_t can be shown to be constant over time, this is equivalent to maximizing:

$$V = \frac{\alpha(1 - \tau) - z}{r - z}. \tag{31}$$

To ensure that the value of the firm is positive, and that the growth rate of the capital stock is positive but bounded from above, z is restricted to the range $0 \le z \le \bar{z} < r$. It is easy to show that the sign of the derivative of V with respect

---

[35]The specification used in (28) is the so-called "AK" technology; its implications for long-run growth are discussed in Chapter 17.

to z is given by the sign of the expression $\alpha(1-\tau)-r$, that is, the excess of the after-tax marginal product of capital over the real interest rate. If this expression is positive, the firm will set z at its maximum value $\bar{z}$. Otherwise, it sets z at its minimum value $z = 0$.

The tax rate τ is determined so as to maintain the government's solvency. Specifically, suppose that the government has an outstanding debt D, and that to maintain its solvency it has to raise resources through distortionary taxation equal in present value to a share θ of its total debt (the remaining resources $(1-\theta)D$ are raised in a nondistortionary fashion). Then the government's intertemporal budget constraint implies:

$$\theta D = \alpha\tau \int_0^\infty K_t e^{-rt} dt = \alpha\tau \int_0^\infty z_t e^{\int_0^s (r-z_s)ds} dt = \frac{\alpha\tau}{r-z}. \tag{32}$$

In turn, this means that the tax rate must be:

$$\tau = (r-z)\theta D/\alpha. \tag{33}$$

Substituting this expression for τ in the firms' objective function, the critical expression governing the behavior of investment becomes:

$$\alpha(1-\tau)-r = \alpha[1-(r-z)\theta D/\alpha]-r = \alpha-(r-z)\theta D-r. \tag{34}$$

Note that the criterion determining the optimal amount of investment depends on the rate of investment itself. A zero-investment (and zero-growth) equilibrium (that is, one with $z = 0$) will be optimal if $\alpha - r(1+\theta D) < 0$, that is, if $\theta D > (\alpha - r)/r$. The intuition is that a high stock of debt requires a high value of the distortionary tax rate, which discourages investment. An equilibrium with the maximum growth rate $\bar{z}$, by contrast, will be optimal if $\alpha - (r-\bar{z})\theta D-r > 0$, or if $\theta D < (\alpha - r)/(r-\bar{z})$. In principle, the growth rate is indeterminate if $(\alpha - r)/r < \theta D < (\alpha - r)/(r-\bar{z})$, because both conditions are satisfied in that range. However, Calvo assumes that in this case coordination among investors will cause the economy to settle on the high-growth equilibrium. Under this assumption the economy's growth rate and level of investment display a discontinuity with respect to the fundamental θD at $\theta D = (\alpha - r)/r$. For debt below this level, the economy is in the high-growth equilibrium $z = \bar{z}$, while if debt is above this level the economy is in the low-growth equilibrium $z = 0$. This has the important implication that for economies that are very close to the threshold $(\alpha - r)/r$, a small decrease in the productivity parameter α or a small increase in the world real interest rate r could cause a discontinuous collapse in the level of investment and rate of growth.

To link this mechanism to sudden stops of capital flows, it is necessary to expand the model to describe the current account of the balance of payments. Suppose that the representative consumer in this economy has a time-separable utility function with a constant rate of time preference that is equal to the world real interest rate r, and let this consumer's instantaneous utility function be denoted as $u(c^T, c^N)$, where the function $u()$ has the usual properties, and c^T and c^N are respectively the consumer's consumption of traded and nontraded goods. Output of nontraded goods, denoted Y^N, is determined by the concave production frontier $Y^N = f(x)$, where x is the portion of total tradables output Y that is used as an input into the production of nontradables. Under these conditions, the budget constraint is given by:

$$r[V - (1 - \theta)D] = c^T + x, \tag{35}$$

given that production and consumption of nontradables must be equal in equilibrium. The consumer's problem is to maximize:

$$u(c^T, f(r[V - (1 - \theta)D] - c^T)), \tag{36}$$

by choosing the level of c^T. This yields the first-order condition:

$$\frac{u_2(c^T, f(r[V - (1 - \theta)D] - c^T))}{u_1(c^T, f(r[V - (1 - \theta)D] - c^T))} = \frac{1}{f'(r[V - (1 - \theta)D] - c^T)} = e^{-1}, \tag{37}$$

where e is the real exchange rate (relative price of traded goods in terms of nontraded goods). Note that this equation implies that c^T and e are both functions of net wealth $V - (1 - \theta)D$. But using (33) and (36), net wealth can be written as:

$$V - (1 - \theta)D = \frac{\alpha - z}{r - z}. \tag{38}$$

By (38), the condition for a high-growth equilibrium to exist requires that $\alpha - z > 0$. This implies that net wealth must be an increasing function of z. If the initial capital stock is equal to unity, as assumed above, gross output of traded goods in this economy is equal to α, and net output of traded goods is $\alpha - x$. Thus, the trade balance is $(\alpha - x) - (c^T + z)$, and the current account is given by:

$$CA = (\alpha - x) - (c^T + z) - rD = -\frac{\alpha - z}{r - z}z. \tag{39}$$

Because $\alpha - \bar{z} > 0$ and $r - \bar{z} > 0$, the current account must be in deficit in the "high growth" equilibrium—that is, when $\theta D < (\alpha - r)/(r - \bar{z})$—and it will be zero when $z = 0$. Thus, a discontinuous elimination of a preexisting current account deficit (a sudden stop) takes place at the transition from a high- to a low-growth equilibrium. Because the collapse in the economy's growth rate at the transition point implies a reduction in net wealth, the demand for nontraded goods must fall. This has the joint implication that real output falls and the real exchange rate depreciates.

5.2 ■ The Role of Reserves and Policy Responses

The model described in the previous subsection is a nonmonetary one. As Calvo shows, however, it can easily be extended to a monetary economy by adding a cash-in-advance motive for holding money:

$$M = S(c^T + e^{-1}c^N), \tag{40}$$

where M is the money supply and S is the nominal exchange rate, assumed fixed initially. Because c^T and c^N both fall over the transition from a high- to a low-growth equilibrium, and the real exchange rate depreciates (e rises), the demand for money falls as well. Consequently, the stock of foreign exchange reserves must also fall. In other words, the sudden stop is accompanied by a speculative attack. If the stock of reserves is sufficiently low initially, this reserve loss could be accompanied by an abandonment of the fixed exchange rate and a transition to a floating rate, as in first-generation models.

The model has another interesting implication for policy. In first-generation models, if the factor driving domestic credit expansion is an ongoing fiscal deficit, a fixed exchange rate can be sustained by making a fiscal adjustment that permits the rate of credit expansion to be reduced. However, in Calvo's sudden-stop model, such a fiscal adjustment may actually trigger the sudden stop and the associated currency crisis if it takes the form of an increase in τ, because an increase in τ, which effectively represents an increase in the share θ of government debt that is serviced through distortionary taxation, may actually take the economy over the threshold from the high- to the low-growth equilibrium. Instead, what is required to avoid the crisis in the present model is a reduction in θD. This implies that what matters is not the fiscal deficit per se, but rather the distortions imposed on the economy by the need to finance the government's activities. Avoiding sudden stops requires either reducing the scale of such activities or adopting less distortionary ways of financing them.

In practice, countries that are susceptible to sudden stops have tended to accumulate sizable international reserves. A rationale for such a (generally expensive) self-insurance strategy is the desire to gain a measure of protection and avoid costly liquidation of investment projects and a drop in output.[36] Aizenman and Lee (2007)

---

[36]Whereas traditional approaches argue that reserves are needed to finance imbalances in the balance of payments under a fixed exchange-rate system, the more recent literature, which emerged after the series of financial crises during the 1990s, focuses on the stock of reserves, which is seen as a "backstop" against financial crises. Both approaches coincide in the view that there exists an adequate level of reserve holdings, which is the outcome of an optimizing behavior of the central bank.

develop a model of the precautionary (and thus voluntary) demand for reserves along these lines. Their analysis suggests that, although hoarding international reserves entails an opportunity cost, a high degree of volatility in capital flows (coupled with limited access to global capital markets) makes the welfare gain from hoarding reserves of a first-order magnitude—even under risk neutrality. Put differently, optimal hoarding of reserves reduces the magnitude of the output cost associated with sudden stops from first to second order. Aizenman et al. (2007) provide empirical evidence that supports the precautionary approach for the case of Korea, in the aftermath of the 1997 Asian crisis. Jeanne and Rancière (2011) also developed a model of the optimal level of international reserves for a small open economy seeking insurance against sudden stops in capital flows. They derived a formula for the optimal level of reserves and showed that plausible calibrations can explain reserves of the order of magnitude observed in some developing countries.

Given the economic costs associated with sudden stops, how should countries manage the likelihood that they may occur? Caballero and Panageas (2008) studied a variety of (optimal) contingent liability management options that countries may consider. In their model, a sudden stop is defined as a probabilistic event which, once triggered, requires the country to reduce the pace of external (net) borrowing significantly. At each point in time, the country faces a signal—for instance, a sharp drop in the price of the country's main commodity export—which describes the likelihood of sudden stop at that time. They characterize formally the impact of changes in this signal on optimal precautionary savings, and the role of different hedging opportunities in reducing the extent of fluctuations due to precautionary contractions and the direct cost of sudden stops. In practice, however, implementing aggregate hedging strategies of the type that they propose remains a challenge; reasons for that include uncertainty about the nature or duration of shocks that policymakers face, and the lack (or inadequate development) of markets from which signals about these shocks can be inferred.

Chapter 15

Banking Crises and Twin Crises

The spate of financial crises that developing countries have undergone over the past two decades has included not just sudden stops and currency crises, as examined in the previous chapter, but a large number of domestic banking crises as well. Banking crises are systemic or near-systemic breakdowns of the domestic financial sector in which a large number of banks find themselves with significant reductions in their net worth, forcing them to go out of business or otherwise severely curtail their activities. Such events severely disrupt domestic financial intermediation, generally involve large fiscal costs, and often have harmful effects on real economic activity. According to Laeven and Valencia (2013), there were 147 banking crises around the world between 1970 and 2011. Many of the most dramatic financial collapses in middle-income developing countries during recent years—including the 1994 Mexican crisis, the 1997–1998 Asian crisis, and the 2001 Argentine crisis (as documented in Supplement D)—included a breakdown of the domestic financial system as an important component. In a formal study of both aggregate and bank-level data for as many as thirty-five countries, Demirgüç-Kunt et al. (2006) found that banking crises are followed by a sharp (albeit short-lived) drop in the growth rate of output and a credit crunch. Tornell and Westermann (2002, 2003) also found that the aftermath of crises is often characterized by a (short-lived) recession and a protracted credit crunch, which affects mostly (small) firms in the nontradables sector and persists long after the resumption of growth. Kroszner et al. (2007), using data for thirty-eight developed and developing countries, found that industries that are highly dependent on external finance tend to experience a substantial contraction of value added during a banking crisis; this adverse effect is magnified in countries with deeper financial systems. One reason for such large effects is the link between credit and the supply side through working-capital needs, as discussed in Chapters 5 and 6.

As those examples suggest, sovereign debt, currency, and banking crises are not independent of each other. A variety of channels exist through which the occurrence of each type of crisis may make one of the others more likely. Indeed, the real domestic costs of currency crises in developing countries may largely depend on the extent to which they trigger a sovereign debt or a domestic banking crisis. Having examined in Chapter 14 the factors associated with the emergence of currency crises, in this chapter we focus on domestic banking crises, as well as on some of the channels through which banking crises may cause currency crises. The next chapter will study the links among banking, currency, and sovereign debt crises.

The increased incidence of banking crises in developing countries in recent years has coincided in timing with domestic financial liberalization in developing countries, which became widespread during the decade of the 1980s (see Chapter 18). Financial liberalization means the removal of the restrictions associated with financial repression, including the freeing of bank interest rates to be determined by market forces, lowering or abolishing reserve and liquidity requirements on banks, removing directed credit regulations, adopting indirect instruments of monetary control (instead of imposing credit ceilings on individual banks), opening up entry into the financial sector (including privatization), and opening up the capital account of the balance of payments. These measures were undertaken to accelerate financial development, prompted in part by the accumulation of evidence that financial development can have important positive effects on economic welfare and growth in developing countries.[1]

However, an important lesson conveyed by the spate of banking crises that have occurred during the post-financial liberalization period in developing countries is that it matters—and matters a lot—how financial reform is carried out. A laissez-faire approach to financial reform would have the government undertake the desired reform measures and then rely on competition and market efficiency to ensure the appropriate functioning of the newly deregulated financial system. There are two fundamental problems with this approach. The first is that in the presence of asymmetric information and opportunistic behavior, there is no necessary presumption that unregulated competitive banking markets will be Pareto efficient, so a laissez-faire approach may result in a systematic misallocation of resources by the liberalized financial system, undermining the growth benefits expected to ensue from financial liberalization. The second is that, even in the absence of the problems of asymmetric information and opportunistic behavior that may tend to undermine microeconomic welfare gains, in contrast with a severely repressed financial system a fully liberalized one may be vulnerable to highly disruptive periodic banking crises. As Carlos Díaz-Alejandro put it in the title of a famous paper on this topic, the post-liberalization situation may be characterized as "good-bye financial repression, hello financial crash" (Diaz-Alejandro, 1985).

In this chapter we will explore how such financial crashes can come about. The next section examines how banking crises can emerge even when problems of asymmetric information and opportunistic behavior are absent—that is, even when

---

[1] For further discussion, see Chapter 17.

a liberalized domestic financial system plays a welfare-enhancing role in the domestic economy. Section 2 examines models that adopt the framework of Section 1 to explore how banking crises may be linked to currency crises, the so-called twin crisis phenomenon. In Section 3 we examine the implications of asymmetric information and opportunistic behavior for both the efficiency of resource allocation by the financial sector and the likelihood of financial crashes. Section 4 concludes the chapter by describing some recent empirical work on the determinants of banking system distress, and their macroeconomic effects, in developing countries.

1   Banks as Maturity Transformers

Explanations of banking crises must take as their point of departure an interpretation of the economic role of banks. One such interpretation views banks primarily as maturity transformers. From this perspective, banks play the valuable social role of allowing individuals who place a high premium on liquidity to nevertheless use their savings to finance illiquid social investments that yield high returns. Banks can achieve this result by offering their individual depositors highly liquid assets and using these resources to fund investments that, while yielding high returns, require a long period to mature. They are able to do this essentially by pooling the idiosyncratic liquidity shocks that their depositors face into an aggregate liability portfolio from which liquidity shocks are effectively eliminated. But precisely because their individual depositors require instant access to their funds while banks' assets take a long time to mature, vulnerability to panic is inherent in the very activity of banking. The key problem is that even solvent banks will not typically have the liquid resources on hand to meet unusual demands for withdrawals by their depositors. Because its long-maturity assets lose value if they are liquidated prematurely, a bank that tries to meet such unusual demands by liquidating assets may find itself becoming insolvent. This means that in the event of unusual demand, some depositors will lose at least some of the value of their claims on the bank. An important feature of the liquid liabilities of banks—that their depositors have access to them on a first come-first served basis (the sequential servicing constraint)—means that depositors who anticipate this loss of value will have an incentive to "run," that is, to withdraw their assets first, even in the absence of a liquidity motive to withdraw funds. The implication is that, precisely because of its illiquid portfolio structure, a run on a bank can be a rational expectations equilibrium.

1.1 ■ The Diamond-Dybvig Framework

The canonical model of such bank liquidity crises was developed by Diamond and Dybvig (1983). The model simultaneously illustrates the welfare gains provided by banks and their vulnerability to panic. Because this model has provided the basis for much subsequent analysis of banking crises, we describe it in some detail in this section.[2]

Consider a three-period world populated by a continuum of initially identical consumers, each of whom receives an endowment of one perfectly divisible good in period 0 and makes consumption decisions in periods 1 and 2 (there is no consumption in period 0). In period 0, any fraction of the good can be costlessly stored or invested in an illiquid production technology, that is, a technology with the property that if production is aborted in period 1 the technology yields one unit of output for each unit of the good invested, while if production is allowed to continue until period 2, it yields $R > 1$ goods for each good invested. Consumers are allowed to enter into contracts to trade current for future consumption in both periods 0 and 1. However, the assumed linear technology fixes the relative price of period 2 consumption in terms of period 1 consumption at R^{-1}, and that of period 1 consumption in terms of period 0 goods at unity.

A motivation for intertemporal trade arises because in this model consumers are only identical in period 0. At the beginning of period 1 each individual consumer may or may not be subjected to an idiosyncratic "liquidity shock." This shock causes a fraction λ of all consumers to turn out to be "type A" consumers who care only about consumption in period 1, while a fraction $(1 - \lambda)$ turn out to be "type B" consumers who care only about consumption in period 2. The utility of consumption for type A consumers in period 1 is given by $u(c_1)$, where c_1 is the period 1 consumption of a type A consumer. The utility function has the properties $u'(\cdot) > 0$, $u''(\cdot) < 0$, and satisfies the Inada conditions. The period 1 value of the utility of type B consumers is given by $\rho u(c_2)$, where c_2 is the period 2 consumption of a type B consumer and $1 > \rho > R^{-1}$, so $\rho R > 1$. The coefficient of relative risk aversion, given by $-cu''/u'$, is assumed to always be greater than unity.

Because consumers are risk averse, they would be willing to pay in period 0 to reduce the uncertainty that they face in this environment. Thus, it would be optimal for them to design insurance contracts in period 0 that distribute their consumption optimally across the two possible states of nature in which they might find themselves in periods 1 and 2 (that is, type A and type B). The resulting optimal equilibrium allocation of consumption for the two types of agent in the two periods would satisfy the conditions:

$$u'(c_1) = \rho R u'(c_2), \tag{1}$$

$$(1 - \lambda)c_2 = R(1 - \lambda c_1). \tag{2}$$

The first condition sets the ratio of marginal utilities across the two states of nature equal to the relative price of consumption in the two states, while the

---

[2]Kawamura (2007) presents a small open-economy, two-good version of the Diamond-Dybvig model with cash constraints and analyzes the implications for banking of different exchange-rate regimes and monetary policies.

second condition reflects the economy's aggregate resource constraint. Achieving this allocation, however, requires that consumers be able to make payments to and receive payments from other consumers in period 1 that are contingent on the consumer's revealed type in that period. To see what form such payments would take, note from the properties of the utility function that in the optimal allocation just described, $c_2 < R$, while $c_1 > 1$. Because their endowments would allow type A consumers to consume one unit of the good in period 1 and type B consumers to consume R units in period 2, the optimal insurance contracts therefore involve period 1 payments from type B to type A consumers. However, a key assumption of the Diamond-Dybvig model is that the consumers' revealed types are private—not public—information. The implication of this assumption is that contracts cannot be written that are contingent on the consumer's type, because that type is unverifiable to the other party in the contract. This means that consumers cannot write insurance contracts that allocate utility optimally across states of nature.

Diamond and Dybvig explore what this constraint implies for the competitive equilibrium of this economy. They argue that because consumers are unable to write state-contingent contracts, no trading would actually take place in a competitive equilibrium. No trading takes place in period 0, because consumers are identical ex ante then, and they cannot write contracts contingent on their revealed differences in period 1. Similarly, no trading takes place after "types" have been revealed in period 1, because while consumers have different preferences about when to consume once they find out what "type" they are, they all have access to the same technology for converting period 1 into period 2 resources, so there is no opportunity for mutually advantageous trades. The upshot is that the competitive equilibrium is autarchic: type A consumers simply abort production and consume their endowments in period 1, attaining utility $u(1)$, with marginal utility $u'(1)$, while type B consumers do not abort production, reaping the higher-return benefit of allowing production to continue until period 2 and achieving utility $\rho u(R)$, with marginal utility $\rho u'(R)$. Diamond and Dybvig show that $\rho R u'(R) < u'(1)$, so the competitive equilibrium does not satisfy the optimality conditions described above.

Banks can provide a solution to this problem that allows the optimal allocation of consumption to be achieved. They can do so by offering deposits in period 0 that are available on demand in period 1 and yield a return that exceeds that of the pure storage technology, making such deposits attractive to all consumers. Such deposits pay a return r_1 if they are withdrawn by the jth agent during period 1, *as long as the bank has the resources to make the payment*, that is, as long as f^j is less than r_1^{-1}, where f^j is the fraction of all deposits withdrawn before the jth individual presents her deposit for withdrawal, and pays 0 if $f^j \geqslant r_1^{-1}$, because the bank's resources would be exhausted before the jth individual tries to withdraw in this case. In period 2, the bank pays out the resources that it has left to its remaining depositors, paying $R(1 - r_1 f)/(1 - f)$ per unit of deposit made in period 0, where f is the fraction of all deposits withdrawn in period 1, unless its resources were exhausted in period 1, in which case it pays 0.

The bank can mimic the complete information equilibrium if it sets $r_1 = c_1$. To see how, note that if type A consumers all withdraw their deposits in period 1, they consume c_1 in period 1, exactly as in the perfect-information equilibrium. The deposits not withdrawn remain invested in the illiquid technology. The bank's payout to the type B consumers in period 2 is given by its resource constraint. It distributes:

$$R(1 - r_1 f)/(1 - f) = R(1 - c_1 \lambda)/(1 - \lambda) = c_2, \tag{3}$$

per unit of deposit in period 2 to the fraction $(1 - \lambda)$ of their depositors who happen to be type B consumers and leave their deposits in the bank until the second period. The equilibrium just described is a rational expectations equilibrium, because type A consumers who withdraw their deposits in period 1 do not regret doing so, while type B consumers who do *not* withdraw in period 1 also do not regret having left their assets in the bank.

Unfortunately, this is not the only possible rational expectations equilibrium. The problem is that there is no guarantee that $f = \lambda$ in period 1. In other words, the fraction of deposits withdrawn in that period may not be limited to those withdrawn by type A consumers. Suppose, in particular, that $f = r_1^{-1}$, so *all* of the bank's deposits are exhausted by first-period withdrawals. For this to happen, some type B consumers must also withdraw their deposits in period 1, taking advantage of the free storage assumption to consume c_1 (the contractual return paid by the bank in period 1) during period 2. It is rational for them to do so, because the sequential service constraint implies that those type B consumers who attempt to withdraw their funds after the bank's resources have been exhausted receive no return at all in period 2, and thus are worse off than if they had been among the lucky few who got their deposits out in time. Thus, an equilibrium in which type B consumers stage a "run" on the bank is also a perfect foresight equilibrium.

In short, banks that provide liquidity services are inherently vulnerable to runs. Because $c_1 < c_2$, it is easy to show that type A consumers can be no better off in the event of a bank run equilibrium, while type B consumers must be worse off, so the bank run equilibrium is strictly inferior to the no-run equilibrium. The intuition for this is that the run forces the premature liquidation of assets, so that de facto the economy as a whole invests in the storage technology, rather than in the production technology. Diamond and Dybvig identify two possible solutions to this problem: the suspension of payments by the bank, and deposit insurance. We will come back to these later.

1.2 ▪ Business Cycles and Banking Crises

The Diamond-Dybvig model does not specify the conditions under which a bank panic is likely to take place. Because both the "run" and "no run" outcomes are rational expectations equilibria, either outcome is possible at any time. However, subsequent research has shown that banking crises are empirically systematically related to a variety of macroeconomic developments. An early finding by Gorton (1988), for instance, was that during the National Banking era in the United States (1863–1914) a systematic relationship existed between business cycles and banking crises: banking crises were much more likely to happen during recessions. This finding can be given a straightforward interpretation in the context of the Diamond-Dybvig model; if business cycle recessions are periods when liquidity shocks are more likely to happen (so that λ increases), or when expectations of future returns on illiquid investments (R) fall, then panics are more likely to happen during recessions. Gorton also found, as suggested by the Diamond-Dybvig analysis, that the creation of a lender of last resort for banks in the United States (in the form of the Federal Reserve System in 1914) and of deposit insurance (in the form of the Federal Deposit Insurance Corporation in 1934) were associated with a reduction in the incidence of bank panics.

Theoretical underpinnings for these findings are provided by Gorton and Huang (2006), who develop a model in which banking panics are not irrational manifestations of multiple equilibria. Rather, these episodes are the outcomes of asymmetric information and depositors monitoring their banks, which are vulnerable to moral hazard problems in certain states of the world. Specifically, depositors lack full information about the value of bank assets, so that during macroeconomic downturns they monitor their banks by withdrawing in a banking panic. Such panics may involve inefficiencies because banks may be liquidated for no good reason: because there is not enough liquidity in the banking system, banks cannot honor the demands of all depositors. Efficiency can be improved by having a central bank that creates liquidity if needed. This also mitigates moral hazard problems.

We will provide a brief review of the evidence on the systematic determinants of banking crises in developing countries in Section 4. Before doing so, however, we turn to a consideration of the relationship between banking and currency crises.

2   Twin Crises

The dramatic concurrence of banking and currency crises in the Southern Cone countries of Latin America during the early 1980s alerted economists to the possibility that these phenomena may exhibit particularly close links in the context of developing countries. An early recognition of these links was in the already-cited paper by Díaz-Alejandro (1985), who first drew attention to the close connection between the two types of crises in the Southern Cone.

Subsequently, Kaminsky and Reinhart (1999) undertook a more systematic relationship of the empirical association between the two types of crises, for which they coined the term "twin crisis." To investigate the relationship between banking and currency crises, they examined a sample of 76 currency and 26 banking crises in 25 countries (20 of which were developing countries) from 1970 to 1995.[3] They found that there was actually little relationship between the two types of crises during the 1970s, before financial liberalization gathered momentum among developing countries, but that they became closely linked in the post-liberalization period. Specifically, though troubles in the banking system tended to predate currency crises (and indeed the occurrence of banking crises helped to predict subsequent currency crises), the outbreak of a currency crisis had the effect of deepening the banking crisis. Both types of crisis tended to be preceded by a deterioration in macroeconomic fundamentals and specifically, consistent with Gorton's historical evidence for the United States, by a recession brought on by a worsening of the terms of trade, an overvalued real exchange rate, or rising cost of credit. Importantly, Kaminsky and Reinhart found that currency and banking crises had much more severe effects on the economy when they occurred jointly than when they appeared in isolation.

In the rest of this section we examine two generations of analytical models that attempt to explain the link between banking and currency crisis. The first, by Velasco (1987), adopts a first-generation currency crisis framework and explains the occurrence of a currency crisis as the result of a government bailout of a troubled banking system. The second, by Chang and Velasco (2001), adopts a third-generation currency crisis perspective (as discussed in the previous chapter) and models the joint occurrence of a banking crisis and a sudden stop of capital inflows as outcomes of simultaneous panic on the part of domestic depositors and the domestic banking system's foreign creditors.

2.1 ■ A Basic Model with Close Linkages

An early model of the relationship between banking and currency crises was developed by Velasco (1987). This model essentially shows how government guarantees of the liabilities of private banks can generate a standard first-generation currency crisis very similar to that analyzed by Krugman (1979) and discussed in Chapter 14. The mechanism is as follows: in the presence of government guarantees for the liabilities of the domestic banking system, a failure of that system causes a deterioration in the government's budget, which is financed through a depletion of foreign exchange reserves. Given a lower bound on such reserves, their steady depletion must result in a first-generation currency crisis.

Velasco begins by describing a simple dynamic economy without banks. In the style of early first-generation balance-of-payments crisis models, he assumes that the domestic economy is small and produces a single traded good, so the domestic price level is determined by PPP as $p_t = s$, where s is the nominal exchange rate (price of

---

[3]Evidence that twin crises tend to occur more frequently in developing countries is also provided by Glick and Hutchison (1999).

foreign currency in terms of domestic currency) and the foreign-currency price of the traded good is normalized to unity. Domestic prices and wages are fully flexible, so domestic output is always at its full employment level y. Uncovered interest parity ensures that the domestic nominal interest rate i is always equal to the foreign rate i^*. The domestic demand for money is given by:

$$m_t = L(i^*)w_t, \tag{4}$$

where w_t is private nonbank wealth. The money supply is fully backed by foreign exchange reserves, which pay interest to the government at the rate i^*. The government is assumed to simply consume the interest earnings on its foreign exchange reserves, so government consumption g is:

$$g_t = i^* R_t. \tag{5}$$

As we will see below, the government's stock of foreign exchange reserves will be constant initially, so government consumption is constant as well. The wealth of the private nonbank sector is defined as:

$$w_t = m_t + b_t^* + y/i^*, \tag{6}$$

where b_t^* denotes domestic private holdings of foreign bonds. Private sector wealth accumulation is accordingly given by:

$$\dot{w}_t = y + i^*b^* - c(w_t) = i^*(w_t - m_t) - c(w_t), \tag{7}$$

where c is real private consumption, taken to be an increasing function of real private wealth, and the second equality follows from substituting (6) into the first part of (7). Substituting (4) into (7), the steady-state level of wealth in the economy is defined implicitly by:

$$0 = i^*[w_t - L(i^*)w_t] - c(w_t). \tag{8}$$

Velasco introduces banks by assuming that the economy's capital stock is held indirectly by the nonbank sector, with banks serving as the financial intermediary, as in Diamond and Dybvig. In effect, the capital stock is transferred by the nonbank private sector to a bank, which in return issues claims on the bank to the nonbank private sector. In this case, however, those claims are in the form of domestic bonds, rather than demand deposits. The present value of the private bonds issued must equal that of the economy's future output, or $b_0 = y/i^*$, so in the presence of banks the private nonbank sector's wealth becomes $w_t = m_t + b_t^* + b_0$. The production of the single traded good is assumed to be subject to economies of scale, allowing the bank to earn monopoly profits equal to π per period, so in the presence of such economies the economy's output becomes $y' = y + \pi$. The banker is assumed to consume all of these excess profits.

The next step is to consider the effects of an exogenous shock to this economy, in the form of a contraction in y. Because the bank is committed to paying out i^*b_0 per period, the private nonbank sector does not perceive a change in its wealth, and therefore does not alter its consumption behavior. If the shock is small enough, the bank can continue to meet its obligations to its private creditors by simply reducing its own income π. But if the shock is sufficiently large that it exceeds what the bank can pay out of its own income, the bank can only continue to meet its obligations by borrowing. Assuming for simplicity that the shock is so large that it drives y' to zero, bank borrowing per period, denoted $\dot{F}_t$, is given by:

$$\dot{F}_t = i^*b_0 + \pi + i^*F_t. \tag{9}$$

Because neither the private sector nor the banker initially changes its consumption behavior, what happens in this situation is that the larger current account deficit caused by the reduction in y' is financed by external borrowing on the part of the bank. However, if this external borrowing has an upper bound, say F_u, then this situation must eventually come to an end. The critical moment T when the bank's borrowing capacity is exhausted, that is, when $F_T = F_u$, is given by:

$$e^{i^*T} = \frac{i^*F_u + i^*b_0 + \pi}{i^*b_0 + \pi}. \tag{10}$$

Velasco assumes that bank deposits and the bank's foreign debt are guaranteed by the government. However, the government is assumed not to have sufficient foreign exchange reserves to simultaneously redeem the private bank's deposits and pay off its external debt. He therefore assumes that the government uses reserves to redeem the bank's deposits, but simply takes on the bank's external debts and continues to service them on schedule. If the government consumed the amount g initially, then its reserves must have been given by g/i^*, and the initial evolution of its reserves over time would have been given by:

$$\dot{R}_t = 0 = g - i^*R_0. \tag{11}$$

When it pays off the bank's depositors, its reserves fall by b_0, so its revenues fall by i^*b_0. In addition, when it assumes the bank's debts, its spending rises by i^*F_u. Thus, the dynamics of reserves become:

$$\dot{R}_{t-T} = i^*R_{t-T} - (i^*F_u + g). \tag{12}$$

The key point of the model is that because $R_T = R_0 - b_0 = g/i^* - b_0$, the bailout of the private bank makes $\dot{R}_{t-T} < 0$ for all $t \geqslant T$. Thus, as in the canonical

Krugman (1979) model, there is an inexorable decrease in the stock of reserves which, assuming a finite lower bound on reserves, must inevitably give rise to a successful speculative attack on the currency. As in the Krugman model, the timing of the attack is predictable, and assuming a zero lower bound on reserves, is given implicitly by:

$$e^{i^*(T^*-T)} = \frac{R_{T^*-T} - (F_u - g/i^*)}{(R_0 - b_0) - (F_u - g/i^*)}. \tag{13}$$

Note that the link between a banking crisis and an eventual currency crisis in this model operates through the government's budget. Consistent with the results of Gorton and Kaminsky-Reinhart, what triggers the banking crisis is a recession, which impairs the value of the bank's assets. Because it guarantees the value of the banking system's liabilities, this shock to the system's net worth is absorbed by the government, which is thereby caused to run a fiscal deficit that eventually forces it to run out of reserves, triggering the currency crisis.

2.2 ■ The Chang-Velasco Framework

In the Velasco (1987) model, causation therefore runs directly from the banking crisis to a currency crisis. In the more recent model by Chang and Velasco (2001), by contrast, domestic and external financial crises occur simultaneously as the result of a joint panic by domestic and external creditors of the domestic banking system. Chang and Velasco build directly on the Diamond-Dybvig model. As in the latter, they adopt a three-period setup in which agents are born in period zero and receive e units of a perfectly divisible endowment good. In period 0, the good can be invested either at home or abroad. Domestic investments are subject to an illiquid technology, which yields a return $r < 1$ per unit invested if the investment is liquidated in the first period, and $R > 1$ if it is held until the second period. The foreign investment, which replaces the storage technology in Diamond and Dybvig, yields one unit of consumption in either period 1 or period 2, depending on when it is liquidated. Domestic agents can also borrow abroad at zero interest in periods 0 and 1, with a ceiling on their total external borrowing equal to f units of the consumption good. As in Diamond and Dybvig, consumers discover in period 1 whether they are type A (who care only about consumption in period 1) or type B (who care only about consumption in period 2), and this is assumed to be private information. The probability of being a type A consumer is λ, while that of type B is $(1-\lambda)$. As of period 0, expected utility is thus given by:

$$\lambda u(c_1) + (1-\lambda)u(c_2), \tag{14}$$

where $u(\cdot)$ now explicitly takes the constant relative risk aversion form $u(c) = c^{1-\sigma}/(1-\sigma)$.

Because domestic agents are risk averse and face idiosyncratic uncertainty about their type, they can benefit from pooling their resources. As in Diamond and Dybvig, Chang and Velasco explore how this superior equilibrium can be achieved by a bank issuing demand deposits subject to a sequential servicing constraint. As a first step in the analysis, consider the problem faced by a planner who cannot observe the individual's type. Under these circumstances, an incentive compatibility constraint has to be satisfied for type B consumers to reveal their true type in period 1.[4] Letting b_0 and b_1 denote net foreign borrowing in periods 0 and 1 respectively, k the amount invested in the illiquid technology, and l the amount of domestic investment liquidated in period 1, the problem is to maximize expected utility as given by (14) subject to:

$$k \leq b_0 + e, \tag{15}$$

$$\lambda c_1 \leq b_1 + rl, \tag{16}$$

$$(1 - \lambda)c_2 + b_0 + b_1 \leq R(k - l), \tag{17}$$

$$b_0 \leq f, \tag{18}$$

$$b_0 + b_1 \leq f, \tag{19}$$

$$c_2 \geqslant c_1, \tag{20}$$

$$c_1, c_2, k, l \geqslant 0. \tag{21}$$

With the exception of (20), these constraints are self-explanatory. Equation (20) is the incentive compatibility constraint referred to earlier. It ensures that type B agents have no incentive to misrepresent their type.

Because the economy faces no aggregate uncertainty, the solution to this problem will imply no liquidation of domestic investment to finance period 1 consumption, because it is cheaper to finance such consumption by borrowing abroad. Thus, the solution must imply $l = 0$ and $\lambda c_1 = b_1$. Because external borrowing is optimal in period 1, constraint (18) cannot bind, and (19) must hold as an equality that determines b_0. From (17), these considerations imply that:

$$R\lambda c_1 + (1 - \lambda)c_2 = Re + (R - 1)f = Rw, \tag{22}$$

---

[4] The incentive compatibility constraint is automatically satisfied for type A consumers, who have no incentive to be paid in period 2.

where $w = e + f(R-1)/R$ is a measure of the economy's wealth. Maximizing expected utility (14) subject to this constraint yields the optimal consumption levels:

$$\lambda c_1^* = \theta w, \, (1-\lambda)c_2^* = (1-\theta)Rw, \tag{23}$$

where $0 \leq \theta \equiv [1 + (1-\lambda)/\lambda R^{(\sigma-1)/\sigma}]^{-1} \leq 1$. It can be readily verified that this solution satisfies the incentive compatibility constraint (20).

Chang and Velasco argue that this equilibrium can be generated by a situation in which in period 0 domestic agents surrender their endowments and their capacity for foreign borrowing to a bank, which in return agrees to invest k in the domestic technology, to borrow b_0 and b_1 abroad respectively in periods 0 and 1, and to pay a return to depositors equal to c_1^* if funds are withdrawn in period 1—at least until the bank's resources are exhausted—and c_2^* if they are withdrawn in period 2. If type A depositors each withdraw c_1^* in period 1 and type B depositors leave their funds in the bank, the resulting equilibrium satisfies the conditions listed above and is a social optimum.

The problem is that, as in Diamond and Dybvig, this is not the only possible equilibrium. In particular, a bank panic, in which withdrawals exceed the resources available to the bank in period 1, resulting in the liquidation of the bank, is also a possible equilibrium. An important question in this regard concerns the conditions under which the bank's resources may be exhausted by period 1 withdrawals. In principle, the bank could meet such withdrawals by borrowing abroad or by liquidating domestic investments. If the bank is committed to servicing its external borrowing, then the maximum amount of domestic investment it can liquidate is given by:

$$l^+ = Rk^* - f, \tag{24}$$

so it will be unable to fulfill its obligations in period 1 if:

$$z^+ = c_1^* - (b_1 + rl^+) > 0. \tag{25}$$

This condition holds when the bank's liquid assets, in the form of external funds and the liquidation value of domestic investments, which together sum to $b_1 + rl^+$, fall short of its demand deposit liabilities c_1^*. If it holds, a bank run in which a sufficient number of type B depositors seek to withdraw funds in period 1 so as to exhaust the bank's resources is also a rational expectations equilibrium, because in the event of a run, type B depositors who are *not* successful in withdrawing funds in period 1 will receive nothing in period 2.

The conditions for a successful run are more likely to be met if a "sudden stop" of capital inflows accompanies the run. To see this, assume that the bank feels obliged to service only its period 0 external debt—and not its period 1 external debt—in the event of a run. If so, the maximum amount of domestic investment that it can liquidate increases to:

$$l^a = Rk^* - b_0 = Rk^* - (f - b_1) = l^+ + b_1. \tag{26}$$

But the critical liquidity condition now becomes:

$$z^a = c_1^* - rl^a = c_1^* - r(l^+ + b_1),$$

that is

$$z^a = z^+ + (1 - r)b_1 > 0. \tag{27}$$

Because $z^a > z^+$, this condition is more likely to be met. The implication of this analysis is that if a run is accompanied by a sudden stop of capital inflows, the conditions for a run to be an equilibrium are more likely to be met. Thus, a sudden stop of capital inflows could trigger a run on the bank. But the converse is also true: a bank run makes a sudden stop of capital inflows more likely, because a run makes it less likely that new external borrowing will be serviced by the bank. Thus, domestic bank runs and "sudden stops" of capital flows (as discussed in the previous chapter) are complementary.[5]

2.3 ■ The Flood-Marion Joint Distribution Approach

Other models of the joint occurrence of banking system and currency collapses include Buch and Heinrich (1999) and Flood and Marion (2004). In the Buch-Heinrich model, as in the model by Velasco (1987), there is a close link between the two types of crises. A banking collapse brings forward the time of a currency collapse. An adverse shock to bank asset returns lowers the net worth of banks and increases their cost of foreign borrowing. Because the government is already monetizing a fiscal deficit and losing international reserves, the decline in foreign borrowing speeds up the inevitable collapse of the fixed exchange rate.

In Flood and Marion (2004), by contrast, bank and currency collapses need not occur together or sequentially. they consider a small open economy with a fixed exchange rate and a banking system that incurs foreign-currency-denominated liabilities. There is a single, economy-wide real shock that affects returns on bank assets, the demands for assets and government financing. A bank collapse occurs when banks' liabilities exceed their assets, whereas a currency collapse occurs when currency speculators rush to purchase all the government's international reserves committed to the defense of the fixed rate. Speculators act the moment the shadow exchange rate exceeds the fixed rate, as in the standard Krugman-Flood-Garber

---

[5] Vaugirard (2007) extends the Chang-Velasco framework to study contagious effects of bank runs.

model (see Chapter 14). Both bank and currency collapses result from bad shocks to fundamentals, and they are therefore related; but because these shocks affect differently the two conditions for collapse, banking and currency crises do not always occur together.

3 Asymmetric Information and Opportunism

The Diamond-Dybvig framework adopted up to now perceives the social role of banks as allowing the economy to undertake highly productive but illiquid investments despite the fact that individual savers have reason to value liquidity. Banks essentially substitute for missing insurance markets. An alternative perspective on the social role of banks views them instead as social innovations to solve information and incentive, rather than insurance, problems.[6] From this perspective, rather than being an unfortunate byproduct of illiquidity, bank runs actually play the socially useful role of reducing principal-agent problems between banks and their depositors.

The key insight of this alternative analytical perspective is that in the presence of asymmetric information and opportunistic behavior, financial transactions are costly. The costs involved are of various types, and are incurred at every step of the financial transaction, from the initial coming together of the two parties to the transaction to its eventual liquidation. First, when information is asymmetric, lenders and borrowers have to search for each other. Matching the two sides of a financial transaction thus involves incurring brokerage costs. Second, in the presence of asymmetric information, adverse selection requires a potential lender to incur loan evaluation costs. Third, the combination of asymmetric information and opportunistic behavior creates principal-agent problems after money has changed hands between lenders and borrowers, because borrowers will have an incentive to use the funds they have acquired to pursue their own interests, rather than those of the lenders. This requires the incurring of monitoring costs. Finally, because contracts are not self-enforcing in a world of opportunistic behavior, financial transactions also involve incurring contract enforcement costs. All of these costs create a wedge between the interest rate paid by borrowers and that received by lenders, known as the external finance premium.

A second key observation is that all such costs are likely to have a substantial fixed component (that is, a component that is independent of the amount of money being transacted). The implication is that the external finance premium would be very high if financial intermediation were conducted by individuals. Institutions that specialize in financial intermediation, however, can achieve lower unit costs by taking advantage of economies of scale in each step of the process of financial intermediation (bringing lenders and borrowers together, evaluating loans, monitoring them, and

---

[6]For an early overview, see Gertler (1988); see also Freixas and Rochet (1997).

enforcing loan contracts), as well as of economies of scope among these activities. As a result, specialized firms can intermediate between borrowers and lenders at significantly lower cost than individuals can. The social contribution of such firms, therefore, is to lower the external finance premium.

This, then, is what banks do. However, because the key advantage of banks is that they can make information-intensive loans at lower costs than individuals, banks will necessarily possess more information about the quality of the assets in their portfolios than any outside agents, including banks' own depositors. Thus, bank's depositors themselves face an adverse selection problem as lenders. Moreover, banks as borrowers are in a principal-agent relationship with their depositors, and they face the same incentives to act in their own interest once entrusted with others' money as other borrowers do. Thus, bank depositors also have to solve a moral hazard problem. This problem is compounded by the fact that monitoring the bank is a public good: as long as monitoring by some depositors keeps the bank—as agent—serving the needs of its depositors—as principals—all depositors benefit, whether they monitor or not.

The issuance of liquid bank liabilities with a sequential service constraint addresses the adverse selection and moral hazard problems confronting bank depositors. The availability of deposits on demand enables depositors to quickly penalize a bank that is perceived to be misusing depositors' money by cutting off the bank's access to funds. The sequential servicing constraint, in turn, addresses the public good character of monitoring. It preserves an incentive for individual depositors to monitor banks, because only well-informed depositors who get their money out early are likely to avoid losses if the bank underperforms. Finally, banking crises that wipe out the bank's equity are the ultimate penalty for misallocation of depositors' funds. From this perspective, then, liquid liabilities, sequential servicing, and bank runs are the enforcement devices through which banks are induced to act in their depositors' interest and which therefore encourage depositors to entrust their savings to banks.[7]

This does not mean, of course, that bank runs are socially beneficial from this perspective. Though the threat of a run that causes a bank to become insolvent plays the socially useful role of aligning the interests of the owners of the bank with that of its depositors, a run that resulted in bank insolvency would nonetheless be destructive from a social perspective. Not only may highly productive but illiquid assets be liquidated, as in the Diamond-Dybvig model, but the failure of a bank also means the loss to society of the private information the bank had acquired about its debtors.

For this reason, last-resort lending and/or deposit insurance arrangements continue to offer social benefits. However, from the asymmetric information perspective, these benefits must be weighed against some potentially serious costs (see Santos, 2006). Specifically, while such arrangements may reduce or even eliminate the likelihood of a costly panic, they also reduce the incentives for depositors to monitor

---

[7] For elaboration, see Calomiris and Gorton (1989).

and may thus aggravate moral hazard problems in banking. The upshot is that the presence of such arrangements creates a case for the government to act as delegated monitor, through the regulation and supervision of banks to prevent moral hazard lending.

4   Determinants of Banking Crises: Evidence

There is no necessary conflict between the views of banks as social innovations to reduce the costs of financial intermediation arising from asymmetric information and opportunistic behavior, on the one hand, and as mechanisms for maturity transformation, on the other. The liquid liabilities that banks are induced to issue to facilitate monitoring by depositors are also attractive to depositors because they satisfy liquidity needs. At the same time, the pooling of many liquid liabilities allows banks to reduce exposure to liquidity risk and thus, in undertaking information-intensive lending, to include in their asset portfolios relatively illiquid projects with high expected returns. This eclectic perspective, however, leaves banks with assets that are simultaneously opaque (at least from the viewpoint of outsiders) as well as relatively illiquid, and with highly liquid liabilities that are subject to a sequential servicing constraint. From this perspective, it may not be surprising that banking crises have become relatively frequent events after domestic financial systems have been liberalized in developing countries.[8] In this section, we review some of the international evidence on the factors that have caused such crises. Three types of evidence are examined: episodic cross-country studies, results from "early warning" indicators, and multivariate econometric evidence.

4.1 ■ Episodic Cross-Country Evidence

An early study of the causes and effects of banking crises in developing countries was summarized in Sundararajan and Baliño (1991), who examined the experiences of seven developing countries, including the Southern Cone crises in Argentina during 1980–1982, Chile in 1981–1983, and Uruguay in 1982–1985, as well as those in the Philippines during 1983–1986, Thailand in 1984–1986, Spain over the period 1978–1983, and Malaysia in 1985–1986. Each of these episodes was preceded by domestic financial liberalization, though the extent of liberalization and the time elapsed between the change in policy regime and the emergence of the banking crisis varied widely among them. In all of them, the crises resulted in the generalized insolvency of domestic banks.

---

[8] For evidence on banking crises in industrial countries and similarities with developing countries, see Schularick and Taylor (2012) and Reinhart and Rogoff (2013).

Because nonperforming loans grew sharply just prior to and during each of these crises, the authors concluded that none of them could be interpreted as a self-fulfilling bank panic, that is, these crises were caused by deterioration in fundamentals. In all of these cases, the crisis occurred after a period of rapid economic growth, with substantial variations in relative performance among sectors, and followed by a slowdown. Adverse movements in asset prices (real estate and stocks) were important elements in some cases, but not all. However, consistent with the subsequent findings of Kaminsky and Reinhart (1999), the outbreak of these crises was associated with major external shocks and balance-of-payments problems. Sharp adjustments in exchange rates and interest rates, reflecting exchange market pressures, occurred around the time of the crises, though in some cases the currency crisis came before, and in others after, the banking crisis. In most countries, however, external imbalances were severe just before the banking crisis. However, in contrast with the findings of Gorton for the National Banking Era in the United States, these crises happened both with and without deposit insurance. Full deposit insurance was abandoned in Argentina in November 1979, and in the Philippines the deposit insurance agency had insufficient funds, causing the settlement of claims to be delayed.

There was a significant shift from deposits into currency and/or a decrease in the interest elasticity of currency demand following the crises in all of these countries. As a result, there were sharp reductions in money multipliers in Argentina, the Philippines, Spain, and Uruguay, though not in Thailand and Chile (in Thailand this is because the crisis affected mainly finance companies, rather than banks). The crises were associated with strong reductions in GDP growth and an initial deceleration of inflation, though the latter was subsequently reversed in some cases. Confidence was restored by last-resort lending (which was used in all of these cases), intervention of some of the troubled institutions, and the reimposition of deposit insurance. Last-resort lending, however, soon gave way to long-term lending at concessional rates, because of the generalized insolvency of financial institutions. Thus, governments wound up subsidizing failed institutions, as modeled by Velasco (1987). The losses to depositors were minimal in all cases (though Argentina and Thailand permitted some losses) and the fates of troubled banks differed across countries (they were liquidated in some cases, merged or restructured in others, and nationalized, or subsidized in still others). Bank borrowers were assisted with financial support, technical assistance, and debt-equity conversions.

A more comprehensive study that provided a dataset used in many subsequent contributions is that of Caprio and Klingebiel (2003). Defining a systemic banking crisis as occurring when the banking system reports nonperforming loans in excess of 5 percent of total loans, these authors identified a total of 112 systemic banking crisis episodes in 88 countries from 1975 to 2001.[9] As did Baliño and Sundararajan, they

---

[9] More recent studies have made use of the database described by Laeven and Valencia (2013).

found that the pre-crisis period in these cases tended to be characterized by unusually rapid credit growth as well as macroeconomic volatility (measured in this case by variability in GDP growth, inflation and the terms of trade). Even more prevalent than macroeconomic problems, however, were microeconomic factors such as poor supervision and regulation of banks, political interference, connected lending, and poor bank management. This provides strong support for the empirical importance of the asymmetric information and opportunistic behavior perspective of Section 3.

Joyce and Nabar (2009) and Dwyer et al. (2013) are two other studies on the effects of banking crises. The first study found that the adverse effect of banking crises on investment is magnified in a financially open economy. In a study for twenty-one industrial and developing countries over long periods (1870 to 2009 for many, and starting in 1901 for the others), Dwyer et al. (2013) found that 25 percent of countries experience no decrease in real GDP per capita in the year of a banking crisis or the following two years. Some countries see an increase in long-run growth after a crisis while others see a fall, with no clear overall pattern.

4.2 ■ Signaling Approach

Two dominant empirical approaches have been adopted for the more systematic investigation of the factors driving banking crises in developing countries: a "signaling" approach, and a multivariate approach typically based on the estimation of logit or probit regressions.

The signaling approach consists of trying to identify "early warning indicators" of future banking sector difficulties. The Kaminsky-Reinhart "twin crises" paper cited previously pioneered this approach in the context of developing-country banking crises. The approach consists essentially of specifying a comprehensive list of possible crisis determinants suggested by theory, and examining the extent to which unusual movements in each of these variables help to predict a future banking crisis. More concretely, Kaminsky and Reinhart considered whether each potential crisis determinant crossed a critical threshold in the period before the crisis. If it did, it was interpreted as emitting a signal of a future crisis. The critical threshold for each variable was chosen empirically, so as to minimize the signal-to-noise ratio within the sample for that variable (that is, the ratio of correct predictions to false positives). Kaminsky and Reinhart found that the most reliable early warning signals of impending crises were emitted by the behavior of the real exchange rate (an extreme real appreciation portends a future banking crisis), of stock prices (an extreme decline signals a future crisis), and the money multiplier (again, an extreme decline signals an upcoming crisis).

Kaminsky (1999) further developed the signaling approach, by combining the information contained in several indicators in a manner that gives relatively more weight to the more effective indicators. Her approach consisted of constructing a composite indicator consisting of the number of indicators that emit a positive signal at any moment of time, weighted by the signal-to-noise ratio of each indicator. The composite indicator turned out to be better than any single indicator at predicting banking crises, though it displayed a greater tendency for false positives. Further extensions are provided by Edison (2003), but with mixed results.

4.3 ■ Econometric Investigations

There have been a large number of econometric investigations of the empirical determinants of banking crises in recent years, typically applying logit or probit estimation to a qualitative crisis–non-crisis-dependent variable. The pioneering study was by Demirgüç-Kunt and Detragiache (1998). In this paper the authors sought to explain the empirical determinants of banking crises using annual data drawn from samples of 45–65 countries (depending on data availability for specific equation specifications), over the period 1980–1994. Demirgüç-Kunt and Detragiache classified a given year as a crisis observation if the ratio of nonperforming loans to total assets in the banking system exceeded 10 percent, if there was a bank rescue operation with fiscal costs in excess of 2 percent of GDP, if there were widespread bank nationalizations specifically as the result of banking sector problems, whether extensive bank runs, deposit freezes, or prolonged bank holidays took place in that year, or if generalized deposit insurance was enacted in response to such problems. On the basis of these criteria, they classified 31 out of the 546 observations in their sample as banking crisis episodes.

Using a logit procedure, they investigated the factors that affected the probability that any given observation in the sample would be classified as a crisis observation. Among macroeconomic variables, slow domestic GDP growth, poor performance of the country's terms of trade, and high domestic nominal and real interest rates tended to be associated with banking crises, but exchange-rate depreciation and fiscal variables were not. There was weak evidence that rapid growth of credit to the private sector—such as would emerge in a liberalized environment with inappropriate regulation of banks—predicted subsequent crises. Consistent with the Chang-Velasco emphasis on bank vulnerability to depositor and external creditor panic, a high ratio of M2 to the central bank's stock of foreign exchange reserves increased the likelihood of a crisis. Finally, Demirgüç-Kunt and Detragiache found that a low value of the law and order index that they used to indicate the adequacy of the domestic institutional environment helped predict subsequent crises, and that the presence of deposit insurance *increased* the probability of a crisis in their sample. This result was confirmed in a subsequent study by the authors (Demirgüç-Kunt and Detragiache, 2002), based on a sample of sixty-one countries over the period 1980–1997.

A similar study by Hutchinson and McDill (1999) supplemented a statistical study of determinants of banking crises in a large sample of countries with an examination of the "typical" time series behavior of macroeconomic variables and financial variables in crisis countries. They found that in crisis countries, as compared to the others, the pre-crisis period was characterized by a faster rate of currency depreciation, a higher rate of inflation, and a higher ratio of M2 to foreign exchange reserves. Stock prices were somewhat higher in crisis countries, but fiscal performance showed no noticeable differences. In economies that had crises, real output growth experienced a boom before a crisis, but slowed gradually prior to the crisis. It dropped sharply at the onset of the crisis, and gradually recovered. Credit growth was strong prior to the crisis, contracted during the first year, and then rebounded slowly. Exchange-rate depreciation jumped significantly at the onset of the crisis, and stock prices dropped markedly. In their formal statistical analysis, Hutchinson and McDill found that slower growth of real GDP and lower stock prices all increased the likelihood of a subsequent crisis, as did financial liberalization, deposit insurance, and their interaction. By contrast, greater central bank independence reduced susceptibility to banking crises.

One problem with studies of this sort is that, because they typically start with a large number of possible crisis determinants identified on an ex ante basis and identify the set of critical determinants on the basis of theoretically correct signs and statistical significance within a specific sample, their robustness to variations in the set of included variables and the specific sample chosen is difficult to ascertain. Eichengreen and Arteta (2002) focused on the robustness of alternative predictors of banking crises in developing countries. They used the Caprio-Klingebiel crisis dataset to generate the dependent variable for a probit regression to explain crisis incidence. In accordance with much of the empirical literature on banking crises, they found that domestic financial liberalization, rapid prior credit expansion, and a low ratio of central bank foreign exchange reserves to broad money have been the most robust predictors of banking crises in developing countries. This is consistent not just with both of the perspectives on the role of banks reviewed above, but also with the importance of "twin crises," because the reserve/broad money ratio is an indicator of external vulnerability. Despite this, and somewhat surprisingly, Eichengreen and Arteta did not find a stable relationship between the exchange-rate regime and the incidence of banking crises.

Two other findings in the Eichengreen-Arteta study are worth mentioning in association with the issues analyzed in this chapter. First, regarding the role of financial liberalization, as already mentioned, domestic financial liberalization was associated with an increased susceptibility to crises. By contrast, Eichengreen and Arteta did *not* find that opening up the capital account contributed to increasing the likelihood of banking crises, at least on its own. However, capital account liberalization did increase the effect of domestic financial liberalization on the probability of a banking crisis. Second, with respect to deposit insurance, Eichengreen and Arteta obtained results directly opposite to those of both Demirgüç-Kunt and Detragiache and Hutchinson and McDill: the presence of deposit insurance coverage *reduced* the likelihood of banking crises in their sample. Eichengreen and Arteta attributed the difference in results to their use of a larger developing-country sample than earlier investigators. However, they did find, consistent with the asymmetric-information perspective on the role of banks, that the interaction of deposit insurance and weak institutions—interpreted as indicating a weak regulatory and supervisory structure—increased the likelihood of banking crises.

Bussière and Fratzscher (2006) proposed an alternative early-warning system for predicting financial crises, based on a multinomial logit model. They argue that commonly used approaches, which use binomial discrete-dependent-variable models, are subject to a post-crisis bias—which arises because no distinction is made between tranquil periods, when economic fundamentals are largely sound and sustainable, and crisis/post-crisis periods, when economic variables go through an adjustment process before reaching a more sustainable level or growth path. A multinomial logit model, which allows distinguishing between more than two states, allows a substantial improvement in the ability to forecast financial crises for a set of twenty countries over the period 1993–2001.

Chapter 16

Sovereign Debt Crises

In the last two chapters, we examined two types of financial crises that have frequently afflicted developing countries, in the form of currency and banking crises. These were respectively situations in which central-banks became unable or unwilling to honor a commitment to an announced exchange-rate parity, and in which a country's banking system found itself in a generalized state of insolvency, leaving it unable to meet its obligations to its creditors. We also examined the "twin crises" phenomenon, involving the simultaneous occurrence of currency and banking crises. But these are by no means the only types of financial crises that have complicated macroeconomic management in developing countries over the past several decades. In this chapter we consider sovereign debt crises, consisting of situations in which governments find themseleves unable or unwilling to service their debts on contractual terms.

Sovereign debt crises have been common events historically, not just among developing countries, but among today's high-income countries as well. Tomz and Wright (2012), for instance, document 251 cases of default by 107 distinct sovereign entities between 1820 and 2012.[1] Such defaults have often emerged in waves (in the form of nearly synchronous defaults in a large number of countries following a period during which defaults were relatively rare). The most recent of these occurred during the decade of the 1980s and involved many developing countries in Latin America as well as elsewhere. However, public debt defaults among developing countries have not been restricted to those that occurred in the 1980s. There were some well-publicized emerging-market sovereign debt defaults in the late 1990s and early 2000s in Argentina, Ecuador, Pakistan, Russia, Ukraine, and Uruguay. Moreover, the sovereign debt problem has not gone away and has recently not been restricted to emerging and developing economies, as the experience of several countries in

---

[1] Standard and Poor's defines a default as occurring when a government misses a debt service payment stipulated in the original debt contract or when it offers its creditors a restructuring on less favorable terms than the original debt contract. The already-classic reference to the history of such defaults is Reinhart and Rogoff (2009).

the periphery of the EU (for instance, Cyprus, Greece, and Ireland) in the wake of the Great Recession of the late 2000s amply demonstrates. As the recent adverse performance of these economies shows, such crises have frequently been associated with especially severe economic downturns.

This experience has raised a number of analytical and empirical issues. An important question concerns how to determine empirically whether a crisis may be in the offing in the absence of a policy adjustment, that is, whether a government's *current* fiscal strategy is sustainable, in the sense of being consistent with an intention to service debt on contractually agreed terms. Whether the current fiscal strategy is sustainable or not, a second, broader question concerns the conditions under which a government is likely to choose to adopt a sustainable strategy, deviating from the current strategy if necessary to one that is likely to be sustainable, thereby allowing the government to remain solvent. In other words, under what conditions are governments likely to seek to avoid default? This is a similar question to that posed in Chapter 13 about central banks' commitment to continue to defend an announced exchange-rate parity, because it involves a comparison between the benefits and costs of continuing to comply with a previously incurred financial obligation that may not be legally enforceable. A third question, related to the second, concerns the macroeconomic consequences of sovereign default for the country of the defaulting government. As in the case of central banks and the exchange rate, these last two questions are related, because to the extent that default is associated with adverse consequences for the domestic economy, the associated costs to domestic residents would give a government that internalizes such costs a strong incentive to remain solvent. The costs of default are likely to depend, in turn, on the extent to which sovereign default triggers other types of financial crises, such as currency and banking crises. An important question concerns the conditions under which it would be more or less likely to do so.

This chapter will consider all of these issues. It begins by asking what we mean analytically by fiscal solvency, and how we can attempt to determine empirically when a government's solvency is threatened. It subsequently considers the conditions under which a government would voluntarily choose to repay its debt. The closely related question of the cost of default is considered next, followed by a review of how such costs may be affected by links to banking and currency crises. An appendix provides a short survey of the empirical evidence on the determinants of sovereign default.

1 Fiscal Sustainability and Fiscal Solvency

It is useful to begin by sorting out some conceptual issues. First, fiscal *solvency* should be distinguished from fiscal *sustainability*. Solvency implies that the government is expected (by its creditors) to be both able and willing to adopt a future fiscal program (a time path of spending and revenues) that will satisfy its intertemporal budget constraint. Sustainability, on the other hand, implies that it is able to do so without a change in the prevailing fiscal policy regime.

A second issue concerns the scope of public sector activities that should be included in an analysis of fiscal solvency. Buiter (1989*b*) argues that there are two key requirements for inclusion: that the state is ultimately responsible for the relevant public sector entity's debt and that the state appropriates the profits of the entity and makes up its losses. This suggests that the central bank should be included in any analysis of fiscal solvency, as well as the social security and state pension, disability, and insurance funds.[2]

A third issue concerns which specific public sector assets and liabilities should be included. In principle, we would want to include *all* public sector assets and liabilities. Assets should be "marked to market," and where no market exists for the relevant assets, they should be valued by the estimated risk-adjusted present value of the future net cash flows they could generate for the government. Debt, on the other hand, should be valued at its default risk-free value, with concessional debt—common in many low-income developing countries—valued at the present value of its scheduled debt service.

1.1 ■ The Algebra of Fiscal Solvency

The requirements for fiscal solvency were derived in a continuous-time framework in Chapter 3. We repeat the analysis here in condensed form for convenience.

Begin by assuming that all government debt is of equal seniority, that is, in making debt service payments, the government does not privilige any type of its outstanding debt over any other. Suppose that the government issues instant-maturity debt, some share of which is denominated in foreign currency. The nominal interest rates on domestic and foreign-currency debt can potentially differ, with the former paying an interest rate i and the latter i^*. Let the actual and expected rate of depreciation of the domestic currency be given by ε. Under these conditions, with neither type of debt senior to the other and risk-neutral creditors, we would expect that the two types of debt would yield equal returns when expressed in a common currency, that is, $i = i^* + \varepsilon$. In continuous time the flow budget constraint of the consolidated public sector (referred to for convenience as the "government" henceforth) can be written as:

$$\dot{\Delta} = -(\sigma + s) + [i - (i_F + \varepsilon)]f) + (r - n)\Delta, \tag{1}$$

where Δ is the ratio of government's net commercial debt to GDP and $\dot{\Delta}$ is its time derivative, σ is the ratio of its primary surplus (non-interest revenues minus

---

[2] In what follows, therefore, the term "government" will refer to the consolidated public sector, including the central bank and these other public sector agencies.

non-interest expenditures) to GDP, s is the ratio of seignorage revenue to GDP, i_F is the rate of return that the central bank receives on its holding of foreign exchange reserves, f is the domestic-currency value of those reserves, r is the real interest rate on domestic-currency debt, and n is the rate of growth of GDP. Define the *adjusted primary surplus*, $\hat{\sigma}$, as:

$$\hat{\sigma} = \sigma + s - [i - (i_F + \varepsilon)] f. \tag{2}$$

The evolution of $\hat{\sigma}$ over time depends on the path of non-interest spending, non-interest revenues, seignorage, and reserve accumulation over time. Thus, we can refer to it as the government's fiscal-monetary *program*. Now suppose there is a set of alternative fiscal and monetary programs $\hat{\sigma}$ that the government would be economically able and politically willing to implement, if they could be financed. We can define *feasible* programs as those that would be voluntarily financed by private creditors on market terms. We can then say that a government is solvent if its set of potential fiscal-monetary programs contains at least one member that is feasible.

How do we know whether a program is feasible? The answer is that private creditors will be willing to finance the government's fiscal-monetary program as long as the present value of the government's anticipated future debt service payments under the program, discounted at the risk-free interest rate that creditors could earn elsewhere, is at least as large as the value of the government's debt. Thus, any program that meets this condition is a feasible program. To see what this entails, use (2) to write the flow budget constraint as:

$$\dot{\Delta} = -\hat{\sigma} + (r - n)\Delta.$$

Notice that $\hat{\sigma} = (r - n)\Delta - \dot{\Delta}$ is the flow of debt service payments that the government makes to its creditors each period. Thus, by the definition above (and assuming a constant real interest rate for simplicity), a fiscal-monetary program will be feasible if it satisfies:

$$\Delta_t \leq \int_t^{\infty} \hat{\sigma}_s e^{-(r-n)(s-t)} ds.$$

Alternatively, solving the flow budget constraint forward:

$$\Delta_t = \int_t^{\infty} \hat{\sigma}_s e^{-(r-n)(s-t)} ds + \lim_{s \to \infty} \Delta_t e^{-(r-n)(s-t)},$$

so

$$\Delta_t - \int_t^{\infty} \hat{\sigma}_s e^{-(r-n)(s-t)} ds = \lim_{s \to \infty} \Delta_t e^{-(r-n)(s-t)}.$$

The condition $\Delta_t \leq \int_t^{\infty} \hat{\sigma}_s e^{-(r-n)(s-t)} ds$ is thus equivalent to $\lim_{s \to \infty} \Delta_t e^{-(r-n)(s-t)} \leq 0$. Intuitively, unless the government's debt grows at a rate that is slower than the growth-adjusted real interest rate, creditors would not be earning a market rate of return on their lending to the government, and thus would not finance the associated fiscal-monetary program.

1.2 ■ Implications for Fiscal Policy

To see the constraints that intertemporal solvency imposes on fiscal policy, begin by noting that Barro (1979) has suggested that optimal fiscal policy should feature constant tax rates over time, for two reasons. First, variations in tax rates over time would tend to distort intertemporal decisions, inducing agents to move economic activities from periods with high tax rates to those with low tax rates. Second, if tax collection costs are convex, fluctuating tax rates would tend to increase the excess burden of taxation. This leaves open the question, however, of the level at which the constant tax rate should be set. Note that the intertemporal budget constraint will be satisfied if:

$$\Delta_t \leq \hat{\sigma}_P/(r_P - n_P), \tag{3}$$

where $\hat{\sigma}_P = (r_P - n_P) \int_t^\infty \hat{\sigma}_s e^{-(r-n)(s-t)} ds$ is the annuity (permanent) value of the adjusted primary surplus. Letting τ_P and g_P respectively denote the permanent values of the ratios of government revenue and government noninterest spending to GDP, this is given by $\hat{\sigma}_P = \tau_P - g_P$. The permanent tax rate should therefore satisfy:

$$\tau_P = g_P + (r_P - n_P)\Delta_t,$$

which Buiter (2004) refers to as the *permanent balance* rule. Note what this implies for the behavior of the fiscal deficit. Because the actual fiscal deficit is given by $d_t = \dot{\Delta}_t + (n + \pi)\Delta_t$, we can rewrite it as:[3]

$$d_t = (n + \pi)\Delta_t + \{(g - \tau_P) + (r - n)\Delta_t\},$$

or

$$d_t = (n + \pi)\Delta_t + \{g - [g_P + (r_P - n_P)\Delta_t] + (r - n)\Delta_t\},$$

or again

$$d_t = (n + \pi)\Delta_t + (g - g_P) + [(r - r_P) - (n - n_P)]\Delta_t.$$

This permanent balance rule has several attractive properties:

- It ensures the solvency of the government and the sustainability of its fiscal-monetary program.

---

[3]For simplicity, we are ignoring seigniorage and differences between the interest rate on commercial debt and on foreign exchange reserves, that is, we are setting $s = i - (i_F + \varepsilon) = 0$, so $\hat{\sigma} = \sigma$.

- It respects intertemporal tax smoothing.
- It is *inflation and real growth corrected*, that is, it takes into account the effects of inflation and growth on the sustainable value of the deficit. Specifically, if g, r, and n are at their permanent levels, then this rule sets the deficit at $d_t = (n + \pi)\Delta_t$. For instance, using the "Maastricht" numbers for the stock of debt, as well as the sustainable values of growth and inflation ($b = 0.6$, $n = 0.03$, $\pi = 0.02$) yields a fiscal deficit of $d = 0.03$.
- The permanent balance rule avoids procyclical behavior. It suggests that the deficit should accommodate temporary increases in g and r, as well as temporary reductions in n.
- It does not incorporate the golden rule fallacy that borrowing for public investment is inherently safer than doing so to finance public consumption and transfer payments, because it does not privilege public investment. This is a fallacy in the sense that public investment does not necessarily generate the revenues required to service the debt incurred in financing it.
- Finally, in contrast with the fiscal rules often adopted in monetary unions (such as the Growth and Stability Pact of the Eurozone), it allows for differences in economic structure across countries.

2 ∎ Empirical Tests of Fiscal Sustainability

As indicated above, a fiscal program (or fiscal regime) is sustainable if implementing it does not violate the government's solvency condition. This section reviews various empirical tests that have been designed for assessing the sustainability of a fiscal program.

2.1 ∎ Deterministic Tests

From (3), tests of sustainability can be based on the equation:

$$\Delta_{MAX} = \hat{\sigma}_P / (r_P - n_P).$$

They can proceed in two ways.

2.1.1 *Sustainable Debt*

Projections of the long-run values of $\hat{\sigma}$, r, and n under current policies, given by $\hat{\sigma}_P$, r_P, and n_P, can be based on recent historical values. Substituting these into the equation above would produce an estimate of the maximum level of debt that the government could sustain under current policies. This maximum sustainable level of debt can then be compared to the existing stock of net debt to determine whether current policies are sustainable. They are judged to be sustainable only if the existing stock of net debt falls short of Δ_{MAX}. In its 2003 *World Economic Outlook* exercise, for instance, the IMF conducted such a calculation for a group of both industrial and emerging economies. It found a median value of the sustainable debt/GDP ratio of 0.75 for industrial countries and 0.25 for emerging-market economies. For industrial countries as well as for Asian emerging-market economies, actual debt was below the estimated sustainable value. However, for emerging-market economies as a whole, as well as for those in Latin America, the ratio was 2.5. For emerging-market economies outside of Latin America and Asia, moreover, it was nearly 6. The Fund concluded that the governments of these countries had effectively overborrowed.[4]

2.1.2   *The Sustainable Primary Surplus*

An alternative approach is essentially the mirror image of the previous one: it calculates the sustained value of the adjusted primary surplus required to make the existing level of debt sustainable:

$$\hat{\sigma}_P = (r_P - n_P)\Delta_t.$$

This is then compared to the existing adjusted primary surplus to determine whether fiscal adjustment is required to make the existing stock of debt sustainable, and if so, how much. Montiel (2011) provides a straightforward application of this approach to the 1982 Latin American debt crisis.

2.2 ■ Time-Series Tests

The approaches to testing for sustainability just described assume long-run equilibrium and do not take into account the role of shocks that could affect the public sector's ability to service its debt. The remaining sustainability tests to be described in this section confront these issues. A first set of tests is based on the time-series properties of fiscal variables. To motivate these tests, begin by writing the government's intertemporal budget constraint in discrete time as:

$$\Delta_t = (1 + r_P)\Delta_{t-1} - \hat{\sigma}_t + v_t,$$

or

$$(1 + r_P)^{-1}[\Delta_t + (\hat{\sigma}_t - v_t)] = \Delta_{t-1},$$

where v_t is a catch-all variable representing random shocks to the government's budget. In the formulation above, these shocks would take the form of temporary

---

[4]An econometric analysis of the determinants of overborrowing among these countries linked it to low ratios of government revenue to GDP, a low degree of commercial openness, poor quality of domestic institutions, and the nature of the domestic political system (single-party vs. multiparty coalitions).

deviations of the real interest rate from its sustainable value r_P. Iterating forward:

$$\Delta_t = (1+r_P)^{-j}\Delta_{t+j} + \sum_{i=1}^{j}(1+r)^{-i}(\hat{\sigma}_{t+i} - v_{t+i}).$$

Letting j go to infinity and taking expectations:

$$\Delta_t = \lim_{j\to\infty}(1+r_P)_t^{-j}\mathbb{E}_t\Delta_{t+j} + \mathbb{E}_t\sum_{i=1}^{\infty}(1+r_P)^{-i}(\hat{\sigma}_{t+i} - v_{t+i}).$$

Solvency requires:

$$\Delta_t = \mathbb{E}_t\sum_{i=1}^{\infty}(1+r_P)^{-i}(\hat{\sigma}_{t+i} - v_{t+i}),$$

or

$$\lim_{j\to\infty}(1+r_P)^{-j}\mathbb{E}_t\Delta_{t+j} = 0,$$

if r_P is constant. The transversality condition captured in the last equation reveals the restrictions that solvency imposes on the behavior of the debt/GDP ratio: it does not require Δ_t to be stationary, just that it grow at a rate that is smaller than the rate of interest.

2.2.1   Hamilton and Flavin (1986)

Hamilton and Flavin (1986) devised a test of fiscal sustainability that essentially tests the hypothesis that the debt is growing at less than the rate of interest (implying that the government remains solvent under the current fiscal program) against the alternative that it grows at the rate of interest, which would mean that interest is being capitalized and debt is not being serviced, so the present value of the future debt stock converges to a positive constant, say a (implying insolvency under current policies).

To see what the latter would imply for the transversality condition, let $N = t + j$ and write the transversality condition as:

$$\lim_{j\to\infty}(1+r_P)^{-j}\mathbb{E}_t\Delta_{t+j} = \lim_{N\to\infty}(1+r_P)^{-(N-t)}\mathbb{E}_t\Delta_N$$

$$= (1+r_P)^t\lim_{N\to\infty}(1+r_P)^{-N}\mathbb{E}_t\Delta_N,$$

or, equivalently,

$$\lim_{j\to\infty}(1+r_P)^{-j}\mathbb{E}_t\Delta_{t+j} = a(1+r_P)^t > 0.$$

That is, from the perspective of period t, interest capitalization would cause the present value of the stock of debt to converge to whatever the debt happens to be at time t. Hamilton and Flavin propose two ways of conducting the test. First, notice that if the alternative is true, the forward iteration becomes:

$$\Delta_t = \mathbb{E}_t \sum_{i=1}^{\infty} (1+r)^{-i} (\hat{\sigma}_{t+i} - v_{t+i}) + a(1+r)^t.$$

Now if $\hat{\sigma}_t$ is stationary, then because $\sum_{i=1}^{\infty} (1+r)^{-i} v_{t+i}$ can be expected to be stationary, the only way that Δ_t can be stationary as well is if $a = 0$. So the first test consists of testing for the stationarity of $\hat{\sigma}_t$, and if this is stationary, testing for the stationarity of Δ_t. If both are stationary, then it must be the case that $a = 0$ and the solvency condition therefore holds in the data.

The second test is based on the previous equation. Assuming that expected future values of $\hat{\sigma}_t$ are based on lagged values of Δ_t and $\hat{\sigma}_t$, consider estimating the coefficients α_i, β_i and a in the regression:

$$\Delta_t = \sum_{i=0}^{A} \alpha_i \hat{\sigma}_{t-i} + \sum_{i=1}^{B} \beta_i \Delta_{t-i} + a(1+r)t.$$

Hamilton and Flavin's second test consists of testing whether $a = 0$ in this regression.

The Hamilton and Flavin tests are subject to several limitations:

- They assume a constant expected real interest rate.
- They specify a restrictive alternative hypothesis (that is, that a is constant).
- The tests only work for the case where $\hat{\sigma}_t$ is stationary, yet the stationarity of $\hat{\sigma}_t$ is not a requirement of solvency.

2.2.2   Trehan and Walsh (1991)

Several modifications of the Hamilton-Flavin tests proposed by Trehan and Walsh (1991) address these problems. First, Trehan and Walsh show that the first version of the Hamilton-Flavin test holds when the term $a(1+r)^t$ is replaced by a more general ARIMA process, so the test remains valid for less restrictive alternative hypotheses than supposed by Hamilton and Flavin. The bottom line is that if $\hat{\sigma}_t$ is stationary, then fiscal sustainability requires Δ_t to be stationary as well. Second, they deal with the case of nonstationary $\hat{\sigma}_t$. They show that, if $\hat{\sigma}_t$ is difference stationary, the transversality condition required for solvency is satisfied if and only if the interest-inclusive deficit is stationary, that is, if Δ_t and $\hat{\sigma}_t$ are cointegrated with cointegrating vector $(r, -1)$. If $\hat{\sigma}_t$ is nonstationary with a root between 1 and $1 + r$, then Δ_t and $\hat{\sigma}_t$ have to be cointegrated. Intuitively, this is because when the interest-inclusive deficit is stationary, increases in debt are associated with increases in the primary surplus plus seigniorage, which implies that the debt is being serviced on market terms. Finally, regarding the assumption in Hamilton and Flavin of a constant expected real interest rate, they show that as long as the stochastic process driving the real interest rate is bounded from below by zero (real interest rates are always positive), a sufficient condition for solvency is that the change in the debt is stationary. The reason is that if the change in the debt is stationary, the debt can contain at most a linear trend, so it can grow at most linearly. But if the expected real interest rate is positive, the discount factor must grow exponentially, so the present value of the debt must converge to zero and the transversality condition must hold.

2.3 ■ Fiscal Reaction Functions

Bohn (1998) argues that time-series tests such as those just described are problematic, because their low power tends to suggest that debt is nonstationary, when it may simply be stationary and persistent. He proves that a positive linear response of the surplus ratio to the debt ratio above some threshold of the debt ratio is sufficient to guarantee intertemporal solvency under fairly general conditions (specifically, as long as the present value of GDP is finite—which will be true under dynamic efficiency— and the other determinants of the surplus are bounded). If the surplus and the debt ratio are both nonstationary and the other determinants of the surplus are stationary, this could be tested as a cointegrating relationship between the surplus and the debt. If they are both stationary, however, then the method requires the estimation of a regression that controls for other determinants of the surplus.

Bohn applies his method to the United States. Because he finds the surplus and the debt both to be stationary, he controls for other determinants of the surplus with with a model based on Barro's optimal tax smoothing story:

$$\hat{\sigma}_t = \rho \Delta_{t-1} + \alpha_0 + \alpha_1 GVAR_t + \alpha_2 YVAR_t + \varepsilon_t.$$

From the equation above and the budget constraint $\Delta_t - \Delta_{t-1} = (r - n)\Delta_{t-1} - \hat{\sigma}_t$ it follows that $\Delta_t - \Delta_{t-1} = (r - n)\Delta_{t-1} - \rho \Delta_{t-1} + \mu_t = (r - n - \rho)\Delta_{t-1} + \mu_t$, where $\mu_t = \alpha_0 + \alpha_1 GVAR_t + \alpha_2 YVAR_t + \varepsilon_t$, a stationary variable. This suggests that the debt ratio would be stationary if $-1 < (r - n - \rho) < 0$. Bohn also shows that his test is more general than others, because it does not depend on assumptions of constant real interest rates and the absence of uncertainty.

The IMF's April 2003 *World Economic Outlook* provides a wider international application of this method. It finds that adjustment of the primary balance to debt is nonlinear among both emerging-market countries and industrial countries, but:

- For industrial countries, the response of the primary surplus to the debt ratio actually increases as the debt ratio increases.

- However, for emerging-market countries the adjustment coefficient becomes *weaker* as the debt ratio rises, and stops altogether when the debt/GDP ratio hits 50 percent. Because solvency requires a positive coefficient, the implication is that debt/GDP ratios in excess of 50 percent of GDP may not be compatible with fiscal solvency in emerging economies.

2.4 ■ Tests of Fiscal Vulnerability

Time-series tests do not connect the sources of underlying macroeconomic uncertainty with the dynamics of public debt in order to produce forward-looking measures of fiscal vulnerability. In other words, they tell us whether the government's fiscal behavior is sustainable if the future looks like the past, but don't tell how different the future would have to be for the government's behavior to result in insolvency. Tests of fiscal vulnerability address this issue. Mendoza and Oviedo (2004), for instance, note that countries with more stable ratios of revenues to GDP and more stable GDP growth rates seem to be able to support higher debt ratios. This observation suggests that the stochastic environment matters in assessing sustainability. We now examine two approaches that take this into account.

2.4.1   Value at Risk

One approach mimics the value-at-risk approach used to assess the soundness of bank balance sheets. Suppose that the change in the government's net worth is given by $\Delta_t - \Delta_{t-1} = (r - n)\Delta_{t-1} - \hat{\sigma}_t + \mu_t$, where μ_t represents the effects of one-time debt shocks ("skeletons" such as exercised guarantees, or privatizations). The value-at-risk methodology for assessing fiscal vulnerability involves the following steps:

Step 1: Identify the key macro variables that affect the government's net worth. That would include those listed above (that is, the real interest rate, the growth rate, the primary deficit, and debt shocks), but possibly others as well [for instance, Garcia and Rigobon (2004), include the real exchange rate z_t and the inflation rate π_t].

Step 2: Derive the relationship between changes in these variables and changes in the government's net worth. For r, n, $\hat{\sigma}_t$, and μ_t that relationship is direct, because they appear in the flow budget constraint. For variables such as the real exchange rate and the inflation rate, the effect is indirect: these variables do not appear in the flow budget constraint, but innovations in these variables may affect the variables that do enter directly.

Step 3: Assume that these variables have a joint normal distribution. Use a VAR to estimate the joint probability distribution of changes in these underlying variables. The model is $X_t = c + B(L)X_t + \upsilon_t$, where $X_t = (r_t, n_t, \hat{\sigma}_t, \mu_t, z_t, \pi_t)$ and $\upsilon_t \backsim N(0, \Omega)$. This VAR yields estimates of c, $B(L)$, and Ω.

Step 4: Use the results of steps 2 and 3 to derive a probability distribution for the change in the government's net worth between now and some specified date in the future. The procedure is as follows: take a six-variable random drawing to derive a realization of v_{t+1} from the distribution $N(0, \Omega)$, use this to update X_t to X_{t+1}. Do this again for v_{t+2} and so on until the desired period T. Given this simulated future path of the vector X, the associated future path of the government's net worth can be derived. Repeat this procedure a large number of times (say N times) to derive N possible future values of the government's net worth. The Value@risk is the 5 percent critical value in the left-hand tail of this distribution. The value at risk is thus the maximum loss in net worth with at least a 5 percent chance of being observed. The smaller the value at risk relative to the government's initial net worth, the safer the government's solvency.

This approach has the virtue of taking into account the covariation among the macro and fiscal variables that affect the government's budgetary outcome. Applications include Barnhill and Kopits (2003) for Ecuador, and Garcia and Rigobon (2004) for Brazil. One problem with the Value@Risk approach, however, is that, because it relies on nonstructural methods, it is vulnerable to the Lucas critique. That is, it assumes the government will behave in the same way in the future as it has in the past. Thus, it is not clear that the relationships among the variables included in the VAR would remain invariant in the face of realization of the shocks that might trigger a change in the policy regime.

2.4.2   *Mendoza and Oviedo (2004)*

This observation led Mendoza and Oviedo (2004) to propose a structural approach. Their method investigates the maximum level of debt that the government can guarantee to pay in all states of nature (they refer to this as the natural debt limit, or NDL), under specific assumptions about its behavior. Specifically, suppose that the government's revenues are stochastic, described by a Markov chain (that is, with a set of finite discrete outcomes and fixed transition probabilities among them, given by a transition matrix). The ratio of the government's revenue to GDP is bounded from below, however, at some value $\underline{t}$. Mendoza and Oviedo estimate the lower bound to this ratio empirically as the value of the ratio that is two standard deviations below the average ratio for the country. They assume that the government wants to smooth public consumption as long as it can, but is willing to cut it to some lower bound $\underline{g}$ if it finds itself in a "fiscal crisis," that is, if its revenues are at their lower bound and its debt reaches an upper bound. So if its tax revenues reach a lower bound and the worst happens—they stay there period after period—the government keeps public consumption at its desired level as long as it can, financing it by accumulating debt. But when its debt reaches a maximum, it finally cuts public consumption to its lowest feasible value. Under these conditions, the maximum level of debt that the government can credibly promise to repay under all circumstances is equal to the present value of the primary surplus when both revenues and spending are at their lower bounds. It is therefore given by:

$$\Delta_{MAX} = (\underline{t} - \underline{g})/(r - n).$$

This NDL is lower for governments that:

- Have lower revenue ratios and greater variability in revenues.
- Have less flexibility to adjust spending.
- Face higher borrowing rates and/or have lower growth rates.

To determine whether a given level of debt is sustainable, Mendoza and Oviedo ask how large a commitment to contract the ratio of public expenditures to GDP the government would have to make in order to service this debt in the event of a fiscal crisis (that is, when revenues fall to their lower bound), and compare this to the standard deviation of the public expenditure ratio.

3   Fiscal Solvency and Debt Repayment

The two previous sections have drawn out the implications of fiscal solvency for fiscal programs, and considered empirical tests of whether prevailing fiscal programs are sustainable, in the sense that they are consistent with solvency. But this begs a key question: what incentives does the government have to undertake fiscal programs that are consistent with solvency? This question is not an idle one, because as already indicated, sovereign defaults have not been uncommon in the international experience. Indeed, one might wonder why they are not *more* common, because governments that seek to maximize the welfare of their constituents have an incentive to repudiate debt in order to make use of the resources that they would otherwise have to transfer to their creditors. To answer this question, it is convenient to distinguish between government debt held by domestic residents (domestic debt) and that held by foreign residents (external debt).[5] Domestic residents may be able to enforce repayment on the government by appealing to the domestic legal system or through the political sanctions that they can impose on a defaulting government. But foreign creditors do not have access to either mechanism to enforce their claims, because a defaulting government may be able to deny foreigners access to its domestic legal system and because foreigners don't vote. Moreover, while foreigners may be able to pursue legal remedies in their own courts against defaulting governments (for instance, seizing the defaulting government's financial and real assets), such governments may have few assets overseas that can be seized by creditors. Alternatively, foreign creditors may appeal to their own governments to exert pressure on defaulting governments in order to induce them to meet their debt obligations. But while this mechanism may have played a role historically, it has ceased to be operative in modern

---

[5]In fact, as noted by Panizza (2008) the distinction between domestic and external debt is problematic. "External" debt could refer to debt that is denominated in foreign currency, that is held by foreign residents, or that is to be adjudicated in foreign legal jurisdictions. For the purposes of this section, we will consider external debt to be debt held by foreign residents *and* issued in foreign jurisdictions.

times. The question then becomes: why do governments adopt fiscal programs that allow them to repay their external debts?

Because foreign creditors are aware of the government's incentive to repudiate external debt, the puzzle is how, in light of such incentives, it is ever possible to sustain an equilibrium with positive levels of government external debt. Clearly, repudiation must entail costs that induce the government to continue to service such debt. Unless repudiation is costly, governments may not be able to borrow. The question is what such costs might be.

This issue has dominated the analytical literature on sovereign debt since the early 1980s, when most voluntary lending to developing-country governments was indeed done by foreign creditors.[6] One traditional explanation, due to Eaton and Gersovitz (1981) is based on the notion that nonrepayment by the government may trigger a long-lasting loss of access by the country to external financial markets. In the Eaton and Gersovitz framework, which is typical of the sovereign debt literature that arose in the midst of the debt crises of the 1980s, the government is the only domestic agent that can borrow externally, and it does not issue domestic debt. Thus all government debt is external, and all external debt is public. Key features of the framework are that the governnment is benevolent (its objective is to maximize the intertemporal utility of a representative domestic agent), the motivation for external borrowing is to smooth domestic consumption, and the cost of default is permanent exclusion from international capital markets. A simple version of the model, which has become the canonical model of sovereign default, can be described as follows.[7]

The government of a small endowment economy maximizes household intertemporal utility arising from consumption. It enters the current period with an outstanding stock of debt Δ consisting of one-period bonds promising to pay one unit of output, and a stochastically determined endowment of output y. In making the decision whether to service its debt, it maximizes a value function that depends on these two variables:

$$V(\Delta, y) = \max\{V^D(y), V^{ND}(\Delta, y)\},$$

where the superscripts D and ND refer respectively to *default* and *no default*. A default causes the country to permanently lose access to international capital markets. If the government defaults at time t, therefore, the value function is given by the country's lifetime utility of consumption under autarky, with time preference

---

[6]Domestic capital markets were poorly developed among developing countries at the time, and the domestic banking systems of such countries operated under conditions of financial repression, which imposed mandatory holdings of government debt by banks.

[7]The simplified version of the Eaton-Gersovitz model described here is taken from Aguiar (2011). See also Aguiar and Amador (2013).

factor β:

$$V^D(y) = E_y \sum_{s=t}^{\infty} \beta^{s-t} u(y_s).$$

On the other hand, if the government services its debt, the country retains access to the world capital market. In this case, the value function is given by the solution to the intertemporal utility maximization problem:

$$V^{ND}(\Delta, y) = \max_{c, \Delta'} u(c) + \beta E_y V(\Delta', y'),$$

subject to:

$$c + \Delta \leq y + q(\Delta'; y)\Delta',$$

where y' is next period's output, Δ' is next period's debt, and $q(\Delta'; y)$ is the price of a bond issue of size Δ' given the current output endowment y. The latter, in turn, is determined by an arbitrage relationship that links the price of the bond issue to the probability of repayment in the next period and the risk-free interest rate that risk-neutral creditors could earn elsewhere:

$$q(\Delta'; y) = \Pr\{V^{ND}(\Delta', y') \geq V^D(y') \mid y\}/(1+r).$$

In this model, the incentive to repay arises from households' desire to smooth consumption. This reduces the value function under autarky, because autarky causes household consumption to be tied to the stochastically fluctuating domestic income stream. The incentive to default, on the other hand, arises from the negative effect on the no-default value function of the reduction in current consumption required to service the inherited debt. The government is more likely to default when it suffers a particularly poor draw of current income, when it enters the current period with a large stock of debt, and when the world interest rate is high. These conditions make the resources that can be diverted from creditors through nonpayment particularly valuable and the terms on new debt particularly unattractive.

While this framework has been widely adopted in the sovereign debt literature, it is subject to several analytical and empirical shortcomings. An important analytical problem is that it relies on the assumption that external borrowing is motivated by consumption-smoothing considerations. As noted by Panizza et al. (2009), this creates a *permanent* benefit from external borrowing, which implies that future exclusion from such borrowing would indeed be costly for the debtor country. But if the benefit from external borrowing is transitory, such as when such borrowing is motivated by impatience to consume or by the acceleration of capital accumulation, the possibility of a future loss of access would not induce a debtor to repay.

A second problem has to do with the effectiveness of exclusion as an enforcement device. The Eaton-Gersovitz framework leaves unexplained why the country loses access to international capital markets in the event of default. Implicitly, the assumption is that creditors retaliate against a defaulter by denying future loans. However, this may not be feasible. The reason is that it may not be in any individual creditor's interest to participate in such sanctions if lending to the government is perceived to be profitable in the future. A mechanism is required to coordinate the actions of present and all potential future creditors. The absence of such a mechanism would make the threat of future exclusion from capital markets time-inconsistent. Moreover, even if it were possible to enforce it, exclusion may not have much "bite" as a penalty on creditor governments if they have other means available to smooth future consumption, such as by accumulating foreign assets or by purchasing insurance (Bulow and Rogoff, 1989). All of this being said, it is possible to imagine alternative mechanisms that could render exclusion effective. Exclusion could be sustained, for instance, if funds temporarily deposited abroad on account of new credits extended to a defaulting government become subject to seizure by the creditors affected by the default. This would certainly discourage new lending. Moreover, funds deposited abroad by a defaulting government to provide self-insurance against future income fluctuations could also be subject to seizure (see Wright, 2011).

A third analytical problem with the framework is its omission of external borrowing by the private sector. Allowing for the possibility of external borrowing by the private sector would obviate the need for consumption smoothing by the government, because in that case the private sector could perform that function for itself. However, once again this is not a fatal problem. It would still be possible to motivate countercyclical government borrowing (both domestic and external) as the result of intertemporal tax smoothing. To the extent that some such borrowing is external, government repayment of external debt could in turn be motivated through the possibility of the exclusion of *all* domestic agents from international capital markets in the event of a government default.[8]

The empirical shortcomings of the Eaton-Gersovitz framework appear to be more serious. In particular, the consumption-smoothing motive suggests that external borrowing should be countercyclical, which contradicts the repeated finding that capital flows to emerging and developing countries tend to be procyclical (see, for instance, Kaminsky et al., 2004).

Moreover, the empirical evidence on costs of default indicates that exclusion of defaulting governments from international capital markets has been temporary. Sovereigns have been excluded from borrowing during the duration of the default episode, but have subsequently regained market access relatively quickly. Risk premiums also do not seem to stay at inordinately high levels for long periods of time after

---

[8] For the effects of sovereign defaults on external credit to the private sector, see Arteta and Hale (2008).

a default episode. As noted by Panizza et al. (2009), access to international capital markets appears empirically to be restored relatively quickly after the negotiation of a restructuring of defaulted debt.[9] Not only access, but even the terms on which governments can access capital markets, appear to be only temporarily affected negatively by a default. Borenzstein and Panizza (2009) for instance show that while credit ratings and risk premia are indeed affected by default, such effects tend to be highly transitory. Although these results have recently been questioned by Cruces and Trebesch (2013), who argue that the effects of default on the duration of exclusion as well as on subsequent borrowing costs depend on the size of the losses (*haircuts*) experienced by creditors, Cruces and Trebesch do not claim to establish a causal relationship between larger haircuts and subsequent adverse borrowing conditions, as in the theory reviewed above. The empirical relationship they uncover may be driven by other factors (for instance, information revelation: governments of countries that are in worse shape produce larger haircuts and have more difficulty accessing capital markets). They simply question the conventional empirical wisdom that defaults are not associated with more adverse subsequent conditions of access.

Finally, calibrated versions of the Eaton-Gerovitz framework have difficulty matching several stylized facts associated with sovereign borrowing and default. For instance, the levels of debt that calibrated models are able to explain solely through the threat of even permanent exclusion are much lower than those actually observed, requiring such models to assume additional exogenous output costs of default in order to account for the existence of debt levels such as those observed in practice.[10] In addition, such models tend to predict that a much larger fraction of defaults would occur in bad times (that is, during recessions) than has historically been the case (see Tomz and Wright, 2007).

In short, the threat of potential exclusion from international financial markets does not appear to be the key mechanism inducing debt repayment.

4 Costs of Default

If the threat of future exclusion does not appear to be sufficient to explain external debt repayment, how is it possible for governments to sustain positive levels of external debt? Under the benevolent-government assumption of the Eaton-Gerovitz framework, debt repayment is induced by the likelihood that default may impose costs on the domestic economy, but such costs need not be limited to capital market exclusion. Two other types of costs have been proposed in the literature: the costs

---

[9] See also Gelos et al. (2011). The fact that many developing countries were excluded from international capital markets for several decades after the defaults of the 1930s does not contradict this statement, since exclusion affected both defaulters and nondefaulters equally (see Borensztein and Panizza, 2009).

[10] See Alfaro and Kanczuk (2005), as well as Hatchondo et al. (2007).

of default on *domestic* creditors and the likelihood that default will result in a contraction of real output.

4.1 ■ Default and Domestic Debt

The existence of domestic debt creates an alternative mechanism inducing debt repayment by the government: an inability by defaulting governments to default selectively on debt owed to foreign creditors, rather than domestic ones. This would be true, for instance, if existing debt takes the form of assets that can be actively traded on secondary markets, making it difficult to determine which debt is owed to foreign creditors (Broner et al., 2006). This may reduce the appeal of default for a government that cares directly about the welfare of its own residents, or may dissuade a less benevolent potential defaulter if the involvement of domestic creditors in the default increases the costs that creditors can collectively impose on the defaulting government.

For instance, if domestic debt is potentially impaired by the default, the government may lose *all* access to market financing (not merely to external financing). The inability to issue debt may require the full tax financing of government expenditures. Full tax financing of government expenditures, in turn, would tend to increase the present value of the excess burden associated with the financing of a given program of exhaustive government spending if the excess burden associated with each dollar of tax revenue is an increasing function of the tax ratio (Barro, 1979). Full tax financing, by causing tax rates to vary intertemporally with government expenditures, may also distort the intertemporal allocation decisions of economic agents by inducing them to redistribute their production and spending decisions over time. Moreover, it would involve raising tax rates during cyclical downturns and lowering them during booms, thus causing fiscal policies to behave procyclically. Finally, full tax funding forces the current generation to bear the burden of public sector capital expenditures that will benefit future generations, thus violating the "benefit principle" of public finance. The alternative of financing deficits by printing money runs the risk of subjecting the economy to high and unstable inflation. The increased transaction costs, and the instability of intratemporal and intertemporal relative prices that this entails, have adverse consequences for efficiency and equity that have typically (but not always!) rendered pure money financing unacceptable. All of these adverse effects on the domestic economy emenating from loss of government access to capital markets would cause the government to internalize the costs of default through the political system.

4.2 ■ Default and Real Output

Several observers have argued that the main cost of default that induces repayment and is thus able to sustain positive levels of debt is that default tends to be associated with severe, albeit temporary, output contractions in the defaulting country (see for instance Dooley, 2000). Such economy-wide costs would directly affect domestic agents, who can penalize the defaulting government through the domestic political system.

There is indeed substantial empirical evidence that the output costs of defaults have been significant in practice, suggesting that incentives for repayment are substantial. Sturzenegger (2004) examined the costs of sovereign defaults in one-hundred countries during the period 1974–1999, using two empirical approaches based respectively on cross-section and annual data.[11] In the cross-section exercise, he looked at the effect of default on average growth performance over the sample period, controlling for a large number of potential growth determinants (initial GDP per capita, population, the share of investment in GDP, the rate of growth of the population, the rate of growth of government consumption, the initial level of education, an indicator of civil unrest, changes in the terms of trade, a measure of openness, the average inflation over the sample period, a measure of inflation volatility, and the incidence of banking crises). Two measures of default were used: a dummy variable indicating whether the country ever defaulted over the sample, and a dummy variable that took the value of 1 if the country defaulted in the 1980s or 1990s, 2 if it defaulted in both decades, and 0 otherwise. In cross-section, the defaulters in his sample grew by 0.6 percent per year slower than nondefaulters. Annual data were used to address the possibility that the incidence of default in the cross-section may proxy for omitted poor country characteristics. These characteristics were captured by fixed effects in the annual panel. Two new default dummies were used: the first took on the value of 1 in the default year as well as the subsequent year, and the second was 1 in the default year and for next five years. Separate dummies were created for the decades of the 1980s and 1990s. The key finding was that the short-run dummy was associated with lower growth by 2 percent per year, the longer one by 0.8 percent per year.

Recent studies have derived similar results. Using Standard and Poor's definition of default, and looking at the experience of eighty-three countries over the 1972–2000 period, Borensztein and Panizza (2009), for instance, find that default is associated with an average reduction in growth of 1.2 percent per year in the year of the default. Similarly, Panizza et al. (2009) find that default has been associated with a reduction in growth rates of some 1.3 percent of GDP in the year of default over the 1970–2006 period, with significant negative effects on growth in the vicinity of 1 percent of GDP for both predicted as well as unpredicted defaults, indicating that actual default matters for growth, not just the anticipation of a potential default.[12] More recent work has suggested that the adverse output consequences of default may

---

[11] See also Chuhan and Sturzenegger (2005).

[12] As noted by Levy Yeyati and Panizza (2011), there is an important distinction to be drawn between effective insolvency and the formal act of default. Using quarterly data, Levy Yeyati and Panizza note that the formal act of default typically represents an inflection point at which real ouput begins to recover, suggesting that output contraction is associated with the anticipation of default, that is, with effective fiscal insolvency, rather than with

be both large and long-lasting. Gornemann (2013), for instance, based on a sample of sixty defaults from 1970 to 2007, finds that ten years after a default event real output remains 6 percent below what it would have been otherwise. In a simulation model, sustained output losses on this scale permit him to explain the existence of debt/GDP ratios that approximate much more closely those that are empirically observed than models based on foregone consumption smoothing opportunities can do.

This leaves open the question, however, of what the precise mechanisms may be through which sovereign defaults exert such adverse effects on aggregate economic performance. Several candidates have been proposed.

4.2.1   Debt Overhangs

Default episodes can be prolonged, as creditors' ability to potentially extract additional payments from the defaulting government provides them an incentive to refuse to relinquish their claims. During the period between the time when a default event becomes anticipated and when the debt is eventually restructured, the status of the outstanding debt is uncertain, creating a "debt overhang" problem that potentially distorts intertemporal relative prices in the domestic economy by creating the possibility that future income gains may effectively be taxed away by creditors to service debt (see, for instance, Sachs 1988, and Krugman, 1988). At the aggregate level this would discourage pro-growth policies, to the detriment of domestic macroeconomic performance, because the sacrifices entailed would be borne by domestic residents, while a share of the fruits would go to creditors. But aside from the effects on the incentives facing policymakers, debt overhangs would tend to discourage investment directly to the extent that any additional payments to creditors potentially are financed from the taxation of returns to investment (Helpman, 1989). Other costs may emerge through the impairment of international trade, through signaling, or through adverse effects on the domestic financial system (see below).

4.2.2   Effects on International Trade

As noted by Rose (2005), sovereign default may discourage trade either because creditors seek to punish defaulting governments by denying trade benefits to their countries or because default tends to dry up trade credit. There is indeed evidence that defaults tend to be associated with decreased international trade. Rose, for instance, using a gravity model, finds rather dramatic effects: default results in a reduction in bilateral trade with creditor countries of about 8 percent per year, and the effect lasts for about fifteen years. Similarly, Borenzstein and Panizza (2009) find that sovereign defaults tend to have disproportionately negative effects on the

---

the first instance of missing a debt service payment or seeking restructured terms on debt. Their interpretation is that the anticipation of a default event causes low growth and the validation of those expectations does not entail additional costs.

growth rates of export-oriented industries in the defaulting economy, although they find these effects to be more transitory than the effects on trade suggested by Rose. However, as Panizza et al. (2009) note, the precise channels that generate this link are not clear. There are no obvious empirical episodes in which the country of the affected creditors imposed trade sanctions on a defaulting country in retaliation for the default. At the same time, while they find that default does seem to adversely affect trade credit, Borenzstein and Panizza (2009) also find that including trade credit in Rose-type gravity equations for bilateral trade does not alter the negative coefficient of default on trade, suggesting that the contraction of trade credit is not the channel that produces this effect.

4.2.3 *Signaling*

A separate mechanism by which a default may exert effects on real output is through information revelation. As noted by Sandleris (2008), in a setting in which the government has information about the economic fundamentals that is not available to private agents—for instance, about the true state of the economy or about the government's future policy intentions—and in which the decision to service debt depends on the government's private information, such that more favorable fundamentals make it more likely that the government will service its debt, the government's debt servicing decision allows the private sector to make inferences about the information that the government possesses. Under these circumstances, a default on sovereign debt would tend to reveal negative information to the domestic and foreign private sectors about the fundamentals. To the extent that such information affects private sector decisions such as the decision to invest or the decision to extend credit, a default could induce the private sector to behave in a way that results in a contraction in domestic output.

5   Sovereign Debt Crises and Banking Crises

In making the case that severe output contractions induced by default were the key mechanisms that induce governments to service their debts, Dooley (2000) emphasized a different mechanism: he argued that default would result in a breakdown in domestic financial intermediation. If sovereign debt crises tend to trigger other types of financial crises that themselves cause output contractions, then the output losses associated with sovereign debt crises would tend to be magnified. It follows that the output costs of specific default episodes depend on whether they are accompanied by other types of financial crises, such as banking and/or currency crises. De Paoli et al. (2006) found that the output losses associated with sovereign debt crises in emerging economies are much larger when such crises are accompanied by banking and/or currency crises. Looking at forty-five sovereign debt crises from 1970 to 2000, they found a median annual shortfall in output during a crisis episode of 6.9 percent relative to what they projected it to have been in the absence of the crisis, but of 22 percent in the twenty-one cases in their sample in which banking and currency crises occurred during the period of the sovereign debt crisis.[13] This section and the one that follows examine the potential links between between sovereign debt crises and banking and currency crises, respectively.

Reinhart and Rogoff (2009) provide evidence that sovereign debt crises have often been accompanied historically by banking crises. However, this does not necessarily imply that sovereign defaults tend to trigger banking crises, because in principle there are several possible channels of transmission between the two types of crises. Some illustrative examples include the following.

Common Causes

- An adverse demand or supply shock to the domestic economy that results in a decline in domestic economic activity could trigger simultaneous sovereign and banking crises by at the same time causing a reduction in government tax revenues as well as in the capacity of bank borrowers to service their debts.
- A sharp depreciation of the currency could trigger a deterioration in the balance sheets of both the government and the banks to the extent that the two types of agents have significant foreign currency exposure.

Causation from Sovereign Debt Crises to Banking Crises

- A banking crisis may be triggered directly by a sovereign debt crisis if banks hold a large amount of government debt relative to the value of bank capital (see Bolton and Jeanne, 2011).
- If sovereign debt crisis result directly in contractions in domestic economic activity through any of the channels mentioned previously, that contraction in activity is likely to hamper the profitability of banks, increasing the probability of a banking crisis.
- To the extent that a sovereign debt crisis impairs not just the value of the government's debt but potentially also that of all assets within the government's political jurisdiction, the emergence of a sovereign debt crisis may trigger capital flight that may take the form of a run on banks, triggering a banking crisis.

Causation from Banking Crises to Sovereign Debt Crises

- A direct channel of transmission from banking crises to sovereign debt crises is through the fiscal costs of restoring solvency to the banking system.

---

[13] As noted by the authors, these numbers appear large. They may confound the effects of the default with those of the shock(s) that triggered it, so that the counterfactual no-default scenario may be overoptimistic. They emphasize instead the relative costs with and without the involvement of other types of financial crises.

The cost of re-capitalizing the banks after an episode of widespread insolvency in the banking system typically implies a large increase in the stock of public sector debt that can impair the solvency of the government.

- An additional indirect channel of transmission linking banking crises to sovereign debt crises operates through the effects of banking crises on real economic activity. Because banks are the key financial intermediaries in many economies, a banking crisis is likely to be associated with a credit crunch that results in a severe contraction in the affected economy. That contraction reduces the government's revenues, impairing the government's fiscal situation and thereby increasing the likelihood of a sovereign debt crisis.

Borensztein and Panizza (2009) provide direct evidence on the frequency with which these different mechanisms may be operative. In a sample of 149 countries over the period 1975 to 2000, they identified 111 banking and 85 sovereign debt crises. They found that the probability of a banking crisis conditional on a sovereign debt crisis was significantly (both statistically and economically) higher than the unconditional probability of a banking crisis, while the probability of a sovereign debt crisis conditional on a banking crisis was only marginally larger than the unconditional probability, and the difference was not statistically significant. Thus, it appears that a sovereign debt crisis is much more likely to trigger a banking crisis than vice versa. The channel highlighted by observers such as Bolton and Jeanne (2011) and Sosa Padilla (2013) is extensive bank holdings of sovereign debt. Sosa Padilla, for instance, finds that in emerging economies the ratio of banking sector credit to the government to total banking sector assets averages 30 percent, and that episodes of sovereign default tend to be associated with sharp contractions in credit to the *private* sector from the domestic banking system. He builds in a model in which the output costs created by sovereign default operate through the consequences of default for the domestic banking system. By rendering bank holdings of government liabilities worthless (or at least, by reducing their value), the default reduces the resources that the banking system has available to lend to domestic firms in the form of working capital. This increases the cost of working capital to firms and induces them to contract output. Calibrated to the Argentine economy, the model is able to reproduce the output contraction associated with the Argentine default of 2001.

6   Sovereign Debt Crises and Currency Crises

Another mechanism through which sovereign debt crises may generate output contraction is by inducing a currency crisis in the economy of the defaulting government. As described in Chapter 14, there are a variety of mechanisms through which a steep depreciation of the currency may prove to be contractionary on its own, so a sovereign default that triggers a currency crisis may have a magnified negative effect on real output. However, as in the case of banking crises, causation is not necessarily unidirectional from sovereign debt to currency crises. Sovereign debt crises and currency crises may interact in a variety of ways, which complicates the task of ascertaining the extent to which debt defaults tend to trigger currency crises. In first-generation currency crisis models, for instance, a currency crisis could be an alternative to a debt crisis, because such crises emerge when the government satisfies its flow budget constraint by printing money, rather than defaulting.

However, currency and debt crises may be complements, rather than substitutes. As in the case of sovereign debt and banking crises, this can happen through a variety of channels.

Common Causes

- An exogenous contraction in aggregate demand could give rise to a currency crisis through a second-generation currency crisis mechanism (for instance, high unemployment caused by the negative demand shock would put pressure on the central bank to devalue the currency to stimulate demand), while at the same time increasing the government's primary deficit, reducing the resources it has available to service debt.
- An increase in the international real interest rate would have similar effects on the domestic economy, and thus on the likelihood of simultaneous sovereign debt and currency crises. Its effects on the budget—and therefore on the likelihhod of a sovereign debt crisis—would be magnified through direct effects on debt service obligations.
- An exogenous "sudden stop" in capital inflows may trigger a currency crisis in a country with a large current account deficit, a large stock of short-maturity external debt, and an insufficient stock of foreign exchange reserves. To the extent that the government is exposed to liquidity risk on its foreign-currency-denominated debt, it may be unable to continue to service its debt, resulting in a debt crisis.

Causation from Sovereign Debt Crises to Currency Crises

- Even short of an actual default, a precarious fiscal position for the domestic government is likely to create the fear of some type of capital levy on assets located within the domestic political jurisdiction, inducing investors to withdraw funds from the country, potentially culminating in a currency crisis.
- An actual default may be interpreted as a signal by markets that the domestic economy is weaker than had previously been thought (as in the signaling mechanism described above), leading to capital outflows and potential currency crises.

- Moreover, an actual default may itself create such weakness, by causing a severe recession through increases in domestic interest rates and a fiscal contraction. Again, this could give rise to a currency crisis through a second-generation channel, as described above.

Causation from Currency Crises to Sovereign Debt Crises

- Speculative attacks tend to raise domestic interest rates as the central bank attempts to support the domestic currency. This puts pressure on the budget, threatening the government's ability to service its debt, both by increasing the cost of servicing the government's short-term debt as well as through the adverse effects of recession on government revenues.
- Using the simple test of debt sustainability that compares Δ to Δ_{MAX}, a real exchange rate devaluation produced by a currency crisis could call the government's solvency into question through debt valuation effects. The sustainability calculation is affected as follows. The maximum value of the government's adjusted primary surplus may be a function of the real exchange rate, depending on the traded-nontraded composition of the government's expenditures and revenues, so $\Delta_{MAX} = \Delta_{MAX}(e) = \hat{\sigma}_{MAX}(e)/(r-n)$. A government with primarily domestic currency-denominated revenues, but with substantial expenditures in foreign exchange, would therefore find its maximum sustainable debt contracting in the event of a real exchange-rate depreciation. At the same time, the actual debt/GDP ratio is given by $\Delta = (B + eB^*)/(Y_N + eY_T)$, where B and B^* are respectively the government's domestic- and foreign currency-denominated debt, while Y_N and Y_T are respectively domestic production of nontraded and traded goods. Thus, if the government has a large stock of debt denominated in foreign currency and the economy is relatively closed (has a small traded goods sector), the debt to GDP ratio will rise, potentially exceeding Δ_{MAX}.

The upshot is that through several of these mechanisms, currency crises and sovereign debt crises are likely to be closely related. Dreher et al. (2006) provide empirical evidence on the strength of these links, based on a panel of eighty developing countries, using data spanning the period 1975–2000. Their indicator of debt servicing problems was an index based on the ratio of interest and principal arrears relative to total debt service due, while their indicator of currency crises was based on an index of exchange market pressure. They defined a debt crisis as occurring when interest and principal arrears were at least 75 percent of debt service due, and a currency crisis as a situation where the exchange market pressure index was more than one standard deviation from its mean. This resulted in 280 debt and 179 currency crises in their sample, with 34 cases of both at the same time.

Dreher et al. noted that sovereign debt and currency crises were closely related in their sample, with causality tests revealing bidirectional causality between the two types of crises. They set out to examine whether this was due to common factors driving both types of crises or from causation running from one type of crisis to the other. To do so, they began by exploring the factors that tended to predict each type of crisis. They initially considered fifty-one potential explanatory variables for the incidence of debt and currency crises, but factor analysis revealed that these variables tended to fall into four main categories: (*a*) checks and balances in the political system, (*b*) economic policy and outcomes, (*c*) the amount and structure of debt, and (*d*) trade. They adopted a fixed effects panel estimation procedure using annual observations to explain the incidence of each type of crisis separately. They followed an iterative procedure to find the best specification: they chose two members from each of the four categories of variables initially, replaced them with other covariates from the group, and retained those with the highest number of significant coefficients. They dropped variables that did not have a coefficient that was significant at the 5 percent level in more than a third of the regressions.

This procedure led to the selection of very different determinants of debt and currency crises, pointing to the conclusion that their correlation is *not* driven by common causes. Currency crises tended to be predicted by contemporaneous debt problems, by the ratio of the government's budget balance to GDP, the black market premium, the ratio of public and guaranteed debt to GDP, the ratio of debt service to exports, a dummy for a military chief executive, and a dummy for whether the observation was for an election year. Sovereign debt crises, on the other hand, were explained by exchange market pressure, by the share of multilateral debt in total debt (with a positive sign), by the ratio of debt to GDP, the ratio of exports to GDP, the presence of capital account restrictions (with a positive sign), the number of years the chief executive had been in office, an index of polarization between the party controlling the executive and the other principal parties in the legislature, and by the degree of democracy (with a positive sign). Overall, their findings suggested that sovereign debt crises helped explain currency crises and vice versa, rather than that both types of crises resulting from common shocks.

Appendix
Determinants of Sovereign Debt Crises: The Evidence

There is a large literature that examines the empirical determinants of sovereign defult episodes based on panel data. Because, as suggested in this chapter, the benefits and costs of defaulting may both depend in complicated ways of a large number of economic and political variables, this literature has, not surprisingly, found a large number of potential correlates of default. In this appendix we provide a brief overview of this literature.

As noted in section 2, theory suggests that solvency depends on the level of debt Δ, as well as on the factors that affect the maximum amount of debt that the government can sustain under normal conditions, Δ_{MAX}. In turn, the latter consist of the interest rate at which the government can borrow r, the economy's long-run growth rate n, and the factors that affect the government's long-run fiscal and monetary program, $\hat{\sigma}$. Notice some implications:

- The ratio of gross debt to GDP is a poor indicator of solvency, because it excludes government assets and neglects the determinants of Δ_{MAX}.
- The ratio of *net* government debt to GDP is also not a good indicator, because it neglects the determinants of Δ_{MAX}.
- Because solvency depends on ability as well as willingness to pay, the range of potential solvency "fundamentals" influencing the default decision is broad, encompassing both economic and political factors.

Given the debt/GDP ratio, therefore, a large class of "deep" variables could in principle affect fiscal solvency. These include (*a*) domestic political economy variables, such as inequality, ethnic fragmentation, the electoral system (winner-take-all vs. proportional representation), and the electoral cycle (years till next presidential election); (*b*) institutional structure, including fiscal institutions (hierarchical vs. collegial budget formulation and approval) and fiscal dominance (central bank independence, exchange rate regime); (*c*) structural economic variables, including commercial openness, the composition of expenditures (productive vs. unproductive), the efficiency of the tax system, and the composition of government debt (maturity, currency composition); (*d*) fiscal history, including past history of default and past history of inflation; and (*e*) the external economic environment, including the nternational risk-free interest rate, the international price of risk, and the terms of trade.

Before turning to the evidence, it is useful to review some stylized facts. The IMF's April 2003 WEO made the following empirical observations:

a. As of that time, there had been no industrial-country defaults in the post-war period. The global financial crisis has since made it clear, however, that high-income countries are not invulnerable to default.
b. Among developing-country defaulters, debt-to-GDP ratios have often been low at the time of default. Over the preceding thirty years, 55 percent of defaults occurred with debt-to-GDP ratios below 0.6, and 35 percent with ratios below 0.4. The median ratio in the year of default was 0.5.
c. Although debt ratios have often been low at the time of default, defaulters have tended to have higher debt ratios than nondefaulters, higher ratios of debt to government revenues, higher ratios of external to total debt, and lower ratios of M2 to GDP (as a measure of financial development).

A more systematic study was conducted by Reinhart et al. (2003), who coined the term *debt intolerance* to refer to country characteristics that made it unlikely that a government would be able to sustain high levels of public sector debt. They argued that sustainable debt-to-GDP ratios are determined by two key variables: the country's past history of default and its history of high inflation. Reinhart et al. maintained that previous defaults and a history of past inflation made countries unable to sustain high levels of debt (thus rendering them "debt intolerant"), because creditors would not be confident that the governments involved would be willing to make the fiscal sacrifices necessary to service high levels of debt. This would be true whether these characteristics served as indicators of endemically weak fiscal discipline, or whether they reflected the implications of past crises for growth and tax revenues. They claimed that these two variables explained why emerging-market economies were forced to sustain lower debt levels than industrial countries.

Other types of evidence rely on measures of ex ante risk in the form of sovereign bond spreads and credit ratings. An early and well-known study by Borio and Packer (2004), for instance, sought to explain the variation in sovereign credit ratings across countries and over time for fifty-two countries, using annual data from 1996 to 2003. They found that ratings were affected by income per capita, inflation, the growth rate, an index of corruption, an index of political risk, the country's default history (the number of years since the last default), its high inflation history (the number of years in the past twenty-five with inflation above 40 percent), country size (potentially an indicator of diversification or liquidity), and a proxy for currency mismatches. The debt to GDP and external debt to export ratios mattered only for emerging market economies.

Another approach has consisted of attempts to explain the default experience ex post, in the form of default prediction equations. Several studies draw their data from eighty-four episodes of foreign default (missed interest and/or principal payments, outright repudiation) identified by Standard and Poors from 1974 to 2002. Several prominent studies provide the flavor of the relevant findings.

Ades et. al. (2000) examined the experience of fifteen emerging economies with data after 1996. They found that the probability of default was influenced both by solvency-related indicators as well as by liquidity-related ones. Among the solvency indicators, measures of real GDP growth, of the government's budget balance and of the ratio of exports to GDP all reduced the probability of default, while the ratio of debt to GDP, a measure of real exchange-rate overvaluation, and a past history of default all increased it. Among liquidity indicators, measures of global liquidity (as measured by international interest rates) reduced the probability of default, while the country's ratio of external debt amortization to reserves increased it.

Easterly (2001) looked directly at the size of the required fiscal adjustment as a determinant of debt crises (defined as reschedulings), rather than looking at "deep" determinants as in Borio and Packer. He used a cross-section sample of forty-nine developing countries. His dependent variable was the number of debt reschedulings from 1980 to 1994. He regressed this on the actual adjusted primary surplus ratio (including aid, the grant element of concessional financing, and seigniorage), and on a constant times the debt to GDP ratio and the product of the growth rate and the debt to GDP ratio. He instrumented for the primary surplus and for the product of growth and the debt to GDP ratio using initial debt, partner-country growth, and dummies for Africa and Latin America. All three variables carried the predicted signs and proved to be statistically significant in GMM estimates, but not always in the single-equation estimates.

Detragiache and Spilimbergo (2002) examined the experience of sixty-nine high-income and developing countries over the period 1971–1998. They classified an observation as a default episode when arrears on obligations toward commercial creditors exceeded 5 percent of commercial debt and there was a rescheduling or debt restructuring agreement. Like Ades et al., they found that both solvency and liquidity measures proved statistically significant in explaining the incidence of such episodes in their sample. The former included the ratio of debt to GDP, a measure of real exchange rate overvaluation, and the ratio of multilateral debt in total debt, all of which increased the probability of default, which was also increased by liquidity measures such as the magnitudes of short-term debt and of debt service due. On the other hand, a higher level of foreign exchange reserves tended to reduce the probability of default.

Manasse et al. (2003) considered governments to be in default if they were classified that way by Standard and Poors or if the relevant country was granted access to nonconcessional IMF loans in excess of 100 percent of its quota with the Fund. Based on the experience of forty-seven countries since 1970, they found that solvency indicators such as the ratio of debt to GDP and of debt to reserves were statistically significant in explaining default episodes, as was the amount of interest due on short-term debt as a liquidity indicator. Manasse et al. also looked at the effects of other country characteristics, finding that the probability of default was increased by past inflation volatility, by the number of years with inflation rates in excess of 50 percent, and by whether a presidential election was being held in the year in question. On the other hand, greater commercial openness tended to reduce the probability of default.

Pescatori and Sy (2004) also classified governments as in default if they were classified as being in default by Standard and Poors, but they also treated instances in which sovereign bond spreads exceeded a threshold (usually 1,000 basis points) as default episodes. Like others, they found that the ratio of debt to GDP, a measure of overvaluation, and a high ratio of short-term debt to reserves all increased the probability of default, while higher real GDP growth and a higher degree of commercial openness reduced it. They also found that past defaults were predictors of future defaults.

Finally, Manasse and Roubini (2005) defined a debt crisis year as one in which Standard and Poors classified a government as in default on interest or principal, or in which the country drew on nonconcessional Fund resources in excess of 100 percent of quota (first disbursement). Using annual observations for the period 1970–2002 for forty-seven developing countries, they found ten variables that proved to be significant predictors of default. The ratio of external debt to GDP, the ratio of government external debt to revenues, measures of real exchange rate overvaluation and of exchange rate volatility, the rate of inflation, the ratios of short-term debt as well as of the current account deficit to reserves, and the U.S. Treasury bill rate, all tended to increase the probability of default, while the growth rate and the number of years until the next presidential election tended to reduce it.

These diverse studies thus provide fairly consistent evidence: higher probabilities of default are associated with larger debt stocks as measured by debt to GDP or debt to export ratios, with larger fiscal deficits, with a prior history of difficulty in making fiscal adjustments, as indicated by high inflation rates or previous defaults, with overvalued real exchange rates (which may be associated with high real interest rates), with inadequate liquidity in the form of high ratios of short-term debt and current account deficits to reserves, with political pressures created by upcoming elections, and with an adverse external environment in the form of high international interest rates.

Chapter 17

Macroeconomic Policies and Growth

The wide dispersion of output growth rates across countries, rich and poor, is a well-documented economic fact. Countries that at one time had similar levels of per capita income have subsequently followed very divergent patterns, with some seemingly caught in an "underdevelopment trap," or long-term stagnation, and others able to sustain high growth rates. The contrast between the postwar experiences of the developing countries of Asia and Africa is particularly striking in this regard. In 1960, average real per capita incomes in Asian and African countries were roughly similar. Thirty years later, income per capita had more than tripled in Asia while it had risen only moderately in Africa.[1] Within developing regions, disparities have also continued to widen across countries.

Traditional neoclassical approaches, which attribute growth to exogenous technological progress, are incapable of explaining the wide disparities in the pace of economic growth across countries. Since the late 1980s, considerable effort has been devoted to understanding the sources of growth and explaining the divergent patterns observed across countries. This research has highlighted the existence of a variety of "endogenous" mechanisms that foster economic growth, and has suggested new roles for public policy.[2] This literature has expanded at a rapid pace, and it is impossible within the context of this book to provide a comprehensive overview of the different approaches that have been developed.[3] We review in this chapter some of the salient features of the "new growth" literature and its implications for

---

[1] Among the "Four Tigers" (Hong Kong, South Korea, Singapore, and Taiwan) alone, real income per capita increased more than fourfold between 1960 and 1990.

[2] The revival of growth theory can be attributed largely to the influential contributions of Lucas (1988), Grossman and Helpman (1991), and Romer (1986).

[3] Barro and Sala-i-Martin (2003) provide a comprehensive overview of the new economics of growth, whereas Agénor (2004*b*) offers a discussion that is more focused on the experience of (and challenges faced by) developing countries.

the effects of macroeconomic policies on the growth process. Section 1 provides a brief review of the neoclassical growth model and examines the available evidence, based on the methodology derived from the neoclassical approach, on the sources of growth in developing countries. Section 2 presents the so-called AK model of endogenous growth, which assumes constant returns to scale in capital. Section 3 discusses interactions between human capital, knowledge, and growth. The links between government spending (and capital), taxes, and growth are taken up in Section 4. Interactions between financial intermediation and growth, and between inflation, macroeconomic volatility, and growth, are discussed in Sections 5, 6, and 7. The final section reviews the recent literature on middle-income growth traps—an issue that has attracted much attention in recent years. In the process, some of the relevant econometric evidence is reviewed, and a short methodological comment on the empirical literature is offered in conclusion.

1   The Neoclassical Growth Model

The neoclassical growth model was developed by Solow (1956) and Swan (1956). It is built upon an aggregate, constant-returns-to-scale production function that combines labor and capital (with diminishing marginal returns) in the production of a composite good. Savings are assumed to be a fixed fraction of output, and technology improves at an exogenous rate. Let Y denote total output, L the number of workers employed in the production process, K the capital stock, and suppose that the production function is Cobb-Douglas, so that

$$Y = AK^{\alpha}L^{1-\alpha}, \quad 0 < \alpha < 1,$$

where A measures the level of technology. Output per worker, $y = Y/L$, is thus given by

$$y = Ak^{\alpha}, \tag{1}$$

where k denotes the capital-labor ratio.

Capital accumulation is given by

$$\dot{k} = sy - (n + \delta)k, \quad 0 < s, \delta < 1, \tag{2}$$

where s denotes the propensity to save, $n > 0$ the exogenous rate of population growth, and δ the rate of depreciation of physical capital. Equation (2) incorporates the equilibrium condition of the goods market or, equivalently, the equality between investment I and saving, $I = sy$.

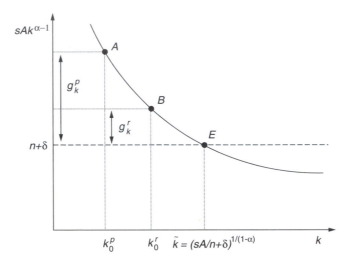

Figure 17–1 ▪ Capital Accumulation in the Solow-Swan Growth Model

Suppose for the moment that A is constant over time. Substituting (1) in (2) and dividing both sides of the resulting expression by k yields the growth rate of the capital-labor ratio, g_k:

$$\mathbf{g_k} \equiv \dot{k}/k = s\,Ak^{\alpha-1} - (n+\delta), \tag{3}$$

from which the rate of growth of output per worker can be derived as

$$\mathbf{g_y} \equiv \dot{y}/y = \alpha\dot{k}\,Ak^{\alpha-1}/Ak^{\alpha} = \alpha g_k.$$

The behavior of the capital stock per worker is illustrated in Figure 17.1. The horizontal line at $n+\delta$ is the *depreciation line*, whereas the curve $s\,Ak^{\alpha-1}$ can be labeled the *savings curve*. The assumption of decreasing marginal returns to capital ensures that the savings curve is downward-sloping. As implied by (3), the growth rate of the capital-labor ratio is the difference between the two curves. The point of intersection of the two curves determines the steady-state value of the capital-labor ratio.[4]

More generally, if technology (like population) grows at a constant rate, it can be shown that in the Solow-Swan model the steady-state values of output per effective worker and the capital/effective labor ratio are also constant and proportional to the rate of (labor-augmenting) technological change. Although the saving rate has no effect in the long run on the growth rate per capita, it affects (positively) the *level* of

---

[4]Under the standard *Inada conditions*, the savings curve is vertical at $k = 0$ and approaches the horizontal axis for $k \to \infty$. Because the savings curve takes all values between zero and infinity, it must cross the depreciation line at least once; and because the savings curve is downward-sloping over the entire interval $(0, \infty)$, it crosses the depreciation line only once. See Agénor (2004b, chapter 11) for more details.

per capita income in the steady state.[5] In addition, the model implies that countries with similar production technologies as well as comparable saving and population growth rates should converge to similar steady-state levels of per capita income. This convergence property means that poor countries starting with a relatively low standard of living and a lower capital/labor ratio will grow faster during the transition as they catch up with the rich countries, but ultimately both groups will arrive at the same level of per capita income.[6] As illustrated in Figure 17.1, a "poor" country starting with a capital stock of k_0^p has a higher initial growth rate (as given by the distance $\mathbf{g}_k^p$) than a "rich" country starting with a capital stock of k_0^r and a growth rate of $\mathbf{g}_k^r$. The poor country will grow faster than the rich country during the transition. Nevertheless, if both countries possess the same level of technology, A, the same saving rate, s, the same depreciation rate, δ, and the same population growth rate, n, they will both converge to the same steady-state level of the capital stock, $\bar{k}$ (point E). Intuitively, convergence occurs because, with diminishing marginal returns to capital, each increment to the capital stock generates large additions to output when the capital stock is initially small. The reverse holds when the capital stock is initially large.

The neoclassical growth model led to the "sources-of-growth" approach, a popular empirical methodology aimed at analyzing the determinants of changes in output. The approach uses an aggregate production function to decompose growth into "contributions" from different sources, namely, the growth rates of factor inputs weighted by their competitive factor shares (the "contribution" of factors), plus a residual. This residual is often labeled "technical progress," but it is more adequately described as the difference between the growth of output and a weighted sum of the growth of inputs, that is, the growth in total factor productivity.

Formally, assume that the production function takes the form $y = Af(k, n)$.[7] In terms of percentage changes, we have

$$\mathbf{g} \equiv \dot{y}/y = \frac{\dot{A}}{A} + Af_k\frac{\dot{k}}{y} + Af_n\frac{\dot{n}}{y} = \mathbf{g}_A + \alpha_k\mathbf{g}_k + \alpha_n\mathbf{g}_n, \tag{4}$$

where $\alpha_h = f_h h/y$ (for $h = k, n$) denotes the elasticity of output with respect to input h. In this expression, $\mathbf{g}_A$ is the rate of growth of total factor productivity

---

[5] Changes in the saving rate also affect the rate of growth in the short run. But in the long run, a rise in the saving rate leads only to a proportional increase in the capital/output ratio.

[6] This implication of the neoclassical growth model holds regardless of whether countries are closed or open to international trade. The model also predicts that convergence may occur more rapidly if countries are open and have access to international capital markets. The relative scarcity of capital and the lower capital-labor ratio in poor countries entails a higher rate of return to capital, leading to capital inflows, accelerated capital accumulation, and higher growth. But if a country can only borrow to finance part of its capital (for instance, if investment in human capital must be financed by domestic savings), the open-economy version of the neoclassical growth model yields essentially the same convergence rate as the closed-economy model. See Barro and Sala-i-Martin (2003).

[7] Technical progress is thus assumed to be "Hicks neutral," in the sense that it raises the output achievable with a given combination of capital and labor without affecting their relative marginal products.

and is derived as a residual. Under conditions of competitive equilibrium, factors are paid their marginal products. The coefficient α_n (α_k) is thus equal to the share of labor (capital) income in total output. In the presence of constant returns to scale, the sum of all share coefficients must be equal to unity. With a Cobb-Douglas production technology as described in (1), assuming that factors of production are paid their marginal products implies that $\alpha = \alpha_k = 1 - \alpha_n$, and that labor's share α_n corresponds to the parameter $1 - \alpha$.

The hypotheses of a constant-returns-to-scale aggregate production function and competitive (and integrated) factor markets are restrictive, particularly in a developing-country context. But although growth accounting techniques cannot be taken too literally, they can be suggestive. In fact, a large number of studies based on the sources-of-growth methodology have been conducted in industrial and developing nations over the years. Elías (1992), for instance, examines the growth process in seven Latin American countries (Argentina, Brazil, Chile, Colombia, Mexico, Peru, and Venezuela) over the period 1940–1985. His study considers different kinds of labor and capital inputs, and he defines a gross and quality component for each of them. In the case of labor, the gross component is the arithmetic sum of employment across characteristics (such as education, sex, and age), whereas for capital it is the arithmetic sum of different categories of capital. The quality component of each input is established by considering their diverse characteristics.[8] The quality component thus captures changes in the composition of factors of production over time. Evidence for a broader group of developing countries is provided by Bosworth and Collins (2003), whereas Bosworth and Collins (2008) use the growth-accounting methodology to perform a comparative analysis of the growth performance of China and India during the period 1978–2004.

In the neoclassical growth model reviewed above, capital exhibits diminishing marginal returns in the production process. This feature of the model prevents it from providing an explanation for the wide and persistent variations across countries in growth rates mentioned earlier. Indeed, the neoclassical growth model predicts only *conditional* convergence, that is, a tendency for per capita income to converge across countries only after controlling for the determinants of the steady-state level of income-saving and population growth rates. The absence of a significant correlation between the growth rate of per capita income and the level of income at a base period cannot, therefore, be construed as evidence against the convergence hypothesis. In fact, recent work has found significant evidence in support of conditional convergence; see Barro and Sala-i-Martin (2003) for a review and Barro (2012), who finds a conditional convergence rate of around 2 percent per annum. However, Quah (1996), and more recently Huang (2005),

---

[8]The rate of change of the quality of labor is determined as the weighted sum of the rates of change in each characteristic considered for the composition of the labor force. The weights are the ratio of the unit wage of each kind of labor to the average wage rate for the whole labor force. A similar procedure is used to derive the rate of change of the quality component of the capital stock.

using nonlinear estimation techniques, suggest that countries tend to converge in groups (convergence clubs), in contrast to results obtained based on linear cross-country growth regressions.

In addition, in the neoclassical model output growth in the long run is independent of the saving rate and determined only by demographic factors (the rate of population growth) and the rate of technological progress. But because population growth and technological change are assumed exogenous, the model does not explain the mechanisms that generate steady-state growth, and therefore does not allow an evaluation of the mechanisms through which government policies can potentially influence the growth process. The assumption that the rate of growth of output is independent of the saving rate is also at variance with the evidence, which suggests that high-growth developing countries tend to have markedly higher saving rates (as well as higher investment rates and higher export volume growth rates) than middle- and low-growth countries (see Agénor, 2004b, chapter 10).

The new growth literature addresses these limitations of the neoclassical model by proposing a variety of channels through which steady-state growth arises endogenously. We begin by discussing the role of externalities and the assumption of constant returns to scale in the new theories. We then focus on the role of human capital and knowledge accumulation; the interactions between economic growth and financial development; public policy and growth; and macroeconomic stability, volatility, and growth.

2 The *AK* Model of Endogenous Growth

Two broad approaches have been followed in the new growth literature to relax the assumption of diminishing returns to capital imposed in the basic neoclassical growth model. The first consists of viewing all production inputs as some form of reproducible capital, including not only physical capital (as emphasized in the basic neoclassical framework), but other types as well, especially human capital (Lucas, 1988) or the "state of knowledge" (Romer, 1986). A simple growth model along these lines is the so-called *AK* model proposed by Rebelo (1991), which results from setting $\alpha = 0$ in (1):

$$y = Ak, \tag{5}$$

where $k = K/L$ as before, but K now is interpreted as a broad measure of capital—a composite measure of the physical and human capital stock. The production function is thus linear and exhibits constant returns to scale. A is again a parameter that captures factors affecting the level of technology.[9]

---

[9]Another route to obtaining an equation like (5) is to postulate that an increasing variety or quality of machinery or intermediate inputs offsets the propensity to diminishing returns. In this interpretation, K now represents the

Using the capital accumulation (2), the steady-state growth rate of the capital stock per worker can be shown to be equal to

$$\mathbf{g}_k = sA - (n + \delta),$$

with the steady-state growth rate per capita given by

$$\mathbf{g}_y = sA - (n + \delta), \tag{6}$$

which implies that the growth rate is, for $sA > n + \delta$, positive (and constant over time) and that the *level* of income per capita rises without bound. An important implication of the AK model is thus that, in contrast to the neoclassical model, an increase in the saving rate permanently raises the growth rate per capita. In addition—and again in contrast with the neoclassical growth model, which predicts as shown earlier that poor countries should grow faster than rich countries—the AK model implies that poor nations whose production process is characterized by the same degree of technological sophistication as other nations always grow at the same rate as rich countries, regardless of the initial level of income. The AK model thus does *not* predict convergence even if countries share the same technology and are characterized by the same pattern of saving, a result that seems to accord well with the empirical evidence.

The AK model has proved very popular in the endogenous growth literature and has been extended in various directions. Rebelo (1991), for instance, examined the implications of considering separately the production of consumption goods, physical capital, and human capital goods. His analysis demonstrates, in particular, that endogenous steady-state growth obtains if a "core" of capital goods is produced according to a constant-returns-to-scale technology and without the use of nonreproducible factors. Put differently, to obtain positive growth requires only that there exist a subset of capital goods whose production takes place under constant returns to scale and does not require the use of nonreproducible inputs.

The second approach to generating growth endogenously consists of introducing spillover effects or externalities in the growth process. The presence of externalities implies that if, say, one firm doubles its inputs, the productivity of the inputs of other firms will also increase. Introducing spillover effects leads to a relaxation of the assumption of diminishing returns to capital.[10] In most models, externalities take the form of general technological knowledge that is available to all firms, which use it

---

variety or quality of inputs. Research and development are necessary to obtain this variety, and firms devote skilled labor to this activity. In order to ensure that outlays for research and development that generate these inputs are recuperated (in the form of rents) by firms that engage in such activities, markets are assumed to be monopolistically competitive. See Grossman and Helpman (1991) and Romer (1990).

[10] A critical difference between this class of models and those based on reproducible capital is that the existence of externalities often results in suboptimality of the competitive equilibrium, creating the scope for welfare-improving government intervention. See the subsequent discussion of the Lucas model.

to develop new methods of production. An exception to this specification is Lucas (1988), where externalities take the form of public learning, which increases the stock of human capital and affects the productivity of all factors of production.[11] Another exception is Barro (1990), who introduces externalities associated with public spending (or public capital, as discussed later).

The presence of externalities is closely associated with the existence of increasing returns to scale in the production function. However, an important implication of the above description is that in models exhibiting spillover effects and externalities, sustained growth does not result from the existence of external effects, but rather from the assumption of constant returns to scale in all production inputs that can be accumulated. As emphasized by Rebelo (1991), increasing returns are thus neither necessary nor sufficient to generate endogenous growth.

3 ▪ Human Capital, Knowledge, and Growth

3.1 ▪ The Production of Human Capital

One particular source of externalities that has been emphasized in the recent growth literature is the accumulation of human capital and its effect on the productivity of the economy. The evidence suggests indeed that human capital per worker—measured by average years of educational attainment—has risen dramatically throughout the world (Jones and Romer, 2010). Lucas (1988) provides one of the best-known attempts to incorporate the spillover effects of human capital accumulation, in a model built upon the idea that individual workers are more productive, regardless of their skill level, if other workers have more human capital.

A simplified presentation of Lucas's model is as follows.[12] Human capital is accumulated through explicit "production": a part of individuals' working time is devoted to accumulation of skills. Formally, let k denote physical capital per worker and h human capital per worker or, more generally, "knowledge" capital. The production process is described by

$$y = Ak^{\sigma}[uh]^{1-\sigma}, \quad 0 < u < 1, \tag{7}$$

where u denotes the fraction of time that individuals devote to producing goods, with the remainder, $1 - u$, allocated to producing human capital. As before, the growth of

---

[11] A taxonomic presentation of the alternative approaches aimed at incorporating externalities and increasing returns to scale in the growth literature is provided by Verspagen (1992). He also discusses various approaches to modeling the innovation process, among others the "quality ladder" concept of Grossman and Helpman (1991).

[12] Lucas's (1988) original formulation is cast in an optimizing framework in which private agents determine their consumption path by maximizing their utility subject to an intertemporal resource constraint. The main point of his analysis, however, can be made by assuming a constant saving rate, as in Lucas (1993).

physical capital depends on the saving rate ($I = sy$), while the growth rate of human capital is determined by the amount of time devoted to its production:

$$\dot{h}/h = \alpha(1-u), \quad \alpha > 0. \tag{8}$$

In this economy, the long-run growth rate of both capital and output per worker is $\alpha(1-u)$, the rate of human capital growth, and the ratio of physical to human capital converges to a constant. In the long run, the level of income is proportional to the economy's initial stock of human capital. In this particular formulation, the saving rate has no effect on the growth rate.

The important implication of the external effect captured in the model presented by Lucas (1988) is that under a purely competitive equilibrium its presence leads to an underinvestment in human capital because private agents do not take into account the external benefits of human capital accumulation. The equilibrium growth rate is thus smaller than the optimal growth rate, due to the existence of externalities. Because the equilibrium growth rate depends on the rate of investment in human capital, the externality implies that growth would be higher with more investment in human capital. This leads to the conclusion that government policies (subsidies) are necessary to increase the equilibrium growth rate up to the level of the optimal growth rate. A government subsidy to human capital formation or schooling could potentially result in a substantial increase in the rate of economic growth.[13]

3.2 ■ The Production of Knowledge

An alternative approach to assessing the role played by external effects in the growth process was proposed by Romer (1986). In his framework the source of the externality is the stock of knowledge rather than an aggregate stock of human capital. Knowledge is produced by individuals, but because newly produced knowledge can be, at best, only partially and temporarily kept secret, the production of goods and services depends not only on private knowledge but also on the aggregate stock of knowledge.[14] Firms or individuals only partially reap the rewards to the production of knowledge, and so a market equilibrium results in an underinvestment in knowledge accumulation. To the extent that knowledge can be related to the level of technology, Romer's framework can be viewed as an attempt to determine endogenously the rate of technological progress. In subsequent work, Romer (1990) also explained endogenously the decision to invest in technological change, using a model based on a

---

[13]Lucas (1988) also develops a second model that assumes a different structure of technological change. In this alternative framework all human capital accumulation occurs through on-the-job training, or learning by doing, rather than through the time allocated by workers to this accumulation. Thus, it is the time devoted directly to production activities that determines the rate of growth.

[14]The existence of knowledge externalities poses the question of whether there is an incentive to produce innovation. Romer assumes that firms or individuals engaged in the production of knowledge enjoy some degree of monopoly power (through, say, patent protection) that ensures temporary appropriability.

distinction between a research sector and the rest of the economy. In that framework, firms cannot appropriate all the benefits of knowledge production, implying that the social rate of return exceeds the private rate of return to certain forms of capital accumulation. A tax and subsidy scheme can thus be utilized to raise the rate of growth. As shown by David Romer (2000*b*, chapter 3) in a simplified version of Romer's (1990) model, accounting for the existence of a knowledge-producing sector may help explain the positive correlation between savings rates and the rate of economic growth suggested by the empirical evidence—a phenomenon that, as noted earlier, the standard Solow-Swan model is unable to explain.

4   Government Spending, Taxes, and Growth

As emphasized in the third part of this book, inflation stabilization implies the need for the reduction of fiscal deficits. But deficits also affect growth. Adam and Bevan (2005), for instance, using panel data for forty-five low- and middle-income developing countries over the period 1970–1999, found a nonlinear relationship between these two variables. Payoffs tend to be significant when reducing deficits from above a threshold level of 1.5 percent of GDP. The magnitude of this payoff depends in part on how deficits are reduced, that is, by decreasing expenditures or increasing revenue. The difference between these two approaches to fiscal adjustment is, of course, the resulting size of the government sector. Does it make a difference for the subsequent performance of long-run economic growth which of the two approaches is undertaken—that is, does the size of government have any direct relationship with the long-run rate of economic growth?

There are analytical reasons to believe that it might. In particular, holding the fiscal deficit constant, larger government expenditures imply the need for additional revenues. Because such revenues would be raised through distortionary taxation, this would be expected to reduce the rate of growth through adverse effects on the efficiency of resource allocation. At the same time, some government expenditure may be directly productive. Government expenditures on health and education, for instance, may best be interpreted as investments in human capital. Other government expenditures may represent investment in "social capital" in the form of institutions that safeguard property rights. This reasoning suggests that both the level and composition of government expenditures may matter for long-term growth. Moreover, to the extent that productive expenditures are financed through distortionary taxes, the effect of larger government on long-term growth is theoretically ambiguous.

The accumulation of physical capital by the government can have important effects on growth. One possible channel through which such effects may occur is through the complementarity between some components of public capital (most importantly in infrastructure, as noted in Chapter 2) and private investment. In this section we present two models that illustrate well the role of fiscal policy in promoting growth. The first is a seminal contribution by Barro (1990), which treats public spending (say, infrastructure services) as a flow input in private production. The second is a simplified version of a more complex endogenous growth model due to Agénor (2008), which accounts for accumulation of both public and private capital. The model builds on Barro's contribution and also treats infrastructure services as a flow rather than a stock (which would include roads, airports, etc.).[15] In addition, however, public spending on infrastructure has an impact on growth by affecting health outcomes, and health in turn affects the productivity of workers in production. The evidence does suggest that access to clean water and sanitation, in particular, helps to improve health and thereby productivity. By reducing the cost of boiling water, and reducing the need to rely on smoky traditional fuels (such as wood, crop residues, and charcoal) for cooking, access to electricity also helps to improve hygiene and health—in the latter case by reducing indoor air pollution and the incidence of respiratory illnesses. Availability of electricity is essential as well for the functioning of hospitals (storing some types of vaccines requires continuous and reliable refrigeration, for instance) and the delivery of health services. Better transportation networks (particularly in rural areas) make it easier to access health care and to attract (or retain) qualified medical workers.

After describing the model (assuming initially that health services are produced using flow spending on health) we solve for the decentralized equilibrium. We then solve for optimal policies, that is, the growth- and welfare-maximizing tax rate and spending allocation between health and infrastructure. We then extend the analysis to treat the production of health services as a function of public capital in health, and show how the model can generate transitional dynamics. Finally, we examine the growth effects of a revenue-neutral shift in government spending from health to infrastructure.

4.1 ■ The Barro Model

Barro (1990) developed a model that illustrates well the dual effects of taxation on growth. The key idea of the model is that the flow of government spending, G, has a positive effect on private production. Assuming that employment is constant and normalized at unity, the production function for each individual (and identical) firm can be specified as

$$Y = AG^\alpha K^{1-\alpha}, \quad 0 < \alpha < 1, \tag{9}$$

where K is the capital stock. This specification implies that for each firm h, the production function exhibits constant returns to G and K_h.

---

[15]Futagami et al. (1993) extended Barro's analysis to include the *stock* of public capital, rather than the flow of government spending, in the production function.

Suppose that the government runs a balanced budget financed by a proportional tax on output, $\tau \in (0, 1)$. Normalizing the number of firms to unity, the government budget constraint is

$$G = \tau Y. \tag{10}$$

The household maximizes the discounted present value of utility

$$\max_C V = \int_0^\infty \frac{C^{1-1/\sigma}}{1 - 1/\sigma} \exp(-\rho t) dt, \tag{11}$$

subject to the resource constraint

$$C + \dot{K}_P = (1 - \tau)Y, \tag{12}$$

where C denotes consumption and K_P the private capital stock. $\sigma > 0$ is the intertemporal elasticity of substitution. For simplicity, the depreciation rate of private capital is assumed to be zero.

Given that G rises along with the aggregate private capital stock and that the individual firm's production function exhibits constant returns to G and K, the model produces endogenous steady-state growth. Barro shows that in fact the economy's growth rate of output is given by

$$\mathbf{g} = \sigma [\alpha A^{1/(1-\alpha)} \tau^{\alpha/(1-\alpha)} (1 - \tau) - \rho], \tag{13}$$

where ρ is the subjective rate of time preference. Equation (13) shows that the effect of government spending on growth operates through two channels:[16] the term $1 - \tau$, which represents the negative effect of taxation on the after-tax marginal product of capital; and the term $\tau^{\alpha/(1-\alpha)}$, which represents the positive effect of the provision of public services on the after-tax marginal product of capital.

Expression (11) implies therefore that the growth rate rises at first with increases in the tax rate (with the positive effect dominating the negative effect), reaches a maximum at τ^*, and then begins to decrease with further rises in the tax rate, as illustrated in Figure 17.2. Thus, for $\tau > \tau^*$, taxation and government expenditure are inefficient.

The optimal tax rate is such that it maximizes the growth rate given in (13), that is, $d\mathbf{g}/d\tau = 0$. The condition that determines τ^* is thus

$$\frac{d\mathbf{g}}{d\tau} = \alpha A^{1/(1-\alpha)} \tau^{\alpha/(1-\alpha)} \left[\frac{\alpha(1 - \tau)}{(1 - \alpha)\tau} - 1 \right] = 0,$$

which yields

$$\tau^* = \alpha. \tag{14}$$

---

[16]Empirical evidence on these two effects is provided by Cashin (1995).

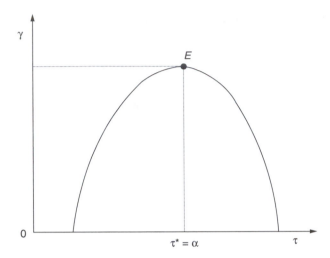

Figure 17–2 ▪ Growth and the Tax Rate in Barro's Model

Thus, the "Barro rule" requires setting the tax rate equal to the elasticity of output with respect to the flow supply of public infrastructure services to maximize growth. Note that, in this model, the optimal tax rate and the optimal share of spending are one and the same, given that there is only one component of public expenditure.

4.2 ▪ Infrastructure, Health, and Growth

Following Agénor (2008), we now extend the foregoing analysis to account for another type of externality associated with public infrastructure, namely, an effect on health outcomes.

Consider an economy with a constant population and an infinitely lived representative household who produces and consumes a single traded good. The good can be used for consumption or investment. The government spends on infrastructure and produces health services, free of charge. It levies a flat tax on output to finance its expenditure.

4.2.1 *Production*

Output, Y, is produced with private physical capital, K_P, public infrastructure services, G_I (consisting of spending on power plants, roads, and so on), and "effective" labor, defined as the product of the quantity of labor and productivity, A. With zero population growth, and the population size normalized again to unity, assuming that the technology is Cobb-Douglas yields

$$Y = G_I^\alpha A^\beta K_P^{1-\alpha-\beta}, \tag{15}$$

where $\alpha, \beta \in (0, 1)$. Health is thus labor-augmenting, as often assumed in micro-level studies of nutrition and labor productivity.

Productivity depends linearly on the supply of health services, H:

$$A = H. \tag{16}$$

Combining (15) and (16) yields

$$Y = \left(\frac{G_I}{K_P}\right)^{\alpha} \left(\frac{H}{K_P}\right)^{\beta} K_P, \tag{17}$$

which implies that in the steady state, with constant ratios of G_I/K_P and H/K_P, the output-capital ratio is also constant; the model therefore behaves as a standard AK framework (see Section 2).

4.2.2 Household Preferences

With C denoting consumption, the household's instantaneous utility function is now given by

$$U = \frac{(C^{\kappa} H^{1-\kappa})^{1-1/\sigma}}{1 - 1/\sigma}, \quad \kappa \in (0, 1), \sigma \neq 1, \tag{18}$$

where $1 - \kappa$ measures the relative contribution of health to utility and $\sigma > 0$ is the intertemporal elasticity of intertemporal substitution. Utility is thus nonseparable in consumption and health services.[17]

The household maximizes the discounted present value of utility

$$\max_C V = \int_0^{\infty} U \exp(-\rho t)dt, \tag{19}$$

subject to a resource constraint similar to (12):

$$C + \dot{K}_P = (1 - \tau)Y, \tag{20}$$

where $\tau \in (0, 1)$ is again the tax rate on income. For simplicity, the depreciation rate of private capital is also assumed to be zero. As in Agénor (2010), the rate of time preference could be assumed to be inversely related to consumption of health services, to capture the fact that healthier individuals are less myopic and tend to value the future more; for simplicity, here we treat ρ as constant.

---

[17]To ensure that the instantaneous utility function has the appropriate concavity properties in C and H, the restriction $\kappa(1 - 1/\sigma) < 1$ must be imposed on σ and κ.

4.2.3 *Production of Health Services*

Production of health services requires combining government spending on both infrastructure and health, G_I and G_H, respectively, with the latter consisting of compensation of medical workers, spending on medicines, and so on. Assuming also a Cobb-Douglas technology yields

$$H = G_I^{\mu} G_H^{1-\mu}, \tag{21}$$

where $\mu \in (0, 1)$. The provision of health services takes place therefore under constant returns to scale.

4.2.4 *Government*

The government spends on infrastructure and health services, and levies a flat tax on output at the rate τ. It cannot issue debt claims and therefore must keep a balanced budget at each moment in time. The government budget constraint is thus given by

$$G_H + G_I = \tau Y. \tag{22}$$

Both categories of spending are taken to be a constant fraction of tax revenue:

$$G_h = \upsilon_h \tau Y, \quad \text{for } h = H, I. \tag{23}$$

The government budget constraint can thus be rewritten as

$$\upsilon_H + \upsilon_I = 1. \tag{24}$$

4.3 ■ The Decentralized Equilibrium

In the present setting, a decentralized equilibrium is a set of infinite sequences for the quantities $\{C, K_P\}_{t=0}^{\infty}$, such that $\{C, K_P\}_{t=0}^{\infty}$ maximizes (19) subject to (20), and the path $\{K_P\}_{t=0}^{\infty}$ satisfies (20), for given values of the tax rate, τ, and the spending shares υ_h, with $h = H, I$, which must also satisfy constraint (24).

This equilibrium can be characterized as follows. The household solves problem (19) subject to (18) and (20), taking the tax rate, τ, and the supply of health services, H, as given. Using (16) and (15), the current-value Hamiltonian for this problem can be written as

$$L = \frac{(C^{\kappa} H^{1-\kappa})^{1-1/\sigma}}{1 - 1/\sigma} + \lambda \left\{ (1 - \tau) \left(\frac{G_I}{K_P} \right)^{\alpha} \left(\frac{H}{K_P} \right)^{\beta} K_P - C \right\},$$

where λ is the costate variable associated with constraint (20). From the first-order condition $dL/dC = 0$ and the co-state condition $\dot{\lambda} = -dL/dK_P + \rho\lambda$, optimality conditions for this problem can be written as, with $s \equiv (1 - \tau)(1 - \alpha - \beta)$,

$$\kappa \left(\frac{H}{C} \right)^{1-\kappa} (C^\kappa H^{1-\kappa})^{-1/\sigma} = \lambda, \tag{25}$$

$$s \left(\frac{G_I}{K_P} \right)^\alpha \left(\frac{H}{K_P} \right)^\beta = s \left(\frac{Y}{K_P} \right) = \rho - \dot{\lambda}/\lambda, \tag{26}$$

together with the budget constraint (20) and the transversality condition

$$\lim_{t \to \infty} \lambda K_P \exp(-\rho t) = 0. \tag{27}$$

Equation (25) can be rewritten as

$$C = (\kappa/\lambda)^{1/[1-\kappa(1-1/\sigma)]} H^{(1-\kappa)(1-1/\sigma)/[1-\kappa(1-1/\sigma)]}.$$

Taking logs of this expression and differentiating with respect to time yields

$$\frac{\dot{C}}{C} = -v_1 \left(\frac{\dot{\lambda}}{\lambda} \right) + v_2 \left(\frac{\dot{H}}{H} \right), \tag{28}$$

where $v_1 \equiv 1/[1 - \kappa(1 - 1/\sigma)] > 0$, and $v_2 \equiv (1 - \kappa)(1 - 1/\sigma)v_1$. Thus, if $\kappa = 1$, this equation yields the familiar result $\dot{C}/C = -\sigma \dot{\lambda}/\lambda$. Note also that $v_2 < 1 \, \forall \sigma \neq 1$, and that $v_1 < 1$, $v_2 < 0$ if $\sigma < 1$.

From (15),

$$\frac{\dot{Y}}{Y} = \alpha \left(\frac{\dot{G}_I}{G_I} \right) + \beta \left(\frac{\dot{H}}{H} \right) + (1 - \alpha - \beta) \left(\frac{\dot{K}_P}{K_P} \right).$$

Using (21), which implies that $\dot{H}/H = \dot{Y}/Y$ (as a result of constant returns to scale) and (23), which also implies that $\dot{G}_I/G_I = \dot{Y}/Y$, yields $\dot{Y}/Y = \dot{K}_P/K_P$. Substituting this result in (28), together with (26), yields

$$\frac{\dot{C}}{C} = v_1 \left\{ s \left(\frac{Y}{K_P} \right) - \rho \right\} + v_2 \left(\frac{\dot{K}_P}{K_P} \right), \tag{29}$$

which can be rewritten as, with $c = C/K_P$:

$$\frac{\dot{c}}{c} = v_1 \left\{ s \left(\frac{Y}{K_P} \right) - \rho \right\} - (1 - v_2) \left(\frac{\dot{K}_P}{K_P} \right). \tag{30}$$

Now, from (17),

$$\frac{Y}{K_P} = \left(\frac{G_I}{Y}\right)^{\alpha/(1-\alpha-\beta)} \left(\frac{H}{Y}\right)^{\beta/(1-\alpha-\beta)},$$

which can be combined with the budget constraint (20) to give

$$\frac{\dot{K}_P}{K_P} = \frac{(1-\tau)Y}{K_P} - c = (1-\tau)\left(\frac{G_I}{Y}\right)^{\alpha/\eta}\left(\frac{H}{Y}\right)^{\beta/\eta} - c, \tag{31}$$

where $\eta \equiv 1 - \alpha - \beta \in (0, 1)$. From (21) and (23),

$$H = (v_I^\mu v_H^{1-\mu})\tau Y, \tag{32}$$

which can be substituted in (31), together with (23), to give

$$\frac{\dot{K}_P}{K_P} = (1-\tau)(v_I\tau)^{\alpha/\eta}[(v_I^\mu v_H^{1-\mu})\tau]^{\beta/\eta} - c = \Lambda - c. \tag{33}$$

Substituting this result in (30) yields the following nonlinear differential equation in c:

$$\frac{\dot{c}}{c} = (1-v_2)c + \left[\frac{s}{1-\tau}v_1 - (1-v_2)\right]\Lambda - v_1\rho. \tag{34}$$

This equation, together with the transversality condition (27), determines the dynamics of the decentralized economy.

On the balanced-growth path (BGP), consumption and the stock of private capital grow at the same constant rate $\gamma = \dot{C}/C = \dot{K}_P/K_P$, so $\dot{c} = 0$. But, given that $v_2 < 1$, the equilibrium is (globally) unstable. Thus, to be on the BGP, the economy must start there.

Setting $\dot{c} = 0$ in (34) yields the economy's steady-state level of the consumption-capital ratio:

$$\tilde{c} = \Lambda + \frac{v_1(\rho - \eta\Lambda)}{1 - v_2}.$$

Substituting this result in (33) yields the steady-state growth rate as

$$\mathbf{g} = \frac{v_1}{1 - v_2}(\eta\Lambda - \rho), \tag{35}$$

which is positive as long as $\rho < \eta\Lambda$. Thus, the model has no transitional dynamics; following a shock, the consumption-capital ratio must jump immediately to its new equilibrium value. It then follows from (35) that the economy is always on its steady-state growth path. Because H/C is constant and $\dot{H}/H = \dot{K}_P/K_P$ along that path, (25) implies that $\dot{\lambda}/\lambda = -\gamma/\sigma$. Thus, the transversality condition (27) is satisfied along the BGP if $\mathbf{g}(1 - 1/\sigma) - \rho < 0$, that is,[18]

$$\rho > \left\{ 1 + \frac{v_1(1 - 1/\sigma)}{1 - v_2} \right\}^{-1} \frac{v_1\eta\Lambda(1 - 1/\sigma)}{1 - v_2}.$$

Noting that $v_1(1 - 1/\sigma)/(1 - v_2) = \sigma - 1$, this expression can be rewritten as

$$\rho > \sigma^{-1}(\sigma - 1)\eta\Lambda. \tag{36}$$

Condition (36) is automatically satisfied if $\sigma \in (0, 1)$. If $\sigma > 1$, it imposes an upper bound on the admissible value of the tax rate or one of the spending shares. Given the evidence discussed in Chapter 11, it will be assumed in what follows that $\sigma < 1$. The transversality condition (27) therefore holds irrespective of the particular values obtained from the analysis of optimal public decisions.

4.4 ▪ Optimal Policies

Consider now the growth and welfare effects of an increase in the tax rate, taking the composition of spending as constant (that is, $d\tau > 0$ and $dv_I = dv_H = 0$), as well as a revenue-neutral shift in government spending from health to infrastructure (that is, $d\tau = 0$ and $dv_I = -dv_H$), assuming that the allocation of spending is set arbitrarily.

Consider first the growth effects. From (35),

$$\text{sg}\left\{ \left. \frac{d\mathbf{g}}{d\tau} \right|_{dv_h=0} \right\} = \text{sg}\left\{ -1 + (1 - \tau)\left(\frac{\alpha + \beta}{\tau\eta} \right) \right\}, \quad h = I, H \tag{37}$$

$$\text{sg}\left\{ \left. \frac{d\mathbf{g}}{dv_I} \right|_{d\tau=0} \right\} = \text{sg}\left\{ \left(\frac{\alpha + \mu\beta}{v_I} \right) - \frac{\beta(1 - \mu)}{v_H} \right\}. \tag{38}$$

Both of these expressions are in general ambiguous. The reason, in the case of an increase in the tax rate, is the trade-off examined by Barro (1990), and discussed earlier, which implies a hump-shaped relationship between τ and γ: at first, a

---

[18]The condition $\rho > \gamma(1 - 1/\sigma)$ is also necessary to guarantee that the integral in (19) remains bounded.

higher tax rate tends to increase growth, because it increases the resources that the government can spend productively. Beyond a certain point, however, further increases in the tax rate tend to deter private capital accumulation and thus to adversely affect the growth rate.

Equation (37) implies that the growth-maximizing tax rate is given by

$$\tau^* = \alpha + \beta. \tag{39}$$

Thus, formula (39) generalizes Barro's tax-and-spending rule (14) to the case where spending on health has a positive effect on the marginal product of capital (by increasing labor productivity), in addition to infrastructure services. It accounts therefore for both *direct* and *indirect* effects of government spending on production.

Consider now a revenue-neutral increase in the share of spending on infrastructure. The ambiguous impact on growth results from two conflicting effects. A rise in the share of spending on infrastructure tends to raise the marginal product of capital, which raises investment and growth, *both* directly and indirectly, through its effect on the production of health services. At the same time, the reduction in public spending on health lowers growth by reducing labor productivity. The net effect depends on the parameters characterizing the technology for producing goods and health services. With $\mu = 0$, for instance, an increase in spending in infrastructure would raise growth if the initial composition of spending υ_I/υ_H exceeds the ratio of elasticities in the production of goods, α/β.

From the budget constraint (24) and (38), the growth-maximizing share of spending on infrastructure can be shown to be

$$\upsilon_I^* = \frac{\alpha + \mu\beta}{\alpha + \beta}, \tag{40}$$

which is in general greater than α. The "strict" Barro rule—which relates the share of spending only to the elasticity of output with respect to infrastructure services, α, as in (14))—is thus suboptimal. In the particular case where $\mu = 0$, that is, the "standard" case where health services are produced only with government spending on health, $\upsilon_I^* = \alpha/(\alpha + \beta)$, which is also greater than α; and with $\mu = 1$, all spending should be allocated to infrastructure ($\upsilon_I^* = 1$).[19] Naturally enough, the higher is the elasticity of output of health services with respect to spending on infrastructure (the higher μ is), the lower should be the share of spending on health.

Consider now the welfare-maximizing allocation. From (20) and (22), the economy's consolidated budget constraint can be written as

$$Y = C + \dot{K}_P + (G_H + G_I),$$

---

[19] See Agénor (2011) for a more detailed discussion of these growth-maximizing rules in a related model with human capital accumulation.

that is, using (22),

$$\dot{K}_P = (1-\tau)Y - C. \tag{41}$$

From (15) and (21), $Y = G_I^{\alpha+\mu\beta} G_H^{\beta(1-\mu)} K_P^{\eta}$. Using again (23), as well as (32), yields

$$Y = \tau^{(\alpha+\beta)/\eta} \upsilon_I^{(\alpha+\mu\beta)/\eta} \upsilon_H^{\beta(1-\mu)/\eta} K_P. \tag{42}$$

Using this result, together with (19) and (32), taking into account the fact that, from the government budget constraint, $\upsilon_H = 1 - \upsilon_I$, and denoting by ζ_P the co-state variable associated with (41), the government's problem is therefore to maximize

$$L = \frac{\{C^{\kappa}[\{\upsilon_I^{\mu}(1-\upsilon_I)^{1-\mu}\}\tau Y]^{1-\kappa}\}^{1-1/\sigma}}{1-1/\sigma} + \zeta_P[(1-\tau)Y - C],$$

with respect to C, υ_I, τ, and K_P, subject to (42). The first-order optimality conditions with respect to C, υ_I, and τ are given by

$$\kappa\left(\frac{H}{C}\right)^{1-\kappa}[C^{\kappa}H^{1-\kappa}]^{-1/\sigma} = \zeta_P, \tag{43}$$

$$(1-\kappa)\left(\frac{C}{H}\right)^{\kappa}[C^{\kappa}H^{1-\kappa}]^{-1/\sigma}\left\{\frac{\alpha(1-\mu)+\mu}{\eta\upsilon_I} - \frac{(1-\mu)(1-\alpha)}{\eta(1-\upsilon_I)}\right\}H \tag{44}$$

$$= -\zeta_P(1-\tau)Y\left\{\frac{\alpha+\mu\beta}{\eta\upsilon_I} - \frac{\beta(1-\mu)}{\eta(1-\upsilon_I)}\right\},$$

$$(1-\kappa)\left(\frac{C}{H}\right)^{\kappa}[C^{\kappa}H^{1-\kappa}]^{-1/\sigma}\left(\frac{H}{\eta\tau}\right) = \zeta_P Y\left\{1-(1-\tau)\frac{(\alpha+\beta)}{\eta\tau}\right\}. \tag{45}$$

Dividing (43) and (45) by (44), yields, after manipulations,

$$\tau^{**} = (\alpha+\beta) + \frac{1-\kappa}{\kappa}\left(\frac{C}{Y}\right), \tag{46}$$

$$v_I^{**} = \frac{1}{1+\Omega} \left\{ \frac{\alpha + \mu\beta}{\alpha + \beta} + [\alpha(1-\mu) + \mu]\Omega \right\} \in (0, 1), \qquad (47)$$

where

$$\Omega \equiv \frac{1-\kappa}{\kappa(1-\tau)(\alpha+\beta)} \left(\frac{C}{Y}\right) > 0,$$

and C/Y is constant in the steady state.[20]

In the particular case where $\kappa = 1$, so that utility does not depend on the (flow) supply of health services, $\Omega = 0$ and formulas (46) and (47) are identical to (39) and (40). In general, however, this is not the case. The utility-maximizing tax rate exceeds the growth-maximizing rate. The magnitude of the wedge depends on κ; because $d\tau^{**}/d\kappa < 0$, the greater the role of health services in utility, the larger the difference between the two rates. Note also that the welfare-maximizing tax rate does *not* depend on the technology for producing health services.

Using (40), formula (47) can be rewritten as

$$v_I^{**} = \frac{v_I^* + [\alpha(1-\mu) + \mu]\Omega}{1+\Omega} \in (0, 1) \qquad (48)$$

from which it can readily be verified that $v_I^{**} < v_I^*$. Thus, the welfare-maximizing share of spending on infrastructure is lower than the growth-maximizing share.

Intuitively, spending on health services is now more "valuable" to the central planner, given its complementarity with consumption. Choosing an income tax rate that exceeds the growth-maximizing rate entails a fall in the balanced growth rate, which tends, on the one hand, to lower welfare. On the other, however, an increase in the tax rate induces the household to shift resources from investment to consumption, as well as produces a higher output of health services [see (32)]. This tends to increase welfare. With $\kappa < 1$, the positive effect dominates if the optimal tax rate is higher than the growth-maximizing value.

Similarly, choosing a share of spending on infrastructure that is lower than the growth-maximizing rate reduces the growth rate but also leads to a reallocation of government outlays toward health services. If μ is not too high, this reallocation leads to a higher output of health services, and thus higher productivity, which tends to mitigate the drop in public outlays in infrastructure. In turn, with $\kappa < 1$, the increase in output of health services translates into a higher level of consumption (and thus lower investment) and an increase in welfare. This positive welfare effect dominates the negative effect of a lower growth rate. The higher μ is, the smaller the difference

---

[20]The solution for τ is admissible only if the steady-state value of the consumption-output ratio is not too high, whereas v_I^{**} is always less than unity [see (48)]. Note also that the complete dynamics of the model under a centralized planner are not fully characterized here; this can be done along the lines discussed in the previous section and the Appendix to this chapter.

between the two solutions. In the limit case where $\mu = 1$, formula (40) yields $v_I^* = 1$, so that, from (48),

$$v_I^{**} = \frac{v_I^* + \Omega}{1 + \Omega} = 1,$$

which shows that both the growth- and welfare-maximizing solutions imply that all tax resources should be allocated to infrastructure.

4.5 ■ A Stock Approach

The foregoing analysis can be extended to consider the case where the flow of health services is proportional to the *stock* of capital in health, K_H, which is itself augmented by combining government spending on infrastructure with spending on health. Specifically, (16) is replaced by

$$H = K_H, \tag{49}$$

whereas the production function becomes

$$Y = G_I^\alpha K_H^\beta K_P^{1-\alpha-\beta} = \left(\frac{G_I}{K_P}\right)^\alpha \left(\frac{K_H}{K_P}\right)^\beta K_P. \tag{50}$$

The production of public capital in health is given by, using (23),

$$\dot{K}_H = G_I^\mu G_H^{1-\mu} = (v_I^\mu v_H^{1-\mu})\tau Y, \tag{51}$$

where, for the sake of simplicity, a zero depreciation rate is assumed. Thus, to accumulate health capital requires spending not only on health per se, but also on infrastructure. Health capital can therefore be thought of as a composite asset. It comprises, for instance, not only a hospital building in a particular location, but also the road (or portion of road) that provides access to it. The "conventional" treatment corresponds, again, to $\mu = 0$.

The instantaneous utility function in (18) also has K_H replacing H. The budget constraints, (20) and (24), remain the same.

As shown by Agénor (2008), the model can be manipulated to give a system of two nonlinear differential equations in $c = C/K_P$ and $k_H = K_H/K_P$:

$$\frac{\dot{c}}{c} = (1-\tau)v(v_I\tau)^{\alpha/(1-\alpha)}k_H^{\beta/(1-\alpha)} + v_2\tau^{1/(1-\alpha)}v_H^{1-\mu}v_I^\omega k_H^{-\eta/(1-\alpha)} - v_1\rho + c, \tag{52}$$

$$\frac{\dot{k}_H}{k_H} = \tau^{1/(1-\alpha)}v_H^{1-\mu}v_I^\omega k_H^{-\eta/(1-\alpha)} - (1-\tau)(v_I\tau)^{\alpha/(1-\alpha)}k_H^{\beta/(1-\alpha)} + c, \tag{53}$$

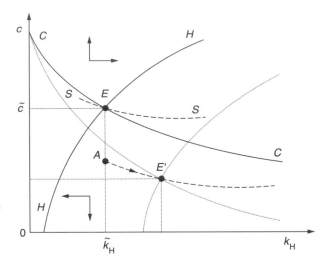

Figure 17–3 ▪ Balanced Growth Path and Revenue-Neutral Shift in Spending from Health to Infrastructure
Source: Agénor (2008).

with $v \equiv \eta v_1 - 1 < 0$, given that $v_1 < 1$ for $\sigma < 1$, and $\eta < 1$. These equations, together with the initial condition k_H^0, and the transversality condition (27), determine now the dynamics of the decentralized economy. The BGP is now a set of sequences $\{c, k_H\}_{t=0}^{\infty}$, such that for the initial condition k_H^0, and for given spending shares and tax rate, (52) and (53) and the transversality condition (27) are satisfied, with consumption and the stocks of private capital and public capital in health all growing at the same constant rate $\mathbf{g} = \dot{C}/C = \dot{K}_H/K_H = \dot{K}_P/K_P$.

The economy's growth rate can be written in the equivalent forms

$$\mathbf{g} = \tau^{1/(1-\alpha)} v_H^{1-\mu} v_I^{\omega} \tilde{k}_H^{-\eta/(1-\alpha)}, \tag{54}$$

$$\mathbf{g} = \frac{v_1 s}{1 - v_2} (v_I \tau)^{\alpha/(1-\alpha)} \tilde{k}_H^{\beta/(1-\alpha)} - \frac{v_1}{1 - v_2} \rho, \tag{55}$$

where $\tilde{k}_H$ denotes the steady-state value of k_H and $\omega = \mu + \alpha/(1 - \alpha)$. The equilibrium is saddlepoint stable and the BGP is unique; the model is thus locally determinate.

Transitional dynamics can be analyzed using the phase diagram depicted in Figure 17.3. The upward-sloping curve HH corresponds to combinations of (c, k_H) for which $\dot{k}_H = 0$, whereas the downward-sloping curve CC corresponds to combinations of (c, k_H) for which $\dot{c} = 0$. The saddlepath, SS, has a negative slope. As before, a budget-neutral shift in spending toward infrastructure has an ambiguous effect on the growth rate and the consumption-private capital ratio, c. In the "standard" case where $\mu = 0$, it also lowers unambiguously the ratio of health capital to private capital, k_H. But in general, if μ is sufficiently high, the steady-state value of k_H may actually increase. The positive effect of an increase in infrastructure spending may thus outweigh the negative effect of lower spending on health services on the stock of health per capita. Graphically, CC always shifts to the left, whereas HH can shift in either direction, depending on the parameters of the model. The case depicted in the figure corresponds to the case where μ and α/β are relatively high, so that curve HH shifts to the right. At the new equilibrium, the public-private capital ratio is higher, whereas the consumption-capital ratio is lower. The adjustment path corresponds to the sequence $E\,AE'$.[21]

As discussed at length by Agénor (2012*b*), there are a number of other channels through which public capital in infrastructure may affect growth. In particular, there is significant evidence of direct linkages between education outcomes and access to electricity, roads, and sanitation. Electricity allows for more studying and greater access to technology. Studies have shown that the quality of education tends to improve with better transportation networks in rural areas, whereas attendance rates for girls tend to increase with access to sanitation in schools. At the same time, there is also evidence that health affects both the quantity and quality of human capital—and thus indirectly growth. Healthier children, for instance, tend to do better in school. Agénor and Neanidis (2011) develop a general endogenous growth framework that captures these interactions between infrastructure, health, and education, and solve for growth- and welfare-maximizing spending allocation rules.

5   Financial Intermediation and Growth

Development economists have long emphasized the importance of financial development for economic growth. But while the early literature recognized this link—see McKinnon (1973), Shaw (1973), and the discussion in Chapter 18—a rigorous formulation of the interactions between financial factors and growth has begun to take shape only recently, in the context of the new generation of endogenous growth theories.[22]

A simple way to introduce financial factors in a growth model is, following Pagano (1993), to assume that a fraction $1 - \mu$ of saving is "lost" as a result of inefficient financial intermediation activities:

$$\mu s\, y = I, \quad 0 < \mu < 1. \tag{56}$$

---

[21] From (54) and (55), it can readily be established that the growth-maximizing tax rate and share of spending on infrastructure are again given by (39) and (40). Thus, the growth-maximizing allocation of government expenditure does not depend on whether it is the flow of spending on health, or the stock of health capital, that matters in determining household utility and productivity.

[22] See Levine (2005) and Ang (2008) for an overview of the literature on financial development and economic growth, and Temple (1999) for an earlier assessment.

Assuming that the production technology is described by constant returns to scale to capital as in Rebelo's model, the steady-state growth rate per capita is now equal to

$$\mathbf{g} = s\mu A - \delta. \tag{57}$$

Equation (57) provides a convenient framework for discussing the different channels through which financial development can affect economic growth. First, financial development may raise the saving rate, s. Second, it may raise A, the marginal productivity of the capital stock. Third, it may lead to an increase in the proportion of saving allocated to investment (or, equivalently, an increase in μ), a phenomenon that—in the spirit of McKinnon (1973), who emphasized the use of cash and bank deposits as a channel for capital accumulation by credit-constrained enterprises—we may call the "conduit" effect.

5.1 ■ Effects on the Saving Rate

While the early development literature emphasized the existence of an unambiguously positive effect of financial development on the saving rate, the new growth literature has shown that the direction of this effect is not unambiguous. The development of financial markets offers households the possibility of diversifying their portfolios and increases their borrowing options—affecting, therefore, the proportion of agents subject to liquidity constraints, which may in turn affect the saving rate (Jappelli and Pagano, 1994). Financial development also tends to reduce the overall level, and to modify the structure, of interest rates, the latter by reducing the spread between the rate paid by borrowers (typically firms) and that paid to lenders (households). Although these factors are bound to affect saving behavior, in each case the effect is ambiguous. For instance, an increase in the overall level of interest rates may have a positive or negative effect on the saving rate. The net effect depends, in particular, on banks' and portfolio holders' attitude toward risk.[23]

The ambiguous effect of financial intermediation on the saving rate may be compounded when all partial effects associated with financial development are taken into account. For instance, Bencivenga and Smith (1991) demonstrate that the direct effect of the emergence of banking activities may be a reduction in the saving rate. However, if at the same time the positive impact of financial development on the productivity of capital and the efficiency of investment is taken into account (see the following discussion), the net effect on growth may well be positive.

---

[23] The evidence reviewed in Chapter 2 on saving in developing countries suggests that the link between interest rates and saving rates is, at best, tenuous. It is worth noting that in his more recent writings, McKinnon (1993) seems to adopt the view that the positive effect of high real interest rates on growth stems from the improved efficiency of investment, rather than higher saving rates.

5.2 ■ Effects on the Allocation of Capital

In a growth context, the role of financial intermediaries can be viewed as facilitating the efficient allocation of resources to investment projects that provide the highest marginal return to capital. In the above framework, financial intermediation increases the average productivity of capital A (and thus the growth rate) in two ways: by collecting, processing, and evaluating the relevant information on alternative investment projects; and by inducing entrepreneurs, through their risk-sharing function, to invest in riskier but more productive technologies.

The link between the informational role of financial intermediation and productivity growth has been emphasized by Greenwood and Jovanovich (1990). In their model, capital may be invested in a safe, low-yield technology or a risky, high-yield one. The return to the risky technology is affected by two types of shocks: an aggregate shock, which affects all projects alike, and a project-specific shock. Unlike individual entrepreneurs, financial intermediaries with their large portfolios can identify the aggregate productivity shock, and thus induce their customers to select the technology that is most appropriate for the current realization of the shock. The more efficient allocation of resources channeled through financial intermediaries raises the productivity of capital and thus the growth rate of the economy.

Another critical function of financial intermediation is that it enables entrepreneurs to pool risks (Pagano, 1993). This "insurance" function results from the fact that financial intermediaries allow investors to share the uninsurable risk (resulting from, say, liquidity shocks) and the diversifiable risk deriving from the variability of the rates of return on alternative assets. The possibility of risk sharing affects saving behavior (as discussed above) as well as investment decisions. In the absence of banks, households can guard against idiosyncratic liquidity shocks only by investing in productive assets that can be promptly liquidated, thus frequently foregoing investments that are more productive but also more illiquid (see Chapter 15). This inefficiency can be considerably reduced by banks, which pool the liquidity risk of depositors and invest most of their funds in more illiquid and more productive projects. This effect is captured in an endogenous growth framework by Bencivenga and Smith (1991). They show that banks increase the productivity of investment both by directing funds to illiquid, high-yield technology and by reducing the investment waste due to premature liquidation. As in Greenwood and Jovanovich (1990), the productivity gain leads to a higher growth rate.[24]

---

[24] Alternatively, consumers' liquidity risk can be shared via a stock market. In the model developed by Greenwood and Jovanovich (1990), for instance, the stock market allows agents to reduce rate-of-return risk by fostering portfolio diversification.

5.3 ■ Intermediation Costs and Efficiency

Financial intermediation operates as a tax—at the rate $1- \mu$ in (57)—in the transformation of saving into investment. Financial intermediation thus has a growth-deterring effect because intermediaries appropriate a share of private saving. To a large extent, the costs associated with financial intermediation represent payments (such as fees and commissions) that are received by intermediaries in return for their services. An important issue in developing countries, however, may be that such absorption of resources results from explicit and implicit taxation—such as high rates of reserve requirements—and from excessive regulations, which lead to higher costs and therefore inefficient intermediation activities.[25] In addition, constraints on bank portfolio choices may reduce the volume and productivity of investment—by reducing the volume of funds channeled to deposit-taking financial intermediaries and causing a less efficient distribution of any given volume of such funds—thus impeding growth (Courakis, 1984). As emphasized in Chapter 18, to the extent that reforms of the financial system lead to a reduction in the cost and inefficiencies associated with the intermediation process (that is, leading to a rise in μ), the result will be an increase in the growth rate.

However, there are conditions under which financial development does not necessarily lead to faster economic growth. Moreover, its growth effects may vary with the state of economic development. Deidda (2006) develops these arguments in a model with costly financial intermediation. Financial development occurs endogenously as the economy reaches a critical level of income. Compared to financial autarky, financial intermediaries allocate savings, net of their costs of operation, to more productive investments. Whenever the technology financed by intermediaries is more capital-intensive than that operated in autarky, the growth effect of financial development is ambiguous. The key reason is that households might prefer to save through intermediaries instead of self-financing their investment needs, even when consumption of resources by the financial sector yields a growth rate lower than under financial autarky.

The *nature* of financial development may also matter from a growth perspective. Chakraborty and Ray (2006) develop a growth model where a financial system emerges endogenously from firms' financing choices. They show that two countries with different financial regimes may enjoy similar rates of growth; what matters for growth is the efficiency of the country's financial and legal institutions, rather than the type of its financial system. But from the perspective of developing a traditional economy into a modern, industrialized one, a bank-based system (in which banks are engaged in project selection, monitoring firms, and identifying successful entrepreneurs) outperforms a market-based one. The reason, essentially,

---

[25]Note that even if the rents or implicit taxes extracted by financial intermediaries and the government were spent on investment rather than consumption, the absorption of resources may still have an adverse effect on growth, particularly if the productivity of capital in the private sector is higher than elsewhere.

is that bank monitoring substitutes for entrepreneurs' initial wealth (with wealthier entrepreneurs relying more on market finance, as they face less of an information gap). It thus enables all modern-sector firms to make larger investments than would be possible under purely unintermediated finance. It also lowers the minimum entrepreneurial wealth required to obtain external finance, so that the traditional sector tends to be smaller under a bank-based system.

6 | Inflation and Growth

High rates of inflation can be expected to reduce economic growth through a variety of mechanisms which can influence both the rate of capital accumulation and the rate of growth of total factor productivity. For instance, Fischer (1993) has argued that, because very high inflation serves no useful economic purpose but may do much economic harm, a government that tolerates high inflation is one that has lost macroeconomic control, and this circumstance is likely to deter domestic investment in physical capital. Others have argued that high inflation means unstable inflation and volatile relative prices, reducing the information content of price signals and thus distorting the efficiency of resource allocation, which may have deleterious effects on growth. At the same time, however, inflation variability may have a *positive* effect on economic growth through increased savings: risk-averse agents may save more during periods of uncertainty. This extra pool of savings will then translate, via higher investment, into higher output growth (Grier and Grier, 2006). In countries where collecting conventional taxes is costly, governments may choose to repress their financial systems to increase revenue, even though they recognize the detrimental growth effects of such policies. From that perspective, inflation can be viewed as a proxy for financial repression (Roubini and Sala-i-Martin, 1995), with adverse consequences on investment and growth.[26]

Gillman and Kejak (2005) offer a broad overview of the channels through which inflation can have an adverse effect on growth. In what follows we present a simplified version of a model developed by De Gregorio (1993), which captures the link between inflation—which depends inversely on the degree of efficiency of the tax system—and growth.

Consider a closed economy consisting of households, firms, and the government. Households hold no money but hold an indexed bond issued by the government.[27] Capital is the only input in the production process, which takes place under constant

---

[26] As noted in Chapter 3, however, this interpretation may not be valid because in general the inflation tax and the financial repression tax may be substitutable fiscal instruments.

[27] The assumption that households hold no money is made for simplicity only. As shown by De Gregorio, in the setup considered here, households' behavior with respect to inflation has no effect on the growth rate. In fact, if only consumers faced transactions costs, the marginal productivity of capital and thus the real rate of interest would not depend on the inflation rate, and there would be no effect of inflation on growth.

returns to scale. Firms hold money because it reduces transactions costs associated with purchases of new equipment. Capital mobility is precluded, so that domestic investment must equal domestic saving. Inflation is, for the moment, assumed exogenous.

The representative household maximizes the present value of utility stream

$$\int_0^\infty \frac{c^{1-\eta}}{1-\eta} e^{-\rho t} dt, \quad 0 < \eta < 1, \tag{58}$$

subject to the flow budget constraint

$$\dot{b} = (1-\iota)(y+rb) - c - \tau, \tag{59}$$

where $\sigma \equiv 1/\eta$ denotes the elasticity of intertemporal substitution, b the real stock of government indexed bonds, $0 < \iota < 1$ the income tax rate, r the real rate of return on bonds, y total factor income, and τ net lump-sum taxes paid by households. For simplicity, income taxes are levied at the same rate on all components of gross income.

Maximization of (58) subject to (59) yields

$$\dot{c}/c = \sigma[(1-\iota)r - \rho]. \tag{60}$$

As in the AK model discussed earlier, production is assumed to exhibit constant returns to scale:

$$y = Ak. \tag{61}$$

Firms require money to purchase new capital goods. The (gross) cost of investing I units is thus equal to $I[1 + \upsilon(m/I)]$, where m denotes firms' real money holdings. The properties of the function $\upsilon(\cdot)$ that characterize the transactions technology are $\upsilon' < 0$ and $\upsilon'' > 0$: holding money reduces transactions costs but entails diminishing returns. The representative firm maximizes the present discounted value of its cash flow, net of the opportunity cost of its holdings of money balances. The latter is given by $(r + \pi)m$, where π is the inflation rate. Thus, the firm maximizes:

$$\int_0^\infty \left[Ak - \left\{ 1 + \upsilon\left(\frac{m}{I}\right) \right\} I - (r + \pi)m - \dot{m} \right] e^{-rt} dt, \tag{62}$$

subject to $\dot{k} = I$. The solution yields

$$-\upsilon'\left(\frac{m}{I}\right) = r + \pi \Rightarrow m = \Phi(r+\pi)I, \quad \Phi' = -1/\upsilon'' < 0, \tag{63}$$

$$\dot{q}/q = r - (A/q), \tag{64}$$

$$q = 1 + \upsilon\left(\frac{m}{I}\right) - \frac{m}{I}\upsilon'\left(\frac{m}{I}\right), \tag{65}$$

where q denotes the shadow price of capital (see Abel, 1990). Equation (63) defines the firm's demand for money. Because cash flows are not subject to direct taxation, the opportunity cost of holding money is given by the sum of the before-tax real interest rate plus the inflation rate. The arbitrage equation (64) can be solved (after imposing the relevant transversality condition) to show that the shadow price of capital is equal to the present discounted value of the marginal product of capital. Equation (65) indicates that q exceeds unity (the price of the composite good) because of the existence of transactions costs incurred in buying a new unit of capital.

Substituting (63) in (65) yields

$$q = 1 + \upsilon[\Phi(\cdot)] + (r+\pi)\Phi(\cdot) = q(r+\pi), \tag{66}$$

where $q' > 0$. Equation (66) indicates that q is constant—at, say, $\tilde{q}$—if the inflation rate is constant. From (64), the real interest rate is in this case equal to

$$\tilde{r} = A/\tilde{q}. \tag{67}$$

The government budget constraint is given by

$$\dot{m} + \dot{b} = g - \iota y - \tau - \pi m, \tag{68}$$

where g denotes public expenditure, which is taken to be a constant fraction of output. In what follows we also assume that the government foregoes the use of bonds to finance its deficit ($\dot{b} = 0$), and instead adjusts lump-sum taxes continuously to maintain fiscal equilibrium.

The aggregate resource constraint of the economy is given by

$$y = c + \left\{1 + \upsilon\left(\frac{m}{I}\right)\right\}I + g. \tag{69}$$

Using the above system of equations, it can be established that consumption, output, and capital grow at a constant rate in the steady state, which is equal to[28]

$$\mathbf{g} = \sigma[(1 - \iota)\tilde{r} - \rho], \tag{70}$$

which is also the rate of growth of real money balances. The model has no transitional dynamics; that is, the economy grows continuously at the rate given by (70).

This model generates an inverse relationship between output growth and the rate of inflation, as can be verified from (66), (67), and (70). This relationship is due to the negative effect of inflation on the profitability of investment. A higher rate of inflation raises the "effective" price of capital goods, which (in addition to its market price) incorporates the opportunity cost of holding money to facilitate purchases of capital goods. The increase in transactions costs raises the shadow value of installed capital, dampens investment, and reduces the growth rate.[29]

Finally, it is also worth noting that the relationship between inflation and growth may take a nonlinear form. Some of the evidence reviewed in Gillman and Kejak (2005) found that there is a threshold rate of inflation, below which the relationship is insignificant, and above which it becomes strongly significant and negative. More recently, in a study of forty developing countries over the period 1960–2004, Bick (2010) found that below 12 percent inflation may have a positive effect on growth, whereas above that value it has a negative impact on growth. This threshold appears to be significantly higher than for industrial countries.

7   Macroeconomic Volatility and Growth

As discussed in Chapter 1, a well-documented feature of developing countries is their greater exposure to aggregate domestic and external shocks. Instability has both external and internal roots; in particular, "stop-and-go" macroeconomic policies, a tendency for government expenditure and fiscal deficits to increase during periods of economic expansion and to fall during recessions, and terms-of-trade shocks, have been a recurrent source of macroeconomic volatility in many of these countries (see, for instance, Caballero, 2000). At a deeper level perhaps, Acemoglu et al. (2003) have argued that the main cause of macroeconomic volatility is not "bad" policies (such as excessive government spending, high inflation, and overvalued exchange rates) per se, but, rather, underlying institutional weaknesses. Weak institutions (including political institutions that do not constrain politicians and political elites, ineffective enforcement of property rights for investors, widespread corruption, and a high

---

[28] See De Gregorio (1993) for details. To ensure positive growth, we assume that $(1 - \iota)\tilde{r} > \rho$.
[29] De Gregorio (1993) also develops a framework in which inflation affects the efficiency, rather than the level, of investment.

degree of political instability) foster the adoption of distortionary macroeconomic policies, which in turn lead to macroeconomic volatility.

One important implication of macroeconomic volatility has been unstable growth rates, with possibly some adverse effects on poverty.[30] In the analytical literature, several contributions have attempted to identify the channels through which this short-run volatility may affect long-run growth. This relationship has been shown to depend on a number of factors, most notably the underlying source of shocks and the parameters governing attitudes toward risk and uncertainty. Blackburn and Pelloni (2004), for instance, showed that the correlation between the mean and variance of output growth depends fundamentally on the impulse source of fluctuations (real or nominal shocks). A correlated increase in the mean and variance of inflation, for instance, may cause either an increase or decrease in the mean of output growth due to offsetting effects through precautionary savings (which tend to spur growth) and the inflation tax on real money balances (which has an adverse effect).

Other results that are highly relevant for developing countries include those of Aizenman and Marion (1993), Turnovsky and Chattopadhyay (2003), García-Peñalosa and Turnovsky (2005), Aghion et al. (2005), and Kose et al. (2006). Aizenman and Marion (1993) for instance studied the impact of policy uncertainty in an endogenous growth model and showed that this may have an adverse effect on growth. This result is consistent with the view that countries with high levels of macroeconomic volatility tend to have weaker political coalitions, and a higher level of political instability which, in turn, are often reflected in suboptimal policies that further increase macroeconomic volatility.[31] Another reason is that volatility may be harmful to growth through its adverse effect on private investment in physical capital. This could occur if irreversibility effects (as discussed in Chapter 2) are important. Turnovsky and Chattopadhyay (2003) perform a variety of numerical experiments with a stochastic endogenous growth model and perform an extensive set of cross-country regressions; their results suggest also that terms-of-trade variability and government expenditure volatility may have large quantitative effects on the growth rate of output. García-Peñalosa and Turnovsky (2005), for their part, argue that because volatility may have an adverse effect on income distribution (or, more precisely, factor shares), it may also have an indirect negative impact on growth. Aghion et al. (2005), suggest that poorly developed financial markets (as measured by a high incidence of binding constraints on borrowing) tend to magnify the impact of volatility on growth.

Another idea that has not yet been exploited (as far as we know) is that a high degree of volatility may create uncertainty about the future returns to education;

---

[30] See Agénor (2004c) for a discussion of the various channels through which volatility may have an adverse effect on the poor.

[31] Carmignani (2003) provides an overview of the various channels through which political instability may affect fiscal policy and growth.

to the extent that growth is driven mainly by human capital accumulation (as in Lucas-type endogenous growth models, discussed earlier), a lack of incentives to invest in the acquisition of skills may prevent a country from switching to a high-growth path. From that perspective, therefore, the harm caused by macroeconomic volatility may be permanent—in the sense of keeping the country in a low-growth trap.

Finally, Kose et al. (2006), in a cross-country study covering the period 1960–2000, found that trade and financial integration have tended to weaken the negative correlation between growth and output volatility. This result is less robust, however, for financial integration. Countries that are more open to trade appear to be able to tolerate higher volatility without adverse consequences for long-term growth. Alternatively, in economies that are intrinsically more volatile, the beneficial effects of trade integration on growth appear to be stronger.

8 Middle-Income Growth Traps

Since the 1950s, rapid growth has allowed a significant number of countries to achieve middle-income status. However, very few have made the additional leap needed to become high-income economies. Rather, many have gotten stuck in what has been called a middle-income trap—or more appropriately perhaps, an imitation trap, as discussed later—characterized by a sharp deceleration in growth.[32] Most countries in Latin America and the Middle East for instance reached middle-income status during the 1960s and 1970s, and have remained there ever since. According to the World Bank (2012), of 101 middle-income economies in 1960, only 13 had become high income by 2008: Equatorial Guinea; Greece; Hong Kong, China; Ireland; Israel; Japan; Mauritius; Portugal; Puerto Rico; South Korea; Singapore; Spain; and Taiwan, China.

In Asia, Malaysia and Thailand provide good examples of the growth slowdown that characterizes a middle-income trap. Despite the financial crisis of 1997–1998, they ended the century with productivity levels that stood significantly closer to those recorded in advanced countries. However, the pattern of labor-intensive production and exports in these countries has remained broadly unchanged for the past two decades. At the same time, they have faced growing competition from low-cost producers, first China and India, and more recently Vietnam and Cambodia. Growth has slowed significantly as a result. Moving up the value chain and resuming rapid growth by breaking into fast-growing markets for knowledge and innovation-based products and services has remained elusive—not only for Malaysia and Thailand but also for a number of other middle-income countries (UNIDO, 2009).

---

[32]"Middle income economies" are defined in accordance with the World Bank's classifications by income group, as given in http://data.worldbank.org/about/country-classifications.

In a more formal analysis, Eichengreen et al. (2012) define a growth slowdown based on three conditions. The first requires that prior to the slowdown the seven-year average growth rate is 3.5 percent per annum or greater. The second identifies a growth slowdown with a decline in the seven-year average growth rate by at least 2 percentage points. The third condition limits slowdowns to cases in which per capita GDP is greater than $10,000 in 2005 prices—thereby ruling out episodes related to countries that have not yet successfully developed. They found that growth slowdowns typically occur at per capita incomes of about $15,000 at 2005 constant international PPP prices. At that point, the growth rate of GDP per capita slows by an average of 3.5 percentage points. They also found, using regression and standard growth accounting techniques, that growth slowdowns are essentially *productivity* growth slowdowns—with a drop in TFP growth representing about 85 percent, or 3 percentage points, of the absolute reduction in the growth rate of GDP per capita. However, there are issues with these definitions; a reduction in the growth rate from, say, 8 percent to 6 percent does qualify as a slowdown according to the authors' definition, but it in no way constitutes a trap.[33]

A common explanation of growth slowdowns is based on a Lewis-type development process. In that perspective, factors and advantages that generate high growth during an initial phase of rapid development—low-cost labor and imitation of foreign technology—disappear when middle- and upper-middle-income levels are reached, thereby requiring new sources of growth to maintain sustained increases in per capita income. Indeed, during a first phase, low-income countries can compete in international markets by producing labor-intensive, low-cost products using technologies imported from abroad. These countries can achieve large productivity gains initially through a reallocation of labor from low-productivity agriculture to high-productivity manufacturing. However, once these countries reach middle-income levels, the pool of underemployed rural workers shrinks and wages begin to rise, thereby eroding competitiveness. Productivity growth from sectoral reallocation and technology catch-up are eventually exhausted, while rising wages make labor-intensive exports less competitive on world markets—precisely at the time when other low-income countries themselves engage in a phase of rapid growth. Put differently, growth slowdowns coincide with the point in the growth process where it is no longer possible to boost productivity by shifting additional workers from agriculture to industry and where the gains from importing foreign technology diminish. This process is well supported by the evidence on productivity slowdowns provided by Eichengreen et al. (2012), as indicated earlier. The implication is that to avoid falling into a middle-income trap (with continued reliance on imitation of foreign technology), countries must address its root structural cause early on and find new ways to boost productivity. Observers have argued that the main sources

---

[33] See Im and Rosenblatt (2013) for a critical review of the evidence.

of higher productivity are a shift to high-value services and the promotion of home-grown innovation, possibly through government subsidies to "priority" sectors.

Agénor and Canuto (2012) develop a formal model in which productivity slowdowns may indeed be the source of a middle-income trap. However, it differs from the existing literature in terms of the reasons why productivity growth may be constrained, and what type of public policies can be implemented to promote a broad-based innovation strategy. They emphasize interactions between three determinants of productivity growth: individual decisions to acquire skills, access to different types of public infrastructure, and *knowledge network externalities*—which they define as a situation where a higher share of workers with advanced levels of education has a positive impact on their performance, that is, their ability to take advantage of existing knowledge.

The model distinguishes between two types of labor skills, basic and advanced. In turn, advanced skills are defined as specialized knowledge that can be acquired by devoting a given amount of time to higher education in early adulthood.[34] Individuals with either basic or advanced skills can both work in the production of final goods (or manufacturing), whereas only those with advanced skills can work in the innovation sector (or, more precisely, design activities) in the tradition of Romer (1990). Because labor is relatively more productive in the design sector, an increase in the supply of workers with advanced skills is growth-enhancing. The model also assumes that occupational choices are endogenous; individuals choose to invest in education only if wages in the design sector are high enough, compared to manufacturing. Due to the combination of a knowledge effect and a learning-by-doing effect, this gain is increasing—at least over a certain range.

Agénor and Canuto also consider two types of infrastructure: *basic* infrastructure (which consists of roads, electricity, and basic telecommunications) and *advanced* infrastructure, which consists of advanced information and communication technologies (ICTs) in general, and high-speed communication networks in particular. It is now well established that access to broadband facilitates the buildup of domestic and international knowledge networks, thereby promoting dissemination and research. Broadband networks also provide a platform that other sectors can leverage to develop other platforms (such as distance education and telemedicine) and enable the development of digital content—all of which can help to promote innovation. To highlight the benefit of ICTs, advanced infrastructure is assumed to promote activity only in the design sector. Because labor supply decisions are endogenously related to relative wages, there is therefore a two-way interaction between these activities and the proportion of the population acquiring advanced skills.

The analysis shows that if the marginal benefits associated with nonrival (disembodied) knowledge depend in a nonlinear fashion on the share of the population

---

[34]Thus, in contrast to models with disembodied knowledge and endogenous schooling time allocation, in the Lucas-Uzawa tradition (discussed earlier), human capital cannot be accumulated indefinitely.

involved in design activities (being high for a range of values for that share), as a result of the knowledge network externality alluded to earlier, then multiple equilibria may emerge—one of them (the lower-growth equilibrium) being synonymous with a middle-income trap. The trap is characterized by low productivity growth as well, in line with the evidence discussed earlier. Intuitively, to benefit from existing ideas, there must be enough high-ability individuals involved in the design sector; but if productivity in that sector is low, because access to advanced infrastructure is limited, wages will be low—implying that few high-ability individuals will choose to invest in the advanced skills needed to operate in that sector. Thus, the lower-growth equilibrium is also characterized by a *misallocation of talent*. The analysis also shows that escaping from a middle-income trap may be achieved by a sufficiently large increase in investment in advanced infrastructure. Improving access to this type of infrastructure boosts productivity and wages in the design sector, which draws more labor there and may trigger the shift in labor supply that magnifies (at least temporarily) the benefit associated with exploiting the existing stock of ideas.

In a subsequent contribution, Agénor and Canuto (2014) shifted their emphasis on access to finance. The impact of financial constraints on innovation, in both industrial and developing countries, has been the subject of much debate in recent years. The conventional view is that firms engaged in innovation may suffer from a variety of frictions that may limit their ability to resort to external finance. Assets held by these firms are mainly intangible; as a result, they may lack collateral value. For instance, spending in the form of salaries and wages for scientists and researchers, which often represent a large fraction of innovation-related activities and help to build human capital, cannot be collateralized. Furthermore, to protect their proprietary information over innovation, firms may be unwilling to offer fully transparent signals about the effectiveness of their intended innovation programs to potential lenders. Limited collateral value and information frictions may thus help to explain why some of these firms rely little on debt finance and instead fund most of their investments with their own resources or (at later stages) equity. Indeed, the high degree of information asymmetry that characterizes investment in innovation projects may induce lenders to demand higher rates of return than in the case of investments in physical assets. Thus, although information asymmetries matter for external financing of all types of investments, they may be particularly significant in limiting financing of innovation projects due to the complexity and specificity of the innovation process. Moreover, funding through equity is either costly—especially for firms whose values are determined mainly by their growth potential and hence are severely exposed to asymmetric information frictions—or simply not available, as is often the case for younger and smaller firms. If financing constraints are binding for a sufficient number of innovative firms, economic growth may be adversely affected.

The model in Agénor and Canuto (2014) shows that if research activity involves borrowing from financial intermediaries and monitoring is costly, high intermediation costs may adversely affect innovation. In addition, if monitoring costs are high, fewer individuals may choose to invest in skills and engage in design activities.

The reason is that high monitoring costs lead to lower wages in the design sector, which in turn lead (for a given cost of education) to reduced incentives to invest in skills and thus a lower share of the labor force engaged in research. From that perspective, lack of access to finance not only has a direct, adverse effect on innovation activity and growth, but also an indirect effect that operates in the same direction. Agénor and Canuto show that if unit monitoring costs fall with the number of successful projects (as a result of information externalities, for instance), multiple equilibria may emerge—one of which, a middle-income trap, characterized by low wages in the design sector, a low share of the labor force engaged in innovation activity, and low growth. A sufficiently ambitious policy aimed at alleviating financial constraints—through the development of capital markets rather than government subsidies, which may be difficult to target effectively—may allow a country to move away from such a trap, not only by reducing the cost of finance but also by improving incentives to invest in skills and promoting the production of ideas.

9   A Methodological Note

In this chapter we have discussed a variety of determinants of economic growth, with a particular emphasis on those factors that may be particularly relevant for developing countries. We have not provided any detailed review of the extensive empirical literature on the determinants of growth. Much of that literature, which is reviewed elsewhere (see Barro and Sala-i-Martin, 2003; Agénor, 2004b) is based on cross-country panel regressions. However, it has been argued that panel regressions mask important cross-country differences and suffer from significant measurement, statistical, and conceptual problems. Doubts have been raised about multi-country growth studies because (a) they cannot address the cross-country heterogeneity and thus mask important cross-country differences in the relationship under investigations; (b) the panel and the country-specific parameters (estimates) may not be equivalent, hence limiting the economic value of panel estimates; and (c) various countries in the panel are unlikely to be on the balanced growth path raising concern on pooled regressions.

Indeed, a number of studies have shown the difficulties associated with the lack of balanced growth paths across countries when pooling data, and the possibility of parameter heterogeneity across panel units (countries), and that unless this heterogeneity is addressed, panel estimates may be biased and inconsistent. Some have also showed a lack of correspondence between panel and country-specific estimates; hence, generalizations based on panel results may lead to incorrect inferences for individual countries in the panel. Luintel et al. (2008) for instance use a sample of fourteen low- and middle-income countries and perform country-by-country time series analyses. They also apply a dynamic heterogeneous panel estimator in order to perform tests of equivalence between the time series and panel estimates.

They address the issue of cross-country parameter heterogeneity by explicitly testing for the poolability of cross-country data. They found significant heterogeneity in cross-country parameters and adjustment dynamics; tests show that data cannot be pooled for the countries included in their sample, which reinforces the use of time-series approach. Third, tests also reveal that the panel estimates (parameters) do not correspond to country-specific estimates. Of course, results of this type do not completely invalidate all inferences from the cross-country empirical literature; studies by Baltagi et al. (2009) and Chang et al. (2009), for instance, do go a long way toward addressing some of these shortcomings. But they do suggest that country-specific studies, along the lines for instance of Demetriades and Hussein (1996), may be a more fruitful approach.

Chapter 18

Trade Liberalization, Financial-Sector Reforms, and Sequencing

Recognition of the adverse effects of import substitution strategies has led an increasing number of developing countries to adopt commercial policies conducive to a more liberal external trade regime.[1] A reduction in trade barriers (such as tariffs and import quotas) fosters an adjustment in relative prices and a reallocation of resources toward the sector producing exportables. In the long term, successful trade liberalization leads to an expansion of exports and a contraction of activity in import-competing industries, as well as an overall transfer of resources from sectors producing nontradables toward those producing tradables. The evidence suggests that a more open trade regime may be associated with higher long-term rates of economic growth.

While trade reforms aim at improving the allocation of resources in the long run, macroeconomic management is concerned with the short-term determination of output, inflation, and the balance of payments. Despite this difference in focus, the conduct of macroeconomic policy interacts in significant ways with the design of trade reforms. The adoption of more liberal commercial policies, such as a reduction in nominal protection, typically entails short-run output and employment costs, which may hinder the attainment of macroeconomic objectives or impose severe constraints on the manipulation of macroeconomic policy instruments.

The first part of this chapter reviews some of the theoretical and empirical literature on trade reforms, with an emphasis on their short- and medium-term macroeconomic implications. We begin by reviewing briefly some recent evidence on

---

[1]The adverse effects of import substitution policies have been well documented in the trade and development literature: an industrial structure heavily dependent on imported intermediates and capital goods, slow export growth and recurrent balance-of-payments difficulties, and severe allocative distortions. See, for instance, Bruton (1989).

the impact of trade liberalization on growth and the labor market. We then analyze, using a dynamic macroeconomic model, the output and employment effects of a permanent cut in tariffs.[2]

In Chapter 17, we discussed the analytical case for the proposition that a well-functioning financial system can be a powerful inducement to long-term economic growth, and we reviewed the empirical evidence on this issue. Growing recognition in developing nations of the distortionary effects of government intervention in financial and exchange markets has indeed led many countries to liberalize the domestic financial system, the exchange-rate regime, and international movements of capital. The second part of this chapter reviews the theoretical and empirical literature on financial reforms, with an emphasis on the short- and medium-term macroeconomic implications of policies ultimately intended to promote long-run growth. We discuss in particular the experience of the Southern Cone countries of Latin America in the late 1970s, which has generated a vast literature over the years. Although a large number of other developing countries have taken steps during the past two decades to deregulate the domestic financial markets, many aspects of the Southern Cone experience have been confronted elsewhere in the developing world, and our discussion is organized so as to draw broad policy lessons.

Structural reform programs have raised a variety of substantive issues, regarding most notably the appropriate sequencing of reforms, the optimal pace at which liberalization policies should proceed, and the conduct of short-run macroeconomic policy in an economy undergoing extensive structural adjustment. While the focus of the preceding sections is largely on the short- and medium-term macroeconomic effects of specific reforms (in the trade regime and the domestic financial system), the determination of the appropriate pace of reform and the sequential order of specific policies that policymakers should follow when implementing comprehensive reform programs also raise important practical and conceptual questions. The third part of this chapter examines issues raised by the sequencing of reforms, focusing on the extent to which the success of adjustment programs depends on the order of liberalization. We also discuss the determination of the appropriate pace of reform in the presence of adjustment costs, and discuss the role of credibility and sustainability in this context.

1   Trade Reform

Since the mid-1980s, far-reaching trade reforms have been implemented in developing countries. Prior to reform, extensive barriers to trade (high tariffs, quantitative

---

[2]We do not discuss here in a systematic manner the welfare implications of trade liberalization. See Edwards and van Wijnbergen (1986), Kähkönen (1987), Rodrik (1987), Ostry (1991), and Davidson and Matusz (2006). Rodrik, in particular, examines the welfare effects of trade reform in a model where—as in the framework developed later on in this chapter—price and wage rigidities lead to unemployment.

restrictions on imports, widespread exemptions, and extensive controls on foreign exchange transactions) were in place in most of these countries. Thus, import policy reform consists not only of reduction of average tariffs and their dispersion, but also of dismantling nontariff barriers such as quantitative restrictions and foreign exchange controls, and eliminating exemptions. Export policy reform involves a reduction or elimination of price and quantitative barriers to exports, and the introduction or improvement of incentives for export promotion and diversification. In many countries, average tariff rates (or rates of nominal protection) were reduced dramatically. The degree of openness increased significantly, as a result of an expansion of both exports and imports in real terms. Episodes of trade reform have also usually been preceded by, or associated with, a significant depreciation of the real exchange rate.[3]

The evidence on the impact of trade reform on growth is mixed (see Yanikkaya, 2003). Lee et al. (2004), for instance, found that trade openness has a small positive effect on growth. But the most robust measure of openness in their study is the parallel market premium, which not only captures trade openness per se but also reflects many other economic and policy distortions. Hence, what is conducive to growth appears to be openness in a broad sense (related to the overall economic, policy, and institutional environment), rather than openness to trade by itself.

Most discussions of the costs of trade reforms center on the transitional costs and temporary unemployment that they may entail. Movements of labor and other production inputs across sectors, however, are precisely what allow countries to reap the benefits of trade openness in classical trade models (see Mikić, 1998). In these models, the gains from trade are generated by moving resources toward sectors in which a country has a comparative advantage, itself resulting from relative differences across countries in either technology (as in the Ricardian model) or factor endowments (as in the Heckscher-Ohlin model). In endogenous models of growth and trade where trade openness facilitates the diffusion of technology across nations (as in Grossman and Helpman, 1991), significant shifts in the allocation of labor may occur after trade liberalization if technological transmission affects sectors differently.

The evidence suggests that the impact of trade reform on sectoral labor movements is rather mixed. In a study of twenty-five episodes of trade liberalization, for instance, Wacziarg and Wallack (2004) found that the effects of liberalization on intersectoral shifts in labor differ across countries, in a way related to the scope and depth of reforms, but that overall effects are relatively small in magnitude. However, some of the evidence does seem to suggest that trade liberalization may be associated with significant reductions in employment and a contraction in output in the short run. From a theoretical standpoint, this is not necessarily surprising; there are a variety of potential channels through which such reforms may lead to contractionary

---

[3] See Papageorgiou et al. (1990) for a review of the early evidence, and Li (2004) for more recent work.

effects in the short term.[4] To the extent that such costs may have an adverse effect on the sustainability of the adjustment process, leading possibly to policy reversals or the complete abandonment of the reform effort (as discussed in the next chapter), it is important to understand the mechanisms through which such effects might operate.[5]

1.1 ■ Analytical Framework

A number of studies have found that in the presence of imperfect labor mobility across sectors (due, for instance, to locational preferences or high relocation costs), trade liberalization may lead to higher unemployment. Agénor and Aizenman (1996), in particular, examine the dynamic impact of trade reform on wages, the composition of employment, and aggregate unemployment in the presence of a variety of labor market distortions. In contrast to the existing literature, they explicitly model interactions between wage formation mechanisms across sectors. In what follows we provide a simplified presentation of their analysis.

Consider a small open economy in which there are three types of agents: producers, households, and the government. All firms and households are identical. The economy produces two goods—a nontraded good, which is used only for final domestic consumption, and an export good, whose output is entirely sold abroad and whose price is determined on world markets. The capital stock in each sector is fixed. Labor is homogeneous and imperfectly mobile across sectors.[6]

Firms in the export sector determine both wages and the level of employment. Workers employed in that sector are paid an above-equilibrium real wage in order to reduce turnover costs—which include recruitment, hiring, training, and firing costs—while the wage earned by workers employed in the nontraded goods sector is fully flexible. Although workers who are not hired in the export sector could find job opportunities at the going wage in the nontraded goods sector, imperfect labor mobility prevents an instantaneous reallocation of the labor force.

Households consume nontraded and imported goods, supply labor inelastically and hold a traded bond, which bears a constant rate of return determined on world capital markets. The government consumes only nontraded goods, and collects lump-sum taxes as well as taxes on imported goods. Finally, wage and employment expectations are assumed to depend on prevailing conditions in the labor market.

---

[4]The evidence also suggests that there are large, and persistent, distributional effects associated with trade reforms. In a study of Colombia's experience with trade reform during the period 1984-1998, Attanasio et al. (2004) for instance found that the increased foreign competition to which tariff reductions exposed domestic producers may have fostered skilled-biased technological change and this in turn was the primary driver of the increase in the skill premium (increased returns to education) observed during that period. See also Gonzaga et al. (2006) for the case of Brazil, and Agénor (2004b, chapter 14) and Ripoll (2005) for a broader discussion.

[5]Understanding the role of the labor market structure is important, given the evidence for instance by Chang et al. (2009) suggesting that the effect of trade liberalization on growth is magnified by a high degree of labor market flexibility.

[6]Traca (2004) studies the implications of trade reform in a model with two categories of labor and lower intersectoral mobility costs for skilled workers.

1.1.1 *Output, Turnover Costs, and Wages*

Production in the export sector, y_E, takes place under a Cobb-Douglas technology and is given by

$$y_X = n_X^{\alpha_X},\tag{1}$$

where n_X is employment and $\alpha_X \in (0, 1)$.

In addition to normal costs associated with the use of labor in the production process, firms in the export sector incur a total cost of $\theta q n_X$, in hiring and training new workers, where q is the quit rate and θ the cost incurred in recruiting and training each worker. The quit rate is specified as depending on the product wage in the sector producing exported goods relative to the wage that workers could earn in the nontraded goods sector:

$$q = q(\omega_X/\omega_N),\tag{2}$$

where ω_X denotes the product wage in the export sector, ω_N the real wage in the nontraded goods sector measured in terms of exported goods, and $q' < 0$ and $q'' > 0$.

The export good is used as the numéraire and is set to unity. Firms in the export sector maximize their real profits, given by

$$\Pi_X = n_X^{\alpha_X} - \omega_X n_X - \theta q \left(\frac{\omega_X}{\omega_N} \right) n_X,$$

with respect to ω_X and n_X, for ω_N given. First-order conditions are

$$-\theta q' = \omega_N,\tag{3}$$

$$\alpha n_X^{\alpha_X - 1} = \Omega_X,\tag{4}$$

where $\Omega_X = \omega_X + \theta q$ is unit labor costs in the export sector. Equations (3) and (4) imply that unit labor costs in the export sector increase with the level of wages in the nontraded goods sector:

$$d\Omega_X = d\omega_N = \omega_X/\omega_N.\tag{5}$$

Logarithmic differentiation of (3) implies that

$$d \ln \omega_X = \left(\frac{1}{\eta} - 1 \right) \ln \omega_N, \quad \eta \equiv -q''\omega/q',\tag{6}$$

where $\omega = \omega_X/\omega_N$. To understand this result, note that (3) can be written in the form $1 = -\theta q'/\omega_N$, which can be interpreted as equating the marginal unit labor cost in the exportable sector (which is unity) to the marginal unit labor benefit, which results from a reduction in labor turnover costs. This equation indicates that an increase in the market-clearing wage ω_N has an ambiguous effect on the marginal benefit. On the one hand, it increases the quit rate, thereby raising the marginal benefit resulting from an increase in the wage in the export sector. On the other, it reduces the marginal benefit associated with a rise in the efficiency wage because a unit increase in that wage represents now a smaller percentage improvement in the relative wage (this is captured by $1/\omega_N$). For low values of the market-clearing wage the first effect dominates, while for large values of ω_N the second effect dominates.

To gain further perspective, additional structure must be imposed on the model. Suppose, for instance, that the quit function takes the logistic form, $q = 1/(1 + \beta\omega)$, where $\beta > 0$ depends positively on the net nonpecuniary benefit—such as the proximity of activities from family and friends, and their physical location—associated with employment in the export sector. As shown in Agénor (2006*b*), as long as the quit rate is below one-half, we have $0 < \eta < 0.5$, and the elasticity of the efficiency wage in the export sector with respect to the market-clearing wage will be less than unity ($0 < d \ln \omega_X / d \ln \omega_N < 1$). Henceforth we assume that this condition holds.

Substituting the optimal value of ω_X from (3) in (4) determines the demand for labor in the export sector, n_X^d. Substituting this result in (1) yields

$$y_X^s = y_X^s(\omega_N), \qquad y_X^{s\prime} < 0, \tag{7}$$

which indicates that a rise in the real wage in the nontraded goods sector lowers output in the export sector.

Production in the nontraded goods sector also takes place under decreasing returns to labor, and can be written as

$$y_N = n_N^{\alpha_N}, \tag{8}$$

where $\alpha_N \in (0, 1)$. Real profits in that sector (in terms of the price of exports) are given by

$$\Pi_N = z^{-1} n_N^{\alpha_N} - \omega_N n_N, \tag{9}$$

where z is the real exchange rate (that is, the relative price of exports over nontraded goods). Profit maximization yields the familiar equality between marginal revenue and marginal cost:

$$\omega_N = z^{-1} \alpha_N n_N^{\alpha_N - 1}, \tag{10}$$

from which labor demand can be derived as $n_N^d = n_N^d(z\omega_N)$. Substituting this result in (8) yields

$$y_N^s = y_N^s(z\omega_N), \qquad y_N^{s\prime} < 0, \tag{11}$$

where $z\omega_N$ is the product wage in the nontraded goods sector.

From (7) and (11), real factor income (measured in terms of the price of exported goods) is given by

$$y = z^{-1} y_N^s(z\omega_N) + y_X^s(\omega_N). \tag{12}$$

1.1.2 Consumption and the Market for Nontraded Goods

Households supply a fixed quantity of labor inelastically and consume imported and nontraded goods. Total consumption c (measured in terms of the price of exportables) is given by

$$c = \lambda(y + i^*b) + (1 - \lambda)(\bar{y} + i^*\bar{b}) - T, \tag{13}$$

where $\lambda \in (0, 1)$, i^* is the world interest rate (assumed constant), b the real stock of traded bonds, T real lump-sum taxes (both measured in terms of the price of exported goods), and $\bar{y}$ and $\bar{b}$ the steady-state values of net factor income and bond holdings. Equation (13) indicates that aggregate consumption depends on disposable income, which is given by subtracting lump-sum taxes from "expected" gross income—measured as a weighted average of current resources (net factor income and interest payments) and long-term (or permanent) income. This specification allows us to capture, in a relatively simple and tractable manner, the forward-looking component of consumption behavior that has been emphasized in the optimizing models used elsewhere in this book (see, for instance, Chapter 10).

Setting the world price of imports to unity implies that the domestic price of imported goods, P_I, is given by

$$P_I = 1 + \tau, \tag{14}$$

where $\tau \in (0, 1)$ denotes the ad valorem tariff rate on imports.

Assuming, as in Chapter 10, that the household's instantaneous utility function in terms of domestic and foreign goods is Cobb-Douglas, the optimal allocation of aggregate consumption expenditure is given by

$$c_I = \delta c / (1 + \tau), \quad c_N = (1 - \delta)zc, \tag{15}$$

where c_I denotes consumption of imports, c_N consumption of nontraded goods, and $\delta \in (0, 1)$ the utility weight attached to imported goods.

The flow budget constraint of the household is thus given by

$$\dot{b} = i^* b + y - z^{-1} c_N - (1+\tau)c_I - T. \tag{16}$$

To close the system, we should specify the long-term demand for bonds, $\tilde{b}$. A fully optimizing model that derives the demand for bonds endogenously would lead to a dynamic system with three variables. To avoid the analytical complications involved in this case, the long-term demand for bonds is assumed to be proportional to long-term income ($\tilde{b} = \varphi \tilde{y}$), and to simplify further we assume that $\varphi = 0$.

Using (11) and (15), the equilibrium condition of the market for nontraded goods can be written as

$$y_N^s(z\omega_N) = (1-\delta)zc + g_N, \tag{17}$$

where g_N is the constant level of public spending on nontraded goods.

1.1.3 Government

The government, as indicated earlier, consumes nontraded goods and collects taxes on imported goods as well as lump-sum taxes on households. Its budget constraint can be written as

$$\tau c_I + T = z^{-1} g_N, \tag{18}$$

which indicates that proceeds from tariffs on imported goods are returned to households as lump-sum transfers or tax rebates as long as they exceed government spending on nontraded goods.

The initial equilibrium (which prevails until an instant before $t = 0$) is assumed to be such that lump-sum taxes are zero ($T_{0^-} = 0$), and that the import tax rate is high enough to equilibrate the budget. Using (15), the initial budget constraint is thus

$$\alpha \chi c = z^{-1} g_N, \quad t < 0 \tag{19}$$

where $\chi = \tau/(1+\tau)$ is the percentage tariff rate. Substituting (12), (13), (15), (17), and (19) in (16) yields

$$\dot{b} = i^* b + y_X^s - \delta c/(1+\tau). \tag{20}$$

1.1.4 Labor Market Adjustment

In the labor market, available workers queue up continuously to seek employment in the export sector. As indicated earlier, firms in that sector determine the wage so as to minimize total labor costs. They hire randomly from the queue, up to the point where their optimal demand for labor is satisfied. Although workers who cannot find a job in the export sector could obtain one in the nontraded goods sector, reallocation of the labor force cannot occur instantaneously—owing to, say, relocation and congestion costs.[7] Imperfect labor mobility implies therefore that the distribution of the workforce across sectors is predetermined at any moment in time. Formally, let N be the size of the total labor force in the economy. The equilibrium condition that equates supply and demand for workers in the nontraded goods sector is given by

$$N - n_X^s = n_N(z\omega_N), \tag{21}$$

where n_X^s denotes the supply of labor in the export sector. The mechanism through which workers migrate across sectors follows the Harris-Todaro formulation discussed in Chapters 1 and 4. The expected wage in the export sector is equal to the going wage weighted by the probability of being hired. Because hiring is random, this probability can be approximated by the prevailing employment ratio. The expected wage in the nontraded goods sector is simply the going wage, given that the probability of finding employment is unity in that sector. Thus. the supply of labor in the export sector evolves over time according to

$$\dot{n}_X^s = \kappa \left(\frac{\omega_X n_X^d}{n_X^s} - \omega_N \right), \tag{22}$$

where $\kappa > 0$ denotes the speed of adjustment. Equation (22) implies that in the steady state, with $\dot{n}_X^s = 0$, the wage ratio $\tilde{\omega}$ is equal to the inverse of the employment rate in the export sector.

Before examining the effects of tariff reform, it is convenient to examine first the effect of changes in the dynamic variables (the stock of foreign bonds and labor supply in the export sector) on the short-run equilibrium values of the real exchange rate and the real wage in the nontraded goods sector. From (8) and the labor market equilibrium condition (21), $n_N^s = (N - n_X^s)^{\alpha_N}$. Using this result, together with the profit maximization condition (10) for firms producing nontraded goods and (7), (8), and (13), and $\dot{b} = 0$, the equilibrium condition of the market for nontraded goods (17) can be written as:

$$\Lambda(N - n_X^s)^{\alpha_N} - z(1 - \delta)[(y_X^s + i^*b) + (1 - \lambda)\tilde{y} - g_N = 0,$$

$$z\omega_N - \alpha_N(N - n_X^s)^{\alpha_N - 1} = 0,$$

where $\Lambda \equiv 1 - \lambda(1 - \delta) > 0$. From this system, it can be established that

$$z = z(\overset{-}{b}, \overset{?}{n_X^s}), \quad \omega_N = \omega_N(\overset{+}{b}, \overset{+}{n_X^s}). \tag{23}$$

---

[7]In Furusawa and Lai (1999), for instance, adjustment costs associated with inter-sectoral reallocation of labor consist of "frictional losses," defined as costs associated with training, physical relocation, and temporary unemployment.

Equations (23) indicate that an increase in the stock of bonds raises the market-clearing wage in the nontraded goods sector (because it raises consumption of home goods, and thus output and the demand for labor) and leads to a real exchange rate appreciation—an increase in the relative price of home goods—which helps restore equilibrium between supply and demand. An increase in the labor force in the export sector raises wages in the nontraded goods sector (because it lowers the supply of labor in that sector) but has an ambiguous effect on the real exchange rate. On the one hand, there is a negative supply effect, because the fall in output of nontraded goods induced by the wage increase (initiated in the nontraded goods sector, and then transmitted to the export sector, as a result of efficiency considerations) leads directly to an appreciation of the real exchange rate. On the other, there is a demand effect, which results from the fact that the fall in output in the nontraded goods sector lowers factor income and reduces private expenditure, thus requiring a real depreciation to restore equilibrium in the market for nontraded goods. Formally, we have

$$\text{sg}\left(\frac{\partial z}{\partial n_X^s}\right) = -\text{sg}\left\{\lambda(1-\delta)\left(\frac{1-\alpha_N}{N-n_X^s}\right)y_X^{s'} + \Lambda\right\} \lesseqgtr 0,$$

which indicates that if aggregate consumption responds mainly to permanent rather than current income ($\lambda \to 0$), the supply effect will dominate, and the net effect of an increase in the labor force in the export sector will be an appreciation of the real exchange rate.

Because, as indicated above, $n_N^s = (N - n_X^s)^{\alpha_N}$, the supply of nontraded goods is independent of changes in the stock of foreign bonds. Equations (7) and (23) imply that output of the export sector is inversely related to holdings of foreign bonds and the size of the labor force in the export sector:

$$y_X^s = (\bar{b}, \bar{n}_X^s). \tag{24}$$

Substituting (12), (13), (15), (17), (19), (23), and (24) in (20) yields

$$\dot{b} = \left(1 - \frac{\delta\lambda}{1+\tau}\right)\{i^*b + y_X^s[\omega_X(b, n_X^s)]\} \tag{25}$$

$$-\frac{\delta}{(1+\tau)}\left\{\frac{\lambda y_N^s[z(\cdot)\omega_N(\cdot)]}{z(b, n_X^s)} + (1-\lambda)\tilde{y}\right\},$$

which determines the rate of accumulation of foreign assets. Finally, using (6), substituting out the short-run equilibrium solution (23) and using both results in (22) yields

$$\dot{n}_X^s = J(b, n_X^s), \tag{26}$$

where

$$\frac{\partial J}{\partial b} = \kappa \left(\frac{\partial \omega_N}{\partial b} \right) \left\{ \left(\frac{\partial \omega_X}{\partial \omega_N} \right) \left(\frac{\tilde{n}_X^d}{\tilde{n}_X^s} \right) + \left(\frac{\tilde{\omega}_X}{\tilde{n}_X^s} \right) \left(\frac{\partial n_X^d}{\partial \omega_N} \right) - 1 \right\},$$

$$\frac{\partial J}{\partial n_X^s} = \kappa \left\{ \left(\frac{\partial \omega_N}{\partial n_X^s} \right) \left[\left(\frac{\partial \omega_X}{\partial \omega_N} \right) \left(\frac{\tilde{n}_X^d}{\tilde{n}_X^s} \right) + \left(\frac{\tilde{\omega}_X}{\tilde{n}_X^s} \right) \left(\frac{\partial n_X^d}{\partial \omega_N} \right) - 1 \right] - \frac{\tilde{\omega}_X \tilde{n}_X^d}{(\tilde{n}_X^s)^2} \right\}.$$

Equation (6) implies that the elasticity of ω_X with respect to ω_N is less than unity. Using this result and the fact that the wage ratio is equal to the inverse of the employment ratio in the export sector in the vicinity of the steady state [see (22)] yields

$$\frac{\partial J}{\partial b} = \kappa \left(\frac{\partial \omega_N}{\partial b} \right) \left\{ \left(\frac{\partial \omega_X}{\partial \omega_N} \right) \left(\frac{\tilde{\omega}_N}{\tilde{\omega}_X} \right) - 1 + \left(\frac{\tilde{\omega}_X}{\tilde{n}_X^s} \right) \left(\frac{\partial n_X^d}{\partial \omega_N} \right) \right\} < 0,$$

$$\frac{\partial J}{\partial n_X^s} = \kappa \left\{ \left(\frac{\partial \omega_N}{\partial n_X^s} \right) \left[\left(\frac{\partial \omega_X}{\partial \omega_N} \right) \left(\frac{\tilde{\omega}_N}{\tilde{\omega}_X} \right) - 1 + \left(\frac{\tilde{\omega}_X}{\tilde{n}_X^s} \right) \left(\frac{\partial n_X^d}{\partial \omega_N} \right) - 1 \right] - \frac{\tilde{\omega}_X \tilde{n}_X^d}{(\tilde{n}_X^s)^2} \right\} < 0.$$

Equations (25) and (26) determine the behavior of foreign assets and the size of the workforce in the export sector over time. Substituting the solution values of this system in (23) yields the equilibrium levels of the real wage in the nontraded goods sector and the real exchange rate. A linear approximation to (25) and (26) around the steady state yields

$$\begin{bmatrix} \dot{b} \\ \dot{n}_X^s \end{bmatrix} = \begin{bmatrix} a_{11} & a_{12} \\ \partial J / \partial b & \partial J / \partial n_X^s \end{bmatrix} \begin{bmatrix} b - \tilde{b} \\ n_X^s - \tilde{n}_X^s \end{bmatrix}, \tag{27}$$

where $\tilde{n}_X^s < N$ and the coefficients a_{11} and a_{12} are given by

$$a_{11} = \left(1 - \frac{\delta \lambda}{1 + \tau} \right) \left\{ i^* + y_X^{s\prime} \left(\frac{\partial \omega_N}{\partial b} \right) \right\} + \frac{\delta \lambda}{(1 + \tau)} \left(\frac{\tilde{y}_N^s}{\tilde{z}^2} \right) \left(\frac{\partial z}{\partial b} \right),$$

$$a_{12} = \left(1 - \frac{\delta \lambda}{1 + \tau} \right) y_X^{s\prime} \left(\frac{\partial \omega_N}{\partial n_X^s} \right) - \frac{\delta \lambda}{1 + \tau} \left\{ \tilde{z}^{-1} \left(\frac{\partial y_N^s}{\partial n_X^s} \right) - \left(\frac{\tilde{y}_N^s}{\tilde{z}^2} \right) \left(\frac{\partial z}{\partial n_X^s} \right) \right\}.$$

Assuming that i^* is small, a_{11} is negative. In general, a_{12} is ambiguous. Given that a_{11} and $\partial J / \partial n_X^s$ are both negative, local stability of the system described by (27) requires that its determinant, given by $a_{11}(\partial J / \partial n_X^s) - a_{12}(\partial J / \partial b)$, be positive, to ensure two negative roots. A sufficient (although not necessary) condition for this result to hold is $a_{12} > 0$. We will assume that this is indeed the case in what follows.

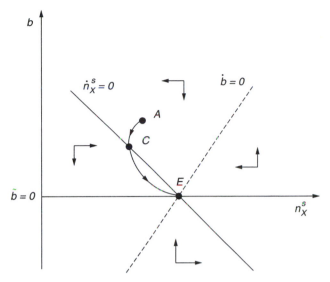

Figure 18–1 ▪ Steady-State Equilibrium
Source: Agénor and Aizenman (1996, p. 274).

The steady-state equilibrium of the model is depicted in Figure 18.1. The upward-sloping locus $[\dot{b} = 0]$ gives the combinations of b and n_X^s for which the stock of foreign assets remains constant, whereas the downward-sloping locus $[\dot{n}_X^s = 0]$ depicts the combinations of b and n_X^s for which the size of the labor force in the export sector does not change over time. The steady-state equilibrium obtains at point E. If the economy's initial position is at, say, point A—characterized by an excess supply of labor in the export sector and a current account surplus— the transition toward the steady state will be nonmonotonic and characterized by a continuous reduction in the stock of foreign assets, associated with an initial reduction of the labor force in the export sector (between points A and C) followed by a gradual increase (between points C and E).

1.2 ▪ Tariffs, Real Wages, and Employment

Consider now a tariff reform implemented at $t = 0$ starting from a situation where, as described earlier, lump-sum taxes are zero and the tariff rate is high enough to generate sufficient revenue to cover government spending on nontraded goods. The reform consists in reducing the percentage tariff rate χ, and simultaneously adjusting lump-sum taxes to equilibrate the government budget.

1.2.1 *Steady-State Effects*

To study the steady-state effects of the tariff reform, let us first consider the system prevailing before the adjustment. From (13), in the steady state, $\tilde{c} = \tilde{y} - \tilde{T}$.

The government budget constraint [equation (18)] can thus be written as

$$\delta\chi(\tilde{y} - \tilde{T}) + \tilde{T} = \tilde{z}^{-1}g_N,$$

or, using (12):

$$\delta\chi(z^{-1}\tilde{y}_N^s + \tilde{y}_X^s) + (1 - \delta\chi)\tilde{T} = \tilde{z}^{-1}g_N. \qquad (28)$$

The steady-state equilibrium condition of the labor market is given by, from (21) and (22):

$$N = n_N^d(\tilde{z}\tilde{\omega}_N) + \tilde{n}_X^s = n_N^d(\tilde{z}\tilde{\omega}_N) + \tilde{\omega}n_X^d(\tilde{\omega}_N), \qquad (29)$$

where, from (6), $\tilde{\omega}_X = \omega_X(\tilde{\omega}_N)$.

Finally, the long-run equilibrium condition of the market for nontraded goods can be written as, using (17),

$$\delta\tilde{y}_N - (1 - \delta)\tilde{z}\tilde{y}_X + (1 - \delta)\tilde{z}\tilde{T} = g_N. \qquad (30)$$

Equations (28)–(30) can be solved in terms of $\tilde{z}$, $\tilde{\omega}_N$, and $\tilde{T}$. Tedious but straightforward calculations show that

$$\frac{d\tilde{T}}{d\chi} < 0, \quad \frac{d\tilde{\omega}_N}{d\chi} < 0, \quad \frac{d\tilde{z}}{d\chi} < 0, \quad \frac{d\tilde{z}\tilde{\omega}_N}{d\chi} < 0.$$

A reduction in the percentage tariff rate raises lump-sum taxes, exerting a negative income effect on total consumption. The induced reduction in private spending on nontraded goods requires a depreciation of the real exchange rate to maintain market equilibrium. The real depreciation tends to increase the product wage in the nontraded goods sector, thereby lowering output and the demand for labor in that sector. The reduction in labor demand puts downward pressure on the market-clearing wage, thus partly offsetting the effect of the real depreciation. But because the real exchange-rate depreciation is proportionally larger than the reduction of the real wage in the nontraded goods sector, the product wage rises and lowers output and employment in that sector. By contrast, the reduction in the real wage in the nontraded goods sector leads to a fall in the product wage in the export sector, which stimulates output and employment. The net effect on total employment is in general ambiguous, because employment rises in the export sector and falls in the nontraded goods sector. Aggregate output measured in terms of traded goods, nevertheless, is likely to rise.

To determine how the relative wage ratio evolves, note that

$$\frac{d\tilde{\omega}}{d\chi} = \left(\frac{\tilde{\omega}}{\tilde{\omega}_N}\right)\left(\frac{d\tilde{\omega}_N}{d\chi}\right)\left(\frac{d\omega_X/\omega_X}{d\omega_N/\omega_N} - 1\right), \tag{31}$$

which implies that, if the elasticity of the efficiency wage relative to the market-clearing wage is less than unity, the wage ratio increases $(d\omega/d\chi < 0)$ as a result of tariff reform. Equivalently, wages in the export sector fall proportionally less than the market-clearing wage. From this result, the effect of the tariff reform on the supply of labor in the export sector can also be determined. From (22), $\tilde{n}^s_X = \tilde{\omega}_X \tilde{n}^d_X/\tilde{\omega}_N$; this implies that

$$\frac{d\tilde{n}^s_X}{d\chi} = \left(\frac{d\tilde{\omega}_N}{d\chi}\right)\left\{\tilde{\omega}\left(\frac{d\tilde{n}^d_X}{d\chi}\right) + \tilde{n}^d_X\left(\frac{\tilde{\omega}}{\tilde{\omega}_N}\right)\left(\frac{d\tilde{\omega}_X/\omega_X}{d\tilde{\omega}_N/\omega_N} - 1\right)\right\}. \tag{32}$$

Given that the demand for labor rises in the export sector $(d\tilde{n}^d_X/d\chi < 0)$ and that the wage elasticity is less then unity, (32) indicates that the tariff reform raises the size of the labor force in that sector $(d\tilde{n}^s_X/d\chi < 0)$. Moreover, as implied by (31) and the equilibrium condition $\tilde{\omega} = \tilde{n}^s_X/\tilde{n}^d_X$, labor supply rises by more than demand, lowering the employment ratio. To the extent that tariff reform leads to a transfer of labor from the nontraded goods sector (where it earns its marginal product) to the export sector (where it is paid more than its marginal product), the use of production factors becomes less efficient.

The (sectoral) unemployment rate, u_X, can be defined as $u_X = (n^s_X - n^d_X)/n^s_X$, so that in the steady state, using (22), $\tilde{u}_X = 1 - (\tilde{\omega}_N/\tilde{\omega}_X)$. Using the results derived earlier, it can be established that

$$\frac{d\tilde{u}_X}{d\chi} = \tilde{\omega}_X^{-1}\left(\frac{d\tilde{\omega}_N}{d\chi}\right)\left(\frac{d\omega_X/\omega_X}{d\omega_N/\omega_N} - 1\right), \tag{33}$$

which shows that a reduction in tariffs raises the unemployment rate in the steady state $(d\tilde{u}_X/d\chi < 0)$ if the elasticity of the efficiency wage with respect to the market-clearing wage is less than unity. In such a case, the increase in labor demand and actual employment in that sector is more than offset by the rise in the size of the labor force seeking employment in the export sector.

Finally, it can be shown that the purchasing power of workers' earnings in both sectors rises in terms of nontraded goods. However, the net welfare effect of tariff reform is in general ambiguous and depends on the magnitude of the wage differential across sectors.

1.2.2 Short-Run Dynamics

To examine the short-run dynamic behavior of the model after reform, note that (25) becomes, after implementation of the tariff-cum-fiscal adjustment:

$$\dot{b} = i^*b + y_X^s(\cdot) - \frac{\delta}{1+\tau}\lambda[i^*b + y_X^s(\cdot) + z(\cdot)^{-1}y_N^s(\cdot)] - T + (1-\lambda)\bar{y}\}, \quad (34)$$

where, from (18), $T = z^{-1}g_N$. The dynamic system consists now of (26) and (34), and can be linearized to study its properties.

The impact effect of the trade liberalization program on wages, employment, and output (given that the stock of bonds and the labor force in the export sector cannot change instantaneously) is in general indeterminate and depends on the degree to which consumption responds to long-run income or transitory income. Regardless of the value of λ, however, because labor reallocation across sectors cannot occur instantaneously, the product wage in the nontraded goods sector must remain constant on impact as a result of offsetting movements in the real wage and the real exchange rate:[8]

$$\frac{d[z_0\omega_N(0)]}{d\chi} = 0. \quad (35)$$

This result implies therefore [see (11)] that output and employment in the nontraded goods sector do not change on impact. The instantaneous effect on total factor income—measured in terms of the price of exports—thus depends only on the direction of the initial effect on output of exported goods:

$$\text{sg}\left(\frac{dy_0}{d\chi}\right) = \text{sg}\left(\frac{dy_X^s(0)}{d\chi}\right) = y_E^{s'}\text{sg}\left(\frac{d\omega_N(0)}{d\chi}\right). \quad (36)$$

For instance, if the consumption behavior of households responds essentially to changes in current resources ($\lambda \to 1$), we have $dz_0/d\chi < 0$ and $d\omega_N(0)/d\chi > 0$, which indicate that the reduction in tariffs lowers wages in the nontraded goods sector (and thus in the export sector as well) and leads to a depreciation of the real exchange rate. This result obtains because the impact effect of tariff reform is an increase in lump-sum taxes and a reduction in consumption of both domestic and imported goods. As a result, the real exchange rate must depreciate to maintain equilibrium in the market for nontraded goods. Because, as shown in (35), the product wage cannot change on impact in the nontraded goods sector, the market-clearing wage measured in terms of export goods must fall—thereby reducing the efficiency wage and raising the demand for labor and output in the export sector.

---

[8]See Chapter 4, Section 5, for a similar result.

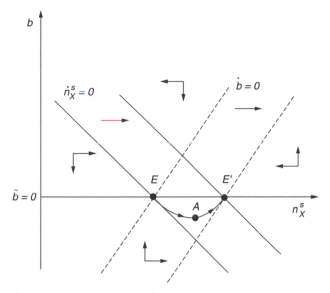

Figure 18–2 ▪ Adjustment to Tariff Reform
Source: Agénor and Aizenman (1996, p. 278).

The increase in exports—which translates, as shown in (36), into an equivalent increase in net factor income—dampens the initial adverse effect of taxes on private expenditure. The short-run effect on the unemployment rate is

$$\frac{du_X(0)}{d\chi} = -\left[\frac{n_X^{d\prime}}{n_X^s(0)}\right]\left[\frac{d\omega_N(0)}{d\chi}\right] > 0,$$

which shows that, as a result of the increase in labor demand and employment in the export sector, the unemployment rate in that sector falls on impact. Thus, while the steady-state effect of tariff reform on unemployment may be negative (if the elasticity of the efficiency wage relative to the market-clearing wage is less than unity), the short-run effect may be positive—assuming that consumption depends mostly on current income.

The dynamic adjustment path is shown in Figure 18.2. Suppose that the economy is initially located at the steady-state point E. The reduction in the tariff rate shifts both curves $[\dot{n}_X^s = 0]$ and $[\dot{b} = 0]$ to the right. In the case shown in the figure, the reduction in the percentage tariff rate raises consumption of imported goods during the transition period. The economy runs a current account deficit during the first stage of the adjustment process (between points E and A) and accumulates foreign debt ($\dot{b} < 0$), whereas in a second stage (between points A and E') it generates a current account surplus which reduces foreign debt ($\dot{b} > 0$). The new equilibrium, which obtains at E', is again characterized by a zero steady-state level of foreign bonds and an increase in the size of the labor force in the export sector.

The foregoing results differ significantly from the conventional view of trade reform, which rests on the assumptions of perfect flexibility of wages and prices, and perfect labor mobility across sectors. Under such conditions, a reduction in tariff protection leads to changes in relative prices that affect both supply and demand, and to a full and instantaneous reallocation of resources across sectors. The cut in tariffs is associated with an overall transfer of labor from sectors producing nontradables toward those producing tradables, thus reducing employment in the former sector and mitigating the fall in employment in the import-competing industries. Unemployment cannot emerge, because workers are perfectly mobile across sectors and wages adjust continuously to clear the labor market.

By contrast, the foregoing results are based on three major assumptions: turnover costs are significant only in the export sector; the elasticity of the wage in the export sector relative to the wage in the nontraded goods sector is less than unity; and labor reallocation across sectors is gradual and follows the Harris-Todaro approach. The latter plays a critical role in deriving the short- and long-run effects of trade liberalization: it prevents an instantaneous reallocation of the labor force across sectors and requires the wage ratio to be equal in the steady state to the inverse of the employment rate in the export sector. Moreover, in the general form in which (31)–(33) are written, they clearly indicate that the steady-state effects of tariff reform on the labor market depend critically on the elasticity of the efficiency wage in the export sector relative to the market-clearing wage in the nontraded goods sector. The quit function specified earlier—which can be derived from proper microeconomic principles—implies that the wage elasticity is less than unity. As a result, labor supply in the export sector rises by more than labor demand, and the unemployment rate rises. Thus, an alternative (and perhaps equally plausible) specification of the quit function that would yield a wage elasticity *higher* than unity would imply a reduction in steady-state unemployment—as emphasized in the conventional view—whereas an elasticity exactly equal to unity would imply no long-run effect at all. A unit elasticity (or equivalently, a constant relative wage ratio) could be generated in the present framework by modeling efficiency considerations through a wage-productivity link, as derived by Agénor and Aizenman (1999a).

In general, therefore, the direction of the long-run effects of tariff reform on the labor market depends crucially on the characteristic of the migration process and the wage formation mechanism. In addition, fixed labor supply in the export sector has important consequences for the short-run effects of trade reform. Although most of these effects are ambiguous in general, we showed that "perverse" results can be obtained when consumption reacts mostly to changes in current disposable income. Put differently, the assumption that labor is imperfectly mobile across sectors alters fundamentally the conventional transmission mechanism of trade reform, because the reallocation of resources in response to relative price signals can only take place over time.

In sum, although the evidence does not suggest that trade reforms have had a large adverse effect on employment in the short run, the above discussion indicates that the interactions between the process of wage formation and the structure of production activities may well lead to undesirable macroeconomic outcomes in the short *and* the long run. Other studies have also found that trade reform may have adverse effects on the labor market; these include Buffie (1984*b*), Batra and Beladi (1999), and Geide-Stevenson (2000). Some of these papers incorporate, as was done here, various types of labor market distortions—although in the Batra-Beladi study, the condition for unemployment to emerge depends solely on the endogeneity of labor supply and on whether the production of importables is more labor-intensive than the production of exportables.

At the same time, however, it is important to realize that even if trade liberalization entails short-run adjustment costs, it may still be beneficial in the long run, because elasticities of substitution between production inputs are generally higher than in the short run.[9] It is nevertheless important to weigh carefully potential short-run costs and devise the reform process so as to minimize them. We will examine later in this chapter the implication of this general principle for the sustainability and the optimal pace of reform, taking into account political factors and the need to maintain credibility in the adjustment process.

2 Financial Liberalization

As indicated in previous chapters, financial repression, involving a broad panoply of legal restrictions on the behavior of banks—such as ceilings on interest rates, restrictions on competition in the banking industry and the composition of bank portfolios—has long characterized the financial system of many developing countries. In the past two decades, however, many of these countries (poor and middle-income alike) have moved away from these regimes and engaged in ambitious reforms, directed at removing these restrictions on bank behavior. Financial liberalization has taken the form of privatization of public financial institutions, the removal of restrictions to entry into banking (including those preventing access by foreign banks), measures aimed at spurring competition in financial markets, the reduction of legal reserve requirements and liquidity ratios, the elimination of directed lending, in addition to the freeing of official interest rates.

This section provides a brief review of the analytics and the empirical evidence on the effects of financial sector reform as a structural policy—that is, as a policy designed to enhance medium-term economic growth by promoting the accumulation and efficient use of productive assets—as well as on the lessons that have emerged from the experience of developing countries.

---

[9]Note also that trade liberalization may induce the creation of new production activities over time, thereby increasing the demand for labor. Thus, our steady-state results may best be characterized as related to the "medium-run" rather than the "long-run" effects of trade liberalization on wages and unemployment.

2.1 ■ Deregulation of Interest Rates

The arguments for freeing interest rates as a structural policy conducive to a higher growth path are due to McKinnon (1973) and Shaw (1973). They can be summarized briefly as follows: In a context in which the saving instruments available in the financial system are limited to cash, demand deposits, and time deposits, raising controlled interest rates to near-equilibrium levels may induce an increase in the saving rate as well as a portfolio shift out of inventories, precious metals, foreign exchange, and curb market lending into the formal financial system. The high real interest rates resulting from the reform would actually increase rather than reduce investment in the aggregate, either because the need to accumulate funds to undertake lumpy investments makes money and capital complementary rather than substitute assets (stressed by McKinnon), or because of a "credit availability" effect (the channel emphasized by Shaw). The latter works as follows: when interest rates are at below-equilibrium levels, total investment is limited to the available saving. By increasing total saving and attracting it into the banking system, higher real interest rates would increase investment through enhanced credit availability.[10] Moreover, many high-return projects not previously funded would be undertaken after freeing interest rates, because banks have scale economies relative to the informal market in collecting and processing information on borrowers. Thus, they are more efficient in channeling funds to high-return investment projects than the informal market. The conclusion is that growth is enhanced both because the increase in saving raises investment and because the quality of investment improves.

According to these arguments, then, allowing previously controlled interest rates to increase to their market levels should raise the demand for domestic time and saving deposits, which in turn should increase the quantity, and improve the quality, of domestic investment. A higher rate of capital accumulation would stimulate growth. The evidence on these propositions takes two forms. Econometric studies have looked at each of these propositions separately, and sometimes have examined the link between the immediate policy objective (higher real interest rates) and intermediate or ultimate targets in the form of investment and growth. A separate strand of evidence evaluates the experience of countries that have fostered interest rate deregulation.[11]

The more recent (and, presumably, more rigorous) evidence on the effect of interest rate liberalization on growth is mixed (see Bandiera et al., 2000). Higher real deposit interest rates do not appear to have strong effects on the saving rate.

---

[10] As pointed out by Cho (1986) in a discussion of the Stiglitz-Weiss model, interest rate liberalization does not completely eliminate credit rationing because at sufficiently high interest rates the additional risk may cause banks' expected profits to be lower. The problem may be compounded by the fact that firms may have no alternative opportunity to raise capital resources for investment. Hence, Cho suggests that the development of stock markets should be fostered along with the liberalization of the financial system. A potential difficulty with Cho's conclusions is that stock markets are not widely used as primary sources of capital in developing countries (see Chapter 5).

[11] See Fry (1996) for an overview of the early evidence.

This is not too surprising, given the evidence reviewed in Chapter 2; many studies have found that the real interest elasticity of total savings is not significantly different from zero, and when it is, it tends to be fairly small.

At the same time, portfolio shifts toward domestic financial instruments are apparently induced by interest rate deregulation. Nevertheless, this may not have a large effect on the volume of investment. There is little evidence in favor of the "complementarity" effect, and while the "credit availability" effect is more strongly supported by the data—in the sense that an increase in the supply of credit, other things equal, is positively correlated with the level of investment, as discussed in Chapter 2—the absence of a positive relationship between real deposit rates and investment raises the question of whether this correlation should be interpreted as being in support of the "credit availability" channel. Last, although a positive correlation between real deposit rates and growth seems to be a feature of developing-country data, the interpretation of this relationship is problematic. It may well reflect some contribution of the efficiency effect discussed above, but the real deposit rate may also be serving as a proxy for more general distortions, including the uncertainties associated with high and unstable inflation.

Not surprisingly, the episodic evidence associated with specific-country cases of interest rate deregulation does not provide a clearer verdict, essentially because *ceteris paribus* conditions do not hold. As an illustration, consider the Korean monetary reform of 1965. As described in McKinnon (1976), nominal deposit and lending rates had been pegged at low levels in Korea prior to the reform, yielding strongly negative real rates in 1963–1964. Nominal rates were revised upward, but not freed, in September 1965, and directed credit restrictions were reduced but not eliminated–thus qualifying this episode as a monetary reform rather than a full financial liberalization. Real rates of return rose markedly subsequent to the reform, the ratio of broad money to GDP increased by a factor of 7 between 1964 and 1969, private saving increased, and growth experienced a very strong acceleration. McKinnon interpreted this as supporting the positive effect of monetary reform on growth, through the channels previously mentioned.

Giovannini (1985), however, reached different conclusions. He emphasized that most of the increase in national saving in Korea in the period after 1965 originated in the public sector and resulted from a fiscal correction. He pointed out further that the measured increase in households' surplus after the reform was a one-shot event concentrated in 1966, and that the correlation between this surplus and the real interest rate was negative after that year. He concluded from this evidence that the measured increase in saving may well have been due to the recording of a portfolio shift out of the informal market as a change in saving.

2.2 ■ Broader Aspects of Financial Liberalization

As noted earlier, in addition to interest rate deregulation, financial liberalization entails two other major aspects—the elimination of restrictions on the allocation of credit by commercial banks and the phasing out of restrictions on capital movements (which may entail also providing foreign banks with greater access to domestic financial markets). The evidence on the benefits and costs of international financial openness was discussed in Chapter 13; here we consider briefly the evidence related to the impact of "financial deepening" (as measured by ratios of bank credit or deposits to output) on economic growth.

Here again, the evidence provides a mixed picture. By and large, cross-country and panel data studies find positive effects of financial development on output growth even after accounting for other determinants of growth as well as for potential biases induced by simultaneity, omitted variables, and unobserved country-specific effects. Levine et al. (2000), for instance, found that financial development is positively associated with economic growth. Moreover, they also discovered that differences across countries in legal and accounting systems (such as creditor rights, contract enforcement, and accounting standards) explain to a significant extent differences in the level of financial depth. Based on data for sixty countries for the period 1980–2002, Ranciere et al. (2006) found that financial liberalization tends to spur long-run growth on average, despite the fact that it also increases the probability (and actual occurrences, on occasion) of financial crises.

Using firm-level panel data for twelve developing countries, Galindo et al. (2007) found that financial liberalization (as measured by various indicators of financial depth) led in the majority of cases to an increase in the efficiency of allocation of investment funds (as measured by the share of investment going to firms with a higher marginal return to capital), and thus presumably to higher growth. Aghion et al. (2005) found a significant and sizable negative coefficient on initial per capita GDP (relative to the United States) interacted with financial intermediation, suggesting therefore a strong impact of poorly developed financial systems on the speed of convergence.

By contrast, several studies based on time-series data give opposite results. Demetriades and Hussein (1996) for instance found little systematic evidence in favor of the view that financial depth is a leading factor in the process of economic growth. In addition, they found that for the majority of the countries they examined, causality is bidirectional, whereas in some cases financial development follows economic growth.

However, Christopoulos and Tsionas (2004) have argued that time-series studies may yield unreliable results due to the short time spans of typical datasets used. Instead, they rely on panel unit root tests and panel cointegration analysis to examine the relationship between financial development and growth in developing countries, thereby increasing significantly their sample size. In contrast to the previous studies, they found strong evidence in favor of long-run causality running from financial development (as measured by the ratio of total bank deposits to nominal GDP) to growth and no evidence of bidirectional causality.[12] Furthermore, they find a unique cointegrating vector between financial development and growth in most cases.

---

[12] Some studies have found evidence of reverse causality from growth to financial depth (at least in the long run); see, for instance, Ang and McKibbin (2007) for the case of Malaysia.

2.3 ▪ Role of Regulation and Supervision

The experience of the 1980s and 1990s has made it abundantly clear that financial liberalization, though potentially beneficial, can be risky if undertaken in a fragile financial environment. The high real interest rates that have often been associated with financial liberalization (as a result for instance of greater bank competition for deposits) may make the financial system more vulnerable to crises by worsening the problems of adverse selection and moral hazard, and by raising the incidence of default on loan commitments.[13] Where financial liberalization has led to an easing of liquidity constraints (through easier access to consumer credit, for instance), it has often been accompanied by a temporary expansion of consumption and a reduction, rather than an increase, in saving rates. If financial liberalization (in the form of lower incidence of credit rationing) leads to lower household savings (by reducing the precautionary motive), it may be detrimental to growth—despite having a positive effect on investment (see Hung 2005, for a detailed analysis). In addition, the credit boom has led to asset price bubbles, a weakening of bank balance sheets (because of inflated values of collateral), and greater vulnerability of the financial system to adverse shocks.

At the same time, macroeconomic instability has compounded the impact of financial reform on the performance of the financial system. By increasing the variance of and covariance among projects funded by banks, such instability leads to an increase in the riskiness of bank portfolios. If deposit insurance is absent or incorrectly priced, an analysis along the lines of the Stiglitz-Weiss model of credit rationing under informational asymmetries (see Chapter 5) predicts that banks would reduce interest rates and ration credit more severely. By contrast, with inadequately priced deposit insurance, moral hazard will induce banks to raise interest rates to attract deposits and fund high-risk projects, because they in effect face a one-way bet: if the projects pay off, bank owners reap the profits, whereas if they do not, the government foots the bill to pay off depositors, with bank owners risking only their limited capital. This outcome can be avoided when deposit insurance is priced correctly, because doing so forces banks to pay for the higher risk that their portfolio choices impose on the government, causing them to internalize the consequences of their actions. The same result could be ensured by adequate bank supervision, even when deposit insurance is free or inadequately priced.[14]

For instance, the data compiled by Williamson and Mahar (1998) for more than thirty industrial and developing countries during the 1980s and early 1990s indicated that in more than half of them, financial liberalization was followed by a

---

[13] Even without moral hazard problems, asymmetric information about the quality of loans (with all loans being viewed in the same risk-neutral way by financial institutions) can lead to financial fragility. See van Order (2006) for a formal analysis.

[14] This outcome would be avoided by supervision through the imposition of loan-loss reserves and capital adequacy standards, which increase the potential losses of shareholders when banks undertake risky loans.

financial crisis.[15] At a more formal level, Demirgüç-Kunt and Detragiache (2001) constructed an index of financial liberalization (reflecting mostly the deregulation of bank interest rates) for a group of more than fifty developed and developing countries for the period 1980–1995 and found that, everything else equal, banking crises were more likely to occur in liberalized financial systems. This relationship was stronger in countries where the institutional environment was weak, particularly in the area of prudential regulation and supervision of financial intermediaries and contract enforcement mechanisms. More specifically, in Argentina, Chile, and Uruguay, rapid removal of interest rate ceilings and credit controls in the mid- to late 1970s was accompanied by the relaxation of bank supervision and the extension of either explicit (Argentina) or implicit (Chile) deposit insurance, all in the context of high inflation and unsatisfactory economic performance. Indeed, the financial liberalization measures were accompanied by innovative macroeconomic stabilization programs in all three countries (see online Supplement B). Previous macroeconomic difficulties implied not just the uncertainties associated with the simultaneous undertaking of stabilization programs, but also that bank portfolios already included an unusual number of bad loans, effectively impairing bank capital and increasing the moral hazard problems created by deposit insurance. In all of these countries, lending rates quickly rose to high real levels, distress borrowing by firms ensued, and bankruptcies became common. In each case, the liberalization and stabilization programs collapsed in the midst of a financial crisis during the early 1980s. The Philippine and Turkish liberalizations in the 1980s were carried out under similar circumstances and in a similar fashion. Not surprisingly, they produced similar results.[16]

By contrast, although financial liberalization was carried out rapidly in Malaysia beginning in late 1978, the country had a long tradition of macroeconomic stability and banking supervision. The transition to a liberalized financial system proved to be rather smooth, with only a mild increase in real interest rates and no widespread bankruptcies culminating in financial collapse. At the same time, like the Southern Cone countries, Sri Lanka (in 1977) and Korea (in 1981) both undertook liberalization from initial conditions characterized by unsatisfactory macroeconomic performance. However, unlike the Southern Cone countries, both Asian countries moved to remove restrictions on interest rates gradually while pursuing macroeconomic stability and stronger prudential regulation over banks. Greater flexibility (although not full liberalization) was permitted in both countries only after macroeconomic stability was achieved and the supervisory mechanism strengthened.

---

[15]The link between financial liberalization and financial crises has often been attributed to poorly designed banking systems, an explanation that is largely static. Daniel and Jones (2007), by contrast, propose a dynamic explanation, based on the evolution of the degree of foreign competition, the marginal product of capital, and the bank's own net worth over time.

[16]For a discussion of the financial liberalization experience of Turkey, with particular emphasis on the role of market structure and competition in the banking industry, see Denizer (1997).

The analysis, overall, emphasizes two major preconditions for successful financial sector reform: a stable macroeconomic environment and a proper system of bank prudential regulation and supervision. Indeed, Villanueva and Mirakhor (1990), drawing from the experience of developing countries—primarily the financial reforms undertaken in the Southern Cone countries of Latin America in the late 1970s, as well as the experience of Korea, Malaysia, the Philippines, and Turkey—argued early on that success in financial liberalization requires macroeconomic stability and a strong and effective system of bank supervision as preconditions, and that success is more likely if controls on interest rates are removed gradually while these conditions are established.[17]

At the same time, the foregoing discussion suggests that reforming banking systems in developing countries requires a comprehensive approach addressing not only the immediate stock and flow problems of weak and insolvent banks but also correcting shortcomings in the accounting, legal, regulatory, and supervisory framework. Bank supervision, in particular, needs to be restructured and strengthened before financial liberalization in order to cope with the risks that liberalization entails. The globalization of financial markets and the associated increase in the volatility of capital flows has also underscored the importance of strengthening prudential supervision and related information systems in order to deal effectively with interest rate and exchange-rate risks, as well as other banking risks, particularly in the context of capital account liberalization.

Strengthening prudential supervision entails a variety of institutional reforms, including establishing an exposure limit on lending to connected parties (most importantly owners and affiliated companies), preventing concentration of credit to single borrowers, and raising bank capital to levels commensurate with the volatile macroeconomic environment that many developing countries face. Capital adequacy standards are particularly important to compensate for the effect of deposit insurance in weakening market discipline of financial institutions and may be important in mitigating the incentives to take on excessive risk.[18] Indeed, as discussed in Chapter 15, in the Diamond-Dybvig framework deposit insurance can avoid bank runs. However, if bank behavior is subject to moral hazard problems, Cooper and Ross (2002) showed that deposit insurance must be supplemented by higher capital requirements to ensure that depositors have adequate incentives for monitoring and for banks to avoid investing excessively in risky projects. Exposure to large macroeconomic shocks may also provide a rationale for centralized prudential regulation (that is, capital requirements), as shown by Rochet (2004).

However, it is possible for such requirements to distort banks' investment behavior to such an extent that they could end up making insolvency more, rather

---

[17] See also Galbis (1993), Leite and Sundararajan (1990), Sundararajan and Baliño (1991), and Goldstein and Turner (1996).

[18] For an overview of the literature on market discipline, see De Ceuster and Masschelein (2003).

than less, likely (Rochet, 1992). Moreover, as shown by Rochet (2004), although market discipline (in the form of private monitors) can be helpful, it does not solve the fundamental problem of regulatory forbearance (due to the inability of political authorities to commit); the key, therefore, is to establish independent and accountable banking supervisors.

In addition to prudential supervision, reforming banking systems in developing countries includes a number of other aspects, such as encouraging better public disclosure of banks' financial condition, adopting strict international accounting standards, upgrading banks' internal controls, and legislation to ensure arm's length credit allocation decisions (Bhattacharya et al., 1998). It is also important to bring greater transparency to government involvement or ownership in banking systems and to redesign official safety nets to include safeguards against strong political pressures for regulatory forbearance.

As noted in Chapter 5, one lesson from the global financial crisis is that financial regulation and supervision must adopt a *macroprudential* perspective to identify financial sector weaknesses and mitigate the build-up of systemic vulnerabilities. Doing so is important not only to mitigate macroeconomic fluctuations in the short run (the focus of most of the recent literature on macroprudential regulation) but also in the longer run. By exacerbating volatility in the economy, financial instability may reduce incentives to invest in projects whose returns are highly uncertain, thereby adversely affecting long-run growth. As a result, there has been a major effort, at both the national and international levels, to adjust and strengthen the regulatory and supervisory financial framework. The Basel III Accord, which was adopted in 2011, introduced substantial regulatory changes for banks, with the goal of reducing the frequency of financial crises and increasing the resilience of financial systems (see Basel Committee on Banking Supervision, 2011). The quantity and quality of capital that banks need to hold has been significantly enhanced to ensure that they operate on a safe and sound basis. Minimum capital requirements have been raised. The improvement in the quality of capital aims to ensure that banks are better able to absorb losses on both a going concern and a gone concern basis. The risk coverage has been increased, in particular for trading activities, securitizations, and exposures related to off-balance sheet vehicles and those arising from derivative products. An internationally harmonized minimum leverage ratio is likely to be introduced as well, to serve as a backstop to the risk-based capital measure and to contain the build-up of excessive leverage in the financial system. The Basel Committee has also introduced international standards for bank liquidity and funding, designed to promote the resilience of banks to liquidity shocks. A minimum requirement for the ratio between highquality liquid assets and net liquidity outflows that banks would face over a one-month horizon in stress conditions (the so-called Liquidity Coverage Ratio, LCR) will also be adopted. The minimum LCR will increase gradually in the coming years, so as to ensure that the new liquidity standard will not hinder the ability of the global banking system to finance the recovery. However, further progress is needed in some areas, including on internal risk control arrangements and disincentives to excessive risk taking, on transparency, and on international convergence of accounting standards.

3 ■ Sequencing of Reforms

The existence of adjustment costs and political or administrative constraints usually prevents the most desirable approach to reform: the simultaneous removal of all distortions. Determining the appropriate sequencing of policy reforms is thus an inescapable practical issue for policymakers, and may have a considerable bearing on the success of any adjustment program. The sequencing question normally involves several dimensions: first, the timing of liberalization of the domestic financial market and the capital account of the balance of payments; second, the opening of the trade and capital accounts; and third, the sequencing of macroeconomic adjustment programs and structural reforms.

3.1 ■ Stabilization, Financial Reform, and Capital Account Opening

A large consensus exists among development macroeconomists that weaknesses in the government budget have to be addressed before financial repression can be eliminated, or the loss of financial repression tax revenues may cause the elimination of financial repression to be associated with the emergence of high inflation. Thus, a first principle of sequencing is that macroeconomic stabilization should precede financial reform. Moreover, investor confidence in the permanence of a policy regime safeguarding their property is necessary to prevent capital flight. This suggests that fiscal adjustment should also precede the removal of restrictions on capital outflows. Even in the absence of prospective fiscal insolvency, the reduction in the inflation tax base resulting from the substitution of foreign assets for domestic-currency holdings may lead to an inflation burst if fiscal rigidities prevent adjustment of the primary deficit.[19] This argument can be extended to the relationship between stabilization and capital account liberalization more generally. As argued in Chapter 13, adequate flexibility of policy instruments—especially of fiscal policy—is required to counteract the effects of capital movements, whether these consist of inflows or outflows. If fiscal consolidation is not achieved before the capital account is opened, it may later prove impossible (because of creditor reactions) to adopt looser fiscal policy in response to contractionary shocks such as increases in external interest rates. The implication is that fiscal consolidation should be achieved before both domestic and external financial liberalization.

---

[19] Brock (1984) has argued, however, that opening the capital account does not necessarily lead to a reduction in inflation tax revenue. For instance, higher reserve requirements on bank deposits held by nonresidents may help compensate for a reduction in the inflation tax base (domestic-currency holdings) induced by a higher degree of substitution between domestic and foreign currencies.

A similarly wide consensus exists that the domestic financial system must be reformed—by freeing up domestic interest rates, increasing reliance on indirect instruments for the purposes of monetary control, and strengthening domestic financial institutions and markets—before opening the capital account of the balance of payments. If real domestic interest rates are maintained by government fiat much below world levels, the removal of capital controls will lead to sustained capital outflows and eventually to a balance-of-payments crisis. Uncertainty about the sustainability of reform, which may be particularly acute in the first stages of a liberalization program, may exacerbate the degree of volatility of capital movements and worsen the crisis. This is one of the main lessons drawn from the experience of the Southern Cone countries during the turbulent period covering the end of the 1970s and the beginning of the 1980s (Hanson, 1995).

A second argument for reforming the domestic financial system before opening up the capital account has to do with the avoidance of immiserizing external borrowing. Specifically, if the domestic financial system is repressed, or has been inappropriately liberalized (that is, liberalized without the appropriate institutional mechanisms to ensure adequate regulation and supervision), as argued in Chapter 14, any resulting capital inflows may be misallocated to the extent that they are intermediated through the domestic financial system. The result may be that the social rate of return on the use of these external funds may fall short of the cost of these funds to the domestic economy, leaving domestic residents poorer than they would otherwise have been.

Overall, then, the sequence suggested by these arguments would call for fiscal adjustment first, followed by domestic financial reform, and capital account liberalization only after the first two steps have been completed.

Fischer and Reisen (1994) advocated a more subtle and articulated sequence of reform. Consistent with what has been said above, they argue that fiscal control is needed before the capital account is opened up, because without such control, financial repression will result in capital outflows or inflation. Moreover, the possible loss of monetary autonomy with a fully open capital account would leave no instruments for stabilization policy if fiscal policy cannot be used flexibly. Both of these arguments were made above. But they argue that, even if opening up financially would leave some domestic monetary autonomy (because domestic and foreign assets are imperfect substitutes), capital account opening should nevertheless be delayed, because of the needs both to establish and deepen domestic money and securities markets to permit sterilization of capital inflows and outflows as well as to develop the domestic banking system to ensure that financial opening does not lead to high domestic interest rates and financial overintermediation. The latter means: (*a*) enforcement of competition to foster allocative efficiency in the financial sector; (*b*) strengthening of prudential regulation and supervision, establishment of legal and accounting systems to cope with systemic risks; and (*c*) the removal of excessive bad loans to increase the franchise value of banks.

While Fischer and Reisen thus concur with the view that macroeconomic stabilization and domestic financial reform should precede capital account openness, their proposed sequence of reform does not postpone all steps to open the capital account until stabilization and domestic financial reform have been accomplished. Indeed, they argue that liberalization of foreign direct investment (FDI) and trade finance should come first. These are viewed as essential for development (because of beneficial spillovers from FDI and the benefits of commercial openness), and as likely to pose few macroeconomic and financial-sector problems. Beyond this, they contend that fiscal consolidation is the most important next step for two reasons. First, as argued above, it is needed to do without revenues from financial repression and to provide a stabilization instrument. Second, a healthy fiscal position is required to cope with potential bad loan problems in the reforming financial sector. Next in priority is the implementation of measures for improved bank regulation and supervision. Because this takes time, it should be done early. After macroeconomic stability is achieved, the appropriate institutional mechanisms are in place for the domestic financial sector, and any bad loan problems are resolved, domestic interest rates can be freed. Under these conditions, overintermediation arising from moral hazard problems should not be a serious concern. At the same time that domestic interest rates are freed, the authorities should take steps to foster deepened securities markets. With high-yielding domestic instruments in place and no debt-overhang problems to trigger capital flight, it is then prudent to liberalize capital outflows and complete domestic financial reform (after having freed interest rates and removed bad loans, this essentially means lowering reserve requirements). At this point, the entry of foreign banks into the domestic financial system can be permitted. Finally, with increased bank competition due to free entry, credit market integration promoted by this competition, with banks exercising independent credit judgment after the resolution of bad loan problems, prudential regulation preventing distress borrowing, and lowered interest rates from stabilization, the liberalization process can be completed by opening up to short-term capital inflows. Under this sequence, Fischer and Reisen argue that interest rate convergence will be achieved, new external resources will be allocated efficiently, and crises will be less likely.

There are conditions, however, under which capital account liberalization may not be desirable even after domestic financial reform. The reason is that liberalization itself may affect the efficiency of the financial system. Alessandria and Qian (2005) develop a general equilibrium model of financial intermediation in which the structure of financial contracts and monitoring efficiency (as in the costly state verification framework discussed in Chapter 5) are both endogenous. They find that removing restrictions on international capital flows may have an adverse effect on the efficiency of financial intermediaries. This happens if, upon liberalization, access to global capital markets occurs at high interest rates—which in turn raise financial intermediaries' cost of capital and make it too costly for them to induce agents to invest in good projects. Thus, an efficient financial system under autarky is not sufficient to ensure that capital account liberalization improves welfare.

3.2 ▪ Capital and Current Account Liberalization

The debate on the appropriate sequencing of trade and capital account liberalization was stimulated to a large extent by the experience of Asian countries (most notably Korea and Indonesia) in the 1960s, and the reform programs implemented by the Southern Cone countries of Latin America in the late 1970s.[20] Among the latter group of nations, Argentina and Uruguay opened their capital account before removing impediments to trade transactions. Chile, by contrast, reduced barriers to international trade before lifting capital controls. In the 1960s, Korea also opened its trade account before relaxing controls on capital movements, while Indonesia reduced trade barriers and simultaneously eliminated most controls on capital movements.

Opening the capital account prior to liberalizing the external trade regime is not, in general, a desirable reform strategy. If (as argued earlier) the domestic financial system is liberalized prior to the removal of capital controls, massive capital inflows are likely to occur, leading to a buildup of reserves and, if not sterilized, fostering monetary expansion, domestic inflation, and a sustained appreciation of the real exchange rate.[21] However, as argued earlier, a successful liberalization of the trade account generally requires a real *depreciation* of the domestic currency to offset the adverse effect of cuts in tariff protection on the balance of payments, and thus stimulate exports and dampen imports.[22] The real appreciation that tends to be associated with the removal of capital controls is likely, on the contrary, to reduce profitability in export industries and have an adverse effect on the reallocation of resources, thereby lengthening—or even derailing—the adjustment process. Even if trade and capital account reforms are implemented simultaneously, the slow response of the real sector to changes in relative prices in the short run and the relatively faster response of capital flows means that the net outcome is likely to be an appreciation of the real exchange rate.[23] Opening the current account first is thus desirable, followed by gradual opening of the capital account. Edwards (1984) and McKinnon (1973,

---

[20] A comprehensive discussion of the sequencing debate in light of the experience of the Southern Cone countries is provided by Edwards (1984, 1989*b*). For subsequent overviews, see Falvey and Kim (1992), Galbis (1994), and Hanson (1995).

[21] If the country undergoing liberalization has limited access to international financial markets or if credibility in the reform process is low (because of perceptions of future policy reversals), opening the capital account may lead to capital flight rather than capital inflows, which would be limited by the increased risk of repatriation. Sustained capital outflows would lead to a depreciation of the real exchange rate, whose effect on trade flows may not be large enough to avoid continuous reserves losses, and eventually a balance-of-payments crisis if monetary policy is not tightened (see Park, 1994). This outcome would thus inhibit the trade liberalization process. In practice, however, the more common experience in developing nations following the removal of restrictions on capital flows has been an appreciation of the real exchange rate.

[22] Without a real depreciation, the surge in imports would lead to a deterioration of the current account, which may generate protracted balance-of-payments difficulties or pressure to reimpose tariffs, thus affecting the credibility of the liberalization program.

[23] The econometric evidence provided by Morandé (1988, 1992) supports the view that capital inflows were the main causal factor behind the appreciation of the Chilean Peso in the late 1970s. See also McNelis and Schmidt-Hebbel (1993).

1993) have been the major advocates of the view that tariffs should be reduced prior to lifting capital controls.[24]

Another line of argument supporting the Edwards-McKinnon view rests on the potential output effects of the sequencing of trade and capital account liberalization. As argued by Rodrik (1987), for instance, trade liberalization may have a contractionary effect in the short run if it is preceded or accompanied by capital account liberalization. The mechanism emphasized by Rodrik is the effect of trade reform on the real interest rate. In the absence of restrictions on capital movements, trade liberalization amounts to a rise in the consumption rate of interest if the future price of traded goods is expected to fall relative to its current level. Intertemporal substitution leads private agents to react by switching spending from the present to the future. With unused production capacity and demand-determined output, the result is a contraction in activity and an increase in unemployment. In a medium-term context, Krueger (1985) has argued that liberalizing capital movements in a country where the capital/labor ratio is low reduces the rate of return to capital, the rate of accumulation, and therefore long-term growth. Opening the current account first may stimulate output sufficiently to compensate for this negative effect.

An important issue that has arisen in the debate on the sequencing of trade and capital account reforms—an issue of relevance for *all* the literature dealing with the sequencing of policy reforms—relates to the role of intertemporal considerations, and the effect of various types of distortions prior to reform. Several authors, including Edwards (1989b), Khan and Zahler (1985), and Edwards and van Wijnbergen (1986), have attempted to take into account these features. Not surprisingly, the case for the "current account first, capital account next" sequence is not as clear-cut as described above, and depends on the type and degree of initial distortions. Nevertheless, it has been shown that opening the capital account may not be optimal in many circumstances. Edwards and van Wijnbergen (1986), for instance, have shown that relaxing capital controls in the presence of tariffs amplifies existing distortions, while the reverse sequence is generally neutral or may even be positive.

Intertemporal effects can also result from the lack of credibility in one or several components of the sequencing strategy leading to capital and current account liberalization. This aspect has been emphasized most forcefully by Calvo (1987a, 1989). His analysis suggests that if a given reform is not credible to private agents, adopting other liberalization measures may actually reduce welfare. For instance, liberalizing the capital account at a time when the public believes that a reduction in tariffs will be reversed in the future will lead private agents to use capital inflows to finance large imports of goods, particularly durable goods. Lack of credibility

---

[24]See also Khan and Zahler (1983, 1985). Note that the cross-country evidence of Baltagi et al. (2009) suggests that both types of openness are statistically significant determinants of banking sector development. Thus, both types may not be necessary to promote financial development; opening up the trade account without the capital acount (or vice versa) would still generate gains from that perspective.

thus plays the role of an intertemporal distortion. The capital account should not be liberalized before agents have achieved a sufficient degree of confidence in the sustainability of the trade liberalization program. Thus, credibility affects not only the speed of reform (as discussed below) but also the optimal sequencing strategy.

A significant omission in the sequencing debate is the fact that, as documented in Chapter 13, capital mobility in developing countries may be higher than what is suggested by the intensity of legal restrictions, because agents use alternative, unofficial channels to transfer funds to and from the rest of the world. The de facto opening of the capital account means that removing legal restrictions on capital controls may not have much effect on the portfolio structure of private agents, assuming that the perceived risk involved in transacting through unofficial channels is not too high, and that the surge in capital inflows through official channels may simply be reflecting a diversion of flows that were formerly transiting through illegal (but tolerated) channels. Similarly, to the extent that a large portion of external trade is carried through unofficial illegal channels, the removal of tariffs is likely to affect mostly the distribution of transactions between official and unofficial markets. In such conditions, the question of the appropriate order of sequencing becomes essentially that of determining the real efficiency gains that the economy would achieve under alternative strategies by legalizing previously illegal activities.

3.3 ▪ Macroeconomic Stabilization and Trade Reform

The empirical evidence discussed earlier suggests that successful trade reforms must, in general, be preceded or accompanied by a depreciation of the real exchange rate. Real devaluations ensure the sustainability of the liberalization process by dampening the excess demand for importables that the removal of tariffs induces. While the real exchange rate is not itself a policy variable, it can be influenced by nominal devaluations and restrictive demand policies. Thus, exchange-rate adjustment constitutes a key element of a trade liberalization program. This is precisely the mechanism we used to formalize trade reform in our previous discussion focusing on the short-run output and employment effects of commercial policies.

Stabilization is generally viewed as a precondition for the implementation of a full-fledged trade liberalization program. Three arguments are conventionally advanced to defend this proposition (see Mussa, 1987; Rodrik, 1995). First, macroeconomic instability—which typically translates into high and variable inflation rates—distorts the signals transmitted by changes in relative prices brought by trade reforms. Second, to the extent that trade liberalization takes the form of substantial tariff reductions and may have an adverse effect on tax revenue, large initial macroeconomic imbalances may severely constrain the scope of measures that can be taken and the pace of tariff reductions. Third, the real devaluation that accompanies liberalization is often brought about by large nominal devaluations, which may exacerbate inflation if monetary and fiscal policies are not tight enough. Moreover, devaluations affect the role of the exchange rate as a nominal anchor and may damage the credibility of the stabilization effort. The latter consideration is largely a reflection of the trade-off discussed in Chapter 8 between inflation stabilization and the expansion of output.

Although the adverse effect of macroeconomic instability can hardly be denied, the argument that the decline in revenue from tariffs and export taxes induced by trade liberalization may complicate short-run macroeconomic management because of its impact on the fiscal deficit is not as clear-cut as is often thought. On the one hand, it is correct that in many developing countries taxes on trade (as noted in Chapter 1) are an important source of government revenue. The reduction in revenue in these cases may indeed lead to increased money financing and higher inflation. On the other, however, trade liberalization may also lead to an increase in output and domestic revenue, even in the short run. First, the removal of quantitative restrictions on imports may be such that the increase in the tax base (the volume of imports) more than compensates for the reduction in tariff rates, bringing an overall increase in revenue. Second, reducing tariff rates when they are already very high reduces incentives for smuggling, under-invoicing, and engaging in rent-seeking activities (such as lobbying for import exemptions), to such an extent that tax revenue may rise, as the Laffer curve would predict. In fact, Greenaway and Milner (1991) find no significant relationship between trade reform and the amount of revenue collected from taxes on external trade in developing countries.

Nevertheless, in some countries the fiscal objective may be relatively important in the early stages of the liberalization process, and may affect the pace and extent of tariff reform. In cases where concern over the fiscal impact of trade reform is important, tariff reductions should proceed in steps, through implementation of gradual reductions in the overall level and structure of tariffs, following the pace of progress in expanding the domestic revenue base. As alternative domestic revenue sources develop over time, the relative importance of the fiscal objective will diminish, allowing an acceleration in the pace of trade reform and the removal of tariffs (Falvey and Kim, 1992). Thus, the pace of trade reform in the early stages may be constrained by the scope for fiscal adjustment.

An important element in the timing of trade and macroeconomic reforms is the role of credibility factors. As discussed at length in Chapter 11, the credibility of a disinflation program may be damaged if appropriate structural measures are not implemented prior to the adoption of a restrictive monetary and fiscal stance. Likewise, implementing tariff reforms without much confidence in macroeconomic management will create doubts about the overall sustainability of the reform process.[25] The fact that trade reforms require, as pointed out earlier, a real exchange-rate depreciation is often regarded as a source of conflict from a credibility point of view. When the real depreciation is brought about by a nominal devaluation,

---

[25] In turn, lack of credibility about the sustainability of trade reform may have an adverse effect on private saving and investment. Aizenman (1992) dicusses the signaling role that capital outlays may play in a framework where the risk of policy reversal translates into uncertainty about future tariffs.

the increase in the price of tradables will usually translate into a temporary rise in inflation, which may confuse agents about the policymakers' commitment to macroeconomic stability. However, the trade-off involved in the use of nominal devaluations may not be as acute as it appears. In particular, Rodrik (1995) has argued that in countries where the source of nominal wage rigidity is a lack of confidence in the macroeconomic policy stance, a credible commitment to a fixed exchange rate is likely to attenuate, rather than exacerbate, the potential conflict between trade liberalization (which requires a real devaluation) and exchange-rate stability, which is necessary for the exchange rate to play its role as a nominal anchor for domestic price setters.

In practice, however, two issues arise. First, the lack of fiscal reform does not seem to explain liberalization failures in some developing countries, particularly those of the Southern Cone. Fernández (1985), for instance, argued that the liberalization program implemented in Chile in the late 1970s did not avert a financial crisis, even though the central government budget moved into surplus at the inception of the program. Second, in practice, trade reforms have been implemented in conjunction with macroeconomic stabilization programs rather than after stabilization has been achieved. Bolivia and Mexico (as documented by Ten Kate, 1992) provide two examples. Thus, the question of determining the appropriate timing between structural reforms and macroeconomic adjustment may be to some extent moot. Ensuring the success of trade reforms requires maintaining a supportive macroeconomic environment (tight monetary and fiscal policies), not only at the inception of the program but also in a continuous fashion, to ensure that the associated real depreciation is not eroded by upward pressure on domestic prices. As emphasized in Chapter 11, consistency between macroeconomic policy measures and trade (or, more generally, structural) reforms is essential to foster credibility and ensure success of the *overall* reform program.

4   Adjustment Costs, Credibility, and Speed of Reform

The long-standing debate about gradual versus overnight policy reform was reviewed in Chapter 11, in the context of our discussion on the credibility of stabilization programs. Issues similar to those discussed there also arise in the context of structural reforms. Trade liberalization, for instance, has strong effects on income distribution, because it affects industries differentially. Social conflicts can be exacerbated if there are more "losers" than "winners," depending on the power structure and the relative strength of sectoral lobbies. Reform may have a large output cost in the short run because, for instance, the reallocation of resources across sectors takes time and is limited by the degree of intersectoral labor mobility, which is itself related to the need for workers to acquire different skills.

A particularly large increase in unemployment in the short run may affect endogenously the credibility of reform and weaken political support, forcing the authorities to abandon the liberalization process.[26] Thus, if the political pressure imposed by "losers" as a result of a sudden removal of protection is believed to be strong enough to stop or reverse the reform effort, a government may want to liberalize gradually. More generally, a gradual liberalization program may be the optimal response in a context where policymakers aim at minimizing adjustment costs—or, equivalently, maximizing the probability of sustaining the reform effort.[27] At the same time, however, doubts will be created about the commitment to reform if the adjustment process is too slow. This outcome may encourage political forces opposing liberalization. Providing sustained external assistance, by allowing policymakers to maintain the momentum of the reform effort, may be of crucial importance in such circumstances.

A formal example of how the speed of adjustment affects the magnitude of the transitional cost associated with reform (and consequently support for the reform process) is provided by Mehlum (2001). He considers a closed economy consisting of an efficient modern private sector, an inefficient public sector, and an informal sector. Reform consists of a fiscal adjustment that takes the form of laying off public surplus labor and reducing taxes.

The short-run effect of the reduction in labor demand is a reduction in wages. In turn, lower wages and reduced taxes raise the return to physical capital in the modern private sector, therefore fostering an increase in the private capital stock over time. Labor and capital are (gross) complements and as the private capital stock grows, so does the demand for labor. Wages therefore tend to recover over time, with the exact path followed depending on the speed of reform. A "big bang" or "cold turkey" reform leads to a sharp decline in wages but also to a high return to capital. Hence, the savings response is strong and the recovery in labor demand is relatively fast. By contrast, gradual reform moderates the immediate wage drop, but at the cost of a slower recovery over time.

In the absence of additional constraints, a big bang reform maximizes overall efficiency. However, if the required wage reduction is restricted due to political constraints, an overnight fiscal adjustment may not be feasible. Mehlum assumes, in fact, that reform proposals are subject to a vote before implementation. If implementation implies too drastic an initial cut in wages (and thus consumption) for too large a segment of the population, the reform is rejected and consequently abandoned. In the model, workers in the informal sector may indeed be pushed below subsistence

---

[26] Reform may also elicit political opposition (even though it generates efficiency gains for the economy as a whole) if it has significant distributional consequences. Von Hagen and Zhang (2008) illustrate this effect in the context of capital account liberalization. They also show that, in such conditions, a gradual liberalization is preferable to facilitate a smooth transition.

[27] Froot (1988) examines the effect of credibility factors on the optimal speed of trade reform, while Mussa (1986) discusses the role of adjustment costs on the optimal pace of liberalization. Neither study, however, considers explicitly political feasibility.

if the drop in labor demand in the formal sector is excessive. When this constraint is binding, a big bang reform becomes politically infeasible. By contrast, a sufficiently gradual reform is feasible because it ensures that the initial drop in wages is more moderate.

Mehlum also investigates the possibility that expectations of reform may turn out to be self-fulfilling. If a reform is abandoned, the future return to capital is lower than in a completed reform. The belief that the reform may be abandoned may therefore adversely affect savings and investment and consequently reduce labor demand. The result may be a *self-fulfilling failure*, where expectations about abandoning the reform itself generate an outcome that validates prior beliefs. Conversely, expectations about reform completion may stimulate investment and labor demand, thereby generating a *self-fulfilling success*. Thus, depending on the speed of adjustment, the model may generate dual equilibria. Reforms that are sufficiently gradual in nature ensure that labor demand remains sufficiently high during the transition, regardless of agents' expectations. The possibility of a vicious circle is thus broken, and the reform is sure to be completed. Sufficiently gradual programs have one unique successful equilibrium.

Chapter 19

The Political Economy of Adjustment

Developments in mainstream macroeconomics have emphasized the role of political factors in the determination of government policy decisions.[1] Such decisions are viewed as the outcome of collective actions resulting from a process of aggregation of individual policy preferences through political institutions. In representative democracies, one mechanism through which such preferences are conveyed to policymakers is the electoral process. The focus on presidential elections and macroeconomic outcomes has generated, in industrial countries, an extensive literature on the "political business cycle."

Research on stabilization and structural adjustment programs in developing countries has also emphasized the role of political factors in the outcome of policy reforms. This growing literature has provided much insight regarding the factors that explain the level and instability of inflation, the setting of macroeconomic policy instruments, and the adoption and collapse of disinflation programs and structural reforms. The first section reviews the general approach followed in this literature. Section 2 discusses alternative approaches used to study how conflicts of interest affect the decision to adopt economic reforms. Section 3 reviews various models of election-induced business cycles in developing countries. The final section focuses on the political economy of fiscal rules.

1   Politics, Economic Policy, and Adjustment

Much attention in the analysis of stabilization and structural adjustment programs in developing countries has focused on the political incentives and institutional

---

[1] See, for instance, Alesina (1991) and Whitehead (1990). The effect of political factors on public policy decisions has long been the central issue in the "public choice" literature, particularly in the analysis of rent-seeking behavior. The focus on macroeconomic issues is, however, more recent.

constraints faced by policymakers. The rationale for such scrutiny has been clearly expressed by Bates:

> We must look to the political incentives that shape politicians' economic choices; for . . . politicians are not perfect agents of economic interests but rather have distinctive political incentives of their own. We must therefore understand the nature of the political problems politicians try to solve when making economic policy. We must also look at the ideologies that motivate their interventions. If politicians do take the initiative, we must turn our attention from the economic forces that demand political intervention to the political forces that supply it. (1990, p 44)

Two areas in which the role of political factors has been emphasized recently are the decision to adopt (and sometimes abandon) structural adjustment programs and the effect of political instability on inflation and budget deficits.[2]

1.1 ▪ The Political Economy of Reform

Stabilization and adjustment policies, regardless of their medium- and long-run beneficial effects for the country as a whole, entail the imposition of short-term costs and have important social, political, and distributional implications.[3] Policies typically advocated in the context of structural adjustment programs (such as public sector reform, devaluation, elimination of marketing boards, or reduction of food subsidies) may threaten the constituencies that political leaders rely on. Privatization of public enterprises, for instance, usually entails the loss of jobs—or rent-creating positions—at times when unemployment may already be high. Real exchange-rate adjustment through a nominal devaluation may raise food prices and the cost of imports dramatically, creating hardship for low-income urban households. Increases in agricultural producer prices may also raise the cost of food to urban workers, at least in the short term. A key issue in the political economy of structural adjustment programs has therefore been to determine how these shocks can be absorbed, and which ones different types of governments may have difficulty coping with. Without a proper understanding of the political consequences of structural reforms, the potential alienation of important constituencies may jeopardize the adjustment process at its inception and lead to a return to the "status quo" (Haggard and Kaufman, 1989).

Typically, governments attempt to control economic outcomes in order to create or maintain political support. Politicians rationally advocate government intervention because the imposition of market regulations may facilitate the construction of political organizations. Rulers try to institutionalize their regimes by establishing

---

[2] See Frey and Eichenberger (1994), and Roemer and Radelet (1991). The role of elections per se is examined subsequently.

[3] See Bates (1990), Corden (1990), Nelson (1990), Nelson and Waterbury (1988), and Haggard and Kaufman (1989, 1990). We discussed in Chapter 11 the relation between income distribution, political instability, and the credibility of stabilization programs.

webs of patron-client relations to garner the support necessary for them to remain in power (Bates, 1990). Leaders reward loyal political followers or those deemed important for their continued tenure in office by direct state intervention in the economy (such as subsidies,[4] privileged access to public enterprises, and selective allocation of licenses for foreign trade), which ensures that resources flow to these groups. Intervention of this sort typically leads to systems where goods are allocated through state coercion, a process that inhibits the market from conveying information through price signals. Viewed from this perspective, disastrous economic policies can be seen as "arrangements" by which potential political instability is reduced (Bates, 1990).

By contrast, economic reforms entail significant political changes that may weaken the power structure of existing leaders to an unacceptable level. Bates (1990) has emphasized that structural adjustment creates a volatile political climate in which the threat of even minor disruptions must be taken seriously. A group with close ties to a given leadership may experience a "status reversal" during structural adjustment because its privileged access to public resources may be lost. For instance, raising taxes may eventually be beneficial to growth and employment (if the additional revenue is productively invested) but can also lead to the loss of political support. Similarly, once prices are liberalized, subsidies on foodstuffs or other basic commodities of the urban population can no longer be used to prevent civilian disturbances. But the urban population is important if incumbents want to retain control of the cities and stay in power. Regimes that depend on a combination of coercion and patronage to remain in power become more repressive when undergoing structural adjustment, compared to constitutionally elected governments. Indeed, given that there may be no way to continue previously established clientelistic networks in the new environment, leaders may have no choice but to repress some of their former supporters in order to maintain stability. Therefore, the real repression that results from structural adjustment may not be from quelling food riots when austerity packages are first instituted, but from the elimination of some of the noncoercive measures that governments could previously use to keep potentially threatening groups under control.[5]

Another potentially adverse effect of reforms is that they may breed corruption and poor governance. Blackburn and Forgues-Puccio (2010), in particular, have argued that financial liberalization may foster corruption, partly by providing greater opportunity to loot and hide assets.[6] They develop an endogenous growth model in which the extent to which corruption affects growth depends on the degree of financial openness, and the extent to which openness affects growth depends

---

[4]Governments often set food prices below the "true" market price in order to subsidize urban workers, who may be politically important to the regime.

[5]Nelson and Waterbury (1988) examine political factors leading to the success or failure of adjustment efforts by nineteen governments in thirteen countries during the 1980s.

[6]See Aidt (2003) for an analytical overview of the economics of corruption.

on the extent to which corruption prevails. Corruption is always bad for growth, because the resources available for investment are reduced by efforts to conceal illegal income and the government's effort to detect illegal activity and seize stolen assets. External financial liberalization exacerbates this problem because it offers the opportunity to launder money abroad. At the same time, financial liberalization leads to greater efficiency in production. Thus, when corruption is high (and governance poor), financial liberalization has an ambiguous effect on growth. If corruption is widespread, a low-growth trap may even emerge in equilibrium.

At the empirical level, Giavazzi and Tabellini (2005), using data for 140 countries over the period 1960–2000, found that there are positive feedback effects between economic and political reforms. Causality appears to run more often from political to economic liberalizations, rather than vice versa; many economic liberalizations are preceded by political liberalizations, while the converse is observed less frequently. They also found that there are interaction effects between the two kinds of reforms: countries that enact both reforms have better economic performance compared to countries that enact only one kind of reform, and the effects are not additive. More important, the sequence of reforms matters. Countries that first liberalize and then become democracies do much better than countries that pursue the opposite sequence. The main effect of a transition to democracy is to improve the quality of institutions (protection of property rights and control of corruption)—a critical step for development.

The central message of the literature is that structural adjustment also implies changes in the political system, which may involve a shift not only in the relative power structure but also in the mechanism through which leaders relate to their constituencies. Structural adjustment takes time, and although it may ultimately promote economic growth and improve the well-being of all groups, it implies short-run costs. Adjustment programs, whether efficiency- or welfare-focused, will fail if they do not recognize the interdependence of efficiency, welfare, and political feasibility.[7] Without a proper understanding of the political logic of structural adjustment, it is difficult to understand why long-term reform programs may become unattractive to political leaders beyond a certain point—the so-called adjustment fatigue phenomenon—even if short-term costs are absorbed. Programs therefore not only must be designed to fit particular economic conditions, but must also take into account the political structure.

1.2 ■ Political Instability, Inflation, and Fiscal Deficits

The role of political factors in the determination of inflation and the size of budget deficits in developing countries has been the focus of much attention. Haggard

---

[7]Edwards and Santaella (1993) provide evidence that political instability weakens a government's capacity to implement successful adjustment. See also Williamson and Haggard (1994).

(1991) and Haggard and Kaufman (1990), for instance, have argued that Argentina, Brazil, Uruguay, and Chile (before Pinochet) show patterns of inflation that are correlated with political events, generally combining two or three of the political mechanisms expected to erode stable macroeconomic management: strong labor movements linked to polarized political parties, severe tenure insecurities, and a propensity toward government with strongly redistributive orientations. In the case of Argentina, the failure to stabilize in the face of endemic inflation has gone hand in hand with continued political polarization and instability, and the failure of any group to consolidate its power effectively (Dornbusch and de Pablo, 1989).

The relationship between political instability and budget deficits has been examined by Edwards and Tabellini (1991), Roubini (1991), and Eslava (2006). All of these studies found that governments composed of large, short-lived, and unstable coalitions of political parties are associated with large budget deficits. Roubini (1991), in particular, shows that budget deficits in developing countries are heavily influenced by the degree of political instability (measured by an index of political cohesion and stability in the government, and the probability of military coups) as well as public finance considerations—with no apparent direct effect of elections.[8] Eslava (2006), for her part, found that more fragmented governments (with fragmentation measured by the fraction of seats held by the different parties represented in the legislature) are associated with higher deficits.

2 Conflicts of Interest and Economic Reforms

A key insight of the new political economy is that policy choices reflect the resolution of conflicts of interest between groups with different goals. The issue, then, is to identify the reasons why such conflicts, and the mechanisms by which they are resolved, may lead to delays in the adoption of beneficial reforms. Two basic approaches have been proposed; both stress heterogeneity of interests and some sort of uncertainty about the net benefits of reform, although they do so in quite different ways: the uncertain-benefits approach, and the distributional conflict approach.[9]

2.1 ■ The Uncertain-Benefits Approach

The key idea underlying the uncertain-benefits approach is that some groups may be uncertain about the net benefits they themselves would receive if a reform is adopted. Thus, reforms that could end up benefitting a majority of the population are not adopted and there is status quo bias. A simple example of this type of model

---

[8] It should be emphasized, however, that empirical correlations between political and economic instability do not establish unidirectional causality.

[9] Drazen (1996, 2001) provides an analytical framework that synthesizes the main features of these approaches.

is provided by Fernández and Rodrik (1991), in the context of trade reform. Their key argument is that idiosyncratic uncertainty associated with the effect of reforms (the fact that individual gainers and losers cannot always be clearly identified before implementation) may generate ex ante opposition to them, even if, ex post, everyone should support them.

To illustrate this result in a simple manner, consider the case of an economy populated by 100 workers, employed in two sectors, identified by W and L. Initially, 40 workers operate in sector W and 60 in L:

$$
\begin{array}{c}
L \\
\boxed{\begin{array}{c} 60 \text{ workers} \\ -0.2 \text{ each} \end{array}}
\end{array}
\quad
\begin{array}{c}
20 \text{ workers} \\ \Longrightarrow
\end{array}
\quad
\begin{array}{c}
W \\
\boxed{\begin{array}{c} 40 \text{ workers} \\ +0.2 \text{ each} \end{array}}
\end{array}
$$

Consider now a reform whose outcome is such that each worker in sector W gains 0.2, whereas workers in sector L each lose 0.2. The reform is anticipated to induce 20 workers to move from L to W. If there is full information regarding the identity of the workers moving from L to W, the majority of voters will approve the reform, because 60 will benefit (the original 40 in W plus the 20 that will be relocated in W).

However, suppose that there is individual uncertainty regarding the identity of the workers moving from L to W. Specifically, suppose that the probability of relocation in W is the same for all workers in sector L; this probability can thus be approximated by 20/60, whereas the probability of remaining in L is simply 40/60. In the first case, as indicated earlier, each worker gains 0.2, whereas in the second he or she loses 0.2; the expected gain from the reform is thus the weighted average given by

$$0.2 \cdot (1/3) - 0.2(2/3) < 0,$$

which implies that each worker expects to lose from the reform—implying that the majority of workers in the L sector will rationally vote against it. The paradox is that if a "benevolent" dictator (assuming of course that such dictators exist) were to implement the reform discretionarily, the majority of workers would ex post support it, because ex post individual uncertainty disappears.

As this example shows, status quo bias reduces welfare. Overcoming it requires policies that mitigate personal uncertainty, such as the design of appropriate transfer schemes or more generally the operation of an insurance market, which would allow individuals to protect themselves from uncertain outcomes. In practice, however, asymmetric information problems often prevent the creation of such markets.

2.2 ■ The Distributional Conflict Approach

The distributional conflict approach, due to Alesina and Drazen (1991) and Drazen and Grilli (1993), draws on the basic idea that there is a conflict over how the known cost of policy change will be divided among interest groups, so that what matters is ex post heterogeneity, that is, heterogeneity caused by the change in policy. Although each interest group knows the net benefit it would receive from the change under a proposed allocation of costs, each group is uncertain about the net benefits other groups will enjoy and hence about their willingness to pay for the reform.

Analytically, this approach draws on models of wars of attrition. A war of attrition takes place when two (or more) groups disagree over the burden sharing that needed policy measures (such as government spending cuts) entail. Uncertainty is crucial in this setting—if a group knew it would eventually have to concede, it would be in its interest to do so early on (at the beginning of the reform program), thereby avoiding a costly delay. As time goes by, each group learns about the strength of rival groups (namely, how costly it is for them to concede) or the costs of the status quo. The war ends when one or both groups find the continuation of the status quo more costly than conceding or compromising.

Alesina and Drazen (1991) for instance consider an economy where government deficits are financed by distortionary taxes (a proxy for inflation), which impose welfare losses on consumers. These welfare losses, which differ across consumers' types, are private information and could be avoided if consumers agreed to "stabilize" the economy—that is, if agreement is achieved on higher (but not distortionary) taxes or lower government transfers. The authors assume that the costs of stabilization are borne unevenly, with the group conceding first incurring the largest share. In equilibrium, each faction hesitates to concede, hoping to outlast its rivals. Although a fully informed social planner would stabilize immediately, delay is individually rational.

The model can be summarized as follows. Prior to stabilization, government expenditure is financed by distortionary taxes, τ, and for simplicity, government expenditure per period, g, is constant over time. Therefore, at time t:

$$\tau_t = g.$$

There are two consumers, both earning the same constant income y and paying an equal share of taxes in each period. Besides reducing consumers' disposable incomes, taxes cause distortions that result in utility losses. These losses are assumed to be proportional to the amount of taxes but different across consumers; they are captured by a parameter θ_i, which is private information.

In equilibrium, each player consumes his disposable income. Ignoring the constant income term, the two players' flow utilities in each period (before stabilization) are, with $i = 1, 2$:

$$u_i = -(\theta_i + 0.5)\tau_t = -(\theta_i + 0.5)g.$$

The parameter θ_i lies between known extremes, θ_L and θ_H. Both players estimate the opponent's cost θ according to the density function $f(\theta)$ and cumulative probability distribution function $F(\theta)$.

At the date of stabilization T, nondistortionary taxes become available and are raised so as to cover all fiscal expenditure. These taxes are divided unequally between players, with the player conceding first (the "loser") shouldering a larger tax burden forever. The tax shares of the "loser" and the "winner" are α (greater than 0.5) and $(1-\alpha)$, respectively.

Because taxes are nondistortionary, the only utility loss following stabilization is associated with the reduction in disposable income. Flow utilities at all times after stabilization are

$$U_L = -\alpha g, \quad U_W = -(1-\alpha)g,$$

where L denotes the loser and W the winner. Discounted lifetime utilities evaluated at the date of stabilization are

$$V_L = -\alpha g/r, \quad V_W = -(1-\alpha)g/r,$$

where r is the constant interest rate.

In each period, each player can concede and bring about stabilization by agreeing to pay higher taxes forever. Alternatively, he can wait, hoping that his opponent will concede but enduring distortionary taxes in the interim. The solution of the game is a function $T(\theta_i)$, mapping the idiosyncratic cost of living in the destabilized economy, θ_i, into an optimal time of concession, T. In equilibrium, T is such that the marginal benefit of conceding at T instead of at $T + dt$ equals the marginal benefit of waiting:

$$-u_i + U_L - \frac{dV_L}{dT} = \Omega(T, \theta_j)(V_W - V_L), \tag{1}$$

where $\Omega(T, \theta_j)$ is the probability that the opponent concedes between T and $T + dt$, given that he has not yet conceded, and is given by:[10]

$$\Omega(T, \theta_j) = -\frac{f(\theta_j)}{F(\theta_j)} \cdot \frac{1}{T'(\theta_j)}. \tag{2}$$

---

[10]To derive this expression, let $G[T(\theta)]$ be the cumulative distribution function of the time of concession T, and $g[T(\theta)]$ the corresponding density function. Then, it can be shown that the probability Ω is given by

$$\Omega(T, \theta) = \frac{g[T(\theta)]}{1 - G[T(\theta)]}.$$

But $1 - G[T(\theta)] = F(\theta)$, and differentiating this expression yields $-g[T(\theta)]T'(\theta) = f(\theta)$. Substituting these two expressions in the equation above yields (2). Note also that in (1), $dV_L/dT = 0$.

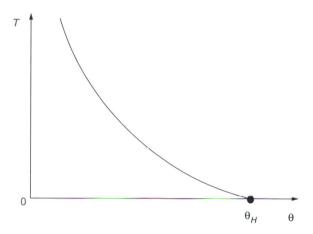

Figure 19–1 ■ The Optimal Concession Time in the War of Attrition Model

Substituting the functional forms assumed above and concentrating on the symmetric equilibrium, equation (1) can be written as

$$T'(\theta) = -\frac{f(\theta)}{F(\theta)} \cdot \frac{(2\alpha - 1)}{r(\theta + 0.5 - \alpha)}. \tag{3}$$

The additional assumption $\theta_L > \alpha - 0.5$ guarantees that all types $\theta > \theta_L$ concede in finite time. As shown by (3), the optimal concession time T depends negatively on θ: the higher is the idiosyncratic cost from distortionary taxation, the earlier a player concedes.

Moreover, the player with the highest possible cost, θ_H, concedes immediately, because he knows that any other type will wait. Thus,

$$T(\theta_H) = 0. \tag{4}$$

The differential equation (3) together with boundary condition (4) completely characterize the symmetric equilibrium. If, for instance, the distribution of θ is uniform between θ_L and θ_H, that is, $f(\theta) = 1/(\theta_H - \theta_H)$, equations (3) and (4) imply

$$T(\theta) = \frac{(2\alpha - 1)}{r(\theta + 0.5 - \alpha)} \left\{ \ln \left[\frac{\theta + 0.5 - \alpha}{\theta_H + 0.5 - \alpha} \right] - \ln \left[\frac{\theta - \theta_L}{\theta_H - \theta_L} \right] \right\},$$

which is illustrated in Figure 19.1.[11]

---

[11] Hsieh (2000) provides an extension of the war of attrition model.

A key factor affecting the length of the period of inaction is an unequal distribution of the burden of adjustment—which delays reform because losing is more costly for at least one group. The war of attrition specification may explain why (without resorting to, say, irrationality of economic agents) governments may at first face little difficulty in implementing a reform package, but then become unable to proceed with further reforms. The empirical results of Alesina et al. (2006), based on a large sample of developed and developing countries, support the main prediction of the war of attrition model, namely, that stabilizations of large fiscal deficits and high inflation are more likely to occur in times of crisis.

3   Political Stabilization Cycles

A dominant theme in the political economy literature in developing countries has been the fragility of political power, despite recent moves in several countries toward democratic systems, and the means that politicians attempt to use to secure reelection. Ames, for instance, writes:

> Latin American executives . . . rarely attain the security and autonomy of their counterparts in industrialized nations. If an executive represents a civilian-competitive regime, the chances of his party electing its successor are slim, and the possibility of implementing a policy package significantly improving those chances is equally poor. When competitively elected leaders face midterm elections, the cost of the political process itself distorts budgets and adds to inflationary pressures. (1987, pp. 98–99)

As argued earlier, contractionary policies designed to reduce inflation impose substantial political costs, particularly when their economic benefits are small and slow to emerge. When an incumbent faces reelection, there is a temptation to manipulate policy instruments for electoral gains, a strategy conducive to the emergence of political business cycles. Generally speaking, a political business cycle refers to policy-induced fluctuations in macroeconomic aggregates (such as output, unemployment, and the inflation rate) that are synchronized with the timing of major elections. Early models viewed these cycles as resulting essentially from a deliberate attempt by incumbent governments to manipulate the economy for electoral gains. Elected officials—or, more generally, the political parties that support politicians in office— have been described as being essentially concerned with maximizing their reelection prospects.[12] These early models of political business cycles were, however, based on several restrictive assumptions, most notably the assumption of an "irrational" electorate. By contrast, more recent analytical approaches have incorporated the assumption of rational and forward–looking voters and have emphasized the role of informational asymmetries among agents. These models yield predictions similar to

---

[12]Nordhaus (1975) provides the first systematic analysis of this type of cycle. See Alesina (1991) and Nordhaus (1989) for recent surveys of this literature.

those of the early literature, but emphasize the synchronization between the timing of elections and cycles in policy instruments, rather than cycles in macroeconomic outcomes. In this section, alternative theories of the political business cycle and their implications for macroeconomic policy instruments are examined. The analysis considers first traditional, "opportunistic" models, and then focuses on more recent, "equilibrium" models with informational asymmetries.

3.1 ▪ Opportunistic Models

Opportunistic models of political business cycles assume that politicians care only about remaining in office. We begin by examining the "traditional" model, which emphasizes the inflation-unemployment trade-off in a closed economy. We then develop a framework that highlights the role of exchange-rate policy and the trade-off between inflation and competitiveness.[13]

3.1.1 Elections, Inflation, and Unemployment

The seminal opportunistic model of political business cycles was developed by Nordhaus (1975). The model relies essentially on an expectations-augmented Phillips curve and backward-looking expectations. Voters have a distribution of preferences that depends on inflation and unemployment. Assume that elections occur every T periods, with T fixed over time for simplicity. The aggregate voting function, which relates the probability of reelection by the incumbent to economic outcomes, is given by

$$V_0(T) = -\int_0^T (u^2/2 + \theta\pi)e^{\rho t}dt, \quad \theta > 0, \tag{5}$$

where u denotes the unemployment rate, π the inflation rate, ρ the rate of "memory loss" by voters, and θ the weight attached to inflation relative to unemployment.[14] For simplicity, the actual inflation rate is assumed to enter linearly in the voting function, and the "desired" inflation rate (related, for instance, to seigniorage considerations) is assumed to be zero. The expectations-augmented Phillips curve is given by

$$\pi = \delta_0 - \delta_1 u + \pi^a, \tag{6}$$

where π^a denotes the expected inflation rate. The assumption of backward-looking expectations, or inertia in voters' preferences, is captured by specifying an adaptive expectational process:

$$\dot{\pi}^a = \alpha(\pi - \pi^a), \quad \alpha > 0. \tag{7}$$

---

[13] Another area where political business cycles may occur is in the use of price controls to stabilize inflation prior to elections; see Agénor and Asilis (1997) for a formal analysis.

[14] The term ρ is a backward-looking, not a forward-looking, rate of discount and corresponds to the rate at which past performance is discounted by voters.

The incumbent maximizes (5) subject to the inflation-unemployment trade-off (6) and the formation of expectations (7). Substituting equation (6) in (5), the decision problem can be written as:

$$\max_{u} V_0(T) = -\int_0^T [u^2/2 + \theta(\delta_0 - \delta_1 u + \pi^a)]e^{\rho t} dt, \tag{8}$$

subject to (7). The Hamiltonian is defined as

$$H(u, \pi^a, \lambda, t) = -[u^2/2 + \theta(\delta_0 - \delta_1 u + \pi^a)]e^{\rho t} + \lambda\alpha(\pi - \pi^a),$$

where λ is the costate variable, which can be interpreted as measuring the marginal electoral gain resulting from a reduction in the expected inflation rate. Necessary conditions for an interior optimum are given by[15]

$$\partial H/\partial u = 0 \Rightarrow u = \delta_1(\theta - \alpha\lambda)e^{-\rho t}, \tag{9}$$

$$\dot{\lambda} = -\partial H/\partial \pi^a \rightarrow \dot{\lambda} = \theta e^{\rho t}, \tag{10}$$

$$\lambda_T = 0, \tag{11}$$

subject to, from (6) and (7),

$$\dot{\pi}^a = \alpha(\delta_0 - \delta_1 u). \tag{12}$$

The terminal condition (11) indicates that at time T there is no further electoral gain from reducing the inflation rate.[16] The solution of the differential equations (10) and (12) subject to (9), the terminal condition (11), and an initial condition on the inflation rate π_0^a, is

$$u = \left(\frac{\theta\delta_1}{\rho}\right)[\rho - \alpha + \alpha e^{-\rho(t-T)}], \tag{13}$$

$$\pi^a = \pi_0^a + \alpha\left[\delta_0 - \frac{\delta_1^2\theta(\rho - \alpha)}{\rho}\right]t - \left(\frac{\alpha\delta_1}{\rho}\right)^2 \theta e^{\rho T}(1 - e^{-\rho t}), \tag{14}$$

$$\lambda = \theta(e^{\rho t} - e^{\rho T})/\rho. \tag{15}$$

---

[15]From concavity, these conditions are also sufficient.

[16]Technically, (11) holds because there is no endpoint condition on the expected inflation rate. See, for instance, Beavis and Dobbs (1990, chapter 7).

Equations (6) and (13)–(15) determine the behavior of inflation and unemployment in the course of an election cycle.[17] Unemployment and inflation fall smoothly in the periods leading to elections (because it is best to reduce these variables at the end of the cycle, so as to exert the maximum impact on voters) and rise sharply after the electoral outcome. Thus, over several electoral cycles, inflation and unemployment display a sawtooth pattern.[18] Assuming that the unemployment rate is inversely related to the level of aggregate demand, the prediction of the model is thus that the incumbent will increase government spending (and therefore aggregate demand) in the periods leading to the election in order to exploit the short-term Phillips curve. Following the elections, a contraction in spending will occur so as to reduce inflation—a policy that at the same time leads to a recession and a rise in unemployment.[19]

The foregoing discussion assumed that the length of the electoral cycle, T, remains fixed. In many countries, however, electoral periods do not have a constant length. Though in general there exists an institutionally defined upper limit on this length, most constitutions also contain provisions allowing incumbent politicians to dissolve prematurely all legislative bodies and call new elections before this limit is reached. Circumstances in which a premature parliamentary dissolution may occur (thereby determining new elections dates) include (a) a presidential decision, as for instance when legislative houses reach an impasse; (b) a request by the prime minister or by the Parliament's majority coalition; and (c) when a vote of censure or no-confidence passes parliament. In such circumstances it is reasonable to assume that the government does not know what the exact length of the electoral cycle is, and instead views it as a random variable (with a well-defined probability law). Lächler (1982) studies such a case in a model similar to the one described above and shows two main results: (a) the amplitude of movements in the unemployment rate is smaller with T uncertain, than in the previous case; and (b) although unemployment is still highest in the aftermath of an election and subsequently smaller, this decline need not be monotonic over the entire electoral period. Put differently, policy-induced business cycles tend to be less pronounced in amplitude as well as in regularity when the length of the electoral period is uncertain.

An alternative case is when the incumbent herself can decide the precise moment at which elections are held. in this case, as shown by Chappell and Peel (1979), the

---

[17]Note that from (13), $\dot{u} = -\alpha\theta\delta_1 e^{-\rho(t-T)}$. Unemployment falls, therefore, from an initial level [obtained by setting $t = 0$ in (13)] of $u_0 = (\theta\delta_1/\rho)(\rho - \alpha + \alpha e^{\rho T})$, to $u_T = \theta\delta_1$. But because, from (6), the natural rate (obtained by setting $\pi = \pi^a$) is given by δ_0/δ_1, the level of unemployment at the end of the electoral cycle will differ in general from the natural rate, implying instability in the inflation rate.

[18]The slope of the time profile of inflation and unemployment is steeper the higher is ρ, and flattens out for $\rho \to 0$, as the incumbent gives more and more weight to the effect of past inflation on the current decision of voters.

[19]It is important to keep in mind that the nature of the cycles depends critically on the structure of voters' preferences. In Nordhaus's model, rather than expanding the economy before an election, the incumbent may follow an anti-inflationary policy (that is, a restrictive fiscal policy) if inflation is perceived by voters as the most pressing economic issue. See, for instance, Neck (1991).

implications are opposite to those obtained with a random electoral cycle: policy-induced business cycles tend to be more regular than with a fixed electoral term.

3.1.2   Elections and Devaluation Cycles

A particularly interesting area in which to look for policy instrument cycles synchronized with electoral cycles in developing countries is exchange-rate policy. In what follows we develop a simple political economy model of devaluation with backward-looking contracts.[20] Consider a small, open economy producing nontraded and traded goods. Let π denote the inflation rate, defined as

$$\pi = \delta \pi_N + (1 - \delta)\varepsilon, \quad 0 < \delta < 1, \tag{16}$$

where π_N is the rate of inflation in nontradable prices and ε the rate of devaluation of the nominal exchange rate. For simplicity, we assume that world inflation is zero. Increases in nontradable prices are determined by the rate of growth of nominal wages, $\pi_N = \omega$. In turn, the rate of growth of nominal wages is set in a manner similar to the backward-looking contract mechanism discussed in Chapter 10, and thus depends only on past inflation rates:

$$\omega = \mu \int_{-\infty}^{t} e^{-\mu(t-h)} \pi_h dh, \quad \mu > 0, \tag{17}$$

where μ is a discount factor. Differentiating (17) with respect to time yields

$$\dot{\omega} = -\mu(\omega - \pi). \tag{18}$$

The incumbent maximizes the aggregate voting function subject to the equilibrium pricing equation and the equation determining the behavior of wages. The incumbent sets the devaluation rate so as to maximize votes on election eve. Elections take place every T periods. Popularity is inversely related to the difference between the rate of growth of real output (which depends on the rate of change of the real exchange rate, $\varepsilon - \pi_N$ and its trend growth rate, as well as inflation).[21] Setting trend output growth to zero, the government's objective is thus to maximize the voting function

$$V_0(T) = -\int_0^T [(\varepsilon - \pi_N)^2/2 + \theta\pi^2/2]e^{\rho t} dt, \tag{19}$$

---

[20] The model is, in many regards, similar to that used to examine the credibility of exchange-rate regimes in Chapter 8. For an alternative model, see van der Ploeg (1989), who emphasizes the role of J-curve effects.

[21] Thus, as before, the desired inflation rate is assumed to be zero.

where θ denotes the relative weight the incumbent attaches to inflation relative to output, and ρ is again the rate of memory loss. Using equation (16) and $\pi_N = \omega$, the decision problem becomes

$$\max_{\varepsilon} - \int_0^T [(\varepsilon - \omega)^2/2 + \theta[\delta\omega + (1-\delta)\varepsilon]^2/2\} e^{\rho t} dt, \tag{20}$$

subject to, from (16) and (18),

$$\dot{\omega} = -\kappa(\omega - \varepsilon), \quad \kappa \equiv (1-\delta)\mu, \tag{21}$$

and an initial condition on ω_0. Forming the Hamiltonian of the system and denoting by λ the costate variable (which measures the marginal electoral gain resulting from a reduction in the rate of growth of wages), necessary (and, from concavity, sufficient) conditions for an optimum are given by

$$\frac{\partial H}{\partial \varepsilon} = [1 + \theta(1-\delta)^2]\varepsilon - [1 - \theta\delta(1-\delta)]\omega + \kappa\lambda = 0, \tag{22}$$

$$\dot{\lambda} = -\rho - \partial H/\partial\omega,$$
$$= [1 - \theta\delta(1-\delta)]\varepsilon - (1 + \theta\delta^2)\omega + (\kappa - \rho)\lambda, \tag{23}$$

$$\lambda_T = 0, \tag{24}$$

subject to (21) and the initial condition on ω_0. The transversality condition (24) indicates that at time T there is no further electoral gain from reducing the rate of growth of nominal wages. Combining equations (22) and (24) yields

$$\varepsilon_T = \frac{1}{1 + \theta(1-\delta)^2}[1 - \theta\delta(1-\delta)]\omega_T \le \omega_T. \tag{25}$$

Taking the time derivative of equation (22), and using (21), (22), and (23) yields the following first-order linear differential equation system in ε and ω:

$$\begin{bmatrix} \dot{\varepsilon} \\ \dot{\omega} \end{bmatrix} = \begin{bmatrix} \kappa - \rho & -\alpha \\ \kappa & -\kappa \end{bmatrix} \begin{bmatrix} \varepsilon \\ \omega \end{bmatrix}, \tag{26}$$

where $\alpha \equiv [1 + \theta(1-\delta)^2]^{-1}[(\kappa - \rho)\{1 - \theta\delta(1-\delta)\} - \kappa\theta\delta]$. We assume here that $\kappa > \rho$.

Equations (26) can be solved subject to a given condition on the rate of change of nominal wages and the terminal condition (25). A necessary and sufficient condition for saddlepath stability to obtain is that the determinant of the coefficient matrix

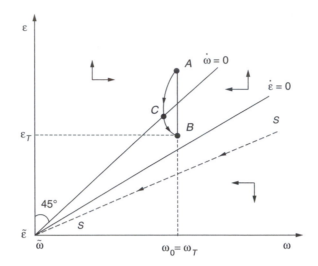

Figure 19–2 ▪ The Electoral Devaluation Cycle, Case I: $\alpha > 0$

appearing in (26) be negative.[22] If α is negative, this condition is always satisfied. If α is positive, we need $\alpha/(\kappa - \rho) < 1$, a condition that is interpreted graphically below. Assuming that this condition holds, the complete solution to (26) is given by

$$\omega = \tilde{\omega} + C_1 e^{v_1 t} + C_2 e^{v_2 t}, \tag{27}$$

$$\varepsilon = \bar{\varepsilon} + \left[\frac{(\kappa - \rho) - v_1}{\alpha}\right] C_1 e^{v_1 t} + \left[\frac{(\kappa - \rho) - v_2}{\alpha}\right] C_2 e^{v_2 t}, \tag{28}$$

where $v_1 < 0$ and $v_2 > 0$ are the roots of the system and $(\tilde{\omega}, \bar{\varepsilon})$ the steady-state solutions. Given that world inflation is zero, both steady-state values are also zero. To ensure the existence of a stationary cycle requires setting $\omega_0 = \omega_T$ in the above expressions. Using the terminal condition (25), equations (27) and (28) can then be solved for the constant terms C_1 and C_2.

The behavior of the devaluation rate and the rate of change of nominal wages during the electoral cycle is represented in Figure 19.2 for $\alpha > 0$, and in Figure 19.3 for $\alpha < 0$. Curves $[\dot{\varepsilon} = 0]$ and $[\dot{\omega} = 0]$ represent combinations of ε and ω for which the devaluation rate and the rate of change of nominal wages, respectively, remain constant. The saddlepath stability condition provided earlier requires that the $[\dot{\omega} = 0]$ curve be steeper (in absolute value) than the $[\dot{\varepsilon} = 0]$ curve. In both figures, the saddlepath is denoted SS. It has a positive slope for $\alpha > 0$ and a negative slope for $\alpha < 0$.

---

[22]The requirement that the system be saddlepath stable ensures that if the length of the electoral cycle tends toward infinity, the system would evolve along a unique path toward the equilibrium values of the devaluation rate and nominal wage growth.

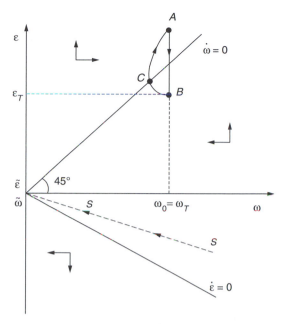

Figure 19-3 ■ The Electoral Devaluation Cycle, Case II: $\alpha < 0$

The path of the devaluation rate during an electoral cycle is depicted in both figures by the sequence ABC. Immediately after assuming office, the incumbent lowers the devaluation rate, which jumps from point A to point B.[23] The inflation rate also jumps downward, and output falls. Because contracts are backward looking, wages cannot change instantaneously. In the periods leading to the electoral contest, with output becoming increasingly important in the eyes of voters, the devaluation rate is increased at an increasing rate. Wages initially fall—up to point C, located on the $[\dot{\omega} = 0]$ curve—to catch up with the initial downward jump in the devaluation rate, and then begin to rise. The economy eventually returns to point A, which is reached an instant before period T, and a new cycle starts again. Note that at T, as indicated by equation (25), the rate of devaluation is maintained below the rate of change in nominal wages. The intuitive interpretation of this result is that a government concerned with its reelection prospects will tend to stimulate output until the last moment before the electoral contest takes place.

The predictions of the opportunistic model of devaluation cycles presented above are therefore qualitatively similar to those predicted by the original Nordhaus model: In the periods leading to the election, the government will increase the rate of

---

[23] The jump in the devaluation rate is finite because of the existence of a positive cost of inflation in the aggregate voting function (parameter θ), which implies that it would be suboptimal to induce an arbitrarily large exchange-rate adjustment at any time during the electoral cycle, as this would carry a correspondingly large cost to voters. But note that the initial downward jump is not large enough to put the economy onto the saddlepath SS. This occurs only if $T \rightarrow \infty$, in which case the economy jumps immediately to its steady-state position.

depreciation of the nominal exchange rate so as to depreciate the real exchange rate and stimulate output. Following the elections, a sharp appreciation of the nominal exchange rate will occur so as to reduce the rate of increase in prices. A recession will consequently occur in the aftermath of the election. However, an important difference (to which we will return below) is that, in the opportunistic model of devaluation cycles, inertial factors are not a reflection of backward-looking expectations by voters (as in the original Nordhaus model), but rather the consequence of institutional wage-setting mechanisms.

3.2 ▪ Models with Informational Asymmetries

Recent research on politico-economic models explains political business cycles on the basis of two key assumptions: First, voters are rational and forward-looking, and second, they are imperfectly informed about the incumbent government's policy preferences and objectives. Both assumptions play an important role in generating electoral cycles in the new theories. In the Nordhaus model described earlier, assuming that voters are rational and forward-looking implies that they will evaluate candidates for office on the basis of their expected *future* performance. The implications of the assumption of perfect foresight can formally be evaluated by setting $\alpha \to \infty$ in the solution equations (13)–(15). This implies, under usual stability conditions, that there will be no "cycle" as such. By itself, therefore, the rationality of expectations in opportunistic models of the Nordhaus type negates the existence of a political business cycle, because agents can "see" beyond the election date the policy shift required to reduce inflation.

In addition to the assumption of rational expectations, recent developments in the theory of political business cycles have emphasized the existence of informational asymmetries between policymakers and voters. The most important models in this class, which rely on a game-theoretic framework, are those of Rogoff and Sibert (1988) and Rogoff (1990).[24] In these models, governments are also opportunistic, in the sense that they are concerned about their reelection prospects, but there is a critical informational asymmetry: voters do not know precisely the "type" of the incumbent (that is, the level of "competence" of the government, defined as its efficiency in reducing "waste" in fiscal decisions and in providing public goods), a characteristic that, to the incumbent, is perfect information. The incumbent government therefore has an incentive to "signal" its competence—because voters rationally prefer more, rather than less, competent policymakers—by manipulating government spending (or, more generally, tax rates, public utility prices, and so on) before elections. An electoral cycle in government expenditures results, therefore,

---

[24]See also Cukierman and Meltzer (1989), who claim that the asymmetry of information between voters and the government results from imperfect monitoring of shocks affecting the economy. Terrones (1989) extends Rogoff's (1990) analysis to account for endogenous election dates.

from an informational asymmetry about the incumbent government's competency in the provision of public goods.[25] Inflationary effects of an expansionary policy are felt after a lag, and therefore occur only after the election has taken place. In addition, in Rogoff's (1990) model, the increase in government spending for signaling purposes may take the form of a preelectoral increase in "consumption" expenditures or highly "visible" transfers–which immediately affect disposable income—and a reduction in "capital" expenditure—which affects individual welfare only with lags. Therefore, spending cycles may also take the form of distortions in the composition of public expenditures. In this type of model, voters judge the performance of the incumbent government by looking at current and past macroeconomic outcomes; they are therefore backward looking, as in Nordhaus-type opportunistic models.

The composition of fiscal adjustment is also important for the electoral prospects of incumbents. Konishi (2006) develops a politico-economic model of fiscal policy in which voters (who have only partial information about the degree of collusion between the incumbent and special interests) base their decisions on past fiscal performance. The model predicts that fiscal adjustment involving sufficiently large spending cuts leads to incumbent reappointment, whereas adjustment involving only tax increases leads to incumbent defeat. The reason is that the political cost of cutting (socially wasteful) expenditure is higher, relative to that of increasing taxes, because incumbents care more about the well-being of special interests. This implies that tax-based fiscal adjustment is likely to produce beliefs among partially informed voters that incumbents are more collusive with special interests. Thus, the former type of adjustment has greater "signaling" power with respect to the incumbent's commitment to fiscal discipline and independence from special interests.

The common implication of both traditional and "rational" political business cycle models is, consequently, the existence of systematic manipulation of policy instruments before elections—in particular, government expenditure.[26] An important difference between opportunistic and "rational" approaches is, however, that the type of budgetary cycles occurring, for instance, in Rogoff's (1990) model need not occur systematically in every election. This result is particularly useful in understanding the lack of robust statistical evidence often observed in empirical analyses, as discussed below. Another important difference is that the "rational" electoral cycle will be reflected in the pattern of policy instruments—but not necessarily in the behavior of output, inflation, and unemployment. Furthermore, as argued by Drazen and Eslava (2005), if incumbents internalize the fact that voters dislike fiscal deficits, the political budget cycle may take the form of large changes in the *composition* of spending or greater targeting of specific groups of voters prior to elections, with little or no changes in the size of the deficit.

---

[25] Note that if there is monetary financing, an expenditure cycle will also be associated with a monetary cycle.

[26] "Rational" theories do not, in fact, provide precise predictions regarding whether a preelectoral fiscal expansion will occur through a reduction in taxes or an increase in government outlays.

This brief review of "old" and "new" theories of the political business cycle leads to several important considerations. First, in developing countries where governments are elected through a democratic process, incumbents may face the same type of incentives for reelection as their counterparts in industrial countries. Thus, at least in principle, the same type of political business cycle phenomenon should be operative. However, the comparative empirical evidence, although limited, is mixed. In a comprehensive study dealing with eighty-five countries over the period 1975–1995, Shi and Svensson (2006) found evidence of political budget cycles (in the sense of higher deficits prior to elections) that is highly significant for developing countries, but much less robust for industrial countries. This result continues to hold when they restrict their sample to elections whose timings are determined by the constitution or announced a year in advance. They find similar results in both groups. One possible explanation is that fiscal policy manipulations are less effective in industrial countries, because voters are better informed in these countries. However, another study by Vergne (2009), using data on forty-two developing countries from 1975 to 2001, found that election-year public spending does appear to shift toward more visible current expenditures (in particular, wages and subsidies) and away from capital expenditures. Thus, electoral cycles do seem to affect the allocation of public expenditures in developing countries.

Second, the inertial factor in opportunistic models may result not from backward-looking expectations per se, but (as explicitly recognized in our model of devaluation cycles) from the nature of labor contracts or other forms of market rigidities, such as sticky prices or inertia in trade flows (van der Ploeg, 1989). In such conditions, even if the private sector is forward-looking and rationally anticipates future economic and political events, a vote-maximizing strategy by the incumbent might still lead to political business cycles. Finally, although in the opportunistic models examined here the ideological orientation of political parties—as well as incumbent governments—matters for the setting of economic policy only through its possible effects on relative weights attached to policy targets in the objective function, recent efforts have attempted to consider a situation where incumbent governments are concerned not only with reelection prospects but also with their ideological commitment (see Nordhaus, 1989). This line of research may be particularly relevant when it is not possible to identify parties with specific ideological preferences.

4   The Political Economy of Fiscal Rules

As discussed in Chapter 3, in recent years an increasing number of countries (industrial and developing alike) have adopted explicit rules aimed at constraining discretion in setting fiscal policy. The particular form chosen for these rules (which have taken the form of maintaining fixed targets for the budget deficit, variously defined, or public debt-to-output ratios), and their implications for reform, have been the subject of much research from a political economy perspective. Two representative contributions in this area are those of Beetsma and Debrun (2004) and Drazen (2004).

From a political economy perspective, the key benefit of fiscal rules, as argued by Drazen (2004), is that they may help governments build a reputation for fiscal discipline. This is so because they help to mitigate the bias toward positive budget deficits and debt accumulation that characterizes the political process of budgeting in many countries—possibly because government resources are viewed as a "common property," out of which interest groups can finance spending on their preferred items (Velasco, 1999). Legislated restrictions can in principle make the goal of achieving fiscal stability more credible relative to simply announcing a commitment to the same goal because they generate a stronger signal about the government's intentions. However, because time inconsistency problems (of the type discussed in Chapter 11) cannot be precluded, particularly if enforcement is perceived to be prohibitively costly or unfeasible, the credibility gain that rules can provide has proved elusive in practice.

Rather than focus on the benefits of rules, Beetsma and Debrun (2004) focus on their potential costs, in a setting where incumbents are concerned about their prospects to remain in office. They argue that many desirable structural reforms (such as tax reforms, welfare reforms, public investment projects, and labor and product market reforms) could require temporarily higher structural deficits and therefore conflict with the requirements of tight budget rules. They use for their analysis a two-period model with electoral uncertainty, which leads the government to discount future economic outcomes at a higher rate than the public, and to spend too much on public good provision, rather than on measures expected to increase future revenues, including structural reforms and productive investment. They show that a temporary relaxation of a deficit cap, conditional on reform efforts, may help lessen the conflict between stability and growth. Fiscal rules may therefore be characterized by an "under-reform bias," which makes their growth and net welfare effects ambiguous.

Epilogue

Rather than summarizing the policy lessons drawn in the previous chapters, we present in this epilogue some final reflections on the state of development macroeconomics as well as some opinions about important directions for future research.

The perspective on development macroeconomics that we have adopted in this book has been motivated by our conviction that, in the old debate between "monetarists" and "structuralists" that dominated the field at its infancy, both sides were ultimately right. As the monetarists claimed, the basic principles of economics are universal and are not suspended in the context of developing countries: macroeconomic outcomes in such countries emerge from the utility- and profit-seeking behavior of individual economic agents who operate subject to technological and resource constraints and interact through markets. At the same time, the structuralists were also right: economic structure matters. Specifically, the environment in which individual agents seek to optimize and in which markets operate affects market outcomes. Most important, this environment tends to be very different in most developing countries from that which is assumed in much modern macroeconomic theorizing focusing on high-income countries. In addition, the issues that have been of concern to policymakers, and of interest to economists, have also often themselves been quite different in developing countries from those in high-income countries. These two observations motivated the writing of this book.

Over the past three decades there has been a proliferation of research aimed at improving our understanding of the macroeconomic issues faced by developing countries. This research has generally taken to heart the special circumstances in which these issues have tended to play out in such countries. In part this explosion of research has been the result of the growing importance and visibility of developing countries on the world stage, and in part of developments in the macroeconomics profession: specifically, the search to improve our understanding of macroeconomic phenomena by exploring their microeconomic foundations. This search has led to a growing appreciation of the important effects that the specific microeconomic context in which agents operate can have on macroeconomic outcomes.

This book has attempted to provide a coherent presentation of some of these developments. We have tried to show that, although many of the principles, methods, and even specific models used in research on development macroeconomics apply equally well to both industrial and developing countries, structural differences between the two groups of countries often require specialized analysis for developing countries, as, for instance, in our study of the monetary transmission mechanism in Chapters 5 and 6. Of course, structural characteristics are not immutable, and features deemed important from a macroeconomic point of view at a given moment in time may lose their relevance as institutions evolve, both as the result of policy choices as well as of technological developments. For instance, as liberalization and structural reforms have continued in most (but not all!) developing countries, some of the issues discussed in previous editions of this book, such as parallel exchange markets and financial repression, are no longer as relevant as they were just a few years ago. However, development is unfortunately not a discontinuous process, so while the structural characteristics of many developing economies have changed, it remains true for the vast majority of them that both the environment in which economic agents operate, as well as the specific macroeconomic issues they face, retain a distinctive flavor.

It therefore remains important that the analytical approaches that we adopt to understand macroeconomic issues in such countries reflect that distinctiveness. As should be evident from the models we have chosen to present in this book, we believe that the search for "first principles" in macroeconomics is far from being of a purely academic and aesthetic nature. Using functional forms with a shaky microeconomic basis may not only invalidate the analytical predictions of a macro model, but may also lead to incorrect policy advice. For instance, in our discussion of first-generation models of currency crises, it appeared that it is not only the elasticity of money demand that determines the shape and effects of such crises, but also the degree of intertemporal substitution—a phenomenon that is hard to isolate without a model with proper microfoundations. Likewise, in our discussion of the boom-recession cycle associated with exchange-rate-based stabilization programs, we indicated that the predictions obtained with arbitrary demand functions and those derived from an optimizing framework are substantially different from each other. However, although the use of dynamic optimizing models with explicit microeconomic foundations has become the standard methodological approach in development macroeconomics, just as it has in macroeconomic analysis focusing on high-income countries, it is vital not to allow modeling choices and analytical tractability to cause us to lose sight of the constraints imposed on agents by the particular environments in which they operate. These specific constraints may well impose restrictions on the specification of these models that condition their outcomes. For instance, liquidity-constrained agents do not behave in the same way as agents who do not face such constraints, and firms operating in a very uncertain environment are likely to respond to standard investment determinants in very different ways than they would in a stable environment. Thus, a key analytical challenge facing development macroeconomists today is to enhance the usefulness of their analysis to policymakers by providing solid microfoundations for models that are faithful to the specific context in which agents operate in developing countries. This may involve modeling not only market imperfections and institutional idiosyncracies of actual economies but also heterogeneities across agents. In many cases, this remains on the to-do list, as realistic models with solid microfoundations often prove intractable. This research agenda is reflected in this book: though we have used micro-founded models whenever possible, at times we have found it necessary to make use of models with postulated behavioral functions. Although we have tried in several instances—particularly in our discussion of the dynamics of monetary and exchange-rate rules—to provide explicit microfoundations for these functions, much remains to be done.

Beyond this general methodological point, we should note that there are several important issues in development macroeconomics that we have written about elsewhere and have not had space to discuss in this book, as well as issues that we believe merit substantial additional attention, though they are difficult to tackle. The former include, in particular, the definition and measurement of equilibrium real exchange rates in developing countries (Hinkle and Montiel, 1999), public sector debt management (Montiel, 2005), the special challenges of monetary transmission in low-income countries (Mishra et al., 2012), and the macroeconomic effects of aid in such countries (including Dutch disease problems), as well as the macroeconomics of poverty reduction (Agénor, 2004c; and Agénor et al., 2006).

The second set of issues includes some that we have touched upon in this book, but to which we have not been able to do full justice and about which much remains to be learned. Most important, we have made reference at various points to the interactions between financial frictions and macroeconomic outcomes, and have devoted a chapter (Chapter 12) to the integration of such frictions in dynamic stochastic general equilibrium models. This is an issue that is at the forefront of current research in macroeconomics in both high-income and developing countries. We have also examined in various places the links between politics and macroeconomics. We argued that the interactions among political factors, the behavior of economic agents, and the setting of policy instruments have played a crucial role in the determination of the degree of credibility of stabilization programs, as well as of macroeconomic policy more generally. A key question in this regard is how macroeconomic institutions can be designed in developing countries such that the outcomes of these complex interactions will result in welfare-enhancing macroeconomic performance. Much more analytical and empirical work is needed both to understand how specific country contexts map unto optimal macroeconomic institutions, as well as to understand the political economy of implementing such institutions. A related area that, while less central in current research, merits increased attention from development macroeconomists, relates to the role of distributional issues in the formulation of macroeconomic policies.[1]

---

[1] The relationship between income inequality and economic growth has been the subject of an extensive literature in development economics. Recent evidence suggests the existence of a positive correlation between growth and a reduction in income inequality (Persson and Tabellini, 1994), particularly in East Asian countries (World Bank,

Our discussion of the new structuralist model of inflation, for instance, emphasized the important role that such considerations may play in the design of a disinflation program. Any shift in relative prices is bound to affect profitability and the distribution of income across sectors and economic groups. Resistance to these changes by various groups in society may exacerbate social conflicts and political instability, affecting the outcome of policy reforms. A meaningful analysis of distributional issues requires relaxing the assumption of representative agents that underlies most of the optimizing models presented in this book. Here again, progress requires focusing on the modeling of heterogeneities across agents.

Despite our emphasis on the analytical basis of macroeconomic policy, we have attempted to review the available empirical evidence on a large number of issues. Although considerable progress has been achieved in the past few years in many areas, the empirical literature is still far from satisfactory in several key areas. For instance, the empirical evidence on the dynamics of real and nominal wages in developing countries remains limited. Similarly, we have at present no convincing way of assessing the effective degree of financial integration of specific developing economies with the world capital market. Isolating and measuring the effects of political factors on the setting of macroeconomic policy instruments has also not commanded the attention it deserves. Techniques for assessing the credibility of macroeconomic reform programs are not well advanced, although some progress has recently been registered in this area. Recent developments in econometrics have provided a large array of new methods for empirical analysis, and their continuous application to the macroeconomic problems faced by developing countries is an essential aspect of future research in this area. The interaction between theoretical constructs and empirical results is, as in most other areas of economics, a key element for future progress.

In closing, we reiterate our central contention that applying theoretical results to real-world settings is a difficult task and requires carefully taking into account individual-country circumstances. Experience suggests that this somewhat obvious point cannot be stressed too much. Proponents of economic reform who ignore structural and institutional constraints can do so only at the cost of repeated failures. We continue to hope that the analytical elements provided in this book will assist policymakers and their advisors in the difficult process of macroeconomic management.

1993). Larraín and Vergara (1993) suggest that investment may be the channel that links income inequality and growth. A more equitable distribution of income reduces social conflict, thus reducing uncertainty and creating a more stable environment for investment.

References

Abel, Andrew B. 1990. "Consumption and Investment." In *Handbook of Monetary Economics* II, edited by Benjamin Friedman and Frank H. Hahn. Amsterdam: North Holland.

Abel, Andrew B., and Janice C. Eberly. 1999. "The Effects of Irreversibility and Uncertainty on Capital Accumulation." *Journal of Monetary Economics* 44 (December): 339–77.

Acemoglu, Daron, Simon Johnson, James Robinson, and Y. Thaicharoen. 2003. "Institutional Causes, Macroeconomic Symptoms: Volatility, Crises and Growth." *Journal of Monetary Economics* 50 (January): 49–123.

Adam, Christopher, and David Bevan. 2005. "Fiscal Deficits and Growth in Developing Countries." *Journal of Public Economics* 89 (April): 571–97.

Ades, Alberto, Federico Kaune, Paulo Leme, Rumi Masih, and Daniel Tenengauzer. 2000. "Introducing GS-ESS: A New Framework for Assessing Fair Value in Emerging Markets Hard-Currency Debt." Global Economics Paper no. 45, Goldman Sachs (June).

Adolfson, Malin, Stefan Laséen, Jesper Lindé, and Lars E. O. Svensson. 2014. "Monetary Policy Trade-Offs in an Estimated Open-Economy DSGE Model." *Journal of Economic Dynamics and Control* 42 (May): 33–49.

Adolfson, Malin, Stefan Laséen, Jesper Lindé, and Mattias Villani. 2008. "Evaluating an Estimated New Keynesian Small Open Economy Model." *Journal of Economic Dynamics and Control* 32 (August): 2690–21.

Agénor, Pierre-Richard. 1994. "Credibility and Exchange Rate Management in Developing Countries." *Journal of Development Economics* 45 (August): 1–16.

——. 1995. "Credibility Effects of Price Controls in Disinflation Programs." *Journal of Macroeconomics* 17 (Winter): 161–71.

——. 1997. *Capital-Market Imperfections and the Macroeconomic Dynamics of Small Indebted Economies*. Study in International Finance no. 82, Princeton University.

——. 1998a. "Wage Contracts, Capital Mobility and Macroeconomic Policy." *Journal of Macroeconomics* 20 (Winter): 1–25.

——. 1998b. "The Behavior of Real Interest Rates in Exchange Rate-Based Stabilization Programs." *Review of Development Economics* 2 (October): 231–49.

——. 1998c. "Capital Inflows, External Shocks, and the Real Exchange Rate." *International Journal of Money and Finance* 17 (October): 713–40.

——. 2002. "Monetary Policy under Flexible Exchange Rates: An Introduction to Inflation Targeting." In *Inflation Targeting: Design, Performance, Challenges*, edited by Norman Loayza and Raimundo Soto. Santiago: Central Bank of Chile.

——. 2004a. "Orderly Exits from Adjustable Pegs and Exchange Rate Bands." *Journal of Policy Reform* 7 (June): 83–108.

——. 2004b. *The Economics of Adjustment and Growth*. 2nd ed. Boston, MA: Harvard University Press.

——. 2004c. "Macroeconomic Adjustment and the Poor: Analytical Issues and Cross-Country Evidence." *Journal of Economic Surveys* 18 (September): 351–409.

——. 2005. "Fiscal Adjustment and Labor Market Dynamics." *Journal of Development Economics* 76 (February): 97–125.

——. 2006a. "Market Sentiment and Macroeconomic Fluctuations under Pegged Exchange Rates." *Economica* 73 (November): 579–604.

——. 2006b. "The Analytics of Segmented Labor Markets." In *Adjustment Policies, Poverty and Unemployment: The IMMPA Framework*, edited by Pierre-Richard Agénor, Alejandro Izquierdo, and Henning Tarp Jensen. Oxford: Blackwell.

——. 2008. "Health and Infrastructure in Models of Endogenous Growth." *Journal of Macroeconomics* 30 (December): 1407-22.

——. 2010. "A Theory of Infrastructure-Led Development." *Journal of Economic Dynamics and Control* 34 (May): 932–50.

——. 2011. "Schooling and Public Capital in a Model of Endogenous Growth." *Economica* 78 (January): 108–32.

——. 2012a. "International Financial Integration: Benefits, Costs, and Policy Challenges." In *Survey of International Finance*, edited by H. Kent Baker and Leigh A. Riddick. Oxford: Oxford University Press.

——. 2012b. *Public Capital, Growth and Welfare*. Princeton, NJ: Princeton University Press.

Agénor, Pierre-Richard, and Joshua Aizenman. 1996. "Trade Liberalization and Unemployment." *Journal of International Trade and Economic Development* 5 (September): 265–86.

——. 1998. "Contagion and Volatility with Imperfect Credit Markets." *IMF Staff Papers* 45 (June): 207–35.

——. 1999a. "Macroeconomic Adjustment with Segmented Labor Markets." *Journal of Development Economics* 58 (April): 277–96.

——. 1999b. "Volatility and the Welfare Costs of Financial Market Integration." In *Financial Crises: Contagion and Market Volatility*, edited by Pierre-Richard Agénor, Marcus Miller, David Vines, and Axel Weber. Cambridge: Cambridge University Press.

——. 2004. "Savings and the Terms of Trade under Borrowing Constraints." *Journal of International Economics* 63 (July): 324–45.

——. 2006. "Investment and Deposit Contracts under Costly Intermediation and Aggregate Volatility." *International Review of Economics and Finance* 15 (September): 263–75.

——. 2011. "Capital Market Imperfections and the Theory of Optimum Currency Areas." *Journal of International Money and Finance* 30 (December): 1659–75.

Agénor, Pierre-Richard, and Koray Alper. 2012. "Monetary Shocks and Central Bank Liquidity with Credit Market Imperfections." *Oxford Economic Papers* 64 (July): 563–91.

Agénor, Pierre-Richard, Koray Alper, and Luiz A. Pereira da Silva. 2012. "Capital Requirements and Business Cycles with Credit Market Imperfections." *Journal of Macroeconomics* 34 (September): 687–705.

——. 2013. "Capital Regulation, Monetary Policy and Financial Stability." *International Journal of Central Banking* 9 (September): 193–238.

——. 2014. "Sudden Floods, Macroprudential Regulation and Stability in an Open Economy." *Journal of International Money and Finance* 48 (November): 68–100.

Agénor, Pierre-Richard, and Carlos Asilis. 1997. "Price Controls and Electoral Cycles." *European Journal of Political Economy* 13 (February): 131–42.

Agénor, Pierre-Richard, and Nihal Bayraktar. 2010. "Contracting Models of the Phillips Curve: Empirical Estimates for Middle-Income Countries." *Journal of Macroeconomics* 32 (June 2010): 555–70.

Agénor, Pierre-Richard, and Otaviano Canuto. 2012. "Middle-Income Growth Traps." Policy Research Working Paper no. 6210, World Bank (September).

——. 2014. "Access to Finance, Product Innovation and Middle-Income Traps." Policy Research Working Paper no. 6767, World Bank (February).

Agénor, Pierre-Richard, and Robert P. Flood. 1994. "Macroeconomic Policy, Speculative Attacks and Balance of Payments Crises." In *The Handbook of International Macroeconomics*, edited by Frederick van der Ploeg. Oxford: Basil Blackwell.

Agénor, Pierre-Richard, Alejandro Izquierdo, and Henning Tarp Jensen, eds. 2006. *Adjustment Policies, Poverty and Unemployment: The IMMPA Framework*. Oxford: Blackwell.

Agénor, Pierre-Richard, Henning Tarp Jensen, Mathew Verghis, and Erinc Yeldan. 2006. "Disinflation, Fiscal Sustainability, and Labor Market Adjustment in Turkey." In *Adjustment Policies, Unemployment and Poverty*, edited by Pierre-Richard Agénor, Alejandro A. Izquierdo, and Henning Tarp Jensen. Oxford: Blackwell.

Agénor, Pierre-Richard, and Mohsin S. Khan. 1996. "Foreign Currency Deposits and the Demand for Money in Developing Countries." *Journal of Development Economics* 50 (June): 101–18.

Agénor, Pierre-Richard, and Paul R. Masson. 1999. "Credibility, Reputation, and the Mexican Peso Crisis." *Journal of Money, Credit, and Banking* 31 (February): 70–84.

Agénor, Pierre-Richard, C. John McDermott, and Eswar Prasad. 2000. "Macroeconomic Fluctuations in Developing Countries: Some Stylized Facts." *World Bank Economic Review* 14 (May): 251–86.

Agénor, Pierre-Richard, C. John McDermott, and Murat E. Ucer. 1997. "Fiscal Imbalances, Capital Inflows, and the Real Exchange Rate: Evidence for Turkey." *European Economic Review* 41 (April): 819–25.

Agénor, Pierre-Richard, and Peter J. Montiel. 2006. "Credit Market Imperfections and the Monetary Transmission Mechanism. Part I: Fixed Exchange Rates." Working Paper no. 76, Centre for Growth and Business Cycle Research, University of Manchester (October).

——. 2007. "Credit Market Imperfections and the Monetary Transmission Mechanism. Part II: Flexible Exchange Rates." Working Paper no. 86, Centre for Growth and Business Cycle Research, University of Manchester (January).

Agénor, Pierre-Richard, and Kyriakos Neanidis. 2011. "The Allocation of Public Expenditure and Economic Growth." *Manchester School* 79 (July): 899–931.

Agénor, Pierre-Richard, and Luiz A. Pereira da Silva. 2013. *Inflation Targeting and Financial Stability: A Perspective from the Developing World*. Washington, DC: Inter-American Development Bank.

——. 2014. "Macroprudential Regulation and the Monetary Transmission Mechanism." *Journal of Financial Stability* 13 (August 2014): 44–63.

Agénor, Pierre-Richard, and Lodovico Pizzatti. 2005. "Disinflation and the Supply Side." *Journal of Macroeconomics* 27 (December): 596–620.

Agénor, Pierre-Richard, and Julio A. Santaella. 1998. "Efficiency Wages, Disinflation, and Labor Mobility." *Journal of Economic Dynamics and Control* 22 (February): 267–91.

Agénor, Pierre-Richard, and Mark P. Taylor. 1993. "Analyzing Credibility in High-Inflation Economies." *Economic Journal* 103 (March): 329–36.

Agénor, Pierre-Richard, and Murat E. Ucer. 1999. "Exchange Market Reform, Inflation, and Fiscal Deficits." *Journal of Policy Reform* 3 (March): 81–96.

Agénor, Pierre-Richard, and Devrim Yilmaz. 2011. "The Tyranny of Rules: Fiscal Discipline, Productive Spending, and Growth." *Journal of Economic Policy Reform* 14 (March): 69–99.

Aghevli, Bijan B. 1977. "Inflationary Finance and Growth." *Journal of Political Economy* 85 (December): 1295–1309.

Aghevli, Bijan B., and Mohsin S. Khan. 1978. "Government Deficits and the Inflationary Process in Developing Countries." *IMF Staff Papers* 25 (September): 383–416.

Aghevli, Bijan B., Mohsin S. Khan, and Peter J. Montiel. 1991. *Exchange Rate Policy in Developing Countries: Some Analytical Issues*. Occasional Paper no. 78, International Monetary Fund (March). Washington, DC: IMF.

Aghion, Philippe, George-Marios Angeletos, Abhijit Banerjee, and Kalina Manova. 2005. "Volatility and Growth: Credit Constraints and Productivity-Enhancing Investment." Working Paper no. 11349, National Bureau of Economic Research (May).

Aghion, Philippe, Philippe Bacchetta, and Abhijit Banerjee. 2000. "A Simple Model of Monetary Policy and Currency Crises." *European Economic Review* 44 (May): 728–38.

——. 2001. "Currency Crises and Monetary Policy in an Economy with Credit Constraints." *European Economic Review* 45 (June): 1121–50.

——. 2004a. "A Corporate Balance-Sheet Approach to Currency Crises." *Journal of Economic Theory* 119 (March): 6–30.

——. 2004b. "Financial Development and the Instability of Open Economies." *Journal of Monetary Economics* 51 (September): 1077–1106.

Aghion, Philippe, Philippe Bacchetta, Romain Rancière, and Kenneth Rogoff. 2009. "Exchange Rate Volatility and Productivity Growth: The Role of Financial Development." *Journal of Monetary Economics* 56 (May): 494–513.

Aghion, Philippe, Peter Howitt, and David Mayer-Foulkes. 2005. "The Effect of Financial Development on Convergence: Theory and Evidence." *Quarterly Journal of Economics* 120 (January): 173–222.

Agosin, Manuel R., and Franklin Huaita. 2012. "Overreaction in Capital Flows to Emerging Markets: Booms and Sudden Stops." *Journal of International Money and Finance* 31 (September): 1140–55.

Aguiar, Mark. 2005. "Investment, Devaluation, and Foreign Currency Exposure: The Case of Mexico." *Journal of Development Economics* 78 (October): 95–113.

——. 2011. "Discussion of Qian, Reinhart and Rogoff's 'On Graduation from Default, Inflation and Banking Crises: Ellusive or Illusion'." In *NBER Macroeconomics Annual 2010*, edited by Daron Acemoglu and Michael Woodford. Chicago: University of Chicago Press.

Aguiar, Mark, and Manuel Amador. 2013. "Sovereign Debt: A Review." Working Paper no. 19388, National Bureau of Economic Research (August).

Ahmed, Shaghil. 2003. "Sources of Economic Fluctuations in Latin America and Implications for the Choice of Exchange Rate Regimes." *Journal of Development Economics* 72 (October): 181–202.

Ahmed, Shaghil, and Andrei Zlate. 2014. "Capital Flows to Emerging Market Economies: A Brave New World?" *Journal of International Money and Finance*. 48 (November): 221–48.

Ahumada, Hildegard. 1992. "A Dynamic Model of the Demand for Currency: Argentina, 1977–1988." *Journal of Policy Modeling* 14 (June): 335–61.

Aidt, Toke S. 2003. "Economic Analysis of Corruption: A Survey." *Economic Journal* 113 (November): 632–52.

Aizenman, Joshua. 1986. "On the Complementarity of Commercial Policy, Capital Controls, and Inflation Tax." *Canadian Journal of Economics* 19 (February): 114–33.

——. 1987. "Inflation, Tariffs and Tax Enforcement Costs." *Journal of International Economic Integration* 2 (Autumn): 12–28.

——. 1989. "Country Risk, Incomplete Information and Taxes on International Borrowing." *Economic Journal* 99 (March): 147–61.

——. 1992. "Trade Reforms, Credibility, and Development." *Journal of Development Economics* 39 (July): 163–87.

Aizenman, Joshua, and Reuven Glick. 2008. "Pegged Exchange Rate Regimes—A Trap?" *Journal of Money, Credit, and Banking* 40 (June): 817–35.

——. 2009. "Sterilization, Monetary Policy, and Global Financial Integration." *Review of International Economics* 17 (September): 777–801.

Aizenman, Joshua, and Ricardo Hausmann. 1995. "The Impact of Inflation on Budgetary Discipline." Working Paper no. 5338, National Bureau of Economic Research (November).

Aizenman, Joshua, Michael Hutchison, and Ilan Noy. 2011. "Inflation Targeting and Real Exchange Rates in Emerging Markets." *World Development* 39 (May): 712–24.

Aizenman, Joshua, and Jaewoo Lee. 2007. "International Reserves: Precautionary vs. Mercantilist Views, Theory and Evidence." *Open Economies Review* (July): 191–214.

Aizenman, Joshua, Yeonho Lee, and Youngseop Rhee. 2007. "International Reserves Management and Capital Mobility in a Volatile World: Policy Considerations and a Case Study of Korea." *Journal of the Japanese and International Economies* 21 (March): 1–15.

Aizenman, Joshua, and Nancy P. Marion. 1993. "Macroeconomic Uncertainty and Private Investment." *Economics Letters* 41 (February): 207–10.

Aizenman, Joshua, and Andrew Powell. 2003. "Volatility and Financial Intermediation." *Journal of International Money and Finance* 22 (October): 657–79.

Akinci, Ozge. 2013. "Global Financial Conditions, Country Spreads and Macroeconomic Fluctuations in Emerging Countries." *Journal of International Economics* 91 (November): 358–71.

Albuquerque, Rui. 2003. "The Composition of International Capital Flows: Risk Sharing through Foreign Direct Investment." *Journal of International Economics* 61 (December): 353–83.

Alesina, Alberto. 1991. "Macroeconomics and Politics." In *NBER Macroeconomics Annual*, edited by Stanley Fischer. Cambridge, MA: National Bureau of Economic Research.

Alesina, Alberto, Silvia Ardagna, and Francesco Trebbi. 2006. "Who Adjusts and When? The Political Economy of Reforms." *IMF Staff Papers* 53 (September): 1–29.

Alesina, Alberto, and Robert J. Barro. 2002. "Currency Unions." *Quarterly Journal of Economics* 107 (May): 409–36.

Alesina, Alberto, and Allan Drazen. 1991. "Why Are Stabilizations Delayed?" *American Economic Review* 81 (December): 1170–88.

Alesina, Alberto, and Roberto Perotti. 1997. "Fiscal Adjustment in OECD Countries: Composition and Macroeconomic Effects." *IMF Staff Papers* 44 (June): 210–48.

Alesina, Alberto, and Guido Tabellini. 1989. "External Debt, Capital Flight, and Political Risk." *Journal of International Economics* 27 (November): 199–220.

Alessandria, George, and Jun Qian. 2005. "Endogenous Financial Intermediation and Real Effects of Capital Account Liberalization." *Journal of International Economics* 67 (September): 97–128.

Alexander, Sidney S. 1952. "Effects of a Devaluation on a Trade Balance." *IMF Staff Papers* 2 (April): 263–78.

Alexius, Annika. 1999. "Inflation Rules with Consistent Escape Clauses." *European Economic Review* 43 (March): 509–23.

Alfaro, Laura, and Fabio Kanczuk. 2005. "Sovereign Debt as a Contingent Claim: A Quantitative Approach." *Journal of International Economics* 65 (March): 297–314.

Ambler, Steve, and Emanuela Cardia. 1992. "Optimal Anti-Inflation Programs in Semi-Industrialized Economies: Orthodox Versus Heterodox Policies." *Journal of Development Economics* 38 (January): 41–61.

Ames, Barry. 1987. *Political Survival: Politicians and Public Policy in Latin America*. Berkeley: University of California Press.

Anand, Ritu, and Sweder van Wijnbergen. 1989. "Inflation and the Financing of Government Expenditure: An Introductory Analysis with an Application to Turkey." *World Bank Economic Review* 3 (March): 17–38.

Andersen, Torben M. 1989. "Credibility of Policy Announcements: The Output and Inflation Costs of Disinflationary Policies." *European Economic Review* 33 (January): 13–30.

Andrés, Javier, and Oscar Arce. 2012. "Banking Competition, Housing Prices and Macroeconomic Stability." *Economic Journal* 122 (December): 1346–72.

Ang, James B. 2008. "A Survey of Recent Development in the Literature on Finance and Growth." *Journal of Economic Surveys* 23 (July): 536–76.

Ang, James B., and Warwick J. McKibbin. 2007. "Financial Liberalization, Financial Sector Development and Growth: Evidence from Malaysia." *Journal of Development Economics* 84 (September): 215–33.

Antunes, António R., and Tiago V. de Cavalcanti. 2007. "Startup Costs, Limited Enforcement, and the Hidden Economy." *European Economic Review* 51 (January): 203–24.

Archer, David. 2006. "Implications of Recent Changes in Banking for the Conduct of Monetary Policy." In *The Banking System in Emerging Economies: How Much Progress Has Been Made?* Document no. 28, Bank for International Settlements (Basel).

Ardagna, Silvia. 2004. "Fiscal Stabilizations: When Do They Work and Why." *European Economic Review* 48 (October): 1047–74.

——. 2007. "Fiscal Policy in Unionized Labor Markets." *Journal of Economic Dynamics and Control* 31 (May): 1498–1534.

Arghyrou, Michael G., and Kul B. Luintel. 2007. "Government Solvency: Revisiting some EMU Countries." *Journal of Macroeconomics* 29 (June): 387–410.

Ariyoshi, Akira, and others. 2000. *Capital Controls: Country Experiences with their Use and Liberalization.* Occasional Paper no. 190. Washington, DC: International Monetary Fund.

Arize, A., John Malindretos, and Elias C. Grivoyannis. 2005. "Inflation-Rate Volatility and Money Demand: Evidence from Less Developed Countries." *International Review of Economics and Finance* 14 (March): 57–80.

Arrau, Patricio, José De Gregorio, Carmen Reinhart, and Peter Wickham. 1995. "The Demand for Money in Developing Countries: Assessing the Role of Financial Innovation." *Journal of Development Economics* 46 (April): 317–40.

Arteta, Carlos, Barry Eichengreen, and Charles Wyplosz. 2001. "When Does Capital Account Liberalization Help More Than It Hurts?" Working Paper no. 8414, National Bureau of Economic Research (August).

Arteta, Carlos, and Galina Hale. 2008. "Sovereign Debt Crises and Credit to the Private Sector." *Journal of International Economics* 74 (January): 53–69.

Ascari, Guido. 2003. "Price/Wage Staggering and Persistence: A Unifying Framework." *Journal of Economic Surveys* 17 (September): 511–40.

Ascari, Guido, and Tiziano Ropele. 2013. "Disinflation Effects in a Medium-Scale New Keynesian Model: Money Supply Rule versus Interest Rate Rule." *European Economic Review* 61 (July): 77–100.

Ascari, Guido, and Lorenza Rossi. 2011. "Real Wage Rigidities and Disinflation Dynamics: Calvo vs. Rotemberg Pricing." *Economics Letters* 110 (February): 126–31.

Asici, Ahmet A., Nadezhda Ivanova, and Charles Wyplosz. 2008. "How to Exit from Fixed Exchange Rate Regimes?" *International Journal of Finance and Economics* 13 (June): 219–46.

Asilis, Carlos M., Patrick Honohan, and Paul D. McNelis. 1993. "Money Demand during Hyperinflation and Stabilization: Bolivia." *Economic Inquiry* 31 (April): 262–73.

Asteriou, Dimitrios, and Simon Price. 2005. "Uncertainty, Investment and Economic Growth: Evidence from a Dynamic Panel." *Review of Development Economics* 9 (June): 277–88.

Athanasoglou, Panayiotis P., Ioannis Daniilidis, and Manthos D. Delis. 2014. "Bank Procyclicality and Output: Issues and Policies." *Journal of Economics and Business* 72 (March): 58–83.

Attanasio, Orazio. 1999. "Consumption." In *Handbook of Macroeconomics*, edited by John B. Taylor and Michael Woodford. Amsterdam: North Holland.

Attanasio, Orazio P., Pinelopi K. Goldberg, and Nina Pavcnik. 2004. "Trade Reforms and Wage Inequality in Colombia." *Journal of Development Economics* 74 (August): 331–66.

Attanasio, Orazio P., and Guglielmo Weber. 2010. "Consumption and Saving: Models of Intertemporal Allocation and their Implications for Public Policy." *Journal of Economic Literature* 48 (September): 693–751.

Auernheimer, Leonardo. 1974. "The Honest Government's Guide to the Revenue from the Creation of Money." *Journal of Political Economy* 92 (May): 598–606.

——. 1987. "On the Outcome of Inconsistent Programs Under Exchange Rate and Monetary Rules." *Journal of Monetary Economics* 19 (March): 279–305.

Auriol, Emmanuelle, and Michael Warlters. 2005. "Taxation Base in Developing Countries." *Journal of Public Economics* 89 (April): 625–46.

Aysun, Uluc, and Adam Honig. 2011. "Bankruptcy Costs, Liability Dollarization, and Vulnerability to Sudden Stops." *Journal of Development Economics* 95 (July): 201–11.

Bacchetta, Philippe. 1990. "Temporary Capital Controls in a Balance-of-Payments Crisis." *Journal of International Money and Finance* 9 (March): 246–57.

Baek, In-Mee. 2006. "Portfolio Investment Flows to Asia and Latin America: Pull, Push, or Market Sentiment?" *Journal of Asian Economics* 17 (April): 363–73.

Bailey, Martin J. 1956. "The Welfare Cost of Inflationary Finance." *Journal of Political Economy* 64 (April): 93–110.

Balakrishnan, Ravi, Sylwia Nowak, Sanjaya Panth, and Yiqun Wu. 2012. "Surging Capital Flows to Emerging Asia: Facts, Impacts, and Responses." Working Paper no. 12/130, International Monetary Fund (May).

Baldwin, Richard, and Rikard Forslid. 2000. "Trade Liberalization and Endogenous Growth." *Journal of International Economics* 50 (April): 497–517.

Ball, Laurence. 1994. "Credible Disinflation with Staggered Price-Setting." *American Economic Review* 84 (March): 282–89.

——. 1999. "Policy Rules for Open Economies." In *Monetary Policy Rules*, edited by John B. Taylor. Chicago: University of Chicago Press.

Baltagi, Badi H., Panicos O. Demetriades, and Siong Hook Law. 2009. "Financial Development and Openness: Evidence from Panel Data." *Journal of Development Economics* 89 (July): 285–96.

Bandiera, Oriana, Gerard Caprio, Jr., Patrick Honohan, and Fabio Schiantarelli. 2000. "Does Financial Reform Increase or Reduce Savings?" *Review of Economics and Statistics* 82 (May): 239–63.

Barajas, Adolfo, Roberto Steiner, and Natalia Salazar. 1999. "Interest Spreads in Banking in Colombia." *IMF Staff Papers* 46 (June): 196–24.

Barnhill, Theodore M., and George Kopits. 2003. "Assessing Fiscal Sustainability under Uncertainty." Working Paper no. 03/79, International Monetary Fund (April).

Barro, Robert J. 1974. "Are Government Bonds Net Wealth?" *Journal of Political Economy* 82 (November): 1095–1117.

——. 1979. "On the Determination of the Public Debt." *Journal of Political Economy* 87 (October): 940–971.

——. 1983. "Inflationary Finance Under Discretion and Rules." *Canadian Journal of Economics* 16 (February): 1–16.

——. 1986. "Reputation in a Model of Monetary Policy with Incomplete Information." *Journal of Monetary Economics* 17 (March): 3–20.

——. 1989. "The Ricardian Approach to Budget Deficits." *Journal of Economic Perspectives* 3 (March): 37–54.

——. 1990. "Government Spending in a Simple Model of Endogenous Growth." *Journal of Political Economy* 98 (Supplement): 103–25.

——. 2012. "Convergence and Modernization Revisited." NBER Working Paper no. 18295, National Bureau of Economic Research (August).

Barro, Robert J., and David B. Gordon. 1983. "A Positive Theory of Monetary Policy in a Natural Rate Model." *Journal of Political Economy* 91 (August): 589–610.

Barro, Robert J., and Xavier Sala-i-Martin. 2003. *Economic Growth*. 2nd ed. New York: MIT Press.

Barry, Frank, and Michael B. Devereux. 1995. "The 'Expansionary Fiscal Contraction' Hypothesis: A Neo-Keynesian Analysis." *Oxford Economic Papers* 47 (April): 249–64.

——. 2003. "Expansionary Fiscal Contraction: A Theoretical Exploration." *Journal of Macroeconomics* 25 (March): 1–23.

Bartolini, Leonardo, and Allan H. Drazen. 1997. "Capital-Account Liberalization as a Signal." *American Economic Review* 87 (March): 138–54.

Basel Committee on Banking Supervision. 2011. "Basel III: A Global Regulatory Framework for more Resilient Banks and Banking Systems." Report no. 189 (June).

Basu, Anupam, and Krishna Srinivasan. 2002. "Foreign Direct Investment in Africa: Some Case Studies." Working Paper no. 02/61, International Monetary Fund (March).

Bates, Robert. 1990. "Macropolitical Economy in the Field of Development." In *Perspectives on Political Economy*, edited by James E. Alt and Kenneth A. Shepsle. Cambridge: Cambridge University Press.

Batra, Ravi, and Hamid Beladi. 1999. "Trade Policies and Equilibrium Unemployment." *Manchester School* 67 (September): 545–56.

Baxter, Marianne, and Robert G. King. 1999. "Approximate Band-Pass Filters for Economic Time Series." *Review of Economics and Statistics* 81 (November): 575–93.

Bayoumi, Tamim. 1994. "A Formal Model of Optimum Currency Areas." *IMF Staff Papers* 41 (December): 537–54.

Beavis, Brian, and Ian Dobbs. 1990. *Optimization and Stability Theory for Economic Analysis*. Cambridge: Cambridge University Press.

Beck, Thorsten, and Asli Demirguc-Kunt. 2006. "Small and Medium-Size Enterprises: Access to Finance as a Growth Constraint." *Journal of Banking and Finance* 30 (November): 2931–43.

Beetsma, Roel M., and Xavier Debrun. 2004. "Reconciling Stability and Growth: Smart Pacts and Structural Reforms." *IMF Staff Papers* 51 (November): 431–56.

Beetsma, Roel M., and Massimo Giuliodori. 2010. "The Macroeconomic Costs and Benefits of the EMU and Other Monetary Unions: An Overview of Recent Research." *Journal of Economic Literature* 48 (September): 603–41.

Bekaert Geert, Campbell R. Harvey, and Christian Lundblad. 2006. "Growth Volatility and Financial Liberalization." *Journal of International Money and Finance* 25 (April): 370–403.

Bencivenga, Valerie R., and Bruce D. Smith. 1991. "Financial Intermediation and Endogenous Growth." *Review of Economic Studies* 58 (April): 195–209.

——. 1992. "Deficits, Inflation, and the Banking System in Developing Countries." *Oxford Economic Papers* 44 (October): 767–90.

Benigno, Pierpaolo, and Alessandro Missale. 2004. "High Public Debt in Currency Crises: Fundamentals versus Signaling Effects." *Journal of International Money and Finance* 23 (March): 165–88.

Bernanke, Ben S., and Alan S. Blinder. 1988. "Is It Money or Credit, or Both, or Neither?" *American Economic Review* 78 (May): 435–39.

Bernanke, Ben S., and Mark Gertler. 1989. "Agency Costs, Net Worth, and Business Fluctuations." *American Economic Review* 79 (March): 14–31.

——. 1995. "Inside the Black Box: The Credit Channel of Monetary Policy Transmission." *Journal of Economic Perspectives* 9 (September): 27–48.

Bernanke, Ben S., Mark Gertler, and Simon Gilchrist. 2000. "The Financial Accelerator in a Quantitative Business Cycle Framework." In *Handbook of Macroeconomics*, edited by John B. Taylor and Michael Woodford. Amsterdam: North Holland.

Bertola, Giuseppe. 1998. "Irreversible Investment." *Research in Economics* 52 (March): 3–37.

Besancenot, Damien, Radu Vranceanu. 2007. "Financial Instability under a Flexible Exchange Rate." *Scandinavian Journal of Economics* 109 (June): 291–302.

Bester, Helmut. 1985. "Screening vs. Rationing in Credit Markets with Imperfect Information." *American Economic Review* 75 (September): 850–55.

Bevan, David, Paul Collier, and Jan W. Gunning. 1993. "Trade Shocks in Developing Countries: Consequences and Policy Responses." *European Economic Review* 37 (April): 557–65.

Bhalla, Surjit. 1980. "The Measurement of Permanent Income and its Application to Saving Behavior." *Journal of Political Economy* 88 (August): 722–43.

Bharucha, Nargis, and Chistopher Kent. 1998. "Inflation Targeting in a Small Open Economy." Discussion Paper no. 9807, Reserve Bank of Australia (July).

Bhattacharya, Sudipto, Arnoud W. Boot, and Anjan V. Thakor. 1998. "The Economics of Bank Regulation." *Journal of Money, Credit, and Banking* 30 (November): 745–70.

Bick, Alexander. 2010. "Threshold Effects of Inflation on Economic Growth in Developing Countries." *Economics Letters* 108 (August): 126–29.

Binici, Mahir, Michael Hutchison, and Martin Schindler. 2010. "Controlling Capital? Legal Restrictions and the Asset Composition of International Financial Flows." *Journal of International Money and Finance* 29 (June): 666–84.

Bird, Richard M., and Eric M. Zolt. 2005. "The Limited Role of the Personal Income Tax in Developing Countries." *Journal of Asian Economics* 16 (December): 928–46.

Blackburn, Keith, and Gonzalo F. Forgues-Puccio. 2010. "Financial Liberalisation, Bureaucratic Corruption and Economic Development." *Journal of International Money and Finance* 29 (November): 1321–39.

Blackburn, Keith, and Alessandra Pelloni. 2004. "On the Relationship between Growth and Volatility." *Economics Letters* 83 (April): 123–28.

Blanchard, Olivier J. 1985. "Credibility, Disinflation, and Gradualism." *Economic Letters* 17 (March): 211–17.

——. 2004. "Fiscal Dominance and Inflation Targeting: Lessons from Brazil." Working Paper no. 10389, National Bureau of Economic Research (March).

Blanchard, Olivier J., and Stanley Fischer. 1989. *Lectures on Macroeconomics*. Cambridge, MA: MIT Press.

Blanchard, Olivier J., and Francesco Giavazzi. 2004. "Improving the SGP through a Proper Accounting of Public Investment." Discussion Paper no. 4220, Centre for Economic Policy Research (February).

Blanco, Herminio, and Peter M. Garber. 1986. "Recurrent Devaluation and Speculative Attacks on the Mexican Peso." *Journal of Political Economy* (February): 148–66.

Bleaney, Michael, and David Fielding. 2002. "Exchange Rate Regimes, Inflation and Output Volatility in Developing Countries." *Journal of Development Economics* 68 (June): 233–45.

Bleaney, Michael, and David Greenaway. 1993a. "Adjustment to External Balance and Investment Slumps in Developing Countries." *European Economic Review* 37 (April): 577–85.

——. 1993b. "Long-Run Trends in the Relative Price of Primary Commodities and in the Terms of Trade of Developing Countries." *Oxford Economic Papers* 45 (July): 349–63.

Blejer, Mario I., and Adrienne Cheasty. 1991. "The Measurement of Fiscal Deficits: Analytical and Methodological Issues." *Journal of Economic Literature* 29 (December): 1644–78.

Blejer, Mario I., and Nissan Liviatan. 1987. "Fighting Hyperinflation: Stabilization Strategies in Argentina and Israel." *IMF Staff Papers* 34 (September): 409–38.

Bohn, Henning. 1990. "Sustainability of Budget Deficits with Lump-Sum and with Income-Based Taxation." *Journal of Money, Credit, and Banking* 23 (August): 580–604.

——. 1998. "The Behavior of US Public Debt and Deficits." *Quarterly Journal of Economics* 113 (August): 949–63.

Bolton, Patrick, and Olivier Jeanne. 2011. "Sovereign Default Risk and Bank Fragility in Financially Integrated Economies." *IMF Economic Review* 59 (June): 162–94.

Borensztein, Eduardo. 1990. "Debt Overhang, Credit Rationing and Investment." *Journal of Development Economics* 32 (April): 315–35.

Borensztein, Eduardo, José De Gregorio, and Jong Wha Lee. 1998. "How Does Foreign Direct Investment Affect Economic Growth?" *Journal of International Economics* 45 (June): 115–35.

Borensztein, Eduardo, and Ugo Panizza. 2009. "The Costs of Sovereign Default." *IMF Staff Papers* 56 (December): 683–741.

Borio, Claudio, and Frank Packer. 2004. "Assessing New Perspectives on Country Risk." *BIS Quarterly Review* (December): 47–65.

Bosworth, Barry P., and Susan M. Collins. 2003. "The Empirics of Growth: An Update." *Brookings Papers on Economic Activity* no. 2 (December): 113–206.

——. 2008. "Accounting for Growth: Comparing China and India." *Journal of Economic Perspectives* 22 (March): 45–66.

Boughton, James M. 1993. "The Economics of the CFA Franc Zone." In *Policy Issues in the Operation of Currency Unions*, edited by Paul R. Masson and Mark P. Taylor. Cambridge: Cambridge University Press.

Brainard, William. 1967. "Uncertainty and the Effectiveness of Policy." *American Economic Review* 57 (May): 411–25.

Branson, William H. 1986. "Stabilization, Stagflation, and Investment Incentives: The Case of Kenya 1979–80." In *Economic Adjustment and Exchange Rates in Developing Countries*, edited by Sebastián Edwards and Liaqat Ahamed. Chicago: University of Chicago Press.

Bravo, Ana B., and Antonio L. Silvestre. 2002. "Intertemporal Sustainability of Fiscal Policies: Some Tests for European Countries." *European Journal of Political Economy* 18 (September): 517–28.

Brock, Philip L. 1984. "Inflationary Finance in an Open Economy." *Journal of Monetary Economics* 14 (July): 37–53.

——. 1989. "Reserve Requirements and the Inflation Tax." *Journal of Money, Credit, and Banking* 21 (February): 106–21.

Brock, Philip L., and Stephen J. Turnovsky. 1994. "The Dependent-Economy Model with Both Traded and Nontraded Capital Goods." *Review of International Economics* 2 (October): 306–25.

Broda, Christian. 2004. "Terms of Trade and Exchange Rate Regimes in Developing Countries." *Journal of International Economics* 63 (May): 31–58.

Broner, Fernando, Tatiana Didier, Aitor Erce, and Sergio L. Schmukler. 2013. "Gross Capital Flows: Dynamics and Crises." *Journal of Monetary Economics* 60 (January): 113–33.

Broner, Fernando, Alberto Martin, and Jaume Ventura. 2006. "Sovereign Risk and Secondary Markets." Working Paper no. 12783, National Bureau of Economic Research (December).

Broto, Carmen, Javier Díaz-Cassou, and Aitor Erce. 2011. "Measuring and Explaining the Volatility of Capital Flows to Emerging Countries." *Journal of Banking and Finance* 35 (August): 1941–53.

Brunnermeier, Markus K., Thomas M. Eisenbach, and Yuliy Sannikov. 2012. "Macroeconomics with Financial Frictions: A Survey." Working Paper no. 18102, National Bureau of Economic Research (May).

Bruno, Michael. 1991. *High Inflation and the Nominal Anchors of an Open Economy.* Princeton Essay in International Finance no. 183. Princeton, NJ: Princeton University.

Bruno, Michael, and Stanley Fischer. 1990. "Seigniorage, Operating Rules, and the High Inflation Trap." *Quarterly Journal of Economics* 105 (May): 353–74.

Bruno, Valentina, and Hyun Song Shin. 2012. "Capital Flows and the Risk-Taking Channel of Monetary Policy." Working Paper no. 400, Bank for International Settlements (December).

Bruton, Henry. 1989. "Import Substitution." In *Handbook of Development Economics* II, edited by Hollis B. Chenery and T. N. Srinivasan. Amsterdam: North Holland.

Brzoza-Brzezina, Michal, Marcin Kolasaz, and Krzysztof Makarski. 2013. "The Anatomy of Standard DSGE Models with Financial Frictions." *Journal of Economic Dynamics and Control* 37 (January): 32–51.

Bubula, Andrea, and Inci Otker-Robe. 2002. "The Evolution of Exchange Rate Regimes since 1990: Evidence from De Facto Policies." Working Paper no. 02/155, International Monetary Fund (September).

Buch, Claudia M., and Ralph P. Heinrich. 1999. "Twin Crises and the Intermediary Role of Banks." *International Journal of Finance and Economics* 4 (October): 313–24.

Budina, Nina, and Sweder van Wijnbergen. 2008. "Quantitative Approaches to Fiscal Sustainability Analysis: A Case Study of Turkey since the Crisis of 2001." *World Bank Economic Review* 23 (March): 119–40.

Buffie, Edward F. 1984*a*. "Financial Repression, the New Structuralists, and Stabilization Policy in the Semi-Industrialized Economies." *Journal of Development Economics* 14 (April): 305–22.

——. 1984*b*. "The Macroeconomics of Trade Liberalization." *Journal of International Economics* 17 (August): 121–37.

——. 1986*a*. "Devaluation and Imported Inputs: The Large Economy Case." *International Economic Review* 27 (February): 123–40.

——. 1986*b*. "Devaluation, Investment and Growth in LDCs." *Journal of Development Economics* 20 (March): 361–79.

——. 1992. "Short- and Long-Run Effects of Fiscal Policy." *World Bank Economic Review* 6 (May): 331–51.

——. 1998. "Public Sector Layoffs, Credibility, and the Dynamics of Inflation in a Simple Macromodel." *Journal of Development Economics* 56 (June): 115–40.

Buffie, Edward E., and Manoj Atolia. 2012. "Resurrecting the Weak Credibility Hypothesis in Models of Exchange-Rate-Based Stabilization." *European Economic Review* 56 (April): 361–72.

Buiter, Willem H. 1980. "Walras' Law and All That: Budget Constraints and Balance Sheet Constraints in Period Models and Continuous Time Models." *International Economic Review* 21 (February): 1–16.

——. 1983. "Measurement of the Public Sector Deficit and Its Implications for Policy Evaluation and Design." *IMF Staff Papers* 30 (June): 306–49.

——. 1985. "A Guide to Public Sector Debt and Deficits." *Economic Policy* no. 1 (November): 13–80.

——. 1987. "Borrowing to Defend the Exchange Rate and the Timing of and Magnitude of Speculative Attacks." *Journal of International Economics* 23 (November): 221–39.

——. 1988. "Structural and Stabilization Aspects of Fiscal and Financial Policy in the Dependent Economy." *Oxford Economic Papers* 40 (June): 220–45.

——. 1989*a*. "Some Thoughts on the Role of Fiscal Policy in Stabilization and Structural Adjustment in Developing Countries." In *Principles of Budgetary and Financial Policy*, edited by Willem H. Buiter. Cambridge, MA: MIT Press.

——. 1989*b*. "The Arithmetic of Solvency." In *Principles of Budgetary and Financial Policy*, edited by Willem H. Buiter. Cambridge, MA: MIT Press.

——. 2004. "Fiscal Sustainability." Unpublished, European Bank for Reconstruction and Development (January).

Buiter, Willem H., and Urjit R. Patel. 1992. "Debt, Deficits and Inflation: An Application to the Public Finances of India." *Journal of Public Economics* 47 (March): 171–205.

Bulow, Jeremy, and Kenneth Rogoff. 1989. "A Constant Recontracting Model of Sovereign Debt." *Journal of Political Economy* 97: 155–178.

Burnside, Craig. 2004. "Currency Crises and Contingent Liabilities." *Journal of International Economics* 62 (January): 25–52.

Burnside, Craig, Martin Eichenbaum, and Sergio Rebelo. 2001. "Prospective Deficits and the Asian Currency Crisis." *Journal of Political Economy* 109 (December): 1155–97.

——. 2004. "Government Guarantees and Self-Fulfilling Speculative Attacks." *Journal of Economic Theory* 119 (November): 31–63.

Burstein, Ariel, Martin Eichenbaum, and Sergio Rebelo. 2005. "Large Devaluations and the Real Exchange Rate." *Journal of Political Economy* 113 (August): 742–84.

Burstein, Ariel, Joao C. Neves, and Sergio Rebelo. 2003. "Distribution Costs and Real Exchange Rate Dynamics during Exchange-Rate-Based Stabilizations." *Journal of Monetary Economics* 50 (September): 1189–1214.

Burton, David. 1983. "Devaluation, Long-Term Contracts, and Rational Expectations." *European Economic Review* 23 (September): 19–32.

Bussière, Matthieu, and Marcel Fratzscher. 2006. "Towards a New Early Warning System of Financial Crises." *Journal of International Money and Finance* 25 (October): 953–73.

Caballero, Ricardo J. 1990. "Consumption Puzzles and Precautionary Savings." *Journal of Monetary Economics* 25 (January): 113–36.

———. 1991. "On the Sign of the Investment-Uncertainty Relationship." *American Economic Review* 81 (March): 279–88.

———. 1999. "Aggregate Investment." In *Handbook of Macroeconomics*, edited by John B. Taylor and Michael Woodford. Amsterdam: North Holland.

———. 2000. "Macroeconomic Volatility in Latin America: A Conceptual Framework and Three Case Studies." Working Paper no. 426, Inter-American Development Bank (August).

———. 2010. "Macroeconomics after the Crisis: Time to Deal with the Pretense-of-Knowledge Syndrome." *Journal of Economic Perspectives* 24 (September): 85–102.

Caballero, Ricardo J., and Arvind Krishnamurthy. 2001. "International and Domestic Collateral Constraints in a Model of Emerging Market Crises." *Journal of Monetary Economics* 48 (December): 513–48.

Caballero, Ricardo J., and Stavros Panageas. 2008. "Hedging Sudden Stops and Precautionary Contractions." *Journal of Development Economics* 85 (February): 28–57.

Calderón, César, Alberto Chong, and Ernesto Stein. 2002. "Trade Intensity and Business Cycle Synchronization: Are Developing Countries Different?" Working Paper no. 195, Central Bank of Chile (December).

Calderón, César, and J. Rodrigo Fuentes. 2014. "Have Business Cycles Changed over the Last Two Decades? An Empirical Investigation." *Journal of Development Economics* 109 (July): 98–123.

Calomiris, Charles W., and Gary Gorton. 1989. "The Origins of Banking Panics: Models, Facts, and Bank Regulation." In *Financial Markets and Financial Crises*, edited by Glenn Hubbard. Chicago: University of Chicago Press.

Calvo, Guillermo A. 1983. "Staggered Contracts and Exchange Rate Policy." In *Exchange Rates and International Macroeconomics*, edited by Jacob A. Frenkel. Chicago: University of Chicago Press.

———. 1986. "Temporary Stabilization: Predetermined Exchange Rates." *Journal of Political Economy* 94 (December): 1319–29.

———. 1987*a*. "On the Cost of Temporary Policy." *Journal of Development Economics* 27 (October): 245–62.

———. 1987*b*. "Balance of Payments Crises in a Cash-in-Advance Economy." *Journal of Money, Credit, and Banking* 19 (February): 19–32.

———. 1989. "Incredible Reforms." In *Debt, Stabilization and Development*, edited by Guillermo A. Calvo, Ronald Findlay, Pentti Kouri, and Jorge Braga de Macedo. Oxford: Basil Blackwell.

———. 1998. "Capital Flows and Capital-Market Crises: The Simple Economics of Sudden Stops." *Journal of Applied Economics* 1 (November): 35–54.

———. 2003. "Explaining Sudden Stop, Growth Collapse, and BOP Crisis: The Case of Distortionary Output Taxes." *IMF Staff Papers* 50 (March): 1–20.

———. 2007. "Interest Rate Rules, Inflation Stabilization, and Imperfect Credibility: The Small Open Economy Case." Unpublished, Columbia University (February).

Calvo, Guillermo A., Oya Celasun, and Michael Kumhoff. 2003. "Inflation Inertia and Credible Disinflation—The Open Economy Case." Working Paper no. 9557, National Bureau of Economic Research (March).

Calvo, Guillermo A., Alejandro Izquierdo, and Luis-Fernando Mejia. 2004. "On the Empirics of Sudden Stops: The Relevance of Balance-Sheet Effects." Working Paper no. 10520, National Bureau of Economic Research (May).

Calvo, Guillermo A., Leonardo Leiderman, and Carmen M. Reinhart. 1996. "Inflows of Capital to Developing Countries in the 1990s: Causes and Effects." *Journal of Economic Perspectives* 10 (Spring): 123–39.

Calvo, Guillermo A., and Enrique G. Mendoza. 1996. "Mexico's Balance-of-Payments Crisis: A Chronicle of a Death Foretold." *Journal of International Economics* 41 (November): 235–64.

Calvo, Guillermo A., and Carmen M. Reinhart. 2002. "Fear of Floating." *Quarterly Journal of Economics* 117 (May): 379–408.

Calvo, Guillermo A., and Carlos A. Rodríguez. 1977. "A Model of Exchange Rate Determination Under Currency Substitution and Rational Expectations." *Journal of Political Economy* 85 (June): 617–25.

Calvo, Guillermo A., and Carlos A. Végh. 1993a. "Exchange Rate-Based Stabilization under Imperfect Credibility." In *Open Economy Macroeconomics*, edited by Helmut Frisch and Andreas Worgotter. New York: St. Martin's Press.

———. 1993b. "Credibility and the Dynamics of Stabilization Policy: A Basic Framework." In *Advances in Econometrics*, edited by Christopher A. Sims. Cambridge: Cambridge University Press.

———. 1994. "Stabilization Dynamics and Backward-Looking Contracts." *Journal of Development Economics* 43 (February): 59–84.

———. 1996. "From Currency Substitution to Dollarization and Beyond: Analytical and Policy Issues." In *Money, Exchange Rates, and Output*, edited by Guillermo A. Calvo. Cambridge, MA: MIT Press.

Canavan, Chris, and Mariano Tommasi. 1997. "On the Credibility of Alternative Exchange Rate Regimes." *Journal of Development Economics* 54 (October): 101–22.

Canova, Fabio, and Evi Pappa. 2006. "The Elusive Costs and the Immaterial Gains of Fiscal Constraints." *Journal of Public Economics* 90 (September): 1391–1414.

Caprio, Gerard, and Daniela Klingebiel. 2003. "Episodes of Systemic and Borderline Financial Crises." World Bank Research Dataset.

Caputo, Rodrigo, Felipe Liendo, and Juan Pablo Medina. 2006. "New Keynesian Models for Chile in the Inflation-Targeting Period: A Structural Investigation." Working Paper no. 402, Central Bank of Chile (December).

Cardoso, Eliana. 1981. "Food Supply and Inflation." *Journal of Development Economics* 8 (June): 269–84.

———. 1993. "Private Investment in Latin America." *Economic Development and Cultural Change* 41 (July): 833–48.

Carlstrom, Charles T., and Timothy S. Fuerst. 2005. "Investment and Interest Rate Policy: A Discrete Time Analysis." *Journal of Economic Theory* 123 (July): 4–20.

Carmichael, Jeffrey, Jerome Fahrer, and John Hawkins. 1985. "Some Macroeconomic Implications of Wage Indexation: A Survey." In *Inflation and Unemployment: Theory, Experience and Policymaking*, edited by Victor E. Argy and John W. Neville. London: G. Allen and Unwin.

Carmignani, Fabrizio. 2003. "Political Instability, Uncertainty and Economics." *Journal of Economic Surveys* 17 (March): 1–54.

Carranza, Luis, José E. Galdon-Sanchez, Javier Gomez-Biscarri. 2009. "Exchange Rate and Inflation Dynamics in Dollarized Economies." *Journal of Development Economics* 89 (May): 98–108.

Carruth, Alan, Andy Dickerson, and Andrew Henley. 2002. "What Do We Know about Investment under Uncertainty?" *Journal of Economic Surveys* 14 (June): 119–53.

Cashin, Paul. 1995. "Government Spending, Taxes, and Economic Growth." *IMF Staff Papers* 42 (June): 237–69.

Cashin, Paul, John McDermott, and Alasdair Scott. 2002. "Booms and Slumps in World Commodity Prices." *Journal of Development Economics* 69 (October): 277–96.

Castiglionesi, Fabio. 2007. "Financial Contagion and the Role of the Central Bank." *Journal of Banking and Finance* 31 (January): 81–101.

Catão, Luis, and Marco E. Terrones. 2005. "Fiscal Deficits and Inflation." *Journal of Monetary Economics* 52 (April): 529–54.

Cavalcanti, Marco Antonio F. 2010. "Credit Market Imperfections and the Power of the Financial Accelerator: A Theoretical and Empirical Investigation." *Journal of Macroeconomics* 32 (March): 118–44.

Cavoli, Tony, and Ramkishen S. Rajan. 2006. "Monetary Policy Rules For Small and Open Developing Economies: A Counterfactual Policy Analysis." *Journal of Economic Development* 31 (June): 89–111.

Ca' Zorzi, Michele, Elke Hahn, and Marcelo Sánchez. 2007. "Exchange Rate Pass-through in Emerging Markets." Working Paper no. 739, European Central Bank (March).

Cecchetti, Stephen G., Hans Genberg, John Lipsky, and Sushil Wadhwani. 2000. *Asset Prices and Central Bank Policy*. London: Centre for Economic Policy Research.

Celasun, Oya. 2006. "Sticky Inflation and the Real Effects of Exchange Rate-Based Stabilization." *Journal of International Economics* 70 (September): 115–39.

Céspedes, Luis F., Roberto Chang, and Andrés Velasco. 2003. "IS-LM-BP in the Pampas." *IMF Staff Papers* 50 (March): 143–56.

———. 2004. "Balance Sheets and Exchange Rate Policy." *American Economic Review* 94 (September): 1183–93.

Chah, Eun Y., Valerie A. Ramey, and Ross M. Starr. 1995. "Liquidity Constraints and Intertemporal Consumer Optimization: Theory and Evidence from Durable Goods." *Journal of Money, Credit, and Banking* 27 (February): 272–87.

Chakraborty, Shankha, and Tridip Ray. 2006. "Bank-Based versus Market-Based Financial Systems: A Growth-Theoretic Analysis." *Journal of Monetary Economics* 53 (March): 329–50.

Chang, P. Kevin, Stijn Claessens, and Robert E. Cumby. 1997. "Conceptual and Methodological Issues in the Measurement of Capital Flight." *International Journal of Finance and Economics* 2 (April): 101–19.

Chang, Roberto, and Andrés Fernández. 2013. "On the Sources of Aggregate Fluctuations in Emerging Economies." *International Economic Review* 54 (November): 1265–93.

Chang, Roberto, Linda Kaltani, and Norman V. Loayza. 2009. "Openness can be Good for Growth: The Role of Policy Complementarities." *Journal of Development Economics* 90 (September): 33–49.

Chang, Roberto, and Giovanni Majnoni. 2002. "Fundamentals, Beliefs, and Financial Contagion." *European Economic Review* 46 (May): 801–08.

Chang, Roberto, and Andrés Velasco. 2000a. "Liquidity Crises in Emerging Markets: Theory and Policy." In *NBER Macroeconomics Annual 1999*, edited by Ben Bernanke and Julio Rotemberg. Cambridge, MA: MIT Press.

———. 2000b. "Banks, Debt Maturity and Financial Crises." *Journal of International Economics* 51 (June): 169–94.

———. 2001. "A Model of Financial Crises in Emerging Markets." *Quarterly Journal of Economics* 116 (May): 489–517.

———. 2002. "Dollarization: Analytical Issues." In *Dollarization*, edited by Federico Sturzenegger and Eduardo Levy-Yeyati. Cambridge, MA: MIT Press.

———. 2006. "Currency Mismatches and Monetary Policy: A Tale of Two Equilibria." *Journal of International Economics* 69 (June): 150–75.

Chappell, D., and David A. Peel. 1979. "On the Political Theory of the Business Cycle." *Economic Letters* 2 (March): 327–32.

Chari, V. V., and Patrick J. Kehoe. 2004. "Financial Crises as Herds: Overturning the Critiques." *Journal of Economic Theory* 119 (November): 128–50.

Chhibber, Ajay, and Mansoor Dailami. 1993. "Fiscal Policy and Private Investment in Developing Countries: Recent Evidence on Key Selected Issues." In *Fiscal Issues in Adjustment in Developing Countries*, edited by Riccardo Faini and Jaime de Melo. New York: St. Martin's Press.

Ching, Stephen, and Michael B. Devereux. 2003. "Mundell Revisited: A Simple Approach to the Costs and Benefits of a Single Currency Area." *Review of International Economics* 11 (September): 674–91.

Chinn, Menzie D., and Hiro Ito. 2006. "What Matters for Financial Development? Capital Controls, Institutions, and Interactions." *Journal of Development Economics* 81 (October): 163–92.

Chirwa, Ephraim W., and Montfort Mlachila. 2004. "Financial Reforms and Interest Rate Spreads in the Commercial Banking System in Malawi." *IMF Staff Papers* 51 (March): 96–122.

Chiu, Ru-Lin. 2001. "The Intratemporal Substitution between Government Spending and Private Consumption: Empirical Evidence from Taiwan." *Asian Economic Journal* 15 (September): 313–24.

Cho, Yoon Je. 1986. "Inefficiencies from Financial Liberalization in the Absence of Well-Functioning Equity Markets." *Journal of Money, Credit, and Banking* 18 (May): 191–99.

Choi, Woon Gyu, and David Cook. 2004. "Liability Dollarization and the Bank Balance Sheet Channel." *Journal of International Economics* 64 (December): 247–75.

Choi, Woon Gyu, and Michael B. Devereux. 2006. "Asymmetric Effects of Government Spending: Does the Level of Real Interest Rates Matter?" *IMF Staff Papers* 53 (September): 147–81.

Chong, Beng Soon, Ming-Hua Liu, and Keshab Shrestha. 2006. "Monetary Transmission via the Administered Interest Rate Channel." *Journal of Banking and Finance* 30 (May): 1467–84.

Choudhry, Nurun N. 1991. "Collection Lags, Fiscal Revenue and Inflationary Financing: Empirical Evidence and Analysis." Working Paper no. 91/41, International Monetary Fund (April).

Chowdhury, Ibrahim, Mathias Hoffmann, and Andreas Schabert. 2006. "Inflation Dynamics and the Cost Channel of Monetary Transmission." *European Economic Review* 50 (May): 995–1016.

Christiano, Lawrence J., and Terry J. Fitzgerald. 2003. "The Band Pass Filter." *International Economic Review* 44 (May): 435–65.

Christiano, Lawrence J., Christopher Gust, and Jorge Roldós. 2004. "Monetary Policy in a Financial Crisis." *Journal of Economic Theory* 119 (November): 64–103.

Christiano, Lawrence J., Roberto Motto, and Massimo Rostagno. 2010. "Financial Factors in Business Cycles." Working Paper no. 1192, European Central Bank (May 2010).

Christiano, Lawrence J., Mathias Trabandt, and Karl Walentin. 2010. "DSGE Models for Monetary Policy Analysis." In *Handbook of Monetary Economics*, edited by Benjamin M. Friedman and Michael Woodford. Amsterdam: North Holland.

———. 2011. "Introducing Financial Frictions and Unemployment into a Small Open Economy Model." *Journal of Economic Dynamics and Control* 35 (December): 1999–2041.

Christopoulos, Dimitris K., and Efthymios G. Tsionas. 2004. "Financial Development and Economic Growth: Evidence from Panel Unit Root and Cointegration Tests." *Journal of Development Economics* 73 (February): 55–74.

Chuhan, Punam, and Federico Sturzenegger. 2005. "Default Episodes in the 1980s and 1990s: What Have We Learned?" In *Managing Economic Volatility and Crises*, edited by Joshua Aizenman and Brian Pinto. Cambridge: Cambridge University Press.

Claessens, Stijn. 1991. "Balance of Payments Crises in an Optimal Portfolio Model." *European Economic Review* 35 (January): 81–101.

Claessens, Stijn, Swati R. Ghosh, and Roxana Mihet. 2013. "Macro-Prudential Policies to Mitigate Financial System Vulnerabilities." *Journal of International Money and Finance* 39 (December): 153–85.

Claessens, Stijn, M. Ayhan Kose, and Marco E. Terrones. 2011. "Recessions and Financial Disruptions in Emerging Markets: A Bird's Eye View." In *Monetary Policy under Financial Turbulence*, edited by Luis F. Céspedes, Roberto Chang, and Diego Saravia. Santiago: Central Bank of Chile.

Clarida, Richard, Jordi Galí, and Mark Gertler. 1999. "The Science of Monetary Policy: A New Keynesian Perspective." *Journal of Economic Literature* 37 (December): 1661–1707.

Clements, Benedict, Rina Bhattacharya, and Toan Q. Nguyen. 2003. "External Debt, Public Investment, and Growth in Low-Income Countries." Working Paper no. 03/249, International Monetary Fund (December).

Coco, Giuseppe. 2000. "On the Use of Collateral." *Journal of Economic Surveys* 14 (June): 191–214.

Coeurdacier, Nicolas, and Hélène Rey. 2013. "Home Bias in Open Economy Financial Macroeconomics." *Journal of Economic Literature* 51 (March): 63–115.

Cohen, Daniel. 1993. "Low Investment and Large LDC Debt in the 1980's." *American Economic Review* 83 (June): 437–49.

Cole, Harold L., and Timothy J. Kehoe. 1996. "A Self-Fulfilling Model of Mexico's 1994–1995 Debt Crisis." *Journal of International Economics* 41 (November): 309–30.

Coles, Melvyn, and Apostolis Philippopoulos. 1997. "Are Exchange Rate Bands Better than Fixed Exchange Rates? The Imported Credibility Approach." *Journal of International Economics* 43 (August): 133–53.

Collard, Fabrice, and Harris Dellas. 2005. "Poole in the New Keynesian Model." *European Economic Review* 49 (May): 887–907.

Connolly, Michael B. 1986. "The Speculative Attack on the Peso and the Real Exchange Rate: Argentina, 1979–81." *Journal of International Money and Finance* 5 (March): 117–30.

Connolly, Michael B., and Arturo Fernández. 1987. "Speculation Against the Pre-Announced Exchange Rate in Mexico: January 1983 to June 1985." In *Economic Reform and Stabilization in Latin America*, edited by Michael Connolly and Claudio González-Vega. New York: Praeger.

Connolly, Michael B., and Dean Taylor. 1984. "The Exact Timing of the Collapse of an Exchange Rate Regime and Its Impact on the Relative Price of Traded Goods." *Journal of Money, Credit, and Banking* 16 (May): 194–207.

Cook, David. 2004. Monetary Policy in Emerging Markets: Can Liability Dollarization Explain Contractionary Devaluation?" *Journal of Monetary Economics* 51 (September): 1155–81.

Cook, David, and Michael B. Devereux. 2006a. "Accounting for the East Asian Crisis: A Quantitative Model of Capital Outflows in Small Open Economies." *Journal of Money, Credit, and Banking* 38 (April): 721–49.

———. 2006b. "Capital Inflows, Fiscal Discretion, and Exchange Rate Policy." *European Economic Review* 50 (November): 1975–92.

Cooper, Richard N. 1971. *Currency Devaluation in Developing Countries*. Essay in International Finance no. 86. Princeton, NJ: Princeton University.

Cooper, Russell, and Thomas W. Ross. 2002. "Bank Runs: Deposit Insurance and Capital Requirements." *International Economic Review* 43 (February): 55–72.

Corden, W. Max. 1984. "Booming Sector and Dutch Disease Economics: Survey and Consolidation." *Oxford Economic Papers* 36 (November): 359–80.

———. 1990. "Macroeconomic Adjustment in Developing Countries." In *Public Policy and Economic Development*, edited by Maurice Scott and Deepak Lal. Oxford: Clarendon Press.

Corden, W. Max, and Ronald Findlay. 1975. "Urban Unemployment, Intersectoral Capital Mobility and Development Policy." *Economica* 42 (February): 59–78.

Cordoba, Juan-Carlos, and Marla Ripoll. 2004. "Credit Cycles Redux." *International Economic Review* 45 (November): 1011–46.

Corsetti, Giancarlo, and Bartosz Maćkowiak. 2006. "Fiscal Imbalances and the Dynamics of Currency Crises." *European Economic Review* 50 (July): 1317–38.

Coudert, Virginie, and Marc Dubert. 2005. "Does Exchange Rate Regime Explain Differences in Economic Results for Asian Countries?" *Journal of Asian Economies* 16 (October): 861–73.

Courakis, Anthony S. 1984. "Constraints on Bank Choices and Financial Repression in Less Developed Countries." *Oxford Bulletin of Economics and Statistics* 46 (November): 341–70.

Cowan, Kevin, Erwin Hansen, and Luis O. Herrera. 2005. "Currency Mismatches, Balance-Sheet Effects and Hedging in Chilean Non-Financial Corporations." Working Paper no. 521, Central Bank of Chile (January).

Cox, W. Michael. 1983. "Government Revenue from Deficit Finance." *Canadian Journal of Economics* 16 (May): 264–74.

Cruces, Juan J., and Christoph Trebesch. 2013. "Sovereign Defaults: The Price of Haircuts." *American Economic Journal—Macroeconomics* 5 (March): 85–117.

Cuddington, John. 1986. *Capital Flight: Estimates, Issues and Explanations*. Study in International Finance no. 58. Princeton, NJ: Princeton University.

Cukierman, Alex. 1988. "The End of the High Israeli Inflation: An Experiment in Heterodox Stabilization." In *Inflation Stabilization*, edited by Michael Bruno et al. Cambridge, MA: MIT Press.

———. 1992. *Central Bank Strategy, Credibility, and Independence*. Cambridge, MA: MIT Press.

Cukierman, Alex, Sebastián Edwards, and Guido Tabellini. 1992. "Seigniorage and Political Instability." *American Economic Review* 82 (June): 537–55.

Cukierman, Alex, and Nissan Liviatan. 1991. "Optimal Accommodation by Strong Policymakers under Incomplete Information." *Journal of Monetary Economics* 27 (February): 99–127.

———. 1992. "Dynamics of Optimal Gradual Stabilizations." *World Bank Economic Review* 6 (September): 439–58.

Cukierman, Alex, and Allan Meltzer. 1989. "A Political Theory of Government Debt and Deficits in a Neo-Ricardian Framework." *American Economic Review* 79 (September): 713–32.

Cukierman, Alex, Yossi Spiegel, and Leonardo Leiderman. 2004. "The Choice of Exchange Rate Bands: Balancing Credibility and Flexibility." *Journal of International Economics* 62 (March): 379–408.

Cumby, Robert E., and Maurice Obstfeld. 1983. "Capital Mobility and the Scope for Sterilization: Mexico in the 1970s." In *Financial Policies and the World Capital Market*, edited by Pedro A. Armella, Rudiger Dornbusch, and Maurice Obstfeld. Chicago: University of Chicago Press.

Cumby, Robert E., and Sweder van Wijnbergen. 1989. "Financial Policy and Speculative Runs with a Crawling Peg: Argentina 1979–1981." *Journal of International Economics* 27 (August): 111–27.

Dabla-Norris, Era, Mark Gradstein, and Gabriela Inchauste. 2008. "What Causes Firms to Hide Output? The Determinants of Informality." *Journal of Development Economics* 85 (February): 1–27.

Daniel, Betty C., and John B. Jones. 2007. "Financial Liberalization and Banking Crises in Emerging Economies." *Journal of International Economics* 72 (May): 202–21.

Darrat, Ali F., and Augustine C. Arize. 1990. "Domestic and International Sources of Inflation in Developing Countries." *International Economic Journal* 4 (Winter): 55–69.

Davidson, Carl, and Steven J. Matusz. 2006. "Trade Liberalization and Compensation." *International Economic Review* 47 (August): 723–47.

Deaton, Angus S. 1989. "Saving in Developing Countries: Theory and Review." *World Bank Economic Review*. Washington, DC: Proceedings of the World Bank Annual Conference on Development Economics.

———. 1992. *Understanding Consumption*. Oxford: Oxford University Press.

Deaton, Angus, and John Muellbauer. 1980. *Economics and Consumer Behavior*. Cambridge: Cambridge University Press.

De Ceuster, Marc J., and Nancy Masschelein. 2003. "Regulating Banks through Market Discipline: A Survey of the Issues." *Journal of Economic Surveys* 17 (December): 749–66.

De Grauwe, Paul. 2012. *Economics of Monetary Union*, 9th ed. Oxford: Oxford University Press.

De Grauwe, Paul, and Magdalena Polan. 2005. "Is Inflation Always and Everywhere a Monetary Phenomenon?" *Scandinavian Journal of Economics* 107 (June): 239–59.

De Grauwe, Paul, and Yuemei Ji. 2014. "How Much Fiscal Discipline in a Monetary Union?" *Journal of Macroeconomics* 39, Part B (March 2014): 348–60.

De Gregorio, José. 1993. "Inflation, Taxation, and Long-Run Growth." *Journal of Monetary Economics* 31 (June): 271–98.

———. 1995. "Policy Accommodation and Gradual Stabilization." *Journal of Money, Credit, and Banking* 27 (August): 727–41.

De Paoli, Bianca, Glenn Hoggarth, and Vistoria Saporta. 2006. "Costs of Sovereign Default." Financial Stability Paper no. 1, Bank of England (July).

Deidda, Luca G. 2006. "Interaction between Economic and Financial Development." *Journal of Monetary Economics* 53 (March): 233–48.

Dellas, Harris, and Alan C. Stockman. 1993. "Self-Fulfilling Expectations, Speculative Attacks, and Capital Controls." *Journal of Money, Credit, and Banking* 25 (November): 721–30.

Demekas, Dimitri G. 1990. "Labor Market Segmentation in a Two-Sector Model of an Open Economy." *IMF Staff Papers* 37 (December): 849–64.

Demetriades, Panicos, and Khaled A. Hussein. 1996. "Does Financial Development Cause Economic Growth? Time-Series Evidence from 16 Countries." *Journal of Development Economics* 51 (December): 387–411.

De Meza, David, and David C. Webb. 1987. "Too Much Investment: A Problem of Asymmetric Information." *Quarterly Journal of Economics* 102 (May): 281–92.

———. 2006. "Credit Rationing: Something's Gotta Give." *Economica* 73 (November): 563–78.

Demirel, Ufuk D. 2010. "Macroeconomic Stabilization in Developing Economies: Are Optimal Policies Procyclical?" *European Economic Review* 54 (April): 409–28.

Demirgüç-Kunt, Asli, and Enrica Detragiache. 1998. "The Determinants of Banking Crises in Developing Countries." *IMF Staff Papers* 45 (March): 81–109.

———. 2001. "Financial Liberalization and Financial Fragility." In *Financial Liberalization: How Far, How Fast?* edited by Gerard Caprio, Patrick Honohan, and Joseph E. Stiglitz. Cambridge: Cambridge University Press.

———. 2002. "Does Deposit Insurance Increase Banking System Stability? An Empirical Investigation." *Journal of Monetary Economics* 49 (October): 1373–1406.

Demirgüç-Kunt, Asli, Enrica Detragiache, and Poonam Gupta. 2006. "Inside the Crisis: An Empirical Analysis of Banking Systems in Distress." *Journal of International Money and Finance* 25 (August): 702–18.

Denizer, Cevdet. 1997. "The Effects of Financial Liberalization and New Bank Entry on Market Structure and Competition in Turkey." Policy Research Working Paper no. 1839, World Bank (November).

Detragiache, Enrica, and Antonio Spilimbergo. 2002. "Crisis and Liquidity: Evidence and Interpretation." Working Paper no. 01/2, International Monetary Fund (January).

Deutsch, Joseph, and Ben-Zion Zilberfarb. 1994. "Inflation Variability and Money Demand in Developing Countries." *International Review of Economics and Finance* 3 (March): 57–72.

Devenow, Andrea, and Ivo Welch. 1996. "Rational Herding in Financial Economics." *European Economic Review* 40 (April): 603–15.

Devereux, Michael B. 2006. "Exchange Rate Policy and Endogenous Price Flexibility." *Journal of the European Economic Association* 4 (December): 737–69.

Devereux, Michael B., Philip R. Lane, and Juanyi Xu. 2004. "Exchange Rates and Monetary Policy in Emerging Market Economies." IIIS Discussion Paper no. 36, University of British Columbia (August).

Devereux, Michael B., and Doris Poon. 2004. "A Simple Model of Optimal Monetary Policy with Financial Constraints." Unpublished, University of British Columbia (March).

Diamond, Douglas W., and Philip H. Dybvig. 1983. "Bank Runs, Deposit Insurance, and Liquidity." *Journal of Political Economy* 91 (June): 401–19.

Díaz-Alejandro, Carlos F. 1963. "A Note on the Impact of Devaluation and the Redistributive Effect." *Journal of Political Economy* 71 (December): 577–80.

———. 1965. *Exchange Rate Devaluation in a Semi-Industrialized Country.* Cambridge, MA: MIT Press.

———. 1985. "Good-Bye Financial Repression, Hello Financial Crash." *Journal of Development Economics* 19 (September): 1–24.

Di Giorgio, Giorgio. 1999. "Financial Development and Reserves Requirements." *Journal of Banking and Finance* 23 (July): 1031–41.

Dincer, N. Nergiz, and Barry Eichengreen. 2014. "Central Bank Transparency and Independence: Updates and New Measures." *International Journal of Central Banking* 10 (March): 189–253.

Disyatat, Piti. 2004. "Currency Crises and the Real Economy: The Role of Banks." *European Economic Review* 48 (February): 75–90.

Disyatat, Piti, and Pinnarat Vongsinsirikul. 2003. "Monetary Policy and the Transmission Mechanism in Thailand." *Journal of Asian Economics* 14 (June): 389–418.

Dixit, Avinash. 1980. "A Solution Technique for Rational Expectations Models with Applications to Exchange Rate and Interest Rate Determination." Unpublished. Department of Economics, Warwick University (November).

——. 1991. "The Optimal Mix of Inflationary Finance and Commodity Taxation with Collection Lags." *IMF Staff Papers* 38 (September): 643–54.

Dixit, Avinash, and Robert S. Pindyck. 1994. *Investment Under Uncertainty*. Princeton, NJ: Princeton University Press.

Dixit, Avinash, and Jospeh E. Stiglitz. 1977. "Monopolistic Competition and Optimum Product Diversity." *American Economic Review* 67 (June): 297–308.

Dixon, Huw, and Engin Kara. 2006. "Understanding Inflation Persistence: A Comparison of Different Models." Working Paper no. 672, European Central Bank (September).

Djankov, Simeon, Oliver Hart, Caralee McLiesh, and Andrei Shleifer. 2010. "Debt Enforcement around the World." *Journal of Political Economy* 116 (December): 1105–49.

Dolado, Juan D., Ramon María-Dolores, and Francisco J. Ruge-Murcia. 2002. "Nonlinear Monetary Policy Rules: Some New Evidence for the U.S." Discussion Paper no. 3405, Centre for Economic Policy Research (June).

Dooley, Michael. 1996. "A Survey of Literature on Controls Over International Capital Transactions." *IMF Staff Papers* 43 (December): 639–87.

——. 2000. "Can Output Losses Following International Financial Crises Be Avoided?" Working Paper no. 7531, National Bureau of Economic Research (February).

Dooley, Michael, Eduardo Fernández-Arias, and Kenneth Kletzer. 1994. "Is the Debt Crisis History? Recent Private Capital Inflows to Developing Countries." Working Paper no. 4792, National Bureau of Economic Research (July).

Dooley, Michael, Jeffrey Frankel, and Donald Mathieson. 1987. "International Capital Mobility: What Do Saving Investment Correlations Tell Us?" *IMF Staff Papers* 34 (September): 503–30.

Dooley, Michael, and Peter Isard. 1980. "Capital Controls, Political Risk, and Deviations from Interest Parity." *Journal of Political Economy* 88 (April): 370–84.

Dornbusch, Rudiger. 1980. *Open-Economy Macroeconomics*. New York: Basic Books.

——. 1982. "PPP Exchange-Rate Rules and Macroeconomic Stability." *Journal of Political Economy* 90 (February): 158–65.

——. 1983. "Real Interest Rates, Home Goods, and Optimal External Borrowing." *Journal of Political Economy* 91 (February): 141–53.

——. 1991. "Credibility and Stabilization." *Quarterly Journal of Economics* 106 (August): 837–50.

——. 1993. "Lessons from Experiences with High Inflation." In *Stabilization, Debt, and Reform*, by Rudiger Dornbusch. Englewood Cliffs, NJ: Prentice Hall.

Dornbusch, Rudiger, and Juan Carlos de Pablo. 1989. "Debt and Macroeconomic Instability in Argentina." In *Developing Country Debt and the World Economy*, edited by Jeffrey D. Sachs. Chicago: University of Chicago Press.

Dornbusch, Rudiger, and Stanley Fischer. 1986. "Stopping Hyperinflations, Past and Present." *Weltwirtschaftliches Archives* 122 (March): 1–47.

——. 1993. "Moderate Inflation." *World Bank Economic Review* 7 (January): 1–44.

Dornbusch, Rudiger, and Mario H. Simonsen. 1988. "Inflation Stabilization: The Role of Incomes Policy and Monetization." In *Exchange Rates and Inflation*, by Rudiger Dornbusch. Cambridge, MA: MIT Press.

Dornbusch, Rudiger, Federico Sturzenegger, and Holger Wolf. 1990. "Extreme Inflation: Dynamics and Stabilization." *Brookings Papers on Economic Activity* no. 1 (March): 1–84.

Drazen, Allan H. 1985. "Tight Money and Inflation: Further Results." *Journal of Monetary Economics* 15 (January): 113–20.

——. 1996. "The Political Economy of Delayed Reform." *Journal of Policy Reform* 1 (March): 25–46.

——. 2001. *Political Economy in Macroeconomics*. Princeton, NJ: Princeton University Press.

——. 2004. "Fiscal Rules from a Political Economy Perspective." In *Rules-Based Fiscal Policy in Emerging Markets*, edited by George F. Kopits. New York: Macmillan.

Drazen, Allan H., and Marcela Eslava. 2005. "Political Budget Cycles with Deficits: How to Play Favorites." Unpublished, University of Maryland (April).

Drazen, Allan H., and Vittorio Grilli. 1993. "The Benefits of Crises for Economic Reforms." *American Economic Review* 83 (June): 598–607.

Drazen, Allan H., and Elhanan Helpman. 1988. "Stabilization Policy with Exchange Rate Management Under Uncertainty." In *Economic Effects of the Government Budget*, edited by Elhanan Helpman, Assaf Razin, and Efraim Sadka. Cambridge, MA: MIT Press.

——. 1990. "Inflationary Consequences of Anticipated Macroeconomic Policies." *Review of Economic Studies* 57 (January): 147–66.

Drazen, Allan H., and Stefan Hubrich. 2006. A Simple Test of the Effect of Interest Rate Defense." *Journal of the Japanese and International Economies* 20 (December): 612–36.

Drazen, Allan H., and Paul R. Masson. 1994. "Credibility of Policies versus Credibility of Policymakers." *Quarterly Journal of Economics* 109 (August): 735–54.

Dreher, Axel, Bernhard Herz, and Volker Karb. 2006. "Is there a Causal Link between Currency and Debt Crises?" *International Journal of Finance and Economics* 11 (October): 305–25.

Driffill, John, and Martin Sola. 2006. "Target Zones for Exchange Rates and Policy Changes." *Journal of International Money and Finance* 25 (October): 912–31.

Duca, John V., and David D. VanHoose. 2004. "Recent Developments in Understanding the Demand for Money." *Journal of Economics and Business* 56 (December): 247–72.

Duffy, John, Maxim Nikitin, and R. Todd Smith. 2006. "Dollarization Traps." *Journal of Money, Credit, and Banking* 38 (December): 2073–97.

Dufrénot, Gilles, Valérie Mignon, and Anne Péguin-Feissolle. 2011. "The Effects of the Subprime Crisis on the Latin American Financial Markets: An Empirical Assessment." *Economic Modelling* 28 (September): 2342–57.

Dutton, Dean S. 1971. "A Model of Self-Generating Inflation: the Argentine Case." *Journal of Money, Credit, and Banking* 3 (May): 245–62.

Dwyer, Gerald P., John Devereux, Scott Baier, and Robert Tamura. 2013. "Recessions, Growth and Banking Crises." *Journal of International Money and Finance* 38 (November): 18–40.

Easterly, William. 2001. "Growth Implosions and Debt Explosions: Do Growth Slowdowns Cause Public Debt Crises?" *Contributions in Macroeconomics* 1 (March): 1–24.

Easterly, William, Paolo Mauro, and Klaus Schmidt-Hebbel. 1995. "Money Demand and Seigniorage-Maximizing Inflation." *Journal of Money, Credit, and Banking* 27 (May): 583–603.

Easterly, William, and Klaus Schmidt-Hebbel. 1994. "Fiscal Adjustment and Macroeconomic Performance: A Synthesis." In *Public Sector Deficits and Macroeconomic Performance*, edited by William Easterly, Carlos A. Rodríguez, and Klaus Schmidt-Hebbel. Oxford: Oxford University Press.

Eaton, Jonathan, and Mark Gersovitz. 1981. "Debt with Potential Repudiation: Theoretical and Empirical Analysis." *Review of Economic Studies* 48 (April): 289–309.

Edison, Hali J. 2003. "Do Indicators of Financial Crises Work? An Evaluation of an Early Warning System." *International Journal of Finance and Economics* 8 (January): 11–53.

Edison, Hali J., Michael W. Klein, Luca A. Ricci, and Torsten Slok. 2004. "Capital Account Liberalization and Economic Performance: Survey and Synthesis." *IMF Staff Papers* 51 (June): 220–56.

Edison, Hali J., Ross Levine, Luca Ricci, and Torsten Slok. 2002. "International Financial Integration and Economic Growth." *Journal of International Money and Finance* 21 (November): 749–76.

Edwards, Sebastián. 1984. *The Order of Liberalization of the External Sector in Developing Countries*. Princeton Essay in International Finance no. 156. Princeton, NJ: Princeton University.

——. 1988. "Terms of Trade, Tariffs and Labor Market Adjustment in Developing Countries." *World Bank Economic Review* 2 (May): 165–85.

——. 1989a. *Real Exchange Rates, Devaluation and Adjustment: Exchange Rate Policies in Developing Countries*. Cambridge, MA: MIT Press.

——. 1989b. "On the Sequencing of Structural Reforms." Working Paper no. 3138, National Bureau of Economic Research (October).

——. 2004. "Financial Openness, Sudden Stops, and Current-Account Reversals." *American Economic Review* (May): 59–64.

——. 2011. "Exchange-Rate Policies in Emerging Countries: Eleven Empirical Regularities from Latin America and East Asia." *Open Economies Review* 22 (September): 533–63.

Edwards, Sebastián, and Mohsin S. Khan. 1985. "Interest Rate Determination in Developing Countries: A Conceptual Framework." *IMF Staff Papers* 32 (September): 377–403.

Edwards, Sebastián, and Eduardo Levy-Yeyati. 2005. "Flexible Exchange Rates and Shock Absorbers." *European Economics Review* 49 (November): 2079–2105.

Edwards, Sebastián, and I. Igal Magdenzo. 2006. "Strict Dollarization and Economic Performance: An Empirical Investigation." *Journal of Money, Credit, and Banking* 38 (February): 269–82.

Edwards, Sebastián, and Peter J. Montiel. 1989. "Devaluation Crises and the Macroeconomic Consequences of Postponed Adjustment in Developing Countries." *IMF Staff Papers* 36 (December): 875–904.

Edwards, Sebastián, and Roberto Rigobon. 2009. "Capital Controls on Inflows, Exchange Rate Volatility and External Vulnerability." *Journal of International Economics* 78 (July): 256–67.

Edwards, Sebastián, and Julio A. Santaella. 1993. "Devaluation Controversies in the Developing Countries: Lessons from the Bretton Woods Era." In *A Retrospective on the Bretton Woods System*, edited by Michael D. Bordo and Barry Eichengreen. Chicago: University of Chicago Press.

Edwards, Sebastián, and Guido Tabellini. 1991. "Explaining Fiscal Policies and Inflation in Developing Countries." *Journal of International Money and Finance* 10 (Supplement, March): 16–48.

Edwards, Sebastián, and Sweder van Wijnbergen. 1986. "The Welfare Effects of Trade and Capital Market Liberalization." *International Economic Review* 27 (February): 141–48.

Edwards, Sebastian, and Carlos A. Végh. 1997. "Banks and Macroeconomic Disturbances under Predetermined Exchange Rates." *Journal of Monetary Economics* 40 (November): 239–78.

Eichengreen, Barry, and Carlos Arteta. 2002. "Banking Crises in Emerging Markets: Presumptions and Evidence." In *Financial Policies in Emerging Markets*, edited by Mario I. Blejer and Marko Skreb. Cambridge, MA: MIT Press.

Eichengreen, Barry, Donghyun Park, and Kwanho Shin. 2012. "When Fast Economies Slow Down: International Evidence and Implications for China." *Asian Economic Papers* 11 (March): 42–87.

Eijffinger, Sylvester C., and Bilge Karatas. 2012. "Currency Crises and Monetary Policy: A Study on Advanced and Emerging Economies." *Journal of International Money and Finance* 31 (September): 948–74.

Eijffinger, Sylvester C., and Mewael F. Tesfaselassie. 2007. "Central Bank Forecasts and Disclosure Policy: Why It Pays to Be Optimistic." *European Journal of Political Economy* 23 (March): 30–50.

Elekdag, Selim, Alejandro Justiniano, and Ivan Tchakarov. 2006. "An Estimated Small Open Economy Model of the Financial Accelerator." *IMF Staff Papers* 53 (June): 219–41.

Elías, Victor J. 1992. *Sources of Growth: A Study of Seven Latin American Countries*. San Francisco, CA: ICS Press.

Erbas, S. Nuri. 1989. "The Limits on Bond Financing of Government Deficits under Optimal Fiscal Policy." *Journal of Macroeconomics* 11 (Fall): 589–98.

Erceg, Christopher J. 2002. "The Choice of an Inflation Target Range in a Small Open Economy." *American Economic Review* 92 (May): 85–89.

Esaka, Taro. 2010. "Exchange Rate Regimes, Capital Controls, and Currency Crises: Does the Bipolar View Hold?" *Journal of International Financial Markets, Institutions and Money* 20 (February): 91–108.

Eslava, Marcela. 2006. "The Political Economy of Fiscal Policy: Survey." Working Paper no. 583, Inter-American Development Bank (October).

Estrella, Arturo, and Frederic S. Mishkin. 1997. "Is There a Role for Monetary Aggregates in the Conduct of Monetary Policy?" *Journal of Monetary Economics* 40 (October): 279–304.

Evans, J. L., and George K. Yarrow. 1981. "Some Implications of Alternative Expectations Hypotheses in the Monetary Analysis of Hyperinflations." *Oxford Economic Papers* 33 (March): 61–80.

Faini, Riccardo, and Jaime de Melo. 1992. "Adjustment, Investment and the Real Exchange Rate in Developing Countries." In *Reviving Private Investment in Developing Countries*, edited by Ajay Chhibber, Mansoor Dailami, and Nemat Shafik. Amsterdam: North Holland.

Falvey, Rod, and Cha Dong Kim. 1992. "Timing and Sequencing Issues in Trade Liberalisation." *Economic Journal* 102 (July): 908–24.

Faruqee, Hamid. 1992. "Dynamic Capital Mobility in Pacific Basin Developing Countries: Estimation and Policy Implications." *IMF Staff Papers* 39 (September): 706–17.

Fatás, Antonio, and Ilian Mihov. 2006. "The Macroeconomic Effects of Fiscal Rules in the US States." *Journal of Public Economics* 90 (January): 101–17.

Faust, Jon, and Lars E. Svensson. 2001. "Transparency and Credibility: Monetary Policy with Unobserved Goals." *International Economic Review* 42 (May): 369–97.

Feenstra, Robert C. 1985. "Anticipated Devaluation, Currency Flight and Direct Trade Controls in a Monetary Economy." *American Economic Review* 75 (June): 386–401.

Feldstein, Martin, and Charles Horioka. 1980. "Domestic Saving and International Capital Flows." *Economic Journal* 90 (June): 314–29.

Fernández, Raquel, and Dani Rodrik. 1991. "Resistance to Reform: Status Quo Bias in the Presence of Individual Specific Uncertainty." *American Economic Review* 81 (December): 1146–55.

Fernández, Roque B. 1985. "The Expectations Management Approach to Stabilization in Argentina 1976–82." *World Development* 13 (August): 871–92.

———. 1991. "Exchange Rate Policy in Countries with Hyperinflation: The Case of Argentina." In *Exchange Rate Policies in Developing and Post-Socialist Countries*, edited by Emil-Maria Claassen. San Francisco: ICS Press.

Fernández-Arias, Eduardo. 1996. "The New Wave of Private Capital Inflows: Push or Pull?" *Journal of Development Economics* 48 (March): 389–418.

Fernández-Arias, Eduardo, and Peter J. Montiel. 1996. "The Surge in Capital Inflows to Developing Countries: An Analytical Overview." *World Bank Economic Review* 10 (March): 51–77.

Fiess, Norbert. 2003. "Capital Flows, Country Risk, and Contagion." Policy Research Working Paper no. 2943, World Bank (January).

Fischer, Bernard, and Helmut Reisen. 1994. *Financial Opening: Why, How, When.* Occasional Paper no. 55, International Center for Economic Growth. San Francisco: ICS Press.

Fischer, Stanley. 1983. "Seigniorage and Fixed Exchange Rates: An Optimal Inflation Tax Analysis." In *Financial Policies and the World Capital Market*, edited by Pedro Aspe Armella, Rudiger Dornbusch, and Maurice Obstfeld. Chicago: University of Chicago Press.

———. 1985. "Contracts, Credibility and Disinflation." In *Inflation and Unemployment: Theory, Experience and Policymaking*, edited by Victor E. Argy and John W. Neville. London: G. Allen and Unwin.

———. 1986. "Exchange Rate Versus Money Targets in Disinflation." In *Indexing, Inflation, and Economic Policy.* Cambridge, MA: MIT Press.

———. 1988. "Real Balances, the Exchange Rate and Indexation: Real Variables in Disinflation." *Quarterly Journal of Economics* 103 (March): 27–49.

———. 1993. "The Role of Macroeconomic Factors in Growth." *Journal of Monetary Economics* 32 (December): 485–512.

Fischer, Stanley, and William Easterly. 1990. "The Economics of the Government Budget Constraint." *World Bank Research Observer* 5 (July): 127–42.

Fischer, Stanley, Ratna Sahay, and Carlos A. Végh. 2002. "Modern Hyper- and High Inflations." *Journal of Economic Literature* 40 (September): 837–80.

Fishlow, Albert, and Jorge Friedman. 1994. "Tax Evasion, Inflation and Stabilization." *Journal of Development Economics* 43 (February): 105–23.

Fishlow, Albert, and Samuel Morley. 1987. "Debts, Deficits and Destabilization: The Perversity of High Interest Rates." *Journal of Development Economics* 27 (October): 227–44.

Fitzgerald, E.V.K., Karel Jansen, and Rob Vos. 1994. "External Constraints on Private Investment Decisions in Developing Countries." In *Trade, Aid, and Development*, edited by Jan Willem Gunning, Henk Kox, Wouter Tims, and Ynto de Wit. New York: St. Martin's Press.

Fleming, J. Marcus. 1962. "Domestic Financial Policies Under Fixed and Under Floating Exchange Rates." *IMF Staff Papers* 9 (March): 369–80.

Flood, Robert P., and Peter M. Garber. 1984. "Collapsing Exchange Rate Regimes: Some Linear Examples." *Journal of International Economics* 17 (August): 1–13.

Flood, Robert P., Peter M. Garber, and Charles Kramer. 1996. "Collapsing Exchange Rate Regimes: Another Linear Example." *Journal of International Economics* 41 (November): 223–34.

Flood, Robert P., and Peter Isard. 1989. "Monetary Policy Strategies." *IMF Staff Papers* 36 (December): 612–32.

Flood, Robert P., and Olivier Jeanne. 2005. "An Interest Rate Defense of a Fixed Exchange Rate?" *Journal of International Economics* 66 (July): 471–84.

Flood, Robert P., and Nancy P. Marion. 1999. "Perspectives on the Recent Currency Crisis Literature." *International Journal of Finance and Economics* 4 (January): 1–26.

———. 2004. "A Model of the Joint Distribution of Banking and Currency Crises." *Journal of International Money and Finance* 23 (December): 841–65.

Forbes, Kristin J., and Francis E. Warnock. 2012. "Capital Flow Waves: Surges, Stops, Flight and Retrenchment." *Journal of International Economics* 88 (November): 235–51.

Fountas, Stiliano, and Agapitos Papagapitos. 2001. "The Monetary Transmission Mechanism: Evidence and Implications for European Monetary Union." *Economics Letters* 70 (March): 397–404.

Frankel, Jeffrey A., Carlos A. Végh, and Guillermo Vuletin. 2013. "On Graduation from Fiscal Procyclicality." *Journal of Development Economics* 100 (January): 32–47.

Fratzscher, Marcel. 2012. "Capital Flows, Push Versus Pull Factors and the Global Financial Crisis." *Journal of International Economics* 88 (November): 341–56.

Freitas, M. Lebre de. 2004. "The Dynamics of Inflation and Currency Substitution in a Small Open Economy." *Journal of International Money and Finance* 23 (February): 133–42.

Freitas, M. Lebre de, and Francisco J. Veiga. 2006. "Currency Substitution, Portfolio Diversification, and Money Demand." *Canadian Journal of Economics* 39 (August): 719–43.

Freixas, Xavier, and Jean-Charles Rochet. 1997. *Microeconomics of Banking*. Cambridge, MA: MIT Press.

Frenkel, Jacob A., and Assaf Razin. 1987. "The Mundell-Fleming Model a Quarter Century Later: A Unified Exposition." *IMF Staff Papers* 34 (December): 567–620.

——. 1992. *Fiscal Policies and the World Economy*. 2nd ed. Cambridge, MA: MIT Press.

Frey, Bruno S., and Reiner Eichenberger. 1994. "The Political Economy of Stabilization Programmes in Developing Countries." *European Journal of Political Economy* 10 (May): 169–90.

Frisch, Helmut, and Sylvia Staudinger. 2003. "Inflation Targeting versus Nominal Income Targeting." *Journal of Economics* 78 (March): 113–37.

Froot, Kenneth A. 1988. "Credibility, Real Interest Rates, and the Optimal Speed of Trade Liberalization." *Journal of International Economics* 25 (August): 71–93.

Fry, Maxwell J. 1996. *Money, Interest and Banking in Economic Development*. 2nd ed. Baltimore, MD: Johns Hopkins University Press.

Fuhrer, Jeffrey C. 1997. "Inflation-Output Variance Trade-Offs and Optimal Monetary Policy." *Journal of Money, Credit, and Banking* 29 (May): 214–34.

Fuhrer, Jeffrey C., and Geoffrey R. Moore. 1995. "Inflation Persistence." *Quarterly Journal of Economics* 110 (February): 127–59.

Furusawa, Taiji, and Edwin L. Lai. 1999. "Adjustment Costs and Gradual Trade Liberalization." *Journal of International Economics* 49 (December): 333–61.

Futagami, Koichi, Yuichi Morita, and Akihisa Shibata. 1993. "Dynamic Analysis of an Endogenous Growth Model with Public Capital." In *Endogenous Growth*, edited by Torben M. Andersen and Karl O. Moene. Oxford: Basil Blackwell.

Gagnon, Etienne. 2009. "Price Setting During Low and High Inflation: Evidence from Mexico." *Quarterly Journal of Economics* 124 (August): 1221–63.

Gagnon, Joseph E., and Jane Ihrig. 2004. "Monetary Policy and Exchange Rate Pass-Through." *International Journal of Finance and Economics* 9 (November): 315–38.

Gaiotti, Eugenio, and Alessandro Secchi. 2006. "Is There a Cost Channel of Monetary Policy Transmission? An Investigation into the Pricing Behavior of 2,000 Firms." *Journal of Money, Credit, and Banking* 38 (December): 2013–37.

Galati, Gabriele, and Richhild Moessner. 2013. "Macroprudential Policy—A Literature Review." *Journal of Economic Surveys* 27 (December): 846–78.

Galbis, Vicente. 1993. "High Real Interest Rates Under Financial Liberalization: Is There a Problem?" Working Paper no. 93/7, International Monetary Fund (January).

——. 1994. "Sequencing of Financial Sector Reforms: A Review." Working Paper no. 94/101, International Monetary Fund (September).

Galí, Jordi. 2008. *Monetary Policy, Inflation, and the Business Cycle: An Introduction to the New Keynesian Framework*. Princeton, NJ: Princeton University Press.

Galindo, Arturo J., Alejandro Izquierdo, and Liliana Rojas-Suárez. 2010. "Financial Integration and Foreign Banks in Latin America: How Do They Impact the Transmission of External Financial Shocks?" Working Paper no. 4651, Inter-American Development Bank (January).

Galindo, Arturo, Fabio Schiantarelli, and Andrew Weiss. 2007. "Does Financial Liberalization Improve the Allocation of Investment? Micro-Evidence from Developing Countries." *Journal of Development Economics* 83 (July): 562–97.

Gan, Wee-Beng, and Lee-Ying Soon. 1994. "Rational Expectations, Saving and Anticipated Changes in Income: Evidence from Malaysia and Singapore." *Journal of Macroeconomics* 16 (Winter): 157–70.

Ganelli, Giovanni. 2005. "The New Open Economy Macroeconomics of Government Debt." *Journal of International Economics* 65 (January): 167–84.

Garcia, Carlos J., Jorge E. Restrepo, and Scott Roger. 2011. "How Much Should Inflation Targeters Care about the Exchange Rate?" *Journal of International Money and Finance* 30 (November): 1590–1617.

García, Gustavo. 2012. "Fiscal Rules for Stability and Sustainability." in *The Fiscal Institutions of Tomorrow*. Washington, DC: Inter-American Development Bank.

Garcia, Marcio, and Roberto Rigobon. 2004. "A Risk Management Approach to Emerging Market Sovereign Debt Sustainability with an Application to Brazilian Data." NBER Working Paper 10336.

García-Peñalosa, Cecilia, and Stephen J. Turnovsky. 2005. "Production Risk and the Functional Distribution of Income in a Developing Economy: Tradeoffs and Policy Responses." *Journal of Development Economics* 76 (February): 175–208.

Gavin, Michael, and Roberto Perotti. 1997. "Fiscal Policy in Latin America." In *Macroeconomics Annual 1997,* edited by Julio Rotemberg and Ben Bernanke. Cambridge, MA: MIT Press.

Geide-Stevenson, Doris. 2000. "Labor Unions, Unemployment, and Trade and Capital Liberalization." *Journal of Economic Integration* 15 (March): 76–99.

Gelos, Gaston, Ratna Sahay, and Guido Sandleris. 2011. "Sovereign Borrowing by Developing Countries: What Determines Market Access?" *Journal of International Economics* 83 (March): 243–54.

Genberg, Hans. 1989. "Exchange Rate Management and Macroeconomic Policy: A National Perspective." *Scandinavian Journal of Economics* 91 (June): 439–69.

Geraats, Petra M. 2014. "Monetary Policy Transparency." Working Paper no. 4611, CESifo (January).

Gerali, Andrea, Stefano Neri, Luca Sessa, and Federico M. Signoretti. 2010. "Credit and Banking in a DSGE Model of the Euro Area." *Journal of Money, Credit, and Banking* 42 (September): 107–41.

Gersbach, Hans, and Volker Hahn. 2006. "Signaling and Commitment: Monetary versus Inflation Targeting." *Macroeconomic Dynamics* 10 (November): 595–624.

Gersovitz, Mark. 1988. "Saving and Development." In *Handbook of Development Economics,* edited by Hollis B. Chenery and T. N. Srinivasan. Amsterdam: North Holland.

Gertler, Mark. 1988. "Financial Structure and Aggregate Economic Activity: An Overview." *Journal of Money, Credit, and Banking* (August): 559–88.

——. 1992. "Financial Capacity and Output Fluctuations in an Economy with Multi-Period Financial Relationships." *Review of Economic Studies* 59 (July): 455–72.

Gertler, Mark, Simon Gilchrist, and Fabio M. Natalucci. 2007. "External Constraints on Monetary Policy and the Financial Accelerator." *Journal of Money, Credit and Banking* 39 (March): 295–330.

Ghosh, Amit. 2013. "Exchange Rate Pass Through, Macro Fundamentals and Regime Choice in Latin America." *Journal of Macroeconomics* 35 (March): 163–71.

Ghosh, Atish R., Jun Il Kim, Mahvash S. Qureshi, and Juan Zalduendo. 2014. "Surges." *Journal of International Economics* 92 (March): 266–85.

Giavazzi, Francesco, Tullio Jappelli, and Marco Pagano. 2000. "Searching for Non-Linear Effects of Fiscal Policy: Evidence from Industrial and Developing Countries." *European Economic Review* 44 (June): 1259–89.

Giavazzi, Francesco, Tullio Jappelli, Marco Pagano, and Marina Benedetti. 2005. "Searching for Non-Monotonic Effects of Fiscal Policy: New Evidence." Working Paper no. 2005-E-13, Bank of Japan (September).

Giavazzi, Francesco, and Marco Pagano. 1988. "The Advantage of Tying One's Hands: EMS Discipline and Central Bank Credibility." *European Economic Review* 32 (June): 1055–82.

Giavazzi, Francesco, and Guido Tabellini. 2005. "Economic and Political Liberalizations." *Journal of Monetary Economics* 52 (October): 1297–1330.

Gillman, Max, and Michal Kejak. 2005. "Contrasting Models of the Effect of Inflation on Growth." *Journal of Economic Surveys* 19 (February 2005): 113–24.

Giovannini, Alberto. 1985. "Saving and the Real Interest Rate in LDCs." *Journal of Development Economics* 18 (August): 197–217.

Giovannini, Alberto, and Martha de Melo. 1993. "Government Revenue from Financial Repression." *American Economic Review* 83 (August): 953–63.

Giovannini, Alberto, and Bart Turtelboom. 1994. "Currency Substitution." In *The Handbook of International Macroeconomics,* edited by Frederick van der Ploeg. Oxford: Basil Blackwell.

Glick, Reuven, and Michael Hutchison. 1999. "Banking and Currency Crises: How Common Are the Twins?" In *Financial Crises in Emerging Markets,* edited by Reuven Glick, Ramon Moreno, and Mark M. Spiegel. Cambridge: Cambridge University Press.

——. 2005. "Capital Controls and Exchange Rate Instability in Developing Countries." *Journal of International Money and Finance* 24 (April): 387–412.

Glick, Reuven, and Andrew Rose. 2002. "Does a Currency Union Affect Trade? The Time-Series Evidence." *European Economic Review* 46 (June): 1125–51.

Goderis, Benedikt, and Vasso Ioannidou. 2008. "Do High Interest Rates Defend Currencies During Speculative Attacks? New Evidence." *Journal of International Economics* 74 (January): 158–69.

Goldberg, Linda S. 1994. "Predicting Exchange Rate Crises: Mexico Revisited." *Journal of International Economics* 34 (May): 413–30.

Goldfeld, Stephen M., and Edward D. Sichel. 1990. "The Demand for Money." In *Handbook of Monetary Economics* I, edited by Benjamin Friedman and Frank H. Hahn. Amsterdam: North Holland.

Goldstein, Itay. 2005. "Strategic Complementarities and the Twin Crises." *Economic Journal* 115 (April): 368–90.

Goldstein, Itay, and Assaf Razin. 2013. "Review of Theories of Financial Crises." Working Paper no. 18670, National Bureau of Economic Research (January).

Goldstein, Morris, and Philip Turner. 1996. *Banking Crises in Emerging Economies: Origins and Policy Options.* Economic Paper no. 46, Bank for International Settlements (October).

Gonzaga, Gustavo, Naércio Menezes Filho, and Cristina Terra. 2006. "Trade Liberalization and the Evolution of Skill Earnings Differentials in Brazil." *Journal of International Economics* 68 (March): 345–67.

Goode, Richard. 1984. *Government Finance in Developing Countries.* Washington, DC: Brookings Institution.

Goodfriend, Marvin, and Bennett T. McCallum. 2007. "Banking and Interest Rates in Monetary Policy Analysis: A Quantitative Exploration." *Journal of Monetary Economics* 54 (July): 1480–1507.

Goodhart, Charles E. 2006. "A Framework for Assessing Financial Stability?" *Journal of Banking and Finance* 30 (December): 3415–22.

Gopinath, Gita. 2004. "Lending Booms, Sharp Reversals and Real Exchange Rate Dynamics." *Journal of International Economics* 62 (January): 1–23.

Gornemann, Nils. 2013. "Sovereign Default, Private Investment, and Economic Growth." Unpublished, University of Pennsylvania (June).

Gorton, Gary. 1988. "Banking Panics and Business Cycles." *Oxford Economic Papers* 40 (December): 751–81.

Gorton, Gary, and Lixin Huang. 2006. "Bank Panics and the Endogeneity of Central Banking." *Journal of Monetary Economics* 53 (October): 1613–29.

Gorton, Gary, and Andrew Metrick. 2012. "Getting Up to Speed on the Financial Crisis: A One-Weekend-Reader's Guide." *Journal of Economic Literature* 50 (March): 128–50.

Greenaway, David, and Chris Milner. 1991. "Fiscal Dependence on Trade Taxes and Trade Policy Reform." *Journal of Development Studies* 27 (April): 96–132.

Greene, Joshua, and Delano Villanueva. 1991. "Private Investment in Developing Countries." *IMF Staff Papers* 38 (March): 33–58.

Greene, William. 2003. *Econometric Analysis.* 5th ed. Englewood Cliffs, NJ: Prentice Hall.

Greenwald, Bruce C., and Joseph E. Stiglitz. 1987. "Keynesian, New Keynesian, and New Classical Economics." *Oxford Economic Papers* 39 (March): 119–33.

——. 1993. "Financial Market Imperfections and Business Cycles." *Quarterly Journal of Economics* 108 (February): 77–114.

Greenwood, Jeremy, and Boyan Jovanovich. 1990. "Financial Development, Growth, and the Distribution of Income." *Journal of Political Economy* 98 (October): 1076–107.

Grier, Robin, and Kevin B. Grier. 2006. "On the Real Effects of Inflation and Inflation Uncertainty in Mexico." *Journal of Development Economics* 80 (August): 478–500.

Grier, Kevin B., and Shu Lin. 2010. "Do High Interest Rates Deter Speculative Attacks? Evidence and some Theory." *Journal of International Money and Finance* 29 (September): 938–50.

Grisanti, Alejandro, Ernesto H. Stein, and Ernesto Talvi. 1998. "Institutional Arrangements and Fiscal Performance: The Latin American Experience." Working Paper no. 367, Inter-American Development Bank (January).

Grossman, Gene M., and Elhanan Helpman. 1991. *Innovation and Growth in the World Economy.* Cambridge, MA: MIT Press.

Grubel, Herbert. 2005. "Small Country Benefits from Monetary Union." *Journal of Policy Modeling* 27 (June): 509–23.

Guender, Alfred V. 2006. "Stabilising Properties of Discretionary Monetary Policies in a Small Open Economy." *Economic Journal* 116 (January): 309–26.

Guender, Alfred V., and Julie Tam. 2004. "On the Performance of Nominal Income Targeting as a Strategy for Monetary Policy in a Small Open Economy." *Journal of International Money and Finance* 23 (March): 143–63.

Guidotti, Pablo E., and Carlos A. Rodríguez. 1992. "Dollarization in Latin America." *IMF Staff Papers* 39 (September): 518–44.

Guidotti, Pablo E., Federico Sturzenegger, and Agustín Villar. 2004. "On the Consequences of Sudden Stops." *Economia* 4 (March): 1–44.

Gupta, Poonam. 2005. "Aftermath of Banking Crises: Effects on Real and Monetary Variables." *Journal of International Money and Finance* 24 (June): 675–91.

Gylfason, Thorvaldur, and Marian Radetzki. 1991. "Does Devaluation Make Sense in the Least Developed Countries?" *Economic Development and Cultural Change* 40 (October): 1–25.

Gylfason, Thorvaldur, and Ole Risager. 1984. "Does Devaluation Improve the Current Account?" *European Economic Review* 25 (February): 37–64.

Gylfason, Thorvaldur, and Michael Schmid. 1983. "Does Devaluation Cause Stagflation?" *Canadian Journal of Economics* 16 (November): 641–54.

Haggard, Stephan. 1991. "Inflation and Stabilization." In *Politics and Policy Making in Developing Countries*, edited by Gerald E. Meier. San Francisco: ICS Press.

Haggard, Stephan, and Robert Kaufman. 1989. "The Politics of Stabilization and Structural Adjustment." In *Developing Country Debt and the World Economy*, edited by Jeffrey D. Sachs. Chicago: University of Chicago Press.

———. 1990. "The Political Economy of Inflation and Stabilization in Middle-Income Countries." PRE Working Paper no. 444, World Bank (June).

Haliasos, Michael, and James Tobin. 1990. "The Macroeconomics of Government Finance." In *Handbook of Monetary Economics* II, edited by Benjamin M. Friedman and Frank H. Hahn. Amsterdam: North Holland.

Hamilton, James D., and Marjorie A. Flavin. 1986. "On the Limitations of Government Borrowing: A Framework for Empirical Testing." *American Economic Review* 76 (September): 808–19.

Hanson, James A. 1983. "Contractionary Devaluation, Substitution in Production and Consumption, and the Role of the Labor Market." *Journal of International Economics* 14 (February): 179–89.

———. 1995. "Opening the Capital Account: A Survey of Issues and Results." In *Capital Controls, Exchange Rates and Monetary Policy in the World Economy*, edited by Sebastián Edwards. New York: Cambridge University Press.

Haque, Nadeem U. 1988. "Fiscal Policy and Private Sector Saving Behavior in Developing Economies." *IMF Staff Papers* 35 (June): 316–35.

Haque, Nadeem U., and Peter J. Montiel. 1989. "Consumption in Developing Countries: Test for Liquidity Constraints and Finite Horizons." *Review of Economics and Statistics* 71 (August): 408–15.

———. 1991. "Capital Mobility in Developing Countries: Some Empirical Tests." *World Development* 19 (October): 1391–98.

———. 1994. "The Macroeconomics of Public Sector Deficits: The Case of Pakistan." In *Public Sector Deficits and Macroeconomic Performance*, edited by William Easterly, Carlos A. Rodríguez, and Klaus Schmidt-Hebbel. Oxford: Oxford University Press.

Harris, John, and Michael P. Todaro. 1970. "Migration, Unemployment and Development: A Two-Sector Analysis." *American Economic Review* 60 (March): 126–43.

Hatchondo, Juan Carlos, Leonardo Martinez, and Horacio Sapriza. 2007. "Quantitative Models of Sovereign Default and the Threat of Financial Exclusion." *Federal Reserve Bank of Richmond Economic Quarterly* 93 (June): 251–286.

Hayo, Bernd, and Carsten Hefeker. 2002. "Reconsidering Central Bank Independence." *European Journal of Political Economy* 18 (November): 653–74.

Heinemann, Frank, and Gerhard Illing. 2002. "Speculative Attacks: Unique Equilibrium and Transparency." *Journal of International Economics* 58 (December): 429–50.

Hellwig, Christian, Arijit Mukherji, and Aleh Tsyvinski. 2006. "Self-Fulfilling Currency Crises: The Role of Interest Rates." *American Economic Review* 96 (December): 1769–87.

Helpman, Elhanan. 1988. "Macroeconomic Effects of Price Controls: The Role of Market Structure." *Economic Journal* 98 (June): 340–54.

———. 1989. "Voluntary Debt Reduction: Incentives and Welfare." *IMF Staff Papers* 36 (September): 580–611.

Helpman, Elhanan, and Leonardo Leiderman. 1988. "Stabilization in High-Inflation Countries: Analytical Foundations and Recent Experience." In *Stabilization Policy and Labor Markets*, edited by Karl Brunner and Allan H. Meltzer. Carnegie-Rochester Conference Series on Public Policy, 28. Amsterdam: North Holland.

Helpman, Elhanan, Leonardo Leiderman, and Gil Bufman. 1994. "New Breed of Exchange Rate Bands: Chile, Israel and Mexico." *Economic Policy* 9 (October): 260–306.

Helpman, Elhanan, and Assaf Razin. 1987. "Exchange Rate Management: Intertemporal Tradeoffs." *American Economic Review* 77 (March): 107–23.

Hernández, Leonardo, and Heinz Rudolph. 1994. "Domestic Factors, Sustainability, and Soft Landing in the New Wave of Private Capital Inflows." Unpublished, World Bank (November).

Herrendorf, Berthold. 1997. "Importing Credibility through Exchange Rate Pegging." *Economic Journal* 107 (May): 687–94.

——. 1999. "Transparency, Reputation, and Credibility under Floating and Pegged Exchange Rates." *Journal of International Economics* 49 (October): 31–50.

Herrmann, Sabine, and Dubravko Mihaljek. 2013. "The Determinants of Cross-Border Bank Flows to Emerging Markets: New Empirical Evidence on the Spread of Financial Crises." *Economics of Transition* 21 (July): 1–27.

Heymann, Daniel, and Pablo Sanguinetti. 1994. "Fiscal Inconsistencies and High Inflation." *Journal of Development Economics* 43 (February): 85–104.

Hinkle, Lawrence, and Peter J. Montiel, eds. 1999. *Exchange Rate Misalignment: Concepts and Measurement for Developing Countries*. Oxford: Oxford University Press.

Hnatkovska, Viktoria, Amartya Lahiri, and Carlos A. Végh. 2013. "Interest Rate and the Exchange Rate: A Non-Monotonic Tale." *European Economic Review* 63 (October): 68–93.

Ho, Corinne, and Robert N. McCauley. 2003. "Living with Flexible Exchange Rates: Issues and Recent Experience in Inflation Targeting Emerging Market Economies." Working Paper no. 130, Bank for International Settlements (February).

Hodrick, Robert J., and Edward C. Prescott. 1997. "Postwar U.S. Business Cycles: An Empirical Investigation." *Journal of Money, Credit, and Banking* 29 (February): 1–16.

Hoffmaister, Alexander W., and Jorge E. Roldós. 1997. "Are Business Cycles Different in Asia and Latin America?" Working Paper no. 97/9, International Monetary Fund (January).

——. 2001. "The Sources of Macroeconomic Fluctuations in Developing Countries: Brazil and Korea." *Journal of Macroeconomics* 23 (Spring): 213–39.

Hoffmaister, Alexander W., Jorge E. Roldós, and Peter Wickham. 1998. "Macroeconomic Fluctuations in Sub-Saharan Africa." *IMF Staff Papers* 44 (March): 132–60.

Hoffman, Dennis L., and Chakib Tahiri. 1994. "Money Demand in Morocco: Estimating Long-Run Elasticities for a Developing Country." *Oxford Bulletin of Economics and Statistics* 56 (August): 305–24.

Hoffmann, Mathias. 2007. "Fixed versus Flexible Exchange Rates: Evidence from Developing Countries." *Economica* 74 (August): 425–49.

Hogan, Vincent. 2004. "Expansionary Fiscal Contractions? Evidence from Panel Data." *Scandinavian Journal of Economics* 106 (December): 647–59.

Hong, Kiseok, and Aaron Tornell. 2005. "Recovery from a Currency Crisis: Some Stylized Facts." *Journal of Development Economics* 76 (February): 71–96.

Horn, Henrik, and Torsten Persson. 1988. "Exchange Rate Policy, Wage Formation, and Credibility." *European Economic Review* 32 (October): 1621–36.

Horton, Susan, Ravi Kanbur, and Dipak Mazumdar. 1994. "Overview." In *Labor Markets in an Era of Adjustment*, edited by Susan Horton, Ravi Kanbur, and Dipak Mazumdar. Washington, DC: World Bank.

House, Christopher L. 2006. "Adverse Selection and the Financial Accelerator." *Journal of Monetary Economics* 53 (September): 1117–34.

Hsieh, Chang-Tai. 2000. "Bargaining over Reform." *European Economic Review* 44 (October): 1659–76.

Huang, Haizhou, and Shang-Jin Wei. 2006. "Monetary Policies for Developing Countries: The Role of Institutional Quality." *Journal of International Economics* 70 (September): 239–52.

Huang, Ho-Chuan. 2005. "Diverging Evidence of Convergence Hypothesis." *Journal of Macroeconomics* 27 (June): 233–55.

Hubbard, R. Glenn. 1998. "Capital-Market Imperfections and Investment." *Journal of Economic Literature* 36 (March 1998): 193–225.

Hubbard, R. Glenn, and Kenneth L. Judd. 1986. "Liquidity Constraints, Fiscal Policy, and Consumption." *Brookings Papers on Economic Activity* (June): 1–50.

Hutchison, Michael M., and Kathleen McDill. 1999. "Are All Banking Crises Alike? The Japanese Experience in International Comparison." Working Paper no. 7253, National Bureau of Economic Research (July).

Hutchison, Michael M., and Ilan Noy. 2005. "How Bad Are Twins? Output Costs of Currency and Banking Crises." *Journal of Money, Credit, and Banking* 37 (August): 725–52.

——. 2006. "Sudden Stops and the Mexican Wave: Currency Crises, Capital Flow Reversals and Output Loss in Emerging Markets." *Journal of Development Economics* 79 (February): 225–48.

Hutchison, Michael M., Ilan Noy, and Lidan Wang. 2010. "Fiscal and Monetary Policies and the Cost of Sudden Stops." *Journal of International Money and Finance* 29 (October): 973–87.

Iacoviello, Matteo. 2005. "House Prices, Borrowing Constraints, and Monetary Policy in the Business Cycle." *American Economic Review* 95 (June): 739–64.

Ikeda, Shinsuke, and Ichiro Gombi. 1999. "Habits, Costly Investment, and Current Account Dynamics." *Journal of International Economics* 49 (December): 363–84.

Im, Fernando G., and David Rosenblatt. 2013. "Middle-Income Traps: A Conceptual and Empirical Survey." Policy Research Working Paper no. 6594, World Bank (September).

Imrohoroglu, Ayse, and Krishna B. Kumar. 2004. "Intermediation Costs and Capital Flows." *Review of Economic Dynamics* 7 (July): 586–612.

——. 2012. "The Liberalization and Management of Capital Flows: An Institutional View." Staff Paper (Washington, DC).

——. 2003. *World Economic Outlook* (April). Washington, DC: International Monetary Fund.

Ireland, Peter N. 2001. "Sticky-Price Models of the Business Cycle: Specification and Stability." *Journal of Monetary Economics* 47 (February) 3–18.

Irvine, Ian, and Susheng Wang. 2001. "Saving Behavior and Wealth Accumulation in a Pure Lifecycle Model with Income Uncertainty." *European Economic Review* 45 (February): 233–58.

Irwin, Gregor. 2004. "Currency Boards and Currency Crises." *Oxford Economic Papers* 56 (January): 64–87.

Ishiyama, Yoshihide. 1975. "The Theory of Optimum Currency Areas: A Survey." *IMF Staff Papers* 22 (July): 344–83.

Islam, Shafiqul. 1984. "Devaluation, Stabilization Policies and the Developing Countries." *Journal of Development Economics* 14 (January): 37–60.

Iyigun, Murat F., and Ann L. Owen. 2004. "Income Inequality, Financial Development, and Macroeconomic Fluctuations." *Economic Journal* 114 (April): 352–76.

Iyoha, Milton A. 2000. "An Econometric Analysis of External Debt and Economic Growth in Sub-Saharan African Countries." In *External Debt and Capital Flight in Sub-Saharan Africa*, edited by S. Ibi Ajayi and Mohsin Khan. Washington, DC: International Monetary Fund.

Ize, Alain, and Guillermo Ortiz. 1987. "Fiscal Rigidities, Public Debt, and Capital Flight." *IMF Staff Papers* 34 (June): 311–32.

Jappelli, Tullio, and Marco Pagano. 1994. "Saving, Growth, and Liquidity Constraints." *Quarterly Journal of Economics* 109 (February): 83–110.

Jeanne, Olivier, and Romain Rancière. 2011. "The Optimal Level of International Reserves for Emerging Market Countries: A New Formula and Some Applications." *Economic Journal* 121 (September): 905–30.

Jensen, Henrik. 2002. "Targeting Nominal Income Growth or Inflation?" *American Economic Review* 92 (September): 928–56.

Jones, Charles I., and Paul M. Romer. 2010. "The New Kaldor Facts: Ideas, Institutions, Population, and Human Capital." *American Economic Journal: Macroeconomics* 2 (January): 224–45.

Jonung, Lars. 1990. *The Political Economy of Price Controls*. Brookfield, VT: E. Gower.

Jorgensen, Steen L., and Martin Paldam. 1986. "Exchange Rates and Domestic Inflation: A Study of Price/Wage Inflation in Eight Latin American Countries, 1946–85." Working Paper no. 10, Aarhus University.

Joyce, Joseph P., and Malhar Nabar. 2009. "Sudden Stops, Banking Crises and Investment Collapses in Emerging Markets." *Journal of Development Economics* 90 (November): 314–22.

Kähkönen, Juha. 1987. "Liberalization Policies and Welfare in a Financially Repressed Economy." *IMF Staff Papers* 34 (September): 531–47.

Kalulumia, Pene, and Francine Nyankiye. 2000. "Labor Adjustment Costs, Macroeconomic Shocks and Real Business Cycles in a Small Open Economy." *Journal of Macroeconomics* 22 (September): 671–94.

Kamas, Linda. 1986. "The Balance of Payments Offset to Monetary Policy: Monetarist, Portfolio Balance, and Keynesian Estimates for Mexico and Venezuela." *Journal of Money, Credit, and Banking* 18 (November): 467–81.

Kaminsky, Graciela. 1999. "Currency and Banking Crises: The Early Warnings of Distress." Working Paper no. 99/178, International Monetary Fund (December).

Kaminsky, Graciela L., and Carmen M. Reinhart. 1999. "The Twin Crises: The Causes of Banking and Balance-of-Payments Problems." *American Economic Review* 89 (June): 473–500.

Kaminsky, Graciela, Carmen Reinhart, and Carlos Vegh. 2004. "When It Rains, It Pours: Procyclical Capital Flows and Macroeconomic Policies." In *NBER Macroeconomics Annual 2004*, edited by Mark Gertler and Kenneth S. Rogoff. Cambridge, MA: MIT Press.

Karayalcin, Cem. 2003. "Habit Formation and Government Spending in a Small Open Economy." *Macroeconomic Dynamics* 7 (June): 407–23.

Karras, Georgios. 1994. "Government Spending and Private Consumption: Some International Evidence." *Journal of Money, Credit, and Banking* 26 (February): 9–22.

——. 2007. "Is Africa an Optimum Currency Area? A Comparison of Macroeconomic Costs and Benefits." *Journal of African Economies* 16 (March): 234–58.

Kawai, Masahiro, and Louis J. Maccini. 1990. "Fiscal Policy, Anticipated Switches in Methods of Finance, and the Effects on the Economy." *International Economic Review* 31 (November): 913–34.

——. 1995. "Twin Deficits versus Unpleasant Fiscal Arithmetic in a Small Open Economy." *Journal of Money, Credit, and Banking* 27 (August): 639–58.

Kawamura, Enrique. 2007. "Exchange Rate Regimes, Banking and the Non-Tradable Sector." *Journal of Monetary Economics* 54 (March): 325–45.

Kay, Cristobal. 1989. *Latin American Theories of Development and Underdevelopment*. London: P. Routledge.

Kehoe, Timothy J., and Kim J. Ruhl. 2009. "Sudden Stops, Sectoral Reallocations, and the Real Exchange Rate." *Journal of Development Economics* 89 (July): 235–49.

Kendall, Maurice G., and Alan Stuart. 1967. *The Advanced Theory of Statistics*. London: Griffin.

Khalkhali, Sal Amir, and Atul Dara. 2007. "Trade Openness and Saving-Investment Correlations." *Economic Modelling* 24 (January): 120–27.

Khan, Mohsin S. 1980. "Monetary Shocks and the Dynamics of Inflation." *IMF Staff Papers* 27 (June): 250–84.

Khan, Mohsin S., and Manmohan S. Kumar. 1994. "Determinants of the Current Account in Developing Countries, 1970–1990." Unpublished, International Monetary Fund (March).

Khan, Mohsin S., and J. Saul Lizondo. 1987. "Devaluation, Fiscal Deficits, and the Real Exchange Rate." *World Bank Economic Review* 1 (January): 357–74.

Khan, Mohsin S., and Peter J. Montiel. 1987. "Real Exchange Rate Dynamics in a Small Primary-Exporter Country." *IMF Staff Papers* 34 (December): 687–710.

Khan, Mohsin S., and C. Luis Ramírez-Rojas. 1986. "Currency Substitution and Government Revenue from Inflation." *Revista de Análisis Económico* 1 (June): 79–88.

Khan, Mohsin S., and Roberto Zahler. 1983. "The Macroeconomic Effects of Changes in Barriers to Trade and Capital Flows." *IMF Staff Papers* 30 (June): 223–82.

——. 1985. "Trade and Financial Liberalization Given External Shocks and Inconsistent Domestic Policies." *IMF Staff Papers* 32 (March): 22–55.

Khor, Hoe E., and Liliana Rojas-Suárez. 1991. "Interest Rates in Mexico." *IMF Staff Papers* 38 (December): 850–71.

Kiguel, Miguel A. 1987. "The Non-Dynamic Equivalence of Monetary and Exchange Rate Rules under Imperfect Capital Mobility and Rational Expectations." *Journal of International Money and Finance* 6 (June): 207–14.

——. 1989. "Budget Deficits, Stability and the Dynamics of Hyperinflation." *Journal of Money, Credit, and Banking* 21 (May): 148–57.

Kiguel, Miguel A., and Nissan Liviatan. 1992. "The Business Cycle Associated with Exchange Rate Based Stabilization." *World Bank Economic Review* 6 (May): 279–305.

——. 1994. "A Policy-Game Approach to the High Inflation Equilibrium." *Journal of Development Economics* 45 (October): 135–40.

Kim, Jimill, and Dale W. Henderson. 2005. "Inflation Targeting and Nominal-Income-Growth Targeting: When and Why Are They Suboptimal?" *Journal of Monetary Economics* 52 (November): 1463–95.

Kimbrough, Kent P. 1985. "An Examination of the Effects of Government Purchases in an Open Economy." *Journal of International Money and Finance* 4 (March): 113–33.

——. 1992. "Speculative Attacks: The Roles of Intertemporal Substitution and the Interest Elasticity of the Demand for Money." *Journal of Macroeconomics* 14 (Fall): 689–710.

——. 2006. "Revenue Maximizing Inflation." *Journal of Monetary Economics* 53 (November): 1967–78.

Kimura, Takeshi, and Takushi Kurozumi. 2007. "Optimal Monetary Policy in a Micro-Founded Model with Parameter Uncertainty." *Journal of Economic Dynamics and Control* 31 (February): 399–431.

Kirman, Alan P. 1992. "Whom or What Does the Representative Individual Represent?" *Journal of Economic Perspectives* 6 (Spring): 117–36.

Kiyotaki, Nobuhiro. 1998. "Credit and Business Cycles." *Japanese Economic Review* 49 (March): 18–35.

Kiyotaki, Nobuhiro, and John Moore. 1997. "Credit Cycles." *Journal of Political Economy* 105 (April): 211–48.

Klein, Michael W., and Jay Shambaugh. 2006. "Fixed Exchange Rates and Trade." *Journal of International Economics* 70 (December): 359–83.

Kletzer, Kenneth, and Mark M. Spiegel. 2004. "Sterilization Costs and Exchange Rate Targeting." *Journal of International Money and Finance* 23 (October): 897–915.

Kollmann, Robert. 2001. "The Exchange Rate in a Dynamic-Optimizing Business Cycle Model with Nominal Rigidities: A Quantitative Investigation." *Journal of International Economics* 55 (December): 243–62.

Konishi, Hideki. 2006. "Spending Cuts or Tax Increases? The Composition of Fiscal Adjustment as a Signal." *European Economic Review* 50 (August): 1441–69.

Kose, M. Ayhan. 2002. "Explaining Business Cycles in Small Open Economies: How Much Do World Prices Matter?" *Journal of International Economics* 56 (March): 299–327.

Kose, M. Ayhan, Eswar S. Prasad, and Marco E. Terrones. 2006. "How Do Trade and Financial Integration Affect the Relationship between Growth and Volatility?" *Journal of International Economics* 69 (June): 176–202.

Kose, M. Ayhan, and Raymond Riezman. 2001. "Trade Shocks and Macroeconomic Fluctuations in Africa." *Journal of Development Economics* 65 (June): 55–80.

Krasker, William S. 1980. "The 'Peso Problem' in Testing the Efficiency of Forward Exchange Rate Markets." *Journal of Monetary Economics* 6 (March): 269–76.

Krishnamurthy, Arvin. 2003. "Collateral Constraints and the Amplification Mechanism." *Journal of Economic Theory* 111 (August): 277–292.

Kroszner, Randall S., Luc Laeven, and Daniela Klingebiel. 2007. "Banking Crises, Financial Dependence, and Growth." *Journal of Financial Economics* 84 (April): 187–228.

Krueger, Ann O. 1985. "How to Liberalize a Small, Open Economy." In *The Economics of the Caribbean Basin*, edited by Michael Connolly and John McDermott. New York: Praeger.

Krugman, Paul. 1979. "A Model of Balance of Payments Crises." *Journal of Money, Credit, and Banking* 11 (August): 311–25.

———. 1988. "Financing vs. Forgiving a Debt Overhang." Working Paper no. 2486, National Bureau of Economic Research (January).

———. 1991. "Target Zones and Exchange Rate Dynamics." *Quarterly Journal of Economics* 106 (November): 669–82.

———. 1998. "What Happened to Asia?" Unpublished, MIT (January).

———. 1999. "Balance Sheets, the Transfer Problem, and Financial Crises." In *International Finance and International Crises*, edited by Peter Isard, Assaf Razin, and Andrew K. Rose. Washington, DC: International Monetary Fund.

———. 2008. "The International Finance Multiplier." unpublished, Princeton University (October).

Krugman, Paul, and Lance Taylor. 1978. "Contractionary Effects of Devaluation." *Journal of International Economics* 8 (August): 445–56.

Kwack, Sung Y., and Young S. Lee. 2005. "What Determines Saving Rates in Korea? The Role of Demography." *Journal of Asian Economics* 16 (October): 861–73.

Labán, Raúl, and Felipe Larraín. 1997. "Can a Liberalization of Capital Outflows Increase Net Capital Inflows?" *Journal of International Money and Finance* 16 (June): 415–31.

Laeven, Luc, and Fabián Valencia. 2013. "Systemic Banking Crises Database." *IMF Economic Review* 61 (March): 225–70.

Lahiri, Amartya. 2001. "Exchange Rate Based Stabilizations under Real Frictions: The Role of Endogenous Labor Supply." *Journal of Economic Dynamics and Control* 25 (August): 1157–77.

Lahiri, Amartya, and Carlos A. Végh. 2003. "Delaying the Inevitable: Interest Rate Defense and Balance of Payments Crises." *Journal of Political Economy* 111 (April): 404–24.

Lahiri, Ashok K. 1989. "Dynamics of Asian Savings: The Role of Growth and Age Structure." *IMF Staff Papers* 36 (March): 228–61.

Lane, Philip R. 2001. The New Open Economy Macroeconomics: A Survey." *Journal of International Economics* 54 (August): 235–66.

———. 2003. "The Cyclical Behavior of Fiscal Policy: Evidence from the OECD." *Journal of Public Economics* 87 (December): 2661–75.

Larraín, Felipe, and Rodrigo Vergara. 1993. "Investment and Macroeconomic Adjustment: The Case of East Asia." In *Striving for Growth After Adjustment*, edited by Luis Servén and Andrés Solimano. Washington, DC: World Bank.

Laurens, Bernard. 2005. *Monetary Policy Implementation at Different Stages of Market Development*. Washington, DC: International Monetary Fund.

Layard, Richard, Stephen Nickell, and Richard Jackman. 1991. *Unemployment*. Oxford: Oxford University Press.

Lächler, Ulrich. 1982. "On Political Business Cycles with Endogenous Election Dates." *Journal of Public Economics* 17 (March): 111–17.

———. 1988. "Credibility and the Dynamics of Disinflation in Open Economies." *Journal of Development Economics* 28 (May): 285–307.

Leblebicioglu, Asli. 2009. "Financial Integration, Credit Market Imperfections and Consumption Smoothing." *Journal of Economic Dynamics and Control* 33 (February): 377–93.

Lee, Ha Yan, Luca A. Ricci, and Roberto Rigobon. 2004. "Once Again, Is Openness Good for Growth?" *Journal of Development Economics* 75 (December): 451–72.

Lee, Jeong-Joon, and Yasuyuki Sawada. 2010. "Precautionary Saving under Liquidity Constraints: Evidence from Rural Pakistan." *Journal of Development Economics* 91 (January): 77–86.

Lee, Junhee, and Wooheon Rhee. 2013. "Financial Factors in the Business Cycle of a Small Open Economy: The Case of Korea." *Open Economies Review* 24 (November): 881–900

Lee, Kiseok, and Ronald A. Ratti. 1993. "On Seigniorage, Operating Rules, and Dual Equilibria." *Quarterly Journal of Economics* 108 (May): 543–50.

Leiderman, Leonardo, and Mario I. Blejer. 1988. "Modeling and Testing Ricardian Equivalence." *IMF Staff Papers* 35 (March): 1–35.

Leiderman, Leonardo, and Assaf Razin. 1988. "Testing Ricardian Neutrality with an Intertemporal Stochastic Model." *Journal of Money, Credit, and Banking* 20 (February): 1–21.

Leite, Sérgio P., and Ved Sundararajan. 1990. "Issues in Interest Rate Management and Liberalization." *IMF Staff Papers* 37 (December): 735–52.

Leitemo, Kai. 2006. "Targeting Inflation by Forecast Feedback Rules in Small Open Economies." *Journal of Economic Dynamics and Control* 30 (March): 393–413.

Levchenko, Andrei A. 2005. "Financial Liberalization and Consumption Volatility in Developing Countries." *IMF Staff Papers* 52 (September): 237–59.

Levine, Ross. 1996. "Foreign Banks, Financial Development, and Economic Growth." In *International Financial Markets*, edited by Claude E. Barfield. Washington, DC: American Enterprise Institute Press.

——. 2005. "Finance and Growth: Theory and Evidence." In *Handbook of Monetary Economics* IA, edited by Philippe Aghion and Steven N. Durlauf. Amsterdam: Elsevier B.V.

Levine, Ross, Norman Loayza, and Thorsten Beck. 2000. "Financial Intermediation and Growth: Causality and Causes." *Journal of Monetary Economics* 46 (August): 31–77.

Levy-Yeyati, Eduardo, and Ugo Panizza. 2011. "The Elusive Costs of Sovereign Defaults." *Journal of Development Economics* 84 (January): 85–105.

Levy-Yeyati, Eduardo, and Federico Sturzenegger. 2003. "To Float or to Fix: Evidence on the Impact of Exchange Rate Regimes on Growth." *American Economic Review* 93 (September): 1173–93.

——. 2005. "Classifying Exchange Rate Regimes: Deeds vs. Words." *European Economic Review* 49 (August): 1603–35.

Levy-Yeyati, Eduardo, Federico Sturzenegger, and Iliana Reggio. 2010. "On the Endogeneity of Exchange Rate Regimes." *European Economic Review* 54 (July): 659–77.

Li, Xiangming. 2004. "Trade Liberalization and Real Exchange Rate Movement." *IMF Staff Papers* 51 (September): 553–84.

Licchetta, Mirko. 2011. "Common Determinants of Currency Crises: The Role of External Balance Sheet Variables." *International Journal of Finance and Economics* 16 (July): 237–55.

Lin, Hsin-Yi, and Hao-Pang Chu. 2013. "Are Fiscal Deficits Inflationary?" *Journal of International Money and Finance* 32 (February): 214–33.

Liviatan, Nissan. 1984. "Tight Money and Inflation." *Journal of Monetary Economics* 13 (January): 5–15.

——. 1986. "The Tight Money Paradox—An Alternative View." *Journal of Macroeconomics* 8 (Winter): 105–12.

——. 1988. "On the Interaction between Monetary and Fiscal Policies Under Perfect Foresight." *Oxford Economic Papers* 40 (March): 193–203.

Lizondo, J. Saul, and Peter J. Montiel. 1989. "Contractionary Devaluation in Developing Countries: An Analytical Overview." *IMF Staff Papers* 36 (March): 182–227.

Loayza, Norman V., Klaus Schmidt-Hebbel, and Luis Servén. 2000. "What Drives Private Saving across the World?" *Review of Economics and Statistics* 82 (May): 165–81.

Lohmann, Susan. 1992. "Optimal Commitment in Monetary Policy: Credibility Versus Flexibility." *American Economic Review* 82 (March): 273–86.

Lombardo, Giovanni, and David Vestin. 2008. "Welfare Implications of Calvo Vs. Rotemberg-Pricing Assumptions." *Economics Letters* 100 (August): 275–79.

Lucas, Robert E. Jr. 1976. "Econometric Policy Evaluation: A Critique." In *The Phillips Curve and Labor Markets*, edited by Karl Brunner and Allan H. Meltzer, Carnegie-Rochester Conference Series on Public Policy. Amsterdam: North-Holland.

——. 1988. "On the Mechanics of Economic Development." *Journal of Monetary Economics* 22 (January): 3–42.

——. 1993. "Making a Miracle." *Econometrica* 61 (March): 251–72.

Luintel, Kul B., Mosahid Khan, Philip Arestis, and Konstantinos Theodoridis. 2008. "Financial Structure and Economic Growth." *Journal of Development Economics* 86 (April): 181–200.

MacKenzie, George A. 1998. "The Macroeconomic Impact of Privatization." *IMF Staff Papers* 45 (June): 363–73.

Manasse, Paolo, Nouriel Roubini, and Axel Schimmelpfennig. 2003. "Predicting Sovereign Debt Crises." Working Paper no. 03/221, International Monetary Fund (November).

Manasse, Paolo, and Nouriel Roubini. 2005. " 'Rules of Thumb' for Sovereign Debt Crises." Working Paper no. 05/42, International Monetary Fund (March).

Mansoorian, Arman, and Simon Neaime. 2003. "Durable Goods, Habits, Time Preference, and Exchange Rates." *North American Journal of Economics and Finance* 14 (March): 115–30.

Markusen, James R., and Anthony J. Venables. 1999. "Foreign Direct Investment as a Catalyst for Industrial Development." *European Economic Review* 43 (February): 335–56.

Masson, Paul R. 1985. "The Sustainability of Fiscal Deficits." *IMF Staff Papers* 32 (August): 577–605.

——. 2000. "Multiple Equilibria, Contagion, and the Emerging Market Crises." In *Financial Crises in Emerging Markets*, edited by Reuven Glick, Ramon Moreno, and Mark M. Spiegel. Cambridge: Cambridge University Press.

Mateut, Simona. 2005. "Trade Credit and Monetary Policy Transmission." *Journal of Economic Surveys* 19 (September): 655–70.

Matsuyama, Kiminori. 1991. "On Exchange-Rate Stabilization." *Journal of Economic Dynamics and Control* 15 (January): 7–26.

McCallum, Bennett T. 1984. "Are Bond-Financed Deficits Inflationary? A Ricardian Analysis." *Journal of Political Economy* 92 (February): 123–35.

——. 1997. "Crucial Issues Concerning Central Bank Independence." *Journal of Monetary Economics* 39 (June): 99–112.

——. 1999. "Issues in the Design of Monetary Policy Rules." In *Handbook of Macroeconomics*, edited by John B. Taylor and Michael Woodford. Amsterdam: North Holland.

McCallum, Bennett T., and Edward Nelson. 2000. "Monetary Policy for an Open Economy: An Alternative Framework with Optimizing Agents and Sticky Prices." *Oxford Review of Economic Policy* 16 (December): 74–91.

McKinnon, Ronald I. 1973. *Money and Capital in Economic Development*. Washington, DC: Brookings Institution.

——. 1976. "Saving Propensities and the Korean Monetary Reform in Retrospect." In *Finance in Growth and Development*, edited by Ronald McKinnon. New York: Marcel Dekker.

——. 1993. *The Order of Economic Liberalization*. 2nd ed. Baltimore, MD: Johns Hopkins University Press.

McKinnon, Ronald I., and Donald J. Mathieson. 1981. *How to Manage a Repressed Economy*. Essay in International Finance no. 145, Princeton University.

McKinnon, Ronald I., and Huw Pill. 1999. "Exchange Rate Regimes for Emerging Markets: Moral Hazard and International Overborrowing." *Oxford Review of Economic Policy* 15 (March): 19–38.

McKinnon, Ronald I., and Günther Schnabl. 2005. "The East Asian Dollar Standard, Fear of Floating, and Original Sin." In *Exchange Rates under the East Asian Dollar Standard: Living with Conflicted Virtue*, edited by Ronald I. McKinnon. Cambridge, MA: MIT Press.

McNelis, Paul D., and Liliana Rojas-Suárez. 1996. "Currency Substitution as Behavior toward Risk: The Case of Bolivia and Peru." Unpublished, Department of Economics, Georgetown University (November).

McNelis, Paul D., and Klaus Schmidt-Hebbel. 1993. "Financial Liberalization and Adjustment." *Journal of International Money and Finance* 12 (June): 249–77.

Meh, Césaire, Vincenzo Quadrini, and Yaz Terajima. 2009. "Real Effects of Price Stability with Endogenous Nominal Indexation." Working Paper no. 09–16, Bank of Canada (May).

Mehlum, Halvor. 2001. "Speed of Adjustment and Self-Fulfilling Failure of Economic Reform." *Journal of International Economics* 53 (February): 149–67.

Mendizábal, Hugo R. 2006. "The Behavior of Money Velocity in High and Low Inflation Countries." *Journal of Money, Credit, and Banking* 38 (February): 209–28.

Mendoza, Enrique G., and Katherine A. Smith. 2002. "Margin Calls, Trading Costs, and Asset Prices in Emerging Markets." Working Paper no. 9286, National Bureau of Economic Research (October).

Mendoza, Enrique G., and Martin Uribe. 1996. "The Syndrome of Exchange-Rate Based Stabilizations and the Uncertain Duration of Currency Pegs." Board of Governors of the Federal Reserve System, International Finance Discussion Paper no. 548 (April).

Mendoza, Enrique, and Marcelo Oviedo. 2004. "Public Debt, Fiscal Solvency, and Macroeconomic Uncertainty in Latin America: The Cases of Brazil, Colombia, Costa Rica, and Mexico." Working Paper no. 10637, National Bureau of Economic Research (July).

Mikić, Mia. 1998. *International Trade*. New York: St. Martin's Press.

Minford, Patrick, and David Peel. 2002. *Advanced Macroeconomics*. Northampton, MA: E. Elgar.

Mishkin, Frederic S., and Miguel A. Savastano. 2001. "Monetary Policy Strategies for Latin America." *Journal of Development Economics* 66 (December): 415–44.

Mishkin, Frederic S., and Klaus Schmidt-Hebbel. 2007. "Does Inflation Targeting Make a Difference?" In *Monetary Policy under Inflation Targeting*, edited by Frederic S. Mishkin and Klaus Schmidt-Hebbel. Santiago: Central Bank of Chile.

Mishra, Prachi, Peter J. Montiel, and Antonio Spilimbergo. 2013. "Monetary Transmission in Low-Income Countries: Effectiveness and Policy Implications." *IMF Economic Review* 60 (June): 270–302.

Mizen, Paul, and Serafeim Tsoukas. 2012. "The Response of the External Finance Premium in Asian Corporate Bond Markets." *Journal of Banking and Finance*, 36 (November): 3048–59.

Mlambo K., and Temitope W. Oshikoya. 2001. "Macroeconomic Factors and Investment in Africa." *Journal of African Economies* 10 (September): 12–47.

Mohanty, M. S., and Marc Klau. 2004. "Monetary Policy Rules in Emerging Market Economies: Issues and Evidence." Working Paper no. 149, Bank for International Settlements (March).

Mohanty, M. S., Gert Schnabel, and Pablo Garcia-Lima. 2006. "Banks and Aggregate Credit: What Is New?" In *The Banking System in Emerging Economies: How Much Progress Has Been Made?* BIS Paper no. 28, Bank for International Settlements (Basel).

Mohsin, Mohammed. 2006. "Durability in Consumption and the Dynamics of the Current Account." *Journal of Economic Dynamics and Control* 30 (January): 143–62.

Montiel, Peter J. 1985. "A Monetary Analysis of a Small Open Economy with a Keynesian Structure." *IMF Staff Papers* 32 (June): 179–210.

——. 1986. "Long-Run Equilibrium in a Keynesian Model of a Small Open Economy." *IMF Staff Papers* 33 (March): 685–708.

——. 1987. "Output and Unanticipated Money in the 'Dependent Economy' Model." *IMF Staff Papers* 34 (June): 228–59.

——. 1989. "Empirical Analysis of High-Inflation Episodes in Argentina, Brazil and Israel." *IMF Staff Papers* 36 (September): 527–49.

——. 1994. "Capital Mobility in Developing Countries: Some Measurement Issues and Empirical Estimates." *World Bank Economic Review* 8 (September): 311–50.

——. 1996. "Policy Responses to Surges in Capital Flows: Issues and Lessons." In *Private Capital Flows to Emerging Markets After the Mexican Crisis*, edited by Guillermo A. Calvo, Morris Goldstein, and Eduard Hochreiter. Washington, DC: Institute for International Economics.

——. 2003. "Tight Money in a Post-Crisis Defense of the Exchange Rate: What Have We Learned?" *World Bank Research Observer* 18 (Spring): 1–23.

——. 2005. "Public Debt Management and Macroeconomic Stability: An Overview." *World Bank Research Observer*, 20 (Fall): 259–81.

——. 2011. *Macroeconomics in Emerging Markets,* 2nd ed. Cambridge: Cambridge University Press.

——. 2013a. "The Simple Analytics of Sudden Stops." *Open Economies Review* 24 (April): 267–81.

——. 2013b. *Ten Crises*. London: Routledge.

Montiel, Peter J., and Carmen Reinhart. 1999. "Do Capital Controls and Macroeconomic Policies Influence the Volume and Composition of Capital Flows? Evidence From the 1990s." *Journal of International Money and Finance* 18 (August): 619–635.

Morandé, Felipe G. 1988. "Domestic Currency Appreciation and Foreign Capital Inflows: What Comes First?" *Journal of International Money and Finance* 7 (December): 448–66.

——. 1992. "Dynamics of Real Asset Prices, the Real Exchange Rate, and Foreign Capital Inflows: Chile, 1976–1989." *Journal of Development Economics* 39 (July): 111–39.

Morón, Eduardo, and Diego Winkelried. 2005. "Monetary Policy Rules for Financially Vulnerable Economies." *Journal of Development Economics* 76 (February): 23–51.

Morris, Stephen, and Hyun Song Shin. 1998. "Unique Equilibrium in a Model of Self-Fulfilling Crises." *American Economic Review* 88 (June): 587–97.

Mourmouras, Alex, and José A. Tijerina. 1994. "Collection Lags and the Optimal Inflation Tax." *IMF Staff Papers* 41 (March): 30–54.

Mundell, Robert A. 1961. "A Theory of Optimum Currency Areas." *American Economic Review* 51 (September): 657–65.

———. 1963. "Capital Mobility and Stabilization Policy Under Fixed and Flexible Exchange Rates." *Canadian Journal of Economics and Political Science* 29 (November): 475–85.

Musgrave, Richard A. 1939. "The Nature of Budgetary Balance and the Case for a Capital Budget." *American Economic Review* 29 (June): 260–71.

Musgrove, Phillip. 1979. "Permanent Household Income and Consumption in Urban South America." *American Economic Review* 69 (June): 355–68.

Mussa, Michael. 1986. "The Adjustment Process and the Timing of Trade Liberalization." In *Economic Liberalization in Developing Countries*, edited by Armeane M. Choksi and Demetris Papageorgiou. Oxford: Basil Blackwell.

———. 1987. "Macroeconomic Policy and Trade Liberalization: Some Guidelines." *World Bank Research Observer* 2 (January): 61–77.

Neck, Reinhard. 1991. "The Political Business Cycle Under a Quadratic Objective Function." *European Journal of Political Economy* 7 (December): 439–67.

Nelson, Joan M. 1990. "The Politics of Economic Adjustment in Developing Nations." In *Economic Crisis and Policy Choice*, edited by Joan M. Nelson. Princeton, NJ: Princeton University Press.

Nelson, Joan M., and John Waterbury. 1988. *Fragile Coalitions: The Politics of Economic Adjustment*. New Brunswick, NJ: Transaction Books.

Neumeyer, Pablo A., and Fabrizio Perri. 2005. "Business Cycles in Emerging Economies: The Role of Interest Rates." *Journal of Monetary Economics* 52 (March): 345–80.

Neut, Alejandro, and Andrés Velasco. 2004. "Tough Policies, Incredible Policies?" Working Paper no. 103, Center for International Development (September).

Nicoló, Gianni de, Patrick Honohan, and Alain Ize. 2005. "Dollarization of Bank Deposits: Causes and Consequences." *Journal of Banking and Finance* 29 (July): 1697–1727.

Nordhaus, William. 1975. "The Political Business Cycle." *Review of Economic Studies* 42 (April): 169–90.

———. 1989. "Alternative Models of Political Business Cycles." *Brookings Papers in Economic Activity* no. 1 (March): 1–68.

Nucci, Francesco, and Alberto F. Pozzolo. 2001. "Investment and the Exchange Rate: An Analysis with Firm-Level Panel Data." *European Economic Review* 45 (February): 259–83.

Obstfeld, Maurice. 1981. "Capital Mobility and Devaluation in an Optimizing Model with Rational Expectations." *American Economic Review* 71 (May): 217–21.

———. 1984. "Balance of Payments Crises and Devaluation." *Journal of Money, Credit, and Banking* 16 (May): 208–17.

———. 1985. "The Capital Inflows Problem Revisited: A Stylized Model of Southern Cone Disinflation." *Review of Economic Studies* 52 (October): 605–25.

———. 1986a. "Capital Flows, the Current Account, and the Real Exchange Rate: Consequences of Liberalization and Stabilization." In *Economic Adjustment and Exchange Rates in Developing Countries*, edited by Liaqat Ahmed and Sebastián Edwards. Chicago: University of Chicago Press.

———. 1986b. "Speculative Attacks and the External Constraint in a Maximizing Model of the Balance of Payments." *Canadian Journal of Economics* 19 (March): 1–22.

———. 1994. "Risk-Taking, Global Diversification, and Growth." *American Economic Review* 84 (December): 1310–29.

———. 1996. "Models of Currency Crises with Self-Fulfilling Features." *European Economic Review* 40 (April): 1037–47.

———. 2001. "International Macroeconomics: Beyond the Mundell-Fleming Model." *IMF Staff Papers* 47 (March): 1–39.

———. 2013. "Finance at Center Stage: Some Lessons of the Euro Crisis." Economic Paper no. 493, European Commission (April).

Ogaki, Masao, Jonathan Ostry, and Carmen M. Reinhart. 1996. "Saving Behavior in Low- and Middle-Income Developing Countries: A Comparison." *IMF Staff Papers* 43 (March): 38–71.

Okada, Keisuke. 2013. "The Interaction Effects of Financial Openness and Institutions on International Capital Flows." *Journal of Macroeconomics* 35 (March): 131–43.

Olivera, Julio H. 1967. "Money, Prices and Fiscal Lags: A Note on the Dynamics of Inflation." *Banca Nazionale del Laboro Quarterly Review* 20 (September): 258–67.

Orphanides, Athanasios. 1992. "Credibility and Reputation in Stabilization." Unpublished, Federal Reserve Board, Washington, DC (May).

——. 1996. "The Timing of Stabilizations." *Journal of Economic Dynamics and Control* 20 (March): 257–79.

Orphanides, Athanasios, and Volker Wieland. 2000. "Inflation Zone Targeting." *European Economic Review* 44 (June): 1351–87.

Orphanides, Athanasios, and David W. Wilcox. 2002. "The Opportunistic Approach to Disinflation." *International Finance* 5 (March): 47–71.

Oshikoya, Temitope W. 1994. "Macroeconomic Determinants of Domestic Private Investment in Africa." *Economic Development and Cultural Change* 42 (April): 573–96.

Ostry, Jonathan D. 1991. "Trade Liberalization in Developing Countries." *IMF Staff Papers* 38 (September): 447–79.

Ostry, Jonathan D., Atish R. Ghosh, Marcos Chamon, and Mahvash S. Qureshi. 2012. "Tools for Managing Financial-Stability Risks from Capital Inflows." *Journal of International Economics* 88 (November): 407–21.

Ostry, Jonathan D., and Carment M. Reinhart. 1992. "Private Saving and Terms of Trade Shocks: Evidence from Developing Countries." *IMF Staff Papers* 39 (September): 495–517.

Ozkan, F. Gulcin, and Alan Sutherland. 1998. "A Currency Crisis Model with an Optimising Policymaker." *Journal of International Economics* 44 (April): 339–64.

Paasche, Bernhard. 2001. "Credit Constraints and International Financial Crises." *Journal of Monetary Economics* 48 (December): 623–50.

Pagano, Marco. 1993. "Financial Markets and Growth: An Overview." *European Economic Review* 37 (April): 613–22.

Pallage, Stéphane, and Michel A. Robe. 2003. "On the Welfare Cost of Economic Fluctuations in Developing Countries." *International Economic Review* 44 (May): 677–98.

Pallage, Stéphane, Michel A. Robe, and Catherine Bérubé. 2006. "The Potential of Foreign Aid as Insurance." *IMF Staff Papers* 53 (December): 453–75.

Panizza, Ugo. 2008. "Domestic and External Public Debt in Developing Countries." Discussion Paper no. 188, UNCTAD (March).

Panizza, Ugo, Federico Sturzenegger, and Jeromin Zettelmeyer. 2009. "The Economics and Law of Sovereign Debt and Default." *Journal of Economic Literature* 47 (September): 651–98.

Papademos, Lucas, and Franco Modigliani. 1983. "Inflation, Financial and Fiscal Structure, and the Monetary Mechanism." *European Economic Review* 21 (March): 203–50.

Papageorgiou, Demetris, Armeane M. Choksi, and Michael Michaely. 1990. *Liberalizing Foreign Trade in Developing Countries*. Washington, DC: World Bank.

Park, Daekeun. 1994. "Foreign Exchange Liberalization and the Viability of a Fixed Exchange Rate Regime." *Journal of International Economics* 36 (February): 99–116.

Parkin, Vincent. 1991. *Chronic Inflation in an Industrializing Economy: The Brazilian Inflation*. Cambridge: Cambridge University Press.

Parsley, David C., and Helen A. Popper. 2006. "Exchange Rate Pegs and Foreign Exchange Exposure in East and South East Asia." *Journal of International Money and Finance* 25 (October): 992–1009.

Patinkin, Don. 1993. "Israel's Stabilization Program of 1985, or Some Simple Truths of Monetary Theory." *Journal of Economic Perspectives* 7 (March): 103–28.

Paus, Eva. 1991. "Adjustment and Development in Latin America: The Failure of Peruvian Orthodoxy." *World Development* 19 (May): 411–34.

Payne, James E. 2005. "Savings-Investment Dynamics in Mexico." *Journal of Policy Modeling* 27 (July): 525–34.

Pericoli, Marcello, and Massimo Sbracia. 2003. "A Primer on Financial Contagion." *Journal of Economic Surveys* 17 (September): 571–608.

Perotti, Roberto. 1999. "Fiscal Policy When Things Are Going Badly." *Quarterly Journal of Economics* 114 (November): 1399–1436.

——. 2013. "The 'Austerity Myth': Gain without Pain?" In *Fiscal Policy after the Financial Crisis*, edited by Alberto Alesina and Francesco Giavazzi. Chicago: University of Chicago Press.

Persson, Torsten, and Guido Tabellini. 1994. "Is Inequality Harmful for Growth?" *American Economic Review* 84 (June): 600–621.

Persson, Torsten, and Sweder van Wijnbergen. 1993. "Signalling, Wage Controls, and Monetary Disinflation Policy." *Economic Journal* 103 (January): 79–97.

Pescatori, Andrea, and Amadou Sy. 2004. "Debt Crises and the Development of International Capital Markets." Working Paper no. 04/44, International Monetary Fund (March).

Phelps, Edmund S. 1973. "Inflation in a Theory of Public Finance." *Swedish Journal of Economics* 75 (March): 67–82.

Phylaktis, Kate, and Mark P. Taylor. 1992. "Monetary Dynamics of Sustained High Inflation: Taiwan, 1945–1949." *Southern Economic Journal* 58 (January): 610–22.

———. 1993. "Money Demand, the Cagan Model, and the Inflation Tax: Some Latin American Evidence." *Review of Economics and Statistics* 75 (February): 32–37.

Polackova, Hana. 1998. "Government Contingent Liabilities: A Hidden Risk to Fiscal Stability." Policy Research Working Paper no. 1989, World Bank (October).

Poloz, Stephen S. 1986. "Currency Substitution and the Precautionary Demand for Money." *Journal of International Money and Finance* 5 (March): 115–24.

Poole, William. 1970. "Optimal Choice of Monetary Policy Instruments in a Simple Stochastic Macro Model." *Quarterly Journal of Economics* 84 (May): 197–216.

Popper, Helen A., Alex Mandilaras, and Graham Bird. 2013. "Trilemma Stability and International Macroeconomic Archetypes." *European Economic Review* 64 (November): 181–93.

Pozsar, Zoltan, Tobias Adrian, Adam Ashcraft, and Hayley Boesky. 2010. "Shadow Banking." Staff Report no. 458, Federal Reserve Bank of New York (July).

Prock, Jerry, Gökçe A. Soydemir, and Benjamin A. Abugri. 2003. "Currency Substitution: Evidence from Latin America." *Journal of Policy Modeling* 25 (June): 415–30.

Quah, Danny T. 1996. "Empirics for Economic Growth and Convergence." *European Economic Review* 40 (June): 1353–75.

Raddatz, Claudio. 2007. "Are External Shocks Responsible for the Instability of Output in Low-Income Countries?" *Journal of Development Economics* 84 (September): 155–87.

Rajan, Ramkishen S., and Chung-Hua Chen. 2002. "Are Crisis-Induced Devaluations Contractionary?" Working Paper no. PB0-06 (August).

Rama, Martín. 1993. "Empirical Investment Equations in Developing Countries." In *Striving for Growth After Adjustment*, edited by Luis Servén and Andrés Solimano. Washington, DC: World Bank.

Ranciere, Romain, Aaron Tornell, and Frank Westermann. 2006. "Decomposing the Effects of Financial Liberalization: Crises vs. Growth." *Journal of Banking and Finance* 30 (December): 3331–48.

Ravenna, Federico, and Carl E. Walsh. 2006. "Optimal Monetary Policy with the Cost Channel." *Journal of Monetary Economics* 53 (March): 199–216.

Razin, Assaf, and Efraim Sadka. 2004. "A Brazilian-type Debt Crisis: Simple Analytics." *IMF Staff Papers* 51 (March): 148–53.

Razin, Assaf, Efraim Sadka, and Chi-wa Yuen. 2000. "Excessive FDI under Asymmetric Information." In *Financial Crises in Emerging Markets*, edited by Reuven Glick, Mark Spiegel, and Ramon Moreno. Cambridge: Cambridge University Press.

Rebelo, Sergio. 1991. "Long-Run Policy Analysis and Long-Run Growth." *Journal of Political Economy* 99 (June): 500–521.

Rebelo, Sergio, and Carlos A. Végh. 1997. "Real Effects of Exchange-Rate Based Stabilization: An Analysis of Competing Theories." *NBER Macroeconomics Annual 1996*, edited by Ben S. Bernanke and Julio J. Rotemberg. Cambridge, MA: MIT Press.

Reinhart, Carmen M., and Rogoff, Kenneth S. 2009. *This Time Is Different: Eight Centuries of Financial Folly*. Princeton, NJ: Princeton University Press.

———. 2013. "Banking Crises: An Equal Opportunity Menace." *Journal of Banking and Finance* 37 (November): 4557–73.

Reinhart, Carmen M., and Carlos A. Végh. 1995. "Nominal Interest Rates, Consumption Booms, and Lack of Credibility." *Journal of Development Economics* 46 (April): 357–78.

Reinhart, Carmen M., and Peter Wickham. 1994. "Commodity Prices: Cyclical Weakness or Secular Decline?" *IMF Staff Papers* 41 (June): 175–213.

Reinhart, Carmen, Kenneth Rogoff, and Miguel Savastano. 2003. "Debt Intolerance." NBER Working Paper no. 9908 (August).

Reisen, Helmut, and Helene Yeches. 1993. "Time-Varying Estimates on the Openness of the Capital Account in Korea and Taiwan." *Journal of Development Economics* 41 (August): 285–305.

Rennhack, Robert, and Guillermo Mondino. 1988. "Capital Mobility and Monetary Policy in Colombia." Working Paper no. 88/77, International Monetary Fund (August).

Rhee, Hyuk Jae. 2008. "Money-Based Stabilization in a Small Open Economy." *Journal of Macroeconomics* 30 (March 2008): 462–80.

Riccuiti, Roberto. 2003. "Asessing Ricardian Equivalence." *Journal of Economic Surveys* 17 (March): 55–78.

Ripoll, Marla. 2005. "Trade Liberalization and the Skill Premium in Developing Economies." *Journal of Monetary Economics* 52 (April): 601–19.

Risager, Ole. 1988. "Devaluation, Profitability and Investment." *Scandinavian Journal of Economics* 90 (June): 125–40.

Roberts, John M. 1995. "New Keynesian Economics and the Phillips Curve." *Journal of Money, Credit, and Banking* 27 (November): 975–84.

Robinson, David J., and Peter Stella. 1993. "Amalgamating Central Bank and Fiscal Deficits." In *How to Measure the Fiscal Deficit: Analytical and Methodological Issues*, edited by Mario I. Blejer and Adrienne Cheasty. Washington, DC: International Monetary Fund.

Rochet, Jean-Charles. 1992. "Capital Requirements and the Behavior of Commercial Banks." *European Economic Review* (June): 1137–70.

——. 2004. "Macroeconomic Shocks and Banking Supervision." *Journal of Financial Stability* 1 (September): 93–110.

Rodríguez, Carlos A. 1978. "A Stylized Model of the Devaluation-Inflation Spiral." *IMF Staff Papers* 25 (March): 76–89.

——. 1982. "The Argentine Stabilization Plan of December 20th." *World Development* 10 (September): 801–11.

——. 1991. "The Macroeconomics of the Public Sector Deficit: The Case of Argentina." Working Paper no. 632, World Bank (March).

——. 1993. "Money and Credit Under Currency Substitution." *IMF Staff Papers* 40 (June): 414–26.

Rodríguez, Jorge C., Carla R. Tokman, and Alejandra C. Vega. 2007. "Structural Balance Policy in Chile." Studies in Public Finance, Budget Office of the Finance Ministry, Chile (December).

Rodríguez, Miguel A. 1991. "Public Sector Behavior in Venezuela: 1970–85." In *The Public Sector and the Latin American Debt Crisis*, edited by Felipe Larraín and Marcelo Selowsky. San Francisco: ICS Press.

Rodrik, Dani. 1987. "Trade and Capital Account Liberalization in a Keynesian Economy." *Journal of International Economics* 23 (August): 113–29.

——. 1989. "Credibility of Trade Reforms—A Policymaker's Guide." *World Economy* 12 (March): 1–16.

——. 1991. "Policy Uncertainty and Private Investment in Developing Countries." *Journal of Development Economics* 36 (October): 229–42.

——. 1995. "Trade Liberalization and Disinflation." In *Understanding Interdependence*, edited by Peter B. Kenen. Princeton, NJ: Princeton University Press.

Roemer, Michael, and Steven C. Radelet. 1991. "Macroeconomic Reform in Developing Countries." In *Reforming Economic Systems in Developing Countries*, edited by Dwight H. Perkins and Michael Roemer. Cambridge, MA: Harvard University Press.

Roger, Scott, Carlos J. Garcia, and Jorge E. Restrepo. 2009. "Hybrid Inflation Targeting Regimes."

Rogoff, Kenneth A. 1985. "The Optimal Degree of Commitment to an Intermediate Monetary Target." *Quarterly Journal of Economics* 100 (November): 1169–89.

——. 1989. "Reputational Constraints on Monetary Policy." In *Modern Business Cycle Theory*, edited by Robert J. Barro. Cambridge, Mass.: Harvard University Press.

——. 1990. "Equilibrium Political Budget Cycles." *American Economic Review* 80 (March): 21–36.

Rogoff, Kenneth A., and Anne Sibert. 1988. "Elections and Macroeconomic Policy Cycles." *Review of Economic Studies* 60 (January): 1–16.

Roldós, Jorge. 1995. "Supply-Side Effects of Disinflation Programs." *IMF Staff Papers* 42 (March): 158–83.

——. 1997. "On Gradual Disinflation, the Real Exchange Rate, and the Current Account." *Journal of International Money and Finance* 16 (February): 37–54.

Romer, David. 2000a. "Keynesian Macroeconomics without the LM Curve." *Journal of Economic Perspectives* 14 (March 2000): 149–69.

——. 2000*b*. *Advanced Macroeconomics*. 2nd ed. New York: McGraw Hill.

Romer, Paul. 1986. "Increasing Returns and Long-Run Growth." *Journal of Political Economy* 94 (October): 1002–37.

——. 1990. "Endogenous Technological Change." *Journal of Political Economy* 98 (October): s71-s102.

Rose, Andrew. 2005. "One Reason Countries Pay Their Debts: Renegotiation and International Trade." *Journal of Development Economics* 77 (June): 189–206.

Rosenzweig, Mark. 2001. "Savings Behaviour in Low-Income Countries." *Oxford Review of Economic Policy* 17 (March): 40–54.

Rossi, Nicola. 1988. "Government Spending, the Real Interest Rate, and the Behavior of Liquidity-Constrained Consumers in Developing Countries." *IMF Staff Papers* 35 (March): 104–40.

——. 1989. "Dependency Rates and Private Savings Behavior in Developing Countries." *IMF Staff Papers* 36 (March): 166–81.

Rotemberg, Julio J. 1982. "Monopolistic Price Adjustment and Aggregate Output." *Review of Economic Studies* 49 (October): 517–31.

Roubini, Nouriel. 1991. "Economic and Political Determinants of Budget Deficits in Developing Countries." *Journal of International Money and Finance* 10 (March, Supplement): 49–72.

Roubini, Nouriel, and Xavier Sala-i-Martin. 1995. "A Growth Model of Inflation, Tax Evasion and Financial Repression." *Journal of Monetary Economics* 35 (April): 275–301.

Sachs, Jeffrey. 1988. "Conditionality, Debt Relief, and the Developing Country Debt Crisis." Working Paper no. 2644, National Bureau of Economic Research (July).

——. 1989. "The Debt Overhang of Developing Countries." In *Debt, Stabilization and Development*, edited by Guillermo A. Calvo et al. Oxford: Basil Blackwell.

Sachs, Jeffrey, Aarón Tornell, and Andrés Velasco. 1996. "The Mexican Peso Crisis: Sudden Death or Death Foretold?" *Journal of International Economics* 41 (November): 265–83.

Salter, Walter E. 1959. "Internal and External Balance: The Role of Price and Expenditure Effects." *Economic Record* 35 (August): 226–38.

Samuelson, Paul A., and Subramanian Swamy. 1974. "Invariant Economic Index Numbers and Canonical Duality: Survey and Synthesis." *American Economic Review* 64 (September): 566–93.

Sandleris, Guido. 2008. "Sovereing Defaults: Information, Investment, and Credit." *Journal of International Economics* 76 (December): 267–75.

Santaella, Julio. 1993. "Stabilization Programs and External Enforcement." *IMF Staff Papers* 40 (September): 584–621.

Santos, Joao C. 2006. "Insuring Banks against Liquidity Shocks: The Role of Deposit Insurance and Lending of Last Resort." *Journal of Economic Surveys* 20 (July): 459–82.

Sarantis, Nicholas, and Chris Stewart. 2003. "Liquidity Constraints, Precautionary Saving and Aggregate Consumption: An International Comparison." *Economic Modelling* 20 (December): 1151–73.

Sargent, Thomas J. 1983. "Stopping Moderate Inflations: The Methods of Poincaré and Thatcher." In *Inflation, Debt and Indexation,* edited by Rudiger Dornbusch and Mario H. Simonsen. Cambridge, MA: MIT Press.

Sargent, Thomas J., and Neil Wallace. 1981. "Some Unpleasant Monetarist Arithmetic." *Federal Reserve Bank of Minneapolis Quarterly Review* 5 (Fall): 1–17.

Sbracia, Massimo, and Andrea Zaghini. 2001. "Expectations and Information in Second Generation Currency Crises Models." *Journal of International Economics* 18 (April): 203–22.

Schadler, Susan, Mari Carkovic, Adam Bennet, and Robert Kahn. 1993. *Recent Experiences with Surges in Capital Inflows*. Occasional Paper no. 108. Washington, DC: International Monetary Fund.

Schaling, Eric. 2004. "The Nonlinear Phillips Curve and Inflation Forecast Targeting: Symmetric versus Asymmetric Monetary Policy Rules." *Journal of Money, Credit, and Banking* 36 (June): 361–86.

Schclarek, Alfredo. 2007. "Fiscal Policy and Private Consumption in Industrial and Developing Countries." *Journal of Macroeconomics* 29 (December): 912–39.

Schmid, Michael. 1982. "Stagflationary Effects of a Devaluation in a Monetary Model with Imported Intermediate Goods." *Jahrbütcher fur Nationalokonomie und Statistik* 197 (March): 107–29.

Schmidt-Hebbel, Klaus, and Tobias Muller. 1992. "Private Investment Under Macroeconomic Adjustment in Morocco." In *Reviving Private Investment in Developing Countries*, edited by Ajay Chhibber, Mansoor Dailami, and Nemat Shafik. Amsterdam: North Holland.

Schneider, Friedrich. 2011. "The Shadow Economy Labor Force: What Do We (Not) Know?" *World Economics* 12 (October): 53–92.

Schorfheide, Frank. 2011. "Estimation and Evaluation of DSGE Models: Progress and Challenges." Working Paper no. 11–7, Federal Reserve Bank of Philadelphia (January).

Schubert, Stefan F., and Stephen J. Turnovsky. 2002. "The Dynamics of Temporary Policies in a Small Open Economy." *Review of International Economics* 10 (November): 604–22.

Schularick, Moritz, and Alan M. Taylor. 2012. "Credit Booms Gone Bust: Monetary Policy, Leverage Cycles, and Financial Crises, 1870–2008." *American Economic Review* 102 (June): 1029–61.

Servén, Luis. 1990."Anticipated Real Exchange Rate Changes and the Dynamics of Investment." PRE Working Paper no. 562, World Bank (December).

———. 1997. "Uncertainty, Instability, and Irreversible Investment: Theory, Evidence, and Lessons for Africa." PRE Working Paper no. 1722, World Bank (February).

Servén, Luis, and Andrés Solimano. 1993. "Private Investment and Macroeconomic Adjustment: A Survey." In *Striving for Growth After Adjustment*, edited by Luis Servén and Andrés Solimano. Washington, DC: World Bank.

Shambaugh, Jay C. 2004. "The Effect of Fixed Exchange Rates on Monetary Policy." *Quarterly Journal of Economics* 119 (February): 301–52.

Sharma, Subhash C., Magda Kandil, and Santi Chaisrisawatsuk. 2005. "Currency Substitution in Asian Countries." *Journal of Asian Economics* 16 (June): 489–532.

Shaw, Edward S. 1973. *Financial Deepening in Economic Development*. New York: Oxford University Press.

Shi, Min, and Jakob Svensson. 2006. "Political Budget Cycles: Do They Differ across Countries and Why?" *Journal of Public Economics* 90 (September): 1367–89.

Silver, Mick. 2006. "Core Inflation Measures and Statistical Issues in Choosing Among Them." Working Paper no. 06/97, International Monetary Fund (April).

Simonsen, Mario H. 1983. "Indexation: Current Theory and the Brazilian Experience." In *Inflation, Debt and Indexation*, edited by Rudiger Dornbusch and Mario H. Simonsen. Cambridge, MA: MIT Press.

Sjaastad, Larry A. 1983. "Failure of Economic Liberalization in the Southern Cone of Latin America." *World Economy* 6 (March): 5–26.

Smith, Katherine A., and Diego Valderrama. 2009. "The Composition of Capital Inflows When Emerging Market Firms Face Financing Constraints." *Journal of Development Economics* 89 (July): 223–34.

Soderstrom, Ulf. 2002. "Monetary Policy with Uncertain Parameters." *Scandinavian Journal of Economics* 104 (March): 125–45.

Solow, Robert M. 1956. "A Contribution to the Theory of Economic Growth." *Quarterly Journal of Economics* 50 (February): 65–94.

Sosa Padilla, Cesar. 2013. "Sovereign Default and Banking Crises." Unpublished, McMaster University (February).

Spaventa, Luigi. 1987. "The Growth of Public Debt." *IMF Staff Papers* 34 (June): 374–99.

Srinivasan, T. G., Vincent Parkin, and David Vines. 1989. "Food Subsidies and Inflation in Developing Countries: A Bridge Between Structuralism and Monetarism." Centre for Economic Policy Research, Working Paper no. 334 (August).

Stella, Peter. 2005. "Central Bank Financial Strength, Transparency, and Policy Credibility." *IMF Staff Papers* 52 (September): 335–65.

Stiglitz, Joseph E. 1974. "Alternative Theories of Wage Determination and Unemployment in LDCs: The Labor Turnover Model." *Quarterly Journal of Economics* 98 (May): 194–227.

———. 1982. "Alternative Theories of Wage Determination and Unemployment: The Efficiency Wage Model." In *The Theory and Experience of Economic Development*, edited by Mark Gersovitz, Carlos F. Diaz-Alejandro, Gustav Ranis, and Mark R. Rosenzweig. London: Allen and Unwin.

———. 1992. "Alternative Approaches to Macroeconomics: Methodological Issues and the New Keynesian Economics." In *Macroeconomics: A Survey of Research Strategies*, edited by Alessandro Vercelli and Nicola Dimitri. Oxford: Oxford University Press.

Stiglitz, Joseph E., and Andrew Weiss. 1981. "Credit Rationing in Markets with Imperfect Information." *American Economic Review* 53 (June): 393–410.

———. 1992. "Asymmetric Information in Credit Markets and Its Implications for Macroeconomics." *Oxford Economic Papers* 44 (October): 694–724.

Stockman, Alan C. 1989. "The Cash-in-Advance Constraint in International Economics." In *Finance Constraints and the Theory of Money*, edited by S. C. Tsiang and Meier Kohn. Orlando, FL: Academic Press.

Straub, Stéphane. 2005. "Informal Sector: The Credit Market Channel." *Journal of Development Economics* 78 (December): 299–321.

Sturzenegger, Federico. 2004. "Tools for the Analysis of Debt Problems." *Journal of Reconstructing Finance* 1 (March): 1–23.

Sundararajan, Ved, and Tomás J. Baliño. 1991. "Issues in Recent Banking Crises." In *Banking Crises: Cases and Issues*, edited by Ved Sundararajan and Tomás J. Baliño. Washington, DC: International Monetary Fund.

Sutherland, Alan. 1997. "Fiscal Crises and Aggregate Demand: Can High Public Debt Reverse the Effects of Fiscal Policy?" *Journal of Public Economics* 65 (August): 147–62.

——. 2006. "The Expenditure Switching Effect, Welfare and Monetary Policy in a Small Open Economy." *Journal of Economic Dynamics and Control* 30 (July): 1159–82.

Suzuki, Yui. 2014. "Financial Integration and Consumption Risk Sharing and Smoothing." *International Review of Economics and Finance* 29 (January): 585–98.

Svensson, Lars E. O. 1992. "An Interpretation of Recent Research on Exchange Rate Target Zones." *Journal of Economic Perspectives* 4 (September): 114–19.

——. 1997. "Inflation Forecast Targeting: Implementing and Monitoring Inflation Targets." *European Economic Review* 41 (June): 1111–46.

——. 1999. "Price Level Targeting vs. Inflation Targeting: A Free Lunch?" *Journal of Money, Credit, and Banking* 31 (August): 277–95.

——. 2003. "What Is Wrong with Taylor Rules? Using Judgment in Monetary Policy through Targeting Rules." *Journal of Economic Literature* 41 (June): 426–77.

——. 2010. "Inflation Targeting." In *Handbook of Monetary Economics*, Vol. 3, edited by Benjamin M. Friedman and Michael Woodford. Amsterdam: North Holland.

Swan, Trevor W. 1956. "Economic Growth and Capital Accumulation." *Economic Record* 32 (November): 334–61.

——. 1960. "Economic Control in a Dependent Economy." *Economic Record* 36 (March): 51–66.

Swinburn, Mark, and Marta Castello-Blanco. 1991. "Central Bank Independence and Central Bank Functions." In *The Evolving Role of Central Banks*, edited by Patrick Downes and Reza Vaez-Zadeh. Washington, DC: International Monetary Fund.

Talvi, Ernesto. 1997. "Exchange Rate-Based Stabilization with Endogenous Fiscal Response." *Journal of Development Economics* 54 (October): 59–75.

Tanzi, Vito. 1978. "Inflation, Real Tax Revenue, and the Case for Inflationary Finance: Theory with an Application to Argentina." *IMF Staff Papers* 25 (September): 417–51.

——. 1988. "Lags in Tax Collection and the Case for Inflationary Finance: Theory With Simulations." In *Fiscal Policy, Stabilization, and Growth in Developing Countries*, edited by Mario I. Blejer and Ke-young Chu. Washington, DC: International Monetary Fund.

Tavlas, George, Harris Dellas, and Alan C. Stockman. 2008. "The Classification and Performance of Alternative Exchange-Rate Systems." *European Economic Review* 52 (August): 941–63.

Taylor, Lance. 1979. *Macro Models for Developing Countries.* New York: McGraw Hill.

——. 1983. *Structuralist Macroeconomics.* New York: Basic Books.

——. 1991. *Income Distribution, Inflation and Growth.* Cambridge, MA: MIT Press.

Temple, Jonathan. 1999. "The New Growth Evidence." *Journal of Economic Literature* 37 (March): 112–56.

Ten Kate, Adriaan. 1992. "Trade Liberalization and Economic Stabilization in Mexico: Lessons of Experience." *World Development* 20 (May): 659–72.

Tenreyro, Silvana, and Robert J. Barro. 2007. "Economic Effects of Currency Unions." *Economic Inquiry* 45 (March): 1–23.

Terrones, Marco E. 1989. "Macroeconomic Policy Cycles Under Alternative Electoral Structures." Working Paper no. 8905, University of Western Ontario (April).

Todaro, Michael P., and Stephen C. Smith. 2011. *Economic Development,* 11th ed. Harlow: Pearson Education.

Tomz, Michael, and Mark L. Wright. 2007. "Do Countries Default in 'Bad Times'?." *Journal of the European Economic Association* 5 (April): 352–60.

——. 2012. "Empirical Research on Sovereign Debt and Default." Federal Reserve Bank of Chicago Working Paper no. 2012–06.

Tornell, Aaron, and Andrés Velasco. 1998. "Fiscal Discipline and the Choice of a Nominal Anchor in Stabilization." *Journal of International Economics* 46 (October): 1–30.

Tornell, Aaron, and Frank Westermann. 2002. "Boom-Bust Cycles in Middle Income Countries: Facts and Explanation." *IMF Staff Papers* 49 (March): 111–55.

——. 2003. "Credit Market Imperfections in Middle-Income Countries." Working Paper no. 9737, National Bureau of Economic Research (May).

Tovar, Camilo E. 2005. "The Mechanics of Devaluations and the Output Response in a DSGE Model: How Relevant Is the Balance Sheet Effect?" Working Paper no. 192, Bank for International Settlements (November).

Tovar, Camilo E., Mercedes Garcia-Escribano, and Mercedes Vera Martin. 2012. "Credit Growth and the Effectiveness of Reserve Requirements and Other Macroprudential Instruments in Latin America." Working Paper no. 12/143, International Monetary Fund (June).

Towbin, Pascal, and Sebastian Weber. 2013. "Limits of Floating Exchange Rates: The Role of Foreign Currency Debt and Import Structure." *Journal of Development Economics* 101 (March): 179–94.

Townsend, Robert M. 1979. "Optimal Contracts and Competitive Markets with Costly State Verification." *Journal of Economic Theory* 21 (October): 265–93.

Traca, Daniel. 2004. "Trade Liberalization, Labour Mobility and Wages." *Journal of International Trade and Economic Development* 13 (June): 111–36.

Trehan, Bharat, and Carl E. Walsh. 1991. "Testing Intertemporal Budget Constraints: Theory and Applications to U.S. Federal Budget and Current Account Deficits." *Journal of Money, Credit and Banking* 23 (May): 206–23.

Turnovsky, Stephen J. 1981. "The Effects of Devaluation and Foreign Price Disturbances Under Rational Expectations." *Journal of International Economics* 11 (February): 33–60.

——. 1983. "Wage Formation and Exchange Market Intervention in a Small Open Economy." *Canadian Journal of Economics* 16 (November): 574–92.

——. 1985. "Domestic and Foreign Disturbances in an Optimizing Model of Exchange Rate Determination." *Journal of International Money and Finance* 1 (March): 151–71.

Turnovsky, Stephen J., and A. Basher. 2009. "Fiscal Policy and the Structure of Production in a Two-Sector Developing Economy." *Journal of Development Economics* 88 (March): 205–16.

Turnovsky, Stephen J., and Pradip Chattopadhyay. 2003. "Volatility and Growth in Developing Economies: Some Numerical Results and Empirical Evidence." *Journal of International Economics* 59 (March): 267–95.

Turnovsky, Stephen J., and Partha Sen. 1991. "Fiscal Policy, Capital Accumulation, and Debt in an Open Economy." *Oxford Economic Papers* 43 (January): 1–24.

Uctum, Merih, and Michael Wickens. 2000. "Debt and Deficit Ceilings, and Sustainability of Fiscal Policies: An Intertemporal Analysis." *Oxford Bulletin of Economics and Statistics* 62 (May): 197–222.

UNIDO. 2009. *Breaking In and Moving Up: New Industrial Challenges for the Bottom Billion and the Middle-Income Countries*. Industrial Development Report, United Nations (Vienna).

Uribe, Martín, and Vivian Z. Yue. 2006. "Country Spreads and Emerging Countries: Who Drives Whom?" *Journal of International Economics* 69 (March): 6–36.

van der Ploeg, Frederick. 1989. "The Political Economy of Overvaluation." *Economic Journal* 99 (September): 850–55.

van Gompel, Johan. 1994. "Stabilization with Wage Indexation and Exchange Rate Flexibility." *Journal of Economic Surveys* 8 (September): 252–81.

van Order, Robert. 2006. "A Model of Financial Structure and Financial Fragility." *Journal of Money, Credit, and Banking* 38 (April): 565–85.

van Wijnbergen, Sweder. 1982. "Stagflationary Effects of Monetary Stabilization Policies." *Journal of Development Economics* 10 (April): 133–69.

——. 1986. "Exchange Rate Management and Stabilization Policies in Developing Countries." *Journal of Development Economics* 23 (October): 227–47.

——. 1988. "Monopolistic Competition, Credibility and the Output Costs of Disinflationary Programs." *Journal of Development Economics* 29 (November): 375–98.

——. 1991. "Fiscal Deficits, Exchange Rate Crises, and Inflation." *Review of Economic Studies* 58 (January): 81–92.

Varian, Hal R. 1992. *Microeconomic Analysis*. New York: Norton.

Vaugirard, Victor. 2007. "Informational Contagion of Bank Runs in a Third-Generation Crisis Model." *Journal of International Money and Finance* 26 (April): 403–29.

Végh, Carlos A. 1989a. "The Optimal Inflation Tax in the Presence of Currency Substitution." *Journal of Monetary Economics* 24 (July): 139–46.

——. 1989b. "Government Spending and Inflationary Finance." *IMF Staff Papers* 46 (September): 657–77.

——. 1992. "Stopping High Inflation: An Analytical Overview." *IMF Staff Papers* 39 (September): 626–95.

Veidyanathan, Geetha. 1993. "Consumption, Liquidity Constraints and Economic Development." *Journal of Macroeconomics* 15 (Summer): 591–610.

Veiga, Francisco J. 1999. "What Causes the Failure of Inflation Stabilization Plans?" *Journal of International Money and Finance* 18 (April): 169–94.

Velasco, Andrés. 1987. "Financial Crises and Balance of Payments Crises—A Simple Model of the Southern Cone Experience." *Journal of Development Economics* 17 (October): 263–83.

——. 1993. "Real Interest Rates and Government Debt during Stabilization." *Journal of Money, Credit, and Banking* 25 (May): 251–72.

——. 1996. "Fixed Exchange Rates: Credibility, Flexibility and Multiplicity." *European Economic Review* 40 (April): 1023–35.

——. 1997. "When Are Fixed Exchange Rates Really Fixed?" *Journal of Development Economics* 54 (October): 5–25.

——. 1999. "A Model of Endogenous Fiscal Deficits and Delayed Fiscal Reforms." In *Fiscal Institutions and Fiscal Performance*, edited by James M. Poterba and Jurgen von Hagen. Chicago: University of Chicago Press.

Venegas-Martínez, Francisco. 2001. "Temporary Stabilization: A Stochastic Analysis." *Journal of Economic Dynamics and Control* 25 (September): 1429–49.

Vergne, Clémence. 2009. "Democracy, Elections and Allocation of Public Expenditures in Developing Countries." *European Journal of Political Economy* 25 (March): 63–77.

Verspagen, Bart. 1992. "Endogenous Innovation in Neo-Classical Growth Models: A Survey." *Journal of Macroeconomics* 14 (Fall): 631–62.

Vestin, David. 2006. "Price-Level versus Inflation Targeting." *Journal of Monetary Economics* 53 (October): 1361–76.

Vickers, John. 1986. "Signalling in a Model of Monetary Policy with Incomplete Information." *Oxford Economic Papers* 38 (November): 443–55.

Villanueva, Delano, and Abbas Mirakhor. 1990. "Strategies for Financial Reforms." *IMF Staff Papers* 37 (September): 509–36.

von Hagen, Jürgen, and Haiping Zhang. 2008. "A Welfare Analysis of Capital Account Liberalization." *Review of International Economics* 16 (August): 576–90.

——. 2014. "Financial Development, International Capital Flows, and Aggregate Output." *Journal of Development Economics* 106 (January): 66–77.

Wacziarg, Romain, and Jessica S. Wallack. 2004. "Trade Liberalization and Intersectoral Labor Movements." *Journal of International Economics* 64 (December): 411–39.

Walsh, Carl E. 1995. "Optimal Contracts for Central Bankers." *American Economic Review* 76 (March): 150–67.

——. 1999. "Announcements, Inflation Targeting and Central Bank Incentives." *Economica* 66 (May): 255–69.

Wang, Neng. 2004. "Precautionary Saving and Partially Observed Income." *Journal of Monetary Economics* 51 (November): 1645–81.

Wasmer, Etienne, and Philippe Weil. 2004. "The Macroeconomics of Labour and Credit Market Imperfections." *American Economic Review* 94 (September): 944–63.

Werner, Alejandro M. 1995. "Exchange Rate Target Zones, Realignments, and the Interest Rate Differential: Theory and Evidence." *Journal of International Economics* 39 (November 1995): 353–67.

Wette, Hildegard. 1983. "Collateral in Credit Rationing in Markets with Imperfect Information." *American Economic Review* 73 (June): 442–45.

Whitehead, Laurence. 1990. "Political Explanations of Macroeconomic Management: A Survey." *World Development* 18 (August 1990): 1133–46.

Wickens, Michael. 2011. *Macroeconomic Theory*. 2nd ed. Princeton, NJ: Princeton University Press.

Willett, Thomas D., Manfred W. Keil, and Young Seok Ahn. 2002. "Capital Mobility for Developing Countries May Not Be So High." *Journal of Development Economics* 68 (August): 421–34.

Williamson, John. 1996. *The Crawling Band as an Exchange Rate Regime: Lessons from Chile, Colombia, and Israel*. Washington, DC: Institute for International Economics.

Williamson, John, and Stephan Haggard. 1994. "The Political Conditions for Economic Reform." In *The Political Economy of Economic Reform*, edited by John Williamson. Washington, DC: Institute for International Economics.

Williamson, John, and Molly Mahar. 1998. *A Survey of Financial Liberalization*. Essay in International Finance no. 211, Princeton University (November).

Williamson, Stephen D. 1986. "Costly Monitoring, Financial Intermediation, and Equilibrium Credit Rationing." *Journal of Monetary Economics* 18 (September): 159–79.

Willman, Alpo. 1988. "The Collapse of the Fixed Exchange Rate Regime with Sticky Wages and Imperfect Substitutability between Domestic and Foreign Bonds." *European Economic Review* 32 (November): 1817–38.

Wolpin, Kenneth I. 1982. "A New Test of the Permanent Income Hypothesis: The Impact of Weather on the Income and Consumption of Farm Households in India." *International Economic Review* 23 (October): 583–94.

Wong, David Y. 1990. "What Do Saving-Investment Relationships Tell Us About International Capital Mobility?" *Journal of International Money and Finance* 9 (March): 60–74.

Woo, Jaejoon. 2005. "Social Polarization, Fiscal Instability and Growth." *European Economic Review* 49 (August): 1451–77.

———. 2011. "Growth, Income Distribution, and Fiscal Policy Volatility." *Journal of Development Economics* 96 (November): 289–313.

Woodford, Michael. 2003. *Interest and Prices*. Princeton, NJ: Princeton University Press.

———. 2010. "Financial Intermediation and Macroeconomic Analysis." *Journal of Economic Perspectives* 24 (September): 21–44.

———. 2013. "Macroeconomic Analysis without the Rational Expectations Hypothesis." Working Paper no. 19368, National Bureau of Economic Research (August).

World Bank. 1993. *The East Asian Miracle*. New York: Oxford University Press.

———. 1997. *Private Capital Flows to Developing Countries*. Washington, DC: World Bank.

———. 2012. *China 2030: Building a Modern, Harmonious, and Creative High-Income Society*. Washington, DC: World Bank.

Wright, Mark L. 2011. "The Theory of Sovereign Debt and Default." In *Encyclopedia of Financial Globalization*, edited by Gerard Caprio. Amsterdam: North-Holland.

Yun, Tack. 1996. "Nominal Price Rigidity, Money Supply Endogeneity, and Business Cycles." *Journal of Monetary Economics* 37 (April): 345–70.

Zeldes, Stephen. 1989. "Consumption and Liquidity Constraints: An Empirical Investigation." *Journal of Political Economy* 97 (April): 305–46.

Zuehlke, Thomas W., and James E. Payne. 1989. "Tests of the Rational Expectations-Permanent Income Hypothesis for Developing Economies." *Journal of Macroeconomics* 11 (June): 423–33.

Index of Names

Index of Subjects

accelerator. *See* financial accelerator; flexible accelerator approach

adjustment: alternative policy rules and, 359–60, 359n19, 435–36; costs of, 672–74, 676, 678, 684; credibility and, 420; fiscal, 109, 127–29, 665–67, 671–74, 693; infrastructure spending cuts and, 68; labor market and, 49–51, 128–43, 647–51, 673–74; nominal anchor of stabilization program and, 435–36; political economy of, 675–95; recession associated with, 68; sequencing of reforms and, 420, 431, 489, 665–72; speed of, 431, 672–74; to tariff reform, 655–57; of wages to devaluation, 409–12. *See also* financial liberalization; reforms; structural reforms; trade reform

adjustment fatigue, 678

Africa: capital flows to, 482–83; currency unions proposed for, 279–80; private investment in, 66, 72

aggregate demand: capital flows and, 509; consumption and, 52–53; contractionary effects and, 303–19; devaluation and, 303–19; exchange rates and, 171, 232–33, 296, 301; fiscal contractions and, 128; in New Keynesian model, 455; nominal income targeting and, 239; policy interest rates and, 170; price controls and, 439; private investment and, 65, 66; shocks affecting, 216, 217; sterilization and, 218–19; temporariness model and, 393, 396n18; unemployment and, 47, 51; working-capital costs and, 221–22. *See also* demand shocks

aggregate supply, 18–20; devaluation and, 319–26; exchange rates and, 233–34, 246; in New Keynesian model, 455; output-inflation variability frontier and, 232; policy interest rates and, 170–71; price controls and, 439; working-capital costs and, 221. *See also* supply shocks

agricultural sector, 43, 44, 47, 48; food supply and, 338–43; growth and, 635; incomes in, 55; reform and, 676; tax system and, 93. *See also* food subsidies

aid to low-income countries, 699

AK model, 607–9; infrastructure and, 615

Argentina: Austral Plan of, 404; banking crises in, 566, 567; crisis of early 1980s in, 662; crisis of 2001 in, 550, 594; depreciation in early 1980s, 338n6; inflation correlated with politics in, 679; money demand and, 74; real wages in, 404, 405; sovereign debt default in, 572; stabilization and, 382, 395n17, 426, 679; wage and price controls in, 426. *See also* Southern Cone

Asian crisis of 1997–1998, 486, 490, 540, 549, 550

Asia-Pacific firms, foreign-currency exposure of, 329

asymmetric information. *See* information asymmetry

Austral Plan, 404

balance of payments: banking crises and, 567; in general accounting framework, 32; monetary approach to, 359; in monetary policy model, 205, 208–10, 215; in one-good model, 123. *See also* capital account liberalization; current account

balance-of-payments crises, 76, 405, 515, 666. *See also* currency crises

balance sheet effects: currency crises and, 539–40; devaluation and, 326; of exchange-rate fluctuations, 172, 329; in monetary transmission mechanism, 172–75

band-pass filter, 22

band regimes, 263, 274–79; capital inflows and, 500, 502; de facto, 248, 252; experience with, 278–79; honeymoon effect with, 275–76, 292–93; Krugman model and, 275–77, 291–94; monetary policy credibility and, 277–78, 279; rationale for, 274–77; smooth pasting and, 276, 292, 293

bands, inflationary. *See* target bands, in inflation targeting

banking crises, 550–52; business cycles and, 555–56; cross-country evidence on, 566–68; currency crises and, 550–51, 556–64, 567; determinants of, 566–71; Diamond-Dybvig model and, 552–56; econometric investigations of, 569–71; as enforcement device, 565; financial liberalization and, 662; logit estimation and, 569, 571; probit regression and, 570; signaling approach to, 568–69